THE VIRGIN ENCYCLOPEDIA OF

SIXTIES MUSIC

THIRD EDITION

COMPILED AND
EDITED BY

COLIN LARKIN

In Association with
MUZE UK Ltd

Dedicated to your old mate Brian Matthew

First published in Great Britain in 2002 by
Virgin Books Ltd
Thames Wharf Studios
Rainville Road
London W6 9HA

A catalogue record for this book is available
from the British Library.

ISBN 1 85227 933 8

muze

Written, edited and produced by
MUZE UK Ltd
All editorial enquiries and complaints
should be sent to:
Suite 16, Arcade Chambers, 28 High Street,
Brentwood, Essex, CM14 4AH.
www.muze.com

Editor-In-Chief: Colin Larkin
Assistant Editor: Nic Oliver
Production Editor: Susan Pipe
Typographic Design: Roger Kohn
Design Assistant: Aku Young
Very special thanks to Trev Huxley, Paul Zullo
and Tom Goldsworthy of Muze Inc., and to
KT Forster and Carolyn Thorne of Virgin Books.

Typeset by Set It Again Studios
Printed and bound in Great Britain
by Mackays of Chatham plc, Chatham, Kent

INTRODUCTION

Q UITE SIMPLY the best decade for music, ever. And that is not because it has been fairly cool recently for younger fans to say so, nor because the likes of us oldsters openly weep as to how great it was. The fact is, it just was. You should have been there: British beat, American pop, Motown, Stax soul, San Francisco acid rock, sunshine pop, freakbeat, mod, ska, folk rock, fusion, heavy/prog rock, FM American radio, and the pirates, London and Caroline. Every single one of 'em, born and blossomed in the 60s. I rest my case.

The choice of entries for this book will satisfy most people. There will be a few complaining that so and so is left out. The book represents what I think are certain artists most popular decade. Certainly the Rolling Stones, Bob Dylan and others had massive success outside this decade. Ultimately it is the flavour of the sixties I am trying to conjure up. You will find the companion books *Stage & Film Musicals* and the *Fifties* will cover all the others. *The Virgin Encyclopedia Of Sixties Music* is one of a major series of books taken from the multi-volume *Encyclopedia Of Popular Music*. Other titles already available are:

The Virgin Encyclopedia Of Fifties Music
The Virgin Encyclopedia Of Seventies Music
The Virgin Encyclopedia Of Eighties Music
The Virgin Encyclopedia Of Nineties Music
The Virgin Encyclopedia Of Jazz
The Virgin Concise Encyclopedia Of Popular Music
The Virgin Encyclopedia Of Stage & Film Musicals
The Virgin Encyclopedia Of Indie & New Wave
The Virgin Encyclopedia Of The Blues
The Virgin Encyclopedia Of Country Music
The Virgin Encyclopedia Of R&B And Soul
The Virgin Encyclopedia Of Heavy Rock
The Virgin Encyclopedia Of Dance Music
The Virgin Encyclopedia Of Reggae

ENTRY STYLE

All albums, EPs (extended play 45s), newspapers, magazines, television programmes, films and stage musicals are referred to in italics. All song titles appear in single quotes. We spell rock n' roll like this. There are two main reasons for spelling rock 'n' roll with 'n' as opposed to 'n'. First, historical precedent: when the term was first coined in the 50s, the popular spelling was n'. Second, the 'n' is not simply an abbreviation of 'and' (in which case 'n' would apply) but as a phonetic representation of n as a sound. The ' ', therefore, serve as inverted commas rather than as apostrophes. The further reading section at the end of each entry has been expanded to give

the reader a much wider choice of available books. These are not necessarily recommended titles but we have attempted to leave out any publication that has little or no merit.

We have also started to add videos at the end of the entries, but have decided not to list DVDs, simply because there is not enough time. Again, this is an area that is expanding faster than we can easily cope with, but there are many items in the videography and the filmography. Release dates in keeping with albums attempt to show the release date in the country of origin. We have also tried to include both US and UK titles in the case of a title change.

DATES OF BIRTH

Occasionally we hear from an artist or manager asking us to change the date of birth, usually upwards, to make the artist younger. We have to reluctantly comply with this unless we have sighted birth registration details. We are constantly seeking accurate birth data, and confirmed corrections would be gratefully received.

DISCOGRAPHY

In attempting to put the record label with albums I am very aware that most labels listed are either from the USA or the UK. These will continue to be our prime sources. We have attempted to list the label (and country) where the release was first issued. Because of the continuing CD revolution and the constant repackaging we have listed the most recent reissues. What we have not done is to list the latest label. That would be too much of a task. Once again please refer to the web site www.muze.com for both US and UK labels and catalogue numbers as well as track listings. This book is not meant to be a discographical tool; we are more concerned with the artist's music and career. For the majority of artists in this work, complete discographies have been compiled. However, on occasion, the discography section at the end of an entry is incomplete. This is not due to lack of effort on our behalf but simply to the fact that some artists have had such extensive careers that it is impossible to go back over numerous decades of files. From our experience, most record companies do not retain this detailed information. The aim of the discography is to allow the reader to investigate further the work of a particular artist. We have included, where possible, the regular albums together with the first year of release date in the known country of origin, which is generally in the USA or the UK. In many cases the delay in releasing the record in another country can be years. Some Latin, African, Caribbean and other Third World recordings have been assigned approximate release dates as the labels often do not carry any release date. We do not list bootlegs but one or two may have accidentally crept in.

In the case of recordings made before the general availability of the LP (album), approximately 1950, we have aimed to inform the reader of the date of recordings and the year of release. Since the advent of the compact disc in 1982, and its subsequent popularity, the reissue market has expanded enormously. There are outstanding reissue programs going ahead, usually with bonus tracks or alternative takes. Companies such as Collectables and Rhino in the USA and Ace and Castle in the UK are just two labels putting two-on-one, a fantastic bonus taking advantage of the CD over short-timed vinyl albums from the 50s and 60s. Our MUZE online database contains every CD release since day one.

ALBUM RATINGS

Due to many requests from librarians and readers we continue to rate all albums. All new releases are reviewed either by myself or by our team of contributors. We also take into serious consideration the review ratings of the leading music journals and critics' opinions.

Our system is slightly different to most 5 Star ratings in that we rate according to the artist in question's work. Therefore, a 4 Star album from the Beach Boys may have the overall edge over a 4 Star album by Bobby Vee. Sorry Bob.

Our ratings are carefully made, and consequently you will find we are very sparing with 5 Star and 1 Star albums.

★★★★★
Outstanding in every way.
A classic and therefore strongly recommended.
No comprehensive record collection
should be without this album.

★★★★
Excellent.
A high standard album from this artist
and therefore highly recommended.

★★★
Good.
By the artist's usual standards
and therefore recommended.

★★
Disappointing.
Flawed or lacking in some way.

★
Poor. An album to avoid
unless you are a completist.

PLAGIARISM

In maintaining the largest text database of popular music in the world, we are naturally protective of its content. We license to approved licensees only. It is both flattering and irritating to see our work reproduced without credit. Time and time again over the past few years I have read a newspaper obituary, knowing that I wrote that line or phrase. Secondly, it has come to our notice that other companies attempting to produce their own rock or pop encyclopedias use our material as a core. Flattering this might also be, but highly illegal. We have been making sure over the past two years that the publishers of these maverick music guides will be stopped once and for all from plagiarizing work that has taken us a lifetime to assemble. Having spent many hours with our lawyers taking action, I do know a bit about copyright law. Be careful and mostly, be warned, we usually know who you are. Our text appears on hundreds of websites, mostly unofficial ones. Once again, thanks for the compliment but make sure that you always credit and acknowledge us as your source (copyright MUZE UK or Encyclopedia Of Popular Music), otherwise we will have to shut you down.

CHART POSITIONS & RECORD SALES

The aim of this book is not to document chart positions and record sales. Many are discussed in passing but are ultimately left to the main books available. The reference books we have used were those formerly edited by Gambaccini, Rice and Rice, but now we use the new bible *The Complete Book Of The British Charts, Singles And Albums*, edited by Brown, Kutner and Warwick for the UK. Joel Whitburn's (*Top Pop Singles*, *Top Pop Albums*, *Country Singles*, *R&B Singles* and *Pop Memories*) for the USA are published by Record Research and are absolutely indispensable. Our chart information from 1952 to 1960 was originally taken from the *New Musical Express* and from 1960 to 1968 were gleaned from the *Record Retailer*. While we have adhered to the BMRB in the main we feel that the *New Musical Express* and the recently departed *Melody Maker* charts were accepted more than the dreary *Record Retailer*, as the latter published its chart before the weekly sales were recorded. If we were to have stuck religiously to the *Record Retailer*, then the Beatles would have only had one record entering the chart at number 1. And cor blimey, we can't have that! It is generally known that most of their records reached number 1 on the week of release in the UK, and this was reflected in the main weekly music papers. This aberration fortunately does not occur in the USA, thanks to the longevity and accuracy of *Billboard* and Joel Whitburn's efforts. We now use the UK chart published by *Music Week*.

For the USA, when we refer to a gold disc for singles it signifies sales of 1,000,000 copies pre-

1989 and 500,000 thereafter. The RIAA (Record Industry Association Of America) made this change in 1989, and *Billboard* followed suit. Similarly, when platinum awards were introduced, they initially signified sales of 2,000,000 copies and post-1989 of 1,000,000. For albums from 1958 to 1974, the term gold refers to LPs that sold $1 million worth of units at manufacturers' wholesale prices. Recognizing that due to rising prices the number of units necessary to gain gold status was dropping, the RIAA as of 1 January 1975 added the further proviso that to be gold an LP had to have sold at least 500,000 copies. A platinum LP has to have sold 1,000,000 copies. In the UK the BPI determines – singles: platinum 600,000 units, gold 400,000 and silver 200,000. For albums: platinum 300,000, gold 100,000, silver 60,000. For the recent introduction of CD box sets, a 4-CD box has to sell 250,000 copies to go platinum, although this does not apply to two-disc sets at the present time.

CRITICAL OPINION

The aim was always to strike a balance between being highly opinionated and bland, with a sprinkle of humour. We have attempted to express the generally accepted opinion and have not set out to be controversial (except in some cases where we hope our entries on certain lesser-known artists will lead to a reappraisal of their work).

ACKNOWLEDGEMENTS

Always first and foremost, Johnny Rogan, who continues to be a fair critic and a good friend. He was the first person to hear of my proposal for the original Encyclopedia and agreed to be involved. His great attention to detail shaped the original editorial style-sheet, and he was instrumental in approaching some early contributors. Additionally there is always at the end of a phone the free advice of Pete Frame, Peter Doggett, Johnny Black and Fred Dellar. And if I fancy a weepy chat about how great Brian Wilson or Dylan is, Stuart Batsford is top of the list. Chris Charlesworth is a most agreeable and experienced Bayko builder. Continuing praise for the efforts of Pete 'the hound' Bassett and his Quite Great company, Anita, Louise and Dave. And thanks to my late Dad for getting me hooked in this business by buying me a magic transistor radio, the Fidelity reel-to-reel and the red Dansette.

Appreciation again and again to production editor Susan Pipe; efficient, trustworthy and loyal as ever, a rare thing in this day and age. Similarly invaluable is my non-stop chattering assistant editor Nic Oliver. Michael Kaye continues as our database/software developer, his determination to fix bugs is admirable. Our contributors are further reduced in number, as we now update and amend all our existing text and write most of the new stuff.

Our team over the past year has included: Jim Allen, Ian Bell, Dominic Chadwick, Tony Clayton-Lea, Jurgen Funk, Dave Gil de Rubio, Karen Glossop, David Hemingway, Sam Hendricks, Ben Hogwood, Ed Houghton, Jake Kennedy, Mark Keresman, Siobhan Long, Dan Nosworthy, Joel McIver, Alex Ogg, Jon Staines, Richard Wilson. Alongside, Spencer Leigh, Hugh T. Wilson and Salsri Nyah, continue to supply their specialist knowledge. The 'very necessary' Bruce Crowther continues to produce anything we throw at him, providing it is jazz. And to Carl Newsum and Dennis of Slipped Disc II in Chelmsford. Support your local independent record shop.

Past contributors' work may still appear in this volume, so just in case, I acknowledge with thanks once again: Simon Adams, David Ades, Mike Atherton, Gavin Badderley, Alan Balfour, Michael Barnett, John Bauldie, Johnny Black, Chris Blackford, Pamela Boniface, Keith Briggs, Paul M. Brown, Michael Ian Burgess, Tony Burke, John Child, Linton Chiswick, Rick Christian, Alan Clayson, Paul Cross, Norman Darwen, Roy Davenport, Peter Doggett, Kevin Eden, John Eley, Lars Fahlin, Tim Footman, John Fordham, Per Gardin, Ian Garlinge, Mike Gavin, Andy Hamilton, Mark Hodkinson, Brian Hogg, Mike Hughes, Arthur Jackson, Mark Jones, Max Jones, Simon Jones, Ian Kenyon, Dave Laing, Steve Lake, Paul Lewis, Graham Lock, John Martland, Bernd Matheja, Chris May, Dave McAleer, David McDonald, York Membery, Toru Mitsui, Greg Moffitt, Michael Newman, Pete Nickols, Lyndon Noon, Zbigniew Nowara, James Nye, Ken Orton, Ian Peel, Dave Penny, Alan Plater, Barry Ralph, John Reed, Emma Rees, Jamie Renton, Lionel Robinson, Johnny Rogan, Alan Rowett, Dave Sissons, Neil Slaven, Chris Smith, Steve Smith, Mitch Solomons, Christopher Spencer, Mike Stephenson, Sam Sutherland, Jeff Tamarkin, Ray Templeton, Liz Thompson, Christen Thomsen, Gerard Tierney, John Tobler, Adrian T'Vell, Pete Wadeson, Frank Warren, Ben Watson, Pete Watson, Simon Williams, Val Wilmer, Dave Wilson and Barry Witherden. Others that have been missed are either through my own sloppy error or deliberate intention.

Record Company Press Offices. These invaluable people are often bombarded with my requests for biogs and review copies. A few actually respond, and those that do are very important to us. It always amazes me how some major record companies completely ignore our numerous requests and others of similar stature are right on the button. Thanks this time especially to Matt Wheeler and Rich Dawes at Polydor, Alan Robinson, Dorothy Howe and Matt Sweeting at Sanctuary, Erik James, Florence Halfon, Rick Conrad and Carlos Anaia at Warners, Dave Clark at Quite Great, Sue and Dave Williams at Frontier Promotions, Tones

Sansom and Vanessa Cotton at Triad Publicity, Joe Foster, Andrew Lauder at Evangeline, Bob, Neil Scaplehorn at Ace, Murray Chalmers, Chris Latham and the team at Parlophone/Capitol, Mike Gott at BGO, Tim Wright and Ian McNay at Cherry Red/RPM, Mick Houghton at Brassneck, Zoe Stafford at RCA, Shane O'Neill at Universal, Ted Cummings at MCA, Jonathan Gill at Demon, Paul at Big Moon, Mal Smith at Delta, Darren Crisp at Crisp Productions, Richard Wootten and Pat Tynan at Koch International.

To the few friends who you can trust, colleagues and family who play no direct part in producing these books but make my life more tolerable: Nils von Veh, Fred Nelson, Stuart Batsford, Danny Sperling, Bob Harris, Johnnie Walker, Kathleen Dougherty, Chris Braham, David Gould, Roger Kohn, Roy Sheridan, Kip Trevor, Alan Lynch, John Burton, David Larkin, Sabra Larkin, Kay and Kevin, Sally Decibelle and the four long lost London cousins, Danny, Peter, Michael and John.

To all our colleagues in the USA at Muze Inc., and MUZE UK, who oil the smooth running of our UK unit. And especially, but in no order whatsoever to Gary Geller, Scott Lehr, Ra Ra Raisa Howe, Catherine Hamilton, Justin Sedgmond, Ian Bell, Karien de Witt, Jennifer Rose, Bernadette Elliott, Paul Parrierra (and the Raiders), Jim Allen, Terry Vinyard, Mark Keresman, Phil Antman, Bill Schmitt, Jeanne Petras, Stephanie Jones, Ed Moore, Mike Lupitkin, Michael Kennedy, Mike Doustan, Tom Goldsworthy and of course Marc 'midnight to six' Miller, Paul 'cosmic charlie' Zullo and Trev 'brave new world' Huxley. Finally, love to Kelly and the tins, Dan, Tom and Goldie.

Colin Larkin,
February 2002

A BAND OF ANGELS

Formed in 1964 at Harrow Public School, England, A Band Of Angels consisted of Michael D'Abo (b. 1 March 1944, Betchworth, Surrey, England; vocals, piano), Christian (John) Gaydon (guitar, vocals), John Baker (guitar), David Wilkinson (bass) and James Rugge-Price (drums). The group made great play of their 'upper class' origins, wearing matching sleek suits and straw boater hats in publicity photographs. They signed to United Artists Records in 1964, and recorded 'Me' and 'She'll Never Be You' for the company before switching to Piccadilly Records. 'Leave It To Me' was issued in 1965 and a year later the group completed their last, and finest, single, 'Invitation'. A strong beat and nagging chorus led to its becoming a favourite on the northern soul scene of the 70s. D'Abo replaced Paul Jones in Manfred Mann in 1966, while John Gaydon became a successful entrepreneur in partnership with ex-A Band Of Angels manager David Enthoven. Together they formed EG Records, home of Roxy Music, King Crimson and Brian Eno.

A.B. SKHY

This San Francisco-based quartet included Dennis Geyer (guitar), Howard Wales (keyboards), Jim Marcotte (bass) and Terry Andersen (drums). A seven-piece horn section supported the group on their debut album, a blues-based set modelled on B.B. King and Bobby Bland. Following the departures of Andersen and Wales, the remaining members continued with newcomers Rick Jaeger (drums) and James 'Curley' Cooke (guitar). The latter was a founder member of the Steve Miller Band, and a former colleague of Geyer in an earlier group, Tim Davis And The Chordaires. *Ramblin' On* was produced by the notorious Kim Fowley. This informal collection showcased the group's instrumental muscle and featured cameo performances from guitarist Elvin Bishop and pianist Ben Sidran. However, the group failed to secure a commercial success and broke up during sessions for a projected third album. Founder member Wales later enjoyed a brief association with the Grateful Dead, and recorded 1971's experimental *Hooteroll* with the latter's guitarist, Jerry Garcia.
● ALBUMS: *A.B. Skhy* (MGM 1969) ★★, *Ramblin' On* (MGM 1970) ★★.

ACADEMY

This UK rock quartet comprised Richard Cobby (guitar), Damon J. Hardy (vocals), Polly Perkins (b. England, c.1943; vocals) and Dick Walter (flute). Formed in the late 60s, the group's sound was dominated by the dual male/female vocals of Hardy and Perkins, with Walter's woodwind contribution helping to establish a distinctive sound that clearly incorporated elements of progressive, folk and jazz rock. In 1969 the group released its sole album, *Pop-Lore According To The Academy*, and the single 'Rachel's Dream'/'Munching The Candy'. Neither secured any mainstream interest, however, and by the early 70s the group had disbanded.
● ALBUMS: *Pop-Lore According To The Academy* (Morgan Bluetown 1969) ★★.

ACCENT

Formed in Yorkshire, England, originally as the Blue Blood Group, the Accent relocated to London in 1966. Comprising Pete Beetham (drums), Alan Davies (bass), Rick Birkett (guitar) and John Hebron (vocals, guitar), the group secured a residency at Billy Walker's Upper Cut Club in Forest Gate, east London. Their reputation in the capital partly established, they then recorded their debut single, 'Red Sky At Night'/'Wind Of Change', for Decca Records in 1967. Produced by Mike Vernon, it demonstrated the group's unusual songwriting, with the a-side including a propulsive guitar riff as well as several disorientating sound effects. However, the single did not fulfil Decca's expectations and it proved to be the Accent's sole release. Birkett later released a solo album (credited to Rick Heyward) for Vernon's Blue Horizon Records, before joining Jellybread and the Zombies. 'Red Sky At Night' later became a cult item among UK progressive rock collectors, and was included on several posthumous compilations including *The British Psychedelic Trip Vol. 1*, *Chocolate Soup For Diabetics Vol. III* and *Illusions From The Cracking Void*.

ACCENTS

Comprising Mike Lasman (lead), Shelly Weiss (first tenor), Allan Senzan (second tenor) and Ian Kaye (baritone), doo-wop group the Accents formed at local high schools in Brooklyn, New York, USA, in 1960. Both Weiss and Lasman had already recorded by this time; Lasman as lead for Mike And The Utopians and Weiss with Bobby Roy And The Chord-A-Roys. Practising regularly on street corners, the new quartet was originally named the Dreamers. Their first supporter was Jerry Halperin, who found them a contract with Carlton Records subsidiary label Guaranteed. They picked a pop standard they had played regularly in their boardwalk days for their first release, 'Canadian Sunset', but it did not chart. Subsequently dropped by their record company, the group changed its name to the Accents (a name also employed by at least six separate doo-wop groups) and became more R&B in style. After successfully auditioning for Sultan Records they released their first single under the new title, 'Where Can I Go'. This was a highly unusual doo-wop number, based on an old Jewish ballad with some of the lyrics in Hebrew. However, it was the flip side, 'Rags To Riches', which became a local favourite, though its popularity did not extend beyond state borders. However, after Kaye and Senzan sang backing vocals on Dion's 'Baby Baby' hit, the second Accents' single was their last. 'High On A Hill' saw the band backing Scott English (credited to Scott English And The Accents). After breaking up, Weiss, who also worked with Jay And The Americans, became a music journalist.

ACKLIN, BARBARA

b. 28 February 1944, Chicago, Illinois, USA, d. 27 November 1998, Omaha, Nebraska, USA. A vocalist in the style of Dionne Warwick and Brenda Holloway, Acklin first recorded for Special Agent under the name Barbara Allen. In 1966, following a spell as a backing singer, she worked as a receptionist at the Brunswick Records offices, and submitted some of her own compositions to producer Carl Davis. One of these, 'Whispers', co-written with David Scott (of the Five Dutones), was a major hit for Jackie Wilson, who returned the favour by helping Acklin to secure a recording contract with Brunswick. 'Love Makes A Woman', a US number 15 pop hit in July 1968, was followed by 'Just Ain't No Love' and 'Am I The Same Girl' (a UK Top 25 hit in 1992 for Swing Out Sister), while a duet with Gene Chandler, 'From The Teacher To The Preacher', also charted. Meanwhile, Acklin began writing with Eugene Record from the Chi-Lites, a partnership that resulted in several of that group's finest moments, including 'Have You Seen Her' and 'Stoned Out Of My Mind'. The relationship continued despite Acklin's departure for Capitol Records, but in spite of her early promise with 'Raindrops' (1974), she was dropped from the label in 1975. *Groovy Ideas* collects the cream of her Brunswick recordings.

● ALBUMS: *Love Makes A Woman* (Brunswick 1968) ★★, *Seven Days Of Night* (Brunswick 1969) ★★, *Someone Else's Arms* (Brunswick 1970) ★★, *I Did It* (Brunswick 1971) ★★, *I Call It Trouble* (Brunswick 1971) ★★, *A Place In The Sun* (Capitol 1975) ★★.

● COMPILATIONS: *Groovy Ideas* (Kent 1987) ★★★★, *The Brunswick Singles As And Bs* (Edsel 1999) ★★★.

ACTION

Formed in Kentish Town, London, in 1965, this respected group consisted of Reg King (vocals), Alan 'Bam' King (b. 18 September 1946, Kentish

Town, London, England; guitar), Pete Watson (guitar), Mike Evans (bass) and Roger Powell (drums). For two years prior to this, the quintet was known as the Boys. As such they recorded one single, 'It Ain't Fair', for Pye Records, and served as a backing group for up-and-coming singer Sandra Barry. Rechristened the Action, the band established a reputation as one of the best Mod groups on the booming London circuit and became the subject of a BBC television documentary that examined the travails of life on the road. The Beatles' producer George Martin spotted their talent and supervised their recordings for his newly established independent company, AIR. He bestowed a crystal-clear sound on a succession of excellent singles: 'Land Of 1,000 Dances', 'I'll Keep On Holding On', 'Baby You've Got It', 'Never Ever' and 'Shadows And Reflections', which combined a love of soul music with a growing awareness of US west coast harmony styles. Watson left in 1966, but the group persevered as a quartet until the following year when Ian Whiteman joined. He, in turn, was replaced by ex-Savoy Brown guitarist Martin Stone. The Action failed to secure a hit and a proposed album was duly left unissued. Several completed masters appeared belatedly on *The Ultimate Action!* CD. During their final months the group took a new name, Azoth, before reverting to the Action, but the departure of the charismatic Reggie King brought this period of indecision to a close. He later recorded a solo album while his former colleagues, with Whiteman back in the fold, embraced progressive rock as Mighty Baby. Although credited to the Action, 1985's Dojo Record's compilation *Action Speaks Louder Than* consists of Mighty Baby demo recordings. The group re-formed in 1998 for several live dates.

● COMPILATIONS: *The Ultimate Action!* (Edsel 1980) ★★, *Brain: The Lost Recordings 1967/8* (Autumn Stone Archives 1995) ★★, *Action Packed* (Edsel 2001) ★★.

AD LIBS

This US vocal quintet evolved from New Jersey's Creators (formed in 1962), and consisted of Hugh Harris and Danny Austin, plus Dave Watt, Norman Donegan and lead singer Mary Ann Thomas. Under the aegis of the swing-era veteran John T. Taylor, they had a Top 10 R&B and pop hit in 1965 with 'The Boy From New York City', which was composed by Taylor. Their compelling performance blended contemporary R&B with doo-wop, but the group was unable to repeat the single's impact. Although a subsequent release, 'He Ain't No Angel', was a minor hit, the Ad Libs struggled to sustain any momentum. 'Giving Up' entered the R&B Top 40 in 1969, but this commercial reprieve owed little to the charm of their heyday and proved equally short-lived. The memory of that lone hit was revived in 1981 when Manhattan Transfer took their version into the US Top 10.

ADAM, MIKE AND TIM

This trio from Liverpool, Merseyside, England, was formed in the early 60s and went on to release a succession of singles for Decca Records and Columbia Records without ever recording an album. Comprising Tim Saunders, Mike Sedgewick and Peter 'Adam' Sedgewick, the trio's vocals were supported by studio musicians as the occasion demanded. They made their debut in 1964 with 'Little Baby', a song written by Les Reed and Barry Mason. After 'That's How I Feel' and 'Little Pictures' in 1965, they moved to Columbia from Decca, but neither of their releases in the following year, 'Flowers On The Wall' and a version of Paul Simon's 'A Most Peculiar Man', brought any sort of breakthrough. After the expiry of the group's contract, Mike Sedgewick recorded an unsuccessful solo single in 1968.

ADAMO

b. 1 November 1943, Cosimo, Italy. Salvadore Adamo's family emigrated to Belgium where he balanced bookish excellence and artistic leanings while at school in Jemmapes. An able guitarist and singer, he had already been heard on local radio when, following his victory in a Radio Luxembourg contest, he gained a Philips Records recording contract. He then had hits in the Netherlands with tracks such as 'Sans Toi Mamie' and 'Dolce Paola', a show-stopper at a Brussels concert (attended by the princess to whom the opus was dedicated). Relocating to Paris, a 1965 appearance at Olympia provoked a favourable notice in *France-Soir* that sparked off a string of self-composed Pathe disc successes in France and its colonies. In 1966 he charted with 'Les Filles Du Bord De Mer', 'Mes Mains Sur Tes Hanches' and the yuletide smash, 'Tombe La Neige'. His clean, conservative image garnered a large middle-of-the-road audience but, with a shy smile that belied personal tragedies unknown to his public, Adamo's appeal foreshadowed that of the 70s singer-songwriters – especially when, after a 1967 visit to the Middle East, he penned 'Inch Allah' and 'On Se Bat Toujours Quelque Part', topical anti-war singles that earned the approbation of the blossoming hippie subculture. While he made few inroads into the English-speaking market, 1969's 'Petit Bonheur' sold a million, and Adamo remains a showbusiness institution in Gallic territories.

ADDERLEY, NAT

b. Nathaniel Adderley, 25 November 1931, Tampa, Florida, USA, d. 1 January 2000, Lakeland, Florida, USA. The younger brother of Cannonball Adderley, Nathaniel was a singer until his voice broke and he took up the trumpet. In the early 50s he served in the army with his brother and played in the 36th Army Band. His professional break came in 1954, when Lionel Hampton asked him to join his riotously swinging, R&B-inflected big band; he stayed for only a year. Later he played with Woody Herman and J.J. Johnson. In 1960, he released *Work Song*, a brilliant amalgam of the soul jazz for which he is celebrated and a more 'cool'-style, chamber music instrumentation (including cello and guitar, the latter played by Wes Montgomery). 'Work Song' has since become a classic crossing over to pop/rock genres. Vocal interpretations have been recorded by Nina Simone and Eric Burdon (the Animals). Throughout the 60s and early 70s, he played in his brother's band and since the latter's death in 1975 he kept alive that special brand of warm, rootsy bop, both on his own recordings and in other contexts, such as Nathan Davis' Paris Reunion Band. In 1997, Adderley became artist-in-residence at Florida Southern College. He was a diabetes sufferer and died in January 2000.

● ALBUMS: *That's Nat* (Savoy 1955) ★★★, *Introducing Nat Adderley* (EmArcy 1955) ★★★, *To The Ivy League From Nat* (EmArcy 1956) ★★★, *Branching Out* (Riverside 1958) ★★★, *Much Brass* (Riverside 1959) ★★★, *That's Right!* (Riverside 1960) ★★★, *Work Song* (Riverside 1960) ★★★★, *Naturally!* (Jazzland 1961) ★★★, *In The Bag* (Jazzland 1962) ★★★★, *The Adderley Brothers In New Orleans* (1962) ★★★, *Little Big Horn!* (Riverside 1964) ★★★, *Autobiography* (Atlantic 1965) ★★★, *Sayin' Something* (Atlantic 1966) ★★★, with Cannonball Adderley *Them Adderleys* (Limelight 1966) ★★★, *Live At Memory Lane* (Atlantic 1967) ★★, *The Scavenger* (Milestone 1968) ★★, *Comin' Out Of The Shadows* (1968) ★★, *You, Baby* (A&M 1968) ★★, *Natural Soul* (Milestone 1968) ★★★, *Calling Out Loud* (A&M 1969) ★★, *Zodiac Soul* (1970) ★★, *Soul Of The Bible* (1972) ★★, *Double Exposure* (1974) ★★★, *Don't Look Back* (1976) ★★★, *A Little New York Midtown Music* (Galaxy 1978) ★★, *On The Move* (1983) ★★★, *Blue Autumn* (Theresa 1983) ★★, with Benny Carter, Red Norvo *Benny Carter All Stars, Featuring Nat Adderley & Red Norvo* (Sonet 1985) ★★★ *That's Nat* (Savoy 1985) ★★★, *Blue Autumn* (Theresa 1987) ★★★, *Work Songs* (Fantasy 1987) ★★★, *Talkin' About You* (Landmark 1991) ★★★, *We Remember Cannon* (In & Out 1991) ★★★, *The Old Country* (Enja 1992) ★★★, *Working* (Timeless 1993) ★★★, *Mercy, Mercy, Mercy* (Evidence 1997) ★★★.

● COMPILATIONS: as the Adderley Brothers *The Summer Of '55* (Savoy 2000) ★★★★, *Introducing Nat Adderley* (Verve 2001) ★★★.

● VIDEOS: *Nat Adderley Quartet* (Kay Jazz 1988).

ADLER, LOU

b. 1935, Los Angeles, California, USA. Adler emerged as a potent force in Californian pop as the manager of Jan And Dean and co-writer of their second US Top 10 hit, August 1959's 'Baby Talk'. At this time he also managed and produced Johnny Rivers and formed a songwriting partnership with Herb Alpert. As Barbara Campbell, he co-wrote the pop hits 'Only Sixteen' and 'Wonderful World' for Sam Cooke. Adler was subsequently involved with the Colpix and Dimension Records labels, where he came into contact with several staff songwriters, including Carole King, Steve Barri and P.F. Sloan. The latter pair formed a successful partnership at Adler's publishing house, Trousdale, and supplied material for his several protégés. In 1965 Adler founded Dunhill Records with Jay Lasker and Bobby Roberts. This influential label became the natural outlet for several of the entrepreneur's discoveries, including the Mamas And The Papas and Barry McGuire, and had major hits with Richard Harris and the Grass Roots. The company was later sold to the ABC Records group, whereupon Adler set up a new venture, Ode, and had a huge international hit with Scott McKenzie's 1967 summer-of-love anthem 'San Francisco (Be Sure To Wear Flowers In Your Hair)'. In the same year, Adler was a director of the highly successful Monterey Pop Festival, which served as a world stage for the emergent west coast scene. Ode's subsequent signings included Spirit, Cheech And Chong and Carole King, whose 1971 release, *Tapestry*, which Adler produced, was one of the decade's biggest-selling albums. Adler then became increasingly involved in films and theatre, where his work included *Brewster McCloud*, *The Rocky Horror Picture Show* and *Tommy*, and his subsequent diversification into nightclubs emphasized his disparate interests.

AFTER TEA

Formed in the Hague, Netherlands, in 1967, After Tea evolved from the beat-based group the Tea Set. The revitalized quartet – Hans van Eijck (keyboards, guitar, vocals), Ray Fenwick (guitar, vocals), Rob 'Polle' Eduard (bass, organ, vocals) and Martin Hage (drums) – enjoyed a Dutch hit with 'Not Just A Flower In Your Hair', while a follow-up single, 'We Will Be There After Tea', secured airplay on Britain's pirate radio stations. The latter song was subsequently covered as 'After Tea' by the Spencer Davis Group, whom the English-born Fenwick joined in 1968 upon the expiry of his work permit. Ferry Lever, also ex-Tea Set, replaced him in After Tea, which continued to enjoy popularity in its homeland. However, the departure of chief composer van Eijck in 1969 robbed the band of its individuality as Eduard, Lever, Duitser Uly Grun (organ) and Ilja Gort (drums) rejected flower-pop affectations in favour of a heavier direction. The group broke up following the release of *Joint House Blues*, but Fenwick and organist Hans Jansen joined the final line-up for a one-off single, 'Mexico', in 1975.

● ALBUMS: *After Tea* (Ace Of Clubs 1967) ★★, *National Disaster* aka *Bubblegum Beat Party* (1968) ★★, *Joint House Blues* (1971) ★★.
● COMPILATIONS: *After Tea* (1978) ★★.

AITKEN, LAUREL

b. 1927, Cuba. Of mixed Cuban and Jamaican descent, Laurel, with his five brothers (including the veteran guitarist Bobby Aitken) and sisters, settled in his father's homeland, Jamaica, in 1938. In the 40s he earned a living singing calypso for the Jamaican Tourist Board, as visitors alighted at Kingston Harbour. By the age of 15 Aitken, like many of the early Jamaican R&B and ska singers, including Owen Gray and Jackie Edwards, entered Vere John's Opportunity Hour, an amateur talent contest held on Friday nights at Kingston's Ambassador Theatre. He won the show for several weeks running, and his success there led to his establishment as one of the island's most popular club entertainers. His first sessions were for Stanley Motta's Caribbean Recording Company, where he recorded some calypso songs, the spiritual 'Roll Jordan Roll' and 'Boogie Rock'. The latter was one of the first ever Jamaican R&B/shuffle recordings. In 1958 he recorded 'Little Sheila'/'Boogie In My Bones', one of the first records produced by future Island Records boss Chris Blackwell, using a Jamaican saxophonist and a white Canadian backing band. It emerged on Blackwell's R&B label (where it spent over 12 months in the Jamaican chart), and in the UK on Starlite and, some years later, Island.

Between 1958 and 1960, Aitken made a number of recordings in the pre-ska shuffle mode, including 'Bartender' and 'Brother David' for Ken Khouri, 'Judgement Day', 'More Whisky', 'Mighty Redeemer' and 'Zion' for Duke Reid, and 'Remember My Darling', 'The Saint', 'I Shall Remove', 'What A Weeping'/'Zion City Wall' and 'In My Soul' for Leslie Kong. On the strength of the popularity of these records in the UK, Aitken came to London in 1960, where he recorded a number of songs including 'Sixty Days & Sixty Nights', 'Marylee' and 'Lucille'. These were released on the entrepreneur Emile Shalett's new Blue Beat Records label, created to handle Jamaican music exclusively in the UK, one of its first releases being Aitken's 'Boogie Rock'. Aitken returned to Jamaica in 1963 and recorded 'Weary Wanderer' and 'Zion' for Duke Reid: these, too, were released on Blue Beat.

Back in London, he recorded for Graeme Goodall's Rio Records, which released around 20 titles by Aitken between 1964 and 1966, including 'Adam & Eve', 'Bad Minded Woman', 'Leave Me Standing' and 'We Shall Overcome', other titles appearing on the Ska Beat and Dice labels. In 1969 he enjoyed great success on Nu Beat, a subsidiary of the Palmer brothers' Pama Records group of labels, writing songs for other artists, including 'Souls Of Africa' for the Classics. He also recorded 'Guilty' by Tiger (which was Aitken under a different name), and enjoyed great success with his own exuberant reggae songs such as 'Woppi King', 'Haile Selassie', 'Landlords & Tenants', 'Jesse James', 'Skinhead Train', 'Rise & Fall', 'Fire In Me Wire', and the notorious 'Pussy Price', in which he bemoaned the rising cost of personal services. During this period Aitken's popularity among Britain's West Indian population was matched only by his patronage by white skinhead youths, and it is mainly with successive skinhead and mod revivals that his name and music have been preserved.

The emerging trend towards cultural and religious (i.e., Rasta) themes among a new generation of young UK (and Jamaican) blacks in the early 70s sharply contrasted with Aitken's brand of simple knees-up. It was probably not to his advantage that he spent so long away from Jamaica's rapidly changing music scene, where producers such as Lee Perry and Bunny Lee were coming up with new rhythms and ideas in production almost monthly. Aitken spent the 70s in semi-retirement, gave up regular recording and moved to Leicester, performing the occasional club date, his show-stopping act undiminished despite his advancing years. He has recorded intermittently since, almost achieving a Top 40 hit with 'Rudi Got Married' for Arista in 1981, and riding for all he was worth on the 2-Tone bandwagon. UB40's *Labour Of Love* featured a cover version of 'Guilty', but since then Aitken has largely disappeared from public notice.

● ALBUMS: *Ska With Laurel* (Rio 1965) ★★★, *High Priest Of Reggae* (Nu Beat 1969) ★★★, with Potato 5 *Potato 5 Meet Laurel Aitken* (Gaz's 1987) ★★, *Early Days Of Blue Beat, Ska And Reggae* (Bold Reprive 1988) ★★★, *It's Too Late* (Unicorn 1989) ★★, *Rise And Fall* (Unicorn 1989) ★★, *Sally Brown* (Unicorn 1989) ★★, *The Blue Beat Years* (Moon 1996) ★★.
● COMPILATIONS: *The Pioneer Of Jamaican Music* (Reggae Retro 2000) ★★★★.
● VIDEOS: *Live At Gaz's Rockin' Blues* (Unicorn 1989).

AKENS, JEWEL

b. 12 September 1940, Houston, Texas, USA. Akens sang in a church choir as a child and moved to Los Angeles in the late 50s. There he worked closely with Eddie Daniels as Eddie And The Four Tunes, before making his recording debut with him as Jewel And Eddie for the local Silver label. Akens went on to make records in the early 60s with the Four Dots and the Astro Jets before he linked up with the Hollywood-based Era label in 1965. There, Akens had his moment of glory with the novelty song 'The Birds And The Bees' in 1965. It was composed by Herb Newman under the name of Barry Stuart, co-owner of Era and was both a pop and R&B hit (numbers 3 and 21, respectively) in the USA. The song was also very popular in Europe, reaching number 29 in the UK. The follow-ups, 'Georgie Porgie' and 'Dancing Jennie', were too similar to succeed, although he did record credible versions of 'Little Bitty Pretty One' (Thurston Harris and the Paramounts) and 'You Better Move On'

(Arthur Alexander and the Rolling Stones).
● ALBUMS: *The Birds And The Bees* (Era 1965) ★★.

ALEXANDER, ARTHUR

b. 10 May 1940, Florence, Alabama, USA, d. 9 June 1993, Nashville, Tennessee, USA. Despite his own interpretations, Alexander's recordings are often better recalled for their inspirational quality. 'Anna (Go To Him)', a US R&B Top 10 hit, and 'You Better Move On' were covered, respectively, by the Beatles and the Rolling Stones, while 'A Shot Of Rhythm And Blues' became an essential UK beat staple (notably by Johnny Kidd). Although 'You Better Move On' was recorded at the rudimentary Fame studios, Alexander's subsequent work was produced in Nashville, where his poppier perceptions undermined the edge of his earlier work. Later singles included 'Go Home Girl' and the haunting 'Soldier Of Love', but his fragile personality was particularly susceptible to pressure. This problem bedevilled his move to another label, Sound Stage 7, and although a 1972 album for Warner Brothers Records was promising, the singer's potential once again seemed to wither.

A pop hit was secured on Buddah Records with 'Every Day I Have To Cry Some' (1975), but the success remained short-lived. For many years Alexander was forced to work outside of the music business; he was a bus driver for much of this time. Alexander began to perform again in 1993 as renewed interest arose in his small but important catalogue. *Lonely Just Like Me* was his first album in 21 years and showed a revitalized performer. He signed a new recording and publishing contract in May 1993, suffering the cruellest fate when he collapsed and died the following month, three days after performing in Nashville with his new band. Richard Younger's excellent biography pays overdue respect to this unsung legend.

● ALBUMS: *You Better Move On* (Dot 1962) ★★★, *Alexander The Great* (Dot 1964) ★★★, *Arthur Alexander* i (Dot 1965) ★★★, *Arthur Alexander* ii (Warners 1972) ★★, *Arthur Alexander* iii (Buddah 1975) ★★, *Lonely Just Like Me* (Elektra 1993) ★★★.
● COMPILATIONS: *A Shot Of Rhythm And Soul* (Ace 1985) ★★★, *Soldier Of Love* (Ace 1987) ★★★, *The Greatest* (Ace 1989) ★★★★, *The Ultimate Arthur Alexander* (Razor & Tie 1993) ★★★★, *Rainbow Road: The Warner Bros. Recordings* (Warner Archives 1994) ★★★, *The Monument Years* (Ace 2001) ★★★.
● FURTHER READING: *Get A Shot Of Rhythm & Blues: The Arthur Alexander Story*, Richard Younger.

ALLISON, MOSE

b. Mose John Allison Jnr., 11 November 1927, Tippo, Mississippi, USA. Allison began piano lessons at the age of five, and played trumpet in high school, although he has featured the latter instrument less frequently in recent years. His music is a highly individual mix of blues and modern jazz, with influences on his cool, laconic singing and piano-playing ranging from Tampa Red and Sonny Boy 'Rice Miller' Williamson to Charlie Parker, Duke Ellington, and Thelonious Monk. He moved to New York in 1956 and worked mainly in jazz settings, playing with Stan Getz, Al Cohn, Zoot Sims and Gerry Mulligan, and recording for numerous companies. During the 60s Allison's work was much in evidence as he became a major influence on the burgeoning R&B scene. Pete Townshend, one of his greatest fans, recorded Allison's 'A Young Man's Blues' for the Who's *Live At Leeds*. Similarly, John Mayall was one of dozens who recorded his classic 'Parchman Farm', and Georgie Fame featured many Allison songs in his heyday with the Blueflames (Fame's nasal and understated vocal was similar to Allison's). In the 80s Allison saw a resurgence in his popularity after becoming a hero to the new, young audience hungry for his blend of modern jazz. In 1996 he collaborated with Fame, Van Morrison and Ben Sidran on his own tribute album, *Tell Me Something: The Songs Of Mose Allison*. Ultimately, however, his work is seen as hugely influential on other performers, and this has to a degree limited the profile afforded his own lengthy recording career.

● ALBUMS: *Back Country Suite* (Prestige 1957) ★★★, *Local Color* (Prestige 1958) ★★★, *Young Man Mose* (Prestige 1958) ★★★, *Ramblin' With Mose* (Prestige 1958) ★★★★, *Creek Bank* (Prestige 1959) ★★★, *Autumn Song* (Prestige 1960) ★★★, *The Transfiguration Of Hiram Brown* (Columbia 1960) ★★, *I Love The Life I Live* (Columbia 1960) ★★★, *Take To The Hills* (Epic 1962) ★★, *I Don't Worry About A Thing* (Atlantic 1962) ★★★, *Swingin' Machine* (Atlantic 1962) ★★★, *The World From Mose* (Atlantic 1964) ★★★, *V-8 Ford Blues* (Columbia 1964) ★★★, *Mose Alive!* (Atlantic 1965) ★★★, *Mose Allison* (Prestige 1966) ★★★, *Wild Man On The Loose* (Atlantic 1966) ★★★, *Jazz Years* (Atlantic 1967) ★★, *Mose Allison Plays For Lovers* (Prestige 1967) ★★, *I've Been Doin' Some Thinkin'* (Atlantic 1969) ★★★, *Hello There, Universe* (Atlantic 1969) ★★, *Western Man* (Atlantic 1971) ★★★★, *Mose In Your Ear* (Atlantic 1972) ★★, *Your Mind Is On Vacation* (Atlantic 1976) ★★★★, *Middle Class White Boy* (Elektra 1982) ★★★, *Lessons In Living* (Elektra 1984) ★★, *Ever Since The World Ended* (Blue Note 1987) ★★, *My Backyard* (Blue Note 1990) ★★★, *The Earth Wants You* (Blue Note 1994) ★★, with Georgie Fame, Van Morrison, Ben Sidran *Tell Me Something: The Songs Of Mose Allison* (Verve 1996) ★★, *Gimcracks And Gewgaws* (Blue Note 1998) ★★★, *The Mose Chronicles: Live In London, Volume 1* (Blue Note 2001) ★★★.

● COMPILATIONS: *The Seventh Son – Mose Allison Sings* (Prestige 1963) ★★★★, *Down Home Piano* (Prestige 1966) ★★★, *The Best Of Mose Allison* (Atlantic 1970) ★★★★, *Retrospective* (Columbia 1976) ★★★, *High Jinks! The Mose Allison Anthology* (Columbia/Legacy 1994) ★★★, *Allison Wonderland: The Mose Allison Anthology* (Rhino 1994) ★★★★, *The Best Of Mose Allison* (Sequel 1994) ★★★★, *Jazz Profile* (Blue Note 1997) ★★★★, *The Sage Of Tippo* (32 Jazz 1998) ★★★★.

● FURTHER READING: *One Man's Blues: The Life And Music Of Mose Allison*, Patti Jones.

● FILMS: *The Score* (2001).

ALLISONS

John Alford (b. 31 December 1939, London, England) and Bob Day (b. 2 February 1942, Trowbridge, Wiltshire, England). The pop duo played the rounds of coffee bars and youth clubs before being spotted by impresario Tito Burns, who became their manager. He saw their immediate potential as Everly Brothers lookalikes. Under the guise of brothers John and Bob Allison, they became overnight UK sensations when their self-composed 'Are You Sure' became Britain's entry in the 1961 Eurovision Song Contest. They received a big wave of publicity when their song became runner-up in the competition. The record, produced by Jack Baverstock and arranged by Harry Robinson on Fontana Records, went to number 1 in the UK charts, sold over a million copies in Europe and narrowly missed the US chart (*Billboard* number 102). The latter fact was significant, as UK acts rarely crossed the Atlantic and entering the *Billboard* Hot 100 was a major feat. The duo, who were backed on stage by the Hunters, and who toured with Larry Parnes' stable of acts, never returned to the UK Top 20. Their only other chart entries were their next two releases, 'Words' and 'Lessons In Love' (a song from Cliff Richard's film *The Young Ones*), in 1962. They have occasionally resurfaced over the years as accomplished writers and record producers but have had no further chart success.

● ALBUMS: *Are You Sure* (Fontana 1961) ★★.

ALPERT, HERB

b. 31 March 1935, Los Angeles, California, USA. A trumpet player from the age of eight, Alpert proved an exceptional arranger, songwriter and entrepreneur. In collaboration with Lou Adler, he wrote Sam Cooke's hit 'Wonderful World', then turned to production, enjoying successes with surfing duo Jan And Dean. After a short-lived partnership with Lou Rawls and a failed attempt at acting, Alpert teamed up with promoter/producer Jerry Moss. Together they founded A&M Records, in 1962, and launched Alpert's own first recording career with 'The Lonely Bull'. Backed by the Tijuana Brass, Alpert enjoyed a number of instrumental hits such as 'Taste Of Honey', 'Tijuana Taxi', 'Spanish Flea' and 'Casino Royale'. A regular in the album charts of the 60s, he cleverly cornered the market by signing and producing his easy listening rivals Sergio Mendes And Brasil '66. In 1968, a rare Alpert vocal outing on Burt Bacharach's 'This Guy's In Love With You' became a US chart-topper, and also reached UK number 3. Meanwhile, A&M flourished and by the end of the 60s had ventured into the rock market with signings such as the Flying Burrito Brothers, Joe Cocker, Carole King, and Leon Russell. It was the easy listening, soft rock act the Carpenters, however, who proved the label's most commercially successful act of the early 70s.In spite of Alpert's record company commitments, he sustained his recording career and earned his second US number 1 with the instrumental 'Rise' in 1979.

One of the most successful music business moguls of his era, Alpert finally sold A&M in 1989 for a staggering $500 million. In 1994 Alpert and Moss started a new record label, this time with the even more imaginative title of Almo. Alpert returned to recording in the late 90s with a series of slick jazz/AOR albums. He also exhibited his abstract expressionist paintings and co-produced a number of Broadway shows, including *Angels In America* and *Jelly's Last Jam*. Alpert and Moss sold their music publishing company Rondor, to Universal Group in 2000 for an estimated $400 million.

● ALBUMS: *The Lonely Bull* (A&M 1962) ★★★★, *Tijuana Brass, Volume 2* (A&M 1963) ★★★, *South Of The Border* (A&M 1964) ★★★, *Whipped Cream And Other Delights* (A&M 1965) ★★★, *Going Places* (A&M 1965) ★★★★, *What Now, My Love* (A&M 1966) ★★★, *S.R.O.* (A&M 1966) ★★★, *Sounds Like* (A&M 1967) ★★★, *Herb Alpert's 9th* (A&M 1967) ★★, *Christmas Album* (A&M 1968) ★★, *The Beat Of The Brass* (A&M 1968) ★★★, *The Brass Are Comin'* (A&M 1969) ★★, *Warm* (A&M 1969) ★★, *Down Mexico Way* (A&M 1970) ★★, *Summertime* (A&M 1971) ★★, *America* (A&M 1971) ★★★, *Solid Brass* (A&M 1972) ★★★, *Foursider* (A&M 1973) ★★★, *You Smile – The Song Begins* (A&M 1974) ★★★, *Coney Island* (A&M 1975) ★★, *Just You And Me* (A&M 1976) ★★, *Herb Alpert And Hugh Masekela* (Horizon 1978) ★★★, *Rise* (A&M 1979) ★★★, *Beyond* (A&M 1980) ★★, *Magic Man* (A&M 1981) ★★, *Fandango* (A&M 1982) ★★, *Blow Your Own Horn* (A&M 1983) ★★, *Bullish* (A&M 1984) ★★, *Wild Romance* (A&M 1985) ★★, *Keep Your Eye On Me* (A&M 1987) ★★, *Under A Spanish Moon* (A&M 1988) ★★, *My Abstract Heart* (A&M 1989) ★★, *North On South Street* (A&M 1991) ★★, *Midnight Sun* (A&M 1992) ★★, *Second Wind* (Almo 1996) ★★★, *Passion Dance* (Almo 1997) ★★, *Colors* (Almo 1999) ★★.

● COMPILATIONS: *Greatest Hits* (A&M 1970) ★★★★, *Solid Brass* (A&M 1972) ★★★, *Foursider* (A&M 1973) ★★★, *Greatest Hits Volume 2* (A&M 1973) ★★★, *40 Greatest* (A&M 1977) ★★★★, *Classics Volume 20* (A&M 1987) ★★★★, *The Very Best Of Herb Alpert* (A&M 1991) ★★★, *Definitive Hits* (A&M 2001) ★★★★.

● VIDEOS: *Very Best Of Herb Alpert* (PolyGram Music Video 1992).

● FILMS: *The Ten Commandments* (1956), *Rowan & Martin At The Movies* (1968).

ALTAMONT FESTIVAL

The free festival at the Altamont Raceway, California on 6 December 1969 was the first major musical event since the peaceful 'happening' at the Woodstock Festival earlier in the year. Altamont tarnished the reputation of the new music revolution. Until then, all events had been free of violence and had allowed the older generation to reluctantly reappraise their perception of pop music and its cultural trappings, even though the conventional press still regarded Woodstock as a disaster. The festival spirit died when Meredith Hunter, an 18-year-old black spectator, was beaten and stabbed to death by a group of Hell's Angels while the Rolling Stones were onstage. Mick Jagger, only yards away, was oblivious to what was happening at his feet. When he finally realized and called for help, it was too late to save Hunter's life. The Angels had become involved in the festival after being recruited by the organizers to keep the peace as 'security' guards: their fee was as much alcohol and drugs as they could consume, and consequently, it was later claimed that they were not in control of their horrific actions. Tempers had earlier become frayed when Santana's performance had been interrupted by a scuffle. Jefferson Airplane, who followed, had their singer Marty Balin knocked unconscious by a blow from one of the Angels when he tried to stop another disturbance. Although the Angels were ultimately deemed responsible, they had themselves become victims of appalling organization. Singer David Crosby defended their actions in a lengthy *Rolling Stone* interview, and Mick Jagger became the focus of a great deal of resentment from certain Hell's Angels groups who accused the singer of shirking any responsibility for the incident and quickly shifting the blame towards them. Although it appeared that, by continuing to perform, Jagger did not act responsibly, the singer still claims he was unaware of what was happening. As a result of the incident, Jagger received numerous death threats, and there is reportedly still a 'contract' out on his life. Other artists appearing in front of the unmanageable crowd of 300,000 included Crosby, Stills, Nash And Young and the Flying Burrito Brothers. Although the Grateful Dead were members of the organizing committee, they did not ultimately perform. The film *Gimme Shelter* ends with the Altamont tragedy and is an interesting, if gory, piece of celluloid rock history.

● FURTHER READING: *Altamont*, Jonathan Eisen (ed.).

● FILMS: *Gimme Shelter* (1970).

AMBOY DUKES

Originally from Detroit, Michigan, USA, the Amboy Dukes – John Drake (vocals), Ted Nugent (b. 13 December 1948, Detroit, Michigan, USA; lead guitar), Steve Farmer (rhythm guitar), Rick Lorber (keyboards), Bill White (bass) and Dave Palmer (drums) – achieved notoriety for their rendition of 'Journey To The Center Of The Mind', which featured Nugent's snarling guitar and reached the US Top 20 in 1968. The brashness of their version of Them's 'Baby Please Don't Go' set the tone for the band's subsequent albums on which Farmer's rather pretentious lyrics often undermined the music on offer. The band were highly competent on instrumentals, however, such as the evocative 'Scottish Tea'. Frequent changes in personnel (Drake, Lorber and White were replaced, in turn, by Rusty Day, Andy Solomon and Greg Arama) made little difference to the Amboy Dukes' development, as the band increasingly became an outlet for Nugent's pyrotechnics. He unveiled a new line-up in 1974 with Call Of The Wild, the first of two albums recorded for Frank Zappa's DiscReet label. The guitarist then abandoned the band's name altogether and embarked on a highly successful solo career.

● ALBUMS: The Amboy Dukes (Mainstream 1967) ★★★, Journey To The Center Of The Mind (Mainstream 1968) ★★★, Migration (Mainstream 1969) ★★★, Marriage On The Rocks/Rock Bottom (Polydor 1969) ★★, Survival Of The Fittest/Live (Polydor 1971) ★★, as Ted Nugent And The Amboy Dukes Call Of The Wild (DiscReet 1974) ★★, as Ted Nugent And The Amboy Dukes Tooth, Fang And Claw (DiscReet 1975) ★★.

● COMPILATIONS: The Best Of The Original Amboy Dukes (Mainstream 1969) ★★★, Loaded For Bear: The Best Of Ted Nugent & The Amboy Dukes (Sony 1999) ★★★.

AMEN CORNER

Formed in Cardiff, Wales, in 1966, this R&B-styled septet comprised Andy Fairweather-Low (b. 8 August 1950, Ystrad Mynach, Hengoed, Wales; vocals), Derek 'Blue Weaver' (b. 3 March 1949, Cardiff, Wales; organ), Neil Jones (b. 25 March 1949, Llanbradach, Wales; guitar), Clive Taylor (b. 27 April 1949, Cardiff, Wales; bass), Alan Jones (b. 6 February 1947, Swansea, Wales; baritone sax), Mike Smith (b. 4 November 1947, Neath, Derbyshire, Wales; tenor sax) and Dennis Byron (b. 14 April 1949, Neath, Wales; drums), all of whom were veterans of local Welsh bands. The band signed to Deram Records in May 1967. After hitting the UK Top 20 with the classic 'Gin House Blues' three months later, Fairweather-Low became a pin-up and the band swiftly ploughed more commercial ground with a succession of UK hits including 'World Of Broken Hearts' (number 24), a cover version of the American Breed's 'Bend Me, Shape Me' (number 3) and 'High In The Sky' (number 6).

What the pop press failed to reveal was the intense power struggle surrounding the proprietorship of the band and the menacingly defensive tactics of their manager Don Arden. After all the drama, the band moved from Decca Records to Andrew Oldham's Immediate Records label and enjoyed their only UK number 1 with '(If Paradise Is) Half As Nice' in early 1969. Following one final UK Top 5 hit, the energetic 'Hello Suzie', they split. Ironically, their pop career ended on an anti-climactic note with the inappropriately titled Beatles cover version, 'Get Back'. Fairweather-Low, Weaver, Byron, Taylor and Neil Jones formed Fairweather, before the lead singer embarked on a solo career. Blue Weaver found his way into the Strawbs, where his keyboard work on 1972's Grave New World was particularly noteworthy. The brass section, Alan Jones and Smith, formed Judas Jump with Andy Bown.

● ALBUMS: Round Amen Corner (Deram 1968) ★★★, National Welsh Coast Live Explosive Company (Immediate 1969) ★★★, Farewell To The Real Magnificent Seven (Immediate 1969) ★★, Return Of The Magnificent Seven (Immediate 1976) ★.

● COMPILATIONS: World Of Amen Corner (Decca 1969) ★★★, Greatest Hits (Immediate 1978) ★★★, The Best Of Amen Corner (Repertoire 1999) ★★★, If Paradise Was Half As Nice: The Immediate Anthology (Sanctuary/Immediate 2000) ★★★.

AMERICAN BREED

Originally known as Gary And The Nite Lites, this Chicago-born quartet was a popular attraction throughout America's Midwest prior to achieving national fame in 1967. Gary Loizzo (b. 16 August 1945; lead vocals, guitar), Al Ciner (b. 14 May 1947; guitar, vocals), Charles Colbert (b. 29 August 1944; bass/vocals, ex-Daylighters) and Lee Graziano (b. 9 November 1943; drums) enjoyed a US Top 30 hit with 'Step Out Of Your Mind', before securing a gold disc for 'Bend Me, Shape Me'. Here the group's tight harmonies were perfectly offset by arranger Eddie Higgins' purposeful horn arrangement, but this excellent single failed to emulate its US success in Britain, where it was overshadowed by Amen Corner's opportunistic rendition. The American Breed enjoyed further success in their homeland with 'Green Light' (1968), but their amalgamation of pop, bubblegum and soul failed to retain its appeal. Kevin Murphy joined in 1968 to add keyboards and Al Ciner, who was also briefly with the band, evolved into the first version of Ask Rufus, later truncated to Rufus.

● ALBUMS: American Breed (Acta 1967) ★★, Bend Me, Shape Me (Acta 1968) ★★, Pumpkin, Powder, Scarlet And Green (1968) ★, Lonely Side Of The City (1968) ★.

● COMPILATIONS: Bend Me, Shape Me: The Best Of The American Breed (1970) ★★★.

AMES, ED

b. Ed Urick, 9 July 1927, Malden, Massachusetts, USA. Ames was a member of the very successful 50s vocal group, the Ames Brothers, who disbanded in 1959. In the early 60s he studied acting in New York. He appeared in several stage productions including *The Crucible*, *The Fantasticks* and *One Flew Over The Cuckoo's Nest* before playing an Indian, Mingo, in the popular US television series *Daniel Boone*. He returned to recording in 1964 with an album of Broadway songs for RCA Records, and one of the tracks, 'Try To Remember' (1965, from *The Fantasticks*), became the first of seven US hits for him in the 60s. His biggest solo record success came with 'My Cup Runneth Over' (from the musical *I Do! I Do!*), a US Top 10 hit in 1967. Ames also had a Top 20 hit with 'Who Will Answer?', a protest song, which seemed quite out of character for the MOR balladeer. He continued to work successfully on the supper-club circuit after the hits dried up, and settled in Los Angeles.

● ALBUMS: *The Ed Ames Album* (RCA Victor 1964) ★★★, *My Kind Of Songs* (RCA Victor 1965) ★★★, *It's A Man's World* (RCA Victor 1966) ★★★, *More I Cannot Wish You* (RCA 1966) ★★★, *My Cup Runneth Over* (RCA 1967) ★★★, *Time, Time* (RCA 1967) ★★, *When The Snow Is On The Roses* (RCA 1967) ★★★, *Who Will Answer? And Other Songs of Our Time* (RCA 1968) ★★, *Apologize* (RCA 1968) ★★, *The Hits Of Broadway And Hollywood* (RCA 1968) ★★★, *A Time For Living, A Time For Hope* (RCA 1969) ★★, *The Windmills Of Your Mind* (RCA 1969) ★★, *Love Of The Common People* (RCA 1970) ★★★, *Sing Away The World* (RCA 1970) ★★, *The Songs Of Bacharach And David* (RCA 1971) ★★★.

● COMPILATIONS: *The Best Of Ed Ames* (RCA 1969) ★★★.

AMORY KANE

b. *c.*1947, San Francisco, California, USA. Singer songwriter Kane moved to England in 1967, having previously toured Europe. He had failed an audition with Family Dogg, not through lack of ability, but because producer Steve Rowland felt he should carve a solo career. Unfortunately, this course never reached the heights his introspective, yet lyrically strong, material deserved. His debut *Memories Of Time Unwound* found few takers other than interested critics.

● ALBUMS: *Memories Of Time Unwound* (MCA 1968) ★★, *Just To Be There* (Columbia 1970) ★★.

ANDREWS, CHRIS

b. 1938, Romford, Essex, England. Originally lead singer in the early 60s band Chris Ravel And The Ravers, Andrews found greater success as a songwriter. Signed by manager Eve Taylor, he composed hits for her artists Adam Faith ('The First Time', 'We Are In Love', 'If He Tells

Me', 'I Love Being In Love With You', 'Stop Feeling Sorry For Yourself', 'Someone's Taken Maria Away') and Sandie Shaw ('Girl Don't Come', 'Long Live Love' and 'Message Understood'). He achieved UK chart success in his own right during 1965-66 with two catchy, upbeat numbers, 'Yesterday Man' (number 3) and 'To Whom It Concerns' (number 13). Although he occasionally recorded additional solo singles, no further hits were forthcoming. He subsequently continued his career as a songwriter.

● ALBUMS: *Yesterday Man* (Decca 1965) ★★.

● COMPILATIONS: *20 Golden Pieces* (Bulldog 1987) ★★, *Swinging Sixties Hit Man: The Definitive Anthology* (Repertoire 1996) ★★★.

ANDROMEDA

Andromeda evolved from the final line-up of UK flower-power pop group the Attack. John Cann (guitar, vocals), Richard Sherman (vocals), Roger Deane (bass) and Keith Hodge (drums) provided Andromeda's first incarnation, which dissolved within weeks of formation. Mick Hawksworth (bass, vocals) and Ian McClane (drums, vocals) then joined Cann in the line-up that recorded for RCA Records. Although their sole album has become a cherished example of UK progressive rock, it was not a success and the trio broke up in 1970 when the guitarist joined Atomic Rooster. Hawksworth subsequently formed the much-lauded Fuzzy Duck and collaborated with Matthew Fisher (ex-Procol Harum) on his solo album *Journey's End*. The bassist latterly appeared in Ten Years Later, a half-hearted conglomeration led by former Ten Years After guitarist Alvin Lee.

● ALBUMS: *Andromeda* (RCA 1969) ★★★.

● COMPILATIONS: *Anthology 1966-1969* (Kissing Spell 1995) ★★★, *Definitive Collection* (Angel Air 2000) ★★★.

ANDWELLA'S DREAM

Formed in Northern Ireland and originally known as Method, this melodic rock band initially comprised Dave Lewis (guitar, keyboards, vocals), Nigel Smith (bass, vocals) and Gordon Barton (drums). They took the name Andwella's Dream upon moving to London, England, in 1968. *Love And Poetry* featured the assistance of jazz musician Bob Downes (saxophone, flute). This impressive set captured the transformation from psychedelic to progressive styles, notably on 'The Day Grew Longer' and 'Sunday', which featured excellent guitar passages. Lewis, who composed all of the material, then recorded a privately pressed album on Ax Records in 1970. *The Songs Of Dave Lewis* included new versions of two songs from *Love And Poetry*, as well as other impressive selections featuring simple piano and guitar accompaniment. Dave McDougall joined the group for *World's End*, by which time they were known simply as Andwella. Here the tracks were more mainstream, with orthodox brass and string arrangements replacing their previous inventiveness. Dave Struthers (bass, vocals) and Jack McCulloch (drums, ex-Thunderclap Newman) augmented Andwella for *People's People*, which echoed the style of its predecessor. Unable to maintain their early promise, Andwella split up in 1972.

● ALBUMS: *Love And Poetry* (Columbia 1968) ★★★, *World's End* (Reflection 1970) ★★, *People's People* (Reflection 1971) ★★.

ANIMALS

This leading UK R&B band was formed in Newcastle-upon-Tyne, England, in 1963, when vocalist Eric Burdon (b. 11 May 1941, Walker, Newcastle-upon-Tyne, Tyne & Wear, England), joined local R&B band the Alan Price Combo. The Animals comprised Alan Price (b. 19 April 1941, Fairfield, Co. Durham, England; piano), Hilton Valentine (b. 22 May 1943, North Shields, Tyne And Wear, England; guitar), John Steel (b. 4 February 1941, Gateshead, Co. Durham, England; drums) and Chas Chandler (b. Bryan James Chandler, 18 December 1938, Heaton, Tyne And Wear, England, d. 17 July 1996; bass). Valentine had previously played with the Gamblers, while Burdon had played trombone, together with Steel on trumpet, in college jazz bands.

With their raucous and exciting stage act, the Animals quickly attracted the attention of several music business entrepreneurs. R&B legend Graham Bond recommended them to his manager Ronan O'Rahilly. The band became stars at the legendary Club A-Go-Go in Newcastle. On one occasion they performed with Sonny Boy 'Rice Miller' Williamson (an album of this explosive gig was released many years later). By the end of 1963 they had moved to London and became an integral part of the fast-burgeoning club scene. After signing with producer Mickie Most, they debuted with the energetic 'Baby Let Me Take You Home' (a version of Eric Von Schmidt's blues standard, 'Baby Let Me Follow You Down'), which became a respectable hit. Their next release was to be both controversial and memorable. This four-and-a-half-minute pop song, about a New Orleans brothel, was at first resisted by their record company Columbia Records as being too long for radio play. Upon release, the record, Josh White's 'The House Of The Rising Sun', leapt to the top of the charts all over the world, and eventually sold several million copies. The combination of Valentine's now legendary but simplistic guitar introduction and Price's shrill organ complemented Burdon's remarkably mature and bloodcurdling vocal.

Over the next two years the Animals had seven further substantial hits on both sides of the Atlantic. Their memorable and dramatic version of a song popularized by Nina Simone, 'Don't Let Me Be Misunderstood', featured the autobiographical 'Club A-Go-Go' on the b-side. Their choice of material was exemplary and many of their hits featured thought-provoking lyrics, from the angst-ridden 'I'm Crying' to the frustration and urban despair of Cynthia Weil and Barry Mann's 'We Gotta Get Out Of This Place'. Their albums contained stirring renditions of classics by Chuck Berry, Sam Cooke, Jimmy Reed and Burdon's hero, Ray Charles. During this time Price departed (allegedly suffering from a fear of flying), and was replaced by Dave Rowberry from the Mike Cotton Sound. Burdon maintains that Price's departure was because he had taken ownership of the lucrative publishing rights to 'The House Of The Rising Sun' and was therefore financially secure. Steel left in 1966, replaced by Nashville Teens drummer Barry Jenkins (b. 22 December 1944, Leicester, England). The new band found success with the brilliant 'It's My Life' and the adventurous 'Inside Looking Out'.

By 1967 Burdon and Valentine had become totally immersed in psychedelia, both musically and chemically. This alienated them from the rest of the band (who preferred good old-fashioned alcohol), and led to its disintegration. Chandler went on to discover and manage the Jimi Hendrix Experience. Burdon, however, retained the name and immediately re-emerged as Eric Burdon And The New Animals. They found greater favour in the USA where they were domiciled, and courted the west coast sound and school of bands from that period. 'San Franciscan Nights' perfectly echoed the moment, with the lyrics: 'Strobe lights beam creates dreams, walls move, minds do too, on a warm San Franciscan night'. Burdon further encapsulated his reverence in the song 'Monterey', cleverly eulogizing the epic Monterey Pop Festival of 1967. A number of interesting musicians passed through various line-ups of the New Animals, notably John Weider, Vic Briggs (formerly of Steam Packet), Danny McCulloch, Zoot Money and future Police guitarist Andy Summers.

The tamed Burdon was now writing introspective and thought-provoking lyrics, although many of his fans found it difficult to take the former raver seriously. Long improvisational pieces began to appear in their live performances, with watered-down versions to be found on the albums *Winds Of Change*, *The Twain Shall Meet*, *Everyone Of Us* and *Love Is*. The group eventually disbanded at the end of 1968. The original line-up regrouped twice, in 1977 and 1983, but on both occasions new albums were released to an indifferent public. For the 1983 revival tour it was reported that Valentine had become so rusty on the guitar that a lead guitarist was recruited. Valentine and Steel continue to gig on the pub circuit as Animals II.

The Animals' contribution to the 60s was considerable and at times their popularity threatened even the Beatles and Rolling Stones. 'The House Of The Rising Sun' gave them musical immortality, and will no doubt continue to be re-released at regular intervals. It is surprising therefore that in the new millennium their standing is noticeably low.

● ALBUMS: *The Animals* (Columbia 1964) ★★★★, *The Animals On Tour* (MGM 1965) ★★★, *Animal Tracks* (Columbia 1965) ★★★, *Most Of The Animals* (Columbia 1966) ★★★★, *Animalization* (MGM 1966) ★★★, *Animalisms* (Decca 1966) ★★★, *Eric Is Here* (MGM 1967) ★★★, *Winds Of Change* (MGM 1967) ★★★, *The Twain Shall Meet* (MGM 1968) ★★★, *Everyone Of Us* (MGM 1968) ★★★, *Love Is* (MGM 1968) ★★★, *In Concert From Newcastle* (DJM 1976) ★★, *Before We Were Rudely Interrupted* (United Artists 1977) ★, *The Ark* (I.R.S. 1983) ★, *Rip It To Shreds – The Animals Greatest Hits Live!* (I.R.S. 1984) ★★, *The Animals With Sonny Boy Williamson* (Decal/Charly 1988) ★★★.

● COMPILATIONS: *The Best Of The Animals* (MGM 1966) ★★★, *The Best Of Eric Burdon And The Animals Volume 2* (MGM 1967) ★★★, *The Greatest Hits Of Eric Burdon And The Animals* (MGM 1969) ★★★, *The EP Collection* (See For Miles 1988) ★★★★, *The Complete Animals* (EMI 1990) ★★★★, *Trackin' The Hits* (Decal/Charly 1990) ★★★, *The Very Best Of The Animals* (Spectrum 1998) ★★★, as Eric Burdon And The New Animals *Psychedelic World* (Edsel 2001) ★★★.

● FURTHER READING: *I Used To Be An Animal But I'm All Right Now*, Eric Burdon. *Wild Animals*, Andy Blackford. *The Last Poet: The Story Of Eric Burdon*, Jeff Kent. *Good Times: The Ultimate Eric Burdon*, Dionisio Castello. *Animal Tracks: The Story Of The Animals*, Sean Egan.

● FILMS: *Get Yourself A College Girl* (1964), *It's A Bikini World* (1967).

ANNETTE

b. Annette Funicello, 22 October 1942, Utica, New York, USA. Initially billed as 'Annette', this singer/actress rose to fame under the aegis of the Walt Disney organization. A one-time Mouseketeer – the last of the original group who appeared on *The Mickey Mouse Club* – she enjoyed several hit singles between 1959 and 1961 which included two US Top 10 entries, 'Tall Paul' and 'O Dio Mio', as well as the enduring 'Pineapple Princess'. During the 60s Annette starred alongside Frankie Avalon in a series of 'quickie' beach films, including *Beach Party*, *Bikini Beach* (both 1964) and *How To Stuff A Wild Bikini* (1965), which combined slim plots, teenage themes and cameos from pop stars. *The Monkey's Uncle* (1964) drew its appeal from an appearance by the Beach Boys and musical contributions from their leader, Brian Wilson. The latter assisted songwriter/producer Gary Usher in creating material for *Muscle Beach Party*, Annette's strongest album, which also featured back-up from the all-female group the

Honeys. She later appeared in the Monkees' cult film *Head* (1968), but subsequently devoted more time to her growing family, making occasional personal appearances, television commercials, and guest shots in series such as *Hondo*, *Love – American Style*, *Fantasy Island*, *The Love Boat*, *Full House*, and *Frasier*. In 1987 she and Avalon returned to the big screen in *Back To The Beach*, an amusing spoof of their earlier successes together. Five years later, after revealing that she had been fighting multiple sclerosis, the actress formed The Annette Funicello Teddy Bear Company and introduced the perfume 'Cello, by Annette'. A percentage of the profits from the latter line go to the Annette Funicello Research Fund for Neurological Diseases. The tribute programme, *A Dream Is A Wish Your Heart Makes: The Annette Funicello Story*, aired on US television in 1995.

● ALBUMS: *Annette* (Buena Vista 1959) ★★, *Songs From Annette And Other Walt Disney Serials* (Mickey Mouse 1959) ★, *Annette Sings Anka* (Buena Vista 1960) ★, *Italiannette* (Buena Vista 1960) ★, *Hawaiiannette* (Buena Vista 1960) ★, *Dance Annette* (Buena Vista 1961) ★, *The Parent Trap* (Buena Vista 1961) ★, *Babes In Toyland* (Buena Vista 1961) ★, *The Story Of My Teens* (Buena Vista 1962) ★, *Teen Street* (Buena Vista 1962) ★, *Muscle Beach Party* (Buena Vista 1963) ★★★, *Annette's Beach Party* (Buena Vista 1963) ★★, *Annette On Campus* (Buena Vista 1964) ★, *Annette At Bikini Beach* (Buena Vista 1964) ★, *Pajama Party* (Buena Vista 1964) ★, *Annette Sings Golden Surfin' Hits,* (Buena Vista 1964) ★, *Something Borrowed, Something Blue* (Buena Vista 1964) ★, *Walt Disney's Wonderful World Of Color* (Disneyland 1964) ★, *The Beast Of Broadway* (Disneyland 1965) ★, *Tubby The Tuba And Other Songs About Music* (Disneyland 1966) ★, *State And College Songs* (Disneyland 1967) ★, *Thunder Alley* (Sidewalk 1967) ★, *Annette Funicello* (Buena Vista 1972) ★, *Annette: A Musical Reunion With America's Girl Next Door* 2-CD set (Walt Disney 1993) ★★★.

● FILMS: *Annette* (1958), *The Shaggy Dog* (1959), *Babes In Toyland* (1961), *Beach Party* (1963), *Pajama Party* (1964), *Muscle Beach Party* (1964), *Bikini Beach* (1964), *The Misadventures Of Merlin Jones* (1964), *How To Stuff A Wild Bikini* (1965), *Beach Blanket Bingo* (1965), *Ski Party* cameo (1965), *Dr. Goldfoot And The Bikini Machine* guest (1965), *The Monkey's Uncle* (1965), *Fireball 500* (1966), *Thunder Alley* (1967), *Head* (1968), *Back To The Beach* (1987), *Troop Beverly Hills* as herself (1989).

ANTHONY, RICHARD

b. Richard Anthony Bush, 13 January 1938, Cairo, Egypt. Anthony forsook higher education in Paris to become a singer but was obliged to make ends meet with a variety of jobs and as a session saxophonist. He signed to Pathe-Marconi in 1958, but his debut single, 'La Rue

Des Coeurs Perdus', fared poorly. However, he became popular with his native reproductions of US smashes such as Buddy Holly's 'Peggy Sue' and Lloyd Price's 'Personality'. He came into his own, however, during the twist craze with 'C'est Ma Fête' ('It's My Party'), and an untranslated 'Let's Twist Again' established him as a rival to Johnny Halliday (the Gallic 'answer' to Elvis Presley). After a million-selling French cover version of Peter, Paul And Mary's '500 Miles Away From Home', he secured a UK chart entry in 1963 with 'Walking Alone' and reached the Top 20 with 'If I Loved You'. His admirable revival of the Everly Brothers' 'Crying In The Rain' narrowly missed the charts. Concentration on this market adversely affected his domestic standing, until 1966's 'Fille Sauvage' (the Rolling Stones' 'Ruby Tuesday') brought him in from the cold. Both on tour and in the studio, he was backed for some time by the Roulettes, who impressed him with their playing on a French version of 'Concrete And Clay'. Anthony's career continued its ups and downs and his total record sales exceeded 12 million.

● ALBUMS: *Disque D'Or* (70s) ★★★.

AORTA

Formed in Chicago, Illinois, USA, in 1967, Aorta initially consisted of Jim Donlinger (guitar, vocals), Jim Nyholt (piano, organ), Dan Hoagland (tenor saxophone), Bobby Jones (bass, vocals) and William Herman (drums). In February 1968, Hoagland left to join the Chicago Transit Authority, later known as Chicago. The remaining quartet was then signed to the local Dunwich production company who leased Aorta's first single, 'The Shape Of Things To Come', to Atlantic Records. The song, which provided the theme to the movie *Wild In The Streets*, was originally recorded by Max Frost And The Troopers. *Aorta* revealed a band fusing rock textures with melody, drawing comparisons with fellow Chicagoans H.P. Lovecraft. This stylish blend was equally apparent on the now dated *Aorta 2*, despite the defections of Herman, who joined the New Colony Six, and Jones. Michael Been (bass, guitar, vocals) and Tom Donlinger (drums) were featured on this second selection, but Aorta broke up soon after its release. Unsurprisingly, given their common musical styles, Jim Donlinger and Been quickly resurfaced in a revamped H.P. Lovecraft, now known simply as Lovecraft. Been formed several subsequent bands and during the 80s led the Call.

● ALBUMS: *Aorta* (Columbia 1969) ★★, *Aorta 2* (Happy Tiger 1970) ★★.

APHRODITE'S CHILD

Formed in Greece during 1967, the Papathanassiou Set comprised Demis Roussos (b. Artemios Ventouris Roussos, 15 June 1946, Alexandria, Egypt; vocals), Vangelis

Papathanassiou (b. Evanghelos Odyssey Papathanassiou, 29 March 1943, Volos, Greece; keyboards), Anargyros 'Silver' Koulouris (guitar) and Lucas Sideras (b. 5 December 1944, Athens, Greece; drums). After recording two demos for the Greek branch of Philips Records, the group was invited to record an album in England. Minus Koulouris, who was obliged to stay in Greece to complete military service, they set off for London but were trapped in Paris by a transport strike. However, the local Philips producer Pierre Sbarro recorded the trio's adaptation of Johann Pachelbel's baroque piece 'Canon'. Renamed Aphrodite's Child, they enjoyed a massive European hit with this track, 'Rain And Tears', a haunting ballad memorable for Roussos' nasal, almost sobbing, falsetto. In France, the single spent 14 weeks at the top of the charts. The single made little impression in the UK, but in Europe their subsequent releases, including 'I Want To Live' and 'Let Me Love, Let Me Live', were massive hits. The group did court a cultish popularity in Britain, particularly in the wake of a second album, *It's Five O'Clock*.

Following the album's release, Papathanassiou began to spend more time in the studio writing television and film scores, exploring new sounds on the synthesizer. He took control of the band's final release, 1972's *666: The Apocalypse Of John*, which saw the return of original guitarist Koulouris. A double set based around *The Book Of Revelations*, the album was applauded for its ambition and execution. 'Break' almost became a hit later that year, but by then the band had gone their separate ways. Roussos subsequently found international fame as a purveyor of sweet, MOR material while Papathanassiou achieved notable solo success under the name of Vangelis. His instrumental and compositional dexterity reached its zenith with the soundtrack to the Oscar-winning UK film, *Chariots Of Fire*.

● ALBUMS: *End Of The World/Rain And Tears* (Mercury 1968) ★★, *It's Five O'Clock* (Mercury 1969) ★★, *666: The Apocalypse Of John* (Vertigo 1972) ★★★.

● COMPILATIONS: *Rain And Tears: The Best Of Aphrodite's Child* (Philips 1975) ★★★, *Greatest Hits* (Mercury 1981) ★★★, *The Complete Collection* (Mercury 1996) ★★★.

APPLEJACKS

Formed in Solihull, West Midlands, this early 60s UK pop group comprised Martin Baggott (b. 20 October 1947, Birmingham, England; guitar), Philip Cash (b. 9 October 1947; guitar), Megan Davies (b. 25 March 1944, Sheffield, Yorkshire, England; bass), Don Gould (b. 23 March 1947; organ), Al Jackson (b. 21 April 1945; vocals) and Gerry Freeman (b. 24 May 1947, Solihull, England; drums). Signed by Decca A&R representative Mike Smith, they found Top 10 UK chart success in 1964 with the memorable

'Tell Me When'. The grand follow-up, 'Like Dreamers Do', was a song taken from the famous John Lennon and Paul McCartney Decca audition tape. It barely scraped the Top 20 in spite of its pedigree and the next single, 'Three Little Words', did no better. Always capable of finding a first-class demo, the group turned to the Kinks' catalogue for Ray Davies's moody 'I Go To Sleep'. Its failure effectively signalled the Applejacks' doom and they duly returned to the northern club scene.

● ALBUMS: *The Applejacks* (Decca 1964) ★★.
● COMPILATIONS: *Tell Me When* (Deram 1990) ★★.

APPLETREE THEATRE

Brothers John and Terence Boylan created this highly imaginative unit in 1968. Their sole release, *Playback*, was completed with the aid of several session musicians, including Eric Gale, Chuck Rainey and Larry Coryell. An original, and indeed pioneering, concept album, the set balanced memorable songs with experimental sound collages, wherein the duo's soft, ethereal harmony work enhanced a spirit of adventure. Although *Playback* became a cult favourite, it was not a commercial success and its protagonists later embarked on contrasting solo careers. Terry Boylan completed a series of well-crafted albums, the latter of which were redolent of Jackson Browne, while John became a highly respected producer for the Eagles, Linda Ronstadt and, in 1991, for the cartoon 'group', the Simpsons.

● ALBUMS: *Playback* (Verve Forecast 1968) ★★★.

ARCADIUM

Miguel Sergides (vocals, guitar), Robert Ellwood (vocals, guitar), Alan Ellwood (keyboards, vocals), Graham Best (bass, vocals) and John Albert Parker (drums) formed this short-lived, but inventive, group, active in 1969. *Arcadium (Breathe Awhile)*, released on Middle Earth Records, captured their highly original style, particularly on 'I'm On My Way', the impressive opening track, which features inspired, emotional guitarwork. The remainder of the set, all of which was composed by Sergides, combines introspective lyrics with densely packed arrangements, resulting in a sense of tense claustrophobia. Despite undoubted promise, Arcadium split soon after the album's release.

● ALBUMS: *Arcadium (Breathe Awhile)* (Middle Earth 1969) ★★.

ARCHIES

Created for mass consumption by bubblegum-pop genius Don Kirshner (the man who gave us the Monkees), the Archies were the ultimate manufactured pop group. They existed on television and on their record sleeves as pure animations, based on the comic book characters of the same name. The voices behind the singing cartoon characters were vocalists Ron Dante (b. Carmine Granito, 22 August 1945, Staten Island, New York, USA), Toni Wine and Andy Kim, who were later called upon for touring purposes. Kirshner was astute enough to employ solid commercial writers of some standing, including Jeff Barry and Ellie Greenwich. After several minor successes, the group released one of the biggest-selling singles in the history of RCA Records. 'Sugar Sugar' became a transatlantic number 1, hogging the top spot in Britain for over two months. Back in the USA, where the television series was extremely popular, the group enjoyed another Top 10 hit with 'Jingle Jangle' before suffering the sharp plunge into obscurity common to animated creations. Aside from the numerous compilation releases, their albums have been repackaged several times under different titles.

● ALBUMS: *The Archies* (Calendar 1968) ★★★, *Everything's Archie* (Calendar 1969) ★, *Jingle Jangle* (Kirshner 1969) ★, *Sunshine* (Kirshner 1970) ★, *This Is Love* (Kirshner 1971) ★.
● COMPILATIONS: *The Archies' Greatest Hits* (Kirshner 1970) ★★★, *Sugar, Sugar ...* (Repertoire 1999) ★★★.

ARDEN, DON

b. Harry Levy, January 1926, Manchester, England. After attending the Royal College of Music as a singer, Levy changed his name to Arden in 1944. He worked as a compere/comedian on the music-hall circuit and switched to promotion during the 50s. As well as bringing acts such as Billy Eckstine and Eddie Fisher to Britain, Arden was also heavily involved in rock 'n' roll. During 1959, he compered Gene Vincent's first UK tour and went on to manage the uproarious Virginian. Their rocky association lasted until 1965, when they parted amid much acrimony. By that time, Arden was moving away from rock 'n' roll and taking advantage of the beat group scene. After promoting the Rolling Stones during 1963, he became agent for the Animals and claims to have introduced them to producer Mickie Most. Arden lost the band following a fracas with their controversial manager Mike Jeffrey. Undeterred, he wasted no time in signing the Nashville Teens. Several hits followed, but the outfit failed to sustain their original promise.

A far more lucrative acquisition for Arden was the Small Faces. He later claimed to have helped their first single 'What'cha Gonna Do About It' into the UK Top 20, along with other singles from his short-lived Contemporary Records roster. Among these was his own recording of 'Sunrise, Sunset', which failed to reach the Top 50. After a series of regular hits with the Small Faces, including the chart-topping 'All Or Nothing', which Arden produced, the entrepreneur lost the band to his managerial rival Andrew Oldham. Arden continued to thrive with his agency

Galaxy Entertainments, whose roster included such acts as the Applejacks, the Action, the Attack, Neil Christian, the Fairytale and the Skatellites. His next major find was Amen Corner, whose management he inherited from agent Ron King. By this time Arden was already notorious as an intimidating character and, as during his association with the Small Faces, threats against rival poaching managers were commonplace. Amid the drama, Arden lost the band and a similar fate befell his next find, Skip Bifferty. The 60s ended for Arden with the inheritance of the celebrated Move, but this proved another unhappy association involving a serious dispute with manager Peter Walsh.

By the early 70s, Arden at last found a near perfect manager/artist relationship with the Electric Light Orchestra and various offshoots such as Roy Wood's Wizzard. With the formation of Jet Records, Arden increasingly spent time in the USA and found his niche in stadium rock. Among the acts he oversaw in the 70s were Black Sabbath, Ozzy Osbourne (who married his daughter, Sharon) Lynsey De Paul and Air Supply. Despite his many successes as a promoter and manager, Arden's career has been punctuated by countless legal battles (he even attempted to sue his son-in-law over Black Sabbath's Live Aid appearance) and tales of intimidation and alleged violence. In 1987 he stood trial at the Old Bailey for allegedly falsely imprisoning and blackmailing his own accountant. The jury found him not guilty and he left the court a free man, after which he set about reviving his record label Jet.

● FURTHER READING: *Starmakers And Svengalis - The History Of British Pop Management*, Johnny Rogan.

ARDLEY, NEIL

b. 26 May 1937, Carshalton, Surrey, England. After graduating from Bristol University, Ardley studied composition and arranging under Raymond Premru and Bill Russo. In the mid- to late 60s he led the New Jazz Orchestra, and throughout the 70s continued to lead his own orchestra for recording dates, concerts and occasional tours. During this time he was able to impart his Gil Evans and Duke Ellington influences to a more contemporary audience. His groups included important musicians such as Harry Beckett, Ian Carr, Mike Gibbs, Don Rendell and Barbara Thompson. Ardley composed much of the music played by his orchestras but his sidemen were also encouraged to write. He has also written for television and is the author of numerous books on a wide range of subjects including music and several of the sciences. A much lower musical profile in recent years has resulted in his work being neglected, but, with Mike Gibbs and Mike Westbrook, he still remains an important figure in the development of 'progressive' orchestrated jazz in the 60s.

● ALBUMS: *Western Reunion* (Decca 1965) ★★★, *Le Déjeuner Sur L'Herbe* (Verve 1968) ★★★★, *The Greek Variations* (Columbia 1969) ★★★★, *A Symphony Of Amaranths* (Regal Zonophone 1971) ★★★, *Will Power* (Argo 1974) ★★★, *Kaleidoscope Of Rainbows* (Gull 1975) ★★★★, *The Harmony Of The Spheres* (Decca 1978) ★★★★.

AREA CODE 615

After Bob Dylan's *Nashville Skyline* in 1969, it became fashionable to record in Nashville. Hence, New York record producer Elliot Mazer went to Nashville and took four noted sessionmen – Kenneth Buttrey (drums), David Briggs (keyboards), Mac Gayden (guitar) and Norbert Putnam (bass) – into a studio to record some instrumentals. Mazer felt that the sessions needed more of a country feel so he then added Charlie McCoy (b. 28 March 1941, Oak Hill, West Virginia, USA; harmonica), Wayne Moss (guitar), Ken Lauber (piano), Weldon Myrick (steel guitar), Buddy Spicher (fiddle) and Bobby Thompson (banjo). These leading session musicians began recording in their own right following interest generated by *Nashville Skyline*, on which McCoy and Buttrey appeared. Area Code 615 was never intended as a permanent vehicle. The sessions came alive when Spicher and Thompson developed a bluegrass arrangement of 'Hey Jude', and the concept of recording familiar tunes, with the lead instruments playing country and the rhythm section playing rock 'n' roll, was born. They named themselves Area Code 615 after the telephone code for Nashville. McCoy and Buttrey alone developed 'Stone Fox Chase', which became the theme for BBC Television's long-running rock programme *The Old Grey Whistle Test*. The musicians returned to individual session work, although Moss, Gayden, Buttrey, and occasionally McCoy worked as Barefoot Jerry.

● ALBUMS: *Area Code 615* (Polydor 1969) ★★★★, *Trip In The Country* (Polydor 1970) ★★★.

ARNOLD, P.P.

b. Patricia Arnold, 1946, Los Angeles, California, USA. This former singer in a church choir and talented session singer first came to notice in 1966 as a member of Ike And Tina Turner's backing group, the Ikettes. Relocating to England, she was signed to Andrew Loog Oldham's Immediate Records label, and was backed on tour by the Nice. Her exceptional version of the Cat Stevens ballad 'The First Cut Is The Deepest', was a UK Top 20 hit in 1967 and she enjoyed a second major hit the following year with Chip Taylor's 'Angel Of The Morning', which was arranged by future Led Zeppelin bassist John Paul Jones. Highly regarded among her musical peers for the sheer power and clarity of her voice, her first two albums were produced by Mick Jagger (the second in conjunction with Steve Marriott). Arnold repaid

Marriott's production work by contributing some powerful vocals to the Small Faces' hit, 'Tin Soldier'. Never quite hitting the big time, Arnold increasingly concentrated on acting, appearing in such musicals as Jack Good's *Catch My Soul*, Tim Rice and Andrew Lloyd Webber's *Jesus Christ Superstar* and Lloyd Webber's *Starlight Express*. A session singer for many artists ranging from Dr. John, Roger Waters to Nils Lofgren and Freddie King, she returned to the UK charts in 1989, fronting the Beatmasters on 'Burn It Up', and in 1998 with retro-popsters Ocean Colour Scene. Recent session work includes albums with Paul Weller and Oasis.
● ALBUMS: *First Lady Of Immediate* (Immediate 1967) ★★★, *Kafunta* (Immediate 1968) ★★.
● COMPILATIONS: *Greatest Hits* (Immediate 1978) ★★, *The P.P. Arnold Collection* (See For Miles 1988) ★★★, *P.P. Arnold's Greatest Hits* (Castle 1998) ★★★, *The Best Of P.P. Arnold* (Repertoire 1999) ★★★, *The First Cut* (Immediate 2001) ★★★.
● FILMS: *Pop Pirates* (1984).

ARS NOVA

This unusual, but enchanting, sextet featured former students from New York's Mannes College Of Music, at the time one of America's finest conservatories. The ensemble comprised Wyatt Day (guitar, keyboards, vocals), Jon Pierson (trombone, vocals), Bill Folwell (trumpet, bass, vocals), Jonathan Raskin (bass, vocals, guitar), Giovanni Papalia (guitar) and Maury Baker (percussion, vocals). They were discovered by producer Paul A. Rothschild, who signed the group to Elektra Records, declaring them 'the most exciting thing since the Doors'. Ars Nova's debut album was a curious hybrid of medieval styles and contemporary rock. Although some of the results were lightweight, others, including 'Pavan For My Lady' and 'I Wrapped Her In Ribbons (After Ibiza)', were genuinely moving. However, this line-up fell apart following a disastrous performance at the Fillmore East and the group was dropped by its label. Pierson and Day secured a replacement contract and found new colleagues in Sam Brown (guitar), Warren Bernhardt (keyboards), Jimmy Owens (trumpet), Art Keonig (bass) and Joe Hunt (drums). A major piece in *Life* magazine celebrated their inventiveness, but a second collection, *Sunshine And Shadows*, lacked the inspiration of its predecessor and Ars Nova broke up soon after its release.
● ALBUMS: *Ars Nova* (Elektra 1968) ★★, *Sunshine And Shadows* (Elektra 1969) ★.

ART

Although formed in London, England, in 1967, the origins of this excellent act lay in a Carlisle-based R&B band, the VIPs, who recorded three singles before December 1966. When three founding members then left the line-up, Mike Harrison (b. 3 September 1945, Carlisle,

Cumberland, England; vocals) and Greg Ridley (b. 23 October 1947, Cumberland, England; bass) regrouped the VIPs around ex-Deep Feeling and ex-Hellions member Luther Grosvenor (b. 23 December 1949, Evesham, Worcestershire, England; guitar), Mike Kellie (b. 24 March 1947, Birmingham, England; drums) and Keith Emerson (b. 1 November 1944, Todmorden, Lancashire, England; keyboards). Emerson left to found the Nice following the release of 'Straight Down To The Bottom' and a French-only EP, after which the remaining quartet rechristened themselves Art. Aided by maverick producer Guy Stevens, they completed *Supernatural Fairy Tales*, which blended R&B, pop and psychedelia in a genuinely innovatory manner. Harrison's gritty vocals and Grosvenor's blistering guitar work are particularly of merit. Stevens was also involved in a concurrent project, Hapshash And The Coloured Coat, which featured designers Michael English and Nigel Weymouth, who were responsible for *Supernatural Fairy Tales'* distinctive sleeve. Reciprocally, the band supplied accompaniment to the trio's experimental album debut. Stevens was also instrumental in suggesting Art required another keyboard player, and, having added US singer Gary Wright (b. 26 April 1945, Englewood, New Jersey, USA) to the line-up, the band became known as Spooky Tooth.
● ALBUMS: *Supernatural Fairy Tales* (Island 1967) ★★.

ARTWOODS

The collectability of the Artwoods' rare recorded works has increased considerably over the past three decades. This competent UK-based R&B band had a brief moment of glory during the early 60s UK beat group club scene. The band were led by Arthur 'Art' Wood (b. 7 July 1935, Middlesex, England; vocals/harmonica), the older brother of Ron Wood. The line-up was completed by Keef Hartley (b. 8 March 1944, Preston, Lancashire, England; drums), Jon Lord (b. 9 June 1941, Leicester, Leicestershire, England; organ), Derek Griffiths (guitar) and Malcolm Pool (bass). Their only album contained workmanlike cover versions of regular R&B songs such as 'Can You Hear Me?' and 'If You've Got To Make A Fool Of Somebody', alongside bolder arrangements, including Jimmy Smith's 'Walk On The Wild Side'. Lord demonstrated the seeds of what became a powerful organ style with Deep Purple. Hartley, a technically brilliant drummer, found limited success with John Mayall and his own unit, the Keef Hartley Band. Leader Wood disappeared from the music world.
● ALBUMS: *Art Gallery* (Decca 1965) ★★★.
● COMPILATIONS: *The Artwoods* (Spark 1973) ★★★, *100 Oxford Street* (Edsel 1983) ★★★.

ASSOCIATION

One of the most attractive pop/psychedelic harmony bands of the mid-60s, the Association was formed by Gary Alexander (lead vocals), Russ Giguere (vocals, guitar), Brian Cole (d. 2 August 1972; vocals, bass), Jim Yester (vocals, guitar), Ted Bluechel (drums) and Terry Kirkman (keyboards). After releasing two singles on small labels, 'Babe I'm Gonna Leave You' and a folk rock version of Bob Dylan's 'One Too Many Mornings', they found success with Tandyn Almer's evocative 'Along Comes Mary'. Its ascent to number 7 in the US charts in June 1966 coincided with allegations that it was a drugs song. The Association's image was ambiguous: genuinely psychedelic in spirit, they also sang ballads and appeared in smart suits. With their strong line-up of singers/composers, they largely wrote their own material for albums. Terry Kirkman gave them a US number 1 single in August with 'Cherish', while their debut album, *And Then ... Along Comes*, produced by Curt Boettcher, displayed their harmonic talent to extraordinary effect. Singles success followed with another US chart-topper, 'Windy' (May 1967), and a number 2 with 'Never My Love' (August 1967).

Their smooth balladeering was consistently balanced by aberrations such as the genuinely weird 'Pandora's Golden Heebie Jeebies', which the band released as a follow-up single to 'Cherish'. Never candidates for the hip elite, the band failed to attract a devoted following and by the late 60s their sales were dwindling, with 'Everything That Touches You' (number 10, February 1968) their last Top 20 single. Gary Alexander left briefly for a trip to India and returned with a new name, 'Jules', while their long-standing producer Jerry Yester, brother of Jim, replaced Zal Yanovsky in the Lovin' Spoonful. Soldiering on, the Association continued to release accomplished singles such as 'Time For Livin'', but soon lost ground and major label status. They released a soundtrack for the movie *Goodbye Columbus* in 1969. Giguere was replaced by keyboard player Richard Thompson the following year. A reasonable 'comeback' album, *Waterbeds In Trinidad* (1972), brought new hope, but the death of founder-member Brian Coles from drug abuse accelerated their eventual move onto the revivalist circuit.

● ALBUMS: *And Then ... Along Comes The Association* (Valiant 1966) ★★★★, *Renaissance* (Valiant 1967) ★★, *Insight Out* (Warners 1967) ★★, *Birthday* (Warners 1968) ★★, *The Association* (Warners 1969) ★★, *Live* (Warners 1970) ★, *Stop Your Motor* (Warners 1971) ★★, *Waterbeds In Trinidad* (Columbia 1972) ★★. Solo: Russ Giguere *Hexagram II* (Warners 1971) ★★.

● COMPILATIONS: *Greatest Hits* (Warners 1968) ★★★★, *Golden Heebie Jeebies* (Edsel 1988) ★★★, *Ten Best* (Cleopatra 2000) ★★★.

ASYLUM CHOIR

This short-lived duo comprised Leon Russell (b. 2 April 1941, Lawton, Oklahoma, USA; piano, vocals) and Marc Benno (b. Benny Darron, 1 July 1947, Dallas, Texas, USA; guitar). Although the latter was relatively unknown, Russell was an established figure in the Los Angeles session hierarchy through his work with disparate figures such as Phil Spector, the Byrds, Frank Sinatra, Herb Alpert and Gary Lewis And The Playboys. *Look Inside The Asylum Choir* received enthusiastic reviews, but when its marriage of psychedelia and white R&B was not a commercial success, the duo's label refused to issue a follow-up album. Russell later purchased the master tape and released the set on his own label, Shelter Records, in the wake of his fame as a solo act. Benno also embarked on an independent career, playing bass on the Doors' *L.A. Woman* and releasing several unexceptional solo albums.

● ALBUMS: *Look Inside The Asylum Choir* (Mercury 1968) ★★★, *Asylum Choir II* (Shelter 1971) ★★.

ATKINS, CHET

b. Chester Burton Atkins, 20 June 1924, Luttrell, Tennessee, USA, d. 30 June 2001, Nashville, Tennessee, USA. The man known as 'Mister Guitar' was one of the most influential and prolific guitarists of the twentieth century, as well as an important producer and an RCA Records executive. The son of a music teacher and brother of guitarist Jim Atkins (who played with Les Paul), Atkins began as a fiddler in the early 40s, with the Dixieland Swingers in Knoxville, Tennessee. He also played with artists including Bill Carlisle and Shorty Thompson. He moved to Cincinnati, Ohio, in 1946 and his first recording session took place that year, for Jim Bullet. In 1947 Atkins was signed to RCA, recording 16 tracks on 11 August, including a number of vocals. Atkins first performed at the *Grand Ole Opry* in Nashville in 1948, working with a band that included satirists Homer And Jethro. He toured with Maybelle Carter in 1949 and recorded as an accompanist with the Carter Family the following year. At that time he made a decision to concentrate on session work, encouraged and often hired by music publisher Fred Rose. During this period, Atkins recorded largely with MGM Records artists such as Red Sovine and the Louvin Brothers, and most notably on 24 of Hank Williams' tracks for the label. He also recorded on several of the Everly Brothers' Cadence Records hits later in the 50s.

In 1952 RCA executive Steve Sholes, who had signed Atkins for session work, gave him authority to build up the label's roster, and Atkins began a second career as a talent scout. By the mid-50s he was recording his own albums and producing 30 artists a year for RCA. Atkins' first album, *Chet Atkins' Gallopin' Guitar*, was issued in 1953, and his discography eventually comprised over 100 albums under his own name. Among the other artists with whom he worked at RCA were Elvis Presley, Jim Reeves, Don Gibson, Charley Pride, Waylon Jennings, Hank Snow, Jerry Reed and Perry Como, and he is generally regarded as the chief architect of the pop-orientated 'Nashville Sound'. His trademark guitar was a Gretsch, which was later manufactured as the 'Chet Atkins Country Gentleman'. George Harrison endorsed this instrument, and this led to a huge increase in sales for the company during the 60s. During this decade Atkins recorded the first of a series of guitar duet albums, including works with Snow, Reed, Merle Travis, Les Paul and Doc Watson. Atkins was named an RCA vice-president in 1968 and remained in that position until 1981. The following year he left RCA for Columbia Records and continued to record for that company into the following decade. Atkins won several Grammy awards and was elected to the Country Music Hall of Fame in 1973. In the 90s he collaborated with Suzy Bogguss and Mark Knopfler and went full circle in 1996 with a true solo work, *Almost Alone*, which contained tributes to the aforementioned artists. For over five decades Atkins was the consummate professional musician who was greatly respected and liked by all who ever worked with him.

● ALBUMS: *Chet Atkins' Gallopin' Guitar* 10-inch album (RCA Victor 1953) ★★★, *Stringin' Along With Chet Atkins* 10-inch album (RCA Victor 1953) ★★★, *A Session With Chet Atkins* (RCA Victor 1954) ★★★, *Chet Atkins In 3 Dimensions* (RCA Victor 1955) ★★★, *Finger Style Guitar* (RCA Victor 1956) ★★, *Hi-Fi In Focus* (RCA Victor 1957) ★★★, *Chet Atkins At Home* (RCA Victor 1958) ★★★, *Mister Guitar* (RCA Victor 1959) ★★★, *Hummm And Strum Along With Chet Atkins* (RCA Victor 1959) ★★★, *Chet Atkins In Hollywood* (RCA Victor 1959) ★★, *The Other Chet Atkins* (RCA Victor 1960) ★★★, *Teensville* (RCA Victor 1960) ★★★, *Chet Atkins' Workshop* (RCA Victor 1961) ★★, *The Most Popular Guitar* (RCA Victor 1961) ★★★, *Christmas With Chet Atkins* (RCA Victor 1961) ★★, *Down Home* (RCA Victor 1961) ★★★, *Plays Back Home Hymns* (RCA Victor 1962) ★★★, *Caribbean Guitar* (RCA Victor 1962) ★★, *Our Man In Nashville* (RCA Victor 1963) ★★★, *Teen Scene* (RCA Victor 1963) ★★★, *Travelin'* (RCA Victor 1963) ★★★, *The Guitar Genius* (RCA Camden 1963) ★★★, *Guitar Country* (RCA Victor 1964) ★★★, *Progressive Pickin'* (RCA Victor 1964) ★★★, with Hank Snow *Reminiscing* (RCA Victor 1964) ★★★, *My Favorite Guitars* (RCA Victor 1965) ★★★, *More Of That Guitar Country* (RCA Victor 1965) ★★★, *Chet Atkins Picks On The Beatles* (RCA Victor 1966) ★★, *From Nashville With Love* (RCA Victor 1966) ★★★, with Boston Pops, Arthur Fiedler *The "Pops" Goes Country* (RCA Victor 1966) ★★, *Music From Nashville, My Hometown* (RCA Camden 1966) ★★★, *It's A Guitar World* (RCA Victor 1967) ★★★, *Chet Atkins Picks The Best* (RCA Victor 1967) ★★, *Class Guitar* (RCA Victor 1967) ★★★, *Chet* (RCA Camden 1967) ★★★, *Solo Flights* (RCA Victor 1968) ★★★, *Solid Gold '68* (RCA Victor 1968) ★★★, *Play Guitar With Chet Atkins* (Dolton/Liberty 1968) ★★★, *Hometown Guitar* (RCA Victor 1968) ★★★, *Relaxin' With Chet* (RCA Camden 1969) ★★★, *Lover's Guitar* (RCA Victor 1969) ★★★, *Solid Gold '69* (RCA Victor 1969) ★★★, with Hank Snow *C.B. Atkins And C.E. Snow By Special Request* (RCA Victor 1969) ★★★, with Boston Pops, Arthur Fiedler *Chet Atkins Picks On The Pops* (RCA Victor 1969) ★★★, *Yestergroovin'* (RCA Victor 1970) ★★, with Jerry Reed *Me And Jerry* (RCA Victor 1970) ★★, *Pickin' My Way* (RCA Victor 1970) ★★★, *This Is Chet Atkins* (RCA Victor 1970) ★★★, *Mr. Atkins, Guitar Picker* (RCA Camden 1971) ★★★, *For The Good Times* (RCA Victor 1971) ★★★, with Floyd Cramer, 'Boots' Randolph *Chet, Floyd, Boots* (RCA Camden 1971) ★★★, with Jerry Reed *Me And Chet* (RCA Victor 1972) ★★, *Now And ... Then* (RCA Victor 1972) ★★★, *Nashville Gold* (RCA Camden 1972) ★★★, *Chet Atkins Picks On The Hits* (RCA Victor 1973) ★★, *Finger Pickin' Good* (RCA Camden 1973) ★★★, with Jerry Reed *Chet Atkins Picks On Jerry Reed* (RCA Victor 1974) ★★, *Superpickers* (RCA Victor 1974) ★★★, with Merle Travis *The Atkins-Travis Traveling Show* (RCA Victor 1974) ★★★, *In Concert* (RCA Victor 1975) ★★★, *Alone* (RCA Victor 1975) ★★★, with Les Paul *Chester & Lester* (RCA Victor 1975) ★★★, *Chet Atkins Goes To The Movies* (RCA Victor 1975) ★★★, *Love Letters* (RCA Camden 1976) ★★★, *Me And My Guitar* (RCA Victor 1977) ★★★, with Floyd Cramer, Danny Davis *Chet, Floyd & Danny* (RCA Victor 1977) ★★★★, *A Legendary Performer* (RCA Victor 1977) ★★★, with Les Paul *Guitar Monsters* (RCA Victor 1978) ★★★, *The First Nashville Guitar Quartet* (RCA Victor 1979) ★★, *The Best Of Chet On The Road ... Live* (RCA Victor 1980) ★★, with Doc Watson *Reflections* (RCA Victor 1980) ★★★, *Country After All These Years* (RCA Victor 1981) ★★★, with Lenny Breau *Standard Brands* (RCA Victor 1981) ★★★, *Work It Out With Chet Atkins C.G.P.* (Columbia 1983) ★★, *East Tennessee Christmas* (Columbia 1983) ★★, *Stay Tuned* (Columbia 1985) ★★★, *Street Dreams* (Columbia 1986) ★★★, *Sails* (Columbia 1987) ★★★★, *C.G.P.* (Columbia 1988) ★★★, with Mark Knopfler *Neck And Neck* (Columbia 1990) ★★★, with Jerry Reed *Sneakin' Around* (Columbia 1992) ★★★, with Suzy Bogguss *Simpatico* (Liberty 1994) ★★★, *Read My Licks* (Columbia 1994) ★★★★, *Almost Alone* (Columbia 1996) ★★★, with Timmy Emmanuel *The Day Finger Pickers Took Over The World* (Sony 1997) ★★★.

● COMPILATIONS: *The Best Of Chet Atkins* (RCA Victor 1964) ★★★★, *The Early Years Of Chet Atkins And His Guitar* (RCA Camden 1964) ★★★, *The Best Of Chet Atkins Volume 2* (RCA

Victor 1966) ★★★★, *Country Pickin'* (Pickwick 1971) ★★★★, *The Golden Guitar Of Chet Atkins* (RCA Victor 1975) ★★★★, *The Best Of Chet Atkins & Friends* (RCA 1976) ★★★, *Solid Gold Guitar* (RCA 1982) ★★★, *Great Hits Of The Past* (RCA 1983) ★★★, *Tennessee Guitar Man* (Pair 1984) ★★, *A Man & His Guitar* (RCA 1985) ★★★, *Collector's Series* (RCA 1985) ★★★, *20 Of The Best* (RCA 1986) ★★★★, *Pickin' On Country* (Pair 1988) ★★★, *Guitar For All Seasons* (Pair 1988) ★★★★, *Pickin' The Hits* (Pair 1989) ★★★, *The Magic Of Chet Atkins* (Heartland 1990) ★★★, *Country Gems* (Pair 1990) ★★★, *The RCA Years* 2-CD box set (RCA 1992) ★★★★, *Galloping Guitar: The Early Years 1945-54* 4-CD box set (Bear Family 1993) ★★★★, *The Essential Chet Atkins* (RCA 1996) ★★★★, *Super Hits* (RCA 1998) ★★★★.
● VIDEOS: *Get Started On The Guitar* (MMG Video 1987), *Chet Atkins & Friends* (MMG Video 1991), *The Guitar Of Chet Atkins* (Stefan Grossman's Guitar Workshop 1996), *Rare Performances 1955-75* (Stefan Grossman's Guitar Workshop 1996).
● FURTHER READING: *Country Gentleman*, Chet Atkins with Bill Neeley. *Chet Atkins: Me And My Guitars*, Russ Cochran and Michael Cochran.

ATTACK

This mid-60s mod-influenced UK pop act, formerly known as the Soul System, comprised Gerry Henderson (bass), Richard Sherman (vocals), David O'List (b. 13 December 1948, Chiswick, London, England; guitar) and Alan Whitehead (b. 24 July 1946, Oswestry, Shropshire, England; drums). They were signed to entrepreneur Don Arden's agency, Galaxy Entertainments, in the hope of emulating the success of his other protégés, the Small Faces. Not to be confused with the US band of the same name who issued one single 'Washington Square', the Attack's debut for the Decca Records label was a cover version of the Standells' 'Try It'. Several further unremarkable singles ('Colour Of My Mind'/'Created By Clive', 'Neville Thumbcatch') on Decca demonstrated a new psych-pop sound. The line-up was ever-changing and at one time included future Nice drummer Brian 'Blinky' Davidson, and future Andromeda and Atomic Rooster member John Cann (vocals/guitar). They failed to chart but became embroiled in a war of words with Jeff Beck after recording a cover version of his hit 'Hi-Ho Silver Lining' in 1967. An album *Roman Gods Of War* was ready for release but never appeared. That same year, the Attack folded but their talented guitarist David O'List later found a degree of fame as a member of the Nice and Whitehead joined Marmalade.
● COMPILATIONS: *Magic In The Air* (Reflection 1990) ★★, *Final Daze* (Angel Air 2001) ★★.

AU GO-GO SINGERS

Evolving from New York group the New Choctawquins, this nine-piece vocal ensemble

was formed in Greenwich Village in 1964. Heavily influenced by the New Christy Minstrels and other commercialized folk aggregations of the period, the Au Go-Go Singers sang in an off-Broadway musical, toured the southern states and recorded one album before fragmenting in 1965. Among their alumni were Stephen Stills and Richie Furay, who formed the hit group Buffalo Springfield the following year.
● ALBUMS: *They Call Us The Au Go-Go Singers* (Roulette 1964) ★★.

AUM

This minor San Francisco blues-rock trio formed in 1968 and lasted two years. The group consisted of Wayne Ceballos (guitar, piano, lead vocals), Kenneth Newell (bass, vocals) and Larry Martin (drums, vocals). By early 1969 Aum began appearing as an opening act at Bill Graham's Fillmore West. That summer found the band touring the east coast, where it played the Atlantic City Pop Festival and opened for Creedence Clearwater Revival at the Fillmore East. Immersed in the San Francisco tradition, the band tended to inject diverse influences, such as gospel, into its sound and improvised on stage. Aum released one album on the Sire label in 1969 and a follow-up for Graham's Fillmore label in 1970, after which they disbanded.
● ALBUMS: *Bluesvibes* (Sire 1969) ★★★, *Resurrection* (Fillmore 1970) ★★.

AUTOSALVAGE

One of the more enigmatic groups to emerge from New York's post-folk/rock circuit, Autosalvage consisted of Rick Turner (guitar, banjo, dulcimer), Thomas Danaher (vocals, guitar), Skip Boone (bass, piano) and Darius LaNoue Davenport (vocals, oboe, piano, drums). Skip was the brother of Steve Boone, bassist in the Lovin' Spoonful, one of several groups influencing the above quartet. *Autosalvage*, the band's sole album, was released in 1968 to universal critical acclaim. Traditional themes were mixed with jugband music, while the adventurous, quirky compositions blended shimmering guitar with textured instrumentation. Commercial indifference doomed their continuation and by the end of the decade Autosalvage had broken up.
● ALBUMS: *Autosalvage* (RCA Victor 1968) ★★★.

AVONS

Sisters-in-law Valerie (b. 1936, Willesden, London, England) and Elaine Murtagh (b. 1940, County Cork, Eire) originally performed as the Avon Sisters. After being discovered singing at the 1958 BBC Radio Exhibition, they signed to UK Columbia Records where they recorded with producer Norrie Paramor. Their debut was 'Which Witch Doctor?' with the Mudlarks and their debut solo release was a cover version of 'Jerri O' – both songs failed to chart. They added

Ray Adams (b. 1938, Jersey, Channel Islands), whom they spotted singing with Nat Gonella's Band, and then changed their name to the Avons. Their first single under the new name, a cover version of Paul Evans' 'Seven Little Girls Sitting In The Back Seat' in 1959, gave them their only UK Top 20 chart entry. The light-pop trio had three minor hits and last charted with a cover version of 'Rubber Ball' in 1961. In 1962 a song they had written, 'Dance On', became a UK number 1 instrumental hit for the Shadows and it returned to the Top 20 the following year with a powerful vocal version by Kathy Kirby. They recorded for Decca Records in 1963 and Fontana Records in 1964 but had no other hits. Valerie continued to have success as a writer and is still a well-known behind-the-scenes figure in the UK music business. Their only album is now much sought after, fetching high prices in the collector's market
● ALBUMS: *The Avons* (Columbia/Hull 1960) ★★.

AZNAVOUR, CHARLES

b. Chahnour Varenagh Aznavourian, 22 May 1924, Paris, France. This premier singer-songwriter has carried the torch for the French chanson tradition for over six decades and remains one of popular music's last great stylists. He also established a film career as a leading character actor.
Aznavour's parents fled from Armenia after the Turkish massacre. A later composition, 'They Fell', expressed the bewilderment felt by all Armenians, and Aznavour has stated: 'I am Armenian. Everybody figures out that I am a Frenchman because I sing in French, I act like a Frenchman and I have all the symptoms of a Frenchman.' His father had a small restaurant but Aznavour himself was preoccupied with music. When aged only 15, he wrote a one-man show, and soon after adopted the stage name Aznavour. In 1942 he formed a performing and songwriting partnership with Pierre Roche and the duo had success in Canada between 1948 and 1950. Aznavour's first hit was the drinking song 'J'ai Bu', recorded by Charles Ulmer. In 1950, Aznavour became a solo performer ('I was small and undistinguished, so I had to become rich and famous').
Aznavour often opened for Edith Piaf, who recorded several of his songs, including 'Il Pleut' and 'Le Feutre Tropez', as well as a translation of 'Jezebel'. 'When I gave 'Je Hais Les Dimanches' to her, she laughed in my face and told me to give it to an existentialist singer', he recalled. 'I took her at her word and gave it Juliette Greco. She said, "You idiot! You've given my song to that girl. Now I'll have to record it to show her how to sing it."' Aznavour has written numerous songs about ageing, notably 'Hier Encore', which was translated into English by Herbert Kretzmer as 'Yesterday When I Was Young'. 'Les Plaisirs Demodes' ('The Old-Fashioned Way')

was an antidote to rock 'n' roll, but ironically in the movie *And Then There Was None*, the character he played was poisoned after singing it. His film appearances have included the title role in François Truffaut's meritorious *Shoot The Pianist* (1960), and he has also featured in popular movies including *Candy*, *The Adventurers* and *The Games*.
Matt Monro made the UK charts with the maudlin 'For Mama', while Jack Jones recorded a tribute album, *Write Me A Love Song, Charlie*. In 1974 Aznavour had a UK number 1 of his own with 'She', the theme for the ITV television series, *The Seven Faces Of Woman*. Although small (5 feet 3 inches), slight and with battered, world-weary features, he is nonetheless an imposing concert performer, acting his songs with the ability of a leading mime artist. Aznavour starred in the 1975 Royal Command Performance, and was parodied by UK comedy troupe the Goodies as Charles Aznovoice. He rarely records anything other than his own songs and his inventive compositions have included 'You've Let Yourself Go', in which his woman is overweight and argumentative, 'What Makes A Man' about a transvestite, 'Pretty Shitty Days' about an English word that amused him, and the account of a disastrous wedding anniversary in 'Happy Anniversary'. His range encompasses novelty tunes, pastiches, ballads, bittersweet love songs, and narrative and character sketches. He has been quoted as saying, 'Songs mature inside of me and then take their life on paper. A song may take me five minutes to write but it also takes 40 years of living.' Though remaining active as a recording artist, Aznavour performed a series of farewell concerts at the Palais des Congrès in Paris between October and December 2000.
● ALBUMS: including *Charles Aznavour Sings* (Barclay 1963) ★★★★, *Qui?* (Barclay 1964) ★★★, *Et Voici* (Barclay 1964) ★★★, *Aznavour Sings His Love Songs In English* (Barclay 1965) ★★★, *Charles Aznavour '65* (Barclay 1965) ★★★, *Encore* (Barclay 1966) ★★★, *De T'Avoir Aimée* (Barclay 1966) ★★★, *Aznavour Sings Aznavour, Volume 1* (Barclay 1970) ★★★★, *Aznavour Sings Aznavour, Volume 2* (Barclay 1971) ★★★, *Désormais* (Barclay 1972) ★★★, *Aznavour Sings Aznavour, Vol. 3* (Barclay 1973) ★★★, *Chez Lui A Paris* (Barclay 1973) ★★★, *A Tapestry Of Dreams* (Barclay 1974) ★★★, *I Sing For ... You* (Barclay 1975) ★★★, *Charles Aznavour Esquire* (Barclay 1978) ★★★, *A Private Christmas* (Barclay 1978) ★★, *Guichets Fermés* (Barclay 1978) ★★★★, *In Times To Be* (Barclay 1983) ★★★, *You And Me* (EMI 1995) ★★★, *Plus Bleu* (EMI 1997) ★★★, *Jazznavour* (EMI 1999) ★★★★, *Aznavour Live: Palais Des Congres* (EMI 1999) ★★★★, *Aznavour 2000* (EMI 2000) ★★★.
● COMPILATIONS: *Best Of Charles Aznavour* (Barclay 1979) ★★★★, *His Greatest Love Songs* (K-Tel 1980) ★★★, *Charles Aznavour Collection 1*

(Barclay 1982) ★★★★, *Charles Aznavour Collection 2* (Barclay 1982) ★★★, *She: The Best Of Charles Aznavour* (EMI Premier 1996) ★★★★, *Greatest Golden Hits* (EMI 1996) ★★★.
● VIDEOS: *An Evening With Charles Aznavour* (RCA 1984).
● FURTHER READING: *Aznavour By Aznavour: An Autobiography*, Charles Aznavour. *Yesterday When I Was Young*, Charles Aznavour. *Charles Aznavour*, Y. Salgues.
● FILMS: *Adieu Chérie* (1945), *Entrez Dans La Danse* (1948), *Une Gosse Sensass'* (1957), *Paris Music Hall* (1957), *C'est Arrivé À 36 Chandelles* (1957), *La Tête Contre Les Murs* aka *The Keepers* (1958), *Les Dragueurs* aka *The Chasers* (1959), *Porquoi Viens-Tu Si Tard?* (1959), *Le Testament D'Orphée* (1960), *Un Taxi Pour Tobruk* aka *Taxi For Tobruk* (1960), *Tirez Sur Le Pianiste* aka *Shoot The Pianist* (1960), *Le Passage Du Rhin* aka *The Crossing Of The Rhine* (1960), *Horace 62* (1962), *Le Diable Et Les Dix Commandements* aka *The Devil And The Ten Commandments* (1962), *Le Rat D'Amérique* (1962), *Les Quatre Vérités* aka *Three Fables Of Love* (1962), *Pourquoi Paris?* (1962), *Esame Di Guida – Tempo Di Roma* aka *Destination Rome* (1962), *Les Vierges* aka *The Virgins* (1963), *Cherchez L'Idole* aka *The Chase* (1963), *Thomas L'Imposteur* aka *Thomas The Imposter* (1964), *Alta Infedeltà* aka *High Infidelity* (1964), *La Métamorphose Des Cloportes* aka *Cloportes* (1965), *Paris Au Mois D'Août* aka *Paris In August* (1965), *Le Facteur S'En Va-T-En Guerre* aka *Postman Goes To War* (1966), *Caroline Chérie* aka *Dear Caroline* (1967), *Candy* (1968), *Le Temps Des Loups* aka *The Heist* (1969), *The Adventurers* (1970), *Un Beau Monstre* aka *Love Me Strangely* (1970), *The Games* (1970), *La Part Des Lions* (1971), *Les Intrus* aka *The Intruders* (1972), *The Blockhouse* (1973), *And Then There Were None* aka *Ten Little Indians* (1974), *Folies Bourgeoises* aka *The Twist* (1975), *Die Blechtrommel* aka *The Tin Drum* (1979), *Ciao, Les Mecs* aka *Ciao, You Guys* (1979), *Une Jeunesse* (1981), *Qu'est-ce Qui Fait Courir David?* aka *What Makes David Run?* (1981), *Les Fantômes Du Chapelier* aka *The Hatter's Ghost* (1982), *Der Zauberberg* aka *The Magic Mountain* (1982), *Édith Et Marcel* (1983), *Viva La Vie!* aka *Long Live Life* (1984), *Yiddish Connection* aka *Safe Breaker* (1986), *Mangeclous* (1988), *Il Maestro* aka *The Maestro* (1989), *Les Années Campagne* aka *The Country Years* (1992), *Pondichéry, Dernier Comptoir Des Indes* aka *Last Trading Post In India* (1997), *Edith And Marcel* (1983), *Le Comédien* (1997).

B. BUMBLE AND THE STINGERS

This short-lived act was one of several US acts formed by pop svengali Kim Fowley (b. 27 July 1942, Los Angeles, California, USA) as an outlet for his production/songwriting talents at Rendezvous Records. Their 1961 release, 'Bumble Boogie' (featuring Ernie Freeman at the piano), an adaptation of Nicolai Rimsky-Korsakov's 'The Flight Of The Bumble Bee', reached number 21 in the US chart. It was, however, the following year's 'Nut Rocker' (with pianist Lincoln Mayorga) that brought them lasting fame. Although it only reached number 23 in the USA, this propulsive instrumental, an irreverent boogie-woogie reading of Pyotr Ill'yich Tchaikovsky's *Nutcracker Suite*, fared much better in the UK where it soared to number 1 and, 10 years later, again reached the Top 20 on reissue. The band – B. Bumble (who at this juncture was R.C. Gamble (b. Spiro, Oklahoma, USA)), Terry Anderson (b. Harrison, Arkansas, USA; guitar), Jimmy King (rhythm guitar) and Don Orr (drums) – completed a UK tour in 1962. Although only compilations are available featuring variations on the same theme, 'Bumble Boogie', 'Apple Knocker' and 'Bee Hive', their one major original hit remains 'Nut Rocker' – it is set for immortality.
● COMPILATIONS: *Best O'B Bumble* (One Way 1995) ★★★, *Golden Classics Edition* (Collectables 1996) ★★★, *Nut Rocker And All The Classics* (Ace 1996) ★★★.

BACHARACH, BURT

b. 12 May 1928, Kansas City, Missouri, USA. As a composer and arranger, Bacharach is rightly regarded as one of the most important figures in contemporary pop music. Although his father was a journalist, it was music rather than lyrics that was to prove Bacharach's forte. Raised in New York, he was a jazz aficionado and played in various ensembles during the 40s. He studied musical theory and composition at university and served in the US Army between 1950 and 1952. Following his discharge, he worked as a pianist, arranger and conductor for a number of artists, including Vic Damone, Steve Lawrence, Polly Bergen and the Ames Brothers. From 1956-58, Bacharach worked as musical director for Marlene Dietrich, a period in which he also registered his first hit as a composer. The song in question was the Five Blobs' 'The Blob', a tune written for a horror b-movie. Bacharach's co-composer on that hit was Mack David, but a more fruitful partnership followed when Burt was introduced to his collaborator's brother, Hal David. In 1958, Bacharach/David enjoyed their first hit with 'The Story Of My Life', a US Top 20 for Marty Robbins. In the UK, the song became an instant standard, courtesy of the chart-topping Michael Holliday and three other hit versions by Gary Miller, Alma Cogan and Dave King. Even greater success followed with Perry Como's reading of the engagingly melodic 'Magic Moments', which topped the UK charts for an astonishing eight weeks (number 4 in the USA).

Despite their chart-topping songwriting success, the Bacharach/David team did not work together exclusively until as late as 1962. In the meantime, Bacharach found a new songwriting partner, Bob Hilliard, with whom he composed several songs for the Drifters. They also enjoyed minor success with Chuck Jackson's beautifully sparse 'Any Day Now' (later recorded by Elvis Presley). It was during the early 60s that the Bacharach/David team recommenced their collaboration in earnest and many of their recordings brought success to both US and UK artists. Frankie Vaughan's 'Tower Of Strength' gave them their third UK number 1, as well as another US Top 10 hit in a version by Gene McDaniels. The highly talented Gene Pitney, himself a songwriter, achieved two of his early hits with the duo's '(The Man Who Shot) Liberty Valance' and 'Twenty Four Hours From Tulsa'. Other well-known Bacharach/David standards from the early/mid-60s included 'Wives And Lovers' and 'What The World Needs Now Is Love' (successfully covered by Jack Jones and Jackie DeShannon, respectively).

From 1962 onwards the formidable Bacharach/David writing team steered the career of songstress Dionne Warwick with a breathtaking array of high-quality hit songs, including 'Don't Make Me Over', 'Anyone Who Had A Heart', 'Walk On By', 'You'll Never Get To Heaven (If You Break My Heart)', 'Reach Out For Me', 'Are You There (With Another Girl)', 'Message To Michael', 'Trains And Boats And Planes', 'I Just Don't Know What To Do With Myself', 'Alfie', 'The Windows Of The World', 'I Say A Little Prayer', 'Valley Of The Dolls' and 'Do You Know The Way To San Jose?'. Interestingly, the songwriting duo maintained a quotient of number 1 singles in the UK, thanks to first-class cover versions by Cilla Black ('Anyone Who Had A Heart'), Sandie Shaw ('(There's) Always Something There To Remind Me'), the Walker Brothers ('Make It Easy On Yourself') and Herb Alpert ('This Guy's In Love With You'). Looking back at this remarkable series of hits, one notices the strength of Bacharach's melodies and the deftness of touch that so neatly complemented David's soul-tortured, romantic lyrics. After writing the theme song to *The Man Who Shot Liberty Valance*, Bacharach/David were popular choices as composers of film scores. The comedy *What's New, Pussycat* brought them an Oscar nomination and another hit when the title song was recorded by Tom Jones. Dusty Springfield recorded numerous Bacharach songs on her albums throughout the 60s and, together with Warwick, was arguably the best interpreter of his material. Further hits and Academy Award nominations followed between 1967 and 1968 for the movies *Alfie* and *Casino Royale* (which featured 'The Look Of Love'). Finally, in 1969, a double Oscar celebration was achieved with the score from *Butch Cassidy And The Sundance Kid* and its award-winning standard 'Raindrops Keep Fallin' On My Head'. Although there were opportunities to write further film material during the late 60s, the duo were determined to complete their own musical, *Promises, Promises*. The show proved enormously successful and enjoyed a lengthy Broadway run.

Although Bacharach's reputation rests mainly on his songwriting, he has had a sporadic career as a recording artist. After a minor US hit with 'Saturday Sunshine' in 1963, he outmanoeuvred Billy J. Kramer And The Dakotas in the 1965 chart race involving 'Trains And Boats And Planes'. Personal appearances at such prestigious venues as the Greek Theatre in Los Angeles and the Riviera Hotel in Las Vegas have produced 'standing room only' notices, while television specials based on his songs proved very popular.

By 1970, Bacharach seemed blessed with the hit Midas touch, and the Carpenters' beautiful reading of 'Close To You' suggested that further standards would follow. Remarkably, however, this inveterate hitmaker did not enjoy another chart success for over 10 years. An acrimonious split from partner Hal David broke the classic songwriting spell. A barren period was possibly exacerbated by the concurrent break-up of Bacharach's marriage to actress Angie Dickinson and the loss of his most consistent hitmaker Dionne Warwick. Bacharach's desultory decade was alleviated by a series of albums for A&M Records, which featured his own readings of his compositions. Although the late 60s recording *Make It Easy On Yourself* and the 1971 *Burt Bacharach* were chart successes, the curse of the 70s was once more evident when *Living Together* sold poorly. Worse followed when his musical *Lost Horizon* emerged as a commercial disaster. His succeeding albums, *Futures* and *Woman*, also fared badly and none of his new compositions proved chartworthy.

It was not until 1981 that Bacharach's dry run ended. At last he found a lyricist of genuine commercial fire in Carole Bayer Sager. Their Oscar-winning 'Arthur's Theme' (co-written with Peter Allen and singer Christopher Cross) returned Bacharach to the charts and in 1982 he married Sager. Together, they provided hits for Roberta Flack ('Making Love') and Neil Diamond ('Heartlight'). In 1986 Bacharach enjoyed the level of success so familiar during the late 60s, with two US number 1 hits, 'That's What Friends Are For' (an AIDS charity record by Warwick and 'Friends' – Elton John, Gladys Knight and Stevie Wonder) and 'On My Own' (a duet between Patti Labelle and Michael McDonald). In the late 80s Bacharach collaborated with Sager on film songs such as 'They Don't Make Them Like They Used To' (for *Tough Guys*), 'Everchanging Time' (with Bill Conti for *Baby Boom*), and 'Love Is My Decision' (for *Arthur 2: On The Rocks*). He also wrote the score for the latter. In 1989 the American vocalist Sybil revived 'Don't Make Me Over', Warwick's first hit with a Bacharach/ David song, and a year later the UK band Deacon Blue went to number 2 with their *Four Bacharach And David Songs* EP. In 1992, some months after Bacharach had announced that his nine-year marriage to Sager was over, he and David finally reunited to write songs, including 'Sunny Weather Lover' for Dionne Warwick's new album. In the following year, Bacharach extended his publishing empire in collaboration with veteran publishing executive Bob Fead, and subsequently wrote with John Bettis ('Captives Of The Heart'), Will Jennings and Narada Michael Walden. In 1994, a musical revue entitled *Back To Bacharach And David* opened in New York, and in the following year, BBC Television transmitted a major film profile, *Burt Bacharach: ... This Is Now*, which was narrated by Dusty Springfield. Naturally, she was represented (with 'I Just Don't Know What To Do With Myself') on the 23-track celebratory *The Look Of Love: The Classic Songs Of Burt Bacharach* (1996), which also contained other significant versions of the composer's immortal melodies, such as 'Walk On By' (Dionne Warwick), 'Raindrops Keep Fallin' On My Head' (B.J. Thomas), 'This Guy's In Love With You' (Herb Alpert) and 'Make It Easy On Yourself' (Walker Brothers). That album, along with Bacharach's *Reach Out* (originally released in 1967) and *The Best Of Burt Bacharach* (on which he plays instrumental versions of 20 of his hits) were issued in the UK in response to a tremendous upsurge of interest in easy-listening music among young people in the mid-90s. Suddenly, Bacharach was considered 'hip' again. Noel Gallagher of Oasis declared himself a great admirer, and leading figures in contemporary popular music such as Jarvis Cocker of Pulp, Michael Stipe of R.E.M., and Paul Weller all covered his songs. Welcomed by many critics as 'a backlash against the hard rhythms of the dance/house stuff', the phenomenon also dismayed others, one of whom groaned: 'And to think we went through two Woodstocks for this.'

Bacharach's music is now hip with the young, so much so that he made a cameo appearance in the Mike Myers movie *Austin Powers: International Man Of Mystery*. In 1998, Bacharach collaborated with Elvis Costello on *Painted From Memory*, a finely crafted collection of ballads bearing the unmistakable trademarks of its creators: Bacharach's deft romantic touch, coupled with the quirky, realistic style of Costello. Among the album's highlights were 'God Give Me Strength', which featured in the 1996 movie, *Grace Of My Heart*, 'This House Is Empty Now', and an impressive showcase for Costello's lyrics, 'Toledo'. Another of the numbers, 'I Still Have That Other Girl', won a 1999 Grammy Award. In the same year, Bacharach and David contributed some songs to the Bette Midler movie *Isn't She Great*.

● ALBUMS: *Hit Maker – Plays The Burt Bacharach Hits* (London 1965) ★★★, *Casino Royale* film soundtrack (RCA 1967) ★★★, *Reach Out* (A&M 1967) ★★★, *Make It Easy On Yourself* (A&M 1969) ★★, *Butch Cassidy And The Sundance Kid* film soundtrack (A&M 1970) ★★★, *Burt Bacharach* (A&M 1971) ★★, *Living Together* (A&M 1973) ★★, *In Concert* (A&M 1974) ★★, *Futures* (A&M 1977) ★★, *Woman* (A&M 1979) ★★, with Elvis Costello *Painted From Memory: The New Songs Of Bacharach & Costello* (Mercury 1998) ★★★, *One Amazing Night* (Edel 1998) ★★.

● COMPILATIONS: *Portrait In Music* (A&M 1971) ★★★, *Portrait In Music Volume 2* (A&M 1973) ★★★, *Burt Bacharach's Greatest Hits* (A&M 1974) ★★★★, *The Best Of Burt Bacharach* (A&M 1996) ★★★★, *The Burt Bacharach Songbook* (Varèse Sarabande 1997) ★★★, *A Man And His Music* (Spectrum 1998) ★★★, *The Look Of Love: The Burt Bacharach Collection* 3-CD box set (Rhino 1998) ★★★★, *More From The Bacharach Songbook* (Varèse Vintage 1999) ★★★★, *The Love Songs Of Burt Bacharach* (PolyGram 1999) ★★★, *Trains & Boats & Covers: The Songs Of Burt Bacharach* (Sequel 1999) ★★★★, *The Look Of Love: The Burt Bacharach Collection* (Warner ESP 2001) ★★★★.

● VIDEOS: *A Tribute To Burt Bacharach & Hal David* (Aviva International 2001).

● FILMS: *Austin Powers: International Man Of Mystery* (1997), *Austin Powers: The Spy Who Shagged Me* (1999), *Listen With Your Eyes* (2000).

BACHELORS

Formed in Dublin, Eire, in 1958, the Bachelors were originally known as both the Harmony Chords and Harmonichords and featured brothers Conleth (b. 18 March 1941) and Declan Cluskey (b. 12 December 1942) and John Stokes (b. Sean James Stokes, 13 August 1940). The Dublin-born trio initially worked as a mainstream folk act, all three playing harmonicas. In 1961, they were discovered in Scotland by entrepreneur Phil Solomon and his wife Dorothy. After a further period of struggle Solomon introduced them to Decca Records' A&R head Dick Rowe who recalls: 'They all played harmonicas and sang folk songs. They weren't an act you could sign to a pop record company. We went backstage afterwards and there were these three boys who looked at me as if I'd come from heaven and was going to open the door for them to walk in. I said, "God be with me at this moment", and I meant it.' After signing the trio, Rowe suggested a name change: 'I said, "What do girls like, Philip? . . . Bachelors!"' With the assistance of producer Shel Talmy, the group enjoyed a UK Top 10 hit with a revival of the Lew Pollack and Erno Rapee song 'Charmaine' in the summer of 1963. After three unsuccessful follow-ups ('Far Away', 'Whispering' and 'I'll See You') they struck again with a string of easy listening pop hits including several revivals suggested by Rowe: 'Diane', 'I Believe', 'Ramona', 'I Wouldn't Trade You For The World' and 'No Arms Can Ever Hold You'. In 1966, they revealed their former folk roots and, surprisingly, completely out-manoeuvred Simon And Garfunkel by taking 'The Sound Of Silence' to number 3 in the UK charts.

Working primarily with agent Dorothy Solomon, the Bachelors achieved great success on the cabaret circuit with a line-up that remained unchallenged for 25 years. However, in 1984, a dispute arose between the members and John Stokes was asked to leave. He duly took legal action against the brothers and the company Bachelors Ltd. During the hearing, Stokes' voice was likened to that of a 'drowning rat' but he received compensation and left with plans to form a duo. He was replaced by Peter Phipps who was inducted into the second generation New Bachelors, staying with the Cluskey brothers until 1993. The brothers have continued to tour and record as a duo. As Philip Solomon concluded: 'The Bachelors never missed a date in their lives. One of them even had an accident on their way to do a pantomime in Bristol and went on with his leg in plaster and 27 stitches in his head. That is professionalism.'

● ALBUMS: *The Bachelors* (Decca 1963) ★★★, *The Bachelors Second Album* (Decca 1964) ★★, *Presenting: The Bachelors* (Decca 1964) ★★★, *The Bachelors And Sixteen Great Songs* (Decca 1964) ★★★, *No Arms Can Ever Hold You* (Decca 1965) ★★★, *Marie* (Decca 1965) ★★★, *More Great Song Hits From The Bachelors* (Decca 1965) ★★★, *Hits Of The Sixties* (Decca 1966) ★★★, *The Bachelors' Girls* (Decca 1966) ★★★, *The Golden All-Time Hits* (Decca 1967) ★★★, *Under & Over (16 Irish Songs)* (Decca 1971) ★★★, *The Bachelors With Patricia Cahill* (Decca 1971) ★★★, *Bachelors 74* (Philips 1974) ★★★, *Singalong Album* (Philips 1975) ★★, *In Love With Love Songs* (Bachelors 2000) ★★.

● COMPILATIONS: *World Of The Bachelors* (Decca 1968) ★★★★, *World Of The Bachelors: Volume Two* (Decca 1969) ★★★★, *World Of The Bachelors: Volume Three* (Decca 1969) ★★★, *World Of The Bachelors: Volume Four* (Decca 1970) ★★★★, *World Of The Bachelors: Volume Five* (Decca 1970) ★★, *The Very Best Of The Bachelors* (Decca 1974) ★★★, *Focus On The Bachelors* (Decca 1979) ★★★, *25 Golden Greats*

(Warwick 1979) ★★★★, *The Best Of The Bachelors* (Decca 1981) ★★★, *The Bachelors Collection* (Pickwick 1985) ★★★, *Bachelors Hits* (Deram 1989) ★★★, *The Decca Years 1962-1972* (Decca 1999) ★★★.
● FILMS: *It's All Over Town* (1964).

BAEZ, JOAN
b. Joan Chandos Baez, 9 January 1941, Staten Island, New York, USA. The often-used cliché – the queen of folk to Bob Dylan's king – her sweeping soprano is one of the most distinctive voices in popular music. An impressive appearance at the 1959 Newport Folk Festival followed the singer's early performances throughout the Boston/New England club scene and established Baez as a vibrant interpreter of traditional material. Her first four albums featured ballads drawn from American and British sources, but as the civil rights campaign intensified, so the artist became increasingly identified with the protest movement. Her reading of 'We Shall Overcome', first released on *In Concert/Part 2*, achieved an anthem-like quality. This album also featured Dylan's 'Don't Think Twice, It's All Right' and Baez then took the emergent singer on tour and their well-documented romance blossomed. Over the years she interpreted many of his songs, several of which, including 'Farewell Angelina' and 'Love Is Just A Four Letter Word', Dylan did not officially release. In the 60s she founded the Institute for the Study Of Nonviolence. Baez also featured early work by other contemporary writers, including Phil Ochs, brother-in-law Richard Farina, Tim Hardin and Donovan, and by the late 60s was composing her own material. The period was also marked by the singer's increasing commitment to non-violence, and she was jailed on two occasions for participation in anti-war rallies. In 1968 Baez married David Harris, a peace activist who was later imprisoned for several years for draft resistance. The couple were divorced in 1972.

Although a cover version of the Band song, 'The Night They Drove Old Dixie Down', gave Baez a hit single in 1971, she found it hard to maintain a consistent commercial profile. Her devotion to politics continued as before and a 1973 release, *Where Are You Now, My Son*, included recordings the singer made in North Vietnam. A 1975 collection, *Diamonds And Rust*, brought a measure of mainstream success. The title track remains her own strongest song. The story of her relationship with Dylan, it presaged their reunion, after ten years apart, in the legendary Rolling Thunder Revue. That, in turn, inspired her one entirely self-penned album, *Gulf Winds*, in which her songwriting continued to develop, often in new and unexpected directions. In 1989, she released an album celebrating 30 years of performing – *Speaking Of Dreams* – which found her duetting with her old friends Paul Simon and Jackson Browne and, surprisingly, with the Gypsy Kings in a rumba-flamenco cover version of 'My Way'. However, she has preferred to concentrate her energies on humanitarian work rather than recording.

In 1979 she founded Humanitas International, a rapid-response human rights group that first persuaded US President Carter to send the Seventh Fleet to rescue boat people. She has received numerous awards and honorary doctorates for her work. In the 80s and 90s Baez continued to divide her time between social activism, undergoing therapy and singing. She found a new audience among the young socially aware Europeans – 'The Children Of The Eighties', as she dubbed them in song. She retains a deserved respect for her early, highly influential releases. At the end of 1992 *Play Me Backwards* was released to universal acclaim; this smooth country rock album put Baez very much in the same bracket as Mary-Chapin Carpenter. She sounded confident flirting with rock and country and in the mid-90s began to dally with African rhythms and sounds. Baez appears a relaxed individual, although still capable of being a prickly interviewee, especially if the subject of Dylan is broached. She remains, largely through her achievements in the 60s, a giant of folk music.

● ALBUMS: *Joan Baez* (Vanguard 1960) ★★★, *Joan Baez 2* (Vanguard 1961) ★★★, *Joan Baez In Concert* (Vanguard 1962) ★★★★, *Joan Baez In Concert Part 2* (Vanguard 1963) ★★★, *Joan Baez 5* (Vanguard 1964) ★★★★, *Farewell Angelina* (Vanguard 1965) ★★★★, *Portrait* (Vanguard 1966) ★★★, *Noel* (Vanguard 1966) ★★, *Joan* (Vanguard 1967) ★★★, *Baptism* (Vanguard 1968) ★★★, *Any Day Now (Songs Of Bob Dylan)* (Vanguard 1968) ★★★, *David's Album* (Vanguard 1969) ★★, *One Day At A Time* (Vanguard 1970) ★★★, *Blessed Are* (Vanguard 1971) ★★★, *Carry It On* (Vanguard 1971) ★★★, *Sacco And Vanzetti* (RCA Victor 1971) ★★, *Come From The Shadows* (A&M 1972) ★★★, *Where Are You Now, My Son?* (Vanguard 1973) ★★, *Gracias A La Vida (Here's To Life)* (A&M 1974) ★★, *Diamonds And Rust* (A&M 1975) ★★★, *Live In Japan* (Vanguard 1975) ★★★, *From Every Stage* (A&M 1976) ★★, *Gulf Winds* (A&M 1976) ★★, *Blowing Away* (Portrait 1977) ★★★, *Honest Lullaby* (Portrait 1979) ★★, *The Night They Drove Old Dixie Down* (Vanguard 1979) ★★★★, *Country Music Album* (Vanguard 1979) ★★★, *European Tour* (Portrait 1981) ★★, *Live Europe 83* (Ariola 1983) ★★, *Recently* (Gold Castle 1988) ★★★, *Diamonds And Rust In The Bullring* (Gold Castle 1989) ★★, *Speaking Of Dreams* (Gold Castle 1989) ★★★, *No Woman No Cry* (Laserlight 1989) ★★★, *Brothers In Arms* (Gold Castle 1991) ★★★, *Play Me Backwards* (Virgin 1992) ★★★, *Ring Them Bells* (Grapevine 1995) ★★★, *Gone From Danger* (Guardian 1997) ★★★.

● COMPILATIONS: *The First Ten Years* (Vanguard 1970) ★★★★, *The Ballad Book* (Vanguard 1972) ★★★, *The Contemporary Ballad Book* (Vanguard 1974) ★★★, *The Love Song Album* (Vanguard 1975) ★★★, *Hits Greatest And Others* (Vanguard 1976) ★★★, *The Best Of Joan Baez* (A&M 1977) ★★★, *Spotlight On Joan Baez* (Spotlight 1980) ★★★, *Very Early Joan Baez* (Vanguard 1983) ★★★, *Rare, Live And Classic* 3-CD box set (Vanguard 1994) ★★★★, *Diamonds* (PolyGram Chronicles 1996) ★★★, *The Best Of Joan Baez: The Millennium Collection* (PolyGram 1999) ★★★★.

● VIDEOS: *Joan Baez In Concert* (Old Gold 1990).

● FURTHER READING: *Daybreak: An Intimate Journey*, Joan Baez. *The Playboy Interviews: Joan Baez*, no editor listed. *Joan Baez, A Bio-Disco-Bibliography: Being A Selected Guide To Material In Print*, Peter Swan. *Diamonds And Rust: A Bibliography And Discography Of Joan Baez*, Joan Swanekamp. *And A Voice to Sing With*, Joan Baez. *Positively 4th Street: The Lives And Times Of Joan Baez, Bob Dylan, Mimi Baez Fariña And Richard Fariña*, David Hajdu.

● FILMS: *Don't Look Back* (1967), *Woodstock* (1970), *Carry It On* aka *Joan* (1970), *Dynamite Chicken* (1971), *Banjoman* (1975), *Renaldo And Clara* (1976), *In Remembrance Of Martin* (1986), *The Return Of Bruno* (1988), *The Life And Times Of Allen Ginsberg* (1993).

BAKERLOO

Originally the Bakerloo Blues Line, this late 60s power-blues trio from Tamworth, Staffordshire, England, were briefly compared to Cream. Ironically, the band's leader, Dave Clempson (b. 5 September 1949, Tamworth, Staffordshire, England), found himself singing Cream numbers many years later as a member of Jack Bruce's band. The original Bakerloo comprised Clempson (guitar, vocals), Terry Poole (bass) and Keith Baker (drums). Their self-titled album is a collector's item, both as one of the initial Harvest fold-out sleeves and for the music therein. The extended 'Moonshine' gave each member the opportunity to demonstrate his musical dexterity. Clempson was soon tempted away to join Jon Hiseman's Colosseum, and Bakerloo was terminated. Keith Baker re-emerged in one of the early line-ups of Uriah Heep, later teaming up again with Terry Poole in May Blitz. An overlooked album from the blues/rock era.

● ALBUMS: *Bakerloo* (Harvest 1969) ★★★.

BALDRY, LONG JOHN

b. 12 January 1941, London, England. Beginning his career playing folk and jazz in the late 50s, Baldry toured with Ramblin' Jack Elliott before moving into R&B. His strong, deep voice won him a place in the influential Blues Incorporated, following which he joined Cyril Davies' R&B All Stars. After Davies' death, Long John fronted the Hoochie Coochie Men, which also included future superstar Rod Stewart, who later joined Baldry in Steam Packet (featuring

Brian Auger and Julie Driscoll). After a brief period with Bluesology (which boasted a young Elton John on keyboards), Baldry decided to go solo and record straightforward pop. Already well known on the music scene, he nevertheless appeared an unusual pop star in 1967 with his sharp suits and imposing 6 foot 7 inch height. Composer/producer Tony Macauley and his partner John McLeod presented him with the perfect song in 'Let The Heartaches Begin', a despairing ballad which Baldry took to number 1 in the UK in 1967.

His chart career continued with the Olympic Games theme, 'Mexico', the following year, which also made the Top 20. By the end of the 60s, however, the hits had ceased and another change of direction was ahead. Furs and a beard replaced the suits and the neat, short haircut, as Long John attempted to establish himself with a new audience. With production assistance from former colleagues Rod Stewart and Elton John, he recorded a strong album, It Ain't Easy, but it failed to sell. After a troubled few years in New York and Los Angeles he emigrated to Vancouver, Canada, where he performed on the club circuit. In the early 90s his voice was used as Robotnik on the Sonic The Hedgehog computer game. After many years a new Baldry album was released in 1993, subtly titled It Still Ain't Easy. Since then from his base in the USA he has continued to perform in blues clubs, recording occasionally.

● ALBUMS: as Hoochie Coochie Men Long John's Blues (United Artists 1964) ★★★, Lookin' At Long John (United Artists 1966) ★★★, Let The Heartaches Begin (Pye 1968) ★★, Wait For Me (Pye 1969) ★, It Ain't Easy (Warners 1971) ★★, Everything Stops For Tea (Warners 1972) ★, Good To Be Alive (GM 1976) ★★, Welcome To The Club (Casablanca 1977) ★★, Baldry's Out! (A&M 1979) ★★, Rock With The Best (A&M 1982) ★★, Silent Treatment (Capitol 1986) ★★, It Still Ain't Easy (Stony Plain 1991) ★★, Right To Sing The Blues (Stony Plain 1997) ★★★, Live (Stony Plain 2000) ★★★, Silent Treatment (BMG 2000) ★★★, Evening Conversation (Hyperion 2000) ★★★.

● COMPILATIONS: Let The Heartaches Begin: The Best Of John Baldry (PRT 1988) ★★★, The Best Of Long John Baldry (Castle 1991) ★★★★, Mexico (Spectrum 1995) ★★, The Very Best Of Long John Baldry (Music Club 1997) ★★★★.

BALFA BROTHERS

The Balfa family name is legendary in Cajun music. They grew up in abject poverty in Bayou Grand Louis, near Big Mamou, Louisiana, USA, where their father, from whom they gained their musical interest, worked as a sharecropper. The music offered a means of escape and relief and in the mid-40s, brothers Will (b. c.1920, d. 6 February 1979; fiddle), Harry (b. 1931; accordion) and Dewey (b. 20 March 1927, d. 17 June 1992; fiddle, harmonica, accordion, guitar and sundry other minor instruments) began to play for local dances. In 1951, they made their first recording on home recording equipment, but during the 50s Dewey frequently played and recorded with Nathan Abshire. He also appeared at the Newport Folk Festival in 1964, playing guitar with Gladius Thibodeaux (accordion) and Louis Lejeune (fiddle). In 1967, Dewey was joined by Will, Rodney (b. 1934, d. 6 February 1979; guitar, harmonica, vocals), daughter Nelda and Hadley Fontenot (an accordion-playing local farmer) and the unit toured extensively both in the USA and Europe as the Balfa Brothers (incidentally, Will always preferred to spell his name as Bolfa). In the late 60s, they recorded for Swallow and their recording of 'Drunkard's Sorrow Waltz' was a bestselling Cajun single in 1967.

In 1968, they appeared in Mexico City at music festivals run in conjunction with the Olympic Games. They played music for and appeared in the 1972 film on Cajun life, Spend It All. Dewey also formed his nightclub orchestra, which comprised himself and Rodney (fiddle, guitar, vocals), Nathan Menard (accordion), Ervin 'Dick' Richard (fiddle), J.W. Pelsia (steel guitar), Austin Broussard (drums) and Rodney's son, Tony (bass guitar). In the mid-70s, they made further recordings (with Nathan Abshire) for Swallow and Sonet Records and appeared in a documentary on Cajuns. On 6 February 1979, Will and Rodney were killed in a car accident. Dewey continued to perform and record as the Balfa Brothers with other musicians, including Tony, his daughter Christine (triangle), Tony, Ally Young (accordion), Dick Richard, Mark Savoy (b. 1940; accordion), Robert Jardell (accordion) and Peter Schwartz (bass, fiddle, piano) (Schwartz, who first played with the group in his early teens, was Tracy Schwartz's son). Many of the Swallow and other recordings made by the Balfa Brothers have been reissued in the UK by Ace Records. Dewey Balfa later ran a furniture business but remained active in music until his death in June 1992. After his death his daughters, Christine and Nelda, continued the family tradition by playing and recording with other Cajun musicians, including Mike Chapman, Dick Powell and Kevin Wimmer, as Balfa Toujours.

● ALBUMS: Balfa Brothers Play Traditional Cajun Music (Swallow 1965) ★★★★, Balfa Brothers Play More Cajun Music (Swallow 1968) ★★★, with Nathan Abshire The Cajuns (Sonet 1972) ★★★, Cajun Fiddle Tunes By Dewey Balfa (Folkways 1974) ★★★, with Abshire The Good Times Are Killing Me (Swallow 1975) ★★★, J'ai Vu Le Loup, Le Renard Et La Belette (Cezeno/Rounder 1975) ★★★, The New York Concerts (Swallow 1980) ★★, Dewey Balfa, Marc Savoy, D.L. Menard: Under The Green Oak Tree (Arhoolie 1982) ★★★, The New York Concerts Plus (Ace 1991) ★★★, as Balfa Toujours New Cajun Tradition (Ace 1995) ★★★.

● COMPILATIONS: The Balfa Brothers Play

Traditional Cajun Music Volumes 1 & 2 (Swallow/Ace 1987) ★★★★, *Dewey Balfa & Friends* (Ace 1991) ★★★★.

BALL, KENNY

b. 22 May 1930, Ilford, Essex, England. The most successful survivor of the early 60s 'trad boom', Ball played the harmonica and bugle in a local band before switching to the trumpet. Having previously played alongside Charlie Galbraith for a BBC radio broadcast and deputized for Britain's leading dixieland trumpet player, Freddy Randall, Ball joined clarinettist Sid Phillips' band in 1954 and formed his own dixieland-styled Jazzmen four years later, between which times he worked with Eric Delaney, George Chisholm, Terry Lightfoot and Al Fairweather. The Jazzmen did not record until the summer of 1959, resulting in the single 'Waterloo'/'Wabash Cannonball'. Signed to Pye Records, his first hit was in 1961 with Cole Porter's 'Samantha', originally from the Bing Crosby/Frank Sinatra movie *High Society*. This was followed by the million-selling 'Midnight In Moscow', which reached number 2 in the UK and US charts, 'March Of The Siamese Children' from *The King And I*, 'The Green Leaves Of Summer', 'Sukiyaki', and several more hits throughout the 60s. Ball featured alongside Chris Barber and Acker Bilk on a compilation album of the best of British dixieland/trad jazz, *The Best Of Ball, Barber And Bilk*, which reached UK number 1 in 1962. The band made its film debut in 1963 in *Live It Up* with Gene Vincent, and appeared in *It's Trad, Dad!*. In the same year Ball was made an honorary citizen of New Orleans. For three years, from 1962-64, he received the Carl Alan Award for the Most Outstanding Traditional Jazz Band, and in 1968 the band appeared with Louis Armstrong on his last European visit.

Throughout the 70s and 80s Ball extensively toured abroad while maintaining his UK popularity with regular concerts, featuring guests from the 'old days' such as Acker Bilk, Kenny Baker, Lonnie Donegan and George Chisholm. Ball claims his career peaked in 1981 when he and the Jazzmen played at the reception following the wedding of Prince Charles and Princess Diana. Members of the Jazzmen during the following decade included founder member John Bennett (trombone), Andy Cooper (clarinet, ex-Charlie Galbraith and Alan Elsdon bands), John Benson (bass, vocals, ex-Monty Sunshine Band), John Fenner (guitar, vocals), Hugh Ledigo (piano, ex-Pasadena Roof Orchestra), Ron Bowden (drums, ex-Ken Colyer; Lonnie Donegan and Chris Barber bands), and Nick Millward (drums).

● ALBUMS: *Kenny Ball And His Jazzmen* (Pye 1961) ★★★, *Recorded Live!* (Kapp 1962) ★★★, *Midnight In Moscow* (Kapp 1962) ★★★★, *It's Trad* (Kapp 1962) ★★★, *The Big Ones – Kenny Ball Style* (Pye 1963) ★★★, *Colonel Bogey And Eleven*

Japanese Marches Japan only release (Phonogram 1964) ★, *Kenny Ball Plays For The Jet Set* US only release (Kapp 1964,) ★★★, *Tribute To Tokyo* (Pye 1964) ★★, *Kenny Ball And His Jazzmen Live In Berlin* German release (Amiga 1968) ★★★, *King Of The Swingers* (Fontana 1969) ★★, *At The Jazz Band Ball* (Pye 1970) ★★★, *Fleet Street Lightning* (Pye 1970) ★★, *Saturday Night With Kenny Ball And His Band* (Pye 1970) ★★★, *Pixie Dust (A Tribute To Walt Disney)* (Pye 1971) ★★, *My Very Good Friend ... Fats Waller* (Pye 1972) ★★★, *Have A Drink On Me* (Pye 1972) ★★★, *Let's All Sing A Happy Song* (Pye 1973) ★★, with the Johnny Arthey Orchestra and the Eddie Lester Singers *A Friend To You* (Pye 1974) ★★★, *Titillating Tango* (Pye 1976) ★★★, *Saturday Night At The Mill* (Spiral 1977) ★★★, *Way Down Yonder* (Top Rank 1977) ★★★, with Bob Barnard *Bulldogs & Kangaroos* (Broad 1977) ★★★, *In Concert* (Nevis 1978) ★★, *Kenny In Concert In The USA* (Jazzology 1979) ★★★, *Soap* (AMI 1981) ★★★, with Chris Barber, Acker Bilk *Ball, Barber And Bilk Live At The Royal Festival Hall* (Cambra 1984) ★★★, *Greensleeves* (Timeless 1986) ★★★, *Kenny Ball And His Jazzmen Play The Movie Greats* (MFP 1987) ★★, *On Stage* (Start 1988) ★★★, *Dixie* (Pickwick 1989) ★★★, *Kenny Ball Plays British* (MFP 1989) ★★★, *Steppin' Out* (Castle 1992) ★★★, *Strictly Jazz* (Kaz 1992) ★★★, *Lighting Up The Town* (Intersound 1993) ★★★.

● COMPILATIONS: with Chris Barber, Acker Bilk *The Best Of Ball, Barber And Bilk* (Pye Golden Guinea 1962) ★★★★, *Kenny Ball's Golden Hits* (Pye Golden Guinea 1963) ★★★★, *Golden Hour* (Golden Hour 1971) ★★★★, *Golden Hour Presents Kenny Ball 'Hello Dolly'* (Golden Hour 1973) ★★, *Golden Hits* (PRT 1986) ★★★★, *Kenny Ball's Cotton Club* (Conifer 1986) ★★★, *The Singles Collection* (PRT 1987) ★★★, *Images* (Images 1990) ★★★, *The Collection* (Castle 1990) ★★★★, *Hello Dolly* (Spectrum 1995) ★★★, *Greatest Hits* (Pulse 1997) ★★★, *Kenny Ball And His Jazzmen 1960-1961* (Lake 1997) ★★★, *Back At The Start* (Lake 1998) ★★★★, *The Pye Jazz Anthology: Kenny Ball And His Jazzmen* (Castle 2001) ★★★★.

BALLARD, FLORENCE

b. 30 June 1943, Detroit, Michigan, USA, d. 22 February 1976. In her teens, Ballard formed the vocal group the Primettes with school friends Mary Wilson and Betty Travis. Diana Ross completed the line-up in 1960. The following year, the Primettes were signed by Motown, who renamed them the Supremes. As the group's acknowledged leader, Ballard was the featured vocalist on their early Motown singles, but label boss Berry Gordy insisted that Diana Ross become the lead singer in 1963. Thereafter, Ballard was allowed few opportunities to take the limelight, either on record or in concert. Unhappy with her diminishing role in the Supremes, she repeatedly complained to Gordy and his executives, and the resulting friction led to her being ousted from the group in 1967. Throughout the drama, Motown maintained that she was retiring because of the strain of constant touring. The label annulled Ballard's contract, and she signed with ABC, for whom she made two singles under the direction of ex-Satintone Robert Bateman. Ballard was legally barred from capitalizing on her glorious past with the Supremes, and while her former group went from strength to strength, her solo releases flopped. Her contract with ABC was terminated. Other labels were wary of offending Gordy by signing her up, and Ballard became an increasingly embittered figure, ignored by the Detroit music scene in which she had played such a pivotal role. By the early 70s, Ballard was living in extreme poverty on a Detroit housing project. Her reliance on a lethal cocktail of alcohol and diet pills had weakened her health, and in February 1976 her tragic career ended when she suffered a cardiac arrest. Ironically, her contribution to the success of the Supremes has now been recognized, and her fate has been described as a telling verdict on the way in which Motown handled its more uncompromising artists.

BANKS, DARRELL

b. Darrell Eubanks, 1938, Mansfield, Ohio, USA, d. March 1970, Detroit, Michigan, USA. Banks sprang to fame in 1966 with his magnificent debut single, 'Open The Door To Your Heart', one of the finest non-Motown releases to emerge from Detroit. A second hit, 'Somebody (Somewhere) Needs You', followed that same year, but the singer's progress was undermined by an inability to remain with one label for any length of time. By 1967, he had signed to Atco Records and in 1969 to Stax (Volt). Banks' later work included superb performances in 'I'm The One Who Loves You' and 'No One Blinder (Than A Man Who Won't See)', but he was tragically shot dead in March 1970 during a gun duel with a policeman who had been having an affair with his girlfriend.
● ALBUMS: *Darrell Banks Is Here* (Atco 1967) ★★★, *Here To Stay* (Volt 1969) ★★.
● COMPILATIONS: *Don Davis Presents The Sound Of Detroit* (1993) ★★★, *The Lost Soul* (Goldmine/Soul Supply 1997) ★★★★, *The Best Of Darrell Banks* (Connoisseur 2000) ★★★.

BANKS, HOMER

b. 2 August 1941, Memphis, Tennessee, USA. A former member of the Soul Consolidators gospel group, in the late 50s Banks worked as a clerk in the offices of the Satellite Studio in Memphis, hoping that the emergent label, later to become Stax Records, would recognize his talent as a singer and songwriter. At first his talents went largely unnoticed at Stax, although Isaac Hayes and David Porter were

instrumental in setting up Banks' own solo recording debut for the Genie label in 1964, and in 1966 they wrote one of his early songs for the recently reactivated Minit label, '60 Minutes Of Your Love'. Banks recorded five singles for Minit between 1966 and 1968, including the co-penned 'A Lot Of Love', the strident riff of which was later borrowed by the Spencer Davis Group for 'Gimme Some Lovin''. Meanwhile, Banks, still a Memphis resident, had maintained his connections with Stax Records, and by the 70s, was writing many hits with regular collaborators such as Raymond Jackson, Carl Hampton and Bettye Crutcher, including 'Who's Making Love' for Johnnie Taylor, 'Be What You Are' and 'If You're Ready (Come Go With Me)' for the Staple Singers, and '(If Loving You Is Wrong) I Don't Want To Be Right' for the Koko Records artist Luther Ingram, a 1972 million-seller, later covered by Millie Jackson, Isaac Hayes and Rod Stewart. Banks also co-wrote Shirley Brown's 1974 hit on the Truth label, 'Woman To Woman'. After the demise of Stax, Banks went on to write for and/or produce artists on labels including TK, Sound Town, Parachute and Malaco. He also formed a Memphis-based partnership with Lester Snell called Two's Company, which has released albums on the Platinum Blue label, including 1993 sets from J. Blackfoot and Ann Hines.

BAR-KAYS

The Bar-Kays, formed in Memphis, Tennessee, USA by Jimmy King (guitar), Ronnie Caldwell (organ), Phalon Jones (saxophone), Ben Cauley (trumpet), James Alexander (bass) and Carl Cunningham (drums), were originally known as the River Arrows. Signed to Stax Records, the Bar-Kays were groomed as that label's second-string house band by Al Jackson, drummer in Booker T. And The MGs. They were employed as Otis Redding's backing group on tour, and the tragic plane crash in 1967 that took his life also claimed King, Caldwell, Jones and Cunningham. Alexander, who missed the flight, put together a new line-up with Cauley, the sole survivor of the accident, recruiting Harvey Henderson (saxophone), Ronnie Gordon (keyboards), Michael Toles (guitar), Willie Hall (drums) and Roy Cunningham (drums). By 1970 Cunningham and Gordon had left the band, with Winston Stewart replacing the latter. Primarily a session group, the Bar-Kays provided the backing on many releases, including Isaac Hayes' *Shaft* and several of Albert King's 70s recordings.
The group pursued a funk-based direction on their own releases with the addition of vocalist Larry Dodson, who was first featured on the excellent *Black Rock* album. Further personnel upheaval saw Cauley and Toles replaced by Charles Allen and Vernon Burch respectively. Although 'Son Of Shaft' reached the US R&B Top 10 in 1972, consistent success was only

secured on their move to Mercury Records. Later singles, including 'Shake Your Rump To The Funk' (1976), 'Move Your Boogie Body' (1979) and 'Freakshow On The Dancefloor' (1984), were aimed squarely at the disco market. The stable line-up during this period featured Alexander, Allen, Dodson, Henderson, Stewart, Lloyd Smith (guitar), Frank Thompson (trombone) and Michael Beard (drums), with Sherman Guy (percussion, vocals) and Mark Bynum (keyboards) recruited following the release of the successful *Flying High On Your Love*. Guy and Allen left in 1983 as the band's fortunes began to wane, and on 1987's *Contagious* the line-up was reduced to Dodson, Henderson and Stewart. The latter two called it a day in 1993, leaving Dodson to carry on with original member James Alexander and several new recruits.

● ALBUMS: *Soul Finger* (Volt 1967) ★★★★, *Gotta Groove* (Volt 1969) ★★★, *Black Rock* (Volt 1971) ★★, *Do You See What I See?* (Polydor 1972) ★★★, *Cold Blooded* (Stax 1974) ★★, *Too Hot To Stop* (Mercury 1976) ★★, *Flying High On Your Love* (Mercury 1977) ★★★, *Money Talks* (Stax 1978) ★★, *Light Of Life* (Mercury 1978) ★★, *Injoy* (Mercury 1979) ★★, *As One* (Mercury 1980) ★★★, *Nightcruising* (Mercury 1981) ★★★, *Propositions* (Mercury 1982) ★★, *Dangerous* (Mercury 1984) ★★, *Banging The Wall* (Mercury 1985) ★★, *Contagious* (Mercury 1987) ★★★, *Animal* (Mercury 1989) ★★★, *48 Hours* (Basix 1994) ★★.

● COMPILATIONS: *The Best Of The Bar-Kays* i (Stax 1988) ★★★★, *The Best Of The Bar-Kays* ii (Mercury 1993) ★★★, *The Best Of The Bar-Kays Volume 2* (Mercury 1996) ★★, *Greatest Hits* (Masters 2001) ★★★.

● FILMS: *Breakdance – The Movie* (1984).

BARBARIANS

Formed in 1964 in Provincetown, Massachusetts, USA, the Barbarians consisted of Jeff Morris, Jerry Causi, Bruce Benson and 'Moulty' Molten. They made their recording debut with 'Hey Little Bird', issued on the local Joy Records, prior to signing a contract with Laurie Records. In 1965 the Barbarians enjoyed a minor US hit with 'Are You A Boy Or Are You A Girl?', a brilliant garage-styled single about long hair fashions. It was succeeded by 'Moulty', a monologue from the group's one-armed drummer about his disability, interspersed with a call-and-response chorus. His story enshrined forever, Molten left the Barbarians in 1967. The remaining trio moved to San Francisco, California, USA, where they formed Black Pearl.

● ALBUMS: *Are You A Boy Or Are You A Girl?* (Laurie 1966) ★★.

BARNES, J.J.

b. James Jay Barnes, 30 November 1943, Detroit, Michigan, USA. Barnes built his reputation with a classic series of hard-driving Detroit soul records in the 60s, and is better known on the British 'northern soul' scene than he is in his native America. A former member of the Halo Gospel Singers, Barnes' first single was 'Won't You Let Me Know' (1960) for Kable, and later singles followed on Mickays and Ring with no success. He signed with Ric Tic in 1965 and three remarkable releases followed: 'Please Let Me In' (1965), 'Real Humdinger' (1966, US R&B Top 20 and pop number 60) and 'Day Tripper' (1966), the latter a George Clinton production of the Beatles classic. In 1966, Barnes, as part of Holidays, an *ad hoc* group that also included Edwin Starr and Steve Mancha, had a big hit with 'I'll Love You Forever' (US R&B Top 10). Barnes' contract and masters were acquired by Motown Records in 1966 but the company never released any of his recordings. In 1967, he moved to Don Davis' Groovesville, where he achieved two hits, 'Baby Please Come Back Home' (US R&B Top 10) and 'Now That I Got You Back' (US R&B Top 50), sounding uncannily like Marvin Gaye. In 1968, Barnes switched to a companion label, Revilot, which yielded a northern soul favourite, 'Our Love (Is In The Pocket)'. Recognition in northern soul circles resulted in an album and a batch of singles recorded in the UK in the late 70s and early 80s that were of much lesser merit than his Detroit output. In 1991 he released two singles and *Try It One More Time* for Ian Levine's Motor City label.

● ALBUMS: *Born Again* (Perception 1973) ★★★, *Sara Smile* (Contempo 1978) ★★, *Try It One More Time* (Motor City 1991) ★★★, *King Of Northern Soul* (Motor City 1996) ★★★.

● COMPILATIONS: *Ric Tic Relics* 5 tracks (1968) ★★★, *Rare Stamps* one side by Steve Mancha (Stax 1969) ★★★, *The Groovesville Masters* (Contempo 1975) ★★★, *Free To Be Me* (1982) ★★, *Don Davis Presents The Sound Of Detroit* 6 tracks (1993) ★★, *Born Again Again* (Sequel 1997) ★★★, *Best Of J.J. Barnes* (Connoisseur 2000) ★★★.

BARRETT, SYD

b. Roger Keith Barrett, 6 January 1946, Cambridge, England. One of English pop's most enigmatic talents, Barrett embraced music in the early 60s as a member of Geoff Mutt and the Mottoes, a local group modelled on Cliff Richard And The Shadows. He acquired his 'Syd' sobriquet while attending Cambridge High School where his friends included Roger Waters and David Gilmour. Gilmour joined Barrett on a busking tour of Europe where their folk-based repertoire was peppered with songs by the Rolling Stones. Barrett then took up a place at London's Camberwell School Of Art, alternating his studies with a spell in an aspiring R&B act, the Hollering Blues. Waters, a student of architecture at Regent Street Polytechnic, had meanwhile formed his own group, at that point dubbed the (Screaming) Abdabs. In 1965 he invited Barrett to join his group, which took the name the Pink Floyd Sound, at Syd's suggestion, from an album featuring Georgia blues musicians Pink Anderson and Floyd Council. Having dropped their now-superfluous suffix, Pink Floyd became a linchpin of London's nascent 'underground' scene. Barrett emerged as their principal songwriter and undisputed leader, composing their early hit singles, 'Arnold Layne' and 'See Emily Play' (both 1967), as well as the bulk of *The Piper At The Gates Of Dawn*. Barrett's childlike, often naïve compositional style was offset by his highly original playing style. An impulsive, impressionistic guitarist, his unconventional use of feedback, slide and echo did much to transfer the mystery and imagery of Pink Floyd's live sound into a studio equivalent. However, the strain of his position proved too great for a psyche dogged by instability and an indulgence in hallucinogenic drugs. The group's brilliant, but erratic, third single, 'Apples And Oranges', reflected Barrett's disintegrating mental state. During a 1967 US tour he refused to mime on Dick Clark's influential television show, *American Bandstand* – 'Syd wasn't into moving his lips that day' – and, on a corresponding programme, Pat Boone's vacuous repartee was greeted by stony silence. Dave Gilmour was drafted into the line-up in February 1968, prompting suggestions that Barrett would retire from live work and concentrate solely on songwriting. This plan did not come to fruition and Barrett's departure from Pink Floyd was announced the following April. The harrowing 'Jugband Blues' on *Saucerful Of Secrets* was his epitaph to this period.

Within a month Barrett had repaired to the Abbey Road studios to begin a solo album. Work continued apace until July, but sessions were then suspended until April 1969 when, with Malcolm Jones as producer, Barrett opted to begin work anew. Several tracks were completed with the aid of Willie Wilson, former bassist with an early Gilmour group, Joker's Wild, and Humble Pie drummer, Jerry Shirley. On one selection, 'No Use Trying', Barrett was supported by the Soft Machine – Mike Ratledge, Hugh Hopper and Robert Wyatt. Dave Gilmour had been taking a keen interest in the sessions. In June he suggested that he and Waters should also produce some tracks, and the rest of the album was completed in three days. These particular recordings were left largely unadorned, adding poignancy to already haunting material. The resultant set, *The Madcap Laughs*, was an artistic triumph, on which Barrett's fragile vocals and delicate melodies created a hypnotic, ethereal atmosphere. It contained some of his finest performances, notably 'Octopus', which was issued as a single, and 'Golden Hair', a poem from James Joyce's *Chamber Music* set to a moving refrain. In January 1970, Barrett began recording a second album, again with Gilmour

as producer. Sessions continued intermittently until July, wherein the 'best' take, featuring Barrett on guitar and vocals, was overdubbed by a combo of Gilmour, Shirley and Pink Floyd keyboard player, Rick Wright. Released in November that year, housed in a sleeve sporting a Barrett painting, *Barrett* was largely more assertive, but less poignant, than its predecessor. It did include the chilling 'Rats', one of the singer's most vitriolic performances, but Gilmour later recalled that Barrett seemed less prepared for recording than before: 'He'd search around and eventually work something out.'

Barrett then completed a session for BBC Radio 1's 'Sounds Of The Seventies', but despite declaring himself 'totally together' in an interview for *Rolling Stone* (December 1971), in truth he was slipping into the life of a recluse. The following year he did put together a group with bassist Jack Monk (ex-Delivery) and former Pink Fairies/Pretty Things drummer Twink. They supported Eddie 'Guitar' Burns at King's College Cellar in Cambridge and, although reportedly 'chaotic', the same group, now dubbed Stars, subsequently shared a bill with the MC5 at the nearby Corn Exchange. Barrett failed to surface for their next proposed date and ensuing shows were cancelled. He remained the subject of interest and speculation, but a disastrous attempt at recording, undertaken in September 1974, suggested that the artist's once-bright muse had completely deserted him. He gained a high profile when Pink Floyd included a tribute – 'Shine On You Crazy Diamond' on their best-selling *Wish You Were Here* (1975), but Barrett's precarious mental state precluded any further involvement in music.

Opel, a 1988 release comprising unissued masters and alternate takes, enhanced his reputation for startling, original work, as evinced by the affecting title track, bafflingly omitted from *The Madcap Laughs*. Barrett, by now living back in Cambridge with his mother, pronounced his approval of the project. Although he suffers from diabetes, rumours of Barrett's ill health tend to be exaggerated. He simply lives quietly and prefers to forget his past musical career.

● ALBUMS: *The Madcap Laughs* (Harvest 1970) ★★★, *Barrett* (Harvest 1970) ★★★, *The Peel Sessions* (Strange Fruit 1995) ★★★.
● COMPILATIONS: *Opel* (Harvest 1988) ★★★, *Crazy Diamond* 3-CD box set (Harvest 1993) ★★★, *Wouldn't You Miss Me? The Best Of Syd Barrett* (Harvest 2001) ★★★.
● VIDEOS: *Syd Barrett's First Trip* (Vex 1993).
● FURTHER READING: *Crazy Diamond: Syd Barrett And The Dawn Of Pink Floyd*, Mike Watkinson and Pete Anderson. *Syd Barrett: The Madcap Laughs*, Pete Anderson and Mick Rock. *A Fish Out Of Water*, Luca Ferrari. *Lost In The Woods: Syd Barrett And The Pink Floyd*, Julian Palacios. *Random Precision: Recording The Music Of Syd Barrett 1965-1974*, David Parker.

BARRI, STEVE

Barri's long, diverse career began in the USA in 1959 when his composition, 'Suzie Jones', was recorded by the Nortones. Several solo singles followed before the songwriter forged a partnership with Carol Connors, a former member of the Teddy Bears. When singles under the latter's name proved unsuccessful, the duo formed the Storytellers with Carol's sister Cheryl. Their debut single, 'When Two People (Are In Love)' (1963), was acquired for Dimension Records by producer Lou Adler. This successful entrepreneur then paired Barri with protégé (Phil) P.F. Sloan and together the new team began creating material for many of Adler's acts. Jan And Dean, Johnny Rivers and Terry Black were among those benefiting from Sloan/Barri songs, while the duo also recorded in their own right under various pseudonyms, notably the surfing act the Fantastic Baggys. Their talents as songwriters, producers and arrangers flourished more fully at Adler's Dunhill Records label, the hub of the west coast folk-rock and protest movement. Sloan's solo releases notwithstanding, the partners made particular contributions to the careers of Barry McGuire, Herman's Hermits, the Searchers and the Turtles. They also recorded together as part of another 'backroom' group, the Grass Roots, and when 'Where Were You When I Needed You?' reached the US Top 30 in 1966, the pair put an official band together to carry on the name. Their relationship was severed in 1967, following which Barri became director of A&R at the newly amalgamated ABC/Dunhill. He signed several major acts, including Steppenwolf and Three Dog Night, and was responsible for revitalizing the career of Bobby Bland. Barri then moved to Warner Brothers Records where he produced, among others, John Sebastian's *Welcome Back* and the theme to television's *Happy Days*, before joining the staff of Motown Records during the 80s. In 1991, he co-produced the debut album by teenage girl-group the Triplets, which featured a version of 'Where Were You When I Needed You'.

BARRON KNIGHTS

Formed in Leighton Buzzard, Bedfordshire, England, the Barron Knights rose from comparative obscurity following their appearance on the bill of the Beatles' 1963 Christmas Show. Duke D'mond (b. Richard Palmer, 25 February 1945, Dunstable, Bedfordshire, England; vocals, rhythm guitar), Butch Baker (b. Leslie John Baker, 16 July 1941, Amersham, Buckinghamshire, England; guitar, banjo, vocals), 'P'nut' Langford (b. Peter Langford, 10 April 1943, Durham, Co. Durham, England; guitar, vocals), Barron Antony (b. Antony Michael John Osmond, 15 June 1940, Abingdon, Berkshire, England; bass, vocals) and Dave Ballinger (b. 17 January 1941, Slough, Buckinghamshire, England; drums) enjoyed a UK Top 3 hit the following year with 'Call Up The Groups', a parodic medley of contemporary releases by, among others, the Rolling Stones, the Searchers and the Dave Clark Five, based on the Four Preps' US release, 'Big Draft'. Two similarly styled singles, 'Pop! Go The Workers' and 'Merrie Gentle Pops', reached numbers 5 and 9, respectively, in 1965, but the group failed to emulate this success with conventional releases. The group also became the subject of one of the most bizarre high court actions in pop history when their original drummer, who had been hospitalized, sued the Barron Knights for engaging Ballinger. The Barron Knights pursued a lucrative career on the cabaret circuit throughout the late 60s and early 70s, before reviving the pastiche formula with two further Top 10 hits, 'Live In Trouble' (1977) and 'A Taste Of Aggro' (1978). A slick, showbusiness professionalism had now replaced the quintet's original perkiness, but they established themselves as one of Britain's most popular MOR attractions. Still featuring founder members Palmer, Baker and Langford, the Barron Knights remain a lucrative draw on the cabaret circuit.

● ALBUMS: *Call Up The Groups* (Columbia 1964) ★★★, *The Barron Knights* (Columbia 1966) ★★★, *Scribed* (Columbia 1967) ★★★, *The Two Sides Of The Barron Knights* (Pickwick 1971) ★★, *Live In Trouble* (Epic 1977) ★★, *Knight Gallery* (Epic 1978) ★★, *Teach The World To Laugh* (Epic 1979) ★★, *Jesta Giggle* (Epic 1980) ★★, *Twisting The Knights Away* (Epic 1981) ★★★, *Funny In The Head* (Epic 1984) ★★.

● COMPILATIONS: *Knights Of Laughter* (Hallmark 1979) ★★★, *Barron Knights* (Contour 1982) ★★★, *The Best Of The Barron Knights* (Warwick 1982) ★★★.

● FURTHER READING: *Once A Knight: History Of The Barron Knights*, Pete Langford.

BARRY, JEFF

b. 3 April 1938, Brooklyn, New York, USA. Barry began his music career as a singer, completing several singles for RCA Records and Decca Records between 1959 and 1962. He also enjoyed concurrent success as a songwriter, most notably with 'Tell Laura I Love Her', a US Top 10 hit for Ray Peterson and a UK number 1 for Ricky Valance. In 1961 Barry was contracted to Trinity Music, for whom he completed over 100 compositions and gained valuable experience in arranging, producing and recording demos. Although Barry collaborated with several partners, his relationship with Ellie Greenwich would prove to be the most enduring. Together they wrote for Leslie Gore ('Maybe I Know'), the Four Pennies ('When The Boy's Happy') and the Exciters/Manfred Mann ('Do Wah Diddy Diddy') and, as the Raindrops, recorded a US Top 20 hit, 'The Kind Of Boy You Can't Forget'. However, the couple, who were now married, are best recalled for their classic work with Phil Spector, which included the joyous 'Da Doo Ron Ron' and 'Then He Kissed Me' for the Crystals, 'Be My Baby' and 'Baby, I Love You' for the Ronettes and the monumental 'River Deep – Mountain High' for Ike And Tina Turner. Greenwich and Barry also wrote, and co-produced, releases on the Red Bird Records label for the Dixie Cups, Shangri-Las and Jelly Beans. It was also during this period that the duo 'discovered' Neil Diamond, whose early work they produced, but despite this professional commitment, their marriage ended in 1965. Barry then resumed his recording career with singles for United Artists Records and A&M Records, but achieved a greater degree of success in partnership with singer Andy Kim, writing, producing and performing for the Archies' cartoon series. The work with Greenwich has rightly stood the test of time, having reached the pinnacle of stylish pop music during the 60s.

BARRY, LEN

b. Leonard Borisoff, 6 December 1942, Philadelphia, Pennsylvania, USA. Barry began his career as the anonymous vocalist on the Bosstones' 1958 single 'Mope-Itty Mope' before joining the Dovells between 1961 and 1963. As a solo artist, his white soul vocals were best exemplified on the scintillating chart-topper '1-2-3' and the similarly paced 'Like A Baby'. With his sharp suits and clean-cut image, Barry seemed a Philadelphia teen-idol chronologically cut adrift in 1965, and his contention that long-haired groups were on the way out caused a few ripples in the pop press. Although he enjoyed another minor hit in the USA with the *West Side Story* anthem 'Somewhere', the song had already charted in the UK courtesy of P.J. Proby. During the psychedelic boom of the late 60s, Barry went out of fashion and gradually toned down his lively stage act for cabaret purposes. By the end of the decade and through the 70s, he moved into production work.
● ALBUMS: *1-2-3* (Decca 1965) ★★, *My Kind Of Soul* (RCA Victor 1967) ★★.
● COMPILATIONS: *The Very Best Of …* (Taragon 1995) ★★★.

BART, LIONEL

b. Lionel Begleiter, 1 August 1930, London, England, d. 3 April 1999, London, England. The comparative inactivity of Bart for many years tended to cloud the fact that he was one of the major songwriters of twentieth-century popular song. The former East-End silk-screen printer, was at the very hub of the rock 'n' roll and skiffle generation that came out of London's Soho club scene in the mid-50s. As a member of the Cavemen with Tommy Steele he later became Steele's main source of non-American song material. In addition to writing the pioneering 'Rock With The Cavemen' he composed a series of glorious singalong numbers, including 'A Handful Of Songs', 'Water Water' and the trite but delightfully innocent 'Little White Bull'. Much of Bart's work was steeped in the English music-hall tradition, diffused with a strong working-class pride, and it was no surprise that he soon graduated into writing songs for full-length stage shows. *Lock Up Your Daughters* and *Fings Ain't Wot They Used T'Be* were two of his early successes, both appearing during 1959, the same year he wrote the classic 'Living Doll' for Cliff Richard. 'Living Doll' was a fine example of simplicity and melody working together perfectly. Bart could mix seemingly incompatible words such as 'gonna lock her up in a trunk, so no big hunk can steal her away from me', and they would come out sounding as if they were meant to be together. Bart was also one of the first writers to introduce mild politics into his lyrics, beautifully transcribed with topical yet humorously ironic innocence, for example: 'They've changed our local Palais into a bowling alley and fings ain't wot they used to be.'

As the 60s dawned Bart unconsciously embarked on a decade that saw him reach dizzy heights of success and made him one of the musical personalities of the decade. During the first quarter of the year he topped the charts with 'Do You Mind' for Anthony Newley, a brilliantly simple and catchy song complete with Bart's own finger-snapped accompaniment. The best was yet to come when that year he launched *Oliver!*, a musical based on Dickens' *Oliver Twist*. This became a phenomenal triumph, and remains one of the most successful musicals of all time. Bart's knack of simple melody, combined with unforgettable lyrics, produced many classics, including the pleading 'Who Will Buy', the rousing 'Food Glorious Food' and the poignant 'As Long As He Needs Me' (also a major hit for Shirley Bassey, although she reputedly never liked the song). Bart was a pivotal figure throughout the swinging London scene of the 60s, although he maintained that the party actually started in the 50s. Bart befriended Brian Epstein, the Beatles, the Rolling Stones, became an international star following *Oliver!*'s success as a film (winning six Oscars), and, although he was homosexual, was romantically linked with Judy Garland and Alma Cogan. Following continued, although lesser, success with *Blitz!* and *Maggie May*, Bart was shaken into reality when the London critics damned his 1965 musical *Twang!!*, based upon the life of Robin Hood. Bart's philanthropic nature made him a prime target for business sharks and he lost much of his fortune as a result.

By the end of the 60s the cracks were beginning to show; his dependence on drugs and alcohol increased and he watched many of his close friends die in tragic circumstances – Cogan with cancer, Garland through drink and drugs and Epstein's supposed suicide. In 1969, *La Strada* only had a short run in New York before Bart retreated into himself, and for many years maintained a relatively low profile, watching the 70s and 80s pass almost as a blur, only making contributions to *The Londoners* and *Costa Packet*. During this time the gutter press was eager for a kiss-and-tell story but Bart remained silent, a credible action considering the sums of money he was offered. During the late 80s Bart finally beat his battle with alcohol and ended the decade a saner, wiser and healthier man. His renaissance started in 1989 when he was commissioned by a UK building society to write a television jingle. The composition became part of an award-winning advertisement, featuring a number of angelic children singing with Bart, filmed in pristine monochrome. The song 'Happy Endings' was a justifiable exhumation of a man who remained an immensely talented figure and whose work ranks with some of the greatest of the American 'musical comedy' songwriters.

In the early 90s his profile continued to be high, with revivals by the talented National Youth Theatre of *Oliver!*, *Maggie May* and *Blitz!* (the latter production commemorating the 50th anniversary of the real thing), and the inclusion of one of his early songs, 'Rock With The Caveman', in the blockbuster movie *The Flintstones*, in a version by Big Audio Dynamite. In December 1994 Lionel Bart's rehabilitation was complete when producer Cameron Mackintosh presented a major new production of *Oliver!* at the London Palladium, initially starring Jonathan Pryce. In a gesture rare in the cut-throat world of showbusiness, Mackintosh returned a portion of the show's rights to the composer (Bart had sold them during the bad old days), thereby assuring him an 'income for life'. With *Oliver!* set to make its North American debut in Toronto, Bart died in April 1999 shortly after overseeing the first major revival of *Fings Ain't Wot They Used T'Be* at the Queen's Theatre, Hornchurch, in England. He spent his last few years living alone in his apartment in Acton, West London and died after losing his battle with cancer. He had been able to experience a just and well-deserved reappraisal during his last years, with *Oliver* destined to continue in perpetuity.

● FURTHER READING: *Bart!: The Unauthorized Life & Times, Ins & Outs, Ups & Downs Of Lionel Bart*, David Roper.

BASS, FONTELLA

b. 3 July 1940, St. Louis, Missouri, USA. The daughter of gospel luminary Martha Bass, Fontella toured as keyboard player and singer with the Little Milton band during the early 60s. Simultaneously, she made several solo records, including one for Ike Turner's Prann label. When Milton's bandleader, Oliver Sain, left to form his own group, he took Bass with him, and teamed her with another featured vocalist, Bobby McClure. The duo was subsequently signed to Checker Records, on which 'Don't Mess Up A Good Thing' and 'You'll Miss Me (When I'm Gone)' were hits in 1965. 'Rescue Me', a driving song, gave Fontella success in her own right that same year with an R&B number 1 and a UK/US Top 20 hit. Other solo hits, including 'Recovery', followed, but by the end of the decade she had moved to Paris with her husband, jazz trumpeter Lester Bowie. When they later returned to America, Fontella recorded a series of fine records for the Shreveport-based Ronn/Jewel/Paula complex. She has also worked with Bowie's *avant garde* group, the Art Ensemble Of Chicago. In Milan in 1980, Bass recorded a real 'back to basics' gospel album in the company of her mother Martha, her brother and fellow soul artist David Peaston, and Amina Myers. She has subsequently recorded in the gospel field, and worked on the occasional project with Sain and Bowie.

● ALBUMS: *The New Look* (Checker/Chess 1966) ★★★, *Free* (Paula/Mojo 1972) ★★★, *No Ways Tired* (Nonesuch 1995) ★★★, *Now That I Found A Good Thing* (Jewel 1996) ★★★, with the Voices Of St. Louis *Travelin'* (Justin Time 2001) ★★.

● COMPILATIONS: *Sisters Of Soul* 14 tracks Fontella Bass/12 tracks Sugar Pie DeSanto (Roots 1990) ★★★, *Rescued: The Best Of Fontella Bass* (Chess 1992) ★★★.

BASSEY, SHIRLEY

b. 8 January 1937, Tiger Bay, Cardiff, Wales. A thrilling, highly emotional singer, whose career has spanned some 40 years. Her early jobs included work in a factory's wrapping and packing department, while playing working men's clubs at weekends. After touring the UK in revues and variety shows, Lancashire comedian Al Read included her in his 1955 Christmas Show at London's Adelphi Theatre, and his revue, *Such Is Life*, which ran for a year. Her first hit, in 1957, was the calypso-styled 'Banana Boat Song', followed by 'Kiss Me Honey Honey, Kiss Me' nearly two years later. With her powerful voice (she was sometimes called 'Bassey the Belter'), the unique Bassey style and phrasing started to emerge in 1959 with 'As I Love You' which topped the UK chart, and continued through to the mid-70s via such heart-rending ballads as Lionel Bart's 'As Long As He Needs Me' (Nancy's big song from *Oliver!*), 'You'll Never Know', 'I'll Get By', 'Reach For The Stars'/'Climb Ev'ry Mountain', 'What Now My Love', 'I (Who Have Nothing)', George Harrison's 'Something', 'For All We Know', and an Italian hit with a new lyric by Norman Newell, 'Never, Never, Never'.

Her singles sales were such that, even into the 90s, her records had spent more weeks on the UK chart than those of any other British female performer, and 29 of her albums registered in the UK bestsellers between 1961 and 1991. In 1962 she was accompanied on *Let's Face The*

Music by top US arranger/conductor Nelson Riddle. In live performances her rise to the top was swift and by the early 60s she was headlining in New York and Las Vegas. In 1964 Bassey had a big hit in the USA with 'Goldfinger', one of three songs she has sung over the title sequences of James Bond movies (the others were 'Diamonds Are Forever' and 'Moonraker'). In 1969 she moved her base to Switzerland but continued to play major concert halls throughout the world. The American Guild Of Variety Artists voted her Best Female Entertainer for 1976, and in the same year she celebrated 20 years as a recording artist with a 22-date British tour. In 1977, she received a Britannia Award for the Best Female Solo Singer In The Last 50 Years.

In 1981, Bassey withdrew to her Swiss home and announced her semi-retirement, but continued to emerge occasionally throughout the 80s for television specials, concert tours, and a few albums including *Love Songs* and *I Am What I Am*. In one of pop's more unlikely collaborations, she was teamed with Yello in 1987 for the single 'The Rhythm Divine'. In the 90s, with her provocative body language, ever more lavish gowns, and specialities such as 'Big Spender', 'Nobody Does It Like Me', 'Tonight' and 'What Kind Of Fool Am I' – together with more contemporary material – the 'Tigress Of Tiger Bay' has shown herself to be an enduring, powerful and exciting performer. In 1993 she was awarded the CBE, and a new cabaret club named 'Bassey's' was opened in Cardiff. In the following year her 40th Anniversary UK concert tour attracted favourable reviews, even from some hardened rock critics, and in 1995 Bassey was named 'Show Business Personality of the Year' by the Variety Club of Great Britain. In the following year, after celebrating her 60th birthday with nine sell-out concerts at London's Royal Festival Hall (among other locations), and on television in *Happy Birthday, Shirley*, she duetted with Chris Rea on the clubland hit "'Disco' La Passione'. It was the title song from her first feature film, written and scored by Rea, in which she played herself. In 1997 Bassey reinvented herself once more, and was back in the UK Top 20 with 'History Repeating', a collaboration with big beat artists, the Propellerheads. Two years later, *The Birthday Concert* album was nominated for a Grammy Award. In the year 2000, Bassey embarked on her Millennium Tour and also played Las Vegas for the first time in a decade. In the same year she was created a Dame Commander of the Most Excellent Order of British Empire.

● ALBUMS: *Born To Sing The Blues* (Philips 1958) ★★★, *The Bewitching Miss Bassey* (MGM 1959) ★★★, *The Fabulous Shirley Bassey* (MGM 1960) ★★★, *Shirley* (Columbia 1961) ★★★★, *Shirley Bassey* (United Artists 1962) ★★★, *Shirley Bassey Sings The Hit From 'Oliver' (And 11 Other Musical Tunes)* (United Artists 1962) ★★★, *Let's Face The Music* (Columbia 1962) ★★★, *Shirley Bassey At The Pigalle* (Columbia 1965) ★★★★, *Shirley Bassey Belts The Best!* (Columbia 1965) ★★★, *I've Got A Song For You* (United Artists 1966) ★★★, *Twelve Of Those Songs* (Columbia 1968) ★★★, *Live At The Talk Of The Town* (United Artists 1970) ★★★, *Something* (United Artists 1970) ★★★, *Something Else* (United Artists 1971) ★★★, *Big Spender* (United Artists 1971) ★★★, *It's Magic* (United Artists 1971) ★★★, *What Now My Love?* (United Artists 1971) ★★★, *I Capricorn* (United Artists 1972) ★★★, *And I Love You So* (United Artists 1972) ★★★, *Never, Never, Never* (United Artists 1973) ★★★, *Live At Carnegie Hall* (United Artists 1973) ★★★★, *Broadway, Bassey's Way* (United Artists 1973) ★★★, *Nobody Does It Like Me* (United Artists 1974) ★★, *Good, Bad But Beautiful* (United Artists 1975) ★★★, *Love, Life And Feelings* (United Artists 1976) ★★, *Thoughts Of Love* (United Artists 1976) ★★★, *You Take My Heart Away* (United Artists 1977) ★★★, *The Magic Is You* (United Artists 1979) ★★★, *As Long As He Needs Me* (Ideal 1980) ★★★, *As Time Goes By* (MFP 1980) ★★★, *I'm In The Mood For Love* (MFP 1981) ★★, *Love Songs* (Applause 1982) ★★, *All By Myself* (Vogue 1984) ★★, *I Am What I Am* (Towerbell 1984) ★★★, *Playing Solitaire* (President 1985) ★★★, *I've Got You Under My Skin* (Astan 1985) ★★★, *Sings The Songs From The Shows* (Hour Of Pleasure 1986) ★★★, *Let Me Sing And I'm Happy* (EMI 1988) ★★★, *Her Favourite Songs* (EMI 1988) ★★, *Keep The Music Playing* (Freestyle 1991) ★★★, *Sings Andrew Lloyd Webber* (Premier 1993) ★★, *Sings The Movies* (PolyGram 1995) ★★★, *The Show Must Go On* (PolyGram 1996) ★★★, *The Birthday Concert* (Artful 1998) ★★★★.

● COMPILATIONS: *Golden Hits Of Shirley Bassey* (Columbia 1968) ★★★, *The Shirley Bassey Collection* (United Artists 1972) ★★★, *The Shirley Bassey Singles Album* (United Artists 1975) ★★★★, *25th Anniversary Album* (United Artists 1978) ★★★, *21 Hit Singles* (EMI 1979) ★★★, *Tonight* (MFP 1984) ★★★★, *Diamonds – The Best Of Shirley Bassey* (EMI 1988) ★★★, *The Best Of Shirley Bassey* (Dino 1992) ★★★, *The Definitive Collection* (Magnum 1994) ★★★, *The EMI/UA Years 1959-1979* 5-CD box set (EMI 1994) ★★★★, *The Magic Of Shirley Bassey* (Mercury 1998) ★★★, *The Diamond Collection: Greatest Hits 1958-1998* (EMI 1998) ★★★, *The Remix Album ... Diamonds Are Forever* (EMI 2000) ★★★, *This Is My Life: The Greatest Hits* (EMI 2000) ★★★★.

● VIDEOS: *Shirley Bassey Live* (Video Gems 1988), *Live In Cardiff* (BBC 1995), *Divas Are Forever* (Eagle Rock 1998).

● FURTHER READING: *Shirley: An Appreciation Of The Life Of Shirley Bassey*, Muriel Burgess.

● FILMS: *La Passione* (1997).

BATTERED ORNAMENTS

Formed in 1969 by poet and lyricist Pete Brown (b. 25 December 1940, London, England), this innovative group was initially completed by Graham Layden (vocals), Chris Spedding (b. 17 June 1944, Sheffield, Yorkshire, England; guitar), Charlie Hart (organ, violin), George Khan (tenor saxophone), Butch Potter (bass), Rob Tait (drums) and Pete Bailey (percussion). Brown's early intention to play trumpet rather than sing ended on Layden's departure, but the leader's gruff, untutored delivery added considerable empathy to the unit's excellent debut single, 'The Week Looked Good On Paper', and their subsequent album, *A Meal You Can Shake Hands With In The Dark*. This eclectic set drew its inspiration from Graham Bond, jazz and oriental modes and included 'Politician', Brown's acerbic view of parliamentarians also recorded by Cream. However, strained relations between Brown and Spedding culminated in a disingenuous *putsch* when the former was fired on the eve of the Rolling Stones' famed Hyde Park free concert of 1969. *Mantlepiece* had been completed prior to this development, but the original vocal was wiped and replaced prior to release. Brown then formed the highly regarded Piblokto!, which included Rob Tait, and the Battered Ornaments split when Spedding embarked on an independent career.

● ALBUMS: as Pete Brown And His Battered Ornaments *A Meal You Can Shake Hands With In The Dark* (Harvest 1969) ★★★, as the Battered Ornaments *Mantlepiece* (Harvest 1969) ★★.

BATTISTE, HAROLD

b. New Orleans, Louisiana, USA. A former jazz pianist, Battiste turned to production on joining the staff at Specialty Records. Initially based in Los Angeles, he returned to his home town in 1956 to administer a newly founded wing, but the venture floundered upon head-office intransigence. In 1960 Battiste switched to Ric, where he produced Joe Jones's US Top 3 hit 'You Talk Too Much', and arranged several sessions for Lee Dorsey, including the singer's debut hit 'Ya Ya'. Battiste also established the ambitious musicians' collective AFO (All For One). The house band included pianist Allen Toussaint, but although the label enjoyed chart entries with Prince La La and Barbara George, recurring arguments with distributors brought about its downfall. Having returned to Los Angeles, Battiste secured work as an arranger with Phil Spector, and became reacquainted with Sonny Bono. A former colleague at Specialty, Bono later formed a singing duo with his wife and invited Battiste to assist with production. Initial releases by Sonny And Cher, as well as attendant solo singles, proved highly popular, but a rift developed when Battiste's contributions were largely uncredited. However, a new partnership with fellow New Orleans exile Mac Rebennack resulted in the creation of the moniker Dr. John. Battiste matched the singer's husky inflections with a skilful blend of voodoo incantations and classic 'Crescent City'

rhythms, exemplified on the highly popular *Gris Gris* (1968).

BEACH BOYS

The seminal line-up comprised Brian Wilson (b. 20 June 1942, Hawthorne, California, USA), Carl Wilson (b. 21 December 1946, Hawthorne, California, d. 6 February 1998, Los Angeles, USA), Dennis Wilson (b. 4 December 1944, Hawthorne, California, USA, d. 28 December 1983), Al Jardine (b. 3 September 1942, Lima, Ohio, USA) and Mike Love (b. 15 March 1941, Baldwin Hills, California, USA). When the aforementioned three brothers, one cousin and a schoolfriend formed a casual singing group in Hawthorne in 1961, they unconsciously created one of the longest-running, compulsively fascinating and bitterly tragic sagas in popular music. As Carl And The Passions, the Pendletones and Kenny And The Cadets, they rehearsed and played high-school hops while elder brother Brian began to demonstrate his songwriting ability. He was already obsessed with harmonics and melody, and would listen for hours to close-harmony groups, especially the Four Freshmen and the Hi-Lo's. One of his earliest songs, 'Surfin'' (written at the suggestion of keen surfing brother Dennis), was released on a local label, and the topical name 'Beach Boys' was innocently adopted. The domineering father of the brothers, Murry Wilson, immediately seized on their potential and appointed himself as manager, publicist and producer. After his own abortive attempts at a career in music, he began to live his frustrated career dreams through his sons. 'Surfin'', with Murry's efforts, became a sizeable local hit, and made the *Billboard* Hot 100 (number 75). His continuing efforts gained them a recording contract with Capitol Records during the summer of 1962. In addition to the developing group's conflicts, Nik Venet (the producer at Capitol) became embroiled immediately with Murry, and their ideas clashed.

Over the next 18 months the Beach Boys had 10 US hits and released four albums of surfing and hot-rod songs (each cover showed the photograph of neighbourhood friend David Marks, who had temporarily replaced Al Jardine while he attended dentistry college). The Beach Boys' punishing workload began to affect the main songwriter, Brian, who was additionally writing similar material for fellow surf/hot-rodders Jan And Dean. In 1963 the Beach Boys phenomenon reached the UK in the shape of the single 'Surfin' USA', which mildly interrupted the Merseybeat domination. The predominantly working-class image of the British beat group scene was at odds with the perception of the clean and wholesome west coast, blessed with permanent sunshine, fun and beautiful girls. During 1964 a further four albums were released, culminating in the *Christmas Album*. This represented a staggering eight albums in just over two years, six of which were arranged and produced by Brian, in addition to his having written 63 out of a total of 84 songs. In America, the Beatles had begun their unmatched domination of the charts, and in their wake came dozens of groups as the British invasion took place. The Beach Boys, more especially Brian, could only stand back in amazement. He felt so threatened that it drove him to compete against the Beatles. Eventually, Brian gained some pyrrhic revenge, when in 1966 the Beach Boys were voted number 1 group in the world by the UK music press, pushing the Fab Four into second place.

Wilson's maturity as a composer was developing at a staggering pace with classic hits such as 'I Get Around', 'California Girls' and 'God Only Knows'. The overall quality of albums such as *Summer Days And Summer Nights!!* and *Today* was extremely high. Many of Wilson's songs described his own insecurity as an adolescent. Songs such as 'In My Room', 'Wouldn't It Be Nice' and 'Girl Don't Tell Me' found a receptive audience who could immediately relate to the lyrics. While the group's instrumental prowess was average, the immaculate combination of the members' voices delivered a sound that was unmistakable. Both Carl and Brian had perfect pitch, even though Brian was deaf in one ear (reputedly caused through his father's beatings). In private, the 'musical genius' was working on what was to be his masterpiece, *Pet Sounds*. Released in August 1966, the high-profile pre-publicity proved deserved and the reviews were outstanding. The music on *Pet Sounds* was staggering, but for some inexplicable reason, the album sold poorly compared to previous Beach Boys releases. It was later reported that Brian was devastated by the comparative commercial failure of *Pet Sounds* in his own country (US number 10), and felt mortified a year later when the Beatles' *Sgt. Pepper's Lonely Hearts Club Band* was released. It was not widely known that Brian had already experienced two nervous breakdowns, retired from performing with the group and had begun to depend on barbiturates. Even less public was the breakdown of his relationship with his father and the festering tension within the band.

The brief recruitment of Glen Campbell, followed by Bruce Johnston (b. c.1943, Los Angeles, California, USA), filled Brian's place in public. Through all this turmoil the Beach Boys rose to their peak at the end of 1966 with arguably their greatest achievement, 'Good Vibrations'. This glorious collage of musical patterns, with its changes of tempo, unusual lyrics and incredible dynamics, earned Brian and the band the respect of every musician. The group embarked on a major tour of Europe with a new single, 'Heroes And Villains', another innovative excursion with intriguing lyrics by Van Dyke Parks. Brian, meanwhile, attempted a counter-attack on the Beatles, with a project to be

known as 'Smile'. This became the band's albatross, although it was never officially released. The painstaking hours spent on this project now form one of pop's legendary tales. Parts of the material surfaced on their next three albums, and further tracks appeared on other collections up until 1971.

The conflict between Brian Wilson and the other band members was surfacing more regularly. Mike Love, in particular, wanted the other Beach Boys to continue with their immaculate pop music, and argued that Brian was becoming too 'far out'. Indeed, Brian's reclusive nature, fast-increasing weight and growing dependence on drugs added fuel to Love's argument. Observers felt that the band could not raise themselves to the musical level visualized in Brian's present state of mind. *Smiley Smile* in 1967 and *Wild Honey* the following year were comparative failures in the charts by previous Beach Boys standards. Their music had lost its cohesiveness and their mentor and guiding light had by now retreated to his bed, where he stayed for many years. In Europe the group were still having hits, and even had a surprise UK chart-topper in 1968 with 'Do It Again', with Love's nasal vocals taking the lead on a song harking back to better times. Love had by this time become a devotee of the Maharishi Mahesh Yogi, while Dennis Wilson, who was emerging as a talented songwriter, became dangerously involved with Charles Manson, later jailed for his involvement in the murders of nine people between 8 and 10 August 1969. Dennis was drained of money, parted from his home and ultimately threatened with his life by Manson and his followers. Manson and Wilson collaborated on a number of songs, notably 'Never Learn Not To Love', which, although a Beach Boys b-side, had the ironic distinction of putting Charles Manson in the charts. To highlight their discontent, three of their next four singles were extraneous compositions, namely 'Bluebirds Over The Mountain', and a competent version of Lead Belly's 'Cottonfields'. The third non-original was the Phil Spector/Jeff Barry/Ellie Greenwich opus 'I Can Hear Music', featuring a passionate lead vocal from Carl, confirming his status as acting leader.

He struggled to maintain this role for many years to come. In April 1969 the Beach Boys left Capitol in a blaze of litigation. No new product surfaced until August the following year, apart from 'Add Some Music To Your Day' in March 1970. They had the ignominy of having an album rejected prior to that. *Sunflower* was an artistic triumph but a commercial disaster, on which Dennis contributed four excellent songs including the sublime 'Forever'. Throughout the subsequent 12 months they set about rebuilding their credibility in the USA, having lost much ground to the new-wave bands from San Francisco. They started to tour constantly, even appearing with unlikely compatriots the Grateful Dead. Through determination and hard work they did the seemingly impossible and allied themselves with the hip cognoscenti. The arrival of *Surf's Up* in July 1971 completed their remarkable renaissance. The title track, with surreal lyrics by Van Dyke Parks, was another masterpiece, while on the rest of the album it was Carl's turn to offer strong contributions with the beautiful 'Feel Flows' and 'Long Promised Road'. The record's strong ecological stance was years ahead of its time, and the critics were unanimous in favourably reassessing them. As Dennis co-starred with James Taylor in the cult road movie *Two-Lane Blacktop*, so Brian's life was deteriorating into mental instability. Miraculously, the band were able to maintain their career, which at times included only one Wilson, Carl, and no longer featured the presence of the long-serving Bruce Johnston. The addition of Ricky Fataar, Blondie Chaplin and Daryl Dragon nevertheless gave the depleted band a fuller sound. One further album appeared before the outstanding *Holland* came in 1973. For this project the entire Beach Boys organization, including wives and children, moved to Holland for eight months of recording. Thankfully, even Brian was cajoled into going, and his composition 'Sail On Sailor' was a high point of the album.

Murry Wilson died of a heart attack in June 1973, but Brian and Dennis declined to attend the funeral. At the same time, the group's fortunes were once again in the descendent as a double live album was badly received, but a year later the compilation *Endless Summer*, put together by Mike Love, unexpectedly rocketed to the top of the US charts. It spent 71 weeks on the lists, disappeared and returned again the following year, staying for a further 78 weeks. This unparalleled success reinforced Love and Jardine's theory that all anybody wanted of the Beach Boys was surfing and car songs. With the addition of James William Guercio, formerly of Chicago and ex-producer of Blood Sweat And Tears, the band enjoyed extraordinary concert tour success, and ended 1974 being voted 'Band of the Year' by *Rolling Stone* magazine. *Spirit Of America* (1975), another compilation of earlier tracks, enjoyed further success, staying on the American charts for almost a year. Meanwhile, Brian's condition had further deteriorated and he underwent treatment with controversial therapist Eugene Landy. The album *15 Big Ones*, released in July 1976, gave them a big hit with a cover version of Chuck Berry's 'Rock And Roll Music'. The publicity centred on a tasteless 'Brian Is Back' campaign, the now obese Wilson being unwillingly pushed into the spotlight. It seemed obvious to all that Brian was a sick, confused and nervous man being used as a financial tool.

Subsequent albums, *The Beach Boys Love You* and *M.I.U. Album*, attempted to maintain Brian's high profile as producer, but close observers were well aware that this was a complete sham. The material was of below average quality, although the former showed strong glimpses of Wilson's fascination with childlike innocence. In 1977 they signed a recording contract with CBS Records reputedly worth $8,000,000, on the terms that Brian Wilson contributed at least four new songs and a total of 70 per cent of all the material for each album. The first album under this contract was the patchy *LA (Light Album)*, with Bruce Johnston recalled to bail them out on production duties. The album did manage to produce a sizeable hit with Al Jardine's 'Lady Lynda'. The most controversial track, however, was a remake of 'Here Comes The Night'; this previously innocuous R&B song from *Wild Honey* was turned into an 11-minute extended disco extravaganza, and alone cost $50,000 to produce. By this time, Dennis had developed a serious cocaine habit, which hampered the recording of his own solo album, *Pacific Ocean Blue*. However, he was rewarded with excellent reviews, and, now openly, verbally abused the other members of the band except for Brian, whom he defended resolutely. When Carl became addicted to cocaine and alcohol, the fragmentation of the group was at its height.

The next official Beach Boys release was *Keeping The Summer Alive*, a poor album (with an even poorer cover), without the presence of Dennis, who had acrimoniously left the group. He was now living with Christine McVie of Fleetwood Mac. During 1980 only Love and Jardine were present from the original group. Carl delivered his first solo album, a beautifully sung, well-produced record that flopped. One track, 'Heaven', later became a regular part of the Beach Boys' repertoire and was dedicated to Dennis during the 80s. In 1982, Brian Wilson was officially dismissed, and was admitted to hospital for detoxification, weighing a massive 320 pounds. In December 1983, Dennis Wilson tragically drowned while diving from his boat. Ironically, his death reportedly snapped Brian out of his stupor, and he gradually re-emerged to participate onstage. A clean and healthy-looking band graced the back of the 1985 Steve Levine-produced *The Beach Boys*. Following this collection they found themselves without a recording contract, and decided to concentrate purely on being a major concert attraction, travelling the world. While no new albums appeared, they concentrated on singles, including an energetic, well-produced 'Rock And Roll To The Rescue', followed by their version of the Mamas And The Papas' classic 'California Dreaming', with Roger McGuinn featured on 12-string guitar. In 1987, they teamed up with rap act the Fat Boys for a remake of the Surfaris' 'Wipe Out'.

In 1988, a phoenix-like Brian Wilson returned with the solo album that his fans had awaited for over 20 years. The critics and fans loved it, but the album sold only moderately well. At the same time, the Beach Boys released 'Kokomo', which was included in the Tom Cruise film *Cocktail*, and unexpectedly found themselves at the top of the US charts for many weeks. In May 1990, the Beach Boys took Brian Wilson to court in an alleged attempt to wrest his $80 million fortune from him, maintaining that he was insane and unable to look after himself. His medical condition was confirmed (extreme introversion, pathological shyness and manic depression). Wilson defended the case but reluctantly accepted a settlement by which he severed his links with Eugene Landy. Wilson was then officially sacked/resigned and proceeded to recoup monies that had been pouring in from his back catalogue. Murry Wilson had sold his son's company, Sea Of Tunes, to another publisher in 1969, and during this latest court case, Wilson testified that he was mentally ill and a casualty of drug abuse at the time. Wilson won the case and received substantial back royalties. The dust had barely settled when Mike Love issued a writ to Brian Wilson claiming he co-wrote 79 songs with him, including 'California Girls', 'I Get Around' and 'Surfin' USA' (the latter was 'borrowed' from Chuck Berry). In 1993 the band continued to tour, although their show was merely an oldies package. During 1994 mutterings were heard that the pending lawsuit would be settled, as Love and Brian were at least speaking to each other. Late that year it was announced that a substantial settlement had been made to Love, effectively confirming all his claims. In February 1995 a thin, handsome, recently remarried Wilson and a neat, lively-looking Love met at the latter's home. Not only had they mended the rift but they were writing songs together. Early reports indicated both enthusiasm and a desire to make up for many years of wasted time. Instead they released *Stars And Stripes Vol. 1*, a lacklustre album of old Beach Boys songs featuring various country artists on lead vocals. Wilson's collaboration with songwriter Andy Paley (who co-wrote material on *Brian Wilson*) produced several much-hyped tracks, and kindred spirit Sean O'Hagan from the High Llamas was flown over to co-ordinate the mooted album. The sessions ended in confusion and discord, however, and no new material has been forthcoming, with Brian going on to record a second solo album. Carl Wilson began treatment for cancer in 1997 and, with Al Jardine, decided to take action against Brian Wilson for statements made in his autobiography. Carl's health steadily deteriorated, and his death in February 1998 robbed the band of their sweetest voice. Since Wilson's death there have been two rival bands touring under the Beach Boys moniker, one led by Mike Love with Bruce Johnston. The other goes under the banner, Beach Boys, Family And Friends, and is led by Al Jardine together with Brian's daughters Wendy and Carnie and Jardine's two sons Matt and Adam. Ed Carter is also a member of this band. Jardine started

litigation in 2001 claiming that Love has no right to use the name 'Beach Boys'. The continuing absence of Brian, who is now concentrating on his solo career, casts a major shadow on the group. The Beach Boys without a Wilson is like surfing without any waves.

Much has been written about the band, and to those wishing to study this institution, David Leaf's book is highly recommended. Timothy White's book adds information that had previously never surfaced, and is a well-written documentary of California life. Adam Webb's *Dumb Angel* is an excellent biography of Dennis Wilson. Their career has been rolling, like the tide their great songs evoked, constantly in and out, reaching incredible highs and extraordinary troughs. Through all these appalling experiences, however, they still reign supreme as the most successful American group in pop history.

● ALBUMS: *Surfin' Safari* (Capitol 1962) ★★, *Surfin' USA* (Capitol 1963) ★★★, *Surfer Girl* (Capitol 1963) ★★★, *Little Deuce Coupe* (Capitol 1963) ★★★, *Shut Down Vol. 2* (Capitol 1964) ★★★★, *All Summer Long* (Capitol 1964) ★★★★, *Beach Boys Concert* (Capitol 1964) ★★★, *The Beach Boys' Christmas Album* (Capitol 1964) ★★★, *The Beach Boys Today!* (Capitol 1965) ★★★★, *Summer Days (And Summer Nights!!)* (Capitol 1965) ★★★★, *The Beach Boys' Party!* (Capitol 1965) ★★, *Pet Sounds* (Capitol 1966) ★★★★★, *Smiley Smile* (Capitol 1967) ★★★★, *Wild Honey* (Capitol 1967) ★★★, *Friends* (Capitol 1968) ★★★★, *Stack-O-Tracks* (Capitol 1968) ★★, *20/20* (Capitol 1969) ★★★, *Live In London* (Capitol 1970) ★★, *Sunflower* (Brother 1970) ★★★★★, *Surf's Up* (Brother 1971) ★★★★★, *Carl And The Passions-So Tough* (Brother 1972) ★★★, *Holland* (Brother 1973) ★★★★, *The Beach Boys In Concert* (Brother 1973) ★★, *15 Big Ones* (Brother 1976) ★★★, *The Beach Boys Love You* (Brother 1977) ★★★, *M.I.U. Album* (Brother 1978) ★, *LA (Light Album)* (Caribou 1979) ★★★, *Keepin' The Summer Alive* (Caribou 1980) ★, *Rarities* (Capitol 1983) ★★★, *The Beach Boys* (Caribou 1985) ★★★, *Still Cruisin'* (Capitol 1989) ★, *Summer In Paradise* (Brother 1992) ★, *Stars And Stripes Vol. 1* (River North 1996) ★, *Ultimate Christmas* 1964/1977 recordings (Capitol 1998) ★★.

● COMPILATIONS: *Endless Summer* (Capitol 1974) ★★★★★, *Spirit Of America* (Capitol 1975) ★★★★, *20 Golden Greats* (Capitol 1976) ★★★★, *Sunshine Dream* (Capitol 1982) ★★★, *The Very Best Of The Beach Boys* (Capitol 1983) ★★★, *Made In The USA* (Capitol 1986) ★★★★, *Summer Dreams* (Capitol 1990) ★★★★, *Good Vibrations: Thirty Years Of The Beach Boys* 5-CD box set (Capitol 1993) ★★★★★, *The Pet Sounds Sessions* 4-CD box set (Capitol 1997) ★★★★★, *Endless Harmony* (Capitol 1998) ★★★★, *The Greatest Hits Volume 1: 20 Good Vibrations* (Capitol 1999) ★★★★★, *The Greatest Hits Volume 2: 20 More Good Vibrations* (Capitol 1999) ★★★★, *The Greatest Hits Volume Three: Best Of The Brother*

Years (Capitol 2000) ★★★★, *Hawthorn CA, Birthplace Of A Musical Legacy* (Capitol 2001) ★★★.

● VIDEOS: *Beach Boys: An American Band* (Vestron Music Video 1988), *Summer Dreams* (PolyGram Music Video 1991), *Nashville Sounds* (Feedback Fusion 1997).

● FURTHER READING: *The Beach Boys: Southern California Pastoral*, Bruce Golden. *The Beach Boys: A Biography In Words & Pictures*, Ken Barnes. *The Beach Boys*, John Tobler. *The Beach Boys And The California Myth*, David Leaf. *The Beach Boys: The Authorized Illustrated Biography*, Byron Preiss. *Surf's Up!: The Beach Boys On Record, 1961 - 1981*, Brad Elliott. *The Beach Boys*, Dean Anthony. *The Beach Boys: Silver Anniversary*, John Millward. *Heroes And Villains: The True Story Of The Beach Boys*, Steven Gaines. *Look! Listen! Vibrate! SMILE*, Dominic Priore. *Denny Remembered, Dennis Wilson In Words And Pictures*, Edward L. Wincentsen. *Wouldn't It Be Nice: My Own Story*, Brian Wilson and Todd Gold. *In Their Own Words*, Nick Wise (compiler). *The Nearest Faraway Place: Brian Wilson, The Beach Boys & The Southern California Experience*, Timothy White. *The Rainbow Files: The Beach Boys On CD*, Rene Hultz and Hans Christian Skotte. *Back To The Beach: A Brian Wilson And The Beach Boys Reader*, Kingsley Abbott (ed.). *Add Some Music To Your Day: Analyzing And Enjoying The Music Of The Beach Boys*, Don Cunningham (ed.) and Jeff Bleiel (ed.). *Dennis Wilson: The Real Beach Boy*, Jon Stebbins. *Dumb Angel* , Adam Webb.

● FILMS: *Girls On The Beach* (1965), *Americation* (1979).

BEACON STREET UNION

One of the bands included as part of MGM Records' over-hyped 'Bosstown Sound' advertising campaign of 1968, Beacon Street Union managed to survive for two years and two albums despite a lack of critical support. The band consisted of vocalist John Lincoln Wright, Paul Tartachny (guitar), Robert Rhodes (keyboards), Wayne Ulaky (bass) and Richard Weisberg (percussion). Formed in Boston, Massachusetts, USA, around 1967, the group was signed to MGM along with such bands as Ultimate Spinach and Orpheus – the label's ill-fated intention was to create a Boston music scene to parallel San Francisco's. The group recorded two albums, both of which were hard folk rock albums with jazz and blues leanings and ambitious, often pretentious lyrics. The debut album reached number 75 in the USA and the follow-up number 173 before the band regrouped in 1970 as Eagle.

● ALBUMS: *The Eyes Of The Beacon Street Union* (MGM 1968) ★★, *The Clown Died In Marvin Gardens* (MGM 1968) ★★.

● COMPILATIONS: *State Of The Union* 3-CD box set (Phantom 2001) ★★★.

BEATLES

The origin of the phenomenon that became the Beatles can be traced to 1957 when Paul McCartney (b. James Paul McCartney, 18 June 1942, Liverpool, England) successfully auditioned at a church fête in Woolton, Liverpool, for the guitarist's position in the Quarry Men, a skiffle group led by John Lennon (b. John Winston Lennon, 9 October 1940, Liverpool, England, d. 8 December 1980, New York, USA). Within a year, two more musicians had been brought in, the 15-year-old guitarist George Harrison (b. 25 February 1943, Liverpool, England, d. 29 November 2001, Los Angeles, California, USA) and an art school friend of Lennon's, Stuart Sutcliffe (b. 23 June 1940, Edinburgh, Scotland, d. 10 April 1962, Hamburg, Germany). After a brief spell as Johnny And The Moondogs, the band rechristened themselves the Silver Beetles, and, in April 1960, played before impresario Larry Parnes, winning the dubious distinction of a support slot on an arduous tour of Scotland with autumnal idol Johnny Gentle. By the summer of 1960 the group had a new name, the Beatles, dreamed up by Lennon who said 'a man in a flaming pie appeared and said you shall be Beetles with an a'. A full-time drummer, Pete Best (b. 1941, Liverpool, England), was recruited and they secured a residency at Bruno Koschminder's Indra Club in Hamburg. It was during this period that they honed their repertoire of R&B and rock 'n' roll favourites, and during exhausting six-hour sets performed virtually every song they could remember. Already, the musical/lyrical partnership of Lennon/ McCartney was bearing fruit, anticipating a body of work unparalleled in modern popular music. The image of the group was changing, most noticeably with their fringed haircuts or, as they were later known, the 'mop-tops', the creation of Sutcliffe's German fiancée Astrid Kirchherr. The first German trip ended when the under-age Harrison was deported in December 1960 and the others lost their work permits. During this turbulent period, they also parted company with manager Allan Williams, who had arranged many of their early gigs. Following a couple of months' recuperation, the group reassembled for regular performances at the Cavern Club in Liverpool and briefly returned to Germany where they performed at the Top Ten club and backed Tony Sheridan on the single 'My Bonnie'. Meanwhile, Sutcliffe decided to leave the group and stay in Germany as a painter. The more accomplished McCartney then took up the bass guitar. This part of their career is well documented in the 1994 feature film *Backbeat*.

In November 1961, Brian Epstein, the manager of North End Music Store, a record shop in Liverpool, became interested in the group after he received dozens of requests from customers for the Tony Sheridan record, 'My Bonnie'. He went to see the Beatles play at the Cavern and soon afterwards became their manager. Despite Epstein's enthusiasm, several major record companies passed on the Beatles, although the group were granted an audition with Decca Records on New Year's Day 1962. After some prevarication, the A&R department, headed by Dick Rowe, rejected the group in favour of Brian Poole And The Tremeloes. Other companies were even less enthusiastic than Decca, which had at least taken the group seriously enough to finance a recording session. On 10 April, further bad news was forthcoming when the group heard that Stuart Sutcliffe had died in Hamburg of a brain haemorrhage. The following day, the Beatles flew to Germany and opened a seven-week engagement at Hamburg's Star Club. By May, Epstein had at last found a Beatles convert in EMI Records producer George Martin, who signed the group to the Parlophone Records label. Three months later, drummer Pete Best was sacked; although he had looked the part, his drumming was poor. An initial protest was made by his considerable army of fans back in Liverpool.

His replacement was Ringo Starr (b. Richard Starkey, 7 July 1940, Dingle, Liverpool, England), the extrovert and locally popular drummer from Rory Storm And The Hurricanes. Towards the end of 1962, the Beatles broke through to the UK charts with their debut single, 'Love Me Do', and played the Star Club for the final time. The debut was important, as it was far removed from the traditional 'beat combo' sound, and Lennon's use of a harmonica made the song stand out. At this time, Epstein signed a contract with the music publisher Dick James, which led to the formation of Northern Songs. On 13 February 1963 the Beatles appeared on UK television's *Thank Your Lucky Stars* to promote their new single, 'Please Please Me', and were seen by six million viewers. It was a pivotal moment in their career, at the start of a year in which they would spearhead a working-class assault on music, fashion and the peripheral arts. 'Please Please Me', with its distinctive harmonies and infectious group beat, soon topped the UK charts. It signalled the imminent overthrow of the solo singer in favour of an irresistible wave of Mersey talent. From this point, the Beatles progressed artistically and commercially with each successive record. After seven weeks at the top with 'From Me To You', they released the strident, wailing 'She Loves You', a rocker with the catchphrase 'Yeah, Yeah, Yeah' that was echoed in ever more frequent newspaper headlines. 'She Loves You' hit number 1, dropped down, then returned to the top seven weeks later as Beatlemania gripped the nation. It was at this point that the Beatles became a household name. 'She Loves You' was replaced by 'I Want To Hold Your Hand', which had UK advance sales of over one million and entered the charts at number 1.

Until 1964, America had proven a barren ground for aspiring British pop artists, with only the occasional record such as the Tornados' 'Telstar' making any impression. The Beatles changed that abruptly and decisively. 'I Want To Hold Your Hand' was helped by the band's television appearance on the top-rated *Ed Sullivan Show* and soon surpassed UK sales. The Beatles had reached a level of popularity that even outshone their pre-eminence in Britain. By April, they held the first five places in the *Billboard* Hot 100, while in Canada they boasted nine records in the Top 10. Although the Beatles' chart statistics were fascinating in themselves, they barely reflected the group's importance. They had established Liverpool as the pop music capital of the world and the beat boom soon spread from the UK across to the USA. In common with Bob Dylan, the Beatles had taught the world that pop music could be intelligent and was worthy of serious consideration beyond the screaming hordes of teendom. Beatles badges, dolls, chewing gum and even cans of Beatle breath showed the huge rewards that could be earned with the sale of merchandising goods. Perhaps most importantly of all, however, they broke the Tin Pan Alley monopoly of songwriting by steadfastly composing their own material. From the moment they rejected Mitch Murray's 'How Do You Do It?' in favour of their own 'Please Please Me', Lennon and McCartney set in motion revolutionary changes in the music publishing industry.

They even had sufficient surplus material to provide hits for fellow artists such as Billy J. Kramer, Cilla Black, the Fourmost and Peter And Gordon. As well as providing the Rolling Stones with their second single, 'I Wanna Be Your Man', the Beatles encouraged the Stones to start writing their own songs in order to earn themselves composers' royalties. By 1965, Lennon and McCartney's writing had matured to a startling degree and their albums were relying less on outside material. Previously, they had recorded compositions by Chuck Berry, Buddy Holly, Carl Perkins, Bacharach And David, Leiber And Stoller and Goffin And King, but with each successive release the group were leaving behind their earlier influences and moving towards uncharted pop territory. They carried their audience with them, and even while following traditional pop routes they always invested their work with originality. Their first two films, *A Hard Day's Night* and *Help!*, were not the usual pop celluloid cash-ins but were witty and inventive, and achieved critical acclaim as well as box office success. The national affection bestowed upon the loveable mop-tops was best exemplified in 1965, when they were awarded MBEs for services to British industry. The year ended with the release of their first double-sided number 1 single, 'We Can Work It Out'/'Day Tripper', the coupling indicating how difficult it had become to choose between a- and b-sides. At Christmas 1965 the Beatles released *Rubber*

Soul, an album that was not a collection of would-be hits or favourite cover versions, as the previous releases had been, but a startlingly diverse collection, ranging from the pointed satire of 'Nowhere Man' to the intensely reflective 'In My Life'. As ever with the Beatles, there were some pointers to their future styles, including Harrison's use of sitar on the punningly titled tale of Lennon's infidelity, 'Norwegian Wood'. That same year, the Byrds, Yardbirds and Rolling Stones incorporated Eastern-influenced sounds into their work, and the music press tentatively mentioned the decidedly unpoplike Ravi Shankar. Significantly, Shankar's champion, George Harrison, was allowed two writing credits on *Rubber Soul*, 'Think For Yourself' and 'If I Needed Someone' (also a hit for the Hollies). During 1966, the Beatles continued performing their increasingly complex arrangements before scarcely controllable screaming fans, but the novelty of fandom was wearing frustratingly thin. In Tokyo, the group incurred the wrath of militant students who objected to their performance at Budokan. Several death threats followed and the group left Japan in poor spirits, unaware that worse was to follow. A visit to Manila ended in a near riot when the Beatles did not attend a party thrown by President Ferdinand Marcos, and before leaving the country they were set upon by angry patriots. A few weeks later Beatles records were being burned in the redneck southern states of America because of Lennon's flippant remark that: 'We are more popular than Jesus now'. Although his words passed unnoticed in Britain, their reproduction in an American magazine instigated assassination threats and a massed campaign by members of the Ku Klux Klan to stamp out the Beatle menace. By the summer of 1966, the group were exhausted and defeated and played their last official performance at Candlestick Park, San Francisco, USA, on 29 August.

The controversy surrounding their live performances did not detract from the quality of their recorded output. 'Paperback Writer' was another step forward, with its gloriously elaborate harmonies and charmingly prosaic theme. It was soon followed by a double-sided chart-topper, 'Yellow Submarine'/'Eleanor Rigby', the former a self-created nursery rhyme sung by Starr, complete with mechanical sounds, and the latter a brilliantly orchestrated narrative of loneliness, untainted by mawkishness. The attendant album, *Revolver*, was equally varied, with Harrison's caustic 'Taxman', McCartney's plaintive 'For No One' and 'Here, There And Everywhere', and Lennon's drug-influenced 'I'm Only Sleeping', 'She Said She Said' and the mantric 'Tomorrow Never Knows'. The latter has been described as the most effective evocation of a LSD experience ever recorded. After 1966, the Beatles retreated into the studio, no longer bound by the restriction of having to perform live. Their image as pin-up pop stars was also undergoing a metamorphosis and when they next appeared in photographs, all four had moustaches, and Lennon even boasted glasses, his short-sightedness previously concealed by contact lenses. Their first recording to be released in over six months was 'Penny Lane'/'Strawberry Fields Forever', which broke their long run of consecutive UK number 1 hits, as it was kept off the top by Engelbert Humperdinck's schmaltzy 'Release Me'. Nevertheless, this landmark single brilliantly captured the talents of Lennon and McCartney and is seen as their greatest pairing on disc. Although their songwriting styles were increasingly contrasting, there were still striking similarities, as both songs were about the Liverpool of their childhood. Lennon's lyrics to 'Strawberry Fields Forever', however, dramatized a far more complex inner dialogue, characterized by stumbling qualifications ('That is, I think, I disagree'). Musically, the songs were similarly intriguing, with 'Penny Lane' including a piccolo trumpet and shimmering percussive fade-out, while 'Strawberry Fields Forever' fused two different versions of the same song and used reverse-taped cellos to eerie effect.

It was intended that this single would be the jewel in the crown of their next album, but by the summer of 1967 they had sufficient material to release 13 new tracks on *Sgt. Peppers Lonely Hearts Club Band*. *Sgt. Pepper* turned out to be no mere pop album but a cultural icon embracing the constituent elements of the 60s' youth culture: pop art, garish fashion, drugs, instant mysticism and freedom from parental control. Although the Beatles had previously experimented with collages on *Beatles For Sale* and *Revolver*, they took the idea further on the sleeve of *Sgt. Peppers Lonely Hearts Club Band*, which included photos of every influence on their lives that they could remember. The album had a gatefold sleeve, cardboard cut-out figurines, and, for the first time on a pop record, printed lyrics. The music, too, was even more extraordinary and refreshing. Instead of the traditional breaks between songs, one track merged into the next, linked by studio talk, laughter, electronic noises and animal sounds. A continuous chaotic activity of sound ripped forth from the ingenuity of their ideas translator, George Martin. The songs were essays in innovation and diversification, embracing the cartoon psychedelia of 'Lucy In The Sky With Diamonds', the music-hall pastiche of 'When I'm Sixty-Four', the circus atmosphere of 'Being For The Benefit Of Mr Kite', the eastern philosophical promise of 'Within You, Without You' and even a modern morality tale in 'She's Leaving Home'. Audio tricks and surprises abounded, involving steam organs, orchestras, sitars, and even a pack of foxhounds in full cry at the end of 'Good Morning, Good Morning'. The album closed with the epic 'A Day In The Life', the Beatles' most ambitious work to date, featuring what Lennon described as 'a sound building up from nothing to the end of the world'. As a final gimmick, the orchestra was recorded beyond a 20,000 hertz frequency, meaning that the final note was audible only to dogs. Even the phonogram was not allowed to interfere with the proceedings, for a record groove was cut back to repeat slices of backwards-recorded tape that played on into infinity.

While *Sgt. Peppers Lonely Hearts Club Band* topped the album charts, the group appeared on a live worldwide television broadcast, playing their anthem of the period, 'All You Need Is Love'. The following week it entered many of the world's charts at number 1, echoing the old days of Beatlemania. There was sadness, too, that summer, for on 27 August 1967, Brian Epstein was found dead, the victim of a cumulative overdose of the drug Carbitrol, together with hints of a homosexual scandal cover-up. With spiritual guidance from the Maharishi Mahesh Yogi, the Beatles took Epstein's death calmly and decided to look after their business affairs without a manager. The first fruit of their post-Epstein labour was the film *Magical Mystery Tour*, first screened on national television on Boxing Day 1967. While the phantasmagorical movie received mixed reviews, nobody could complain about the music, initially released in the unique form of a double EP, featuring six well-crafted songs. The EPs reached number 2 in the UK, making chart history in the process. Ironically, the package was robbed of the top spot by the traditional Beatles Christmas single, this time in the form of 'Hello Goodbye'.

In 1968, the Beatles became increasingly involved with the business of running their company, Apple Corps. A mismanaged boutique near Baker Street came and went. The first Apple single, 'Hey Jude', was a warm-hearted ballad that progressed over its seven-minute duration into a rousing singalong finale. Their next film, *Yellow Submarine*, was a cartoon, and the graphics were acclaimed as a landmark in animation. The soundtrack album was half instrumental, with George Martin responsible for some interesting orchestral work. Only four genuinely new Beatles tracks were included, with Lennon's biting 'Hey Bulldog' being the strongest. Harrison's swirling 'Only A Northern Song' had some brilliant Pepperesque brass and trumpets. Although 'It's All Too Much' was flattered by the magnificent colour of the animation in the film, it was not a strong song. With their prolific output, the group crammed the remainder of their most recent material onto a double album, *The Beatles* (now known as 'The White Album'), released in a stark white cover. George Martin's perceptive overview many years later was that it would have made an excellent single album. It had some brilliant moments that displayed the broad sweep of the

Beatles' talent, from 'Back In The USSR', the affectionate tribute to Chuck Berry and the Beach Boys, to Lennon's tribute to his late mother, 'Julia', and McCartney's excellent 'Blackbird'. Harrison contributed 'While My Guitar Gently Weeps', which featured Eric Clapton on guitar. Marmalade took 'Ob-La-Di, Ob-La-Da' to number 1 in the UK, while 'Helter Skelter' took on symbolic force in the mind of the mass murderer Charles Manson. There were also a number of average songs that seemed still to require work, plus some ill-advised doodlings such as 'Revolution No. 9' and 'Goodnight'.

The Beatles revealed that the four musicians were already working in isolated neutrality, although the passage of time has now made this work a critics' favourite. Meanwhile, the Beatles' inability as business executives was becoming apparent from the parlous state of Apple, to which Allen Klein attempted to restore some order. The new realism that permeated the portals of their headquarters was even evident in their art. Like several other contemporary artists, including Bob Dylan and the Byrds, they chose to end the 60s with a reversion to less complex musical forms. The return-to-roots minimalism was spearheaded by the appropriately titled number 1 single 'Get Back', which featured Billy Preston on organ. Cameras were present at their next recording sessions, as they ran through dozens of songs, many of which they had not played since Hamburg. When the sessions ended, there were countless spools of tape that were not reassembled until the following year. In the meantime, a select few witnessed the band's last 'public' performance on the rooftop of the Apple headquarters in Savile Row, London. Amid the uncertainty of 1969, the Beatles enjoyed their final UK number 1 with 'Ballad Of John And Yoko', on which only Lennon and McCartney performed.

In a sustained attempt to cover the cracks that were becoming increasingly visible in their personal and musical relationships, they reconvened for *Abbey Road*. The album was dominated by a glorious song cycle on side 2, in which such fragmentary compositions as 'Mean Mr. Mustard', 'Polythene Pam', 'She Came In Through The Bathroom Window' and 'Golden Slumbers'/'Carry That Weight' gelled into a convincing whole. The accompanying single coupled Lennon's 'Come Together' with Harrison's 'Something'. The latter song gave Harrison the kudos he deserved, and rightly became the second most covered Beatles song ever, after 'Yesterday'. The single only reached number 4 in the UK, the group's lowest chart position since 'Love Me Do' in 1962. Such considerations were small compared to the fate of their other songs. The group could only watch helplessly as a wary Dick James surreptitiously sold Northern Songs to ATV. The catalogue continued to change hands over the following years and not even the combined financial force of McCartney and Yoko Ono could eventually wrest it from superstar speculator Michael Jackson.

With various solo projects on the horizon, the Beatles stumbled through 1970, their disunity betrayed to the world in the depressing film *Let It Be*, which shows Harrison and Lennon clearly unhappy about McCartney's attitude towards the band. The subsequent album, finally pieced together by producer Phil Spector, was a controversial and bitty affair, initially housed in a cardboard box containing a lavish paperback book, which increased the retail price to a prohibitive level. Musically, the work revealed the Beatles looking back to better days. It included the sparse 'Two Of Us' and the primitive 'The One After 909', a song they used to play as the Quarrymen, and an orchestrated 'The Long And Winding Road', which provided their final US number 1, although McCartney pointedly preferred the non-orchestrated version in the film. There was also the aptly titled last official single, 'Let It Be', which entered the UK charts at number 2, only to drop to number 3 the following week. For many it was the final, sad anti-climax before the inevitable, yet still unexpected, split. The acrimonious dissolution of the Beatles, like that of no other group before or since, symbolized the end of an era that they had dominated and helped to create.

It is inconceivable that any group in the future can shape and influence a generation in the same way as these four individuals. More than 30 years on, the quality of the songs is such that none show signs of sounding either lyrically or musically dated. Since the break-up of the band, there have been some important releases for Beatles fans. In 1988, the two *Past Masters* volumes collected together all the Beatles tracks not available on the CD releases of their original albums. The first volume has 18 tracks from 1962-65; the second, 15 from the subsequent years. *Live At The BBC* collected together 56 tracks played live by the Beatles for various shows on the BBC Light Programme in the infancy of their career. Most of the songs are cover versions of 50s R&B standards, including nine by Chuck Berry. The first volume of *Anthology*, released in November 1995, collected 52 previously unreleased out-takes and demo versions recorded between 1958 and 1964, plus eight spoken tracks taken from interviews. The album was accompanied by an excellent six-part television series that told the complete story of the band, made with the help of the three remaining Beatles, and by the single release of 'Free As A Bird', the first song recorded by the band since their break-up. This consisted of a 1977 track sung by Lennon into a tape recorder, and backed vocally and instrumentally in 1995 by the other three Beatles and produced by Jeff Lynne. It narrowly failed to reach number 1 on both sides of the Atlantic, as did the slightly inferior 'Real Love' in March 1996.

The reaction to *Anthology 2* was ecstatic. While it was expected that older journalists would write favourably about *their* generation, it was encouraging to see younger writers offering some fresh views. David Quantick of the *New Musical Express* offered one of the best comments in recent years: 'The Beatles only made – they could only make – music that referred to the future. And *that* is the difference between them and every other pop group or singer ever since'. *Anthology 3* could not improve upon the previous collection but there were gems to be found. The acoustic 'While My Guitar Gently Weeps' from Harrison is stunning. 'Because', never an outstanding track when it appeared on *Abbey Road*, is given a stripped *a cappella* treatment. The McCartney demo of 'Come And Get It' for Badfinger begs the question of why the Beatles chose not to release this classic pop song themselves.

In 1999, more mass media coverage came with the release of a remixed *Yellow Submarine*. The remastered film delighted a new audience stunned by its still incredibly original effects. The accompanying album dispensed with the George Martin instrumentals and instead reverted to the order of tracks featured in the film. Later in the year they were confirmed as the most successful recording act of the twentieth century in the USA, with album sales of over 106 million. The following year saw further Beatles activity. The long awaited but overpriced *Anthology* book, on which all three surviving Beatles collaborated with Yoko Ono, was published in October. A month later, their 27 number 1 hits were compiled on *1*. Though the compilation was a huge commercial success, close scrutiny reveals that classic tracks such as 'Please Please Me' and the magnificent 'Strawberry Fields Forever' have to be omitted as they never reached the top of the UK or US charts.

In the course of history the Rolling Stones and countless other major groups are loved, but the Beatles are universally and unconditionally adored. This was further proved in November 2001 when George Harrison lost his battle with cancer. The worldwide mourning resulted in massive coverage in the press and on radio and television. After this, Lennon's famously flippant 1966 comment about the Beatles being more popular than Jesus Christ should be taken very seriously indeed.

● ALBUMS: *Please Please Me* (Parlophone 1963) ★★★★, *With The Beatles* (Parlophone 1963) ★★★★, *A Hard Day's Night* (Parlophone 1964) ★★★★★, *Beatles For Sale* (Parlophone 1964) ★★★★, *The Savage Young Beatles* (USA) (Savage 1964) ★, *Ain't She Sweet* (USA) (Atco 1964) ★, *The Beatles With Tony Sheridan & Their Guests & Others* (USA) (MGM 1964) ★, *Meet The Beatles* (USA) (Capitol 1964) ★★★, *The Beatles Second Album* (USA) (Capitol 1964) ★★★, *Something New* (USA) (Capitol 1964) ★★★, *Beatles '65*

(USA) (Capitol 1965) ★★★, *The Early Beatles*
(USA) (Capitol 1965) ★★, *Beatles VI* (USA)
(Capitol 1965) ★★, *Help!* (Parlophone 1965)
★★★★★, *Rubber Soul* (Parlophone 1965)
★★★★★, *Yesterday And Today* (Capitol 1966)
★★★, *Revolver* (Parlophone 1966) ★★★★★, *Sgt.
Peppers Lonely Hearts Club Band* (Parlophone
1967) ★★★★★, *Magical Mystery Tour* (Capitol
1968) ★★★★, *The Beatles* (Apple 1968)
★★★★★, *Yellow Submarine* (Apple 1969) ★★,
Abbey Road (Apple 1969) ★★★★★, *Let It Be*
(Apple 1970) ★★★, *Hey Jude* (Capitol 1970)
★★★, *The Beatles At The Hollywood Bowl*
(Parlophone 1977) ★★, *Yellow Submarine
Songtrack* (Parlophone 1999) ★★★★.
● COMPILATIONS: *A Collection Of Beatles Oldies*
(Parlophone 1966) ★★★★, *The Early Years*
(Contour 1971) ★★, *The Beatles 1962-1966* (Apple
1973) ★★★★★, *The Beatles 1967-1970* (Apple
1973) ★★★★★, *Rock & Roll Music* (EMI 1976)
★★★★, *Love Songs* (EMI 1977) ★★★★, *Rarities*
(Parlophone 1979) ★★★★, *Past Masters Volume 1*
(Parlophone 1988) ★★★★★, *Past Masters
Volume 2* (Parlophone 1988) ★★★★★, *Live At
The BBC* (Apple 1994) ★★★★, *Anthology 1*
(Apple 1995) ★★★★, *Anthology 2* (Apple 1996)
★★★★, *Anthology 3* (Apple 1996) ★★★, *1*
(Parlophone/Capitol 2000) ★★★★.
● CD-ROMS: *At The Movies/Scenes From A
Career* (UFO 1998).
● VIDEOS: *Ready Steady Go Special* (PMI 1985),
A Hard Days Night (Vestron Video 1986), *The
Compleat Beatles* (MGM 1986), *Magical Mystery
Tour* (PMI 1989), *Help!* (PMI 1989), *On The Road*
(MMG Video 1990), *Alone And Together* (Channel
5 1990), *The First U.S. Visit* (1993), *Beatles Firsts*
(Goodtimes 1995), *The Making Of A Hard Day's
Night* (VCI 1995), *The Beatles Anthology Volumes
1-8* (PMI 1996), *Alf Bicknell's Personal Beatles
Diary* (Simitar Entertainment 1997), *Yellow
Submarine* (MGM 1999).
● FURTHER READING: There have been
hundreds of books published of varying quality.
Our four recommendations are: *The Complete
Beatles Chronicle* by Mark Lewisohn, an accurate
and definitive career and recording history by
their greatest historian; *The Beatles After The
Break-Up 1970-2000*, by Keith Badman; *Shout! The
True Story Of The Beatles* by Philip Norman, the
most readable and objective biography;
Revolution In The Head by Ian MacDonald, a
beautifully written authoritative study of every
song. Others are:
The True Story Of The Beatles, Billy Shepherd.
The Beatles Book, Norman Parkinson and
Maureen Cleave. *A Cellarful Of Noise*, Brian
Epstein. *The Beatles: A Hard Day's Night*, John
Burke. *Love Me Do: The Beatles' Progress*, Michael
Braun. *The Beatles In Help*, Al Hine. *The Beatles:
Words Without Music*, Rick Friedman. *The
Beatles*, Hunter Davies. *Get Back*, Ethan Russell
(photographs). *The Beatles Illustrated Lyrics
Volume 2*, Alan Aldridge (ed.). *Apple To The Core:
The Unmaking Of The Beatles*, Peter McCabe and

Robert D. Schonfeld. *The Longest Cocktail Party*,
Richard DiLello. *As Time Goes By: Living In The
Sixties*, Derek Taylor. *Twilight Of The Gods: The
Beatles In Retrospect*, Wilfred Mellers. *The Man
Who Gave The Beatles Away*, Allan Williams. *The
Beatles: An Illustrated Record*, Roy Carr and Tony
Tyler. *All Together Now: The First Complete Beatles
Discography 1961-1975*, Harry Castleman and
Walter J. Podrazik. *The Beatles: Yesterday, Today,
Tomorrow*, Rochelle Larkin. *Beatles In Their Own
Words*, Miles. *The Beatles: A Day In The Life: The
Day By Day Diary 1960-1970*, Tom Schultheiss.
*The Boys From Liverpool: John, Paul, George,
Ringo*, Nicholas Schaffner. *The Beatles Illustrated
Lyrics*, Alan Aldridge (ed.). *The Beatles Apart*,
Bob Woffinden. *Shout! The True Story Of The
Beatles*, Philip Norman. *The Beatles: An
Illustrated Discography*, Miles. *Thank U Very
Much: Mike McCartney's Family Album*, (Peter)
Michael McCartney. *All You Needed Was Love:
The Beatles After The Beatles*, John Blake. *The
Long And Winding Road: A History Of The Beatles
On Record*, Neville Stannard. *Abbey Road: The
Story Of The World's Most Famous Recording
Studios*, Brian Southall. *The Complete Beatles
Lyrics*, no author listed. *The Beatles At The Beeb
62-65: The Story Of Their Radio Career*, Kevin
Howlett. *With The Beatles: The Historic
Photographs*, Dezo Hoffman. *Beatles' England*,
David Bacon and Norman Maslov. *Working Class
Heroes: The History Of The Beatles' Solo
Recordings*, Neville Stannard. *The Beatles: An
Illustrated Diary*, H.V. Fulpen. *The Love You
Make: An Insider's Story Of The Beatles*, Peter
Brown and Steven Gaines. *John Ono Lennon
1967-1980*, Ray Coleman. *John Winston Lennon
1940-1966*, Ray Coleman. *Beatlemania: An
Illustrated Filmography*, Bill Harry. *Paperback
Writers: An Illustrated Bibliography*, Bill Harry.
The End Of The Beatles, Harry Castleman and
Wally Podrazik. *Beatle! The Pete Best Story*, Pete
Best and Patrick Doncaster. *The Beatles Live*,
Mark Lewisohn. *It Was Twenty Years Ago*, Derek
Taylor. *Yesterday: The Beatles Remembered*,
Alistair Taylor. *All Our Loving: A Beatle Fan's
Memoir*, Carolyn Lee Mitchell and Michael
Munn. *The Beatles: 25 Years In The Life*, Mark
Lewisohn. *Brian Epstein: The Man Who Made
The Beatles*, Ray Coleman. *The Beatles Album File
And Complete Discography*, Jeff Russell. *How
They Became The Beatles: A Definitive History Of
The Early Years 1960-1964*, Gareth L. Pawlowski.
*Complete Beatles Recording Sessions: The Official
Story Of The Abbey Road Years*, Mark Lewisohn.
Day By Day, Mark Lewisohn. *Speak Words Of
Wisdom: Reflections On The Beatles*, Spencer
Leigh. *In Their Own Words: The Beatles After The
Break-Up*, David Bennahum. *The Complete
Beatles Chronicle*, Mark Lewisohn. *Ultimate
Beatles Encyclopedia*, Bill Harry. *Tomorrow Never
Knows: Thirty Years Of Beatles Music &
Memorabilia*, Geoffrey Giuliano. *The Ultimate
Recording Guide*, Allen J. Wiener. *Beatles*, John
Ewing. *It Was Thirty Years Ago Today*, Terence

Spencer. *The Summer Of Love*, George Martin. *A Hard Day's Write*, Steve Turner. *Revolution In The Head: The Beatles Records And The Sixties*, Ian MacDonald. *Backbeat*, Alan Clayson and Pauline Sutcliffe. *The Essential Guide To The Music Of ...*, John Robertson. *The Beatles' London*, Piet Schreuders, Mark Lewisohn and Adam Smith. *A Day In The Life: The Music And Artistry Of The Beatles*, Mark Hertsgaard. *The Beatles: Not For Sale*, Jim Belmo. *The Encyclopedia Of Beatles People*, Bill Harry. *Beatles – From Cavern To Star Club*, Hans Olaf Gottfridsson. *The Beatles Movies*, Bob Neaverson. *Hamburg: The Cradle Of British Rock*, Alan Clayson. *The Complete Idiot's Guide To The Beatles*, Richard Buskin. *Classic Rock Albums: Abbey Road/Let It Be*, Peter Doggett. *The Beatles: A Diary*, Miles. *Beatles Undercover*, Kristofer Engelhardt. *Drummed Out! The Sacking Of Pete Best*, Spencer Leigh. *Get Back: The Beatles' Let It Be Disaster*, Doug Sulphy and Ray Schweighardt. *The Beatles: Inside The One And Only Lonely Hearts Club Band*, David Pritchard and Alan Lysaght. *The Beatles After The Break-Up: 1970-2000*, Keith Badman. *The Rocking City: The Explosive Birth Of The Beatles*, Sam Leach. *Beatletoons: The Real Story Behind The Cartoon Beatles*, Mitch Axelrod. *The Beatles' Story On Capitol Records: Beatlemania & The Singles*, Bruce Spizer (ed.). *The Beatles Anthology*, the Beatles. *The Beatles Off The Record*, Keith Badman. *The Beatles In Rishikesh*, Paul Saltzman. *The Beatles, Popular Music And Society: A Thousand Voices*, Ian Inglis (ed.). *The Beatles Uncovered: 1,000,000 Mop-Top Murders By The Fans And The Famous*, Dave Henderson. *The Beatles Mixes*, Holger Schoeler & Thorsten Schmidt. *Mania Days*, Curt Gunther (photographer). *Sgt. Pepper's Lonely Hearts Club Band: The Album Collection Vol. 8*, Azing Moltmaker. *The Quarrymen*, Hunter Davies.

● FILMS: *A Hard Day's Night* (1964), *Help!* (1965), *Magical Mystery Tour* (1967), *Yellow Submarine* (1968), *Let It Be* (1970).

BEATSTALKERS

Formed in Glasgow, Scotland, in 1962, the Beatstalkers originally comprised Davie Lennox (vocals), Eddie Campbell (guitar), Alan Mair (bass) and 'Tudge' Williamson (drums). Within weeks Ronnie Smith (rhythm guitar) had been added to the line-up. By 1964 the Beatstalkers had become a leading attraction, specializing in cover versions of hitherto obscure soul and R&B songs. Such was their popularity, the group was dubbed 'Scotland's Beatles' and in 1965 an open-air concert in Glasgow's George Square was abandoned when fans rioted. The Beatstalkers then secured a recording contract with Decca Records. 'Everybody's Talkin' 'Bout My Baby', 'Left Right Left' and 'A Love Like Yours' followed in succession, but although worthwhile in their own right, these records failed to capture the group's true mettle. The Beatstalkers moved to London in 1967 where they secured a residency at the famed Marquee Club. However, despite switching to CBS Records, the group was still unable to achieve a major breakthrough, in part because they relied on outside material. Their new manager Ken Pitt suggested that the Beatstalkers record songs by his best-known charge, David Bowie. Three of his compositions, 'Silver Tree Top School For Boys', 'Everything Is You' and 'When I'm Five', were released in succession, although only the first title was issued as an a-side. The experiment was neither an artistic nor commercial success, and, as Alan Mair later recalled, 'It was pitiful to watch Davie Lennox rehearse the songs in an English accent.' The Beatstalkers split up in 1969 when their equipment was stolen. Late-period drummer Jeff Allen joined East Of Eden, while Mair was later a member of the critically acclaimed Only Ones.

BEAU BRUMMELS

Formed in San Francisco in 1964, the Beau Brummels provided a vital impetus to the city's emergent rock circuit. Vocalist Sal Valentino (b. Sal Spampinato, 8 September 1942, San Francisco, California, USA) had previously led his own group, Sal Valentino And The Valentines, which issued 'I Wanna Twist'/'Lisa Marie' in 1962. Ron Elliott (b. 21 October 1943, Healdsburg, California, USA; guitar, vocals), Ron Meagher (b. 2 October 1941, Oakland, California, USA; bass) and John Petersen (b. 8 January 1942, Rudyard, Michigan, USA; drums), formerly of the Sparklers, joined him in a new act, taking the name Beau Brummels in deference to their love of British beat music. Playing a staple diet of current hits and material by the Beatles and Searchers, the quartet enjoyed a committed following within the city's Irish community prior to adding Declan Mulligan (b. County Tipperary, Eire; guitar) to the line-up. Local entrepreneurs Tom Donahue and Bob Mitchell saw their obvious topicality and signed the band to their fledgling Autumn Records label. 'Laugh Laugh', the Beau Brummels' debut single, broached the US Top 20 in 1964, while its follow-up, 'Just A Little', reached number 8 early the following year. Both songs, which were original compositions, bore an obvious debt to UK mentors, but later, more adventurous releases, including 'You Tell Me Why' and 'Don't Talk To Strangers', emphasized an American heritage, presaging the 'West Coast' sound.

The band's first two albums offered elements of folk, country and R&B. Producer Sylvester Stewart, later known as Sly Stone, sculpted a clear, resonant sound that outstripped that of many contemporaries. Elliott emerged as a distinctive songwriter, while Valentino's deep, tremulous delivery provided an unmistakable lead. Mulligan's premature departure in March 1965 did little to undermine this progress. Autumn Records was wound up in 1966 and the and's contract was sold to Warner Brothers Records. A new member, Don Irving, was featured on their next collection, *Beau Brummels 66*, but this sorry affair was a marked disappointment, consisting of throwaway readings of current hits. The release undermined the quintet's credibility. Irving then left, and, as the band now eschewed live appearances, Petersen opted for another local attraction, the Tikis, who later became Harpers Bizarre. The remaining trio completed the exquisite *Triangle*, one of the era's most cultured and delicate albums, but the loss of Meagher in September 1967 reduced the band to the central duo of Elliott and Valentino. The former undertook several 'outside' projects, producing and/or writing singles for Butch Engle And The Styx, before donating songs and/or arranging skills on albums by Randy Newman, the Everly Brothers and the aforementioned Harpers Bizarre. In 1968 the Beau Brummels duo completed *Bradley's Barn*, an early and brave excursion into country rock, before embarking on separate careers. Valentino issued three solo singles before founding Stoneground. Elliott completed the gorgeous *The Candlestickmaker*, formed the disappointing Pan, then undertook occasional session work, including a cameo on Little Feat's *Sailin' Shoes*.

The original Beau Brummels regrouped in 1974 but Meagher was an early casualty. He was replaced by Dan Levitt, formerly of Pan and Levitt And McClure. *Beau Brummels* was an engaging collection, but progress halted in 1975 when Petersen opted to assist in a Harpers Bizarre reunion. Peter Tepp provided a temporary replacement, but the project was latterly abandoned. Since then the Beau Brummels have enjoyed several short-lived resurrections, but conflicting interests, coupled with Elliott's ill health, have denied them a long-term future. Numerous archive recordings, many previously unreleased, have nonetheless kept the band's name and music alive.

● ALBUMS: *Introducing The Beau Brummels* (Autumn/Pye International 1965) ★★★, *Beau Brummels, Volume 2* (Autumn 1965) ★★★, *Beau Brummels 66* (Warners 1966) ★★, *Triangle* (Warners 1967) ★★★★, *Bradley's Barn* (Warners 1968) ★★★★, *Volume 44* (Vault 1968) ★★, *The Beau Brummels* (Warners 1975) ★★.

● COMPILATIONS: *The Best Of The Beau Brummels* (Vault 1967) ★★★, *The Beau Brummels Sing* (Post 1972) ★★★, *The Original Hits Of The Beau Brummels* (JAS 1975) ★★★, *The Best Of The Beau Brummels 1964-68* recordings (Rhino 1981) ★★★, *From The Vaults* (Rhino 1982) ★★★, *Autumn In San Francisco* (Edsel 1985) ★★★, *The Autumn Of Their Years* (Big Beat/Nuggets From The Golden Era 1995) ★★★, *San Fran Sessions* 3-CD set (Sundazed 1996) ★★, *Greatest Hits* (Classic World 2000) ★★★.

BEDROCKS

Formed in Leeds, England, in late 1967, this West Indian sextet comprised Trevor Wisdom (b. 1945, Jamaica; organ), Owen Wisdom (b. 1948, Jamaica; bass guitar), Leroy Mills (b. 1949, St. Kitts; trumpet), Reg Challenger (b. 1948, St. Kitts; drums), William Hixon (b. 1951, Monseratt; lead guitar), Paul Douglas (b. 1947, Jamaica; tenor saxophone). Their big break came in 1968 when they were offered the opportunity to record at EMI with producer Norman Smith (later Hurricane Smith). After borrowing £25 to hire a van for the trip, they completed a single within a day. Two days later, their topical cover version of the Beatles' 'Ob-La-Di, Ob-La-Da' was issued and a fortnight later it was in the UK Top 20. Unfortunately, their ethnic reading was outsold by Marmalade's chart-topping version. For their follow-up, the Bedrocks recorded a version of the rugby song 'The Lovedene Girls', but the single received little airplay and failed to chart. It was to prove their last chance of commercial success.

BEGGARS OPERA

Glasgow, Scotland, rock band Beggars Opera was formed in the late 60s by Marshall Erskine (bass, flute), Ricky Gardiner (guitar, vocals), Martin Griffiths (vocals, percussion), Alan Park (keyboards) and Raymond Wilson (drums). The group's grandiose ambition was to fuse classical and progressive rock elements, an accommodation they achieved but only to moderate critical and commercial interest. Signed to Vertigo Records, they made their debut in 1970 with *Act One*, released concurrently with 'Sarabande'. The single was the most successful of the two releases, charting in several mainland European countries. The album included a preposterous rendition of 'Classical Gas', which was eventually released as a single in its own right four years later. The group then expanded to a quintet with the addition of multi-instrumentalist Gordon Sellar (bass, guitar, vocals) for the follow-up collection, *Waters Of Change*. Abandoning some of the progressive rock elements of earlier recordings, the group pursued a more melodious rock direction on this album, heavily indebted to musical developments on America's west coast. Erskine had left the group by the time they recorded 1972's *Pathfinder*, which included a cover version of Richard Harris's 'MacArthur Park'. Their final effort, 1973's *Get Your Dog Off Me*, was completed as a trio, with Sellar joined by founder-members Gardiner and Park. Unfortunately, this again proved unsuccessful, and with Vertigo wary of further investment in the group, they broke up in 1974. Sellar attempted a re-formation in the mid-70s when two further albums were issued in Germany – still the group's most receptive market. Gardiner enjoyed greater success as a member of David Bowie's touring band.

● ALBUMS: *Act One* (Vertigo 1970) ★★★, *Waters Of Change* (Vertigo 1971) ★★★, *Pathfinder* (Vertigo 1972) ★★, *Get Your Dog Off Me* (Vertigo 1973) ★★.

BEL-AIRS

Formed in Redondo Beach, California, USA, in 1961, the Bel-Airs were an instrumental surf group best known for their first single, 'Mr. Moto', on Arvee Records. The record never reached the national charts but was a popular local hit in the Los Angeles region and subsequently became a staple of the repertoires of many other surf bands. The group consisted of Paul Johnson (guitar), Richard Delvy (drums), Jim Roberts (piano), Chaz Stewart (saxophone) and Eddie Bertrand (guitar). Delvy later formed the similar sounding Challengers in 1964. A later member was drummer Dick Dodd, who went on to play drums and sing lead vocals for the Standells. The Bel-Airs broke up in 1963, having never recorded an album. Their recorded material was finally compiled by Sundazed in 2001.

● COMPILATIONS: *Volcanic Action* (Sundazed 2001) ★★★.

BELAFONTE, HARRY

b. Harold George Belafonte Jnr., 1 March 1927, Harlem, New York City, New York, USA. In recent years, the former 'King Of Calypso' has become better known for his work with UNICEF and his enterprise with the charity organization USA For Africa. Prior to that, Belafonte had an extraordinarily varied life. His early career was spent as an actor, until he had time to demonstrate his silky smooth and gently relaxing singing voice. He appeared as Joe in Oscar Hammerstein's *Carmen Jones*; an adaptation of *Carmen* by Bizet, and in 1956 he was snapped up by RCA-Victor Records. Belafonte was then at the forefront of the calypso craze, which was a perfect vehicle for his happy-go-lucky folk songs. Early hits included 'Jamaica Farewell', 'Mary's Boy Child' and the classic transatlantic hit 'Banana Boat Song' with its unforgettable refrain: 'Day-oh, dayyy-oh, daylight come and me wanna go home'. *Calypso* became the first ever album to sell a million copies, and spent 31 weeks at the top of the US charts. Belafonte continued throughout the 50s with incredible success. He was able to cross over into many markets appealing to pop, folk and jazz fans, as well as to the ethnic population with whom he became closely associated, particularly during the civil rights movement. He appeared in many movies including *Island In The Sun*, singing the title song, and *Odds Against Tomorrow*. His success as an album artist was considerable; between 1956 and 1962 he was hardly ever absent from the album chart. *Belafonte At Carnegie Hall* spent over three years in the charts, and similar success befell *Belafonte Returns To Carnegie Hall*,

featuring Miriam Makeba, the Chad Mitchell Trio and Odetta, with a memorable recording of 'There's A Hole In My Bucket'.

Throughout the 60s Belafonte was an ambassador of human rights and a most articulate speaker at rallies and on television. His appeal as a concert-hall attraction was immense; no less than seven of his albums were recorded in concert. Although his appearances in the bestseller lists had stopped by the 70s he remained an active performer and recording artist, and continued to appear on film, although in lightweight movies such as *Buck And The Preacher* and *Uptown Saturday Night*. In the mid-80s he was a leading light in the USA For Africa appeal and sang on 'We Are The World'. His sterling work continued into the 90s with UNICEF. Belafonte was one of the few black artists who broke down barriers of class and race, and should be counted alongside Dr Martin Luther King as a major figure in achieving equal rights for blacks in America through his work in popular music. He researched and produced an impressive box set of early African recordings in 2001. *The Long Road To Freedom: An Anthology Of Black Music* was another landmark in an impressive career.

● ALBUMS: *Mark Twain And Other Folk Favorites* (RCA Victor 1955) ★★★, *Belafonte* (RCA Victor 1956) ★★★★, *Calypso* (RCA Victor 1956) ★★★★, *An Evening With Belafonte* (RCA Victor 1957) ★★★★, *Belafonte Sings Of The Caribbean* (RCA Victor 1957) ★★★, *Belafonte Sings The Blues* (RCA Victor 1958) ★★★, *Love Is A Gentle Thing* (RCA Victor 1959) ★★★, with Lena Horne *Porgy And Bess* film soundtrack (RCA Victor 1959) ★★★★, *Belafonte At Carnegie Hall* (RCA Victor 1959) ★★★★, *My Lord What A Mornin'* (RCA Victor 1960) ★★★, *Belafonte Returns To Carnegie Hall* (RCA Victor 1960) ★★★, *Swing Dat Hammer* (RCA Victor 1960) ★★★, *At Home And Abroad* (RCA Victor 1961) ★★★, *Jump Up Calypso* (RCA Victor 1961) ★★★★, *The Midnight Special* (RCA Victor 1962) ★★★, *The Many Moods Of Belafonte* (RCA Victor 1962) ★★★, *To Wish You A Merry Christmas* (RCA Victor 1962) ★★★, *Streets I Have Walked* (RCA Victor 1963) ★★★, *Belafonte At The Greek Theatre* (RCA Victor 1964) ★★★, *Ballads Blues And Boasters* (RCA 1964) ★★, with Miriam Makeba *An Evening With Belafonte/Makeba* (RCA 1965) ★★★★, with Nana Mouskouri *An Evening With Belafonte/Mouskouri* (RCA 1966) ★★★, *In My Quiet Room* (RCA 1966) ★★★, *Calypso In Brass* (RCA 1967) ★★, *Belafonte On Campus* (RCA 1967) ★★, *Homeward Bound* (RCA 1970) ★★, *Play Me* (RCA 1976) ★★★, *Turn The World Around* (Columbia 1977) ★★, *Loving You Is Where I Belong* (Columbia 1981) ★★, *Paradise In Gazankulu* (EMI-Manhattan 1988) ★★, *Belafonte '89* (EMI 1989) ★★, *The Long Road To Freedom: An Anthology Of Black Music* 5-CD box set (Buddah 2001) ★★★★.

● COMPILATIONS: *Pure Gold* (RCA 1975) ★★★★, *A Legendary Performer* (RCA 1978)

★★★, *The Very Best Of Harry Belafonte* (RCA 1982) ★★★, *20 Golden Greats* (Deja Vu 1985) ★★★, *Collection* (Castle 1987) ★★★, *Banana Boat Song* (Entertainers 1988) ★★★, *All Time Greatest Hits, Volume 1* (RCA 1989) ★★★★, *All Time Greatest Hits, Volume 2* (RCA 1989) ★★★, *All Time Greatest Hits, Volume 3* (RCA 1989) ★★★, *Day-O And Other Hits* (RCA 1990) ★★★.
● FURTHER READING: *Belafonte*, A.J. Shaw.
● FILMS: *Bright Road* (1953), *Carmen Jones* (1954), *Island In The Sun* (1957), *The World, The Flesh And The Devil* (1959), *Odds Against Tomorrow* (1959), *The Angel Levine* (1970), *Buck And The Preacher* (1972), *Uptown Saturday Night* (1974), *Free To Be ... You & Me* (1974), *A Veces Miro Mi Vida* (1982), *Roots Of Rhythm* narrator (1984), *We Shall Overcome* narrator (1989), *The Player* (1992), *Prêt-À-Porter* aka *Ready To Wear* (1994), *White Man's Burden* (1995), *Kansas City* (1996).

BELMONTS

The Belmonts were one of the leading American doo-wop groups of the late 50s and comprised Angelo D'Aleo (b. 3 February 1940, Bronx, New York, USA), Carlo Mastrangelo (b. 5 October 1938, Bronx, New York, USA) and Freddie Milano (b. 22 August 1939, Bronx, New York, USA). Their leader was Dion DiMucci (b. 18 July 1939, Bronx, New York, USA), who left for a solo career in 1960. The band soldiered on for three more years after being signed to a new record label, Sabina, with Frank Lyndon replacing Mastrangelo in 1962. They had enough fans to give them six further hits, including a smooth version of the Ink Spots' hit 'Don't Get Around Much Anymore'. They re-formed briefly with Dion in 1967, 1972 and 1973. Their most memorable work remains in the 50s with Dion.
● COMPILATIONS: *The Belmonts' Carnival Of Hits* (Sabina 1962) ★★★, *Carlo & The Belmonts* (Ace 1990) ★★★, *The Laurie, Sabina & United Artists Sides Volume One* (Ace 1995) ★★★★, *The Laurie, Sabina & United Artists Sides Volume Two* (Ace 1999) ★★★.

BENNETT, CLIFF

One of the most accomplished British R&B vocalists of his era, Cliff Bennett (b. 4 June 1940, Slough, England) formed the excellent Rebel Rousers in early 1961. Taking their name from a Duane Eddy hit of the period, the band comprised Mick King (lead guitar), Frank Allen (bass), Sid Phillips (piano, saxophone) and Ricky Winters (drums). With a repertoire of rock 'n' roll, blue-eyed soul and R&B, the band was briefly taken under the wing of madcap producer Joe Meek, with whom they recorded several unsuccessful singles. A succession of R&B cover versions brought no further success and, early in 1964, bassist Frank Allen departed to replace Tony Jackson in the Searchers. The Rebel Rousers continued their busy touring

schedule at home and abroad and were finally rewarded with a Top 10 hit, 'One Way Love', in November 1964. This brassy, upbeat cover version of the Drifters' original augured well for the future, but the follow-up, 'I'll Take You Home', stalled at number 43. Abandoning the Drifters as source material, they covered other R&B artists, without noticeable success.
A move to Brian Epstein's NEMs management secured them the invaluable patronage of the Beatles, and Paul McCartney stepped in to produce their sparkling reading of 'Got To Get You Into My Life' from the recently released *Revolver*. Peaking at number 6, the single was their second and last Top 10 hit. Thereafter, Bennett fell victim to changing musical fashions as beat groups were generally dismissed as anachronistic. The Rebel Rousers changed their name to the more prosaic Cliff Bennett And His Band and briefly sought success with contemporary writers such as Mark London and Roy Wood. By mid-1969, Bennett decided to dissolve his band and reinvent himself for the progressive market. The result was Toe Fat, a short-lived ensemble now best remembered for their tasteless album covers rather than their music. In 1972, Bennett tried again with Rebellion, and, three years later, Shanghai, but without success. Weary of traipsing around the country, he eventually turned to working in the advertising business, but still plays semi-professionally.
● ALBUMS: *Cliff Bennett And The Rebel Rousers* (Parlophone 1965) ★★★, *Drivin' You Wild* (MFP 1966) ★★★, *Cliff Bennett* (Regal 1966) ★★★, *Got To Get You Into Our Lives* (Parlophone 1967) ★★★, *Cliff Bennett Branches Out* (Parlophone 1968) ★★.
● COMPILATIONS: *25 Greatest Hits* (MFP 1998) ★★★, *Abbey Road 1963-1969* (EMI 1998) ★★★★, *Got To Get You Into My Life/Cliff Bennett* (BGO 2000) ★★★★, *Soul Blast* (Castle 2001) ★★★.

BENNETT, DUSTER

b. Anthony Bennett, c.1940, d. 26 March 1976. Bennett was a dedicated British one-man-band blues performer, in the style of Jesse Fuller and Dr Ross. He played the London R&B club circuit from the mid-60s and was signed by Mike Vernon to Blue Horizon Records in 1967, releasing 'It's A Man Down There' as his first single. On his first album he was backed by Peter Green and John McVie of Fleetwood Mac. Bennett also played harmonica on sessions for Fleetwood Mac, Champion Jack Dupree, Memphis Slim, Shusha and Martha Velez. He was briefly a member of John Mayall's Bluesbreakers, and in 1974 recorded for Mickie Most's Rak Records label, releasing a single, 'Comin Home'. He was killed in a road accident, after falling asleep at the wheel, on 26 March 1976 in Warwickshire, England, returning home after performing with Memphis Slim.
● ALBUMS: *Smiling Like I'm Happy* (Blue

Horizon 1968) ★★★, *Bright Lights* (Blue Horizon 1969) ★★★, *12 DBs* (1970) ★★★, *Fingertips* (Rak 1974) ★★.

● COMPILATIONS: *Out In The Blue* (Indigo 1994) ★★★, *Jumpin' At Shadows* (Indigo 1994) ★★, *Blue Inside* (Indigo 1995) ★★★, *I Choose To Sing The Blues* (Indigo 1997) ★★★, *Comin' Home: Unreleased And Rare Studio Recordings, Vol 2, 1971-1975* (Indigo 1999) ★★★★, *Shady Little Baby: Unreleased And Rare Recordings Volume 3* (Indigo 2000) ★★★.

BENNETT, TONY

b. Anthony Dominick Benedetto, 13 August 1926, Astoria, New York, USA. The son of an Italian father and American mother, Bennett studied music and painting at the High School of Industrial Arts. He later became a talented artist, exhibiting under his real name in New York, Paris and London. Originally possessing a tenor voice that would deepen over the years, Bennett sang during service with the US Army's entertainment unit late in World War II. Upon his discharge he worked in clubs before joining a Pearl Bailey revue in Greenwich Village as singer and master of ceremonies under the name of Joe Bari, where he was spotted by Bob Hope, who engaged him to sing in his Paramount show and changed his name to Tony Bennett. In 1950 he successfully auditioned for Columbia Records' producer Mitch Miller, singing 'Boulevard Of Broken Dreams', and a year later topped the US chart with 'Because Of You' and 'Cold, Cold Heart'. Other 50s hits, mostly backed by the Percy Faith Orchestra, included 'Rags To Riches', 'Just In Time', 'Stranger In Paradise' (from *Kismet*), 'There'll Be No Teardrops Tonight', 'Cinnamon Sinner', 'Can You Find It In Your Heart' and 'In The Middle Of An Island'. In 1958, his album *Basie Swings-Bennett Sings* was a precursor to later jazz-based work.

That same year 'Firefly', by the new songwriting team of Cy Coleman and Carolyn Leigh, was Bennett's last US Top 40 entry until 1962, when he made a major comeback with the 1954 song 'I Left My Heart In San Francisco' (which won a Grammy Award) and a sell-out Carnegie Hall concert, which was recorded and released on a double-album set. During this period he continued his long association with pianist/arranger Ralph Sharon, and frequently featured cornet soloist Bobby Hackett. Often quoted as being unable to find suitable new material, Bennett nevertheless made the 60s singles charts with contemporary songs such as 'I Wanna Be Around', 'The Good Life', 'Who Can I Turn To' and 'If I Ruled The World'. Even so, the future lay with concerts and his prolific album output, which included US Top 40 albums such as *I Wanna Be Around*, *The Many Moods Of Tony*, *The Movie Song Album*, and four albums with Canadian composer/conductor Robert Farnon. In the 70s Bennett left Columbia Records and

recorded for various labels including his own, and made albums with jazz musicians Ruby Braff and Bill Evans. His return to Columbia in the mid-80s produced *The Art Of Excellence*, which included a duet with Ray Charles, and *Bennett/Berlin*, a celebration of America's premier songwriter, on which he was accompanied by the Ralph Sharon Trio. He continued to gain excellent reviews at venues such as the Desert Inn, Las Vegas, and in 1991 celebrated 40 years in the business with a concert at London's Prince Edward Theatre. In 1993 and 1994 he was awarded Grammys for 'Best Traditional Pop Performance' for his albums *Perfectly Frank* and *Steppin' Out*. Around the same time, Bennett was 'discovered' by younger audiences following his appearances on the *David Letterman Show*, benefit shows hosted by 'alternative rock' radio stations, and his *Unplugged* session on the US cable channel MTV. The latter teamed him with contemporary artists k.d. lang and Elvis Costello. By the time he had gained two more Grammys and a World Music Award in 1995 for his *MTV Unplugged*, the album had spent 35 weeks at the top of the US Jazz chart. He received a second World Music Award for lifelong contribution to the music industry. Bennett's star continued to shine with *Here's To The Ladies*, a formidable collection of classic songs with particularly impressive versions of 'God Bless The Child' and 'I Got Rhythm'. He expanded his Billie Holiday catalogue with the excellent *Tony Bennett On Holiday: A Tribute To Billie Holiday*. The 90s proved to be his most critically acclaimed decade, especially with his Duke Ellington tribute album. His voice has ripened with age and he appears hip to a much wider and younger audience.

● ALBUMS: *Because Of You* (Columbia 1952) ★★★, *Alone At Last With Tony Bennett* (Columbia 1955) ★★, *Treasure Chest Of Songs* (1955) ★★★, *Cloud Seven* (Columbia 1955) ★★, *Tony* (Columbia 1957) ★★★, *The Beat Of My Heart* (Columbia 1957) ★★★, *Long Ago And Far Away* (Columbia 1958) ★★★, with Count Basie *Basie Swings, Bennett Sings* (Roulette 1958) ★★★★, *Blue Velvet* (Columbia 1959) ★★★, *If I Ruled The World* (Columbia 1959) ★★★★, with Basie *Tony Bennett In Person* (Columbia 1959) ★★★, *Hometown, My Town* (Columbia 1959) ★★★, *To My Wonderful One* (Columbia 1960) ★★, *Tony Sings For Two* (Columbia 1960) ★★★, *Alone Together* (Columbia 1960) ★★★, *A String Of Harold Arlen* (Columbia 1960) ★★★, *My Heart Sings* (Columbia 1961) ★★★, with Basie *Bennett And Basie Strike Up The Band* (Roulette 1962) ★★, *Mr. Broadway* (Columbia 1962) ★★★, *I Left My Heart In San Francisco* (Columbia 1962) ★★★★, *On The Glory Road* (Columbia 1962) ★★, *Tony Bennett At Carnegie Hall* (Columbia 1962) ★★★, *I Wanna Be Around* (Columbia 1963) ★★★★, *This Is All I Ask* (Columbia 1963) ★★★, *The Many Moods Of Tony* (Columbia 1964) ★★★,

When Lights Are Low (Columbia 1964) ★★★, *Who Can I Turn To?* (Columbia 1964) ★★★, *If I Ruled The World – Songs For The Jet Set* (Columbia 1965) ★★★, *The Movie Song Album* (Columbia 1966) ★★★, *A Time For Love* (Columbia 1966) ★★★, *The Oscar* film soundtrack (Columbia 1966) ★★, *Tony Makes It Happen!* (Columbia 1967) ★★, *For Once In My Life* (Columbia 1967) ★★★, *Snowfall/The Tony Bennett Christmas Album* (Columbia 1968) ★★★, *I've Gotta Be Me* (Columbia 1969) ★★, *Tony Sings The Great Hits Of Today!* (Columbia 1970) ★★, *Tony Bennett's 'Something'* (Columbia 1970) ★★★, *Love Story* (Columbia 1971) ★★★, *Get Happy With The London Philharmonic Orchestra* (Columbia 1971) ★★, *Summer Of '42* (Columbia 1972) ★★, *With Love* (Columbia 1972) ★★★, *The Good Things In Life* (MGM/Verve 1972) ★★★, *Rodgers And Hart Songbook* (Columbia 1973) ★★, with Bill Evans *The Tony Bennett/Bill Evans Album* (Original Jazz Classics 1975) ★★★★, with Bill Evans *Together Again* (DRG 1976) ★★★, *Chicago* (DCC 1984) ★★★, *The Art Of Excellence* (Columbia 1986) ★★★, *Jazz* (Columbia 1987) ★★★, *Astoria: Portrait Of The Artist* (Columbia 1990) ★★★, *Perfectly Frank* (Columbia 1992) ★★, *Steppin' Out* (Columbia 1993) ★★★, *MTV Unplugged* (Columbia 1994) ★★★★, *Here's To The Ladies* (Columbia 1995) ★★★, *Tony Bennett On Holiday: A Tribute To Billie Holiday* (Columbia 1997) ★★★, *The Playground* (Columbia 1998) ★★, *Bennett Sings Ellington Hot And Cool* (Columbia 1999) ★★★★, *Playing With My Friends: Bennett Sings The Blues* (Columbia 2001) ★★★.
● COMPILATIONS: *Tony's Greatest Hits* (Columbia 1958) ★★★★, *More Tony's Greatest Hits* (Columbia 1960) ★★★★, *Tony's Greatest Hits, Volume III* (Columbia 1965) ★★★★, *A String Of Tony's Hits* (Columbia 1966) ★★★★, *Tony Bennett's Greatest Hits, Volume IV* (Columbia 1969) ★★★, *Tony Bennett's All-Time Greatest Hits* (Columbia 1972) ★★★, *The Very Best Of Tony Bennett – 20 Greatest Hits* (Warwick 1977) ★★★, *40 Years, The Artistry Of Tony Bennett* 4-CD box set (Legacy 1991) ★★★★, *The Essential Tony Bennett (A Retrospective)* (Columbia 1998) ★★★★.
● VIDEOS: *Tony Bennett In Concert* (Mastervision 1987), *A Special Evening With Tony Bennett* (MIA 1995), *The Art Of The Singer* (SMV 1996).
● FURTHER READING: *What My Heart Has Seen*, Tony Bennett. *The Good Life*, Tony Bennett.

BENT FABRIC

b. Bent Fabricus Bjerre, 7 December 1924, Copenhagen, Denmark. A multi-talented Danish musician, known mainly for his piano work. Bent Fabric first formed a jazz band in the 40s when he was still in his teens. They made some of the first ever jazz recordings in Denmark. In 1950, having moved into the pop music of the day, he took over the Danish record company Metronome where he appointed himself A&R

manager. Bent Fabric also had his own Saturday night television show, *Around A Piano*. In 1962 he sold a million copies worldwide of the tune 'Alley Cat', which he had written under the pseudonym Frank Bjorn. The subsequent album made the US Top 20. He never followed the hit with any success other than the minor hit 'Chicken Feed', the following year, and returned to Denmark and his record company. In recent years he has become one of the most successful music publishers in Europe.
● ALBUMS: *Alley Cat* (1962) ★★★.

BENTON, BROOK

b. Benjamin Franklin Peay, 19 September 1931, Camden, South Carolina, USA, d. 9 April 1988, New York City, New York, USA. A stylish, mellifluent singer, Benton's most ascendant period was the late 50s/early 60s. Although he began recording in 1953, Benton's first major hit came in 1959 on forging a songwriting partnership with Clyde Otis and Belford Hendricks. 'It's Just A Matter Of Time' reached the US Top 3 and introduced a remarkable string of successes, including 'So Many Ways' (1959), 'The Boll Weevil Song' (1961) and 'Hotel Happiness' (1962). Duets with Dinah Washington, 'Baby (You've Got What It Takes)', a million-seller, and 'A Rockin' Good Way (To Mess Around And Fall In Love)', topped the R&B listings in 1960. Benton's warm, resonant delivery continued to prove popular into the early 60s. A versatile vocalist, his releases encompassed standards, blues and spirituals, while his compositions were recorded by Nat 'King' Cole, Clyde McPhatter and Roy Hamilton. Brook remained signed to the Mercury Records label until 1964 before moving to RCA Records, then Reprise Records. Releases on these labels failed to recapture the artist's previous success, but by the end of the decade, Benton rose to the challenge of younger acts with a series of excellent recordings for Atlantic Records' Cotillion subsidiary. His languid, atmospheric version of 'Rainy Night In Georgia' (1970) was an international hit and the most memorable product of an artistically fruitful period. Benton continued to record for a myriad of outlets during the 70s, including Brut (owned by the perfume company), Stax Records and MGM Records. Although his later work was less incisive, the artist remained one of music's top live attractions. He died in April 1988, aged 56, succumbing to pneumonia while weakened by spinal meningitis.
● ALBUMS: *Brook Benton At His Best* (Epic 1959) ★★, *It's Just A Matter Of Time* (Mercury 1959) ★★★, *Brook Benton* (Mercury 1959) ★★★, *Endlessly* (1959) ★★★, *So Many Ways I Love You* (Mercury 1960) ★★★, with Dinah Washington *The Two Of Us* (Mercury 1960) ★★★★, *Songs I Love To Sing* (Mercury 1960) ★★★, *The Boll Weevil Song (& Eleven Other Great Hits)* (Mercury 1961) ★★★, *If You Believe* (Mercury 1961) ★★★,

Singing The Blues – Lie To Me (Mercury 1962) ★★★, *There Goes That Song Again* (Mercury 1962) ★★★, *Best Ballads Of Broadway* (Mercury 1963) ★★, with Jesse Belvin *Brook Benton And Jesse Belvin* (Crown 1963) ★★★, *Born To Sing The Blues* (Mercury 1964) ★★★, *That Old Feeling* (RCA 1966) ★★★, *Laura (What's He Got That I Ain't Got)* (Reprise 1967) ★★, *Do Your Own Thing* (Cotillion 1969) ★★, *Brook Benton Today* (Cotillion 1970) ★★, *Home Style* (Cotillion 1970) ★★★, *The Gospel Truth* (Cotillion 1971) ★★, *Something For Everyone* (MGM 1973) ★★, *Sings A Love Story* (RCA 1975) ★★, *Mr. Bartender* (All Platinum 1976) ★★, *This Is Brook Benton* (All Platinum 1976) ★★★, *Makin' Love Is Good For You* (Olde Worlde 1978) ★★, *Ebony* (Olde Worlde 1978) ★★, *Brook Benton Sings The Standards* (RCA 1984) ★★★.
● COMPILATIONS: *Brook Benton's Golden Hits* (Mercury 1961) ★★★, *Golden Hits Volume Two* (Mercury 1963) ★★★, *Spotlight On Brook Benton* (Philips 1977) ★★★, *The Incomparable Brook Benton: 20 Greatest Hits* (Audio Fidelity 1982) ★★★, *Sixteen Golden Classics* (Unforgettable/ Castle 1986) ★★★, *The Brook Benton Anthology* (Rhino 1986) ★★★★, *His Greatest Hits* (Mercury 1987) ★★★, *40 Greatest Hits* (Mercury 1990) ★★★★, *A Rainy Night In Georgia* (Mainline 1990) ★★★, *Greatest Hits* (Curb 1991) ★★★, *Endlessly: The Best Of Brook Benton* (Rhino 1998) ★★★★, *The Essential MGM And RCA Victor Recordings* (Taragon 2000) ★★★, *Red Hot And Blue* (TKO 2001) ★★★.
● FILMS: *Mister Rock And Roll* (1957).

BERNS, BERT
b. Bertrand Russell Berns, 8 November 1929, New York City, New York, USA, d. 30 December 1967, New York City, New York, USA. This exceptional Bronx-born songwriter and producer was responsible for some of urban, 'uptown' soul's most treasured moments. He began his career as a record salesman, before being drawn into a new role as a copywriter and session pianist. He became a writer for Mellin Music, one of dozens of small publishers residing in the legendary Brill Building at 1650 Broadway. Berns began composing, often under such pseudonyms as 'Bert Russell' and 'Russell Byrd', and in 1960 formed a partnership with Phil Medley, the first of several similar highly successful working relationships (with Jerry Ragovoy, Jeff Barry and Wes Farrell). The first major Berns/Medley success came with 'Twist And Shout', originally recorded by the Top Notes but later transformed into an anthem by the Isley Brothers and regularly performed as a show-stopper by the Beatles before becoming one of the rock 'n' roll standards of the modern era.
Berns' work then appeared on several New York-based outlets, but his next important step came when he replaced the team of Leiber And Stoller as the Drifters' writer/producer. He formed WEB IV along with Jerry Wexler and the Ertegun

brothers in 1965. Now firmly in place at the Atlantic Records label, he was involved with several other artists including Ben E. King and Barbara Lewis, although his finest work was often saved for Solomon Burke and such definitive releases as 'Goodbye Baby', 'Cry To Me', 'Everybody Needs Somebody To Love' and 'The Price'. Berns also forged an exceptional partnership with Jerry Ragovoy which included stellar work for Garnet Mimms and Lorraine Ellison, plus 'Piece Of My Heart' which was recorded by Erma Franklin and later by Janis Joplin.
In addition to the previously mentioned classic Berns was responsible for; 'Tell Him' (the Exciters, Alma Cogan, Hello and Billie Davis), 'A Little Bit Of Soap' (Jarmels, Showaddywaddy, Gene McDaniels, Jimmy Justice), 'It Was Easier To Hurt Her' (Wayne Fontana), 'I Don't Want To Go On Without You' (Drifters, Moody Blues), 'Let The Water Run Down' (PJ Proby), 'I Want Candy' (Strangeloves, Brian Poole, Bow Wow Wow), 'Down In The Valley' (Otis Redding), 'If I Didn't Have A Dime' (Gene Pitney), and 'Hang On Sloopy' (McCoys). A spell in Britain resulted in sessions with Them and Lulu. He composed and produced 'Here Comes The Night' and produced both 'Gloria' and 'Baby Please Don't Go'. Berns returned home to inaugurate the Bang and Shout labels. The former, pop-oriented company boasted a roster including Neil Diamond, the McCoys, the Strangeloves and former Them lead singer Van Morrison, while Shout was responsible for several excellent soul releases by Roy C, Bobby Harris, Erma Franklin and Freddy Scott. An astute individual, Berns once proffered a photograph of the Beatles to writer Nik Cohn: 'These boys have genius. They may be the ruin of us all.' He was referring to an endangered generation of hustling backroom talent, responsible for gathering songs, musicians and arrangements. He did not survive to see his prophecy fulfilled – Berns died of a heart attack in a New York hotel room on 30 December 1967 at the young age of 38. His catalogue remains, littered with unforgettable gems.

BERNSTEIN, ELMER
b. 4 April 1922, New York City, New York, USA. An important and prolific arranger-conductor and composer of over 200 film scores, Bernstein was hailed as a 'musical genius' in the classical field at the age of 12. Despite being a talented actor, dancer and painter, he devoted himself to becoming a concert pianist and toured nationally while still in his teens. His education at New York University was interrupted when he joined the United States Air Force during World War II. Throughout his four years' service he composed and conducted music for propaganda programmes, and produced musical therapy projects for operationally fatigued personnel. After the war he attended the Juilliard School of Music and studied composition with the

distinguished composer, Roger Sessions. Bernstein moved to Hollywood and started writing film scores in 1950, and two years later wrote the background music for *Sudden Fear*, a suspense thriller starring Joan Crawford and Jack Palance. Agent and producer Ingo Preminger, impressed by Bernstein's music, recommended him to his brother Otto for the latter's 1955 project, *The Man With The Golden Arm*.

A tense, controversial movie, its theme of drug addiction, accompanied by the Bernstein modern jazz score, played by top instrumentalists such as Shelly Manne, Shorty Rogers, Pete Candoli and Milt Bernhart, caused distribution problems in some American states. The movie won Oscar nominations for the star, Frank Sinatra, and for Bernstein's powerful, exciting music score. Bernstein made the US Top 20 with his record of the film's 'Main Title', and Billy May entered the UK Top 10 with his version. In 1956, Bernstein wrote the score for Cecil B. De Mille's epic *The Ten Commandments*. Thereafter, he has provided the background music for an impressive array of movies with varied styles and subjects, including *Fear Strikes Out* (1957), *Sweet Smell Of Success* (1957), *God's Little Acre* (1958), *Some Came Running* (1958), *The Rat Race* (1960), *Birdman Of Alcatraz* (1962), *The Great Escape* (1963), *I Love You, Alice B. Toklas!* (1968), *The Shootist* (1976), *Animal House* (1978), *An American Werewolf In London* (1981), *Ghostbusters* (1984), *Three Amigos!* (1986), *Amazing Grace And Chuck* (1987), *Slipstream* (1989), *My Left Foot* (1989), *The Grifters* (1990), *The Field* (1990), *Rambling Rose* (1991), *Oscar* (1991), *A Rage In Harlem* (1991), *The Babe* (1992), *Mad Dog And Glory* (1993), *Lost In Yonkers* (1993), *Bulletproof* (1996), *The Rainmaker* (1997), *Wild Wild West* (1999), *Bringing Out The Dead* (1999), *Keeping The Faith* (2000), and *Gangs Of New York* (2001).

In 1991, Bernstein was the musical director and arranger of Bernard Herrman's original score for the 1962 classic, *Cape Fear*. He has received Academy Award nominations for his work on *The Magnificent Seven* (1960); *Summer And Smoke* (1961), the title song for *Walk On The Wild Side* (1961), with a lyric by Mack David; *To Kill A Mockingbird* (1962), said to be Bernstein's favourite of his own scores; the scores for *Return Of The Seven* (1966), and *Hawaii* (1966) (and a song from *Hawaii*, 'Wishing Doll', lyric by Mack David); the title song from *True Grit* (1969) lyric by Don Black; a song from *Gold* (1974), 'Wherever Love Takes Me', lyric by Don Black; and *Trading Places* (1983). Bernstein won an Oscar for his original music score for the 20s spoof, *Thoroughly Modern Millie* (1967). Coincidentally, Bernstein was the musical arranger and conductor at the Academy Awards ceremony when his award was announced, and had to relinquish the baton before going on stage to receive his Oscar. Bernstein also worked extensively in television: in 1958 he signed for US Revue Productions to provide background music for television dramas. One of his most notable scores was for *Staccato* (1959) (later retitled *Johnny Staccato*), a series about a jazz musician turned private eye, starring John Cassavetes. The shows were extremely well received in the UK, where Bernstein's recording of 'Staccato's Theme' rose to Number 4 in the singles chart in 1959, and re-entered the following year. On a somewhat larger scale instrumentally, an 81-piece symphony orchestra was contracted to record Bernstein's score for Martin Scorsese's 1993 movie, *Age Of Innocence*.

● COMPILATIONS: *Great Composers* (Varèse Sarabande 1999) ★★★.

BERNSTEIN, LEONARD

b. Louis Bernstein, 25 August 1918, Lawrence, Massachusetts, USA, d. 14 October 1990, New York City, New York, USA. Bernstein was a major and charismatic figure in modern classical music and the Broadway musical theatre. He was also a conductor, composer, pianist, author and lecturer. A son of immigrant Russian Jews, Bernstein started to play the piano at the age of 10. In his teens he showed an early interest in the theatre, organizing productions such as *The Mikado*, and an unconventional adaptation of *Carmen*, in which he played the title role. Determined to make a career in music, despite his father's insistence that 'music just keeps people awake at night', Bernstein eschewed the family beauty parlour business. He went on to study first with Walter Piston and Edward Burlingaunt Hill at Harvard, then with Fritz Reiner, Isabella Vengerova and Randall Thompson at the Curtis Institute in Philadelphia, and finally with Serge Koussevitzky at the Berkshire Music Institute at Tanglewood. Bernstein had entered Harvard regarding himself as a pianist, but became influenced by Dimitri Mitropoulos and Aaron Copland. They inspired him to write his first symphony, *Jeremiah*. In 1943 he was chosen by Artur Rodzinski to work as his assistant at the New York Philharmonic. On 14 November 1943, Bernstein deputized at the last minute for the ailing Bruno Walter, and conducted the New York Philharmonic in a concert that was broadcast live on network radio. The next day, he appeared on the front pages of the newspapers and became a celebrity overnight.

In the same year he wrote the music for *Fancy Free*, a ballet, choreographed by Jerome Robbins, about three young sailors on 24 hours' shore leave in New York City. It was so successful that they expanded it into a Broadway musical, with libretto and lyrics by Betty Comden and Adolph Green. Retitled *On The Town* and directed by George Abbott, it opened in 1944, with a youthful, vibrant score which included the memorable anthem 'New York, New York', 'Lonely Town', 'I Get Carried Away' and 'Lucky To Be Me'. The 1949 film version, starring Frank Sinatra and Gene Kelly, and directed by Kelly and Stanley Donen, is often regarded as innovatory in its use of real New York locations, although Bernstein's score was somewhat truncated in the transfer. In 1950 Bernstein wrote both music and lyrics for a musical version of J. M. Barrie's *Peter Pan*, starring Jean Arthur and Boris Karloff. His next Broadway project, *Wonderful Town* (1953), adapted from the play *My Sister Eileen*, by Joseph Fields and Jerome Chodorov, again had lyrics by Comden and Green, and starred Rosalind Russell, returning to Broadway after a distinguished career in Hollywood. Bernstein's spirited, contemporary score, for which he won a Tony Award, included 'Conversation Piece', 'Conga', 'Swing', 'What A Waste', 'Ohio', 'A Quiet Girl' and 'A Little Bit Of Love'.

The show had a successful revival in London in 1986, with Maureen Lipman in the starring role. *Candide* (1956) was one of Bernstein's most controversial works. Lillian Hellman's adaptation of the Voltaire classic, sometimes termed a 'comic operetta', ran for only 73 performances on Broadway. Bernstein's score was much admired, however, and one of the most attractive numbers, 'Glitter And Be Gay', was sung with great effect by Barbara Cook, one year before her Broadway triumph in Meredith Willson's *The Music Man*. *Candide* has been revived continually since 1956, at least twice by producer Hal Prince. It was his greatly revised production, which included additional lyrics by Stephen Sondheim and John Latouche (original lyrics by Richard Wilbur), that ran for 740 performances on Broadway in 1974. The Scottish Opera's production, directed by Jonathan Miller in 1988, is said to have met with the composer's approval, and Bernstein conducted a concert version of the score at London's Barbican Theatre in 1989, which proved to be his last appearance in the UK.

Bernstein's greatest triumph in the popular field came with *West Side Story* in 1957. This brilliant musical adaptation of Shakespeare's *Romeo And Juliet* was set in the streets of New York, and highlighted the violence of the rival gangs, the Jets and the Sharks. With a book by Arthur Laurents, lyrics by Sondheim in his first Broadway production, and directed by Jerome Robbins, Bernstein created one of the most dynamic and exciting shows in the history of the musical theatre. The songs included 'Jet Song', 'Something's Coming', 'Maria', 'Tonight', 'America', 'Cool', 'I Feel Pretty', 'Somewhere' and 'Gee, Officer Krupke!'. In 1961, the film version gained 10 Academy Awards, including 'Best Picture'. Bernstein's music was not eligible for an award because it had not been written for the screen. In 1984, he conducted the complete score of *West Side Story* for the first time, in a recording for Deutsche Grammophon, with a cast of opera singers including Kiri Te Kanawa, José Carreras, Tatania Troyanos and Kurt Allman. Bernstein's last Broadway show, *1600*

Pennsylvania Avenue (1976), was an anticlimax. A story about American presidents, with book and lyrics by Alan Jay Lerner, it closed after only seven performances. Among Bernstein's many other works was the score for the Marlon Brando movie, *On The Waterfront* (1954), for which he was nominated for an Oscar; a jazz piece, 'Prelude, Fugue and Riffs', premiered on US television by Benny Goodman in 1955; and 'My Twelve Tone Melody' written for Irving Berlin's 100th birthday in 1988.

In his celebrated classical career, which ran parallel to his work in the popular field, Bernstein was highly accomplished and prolific, composing three symphonies, a full-length opera, and several choral works. He was musical director of the New York Philharmonic from 1958-69, conducted most of the world's premier orchestras, and recorded many of the major classical works. In the first week of October 1990, he announced his retirement from conducting because of ill health, and expressed an intention to concentrate on composing. He died one week later on 14 October 1990. In 1993, BBC Radio marked the 75th anniversary of his birth by devoting a complete day to programmes about his varied and distinguished career. A year later, *The Leonard Bernstein Revue: A Helluva Town*, played the Rainbow & Stars in New York, and, on a rather larger scale, in June of that year the New York Philharmonic presented their own celebration entitled *Remembering Lenny*. Further contrasting interpretations of Bernstein's work were heard in 1994 when television coverage of the World Cup used his 1984 recording of 'America' as its theme, while the new pop band, Thunderballs, 'viciously mugged' the song (with permission from the Bernstein estate) under the title of '1994 America'.

● COMPILATIONS various artists *Leonard Bernstein's New York* (Nonesuch 1996) ★★★, *The Essential Bernstein* (Sony Classical 1999) ★★★★.
● FURTHER READING: *The Joy Of Music*, Leonard Bernstein. *Leonard Bernstein*, John Briggs. *Leonard Bernstein*, Peter Gadenwitz. *Leonard Bernstein*, Joan Peyser. *Leonard Bernstein*, Humphrey Burton. *Leonard Bernstein – A Life*, Meryle Secrest. *Leonard Bernstein*, Paul Myers.

BERRY, CHUCK

b. Charles Edward Anderson Berry, 18 October 1926, San Jose, California, USA (although Berry states that he was born in St. Louis, Missouri). A seminal figure in the evolution of rock 'n' roll, Chuck Berry's influence as songwriter and guitarist is incalculable. His cogent songs captured adolescent life, yet the artist was 30 years old when he commenced recording. Introduced to music as a child, Berry learned guitar while in his teens, but this period was blighted by a three-year spell in Algoa Reformatory following a conviction for armed robbery. On his release Berry undertook several lue-collar jobs while pursuing part-time spots in 5t. Louis bar bands. Inspired by Carl Hogan, guitarist in Louis Jordan's Timpani Five, and Charlie Christian, he continued to hone his craft and in 1951 purchased a tape recorder to capture ideas for compositions. The following year Berry joined Johnnie Johnson (piano) and Ebby Hardy (drums) in the house band at the Cosmopolitan Club. Over the ensuing months the trio became a popular attraction, playing a mixture of R&B, country/hillbilly songs and standards, particularly those of Nat 'King' Cole, on whom Berry modelled his cool vocal style. The guitarist also fronted his own group, the Chuck Berry Combo, at the rival Crank Club, altering his name to spare his father's embarrassment at such worldly pursuits.

In 1955, during a chance visit to Chicago, Berry met bluesman Muddy Waters, who advised the young singer to approach the Chess Records label. Berry's demo of 'Ida May', was sufficient to win a recording contract and the composition, retitled 'Maybellene', duly became his debut single. This ebullient performance was a runaway success, topping the R&B chart and reaching number 5 on the US pop listings. Its lustre was partially clouded by a conspiratorial publishing credit that required Berry to share the rights with Russ Fratto and disc jockey Alan Freed, in deference to his repeated airplay. This situation remained unresolved until 1986. Berry enjoyed further US R&B hits with 'Thirty Days' and 'No Money Down', but it was his third recording session that proved even more productive, producing a stream of classics, 'Roll Over Beethoven', 'Too Much Monkey Business' and 'Brown-Eyed Handsome Man'. The artist's subsequent releases read like a lexicon of pop history – 'School Days' (a second R&B number 1), 'Rock And Roll Music' (all 1957), 'Sweet Little Sixteen', 'Reelin' And Rockin', 'Johnny B. Goode', Around And Around', 'Memphis Tennessee' (all 1958), 'Little Queenie', 'Back In The USA', 'Let It Rock' (all 1959), 'Bye Bye Johnny', 'Jaguar And Thunderbird' (all 1960), 'Nadine', 'You Never Can Tell', No Particular Place To Go' and 'The Promised Land' (all 1964) are but a handful of the peerless songs written and recorded during this prolific period. In common with contemporary artists, Berry drew from both country and R&B music, but his sharp, often piquant, lyrics, clarified by the singer's clear diction, introduced a new discipline to the genre. Such incomparable performances not only defined rock 'n' roll, they provided a crucial template for successive generations.

Both the Beatles and Rolling Stones acknowledged their debt to Berry. The former recorded two of his compositions, taking one, Roll Over Beethoven', into the US charts, while the latter drew from his empirical catalogue on many occasions. This included 'Come On', their debut single, 'Little Queenie', 'You Can't Catch Me' and 'Around And Around', as well as non-

Berry songs that nonetheless aped his approach. The Stones' readings of 'Route 66', 'Down The Road Apiece' and 'Confessin' The Blues' were indebted to their mentor's versions, while Keith Richards' rhythmic, propulsive guitar figures drew from Berry's style. Elsewhere, the Beach Boys rewrote 'Sweet Little Sixteen' as 'Surfin' USA' to attain their first million-seller, while countless other groups scrambled to record his songs, inspired by their unique combination of immediacy and longevity.

Between 1955 and 1960, Berry seemed unassailable. He enjoyed a run of 17 R&B Top 20 entries, appeared in the movies *Go, Johnny, Go!*, *Rock, Rock, Rock* and *Jazz On A Summer's Day*, the last of which documented the artist's performance at the 1958 *Newport Jazz Festival*, where he demonstrated the famed 'duckwalk' to a bemused audience. However, personal impropriety undermined Berry's personal and professional life when, on 28 October 1961, he was convicted under the Mann Act of 'transporting an underage girl across state lines for immoral purposes'. Berry served 20 months in prison, emerging in October 1963 just as 'Memphis, Tennessee', recorded in 1958, was providing him with his first UK Top 10 hit. He wrote several compositions during his incarceration, including 'Nadine', 'No Particular Place To Go', 'You Never Can Tell' and 'Promised Land', each of which eventually reached the UK Top 30. Such chart success soon waned as the R&B bubble burst, and in 1966 Berry sought to regenerate his career by moving from Chess to Mercury Records. However, an ill-advised *Golden Hits* set merely featured re-recordings of old material, while attempts to secure a contemporary image on *Live At The Fillmore Auditorium* (recorded with the Steve Miller Band) and *Concerto In B. Goode* proved equally unsatisfactory.

He returned to Chess Records in 1969 and immediately re-established his craft with the powerful 'Tulane'. *Back Home* and *San Francisco Dues* were cohesive selections and in-concert appearances showed a renewed purpose. Indeed, a UK performance at the 1972 Manchester Arts Festival not only provided half of Berry's *London Sessions* album, but also his biggest-ever hit. 'My Ding-A-Ling', a mildly ribald *double entendre* first recorded by Dave Bartholomew, topped both the US and UK charts, a paradox in the light of his own far superior compositions, which achieved lesser commercial plaudits. It was his last major hit, and despite several new recordings, including *Rockit*, a much-touted release on Atco Records, Berry became increasingly confined to the revival circuit. He gained an uncomfortable reputation as a hard, shrewd businessman and disinterested performer, backed by pick-up bands with whom he refused to rehearse. Tales abound within the rock fraternity of Berry's refusal to tell the band which song he was about to launch into. Pauses and changes would come about by the musicians watching Berry closely for an often disguised signal. Berry has insisted for years upon pre-payment of his fee, usually in cash, and he will only perform an encore after a further negotiation for extra payment.

Berry's continued legal entanglements resurfaced in 1979 when he was sentenced to a third term of imprisonment following a conviction for income tax evasion. Upon release he embarked on a punishing world tour, but the subsequent decade proved largely unproductive musically and no new recordings were undertaken. In 1986, the artist celebrated his 60th birthday with gala performances in St. Louis and New York. Keith Richards appeared at the former, although relations between the two men were strained, as evinced in the resultant documentary *Hail! Hail! Rock 'N' Roll*, which provided an overview of Berry's career. Berry was inducted into the Rock And Roll Hall Of Fame the same year. Sadly, the 90s began with further controversy and allegations of indecent behaviour at the singer's Berry Park centre. Although the incident served to undermine the individual, Berry's stature as an essential figure in the evolution of popular music cannot be overestimated.

● ALBUMS: *After School Session* (Chess 1958) ★★★★, *One Dozen Berrys* (Chess 1958) ★★★★★, *Chuck Berry Is On Top* (Chess 1959) ★★★★, *Rockin' At The Hops* (Chess 1960) ★★★★, *New Juke-Box Hits* (Chess 1961) ★★★, *Chuck Berry Twist* (Chess 1962) ★★★, *More Chuck Berry* UK release (Pye 1963) ★★★, *Chuck Berry On Stage* (Chess 1963) ★★, *The Latest And The Greatest* (Chess 1964) ★★★, *You Never Can Tell* (Chess 1964) ★★★, with Bo Diddley *Two Great Guitars* (Chess 1964) ★★★, *St. Louis To Liverpool* (Chess 1964) ★★★★, *Chuck Berry In London* (Chess 1965) ★★★, *Fresh Berry's* (Chess 1965) ★★★, *Golden Hits* new recordings (Mercury 1967) ★★, *Chuck Berry In Memphis* (Mercury 1967) ★★★, *Live At The Fillmore Auditorium* (Mercury 1967) ★★, *From St. Louis To Frisco* (Mercury 1968) ★★, *Concerto In B. Goode* (Mercury 1969) ★★, *Back Home* (Chess 1970) ★★, *San Francisco Dues* (Chess 1971) ★★, *The London Chuck Berry Sessions* (Chess 1972) ★★, *Bio* (Chess 1973) ★★, *Chuck Berry* (Chess 1975) ★★, *Live In Concert* (Magnum 1978) ★★★, *Rockit* (Atco 1979) ★★★★, *Rock! Rock! Rock 'N' Roll!* (Atco 1980) ★★, *Hail! Hail! Rock 'N' Roll* film soundtrack (MCA 1987) ★★, *Live 1982 recording* (Columbia River 2000) ★★.

● COMPILATIONS: *Chuck Berry's Greatest Hits* (Chess 1964) ★★★★★, *Chuck Berry's Golden Decade* (Chess 1967) ★★★★★, *Golden Decade, Volume 2* (Chess 1973) ★★★★, *Golden Decade, Volume 3* (Chess 1974) ★★★★, *Motorvatin'* (Chess 1977) ★★★, *Spotlight On Chuck Berry* (PRT 1980) ★★★, *The Great Twenty-Eight* (Chess/MCA 1982) ★★★★★, *Chess Masters* (Chess 1983) ★★★, *Reelin' And Rockin' (Live)* (Aura 1984) ★★, *Rock 'N' Roll Rarities* (Chess/MCA 1986) ★★, *More Rock 'N' Roll Rarities* (Chess/MCA 1986) ★★★, *Chicago Golden Years* (Vogue 1988) ★★★, *Decade '55 To '65* (Platinum 1988) ★★★, *Chess Box* 3-CD box set (Chess/MCA 1989) ★★★★, *Missing Berries: Rarities, Volume 3* (Chess/MCA 1990) ★★★, *The Chess Years* 9-CD box set (Charly 1991) ★★★★★, *On The Blues Side* (Ace 1993) ★★★★, *Oh Yeah!* (Charly 1994) ★★★, *Poet Of Rock 'N' Roll* 4-CD box set (Charly 1995) ★★★★★, *His Best Volume 1* (Chess 1997) ★★★★, *The Best Of Chuck Berry: The Millennium Collection* (PolyGram 1999) ★★★★, *Chuck Berry: The Anthology* (MCA 2000) ★★★★.

● VIDEOS: *The Legendary Chuck Berry* (Channel 5 1987), *Hail! Hail! Rock 'N' Roll* (CIC Video 1988), *Live At The Roxy* (Old Gold 1990), *Rock 'N' Roll Music* (BMG Video 1991).

● FURTHER READING: *Chuck Berry: Rock 'N' Roll Music*, Howard A. De Witt. *Chuck Berry: Mr Rock 'N' Roll*, Krista Reese. *Chuck Berry: The Autobiography*, Chuck Berry. *Long Distance Information: Chuck Berry's Recorded Legacy*, Fred Rothwell.

● FILMS: *Rock, Rock, Rock* (1956), *Mister Rock And Roll* (1957), *Go, Johnny, Go!* (1958), *Jazz On A Summer's Day* (1959), *Alice In Den Städten* aka *Alice In The Cities* (1974), *American Hot Wax* (1978), *Class Reunion* (1982), *Hail! Hail! Rock 'N' Roll* (1987).

BERRY, DAVE

b. David Holgate Grundy, 6 February 1941, Woodhouse, Sheffield, Yorkshire, England. With his long-serving backing group, the Cruisers, Berry was signed to Danny Betesh's Manchester-based Kennedy Street Enterprises, and, after signing to Decca Records, found success with a version of Chuck Berry's 'Memphis Tennessee' in 1963. Cover versions of Arthur Crudup's 'My Baby Left Me' and Burt Bacharach's 'Baby It's You' were also minor hits, but the band's breakthrough came with Geoff Stevens' 'The Crying Game', which reached the UK Top 5 in August 1964. Berry's stage act and image was strong for the period and featured the singer dressed in black, erotically contorting his body and playing with the microphone as though it were a writhing snake. Bobby Goldsboro's chirpy 'Little Things' and Ray Davies' 'This Strange Effect' – which became the Netherlands' biggest-selling record ever – provided further chart success, which concluded with the much-covered B.J. Thomas opus, 'Mama', in 1966. In the late 70s, Berry was one of the few 60s stars held in any esteem in punk circles, epitomised by the Sex Pistols' revival of 'Don't Gimme No Lip Child', one of Berry's 1964 b-sides. The next decade saw a resumption of his recording career and he continues to tour abroad, appearing regularly on the cabaret/revivalist circuit.

● ALBUMS: *Dave Berry* (Decca 1964) ★★★, *The Special Sound Of Dave Berry* (Decca 1966) ★★★, *One Dozen Berrys* (Ace Of Clubs 1966) ★★★,

Dave Berry '68 (Decca 1968) ★★, *Hostage To The Beat* (Butt 1986) ★★.
● COMPILATIONS: *Berry's Best* (Ace 1988) ★★★, *The Very Best Of Dave Berry* (Spectrum 1998) ★★★.

BERRY, MIKE

b. Michael Bourne, 24 September 1942, Northampton, England. Buddy Holly-influenced singer whose Joe Meek-produced recording debut was a Hollyesque cover version of the Shirelles' 'Will You Still Love Me Tomorrow?' on Decca Records. He narrowly missed reaching the UK Top 20 in 1961 with his heartfelt 'Tribute To Buddy Holly' on HMV Records, a song supposedly given the seal of approval by Buddy at a seance! Berry was backed on this and other early recordings by the Outlaws, a noted group that included Ritchie Blackmore and Chas Hodges. Berry's biggest hit came in 1963 with the first of his two UK Top 10 hits, 'Don't You Think It's Time?', again written by spiritualist/songwriter Geoff Goddard and produced by Meek. Berry's records were picked up in the USA by Holly's old label, Coral Records, but did not reach the charts. In the 70s he became a television actor, appearing regularly in television programmes such as the top children's show, *Worzel Gummidge*. In 1980, after a 17-year gap, he returned to the UK Top 10 on Polydor Records with a MOR revival of 'The Sunshine Of Your Smile', produced by his old colleague Chas Hodges, now of Chas And Dave.
● ALBUMS: *Drifts Away* (1972) ★★, *Rocks In My Head* (1976) ★★, *I'm A Rocker* (1980) ★, *Sunshine Of Your Smile* (Polydor 1980) ★★, *Memories* (Polydor 1982) ★★, *Rock N Roll Daze* (Roller Coaster 2000) ★★.
● COMPILATIONS: *Sounds Of The Sixties* (Rollercoaster 1989) ★★★.

BERRY, RICHARD

b. 11 April 1935, Extension, Louisiana, USA, d. 23 January 1997, USA. Berry was raised in Los Angeles, where he learned piano, playing along with the records of Joe Liggins and his Honeydrippers. In high school he formed a vocal group and began recording in 1953 under various names (the Hollywood Blue Jays, the Flairs, the Crowns, the Dreamers, the Pharaohs), as well as doing solo sessions for Modern's Flair subsidiary. His most famous moments on record are his bass vocal contributions to the Robins' 'Riot In Cell Block No. 9' and as 'Henry', Etta James' boyfriend, on her early classic 'Roll With Me Henry (The Wallflower)'. His main claim to fame is composing rock 'n' roll's famous standard 'Louie Louie', which he recorded in 1956 on Flip Records, but he had to wait seven years for its success with the Kingsmen's hit. The song spawned over 300 cover versions, including those by the Kinks, the Beach Boys and Paul Revere And The Raiders, none of which approached the Kingsmen's definitive recording.

The sensual rhythm and theme of the song led to Berry's being accused of writing pornographic lyrics, but as they were virtually unintelligible, Berry took their secret to the grave with him. During the 60s and 70s, Berry, inspired by Bobby Bland and his wife Dorothy (herself a recording artist), became a soul singer. He recorded for myriad west coast labels (including his debut album for Johnny Otis' Blues Spectrum label) and continued performing into the 90s until his death.
● ALBUMS: *Richard Berry And The Dreamers* (Crown 1963) ★★★, with the Soul Searchers *Live From H.D. Hover Century Restaurant* (Pam 1968) ★★, with the Soul Searchers *Wild Berry* (Pam 1968) ★★, *Great Rhythm & Blues Oldies* (Blues Spectrum 1977) ★★★.
● COMPILATIONS: *Get Out Of The Car* (Ace 1982) ★★★★, *Louie, Louie* (Earth Angel 1986) ★★.

BEST, PETE

b. Liverpool, England, 1941. A founder-member of the Beatles, the luckless drummer was fired from the group in August 1962, prior to their official recording debut. He then joined Lee Curtis And The All-Stars, a group that became the Pete Best All-Stars on its erstwhile leader's departure. The artist enjoyed a temporary notoriety in the wake of the Beatles' success and his group, now known as the Pete Best Four, secured a contract with Decca Records. A perfunctory reading of 'I'm Gonna Knock On Your Door' was the act's sole British release on Decca, but they pursued a career in the USA and Canada under various guises, including the Pete Best Combo and Best Of The Beatles. Singles appeared on a variety of often dubious outlets, the most opportunistic of which was their reading of 'This Boy', a song associated with Ringo Starr. Many of these recordings were collected on a subsequent album, *Best Of The Beatles*. This somewhat tawdry affair ended, against the odds, in 1966 with the excellent 'Carousel Of Love'. The group was then dissolved, but although former members Tony Waddington and Wayne Bickerton achieved success in the 70s with their work for the Rubettes and Flirtations, Best was unable to pursue a full-time career in music, although rumours persisted of a new band being formed. As a result of the Beatles' *Anthology* series, the first CD of which was issued in 1995, Best was set to earn millions in royalties, as a number of early tracks featured him on drums: a highly satisfactory redundancy payment 30 years on.
● ALBUMS: *Best Of The Beatles* (Savage 1965) ★, as the Pete Best Combo *Beyond The Beatles 1963-68* (Cherry Red 1996) ★★, *Live At The Adelphi* (Cherry Red 1996) ★★, *Casbah Coffee Club* (Splash 2000) ★★.
● FURTHER READING: *Beatle! The Pete Best Story*, Pete Best and Patrick Doncaster. *Drummed Out! The Sacking Of Pete Best*, Spencer Leigh.

BIENSTOCK, FREDDY

b. 24 April 1923, Vienna, Austria. The music publishing branch of popular music is often criticized by the very artists the publishers represent. This is not the case for Freddy Bienstock, who has maintained respect and credibility for over five decades in shark-infested waters. A young Ray Davies, who signed with Bienstock's Carlin Music at the age of 19, stated: 'I went to Carlin because I wanted to get paid for what I was doing. Music publishers when I started were all Denmark Street.' Bienstock started out as a young man working at the legendary Brill Building in the stockroom at Chappell Music in New York, where his cousins Jean and Julian Aberbach were executives. They eventually left to form their own music company and Freddy joined them a few years later. His first manna from heaven came in 1955 when he was introduced to Colonel Tom Parker. Over the next few years Bienstock was instrumental in presenting new songs to Elvis Presley via the Hill and Range publishing company. This resulted in classics such as 'Blue Suede Shoes' (Carl Perkins) and 'Jailhouse Rock' (Leiber And Stoller). Bienstock moved to London in 1957 to set up Belinda Music to handle the Aberbachs' catalogue. Freddy eventually bought the list and founded Carlin Music in 1966. He originally wanted to name the company after his daughter Caroline but the Pirate Radio ship owner Ronan O'Rahilly had already registered the name, and so Bienstock removed the letters 'o' and 'e' to evade the Companies House legislation. One of his first signings was the Kinks, and it is to Bienstock's credit that he saw the future potential in the songwriting talent of Raymond Douglas Davies. Bienstock also acquired the Motown, Burt Bacharach and Gamble And Huff catalogues, in addition to many classic songs from the beat group era from Cliff Richard, the Shadows and the Animals. Great writers like Phil Spector, Ellie Greenwich, Jeff Barry, Doc Pomus and Mort Shuman also became part of the Carlin list. In 1980 he added over 100,000 American popular songs with the acquisition of the Redwood catalogue. This contained evergreens such as 'As Time Goes By', 'Sweet Georgia Brown', 'Button Up Your Overcoat' and the Al Jolson perennial, 'My Mammy'. Bienstock was able to purchase Chappells in 1984 on the condition that he agreed to suspend the Carlin operation. Outside purchasers were also taking an interest in Bienstock's Midas touch, and in 1987 his board agreed to sell Chappells to Warner Brothers Records at a huge profit. Bienstock, however, shrewdly retained an outstanding collection with the Carlin catalogue and the company had already established a firm foundation of classic rock 'n' roll, 60s pop, standards of American popular song and 70s progressive rock. Bienstock is publisher to what is probably the finest independent pop music catalogue in the world and remains a peerless entrepreneur in popular music history.

BIENSTOCK, JOHNNY

b. 1 March 1927, Vienna, Austria. The younger brother of Freddie Bienstock has also established himself in the music business. Although his elder sibling has become a music business legend, Johnny has been an instigator, creator and an outstanding administrator, as well as a music publisher. He became the first employee of his cousins Julian and Jean Aberbach's company Biltmore Music in 1945, after leaving the US army. In 1958 he was asked to set up Big Top Records, and oversaw four golden years with a string of hits, including those by Sammy Turner, Johnny And The Hurricanes and Del Shannon. After refusing to accept a gift of a new house from one of his cousins (which would have effectively tied him to them for life), he was sacked in 1966. On the same day, he received a call from Jerry Wexler at Atlantic Records who invited him to the company as his executive assistant. Bienstock was with Atlantic through its golden era, and later managed their subsidiary Atco Records. During his time there (1966-72) he worked closely with Aretha Franklin, Tom Dowd, Iron Butterfly, Bobby Darin and Buffalo Springfield. It was Bienstock who suggested that the *Woodstock* album should be a triple-record set, much to the astonishment of his colleagues. In addition to publishing some of J.J. Cale's work, Bienstock managed RSO Records from their inception in 1972 and dealt with Cream, Eric Clapton, the Bee Gees and Derek And The Dominos. He rejoined his brother at the Carlin Group offices at the Brill Building in 1983 and administers the E.B. Marks publishing company; he is also involved with the Carlin Music Recorded Library. In 1993 he was responsible for the promotion and eventual release of Meat Loaf's *Bat Out Of Hell II*, evidence that even in his sixth decade in the music business, Bienstock still had the Midas touch.

BIG BERTHA

Big Bertha was formed in 1969 by Dennis Ball (bass) and Cozy Powell (drums), two ex-members of the Ace Kefford Stand. Pete French (vocals) and Dave Ball (guitar) completed the original line-up. In 1969 the group made a single for Atlantic Records. Although the a-side, 'The World's An Apple', was a new recording, its instrumental coupling, 'Gravy Booby Jamm', was previously issued as being by the Ace Kefford Stand. A further single, 'Munich City', was only issued in Europe, where Big Bertha often toured. In 1970 Powell left to join Jeff Beck, while French opted for Atomic Rooster. They were replaced, respectively, by Mac Poole and Dave McTavish. Big Bertha split up in 1971. Dave Ball became a member of Procol Harum until 1972, before being reunited with brother Dennis

and former colleague Powell in Bedlam.
● ALBUMS: *Cozy Powell's Big Bertha: Live In Hamburg* 1970 recording (Zoom Club 1999) ★★.

BIG BROTHER AND THE HOLDING COMPANY

Formed in September 1965, this pivotal San Franciscan rock outfit evolved out of 'jam' sessions held in the basement of a communal house. The original line-up featured Sam Andrew (b. 18 December 1941, Taft, California, USA; guitar, vocals), Peter Albin (b. 6 June 1944, San Francisco, California, USA; bass, vocals), Dave Eskerson (guitar) and Chuck Jones (drums), but within months the latter pair had been replaced, respectively, by James Gurley (b. Detroit, Michigan, USA) and Dave Getz (b. Brooklyn, New York City, New York, USA). The restructured quartet initially eschewed formal compositions, preferring a free-form improvisation centred on Gurley's mesmeric fingerpicking style, but a degree of discipline gradually evolved. The addition of Texas singer Janis Joplin (b. 19 January 1943, Port Arthur, Texas, USA, d. 4 October 1970, Los Angeles, California, USA) in June 1966 emphasized this new-found direction, and her powerful, blues-soaked delivery provided the perfect foil to the unit's instrumental power. The band rapidly became one of the Bay Area's leading attractions, but they naïvely struck an immoderate recording contract with the Chicago-based Mainstream label. Although marred by poor production, *Big Brother And The Holding Company* nevertheless contains several excellent performances, notably 'Bye Bye Baby' and 'Down On Me'.

The quintet rose to national prominence in 1967 following a sensational appearance at the Monterey Pop Festival. Joplin's charismatic performance engendered a prestigious management deal with Albert Grossman, who in turn secured their release from all contractual obligations. The band then switched outlets to Columbia Records, for which they completed *Cheap Thrills* (1968). This exciting album topped the US charts, but despite the inclusion of in-concert favourites 'Piece Of My Heart' and 'Ball And Chain', the recording was fraught with difficulty. Joplin came under increased pressure to opt for a solo career as critics denigrated the musicians' abilities. The band broke up in November 1968 and while Sam Andrew joined the singer in her next venture, Albin and Getz joined Country Joe And The Fish. The following year the latter duo reclaimed the name and with the collapse of an interim line-up, re-established the unit with ex-colleagues Andrew and Gurley. Several newcomers, including Nick Gravenites (b. Chicago, Illinois, USA; vocals), Kathi McDonald (vocals), David Schallock (guitar) and Mike Finnegan (piano), augmented the quartet on an informal basis, but despite moments of inspiration, neither *Be A Brother* (1970) nor *How*

Hard It Is (1971) recaptured former glories. The group was disbanded in 1972, but reconvened six years later at the one-off Tribal Stomp reunion. In 1987 singer Michel Bastian joined Getz, Gurley, Andrew and Albin in a fully reconstituted Big Brother And The Holding Company line-up, still hoping to assert an independent identity. During the mid-90s, Lisa Battle (vocals) and Tom Finch (guitar) were brought into the line-up. In 1998, the band released *Do What You Love*, their first new studio album in over 25 years.
● ALBUMS: *Big Brother And The Holding Company* (Mainstream/Columbia 1967) ★★★, *Cheap Thrills* (Columbia 1968) ★★★★, *Be A Brother* (Columbia 1970) ★★, *How Hard It Is* (Columbia 1971) ★, *Cheaper Thrills* 1966 recording (Made To Last/Edsel 1984) ★★, *Big Brother And The Holding Company Live* 1966 recording (Rhino 1984) ★★, *Can't Go Home Again* (Legend 1997) ★★, *Do What You Love* (Cheap Thrills 1998) ★★, with Janis Joplin *Live At Winterland '68* (Columbia 1998) ★★★.
● COMPILATIONS: *Joseph's Coat* (Edsel 1986) ★★.
● VIDEOS: *Comin' Home* (BMG 1992), *Live In Studio: San Francisco '67* (Castle Music Pictures 1992).
● FILMS: *American Pop* (1981).

BIG THREE

Formed in Liverpool in 1961 as an offshoot from Cass And The Cassanovas, the Big Three comprised John Gustafson (vocals, bass), Johnny Hutchinson (vocals, drums) and Adrian Barber (guitar). During 1962, Barber relocated to Germany and was replaced by Brian Griffiths, who made his debut at the Star Club, Hamburg. A mini-legend in their native Liverpool, the Big Three were revered as one of the loudest, most aggressive and visually appealing acts on the circuit. After signing with the Beatles' manager Brian Epstein, success seemed assured, but their characteristic unruliness proved to be their undoing. They achieved only two minor hits, a cover version of Ritchie Barrett's R&B standard 'Some Other Guy', and Mitch Murray's 'By The Way'. Although a live EP, *At The Cavern*, gave some indication of their power, their vinyl excursions failed to reveal their true potential. An acrimonious split with Epstein only months into their relationship effectively wrecked their chances. By November 1963, Griffiths and Gustafson found alternative employment with the Seniors; Hutchinson recruited Paddy Chambers and Faron (of the Flamingos) as replacements. Less than a year later, the Big Three disbanded. Gustafson later joined the Merseybeats, Episode Six and then Quatermass, and appeared again in the 70s as the bassist in Roxy Music.
● ALBUMS: *Resurrection* (Polydor 1973) ★★, *Cavern Stomp* (Edsel 1982) ★★★, *I Feel Like Steppin' Out* (Dr. Horse 1986) ★★★.

BIG TOP RECORDS

Although the life of this New York record company was short, its achievements and history are worthy of many after-dinner tales. The company was founded in May 1958 after discussions between Elvis Presley's manager Colonel Tom Parker and the Aberbach Brothers, who, as Hill And Range, published the Presley catalogue. Sheet music revenue was in decline as records began to sell more, and a record company seemed the logical solution. Parker informed the brothers that the contract with RCA Records was coming up for renewal and he mooted the idea of a new record label that could sign Presley. The idea was for the Colonel to demand such an outrageous advance from RCA that they would have to refuse. However, even the Colonel had vastly underestimated the power of Elvis, as RCA agreed to the high advance. It was too late for the Aberbachs; Big Top Records had been formed but had no artists. Even the company name had come from Parker, who had been a circus man in his native Holland. Johnny Bienstock, brother of the legendary Freddie Bienstock, was employed as the label's boss, and he set about finding some talent. The label's first release was Bobby Pedrick's 'White Bucks And Saddle Shoes', which was produced by Leiber And Stoller. The first hits came in 1959 with Sammy Turner's 'Sweet Annie Laurie' (US number 100), 'Lavender Blue' (US number 3), 'Always' (US number 19) and 'Symphony' (US number 82). All these, plus a further success with 'Paradise', were produced by Leiber And Stoller. Bienstock, meanwhile, was still searching for talent, and through a Michigan DJ colleague, Ollie McLaughlan, he was introduced to Harry Balk and Irving Mickanich, who managed Johnny Paris and Charles Westover. These two performers turned Big Top into a highly successful operation; Paris became Johnny And The Hurricanes and Westover, adopting a much more commercial name, became Del Shannon. At the momentous recording session that produced tracks from Max Crook ('The Snake') and Shannon's 'Jody', together with another catchy number 'Runaway', Bienstock and Balk knew they had at least one hit. In the case of the latter song, however, Shannon was singing flat on the falsetto, and that night in the recording studio, Bienstock and Balk sped up the master tape, thereby shortening the song by 10 seconds and correcting the flat notes. Nobody else (including Shannon) was ever made aware of this. Shannon went on to become the label's brightest star. During this time, Big Top distributed Dunes Records recordings (notably Ray Peterson's 'Corrine Corrina' and 'Pretty Little Angel Eyes' by Curtis Lee). Big Top became a publishing company in the early 60s, by which time Bienstock had become Jerry Wexler's executive assistant at Atlantic Records.

BIKEL, THEODORE

b. 2 May 1924, Vienna, Austria. Bikel is a prolific stage and screen actor as well as a respected folk singer and musician. He left Austria with his parents in 1937, and was raised in Palestine. Though he was a talented linguist, Bikel opted to join the Habimah Theatre and later co-founded the Israeli Chamber Theatre. In 1946 he entered the Royal Academy of Dramatic Art in London, England. He arrived in the USA in the late 40s. In 1951 he landed his first big film role, appearing as the First Officer in John Huston's *The African Queen*. Eight years later he appeared as Captain Von Trapp with Mary Martin in the Broadway production of *The Sound Of Music*. His other stage appearances have included national starring roles in *Zorba* and *Fiddler On The Roof*. Bikel's Jewish background enabled him to build up a comprehensive repertoire of Eastern European, Russian and Yiddish songs, and he is also fluent in over half a dozen European and middle eastern languages. One of his first albums for Elektra Records was appropriately titled *Folk Songs From Just About Everywhere*. Bikel's versatility stretches to his musical skills, with guitar, mandolin, harmonica and balalaika among the instruments he plays on his folk recordings. Bikel co-founded the Newport Folk Festival, and also presented his own radio show, *At Home With Theodore Bikel*. He was also a regular on the early 60s television show, *Hootenanny*. During this decade Bikel established himself as one of Hollywood's most versatile actors, and though he often played the villain of the movie his mastery of languages and accents prevented his characters from descending into cliché. Ironically he was often cast as a German, but among his most notable roles are General Jouvet in *The Pride And The Passion* (1957), Sheriff Max Muller in *The Defiant Ones* (1958), Zolton Karpathy in *My Fair Lady* (1964), and Rance Muhammitz in *200 Motels* (1971). His television appearances have included roles in *All In The Family*, *Murder, She Wrote* and *Babylon 5*.

Despite the success of his acting career, Bikel has maintained a busy performing and recording schedule and continues to campaign for political causes around the world. In 1977, he was appointed by President Jimmy Carter to the National Council For The Arts, a position he held until 1982. He currently serves as the president of the Associated Actors and Artistes of America.

● ALBUMS: *Israeli Folk Songs* (Elektra 1955) ★★★, *An Actor's Holiday* (Elektra 1956) ★★★, with Cynthia Gooding *A Young Man And A Maid* (Elektra 1956) ★★★, *Folk Songs Of Israel* (Elektra 1958) ★★★, *Jewish Folk Songs* (Elektra 1958) ★★★, *Songs Of A Russian Gypsy* (Elektra 1958) ★★★, with Geula Gill *Folk Songs From Just About Everywhere* (Elektra 1958) ★★★, *More Jewish Folk Songs* (Elektra 1959) ★★★, *Bravo Bikel!* (Elektra 1959) ★★★, with Gill *Songs Of Russia*

Old And New (Elektra 1960) ★★★, From Bondage To Freedom (Elektra 1961) ★★★, A Harvest Of Israeli Folk Songs (Elektra 1962) ★★★, The Poetry And Prophecy Of The Old Testament (Elektra 1962) ★★★, On Tour (Elektra 1963) ★★★, A Folksinger's Choice (Elektra 1964) ★★★, Yiddish Theatre And Folk Songs (Elektra 1964) ★★★, with the Pennywhistlers Songs Of The Earth (Elektra 1967) ★★★, Is Tevye (Elektra 1968) ★★★, A New Day (Reprise 1970) ★★★, Silent No More (Star 1972) ★★★, For The Young (Peter Pan 1973) ★★, Sings Jewish Holiday Songs (Western Wind 1987) ★★★★, A Passover Story (Western Wind 1991) ★★★, A Chanukkah Story (Western Wind 1992) ★★★, A Taste Of Passover (Rounder 1998) ★★★.
● COMPILATIONS: The Best Of Bikel (Elektra 1962) ★★★★.
● FURTHER READING: Folksongs And Footnotes, Theodore Bikel. Theo, Theodore Bikel.
● FILMS: Ein Breira aka No Alternative narrator (1949), The African Queen (1951), Moulin Rouge (1952), Desperate Moment (1953), Never Let Me Go (1953), Melba (1953), The Kidnappers aka The Little Kidnappers (1953), A Day To Remember (1953), The Young Lovers aka Chance Meeting (1954), The Love Lottery (1954), Forbidden Cargo (1954), The Divided Heart (1954), The Colditz Story (1955), Above Us The Waves (1955), Flight From Vienna (1956), The Pride And The Passion (1957), The Vintage (1957), The Enemy Below (1957), Fräulein (1958), The Defiant Ones (1958), I Want To Live! (1958), I Bury The Living (1958), The Angry Hills (1959), Woman Obsessed (1959), The Blue Angel (1959), A Dog Of Flanders (1959), Man On The Run aka The Kidnappers (1963), My Fair Lady (1964), Sands Of The Kalahari (1965), The Russians Are Coming, The Russians Are Coming (1966), Sweet November (1968), The Desperate Ones aka Beyond The Mountains (1968), My Side Of The Mountain (1969), Darker Than Amber (1970), 200 Motels (1971), The Little Ark (1972), Prince Jack (1984), Very Close Quarters (1986), Dark Tower (1987), See You In The Morning (1989), Lodz Ghetto voice only (1989), Shattered (1991), Crisis In The Kremlin aka The Assassination Game (1992), Benefit Of The Doubt (1993), My Family Treasure (1993), Shadow Conspiracy (1997), Second Chances (1998), Trickle (1998), Crime And Punishment (2000).

BILK, ACKER

b. Bernard Stanley Bilk, 28 January 1929, Pensford, Somerset, England. A self-taught clarinettist, Bilk made his first public appearance in 1947 while on National Service in Egypt. On his return to the UK, he played as a semi-professional around the Bristol area, before gaining his big break with the Ken Colyer band in 1954. Four years later, under the name 'Mr' Acker Bilk, he enjoyed his first UK Top 10 hit with 'Summer Set'. Backed by the Paramount Jazz Band, and promoted by his Bilk Marketing Board, he was at the forefront of the British traditional jazz boom of the early 60s. With their distinctive uniform of bowler hats and striped waistcoats, Bilk and company enjoyed a number of jazzy UK hits in the 60s, including 'White Cliffs Of Dover', 'Buona Sera', 'That's My Home', 'Stars And Stripes Forever', 'Frankie And Johnny', 'Gotta See Baby Tonight' and 'A Taste Of Honey'. However, it was with the Leon Young String Chorale that Bilk achieved his most remarkable hit. 'Stranger On The Shore' was a US number 1 in May 1962, and peaked at number 2 in the UK, staying for a record-breaking 55 weeks in the bestsellers. Although the beat boom all but ended the careers of many traditional jazzmen, Bilk has continued to enjoy a successful career in cabaret and concerts, and returned to the Top 10 in 1976, again with a string backing, with 'Aria'. He continues to tour regularly alongside contemporaries such as Kenny Ball and Chris Barber. The trio had a number 1 album, The Best Of Ball, Barber And Bilk, in 1962. Bilk remains a major figure in traditional jazz, and more than 30 years after 'Stranger On The Shore' gained an Ivor Novello Award for 'Most Performed Work'.
● ALBUMS: Mr. Acker Requests (Pye 1958) ★★★, Mr. Acker Marches On (Pye 1958) ★★★, Mr. Acker Bilk Sings (Pye 1959) ★★, Mr. Acker Bilk Requests (Part One) (Pye 1959) ★★★, Mr. Acker Bilk Requests (Part Two) (Pye 1959) ★★★, The Noble Art Of Mr. Acker Bilk (Pye 1959) ★★★, Seven Ages Of Acker (Columbia 1960) ★★★★, Mr. Acker Bilk's Omnibus (Pye 1960) ★★★, Acker (Columbia 1960) ★★★, A Golden Treasury Of Bilk (Columbia 1961) ★★★★, Mr. Acker Bilk's Lansdowne Folio (Columbia 1961) ★★★, Stranger On The Shore (Columbia 1961) ★★★★, Above The Stars And Other Romantic Fancies (Columbia 1962) ★★★, A Taste Of Honey (Columbia 1963) ★★★★, Great Themes From Great European Movies (Columbia 1965) ★★, Acker In Paris (Columbia 1966) ★★★, with Stan Tracey Big Brass Blue Acker (Columbia 1968) ★★★★, with Stan Tracey Strings Horn Of Plenty (Columbia 1971) ★★★, Some Of My Favourite Things (PRT 1973) ★★★, That's My Desire (PRT 1974) ★★★, Serenade (PRT 1975) ★★★, The One For Me (PRT 1976) ★★★, Invitation (PRT 1977) ★★★, Meanwhile (PRT 1977) ★★★, Sheer Magic (Warwick 1977) ★★★, Extremely Live In Studio 1 (PRT 1978) ★★, Free (PRT 1978) ★★★, When The Lights Are Low (PRT 1978) ★★★, with Max Bygraves Twogether (Piccadilly 1980) ★★, Unissued Acker (PRT 1980) ★★★, Made In Hungary (PRT 1980) ★★★, The Moment I'm With You (PRT 1980) ★★★, Mama Told Me So (PRT 1980) ★★★, Relaxin' (PRT 1981) ★★★, Wereldsuccessen (Philips 1982) ★★★, I Think The Best Thing About This Record Is The Music (Bell 1982) ★★, Acker Bilk In Holland (Timeless 1985) ★★, Nature Boy (PRT 1985) ★★★, Acker's Choice (Teldec 1985) ★★★, John, Paul And Acker (PRT 1986) ★★, Love Songs My Way (Topline 1987)

, *On Stage* (Start 1988) *, with Ken Colyer *It Looks Like A Big Time Tonight* (Stomp Off 1988) ***, *That's My Home* (Pickwick 1988) ***, *The Love Album* (Pickwick 1989) ***, *Imagine* (Pulse 1991) **, *Blaze Away* (Timeless 1990) ****, *Heartbeats* (Pickwick 1991) ***, with Humphrey Lyttelton *At Sundown* (Calligraph 1992) ****, with Lyttelton *Three In The Morning* (Calligraph 1995) ****, *Chalumeau That's My Home* (Apricot 1995) ****, *Oscar Winners* (Carlton 1995) **.
● COMPILATIONS: *The Best Of Ball, Barber And Bilk* (Pye 1962) ****, *Golden Hour Of Acker Bilk* (Knight 1974) ****, *Evergreen* (Warwick 1978) ***, *The Acker Bilk Saga* (Polydor 1979) ***, *Spotlight On Acker Bilk* (PRT 1980) ***, *100 Minutes Of Bilk* (PRT 1982) ****, *Spotlight On Acker Bilk Volume 2* (PRT 1982) ***, *I'm In The Mood For Love* (Philips 1983) ***, *Finest Moments* (Castle 1986) ***, *Magic Clarinet Of Acker Bilk* (K-Tel 1986) ***, *16 Golden Memories* (Spectrum 1988) ***, *Best Of Acker Bilk His Clarinet And Strings* (PRT 1988) ***, *Hits Blues And Classics* (Kaz 1988) ***, *The Collection* (Castle 1989) ***, *Images* (Knight 1989) ***, *After Midnight* (Pickwick 1990) **, *In A Mellow Mood* (Castle 1992) ***, *Reflections* (Spectrum 1993) ***, *Acker Bilk Songbook* (Tring 1993) ***, *Bridge Over Troubled Water* (Spectrum 1995) **, *All The Hits Plus More* (Prestige 1997) ***, *Mr. Acker Bilk And His Paramount Jazz Band* (Castle 2001) ****.
● FURTHER READING: *The Book Of Bilk*, P. Leslie and P. Gwynn-Jones.
● FILMS: *It's Trad, Dad!* (1962), *It's All Over Town* (1964).

BIRDS

Formed in Yiewsley, Middlesex, England, in 1964, Ali McKenzie (vocals), Tony Munroe (guitar, vocals), Ron Wood (b. Ronald David Wood, 1 June 1947, Hillingdon, Middlesex, England; guitar, vocals), Kim Gardner (b. 27 January 1946, Dulwich, London, England; bass, vocals) and Bob Langham (drums) were originally known as the Thunderbirds, but truncated their name to avoid confusion with Chris Farlowe's backing group. Langham was soon replaced by Pete Hocking, who changed his name to Pete McDaniel. One of the era's most powerful R&B groups, the Birds' legacy is confined to a mere four singles, but the energy displayed on 'Leaving Here' and 'No Good Without You Baby' (both 1965 singles released on Decca Records) shows that their reputation is deserved. However, the group is better known for a scurrilous publicity stunt, wherein seven writs were served on the American Byrds, demanding that they change their name and claiming loss of income. The US group naturally ignored the charges and the UK unit was latterly known as Bird's Birds, releasing September 1966's 'Say Those Magic Words' on Robert Stigwood's Reaction label. They broke up in

October 1966 when Gardner joined Creation. Wood was also a member of the latter between his two spells with the Jeff Beck Group. Gardner achieved temporary fame in the 70s with Ashton, Gardner And Dyke and Badger, but it was Wood who enjoyed the greater profile, first with the Faces, and latterly, the Rolling Stones.
● COMPILATIONS: *The Collectors' Guide To Rare British Birds* (Deram 1999) ***.
● FURTHER READING: *Rock On Wood: The Origin Of A Rock & Roll Face*, Terry Rawlings.

BIRKIN, JANE

b. 14 December 1946, London, England. The unlikely recording success of actress Jane Birkin came about in 1969 as a result of her romantic association with French composer Serge Gainsbourg. He had originally recorded a track with Brigitte Bardot titled 'Je T''Aime … Moi Non Plus', but, as he explained at the time, 'She thought it was too erotic and she was married'. Birkin, who by this time had married and divorced soundtrack composer John Barry and appeared in Michelangelo Antonioni's controversial *Blowup*, had no such reservations and expertly simulated the sensual heavy breathing and loving moans that gave the disc its notoriety. Originally released in the UK by Fontana Records, the company disassociated itself from the disc's controversial matter by ceasing production while the record was number 2 in the charts. The ever-opportunistic entrepreneur Phil Solomon gratefully accepted the banned composition, which was reissued on his Major Minor label and reached number 1 in late 1969. An album, which included such sensual numbers as '69 Année Erotique' and '18-39', was subsequently issued before Gainsbourg reverted to less newsworthy recording ventures. 'Je T'Aime . . .' re-entered the UK charts in 1974. Birkin separated from Gainsbourg in 1980. In 1996 she released an album of songs composed by her ex-partner, who had died five years previously.
● ALBUMS: with Serge Gainsbourg *Jane Birkin And Serge Gainsbourg* (Fontana 1969) ***, *Jane B* (Phonogram 1974) ***, *Di Doo Dah* (Phonogram 1975) **, *Versions Jane* (Discovery 1996) ***.
● COMPILATIONS: *The Best Of Jane Birkin* (Mercury 1997) ***, *Talent Of The Century* (Universal 2000) ***.
● FILMS: *Blowup* (1966), *Kaleidoscope* aka *The Bank Breaker* (1966), *La Piscine* aka *The Swimming Pool* (1969), *Wonderwall: The Movie* (1969), *Les Chemins De Katmandou* aka *The Road To Katmandu* (1969), *Cannabis* aka *The Mafia Wants Your Blood* (1969), *Trop Petit Mon Ami* aka *Too Small My Friend* (1970), *Sex Power* (1970), *Alba Pagana (May Morning In Oxford)* (1970), *Romance Of A Horsethief* (1971), *19 Djevojaka I 1 Mornar* (1971), *Trop Jolies Pour Être Honnêtes* aka *Too Pretty To Be Honest* (1972), *Don Juan 73* (1973), *Projection Privée* aka *Private Projection*

973), *La Morte Negli Occhi Del Gatto* aka *Seven Deaths In The Cat's Eye* (1973), *Le Mouton Enragé* aka *The French Way Is* (1974), *Sérieux Comme Le Plaisir* aka *Serious As Pleasure* (1974), *La Moutarde Me Monte Au Nez* aka *Lucky Pierre* (1974), *Dark Places* (1974), *Comment Réussir Dans La Vie Quand On Est Con Et Pleurnichard* (1974), *La Course À L'Échalote* aka *The Wild Goose Chase* (1975), *Catherine Et Cie* aka *Catherine & Co.* (1975), *Sept Morts Sur Ordonnance* aka *Bestial Quartet* (1975), *Je T'Aime, Moi Non Plus* aka *I Love You, I Don't* (1975), *Le Diable Au Coeur* aka *The Devil In The Heart* (1975), *Bruciati Da Cocente Passione* aka *Burnt By Scalding Passion* (1976), *L'Animal* (1977), *Death On The Nile* (1978), *Au Bout Du Bout Du Banc* aka *Make Room For Tomorrow* (1978), *La Miel* aka *Honey* (1979), *Melancholy Baby* (1979), *La Fille Prodigue* (1981), *Rends-Moi La Clé!* (1981), *Nestor Burma, Détective De Choc* (1981), *Egon Schile – Exzesse* (1981), *Evil Under The Sun* (1982), *Circulez Y'A Rien À Voir* (1983), *L'Ami De Vincent* aka *A Friend Of Vincent* (1983), *Le Garde Du Corps* (1984), *La Pirate* (1984), *L'Amour Par Terre* aka *Love On The Ground* (1984), *Dust* (1985), *Le Neveu De Beethoven* aka *Beethoven's Nephew* (1985), *Leave All Fair* (1985), *La Femme De Ma Vie* aka *Women Of My Life* (1986), *Comédie!* (1987), *Soigne Ta Droite* aka *Keep Up Your Right* (1987), *Kung Fu Master* (1987), *Jane B. Par Agnès* (1987), *Daddy Nostalgie* (1990), *La Belle Noiseuse* aka *The Beautiful Troublemaker* (1991), *Contre L'Oubli* (1991), *Les Cent Et Une Nuits* (1995), *Noir Comme Le Souvenir* aka *Black For Remembrance* (1995), *Between The Devil And The Deep Blue Sea* voice only (1995), *On Connait La Chanson* aka *The Same Old Song* (1997), *A Soldier's Daughter Never Cries* (1998), *The Last September* (1999).

BLACK CAT BONES

The original line-up of this London-based blues band included Paul Kossoff (b. 14 September 1950, Hampstead, London, England, d. 19 March 1976; guitar), Stuart Brooks (bass) and Simon Kirke (b. 28 July 1949, Shrewsbury, Shropshire, England; drums). Producer Mike Vernon invited the group to back pianist Champion Jack Dupree on his 1969 release, *When You Feel The Feeling*, and attendant live appearances, but momentum faltered when Kossoff and Kirke left to form Free. A restructured Black Cat Bones – Brian Short (vocals), Derek Brooks (guitar), Rod Price (guitar, vocals) and Phil Lenoir (drums) – joined Stuart Brooks for *Barbed Wire Sandwich*, but the revised unit failed to capture the fire of its predecessor.

● ALBUMS: *Barbed Wire Sandwich* (Nova 1970) ★★.

BLACK, BILL

William Patton Black, 17 September 1926, Memphis, Tennessee, USA, d. 21 October 1965, Memphis, Tennessee, USA. Black was the bass-playing half of the Scotty And Bill team that backed Elvis Presley on his earliest live performances. After leaving Presley, Black launched a successful career of his own as leader of the Bill Black Combo. Initially playing an acoustic stand-up bass, Black was hired as a session musician by Sun Records, where he met Presley in 1954. He played on the earliest Sun tracks, including 'That's All Right'. Black toured with Presley alongside guitarist Scotty Moore; later, drummer D.J. Fontana was added to the group. Black and Moore left Presley's employment in 1957 owing to what they felt was unfair payment. The Bill Black Combo was formed in 1959, with Black (electric bass guitar), Reggie Young (guitar), Martin Wills (saxophone), Carl McAvoy (piano) and Jerry Arnold (drums). Signed to Hi Records in Memphis, the group favoured an instrumental R&B-based sound tempered with jazz. Their first chart success was 'Smokie Part 2' in late 1959, but it was the follow-up, 'White Silver Sands', in the spring of 1960, that gave the group its biggest US hit, reaching number 9. Black retired from touring in 1962, and the group continued performing under the same name without him, with Bob Tucker playing bass. The group also backed other artists, including Gene Simmons on the 1964 number 11 hit 'Haunted House'. Saxophonist Ace Cannon was a member of the group for some time. The group continued playing even after Black died of a brain tumour in October 1965. The Bill Black Combo achieved a total of 19 US chart singles and was still working under the leadership of Tucker decades later.

● ALBUMS: *Smokie* (Hi 1960) ★★★, *Saxy Jazz* (Hi 1960) ★★★, *Solid And Raunchy* (Hi 1960) ★★★★, *That Wonderful Feeling* (Hi 1961) ★★★, *Movin'* (Hi 1961) ★★★, *Bill Black's Record Hop* (Hi 1962) ★★★, *Let's Twist Her* (Hi 1962) ★★★★, *The Untouchable Sound Of Bill Black* (Hi 1963) ★★★, *Bill Black Plays The Blues* (Hi 1964) ★★★, *Bill Black Plays Tunes By Chuck Berry* (Hi 1964) ★★, *Bill Black's Combo Goes Big Band* (Hi 1964) ★★, *More Solid And Raunchy* (Hi 1965) ★★, *All Timers* (Hi 1966) ★★, *Black Lace* (Hi 1967) ★★, *King Of The Road* (Hi 1967) ★★, *The Beat Goes On* (Hi 1968) ★★, *Turn On Your Lovelight* (London 1969) ★★, *Solid And Raunchy The 3rd* (Hi 1969) ★★, *Soulin' The Blues* (London 1969) ★★.

● COMPILATIONS: *Greatest Hits* (Hi/London 1963) ★★★, *Hi Rollin': The Story Of Bill Black's Combo (1960-65)* (Edsel 1998) ★★★, *Best Of Bill Black's Combo: The Hi Records Years* (Right Stuff 2001) ★★★, *Bill Black's Greatest Hits/Bill Black Combo Goes West* (Hi 2001) ★★★.

BLACK, CILLA

b. Priscilla White, 27 May 1943, Liverpool, England. While working as a part-time cloakroom attendant at Liverpool's Cavern club in 1963, Priscilla appeared as guest singer with various groups, and was brought to the attention of Brian Epstein. The Beatles' manager changed her name and during the next few years ably exploited her girl-next-door appeal. Her first single, under the auspices of producer George Martin, was a brassy powerhouse reworking of the Beatles' unreleased 'Love Of The Loved', which reached the UK Top 40 in late 1963. A change of style with Burt Bacharach's 'Anyone Who Had A Heart' saw Black emerge as a ballad singer of immense power and distinction. 'You're My World', a translation of an Italian lyric, was another brilliantly orchestrated, impassioned ballad that, like its predecessor, dominated the UK number 1 position in 1964. In what was arguably the most competitive year in British pop history, Black was outselling all her Merseyside rivals except the Beatles. For her fourth single, Paul McCartney presented 'It's For You', a fascinating jazz waltz ballad that seemed a certain number 1, but it stalled at number 8.

By the end of 1964, she was one of the most successful female singers of her era and continued to release cover versions of superb quality, including the Righteous Brothers' 'You've Lost That Lovin' Feelin'' and an excellent reading of Randy Newman's 'I've Been Wrong Before'. A consummate rocker and unchallenged mistress of the neurotic ballad genre, Black was unassailable at her pop peak, yet her chosen path was that of an 'all-round entertainer'. For most of 1965, she ceased recording and worked on her only feature film, *Work Is A Four Letter Word*, but returned strongly the following year with 'Love's Just A Broken Heart' and 'Alfie'. The death of Brian Epstein in 1967 and a relative lull in chart success might have blighted the prospects of a lesser performer, but Black was already moving into television work, aided by her manager/husband Bobby Willis (b. 25 January 1942, England, d. 23 October 1999, England). Her highly rated television series was boosted by the hit title theme 'Step Inside Love', donated by Paul McCartney. Throughout the late 60s, she continued to register Top 10 hits, including the stoical 'Surround Yourself With Sorrow', the oddly paced, wish-fulfilling 'Conversations' and the upbeat 'Something Tells Me (Something Is Gonna Happen Tonight)'.

Like many of her contemporaries, Black wound down her recording career in the 70s and concentrated on live work and television commitments. While old rivals such as Lulu, Sandie Shaw and Dusty Springfield were courted by the new rock élite, Black required no such patronage and entered the 90s as one of the highest paid family entertainers in the British music business, with two major UK television shows, *Blind Date* and *Surprise! Surprise!* In 1993, she celebrated 30 years in showbusiness with an album, full-length video, book and television special, all entitled *Through The Years*. Two years

later she received a BAFTA award on behalf of *Blind Date*, in recognition of her contribution to this 'significant and popular programme'. Her future as an entertainer on UK television is guaranteed: as long as there is television, there will always be a 'Misssa Cillaaa Blaaaaaack'.

● ALBUMS: *Cilla* (Parlophone 1965) ★★★, *Cilla Sings A Rainbow* (Parlophone 1966) ★★★, *Sher oo!* (Parlophone 1968) ★★★, *Surround Yourself With Cilla* (Parlophone 1968) ★★, *Sweet Inspiration* (Parlophone 1969) ★★★, *Images* (Parlophone 1970) ★★, *Day By Day With Cilla* (Parlophone 1973) ★★, *In My Life* (EMI 1974) ★★★, *It Makes Me Feel Good* (EMI 1976) ★★, *Modern Priscilla* (EMI 1978) ★★★, *Especially For You* reissued as *Love Songs* (K-Tel 1980) ★★★, *Surprisingly Cilla* (Towerbell 1985) ★★, *Cilla's World* Australia only (Virgin 1990) ★★, *Through The Years* (Columbia 1993) ★★★.

● COMPILATIONS: *The Best Of Cilla Black* (Parlophone 1968) ★★★, *You're My World* (Regal Starline 1970) ★★★, *The Very Best Of Cilla Black* (EMI 1983) ★★★, *25th Anniversary Album* (MFP 1988) ★★★, *The Best Of The EMI Years* (EMI 1991) ★★★★, *Love, Cilla* (EMI 1993) ★★★, *1963-1973: The Abbey Road Decade* 3-CD box set (EMI 1997) ★★★, *The Essential Cilla Black 1963-1978* (EMI 1999) ★★★★.

● VIDEOS: *Through The Years: The Cilla Black Story* (SMV 1993).

● FILMS: *Ferry Across The Mersey* (1965), *Work Is A Four Letter Word* (1965).

BLACK, DON

b. 21 June 1938, Hackney, London, England. A prolific lyricist for film songs, stage musicals and Tin Pan Alley. One of five children, Black worked part-time as an usher at the London Palladium before finding a job as an office boy and sometime journalist with the *New Musical Express* in the early 50s. After a brief sojourn as a stand-up comic in the dying days of the music halls, he gravitated towards London's Denmark Street, the centre of UK music publishing, where he worked as a song plugger for firms owned by Dave Toff and Joe 'Mr. Piano' Henderson. He met Matt Monro in 1960, shortly before the singer made his breakthrough with Cyril Ornadel and Norman Newell's 'Portrait Of My Love'. Encouraged by Monro, Black began to develop his talent for lyric writing. Together with another popular vocalist, Al Saxon, Black wrote 'April Fool', which Monro included on his *Love Is The Same Anywhere*. In 1964 Black collaborated with the German composer, Udo Jurgens, and together they turned Jurgens' Eurovision Song Contest entry, 'Warum Nur Warum', into 'Walk Away', which became a UK Top 5 hit for Monro. The singer also charted with 'For Mama', which Black wrote with Charles Aznavour.

The song was also popular for Connie Francis and Jerry Vale in the USA. In 1965 Black made his break into films with the lyric of the title song for *Thunderball*, the fourth James Bond movie. The song was popularized by Tom Jones, and it marked the beginning of a fruitful collaboration with composer John Barry. As well as providing Bond with two more themes, 'Diamonds Are Forever' (1971, Shirley Bassey, and for which they received an Ivor Novello Award) and 'The Man With The Golden Gun' (1974, Lulu), the songwriters received a second 'Ivor' and an Academy Award for their title song to *Born Free* in 1966. Black has been nominated on four other occasions: for 'True Grit' (with Elmer Bernstein, 1969), 'Ben' (Walter Scharf, a US number 1 for Michael Jackson in 1972, and a UK hit for Marti Webb in 1985), 'Wherever Love Takes Me', from *Gold* (Bernstein, 1972), and 'Come To Me', from *The Pink Panther Strikes Again* (Henry Mancini, 1976).

It has been estimated that Black's lyrics have been heard in well over 100 movies, including *To Sir With Love* (title song, with Mark London, 1972, a US number 1 for Lulu), *Pretty Polly* (title song, Michel Legrand, 1967), *I'll Never Forget What's 'Is Name* ('One Day Soon', Francis Lai, 1968), *The Italian Job* ('On Days Like These', Quincy Jones, 1969), *Satan's Harvest* ('Two People', Denis King, 1969), *Hoffman* ('If There Ever Is A Next Time', Ron Grainer, 1970), *Mary Queen Of Scots* ('Wish Was Then', John Barry, 1971), *Alice's Adventures In Wonderland* (several songs with Barry, 1972), *The Tamarind Seed* ('Play It Again', Barry, 1974), *The Dove* ('Sail The Summer Winds', Barry, 1974), and *The Wilby Conspiracy* ('All The Wishing In The World', Stanley Myers, 1975). In 1970, Matt Monro invited Don Black to become his manager, and he remained in that role until the singer died in 1985. Black considered Monro to be one of the finest interpreters of his lyrics, particularly with regard to 'If I Never Sing Another Song', which Black wrote with Udo Jurgens in 1977. It was featured on *Matt Monro Sings Don Black* which was released in 1990. The song became a favourite closing number for many artists, including Johnnie Ray and Eddie Fisher.

In 1971, Black augmented his already heavy workload by becoming involved with stage musicals. His first score, written with composer Walter Scharf, was for *Maybe That's Your Problem*, which had a limited run (18 performances) at London's Roundhouse Theatre. The subject of the show was premature ejaculation (Black says that his friend, Alan Jay Lerner, suggested that it should be called *Shortcomings*, but the critics regarded it as 'a dismal piece'). However, one of the performers was Elaine Paige, just seven years before her triumph in *Evita*. Paige was also in *Billy*, London's hit musical of 1974. Adapted from the play *Billy Liar*, which was set in the north of England, Black and John Barry's score captured the 'feel' and the dialect of the original. The songs included 'Some Of Us Belong To The Stars', 'I Missed The Last Rainbow', 'Any Minute

Now', and 'It Were All Green Hills', which was subsequently recorded by Stanley Holloway. *Billy* ran for over 900 performances and made a star of Michael Crawford in his musical comedy debut. Black's collaborator on the score for his next show, *Bar Mitzvah Boy* (1978), was Jule Styne, the legendary composer of shows such as *Funny Girl* and *Gypsy*, among others. Although *Bar Mitzvah Boy* had a disappointingly short run, it did impress Andrew Lloyd Webber, who engaged Black to write the lyrics for his song cycle, *Tell Me On Sunday*, a television programme and album that featured Marti Webb. Considered too short for theatrical presentation, on the recommendation of Cameron Mackintosh it was combined with Lloyd Webber's *Variations* to form *Song And Dance*, a two-part 'theatrical concert', and featured songs such as 'Take That Look Off Your Face', which gave Marti Webb a UK Top 5 hit and gained Black another Ivor Novello Award, 'Nothing Like You've Ever Known', 'Capped Teeth And Caesar Salad', and 'Tell Me On Sunday'. The show ran in the West End for 781 performances before being remodelled and expanded for Broadway, where it starred Bernadette Peters, who received a Tony Award for her performance.

Black teamed with Benny Andersson and Bjorn Ulvaeus, two former members of Abba, for the aptly titled *Abbacadabra*, a Christmas show that played to packed houses in 1983. Earlier that year, he had written the score for *Dear Anyone* with Geoff Stephens, a successful composer of pop hits such as 'Winchester Cathedral', 'You Won't Find Another Fool Like Me' and 'There's A Kind Of Hush'. The show first surfaced as a concept album in 1978, and one of its numbers, 'I'll Put You Together Again', became a Top 20 hit for the group Hot Chocolate. The 1983 stage presentation did not last long, and neither did *Budgie* (1988). Against a background of 'the sleazy subculture of London's Soho', this show starred Adam Faith and Anita Dobson. Black's lyrics combined with Mort Shuman's music for songs such as 'Why Not Me?', 'There Is Love And There Is Love', 'In One Of My Weaker Moments', and 'They're Naked And They Move', but to no avail – Black, as co-producer, presided over a '£1 million flop'. Two years earlier, Anita Dobson had achieved a UK hit with 'Anyone Can Fall In Love', when Black added a lyric to Simon May and Leslie Osborn's theme for BBC Television's *EastEnders*, one of Britain's top television soap operas. He collaborated with the composers again for 'Always There', a vocal version of their theme for *Howard's Way*, which gave Marti Webb a UK hit. In 1989, Black resumed his partnership with Andrew Lloyd Webber for *Aspects Of Love*. Together with *Phantom Of The Opera* lyricist Charles Hart, they fashioned a musical treatment of David Garnett's 1955 novel that turned out to be more intimate than some of Lloyd Webber's other works, but still retained the operatic form. The show starred Michael Ball and Ann Crumb; Ball took the big ballad, 'Love Changes Everything', to number 2 in the UK, and the score also featured the 'subtle, aching melancholy' of 'The First Man You Remember'. *Aspects of Love* was not considered a hit by Lloyd Webber's standards – it ran for three years in the West End, and for one year on Broadway – but the London Cast recording topped the UK album chart.

In the 90s Black's activities remained numerous and diverse. In 1992, together with Chris Walker, he provided extra lyrics for the London stage production of *Radio Times*; wrote additional songs for a revival of *Billy* by the National Youth Music Theatre at the Edinburgh Festival; renewed his partnership with Geoff Stephens for a concept album of a 'revuesical' entitled *Off The Wall*, the story of 'six characters determined to end it all by throwing themselves off a ledge on the 34th storey of a London highrise building'; collaborated with Lloyd Webber on the Barcelona Olympics anthem, 'Friends For Life' ('Amigos Para Siempre'), which was recorded by Sarah Brightman and Jose Carreras; and worked with David Dundas on 'Keep Your Dreams Alive', for the animated feature, *Freddie As F.R.O.7*. He spent a good deal of the year co-writing the book and lyrics, with Christopher Hampton, for Lloyd Webber's musical treatment of the Hollywood classic, *Sunset Boulevard*. The show, which opened in London and on Broadway in 1993, brought Black two Tony Awards. He adapted one of the hit songs, 'As If We Never Said Goodbye', for Barbra Streisand to sing in her first concert tour for 27 years. Black has held the positions of chairman and vice-president of the British Academy of Songwriters, Composers and Authors, and has, for the past few years, been the genial chairman of the voting panel for the Vivian Ellis Prize, a national competition to encourage new writers for the musical stage. In 1993, 22 of his own songs were celebrated on *The Don Black Songbook*, and in the following year Black branched out into broadcasting, interviewing Elmer Bernstein, and presenting the six-part *How To Make A Musical* on BBC Radio 2. In 1995 he was presented with the Jimmy Kennedy Award at the 40th anniversary Ivor Novello Awards ceremony. In 1996 he received a Lifetime Achievement Award from BMI, and in the following year provided the lyric for 'You Stayed Away Too Long', a song that made the last four of the British heats of the Eurovision Song Contest, but failed to progress further. Another disappointment in 1997 came when the London production of the flop Broadway musical, *The Goodbye Girl*, for which Black wrote seven new songs with composer Marvin Hamlisch, departed after a brief run.

BLACK, ROY

b. Gerd Hoellerich, 25 January 1943, Augsburg, Germany, d. 10 October 1991. As a teenager,

Black fronted the Canons, a beat group modelled to Merseybeat specifications, often playing Hamburg clubs, but he was uncomfortable with this style. He was signed to Polydor as a solo balladeer after a well-received performance in a televised song festival. Composed by Henry Arland and Kurt Hertha, 1965's 'Du Bist Nicht Allein' ('You Are Not Alone') established him as a national star and ensured sell-out tours and high chart placings until the mid-70s. In 1966, 'Ganz In Weiss' ('All In White') was a German number 1 for six weeks, and his second album had advance orders of 50,000. Disinclined to attempt any breakthrough into the English language market, he consolidated his domestic success with 'Deine Schonstes Geschenk', which, in 1970, stayed at the top of the charts even longer than 'Ganz In Weiss'. Identified with and dependent on a particular sound, he lost the knack of consistently picking hits, but wisely invested his royalties and subsequently worked in cabaret.

● ALBUMS: *Roy Black* (Polydor 1966) ★★★, *Roy Black II* (Polydor 1967) ★★★.

BLAINE, HAL

b. Harold Simon Belsky, 5 February 1929, Holyoke, Massachusetts, USA. Drummer Blaine claims to be the most-recorded musician in history. The Los Angeles-based session musician says he has performed on over 35,000 recordings (c.1991), including over 350 that have reached the US Top 10. Blaine began playing drums at the age of seven, owning his first drum set at 13. A fan of big-band jazz, he joined the high school band when his family moved to California in 1944. After a stint in the army, he became a professional drummer, first with a band called the Novelteers (also known as the Stan Moore Trio) and then with singer Vicki Young, who became the first of his several wives. At the end of the 50s he began working with teen-idol Tommy Sands, then singer Patti Page. At the recommendation of fellow studio drummer Earl Palmer, Blaine began accepting session work in the late 50s, beginning on a Sam Cooke record. His first Top 10 single was Jan And Dean's 'Baby Talk' in 1960. His huge discography includes drumming for nearly all the important sessions produced by Phil Spector, including hits by the Crystals, Ronettes and Righteous Brothers. He played on many of the Beach Boys' greatest hits and on sessions for Elvis Presley, Frank Sinatra, Nancy Sinatra, the Association, Gary Lewis And The Playboys, the Mamas And The Papas, Johnny Rivers, the Byrds, Simon And Garfunkel, the Monkees, Neil Diamond, the Carpenters, John Lennon, Ringo Starr, George Harrison, Herb Alpert, Jan And Dean, the Supremes, the Partridge Family, John Denver, the Fifth Dimension, Captain And Tennille, Barbra Streisand, Grass Roots, Cher and hundreds of other artists. In the late 70s Blaine's schedule slowed down and by the 80s his involvement in

the LA studio scene drew to a near halt. In 1990 he wrote a book about his experiences, *Hal Blaine And The Wrecking Crew*.
● ALBUMS: *Deuces, "T's", Roadsters & Drums* (RCA Victor 1963) ★★, *Drums! Drums! A Go Go* (Dunhill 1966) ★★, *Psychedelic Percussion* (Dunhill 1967) ★, *Have Fun!!! Play Drums!!!* (Dunhill 1969) ★★, Buh-Doom (Acoustic Disc 1998) ★★★.
● FURTHER READING: *Hal Blaine And The Wrecking Crew*, Hal Blaine.

BLAND, BOBBY
b. Robert Calvin Bland, 27 January 1930, Rosemark, Tennessee, USA. Having moved to Memphis with his mother, Bobby 'Blue' Bland started singing with local gospel groups, including the Miniatures. Eager to expand his interests, he began frequenting the city's infamous Beale Street, where he became associated with an *ad hoc* circle of aspiring musicians, named, not unnaturally, the Beale Streeters. Bland's recordings from the early 50s show him striving for individuality, but his progress was halted by a stint in the US Army. When the singer returned to Memphis in 1954 he found several of his former associates, including Johnny Ace, enjoying considerable success, while Bland's recording label, Duke, had been sold to Houston entrepreneur Don Robey. In 1956, Bland began touring with 'Little' Junior Parker. Initially, he doubled as valet and driver, a role he reportedly performed for B.B. King, but simultaneously began asserting his characteristic vocal style. Melodic big-band blues singles, including 'Farther Up The Road' (1957) and 'Little Boy Blue' (1958), reached the US R&B Top 10, but Bland's vocal talent was most clearly heard on a series of superb early 60s releases, including 'Cry Cry Cry', 'I Pity The Fool' and the sparkling 'Turn On Your Lovelight', which was destined to become a much-covered standard. Despite credits to the contrary, many such classic works were written by Joe Scott, the artist's bandleader and arranger.
Bland continued to enjoy a consistent run of R&B chart entries throughout the mid-60s, but his recorded work was nonetheless eclipsed by a younger generation of performers. Financial pressures forced the break-up of the group in 1968, and his relationship with Scott, who died in 1979, was irrevocably severed. Nonetheless, depressed and increasingly dependent on alcohol, Bland weathered this unhappy period. In 1971, his record company, Duke, was sold to the larger ABC Records group, resulting in several contemporary blues/soul albums including *His California Album* and *Dreamer*. Subsequent attempts at pushing the artist towards the disco market were unsuccessful, but a 1983 release, *Here We Go Again*, provided a commercial lifeline. Two years later Bland was signed by Malaco Records, specialists in traditional southern black music, who offered a

sympathetic environment. One of the finest singers in post-war blues, Bobby Bland has failed to win the popular acclaim his influence and talent perhaps deserve.
● ALBUMS: with 'Little' Junior Parker *Blues Consolidated* (Duke 1958) ★★★, with Parker *Barefoot Rock And You Got Me* (Duke 1960) ★★★, *Two Steps From The Blues* (Duke 1961) ★★★★, *Here's The Man!!!* (Duke 1962) ★★★★, *Call On Me* (Duke 1963) ★★★, *Ain't Nothin' You Can Do* (Duke 1964) ★★★, *The Soul Of The Man* (Duke 1966) ★★★, *Touch Of The Blues* (Duke 1967) ★★, *Spotlighting The Man* (Duke 1968) ★★, *His California Album* (Dunhill 1973) ★★, *Dreamer* (Dunhill 1974) ★★, with B.B. King *Together For The First Time – Live* (Dunhill 1974) ★★★★, *Get On Down With Bobby Bland* (ABC 1975) ★★, with King *Together Again – Live* (ABC 1976) ★★★, *Reflections In Blue* (ABC 1977) ★★, *Come Fly With Me* (ABC 1978) ★★, *I Feel Good I Feel Fine* (MCA 1979) ★★, *Sweet Vibrations* (MCA 1980) ★★, *You Got Me Loving You* (MCA 1981) ★★, *Try Me, I'm Real* (MCA 1981) ★★, *Here We Go Again* (MCA 1982) ★★, *Tell Mr. Bland* (MCA 1983) ★★, *Members Only* (Malaco 1985) ★★, *After All* (Malaco 1986) ★★, *Blues You Can Use* (Malaco 1987) ★★, *Midnight Run* (Malaco 1989) ★★★, *Portrait Of The Blues* (Malaco 1991) ★★★, *Sad Street* (Malaco 1995) ★★★, *Live On Beale Street* (Malaco 1998) ★★, *Memphis Monday Morning* (Malaco 1999) ★★.
● COMPILATIONS: *The Best Of Bobby Bland* (Duke 1967) ★★★★, *The Best Of Bobby Bland Volume 2* (Duke 1968) ★★★★, *Introspective Of The Early Years* (MCA 1974) ★★★, *Woke Up Screaming* (Ace 1981) ★★★, *The Best Of Bobby Bland* (ABC 1982) ★★★, *Foolin' With The Blues* (Charly 1983) ★★★, *Blues In The Night* (Ace 1985) ★★★, *The Soulful Side Of Bobby Bland* (Kent 1986) ★★, *First Class Blues* (Malaco 1987) ★★★, *Soul With A Flavour 1959-1984* (Charly 1988) ★★★, *The '3B' Blues Boy: The Blues Years 1952-59* (Ace 1991) ★★★★, *The Voice: Duke Recordings 1959-1969* (Ace 1992) ★★★★, *I Pity The Fool: The Duke Recordings Vol. 1* (MCA 1992) ★★★★, *That Did It! The Duke Recordings Volume 3* (MCA 1996) ★★★, *Greatest Hits Vol. One: The Duke Recordings* (MCA 1998) ★★★★, *Greatest Hits Vol. Two: The Dunhill Recordings* (MCA 1998) ★★★★, *Not Afraid To Sing The Blues* (Music Club 1998) ★★★, *Best Of Bobby Bland: The Millennium Collection* (MCA 2000) ★★★★, *The Anthology* (MCA 2001) ★★★★.

BLIND FAITH
Formed in 1969 and one of the earliest conglomerations to earn the dubious tag 'supergroup'. The band comprised Eric Clapton (b. 30 March 1945, Ripley, Surrey, England; guitar, vocals), Ginger Baker (b. 19 August 1939, Lewisham, London, England; drums), Steve Winwood (b. 12 May 1948, Birmingham, England; keyboards, vocals) and Ric Grech (b. 1 November 1945, Bordeaux, France, d. 16 March

1990; bass, violin). The band stayed together for one highly publicized, million-selling album and a lucrative major US tour. Their debut was at a free pop concert in front of an estimated 100,000 at London's Hyde Park, in June 1969. The controversial album cover depicted a topless prepubescent girl holding a phallic chrome model aeroplane. The content included only one future classic, Clapton's 'Presence Of The Lord'. Baker's 'Do What You Like' was self-indulgent and overlong and their cover version of Buddy Holly's 'Well All Right' was unspectacular. Buried among the tracks was the beautiful Winwood composition 'Can't Find My Way Home', never afforded the attention it deserved. Further live Blind Faith tracks can be heard on the Winwood box set, *The Finer Things*. The *Deluxe Edition* is an excellent closing of the chapter. The band left many feeling cheated that they were unable to stay together long enough to fulfil their own ambition and so denied fans of what might have been. The *Deluxe Edition* contains everything Blind Faith recorded, including the long studio jams which capture the band in a natural and unrehearsed setting, although too talented for their own good.

● ALBUMS: *Blind Faith* (Polydor 1969) ★★★, *Blind Faith – Deluxe Edition* (Polydor 2001) ★★★★.

BLONDE ON BLONDE

Blonde On Blonde – Ralph Denver (guitar, vocals), Gareth Johnson (guitar), Richard Hopkins (bass, keyboards) and Les Hicks (drums) – came to prominence on BBC Television's short-lived programme *How Late It Is*. Their debut single, 'All Day, All Night/Country Life' (1969), showed considerable promise, but *Contrasts* was a comparative disappointment, demonstrating little of the group's initial imagination. Blonde On Blonde appeared at the 1969 Isle Of Wight Festival, after which Denver and Hopkins left the line-up. Dave Thomas (guitar, vocals) and Richard John (bass) joined for *Rebirth*, on which the group pursued a musical direction reminiscent of the Moody Blues. They added a mellotron player, known only as Kip, for *Reflections On A Life*, which also featured new bassist Graham Davies in place of John. This somewhat pretentious selection was not a success and Blonde On Blonde broke up soon afterwards.

● ALBUMS: *Contrasts* (Pye 1969) ★★, *Rebirth* (Ember 1970) ★★, *Reflections On A Life* (Ember 1971) ★★.

BLOOD, SWEAT AND TEARS

The jazz/rock excursions made by Blood, Sweat And Tears offered a refreshing change to late 60s guitar-dominated rock music. The many impressive line-ups of the band comprised (among others) David Clayton-Thomas (b. David Thomsett, 13 September 1941, Surrey, England; vocals), Al Kooper (b. 5 February 1944, New York, USA; keyboards, vocals), Steve Katz (b. 9 May 1945, New York, USA; guitar), Jerry Weiss, Randy Brecker (b. 27 November 1945, Philadelphia, Pennsylvania, USA; saxophone), Dick Halligan (b. 29 August 1943, New York, USA; trombone, flute, keyboards), Fred Lipsius (b. 19 November 1944, New York, USA; alto saxophone, piano), Bobby Colomby (b. 20 December 1944, New York, USA; drums), Jim Fielder (b. 4 October 1947, Denton, Texas, USA; bass, ex-Buffalo Springfield), Lew Soloff (b. 20 February 1944, Brooklyn, New York, USA; trumpet), Chuck Winfield (b. 5 February 1943, Monessen, Pennsylvania, USA; trumpet), Jerry Hyman (b. 19 May 1947, Brooklyn, New York, USA; trumpet) and Dave Bargeron (b. 6 September 1942, Athol, Massachusetts, USA; trumpet). The band was conceived by Al Kooper, who, together with Katz, had played with the Blues Project, but Kooper departed soon after the debut *Child Is Father To The Man*, which contained two of his finest songs, 'I Can't Quit Her' and 'My Days Are Numbered'.

The record, although cited as a masterpiece by some critics, was ultimately flawed by erratic vocals. Kooper, Brecker and Weiss were replaced by Winfield, Soloff and Clayton-Thomas. The latter took over as vocalist to record *Blood Sweat & Tears*, which is now regarded as their finest work, standing up today as a brilliantly scored and fresh-sounding record. Kooper, although working on the arrangements, missed out on the extraordinary success this record achieved. The album topped the US album charts for many weeks during its two-year stay, sold millions of copies, won a Grammy award and spawned three major worldwide hits: a cover version of Brenda Holloway's 'You've Made Me So Very Happy', 'Spinning Wheel' and 'And When I Die'. The following two albums were both considerable successes, although unoriginal, with their gutsy brass arrangements, occasional biting guitar solos and Clayton-Thomas' growling vocal delivery. Following *BS&T4*, Clayton-Thomas departed for a solo career, resulting in a succession of lead vocalists, including the former member of Edgar Winter's White Trash, Jerry LaCroix (b. 10 October 1943, Alexandria, Louisiana, USA). The band never regained their former glory, even following the return of Clayton-Thomas. *New City* reached the US album charts, but the supper-club circuit ultimately beckoned with the Blood, Sweat And Tears name continuing in one guise or another behind Clayton-Thomas. Nevertheless, the original band deserves a place in rock history as both innovators and brave exponents of psychedelic-tinged jazz/rock.

● ALBUMS: *Child Is Father To The Man* (Columbia 1968) ★★★, *Blood, Sweat & Tears* (Columbia 1969) ★★★★, *Blood, Sweat & Tears 3* (Columbia 1970) ★★★, *BS&T4* (Columbia 1971) ★★★, *New Blood* (Columbia 1972) ★★, *No Sweat* (Columbia 1973) ★★, *Mirror Image* (Columbia

1974) ★★, *New City* (Columbia 1975) ★★, *More Than Ever* (Columbia 1976) ★★, *Brand New Day* (ABC 1977) ★★, *Nuclear Blues* (LAX 1980) ★★, *Live And Improvised* (Columbia 1991) ★★, *Live* (Rhino 1994) ★★.
● COMPILATIONS: *Greatest Hits* (Columbia 1972) ★★★★, *Classic B S T* (Columbia 1980) ★★★, *What Goes Up! The Best Of* (Columbia/Legacy 1995) ★★★★, *Super Hits* (Columbia 1998) ★★★.
● FURTHER READING: *Blood, Sweat & Tears*, Lorraine Alterman.

BLOOM, BOBBY

d. 28 February 1974. New York-based Bloom began his career during the 60s as one of several backroom entrepreneurs, along with Anders And Poncia, Artie Ripp and Levine/Reisnick, central to the Kama Sutra Records/Buddah Records group of labels. He also made several solo recordings, including 'Love Don't Let Me Down' and 'Count On Me', worked with the Imaginations, and later formed a partnership with composer/producer Jeff Barry. Together, they contributed material for the Monkees, notably 'Ticket On A Ferry Ride' and 'You're So Good To Me'. Bloom's singing career blossomed with the effervescent 'Montego Bay' which reached US number 8 and UK number 3 in 1970. This adept combination of bubblegum, calypso and rock was maintained on 'Heavy Makes You Happy' and *The Bobby Bloom Album*, which Barry produced. Bloom was killed in an accidental shooting in February 1974.
● ALBUMS: *The Bobby Bloom Album* (MGM 1970) ★★★.

BLOOMFIELD, MIKE

b. Michael Bernard Bloomfield, 28 July 1944, Chicago, Illinois, USA, d. 15 February 1981, San Francisco, California, USA. For many, both critics and fans, Bloomfield was the finest white blues guitarist America has so far produced. Although signed to Columbia Records in 1964 as the Group (with Charlie Musslewhite and Nick Gravenites), it was his emergence in 1965 as the young, shy guitarist in the Paul Butterfield Blues Band that brought him to public attention. He astonished those viewers who had watched black blues guitarists spend a lifetime trying, but failing, to play with as much fluidity and feeling as Bloomfield. That same year he was an important part of musical history, when folk purists accused Bob Dylan of committing artistic suicide at the Newport Folk Festival. Bloomfield was his lead electric guitarist at that event, and again on Dylan's 60s masterpiece *Highway 61 Revisited.*. On leaving Butterfield in 1967 he immediately formed the seminal Electric Flag, although he had left before the first album's release and their fast decline in popularity. His 1968 album *Super Session*, with Stephen Stills and Al Kooper, became his biggest-selling record. It led to a short but financially lucrative career with Kooper.

The track 'Stop' on the album epitomized Bloomfield's style: clean, crisp, sparse and emotional. The long sustained notes were produced by bending the string with his fingers underneath the other strings so as not to affect the tuning. It was five years before his next satisfying work appeared, *Triumvirate*, with John Hammond and Dr. John, and following this, Bloomfield became a virtual recluse. Subsequent albums were distributed on small labels and did not gain national distribution. Plagued with a long-standing drug habit he occasionally supplemented his income by scoring music for pornographic movies. He also wrote or co-wrote the soundtracks for *The Trip* (1967), *Medium Cool* (1969) and *Steelyard Blues* (1973). Additionally, he taught music at Stanford University in San Francisco, wrote advertising jingles and was an adviser to *Guitar Player* magazine. Bloomfield avoided the limelight, possibly because of his insomnia while touring, but mainly because of his perception of what he felt an audience wanted: 'Playing in front of strangers leads to idolatry, and idolatry is dangerous because the audience has a preconception of you, even though you cannot get a conception of them'. In 1975 he was cajoled into forming the 'supergroup' KGB with Ric Grech, Barry Goldberg and Carmine Appice. The resulting album was an unmitigated disaster and Bloomfield resorted to playing mostly acoustic music. He had an extraordinarily prolific period between 1976 and 1977, the most notable release being the critically acclaimed *If You Love These Blues, Play 'Em As You Please*, issued through *Guitar Player* magazine. A second burst of activity occurred shortly before his tragic death, when another three albums' worth of material was recorded. Bloomfield was found dead in his car from a suspected accidental drug overdose, a sad end to a 'star' who had constantly avoided stardom in order to maintain his own integrity.
● ALBUMS: with Al Kooper, Stephen Stills *Super Session* (Columbia 1968) ★★★, *The Live Adventures Of Mike Bloomfield And Al Kooper* (Columbia 1969) ★★★, with Barry Goldberg *Two Jews Blues* (Buddah 1969) ★★, *It's Not Killing Me* (Columbia 1970) ★★, with Dr. John, John Hammond *Triumvirate* (Columbia 1973) ★★★, with KGB *KGB* (MCA 1976) ★, with Mill Valley Bunch *Mill Valley Session* (Polydor 1976) ★★★, *If You Love These Blues, Play 'Em As You Please* (Guitar Player 1976) ★★★, *Analine* (Takoma 1977) ★★, *Count Talent And The Originals* (Clouds 1978) ★★, *Michael Bloomfield* (Takoma 1978) ★★, with Woody Harris *Bloomfield/Harris* (Kicking Mule 1979) ★★, *Between The Hard Place And The Ground* (Takoma 1979) ★★, *Livin' In The Fast Lane* (Waterhouse 1980) ★★, *Gospel Duets* (Kicking Mule 1981) ★★, *Cruisin' For A Bruisin'* (Takoma 1981) ★★, *Junko Partners* (Intermedia 1984) ★★, *I'm With You Always* 1977 recording (Demon 1987) ★★, *Try It Before You*

Buy It 1973 recording (One Way 1990) ★★, *Blues, Gospel And Ragtime Guitar Instrumentals* (Shanachie 1994) ★★★, *Rx For The Blues* (Eclipse 1996) ★★, *Bloomfield Blues* (Columbia River 2000) ★★★, *Red Hot And Blue* (City Hall 2000) ★★.

● COMPILATIONS: *Bloomfield: A Retrospective* (Columbia 1983) ★★★, *Don't Say That I Ain't Your Man! Essential Blues 1964-1969* (Columbia/ Legacy 1994) ★★★, *The Best Of* (Takoma/Ace 1997) ★★★.

● FURTHER READING: *The Rise And Fall Of An American Guitar Hero*, Ed Ward. *If You Love These Blues*, Jan Mark.

BLOSSOM TOES

Brian Godding (guitar, vocals, keyboards), Jim Cregan (guitar, vocals), Brian Belshaw (bass, vocals) and Kevin Westlake (drums) were initially known as the Ingoes, but became Blossom Toes in 1967 upon the launch of manager Giorgio Gomelsky's Marmalade label. *We Are Ever So Clean* was an enthralling selection, astutely combining English pop with a quirky sense of humour. The grasp of melody offered on 'Love Is' or 'What's It For' was akin to that of the Idle Race or the Beatles, while the experimental flourish on 'What On Earth' or 'Look At Me, I'm You' captures the prevailing spirit of 1967. *If Only For A Moment* marked the departure of Westlake, who was replaced, in turn, by John 'Poli' Palmer, then Barry Reeves. A noticeably heavier sound was shown to great effect on the revered 'Peace Lovin' Man', but the set was altogether less distinctive. The quartet was dissolved in 1970, but while Belshaw and Godding rejoined Westlake in B.B. Blunder, Cregan formed Stud with Jim Wilson and Charlie McCracken, before joining Family. He later found fame with Cockney Rebel and Rod Stewart.

● ALBUMS: *We Are Ever So Clean* (Marmalade 1967) ★★★★, *If Only For A Moment* (Marmalade 1969) ★★★.

● COMPILATIONS: *The Blossom Toes Collection* (Decal/Charly 1989) ★★★★.

BLOSSOMS

The Blossoms began their career in Los Angeles, USA, in 1954 under the name of the Dreamers, with a line-up comprising Fanita Barrett (later James), Gloria Jones, Nanette Williams (later Jackson) and Annette Williams. The following year they recorded as Richard Berry's backing group. Darlene Wright (later Love) then replaced Nanette Williams and by 1957 the quartet were renamed the Blossoms. Releases on Capitol Records (1957-58) and Challenge (1961-62) were interspersed with session work for Duane Eddy and several one-off singles under such pseudonyms as the Coeds And The Playgirls. Love and James were also members of Bob B. Soxx And The Blue Jeans, a trio that worked with Phil Spector. The famed producer used Love on several Crystals sessions and the singer also released several singles under her own name. The Blossoms became a permanent fixture on the *Shindig* US television show. By 1965 the group had been reduced to a trio of Love, James and Jean King. They recorded for Challenge, and 'Son-In Law', a response to Ernie K-Doe's 'Mother-In-Law', was their only single to chart. They had a minor R&B hit in 1967 with 'Good Good Lovin''. The line-up underwent several further changes; Edna Wright (Darlene's sister) and Grazia Nitzsche were also members as the Blossoms progressed through several outlets including Ode (1967), Bell (1969-70) and Lion (1972). Love then left to pursue an intermittent solo career. Of the other ex-members, Jones and Jackson formed the Girlfriends with Carolyn Willis. Jones later recorded the original version of 'Tainted Love', which later became a UK number 1 hit in 1981 for Soft Cell, and achieved a certain notoriety for her marriage to Marc Bolan. Willis subsequently joined Edna Wright in the Honey Cone. Fanita James, meanwhile, continued to lead the Blossoms during the 80s.

● ALBUMS: *Shockwave* (MGM 1972) ★★★.

BLUE CHEER

San Francisco's Blue Cheer, consisting of Dickie Peterson (b. 1948, Grand Forks, North Dakota, USA; vocals, bass), Leigh Stephens (guitar) and Paul Whaley (drums), harboured dreams of a more conventional direction until seeing Jimi Hendrix perform at the celebrated Monterey Pop Festival. Taking their name from a potent brand of LSD, they made an immediate impact with their uncompromising debut album, *Vincebus Eruptum*, which featured cacophonous interpretations of Eddie Cochran's 'Summertime Blues' (US number 14) and Mose Allison's 'Parchman(t) Farm'. A second set, *Outsideinside*, was completed in the open air when the trio's high volume levels destroyed the studio monitors. Stephens left the group during the sessions for *New! Improved! Blue Cheer*, and his place was taken by former Other Half guitarist Randy Holden; they also added Bruce Stephens (bass, ex-Mint Tattoo), and Holden left during the recording sessions. *Blue Cheer* then unveiled a reconstituted line-up of Peterson, Ralph Burns Kellogg (keyboards, ex-Mint Tattoo), and Norman Mayell (drums, guitar), who replaced Whaley. Stephens was then replaced by former Kak guitarist Gary Yoder, for *The Original Human Being*. It featured the atmospheric, raga-influenced 'Babaji (Twilight Raga)', and is widely acclaimed as the group's most cohesive work. The band was dissolved in 1971 but re-formed in 1979 following an emotional reunion between Peterson and Whaley. This line-up made *The Beast Is Back* in 1985 and added guitarist Tony Rainier. Blue Cheer continued to pursue their original bombastic vision, and *Highlights And Lowlives* coupled the group with Anthrax producer Jack Endino. In the early 90s the band vas reappraised, with many of the Seattle grunge rock bands admitting a strong affection or Blue Cheer's groundbreaking work.

● ALBUMS: *Vincebus Eruptum* (Philips 1967) ★★★, *Outsideinside* (Philips 1968) ★★★, *New! mproved! Blue Cheer* (Philips 1969) ★★, *Blue Cheer* (Philips 1969) ★★, *The Original Human 3eing* (Philips 1970) ★★★, *Oh! Pleasant Hope* Philips 1971) ★, *The Beast Is Back* (Megaforce 985) ★, *Blitzkrieg Over Nuremberg* (Thunderbolt 989) ★★★, *Dining With Sharks* (Nibelung 1991) ★★.

COMPILATIONS: *The Best Of Blue Cheer* Philips 1982) ★★★, *Louder Than God* (Rhino 986) ★★★, *Good Times Are So Hard To Find (The History Of Blue Cheer)* (Mercury 1988) ★★★, *Highlights And Lowlives* (Nibelung 1990) ★★, *The 3east Is Back: The Megaforce Years* (Megaforce 996) ★★, *Live & Unreleased* (Captain Trip 1996) ★★.

3LUE, DAVID

●. Stuart David Cohen, 18 February 1941, Providence, Rhode Island, USA, d. 2 December 982, New York City, New York, USA. Having left the US Army, Cohen arrived in Greenwich Village in 1960 hoping to pursue an acting career, but was drawn instead into the nascent olk circle. He joined a generation of younger performers – Eric Anderson, Phil Ochs, Dave 'an Ronk and Tom Paxton – who rose to prominence in Bob Dylan's wake. Blue was signed to the influential Elektra Records label in 965 and released the *Singer/Songwriter Project* album – a joint collaboration with Richard arina, Bruce Murdoch and Patrick Sky. Although Blue's first full-scale collection in 1966 wore an obvious debt to the folk rock style of Dylan's *Highway 61 Revisited*, a rudimentary charm was evident on several selections, notably 3rand Hotel' and 'I'd Like To Know'. Several acts recorded the singer's compositions, but subsequent recordings with a group, American Patrol, were never issued and it was two years before a second album appeared. *These 23 Days In December* showcased a more mellow performer, best exemplified in the introspective reworking of 'Grand Hotel', before a further release recorded in Nashville, *Me, S. David Cohen*, embraced country styles. Another hiatus ended in 1972 when Blue was signed to David Geffen's emergent Asylum Records label, and his first album for the company, *Stories*, was the artist's bleakest, most introspective selection. Subsequent releases included the Graham Nash-produced *Nice Baby And The Angel* and *Com'n Back For More*, but although his song, 'Outlaw Man', was covered by the Eagles, Blue was unable to make a significant commercial breakthrough. During this period, he appeared alongside his old Greenwich Village friend, Bob Dylan, in the Rolling Thunder Revue, which toured North America. Blue resumed acting later in the decade and made memorable appearances

in Neil Young's *Human Highway* and Wim Wenders' *The American Friend*. His acerbic wit was one of the highlights of Dylan's *Renaldo And Clara* movie, but this underrated artist died in 1982 while jogging in Washington Square Park. Reappraisal is long overdue.

● ALBUMS: with Richard Farina *Singer/Songwriter Project* (Elektra 1965) ★★★, *David Blue* (Elektra 1966) ★★★, *These 23 Days In December* (Elektra 1968) ★★, *Me, S. David Cohen* (1970) ★★, *Stories* (Asylum 1971) ★★★, *Nice Baby And The Angel* (Asylum 1973) ★★★, *Com'n Back For More* (Asylum 1975) ★★★, *Cupid's Arrow* (Asylum 1976) ★★★.

● FILMS: *Der Amerikanische Freund* aka *The American Friend* (1977), *Renaldo And Clara* (1978).

BLUES MAGOOS

Formed in the Bronx, New York, USA, in 1964 and initially known as the Bloos Magoos, the founding line-up consisted of Emil 'Peppy' Thielhelm (b. 16 June 1949; vocals, guitar), Dennis LaPore (lead guitar), Ralph Scala (b. 12 December 1947; organ, vocals), Ronnie Gilbert (b. 25 April 1946; bass) and John Finnegan (drums), but by the end of the year LaPore and Finnegan had been replaced by Mike Esposito (b. Delaware, USA) and Geoff Daking (b. Delaware, USA). The group quickly became an important part of the emergent Greenwich Village rock scene and in 1966 secured a residency at the fabled Night Owl club. Having recorded singles for Ganim and Verve Forecast, the band was signed to Mercury Records, where they became the subject of intense grooming. However, Vidal Sassoon-styled haircuts and luminous costumes failed to quash an innate rebelliousness, although the group enjoyed one notable hit when '(We Ain't Got) Nothin' Yet' (1966) reached number 5 in the US chart. Its garage-band snarl set the tone for an attendant album, *Psychedelic Lollipop*, which contained several equally virulent selections.

The Blues Magoos' dalliance with drugs was barely disguised, and titles such as 'Love Seems Doomed' (LSD) and 'Albert Common Is Dead' (ACID) were created to expound their beliefs. By 1968 tensions arose within the group and they broke up following the release of *Basic Blues Magoos*. The management team re-signed the name to ABC Records, and, as Thielhelm had accumulated a backlog of material, suggested he front a revamped line-up. John Leillo (vibes, percussion), Eric Kaz (b. Eric Justin Kaz, Brooklyn, New York City, New York, USA; keyboards), Roger Eaton (bass) and Richie Dickon (percussion) completed *Never Goin' Back To Georgia*, while the same group, except for Eaton, was augmented by sundry session musicians for the disappointing *Gulf Coast Bound*. The Blues Magoos' name was discontinued when Peppy took a role in the musical *Hair*. As Peppy Castro he has since pursued a varied career as a member of Barnaby Bye, Wiggy Bits and Balance, while Cher and Kiss are among the artists who have recorded his songs. Kaz went on to form American Flyer.

● ALBUMS: *Psychedelic Lollipop* (Mercury 1966) ★★★, *Electric Comic Book* (Mercury 1967) ★★★, *Basic Blues Magoos* (Mercury 1968) ★★, *Never Goin' Back To Georgia* (ABC 1969) ★★, *Gulf Coast Bound* (ABC 1970) ★★.

● COMPILATIONS: *Kaleidescopic Compendium: The Best Of The Blues Magoos* (Mercury 1992) ★★★.

BLUES PROJECT

The Blues Project was formed in New York, USA in the mid-60s by guitarist Danny Kalb, and took its name from a compendium of acoustic musicians with whom he played. Tommy Flanders (vocals), Steve Katz (b. 9 May 1945, Brooklyn, New York City, New York, USA; guitar), Andy Kulberg (b. Buffalo, New York, USA; bass, flute), Roy Blumenfeld (drums), plus Kalb, were latterly joined by Al Kooper (b. 5 February 1944, Brooklyn, New York City, New York, USA; vocals, keyboards), fresh from adding the distinctive organ on Bob Dylan's 'Like A Rolling Stone'. The sextet was quickly established as the city's leading electric blues band, a prowess demonstrated on their debut album, *Live At the Cafe Au-Go-Go*.

Flanders then left to pursue a solo career and the resultant five-piece embarked on the definitive *Projections* album. Jazz, pop and soul styles were added to their basic grasp of R&B to create an absorbing, rewarding collection, but inner tensions undermined their obvious potential. By the time *Live At The Town Hall* was issued, Kooper had left the band to form Blood, Sweat And Tears, where he was subsequently joined by Katz. An unhappy Kalb also quit, but Kulberg and Blumenfeld added Richard Greene (b. 9 November 1945, Beverly Hills, California, USA; violin), John Gregory (guitar, vocals) and Don Kretmar (bass, saxophone) for a fourth collection, *Planned Obsolescence*. The line-up owed little to the old band, and in deference to this new direction, changed their name to Seatrain. In 1971, Kalb reclaimed the erstwhile moniker and recorded two further albums with former members Flanders, Blumenfeld and Kretmar. This particular version of the band was supplanted by a reunion of the *Projections* line-up for a show in Central Park, after which the Blues Project name was abandoned. Despite their fractured history, the Blues Project is recognized as one of the leading white R&B bands of the 60s.

● ALBUMS: *Live At The Cafe Au-Go-Go* (Verve/Forecast 1966) ★★★, *Projections* (Verve/Forecast 1967) ★★★★, *Live At The Town Hall* (Verve/Forecast 1967) ★★★, *Planned Obsolescence* (Verve/Forecast 1968) ★★★, *Flanders Kalb Katz Etc.* (Verve/Forecast 1969) ★★, *Lazarus* (Capitol 1971) ★★, *The Blues Project* (Capitol 1972) ★★, *Reunion In Central Park* (Capitol 1973) ★★.

● COMPILATIONS: *The Best Of The Blues Project* (Rhino 1989) ★★★, *Anthology* (Polydor 1997) ★★★★.

BO STREET RUNNERS

Formed in 1964 in Harrow, Middlesex, England, the Bo Street Runners initially comprised John Dominic (vocals), Gary Thomas (lead guitar), Royston Fry (keyboards), Dave Cameron (bass) and Nigel Hutchinson (drums). Within months of forming they recorded a self-financed EP that was sold at Harrow's Railway Hotel, where the group held a residency. When Cameron's mother sent a copy of the disc to the producers of ATV's *Ready, Steady, Go!*, the Bo Street Runners were added to the list of competitors in the show's talent contest, 'Ready, Steady, Win!'. The group won, securing a prized contract with Decca Records. 'Bo Street Runner' duly became their debut single, but despite the publicity, it failed to chart. Glyn Thomas and Tim Hinkley then replaced Hutchinson and Fry, while Dave Quincy was added on saxophone. Two singles for Columbia Records ensued, 'Tell Me What You're Gonna Do' and 'Baby Never Say Goodbye', the latter of which lost out to the original version by Unit Four Plus Two. Thomas was then replaced by Mick Fleetwood, and with Quincy departing for Chris Farlowe, the reshaped Bo Street Runners released a version of the Beatles' 'Drive My Car' in January 1966. Fleetwood was then replaced in turn by Alan Turner and Barrie Wilson, and when Dominic opted to manage the group, Mike Patto joined as vocalist. The Bo Street Runners disbanded late in 1966, after which Patto recorded a solo single, 'Can't Stop Talkin' 'Bout My Baby'. The b-side, 'Love' represented the final Bo Street Runners recording. Patto was reunited with Hinkley in the Chicago Line Blues Band, before joining Timebox, who in turn evolved into Patto. Not to be confused with the American band of the same name.

BOB AND EARL

Formed in Los Angeles, California, USA, in 1960 this duo comprised Bobby Day (b. Bobby Byrd, 1 July 1932, Fort Worth, Texas, USA) and Earl Lee Nelson. Day had previously formed the Hollywood Flames, a group best recalled for the rock 'n' roll hit 'Buzz-Buzz-Buzz' (1957), which featured Nelson on lead vocal. Day then secured a solo hit with 'Rockin' Robin' before briefly joining Nelson in the original Bob And Earl. Bob Relf replaced Day when the latter resumed his own career. The Barry White-produced 'Harlem Shuffle', the pairing's best-known song, was originally released in 1963. A minor hit in the USA, the single proved more durable in Britain. Although it failed to chart when first released, a reissue reached number 7 in 1969. Bob And Earl had meanwhile continued to record excellent singles, although the prophetically titled 'Baby It's Over' (1966) was their only further hit. Nelson recorded under the name of Jay Dee for Warner Brothers Records in 1973, and also as Jackie Lee, charting in the USA with 'The Duck' (1965), 'African Boo-Ga-Loo' (1968) and 'The Chicken' (1970). Relf wrote Love Unlimited's 1974 hit 'Walking In The Rain' and was latterly replaced by Bobby Garrett. The new duo continued to record together, and individually, during the 70s.

● ALBUMS: *Harlem Shuffle* (Tip/Sue 1966) ★★★, *Bob And Earl* (Crestview/B&C 1969) ★★, *Together* (Joy 1969) ★★.

BOB B. SOXX AND THE BLUE JEANS

One of several groups created by producer Phil Spector, this short-lived trio comprised two members of the Blossoms, Darlene Love (b. Darlene Wright, 26 July 1938, Los Angeles, California, USA) and Fanita James, and soul singer Bobby Sheen (b. 1943, St. Louis, Missouri, USA, d. 23 November 2000, Los Angeles, California, USA). The Blue Jeans scored a US Top 10 hit in 1962 with a radical reading of 'Zip-A-Dee-Doo-Dah', wherein the euphoric original was slowed to a snail-like pace. Its success spawned an album which mixed restructured standards ('The White Cliffs Of Dover', 'This Land Is Your Land') with original songs, of which 'Why Do Lovers Break Each Other's Heart?' and 'Not Too Young To Get Married' were also issued as singles. The trio also made a contribution to the legendary *Phil Spector's Christmas Album*.

● ALBUMS: *Zip-A-Dee-Doo-Dah* (Philles 1963) ★★★.

BOETTCHER, CURT

b. 7 January 1944, Eau Claire, Wisconsin, USA, d. 14 June 1987, Los Angeles, USA. This talented individual first drew attention as a member of the GoldeBriars, a Minnesota-based folk group who originally comprised Boettcher, Ron Neilson, Dottie Holmberg and Sheri Holmberg. Formed in 1962, the group expanded to a six-piece and relocated to Los Angeles in 1965, where they issued two albums on Epic Records. He subsequently surfaced in various pop-related units – Summer's Children, Ballroom and Your Gang – before enjoying a fruitful period with the Association. Boettcher produced their debut album which contained two US Top 10 hits, 'Along Comes Mary' and 'Cherish', the latter of which reached number 1. He then founded a production company, Mee Moo, and was the guiding force behind two acts, Millennium and Sagittarius, whose work was marked by distinctive soft, sweet harmonies. In 1970, Boettcher established Together Records with Gary Usher and Keith Olsen, while continuing backroom duties on releases by Tommy Roe and Emitt Rhodes. The artist's solo album, *There's An Innocent Face*, maintained the path of earlier work, but reaped negligible sales, a problem also

bedevilling his 1976 group, California. Boettcher then continued his solo career, but by this point was a neglected talent and his premature death in 1987 was largely unreported.

● ALBUMS: with the GoldeBriars *The GoldeBriars* (Epic 1964) ★★, with the GoldeBriars *Straight Ahead* (Epic 1964) ★★, as Your Gang *The Daily Trip* (Mercury 1967) ★★★, *Friar Tuck And His Psychedelic Guitar* (Mercury 1967) ★★★, *Present Tense* (Columbia 1968) ★★★, *There's An Innocent Face* (Elektra 1973) ★★★.

● COMPILATIONS: *Misty Mirage* (Poptones 2000) ★★★, *California Music* (Poptones 2001) ★★★.

BOND, GRAHAM

b. 28 October 1937, Romford, Essex, England, d. 8 May 1974, London, England. The young Bond was adopted from a Dr Barnardo's children's home and given musical tuition at school; he has latterly become recognized as one of the main instigators of British R&B, along with Cyril Davies and Alexis Korner. His musical career began with Don Rendell's quintet in 1961 as a jazz saxophonist, followed by a stint with Korner's famous ensemble, Blues Incorporated. By the time he formed his first band in 1963 he had made the Hammond organ his main instrument, although he showcased his talent at gigs by playing both alto saxophone and organ simultaneously. The seminal Graham Bond Organisation became one of the most respected units in the UK during 1964, and boasted an impressive line-up of Ginger Baker (drums), Jack Bruce (bass) and Dick Heckstall-Smith (saxophone – replacing John McLaughlin on guitar), playing a hybrid of jazz, blues and rock that was musically and visually stunning. Bond was the first prominent musician in Britain to play a Hammond organ through a Leslie speaker cabinet, and the first to use a Mellotron.

The original Organisation made two superlative and formative albums, *Sound Of '65* and *There's A Bond Between Us*. Both featured original songs mixed with interpretations, such as 'Walk On The Wild Side', 'Wade In The Water' and 'Got My Mojo Working'. Bond's own 'Have You Ever Loved A Woman' and 'Walkin' In The Park' demonstrated his songwriting ability, but despite his musicianship he was unable to find a commercially acceptable niche. The jazz fraternity regarded Bond's band as too noisy and rock-based, while the pop audience found his music complicated and too jazzy. Thirty years later the Tommy Chase Band pursued an uncannily similar musical road, now under the banner of jazz. As the British music scene changed, so the Organisation was penalized for its refusal to adapt to more conventional trends in music. Along the way, Bond had lost Baker and Bruce, who departed to form Cream, although the addition of Jon Hiseman on drums reinforced their musical pedigree. When

Hiseman and Heckstall-Smith left to form Colosseum, they showed their debt to Bond by featuring 'Walkin' In The Park' on their debut album.

Disenchanted with the musical tide, Bond moved to the USA where he made two albums for the Pulsar label. Both records showed a departure from jazz and R&B, but neither fared well and Bond returned to England in 1969. The music press welcomed his reappearance, but a poorly attended Royal Albert Hall homecoming concert must have bitterly disheartened its subject. His new band, the Graham Bond Initiation, featured his wife Diane Stewart. The unlikely combination of astrological themes, R&B and public apathy doomed this promising unit. Bond started on a slow decline into drugs, depression, mental disorder and dabblings with the occult. Following a reunion with Ginger Baker in his ill-fated Airforce project, and a brief spell with the Jack Bruce Band, Bond formed a musical partnership with Pete Brown; this resulted in one album and, for a short time, had a stabilizing effect on Bond's life. Following a nervous breakdown, drug addiction and two further unsuccessful conglomerations, Bond was killed on 8 May 1974 when he fell under the wheels of a London Underground train at Finsbury Park station. Whether Graham Bond could again have reached the musical heights of his 1964 band is open to endless debate; what has been acknowledged is that he was an innovator, a loveable rogue and a major influence on British R&B.

● ALBUMS: *The Sound Of '65* (Columbia 1965) ★★★★, *There's A Bond Between Us* (Columbia 1966) ★★★★, *Mighty Graham Bond* (Pulsar 1968) ★★★, *Love Is The Law* (Pulsar 1968) ★★★, *Solid Bond* (Warners 1970) ★★★★, *We Put The Majick On You* (Vertigo 1971) ★★★, *Holy Magick* (Vertigo 1971) ★★★, with Pete Brown *Bond And Brown: Two Heads Are Better Than One* (Chapter One 1972) ★★★, *This Is Graham Bond* (Philips 1978) ★★★, *The Graham Bond Organisation Live At Klook's Kleek* (Charly 1984) ★★★.

● COMPILATIONS: *Bond In America* (Philips 1971) ★★★★, *Holy Magick/We Put Our Magic On You* (BGO 1999) ★★★, *The Sound Of '65/There's A Bond Between Us* (BGO 1999) ★★★★.

● FURTHER READING: *The Smallest Place In The World*, Dick Heckstall-Smith. *Graham Bond; The Mighty Shadow*, Harry Shapiro.

● FILMS: *Gonks Go Beat* (1965).

BONDS, GARY 'U.S.'

b. Gary Anderson, 6 June 1939, Jacksonville, Florida, USA. Having initially sung in various gospel groups, Bonds embraced secular music upon moving to Norfolk, Virginia. A successful spell in the region's R&B clubs resulted in a recording contract with local entrepreneur Frank Guida, whose cavernous production techniques gave Bonds' releases their distinctive

sound. The ebullient 'New Orleans' set the pattern for the artist's subsequent recordings and its exciting, 'party' atmosphere reached an apogee on 'Quarter To Three', a US chart-topper and the singer's sole million-seller. Between 1961 and 1962 Bonds enjoyed further similar-sounding hits with 'School Is Out', 'School Is In', 'Dear Lady Twist' and 'Twist Twist Senora', but his career then went into sharp decline. He toured the revival circuit until 1978 when long-time devotee Bruce Springsteen joined the singer onstage during a live engagement. Their friendship resulted in *Dedication*, produced by Springsteen and E Street Band associate Miami Steve Van Zandt. The former contributed three original songs to the set, one of which, 'This Little Girl', reached the US Top 10 in 1981. Their collaboration was maintained with *On The Line*, which included Bonds' version of the Box Tops' 'Soul Deep', but he later asserted his independence with the self-produced *Standing In The Line Of Fire*. Little was heard of him in the 90s, other than a cameo appearance with other musical artists in the movie *Blues Brothers 2000*.

● ALBUMS: *Dance 'Til Quarter To Three* (Legrand/Top Rank 1961) ★★★, *Twist Up Calypso* (Legrand/Stateside 1962) ★★★, *Dedication* (EMI America 1981) ★★★, *On The Line* (EMI America 1982) ★★, *Gary 'U.S.' Bonds Meets Chubby Checker* (EMI 1983) ★★, *Standing In The Line Of Fire* (Phoenix 1984) ★★, *At The Stone Pony, Asbury Park, NJ, November 25, 2000* (King Biscuit Flower Hour 2001) ★★★.

● COMPILATIONS: *Greatest Hits Of Gary 'U.S.' Bonds* (Legrand/Stateside 1962) ★★★★, *Certified Soul* (Rhino 1982) ★★, *The School Of Rock 'n' Roll: The Best Of Gary 'U.S' Bonds* (Rhino 1990) ★★★★, *Take Me Back To New Orleans* (Ace 1995) ★★★, *The Best Of Gary U.S. Bonds* (EMI 1996) ★★★★, *The Very Best Of Gary U.S. Bonds* (Varèse Sarabande 1998) ★★★★.

● FILMS: *It's Trad, Dad* aka *Ring-A-Ding Rhythm* (1962), *Blues Brothers 2000* (1998).

BONNEY, GRAHAM

b. 2 July 1945, Stratford, London, England. Vocalist Bonney, a former member of the Expresso Five, was one of six young musicians invited to found the Riot Squad by producer Larry Page. He left the group in the wake of three unsuccessful singles and embarked on a solo career in November 1965 with the release of 'My Little World Is All Blue'. However, it was Bonney's second single, 'Supergirl', that established the artist's brand of superior pop and although this vibrant song barely scraped the UK Top 20, it proved highly popular in Europe, topping the German charts for six weeks and selling in excess of one million copies. An attendant album confirmed the artist's promise, but despite several equally excellent singles, the singer was unable to repeat this early success. In Germany he continued as a star with 14 singles making the German Top 50 between 1966 and

1973. He relocated to Cologne.
● ALBUMS: *Supergirl* (Columbia 1966) ★★★.

BONO, SONNY

b. Salvatore Bono, 16 February 1935, Detroit, Michigan, USA, d. 5 January 1998, Lake Tahoe, California, USA. Although primarily associated with the 60s folk rock boom, Bono's career began the previous decade as director of A&R at Specialty Records. He co-wrote 'She Said Yeah' for Larry Williams, later covered by the Rolling Stones, and penned 'KoKo Joe' for Don & Dewey. Bono also pursued an unsuccessful recording career with the first of several singles bearing numerous aliases, including Don Christy ('Wearing Black'), Sonny Christy and Ronny Sommers ('Don't Shake My Tree (Mama)'), and set-up the ill-fated Rush label. In 1963 he came under the aegis of producer Phil Spector at the Philles label, working as a PR man and studio assistant at the Goldstar Studios, but achieved greater fame when 'Needles And Pins', a collaboration with Spector's engineer Jack Nitzsche, was successfully recorded by Jackie DeShannon and, in 1964, the Searchers. By this time Bono had met and become romantically attached to Cherilyn Sarkisian La Pierre, better known as Cher. Her fledgling career as a Goldstar session singer was subsequently augmented by their work as a duo, firstly as Caesar & Cleo, then Sonny & Cher. In 1965 the couple enjoyed an international smash with 'I Got You Babe', written, arranged and produced by Bono, who resurrected solo ambitions in the wake of its success. Although 'Laugh At Me' reached the Top 10 in the US and UK, 'The Revolution Kind', Bono's disavowal of the counter-culture, failed to emulate this feat. Bono's lone album, *Inner Views*, was an artistic and commercial disaster and he subsequently abandoned solo recordings. A brief resurgence as MOR entertainers in the 70s brought Sonny & Cher their own television series, *The Sonny & Cher Comedy Hour*. They ended their personal partnership in 1974, with Bono briefly hosting his own *Sonny Comedy Revue*. He later concentrated on an acting career, with regular appearances on television and in several films, notably *Hairspray* (1988). A registered Republican, he was voted mayor of Palm Springs, California in 1988, the day after his ex-wife won an Oscar for her role in *Moonstruck*. In 1991 he attempted to run for the US Senate seat in California, losing in the Republican primary, but in 1994 won the House of Representatives seat representing Palm Springs. He was re-elected in 1996, but was killed two years later in a skiing accident in South Lake Tahoe, California.
● ALBUMS: *Inner Views* (Atco 1967) ★.
● FURTHER READING: *Sonny And Cher*, Thomas Braun. *And The Beat Goes On*, Sonny Bono.
● FILMS: *Good Times* (1967), *Hairspray* (1988).

BONZO DOG DOO-DAH BAND

Although this eccentric ensemble was initially viewed as a 20s revival act, they quickly developed into one of the pop era's most virulent satirists. Formed as the Bonzo Dog Dada Band in 1965 by art students Vivian Stanshall (b. 21 March 1943, Shillingford, Oxfordshire, England, d. 5 March 1995, London, England; vocals, trumpet, devices) and Rodney Slater (b. 8 November 1941, Crowland, Lincolnshire, England; saxophone), the group also included Neil Innes (b. 9 December 1944, Danbury, Essex, England; vocals, piano, guitar), Roger Ruskin Spear (b. 29 June 1943, Hammersmith, London, England; props, devices, saxophone) and 'Legs' Larry Smith (b. 18 January 1944, Oxford, England; drums). Various auxiliary members, including Sam Spoons (b. Martin Stafford Ash, 8 February 1942, Bridgewater, Somerset, England), Bob Kerr and Vernon Dudley Bohey-Nowell (b. 29 July 1932, Plymouth, Devon, England), augmented the line-up; the informality was such that no-one knew which members would arrive to perform in the group's early shows.
In 1966, two singles, 'My Brother Makes The Noises For The Talkies' and 'Alley Oop', reflected their transition from trad jazz to pop. *Gorilla*, the Bonzos' inventive debut album, still showed traces of their music-hall past, but the irreverent humour displayed on 'Jollity Farm' and the surrealistic 'The Intro And The Outro' ('Hi there, happy you could stick around, like to introduce you to . . .') confirmed a lasting quality that outstripped that of contemporary 'rivals', the New Vaudeville Band, to whom Kerr, and others, had defected. A residency on the British television children's show, *Do Not Adjust Your Set*, reinforced the group's unconventional reputation and the songs they performed were later compiled on the *Tadpoles* album. The Bonzo Dog Band was also featured in the Beatles' film *Magical Mystery Tour*, performing the memorable 'Death Cab For Cutie', and in 1968 secured a UK Top 5 hit with 'I'm The Urban Spaceman', which was produced by Paul McCartney under the pseudonym Apollo C. Vermouth. Further albums, *The Doughnut In Granny's Greenhouse* and *Keynsham*, displayed an endearing eclecticism that derided the blues boom ('Can Blue Men Sing The Whites?'), suburbia ('My Pink Half Of The Drainpipe') and many points in between, while displaying an increasingly rock-based bent. Newcomers Dennis Cowan (b. 6 May 1947, London, England), Dave Clague and Joel Druckman toughened the group's live sound, but the strain of compressing pre-war English middle-class frivolousness (Stanshall), whimsical pop (Innes) and Ruskin Spear's madcap machinery into a united whole ultimately proved too great. Although a reconvened line-up completed *Let's Make Up And Be Friendly* in 1972, this project was only undertaken to fulfil contractual

obligations. The group had disbanded two years earlier when its members embarked on their inevitably divergent paths.

● ALBUMS: *Gorilla* (Liberty 1967) ★★★★, *The Doughnut In Granny's Greenhouse* (Liberty 1968) ★★★★, *Tadpoles* (Liberty 1969) ★★★, *Keynsham* (Liberty 1969) ★★, *Let's Make Up And Be Friendly* (United Artists 1972) ★★.

● COMPILATIONS: *The History Of The Bonzos* (United Artists 1974) ★★★★, *The Bestiality Of The Bonzo Dog Band* (Liberty 1989) ★★★, *Cornology Volumes 1-3* (EMI 1992) ★★★, *New Tricks* (Right Recordings 2000) ★★★.

● FILMS: *Magical Mystery Tour* (1967), *Adventures Of The Son Of Exploding Sausage* (1969).

BOOKER T. AND THE MGs

Formed in Memphis, Tennessee, USA, in 1962 as a spin-off from the Mar-Keys, this instrumental outfit comprised Booker T. Jones (b. 12 November 1944, Memphis, Tennessee, USA; organ), Steve Cropper (b. 21 October 1941, Willow Spring, Missouri, USA; guitar), Lewis Steinberg (bass) and Al Jackson Jr. (b. 27 November 1934, Memphis, Tennessee, USA, d. 1 October 1975, Memphis, Tennessee, USA; drums). 'Green Onions', their renowned first hit, evolved out of a blues riff they had improvised while waiting to record a jingle. Its simple, smoky atmosphere, punctuated by Cropper's cutting guitar, provided the blueprint for a series of excellent records, including 'Jellybread', 'Chinese Checkers', 'Soul Dressing', 'Mo' Onions' and 'Hip Hug-Her'. Pared to the bone, this sparseness accentuated the rhythm, particularly when Steinberg was replaced on bass in 1965 by Donald 'Duck' Dunn (b. 24 November 1941, Memphis, Tennessee, USA). Their intuitive interplay became the bedrock of Stax Records, the foundation on which the label and studio sound was built. The quartet appeared on all of the company's notable releases, including 'In The Midnight Hour' (Wilson Pickett), 'Hold On I'm Comin'' (Sam And Dave) and 'Walking The Dog' (Rufus Thomas), on which Jones also played saxophone. Although Jones divided his time between recording and studying at Indiana University (he subsequently earned a BA in music), the MGs (Memphis Group) continued to chart consistently in their own right. 'Hang 'Em High' (1968) and 'Time Is Tight' (1969) were both US Top 10 singles, while as late as 1971 'Melting Pot' climbed into the same Top 50. The group split that year; Jones moved to California in semi-retirement, recording with his wife, Priscilla, while his three ex-colleagues remained in Memphis.

In 1973 Jackson and Dunn put together a reconstituted group. Bobby Manuel and Carson Whitsett filled out the line-up, but the resultant album, *The MGs*, was a disappointment. Jackson, meanwhile, maintained his peerless reputation, particularly with work for Al Green

and Syl Johnson, but tragically in 1975, he was shot dead in his Memphis home after disturbing intruders. Cropper, who had released a solo album in 1971, *With A Little Help From My Friends*, set up his TMI studio/label and temporarily seemed content with a low-key profile. He latterly rejoined Dunn, ex-Bar-Kays drummer Willie Hall and the returning Jones for *Universal Language*. Cropper and Dunn also played musicians' roles in the 1980 movie, *The Blues Brothers*. During the late 70s UK R&B revival, 'Green Onions' was reissued and became a Top 10 hit in 1979. The group did, however, complete some British concert dates in 1990, and backed Neil Young in 1993. They were inducted into the Rock And Roll Hall Of Fame in 1992.

● ALBUMS: *Green Onions* (Stax 1962) ★★★★, *Mo' Onions* (Stax 1963) ★★★★, *Soul Dressing* (Stax 1965) ★★★★, *My Sweet Potato* (Stax 1965) ★★★, *And Now!* (Stax 1966) ★★★, *In The Christmas Spirit* (Stax 1966) ★, *Hip Hug-Her* (Stax 1967) ★★★, with the Mar-Keys *Back To Back* (Stax 1967) ★★★, *Doin' Our Thing* (Stax 1968) ★★★, *Soul Limbo* (Stax 1968) ★★★, *Uptight* film soundtrack (Stax 1969) ★★, *The Booker T. Set* (Stax 1969) ★★★, *McLemore Avenue* (Stax 1970) ★★, *Melting Pot* (Stax 1971) ★★, as the MGs *The MGs* (Stax 1973) ★★, *Memphis Sound* (Warners 1975) ★★, *Time Is Tight* (Warners 1976) ★★, *Universal Language* (Asylum 1977) ★.

● COMPILATIONS: *The Best Of Booker T. And The MGs* (Atco 1968) ★★★★, *Booker T. And The MGs Greatest Hits* (Stax 1970) ★★★★, *Booker T And The MGs: The Memphis Sound* (Stax 1975) ★★★★, *Union Extended* (Stax 1976) ★★★★, *The Best Of Booker T And The MGs (Very Best Of)* (Rhino 1993) ★★★★, *Play The Hip Hits* (Stax/Ace 1995) ★★★★, *Time Is Tight* 3-CD box set (Stax 1998) ★★★★.

BOONE, PAT

b. Charles Eugene Patrick Boone, 1 June 1934, Jacksonville, Florida, USA. Boone sold more records during the late 50s than any other artist except Elvis Presley. From 1955 to date, only six artists (Presley, the Beatles, James Brown, Elton John, Rolling Stones and Stevie Wonder) are ranked above him in terms of total singles sales and their relative chart positions. Boone had a total of 60 hits in the US singles charts during his career, six of which reached number 1. A bona fide 'teen-idol', Boone was, however, a personality quite unlike Presley. Where Elvis represented the outcast or rebel, Boone was a clean-cut conformist. He was a religious, married family man, who at one point turned down a film role with Marilyn Monroe rather than having to kiss a woman who was not his wife. While Elvis wore long sideburns and greasy hair, Boone was recognized by his 'white buck' shoes and ever-present smile. Boone even attended college during the height of his career. Accordingly, Boone's music, although considered to be rock 'n' roll during his first few years of popularity, was considerably less manic than that being made by Presley and the early black rockers. Boone, in fact, built his career on 'cover' records, tame, cleaned-up versions of R&B songs originally recorded by black artists such as Fats Domino, Little Richard, Ivory Joe Hunter, the Flamingos and the El Dorados. Boone grew up in the Nashville, Tennessee, area, where he began singing in public at the age of 10. He appeared on the national *Ted Mack Amateur Hour* and *Arthur Godfrey's Talent Scouts* television programmes in the early 50s, and had his own radio programme on Nashville's WSIX. In 1953, he married Shirley Foley, daughter of country star Red Foley. The following year, Boone recorded his first of four singles for the small Republic label in Nashville, all of which failed. That year the Boones moved to Denton, Texas, and began raising a family of four daughters, the third of whom, Debby Boone, had a chart hit in 1977 with the ballad 'You Light Up My Life'. Pat signed to Dot Records and recorded his first single for the company, 'Two Hearts' (originally by R&B group Otis Williams And The Charms) in February 1955. Admittedly unfamiliar with the genre, Boone quickly adapted the raw music to his own crooning style. His second single, Domino's 'Ain't That A Shame', went to number 1, and was followed by a non-stop procession of hits. Boone stayed with the R&B cover versions until 1957. Even today it is a controversial question whether Boone's cover records helped to open the door to the black originators or shut them out of the white marketplace. By 1957, when Presley had established himself as the reigning white rocker, Boone had given up rock and switched to ballads. Among the biggest sellers were 'Friendly Persuasion (Thee I Love)', 'Don't Forbid Me', 'Love Letters In The Sand' and 'April Love'. Some of Boone's recordings by this time were taken from films in which he starred. He also frequently appeared on television, toured the country, and was the subject of magazine articles praising his positive image and outlook. Boone even wrote several books giving advice to teenagers.

From 1957-60, Boone hosted his own television show, *The Pat Boone Chevy Showroom*. Although still popular, by the beginning of the 60s, his place at the top had slipped somewhat lower. 'Moody River' in 1961, and 'Speedy Gonzales', a novelty rock number of the following year, were his last major pop hits.

By 1966 Boone's contract with Dot ended. He drifted from one label to the next, trying his hand at country music and, primarily, gospel. Although he had started recording Christian music as early as 1957, his concentration on that form was near-total by the late 70s; he recorded over a dozen Christian albums during that decade, several with his wife and children as the Boone Family Singers. He continued to make live appearances into the 90s, and became an outspoken supporter of politically conservative and religious causes. By 1991 he had begun discussing the possibility of singing rock music again. In 1993, Boone joined another 50s legend, Kay Starr, on 'The April Love Tour' of the UK. In 1997, Boone recorded with Ritchie Blackmore and Guns N'Roses' Slash for his heavy metal tribute album. Ridiculous although it may seem, Boone tackled classics such as 'The Wind Cries Mary', 'No More Mr Nice Guy', 'Smoke On The Water' and, of course, 'Stairway To Heaven'. In addition he owns his own record company Gold Label, whose featured artists include Glen Campbell.

● ALBUMS: *Pat Boone* (Dot 1956) ★★★, *Howdy!* (Dot 1956) ★★★, *'Pat'* (Dot 1957) ★★★, *Pat Boone Sings Irving Berlin* (Dot 1957) ★★, *Hymns We Love* (Dot 1957) ★★, *Star Dust* (Dot 1958) ★★★, *Yes Indeed!* (Dot 1958) ★★★, *White Christmas* (Dot 1959) ★★★, *He Leadeth Me* (Dot 1959) ★★, *Pat Boone Sings* (Dot 1959) ★★★, *Great Millions* (Dot 1959) ★★★, with Shirley Boone *Side By Side* (Dot 1959) ★★, *Tenderly* (Dot 1959) ★★★, *Hymns We Have Loved* (Dot 1960) ★★, *Moonglow* (Dot 1960) ★★★, *This And That* (Dot 1960) ★★★, *Moody River* (Dot 1961) ★★, *Great! Great! Great!* (Dot 1961) ★★, *My God And I* (Dot 1961) ★★, *I'll See You In My Dreams* (Dot 1962) ★★★, *Pat Boone Reads From The Holy Bible* (Dot 1962) ★, *Pat Boone Sings Guess Who?* (Dot 1963) ★★, *I Love You Truly* (Dot 1963) ★★, *The Star Spangled Banner* (Dot 1963) ★★, *Days Of Wine And Roses* (Dot 1963) ★★★, *Tie Me Kangaroo Down* (Dot 1963) ★★, *Sing Along Without* (Dot 1963) ★★, *Touch Of Your Lips* (Dot 1964) ★★, *Pat Boone* (Dot 1964) ★★, *Ain't That A Shame* (Dot 1964) ★★★, *Lord's Prayer And Other Great Hymns* (Dot 1964) ★★, *Boss Beat* (Dot 1964) ★★, *True Love: My Tenth Anniversary With Dot Records* (Dot 1964) ★★, *Near You* (Dot 1965) ★★★, *Blest Be Thy Name* (Dot 1965) ★★★, *Golden Era Of Country Hits* (Dot 1965) ★, *Pat Boone 1965* (Dot 1965) ★★, *Great Hits Of '65* (Dot 1966) ★★, *Memories* (Dot 1966) ★★★, *Pat Boone Sings Winners Of The Readers Digest Poll* (Dot 1966) ★★, *Wish You Were Here, Buddy* (Dot 1966) ★★, *Christmas Is A Comin'* (Dot 1966) ★★★, *How Great Thou Art* (Dot 1967) ★★, *I Was Kaiser Bill's Batman* (Dot 1967) ★★, *Look Ahead* (Dot 1968) ★★, *Departure* (Dot 1969) ★★★, *The Pat Boone Family In The Holy Land* (Lion & Lamb 1972) ★, *The New Songs Of The Jesus People* (Lion & Lamb 1972) ★, *I Love You More And More Each Day* (MGM 1973) ★★, *Born Again* (Lion & Lamb 1973) ★, *S.A.V.E.D.* (Lion & Lamb 1973) ★, *The Family Who Prays* (Lion & Lamb 1973) ★, *All In The Boone Family* (Lion & Lamb 1973) ★, *The Pat Boone Family* (Lion & Lamb 1974) ★, *Songs From The Inner Court* (Lion & Lamb 1974) ★, *Something Supernatural* (Lion & Lamb 1975) ★, *Texas Woman* (Hitsville 1976) ★★, *Country Love* (Hitsville 1977) ★★, *The Country Side Of Pat Boone* (Motown 1977) ★, *Just The Way I Am*

(Lion & Lamb 1981) ★★, *Songmaker* (Lion & Lamb 1981) ★★, *Whispering Hope* (Lion & Lamb 1982) ★★, *Pat Boone Sings Golden Hymns* (Lion & Lamb 1984) ★★, *Jivin' Pat* (Bear Family 1986) ★★, *Let's Get Cooking, America* (Hunt-Wesson 1987) ★, *Tough Marriage* (Dove 1987) ★★, *With The First Nashville Jesus Band* (Lion & Lamb 1988) ★★, *Pat Boone In A Metal Mood: No More Mr Nice Guy* (Hip-O 1997) ★★.
● COMPILATIONS: *Pat's Great Hits* (Dot 1957) ★★★★, *Pat's Great Hits, Volume 2* (Dot 1960) ★★★, *Pat Boone's Golden Hits* (Dot 1962) ★★★★, *12 Great Hits* (Hamilyon 1964) ★★★, *Sixteen Great Performances* (ABC 1972) ★★★, *The Best Of Pat Boone* (MCA 1982) ★★★, *16 Golden Classics* (MCA 1987) ★★★, *Greatest Hits* (Curb 1990) ★★★, *Golden Greats* (1993) ★★★, *More Golden Hits: The Original Dot Recordings* (Varèse Sarabande 1995) ★★★★, *The EP Collection* (See For Miles 1998) ★★★, *Pat Boone: The Fifties Complete* 12-CD box set (Bear Family 1998) ★★★★, *The Best Of Pat Boone: The Millennium Collection* (MCA 2000) ★★★★, *Pat's 40 Big Ones* (Connoisseur 2001) ★★★★.
● FURTHER READING: *A New Song*, Pat Boone. *Together: 25 Years With The Boone Family*, Pat Boone.
● FILMS: *Bernadine* (1957), *April Love* (1957), *Mardi Gras* (1958), *Journey To The Center Of The Earth* (1959), *All Hands On Deck* (1961), *State Fair* (1962), *The Main Attraction* (1962), *The Yellow Canary* (1963), *The Horror Of It All* (1963), *Goodbye Charlie* (1964), *Never Put It In Writing* (1964), *The Greatest Story Ever Told* (1965), *The Perils Of Pauline* (1967), *The Cross And The Switchblade* (1972), *Roger & Me* (1989), *In A Metal Mood* (1996), *The Eyes Of Tammy Faye* (2000).

BOSTON DEXTERS

Formed in Edinburgh, Scotland, in 1964 by local club owner Brian Waldman. Tam White (vocals) and Toto McNaughton (drums) – two ex-members of the Heartbeats – were joined by John Turnbull (guitar) and Alan Coventry (bass) in an act visually based on US gangsters of the 30s. They wore expensive, pin-striped suits and even carried replica guns onstage. Musically, the Boston Dexters were a gutsy R&B band, although their debut single, 'I've Got Something To Tell You Baby', written by Tin Pan Alley pop stalwart Bill Martin, was musically out of character. An impassioned reading of Ray Charles' 'I Believe To My Soul', tucked away as its b-side, was a better measure of their talent, particularly that of White. Turnbull co-wrote the Curtis Mayfield-inspired follow-up, 'Try Hard', but the original Boston Dexters split up in 1966 following an unsuccessful spell in London. White and Turnbull formed the short-lived Buzz, while McNaughton kept the Boston Dexters' name going for a few months with singer Linnie Patterson, later of Writing On The Wall. White later pursued a solo career as a pop balladeer before finding success as an R&B/jazz singer. His

voice was heard in the acclaimed BBC Television series *Tutti Frutti*.

BOWN!, ALAN, THE

Trumpeter Alan Bown, formerly of the John Barry Seven, formed this respected group in 1965. Originally known as the Alan Bown Set, the septet – Bown, Jess Roden (vocals), Tony Catchpole (guitar), John Goodsall (saxophone), Geoff Bannister (keyboards), Stan Haldane (bass) and Vic Sweeny (drums) – were stalwarts of London's R&B and soul circuit and appeared on the era's seminal selection, *London Swings Live At The Marquee Club*. By 1967 the unit had abandoned soul music in favour of the emergent 'underground' style and truncated its name to The Alan Bown! *Outward Bown* offered such contemporaneous fare as 'Toyland' and 'Technicolour Dream', but the group subsequently pursued a heavier, more progressive direction on *The Alan Bown!* Brown recruited vocalist Robert Palmer from local support act, the Mandrakes. He replaced Jess Roden, who formed Bronco. The group at that time also included John Anthony (b. 15 February 1945, Todmorden, Yorkshire, England) on saxophone, who later changed his name to John Helliwell and joined Supertramp. Before he left, Roden had recorded the vocal tracks for a projected album, and it fell to Palmer to dub his voice over these (however, the US version of the group's self-titled debut retained Roden's contributions). Afterwards, Palmer moved on to Dada, then Vinegar Joe, although The Alan Bown! continued to play sporadic live dates. In the wake of Palmer's subsequent breakthrough, the group's sole album has been reissued twice under different titles by See For Miles Records in 1985 and C5 Records in 1987. Bown continued to lead a fluctuating line-up for two further albums, before dissolving the group. The trumpeter then accepted an A&R appointment with CBS Records.
● ALBUMS: with various artists *London Swings Live At The Marquee Club* (1966) ★★, *First Album – Outward Bown* (Music Factory 1967) ★★★, *The Alan Bown!* (Deram 1968) ★★★, *Listen* (Island 1970) ★★★, *Stretchin' Out* (Island 1971) ★★.
● COMPILATIONS: *Kick Me Out* (See For Miles 1985) ★★★, as Robert Palmer And Alan Bown *The Early Years* (C5 1987) ★★★, *Emergency 999* (Sequel 2000) ★★★.

BOX TOPS

Formed in 1965, this Memphis-based quintet – Alex Chilton (b. 28 December 1950, Memphis, Tennessee, USA; guitar, harmonica, vocals), Gary Talley (b. 17 August 1947, Memphis, Tennessee, USA; lead guitar), Billy Cunningham (b. 23 January 1950, Memphis, Tennessee, USA; rhythm guitar), John Evans (bass) and Danny Smythe (drums) – sprang to fame two years later when their debut single, 'The Letter', became an international hit and a US chart-topper. Although nominally a band, their appeal lay in Chilton's aspy delivery and Dan Penn's complementary production, a combination repeated on further successes, 'Neon Rainbow', 'Cry Like A Baby', 'Soul Deep' and the annoyingly infectious 'Choo Choo Train'. Rick Allen (b. 28 January 1946, Little Rock, Arkansas, USA) replaced Evans in 1968, but the band's gifted singer remained its vocal point. The Box Tops adeptly combined southern soul with pop, but any impetus faltered when their backroom mentors were drawn into other projects. The band broke up in 1969, but Chilton subsequently reappeared in the critically acclaimed Big Star. A one-off reunion took place in Los Angeles at the House of Blues club in 1997.

● ALBUMS: *The Letter/Neon Rainbow* (Bell 1967) ★★★, *Cry Like A Baby* (Bell 1968) ★★★, *Non top* (Bell 1968) ★★★, *Dimensions* (Bell 1969) ★★.

● COMPILATIONS: *The Box Tops Super Hits* (Bell 1968) ★★★, *Greatest Hits* (Rhino 1982) ★★★, *Ultimate Box Tops* (Warners 1988) ★★★, *Soul Deep: The Best Of The Box Tops* (Arista 1998) ★★★★.

BOYCE AND HART

Recalled chiefly for their association with the Monkees, this songwriting team also enjoyed a fruitful independent career. Tommy Boyce (b. 29 September 1944, Charlottesville, Virginia, USA, d. 23 November 1994, Nashville, Tennessee, USA) had recorded several singles during the early 60s, charting briefly with 'I'll Remember Carol', while Bobby Hart (b. Phoenix, Arizona, USA) helped to compose hits for Little Anthony And The Imperials and Tommy Sands. The two were originally cast as members of the Monkees, but secured the musical/production rights when this idea was vetoed. Together they wrote several of the group's early classics, including 'Last Train To Clarksville', 'Valleri' and '(I'm Not Your) Steppin' Stone', but they were latterly supplanted during the backroom machinations surrounding the group's progress. Boyce and Hart then embarked on a performing career. They had several US Top 40 hits, the most successful of which was 'I Wonder What She's Doing Tonite?' which peaked at number 8 in January 1968. Their interest in the Monkees continued with the release of several previously shelved masters, and in 1975 they joined former members Davy Jones and Mickey Dolenz for a nostalgia tour. This, in turn, engendered a handful of new recordings. The songwriters subsequently pursued a myriad of projects. Bobby Hart recorded a solo album, while Tommy Boyce enjoyed a successful career in London, and produced a series of hits for showaddywaddy and Darts.

● ALBUMS: *Test Patterns* (A&M 1967) ★★, *I Wonder What She's Doing Tonite?* (A&M 1968) ★★, *It's All Happening On The Inside* (A&M 1968) ★★, with Mickey Dolenz and Davy Jones *Dolenz, Jones, Boyce And Hart* (1976) ★★, *Concert In Japan, 1976* (1981) ★★, *The Songs Of Tommy Boyce & Bobby Hart* (Varèse Sarabande 1996) ★★★.

BREAKAWAYS

Formed in London, England, in 1962, this vocal act comprised Vikki Haseman, Margot Quantrell and Betty Prescott, all former members of the Vernons Girls. The Breakaways made their debut with a poor rendition of the Crystals' 'He's A Rebel', although their arrangement was modelled on Vikki Carr's cover version, rather than Phil Spector's original production. The single was not a success and the Breakaways began working as session singers for fellow Pye Records artists Joe Brown, Julie Grant and Jimmy Justice. A brief split followed, but in 1963 Haseman and Quantrell were reunited with another ex-Vernons Girl, Jean Ryder. Having adopted a 'tougher' visual image – black sweaters, slacks and spike-heeled boots – the Breakaways proceeded to record two superb 'girl group' singles, 'That Boy Of Mine' and 'That's How It Goes', both of which were produced by Tony Hatch. The Breakaways remained an in-demand session act, appearing on discs by Cilla Black ('Anyone Who Had A Heart', 'You're My World'), Dusty Springfield ('Stay Awhile'), the Walker Brothers ('The Sun Ain't Gonna Shine Anymore') and Burt Bacharach ('Trains And Boats And Planes'). In 1965 the Breakaways' fourth single, 'Danny Boy', was released to little effect and it was 1967 before another disc, 'Sacred Love', was issued. Their final single, 'Santo Domingo', appeared in 1968. Nevertheless, the Breakaways remained an integral part of the music scene into the 70s, working with, among others, Cliff Richard and James Last. However, by the middle of the decade the Breakaways' name was dropped. Quantrell left music altogether, Ryder continued in session work while Hasemen – now Vikki Brown following her marriage to Joe Brown – began a solo career with *From The Inside* (1977) which was produced by Shel Talmy. In 1986 she duetted with George Harrison on 'Shanghai Surprise' and her busy studio-based career continued unabated into the 90s; she died of cancer in 1995.

BREL, JACQUES

b. 8 April 1929, Brussels, Belgium, d. 9 October 1978, Bobigny, Seine-Saint-Denis, France. Brel remained a figurehead of modern songwriting, despite a reluctance either to sing in English or, owing to his bitter opposition to the Vietnam war, perform in North America – or, indeed, anywhere else, after retiring from concert appearances in 1966. Although Flemish, he conversed in French. After studying commercial law, he married and spent several years in the family cardboard merchandising business until, in 1953, nauseated by bourgeois convention, he began a new career in Paris as a singing composer. Buck-toothed and lanky, his lack of obvious mass appeal was thrust aside by impresario Jacques Canetti, who presented him regularly at Pigalle's Theatre Des Trois Baudets, where he was accompanied by his own guitar and a small backing band. A sense of dramatic construction resulted in performances that, embracing fierce anger, open romanticism and world-weariness, captivated the audiences; his popularity increased after 'Quand On N'A Que L'Amour', his first record success. Other domestic hits such as 'La Valse À Mille Temps', 'Les Bourgeois', 'La Dame Patronesse' and 'Les Flamandes' gave vent to social comment via a wryly watchful, literate lyricism.

This remained intrinsically Gallic until US recording manager Nat Shapiro enthused about Brel to his CBS Records superiors, who authorized the issue of 1957's *American Debut*, from which grew a substantial English-speaking following. Brel strongly influenced the output of such diverse wordsmiths as Mort Shuman (an early and lifelong disciple), the Kinks' Ray Davies, Leonard Cohen, David Bowie and – also the foremost interpreter of his work – Scott Walker. Brel was to reach a global market by proxy when his material was translated. However, it was often emasculated, as instanced by Rod McKuen's reinvention of 'Le Moribond' as 'Seasons In The Sun' (a 1964 hit for the Kingston Trio, and a UK number 1 for Terry Jacks a decade later), and the evolution of 'If You Go Away' into a cabaret 'standard'. He played two sell-out Carnegie Hall shows but was keener on developing himself in movies such as *Les Risques Du Métier* and *La Bande À Bonnet* (an account of a French anarchist movement at the turn of the century). After he withdrew to the Polynesian Islands, he returned only fleetingly to Paris for one-take recording sessions: his work remained in the public eye through a three-year Broadway run of the musical *Jacques Brel Is Alive And Well And Living In Paris* (which later became a film), and smaller tributes such as the Sensational Alex Harvey Band's use of 'Next' as the title track of a 1975 album. In 1977, Brel returned to France for treatment for the cancer that killed him the following year – a passing marked by a million-selling compilation album and a posthumous recognition of his popularity.

● ALBUMS: *Jacques Brel* i (Philips 1954) ★★★, *Jacques Brel* ii (Philips 1957) ★★★★, *Jacques Brel* iii (Philips 1958) ★★★★, *Jacques Brel* iv (Philips 1959) ★★★★, *Jacques Brel* v (Philips 1961) ★★★★, *Jacques Brel* vi (Philips 1962) ★★★★, *Jacques Brel* vii (Barclay 1962) ★★★, *Jacques Brel* viii (Barclay 1963) ★★★, *Jacques Brel* ix (Barclay 1964) ★★★★, *Olympia 64* (Barclay 1964) ★★★, *Jacques Brel* x (Barclay 1965) ★★★, *Jacques Brel* xi (Barclay 1967) ★★★, *Jacques Brel* xii (Barclay 1967) ★★★, *Jacques Brel* xiii (Barclay 1968) ★★★★, *L'Homme De La Mancha* (Barclay 1968) ★★★, *L'Histoire De Babar/Pierre Et Le Loup* (Barclay 1969) ★★★, *Jacques Brel* xiv (Barclay

1972) ★★★★, *Brel* (Barclay 1977) ★★★.
● COMPILATIONS: *American Debut* (CBS 1957) ★★★★, *The Complete Works Of Jacques Brel* 15-CD box set (Barclay 1988) ★★★★, *Greatest Hits* (PolyGram 1993) ★★★★, various artists *Ne Me Quitte Pas: Brel Songs* (Irregular 1998) ★★★.
● FURTHER READING: *Jacques Brel: The Biography*, Alan Clayson.
● FILMS: *La Grande Peur De Monsieur Clément* (1956), *Les Risques Du Métier* aka *Risky Business* (1967), *Mon Oncle Benjamin* aka *The Adventures Of Uncle Benjamin* (1969), *La Bande À Bonno* (1969), *Les Assassins De L'Ordre* aka *Law Breakers* (1971), *Mont-Dragon* (1971), *Franz* (1971), *L'Aventure, C'est L'Aventure* (1972), *La Bar De La Fourche* (1972), *Far West* (1973), *L'Emmerdeur* (1973), *Jacques Brel Is Alive And Well And Living In Paris* (1975).

BRENDA AND THE TABULATIONS

This R&B vocal group from Philadelphia, Pennsylvania, USA, consisting of Brenda Payton (d. 14 June 1992), Jerry Jones, Eddie Jackson and Maurice Coates, was recognizable for the fetchingly innocent-sounding vocals of Payton on a series of intensely sung ballads. Their biggest hit was their 1967 debut single on the Dionn label, 'Dry My Eyes' (number 8 US R&B chart, number 20 pop chart). This was followed by further successful records, including a remake of the Miracles' 'Who's Lovin' You' (number 19 R&B, June 1967), 'When You're Gone' (number 27 R&B, December 1967). Bernard Murphy joined the line-up in 1969, and, reorganized in 1970 around Brenda Payton, Pat Mercer, and Deborah Martin, the group achieved a further string of hits including 'The Touch Of You' (number 12 R&B, December 1969), 'And My Heart Sang (Tra La La)' (number 12 R&B, May 1970), 'Don't Make Me Over' (number 15 R&B, August 1970) and 1971's 'Right On The Tip Of My Tongue' (number 10 R&B, number 23 pop), all released on the Top & Bottom label. A stint at Epic Records produced no major hits, but in 1973 their excellent 'One Girl Too Late' (number 43 R&B) deserved far greater recognition and success. The group's last chart success was in 1977.
● ALBUMS: *Dry Your Eyes* (Dionn 1967) ★★★, *Brenda And The Tabulations* (Top & Bottom 1970) ★★, *I Keep Coming Back For More* (Chocolate City 1977) ★★.
● COMPILATIONS: *Right On The Tip Of My Tongue* (Jamie 2000) ★★★.

BRENNAN, WALTER

b. 25 July 1894, Lynn, Massachusetts, USA, d. 21 September 1974. A character actor who specialized in playing the classic ol' timer and 'toothless old men', especially in westerns, Brennan appeared in dozens of films from 1924 onwards. Notable among these were *The Adventures Of Tom Sawyer*, *To Have And Have Not* and *Rio Bravo*. He went on to play Grandpa in *The Real McCoys* television series, which was a forerunner of *The Beverly Hillbillies*. He hit the pop charts with three spoken word singles – 'Dutchman's Gold' (1960), 'Old Rivers' and 'Mama Sang Me A Song' (1962). He was still acting during his 70s in *The Love Bug Rides Again*, but died in 1974.

● ALBUMS: *Dutchman's Gold* (Dot 1960) ★★★, *World Of Miracles* (Everest 1960) ★★★, *The President* (Everest 1960) ★★★, *By The Fireside* (RPC 1962) ★★★, *Old Rivers* (Liberty 1962) ★★★, *Twas The Night Before Christmas Back Home* (Liberty 1962) ★★★, *Mama Sang A Song* (Liberty 1963) ★★★, *Talkin' From The Heart* (Liberty 1964) ★★★, *Gunfight At The OK Corral* (Liberty 1964) ★★★.

● COMPILATIONS: *Old Shep* (Universal 2000) ★★★★.

● FILMS: *King Of Jazz* (1930), *Barbary Coast* (1935), *Come And Get It* (1936), *Banjo On My Knee* (1937), *The Buccaneer* (1938), *Kentucky* (1938), *The Adventures Of Tom Sawyer* (1938), *Stanley And Livingstone* (1939), *Northwest Passage* (1940), *The Westerner* (1941), *Sergeant York* (1941), *Meet John Doe* (1941), *Pride Of The Yankees* (1942), *North Star* (1943), *The Princess And The Pirate* (1944), *To Have And Have Not* (1944), *Dakota* (1945), *Centennial Summer* (1946), *My Darling Clementine* (1946), *Red River* (1948), *Task Force* (1949), *Curtain Call At Cactus Crick* (1950), *Best Of The Badmen* (1951), *Sea Of Lost Ships* (1953), *Bad Day At Black Rock* (1954), *Glory* (1956), *God Is My Partner* (1957), *Rio Bravo* (1958), *Those Calloways* (1965), *The Oscar* (1966), *Who's Minding The Mint* (1967), *The Gnome-Mobile* (1967), *The One And Only Genuine And Original Family Band* (1968), *Support Your Local Sheriff* (1969).

BRICUSSE, LESLIE

b. 29 January 1931, London, England. A composer, lyricist, librettist and screenwriter, Bricusse was influenced by the MGM musicals of the 40s, particularly *Words And Music*, the Richard Rodgers and Lorenz Hart biopic. He originally intended to be a journalist, but, while studying at Cambridge University, started to write, direct and appear in the *Footlights Reviews*. In 1953, he wrote the music and lyrics (with Robin Beaumont) for *Lady At the Wheel*, a musical with the Monte Carlo rally as its setting, which included songs such as 'The Early Birdie', 'Pete Y'Know', 'Love Is' and a comedy tango, 'Siesta'. It was staged at the local Arts Theatre, and, five years later, had a limited run in the West End. From 1954-5, Bricusse had appeared on the London stage himself with a theatrical legend, in *An Evening With Beatrice Lillie*. For a while during the 50s, he was under contract as a writer at Pinewood Film Studios, and in 1954, wrote the screenplay and the songs (with Beaumont) for *Charley Moon*, which starred Max Bygraves. The popular singer/comedian took one of the numbers, 'Out Of Town', into the UK

Top 20, and it gained Bricusse his first Ivor Novello Award: he won several others, including one for 'My Kind Of Girl' (words and music by Bricusse), which was a UK Top 5 hit for Matt Monro in 1961. Bricusse also wrote a good deal of special material for Bygraves, including one of his 'catchphrase' songs, 'A Good Idea – Son!'. Early in 1961, Bricusse went to New York to write for another Beatrice Lillie revue, taking Anthony Newley with him to develop ideas for a show of their own. The result, *Stop The World – I Want To Get Off*, written in around three weeks, opened in London's West End in July of that year, and stayed there until November 1962. It later ran for over 500 performances on Broadway, and was filmed in 1966. Book, music and lyrics were jointly credited to Bricusse and Newley, and the latter starred as the central character, Littlechap, in London and New York. The score included several hit songs, including 'What Kind Of Fool Am I?', 'Once In A Lifetime' and 'Gonna Build A Mountain', as well as other, more specialized numbers, such as 'Lumbered', 'Typically English' and 'Someone Nice Like You'. While Newley went off to appear in the offbeat, parochial movie *The World Of Sammy Lee*, Bricusse collaborated with Cyril Ornadel on the score for the musical *Pickwick* (1963), which starred the 'Goon with the golden voice', Harry Secombe, in the title role. His recording of the show's big ballad, 'If I Ruled The World', was a Top 20 hit in the UK, and, later, after the Broadway production had flopped, it became part of Tony Bennett's repertoire. Reunited in 1964, Bricusse and Newley's next major stage project, *The Roar Of The Greasepaint – The Smell Of The Crowd* (1965), appeared similar to their previous effort, a moral tale of a downtrodden little man, bucking the system. It toured (Bricusse: 'We managed to empty every provincial theatre in England'), but did not play the West End. Bricusse, and others, felt that comedian Norman Wisdom was miscast in the central role, and Newley took over for the Broadway run of 232 performances.

Once again, however, the memorable hit songs were there – in this case, 'Who Can I Turn To?' and 'A Wonderful Day Like Today', plus other items such as 'This Dream', 'The Beautiful Land', 'The Joker', 'Where Would You Be Without Me?', 'Nothing Can Stop Me Now' and 'Feeling Good'. The latter number was popularized in the USA by Joe Sherman, and received an impressive, extended treatment from UK rock band, Traffic, on their live *Last Exit*. In 1964, Bricusse and Newley turned their attention to the big screen, providing the lyric to John Barry's music for the title song to the James Bond movie *Goldfinger* (1964), sung by Shirley Bassey. Bricusse and Barry later wrote another Bond theme for *You Only Live Twice* (1968), popularized by Nancy Sinatra. In 1967, Bricusse contributed the screenplay and the complete song score to *Doctor Dolittle*, which starred Newley, along with Rex Harrison, who sang the Oscar-winning 'Talk To The Animals'. Considered an 'expensive dud', there was no mention of a *Doctor Dolittle II*. Far more to the public's taste was Roald Dahl's *Willy Wonka And The Chocolate Factory* (1971). Bricusse and Newley's score contained 'The Candy Man', a song that gave Sammy Davis Jnr. a US number 1 the following year. Davis was one of the songwriting team's favourite people – Bricusse estimates that he recorded at least 60 of his songs, including a complete album of *Doctor Dolittle*. Davis also starred in a revival of *Stop The World – I Want To Get Off* during the 1978/9 Broadway season.

After writing several numbers for a 1971 US television adaptation of *Peter Pan*, which starred Danny Kaye and Mia Farrow, Bricusse and Newley returned to the stage with *The Good Old Bad Old Days*. Newley directed and starred in the show, which ran for 10 months in London, and included the jolly title song and several other appealing numbers, such as 'I Do Not Love You', 'It's A Musical World', 'The People Tree' and 'The Good Things In Life'. Since then, their back catalogue has been repackaged in productions such as *The Travelling Music Show* (1978), with Bruce Forsyth, and *Once Upon A Song*, in which Newley occasionally appeared when he is not singing for big dollars in Las Vegas. Also in 1978, Bricusse collaborated with composer Armando Trovajoli on *Beyond The Rainbow*, an English language version of the Italian musical *Aggiungi Una Posta Alla Tavola*, which ran for six months in London – a good deal longer than his own *Kings And Clowns*. He also wrote some new songs for a Chichester Festival Theatre production of his film score for *Goodbye, Mr Chips* (1982). By then, he was generally wearing his Hollywood hat, and had received Oscar nominations for his work on *Goodbye, Mr Chips* (1969, original song score, with John Williams), *Scrooge* (1970, original song score with Ian Fraser and Herbert W. Spencer, and his own song, 'Thank You Very Much'), *That's Life* (1986, 'Life In a Looking Glass', with Henry Mancini), *Home Alone* (1990, 'Somewhere In My Memory', with John Williams), and *Hook* (1991, 'When You're Alone', with John Williams).

He won his second Academy Award in 1982, in collaboration with Mancini, for the original song score to *Victor/Victoria*. Bricusse and Newley were inducted into the Songwriters' Hall Of Fame in 1989, a year that otherwise proved something of a disappointment for the partners. For instance, an updated version of *Stop The World*, directed by, and starring Newley, staggered along for five weeks in London, and Bricusse's *Sherlock Holmes*, with Ron Moody and Liz Robertson, opened there as well, to disappointing reviews. *Sherlock Holmes* resurfaced in 1993, and toured the UK with Robert Powell in the title role. In the same year,

Bricusse's stage adaptation of *Scrooge*, with Newley in the title role, was presented for the first time. Also in 1993, Harry Secombe recreated his original role in *Pickwick* at Chichester and in the West End. In October 1995, a stage version of *Victor/Victoria*, starring Julie Andrews, opened on Broadway, to be followed in April 1997 by *Jekyll And Hyde*, on which librettist/lyricist Bricusse collaborated with composer Frank Wildhorn. In July 1998, a stage version of *Doctor Dolittle*, for which Bricusse wrote the book, music and lyrics, opened at the Labatt's Apollo Theatre in West London.

BRILL BUILDING

The Brill Building, situated in Broadway, New York, was the home of Tin Pan Alley, conveyor-belt-produced pop. Housed within the building were tiny cubicles in which some of the leading songwriters of the day provided the soundtrack to a generation of teenage dreams. With talents such as Carole King, Neil Sedaka, Barry Mann, Cynthia Weill, Jeff Barry and Ellie Greenwich, Leiber And Stoller, and Doc Pomus and Mort Shuman, a string of hits in rapid succession seemed almost inevitable. With key bubblegum-pop genius Don Kirshner cracking the whip, a veritable university of young, top-class composers and musicians competed among themselves to produce chart-topping songs. The golden era of New York-based pop lasted from 1960-64 when the emergence of the Beatles and the commercial upsurge of Bob Dylan prompted many artists to compose their own material. Several former Brill Building pupils, including Neil Sedaka and Carole King, re-emerged as major singer-songwriters at the end of the decade.

● COMPILATIONS: *On Broadway: Hit Songs And Rarities From The Brill Building Era* (Westside 1999) ★★★★.

BROGUES

Formed in San Jose, California, USA, in 1964, the Brogues were one of the region's finest garage bands. Their initial line-up comprised Eddie Rodrigues (guitar, vocals), Rick Campbell (guitar, vocals), Bill Whittington (bass, vocals) and Greg Elmore (drums), but their reputation was more fully established upon the addition of Gary Grubb (aka Gary Cole; guitar). The group completed two singles, the best known of which was a riveting reading of 'I Ain't No Miracle Worker', also recorded by the Chocolate Watch Band. The Brogues disbanded in July 1965 when Rodrigues joined the US Army. Whittington then became a founder-member of Family Tree, while Elmore and Grubb, now known as Gary Duncan, joined Quicksilver Messenger Service.

BROOK BROTHERS

Geoffrey Brook (b. 12 April 1943) and Ricky Brook (b. 24 October 1940) were a pop duo from

Winchester, Hampshire, England, who were often called the British Everly Brothers. The pair made their first appearance in a skiffle group in 1956 and started on the road to fame after winning a talent competition on Southern UK television's programme *Home Grown*. They first recorded in 1960 for Top Rank Records and their first single (which was an Italian hit for them) was a cover version of the Brothers Four's US hit 'Greenfields'. They followed it with a double-sided cover, 'Please Help Me, I'm Falling'/'When Will I Be Loved'. They then moved to Pye Records with their producer Tony Hatch, and their second release on that label, 'Warpaint', reached the UK Top 5, with 'Ain't Gonna Wash For A Week' making the Top 20 a few months later. Again, these were cover versions of US records with the originals coming from Barry Mann and Eddie Hodges, respectively. The duo, backed by the Semi-Tones, toured with acts such as Cliff Richard, Bobby Rydell and Jimmy Jones. They had three smaller UK follow-up hits, appeared in the film *It's Trad, Dad!* and recorded on Decca Records as the Brooks before fading from the scene. The crisp production of their canon of hits placed them above many of their contemporaries during their brief days of glory.

● ALBUMS: *Brook Brothers* (Pye 1961) ★★★.
● COMPILATIONS: *War Paint* (Castle 2001) ★★★.
● FILMS: *It's Trad, Dad!* aka *Ring-A-Ding Rhythm* (1961).

BROOKLYN BRIDGE

Johnny Maestro (b. John Mastrangelo, 7 May 1939, Brooklyn, New York, USA) had been the lead singer of the Crests in the 50s, and his voice was behind one of the most memorable doo-wop songs ever, '16 Candles', in 1958. He was also the featured vocalist on follow-up hits such as 'The Angels Listened In', 'Step By Step' and 'Trouble In Paradise'. When Maestro left the group to go solo in 1961, his career took a downturn. In 1968 he formed a new group, Brooklyn Bridge, with singers Les Cauchi, Fred Ferrara, both formerly of the Del-Satins (once the backing group for Dion), and an eight-member backing band, formerly known as the Rhythm Method. The new group fashioned an orchestral, more modernized style of doo-wop, and with the dramatic vocals of Maestro, were signed to Buddah Records. Their first single was a Jimmy Webb song, 'The Worst That Could Happen', which became a number 3 US hit at the beginning of 1969. The group achieved a total of seven chart singles and two albums by the end of 1970. They became a mainstay at revival concerts featuring old rock 'n' roll. Maestro continued to front the band through many personnel changes, and Brooklyn Bridge were still a top concert and club attraction on the east coast in the early 90s.

● ALBUMS: *Brooklyn Bridge* (Buddah 1969) ★★★, *The Second Brooklyn Bridge* (Buddah 1969)

★★, with the Isley Brothers and Edwin Hawkins *Live At Yankee Stadium* (T-Neck 1969) ★★, *Brooklyn Bridge* (1970) ★★, *Bridge In Blue* (1972) ★★.
● COMPILATIONS: *Johnny Maestro And The Brooklyn Bridge: The Greatest Hits* (Collectables 1994) ★★★.

BROWN, ARTHUR

b. 24 June 1944, Whitby, Yorkshire, England. A distinctive, uncompromising vocalist, Brown formed an R&B band – Blues And Brown – while studying philosophy at Reading University. He made his recording debut in 1965 with two contributions to a student 'Rag Week' flexi-disc, before moving to London where he fronted a succession of bands, known variously as the Southwest Five, the Arthur Brown Union and the Arthur Brown Set. In 1966 the singer moved to Paris where he began honing a theatrical and visual image. He was fêted by the city's artisans and contributed two songs to *La Curee*, a Roger Vadim film that starred Jane Fonda. Brown returned to London in 1967 and formed the first Crazy World Of Arthur Brown with Vincent Crane (b. 21 May 1943, Reading, Berkshire, England, d. 14 February 1989; organ), Drachen Theaker (drums) and, later, Nick Greenwood (bass). They were quickly adopted by the 'underground' audience, where Brown's facial make-up, dervish dancing and fiery helmet earned them immediate notoriety. Their popularity engendered a recording contract and the following year the band enjoyed a surprise number 1 hit with the compulsive 'Fire'. The attendant album, *The Crazy World Of Arthur Brown*, contained many stage favourites, including 'Spontaneous Apple Creation' and 'Come And Buy', but was marred by poor production.

Theaker and Crane left the band during a US tour, and although Crane later returned, Carl Palmer (b. 20 March 1947, Birmingham, West Midlands, England), formerly of Chris Farlowe's Thunderbirds, joined as drummer. However, Brown's most successful group ended in 1969 when the newcomer and Crane formed Atomic Rooster. Brown moved to Puddletown in Dorset, where a musically fertile commune had been established. Reunited with Theaker, he completed the experimental set latterly issued as *Strangelands*, before embarking on a new direction with Kingdom Come. This intermittently interesting band recorded three albums before splitting up. The singer resumed a solo career in 1974, but despite a memorable cameo as the Priest in Ken Russell's movie, *Tommy*, subsequent recordings proved highly disappointing. His voice, which once stood comparison with those of 'Screamin' Jay' Hawkins, Little Richard and James Brown, was muted on the tired *Dance* album, and a reconciliation with Crane for *Chisholm In My Bosom* was little better. Brown then went into semi-retirement from the music business and settled in Austin, Texas, where he pursued a career as a carpenter and decorator in partnership with former Mothers Of Invention drummer, Jimmy Carl Black. In 1999 he guested with UK psychedelic revivalists Kula Shaker, still with his helmet of fire.

● ALBUMS: *The Crazy World Of Arthur Brown* (Track 1968) ★★★, *Dance* (Gull 1974) ★, *Chisholm In My Bosom* (Gull 1978) ★, with Vincent Crane *Faster Than The Speed Of Light* (Warners 1980) ★★, *Requiem* (Remote 1982) ★★, *Strangelands* (Reckless 1988) ★★, with Jimmy Carl Black *Brown, Black & Blue* (Voiceprint 1991) ★★★, *Order From Chaos – Live 1993* (Voiceprint 1994) ★★★.

● FILMS: *Tommy* (1975), *Club Paradise* (1986).

BROWN, JAMES

b. 3 May 1928, Barnwell, South Carolina, USA. Brown claims he was born in 1933 in Macon, Georgia. 'The Hardest Working Man In Showbusiness', 'The Godfather Of Soul', 'The Minister Of The New New Super Heavy Funk' – such sobriquets only hint at the protracted James Brown legend. Convicted of theft at the age of 16, he was imprisoned at the Alto Reform School, but secured an early release on the approbation of local singer Bobby Byrd. Brown later joined his group, the Gospel Starlighters, who evolved into the Flames after embracing R&B. In 1955 they recorded a demo of 'Please Please Please' at WIBB, a Macon, Georgia radio station. Local airplay was such that talent scout Ralph Bass signed the group to the King/Federal company. A re-recorded version of the song was issued in March 1956. Credited to 'James Brown And The Famous Flames', it eventually climbed to number 5 in the US R&B list. Further releases fared poorly until 1958, when 'Try Me' rose to number 1 in the same chart. Once again Brown found it difficult to maintain this level of success, but 'I'll Go Crazy' and 'Think' (both 1960) put his progress on a surer footing. From thereon, until 1977, almost every 'official' single charted. However, it was an album, *Live At The Apollo* (1963), that assuredly established the singer. Raw, alive and uninhibited, this shattering collection confirmed Brown as the voice of black America – every track on the album is a breathtaking event. More than 30 years on, with all the advances in recording technology, this album stands as one of the greatest live productions of all time.

His singles continued to enthral: energetic songs such as 'Night Train' and 'Shout And Shimmy' contrasted with such slower sermons as 'I Don't Mind' and 'Bewildered', but it was the orchestrated weepie, 'Prisoner Of Love' (1963), that gave Brown his first US Top 20 pop single. Such eminence allowed Brown a new manoeuvrability. Dissatisfied with King Records, he ignored contractual niceties and signed with Smash Records. By the time his former outlet

had secured an injunction, 'Out Of Sight' had become another national hit. More importantly, however, the single marked the beginning of a leaner, tighter sound that would ultimately discard accepted western notions of harmony and structure. This innovative mid-60s period is captured on film in his electrifying performance on the *TAMI Show*.

Throughout the 60s, Brown proclaimed an artistic freedom with increasingly unconventional songs, including 'Papa's Got A Brand New Bag', 'I Got You (I Feel Good)', 'It's A Man's Man's Man's World' (with a beautifully orchestrated string section) and 'Money Won't Change You'. In 1967 Alfred Ellis replaced Nat Jones as Brown's musical director and 'Cold Sweat' introduced further radical refinements to the group's presentation. With Clyde Stubblefield on drums, 'Say It Loud – I'm Black And I'm Proud' (1968), 'Mother Popcorn' (1969), and 'Get Up (I Feel Like Being A) Sex Machine' (1970) were each stripped down to a nagging, rhythmic riff, over which the singer soared, sometimes screaming, sometimes pleading, but always with an assertive urgency. In 1971 Brown moved to Polydor Records and unveiled a new backing band, the JBs. Led by Fred Wesley, it featured such seasoned players as Maceo Parker and St. Clair Pinckney, as well as a new generation of musicians. Elsewhere, former bassist Bootsy Collins defected with other ex-members to George Clinton's Funkadelic. Such changes, coupled with Sly Stone's challenge, simply reinforced Brown's determination. He continued to enjoy substantial hits; in 1974 he had three successive number 1 R&B singles in 'The Payback', 'My Thang' and 'Papa Don't Take No Mess (Part 1)', and Brown also scored two movie soundtracks, *Black Caesar* and *Slaughter's Big Rip Off*. However, as the decade progressed, his work became less compulsive, suffering a drop in popularity with the advent of disco. A cameo role in the movie *The Blues Brothers* marked time, and in 1980 Brown left the Polydor label. Subsequent releases on such smaller labels as TK, Augusta Sound and Backstreet were only marginally successful.

However, Brown returned with a vengeance in 1986 (the year he was inducted into the Rock And Roll Hall Of Fame) with 'Living In America', the theme song from the *Rocky IV* soundtrack. An international hit single, it was followed by two R&B Top 10 entries, 'How Do You Stop' (1987) and 'I'm Real' (1988), the latter of which inspired a compulsive album of the same name. The Brown resurrection was abruptly curtailed that same year when the singer was arrested after a high-speed car chase. Charged with numerous offences, including illegal possession of drugs and firearms, aggravated assault and failure to stop for the police, he was sentenced to six and a half years' imprisonment at the State Park Correctional Centre. He was released in February 1991, having reportedly written new material while incarcerated. During the 90s he continued to have further problems with the law and a continuing battle to quit drugs; in 1995 he was forced to cope with a tragic medical accident when his ex-wife Adrienne died during surgery for 'liposuction'. In January 1998 there were new fears for his own health, and he was treated in hospital for addiction to painkillers. Shortly afterwards he was arrested and charged for possession of marijuana and unlawful use of a firearm.

Brown's considerable influence has increased with the advent of hip-hop. New urban-based styles are indebted to the raw funk espoused by 'The Godfather of Soul', while Stubblefield's rhythmic patterns, particularly those on 1970's 'Funky Drummer', have been heavily sampled, as have Brown's notorious whoops, screams, interjections and vocal improvisations. Artists as disparate as Public Enemy, George Michael, Sinéad O'Connor and Candy Flip have featured beats taken from Brown's impressive catalogue. Despite his ongoing personal problems, he is still seen as one of the most dynamic performers of the century and a massive influence on most forms of black music – soul, hip-hop, funk, R&B and disco.

● ALBUMS: *Please Please Please* (King 1959) ★★★, *Try Me* (King 1959) ★★, *Think* (King 1960) ★★★, *The Amazing James Brown* (King 1961) ★★★, *James Brown Presents His Band/Night Train* (King 1961) ★★★, *Shout And Shimmy* (King 1962) ★★★, *James Brown And His Famous Flames Tour The USA* (King 1962) ★★, *Excitement Mr Dynamite* (King 1962) ★★★, *Live At The Apollo* (King 1963) ★★★★★, *Prisoner Of Love* (King 1963) ★★★, *Pure Dynamite! Live At The Royal* (King 1964) ★★★, *Showtime* (Smash 1964) ★★, *The Unbeatable James Brown* (King 1964) ★★★, *Grits And Soul* (Smash 1964) ★★, *Out Of Sight* (Smash 1964) ★★★, *Papa's Got A Brand New Bag* (King 1965) ★★★, *James Brown Plays James Brown Today And Yesterday* (Smash 1965) ★★, *I Got You (I Feel Good)* (King 1966) ★★★, *Mighty Instrumentals* (King 1966) ★★, *James Brown Plays New Breed (The Boo-Ga-Loo)* (Smash 1966) ★★, *Soul Brother No. 1: It's A Man's Man's Man's World* (King 1966) ★★★, *James Brown Sings Christmas Songs* (King 1966) ★★, *Handful Of Soul* (Smash 1966) ★★, *The James Brown Show* (Smash 1967) ★★, *Sings Raw Soul* (King 1967) ★★★, *James Brown Plays The Real Thing* (Smash 1967) ★★★, *Live At The Garden* (King 1967) ★★, *Cold Sweat* (King 1967) ★★★, *James Brown Presents His Show Of Tomorrow* (King 1968) ★★★, *I Can't Stand Myself (When You Touch Me)* (King 1968) ★★, *I Got The Feelin'* (King 1968) ★★★, *Live At The Apollo, Volume 2* (King 1968) ★★★★, *James Brown Sings Out Of Sight* (King 1968) ★★★, *Thinking About Little Willie John And A Few Nice Things* (King 1968) ★★★, *A Soulful Christmas* (King 1968) ★★, *Say It Loud, I'm Black And I'm Proud* (King 1969) ★★★★, *Gettin' Down To It* (King 1969) ★★★, *The Popcorn* (King 1969) ★★★, *It's A Mother* (King 1969) ★★★, *Ain't It Funky* (King 1970) ★★★, *Soul On Top* (King 1970) ★★★, *It's A New Day – Let A Man Come In* (King 1970) ★★★, *Sex Machine* (King 1970) ★★★, *Hey America* (King 1970) ★★★, *Super Bad* (King 1971) ★★, *Sho' Is Funky Down Here* (King 1971) ★★, *Hot Pants* (Polydor 1971) ★★, *Revolution Of The Mind/Live At The Apollo, Volume 3* (Polydor 1971) ★★★, *There It Is* (Polydor 1972) ★★★, *Get On The Good Foot* (Polydor 1972) ★★★, *Black Caesar* film soundtrack (Polydor 1973) ★★★, *Slaughter's Big Rip-Off* film soundtrack (Polydor 1973) ★, *The Payback* (Polydor 1974) ★★★★, *Hell* (Polydor 1974) ★★★, *Reality* (Polydor 1975) ★★★, *Sex Machine Today* (Polydor 1975) ★★★, *Everybody's Doin' The Hustle And Dead On The Double Bump* (Polydor 1975) ★★, *Hot* (Polydor 1976) ★★★, *Get Up Offa That Thing* (Polydor 1976) ★★, *Bodyheat* (Polydor 1976) ★★, *Mutha's Nature* (Polydor 1977) ★★★, *Jam/1980's* (Polydor 1978) ★★★, *Take A Look At Those Cakes* (Polydor 1979) ★★★, *The Original Disco Man* (Polydor 1979) ★★★, *People* (Polydor 1980) ★★★, *James Brown ... Live/Hot On The One* (Polydor 1980) ★★, *Soul Syndrome* (TK 1980) ★★★★, *Nonstop!* (Polydor 1981) ★★★, *Live In New York* (Audio Fidelity 1981) ★★★, *Bring It On* (Churchill 1983) ★★★, *Gravity* (Scotti Bros 1986) ★★★, *James Brown And Friends* (Scotti Bros 1988) ★★★, *I'm Real* (Scotti Bros 1988) ★★★, *Soul Session Live* (Scotti Bros 1989) ★★★★, *Love Overdue* (Scotti Bros 1991) ★★★, *Universal James* (Scotti Bros 1993) ★★, *Live At The Apollo 1995* (Scotti Bros 1995) ★★★, *I'm Back* (Private I 1998) ★★.

● COMPILATIONS: *James Brown Soul Classics* (Polydor 1973) ★★★, *Soul Classics, Volume 2* (Polydor 1974) ★★★, *Soul Classics, Volume 3* (Polydor 1975) ★★★, *Solid Gold* (Polydor 1977) ★★★, *The Fabulous James Brown* (HRB 1977) ★★★, *Can Your Heart Stand It?* (Solid Smoke 1981) ★★★, *The Best Of James Brown* (Polydor 1981) ★★★★, *The Federal Years, Part 1* (Solid Smoke 1984) ★★★★, *The Federal Years, Part 2* (Solid Smoke 1984) ★★★, *Roots Of A Revolution* (Polydor 1984) ★★★, *Ain't That A Groove: The James Brown Story 1966-1969* (Polydor 1984) ★★★, *Doing It To Death: The James Brown Story 1970-1973* (Polydor 1984) ★★★, *Dead On The Heavy Funk: The James Brown Story 1974-1976* (Polydor 1985) ★★★, *The CD Of JB: Sex Machine And Other Soul Classics* (Polydor 1985) ★★★★, *James Brown's Funky People* (Polydor 1986) ★★★★, *In The Jungle Groove* (Polydor 1986) ★★★, *The CD Of JB II: Cold Sweat And Other Soul Classics* (Polydor 1987) ★★★★, *James Brown's Funky People (Part 2)* (Polydor 1988) ★★★, *Motherlode* (Polydor 1988) ★★★, *Messing With The Blues* (Polydor 1990) ★★★, *20 All-Time Greatest Hits!* (Polydor 1991) ★★★★, *Star Time* 4-CD box set (Polydor 1991) ★★★★★, *Sex Machine (The Very Best Of James Brown, Volume 1)* (Polydor 1991) ★★★★, *The Greatest Hits Of The Fourth Decade* (Scotti Brothers 1992) ★★★,

Soul Pride (The Instrumentals 1960-1969) (Polydor 1993) ★★★, *Funky President (The Very Best Of James Brown, Volume 2)* (Polydor 1993) ★★★, *40th Anniversary Collection* (Polydor 1996) ★★★★, *Foundations Of Funk (A Brand New Bag: 1964-1969)* (Polydor 1997) ★★★★★, *On Stage* (Charly 1997) ★★★, *Dead On The Heavy Funk: 1975-1983* (Polydor 1998) ★★★★, *James Brown's Original Funky Divas* (Polydor 1998) ★★★, the JBs *The JBs Funky Good Time: The Anthology* (Polydor 1998) ★★★.
● VIDEOS: *Video Biography* (Virgin Vision 1988), *Live In London: James Brown* (Virgin Vision 1988), *James Brown And Friends* (Video Collection 1988), *Live In Berlin* (Channel 5 1989), *Soul Jubilee* (MMG Video 1990), *Live On Stage (With Special Guest B.B. King)* (Old Gold 1990), *Sex Machine (The Very Best Of James Brown)* (PolyGram Music Video 1991), *The Lost Years (Live In Santa Cruz)* (BMG Video 1991), *Live In New York* (Enteleky 1991), *James Brown Live* (MIA 1995). *Live From The House Of Blues* (Aviva 2001).
● FURTHER READING: *James Brown: The Godfather Of Soul*, James Brown with Bruce Tucker. *Living In America: The Soul Saga Of James Brown*, Cynthia Rose. *James Brown: A Biography*, Geoff Brown.
● FILMS: *The Blues Brothers* (1980).

BROWN, JOE

b. Joseph Roger Brown, 13 May 1941, Swarby, Lincolnshire, England. Brown has sustained a career for over 40 years as a cheerful 'cockney' rock 'n' roll singer and guitarist. He was a popular live and television performer in the late 50s, a major UK recording star in the early 60s and is still a well-loved personality into the new millennium. In 1956, this east London-based performer formed the Spacemen skiffle group, which became the backing group on Jack Good's top-rated television series *Boy Meets Girl* in 1959. At this point in his career, Brown was generally regarded as one of the finest guitarists in the UK and his services were frequently in demand. Rechristened Joe Brown And The Bruvvers, the group joined Larry Parnes' successful stable of artists (Parnes allegedly tried to rename him Elmer Twitch!) and signed to Decca Records. He first charted with a unique treatment of 'The Darktown Strutters Ball' in 1960 and had a trio of UK Top 10 hits on the Piccadilly label in 1962-63 with 'A Picture Of You', 'It Only Took A Minute' and 'That's What Love Will Do'. Being a happy and cheeky 'character' with a regional accent, it is likely that he could have had success in the USA in the way that Herman's Hermits did (Brown actually recorded 'I'm Henry The VIII, I Am' first). Brown was just two years early, and arrived before the USA was completely receptive to the 'British Invasion'. As it was, his major hits were covered in the USA by acts such as Paul Evans, the Kalin Twins and Bobby Goldsboro. He was voted 'Top UK Vocal Personality' in the *New Musical Express* poll in 1962 and 1963. He appeared in the film *What A Crazy World* and in the mid-60s starred in the hit musical *Charlie Girl*, as well as fronting his own UK television shows *Joe & Co* and *Set 'Em Up Joe*. Brown has recorded sporadically since then on a variety of labels. During the early 70s, he put together the country rock band Home Brew, which originally featured his wife Vicki, Dave Hynes (drums), Ray Mynott (guitar), Kirk Duncan (keyboards) and Jeff Peters (bass). A second line-up featured the Browns and Hynes joined by Tony Williams (piano/vocals), Joe Fagin (bass, vocals), and Roger McKew (guitar). Vicki was one of Britain's most successful and prolific backing session vocalists until her career was tragically curtailed by illness. She died from cancer in June 1991. Three albums released in the 90s marked a small step in the direction of reaffirming Brown's real talent, and he makes regular trips to Nashville to write for the country market and latterly to record his own material. Brown has also earned acclaim for his work on BBC Radio, presenting a 1997 documentary dealing with skiffle music called *The Rock Island Line*, and a series the following year called *Let It Rock* which dealt with the early years of rock 'n' roll. He also collaborated with songwriter Roger Cook on the stage musical *Skiffle*. Brown has occasionally appeared on other artists' recordings, including a guest slot on George Harrison's *Gone Troppo*, while his daughter Sam Brown has forged a notable singing career. Although Brown's own career has often suffered from him being perceived as a 'cor blimey mate, what a lovely bloke' stereotype, in reality he is a masterful guitarist and singer who commands respect and admiration from a wide spectrum of artists.
● ALBUMS: *A Picture Of You* (Pye Golden Guinea 1962) ★★★, *Joe Brown Live* (Piccadilly 1963) ★★★, *Here Comes Joe!* (Pye 1967) ★★, *Joe Brown* (MCA 1968) ★★★, *Browns Home Brew* (Vertigo 1972) ★★★, *Together* (Vertigo 1974) ★★★, *Joe Brown Live* (Power 1977) ★★★, *Come On Joe* (Power 1993) ★★★, *Fifty Six & Taller Than You Think* (Demon 1997) ★★★, *On A Day Like This* (Round Tower 1999) ★★★★.
● COMPILATIONS: *Joe Brown Collection* (Pye 1974) ★★★, *Hits 'N' Pieces* (PRT 1988) ★★, *The Joe Brown Story* (Sequel 1993) ★★★★.
● VIDEOS: *Joe Brown In Concert* (1994).
● FURTHER READING: *Brown Sauce: The Life And Times Of Joe Brown*, Joe Brown.
● FILMS: *What A Crazy World* (1963), *Three Hats For Lisa* (1965), *Hostile Guns* (1967), *Lionheart* (1968), *Mona Lisa* (1986).

BROWN, MAXINE

b. 27 April 1932, Kingstree, South Carolina, USA. Having sung in two New York gospel groups, the Manhattans and the Royaltones, Brown made her recording debut on Nomar with 'All In My Mind'. A US Top 20 hit in 1961, this uptown soul allad was followed by another hit single, 'Funny'. A period at ABC-Paramount then passed before Brown signed to Wand Records and proceeded to make a series of excellent singles. She is best recalled for the US Top 30 hit 'Oh No Not My Baby' (1964), a beautifully written Gerry Goffin and Carole King song that was later covered by Manfred Mann, Rod Stewart and Aretha Franklin. Brown also recorded with Chuck Jackson – their version of 'Something You Got' made the US R&B Top 10 – but her position at Wand was undermined by the company's preoccupation with Dionne Warwick. Releases on a new outlet, Commonwealth United, resulted in two R&B chart entries, including the acclaimed 'We'll Cry Together' (1969). Maxine signed with Avco in 1971, but her work there failed to re-establish her former profile.

● ALBUMS: *The Fabulous Sound Of Maxine Brown* (Wand 1962) ★★★, *Spotlight On Maxine Brown* (Wand 1964) ★★★, *We'll Cry Together* (Common 1969) ★★★.

COMPILATIONS: *Maxine Brown's Greatest Hits* (Wand 1964) ★★★, *One In A Million* (Kent/Ace 1984) ★★★, *Like Never Before* Wand recordings (Kent/Ace 1985) ★★★, *Oh No Not My Baby: The Best Of Maxine Brown* (Kent/Ace 1990) ★★★★, *Golden Classics* (Collectables 1991) ★★★, *Maxine Brown's Greatest Hits* (Tomato 1995) ★★★★, *Greatest Hits* (Curb 1996) ★★★.

BROWN, OSCAR, JNR.

b. 10 October 1926, Chicago, Illinois, USA. Brown is a witty songwriter operating on the borders of soul and jazz. The son of a lawyer, Brown acted in a radio soap opera as a child and did a variety of jobs (copywriter, publicist, realtor) before serving in the US Army in 1954-56. Afterwards, he turned to professional songwriting and performing. The first of his compositions to be recorded was 'Brown Baby' by Mahalia Jackson. In 1961, his stage musical, *Kicks And Company*, was performed in Chicago, containing numerous songs that he later used in his stage act. Brown made his first album for CBS Records in 1960. It included some of his most well-known pieces, such as 'Signifyin' Monkey', and versions of Bobby Timmons' soul jazz tune, 'Dat Dere', and Herbie Hancock's 'Watermelon Man', to which Brown set lyrics. Later records contained such originals as 'Forbidden Fruit' (also recorded by Nina Simone) and 'The Snake', two hipster's versions of the biblical story of Adam and Eve. Brown's most popular setting of lyrics to a jazz instrumental was 'Work Song', composed by Nat Adderley and covered by Georgie Fame in Britain, where Brown's slick lyrics had a minor vogue among the more jazz-inspired R&B groups, and both the Mark Leeman Five and the Nashville Teens issued 'Forbidden Fruit' as a single in 1966. *Movin' On* was made for Atlantic Records and included Bernard Purdie, Richard

Tee and Cissie Houston among the backing musicians. In the late 80s, Brown appeared at nightspots with his son, Oscar Brown III (d. 12 August 1996, Chicago, Illinois, USA), and daughter Maggie. He returned to recording in the mid-90s with *Then & Now*, which included reworkings of material from his first two albums.

● ALBUMS: *Sin & Soul* (Columbia 1960) ★★★★, *Between Heaven And Hell* (Columbia 1961) ★★★, *In A New Mood* (Columbia 1962) ★★★, *Tells It Like It Is* (Columbia 1963) ★★★★, *Mr. Oscar Brown Jr. Goes To Washington* (Fontana 1964) ★★★, with Luiz Henrique *Finding A New Friend* (Fontana) ★★★, with Jean Pace, Sivuca *Joy* (RCA 1970) ★★★, *Movin' On* (Atlantic 1972) ★★★, *Brother Where Are You* (Atlantic 1973) ★★★, *Fresh* (Atlantic 1974) ★★★, *Then & Now* (Weasel 1995) ★★★, *Live Every Minute* (Minor 1998) ★★★.

BROWN, PETE

b. 25 December 1940, London, England. During the early 60s Brown was one of the UK's leading beat poets, with his recitals at jazz fraternity gatherings and small clubs making him an important figure on the burgeoning underground scene. His work came to national prominence as lyricist with late 60s power rock trio Cream. No-one before or since has captured more effectively the essence of the drug experience, all the more remarkable since Brown had stopped all drug-taking and drinking by the time he began writing for the band. On 1967's *Disraeli Gears*, Brown's outstanding, nonsensical tales contributed to its prodigious success; lines such as, 'Its getting near dark, when light close their tired eyes' in 'Sunshine Of Your Love', and the powerful surrealism of 'SWLABR', were but two examples of Brown's fertile hallucinogenic imagination. The superlative 'White Room' from *Wheels Of Fire* has stood the test of time, and along with much of the Cream catalogue has enabled Brown to receive continuing financial reward for a series of classic rock songs. Some of his finest lyrics are to be found on Jack Bruce's *Songs For A Tailor* and *How's Tricks*, the former including the evocative 'Theme For An Imaginary Western' and the quirky 'Weird Of Hermiston'. During his most prolific period in the late 60s, he also formed two bands that have received belated critical acclaim. The Battered Ornaments featured the explorative guitar of Chris Spedding, while Piblokto! recorded two albums that are valuable collector's items.

Brown also worked with the pivotal R&B pioneer Graham Bond in a partnership known as Bond And Brown. Brown became more involved with writing film scripts during subsequent decades, but recently returned to the music scene. His contributions have lost none of their surreal sharpness, as demonstrated on Bruce's *A Question Of Time* in

1990. Brown has also continued to work with former Piblokto! colleague Phil Ryan, frequently on musicals and film scores. In the 90s Brown reunited with Bruce for the album *Cities Of The Heart* and was part of Calvin Owens' band for UK gigs. He became a credible record producer, producing Dick Heckstall-Smith's *Where One Is* and worked with a rejuvenated Peter Green and former Keef Hartley Band singer Miller Anderson. Brown is a true original, retaining all the best qualities, humour and aspirations of the 60s underground scene without the drugs and alcohol.
● ALBUMS: with Graham Bond *Bond And Brown: Two Heads Are Better Than One* (Chapter One 1972) ★★★, *The 'Not Forgotten' Association* spoken word (Deram 1973) ★★, with Ian Lynn *Party In The Rain* (Discs International 1983) ★★, *Ardours Of The Lost Rake* (Aura 1991) ★★, with Phil Ryan *The Land That Cream Forgot* (Viceroy 1997) ★★★.
● COMPILATIONS: *Before Singing Lessons 1969-1977* (Decal 1987) ★★★.

BRUCE AND TERRY
Based in Los Angeles, California, USA, this duo comprised Terry Melcher (b. 8 February 1942, New York City, New York, USA, d. 1991; vocals) and Bruce Johnston (b. 27 June 1944, Peoria, Illinois, USA; vocals). They met in 1959 when Johnston recorded for the Arwin label which was co-owned by Melcher's mother, Doris Day. Within three years Melcher had become a staff producer at Columbia Records where he oversaw, among others, Johnston's *Surfin' Around The World*. The pair began working together in 1963 as the Hot Doggers, before enjoying chart success as the Rip Chords. They made their chart debut as Bruce And Terry in February 1964 with 'Custom Machine', written by Brian Wilson of the Beach Boys. It was succeeded by 'Summer Means Fun', the first of several P.F. Sloan/Steve Barri songs the duo recorded. Bruce and Terry parted company in 1965 as Melcher's production commitments to the Byrds and Paul Revere And The Raiders took precedence. In April 1965 Johnston joined the Beach Boys, with whom he still plays. However, he resumed a partnership with Melcher in 1976 when the pair founded a short-lived record label, Equinox Productions.
● COMPILATIONS: *The Best Of Bruce And Terry* (Sundazed 1998) ★★★.

BRUCE, ED
b. William Edwin Bruce, 29 December 1939, Keiser, Arkansas, USA. His family moved to Memphis and Bruce was to spend many years promoting tourism as 'the Tennessean'. He loved the early Sun records of Carl Perkins and, after graduating in 1957, was given the money to make a demo, and so impressed Sun's engineer, Jack Clement, that he was signed to the label. His singles, 'Rock Boppin' Baby' and 'Sweet

Woman', under the name of Edwin Bruce are collector's items, but they are also included, along with previously unreleased Sun tracks, on the 1986 Bear Family collection. He had his first financial success when he wrote 'Save Your Kisses', the b-side of Tommy Roe's chart-topping 'Sheila'. He also wrote 'See The Big Man Cry', a solo hit for Charlie Louvin, and 'Northeast Arkansas Mississippi County Bootlegger' for Kenny Price. Bruce had a minor country hit with the Monkees' 'Last Train To Clarksville' and found himself a country star with 'The Last Cowboy Song' and 'You're The Best Break This Old Heart Ever Had', his only number 1. Bruce regards himself primarily as a songwriter and 'Mammas, Don't Let Your Babies Grow Up To Be Cowboys', for Waylon Jennings and Willie Nelson, became the anthem of outlaw country (Nelson added a final chorus to his 1980 version of 'The Last Cowboy Song'. Other songs include 'The Man That Turned My Mama On' (Tanya Tucker), 'Workingman's Prayer' (Arthur Prysock, Tex Ritter), 'Restless' (Crystal Gayle) and 'Too Much Love Between Us' (Kitty Wells). Many songs were co-written with his former wife and manager, Patsy. Bruce starred as Tom Guthrie alongside James Garner in the US television series *Maverick* and recorded 'Theme From Bret Maverick'.
● ALBUMS: *If I Could Just Go Home* (RCA 1968) ★★★, *Shades Of Ed Bruce* (Monument 1969) ★★★★, *Ed Bruce* (United Artists 1976) ★★, *The Tennessean* (Epic 1977) ★★★, *Cowboys And Dreamers* (Epic 1978) ★★★, *Ed Bruce* (MCA 1980) ★★★, *One To One* (MCA 1981) ★★★, *Last Train To Clarksville* (RCA International 1982), *Write It Down* (MCA 1982) ★★, *You're Not Leavin Here Tonight* (MCA 1983) ★★★ *Tell 'Em I've Gone Crazy* (MCA 1984) ★★★, *Homecoming* (RCA 1984) ★★★, *Night Things* (RCA 1986) ★★.
● COMPILATIONS: *Rockin' And Boppin' Baby* (Bear Family 1986) ★★★★, *Greatest Hits* (MCA 1986) ★★★★, *The Best Of Ed Bruce* (Varèse Sarabande 1995) ★★★★, *Puzzles* (Bear Family 1995) ★★★.

BRUCE, TOMMY
b. 1939, London, England. This 60s rock 'n' roll vocalist possessed an extraordinary voice that was described as a subtle blending of a corncrake, steam hammer and gravel polisher Orphaned at the age of 10, he worked for some years as a driver's mate in London's famous Covent Garden fruit market, before his neighbour, the then actor and later successful songwriter, Barry Mason, encouraged him to make the demo record that secured him a contract with Norrie Paramor at Columbia Records in 1960. His first release, the Fats Waller oldie 'Ain't Misbehavin'', was a UK number 2 hit and his follow-up, another standard, 'Broken Doll', also reached the UK Top 40, but was his last record to do so. The singer, who was either loved or hated, was often accused of emulating

the Big Bopper. He hotly disputed this claim, saying he was not particularly familiar with the late singer's work. Together with his group the Bruisers, he appeared on television programmes such as *Wham!!* and on many live shows, often under the auspices of impresario Larry Parnes. This unique cockney performer, who never claimed that he could actually sing, also recorded on Polydor in 1965, RCA in 1966 and CBS in 1969. Bruce is still to be found singing in rock 'n' roll revival and 60s nostalgia shows.
● COMPILATIONS: *Greatest Hits* (Autograph 1985) ★★★.

BRYANT, ANITA
b. 25 March 1940, Barnsdale, Oklahoma, USA. Bryant has had a unique series of career changes: a beauty queen turned hitmaker, turned religious singer and spokesperson against gay liberation. Her first stage appearance was at the age of six and at nine she won her first talent show. She became known as 'Oklahoma's Red Feather Girl', and local television and radio appearances brought her to the attention of Arthur Godfrey, who put her on his television talent show where she won first prize. Her first record was 'Sinful To Flirt' in early 1956. In 1958 she became 'Miss Oklahoma' and at that year's 'Miss America Pageant', where she also sang, she came third. Her first chart entry was her second single on Carlton, a version of 'Till There Was You' (from the musical *The Music Man*), in 1959. She had three US Top 20 singles in 1960-61 with 'Paper Roses', 'In My Little Corner Of The World' (both minor UK hits and both revived later by Marie Osmond) and the vocal version of Bert Kaempfert's number 1 hit, 'Wonderland By Night'. She joined Columbia Records in 1962 and later recorded religious material for Myrrh and Word. Still a well-known figure in the USA, she continues to reside in California and performs regularly at the Anita Bryant Theater in Branson, Missouri, but is now best known for her outspoken views on the gay community.
● ALBUMS: *Anita Bryant* (Carlton 1959) ★★★, *Hear Anita Bryant In Your Home Tonight* (Carlton 1960) ★★★, *In My Little Corner Of The World* (Carlton 1961) ★★★★, *In A Velvet Mood* (Columbia 1962) ★★★, *Mine Eyes Have Seen The Glory* (Columbia 1967) ★★, *Love Lifted Me* (Word 1972) ★★★, *Miracle Of Christmas* (Word 1972) ★★, *Battle Hymn Of The Republic* (Word 1973) ★★, *Abide With Me* (Columbia 1975) ★★.
● COMPILATIONS: *Paper Roses: Golden Classics* (Collectables 1995) ★★★.

BUBBLE PUPPY
One of the last groups signed to the legendary International Artists label, Bubble Puppy also gave the company its most substantial hit, 'Hot Smoke And Sasafrass'. Originally known as the New Seeds, the Austin, Texas, USA-based quartet comprised Todd Potter (guitar), Roy Cox (bass), Rod Prince (guitar) and M. Taylor (drums) and

derived their new name from Aldous Huxley's *Brave New World*. More mainstream than many of their contemporaries, their debut album, *A Gathering Of Promises*, showed traces of Jimi Hendrix, Cream and Moby Grape. An unstable unit, Bubble Puppy moved labels to ABC Records in 1970 and changed their name to Demian. Their eponymous album relied on progressive styles at the expense of melody and this aggregation was allowed to wither away. Rod Prince, the Puppy's lead guitarist, re-established the group in 1977 under the title Sirius, and the resultant release, *Electric Flow*, recalled something of the old group's erstwhile fire. Ten years later he re-emerged with a reconstituted Bubble Puppy and an album, *Wheels Go Round*, which bore a kinship with ZZ Top.
● ALBUMS: *A Gathering Of Promises* (International Artists 1969) ★★, as Demian *Demian* (ABC 1971) ★★, as Sirius *Electric Flow* (1977) ★★, *Wheels Go Round* (One Big Guitar 1987) ★★.
● COMPILATIONS: *Sirius Rising* (1999) ★★★.

BUCKINGHAMS
Formed in Chicago, Illinois, USA, in 1966, the Buckinghams originally consisted of Dennis Tufano (b. 11 September 1946, Chicago, Illinois, USA; vocals), Carl Giammarese (b. 21 August 1947, Chicago, Illinois, USA; lead guitar), Dennis Miccoli (organ), Nick Fortuna (b. 1 May 1946, Chicago, Illinois, USA; bass) and Jon Poulos (b. 31 March 1947, Chicago, Illinois, USA, d. 26 March 1980; drums). Although their first hit, the US chart-topper 'Kind Of A Drag', was their only gold disc, the band enjoyed a consistent run of US chart successes throughout 1967, achieving two further US Top 10 entries with 'Don't You Care' and 'Mercy, Mercy, Mercy'. Miccoli was latterly replaced by Marty Grebb (b. 2 September 1946, Chicago, Illinois, USA) before the Buckinghams' staid image was deemed *passé* by a more discerning audience. Nevertheless, despite those slick, commercial singles, their albums showed a desire to experiment. Produced and directed by Jim Guercio, such releases hinted at the brass arrangements this talented individual later brought to protégés Chicago. Unable to reconcile their image and ambitions, the quintet split up in 1970. Poulos later managed several local acts, but died of drug-related causes in 1980. Tufano and Giammarese continued to work as a duo, while Grebb later worked with Chicago. Fortuna and Giammarese subsequently revived the Buckinghams for nostalgia tours, making an occasional return to the recording studio.
● ALBUMS: *Kind Of A Drag* (USA 1967) ★★★, *Time And Changes* (Columbia 1967) ★★★, *Portraits* (Columbia 1968) ★★★, *In One Ear And Gone Tomorrow* (Columbia 1968) ★★, *Made In Chicago* (Columbia 1969) ★★★, *Terra Firma* (Nation 1998) ★★.

● COMPILATIONS: *The Buckinghams' Greatest Hits* (Columbia 1969) ★★★, *Mercy Mercy Mercy: A Collection* (Columbia 1991) ★★★.

BUFFALO SPRINGFIELD

A seminal band in the development of American country-rock and folk-rock, although short-lived, the monumental influence of Buffalo Springfield rivals that of the Byrds. Despite the line-up constantly changing, the main members throughout the band's three turbulent years were Stephen Stills (b. 3 January 1945, Dallas, Texas, USA; guitar, vocals), Neil Young (b. 12 November 1945, Toronto, Canada; guitar, vocals), Richie Furay (b. 9 May 1944, Yellow Springs, Ohio, USA; guitar, vocals), Dewey Martin (b. 30 September 1942, Chesterville, Canada; drums), Bruce Palmer (b. 1947, Liverpool, Canada) and Jim Messina (b. 5 December 1947, Maywood, California, USA). Furay and Stills worked together in the Au Go-Go Singers in the mid-60s, where they met Young, who at that time was a solo singer, having previously worked with Palmer in the Mynah Birds. Furay and Stills had moved to Los Angeles to start a band, and decided to seek out the enigmatic Young, eventually spotting his distinctive funeral hearse while driving along Sunset Strip. They formed a band in 1966 and, following a series of successful gigs at the prestigious *Whisky A Go-Go*, and boosted by verbal endorsements from the Byrds' Chris Hillman and David Crosby, were signed by Ahmet Ertegun to his Atco Records label. Any band containing three main songwriters who could all play lead guitar was heading for trouble, and soon their egos and fists clashed. The main antagonists were Stills and Young, but their problems were compounded by the continual immigration and drug problems of Palmer, with their road manager Dick Davis even having to masquerade as the bass player for a television appearance. Eventually, Young's former associate, Ken Koblun, was recruited as a replacement. He, in turn, was replaced by Jim Fielder (b. 4 October 1947, Denton, Texas, USA) from the Mothers Of Invention, but Fielder only lasted a couple of months.

The band's only major hit was 1967's 'For What It's Worth'. The song remains one of the finest protest anthems of the 60s, and exemplified the phenomenon of the 'right song at the right time'. Stills' plaintive yet wry and lethargic plea for tolerance was written after the police used heavy-handed methods to stop a demonstration outside a club, Pandora's Box, on Sunset Strip in 1966. They were protesting about the curfew times imposed. The chorus of 'Stop children, what's that sound everybody look what's going down' became an anthem for west coast students in their protests against the government.

The band always seemed doomed throughout their brief time together. Neil Young's unpredictability also meant that he sometimes did not arrive for gigs, or quite simply left the band for long periods. His main replacement was ex-Daily Flash guitarist Doug Hastings (b. 21 June 1946, Seattle, Washington, USA). Two official albums were released (a third, *Stampede*, was planned but only appeared later as a compilation bootleg). *Last Time Around* was patched together by producer and latter-day bass player Jim Messina, after the band had broken up for the final time. *Buffalo Springfield Again* remains their finest work and is still highly favoured by the *cognoscenti*. The album demonstrated the developing talents of Stills and Young as major songwriters. Young's superb, surreal mini-epics 'Expecting To Fly' and 'Broken Arrow' were equalled by Stills' immaculate 'Everydays' and the lengthy 'Bluebird' (about Judy Collins). Furay also contributed strong material, including the heavily countrified 'A Child's Claim To Fame' and 'Sad Memory'. Both the band's and the album's essence, however, was encapsulated in one short track, 'Rock And Roll Woman', a brilliant Stills song written about the Jefferson Airplane's stunning Grace Slick, and co-written by an uncredited David Crosby, who briefly appeared with the band as Young's substitute at the 1967 Monterey Pop Festival. The three lead guitars duelled together and the three lead vocals enmeshed brilliantly to enshrine, for a brief moment, the brilliance of a band who could have been America's greatest rivals to the Beatles.

Following the band's split, Furay formed the highly respected Poco, continuing down the road to country rock. Messina joined with Furay and later with Kenny Loggins as Loggins And Messina. Fielder became highly respected as part of Blood, Sweat And Tears, while Hastings joined Rhinoceros. Dewey Martin formed the ill-fated New Buffalo Springfield only to be forced to change the name to New Buffalo. Together with Bruce Palmer, they continued on the nostalgia circuit under the banner of Buffalo Springfield Again. Young and Stills went on to mega-stardom as members of Crosby, Stills, Nash And Young and high profile solo careers. More than thirty years later, the massive contribution and importance of the band is recognized as having been the most fertile training school of the era. The magnificent box set issued in 2001 is a fitting tribute to their huge influence.

● ALBUMS: *Buffalo Springfield* (Atco 1967) ★★★★, *Buffalo Springfield Again* (Atco 1967) ★★★★★, *Last Time Around* (Atco 1968) ★★★.
● COMPILATIONS: *Retrospective* (Atco 1969) ★★★★, *Expecting To Fly* (Atlantic 1970) ★★★★, *Buffalo Springfield* (Atco 1973) ★★★★, *Buffalo Springfield* 4-CD box set (Rhino 2001) ★★★★.
● FURTHER READING: *Neil Young: Here We Are In The Years*, Johnny Rogan. *Crosby, Stills, Nash & Young: The Visual Documentary*, Johnny

Rogan. *Crosby, Stills & Nash: The Biography*, Dave Zimmer and Henry Diltz. *For What It's Worth: The Story Of Buffalo Springfield*, John Einarson and Richie Furay. *Prisoner Of Woodstock*, Dallas Taylor.

BURDON, ERIC

b. 11 May 1941, Walker, Newcastle-upon-Tyne, Tyne & Wear, England. Burdon originally came to prominence as the lead singer of the Animals in 1963. His gutsy, distinctive voice was heard on their many memorable records in the 60s. Following the demise of the latter-day Eric Burdon And The New Animals, it was announced that he would pursue a career in films. By 1970 no offers from Hollywood were forthcoming so he linked up with the relatively unknown black jazz/rock band Nite Shift, and, together with his friend Lee Oskar, they became Eric Burdon And War. A successful single, 'Spill The Wine', preceded the well-received *Eric Burdon Declares War*. In the song Burdon parodied himself with the lyrics: 'Imagine me, an overfed, long-haired leaping gnome, should be a star of a Hollywood movie.' Both this and the follow-up, *Black Man's Burdon*, combined ambitious arrangements mixing flute with Oskar's harmonica. Eventually the jazz/rock/funk/blues/soul mix ended up merely highlighting Burdon's ultra pro-black stance. While his intentions were honourable, it came over to many as inverted racism. Burdon received a great deal of press in 1970 when he was still regarded as an influential spokesperson of the hippie generation. At the time of Jimi Hendrix's death, he claimed to possess a suicide note, the contents of which he refused to divulge. After parting company, War went on to become hugely successful in the early 70s, while Burdon's career stalled. He teamed up with Jimmy Witherspoon on *Guilty* and attempted a heavier rock approach with *Sun Secrets* and *Stop*. The ponderous Hendrix-influenced guitar style of the last two albums did not suit reworked versions of early Animals hits, and the albums were not successful. In 1980 Burdon formed Fire Dept in Germany, making one album, *Last Drive*. He finally fulfilled his long-standing big-screen ambitions by appearing in the movie *Comeback*, albeit as a fading rock star.
Throughout the 80s Burdon continued to perform with little recorded output, while experiencing drug and alcohol problems. His 1977 and 1983 reunion albums with the original Animals were not well received. Burdon's popularity in Germany continued, while his profile in the UK and USA decreased. His confessional autobiography was published in 1986. Burdon continued to tour throughout the 90s, playing with his own I Band and Alvin Lee's The Best Of British Blues, and re-forming the New Animals in 1999. Ultimately, Burdon remains one of the finest white blues vocalists of our time, although remaining typecast as the man who sang 'House Of The Rising Sun'.
● ALBUMS: as Eric Burdon And War *Eric Burdon Declares War* (Polydor 1970) ★★★, as Eric Burdon And War *Black Man's Burdon* (Liberty 1971) ★★★, with Jimmy Witherspoon *Guilty!* (United Artists 1971) ★★★, *Ring Of Fire* (Capitol 1974) ★★★, *Sun Secrets* (Capitol 1975) ★★, *Stop* (Capitol 1975) ★★, *Survivor* (Polydor 1978) ★★, *Darkness – Darkness* (Polydor 1980) ★★, as Eric Burdon's Fire Department *The Last Drive* (Ariola 1980) ★★, *Comeback* (Line 1982) ★★ reissued as *The Road* (Thunderbolt 1984), as The Eric Burdon Band *Comeback* new songs from 1982 session (Blackline 1983) ★★, *Power Company* aka *Devil's Daughter* new songs from 1982 session (Carrere 1983) ★★, as The Eric Burdon Band *That's Live* (In-Akustik 1985) ★★, *I Used To Be An Animal* (Striped Horse 1988) ★★, *Wicked Man* reissue of *Comeback/Power Company* material (GNP Crescendo 1988) ★★, *The Unreleased Eric Burdon* (Blue Wave 1992) ★★, *Crawling King Snake* (Thunderbolt 1992) ★★, with Brian Auger *Access All Areas* (SPV 1993) ★★, *Misunderstood* (Aim 1995) ★★, *Live At The Roxy* 1976 recording (Magnum 1997) ★★, *F#ck Me!!! I Thought I Was Dead: Greatest Hits Alive* (One Way 1999) ★★, *Lost Within The Halls Of Fame* (Mooncrest 2000) ★★★.
● COMPILATIONS: War featuring Eric Burdon *Love Is All Around* (ABC 1976) ★★, *The Touch Of Eric Burdon* (K-Tel 1983) ★★, *Star Portrait* (Polydor 1988) ★★★, *Sings The Animals Greatest Hits* (Avenue 1994) ★★.
● VIDEOS: *Finally* (Warners 1992).
● FURTHER READING: *Wild Animals*, Andy Blackford. *I Used To Be An Animal But I'm All Right Now*, Eric Burdon. *The Last Poet: The Story Of Eric Burdon*, Jeff Kent. *Good Times: The Ultimate Eric Burdon*, Dionisio Castello. *Animal Tracks: The Story Of The Animals*, Sean Egan
● FILMS: *Pop Gear* aka *Go Go Mania* (1965), *Tonite Let's All Make Love In London* aka *The London Scene* (1967), *Monterey Pop* (1969), *Comeback* (1982), *The Doors* (1991), *Schee In Der Neujahrsnacht* aka *Snow On New Year's Eve* (1999), *Plaster Caster* (2001).

BURKE, SOLOMON

b. 1936, Philadelphia, Pennsylvania, USA. The former 'Wonder Boy Preacher', Burke's first recordings appeared on the New York-based Apollo label. From 1955-59 he attempted various styles until a brisk rocker, 'Be Bop Grandma', attracted the attention of Atlantic Records. An eclectic performer, his reading of a sentimental country song, 'Just Out Of Reach' (1961), was a US Top 30 hit, but the following year, the 'King of Soul' began asserting a defined soul direction with 'Cry To Me'. Burke's sonorous voice was then heard on a succession of inspired singles, including 'If You Need Me' (1963), 'Goodbye Baby (Baby Goodbye)' and the declamatory 'Everybody Needs Somebody To Love' (both 1964). This exceptional period culminated with

'The Price', an impassioned release that marked the end of Burke's relationship with producer Bert Berns. Although further strong records appeared (indeed, in 1965, 'Got To Get You Off My Mind' became his biggest hit), they lacked the drama of the earlier era. Still based in New York, Burke was now overshadowed by Otis Redding, Sam And Dave and other acts who recorded at Stax Records and Fame. A belated Memphis session did provide a US Top 50 entry in 'Take Me (Just As I Am)', but Burke left Atlantic for Bell Records in 1968. The ensuing album, *Proud Mary*, was a southern soul classic, while the title track, written by John Fogerty, charted as a single in the USA.

The 70s saw a move to MGM Records, but his work there was marred by inconsistency. The same was true of his spells at Dunhill Records and Chess Records, although his collaborations with Swamp Dogg collected on *From The Heart* recalled his old power. Following several strong gospel albums for Savoy, Burke's rebirth continued on *Soul Alive*, where, recorded in concert, he sounded inspired, infusing his 'greatest hits' with a new-found passion. A strong studio collection, *A Change Is Gonna Come*, followed 1987's European tour and displayed Burke's enduring talent. Two albums, *The Best Of Solomon Burke* (1965) and *Cry To Me* (1984), compile his Atlantic singles, while *The Bishop Rides South* (1988) adds four extra tracks to the original *Proud Mary* album. Burke carried on recording during the 90s, releasing several worthy albums.

● ALBUMS: *Solomon Burke* (Apollo 1962) ★★★, *If You Need Me* (Atlantic 1963) ★★★, *Rock 'N' Soul* (Atlantic 1964) ★★★, *I Wish I Knew* (Atlantic 1968) ★★★, *King Solomon* (Atlantic 1968) ★★★, *Proud Mary* (Bell 1969) ★★★★, *Electronic Magnetism* (Polydor 1972) ★★, *King Heavy* (Polydor 1972) ★★, *We're Almost Home* (Polydor 1972) ★★, *I Have A Dream* (Dunhill 1974) ★★, *Midnight And You* (Dunhill 1975) ★★, *Music To Make Love By* (Chess 1975) ★★, *Back To My Roots* (Chess 1977) ★★, *Please Don't You Say Goodbye To Me* (Amherst 1978) ★★★, *Sidewalks Fences & Walls* (Infinity 1979) ★★, *Lord I Need A Miracle Right Now* (Savoy 1981) ★★, *Into My Life You Came* (Savoy 1982) ★★, *Take Me, Shake Me* (Savoy 1983) ★★, *This Is His Song* (Savoy 1984) ★★, *Soul Alive* (Rounder 1984) ★★, *A Change Is Gonna Come* (Rounder 1986) ★★★, *Love Trap* (PolyGram 1987) ★★★, *Home Land* (Bizarre 1991) ★★★, *Soul Of The Blues* (Black Top 1993) ★★★, *Live At The House Of Blues* (Black Top 1994) ★★★, *Definition Of Soul* (Pointblank/Virgin 1997) ★★★.

● COMPILATIONS: *Solomon Burke's Greatest Hits* (Atlantic 1962) ★★★, *The Best Of Solomon Burke* (Atlantic 1965) ★★★★, *King Of Rock 'N' Soul/From The Heart* (Charly 1981) ★★★, *Cry To Me* (Charly 1984) ★★★★, *You Can Run But You Can't Hide* (Mr R&B 1987) ★★★, *Hold On I'm Coming* (Atlantic 1991) ★★★, *Home In Your*

Heart: The Best Of Solomon Burke (Rhino 1992) ★★★★, *Greatest Hits: If You Need Me* (Sequel 1997) ★★★, *The Very Best Of Solomon Burke* (Rhino 1998) ★★★★, *King Of Blues 'n' Soul* (Fuel 2001) ★★★★.

BUTLER, JERRY

b. 8 December 1939, Sunflower, Mississippi, USA. Jerry, older brother of Billy Butler, moved to Chicago as a child and was later part of the city's burgeoning gospel circuit. He subsequently joined several secular groups, including the Roosters, an aspiring trio of Sam Gooden and Richard and Arthur Brooks. Butler then suggested they add his friend, Curtis Mayfield, on guitar. Now called the Impressions, the quintet secured a Top 3 US R&B hit with the haunting 'For Your Precious Love' (1958). However, the label credit, 'Jerry Butler And The Impressions', caused friction within the group. A second single, 'Come Back My Love', was less successful and Butler left for a solo career. His early releases were minor hits until 'He Will Break Your Heart' reached number 1 in the US R&B and number 7 in the pop charts in 1960. The song was written by Mayfield, who also added guitar and sang backing vocals. Their differences clearly resolved, two subsequent hits, 'Find Another Girl' and 'I'm A Telling You' (both 1961), featured the same partnership. Mayfield's involvement lessened as the Impressions' own career developed, but Butler's chart run continued. 'Make It Easy On Yourself' (1962) and 'I Stand Accused' (1964) were among his finest singles. Butler switched to Mercury Records in 1966 where he honed the style that won him his 'Ice Man' epithet. 'Hey Western Union Man' and 'Only The Strong Survive' topped the soul chart in 1968 and 1969, while duets with Gene Chandler and Brenda Lee Eager punctuated his early 70s recordings. With his brother, Billy Butler, he formed the Butler Writers Workshop, which encouraged aspiring songwriters and musicians, among whom were Marvin Yancey and Chuck Jackson of the Independents and Natalie Cole. Butler's releases on Motown Records preceded a more successful spell with Philadelphia International Records, while the 80s and 90s saw his work appear on Fountain and CTI. Since the mid-80s Butler has balanced his music career with his involvement in politics, and is currently an elected official in Chicago.

● ALBUMS: *Jerry Butler Esquire* (Abner 1959) ★★★, *He Will Break Your Heart* (Vee Jay 1960) ★★★, *Love Me* (Vee Jay 1961) ★★, *Aware Of Love* (Vee Jay 1961) ★★★, *Moon River* (Vee Jay 1962) ★★, *Folk Songs* (Vee Jay 1963) ★★, *Need To Belong* (Vee Jay 1964) ★★★, with Betty Everett *Delicious Together* (Vee Jay 1964) ★★★, *Soul Artistry* (Mercury 1967) ★★★, *Mr. Dream Merchant* (Mercury 1967) ★★★, *Jerry Butler's Golden Hits Live* (Mercury 1968) ★★, *Just Beautiful* (Mercury 1968) ★★★, *The Soul Goes On*

Mercury 1968) ★★★, *The Ice Man Cometh* (Mercury 1968) ★★★★, *Ice On Ice* (Mercury 969) ★★★★, *You & Me* (Mercury 1970) ★★★, *Special Memory* (Mercury 1970) ★★★, *Jerry Butler Sings Assorted Sounds By Assorted Friends And Relatives* (Mercury 1971) ★★★, with Gene Chandler *Gene & Jerry - One & One* (Mercury 971) ★★★, *The Sagittarius Movement* (Mercury 971) ★★★, *The Spice Of Life* (Mercury 1972) ★★★, *Melinda* (Mercury 1972) ★★★, *Introducing The Ice Man Band* (Mercury 1972) ★★★, with Brenda Lee Eager *The Love We Have, The Love We Had* (Mercury 1973) ★★★, *The Power Of Love* (Mercury 1973) ★★★, *Sweet Sixteen* (Mercury 974) ★★★, *Love's On The Menu* (Motown 1976) ★★, *Make It Easy On Yourself* (Motown 1976) ★★, *Suite For The Single Girl* (Motown 1977) ★★, with Thelma Houston *Thelma And Jerry* (Motown 1977) ★★, with Houston *Two To One* (Motown 1978) ★★, *It All Comes Out In My Song* (Motown 1978) ★★, *Nothing Says I Love You Like I Love You* (Philadelphia International 1978) ★★, *Best Love I Ever Had* (Philadelphia International 1981) ★★★, *Ice 'N Hot* (Fountain 982) ★★, *Time & Faith* (Fountain 1993) ★★★, *Simply Beautiful* (Valley Vue 1994) ★★★.

COMPILATIONS: *The Best Of Jerry Butler* (Vee Jay 1962) ★★★, *More Of The Best Of Jerry Butler* (Vee Jay 1965) ★★★, *Best Of Jerry Butler* (Mercury 1970) ★★★★, *The Vintage Years* double album shared with the Impressions (Sire 1977) ★★★, *Up On Love* (1980) ★★★, *Only The Strong Survive (The Legendary Philadelphia Hits)* (Mercury 1984) ★★★★, *Whatever You Want* (Charly 1986) ★★★★, *Soul Workshop* (Charly 1986) ★★★★, *The Legendary Philadelphia Hits* (Mercury 1987) ★★★★, *The Best Of Jerry Butler* (Rhino 1987) ★★★, *Iceman: The Mercury Years* (Mercury 1992) ★★★★, *The Best Of Jerry Butler: The Millennium Collection* (Mercury 2000) ★★★, *The Gamble & Huff Sessions* (Mercury 2001) ★★★.

● FURTHER READING: *Only The Strong Survive: Memoirs Of A Soul Survivor*, Jerry Butler with Earl Smith.

BUTTERFIELD, PAUL

b. 17 December 1942, Chicago, Illinois, USA, d. 3 May 1987, Hollywood, California, USA. As a catalyst, Butterfield helped to shape the development of blues music played by white musicians in the same way that John Mayall and Cyril Davies did in the UK. Butterfield had the advantage of performing with Howlin' Wolf, Muddy Waters and his mentor Little Walter. He sang, composed and led a series of seminal bands throughout the 60s, but it was his earthy Chicago-style harmonica-playing that gained him attention. He was arguably the first white man to play blues with the intensity and emotion of the great black blues harmonica players. Mike Bloomfield, Mark Naftalin, Elvin Bishop, David Sanborn and Nick Gravenites were some of the outstanding musicians that

passed through his bands. His now infamous performance at the 1965 Newport Folk Festival gave him the distinction of being the man who supported Bob Dylan's musical heresy by going electric. In 1973, his new venture Better Days went on the road to a lukewarm response, and during subsequent years he struggled to find success. Ill health plagued him for some time, much of it caused by aggravating stomach hernias caused by his powerful harmonica playing. Butterfield's legacy lives on and most of his catalogue is still available. *East-West* remains his bestselling and most acclaimed work, although the rawness of the debut album also attracts many critical admirers. Later work, by comparison, lacked the energy and rawness of the earlier Elektra recordings. His harmonica playing however was highly accomplished.
● ALBUMS: *The Paul Butterfield Blues Band* (Elektra 1965) ★★★★, *East-West* (Elektra 1966) ★★★★, *The Resurrection Of Pigboy Crabshaw* (Elektra 1968) ★★★, *In My Own Dream* (Elektra 1968) ★★★, *Keep On Movin'* (Elektra 1969) ★★, *Live* (Elektra 1971) ★★, *Sometimes I Just Feel Like Smilin'* (Elektra 1971) ★★, as Better Days *It All Comes Back* (Bearsville 1973) ★★, as Better Days *Better Days* (Bearsville 1973) ★★★, *Put It In Your Ear* (Bearsville 1976) ★★, *North South For Bearsville* (Bearsville 1981) ★★, *The Legendary Paul Butterfield Rides Again* (Amherst 1986) ★★★, *Strawberry Jam* (Winner 1995) ★★, *The Original Lost Elektra Sessions* 1964 recordings (Rhino 1995) ★★★, *East-West Live* 1966/67 recordings (Winner 1997) ★★★★.
● COMPILATIONS: *Golden Butter - Best Of The Paul Butterfield Blues Band* (Elektra 1972) ★★★, *An Anthology: The Elektra Years* (Elektra 1998) ★★★★, *Bearsville Anthology* (Essential 2000) ★★.

BYRDS

Originally formed as a trio, the Jet Set, this seminal band featured Jim (Roger) McGuinn (b. James Joseph McGuinn, 13 July 1942, Chicago, Illinois, USA; vocals, lead guitar), Gene Clark (b. Harold Eugene Clark, 17 November 1941, Tipton, Missouri, USA, d. 24 May 1991; vocals, tambourine, rhythm guitar) and David Crosby (b. David Van Cortlandt, 14 August 1941, Los Angeles, California, USA; vocals, rhythm guitar). Essentially ex-folkies caught up in the Beatles craze of 1964, they were signed to a one-off singles contract with Elektra Records that resulted in the commercially unsuccessful 'Please Let Me Love You', released under the pseudonym Beefeaters. By late 1964, the trio had expanded to include former bluegrass player turned bassist Chris Hillman (b. 4 December 1942, Los Angeles, California, USA) and drummer Michael Clarke (b. Michael Dick, 3 June 1944, Spokane, Washington State, USA, d. 19 December 1993, Treasure Island, Florida, USA). Under the supervision of manager/producer Jim Dickson, they recorded at

Hollywood's World Pacific studios, slowly and painfully perfecting their unique brand of folk rock. In November 1964, they signed to CBS Records as the Byrds, and were placed in the hands of producer Terry Melcher (b. 8 February 1942, New York City, New York, USA).

Their debut single, 'Mr Tambourine Man', was a glorious creation, fusing the lyrical genius of Bob Dylan with the harmonic and melodic ingenuity of the Beatles (McGuinn later described his vocal on the disc as a cross between that of John Lennon and Bob Dylan). The opening guitar sound of a Rickenbacker 12-string is one that has been linked to the Byrds and McGuinn ever since. By the summer of 1965, the single had topped both the US and UK charts and the Byrds found themselves fêted as teen-idols. They fulfilled this image with their immaculately groomed fringed haircuts and pop trappings, including Crosby's green suede cape and McGuinn's rectangular, tinted granny-glasses. To coincide with their UK success, a tour was hastily arranged on which they were promoted as 'America's Answer To The Beatles'. This presumptuous and premature labelling backfired and during their exhausting visit they fell victim to over-expectant fans and tetchy critics. To make matters worse, their second single, 'All I Really Want To Do', suffered split sales due to an opportunistic cover version from folk rock rival Cher. The band's management attempted to compensate for this setback by simultaneously promoting the b-side, 'Feel A Whole Lot Better', a stunning slice of cynical romanticism that swiftly became a stage favourite.

The Byrds' debut album, *Mr Tambourine Man*, was a surprisingly solid work that featured four Dylan cover versions, a striking rearrangement of Pete Seeger's 'Bells Of Rhymney' and some exceptionally strong torch songs from Clark, including 'I Knew I'd Want You', 'Here Without You' and 'You Won't Have To Cry'. There was even a strange reworking of the wartime favourite 'We'll Meet Again', which ended the album on a bizarre yet amusing note. After returning to the USA, the Byrds spent months in the studio before releasing their third single, the biblically inspired 'Turn! Turn! Turn!', which gave them another US number 1. The album of the same name again showed the prolific Gene Clark in the ascendant with the charming 'The World Turns All Around Her' and the densely worded 'Set You Free This Time', their most sophisticated lyric to date and arguably their definitive self-penned folk rock statement. McGuinn's presence was also felt on the driving 'It Won't Be Wrong' and elegiac 'He Was A Friend Of Mine', with lyrics pertaining to the Kennedy assassination. An odd tribute to Stephen Foster closed the album in the form of the sarcastic 'Oh! Susannah'.

By early 1966, the band had parted from producer Melcher and branched out from their stylized folk rock repertoire to embrace raga and jazz. The awesome 'Eight Miles High', with its John Coltrane-inspired lead break and enigmatic lyrics, effectively elevated them to the artistic level of the Beatles and the Rolling Stones, but their chart rewards were severely qualified by a radio ban based on spurious allegations that their latest hit was a 'drugs song'. In fact, the lyric had been written following their visit to England and the unusual imagery was based on their sense of culture shock. The b-side of the disc, 'Why', included some raga-like guitar work from McGuinn, and during a press conference of the period, they were pictured studiously playing a sitar, although none of them had mastered the instrument. The setback over the banning of 'Eight Miles High' was worsened by the abrupt departure of leading songwriter Clark, whose fear of flying and distaste for life on the road had proved intolerable burdens. Continuing as a quartet, the Byrds recorded *Fifth Dimension*, a clever amalgam of hard, psychedelic-tinged pop ('I See You' and 'What's Happening?!?!') and rich, folk rock orchestration ('Wild Mountain Thyme' and 'John Riley'). Their chart fortunes were already waning by this time and neither the quizzically philosophical '5-D (Fifth Dimension)' nor the catchy 'Mr Spaceman' made much impression on the charts. The Byrds, rather than promoting their latest album with endless tours, became more insular and were the subject of speculation that they were on the point of breaking up.

The pivotal year in their career proved to be 1967, commencing with the hit single 'So You Want To Be A Rock 'N' Roll Star', an acerbic observation on the manufacturing of pop stars complete with taped screams from their ill-fated UK tour and a guest appearance from Hugh Masekela on trumpet. Its b-side, 'Everybody's Been Burned', displayed Crosby's songwriting and vocal sensitivity with an exceptionally strong guitar solo from McGuinn and some stupendous jazz-inspired bass work from Hillman. Their fourth album, *Younger Than Yesterday*, proved their best yet, ably capturing the diverse songwriting skills of Crosby McGuinn and Hillman and ranging in material from the raga-tinged 'Mind Gardens' to the country-influenced 'Time Between', the quirky space rock of 'CTA 102' and even an ironically retrospective Dylan cover version, 'My Back Pages'. Their creative ascendancy coincided with intense inter-group rivalry, culminating in the dismissal of the ever-controversial David Crosby, who would later re-emerge as part of the hugely successful Crosby, Stills And Nash. A Crosby told Johnny Rogan: 'They came zooming up my driveway in their Porsches and said that was impossible to work with and I wasn't very good anyway and they'd do much better without me. It hurt like hell and I just said "it's shameful waste, goodbye".' The remaining Byrds meanwhile, recruited former colleague Gene

ark, who lasted a mere three weeks before his
rophobia once more took its toll. Drummer
ichael Clarke was dismissed from the line-up
on afterwards, leaving McGuinn and Hillman
assemble *The Notorious Byrd Brothers*, a classic
ample of artistic endeavour overcoming
lversity. For this album, the Byrds used
cording studio facilities to remarkable effect,
nploying phasing, close microphone
chnique and various sonic experiments to
hieve the sound they desired. Producer Gary
sher, who worked on this and their previous
bum, contributed significantly towards their
cension as one of rock's most adventurous and
novative bands. Once again, however, it was
e songs rather than the studio gimmickry that
ost impressed. Successful readings of Gerry
offin and Carole King's 'Goin' Back' and 'Wasn't
orn To Follow' were placed alongside Byrds
iginals such as 'Change Is Now', 'Dolphin's
nile', 'Tribal Gathering' and 'Draft Morning'.
early 1968, Hillman's cousin Kevin Kelley
ok over on drums and the talented Gram
arsons (b. Ingram Cecil Connor III, 5
ovember 1946, Winter Haven, Florida, USA, d.
September 1973, Joshua Tree, California,
SA) added musical weight as singer, composer
d guitarist. Under Parsons' guidance, the band
unged headlong into country, recording the
uch-acclaimed *Sweetheart Of The Rodeo*. A
rfectly timed reaction to the psychedelic
cesses of 1967, the album predated Dylan's
ashville Skyline by a year and is generally
cepted as the harbinger of country rock.
though Parsons directed the work and
cluded one of his best compositions, 'Hickory
ind', his lead vocals on such country standards
'You Don't Miss Your Water' and 'You're Still
My Mind' were replaced by those of
cGuinn due to contractual complications. It
s not until 1990 that the public heard the
ugh original vocals, which were incorporated
to a retrospective boxed set package. McGuinn
-established the Bob Dylan links on *Sweetheart*
The Rodeo by featuring two songs from the
en unreleased *The Basement Tapes*, 'You Ain't
in' Nowhere' and 'Nothing Was Delivered'.
e critical plaudits heaped upon the Byrds
ere not translated into sales, however, and
rther conflict ensued when Gram Parsons
amatically resigned on the eve of their ill-
vised tour of South Africa in the summer of
68.
om 1965-68, the Byrds had produced some of
e greatest and most memorable work ever
corded in the history of popular music. Their
markable ability to ride trends and incorporate
listically diverse material ranging from folk
d country to raga, jazz and space rock
monstrated a profound vision and a wondrous
irit of adventure and innovation that few of
eir contemporaries could dream of, let alone
atch. Their work from this period still sounds
sh and contemporary, which is a testament to

their pioneering worth. Their achievement is all
the more remarkable given the loss of several
key personnel over the years. Rather than
destroying the Byrds, their frequent and often
inflammatory internal acrimony served as a
creative catalyst, prompting a combative and
proprietorial sense that resulted in some of the
era's most spectacular recordings. Among their
contemporaries only the Beatles could boast a
body of work of such consistency, and the Byrds
were probably unmatched in terms of musical
diversity and eclecticism.

Late 1968 saw them at their lowest ebb, with
Hillman quitting after a dispute with their new
manager Larry Spector. The embittered bassist
soon reunited with the errant Parsons in the
Flying Burrito Brothers. McGuinn, meanwhile,
assumed total control of the Byrds and
assembled an entirely new line-up featuring
Clarence White (b. 7 June 1944, Lewiston,
Maine, USA, d. 14 July 1973; vocals, guitar),
John York (vocals, bass) and Gene Parsons (b.
Eugene Victor Parsons, 4 September 1944, Los
Angeles, California, USA; vocals, drums). This
new phase began promisingly enough with the
single 'Bad Night At The Whiskey', backed by the
McGuinn/Gram Parsons song 'Drug Store Truck
Driving Man'. York lasted long enough to
contribute to two albums, *Dr Byrds & Mr Hyde*
and *Ballad Of Easy Rider*, before being replaced
by journeyman Skip Battin (b. Clyde Battin, 2
February 1934, Galipolis, Ohio, USA). This
unlikely but stable line-up lasted from 1969-72
and re-established the Byrds' reputation with the
hit single 'Chestnut Mare' and the bestselling
album *(Untitled)*. The latter, a two-disc set,
demonstrated just what an excellent live
attraction they had become. McGuinn was given
freedom to expand three-minute songs into sets
that began to resemble the Grateful Dead. Battin
stretched out with bass solos, and White grew in
stature as an exemplary lead guitarist. Regular
concert appearances brought the Byrds a strong
groundswell support, but the quality of their
early 70s output lacked consistency. McGuinn
often took a back seat and his familiar nasal
whine was replaced with inferior vocals from
the other members.

After three successive albums with their first
producer Melcher, they again severed their
connections with him owing to his decision to
include orchestration on *Byrdmaniax*. The Byrds
hurriedly attempted to record a compensatory
work, *Farther Along*, but it only served to
emphasize their disunity. On this final album
some of their worst efforts appeared; even the
dreadful 'B.B. Class Road' was beaten by a song
that tops the poll as the worst Byrds song ever
committed to record, the unbelievably bad
'America's Great National Pastime'. This nadir
was briefly improved by two songs, 'Tiffany
Queen' and White's poignant vocal on 'Buglar'.
McGuinn eventually elected to dissolve the band
after agreeing to participate in a recorded

reunion of the original Byrds for Asylum Records. Released in 1973, *Byrds* received mixed reviews, prompting the band members to revert to their various solo/offshoot ventures. On this perplexing release they attempted Neil Young's 'Cowgirl In The Sand' and Joni Mitchell's 'For Free'. That same year tragedy struck when ex-Byrd Clarence White was killed by a drunken driver. Less than three months later, Gram Parsons died from a drug overdose.

The Byrds' legacy has continued in a host of new acts who either borrowed their Rickenbacker sound or traded off their folk/country roots (Tom Petty in particular). The individual members later featured in a host of offshoot groups such as Dillard And Clark, various permutations of the Flying Burrito Brothers, Manassas, Souther Hillman Furay and, of course, Crosby, Stills, Nash And Young. Ironically, the ex-Byrds (with the exception of Crosby) failed to exploit their superstar potential, even after reuniting as McGuinn, Clark And Hillman. By the 80s, the individual members were either recording for small labels or touring without a record contract. Crosby, meanwhile, had plummeted into a narcotic netherworld of free-base cocaine addiction, and, after several seizures and arrests, was confined to prison. He emerged reformed, corpulent and enthusiastic, and amid a flurry of activity set about resurrecting the Byrds moniker with McGuinn and Hillman. Crosby, for once humble, acknowledged in interviews that 'McGuinn was, is and will always be the very heart of the Byrds', and added that no reunion was possible without his participation. An acrimonious lawsuit with Michael Clarke ended with the drummer assuming the right to the group name. Although a proposed five-way reunion of the Byrds for a live album and world tour was mooted, the old conflicts frustrated its immediate fruition. However, McGuinn, Crosby and Hillman completed four songs in Nashville during August 1990 which were subsequently included on a boxed set featuring 90 songs. The nearest that the Byrds came to a full reunion was when they were each inducted into the Rock And Roll Hall Of Fame in January 1991. The chance of playing together again finally elapsed with the death of Gene Clark later that year and Michael Clarke in 1993.

By the mid-90s the Byrds were acknowledged as one of the most influential bands of the rock era, and, like the Beatles, little of their catalogue sounds dated. This was confirmed in 1996/7 when the first eight albums were expertly remastered and reissued with bonus tracks that had previously only been heard by the Byrds' serious followers. Albums such as *The Notorious Byrd Brothers* and *Younger Than Yesterday* are certified classics, and much of their earlier catalogue is indispensable. McGuinn continues to tour small venues with his Rickenbacker and Martin 12-string acoustic, happy to reprise 'Mr

Tambourine Man' and his devastating solo on 'Eight Miles High'. Crosby has a new kidney and a new baby and the rounder he gets, the sweeter his voice becomes. Hillman is producing some excellent bluegrass with Larry Rice and Herb Pedersen. It is sad that the late Gene Clark, the Byrd's prolific songwriter, is only now receiving universal acclaim. His song 'Feel A Whole Lot Better' is recognized as a classic of the 60s; ironic that it only appeared as a b-side in 1965.

● ALBUMS: *Mr Tambourine Man* (Columbia 1965) ★★★★, *Turn! Turn! Turn!* (Columbia 1965) ★★★★, *Fifth Dimension* (Columbia 1966) ★★★★, *Younger Than Yesterday* (Columbia 1967) ★★★★★, *The Notorious Byrd Brothers* (Columbia 1968) ★★★★★, *Sweetheart Of The Rodeo* (Columbia 1968) ★★★★, *Dr Byrds & Mr Hyde* (Columbia 1969) ★★★, *Ballad Of Easy Rider* (Columbia 1969) ★★★, *The Byrds (Untitled)* (Columbia 1970) ★★★★, *Byrdmaniax* (Columbia 1971) ★★, *Farther Along* (Columbia 1972) ★, *Byrds* (Asylum 1973) ★★★, *Live At The Fillmore February 1969* (Columbia/Legacy 2000) ★★★.
● COMPILATIONS: *Greatest Hits* (Columbia 1967) ★★★★, *Preflyte* (Together 1969) ★★, *Greatest Hits, Volume II* (Columbia 1971) ★★★, *History Of The Byrds* (Columbia 1973) ★★★★, *The Byrds Play Dylan* (Columbia 1979) ★★★, *The Original Singles* (Columbia 1980) ★★★★, *The Original Singles, Volume II* (Columbia 1982) ★★★, *Never Before* (Murray Hill 1989) ★★★, *In The Beginning* (Rhino 1989) ★★★, *The Byrd Collection* (Castle 1989) ★★★, *The Byrds* 4-CD box set (Columbia/Legacy 1990) ★★★★, *20 Essential Tracks* (Columbia 1993) ★★★★, *The Very Best Of The Byrds* (Columbia 1997) ★★★★, *Sanctuary* (Sundazed 2000) ★★★, *Sanctuary II* (Sundazed 2000) ★★★, *Sanctuary III* (Sundazed 2001) ★★★, *The Preflyte Sessions* (Sundazed 2001) ★★★.
● FURTHER READING: *The Byrds*, Bud Scoppa. *Timeless Flight: The Definitive Biography Of The Byrds*, Johnny Rogan. *Timeless Flight Revisited: The Sequel*, Johnny Rogan.

BYSTANDERS

Formed in Merthyr Tydfil, Mid-Glamorgan, Wales, in 1962, the Bystanders initially comprised Lynn Mittell (vocals), Mickey Jones (b. Mike Jones, 7 June 1946, Merthyr Tydfil, Mid-Glamorgan, Wales; guitar), Clive John (organ), Ray Williams (bass) and Jeff Jones (drums), but Mittell was later replaced by Vic Oakley. The band became a fixture on the small but thriving, Welsh club circuit and their debut release, 'That's The End' (1965), was issued on a Swansea-based independent label. This promising single engendered a contract with Pye Records/Piccadilly. An excellent and versatile harmony act, the Bystanders' career was plagued by misfortune. Although their attractive reading of '98.6' was a minor hit in February 1967, it was outstripped by Keith's original version, while the following year the quintet's haunting ballad, 'When Jesamine Goes', flopped. The song was then recorded by the Casuals, and, as 'Jesamine', it reached number 2 in the UK and enjoyed massive success in Europe. However, the Bystanders were growing increasingly tired of their pop image, and experimented with more imaginative original material on their b-sides. Oakley left the band in 1968, unsettled by this new direction, and was replaced by Deke Leonard (b. Roger Leonard, Wales), from fellow Welsh band the Dream. The reconstituted quintet then embraced progressive rock under a new name, Man.

● COMPILATIONS: *Birth Of Man* (See For Miles 1990) ★★★, *Pattern People: The Pye Anthology* (Castle 2001) ★★★.

C

C., ROY

b. Roy Charles Hammond, 1943, New York City, New York, USA. A member of the Genies, with whom he recorded for several labels, Roy C's most enduring moment came with 'Shotgun Wedding' (1965). A US R&B Top 20 hit, it proved even more popular in the UK, reaching number 6 the following year, and made the Top 10 again in 1972. The singer later recorded, without success, for Black Hawk and Shout, but 'Got To Get Enough (Of Your Sweet Love Stuff)' was a soul hit in 1971. Released on C's own Alaga label, he subsequently secured further success on Mercury Records. He also wrote 'Honey I Still Love You', a 1972 bestseller for the Mark IV.

● ALBUMS: *Sex And Soul* (1973) ★★★, *More Sex And Soul* (1977) ★★.

CADETS

The Cadets were one of the more colourful Irish showbands of the early to mid-60s. The original line-up comprised Eileen Reid (vocals), Patrick Murphy (harmonica), Jas Fagan (trombone), Paddy Burns (vocals, trumpet), Gerry Hayes (piano), Brendan O'Connell (lead guitar), Jimmy Day (tenor saxophone, guitar) and Willie Devey (drums). The band played the usual showband fare of C&W and cover hits, but gained considerable attention for their fancy naval-inspired uniforms and exotic lead vocalist. Eileen Reid, with her enormous beehive haircut, was an instant hit with audiences, and before long the Cadets were attracting record company interest. After a false start with 'Hello Trouble' on Decca, they switched to Pye Records and were soon number 1 in Eire with their version of Jim Reeves' 'Fallen Star'. During this period, they also toured America and appeared on the UK television show *Thank Your Lucky Stars*. They were even given their own show on Radio Eireann, *Carnival Time With The Cadets*. In late 1964, they charted with their most famous song, 'I Gave My Wedding Dress Away'. For this melancholic C&W ballad Reid regularly appeared onstage dressed in a wedding dress, which caused a minor sensation at the time. The Cadets continued to tour the showband circuit and notched up an impressive run of hits including 'Right Or Wrong', 'If I Had My Life To Live Over', 'More Than Yesterday', 'At The Close Of A Long Day' and 'Land Of Gingerbread'. The group split in 1970, just before the showband scene went into a sharp decline.

● ALBUMS: *The Cadets* (Pye 1966) ★★★.

CAIOLA, AL

b. Alexander Emil Caiola, 7 September 1920, Jersey City, New Jersey, USA. A highly respected studio guitarist, Caiola played with many renowned musical directors such as Percy Faith, Hugo Winterhalter and Andre Kostelanetz. After serving as musical arranger and conductor for United Artists Records, Caiola released several singles on RCA during the 50s, including 'Delicado', a Brazilian song written by Walter Azevedo, which became a hit for Percy Faith, Stan Kenton, Ralph Flanagan and Dinah Shore. Caiola also released *Serenade In Blue* and *Deep In A Dream*, recorded by his Quintet. In 1961 he entered the US Top 40 charts with the movie theme *The Magnificent Seven* and *Bonanza*, the title music from the popular western television series; he had his own television show for a short time in the USA.

● ALBUMS: *Deep In A Dream* (Savoy/London 1955) ★★, *Serenade In Blue* (Savoy/London 1956) ★★★, *High Strung* (RCA Victor 1959) ★★★, *Music For Space Squirrels* (Atco 1960) ★★, with Don Arnone *Great Pickin'* (Chancellor 1960) ★★★, *Salute Italia* (Roulette 1960) ★★, *Percussion Espanol* (Time 1960) ★★★, *Spanish Guitars* (Time 1960) ★★★, *Gershwin And Guitars* (Time 1961) ★★★, *Soft Guitars* (1962) ★★★, *Guitar Of Plenty* (1962) ★★★, *Cleopatra And All That Jazz* (United Artists 1963) ★★★, *Tough Guitar* (United Artists 1964) ★★, *Music To Read James Bond By* (1965) ★★★, *Sounds For Spies And Private Eyes* (United Artists 1965) ★★★.

● COMPILATIONS: *Italian Gold: Treasured Collection* (Alanna 2000) ★★★, *Encore Oro Italiano* (Alanna 2001) ★★★, *Guitar For Latin Lovers* (Alanna 2001) ★★★.

CAMPBELL, ALEX

b. 1923 (or 1928), d. January 1987, Denmark. Campbell, nicknamed 'Big Daddy', and 'Le Cowboy d'Ecosse' in Europe, learned his trade by busking in London and Paris. Although he was not a 'technical' folk-singer, he sang from experience and with feeling. He built up a strong European following, and consequently worked extensively in Scandinavia and Germany, establishing himself as one of the leading figures in the European folksong revival. Campbell is believed to have recorded over 100 albums, and one of his early songs, 'Been On The Road Too Long', is regarded by many as a classic. Several of his recordings are still used for guitar tuition. Standouts among the many songs Campbell covered during his long recording career included Eric Bogle's 'And The Band Played Waltzing Matilda', Tom Rush's 'No Regrets', and Allan Taylor's 'Old Joe'. Campbell was renowned for his drinking habits, which contributed to his death in 1987, although since the early 80s throat cancer had curtailed his performing career.

● ALBUMS: *Chansons Populaires Des Etats-Unis* (1958) ★★★, *Chansons Populaires Des Etats-Unis 2* (1958) ★★, *Bahama's Songs* (1958) ★★★, *La Contrescarpe* (1958) ★★★, *American's Square Dance* (1959) ★★★★, *Let's Sing While We Work And Play* (1960) ★★★, *Songs And Stories Of The West* (1960) ★★★★, *Let's Listen And Sing To American Folksongs* (1960) ★★★, *Let's Visit Great Britain* (1960) ★★★★, *Way Out West With Alex Campbell* (Society 1963) ★★★, *Alex Campbell Sings Folk* (Society 1964) ★★★★, *My Old Gibson Guitar* (Transatlantic 1964) ★★★★, *Alex Campbell* (Transatlantic 1965) ★★★★, *Alex Campbell In Copenhagen* (Storyville 1965) ★★, *Yours Aye, Alex* (1966) ★★★, *Alex Campbell And His Friends* (Saga 1967) ★★★, *Alex Campbell Live* (1968) ★★★, *The Scottish Breakaway* (Hallmark 1968) ★★★, *This Is Alex Campbell 1* (Ad-Rhythm-Tepee 1971) ★★★★, *This Is Alex Campbell 2* (Ad-Rhythm-Tepee 1971) ★★★★, *Life Is Just That Way* (1972) ★★★, *Alex Campbell At His Best* (Boulevard 1972) ★★★★, *Goodbye Booze* (Scan 1976) ★★★, *Big Daddy Of Folk Music* (Antagon 1976) ★★★, *No Regrets* (Golcar 1976) ★★★★, *Traditional Ballads Of Scotland* (Sweet Folk All 1977) ★★★, with Dougie MacLean, Alan Roberts *CRM* (Burlington 1979) ★★★, *Dt Er Godt At Se Dig* (1979) ★★★, *Live And Studio* (Happy Bird 1979) ★★.

● COMPILATIONS: *Alex Campbell Sampler* (Transatlantic 1969) ★★★★, *With The Greatest Respect* (Sundown 1987) ★★★★.

CAMPBELL, IAN, FOLK GROUP

This highly respected UK folk group was formed in Birmingham, West Midlands, in 1956, originally as the Clarion Skiffle Group. Campbell had moved with his parents from his hometown of Aberdeen, Scotland, to Birmingham in 1946. The original line-up comprised Campbell (b. 10 June 1933, Aberdeen, Scotland; guitar, vocals), his sister Lorna Campbell (b. Aberdeen, Scotland; vocals), Dave Phillips (guitar) and Gordon McCulloch (banjo). In 1958, they became the Ian Campbell Folk Group, but McCulloch departed the following year and was replaced by John Dunkerley (b. 1942; d. 1977; banjo, guitar, accordion). In 1960, Dave Swarbrick (b. 5 April 1941, New Malden, Surrey, England; fiddle, mandola) joined the group. Issued in 1962, *Ceilidh At The Crown* was the first ever live folk club recording to be released on vinyl. In 1963, the group signed to Transatlantic Records and Brian Clark (guitar, vocals) joined the line-up as a replacement for Phillips. Clark also became a long-term member, staying until 1978.

During the early 60s, the group appeared on television programmes such as the *Hootenanny Show*, *Barn Dance* and *Hullabaloo*. In addition, they regularly played to full houses in concert at venues such as the Royal Albert Hall, and the Royal Festival Hall in London. In 1964, they were invited to perform at the Newport Folk Festival in the USA, and in 1965, they became the first non-US group to record a Bob Dylan song; their cover version of 'The Times They Are A-Changin'' reached the UK Top 50 in March 1965. The group added bass player Mansell Davies in 1966, but he emigrated to Canada three years later, and later became an organizer of Canadian festivals such as Calgary. After Swarbrick's departure in 1966, the group worked with George Watts (flute), who appeared on only two albums, *New Impressions Of The Ian Campbell Folk Group* and *The Ian Campbell Folk Group*, the latter recorded in Czechoslovakia. Unfortunately, due to the prevailing political climate of the time, the record was never released outside the country, and the group did not receive royalties. Watts left in 1968, but a year earlier the group took on bassist Dave Pegg (b. 2 November 1947, Birmingham, England), who remained with them for three years before joining Fairport Convention.

In 1969, Andy Smith (banjo, mandolin, guitar, fiddle) joined, leaving in 1971. That same year, Mike Hadley (bass) joined the ever-changing line-up, leaving in 1974. In 1976, Campbell wrote the 12-song suite *Adam's Rib* for his sister Lorna; the songs dealt with the different crisis points in a woman's life. By now, John Dunkerley had left the group owing to ill health, and died in 1977 from Hodgkinson's disease, aged just 34. The group disbanded in 1978, with Campbell having taken a place at university as a mature student. As the group still had bookings to honour, various session players were recruited for live performances, including Aiden Ford (banjo, mandola), Colin Tommis (guitar) and Neil Cox (guitar). Many of Ian Campbell's songs are often thought of as traditional, but those such as 'The Sun Is Burning' have been covered by countless others, including Simon And Garfunkel.

● ALBUMS: *Ceilidh At The Crown* mini-album (Topic 1962) ★★★, *This Is The Ian Campbell Folk Group* aka *Presenting The Ian Campbell Folk Group* (Transatlantic 1963) ★★★, *Across The Hills* (Transatlantic 1964) ★★★, *Coaldust Ballads* (Transatlantic 1965) ★★★, *Contemporary Campbells* (Transatlantic 1966) ★★, *New Impressions Of The Ian Campbell Folk Group* (Transatlantic 1966) ★★★, as The Ian Campbell Group *The Circle Game* (Transatlantic 1967) ★★★, *Ian Campbell/Ian Campbell Folk Group/ Dave Swarbrick* (MFP 1969) ★★★, *The Sun Is Burning: The Songs Of Ian Campbell* (Argo 1971) ★★★, *Something To Sing About* (Pye 1972) ★★★, *The Ian Campbell Folk Group Live* (Pye 1974) ★★.

● COMPILATIONS: *The Ian Campbell Group Sampler* (Transatlantic 1969) ★★★★, *The Ian Campbell Group Sampler, Vol. 2* (Transatlantic 1969) ★★★, *And Another Thing* (Celtic Music 1994) ★★★.

CANNED HEAT

This popular, but ill-fated, blues/rock band was formed in 1965 by two Los Angeles-based blues aficionados: Alan Wilson (b. 4 July 1943, Boston, Massachusetts, USA, d. 3 September 1970, USA; vocals, harmonica, guitar) and Bob 'The Bear' Hite (b. 26 February 1943, Torrance, California, USA, d. 5 April 1981, Paris, France; vocals). Wilson, nicknamed 'Blind Owl' in deference to his thick-lens spectacles, was already renowned for his distinctive harmonica work and had accompanied Son House on the veteran bluesman's post-'rediscovery' album, *Father Of Folk Blues*. Wilson's obsession with the blues enabled him to build up a massive archive blues collection by his early 20s. The duo was joined by Frank Cook (drums) and Henry Vestine (b. 25 December 1944, Washington, DC, USA, d. December 1997, Paris, France; guitar), a former member of the Mothers Of Invention. They took the name Canned Heat from a 1928 recording by Tommy Johnson and employed several bassists prior to the arrival of Larry Taylor, an experienced session musician who had worked with Jerry Lee Lewis and the Monkees.

Canned Heat's debut album was promising rather than inspired, offering diligent readings of such 12-bar standards as 'Rollin' And Tumblin'', 'Dust My Broom' and 'Bullfrog Blues'. However, the arrival of new drummer Alfredo Fito (b. Adolfo De La Parra, 8 February 1946, Mexico City, Mexico) coincided with a new found confidence, displayed almost immediately on *Boogie With Canned Heat*. This impressive selection introduced the extended 'Fried Hookey Boogie', a piece destined to become an in-concert favourite, and the hypnotic remake of Jim Oden's 'On The Road Again', which gave the band a UK Top 10 and US Top 20 hit single in 1968. Wilson's distinctive frail, high voice, sitar-like guitar introduction and accompanying harmonica have made this version a classic. A double set, *Livin' The Blues*, includes an enthralling version of Charley Patton's 'Pony Blues' and a 19-minute *tour de force*, 'Parthenogenesis', which captures the quintet at their most experimental. However, it was Wilson's adaptation of a Henry Thomas song, 'Bulldoze Blues', that proved most popular. The singer retained the tune of the original, rewrote the lyric and emerged with 'Goin' Up The Country', whose simple message caught the prevalent back-to-nature attitude of the late 60s. This evocative performance charted in the US and UK Top 20, and was one of the highlights of the successful *Woodstock* movie.

In 1969 and 1970 Canned Heat recorded four more albums, including a spirited collaboration with blues boogie mentor John Lee Hooker, and a fascinating documentary of their 1970 European tour. *Hallelujah* boasted one of artist George Hunter's finest album covers. *Future Blues* marked the arrival of guitarist Harvey Mandel, replacing Vestine, who could no longer tolerate working with Taylor. The reshaped band enjoyed two further UK hits with a cover version of Wilbert Harrison's 'Let's Work Together', which reached number 2, and the Cajun-inspired 'Sugar Bee', but they were then shattered by the suicide of Wilson, whose body was found in Hite's backyard on 3 September 1970. His death sparked a major reconstruction within the band: Taylor and Mandel left to join John Mayall, the former's departure prompting Vestine's return, while Antonio De La Barreda became Canned Heat's new bassist. The new quartet completed *Historical Figures & Ancient Heads*, before Hite's brother Richard replaced Barreda for the band's 1973 release, *The New Age*. The changes continued throughout the decade, undermining the band's strength of purpose. Bob Hite, the sole remaining original member, attempted to keep the band afloat, but was unable to secure a permanent recording contract. Spirits lifted with the release of *Human Condition*, but the years of struggle had taken their toll. On 5 April 1981, following a gig at the Palomino Club, the gargantuan vocalist collapsed and died of a heart attack.

Despite the loss of many key members, the Canned Heat name has survived. Inheritors Larry Taylor and Fito de la Parra completed 1989's *Reheated* album with two new members, James Thornbury (vocals) and Junior Watson (guitar). They now pursue the lucrative nostalgia circuit with various former members coming and going as their health allows. Vestine died in 1997, and Taylor now has a heart condition. Greg Kage (bass) and Robert Lucas (vocals) joined de la Parra and Taylor on 1999's *Boogie 2000*.

● ALBUMS: *Canned Heat* (Liberty 1967) ★★★, *Livin' The Blues* (Liberty 1968) ★★★, *Boogie With Canned Heat* (Liberty 1968) ★★★, *Hallelujah* (Liberty 1968) ★★★★, *Live In Europe* (Liberty 1970) ★★, *Live At Topanga Canyon* (Wand 1970) ★★★, *Future Blues* (Liberty 1970) ★★★, with Memphis Slim *Memphis Heat* (Barclay 1971) ★★★, with John Lee Hooker *Hooker 'N' Heat* (Liberty 1971) ★★★, *Historical Figures & Ancient Heads* (United Artists 1972) ★★★, with Clarence 'Gatemouth' Brown *Gate's On Heat* (Barclay 1973) ★★★, *New Age* (United Artists 1973) ★★, *One More River To Cross* (Atlantic 1974) ★★, *Live At The Topanga Corral* (Wand/DJM 1976) ★★★, *The Human Condition* (Takoma 1978) ★★, with John Lee Hooker *Hooker 'N' Heat – Live* (Rhino 1981) ★★★, *Kings Of The Boogie* (Destiny 1982) ★★, *The Boogie Assault: Live In Australia* (Bedrock 1987) ★★★, *Reheated* (SPV/Chameleon 1988) ★★, *Live At The Turku Rock Festival* (Bear Family 1990) ★★, *Internal Combustion* (River Road 1994) ★★, *In Concert* 1979 recording (King Biscuit Flower Hour 1995) ★★★, *Blues Band* (Mystic 1997) ★★, *The Ties That Bind* 1974 recording (Navarre/Archive 1997) ★★, *Canned Heat Live At The King Biscuit Flower Hour* 1979 recording (King Biscuit 1998) ★★, *Canned Heat Blues Band* (Ruf/Mystic 1997) ★★★, *Boogie 2000* (Ruf/Platinum 1999) ★★, *Live At The Kaleidoscope 1969* (Varèse Sarabande 2000) ★★.

● COMPILATIONS: *Canned Heat Cookbook (The Best Of Canned Heat)* (Liberty 1969) ★★★, *Vintage* (Janus 1970) ★★, *Collage* (Sunset 1971) ★★★, *The Best Of Canned Heat* (EMI 1972) ★★★, *The Very Best Of Canned Heat* (United Artists 1973) ★★★, with John Lee Hooker *Infinite Boogie* (Rhino 1986) ★★★, with John Lee Hooker *Hooker 'N' Heat Volume 2* (Rhino 1988) ★★, *The Best Of Hooker 'N' Heat* (See For Miles 1988) ★★★, *Let's Work Together: The Best Of Canned Heat* (Liberty 1989) ★★★, *Uncanned! The Best Of Canned Heat* (Liberty 1994) ★★★★, *1967-1976: The Boogie House Tapes* (Ruf 2000) ★★★.

● VIDEOS: *Canned Heat – Boogie Assault* (Video Music 1984).

● FURTHER READING: *Living The Blues: Canned Heat's Story Of Music, Drugs, Death, Sex And Survival*, Fito de la Parra with T.W. and Marlene McGarry.

CANNON, FREDDY

b. Freddy Picariello, 4 December 1940, Lynn, Massachusetts, USA. A frantic and enthusiastic vocalist, known as the 'last rock 'n' roll star', Cannon was the link between wild rock 'n' roll and the softer Philadelphia-based sounds that succeeded it. The son of a dance-band leader, he fronted Freddy Karmon And The Hurricanes and played guitar on sessions for the G-Clefs. He was spotted by Boston disc jockey Jack McDermott, who gave a song that Freddy and his mother had written, entitled 'Rock 'N' Roll Baby', to top writing and production team Bob Crewe and Frank Slay; they improved the song, retitled it 'Tallahassee Lassie', and renamed him Freddy Cannon. The record was released in 1959 on Swan, a label part-owned by Dick Clark, who often featured Cannon on his US *Bandstand* television programme and road shows. The single was the first of 21 US hits that 'Boom Boom' (as the ex-truck driver was known) enjoyed over the next seven years. He had five US and four UK Top 20 singles, the biggest being his revival of 'Way Down Yonder In New Orleans' in 1959, and 'Palisades Park', written by television personality Chuck Barris, in 1962. His only successful album was *The Explosive! Freddy Cannon* in 1960, which made history as the first rock album to top the UK charts. During his long career, Cannon also recorded with Warner Brothers Records, Buddah Records, Claridge (where he revived his two biggest hits), We Make Rock 'N' Roll Records, Royal American, MCA, Metromedia and Sire Records. He returned briefly to the charts in 1981 in the company of Dion's old group, the Belmonts, with a title that epitomized his work: 'Let's Put The Fun Back Into Rock 'N' Roll'.

● ALBUMS: *The Explosive! Freddy Cannon* (Swan/Top Rank 1960) ★★★★, *Happy Shades Of Blue* (Swan 1960) ★★★, *Freddy Cannon's Solid Gold Hits* (Swan 1961) ★★★, *Twistin' All Night Long* (Swan 1961) ★★★, *Freddy Cannon At*

Palisades Park (Swan 1962) ★★★, *Freddy Cannon Steps Out* (Swan 1963) ★★, *Freddy Cannon* (Warners 1964) ★★, *Action!* (Warners 1966) ★★.
● COMPILATIONS: *Freddy Cannon's Greatest Hits* (Warners 1966) ★★★★, *Big Blast From Boston! The Best Of Freddy Cannon* (Rhino 1995) ★★★, *The EP Collection* (See For Miles 1999) ★★★.

CAPITOLS

An R&B trio from Detroit, Michigan, USA, originally known as the Three Caps, the Capitols were best known for their 1966 hit 'Cool Jerk'. Originally formed around 1962 as a quintet, the two principal members were Donald Storball (guitar, vocals) and Samuel George (d. 17 March 1982; drums, lead vocals). Discovered by record producer Ollie McLaughlin and signed to his Karen label, their first single was 'Dog And Cat', which failed to have any impact. Four years later, after splitting from the other members, Storball and George added pianist/vocalist Richard McDougall to the line-up and they recorded the soulful dance number 'Cool Jerk', which became their only hit, reaching the US Top 10. The group was unable to produce a successful follow-up and disbanded in 1969. Storball enrolled in the Detroit police force, while George was fatally stabbed in March 1982.
● ALBUMS: *Dance The Cool Jerk* (Atco 1966) ★★, *We Got A Thing That's In The Groove* (Atco 1966) ★★.
● COMPILATIONS: *Their Greatest Recordings* (Solid Smoke 1984) ★★, *Golden Classics* (Collectables 1991) ★★.

CAPRIS (60s)

Formed in Queens, New York, USA, in 1958, this vocal quintet consisted of Nick Santamaria (lead vocals), Mike Mincelli (first tenor), Vinny Nacardo (second tenor), Frank Reins (baritone) and John Apostol (bass). They were best known for the doo-wop ballad 'There's A Moon Out Tonight', a US number 3 single in early 1961. The song was recorded by the Capris in 1958 and released on the small Planet Records label; however, it was not a hit and the group disbanded. Late in 1960, the owners of Lost Nite Records, one of the first labels to specialize in reissuing earlier rock 'n' roll recordings, purchased the master of the recording and re-released it. It was then leased to the larger, more established Old Town Records, and, owing to the revived interest in group harmony singing, the record nearly reached the top of the chart. The group re-formed and recorded further singles for Old Town and the Mr. Peeke label, but although three reached the charts, they never had another hit. The group has stayed together since the early 60s, however, and in 1982 recorded an album for Ambient Sound Records that included an update of their hit.
● ALBUMS: *There's A Moon Out Again* (Ambient Sound 1982)*Juggernaut Live At Century Plaza*

(Concord 1978) ★★, re-released as *Morse Code Of Love* (Collectables 1992) ★★.

CAPTAIN BEEFHEART

b. Don Glen Vliet, 15 January 1941, Glendale, California, USA. As a child Vliet achieved some fame as a talented sculptor, but for more than four decades the enigmatic and charismatic 'Captain', together with his various Magic Bands, has been one of rock music's more interesting subjects. During his teens he met Frank Zappa, who shared the same interest in R&B and blues, and while an attempt to form a band together failed, Zappa (and members of the Mothers Of Invention) reappeared frequently during Beefheart's career. The first Magic Band was formed in 1964, although it was not until 1966 that they secured a record contract. The unit comprised, in addition to Beefheart (now the self-appointed Don Van Vliet), Alex St. Clair Snouffer (guitar), Doug Moon (guitar), Paul Blakely (drums) and Jerry Handley (bass). The ensuing singles, including 'Diddy Wah Diddy', were a commercial disaster and he was dropped by A&M Records. He reappeared on the fledgling Buddah Records label with the pioneering *Safe As Milk* in April 1967, and was immediately adopted by the new music underground scene as a mentor. The album was helped by Ry Cooder's unmistakable guitar and it was a critical success throughout the 'summer of love'. Captain Beefheart found that Europe was more receptive to his wonderfully alliterated lyrics, full of nonsensical juxtaposition that defied the listener to decode them. The follow-up, *Strictly Personal*, has fallen from grace as a critics' favourite, but at the time it was considered one of the most innovative albums of the 60s. It is now regarded as more of a blues-based album, with a heavily phased yet hugely atmospheric recording. Titles such as 'Beatle Bones And Smokin' Stones' and 'Ah Feel Like Ahcid' were seemingly astonishing hallucinogenic voyages.
It was with the remarkable follow-up *Trout Mask Replica* that Captain Beefheart reached his creative peak. The double album, crudely recorded by Frank Zappa, contained a wealth of bizarre pieces, including 'Old Fart At Play', 'Veterans Day Poppy', 'Hair Pie: Bake 1' and 'Neon Meate Dream Of A Octafish'. The singer used his incredible octave range to great effect as he narrated and sang a wealth of lyrical 'malarkey'. The definitive Magic Band were present on this record, consisting of Beefheart's cousin, the Mascara Snake (Victor Haydon; bass clarinet), Antennae Jimmy Semens (Jeff Cotton; guitar), Drumbo (John French; drums), Zoot Horn Rollo (Bill Harkleroad b. 8 January 1949, Long Beach, California, USA; guitar) and Rockette Morton (Mark Boston; bass and vocals). It was reliably reported that the band recorded and played most of the tracks in one studio, while the singer added his lyrics in another (out

of earshot). This was later denied. The structure and sound of many of the pieces was reminiscent of the free jazz of Ornette Coleman. At one stage on the record, Beefheart is heard laconically stating: 'Shit, how did the harmony get in there?'. The listener requires a high tolerance level, and while Beefheart and Zappa may have intended to perpetrate one of the greatest musical jokes of our time, the album is cherished as one of the classic albums from the psychedelic era.

A similar theme was adopted for the much underrated *Lick My Decals Off, Baby* and *The Spotlight Kid*, although the latter had a more structured musical format. This album contained the delightfully perceptive 'Blabber And Smoke', written by Jan Van Vliet commenting on her husband's priorities in life. Beefheart also received considerable attention by contributing the vocals to 'Willie The Pimp' on Zappa's *Hot Rats* in 1969. Following the release of the overtly commercial (by Beefheart standards) *Clear Spot* and a heavy touring schedule, the Magic Band split from Beefheart to form Mallard. Beefheart signed to the UK Virgin Records label, releasing a few albums, including the poor *Unconditionally Guaranteed*. In 1975 Beefheart and Zappa released *Bongo Fury*, a superb live set recorded in Austin, Texas. However, the release of the album resulted in protracted litigation with Virgin, which won an injunction against Warner Brothers Records over the sale of the album in the UK.

Beefheart began to spend more time with his other interest, painting. His colourful oils were in the style of Francis Bacon, and eventually became his main interest. Beefheart toured and recorded only occasionally in the late 70s. His cult status was confirmed with the release of *Ice Cream For Crow* in 1982. This excellent return to form saw him writing and performing with renewed fervour, but reached a desultory number 90 in the UK charts and was completely ignored in his homeland. Since that time there have been no new recordings and Don Van Vliet, as he is now known, is a respected full-time artist, exhibiting regularly; his paintings are now fetching considerable prices. In 1993 it was alleged that Beefheart was suffering from multiple sclerosis, although there have been suggestions of other serious ailments. He is clearly physically unwell, but what genius still ferments in that amazing brain. Captain Beefheart's lyrics are works of genius, masquerading as nonsense, while his music is sometimes not of this world. New students of the man should start with *Safe As Milk*, and work upwards.

● ALBUMS: *Safe As Milk* (Buddah 1967) ★★★★, *Strictly Personal* (Blue Thumb/Liberty 1968) ★★★★, *Trout Mask Replica* (Straight 1969) ★★★★★, *Lick My Decals Off, Baby* (Straight 1970) ★★★★, *The Spotlight Kid* (Reprise 1972) ★★★, *Clear Spot* (Reprise 1972) ★★★, *Mirror Man* (Buddah 1973) ★★★, *Unconditionally Guaranteed* (Virgin 1974) ★★, *Bluejeans And Moonbeams* (Virgin 1974) ★★★, with Frank Zappa *Bongo Fury* (DiscReet 1975) ★★★, *Shiny Beast (Bat Chain Puller)* (Virgin 1978) ★★★, *Doc At The Radar Station* (Virgin 1980) ★★★, *Ice Cream For Crow* (Virgin 1982) ★★★, *Merseytrout: Live In Liverpool 1980* (Ozit 2000) ★★, *I'm Going To Do What I Wanna Do* 1978 live recording (Rhino 2001) ★★★.

● COMPILATIONS: *The Alternate Captain Beefheart: I May Be Hungry But I Sure Ain't Weird* (Sequel 1992) ★★★, *Zig Zag Wanderer: The Best Of The Buddah Years* (Wooden Hill 1997) ★★★, *Electricity* (Camden 1998) ★★★★, *Grow Fins* 5-CD box set (Revenant 1999) ★★★, *The Dust Blows Forward (An Anthology)* (Rhino 1999) ★★★★.

● FURTHER READING: *The Lives And Times Of Captain Beefheart*, no editor listed. *Captain Beefheart: The Man And His Music*, Colin David Webb. *Fast And Bulbous: The Captain Beefheart Story*, Ben Cruickshank. *Lunar Notes: Zoot Horn Rollo's Captain Beefheart Experience*, Bill Harkleroad with Billy James. *Captain Beefheart*, Mike Barnes.

CARAVELLES

Former office workers Lois Wilkinson (b. 3 April 1944, Sleaford, Lincolnshire, England) and Andrea Simpson (b. 1946) achieved international success with their distinctive version of 'You Don't Have To Be A Baby To Cry'. This light, breathy single reached the UK Top 10 in August 1963 where it formed an antidote to the more powerful, emergent British beat. Despite touring the USA, where the single was a number 3 hit, the duo was unable to maintain a consistent profile in spite of recording several excellent, if novelty-bound releases. Wilkinson began a solo career as Lois Lane, while Simpson maintained the Caravelles' name with a series of replacements and was actively performing throughout the 80s.

● ALBUMS: *You Don't Have To Be A Baby To Cry* US release (Smash 1963) ★★, *The Caravelles* UK release (Decca 1963) ★★.

CARR, JAMES

b. 13 June 1942, Coahoma, Mississippi, USA, d. 7 January 2001, Memphis, Tennessee, USA. Carr grew up in Memphis where he sang gospel in the Sunset Travellers and the Harmony Echoes and was discovered by Memphis gospel-group mentor Roosevelt Jamison. This budding manager and songwriter brought Carr to the Goldwax Records label, run by Quinton Claunch. It took four singles to define the singer's style, but the deep, magnificent 'You've Got My Mind Messed Up' burned with an intensity few contemporaries could match. A US Top 10 R&B hit in 1966, 'Love Attack' and 'Pouring Water On A Drowning Man' also followed that year. In 1967 Carr released 'The Dark End Of The Street', outhern soul's definitive guilt-laced 'cheating' ong, which inspired several cover versions. His ater work included 'Let It Happen' and 'A Man Ieeds A Woman', but his fragile personality was ncreasingly disturbed by drug abuse. 'To Love omebody' (1969) was Carr's final hit. Goldwax ecords collapsed the following year and Carr noved to Atlantic Records for 'Hold On' (1971), hich was recorded at Malaco Studios in ackson, Mississippi.

Iis problems worsened until 1977, when a now-npoverished Carr was reunited with Jamison.)ne single, the rather average 'Let Me Be Right', ppeared on the River City label and the singer emporarily disappeared from the scene. Carr esurfaced in 1979 on a tour of Japan, the first oncert of which was a disaster when he 'froze' n stage, having taken too much medication efore his performance. In 1991 he had an Ibum of new material entitled *Take Me To The imit* released by Goldwax Records in the USA Ace Records in the UK), with Quinton Claunch nd Roosevelt Jamison back among the roduction credits. The following year, Carr ppeared at the Sweet Soul Music annual festival 1 northern Italy, and three of his songs were ncluded on a 'live' album of the festival on the alian '103' label. By 1993, Claunch had left oldwax and set up his own Soultrax Records, or which Carr recorded his *Soul Survivor* album again also on UK Ace), the title track of which ad a single release in the USA. Meanwhile, aving lost Carr to Claunch, Goldwax's new resident, E.W. Clark, exhumed some prime late)s Carr material for inclusion on *Volume 1* of le projected (and perhaps optimistically titled) *omplete James Carr* (a US-only release). The nger's troubled life was eventually brought to n end by cancer in January 2001. A truly xceptional singer, Carr's work is deserving of ider appreciation. The original *You Got My Iind Messed Up* remains a forgotten gem though the recent Kent compilation of all his oldwax singles is essential. He is definitely one f soul music's greatest and most underrated)ices.

ALBUMS: *You Got My Mind Messed Up* ;oldwax 1966) ★★★★, *A Man Needs A Woman* ;oldwax 1968) ★★★, *Freedom Train* (Goldwax)68) ★★★, *Take Me To The Limit* (Goldwax)91) ★★★, *Soul Survivor* (Soultrax/Ace 1993) ★★.

COMPILATIONS: *At The Dark End Of The reet* (Blueside 1987) ★★★, *The Complete James arr, Volume 1* (Goldwax 1993) ★★★★, *The ssential* (Razor & Tie 1995) ★★★★, with the ibilee Hummingbirds *Guilty Of Serving God* Ace 1996) ★★★, *The Complete Goldwax Singles* Kent 2001) ★★★★, *24 Karat Soul* (Soultrax 2001) ★.

ARR, VIKKI

Florencia Bisenta De Casillas Martinez ardona, 19 July 1941, El Paso, Texas, USA. The eldest of seven children, Carr made her public debut at the age of four singing 'Silent Night' in Latin at a Christmas concert, before moving to Los Angeles, where she took leading roles in school musicals and studied music. After graduating she auditioned for a job at the Chi Chi Club in Palm Springs where she worked as singer with the 'Irish Mexican' Pepe Callahan Orchestra. With them she travelled to Las Vegas, Hawaii and Reno, where she teamed up with the Chuck Leonard Quartette, before pursuing a solo career. After doing some club work she recorded some demos that enticed Liberty Records to sign her. As part of a host of television variety appearances, she was regularly featured as vocalist on the *Ray Anthony Show* in 1962, and enjoyed a much publicized friendship with Elvis Presley. Her biggest hit was Gilbert Bécaud and Mack David's 'It Must Be Him' ('Seul Sur Son Étoile') in 1967, which sold in excess of a million copies. Follow-up hits in the UK included 'There I Go' and 'With Pen In Hand'. She became a popular MOR concert performer, a flavour of which was captured on the 1969 live album *For Once In My Life*. She also performed live in the White House for Presidents Nixon (1970) and Ford (1974). A Royal Command Performance became the equivalent seal of approval in the UK. As the 70s progressed she became increasingly involved in charity work, setting up a scholarship fund for Chicano children. Her popularity in the 90s was very much in the Latin market, singing in her native language.

● ALBUMS: *Color Her Great* (Liberty 1963) ★★★, *Discovery!* (Liberty 1964) ★★★, *Way Of Today* (Liberty 1967) ★★★, *It Must Be Him* (Liberty 1967) ★★★, *Vikki!* (Liberty 1968) ★★★, *For Once In My Life* (Liberty 1969) ★★★, *Nashville By Carr* (1970) ★★, *Vikki Carr's Love Story* (1971) ★★★, *Superstar* (1971) ★★★, *The First Time Ever (I Saw Your Face)* (1972) ★★★, *Song Sung Blue* (Columbia 1972) ★★★, *En Espanol* (1972) ★★★, *Ms. America* (1973) ★★, *Live At The Greek Theatre* (1973) ★★, *One Hell Of A Woman* (1974) ★★★, *Y El Amor* (1980) ★★★, *Emociones* (PolyGram 1996) ★★★.

● COMPILATIONS: *The Vikki Carr Collection* (United Artists 1973) ★★★, *The Liberty Years – The Best Of Vikki Carr* (Liberty/EMI 1989) ★★★.

CARTER AND LEWIS

John Carter b. John Shakespeare, 20 October 1942, Small Heath, Birmingham, England and Ken Lewis b. Kenneth James Hawker, 3 December 1942, Small Heath, Birmingham, England. They initially found fame leading Carter-Lewis And The Southerners, a country influenced group that briefly included guitarist Jimmy Page and recorded several singles, including So Much In Love (1961), Here's Hoping' (1962) and 'Sweet And Tender Romance' and 'Your Mama's Out Of Town' (both 1963). The duo's ability to create unabashed pop had been confirmed with 'Will I What?', a UK number 1 hit for Mike Sarne, and having disbanded their group, Carter/Lewis compositions were adopted by scores of acts, including the Marauders, Brenda Lee, P.J. Proby and the McKinleys, the last of whom they also produced. In 1964 the songwriters resurrected the idea of a group, forming the Ivy League with Perry Ford (b. Bryan Pugh, 1940, Lincoln, England, d. 29 April 1999, England). This harmony trio enjoyed several hits, but lost momentum when first Carter, then Lewis, left the line-up in 1966. The pair resumed a backroom role with the Flowerpot Men, before scoring further success as composers and/or producers with, among others, White Plains and First Class. Carter and Lewis also pursued joint and individual projects writing for commercials and jingles.

● COMPILATIONS: *Carter-Lewis Story* (Sequel 1993) ★★★.

CASCADES

Formed in the late 50s in San Diego, California, USA, the Cascades were best known for their 1963 number 3 US hit, 'Rhythm Of The Rain'. The group consisted of John Gummoe (vocals, guitar), Eddy Snyder (piano), Dave Stevens (bass), Dave Wilson (saxophone) and Dave Zabo (drums). They were discovered at a club called the Peppermint Stick in 1962 and signed to Valiant Records. Their first single, 'Second Chance', failed but 'Rhythm Of The Rain' became a soft-rock classic that still receives radio airplay in the 90s. One other chart single for Valiant and one for RCA Records charted but the group was unable to repeat its main success. Two more albums recorded in the late 60s did not revive the group's fortunes. They disbanded in 1969, with only one original member remaining at that time.

● ALBUMS: *Rhythm Of The Rain* (Valiant 1963) ★★★, *What Goes On* (Cascade 1968) ★★, *Maybe The Rain Will Fall* (UNI 1969) ★★.

● FILMS: *Catalina Caper* (1967).

CASH, JOHNNY

b. 26 February 1932, Kingsland, Arkansas, USA. Cash has traced his ancestry to seventeenth-century Scotland and has admitted that he fabricated the much-publicized story that he was a quarter Cherokee. Cash's father, Ray, worked on sawmills and the railway; in 1936, the family was one of 600 chosen by the Federal Government to reclaim land by the Mississippi River, known as the Dyess Colony Scheme. Much of it was swampland, and in 1937, they were evacuated when the river overflowed. Cash recalled the circumstances in his 1959 country hit 'Five Foot High And Risin''. Other songs inspired by his youth are 'Pickin' Time', 'Christmas As I Knew It' and 'Cisco Clifton's Filling Station'. Carl Perkins wrote 'Daddy Sang Bass' about Cash's family and the 'little brother' is Jack Cash, who was killed when he fell across

an electric saw. Cash was posted to Germany a a radio-operator in the US Army. Many thin the scar on his cheek is a knife wound but it i the result of a cyst being removed by a drunke doctor, while his hearing was permanently damaged by a German girl playfully sticking pencil down his left ear. After his discharge, h settled in San Antonio with his bride, Vivia Liberto. One of their four children, Rosann Cash, also became a country singer.

Cash auditioned as a gospel singer with San Phillips of Sun Records in Memphis, who tol him to return with something mor commercial. Cash developed his 'boom chick boom' sound with two friends: Luther Perkin (lead guitar) and Marshall Grant (bass). Thei first record, 'Hey Porter'/'Cry! Cry! Cry!' credited to Johnny Cash And The Tennesse Two, was released in June 1955, but Cash wa irritated that Phillips had called him 'Johnny as it sounded too young. 'Cry! Cry! Cry!' mad number 14 on the US country charts and wa followed by 'Folsom Prison Blues', which Casl wrote after seeing a film called *Inside The Wall Of Folsom Prison*. They played shows with Car Perkins (no relation to Luther Perkins). Perkin drummer, W.S. Holland, joined Cash in 1958 t make it the Tennessee Three. Cash encourage Perkins to complete the writing of 'Blue Sued Shoes', while he finished 'I Walk The Line' a Perkins' insistence: 'I got the idea from a Dal Carnegie course. It taught you to keep your eye open for something good. I made a love son out of it. It was meant to be a slow, mournfu ballad but Sam had us pick up the tempo until didn't like it at all.' 'I Walk The Line' reache number 17 on the US pop charts and was th title song for a 1970 film starring Gregory Peck Among his other excellent Sun records an 'Home Of The Blues', which was the name of Memphis record shop, 'Big River', 'Luthe Played The Boogie', 'Give My Love To Rose' an 'There You Go', which topped the US countr charts for five weeks. Producer Jack Clemer added piano and vocal chorus. They achieve further pop hits with the high school tale 'Balla Of A Teenage Queen' (number 14), 'Gues Things Happen That Way' (number 11) and 'Th Ways Of A Woman In Love' (number 24). Whil at Sun Records, Cash wrote 'You're My Bab' and 'Rock 'N' Roll Ruby' which were recorded b Roy Orbison and Warren Smith, respectivel Despite having his photograph taken with Elv Presley, Jerry Lee Lewis and Carl Perkins, h did not take part in the 'million dollar sessio but went shopping instead.

At a disc jockeys' convention in Nashville i November 1957, Sun launched their first eve album release, *Johnny Cash With His Hot An Blue Guitar*, but Phillips was reluctant to recor further LPs with Cash. This, and a unwillingness to increase his royalties, led Cash joining Columbia Records in 1958. H cautionary tale about a gunfighter not listenin to his mother, 'Don't Take Your Guns To Town', sold half a million copies and prompted a response from Charlie Rich, 'The Ballad Of Billy Joe', which was also recorded by Jerry Lee Lewis. Its b-side, 'I Still Miss Someone', is one of Cash's best compositions, and has been revived by Flatt And Scruggs, Crystal Gayle and Emmylou Harris. Cash started to take drugs to help make it through his schedule of 300 shows a year; however, his artistic integrity suffered and he regards *The Sound Of Johnny Cash* as his worst album. Nevertheless, he started on an inspiring series of concept albums about the working man (*Blood, Sweat And Tears*), cowboys (*Ballads Of The True West*) and the American Indian (*Bitter Tears*). The concepts are fascinating, the songs excellent, but the albums are bogged down with narration and self-righteousness, making Cash sound like a history teacher. His sympathy for a maligned American Indian, 'The Ballad Of Ira Hayes', led to threats from the Ku Klux Klan. Cash says, 'I didn't really care what condition I was in and it showed up on my recordings, but *Bitter Tears* was so important to me that I managed to get enough sleep to do it right.'

For all his worthy causes, the drugged-up country star was a troublemaker himself, although, despite press reports, he only ever spent three days in prison. His biggest misdemeanour was starting a forest fire for which he was fined $85,000. He wrecked hotel rooms and toyed with guns. He and his drinking buddy, country singer Carl Smith, rampaged through Smith's house and ruined his wife's Cadillac. Smith's marriage to June Carter of the Carter Family was nearing its end but at that stage, few could have predicted Carter's next marriage. In 1963, Mexican brass was added to the ominous 'Ring Of Fire', written by Carter and Merle Kilgore, which again was a pop hit. Without Cash's support, Bob Dylan would have been dropped by Columbia, and Cash had his first British hit in 1965 with Dylan's 'It Ain't Me Babe'. Their offbeat duet, 'Girl From The North Country', was included on Dylan's *Nashville Skyline*, and the rest of their sessions have been widely bootlegged. Dylan also gave Cash an unreleased song, 'Wanted Man'. Cash said, 'I don't dance, tell jokes or wear my pants too tight, but I do know about a thousand songs.' With this in mind, he has turned his roadshow into a history of country music. In the 60s it featured Carl Perkins (who also played guitar for Cash after Luther Perkins' death in a fire), the Statler Brothers and the Carter Family. The highlight of Cash's act was 'Orange Blossom Special' played with two harmonicas. One night Cash proposed to June Carter on stage; she accepted and they were married in March 1968. Their successful duets include 'Jackson' and 'If I Were A Carpenter'.

In 1968 Columbia finally agreed to record one of Cash's prison concerts, and the invigorating album *Johnny Cash At Folsom Prison* is one of the most atmospheric of all live albums. It remains, arguably, Cash's best album and a contender for the best country record of all time. Cash explains: 'Prisoners are the greatest audience that an entertainer can perform for. We bring them a ray of sunshine and they're not ashamed to show their appreciation.' He included 'Graystone Chapel', written by an inmate, Glen Sherley, which he had been given by the Prison Chaplain. Sherley subsequently recorded an album with Cash's support, but he died in 1978. The Folsom Prison concert was followed by one at San Quentin, which was filmed for a television documentary. Shortly before that concert, Shel Silverstein gave Cash a poem, 'A Boy Named Sue'. Carl Perkins put chords to it and, without any rehearsals, the humorous song was recorded, giving Cash his only Top 10 on the US pop charts and a number 4 success in the UK. Cash's popularity led to him hosting his own television series from 1969-71, but, despite notable guests such as Bob Dylan, the show was hampered by feeble jokes and middle-of-the-road arrangements. Far better was the documentary *Johnny Cash – The Man, His World, His Music*. Cash's catchphrase, 'Hello, I'm Johnny Cash', became so well known that both Elvis Presley and the Kinks' Ray Davies sometimes opened with that remark.

Cash championed Kris Kristofferson, wrote the liner notes for his first album, *Kristofferson*, and recorded several of his songs. 'To Beat The Devil' celebrated Cash overcoming drugs after many years, while 'The Loving Gift' was about the birth of Cash's son John Carter Cash, who has since joined his stage show. Cash has often found strength and comfort in religion and he has recorded many spiritual albums. One of his most stirring performances is 'Were You There (When They Crucified My Lord)?' with the Carter Family. He made a documentary film and double album *The Gospel Road* with Kristofferson, Larry Gatlin and the Statler Brothers but, as he remarked, 'My record company would rather I'd be in prison than in church.' He justified himself commercially when 'A Thing Called Love', written by Jerry Reed, made with the Evangel Temple Choir, became one of his biggest-selling UK records, reaching number 4 in 1972.

Cash is an imposing figure with his huge muscular frame, black hair, craggy face and deep bass voice. Unlike other country singers, he shuns lavish colours and in his song 'Man In Black', he explains that he wears black because of the injustice in the world. In truth, he started wearing black when he first appeared on the *Grand Ole Opry* because he felt that rhinestone suits detracted from the music. With little trouble, Cash could have been a major Hollywood star, particularly in westerns, and he acquitted himself well when the occasion arose. He made his debut in *Five Minutes To Live* in

1960 and his best role was opposite Kirk Douglas in the 1972 film *A Gunfight*, which was financed by Apache money, although religious principles prevented a scene with a naked actress. He was featured alongside Kris Kristofferson and Willie Nelson in a light-hearted remake of *Stagecoach* and starred in a television movie adaptation of his pool-hall song *The Baron*. Cash also gave a moving portrayal of a coalminer overcoming illiteracy in another television movie, *The Pride Of Jesse Hallam*. He recorded the theme for the US television series *The Rebel – Johnny Yuma* and, among the previously unissued tracks released by Bear Family Records, is his submission for a James Bond theme, 'Thunderball'.

By opening his own recording studios, House Of Cash, in 1972, he became even more prolific. His family joined him on the quirky *The Junkie And The Juicehead Minus Me* and his son-in-law J.W. Routh wrote several songs and performed with him on *The Rambler*. He has always followed writers and the inclusion of Nick Lowe, former husband of Carlene Carter, and Rodney Crowell, husband of Rosanne Cash, into his family increased his awareness. His recordings include the Rolling Stones' 'No Expectations', John Prine's 'Unwed Fathers', Guy Clark's 'The Last Gunfighter Ballad' and a touching portrayal of Bruce Springsteen's 'Highway Patrolman'. He showed his humour with 'Gone Girl', 'One Piece At A Time' and 'Chicken In Black'. He said, 'I record a song because I love it and let it become a part of me.' Cash moved to Mercury Records in 1986 and found success immediately with the whimsical 'The Night Hank Williams Came To Town'. He made an all-star album, *Water From The Wells Of Home*, with Emmylou Harris, the Everly Brothers, Paul McCartney and many others. His 60s composition 'Tennessee Flat-Top Box' became a US country number 1 for daughter Rosanne in 1988. In the same year, various UK modern folk artists recorded an album of his songs 'Til Things Are Brighter', with proceeds going to an AIDS charity. Cash particularly enjoyed Sally Timms' waltz-time treatment of 'Cry! Cry! Cry!'. During his late-80s revival, Cash was hampered by pneumonia, heart surgery and a recurrence of drug problems. He returned to the stage, however, either touring with the Carter Family or as part of the Highwaymen with Kristofferson, Waylon Jennings and Nelson, and remained passionate about his beliefs: 'A lot of people think of country singers as right-wing, redneck bigots,' he says, 'but I don't think I'm like that.'

In all, Cash has made over 70 albums of original material, plus countless guest appearances. His music reflects his love of America (a recent compilation was called *Patriot*), his compassion, his love of life, and, what is often lacking in country music, a sense of humour. His limited range is staggeringly impressive on particular songs, especially narrative ones. Like Bo Diddley's 'shave and a haircut' rhythm, he has developed his music around his 'boom chicka boom', and instilled enough variety to stave off boredom. In a genre now dominated by new country, Cash has found it difficult to obtain record contracts of late, but this worked to his advantage with the low-key *American Recordings*, produced by Rick Rubin in 1994. Featuring just his craggy voice and simple guitar, it reaffirmed his talent for storytelling. Among the many excellent songs included Nick Lowe's 'The Beast In Me' (Lowe was a former son-in-law) and Loudon Wainwright's 'The Man Who Couldn't Cry'. An appearance at the Glastonbury Festival in 1994 also introduced him to a new audience, this time indie and new wave rockers. In the USA during 1994 Cash became a media star and was featured on the cover on many magazines (not just music ones). It was an astonishing rebirth of interest. *Unchained* continued his renaissance, with effortless cover versions of Don Gibson's 'Sea Of Heartbreak' and the Dean Martin classic 'Memories Are Made Of This'. His continuing popularity assured, Cash states he heeded the advice he was given during his one and only singing lesson, 'Never change your voice.' More worryingly, Cash announced he was suffering from Parkinson's disease at a Flint, Michigan concert on 25 October 1997, and was hospitalized with double pneumonia soon afterwards. Later he claimed that he had Shydrager syndrome, although this was subsequently stated to be a wrong diagnosis. Nevertheless, he was able to return to the studio to record the third instalment in Rubin's American Recordings series, *Solitary Man*.

Cash's gigantic contribution to country music's history is inestimable and, as he says, 'They can get all the synthesizers they want, but nothing will ever take the place of the human heart.'

● ALBUMS: *Johnny Cash With His Hot And Blue Guitar* (Sun 1957) ★★★, *Johnny Cash Sings The Songs That Made Him Famous* (Sun 1958) ★★★, *The Fabulous Johnny Cash* (Columbia 1958) ★★★, *Hymns By Johnny Cash* (Columbia 1959) ★, *Songs Of Our Soil* (Columbia 1959) ★★, *Now There Was A Song* (Columbia 1960) ★★, *Johnny Cash Sings Hank Williams And Other Favorite Tunes* (Sun 1960) ★★★, *Ride This Train* (Columbia 1960) ★★★★, *Now Here's Johnny Cash* (Sun 1961) ★★★, *The Lure Of The Grand Canyon* (Columbia 1961) ★★, *Hymns From The Heart* (Columbia 1962) ★, *The Sound Of Johnny Cash* (Columbia 1962) ★★, *All Aboard The Blue Train* (Sun 1963) ★★★, *Blood, Sweat And Tears* (Columbia 1963) ★★★★, *The Christmas Spirit* (Columbia 1963) ★★, with the Carter Family *Keep On The Sunny Side* (1964) ★★★, *I Walk The Line* (Columbia 1964) ★★★★, *Bitter Tears (Ballads Of The American Indian)* (Columbia 1964) ★★★, *Orange Blossom Special* (Columbia 1964) ★★★★, *Mean As Hell* (Columbia 1965) ★★, *The Sons Of Katie Elder* film soundtrack (Columbia 1965) ★★, *Johnny Cash Sings Ballads*

Of The True West (Columbia 1965) ★★★, Ballads Of The True West, Volume 2 (Columbia 1965) ★★★, Everybody Loves A Nut (Columbia 1966) ★, Happiness Is You (Columbia 1966) ★★, with June Carter Carryin' On (Columbia 1967) ★★, From Sea To Shining Sea (Columbia 1967) ★★, Old Golden Throat (Columbia 1968) ★★, Johnny Cash At Folsom Prison (Columbia 1968) ★★★★, The Holy Land (Columbia 1968) ★, More Of Old Golden Throat (Columbia 1969) ★★, Johnny Cash At San Quentin (Columbia 1969) ★★★★, Hello I'm Johnny Cash (Columbia 1970) ★★★, The Johnny Cash Show (Columbia 1970) ★★★, with Carl Perkins Little Fauss And Big Halsey (Columbia 1970) ★★, The Man In Black (Columbia 1971) ★★★, with Jerry Lee Lewis Sings Hank Williams (Sun 1971) ★★, A Thing Called Love (Columbia 1972) ★★, with Jerry Lee Lewis Sunday Down South (Sun 1972) ★★★, Christmas And The Cash Family (Columbia 1972) ★★, America (A 200-Year Salute In Story And Song) (Columbia 1972) ★★, Any Old Wind That Blows (Columbia 1973) ★★, The Gospel Road (Columbia 1973) ★★, with June Carter Johnny Cash And His Woman (Columbia 1973) ★★, Ragged Old Flag (Columbia 1974) ★★, The Junkie And The Juicehead Minus Me (Columbia 1974) ★★, Pa Osteraker aka Inside A Swedish Prison (Columbia 1974) ★★★, John R. Cash (Columbia 1975) ★★★, Look At Them Beans (Columbia 1975) ★★, Strawberry Cake (Columbia 1976) ★★★, One Piece At A Time (Columbia 1976) ★★★★, The Last Gunfighter Ballad (Columbia 1977) ★★★, The Rambler (Columbia 1977) ★★★, Gone Girl (Columbia 1978) ★★★, I Would Like To See You Again (Columbia 1978) ★★★, Silver (Columbia 1979) ★★★, A Believer Sings The Truth (Columbia 1979) ★★, Rockabilly Blues (Columbia 1980) ★★★★, The Baron (Columbia 1981) ★★★, with Jerry Lee Lewis, Carl Perkins The Survivors (Columbia 1982) ★★★, The Adventures Of Johnny Cash (Columbia 1982) ★★, Johnny 99 (Columbia 1983) ★★, Rainbow (Columbia 1985) ★★★, with Kris Kristofferson, Waylon Jennings, Willie Nelson Highwayman (Columbia 1985) ★★★★, with Jerry Lee Lewis, Carl Perkins, Roy Orbison The Class Of '55 (1986) ★★★, with Waylon Jennings Heroes (Columbia 1986) ★★★, Believe In Him (Word 1986) ★★, Johnny Cash Is Back In Town (Mercury 1987) ★★★, Water From The Wells Of Home (Mercury 1988) ★★★★, Boom Chicka Boom (Mercury 1989) ★★★, with Jennings, Kristofferson and Nelson Highwayman 2 (Columbia 1990) ★★★, The Mystery Of Life (Mercury 1991) ★★★, Get Rhythm (Sun 1991) ★★★, American Recordings (American 1994) ★★★★, with Jennings, Kristofferson, Nelson The Road Goes On Forever (Liberty 1995) ★★, Unchained (American 1996) ★★★, with Nelson VH1 Storytellers (American 1998) ★★★★, American III: Solitary Man (American 2000) ★★★.
● COMPILATIONS: Johnny Cash's Greatest (Sun 1959) ★★★, Ring Of Fire (The Best Of Johnny Cash) (Columbia 1963) ★★★, The Original Sun Sound Of Johnny Cash (Sun 1965) ★★★, Johnny Cash's Greatest Hits, Volume 1 (Columbia 1967) ★★★, Original Golden Hits, Volume 1 (Sun 1969) ★★★, Original Golden Hits, Volume 2 (Sun 1969) ★★★, Get Rhythm (Sun 1969) ★★★, Story Songs Of The Trains And Rivers (Sun 1969) ★★★, Showtime (Sun 1969) ★★★, The Rough Cut King Of Country Music (Sun 1970) ★★★, The Singing Story Teller (Sun 1970) ★★★, The Legend (Sun 1970) ★★★★, The World Of Johnny Cash (Columbia 1970) ★★★★, Original Golden Hits, Volume 3 (Sun 1971) ★★, Johnny Cash: The Man, The World, His Music (Sun 1971) ★★★, His Greatest Hits, Volume 2 (Columbia 1971) ★★★, Destination Victoria Station (Bear Family 1976) ★★, Superbilly (Sun 1977) ★★, Golden Souvenirs (Plantation 1977) ★★★, The Unissued Johnny Cash (Bear Family 1978) ★★, Greatest Hits, Volume 3 (Columbia 1978) ★★★, Johnny And June (Bear Family 1980) ★★, Tall Man (Bear Family 1980) ★★★, Encore (Greatest Hits, Volume 4) (Columbia 1981) ★★★, Biggest Hits (Columbia 1982) ★★★, Johnny Cash: The Sun Years 5-LP box set (Sun 1984) ★★★★, Up Through The Years, 1955-1957 (Bear Family 1986) ★★★★, Johnny Cash – Columbia Records 1958-1986 (Columbia 1987) ★★★★, Vintage Years: 1955-1963 (Rhino 1987) ★★★, Classic Cash (Mercury 1988) ★★★, The Sun Years (Rhino 1990) ★★★, I Walk The Line And Other Big Hits (Rhino 1990) ★★★, The Man In Black: 1954-1958 5-CD box set (Bear Family 1990) ★★★★, Come Along And Ride This Train 4-CD box set (Bear Family 1991) ★★★, The Man In Black: 1959-1962 5-CD box set (Bear Family 1992) ★★★★, The Essential Johnny Cash 1955-1983 3-CD box set (Columbia/Legacy 1992) ★★★★, Wanted Man (Mercury 1994) ★★★, The Man In Black: The Definitive Collection (Columbia 1994) ★★★★, Get Rhythm: The Best Of The Sun Years (Pickwick 1995) ★★★, Ring Of Fire (Spectrum 1995) ★★★, The Man In Black: 1963-1969 Plus 6-CD box set (Bear Family 1996) ★★★★, All American Country (Spectrum 1997) ★★★, Tennessee Top Cat Live 1955-1965 (Cotton Town Jubilee 1997) ★★★★, Sings The Country Classics (Eagle 1997) ★★★, Hits And Classics (Carlton 1998) ★★★, The Complete Original Sun Singles (Varèse Sarabande 1999) ★★★★, Love God Murder 3-CD set (American/Legacy 2000) ★★★★, Wanted Man: The Very Best Of Johnny Cash (Sony 2000) ★★★★, Johnny Cash, The EP Collection Plus (See For Miles 2000) ★★★, The Very Best Of The Sun Years (Metro 2001) ★★★.
● VIDEOS: Live In London: Johnny Cash (BBC Video 1987), In San Quentin (Vestron Video 1987), Riding The Rails (Hendring Music Video 1990), Johnny Cash Live! (1993), The Tennessee Top Cat Live 1955-1965 (Jubilee 1995), The Man, His World, The Music (1995), Johnny Cash: The Man In Black (IMC 1999).
● FURTHER READING: Johnny Cash Discography And Recording History 1954-1969,

John L. Smith. *A Boy Named Cash*, Albert Govoni. *The Johnny Cash Story*, George Carpozi. *Johnny Cash: Winners Get Scars Too*, Christopher S. Wren. *The New Johnny Cash*, Charles Paul Conn. *Man In Black*, Johnny Cash. *The Johnny Cash Discography 1954-1984*, John L. Smith. *The Johnny Cash Record Catalogue*, John L. Smith (ed.). *Johnny Cash: The Autobiography*, Johnny Cash with Patrick Carr. *The Cash Family Scrapbook*, Cindy Cash. *Johnny Cash*, Frank Moriarty. *I've Been Everywhere: The Complete Johnny Cash Chronicle*, Peter Lewry.

CASHMAN AND WEST

Terry Cashman (b. Dennis Minogue, 5 July 1941) and Tommy West (b. Thomas R. Picardo Jnr., 17 August 1942) were record producers, songwriters and also recording artists. Best known for producing all of the hit recordings by the late Jim Croce, they also recorded under numerous names between the 50s and 70s and produced several other artists. West's musical career began in 1958 when he formed a group called the Criterions (with Tim Hauser, later of Manhattan Transfer) in New Jersey, USA. They recorded four singles, none of which reached the charts. While attending college, the group changed its style to folk and its name to the Troubadours; West also joined the university singing club, where he met Croce. Cashman also started out in a vocal group, the Chevrons, which recorded two singles. After numerous other music business pursuits, Cashman was hired to head ABC Records' publishing department. He met Gene Pistilli, a songwriter, and hired him. The pair wrote 'Sunday Will Never Be The Same', a hit for Spanky And Our Gang and recorded a single under the name Gene and Tommy. In March 1966 the pair met West and the trio soon formed. Together they recorded numerous singles as Cashman, Pistilli and West for ABC in 1966-68. They briefly changed their name to the Buchanan Brothers and recorded several singles and an album for Event Records in 1969, two of which charted, before reverting to the CP&W name in 1969 and recording several other singles and an album for Capitol Records. West persuaded Capitol to sign Croce and his wife Ingrid, and Cashman, Pistilli and West produced the couple's only Capitol album together. In 1970-71, Pistilli recorded with Manhattan Transfer on their first singles and album and left Cashman and West to go with that new outfit. Cashman and West continued as a duo, recording a chart hit as Morning Mist in 1971 and releasing two albums and a number of singles under their own names on Dunhill Records in 1972. Their 'American City Suite' reached number 27 that year. In 1973, Croce's career took off, and Cashman and West concentrated on their work with him. When Croce died in 1973, the duo resumed their own career, releasing a final album together in 1974. (A fourth album was never issued.) By the

following year, they had begun recording solo albums. They also ran the Lifesong Records label, which signed Dion and had a US Top 10 hit with Henry Gross' 'Shannon' in 1976. In 1981, Cashman wrote and recorded 'Talkin' Baseball', a novelty song that did not hit the charts but has become a cult favourite in subsequent years.

● ALBUMS: as Cashman, Pistilli And West *Bound To Happen* (ABC 1967) ★★★, as Cashman, Pistilli And West *For Love Of Ivy* (ABC 1968) ★★, as the Buchanan Brothers *Medicine Man* (Event 1968) ★★, as Cashman, Pistilli And West *Cashman, Pistilli And West* (Capitol 1969) ★★★, as Cashman And West *A Song Or Two* (Dunhill 1972) ★★★, as Cashman And West *Moondog Serenade* (Dunhill 1973) ★★★★, as Cashman And West *Lifesong* (1974) ★★★.
Solo: Tommy West *Hometown Frolics* (Lifesong 1976) ★★. Terry Cashman *Terry Cashman* (Lifesong 1976) ★★★, *Talkin' Baseball – American League* (1982) ★★, *Talkin' Baseball – National League* (1982) ★★, *Passin' It On: America's Baseball Heritage In Song* (Sony 1995) ★★★.

CASINOS

Formed in 1958 in Cincinnati, Ohio, USA, the Casinos originally consisted of Gene and Glenn Hughes, Pete Bolton, Joe Patterson and Ray White. After gaining popularity locally, they signed with the small Terry Records and covered the Carla Thomas R&B ballad 'Gee Whiz', with no success. They then switched to the local Fraternity Records and recorded a series of singles that also failed commercially. The group, still sporting a clean-cut look and a 50s-orientated doo-wop sound, grew to nine members by the mid-60s, including Bob Armstrong, Tom Mathews, Bill Hawkins and Mickey Denton. Finally, in 1967, the group reached the US Top 10 with a cover version of John D. Loudermilk's ballad, 'Then You Can Tell Me Goodbye'. The Casinos continued to record into the 70s and a version of the group was still performing in Cincinnati by the early 90s, but there have been no further hits.

● ALBUMS: *Then You Can Tell Me Goodbye* (Fraternity 1967) ★★★.
● COMPILATIONS: *The Best Of The Casinos Then You Can tell Me Goodbye* (Varèse Sarabande 1997) ★★★.

CASTAWAYS

Formed in Richfield, Minnesota, USA, in 1962 with the express purpose of playing at a fraternity party, the Castaways made one appearance on the US charts in 1965 with 'Liar, Liar', a 'garage-rock' gem marked by overbearing organ and heavily echoed vocals. Roy Hensley (guitar), Denny Craswell (drums) and Dick Roby (bass) originated the band, with Bob Folschow (guitar) and Jim Donna (keyboards) completing the line-up. Their only hit was also their first single, recorded for the

ocal Soma label which was intended to gain the band a better footing from which to sell itself to local club owners. They recorded several other singles but none charted. Denny Craswell left the band to join Crow in 1970, while the remaining four members still performed together in the late 80s and hope eventually to record an album. Meanwhile, 'Liar, Liar' remains popular, having received a boost in 1987 via placement in the movie *Good Morning Vietnam*.
● FILMS: *It's A Bikini World* (1967).
● COMPILATIONS: *Best Of The Castaways: Liar Liar* (Plum 1999) ★★★.

CASTELLS
Based in Santa Rosa, California, USA, this vocal quartet was originally formed as a trio in 1958. By mid-1959 they had become a quartet with the line-up of teenagers Tom Hicks, Chuck Girard, Bob Ussery and Joe Kelly. They were taken to the successful independent label Era Records by west coast disc jockey Dan Dillon. Their first release, 'Little Sad Eyes', was a local hit and in 1961 their second single, 'Sacred', a sweet and innocent semi-religious song, written by Adam Ross and Bill Laundau, gave them their only Top 20 record. This classy, doo-wop-orientated pop vocal quartet also reached the US Top 40 with 'So This Is Love' in 1962. Kelly and Girard were later members of the Hondells. They later recorded unsuccessfully for United Artists Records, Warner Brothers Records, Decca Records, Solomon and Laurie.
● ALBUMS: *So This Is Love* (Era 1962) ★★★.
● COMPILATIONS: *Sweet Sounds Of The Castells* (Collectables 1987) ★★★.

CASUALS
Three times winners on *Opportunity Knocks*, British television's hugely popular talent show of the late 60s, the Casuals subsequently left the UK for Italy, where they became a leading attraction. Alan Taylor (b. Halifax, Yorkshire, England; guitar, bass), Johnny Tebb (b. 1 October 1945, Lincoln, England; organ), Howard Newcombe (b. Lincoln, England; guitar, trumpet) and Robert O'Brien (b. Bridge Of Allan, Central Scotland; drums) were based in Milan for several years before returning to Britain in 1968, when their single, 'Jesamine', entered the charts. The song was originally recorded by the Bystanders as 'When Jesamine Goes', but the Casuals' inherently commercial reading coincided with a prevailing trend for emotional ballads. The single ultimately reached number 2, but later releases were less successful and 'Toy' (1968), which peaked at number 30, was their only other hit. The Casuals continued to record superior pop: Move leader Roy Wood wrote and produced the polished 'Caroline' (1969), but as the decade closed, so their style of music grew increasingly anachronistic.

● ALBUMS: *Hour World* (Decca 1969) ★★★.
● COMPILATIONS: *The Very Best Of The Casuals* (Spectrum 1998) ★★★.

CATTINI, CLEM
b. 28 August 1939, London, England. As pop exponents tend to accelerate and slow down *en bloc* to inconsistencies of tempo in concert, it is not uncommon for drumming on record to be ghosted by someone more technically adept than a given act's regular player. From the 60s onwards, chief among those Britons earning Musicians Union-regulated tea breaks in this fashion was Clem Cattini, one of the first dyed-in-the-wool rock 'n' rollers to be thus employed and heard on countless UK chart hits.
His professional life began in 1959 in the Beat Boys, led by saxophonist Ray McVay, who accompanied Johnny Gentle, Dickie Pride and similar vocalists managed by the celebrated Larry Parnes. Nevertheless, prospects with Johnny Kidd And The Pirates proved more attractive, particularly when a contract with HMV enabled Cattini to drum on all the group's early recordings – including the classic 'Shakin' All Over'. By 1961, however, Cattini left Kidd for an Italian tour with Colin Hicks (Tommy Steele's younger brother) and the Cabin Boys, for which he retained his Pirate stage costume. On returning, he joined the Tornados house band at producer Joe Meek's north London studio, remaining with them throughout their period of greatest celebrity as a respected session unit, and chart entrants in their own right with 'Telstar', 'Globetrotter' *et al*. With flop singles reducing engagement fees, Cattini quit the Tornados – with whom his name would always be synonymous – in March 1965 for a more lucrative post with Division Two who backed the Ivy League, then at the peak of their fame. He was also much in demand for hundreds of record dates by artists from every avenue of pop. His 60s work included Dusty Springfield, the Kinks, P.J. Proby, Herman's Hermits, Marianne Faithfull, Tom Jones, Love Affair, Joe Cocker and Marmalade. The sharp-eyed would also spot stout Clem on television and in prestigious auditoriums 'rattling the traps' behind artists such as Cliff Richard, Roy Orbison, the Everly Brothers and Engelbert Humperdinck.
During the next decade, he was cajoled into oddball album projects under the direction of Slapp Happy, Bob Downes, Beggar's Opera, as well as Hungry Wolf, Edward's Hand, Rumplestiltskin and other obscure 'progressive' acts. As usual, his 'bread-and-butter' was in mainstream pop – notably the Bay City Rollers and Kenny, but he also continued to serve old friends such as Phil Everly, Chris Spedding, Hank Marvin and, from the Meek era, Mike Berry. By the mid 80s, Cattini was seen more often in theatrical productions such as *The Rocky Horror Show*'s West End run in 1989. Two

years later, he was mainstay of a new Tornados with a repertoire that spanned every familiar avenue of his distinguished career.

● ALBUMS: as Rumplestiltskin *Rumplestiltskin* (Bell 1970) ★★.

CHAD AND JEREMY

Chad Stuart (b. 10 December 1943, Durham, England; vocals, guitar, banjo, keyboards, sitar) and Jeremy Clyde (b. 22 March 1944, Buckinghamshire, England; vocals, guitar) met as students at London's Central School of Speech and Drama and soon began performing together with Stuart providing the musical accompaniment to Clyde's lyrics. Their early releases for the Ember label offered a brand of folk-influenced pop similar to that of Peter And Gordon, but the duo was unable to make commercial inroads in the UK. However, their quintessential Englishness inspired four US Top 30 hits, including 'Yesterday's Gone' and 'A Summer Song' the latter of which reached number 7. Their acting ability made them perfect for television, and they guested on many US television shows and sitcoms, including *The Dick Van Dyke Show*, *Hullabaloo*, *Laredo*, *Batman*, and *The Andy Williams Show*. The 1967 concept album *Of Cabbages And Kings* was produced by Gary Usher and signalled a switch to progressive styles, but this ambitious and sadly neglected work was not a commercial success. *The Ark*, a tighter, less symphonic, altogether more successful attempt to modernize their sound, followed before the pair broke up in 1969. Clyde, who made frequent appearances on the popular television show *Rowan And Martin's Laugh-In*, later pursued a successful acting career. Stuart wrote for musical comedies, worked as musical director for *The Smother Brothers Comedy Hour*, and recorded with his wife Jill before moving into radio work. The duo reunited in 1983 to record a new album, and three years later appeared on the *British Reinvasion* tour.

● ALBUMS: *Sing For You* (UK) (Ember 1964) ★★★, *Yesterday's Gone* (US) (World Artists 1964) ★★★, *Chad & Jeremy's Second Album* (UK) (Ember 1965) ★★★, *Sing For You* (US) (World Artists 1965) ★★★, *Before And After* (Columbia 1965) ★★★, *I Don't Want To Lose You Baby* (Columbia 1965) ★★★, *Distant Shores* (Columbia 1966) ★★★, *Of Cabbages And Kings* (Columbia 1967) ★★★, *The Ark* (Columbia 1968) ★★★★, *Three In The Attic* film soundtrack (Sidewalk 1969) ★★, *Chad Stuart & Jeremy Clyde* (Rocshire 1983) ★★.

● COMPILATIONS: *5 + 10 = 15 Fabulous Hits* (Fidu 1966) ★★, *The Best Of Chad & Jeremy* (Capitol/Ember 1966) ★★★, *More Chad & Jeremy* (Capitol 1966) ★★★, *Chad And Jeremy* (Harmony 1969) ★★★, *The Soft Sound Of Chad & Jeremy* (K-Tel 1990) ★★★, *Painted Dayglow Smile: A Collection* (Columbia/Legacy 1992) ★★★★, *Yesterday's Gone* (Drive Archive 1994) ★★★, *A Summer Song* (K-Tel 1995) ★★★, *The Best Of*

Chad & Jeremy (One Way 1996) ★★★, *Best Of Chad And Jeremy* (Quicksilver/Bulldog 1997) ★★, *Greatest Hits* (Laserlight 1999) ★★★, *The Very Best Of Chad & Jeremy* (Varèse Sarabande 2000) ★★★★.

CHAMBERLAIN, RICHARD

b. George Richard Chamberlain, 31 March 1935, Los Angeles, California, USA. The well-known television and film star had a brief spell as a successful recording artist in the early 60s. In 1960, after serving in Korea and attending the LA Conservatory of Music, he had his first television role in *Gunsmoke* and appeared in the film *The Secret Of The Purple Reef*. In 1961 he landed the lead role in the television series *Dr. Kildare*, which made the photogenic fresh-faced actor a top pin-up on both sides of the Atlantic. In 1962, his first single, a vocal version of the television series' theme song, 'Three Stars Will Shine Tonight', became the first of four UK and four US Top 40 singles for the pleasant-voiced MOR/pop singer. His debut album, *Richard Chamberlain Sings*, on which he was accompanied by David Rose's 40-piece orchestra, also shot into the transatlantic Top 10s. Chamberlain, who at the height of his career as Dr. Kildare was reputedly receiving 2,500 letters a day, quickly faded from the pop scene but has gone on to star in many more television programmes and films. In 1993 he starred on Broadway as Henry Higgins in a drastically revised revival of the classic musical *My Fair Lady*.

● ALBUMS: *Richard Chamberlain Sings* (MGM 1963) ★★, *Joy In The Morning* (MGM 1964) ★, *Theme From Dr Kildare And Other Favourites* (MFP 1965) ★★.

CHAMBERS BROTHERS

Born and raised in Lee County, Mississippi, USA, the four brothers, George (b. 26 September 1931; bass), Willie (b. 3 March 1938; guitar), Lester (b. 13 April 1940; harmonica) and Joe (b. 22 August 1942; guitar), moved to Los Angeles during the early 50s. The group's gospel-based origins were evident in their first recordings, which included an unpolished reading of Curtis Mayfield's 'People Get Ready'. In 1965 they were joined by drummer Brian Keenan and an appearance at that year's Newport Folk Festival reinforced the group's 'R&B combo' approach, the basis for their later direction. The title track to a 1968 album, *Time Has Come Today*, with its exciting, extended instrumental break, introduced the Brothers to the white, counter-culture audience. They cultivated a hippie image and part of a subsequent album, *Love Peace And Happiness*, was recorded live at the Fillmore East, then one of rock's prestigious venues. The group continued to maintain their popularity into the 70s, but in embracing such a transient fashion they were unable to secure a committed following when tastes changed. In the 90s their music found a new generation, given the wink by their elders. The band continue to perform the its together with blues standards, and it appears that the Chambers' children have boosted the line-up. 'Time Has Come Today' is still an encore worth waiting for.

● ALBUMS: *Barbara Dane And The Chambers Brothers* (Folkways 1964) ★★, *People Get Ready* (Vault 1966) ★★★, *The Chambers Brothers Now* (Vault 1967) ★★, *The Time Has Come* (Columbia 1967) ★★★★, *The Chambers Brothers Shout* (Vault 1968) ★★★, *A New Time – A New Day* (Columbia 1968) ★★, *Groovin' Time* (Riverside 1968) ★★, *Feelin' The Blues* (Vault 1969) ★★★, with various artists *Love, Peace And Happiness* (Columbia 1969) ★★, *A New Generation* (Columbia 1971) ★★, *Oh My God* (Columbia 1972) ★★, *Unbonded* (Avco 1974) ★★, *Right Move* (Avco 1975) ★★, *Live In Concert On Mars* (Roxbury 1976) ★★★.

COMPILATIONS: *The Chambers Brothers Greatest Hits* (Columbia 1970) ★★★, *Best Of …* (Fantasy 1973) ★★★, *Time Has Come: The Best Of The Chambers Brothers* (Columbia 1996) ★★★.

CHANDLER, CHAS

b. Bryan James Chandler, 18 December 1938, Heaton, Tyne And Wear, England, d. 17 July 1996. Chandler's career can be placed in two distinct sections. In the 60s he was the giant figure wielding a bass guitar with the pioneering R&B group the Animals. Following the break-up of the original Animals in 1967, the businesslike Chandler had the foresight to spot the potential of a black guitarist, whom he had watched playing in a New York club. He brought this young man, now renamed Jimi Hendrix, over to London. After recruiting two further musicians, Noel Redding and Mitch Mitchell, the shrewd Chandler succeeded in making the Jimi Hendrix Experience one of the most talked-about groups since the Beatles. The summer of 1967 was a perfect time to launch psychedelic rock music to the awaiting 'underground' scene. Chandler proved that his Midas-like touch was no fluke, and after selling out his managerial interest in Hendrix to former Animals manager Mike Jeffries, he nurtured Slade. With wily foresight Chandler led them through extraordinary success in the early 70s with no less than six UK chart-toppers.

He built up a mini-empire of companies, including music publishing, agency, management, production and recording studio under the Barn Group banner. In 1977 the original Animals re-formed and recorded their comeback album in his barn in Surrey. Six years later they re-formed once again, prompting Chandler to sell up his business interests and became a musician again. While the obligatory world tour made money, it also opened old wounds and the group collapsed for a third time.

● FURTHER READING: *Wild Animals*, Andy Blackford.

CHANDLER, GENE

b. Eugene Dixon, 6 July 1937, Chicago, Illinois, USA. Recalled for the gauche but irresistible 1962 US number 1, 'Duke Of Earl', Chandler's million-selling single in fact featured the Dukays, a doo-wop quintet he fronted (Eugene Dixon, Shirley Jones, James Lowe, Earl Edwards and Ben Broyles). His record company preferred to promote a solo artist and thus one of soul's most enduring careers was launched. Temporarily bedevilled by his 'dandy' image, the singer was rescued by a series of excellent Curtis Mayfield-penned songs, including 'Rainbow' and 'Man's Temptation'. These were hits in 1963, but the relationship blossomed with 'Just Be True' (1964) and the sublime 'Nothing Can Stop Me' (1965), both US Top 20 singles. Chandler later recorded under the aegis of producer Carl Davis, including '(The) Girl Don't Care', 'There Goes The Lover' and 'From The Teacher To The Preacher', a duet with Barbara Acklin. Switching to Mercury Records in 1970, 'Groovy Situation' became another major hit, while an inspired teaming with Jerry Butler was an artistic triumph. Chandler's career was revitalized during the disco boom when 'Get Down' was an international hit on Chi-Sound (Chandler was also a vice-president for the label). Further releases, 'When You're Number 1' and 'Does She Have A Friend', consolidated such success, while recordings for Salsoul, with Jaime Lynn and Fastfire, continued his career into the 80s.

● ALBUMS: *The Duke Of Earl* (Vee Jay 1962) ★★★★, *Just Be True* (1964) ★★★, *Gene Chandler Live On Stage In '65* (Constellation 1965, reissued as *Live At The Regal*) ★★, *The Girl Don't Care* (Brunswick 1967) ★★★, *The Duke Of Soul* (Checker 1967) ★★★, *There Was A Time* (Brunswick 1968) ★★, *The Two Sides Of Gene Chandler* (Brunswick 1969) ★★, *The Gene Chandler Situation* (Mercury 1970) ★★★, with Jerry Butler *Gene And Jerry – One & One* (Mercury 1971) ★★★, *Get Down* (Chi-Sound 1978) ★★★, *When You're Number One* (20th Century 1979), *'80* (20th Century 1980) ★★★, *Here's To Love* (20th Century 1981) ★★, *Your Love Looks Good On Me* (Fastfire 1985) ★★★.

● COMPILATIONS: *Greatest Hits By Gene Chandler* (Constellation 1964) ★★★, *Just Be True* (1980) ★★★, *Stroll On With The Duke* (Solid Smoke 1984) ★★★, *60s Soul Brother* (Kent/Ace 1986) ★★★, *Get Down* (Charly 1992) ★★★, *Nothing Can Stop Me: Gene Chandler's Greatest Hits* (Varèse Sarabande 1994) ★★★, *Duke Of Soul: The Brunswick Years* (Brunswick 1998) ★★★, *Get Down With The Get Down: The Best Of The Chi-Sound Years 1978-83* (Westside 1999) ★★★, *Best Of Gene Chandler* (Collectables 2000) ★★★.

● FILMS: *Don't Knock The Twist* (1962).

CHANNEL, BRUCE

b. 28 November 1940, Jacksonville, Texas, USA. Born into a musical family, Channel was

actively performing while still in high school. He secured a six-month residency on the prestigious *Louisiana Hayride* show, which in turn resulted in a recording deal with Smash Records. In 1962 the singer scored a US chart-topper with the infectious 'Hey Baby' which also achieved gold record status on climbing to number 2 in the UK. Much of the song's appeal, however, was derived from its distinctive harmonica passage, which was played by Delbert McClinton. His plaintive style influenced that of several subsequent releases, including the Beatles' 'Love Me Do', although John Lennon later denied his influence. Channel's career floundered over the ensuing years and his releases were confined to low-key labels including Le Cam and Mel-O-Dy. He was signed to Mala in 1968, but although this made no difference to his fortunes in America, the singer enjoyed another UK Top 10 hit with the exuberant 'Keep On'. Long-time fans were perplexed by a figure vowing to return with a blues group featuring McClinton and guitarist Bobby Turner, but Channel's new-found success proved short-lived, and the frantic 'Mr. Bus Driver' failed to chart. He has nonetheless continued to perform and in 1988 made a surprise guest appearance while on a visit to the UK, as a disc jockey on BBC Radio 2. He appeared with the Memphis Horns on their self-titled 1995 album.
● ALBUMS: *Hey! Baby (And 11 Other Songs About Your Baby)* (Smash 1962) ★★★, *Goin' Back To Louisiana* (1964) ★★, *Keep On* (Bell 1968) ★★★, *Stand Up* (Icehouse 1997) ★★★.

CHANTAYS
This US-based group was comprised of the Californian Santa Ana High School students Bob Spickard (lead guitar), Brian Carman (guitar, saxophone), Bob Marshall (piano), Warren Waters (bass) and Bob Welsh (drums). They formed the Chantays in 1962, and secured immortality with 'Pipeline' the following year. Initially released as the b-side to a vocal track, this atmospheric surfing instrumental brought a new level of sophistication to an often one-dimensional genre and deservedly became a hit in the USA and Britain. It was a standard the quintet was unable to repeat and although Steve Khan replaced Welsh, the group broke up following a handful of unsuccessful releases. However, a re-formed line-up emerged during the 80s in the wake of a surfing resurgence.
● ALBUMS: *Pipeline* (Downey 1963) ★★★, *Two Sides Of The Chantays* (Dot 1964) ★★★.

CHANTS
Although Liverpool, England is a cosmopolitan city, few black musicians played in the Merseybeat venues. The best-known black act was the male harmony group the Chants, who, on occasion, were backed by the Beatles. They included Joey (b. 1942) and Eddie (b. 1944), who

were brothers of the professional boxer Ro Ankrah. The other members were lead vocalis Nat Smeda (b. 1944), Alan Hardin (b. 1944) an Eddie Amoo (b. 1944), who was also th songwriter for the group. The Chants wer formed at the Stanley House Community Centr and because they came from a deprived part o the city, they were championed by local M Bessie Braddock. Record producer Tony Hatc wrote a sparkling arrangement for their versio of 'I Could Write A Book' from *Pal Joey* and th publicity proclaimed, 'The Beatles say, "It's fab the gear."' They also recorded strong cove versions of the US doo-wop hits 'Come Go Wit Me' and 'A Thousand Stars'. Their best recor was 'She's Mine', although the arrangemen borrowed heavily from Phil Spector's 'He's Sur The Boy I Love'. Eddie Amoo reflects 'Unfortunately, none of our singles eve happened and it's a bit sick when I look at th success of Showaddywaddy and Darts. The were doing exactly what the Chants were doing only not as well.' It's also unfortunate that th Chants never made an album – their onstag favourite, 'Duke Of Earl', should have bee captured on tape.

CHARLATANS (USA)
The first of San Francisco's 'underground' roc acts, the Charlatans were formed in 1964 b George Hunter (autoharp, tambourine), Mik Wilhelm (guitar, vocals) and Richard Olse (bass, clarinet, vocals). They were the augmented by pianist Michael Ferguson, whom Hunter had met in line at an unemploymen office, and Sam Linde (drums). Th incompatible Linde was replaced by Dan Hicks by which time the band had adopted thei striking visual image, reminiscent of turn-of-the century western outlaws. Their waistcoats, stiff necked collars, high boots and long hair s impressed the owner of the Red Dog Saloon, bar in Virginia City, Nevada, that he booke them as his resident house band. It was here tha the band honed their mélange of blues, folk R&B and goodtime music, while Ferguson' artwork for their debut performance i recognized as America's first psychedelic poste The Charlatans returned to San Francisco late i 1965 but their eminent position did not result i a coherent recording career. Demos for the loca Autumn label were rejected, and although th quintet completed an album for Kama Sutra Records, the results were shelved. 'The Shadow Knows', a single issued against the band' preference, was the sole release by thi pioneering line-up. Hicks, Ferguson and Hunte then left, disillusioned at this seeming impasse Olsen and Wilhelm persevered and in 196 completed the Charlatans' self-titled album wit Darrell De Vore (piano) and Terry Wilso (drums). Although the group's erstwhile fire wa muted, glimpses of their legacy appeared i 'Alabama Bound' and 'Fulsom Prison Blues'. Th

Charlatans then dissolved, but its individual members remained active. Hicks formed the impressive Dan Hicks And His Hot Licks, and while Wilhelm fronted Loose Gravel, Ferguson joined Lynne Hughes, barmaid at the Red Dog Saloon, in Tongue And Groove. Olsen became a producer at Pacific High Studios and Hunter, the band's visionary, founded the Globe Propaganda design company. Hunter's artwork graced numerous magnificent covers including *Happy Trails* (Quicksilver Messenger Service), *Hallelujah* (Canned Heat) and *It's A Beautiful Day* (It's A Beautiful Day). Although the Charlatans were denied the acclaim accorded to those in their wake, the élan of San Francisco's renaissance is indebted to their influence.

● ALBUMS: *The Charlatans* (Philips 1969) ★★★, *The Autumn Demos* (Ace 1982) ★★★.
● COMPILATIONS: *The Charlatans* (Ace 1996) ★★★, *The Amazing Charlatans* (Ace/Big Beat 1996) ★★★.

CHARLES, RAY

b. Ray Charles Robinson, 23 September 1930, Albany, Georgia, USA. Few epithets sit less comfortably than that of genius; Ray Charles has borne this title for over 30 years. As a singer, composer, arranger and pianist, his prolific work deserves no other praise. Born in extreme poverty, Charles was slowly blinded by glaucoma until, by the age of seven, he had lost his sight completely. Earlier, he had been forced to cope with the tragic death of his brother, whom he had seen drown in a water tub. He learned to read and write music in braille and was proficient on several instruments by the time he left school. His mother Aretha died when Charles was 15, and he continued to have a shared upbringing with Mary Jane (the first wife of Charles's absent father). Charles drifted around the Florida circuit, picking up work where he could, before moving across the country to Seattle. Here he continued his itinerant career, playing piano at several nightclubs in a style reminiscent of Nat 'King' Cole and a vocal similar to Charles Brown.
Charles began recording in 1949 and this early, imitative approach was captured on several sessions. Three years later, Atlantic Records acquired his contract, but initially the singer continued his 'cool' direction, revealing only an occasional hint of the passions later unleashed. 'It Should've Been Me', 'Mess Around' and 'Losing Hand' best represent this early R&B era, but Charles's individual style emerged as a result of his work with Guitar Slim. This impassioned, almost crude blues performer sang with a gospel-based fervour that greatly influenced Charles's thinking. He arranged Slim's million-selling single, 'Things That I Used To Do', on which the riffing horns and unrestrained voice set the tone for Charles's own subsequent direction. This effect was fully realized in 'I Got A Woman' (1954), a song soaked in the fervour of the Baptist Church, but rendered salacious by the singer's abandoned, unrefined delivery. Its extraordinary success, commercially and artistically, inspired similarly compulsive recordings, including 'This Little Girl Of Mine' (1955), 'Talkin' 'Bout You' (1957) and the lush and evocative 'Don't Let The Sun Catch You Crying' (1959), a style culminating in the thrilling call and response of 'What'd I Say' (1959). This acknowledged classic is one of the all-time great encore numbers performed by countless singers and bands in stadiums, clubs and bars all over the world. However, Charles was equally adept at slow ballads, as his heartbreaking interpretations of 'Drown In My Own Tears' and 'I Believe To My Soul' (both 1959) clearly show. Proficient in numerous styles, Charles's recordings embraced blues, jazz, standards and even country, as his muscular reading of 'I'm Movin' On' attested.
In November 1959 Charles left the Atlantic label for ABC Records, where he secured both musical and financial freedom. Commentators often cite this as the point at which the singer lost his fire, but early releases for this new outlet simply continued his groundbreaking style. 'Georgia On My Mind' (1960) and 'Hit The Road Jack' (1961) were, respectively, poignant and ebullient, and established the artist as an international name. This stature was enhanced further in 1962 with the release of the massive-selling album *Modern Sounds In Country And Western Music*, a landmark collection that produced the million-selling single 'I Can't Stop Loving You'. Its success defined the pattern for Charles's later career; the edges were blunted, the vibrancy was stilled as Charles's repertoire grew increasingly inoffensive. There were still moments of inspiration: 'Let's Go Get Stoned' and 'I Don't Need No Doctor' brought glimpses of a passion now too often muted, while *Crying Time*, Charles's first album since kicking his heroin habit, compared favourably with any Atlantic release. This respite was, however, temporary and as the 60s progressed so the singer's work became less compulsive and increasingly MOR. Like most artists, he attempted cover versions of Beatles songs and had substantial hits with versions of 'Yesterday' and 'Eleanor Rigby'. Two 70s releases, *A Message From The People* and *Renaissance*, did include contemporary material in Stevie Wonder's 'Living In The City' and Randy Newman's 'Sail Away', but subsequent releases reneged on this promise.
Charles's 80s work included more country-flavoured collections and a cameo appearance in the movie *The Blues Brothers*, but the period is better marked by the singer's powerful appearance on the USA For Africa release, 'We Are The World' (1985). It brought to mind a talent too often dormant, a performer whose marriage of gospel and R&B laid the foundations for soul music. His influence is inestimable, and his talent widely acknowledged and imitated by

formidable white artists such as Steve Winwood, Joe Cocker, Van Morrison and Eric Burdon. Charles has been honoured with countless awards during his career including induction into the Rock And Roll Hall Of Fame in 1986, and receiving the Grammy Lifetime Achievement Award in 1987. It was fitting that, in 1992, an acclaimed documentary, *Ray Charles: The Genius Of Soul*, was broadcast by PBS television. *My World* was a return to form, and was particularly noteworthy for his cover versions of Paul Simon's 'Still Crazy After All These Years' and Leon Russell's 'A Song For You', which Charles made his own through the power of his outstanding voice. *Strong Love Affair* continued in the same vein with a balance of ballads matching the up-tempo tracks; however, it was clear that low-register, slow songs such as 'Say No More', 'Angelina' and 'Out Of My Life' should be the focus of Charles' concentration. In 2000 Charles returned to jazz with an excellent contribution to Steve Turre's *In The Spur Of The Moment*.

No record collection should be without at least one recording by this 'musical genius'. His ability to cross over into other musical territories is enviable. He has performed rock, jazz, blues and country with consummate ease, but it is 'father of soul music' that remains his greatest title.

● ALBUMS: *Hallelujah, I Love Her So* aka *Ray Charles* (Atlantic 1957) ★★★, *The Great Ray Charles* (Atlantic 1957) ★★★★, with Milt Jackson *Soul Brothers* (Atlantic 1958) ★★★★, *Ray Charles At Newport* (Atlantic 1958) ★★★★, *Yes Indeed* (Atlantic 1959) ★★★, *Ray Charles* (Hollywood 1959) ★★★★, *The Fabulous Ray Charles* (Hollywood 1959) ★★★, *What'd I Say* (Atlantic 1959) ★★★, *The Genius Of Ray Charles* (Atlantic 1959) ★★★★★, *Ray Charles In Person* (Atlantic 1960) ★★★★, *The Genius Hits The Road* (ABC 1960) ★★★★, *Dedicated To You* (ABC 1961) ★★★, *Genius + Soul = Jazz* (Impulse! 1961) ★★★★★, *The Genius After Hours* (Atlantic 1961) ★★★★, with Betty Carter *Ray Charles And Betty Carter* (ABC 1961) ★★★★, *The Genius Sings The Blues* (Atlantic 1961) ★★★★, with Jackson *Soul Meeting* (Atlantic 1961) ★★★★, *Do The Twist With Ray Charles* (Atlantic 1961) ★★★, *Modern Sounds In Country And Western Music* (ABC 1962) ★★★★★, *Modern Sounds In Country And Western Volume 2* (ABC 1962) ★★★★, *Ingredients In A Recipe For Soul* (ABC 1963) ★★★★, *Sweet And Sour Tears* (ABC 1964) ★★★, *Have A Smile With Me* (ABC 1964) ★★★, *Ray Charles Live In Concert* (ABC 1965) ★★★, *Country And Western Meets Rhythm And Blues* aka *Together Again* (ABC 1965) ★★★, *Crying Time* (ABC 1966) ★★★, *Ray's Moods* (ABC 1966) ★★★, *Ray Charles Invites You To Listen* (ABC 1967) ★★★, *A Portrait Of Ray* (ABC 1968) ★★★, *I'm All Yours, Baby!* (ABC 1969) ★★, *Doing His Thing* (ABC 1969) ★★★, *My Kind Of Jazz* (Tangerine 1970) ★★★, *Love Country Style* (ABC 1970) ★★, *Volcanic Action Of*

My Soul (ABC 1971) ★★★, *A Message From The People* (ABC 1972) ★★★★, *Through The Eyes Of Love* (ABC 1972), *Jazz Number II* (Tangerine 1972) ★★★, *Ray Charles Live* (Atlantic 1973) ★★★, *Come Live With Me* (Crossover 1974) ★★, *Renaissance* (Crossover 1975) ★★, *My Kind Of Jazz III* (Crossover 1975) ★★, *Live In Japan* (Atlantic 1975) ★★★, with Cleo Laine *Porgy And Bess* (RCA 1976) ★★★, *True To Life* (Atlantic 1977) ★★, *Love And Peace* (Atlantic 1978) ★, *Ain't It So* (Atlantic 1979) ★★, *Brother Ray Is At It Again* (Atlantic 1980) ★★, *Wish You Were Here Tonight* (Columbia 1983) ★★, *Do I Ever Cross Your Mind* (Columbia 1984) ★★, *Friendship* (Columbia 1985) ★★★★, *The Spirit Of Christmas* (Columbia 1985) ★★, *From The Pages Of My Mind* (Columbia 1986) ★★, *Just Between Us* (Columbia 1988) ★★, *Seven Spanish Angels And Other Hits* (Columbia 1989) ★★, *Would You Believe* (Warners 1990) ★★, *My World* (Warners 1993) ★★★, *Strong Love Affair* (Qwest/Warners 1996) ★★, *Berlin, 1962* (Pablo 1996) ★★★★.

● COMPILATIONS: *The Ray Charles Story* (Atlantic 1962) ★★★, *Ray Charles' Greatest Hits* (ABC 1962) ★★★★, *A Man And His Soul* (ABC 1967) ★★★, *The Best Of Ray Charles 1956-58* (Atlantic 1970) ★★★★, *A 25th Anniversary In Show Business Salute To Ray Charles* (ABC 1971) ★★★★, *The Right Time* (Atlantic 1987) ★★★, *A Life In Music 1956-59* (Atlantic 1982) ★★★★, *Greatest Hits Volume 1 1960-67* (Rhino 1988) ★★★★, *Greatest Hits Volume 2 1960-72* (Rhino 1988) ★★★★, *Anthology* (Rhino 1989) ★★★★, *The Collection* ABC recordings (Castle 1990) ★★★, *Blues Is My Middle Name 1949-52* recordings (Double Play 1991) ★★★, *The Birth Of Soul: The Complete Atlantic R&B '52-'59* (Rhino/Atlantic 1991) ★★★★★, *The Living Legend* (Atlantic 1993) ★★★, *The Best Of The Atlantic Years* (Rhino/Atlantic 1994) ★★★, *Classics* (Rhino 1995) ★★★, *Genius & Soul* 5-CD box set (Rhino 1997) ★★★★★, *Standards* (Rhino 1998) ★★★★, *The Complete Country & Western Recordings, 1959-1986* 4-CD box set (Rhino 1998) ★★★★★, *The Definitive Ray Charles* (WSM 2001) ★★★★.

● FURTHER READING: *Ray Charles*, Sharon Bell Mathis. *Brother Ray, Ray Charles' Own Story*, Ray Charles and David Ritz. *Ray Charles: Man And Music*, Michael Lydon.

● FILMS: *Blues For Lovers* aka *Ballad In Blue* (1964), *The Blues Brothers* (1980).

CHECKER, CHUBBY

b. Ernest Evans, 3 October 1941, Philadelphia, Pennsylvania, USA. Checker's musical career began in 1959 while working at a local chicken market. His employer introduced the teenager to songwriter Kal Mann, who penned the singer's debut single, 'The Class'. He was given his new name by the wife of the legendary disc jockey Dick Clark as a derivation of Fats Domino. Chubby Checker became one of several artists to enjoy the patronage of Clark's influential *American Bandstand* television show and the successful Cameo-Parkway label. He achieved national fame in 1960 with 'The Twist', a compulsive dance-based performance which outgrew its novelty value to become an institution. The song, initially recorded in 1958 by Hank Ballard And The Midnighters, was stripped of its earthy, R&B connotation as Checker emphasized its carefree quality. 'The Twist' topped the US chart on two separate occasions (1960 and 1961), and twice entered the UK charts, securing its highest position, number 14, in 1962. 'Pony Time' (1961), a rewrite of Clarence 'Pine Top' Smith's 'Boogie Woogie', became Checker's second gold disc and second US number 1, before 'Let's Twist Again' established him as a truly international attraction. A Top 10 hit on both sides of the Atlantic, it became the benchmark of the twist craze, one of the memorable trends of the immediate pre-Beatles era. It inspired competitive releases by the Isley Brothers ('Twist And Shout'), Joey Dee ('Peppermint Twist') and Sam Cooke ('Twistin' The Night Away') while Checker mined its appeal on a surprisingly soulful 'Slow Twistin'' (with Dee Dee Sharp) and 'Teach Me To Twist' (with Bobby Rydell).

Eager for more dance-orientated success, he recorded a slew of opportunistic singles including 'The Fly' (1961) and 'Limbo Rock' (1962), both of which sold in excess of one million copies. However, the bubble quickly burst, and dance-inspired records devoted to the Jet, the Swim and the Freddie were much less successful. Even so, Checker had in a comparatively short time a remarkable run of 32 US chart hits up to 1966. Checker was latterly confined to the revival circuit, reappearing in 1975 when 'Let's Twist Again' re-entered the UK Top 5. The Fat Boys' single, 'The Twist (Yo Twist)', with Chubby guesting on vocals, climbed to number 2 in the UK in 1988. He has continued to perform, record and maintain a profile, particularly in the music trade where he continues to remind and inform the music business that he deserves greater recognition.

● ALBUMS: *Chubby Checker* (Parkway 1960) ★★★, *Twist With Chubby Checker* (Parkway 1960) ★★★, *For Twisters Only* (Parkway 1960) ★★★, *It's Pony Time* (Parkway 1961) ★★★, *Let's Twist Again* (Parkway 1961) ★★★★, *Bobby Rydell/Chubby Checker* (Parkway 1961) ★★★, *Twistin' Round The World* (Parkway 1962) ★★, *For Teen Twisters Only* (Parkway 1962) ★★★, *Don't Knock The Twist* film soundtrack (Parkway 1962) ★★, *All The Hits (For Your Dancin' Party)* (Parkway 1962) ★★★, *Limbo Party* (Parkway 1962) ★★★, *Let's Limbo Some More* (Parkway 1963) ★★, *Beach Party* (Parkway 1963) ★★, *Chubby Checker In Person* (Parkway 1963) ★★, *Chubby's Folk Album* (Parkway 1964) ★, *Chubby Checker With Sy Oliver* (Parkway 1964) ★★, *Discotheque* (Parkway 1965) ★★, *Chequered*

(London 1971) ★★, *The Change Has Come* (MCA 1982) ★★, *The Texas Twist* (Twisted Entertainment 2001) ★★★, *Toward The Light* (Twisted Entertainment 2001) ★★★.
● COMPILATIONS: *Your Twist Party* (Parkway 1961) ★★★, *Chubby Checker's Biggest Hits* (Parkway 1962) ★★★★, *Chubby Checker's Eighteen Golden Hits* (Parkway 1966) ★★★★, *Chubby Checker's Greatest Hits* (ABKCO 1972) ★★★★, *Let's Twist Again* (BMG 1997) ★★★.
● FILMS: *It's Trad, Dad!* aka *Ring-A-Ding Rhythm* (1962), *Don't Knock The Twist* (1962).

CHEROKEES

Sons of Worcester, England, John Kirby (vocals), David Dower (rhythm guitar), Terry Stokes (lead guitar), Mike Sweeney (bass) and drummer Jim Green's moment of glory came in autumn 1964 when their revival of Lonnie Donegan's trudging b-side 'Seven Daffodils' spent five weeks in the UK Top 40, almost outpacing a version by the better-known Mojos. This feat was mostly attributable to generous pirate radio plugging and the production skills of Mickie Most, fresh from a chart-topper with the Animals, an act also signed to EMI Columbia. The Cherokees' future looked rosy but their follow-up, 'Wondrous Face', flopped. Further impetus was lost by procrastination about their next release – 1966's 'Land of 1,000 Dances'. This Chris Kenner opus proved to be an error of judgement as it battled in vain against more simultaneous covers than had 'Seven Daffodils'. By 1967, the Cherokees were back on the Worcester orbit of engagements – a classic local group.

CHESS RECORDS

Polish-born brothers Leonard and Philip Chess were already proprietors of several Chicago nightclubs including the Macomba Lounge when they bought into the Aristocrat label in 1947. Its early repertoire consisted of jazz and jump-blues combos, but these acts were eclipsed by the arrival of Muddy Waters. This seminal R&B performer made his debut with 'I Can't Be Satisfied', the first of many superb releases that helped to establish the fledgling company. Having then secured the services of Sunnyland Slim and Robert Nighthawk, the brothers confidently bought out a third partner, Evelyn Aron, renaming their enterprise Chess in 1950. Initial releases consisted of material from former Aristocrat artists, but the new venture quickly expanded its roster with local signings Jimmy Rogers and Eddie Boyd, as well as others drawn from the southern states, including Howlin' Wolf. Their recordings established Chess as a leading outlet for urban blues, a position emphasized by the founding of the Checker Records subsidiary and attendant releases by Little Walter, Sonny Boy (Rice Miller) Williamson and Elmore James. Other outlets, including Argo and Specialist were also established, and during the mid-50s the Chess empire successfully embraced rock 'n' roll with Chuck Berry and Bo Diddley. White acts, including Bobby Charles and Dale Hawkins, also provided hits, while the label's peerless reputation was sufficient to attract a new generation of virtuoso blues performers, led by Otis Rush and Buddy Guy.

The R&B boom of the 60s, spearheaded by the Rolling Stones and later emphasized by John Mayall and Fleetwood Mac, brought renewed interest in the company's catalogue, but the rise of soul, in turn, deemed as anachronistic. Although recordings at the Fame studio by Etta James, Irma Thomas and Laura Lee matched the artistic achievements of Motown Records and Atlantic Records, ill-advised attempts at aiming Waters and Wolf at the contemporary market with *Electric Mud* and *The New Howlin' Wolf Album*, marked the nadir of their respective careers. The death of Leonard Chess on 16 October 1969 signalled the end of an era and Chess was then purchased by the GRT corporation. Phil left the company to run the WVON radio station, while Leonard's son, Marshall, became managing director of Rolling Stones Records. Producer Ralph Bass remained in Chicago, cataloguing master tapes and supervising a studio reduced to recording backing tracks, but he too vacated the now moribund empire. Chess was later acquired by the All Platinum/Sugarhill companies, then MCA, who, in tandem with European licensees Charly Records, have undertaken a major reissue programme. Chess Records between the late 40s and the late 60s represent a body of American music that is both hugely influential and to this day, still magnificent to listen to.

● COMPILATIONS: *Chess: The Rhythm And The Blues* (1988) ★★★★, *The Chess Story: Chess Records 1954-1969* (1989) ★★★★, *First Time I Met The Blues* (1989) ★★★, *Second Time I Met The Blues* (1989) ★★★, *Chess Blues* 4-CD box set (1993) ★★★★, *Chess Rhythm & Roll* 4-CD box set (MCA 1995) ★★★★, *Chess Blues Guitar 1949-1969* (Chess 1998) ★★★★, *The Chess Blues-Rock Songbook* (Chess 1998) ★★★★, *The Chess Story 1947-1975* 13-CD box set (MCA/Universal 1999) ★★★★.

● FURTHER READING: *The Chess Labels*, Michel Ruppli. *A Discography Of The Rhythm & Blues Artists On The Chess Labels, 1947-75*, Les Fancourt. *The Story Of Chess Records*, John Collis. *A Discography Of The Blues Artists On The Chess Labels, 1947-57*, Les Fancourt. *Spinning Blues Into Gold: The Chess Brothers And The Legendary Chess Records*, Nadine Cohodas.

CHESSMEN

One of the more adventurous Irish showbands of the mid-60s, the Chessmen featured singer Alan Dee, who was also a strong songwriter. It was almost unprecedented for a showband to compose their own material, but Dee penned several hit songs such as 'Fighting' and 'What In

The World Has Come Over You'. His greatest success, however, came with an evocative ballad of emigration, 'Michael Murphy's Boy'. With its haunting chorus ('My name is Patrick Joseph, I'm Michael Murphy's Boy') the song was played frequently on Radio Eireann and reached number 4 in the Irish charts in the summer of 1966. The Chessmen enjoyed the privilege of being managed by Noel Pearson, a talented impresario who wrote and was on the board of the Abbey Theatre and producer of such acclaimed Irish films as *My Left Foot* and *The Field*. Although the Chessmen were a promising act, they felt restricted by the showband routine and fragmented in the late 60s following the departure of Dee.

CHEYNES

Formed in London, England, in July 1963, the Cheynes' founding line-up consisted of Roger Peacock (vocals), Eddie Lynch (lead guitar), Peter Bardens (b. 19 June 1945, Westminster, London, England; organ, vocals), Peter Hollis (bass) and Mick Fleetwood (drums). Within weeks Lynch was replaced by Phil Sawyer. The Cheynes were one of the most popular and exciting R&B acts of their era, but the group was unable to emulate the success of the Yardbirds or Manfred Mann. They made their recording debut in 1963 with a version of the Isley Brothers' 'Respectable'. It was succeeded in 1964 by the gospel-tinged 'Goin' To The River' and in 1965 by the equally confident 'Down And Out'. They disbanded in April 1965. Peacock joined the Mark Leeman Five, Fleetwood joined the Bo Street Runners, Sawyer joined (Les) Fleur De Lys and Bardens joined Them.

CHICKEN SHACK

Chicken Shack was the product of eccentric guitarist Stan Webb, veteran of several R&B outfits including the Blue 4, Sound Five and the Shades Of Blue. The latter, active between 1964 and 1965, included Webb, Christine Perfect (b. 12 July 1943, Grenodd, Lancashire, England; piano, vocals) and Andy Silvester (bass), as well as future Traffic saxophonist Chris Wood. Webb and Silvester formed the core of the original Chicken Shack, who enjoyed a long residency at Hamburg's famed Star Club before returning to England in 1967. Perfect then rejoined the line-up which was augmented by several drummers until the arrival of Londoner Dave Bidwell. Producer Mike Vernon then signed the quartet to his Blue Horizon Records label. *Forty Blue Fingers Freshly Packed And Ready To Serve* was a fine balance between original songs and material by John Lee Hooker and Freddie King, to whom Webb was stylistically indebted. *OK Ken?* emphasized the guitarist's own compositions, as well as his irreverence, as he introduces each track by impersonating well-known personalities, including UK disc jockey John Peel, ex-Prime Minister Harold Wilson and

UK comedian Kenneth Williams. The quartet also enjoyed two minor hit singles with 'I'd Rather Go Blind' and 'Tears In The Wind', the former of which featured a particularly moving vocal from Perfect, who then left for a solo career (later as Christine McVie). Her replacement was Paul Raymond from Plastic Penny.

Ensuing releases, *100 Ton Chicken* and *Accept!*, lacked the appeal of their predecessors and their heavier perspective caused a rift with Vernon, who dropped the band from his blues label. Friction within the line-up resulted in the departure of Raymond and Bidwell for Savoy Brown, a band Silvester later joined. Webb reassembled Chicken Shack with John Glascock (bass, ex-Jethro Tull) and Paul Hancox (drums) and embarked on a period of frenetic live work. They completed the disappointing *Imagination Lady* before Bob Daisley replaced Glascock, but the trio broke up, exhausted, in May 1973, having completed *Unlucky Boy*. The guitarist established a completely new line-up for *Goodbye Chicken Shack*, before dissolving the band in order to join the ubiquitous Savoy Brown for a US tour and the *Boogie Brothers* album. Webb then formed Broken Glass and the Stan Webb Band, but he has also resurrected Chicken Shack on several occasions, notably between 1977 and 1979, and 1980 and 1982, in order to take advantage of the band's continued popularity on the European continent, which, if not translated into record sales, assures this instinctive virtuoso a lasting career. Stan 'The Man' Webb continues to delight small club audiences with his latest incarnation of Chicken Shack.

● ALBUMS: *Forty Blue Fingers Freshly Packed And Ready To Serve* (Blue Horizon 1968) ★★★★, *OK Ken?* (Blue Horizon 1969) ★★★, *100 Ton Chicken* (Blue Horizon 1969) ★★★, *Accept! Chicken Shack* (Blue Horizon 1970) ★★★, *Imagination Lady* (Deram 1972) ★★★, *Unlucky Boy* (Deram 1973) ★★★★, *Goodbye Chicken Shack* (Deram 1974) ★★, *The Creeper* (Warners 1979) ★★, *Chicken Shack* (Gull 1979) ★★, *Roadie's Concerto* (RCA 1981) ★★★, *Chicken Shack On Air* (Band Of Joy 1991) ★★★, *Changes* (Indigo 1992) ★★★, *Webb's Blues* (Indigo 1994) ★★★, *Plucking Good* (Inak 1994) ★★★, *Stan 'The Man' Live* (Indigo 1995) ★★★, *Imagination Lady* (Indigo 1997) ★★, *Private Collection Vol 1* (Gygax 1999) ★★, *Poor Boy: In Concert 1973 & 1981* (Indigo 2000) ★★★. Solo: Stan Webb *Webb* (Indigo 2001) ★★.

● COMPILATIONS: *The Golden Era Of Pop Music* (Columbia 1977) ★★★, *In The Can* (Columbia 1980) ★★★, *Collection: Chicken Shack* (Castle 1988) ★★★, *Black Night* (Indigo 1997) ★★★, *Jersey Lightning* 1975-1978 recordings (Indigo 2000) ★★★.

CHIFFONS

Formed in the Bronx, New York, USA, where all the members were born, erstwhile backing singers Judy Craig (b. 1946), Barbara Lee Jones (b. 16 May 1947, d. 15 May 1992), Patricia Bennett (b. 7 April 1947) and Sylvia Peterson (b. 30 September 1946), are best recalled for 'He's So Fine', a superb girl-group release and an international hit in 1963. The song later acquired a dubious infamy when its melody appeared on George Harrison's million-selling single, 'My Sweet Lord'. Taken to court by the original publishers, the ex-Beatle was found guilty of plagiarism and obliged to pay substantial damages. This battle made little difference to the Chiffons, who despite enjoying hits with 'One Fine Day' (1963) and 'Sweet Talkin' Guy' (1966), were all too soon reduced to the world of cabaret and 'oldies' nights. They did, however, record their own version of 'My Sweet Lord'.

● ALBUMS: *He's So Fine* (Laurie 1963) ★★, *One Fine Day* (Laurie 1963) ★★, *Sweet Talkin' Guy* (Laurie 1966) ★★.

● COMPILATIONS: *Everything You Ever Wanted To Hear ... But Couldn't Get* (Laurie 1981) ★★★, *Doo-Lang Doo-Lang Doo-Lang* (Impact/Ace 1985) ★★★, *Flips, Flops And Rarities* (Impact/Ace 1986) ★★, *Greatest Recordings* (Ace 1990) ★★★★, *The Fabulous Chiffons* (Ace 1991) ★★★, *One Fine Day: 26 Golden Hits* (1994) ★★★★.

CHIMES (USA)

Formed in Brooklyn, New York, in 1959, this vocal quintet consisted of Lenny Cocco (lead), Joe Croce (baritone), Pat DePrisco (first tenor), Rich Mercado (second tenor) and Pat McGuire (bass). Signed to the small Tag label, the group reached the US Top 20 in 1961 with 'Once In Awhile'. A cover version of 'I'm In The Mood For Love' managed a US Top 40 placing the following year but the Chimes had no subsequent hits, disbanding in 1965. They re-formed in 1970 and performed at oldies shows until 1973. Cocco assembled a new Chimes group in 1981, which was still performing in the New York area in the early 90s. 'Once In Awhile' has grown in stature, and routinely features among the 10 all-time favourite hits of listeners to New York's 'oldies' radio station. A re-recording was made in the 80s that did not have the lustre of the original.

● ALBUMS: *Once In Awhile* (Ambient Sound 1987) ★★.

● COMPILATIONS: *Best Of Chimes And Classics* (Rare Bird 1974) ★★★.

CHIPMUNKS

A fictional group, the Chipmunks were three cartoon characters, Alvin, Theodore and Simon, who were created by Ross Bagdasarian (b. 27 January 1919, Fresno, California, USA), a multifaceted performer, who had earlier had an international hit as David Seville with 'Witch Doctor' in early 1958. On that hit, Bagdasarian had manipulated a tape recorder so that normally sung vocals played back at a faster speed. Using the same technique, he

experimented with the sound of three voices harmonizing at that faster speed and it reminded him of the chattering of chipmunks. Bagdasarian had recorded 'Witch Doctor' for Liberty Records (the three Chipmunks were named after Liberty executives), which released 'The Chipmunk Song' for the Christmas 1958 season. It reached number 1 in the USA and was quickly followed by 'Alvin's Harmonica' which climbed to number 3. In all, the Chipmunks placed 15 songs on the US charts between 1958 and 1962, spawning a hit television programme. They continued well into the 60s, recording an album of Beatles songs. Bagdasarian died in January 1972 but the Chipmunks were revived in 1980 by his son, Ross Bagdasarian Jnr., and his partner Janice Karmen, this time recording albums of punk, country and current rock! Warning: An entire album in one sitting by the Chipmunks is excruciating.
● ALBUMS: *Let's All Sing With The Chipmunks* (Liberty 1959) ★, *Sing Again With The Chipmunks* (Liberty 1960) ★, *Christmas With The Chipmunks* (Liberty 1962) ★, *Christmas With The Chipmunks – Volume Two* (Liberty 1963) ★, *The Chipmunks Sing The Beatles Hits* (Liberty 1964) ★, *The Chipmunks Sing With Children* (Liberty 1965) ★, *Chipmunk Punk* (Liberty 1980) ★, *Urban Chipmunk* (Liberty 1981) ★, *A Chipmunk Christmas* (Liberty 1981) ★, *Chipmunk Rock* (Liberty 1982) ★, *Merry Christmas Fun With The Merry Chipmunks* (Liberty 1984) ★, *Chipmunks In Low Places* (Sony 1994) ★, *A Very Merry Chipmunk* (Sony 1994) ★, *When You Wish Upon A Chipmunk* (Sony 1995) ★, *Club Chipmunk: The Dance Mixes* (Sony 1996) ★★.
● COMPILATIONS: *Twenty All-Time Greatest Hits* (Liberty 1982) ★★, *Chipmunks Greatest Christmas Hits* (Capitol 1999) ★★, *Greatest Hits: Still Squeaky After All These Years* (Capitol 1999) ★★.

CHISHOLM, GEORGE

b. 29 March 1915, Glasgow, Scotland, d. 6 December 1997, Milton Keynes, England. In his early 20s Chisholm arrived in London, where he played trombone in the popular dance bands led by Teddy Joyce and Bert Ambrose. Inspired originally by recordings of Jack Teagarden, Chisholm naturally gravitated towards the contemporary jazz scene and was thus on hand for informal sessions and even the occasional recording date with visiting American stars such as Benny Carter, Coleman Hawkins and Fats Waller. During World War II he played with the Royal Air Force's dance band, the Squadronaires, with whom he remained in the post-war years. Later he became a regular studio and session musician, playing with several of the BBC's house bands (including *The Goon Show*). In the late 50s and on through the 60s Chisholm's exuberant sense of humour led to a succession of television appearances in *The Black And White Minstrel Show*, both as musician and comic, and if his eccentric dress, black tights and George Robey-style bowler hat caused jazz fans some displeasure, the music he played was always excellent.

During this period he made many records with leading British and American jazz artists including Sandy Brown and Wild Bill Davison. In the 80s, despite having had heart surgery, Chisholm played on, often working with Keith Smith's Hefty Jazz or his own band, the Gentlemen Of Jazz. He continued to delight audiences with his fluid technique and his ability to blend an urgent attack with a smooth style of playing and endless touches of irreverent humour. He was awarded an OBE in 1984. In 1990 he was still on the road, touring with visiting Americans, such as Spike Robinson. Soon afterwards, however, his state of health forced him to retire from active playing but did nothing to damage his high spirits and sense of humour.
● ALBUMS: *George Chisholm And His Band* (1956) ★★★★, *Stars Play Jazz* (1961) ★★★★, *George Chisholm* (1967) ★★★, with Sandy Brown *Hair At Its Hairiest* (1968) ★★, *Along The Chisholm Trail* (1971) ★★★, *In A Mellow Mood* (1973) ★★★, *Trombone Showcase* (1976) ★★★, *The Swingin' Mr C* (Zodiac 1986) ★★★, *That's A-Plenty!* (Zodiac 1987) ★★★, with John Petters *Swinging Down Memory Lane* (CMJ 1989) ★★★.
● COMPILATIONS: *Early Days 1935-44* (Timeless 1998) ★★★.

CHOCOLATE WATCH BAND

The original line-up of this tempestuous US pop group – Ned Torney (guitar), Mark Loomis (guitar, vocals), Jo Kleming (organ), Richard Young (bass), Danny Phay (lead vocals) and Pete Curry (drums) – was assembled in San Jose, California, USA, in 1964. Gary Andrijasevich replaced Curry within weeks of the quintet's inception. The following year Torney, Kleming and Phay defected to another local outfit, the Topsiders, later known as the Other Side, while the latter's guitarist, Sean Tolby (bass), joined Loomis and Andrijasevich. The revitalized quintet was completed by Dave Aguilar (vocals) and Bill Flores (bass). Producer Ed Cobb, already renowned for his work with the Standells, signed the group in 1966. He matched the Watch Band's instinctive love of British R&B with a tough, metallic sound, and the best of their work – 'Don't Need No Lovin'', 'No Way Out' and 'Are You Gonna Be There (At The Love In)' – is among the finest to emerge from America's garage-band genre. However, the group's potential was undermined by personal and professional problems. Several Chocolate Watch Band masters featured studio musicians, while a substitute vocalist, Don Bennett, was also employed on certain sessions. A disillusioned Aguilar quit the line-up prior to the release of *The Inner Mystique*. Phay resumed his place on *One Step Beyond*, but this album proved disappointing, despite a cameo appearance by Moby Grape guitarist Jerry Miller. The Chocolate Watch Band split up in March 1970.

ALBUMS: *No Way Out* (Tower 1967) ★★★, *The Inner Mystique* (Tower 1968) ★★★, *One Step Beyond* (Tower 1969) ★★, *At The Love-In, Live! 1999 recording* (Roir 2001) ★★.
● COMPILATIONS: *The Best Of The Chocolate Watch Band* (Rhino 1983) ★★★, *44* (Big Beat/Ace 1984) ★★★.

CHRISTIAN, NEIL
b. Christopher Tidmarsh, 14 February 1943, Hoxton, East London, England. With backing group the Crusaders, Christian was one of the pioneering acts of Britain's pre-Beatles era. His first line-up included guitarist Jimmy Page, who was later featured as a session musician in the singer's 1964 release, 'Honey Hush'. Albert Lee, Mick Abrahams and Alex Dmochowski (later of Aynsley Dunbar Retaliation) also graced the Crusaders at various times in its career, while Ritchie Blackmore (guitar), Elmer Twitch (piano), Bibi Blange (bass) and Tornado Evans (drums) supported Christian when he toured to promote 'That's Nice'. This perky single reached the UK Top 20 in 1966, but when the similarly styled 'Oops' failed to chart, the singer moved to Germany where he had attracted a fanatical following. Christian subsequently returned to Britain and continued to record sporadically, but, unable to secure a consistent success, he later retired from active performing.
● COMPILATIONS: *The Best Of Strike Records* (RPM 2001) ★★★.

CHRISTIE, LOU
b. Lugee Alfredo Giovanni Sacco, 19 February 1943, Glen Willard, Pennsylvania, USA. A former student of classical music, Christie moved to New York in 1963 where he sang backing vocals on a variety of sessions. Before beginning his string of hits, Christie recorded unsuccessfully with such groups as the Classics and Lugee and the Lions. Although his high falsetto was reminiscent of an earlier era, and similar to that used successfully by Frankie Valli and Del Shannon, 'The Gypsy Cried', the artist's debut solo single, achieved sales in excess of one million in 1963. The following year 'Two Faces Have I' proved equally successful but, unable to avoid the US military draft, Christie's career was interrupted. He achieved a third golden disc with 'Lightnin' Strikes' (1966), arguably his finest record, which pitted the singer's vocal histrionics against a solid, Tamla/Motown Records-styled backbeat. The single also charted in the UK, where its follow-up, 'Rhapsody In The Rain' (1966), was another Top 20 entry, despite a ban in deference to its 'suggestive lyric'. In 1969, this time signed to Buddah Records, Christie had his final Top 10 hit

with 'I'm Gonna Make You Mine', his style virtually unchanged from the earlier hits. Numerous singles followed on small labels into the 80s, but Christie was unable to regain any commercial ground. A curious, almost anachronistic performer, he has spent most of the past two decades performing on the US rock 'n' roll revival circuit.
● ALBUMS: *Lou Christie* (Roulette 1963) ★★, *Lightnin' Strikes* (MGM 1966) ★★★, *Lou Christie Strikes Back* (Co & Ce 1966) ★★, *Lou Christie Strikes Again* (Colpix 1966) ★★★, *Lou Christie Painter Of Hits* (MGM 1966) ★★, *I'm Gonna Make You Mine* (Buddah 1969) ★★★, *Paint America Love* (Buddah 1971) ★★, *Lou Christie – Zip-A-Dee-Doo-Dah* (CTI 1974) ★★.
● COMPILATIONS: *Beyond The Blue Horizon: More Of The Best Of Lou Christie* (Varèse Sarabande 1995) ★★★, *Gonna Make You Mine* (Camden 1998) ★★★, *The Complete Co & Ce/Roulette Recordings* (Taragon 1998) ★★★.

CIRCUS
Circus was originally known as the Stormsville Shakers, a London-based R&B group led by Philip Goodhand-Tait, which supported Larry Williams on his 1965 UK tour. The band recorded several singles in its own right for the Parlophone label, the last two of which – 'Sink Or Swim' and 'Do You Dream' – featured their newly acquired Circus appellation. The sextet – Goodhand-Tait (vocals, keyboards), Mel Collins (saxophone), Clive Burrows (saxophone, ex-Zoot Money), Ian Jelfs (guitar), Kirk Riddell (bass) and Alan Bunn (guitar) – was then signed to Transatlantic, for whom they completed *Circus* in 1969, which featured a lengthy improvised version of the Beatles' 'Norwegian Wood'. This progressive set was the group's sole album, as Goodhand-Tait then left to pursue a singer-songwriter career in the mode of Elton John. Mel Collins, meanwhile, recorded with King Crimson and Alexis Korner.
● ALBUMS: *Circus* (Transatlantic 1969) ★★★.

CLANCY BROTHERS AND TOMMY MAKEM
Tom (b. 1923, Carrick-on-Suir, Co. Waterford, Eire, d. 7 November 1990, Cork, Eire), Paddy (b. 1922, d. 10 November 1998, Carrick-on-Suir, Co. Waterford, Eire) and Liam Clancy (b. 1936) were among the founders of the New York folk revival during the 50s. From a musical family, Tom and Paddy left for Canada in 1947, but soon crossed (illegally) over the American border. Tom enjoyed success as an actor, playing on Broadway with Orson Welles (*King Lear*) and Helen Hayes (*Touch Of The Poet*), while together the brothers staged Irish plays at the Cherry Lane Theatre in Greenwich Village. With money scarce they began performing concerts, and were soon attracting a bigger following for their music than their plays. Paddy was soon assisting the Folkways and Elektra labels in recording Irish material and in 1956 he set up

his own small label, Tradition Records. This released material by Josh White and Odetta. By now, the younger brother Liam had also moved to America, and was collecting songs in the Appalachian mountains.

He encouraged whistle player Tommy Makem (b. 1932, Keady, Co. Armagh, Northern Ireland) to move to New York. In the late 50s, the quartet began to perform in clubs and at hootenannies, eventually recording collections of Irish material in 1959. Among them were many, including 'Jug Of Punch' and 'The Leaving Of Liverpool', that became widely sung in folk clubs on both sides of the Atlantic. The Clancys attracted a large following with their boisterous approach and gained national prominence through an appearance on Ed Sullivan's television show. The group recorded frequently for Columbia Records throughout the 60s. Their sister, Peg Clancy Power made a solo album of Irish songs in the late 60s. Makem left to follow a solo career in 1969, later recording with producer Donal Lunny for Polydor Records in Ireland. The Clancys continued to make occasional appearances, notably their annual St. Patrick's Day concerts in New York. Louis Killen (b. January 1934, Gateshead, Co. Durham, England), a traditional singer from north-east England joined for a 1973 record of *Greatest Hits* on Vanguard Records. Although Liam left in 1975, there were other albums for Warner Brothers Records in the 70s and the original group re-formed for a 1984 concert and album. Although Tom Clancy died in November 1990, the remaining brothers continued to perform together occasionally in the early 90s, appearing in October 1992 at Bob Dylan's 30th Anniversary Concert at Madison Square Garden. Paddy Clancy died of cancer in November 1998, having worked as a dairy farmer since the group's partial retirement in the 60s.

● ALBUMS: *The Rising Of The Moon* (Tradition 1959) ★★★, *Come Fill Your Glass With Us* (Tradition 1959) ★★★, *The Clancy Brothers And Tommy Makem* (Tradition 1961) ★★★★, *A Spontaneous Performance Recording* (Columbia 1961) ★★★★, *The Boys Won't Leave The Girls Alone* (Columbia 1962) ★★★, *In Person At Carnegie Hall* (Columbia 1964) ★★★★, *Isn't It Grand Boys* (Columbia 1966) ★★★, *The Irish Uprising* (Columbia 1966) ★★★, *Freedom's Sons* (Columbia 1967) ★★★, *Home Boys Home* (Columbia 1968) ★★★, *Sing Of The Sea* (Columbia 1968) ★★★, *Bold Fenian Men* (Columbia 1969) ★★★, *Seriously Speaking* (Warners 1975) ★★★, *Every Day* (Warners 1976) ★★★, *Reunion* (Vanguard 1984) ★★★, *Older But No Wiser* (Vanguard 1990) ★★★, *In Concert* (Vanguard 1992) ★★★.

● COMPILATIONS: *Greatest Hits* (Vanguard 1973) ★★★, *The Best Of The Vanguard Years* (Vanguard 2000).

CLARK, CHRIS

Christine Clark joined Motown Records as a receptionist in 1964 and followed a familiar career structure within the company by graduating from office work to a recording contract. Her strident, bluesy vocals led her to be nicknamed 'The White Negress' by British fans, but this style excluded her from Motown's musical mainstream. After having an R&B hit with 'Love Gone Bad' in 1966 on the VIP subsidiary label, she graduated to Tamla in 1967 where she found some success with 'From Head To Toe'. In 1969 she became the Vice-President of Motown's film division, co-writing the screenplay for *Lady Sings The Blues* in 1971. In 1981 she was appointed Vice-President of Motown Productions, with jurisdiction over the company's creative affairs. Clark left the organization in 1989 and re-recorded 'From Head To Toe' with producer Ian Levine for Motor City Records in 1991. Not to be confused with the electronic/dance artist of the same name.
● ALBUMS: *Soul Sounds* (Tamla 1967) ★★★, *CC Rides Again* (Weed 1969) ★★★.

CLARK, DAVE, FIVE

One of the most popular British beat groups of the mid-60s, especially in the USA, the Dave Clark Five's career stretched back as far as 1958. Originally a backing group for north London singer Stan Saxon, the Five comprised Dave Clark (b. 15 December 1942, London, England; drums, vocals), backed by various musicians whose ranks included bassist Chris Wells and lead guitarist Mick Ryan. After splitting from Saxon, the Five established their own identity and nominated their date and place of formation as the South Grove Youth Club, Tottenham, London in January 1962. The evolving and finally settled line-up featured Mike Smith (b. 6 December 1943, London, England; organ, vocals), Rick Huxley (b. 5 August 1942, Dartford, Kent, England; bass guitar), Lenny Davidson (b. 30 May 1944, Enfield, Middlesex, England; lead guitar) and Denis Payton (b. 8 August 1943, London, England; saxophone). Smith's throaty vocals and Clark's incessant thumping beat were the group's most familiar trademarks.

After losing out to Brian Poole And The Tremeloes with the much covered Contours classic 'Do You Love Me', the group elected to record their own material. The Clark/Smith composition 'Glad All Over' proved one of the most distinctive and recognizable beat songs of its era and reached number 1 in the UK during January 1964. Its timing could not have been more opportune as the record fortuitously removed the Beatles' 'I Want To Hold Your Hand', after its six-week reign at the top. The national press, ever fixated with Beatles stories pronounced in large headlines: 'Has The Five Jive Crushed The Beatles' Beat?' The Five took advantage of the publicity by swiftly issuing the less memorable, but even more boot-thumping

'Bits And Pieces', which climbed to number 2. Over the next couple of years, the group's chart career in the UK was erratic at best, although they enjoyed a sizeable Top 10 hit in 1965 with 'Catch Us If You Can' ('Having A Wild Weekend' in the USA) from the film of the same name in which they starred.

Even as their beat group charm in the UK faded, surprisingly new opportunities awaited them in the USA. A series of appearances on the *Ed Sullivan Show* saw them at the forefront of the mid-60s beat invasion and they racked up a string of million-sellers. A remarkable 17 *Billboard* Top 40 hits included 'Can't You See That She's Mine', 'Because', 'I Like It Like That' and their sole US number 1 'Over And Over'. Back in the UK, they enjoyed a belated and highly successful shift of style with the Barry Mason/Les Reed ballad, 'Everybody Knows'. Slipping into the rock 'n' roll revivalist trend of the early 70s, they charted with the medleys 'Good Old Rock 'N' Roll' and 'More Good Old Rock 'N' Roll', before bowing out in 1971. In reappraising their work, their flow of singles between 1964 and 1966 was of an incredibly high standard, and such was their output that most of the b-sides were quite excellent. In terms of production Clark employed a kitchen sink approach; throw in everything. The remarkable 'Anyway You Want It' is one of the most exciting records of the decade, although many are unaware of its existence. This blockbuster has reverb, echo and treble recorded at number 11 volume, with an ear-shattering result that does not distort.

The simultaneous strength and weakness of the group lay in their no-risk policy and refusal to surrender the hit-making formula for a more ambitious approach. Far from serious rivals to the Beatles, as their initial press implied, they were actually a limited but solid outfit. Smith was the most talented with a huge rasping voice and great songwriting ability. Their astute leader, Clark, had a canny sense of the moment and astute business know-how, which enabled them to enjoy lucrative pickings in the US market long after their beat contemporaries had faded. He subsequently became a successful entrepreneur and multi-millionaire, both in the video market, where he purchased the rights to the pop show *Ready Steady Go!*, and onstage where his musical *Time* (starring Cliff Richard) enjoyed box office success. Clark retains the rights to all the band's material, and by sitting on the catalogue has successfully held out for the most lucrative offer to reissue the hits in the age of CD. This was achieved in fine style with the definitive *The History Of The Dave Clark Five* double CD. Old fans will relish the excellent running order and new fans will be astonished to discover how fresh these 60s pop songs still sound. A highly underrated group.

● ALBUMS: *A Session With The Dave Clark Five* (Columbia 1964) ★★★★, *Glad All Over* (Epic 1964) ★★★, *The Dave Clark Five Return* (Epic 1964) ★★★, *American Tour Volume 1* (Epic 1964) ★★★, *Coast To Coast* (Epic 1965) ★★★, *Weekend In London* (Epic 1965) ★★★, *Catch Us If You Can* (UK) *Having A Wild Weekend* (US) film soundtrack (Columbia 1965) ★★★★, *I Like It Like That* (Epic 1965) ★★★, *Try Too Hard* (Epic 1966) ★★★, *Satisfied With You* (Epic 1966) ★★★, *You Got What It Takes* (Epic 1967) ★★★, *Everybody Knows* (Epic 1968) ★★★, *If Somebody Loves You* (Columbia 1970) ★★★, *Glad All Over Again* (Epic 1975) ★★★.

● COMPILATIONS: *The Dave Clark Five's Greatest Hits* (Columbia 1967) ★★★★, *5x5 – Go!* (Epic 1969) ★★★★, *The Best Of The Dave Clark Five* (Regal Starline 1970) ★★★★, *25 Thumping Great Hits* (Polydor 1977) ★★★★, *The History Of The Dave Clark Five* (Hollywood 1993) ★★★★.

● VIDEOS: *Glad All Over Again* (PMI 1993).

● FILMS: *Get Yourself A College Girl* (1964), *Catch Us If You Can* aka *Having A Wild Weekend* (1965).

CLARK, DEE

b. Delecta Clark, 7 November 1938, Blytheville, Arkansas, USA, d. 7 December 1990, Smyrna, Georgia, USA. Clark had a wonderfully impassioned tenor voice and enjoyed a spate of rock 'n' roll hits in the late 50s and a lesser body of soul work in the 60s. Clark's entertainment career began in 1952 as a member of the Hambone Kids, who, with band leader Red Saunders, recorded a novelty number in which Clark's group patted a rhythm known as the Hambone. Clark later joined a vocal group, the Goldentones, who won first prize in a talent show at Chicago's Roberts Show Lounge. Noted disc jockey Herb 'Kool Gent' Kent then took the group to Vee Jay Records, where they recorded as the Kool Gents. Clark's distinctive stylings soon engendered a solo contract and in 1958 he had a US hit with 'Nobody But You' (R&B number 3 and pop Top 30). 'Just Keep It Up' (R&B number 9 and pop Top 20) and 'Hey Little Girl' (R&B number 2 and pop Top 20) proved equally popular the following year. The artist's major success came in 1962 with 'Raindrops' (R&B number 3 and pop number 2). This plaintive offering, co-written by Clark and Phil Upchurch, eventually sold in excess of one million copies. Sadly, Clark was unable to repeat this feat, but continued on Chicago-based Constellation with a spate of moderate R&B hits, namely, 'Crossfire Time' (1963), 'Heartbreak' (1964), and 'TCB' (1965). His career faded after Constellation went out of business in 1966. In the UK he had a sizeable hit in 1975 with 'Ride A Wild Horse'; in the USA the record failed to chart. Clark died of a heart attack in 1990.

● ALBUMS: *Dee Clark* (Abner 1959) ★★★, *How About That* (Abner 1960) ★★★, *You're Looking Good* (Vee Jay 1960) ★★★, *Hold On, It's Dee Clark* (Vee Jay 1961) ★★★, *Hey Little Girl* (Vee

Jay 1982) ★★★.
● COMPILATIONS: *The Best Of Dee Clark* (Vee Jay 1964) ★★★★, *Keep It Up* (Charly 1980) ★★★, *The Delectable Sound Of Dee Clark* (Charly 1986) ★★★★, *Raindrops* (Charly 1987) ★★★★, *Golden Classics* (Collectables 1997) ★★★★, *Ultimate Collection* (Marginal 1997) ★★★★.

CLARK, PETULA

b. 15 November 1932, Epsom, Surrey, England. Her Welsh mother, a soprano, taught Petula to sing, which enabled her to commence a stage career at the age of seven and a broadcasting career two years later. Her youthful image and crystal-clear enunciation were ideal for radio and by 1943, she had her own programme with the accent on wartime, morale-building songs. She made her first film in 1944 and then signed for the J. Arthur Rank Organization appearing in over 20 feature films, including the *Huggett* series, alongside other young hopefuls such as Anthony Newley and Alec Guinness. By 1949 she was recording, and throughout the 50s had several hits on the Polygon and Nixa labels including 'The Little Shoemaker', 'Suddenly There's A Valley', 'With All My Heart' and 'Alone'. Around this period, Clark's success in France led to many concert appearances in Paris and recordings, in French, for the Vogue label. Eventually, in 1959, at the age of 27 and unhappy with the British audiences' reluctance to see her as anything but a sweet adolescent, she moved to France, where she married Vogue's PR representative, Claude Wolff. At the Olympia Theatre, Paris, in 1960, she introduced her new sound, retaining the ultra-clear vocals, but adding to them electronic effects and a hefty beat. Almost immediately her career took off. She had a massive hit with 'Ya Ya Twist', for which she received the Grand Prix du Disque, and by 1962 was France's favourite female vocalist, ahead even of the legendary Edith Piaf. Meanwhile, in Britain, Clark's versions of 'Romeo', 'My Friend The Sea' and 'Sailor', were chasing Elvis Presley up the charts (the latter reached number 1). Her international breakthrough began in 1964 when the British songwriter/arranger Tony Hatch presented Clark with 'Downtown'. It became a big hit in western Europe, and a year later climbed to the top of the US charts, clinching her popularity in a country where she was previously unknown. The record sold over three million copies worldwide and gained a Grammy Award in the USA as the best rock 'n' roll single. Clark's subsequent recordings of other Hatch songs, frequently written with his lyricist wife, Jackie Trent, including 'My Love', 'I Couldn't Live Without Your Love', 'Don't Sleep In The Subway', all made the US Top 10 ('My Love' reached the top). Her recording of 'This Is My Song', written by Charles Chaplin for the Marlon Brando/Sophia Loren epic, *A Countess From Hong Kong* (1967), reached number 1 in the UK

charts and broke into the US Top 5.
Tours of the USA and television guest shots followed. As well as hosting her own BBC Television series, she was given her own US NBC television special *Petula*, in 1968. This was marred by the programme sponsor's request that a sequence in which she touched the arm of black guest Harry Belafonte should be removed in deference to the southern states. The show was eventually transmitted complete. That same year Clark revived her film career when she appeared as Sharon, the 'Glocca Morra' girl in E.Y. 'Yip' Harburg and Burton Lane's *Finian's Rainbow*, co-starring with Fred Astaire and Tommy Steele. While the film was generally regarded as too old-fashioned for 60s audiences, Clark's performance, with just a touch of the blarney, was well received, as was her partnership with Peter O'Toole in MGM's 1969 remake of *Goodbye, Mr. Chips*, marking her 30 years in showbusiness. She was, by now, not only a major recording star, but an international personality, able to play all over the world, in cabaret and concerts. Between 1981 and 1982 she played the part of Maria in the London revival of Richard Rodgers/Oscar Hammerstein II's *The Sound Of Music*. It ran for 14 months, and was a great personal success. In 1989, PYS Records issued a 'radically remised' version of her 60s hit, 'Downtown', with the original vocal accompanied by an acid house backing track. It went to number 10 in the UK chart.
To date Clark has sold over 30 million records worldwide and has been awarded more gold discs than any other British female singer. From early in her career she has written songs, sometimes under the pseudonym of Al Grant; so it was particularly pleasing for Clark to write the music, and appear in a West End musical, *Someone Like You*. The show opened in March 1990 to mixed reviews, and had only a brief run. Two years later Clark undertook her first concert tour of the UK for 10 years, and in 1993 took over the starring role of Mrs Johnstone in Willy Russell's musical *Blood Brothers* on Broadway, and then toured it through 26 American cities. In 1995, she played the part of Norma Desmond in the London production of *Sunset Boulevard* for six weeks while Elaine Paige was on holiday, and subsequently led the cast until the show closed in April 1997. A few months on, she was created CBE, 'for services to entertainment', in the New Year's Honours List. Early in 1998 Clark embarked on a UK tour and released *Where The Heart Is*, a collection of personal favourites. It featured 11 new tracks including her versions of 'With One Look', 'As If We Never Said Goodbye', and 'The Perfect Year', three numbers from *Sunset Boulevard* which had been previously issued as a CD maxi-single. There was also 'Home Is Where The Heart Is', a song she co-wrote for the ill-fated *Someone Like You*. Late in 1998/9, Clark starred in a 'pared-down' *Sunset Boulevard* on a major national US tour. In 1999, a

radical Ian Levine remix of 'Downtown' failed to trouble the charts.

● ALBUMS: *Petula Clark Sings* (Pye Nixa 1956) ★★★, *A Date With Pet* (Pye Nixa 1956) ★★★, *You Are My Lucky Star* (Pye Nixa 1957) ★★★, *A Christmas Carol* mini-album (Pye Nixa 1958) ★★★, *Petula Clark In Hollywood* (Pye Nixa 1959) ★★★, *Tête A Tête Avec Petula Clark* (Vogue 1961) ★★★, *Rendez-Vous Avec Petula Clark* (Vogue 1961) ★★★, *In Other Words* (Pye 1962) ★★★, *Petula* (Vogue 1962) ★★★, *Ceux Qui Ont Un Coeur* (Vogue 1964) ★★★, *Hello Paris* (Pye/Vogue 1964) ★★★, *Les James Dean* (Pye/Vogue 1964) ★★★, *Downtown* (Pye/Warners 1965) ★★★★, *Uptown With Petula Clark* (Imperial 1965) ★★★, *I Know A Place* (Pye 1965) ★★★, *The International Hits!* (Pye/Warners 1965) ★★★, *Petula '65* (Pye/Vogue 1965) ★★★★, *In Love!* (Laurie 1965) ★★★, *My Love* (Pye/Warners 1966) ★★★★, *I Couldn't Live Without Your Love* (Pye/Warners 1966) ★★★★, *Petula Clark* (Vogue 1966) ★★★, *Le Palmares* (Vogue 1966) ★★★, *Petula Clark's Hit Parade* (Pye 1966) ★★★, *Colour My World/Who Am I?* (Pye/Warners 1967) ★★★, *These Are My Songs* (Pye/Warners/Vogue 1967) ★★★, *C'est Ma Chanson* (Vogue 1967) ★★★, *C'est Le Refrain De Ma Vie* (Vogue 1967) ★★★, *The Other Man's Grass Is Always Greener* (Pye/Warners 1968) ★★★★, *Petula Clark* (Vogue 1968) ★★★, *Portrait Of Petula* (Pye/Warners/Vogue 1969) ★★★, *Just Pet* (Pye/Warners/Vogue 1969) ★★★, *Petula Clark* (Vogue 1969) ★★★, *Memphis* (Pye/Warners 1970) ★★, *The Song Of My Life* UK title *Warm And Tender* US/French title (Pye/Warners/Vogue 1971) ★★★, *Today* (Pye 1971) ★★★, *Petula '71* (Pye 1971) ★★★, *Live At The Royal Albert Hall* 1969 recording (Pye/Vogue 1972) ★★★, *The Petula Clark Album* (Pye 1972) ★★★★, *Now* (Polydor 1972) ★★★, *La Chanson De Marie-Madeleine* (Vogue 1972) ★★★, *Comme Une Priere* (Vogue 1972) ★★★, *Come On Home* (Polydor 1974) ★★★, *Live In London* (Polydor 1974) ★★★, *I'm The Woman You Need* (Polydor 1975) ★★★, *Just Petula* (Polydor 1975) ★★★, *Noël* (Pet Projects 1975) ★★, *Beautiful Sounds* (Pet Projects 1976) ★★, *Je Reviens* (CBS 1977) ★★★, *Destiny* (CBS 1978) ★★★, *An Hour In Concert With Petula Clark And The London Philharmonic Orchestra* (MFP 1983) ★★★, *Where The Heart Is* (Connoisseur Collection 1998) ★★★★, *A Sign Of The Times* (Varèse Sarabande 2001) ★★★.

● COMPILATIONS: *The Best Of Petula Clark* (Pye 1969) ★★★★, *Hits ... My Way* (Warners 1970) ★★★, *The Best Of Petula Clark* (Reader's Digest 1971) ★★★, *The Petula Clark Story Vol. 1* (Golden Hour 1971) ★★★, *12 Succes De Petula Clark* (Mondio/Vogue 1972) ★★★, *12 Succes De Petula Clark, Vol. 2* (Mondio/Vogue 1973) ★★★, *Petula* 3-LP set (RSP 1975) ★★★, *20 All-Time Greatest* (K-Tel 1977) ★★★★, *Spotlight On Petula Clark* (PRT 1980) ★★★, *100 Minutes Of Petula Clark* (PRT 1982) ★★★, *20 Greatest Hits* (Vogue 1984)

★★★, *Greatest Hits Of Petula Clark* (GNP Crescendo 1986) ★★★, *The Early Years* (PRT 1986) ★★★, *The Hit Singles Collection* (PRT 1987) ★★★★, *Love Songs* (Pickwick 1988) ★★★, *Downtown: The Petula Clark Collection* (PRT 1988) ★★★, *My Greatest* (MFP 1989) ★★★, *A Golden Hour Of Petula Clark* (Knight 1990) ★★★, *The EP Collection* (See For Miles 1990) ★★★★, *Downtown* (Castle 1990) ★★, *The Special Collection* (Castle 1990) ★★★, *A Golden Hour Of Petula Clark, Vol. 2* (Knight 1991) ★★★, *Portrait Of A Song Stylist* (Knight 1991) ★★★, *The Best Of Petula Clark* (Castle 1992) ★★★, *Treasures, Volume 1* (Scotti Bros 1992) ★★★, *Jumble Sale: Rarities And Obscurities 1959-1964* 2-CD set (Sequel 1992) ★★★★, *The EP Collection Volume Two* (See For Miles 1993) ★★★, *The Polygon Years, Volume One: 1950-1952* (RPM 1994) ★★★, *The Polygon Years, Volume Two: 1952-1955* (RPM 1994) ★★★, *The Nixa Years, Volume One* (RPM 1994) ★★★★, *The Nixa Years, Volume Two* (RPM 1994) ★★★★, *I Love To Sing* 3-CD box set (Sequel 1995) ★★★★, *Downtown: The Best Of Petula Clark* (Pulse 1995) ★★★, *These Are My Songs* (Start 1996) ★★★, *The Classic Collection* 4-CD box set (Pulse 1997) ★★★, *Petula Clark – Her Greatest Hits* (Snapper 1997) ★★★, *Sings Tony Hatch* (Castle Select 1999) ★★★, *Showstoppers* (Castle Select 1999) ★★★, *The International Collection* 4-CD box set (Bear Family 1999) ★★★★, *Downtown: The Pye Anthology* (Sequel 1999) ★★★, *The Songs Of My Life: The Very Best Of Petula Clark* 3-CD box set (Reader's Digest 1999) ★★★★, *The Petula Clark Anthology: Downtown To Sunset B* (Hip-O 2000) ★★★★, *The Sixties EP Collection* 10-CD box set (Sequel 2000) ★★★★, *En Vogue (Beat En Francais)* (Castle 2001) ★★★★.

● VIDEOS: *Petula Clark Spectacular* (Laserlight 1996).

● FURTHER READING: *This Is My Song: A Biography Of Petula Clark*, Andrea Kon.

● FILMS: *Medal For The General* aka *The Gay Intruders* (1944), *Strawberry Roan* (1945), *Murder In Reverse* aka *Query* (1945), *I Know Where I'm Going!* (1945), *London Town* aka *My Heart Goes Crazy* (1946), *Vice Versa* (1948), *Easy Money* (1948), *Here Come The Huggetts* (1948), *Vote For Huggett* (1949), *The Huggetts Abroad* (1949), *Don't Ever Leave Me* (1949), *The Romantic Age* aka *Naughty Arlette* (1949), *Dance Hall* (1950), *White Corridors* (1951), *Madame Louise* (1951), *The Card* aka *The Promoter* (1952), *Made In Heaven* (1952), *The Runaway Bus* (1954), *The Gay Dog* (1954), *The Happiness Of Three Women* (1954), *Track The Man Down* (1955), *That Woman Opposite* aka *City After Midnight* (1957), *6.5 Special* aka *Calling All Cars* (1958), *À Couteaux Tirés* aka *Daggers Drawn* (1964), *Finian's Rainbow* (1968), *Goodbye, Mr. Chips* (1969), *Droles De Zebres* (1977), *Never Never Land* (1982).

CLASSICS IV

Formed in Jacksonville, Florida, USA, the Classics IV were 'discovered' by entrepreneur

Bill Lowery upon their move to Atlanta in 1967. This strongly commercial quintet comprised Dennis Yost (vocals), James Cobb (b. 5 February 1944, Birmingham, Alabama, USA; lead guitar), Wally Eaton (rhythm guitar), Joe Wilson (bass) and Kim Venable (drums). Seasoned session musicians, they had already worked on records by Lowrey protégés Tommy Roe, Billy Joe Royal and the Tams. Between 1968 and 1969, they enjoyed three soft-rock US hits with 'Spooky' (which sold in excess of one million copies), 'Stormy' and 'Traces', all expertly arranged by producer Buddie Buie. For a time, lead singer Dennis Yost was billed independently of the group, as Gary Puckett and Diana Ross had been in the Union Gap and the Supremes during the same period. Despite expanding the line-up to that of an octet with Dean Daughtry (b. 8 September 1946, Kinston, Alabama, USA), the eventual loss of major songwriter Cobb proved insurmountable. Yost failed to emerge as a star in spite of the new billing and, somewhat adrift in the early 70s, Classics IV enjoyed only one more minor hit, 'What Am I Crying For' (1972). Cobb and Daughtry later formed the Atlanta Rhythm Section.

● ALBUMS: *Spooky* (Liberty 1968) ★★★, *Mamas And Papas/Soul Train* (Liberty 1969) ★★, *Traces* (Liberty 1969) ★★.

● COMPILATIONS: *Dennis Yost And The Classics IV Golden Greats Volume 1* (Liberty 1969) ★★★, *The Very Best Of The Classic IV* (EMI 1975) ★★★, *Greatest Hits* (CEMA 1992) ★★★.

CLAY, JUDY

b. Judy Guion, 12 September 1938, St. Paul, North Carolina, USA, d. 19 July 2001, Fayetteville, North Carolina. Guion began singing in church in St. Paul at a very early age, before moving to Fayetteville, North Carolina, to be raised by her grandmother. A move to Brooklyn in the early 50s saw her join a church choir that also sang on Sunday night radio broadcasts. After her grandmother took Guion back to North Carolina, the young teenager asked to return to New York, where she first stayed with a girlfriend and had a church minister as temporary guardian. Soon, however, Lee Warrick Drinkard of the Drinkard Singers 'adopted' her and, from the age of 14, she became a regular performer with the 'family' gospel group, originally formed in Savannah, Georgia, around 1938, when Emily Drinkard (today better known as Cissy Houston, and Lee's cousin) was only five. The family group had moved to East Orange, New Jersey, and Guion joined them around 1953, at which point the family comprised her adopted mother, Lee, and sometimes (though never on record) Lee's two daughters, Marie Dionne (later just Dionne) Warrick (later Warwick) and Delia, also known as Dee Dee Warrick (Warwick), plus regulars Emily/Cissy Drinkard (whose married name at the time was Garland), Emily's married sisters

Marie Epps and Ann Moss, and their brothers Larry and Nick Drinkard, who often helped out on piano. This invaluable experience honed the young Guion's forceful and interpretive contralto, and she regularly shared lead-vocal duties with the other girls, even on three 50s Drinkard albums (a 1954 Newport Spiritual Stars set on Savoy, a 1957 live set from the Newport Jazz Festival on Verve Records and a 1958 studio set for RCA-Victor Records). After marrying John Houston, Cissy Drinkard went on to form the backing group the Sweet Inspirations.

In the early 60s, Guion began her own secular recording career singing with Cissy and other girls in various backing groups that predated the first incarnation of 'The Sweets'. Her first solo recordings (now as Judy Clay, though her record company had wanted to call her Amanda Knight) comprised two singles for the New York-based Ember label in 1961/2, followed by three 1963 sides (one duet and two solo) for Lavette. Next, she moved across town in early 1964 to Scepter Records, where fellow ex-Drinkard Singer Dionne Warwick had by then already successfully started her own secular career. Four singles appeared in 1964/5, with a later one seeing release after she had moved on. The next port of call was Atlantic Records, where Clay had already done much back-up work, but Jerry Wexler decided to send her south to Stax Records in Memphis, where she recorded 'You Can't Run Away From Your Heart' in mid-1967. A return to New York saw her achieve her first hits via two duets on Atlantic with blue-eyed soulman Billy Vera, 'Storybook Children' (a promo of which Vera had first cut with Nona Hendryx and Patti LaBelle's Bluebelles) and 'Country Girl – City Man', with the Sweet Inspirations on back-ups.

Later in 1968, Clay returned to Stax to record her best-remembered track, the fine duet with William Bell, 'Private Number', which had been originally intended as a vehicle for Otis Redding and Carla Thomas. A solo outing by Clay, 'Bed Of Roses', failed to register, and she returned to duets, this time with Bell again on 'My Baby Specialises', which at least made the R&B chart. Again a solo follow-up, 'It Ain't Long Enough', coupled with the exquisite 'Give Love To Save Love', failed to chart, and Clay's association with Stax ended with a song on Booker T.'s soundtrack for the movie *Uptight* and a lone track on Stax's spring 1969 compilation, *Soul Explosion*. Next, it was back to Atlantic for another, this time non-charting duet with Billy Vera, 'Reaching For The Moon', recorded in Muscle Shoals, where solo sessions were also intended to produce a Judy Clay album. In fact, only two solo singles were released, 'Sister Pitiful' and her one and only solo R&B hit, 'Greatest Love'.

Clay continued working through most of the 70s as a back-up singer but had to have major brain surgery in 1979, before returning briefly to the

scene with one unsuccessful single, a live version of the Bee Gees' 'Stayin' Alive', recorded by Dave Crawford in a Newark club and intended as part of a never-issued album. Clay subsequently satisfied herself with being a wife and mother, although she occasionally travelled up to New Jersey from her North Carolina home for gospel work, including appearances with Cissy Houston's choir at the New Hope Baptist Church in Newark. She became a licensed evangelist in 1990. Clay died in July 2001 following complications after a major car accident.
● ALBUMS: with Billy Vera *Storybook Children* Atlantic 1967) ★★★, with Veda Brown *Private Numbers* (Stax 1993) ★★★.
● COMPILATIONS: *Featuring Storybook Children & Greatest Love* (Ichiban 1995) ★★★.

CLEAR LIGHT

Despite releasing only one album, peaking at number 126 on the *Billboard* chart, Los Angeles-based septet Clear Light sent out ripples across the entertainment business. Their music, heavy rock featuring an innovative early use of double drummers, was intriguing with flashes of potential greatness but, after a cameo appearance in James Coburn's 1967 political satire flick, *The President's Analyst*, they imploded in 1968. After two solo albums, Cliff de Young (vocals) pursued an acting career which continues to this day with regular television credits. Ralph Shuckett (keyboards) joined the Peanut Butter Conspiracy before making a name for himself in television soundtracks. Douglas Lubahn (bass) went into session work, notably for the Doors before joining Dreams and even turning up with Billy Squier in the 80s. Dallas Taylor (drums) became the regular drummer for Crosby, Stills, Nash And Young, and after a brief excursion into the obscure Ohio Knox, worked with Steven Stills Band and Manassas. Danny Kortchmar (lead guitar) and Michael Ney (second drummer) both joined up with Carole King in her early band the City, and Kortchmar remained her regular guitarist for many years and was a mainstay friend and guitarist in James Taylor's career. Only Bob Seal (guitar) seems to have returned to oblivion.
● ALBUMS: *Clear Light* (Elektra 1967) ★★★. NB. Subsequent albums under the name Clear Light belong to a Scandinavian band unconnected to the original).

CLOUDS

As part of the expanding UK progressive music boom in 1969, the musically competent Clouds sadly failed to capture record buyers' imagination. Billy Ritchie (keyboards), Harry Hughes (drums) and Ian Ellis (bass), made the trek to London to find fame and fortune. They had previously been members of various Scottish bands but left their homeland in November 1966 and were signed to Robert Stigwood's NEMS Group as One Two Three. They supported Jimi Hendrix at his famous Saville Theatre gig but were dropped soon afterwards by the tough Stigwood. The Chrysalis agency signed and rechristened them Clouds. They made two interesting albums before they disintegrated, unable to find a niche among an overcrowded progressive music scene.
● ALBUMS: *Scrapbook* (Island 1969) ★★★, *Watercolour Days* (Island 1971) ★★★.

COLLECTORS

Formed in Vancouver, Canada, in 1961 and originally known as the C-Fun Classics, the original line-up – Howie Vickers (vocals), Brian Russell (guitar), Claire Lawrence (saxophone), Glenn Miller (bass) and Gary Taylor (drums) – recorded locally with some success before unveiling a new name, the Collectors, with the single 'Looking At A Baby' in 1967. By this point Russell and Taylor had been replaced by Bill Henderson and Ross Turney. The Collectors were then drawn towards US west coast venues where they established a positive reputation for their complex arrangements, soaring harmonies and extended improvisations. Their debut album, *The Collectors* aka *New Vibrations From Canada* admirably displayed their diverse talents. The group's second album, *Grass And Wild Strawberries*, was a loosely framed concept album. Although their imaginative use of time signatures and woodwind garnered critical plaudits, this was not transferred into sales, and the Collectors' career ebbed with two non-album singles. The departure of Vickers prompted an internal rethink and the remaining quartet abandoned the name and emerged as Chilliwack in 1971.
● ALBUMS: *The Collectors* aka *New Vibrations From Canada* (Warners 1968) ★★★, *Grass And Wild Strawberries* (Warners 1969) ★★★.
● COMPILATIONS: *Seventeenth Summer* (1986) ★★★.

COLLINS, GLENDA

b. London, England. Glenda Collins sang on numerous radio shows and in cabaret at the age of 12. In 1960 she was signed by Decca Records who issued her first three singles, 'Take A Chance', 'Oh, How I Miss You Tonight!' and 'Find Another Fool' (originally written by Barry Mann and Cynthia Weill for the Marcels). In 1962, Collins was introduced to enigmatic producer Joe Meek, who oversaw the rest of her output. 'I Lost My Heart At The Fairground' contains all of Meek's trademarks – sound effects, echo, pulsating beat and strong melody. On this recording Collins was backed by the Tornadoes, whereas the equally powerful follow-up, 'If You've Got To Pick A Baby', featured the Outlaws, with guitarist Ritchie Blackmore adding already distinctive accompaniment. Six more singles followed, the best of which was Collins' final release, 'It's Hard To Believe It', issued in 1966. Her recording career ended when Meek committed suicide in February 1967. Collins persevered on the cabaret circuit until the end of the 60s before opting to retire from music. Although denied commercial success, Collins' records remain among the finest Meek produced.

● COMPILATIONS: *Been Invited To A Party: The Singles 1963-1966* (Document 1990) ★★★, *This Little Girl's Gone Rockin': The Complete Glenda Collins* (RPM 1997) ★★★.

COLLINS, JUDY

b. 1 May 1939, Seattle, Washington, USA. One of the leading female singers to emerge from America's folk revival in the early 60s, Judy Collins was originally trained as a classical pianist. Having discovered traditional music while a teenager, she began singing in the clubs of Central City and Denver, before embarking on a full-time career with engagements at Chicago's Gate Of Horn and New York's famed Gerde's. Signed to Elektra Records in 1961, Collins' early releases emphasized her traditional repertoire. However, by the release of *Judy Collins #3*, her clear, virginal soprano was tackling more contemporary material. This pivotal selection, which included Bob Dylan's 'Farewell', was arranged by future Byrds' guitarist Jim (Roger) McGuinn. *Judy Collins' Fifth Album* was the artist's last purely folk collection. Compositions by Dylan, Richard Farina, Eric Andersen and Gordon Lightfoot had gained the ascendancy, but Collins henceforth combined such talent with songs culled from theatre's bohemian fringes.

In My Life embraced Jacques Brel, Bertolt Brecht, Kurt Weill and the then-unknown Leonard Cohen; on *Wildflowers* she introduced Joni Mitchell and in the process enjoyed a popular hit with 'Both Sides Now'. These releases were also marked by Joshua Rifkin's studied string arrangements, which also became a feature of the singer's work. Collins' 1968 release, *Who Knows Where The Time Goes?* is arguably her finest work. A peerless backing group, including Stephen Stills and Van Dyke Parks, added sympathetic support to her interpretations, while her relationship with the former resulted in his renowned composition, 'Suite: Judy Blue Eyes'. The singer's next release, *Whales And Nightingales*, was equally impressive, and included the million-selling single, 'Amazing Grace'. However, its sculpted arrangements were reminiscent of earlier work and although Collins' own compositions were meritorious, she was never a prolific writer. Her reliance on outside material grew increasingly problematic as the era of classic songwriters drew to a close and the artist looked to outside interests. She remained committed to the political causes born out of the 60s protest movement and fashioned a new career by co-producing *Antonia: A Portrait Of The Woman*, a film documentary about her former classical mentor which was nominated for an Academy Award. Collins did secure another international hit in 1975 with a version of Stephen Sondheim's 'Send In The Clowns'. Although subsequent recordings lack her former perception, and indeed have grown increasingly infrequent, she remains an immensely talented interpreter. In recent years Collins has shown a gift for writing novels, while the new millennium saw her launching her own label, Wildflower Records.

● ALBUMS: *A Maid Of Constant Sorrow* (Elektra 1961) ★★★, *Golden Apples Of The Sun* (Elektra 1962) ★★★★, *Judy Collins #3* (Elektra 1964) ★★★, *The Judy Collins Concert* (Elektra 1964) ★★, *Judy Collins' Fifth Album* (Elektra 1965) ★★★, *In My Life* (Elektra 1966) ★★★★, *Wildflowers* (Elektra 1967) ★★★★, *Who Knows Where The Time Goes* (Elektra 1968) ★★★★, *Whales And Nightingales* (Elektra 1970) ★★★, *Living* (Elektra 1971) ★★★, *True Stories And Other Dreams* (Elektra 1973) ★★★, *Judith* (Elektra 1975) ★★★, *Bread And Roses* (Elektra 1976) ★★★, *Hard Times For Lovers* (Elektra 1979) ★★, *Running For My Life* (Elektra 1980) ★★★, *Times Of Our Lives* (Elektra 1982) ★★, *Home Again* (Asylum/Elektra 1984) ★★, *Trust Your Heart* (Gold Castle 1987) ★★, *Sanity And Grace* (Gold Castle 1989) ★★, *Baby's Bedtime* (Lightyear 1990) ★★★, *Baby's Morningtime* (Lightyear 1990) ★★★, *Fires Of Eden* (Columbia 1990) ★★, *Judy Sings Dylan ... Just Like A Woman* (Geffen 1993) ★★, *Come Rejoice! A Judy Collins Christmas* (Mesa 1994) ★★★, *Shameless* (Mesa 1995) ★★★, *Voices* includes songbook and a memoir (Clarkson Potter 1995) ★★★, *Christmas At The Biltmore Estate* (Elektra 1997) ★★★, *Both Sides Now* (QVC 1998) ★★, *Broadway Classics* (Intersound 1999) ★★★, *Live At Wolf Trap* (Wildflower 2000) ★★★.

● COMPILATIONS: *Recollections* (Elektra 1969) ★★★★, *Colors Of The Day: The Best Of Judy Collins* (Elektra 1972) ★★★★, *So Early In The Spring, The First 15 Years* (Elektra 1977) ★★★★, *Most Beautiful Songs Of Judy Collins* (Elektra 1979) ★★★★, *Both Sides Now* (Pickwick 1981) ★★★, *Amazing Grace* (Telstar 1985) ★★★, *Her Finest Hour* (Pair 1986) ★★★, *Wind Beneath My Wings* (Laserlight 1992) ★★★, *Live At Newport (1959-1966)* (Vanguard 1994) ★★★, *Forever: An Anthology* (Elektra 1997) ★★★★, *The Very Best Of Judy Collins* (Rhino 2001) ★★★★.

● VIDEOS: *Baby's Morningtime* (WEA 1990) *Baby's Bedtime* (WEA 1990).

● FURTHER READING: *The Judy Collins Songbook*, Judy Collins and Herbert Haufrecht. *Judy Collins*, Vivian Claire. *Trust Your Heart*, Judy Collins. *My Father*, Judy Collins. *Shameless*, Judy Collins. *Singing Lessons: A Memoir Of Love, Loss, Hope, And Healing*, Judy Collins.

● FILMS: *La Liga No Es Cosa De Hombres* (1972), *Ninguno De Los Tres Se Llamaba Trinidad*

973), *Busco Tonta Para Fin De Semana* (1973),
e Makes Me Feel Like Dancin' (1983), *Junior*
994), *Earl Robinson: Ballad Of An American*
994).

OLOSSEUM
1e commercial acceptance of jazz rock in the
K was mainly due to Colosseum. The band was
rmed in 1968 from the nucleus of the
usicians who accompanied John Mayall on his
fluential album *Bare Wires*. Colosseum
mprised Jon Hiseman (b. 21 June 1944,
•ndon, England; drums), Dick Heckstall-Smith
26 September 1934, Ludlow, Shropshire,
1gland; saxophone), Dave Greenslade (b. 18
nuary 1943, Woking, Surrey, England;
yboards), Tony Reeves (b. 18 April 1943,
•ndon, England; bass) and James Litherland
6 September 1949, Manchester, England;
itar/vocals). Ex-Graham Bond Organis-ation
embers Heckstall-Smith and Hiseman took
eir former boss's pivotal work and made a
ccess of it. From the opening track of their
ong debut, *Those Who Are About To Die Salute*
u (1969), with Bond's 'Walkin' In The Park',
e band embarked on a brief excursion that
uld showcase each member as a strong
usical talent. Heckstall-Smith, already a
asoned jazz professional, combined with 19-
ar-old Litherland to integrate furious wah-wah
itar with bursting saxophone. Greenslade's
oming Hammond organ intertwined with
eves' melodically inventive bass patterns.
is sparkling cocktail was held together by the
asterful pyrotechnics of Hiseman, whose
los, featuring his dual bass drum pedal
chnique, were incredible.
lentyne Suite the same year maintained the
omentum, notably with the outstanding
eckstall-Smith composition 'The Grass Is
eener'. As with many great things, the end
me too soon, although departing member
therland was replaced with a worthy successor
Dave 'Clem' Clempson (b. 5 September 1949,
mworth, Staffordshire, England). In order to
commodate Clempson's wish to concentrate
guitar they enlisted Greenslade's former boss
the Thunderbirds, Chris Farlowe. His strong
cals gave a harder edge to their work.
llowing the departure of Reeves and the
cruitment of Mark Clarke, their work took a
ore rock-orientated approach. The end came
October 1971 with their last studio album,
ughter Of Time, quickly followed by *Colosseum*
ve. Hiseman and Clarke formed Tempest, but
er two mediocre albums Hiseman resurrected
e name in the shape of Colosseum II in 1975.
1e new version was much heavier in sound
d featured ex-Thin Lizzy guitarist Gary Moore,
ure Whitesnake bassist Neil Murray and
ure Rainbow keyboard player Don Airey.
calist Mike Starrs completed the line-up and
ey progressed through the mid-70s with three
ums, before Colosseum II finally collapsed

through Hiseman's exhaustion, and his wish to
return to his jazz roots. He eventually joined his
wife Barbara Thompson, playing jazz with her
band Paraphernalia. Colosseum will be
remembered for their initial pioneering work in
making jazz rock accessible to a wider market.
In 1997 the majority of the original band
reconvened with Farlowe as vocalist. Although
Hiseman had often mooted the idea of a
reunion, he stated that the time now 'seemed
right'.
● ALBUMS: *Those Who Are About To Die Salute
You* (Fontana 1969) ★★★★, *Valentyne Suite*
(Vertigo 1969) ★★★★, *Daughter Of Time*
(Vertigo 1970) ★★, *Live* (Bronze 1971) ★★★, as
Colosseum II *Strange New Flesh* (1976) ★★, as
Colosseum II *Electric Savage* (MCA 1977) ★★, as
Colosseum II *Wardance* (MCA 1977) ★★, *Bread &
Circuses* (Cloud 9 1998) ★★★.
● COMPILATIONS: *The Grass Is Greener* (1969)
★★★, *Collector's Colosseum* (Bronze 1971) ★★★,
Pop Chronik (1974) ★★★, *Epitaph* (Raw Power
1986) ★★★, *The Golden Decade Of Colosseum*
(Nightriding 1990) ★★★, *The Collection* (Castle
1991) ★★★.

COLTRANE, JOHN
b. John William Coltrane, 23 September 1926,
Hamlet, North Carolina, USA, d. 17 July 1967,
New York, USA. Coltrane grew up in the house
of his maternal grandfather, Rev. William Blair
(who gave him his middle name), a preacher
and community spokesman. While he was
taking clarinet lessons at school, his school band
leader suggested his mother buy him an alto
saxophone. In 1939 his grandfather and then his
father died, and after finishing high school he
joined his mother in Philadelphia. He spent a
short period at the Ornstein School of Music and
the Granoff Studios, where he won scholarships
for both performance and composition, but his
real education began when he started gigging.
Two years' military service was spent in a navy
band (1945-46), after which he toured in the
King Kolax and Eddie 'Cleanhead' Vinson bands,
playing goodtime, rhythmic big-band music. It
was while playing in the Dizzy Gillespie Big
Band (1949-51) that he switched to tenor
saxophone. Coltrane's musical roots were in
acoustic black music that combined swing and
instrumental prowess in solos, the forerunner of
R&B. He toured with Earl Bostic (1952), Johnny
Hodges (1953-54) and Jimmy Smith (1955).
However, it was his induction into the Miles
Davis band of 1955 – rightly termed the Classic
Quintet – that brought him to notice. Next to
Davis' filigree sensitivity, Coltrane sounds
awkward and crude, and Davis received
criticism for his choice of saxophonist. The only
precedent for such modernist interrogation of
tenor harmony was John Gilmore's playing with
Sun Ra.
Critics found Coltrane's tone raw and shocking
after years in which the cool school of Lester

Young and Stan Getz had held sway. It was generally acknowledged, however, that his ideas were first rate. Along with Sonny Rollins, he became New York's most in-demand hard bop tenor player: 1957 saw him appearing on 21 important recordings, and enjoying a brief but fruitful association with Thelonious Monk. That same year he returned to Philadelphia, kicking his long-time heroin habit, and started to develop his own music (Coltrane's notes to the later *A Love Supreme* refer to a 'spiritual awakening'). He also found half of his 'classic' quartet: at the Red Rooster (a nightclub that he visited with trumpeter Calvin Massey, an old friend from the 40s), he discovered pianist McCoy Tyner and bassist Jimmy Garrison.

After recording numerous albums for the Prestige label, Coltrane signed to Atlantic Records and, on 15 August 1959, he recorded *Giant Steps*. Although it did not use the talents of his new friends from Philadelphia, it featured a dizzying torrent of tenor solos that harked back to the pressure-cooker creativity of bebop, while incorporating the muscular gospel attack of hard bop. Pianist Tommy Flanagan (later celebrated for his sensitive backings for singers such as Ella Fitzgerald and Tony Bennett) and drummer Art Taylor provided the best performances of their lives. Although this record is rightly hailed as a masterpiece, it encapsulated a problem: where could hard bop go from here? Coltrane knew the answer; after a second spell with Davis (1958-60), he formed his best-known quartet with Tyner, Garrison and the amazing polyrhythmic drummer Elvin Jones. Jazz has been recovering ever since.

The social situation of the 60s meant that Coltrane's innovations were simultaneously applauded as *avant garde* statements of black revolution and efficiently recorded and marketed. The Impulse! label, to which he switched from Atlantic in 1961, has a staggering catalogue that includes most of Coltrane's landmark records, plus several experimental sessions from the mid-60s that still remain unreleased (although they missed *My Favorite Things*, recorded in 1960 for Atlantic, in which Coltrane helped re-establish the soprano saxophone as an important instrument). Between 1961 and his death in 1967, Coltrane made music that has become the foundation of modern jazz. For commercial reasons, Impulse! Records had a habit of delaying the release of his music; fans emerged from the live performances in shock at the pace of his evolution. A record of *Ballads* and an encounter with Duke Ellington in 1962 seemed designed to deflect criticisms of coarseness, although Coltrane later attributed their relatively temperate ambience to persistent problems with his mouthpiece. *A Love Supreme* was more hypnotic and lulling on record than in live performance, but nevertheless a classic.

After that, the records became wilder and wilder. The unstinting commitment to new horizons led to ruptures within the group. Elvin Jones left after Coltrane incorporated a second drummer (Rashied Ali). McCoy Tyner was replaced by Alice McLeod (who married Coltrane in 1966). Coltrane was especially interested in new saxophone players and *Ascension* (1965) made space for Archie Shepp, Pharoah Sanders, Marion Brown and John Tchicai. Eric Dolphy although he represented a different tradition of playing from Coltrane (a modernist projection of Charlie Parker), had also been a frequent guest player with the quartet in the early 60s, touring Europe with them in 1961. *Interstellar Space* (1967), a duet record, pitched Coltrane's tenor against Ali's drums, and provides a fascinating hint of new directions.

Coltrane's death in 1967 robbed *avant garde* jazz of its father figure. The commercial ubiquity of fusion in the 70s obscured his music and the 80s jazz revival concentrated on his hard bop period. Only Reggie Workman's Ensemble and Ali's Phalanx carried the huge ambition of Coltrane's later music into the 90s. As soloists, however, few tenor players have remained untouched by his example. It is interesting that the saxophonists Coltrane encouraged did not sound like him; since his death, his 'sound' has become a mainstream commodity, from the Berklee College Of Music style of Michael Brecker to the 'European' variant of Jan Garbarek. New stars such as Andy Sheppard have established new audiences for jazz without finding new ways of playing. Coltrane's music – like that of Jimi Hendrix – ran parallel with a tide of mass political action and consciousness. Perhaps those conditions are required for the creation of such innovative and intense music. Nevertheless, Coltrane's music reached a wide audience, and was particularly popular with the younger generation of listeners who were also big fans of rock music. *A Love Supreme* sold sufficient copies to win a gold disc, while the Byrds used the theme of Coltrane's tune 'India' as the basis of their hit single 'Eight Miles High'. Perhaps by alerting the rock audience to the presence of jazz, Coltrane can be said to have inadvertently – prepared the way for fusion. Coltrane's work has some challenging moments and if you are not in the right mood, he can sound irritating. What is established without doubt is his importance as a true messenger of music. His jazz came from somewhere inside his body. Few jazz musicians have reached the nirvana, and still have absolute control over their instrument.

● ALBUMS: with Paul Chambers *High Step* 1955-1956 recordings (Blue Note 1956) ★★★, with Elmo Hope *Informal Jazz* reissued as *Two Tenors* (Prestige 1956) ★★★, with various artists *Tenor Conclave* (Prestige 1957) ★★★, *Dakar* (Prestige 1957) ★★★, *Coltrane* reissued as *The First Trane* (Prestige 1957) ★★★, *John Coltrane With The Red Garland Trio* reissued as *Traneing In* (Prestige 1957) ★★★, with various artists *Wheelin'* An-

Dealing (Prestige 1957) ★★★, Blue Train (Blue Note 1957) ★★★★★, with Thelonious Monk Thelonious Monk With John Coltrane (Jazzland 1957) ★★★★, with Miles Davis Miles And Coltrane (Columbia 1958) ★★★★, Lush Life (Prestige 1958) ★★★, Soultrane (Blue Note 1958) ★★★★, John Coltrane (Prestige 1958) ★★★★, Settin' The Pace (Prestige 1958) ★★★, with Paul Quinichette Cattin' With Coltrane And Quinichette (Prestige 1959) ★★★, Coltrane Plays For Lovers (Prestige 1959) ★★★, The Believer (Prestige 1959) ★★★, Black Pearls (Prestige 1959) ★★, The Stardust Session (Prestige 1959) ★★★, Standard Coltrane (Prestige 1959) ★★★, Bahia (Prestige 1959) ★★★, Giant Steps (Atlantic 1959) ★★★★★, Coltrane Jazz (Atlantic 1960) ★★★★, with Don Cherry The Avant-Garde (Atlantic 1960) ★★★, with Milt Jackson Bags And Trane (Atlantic 1961) ★★★★, My Favorite Things (Atlantic 1961) ★★★★, Olé Coltrane (Atlantic 1961) ★★★, Africa/Brass: Volumes 1 & 2 (Impulse! 1961) ★★★★, with Kenny Burrell Kenny Burrell With John Coltrane (New Jazz 1962) ★★★★, Live At The Village Vanguard (Impulse! 1962) ★★★, Coltrane Plays The Blues (Atlantic 1962) ★★★★, Coltrane Time originally released as Cecil Taylor's Hard Driving Jazz (United Artists 1962) ★★★, Coltrane (Impulse! 1962) ★★★★, with Duke Ellington Duke Ellington And John Coltrane (MCA/Impulse! 1962) ★★★★, Ballads (Impulse! 1962) ★★★★, with Johnny Hartman John Coltrane And Johnny Hartman (Impulse! 1963) ★★★★, Coltrane Live At Birdland (Impulse! 1963) ★★★, Impressions (Impulse! 1963) ★★★★, Coltrane's Sound 1960 recording (Atlantic 1964) ★★★★, Crescent (Impulse! 1964) ★★★, with Cannonball Adderley Cannonball And Coltrane (Limelight 1964) ★★★, The Last Trane (Prestige 1965) ★★★, A Love Supreme (Impulse! 1965) ★★★★★, The John Coltrane Quartet Plays (Impulse! 1965) ★★★, with Archie Shepp New Thing At Newport (Impulse! 1965) ★★★, Ascension – Edition 1 (Impulse! 1965) ★★★★, Transition (Impulse! 1965) ★★★★, Ascension – Edition 2 (Impulse! 1966) ★★★★, Kulu Se Mama (Impulse! 1966) ★★★, Meditations (Impulse! 1966) ★★★★, Expression (Impulse! 1967) ★★★, Live At The Village Vanguard Again! (Impulse! 1967) ★★★, Om (Impulse! 1967) ★★, Selflessness 1963, 1965 recordings (Impulse! 1969) ★★★, Sun Ship 1965 recording (1971) ★★★, Dear Old Stockholm (Impulse! 1965) ★★★, Live In Seattle 1965 recording (Impulse! 1971) ★★★, Africa Brass, Volume Two 1961 recording (1974) ★★★★, Interstellar Space 1967 recording (Impulse! 1974) ★★★, First Meditations – For Quartet 1965 recording (Impulse! 1977) ★★★, The Other Village Vanguard Tapes 1961 recording (1977) ★★★, Afro-Blue Impressions 1962 recording (Pablo 1977) ★★★, The Paris Concert 1962 recording (Pablo 1979) ★★★, The European Tour 1962 recording (Pablo 1980) ★★★, Bye Bye Blackbird 1962 recording (1981) ★★★, Live At

Birdland – Featuring Eric Dolphy 1962 recording (Impulse! 1982) ★★★, Stellar Regions 1967 recording (Impulse! 1995) ★★★, The Olatunji Concert: The Last Live Recording (Impulse! 2001) ★★★.

● COMPILATIONS: The Best Of John Coltrane (Atlantic 1969) ★★★★, The Best Of John Coltrane – His Greatest Years (1961-1966) (MCA/Impulse! 1972) ★★★★, The Best Of John Coltrane – His Greatest Years, Volume 2 (1961-1967) (MCA/Impulse! 1972) ★★★★, The Mastery Of John Coltrane, Volumes 1-4 (1978) ★★★★, The Art Of John Coltrane (The Atlantic Years) (Pablo 1983) ★★★★, The Gentle Side Of John Coltrane (Impulse! 1992) ★★★★, The Major Works Of John Coltrane (Impulse! 1992) ★★★★, The Impulse! Years (Impulse! 1993) ★★★★, The Heavyweight Champion: The Complete Atlantic Recordings 7-CD box set (Rhino/Atlantic 1995) ★★★★★, The Complete 1961 Village Vanguard Recordings 4-CD box set (Impulse! 1997) ★★★★, The Classic Quartet – Complete Impulse! Studio Recordings 8-CD box set (Impulse! 1998) ★★★★★, The Bethlehem Years (Charly 1998) ★★★, The Very Best Of John Coltrane (Rhino 2000) ★★★★, with Miles Davis The Complete Columbia Recordings 1955-1961 (Columbia/Legacy 2000) ★★★★, Ken Burns Jazz: The Definitive John Coltrane (Verve 2000) ★★★, Coltrane For Lovers (Impulse! 2001) ★★★.

● CD ROM: John Coltrane – The Ultimate Blue Train (Blue Note 1997).

● VIDEOS: The World According To John Coltrane (1993), Ralph Gleason's Jazz Casual: John Coltrane (Rhino Home Video 1999).

● FURTHER READING: The Style Of John Coltrane, William Shadrack Cole. Trane 'N' Me, Andrew Nathaniel White. About John Coltrane, Tim Gelatt (ed.). John Coltrane, Discography, Brian Davis. The Artistry Of John Coltrane, John Coltrane. Chasin' The Trane, J.C. Thomas. Coltrane, Cuthbert Ormond Simpkins. As Serious As Your Life: John Coltrane And Beyond, Valerie Wilmer. John Coltrane, Brian Priestley. John Coltrane, Bill Cole. Ascension: John Coltrane And His Quest, Eric Nisenson. John Coltrane: A Sound Supreme, John Selfridge.

CONLEY, ARTHUR

b. 4 January 1946, Atlanta, Georgia, USA. Recalled as something of a one-hit-wonder, this Otis Redding protégé remains underrated. Conley first recorded for the NRC label as Arthur And The Corvets. After signing to his mentor Otis Redding's Jotis label, further singles were leased to Volt and Stax Records before 'Sweet Soul Music' (1967) hit both the US R&B and pop charts. A thin reworking of Sam Cooke's 'Yeah Man' saw the song's original lyrics amended to pay homage to several contemporary soul singers. Although 'Funky Street' was a US Top 20 hit, Redding's tragic death forestalled Conley's progress. Minor successes followed throughout 1968 and 1969 before the singer switched to the

Capricorn label in 1971. His debut album, *Sweet Soul Music*, is a strong collection, highlighted by each of his first five singles and two Redding originals. Later, Conley had a set of recordings for Swamp Dogg released, and then, having relocated to Europe, a live album recorded in Amsterdam in 1980 under his pseudonym of Lee Roberts finally emerged some eight years later.

● ALBUMS: *Sweet Soul Music* (Atco 1967) ★★★★, *Shake, Rattle And Roll* (Atco 1967) ★★★, *Soul Directions* (Atco 1968) ★★★, *More Sweet Soul* (Atco 1969) ★★★, *One More Sweet Soul Music* (Warners 1988) ★★, as Lee Roberts And The Sweater *Soulin'* (Blue Shadow 1988) ★★★.

● COMPILATIONS: *Arthur Conley* (Atlantic 1988) ★★★, *Sweet Soul Music: The Best Of Arthur Conley* (Ichiban 1995).

● FURTHER READING: *Sweet Soul Music*, Peter Guralnick.

CONNIFF, RAY

b. 6 November 1916, Attelboro, Massachusetts, USA. Taught to play the trombone by his father, Conniff studied arranging with the aid of a mail-order course while still at college. In 1934, after graduation, he worked with small bands in Boston before joining Bunny Berigan as trombonist/arranger in 1936. After a spell with Bob Crosby's Bobcats, Conniff spent four years with Artie Shaw and featured on several successful records including 'Concerto For Clarinet', 'Dancing In The Dark' and 'St James Infirmary'. During this period he was also studying at the New York Juilliard School of Music in New York. After army service in World War II Conniff spent some time as an arranger with Harry James, then freelanced while searching for a successful formula for producing hit records. He joined Columbia Records in 1954 and worked with several of their artists, including Johnnie Ray, Rosemary Clooney, Guy Mitchell and Marty Robbins. In 1954 he provided the arrangement for Don Cherry's million-seller, 'Band Of Gold', and in 1956 was given the chance, by Columbia producer Mitch Miller, to make an album featuring his 'new sound'.

The successful result, *'S Wonderful!*, was a set of familiar songs with an orchestra, and a cleverly blended mixed chorus of wordless voices, sometimes used as extra instruments within the songs' arrangements. *'S Wonderful!* was followed, naturally, by *'S Marvellous* and *'S Awful Nice*, all in the same vein. *It's The Talk Of The Town*, in 1960, featured a larger chorus, and for the first time they sang words. From 1957-68 Conniff had 28 albums in the US Top 40, including *Say It With Music (A Touch Of Latin)*, *Memories Are Made Of This*, and in 1966, the million-seller, *Somewhere My Love*. The album's title track, 'Lara's Theme' from the film *Doctor Zhivago* (1965), also made the US Top 10 singles chart. In 1969 he topped the UK album charts

with *His Orchestra, His Chorus, His Singers, His Sound*, and in 1974 became the first American popular musician to record in Russia, where he made *Ray Conniff In Moscow*, using a local chorus. More recent albums have included three Spanish sets, *Amor, Amor, Exclusivamente Latino* and *Fantastico*, and *The Nashville Collection* with country guest stars including Barbara Mandrell, George Jones and Charly McClain who featured on songs as diverse as 'Oh, Lonesome Me' and 'Smoke Gets In Your Eyes'.

● ALBUMS: with Don Cherry *Swingin' For Two* (Columbia 1956) ★★★, *'S Wonderful!* (Columbia 1957) ★★★★, *'S Marvelous* (Columbia 1957) ★★★★, *'S Awful Nice* (Columbia 1958) ★★★★, *Concert In Rhythm* (Columbia 1958) ★★★, *Broadway In Rhythm* (Columbia 1959) ★★★, *Hollywood In Rhythm* (Columbia 1959) ★★★, with Billy Butterfield *Conniff Meets Butterfield* (Columbia 1959) ★★★, *Christmas With Conniff* (Columbia 1959) ★★★, *It's The Talk Of The Town* (Columbia 1960) ★★★, *Concert In Rhythm – Volume II* (Columbia 1960) ★★★, *Young At Heart* (Columbia 1960) ★★★, *Hi-fi Companion Album* (Columbia 1960) ★★★★, *Say It With Music (A Touch Of Latin)* (Columbia 1960) ★★★, *Memories Are Made Of This* (Columbia 1961) ★★★, *Somebody Loves Me* (Columbia 1961) ★★★, *So Much In Love* (Columbia 1962) ★★★, *'S Continental* (Columbia 1962) ★★★★, *Rhapsody In Rhythm* (Columbia 1962) ★★★★, *We Wish You A Merry Christmas* (Columbia 1962) ★★★, *The Happy Beat* (Columbia 1963) ★★★, with Butterfield *Just Kiddin' Around* (Columbia 1963) ★★★, *You Make Me Feel So Young* (Columbia 1964) ★★★★, *Speak To Me About Love* (Columbia 1964) ★★★, *Invisible Tears* (Columbia 1964) ★★★, *Friendly Persuasion* (Columbia 1965) ★★★, *Music From Mary Poppins, The Sound Of Music, My Fair Lady & Other Great Movie Themes* (Columbia 1965) ★★, *Love Affair* (Columbia 1965) ★★★, *Happiness Is* (Columbia 1966) ★★★, *Somewhere My Love* (Columbia 1966) ★★★, *Ray Conniff's World Of Hits* (Columbia 1967) ★★★, *En Espanol!* (Columbia 1967) ★★★, *This Is My Song* (Columbia 1967) ★★★, *Hawaiian Album* (Columbia 1967) ★★, *It Must Be Him* (Columbia 1968) ★★★, *Honey* (Columbia 1968) ★★★, *Turn Around Look At Me* (Columbia 1968) ★★★, *I Love How You Love Me* (Columbia 1969) ★★★, *Jean* (Columbia 1969) ★★★, *Bridge Over Troubled Water* (Columbia 1970) ★★, *Concert In Stereo/Live At The Sahara/Tahoe* (Columbia 1970) ★★★, *We've Only Just Begun* (Columbia 1970) ★★★★, *Love Story* (Columbia 1971) ★★★, *Great Contemporary Instrumental Hits* (Columbia 1971) ★★★, *I'd Like To Teach The World To Sing* (Columbia 1972) ★★, *Love Theme From The 'Godfather'* (Columbia 1972) ★★★, *Alone Again (Naturally)* (Columbia 1972) ★★★, *I Can See Clearly Now* (Columbia 1973) ★★★, *You Are The Sunshine Of My Life* (Columbia 1973) ★★★,

Harmony (Columbia 1973) ★★★, *Evergreens* (Columbia 1973) ★★★, *Love Will Keep Us Together* (Columbia 1975) ★★★, *Plays The Carpenters* (Columbia 1975) ★★★, *Laughter In The Rain* (Columbia 1975) ★★★, *Send In The Clowns* (Columbia 1976) ★★★, *I Write The Songs* (Columbia 1976) ★★★, *Smoke Gets In Your Eyes* (Columbia 1977) ★★★, *If You Leave Me Now* (Columbia 1977) ★★★, *Sentimental Journey* (Columbia 1978) ★★★, *I Will Survive* (Columbia 1979) ★★★, *The Perfect Ten Classics* (Columbia 1981) ★★★, *The Nashville Connection* (Columbia 1982) ★★★, *Amor, Amor* (Columbia 1984) ★★★, *Exclusivamente Latino* (Columbia 1984) ★★★, *Fantastico* (Columbia 1984) ★★★, *Smoke Gets In Your Eyes* (Columbia 1984) ★★★, *Always In My Heart* (Columbia 1988) ★★.
● COMPILATIONS: *Ray Conniff's Greatest Hits* (Columbia 1969) ★★★★, *His Orchestra, His Chorus, His Singers, His Sound* (Columbia 1969) ★★★★, *Happy Beat Of Ray Conniff* (Columbia 1975) ★★★, *The Ray Conniff Songbook* (Columbia 1984) ★★★★, *16 Most Requested Songs* (Columbia 1991) ★★★, *Memories Are Made Of This* (Sony 1992) ★★★.

CONRAD, JESS
b. 1935, Brixton, London, England. Christened Jesse James, Conrad began his career as a repertory actor and film extra before being cast as a pop singer in a television play, *Rock-A-Bye Barney*. Initially, his singing voice was overdubbed by that of Gary Mills, but before long life imitated art and Conrad was transformed into a pop adonis. Championed by television producer Jack Good, he appeared in *Oh Boy!*, *Wham!* and *Boy Meets Girl*, which led to a recording contract with Decca Records and some minor early 60s hits with 'Cherry Pie', 'Mystery Girl' and 'Pretty Jenny'. When his recording career waned, he continued acting in low budget movies and pantomime, and in the 70s appeared in the musicals *Joseph And The Amazing Technicolor Dreamcoat* and *Godspell* as well as taking a cameo part in the Sex Pistols' celluloid excursion, *The Great Rock 'N' Roll Swindle*. One of Conrad's early singles, 'This Pullover', was belatedly named the worst single ever made in a novelty compilation of pop atrocities. Conrad continued to work throughout the 80s, and, in 1993, shed his 'squeaky-clean' image when he appeared as Prince Charming, with comedians Charlie Drake and Jim Davidson, in Davidson's 'blue' pantomime, *Sinderella*.
● ALBUMS: *Jess For You* (Decca 1961) ★.

CONTOURS
The Contours formed as an R&B vocal group in Detroit in 1959, featuring lead vocalist Billy Gordon, Billy Hoggs, Joe Billingslea and Sylvester Potts. Hubert Johnson (d. 11 July 1981) joined the line-up in 1960, and it was his cousin Jackie Wilson who secured the group an audition and then a contract with Motown Records in 1961. Initial singles proved unsuccessful, but in 1962 the dance-orientated number 'Do You Love Me' became one of the label's biggest hits to date, topping the R&B charts and reaching number 3 in the US pop listing. The same frantic blend of R&B and the twist dance craze powered the follow-up, 'Shake Sherry', in 1963. Both songs heavily influenced the British beat group scene, with 'Do You Love Me' being covered by Brian Poole And The Tremeloes, Faron's Flamingos and the Dave Clark Five. Unfortunately, the Contours were unable to capitalize on their early success, and their exciting, slightly chaotic sound lost favour at Motown, usurped by the choreographed routines and tight harmonies of acts such as the Temptations and the Four Tops.
As the Contours' line-up went through a rapid series of changes, they had occasional R&B successes with 'Can You Jerk Like Me', Smokey Robinson's witty 'First I Look At The Purse', and the dance number 'Just A Little Misunderstanding'. Although 'It's So Hard Being A Loser' (1967) was the Contours' last official single, posthumous releases, particularly in Britain, kept their name alive. Former lead vocalist Dennis Edwards later enjoyed consistent success with the Temptations, and as a soloist. Versions of the Contours appeared on the revival circuit from 1972 onwards, and while Johnson committed suicide on 11 July 1981, a trio consisting of Billingslea, Potts and Jerry Green were still performing into the 80s. In 1988, 'Do You Love Me' returned to the US Top 20 on the strength of its inclusion in the film *Dirty Dancing*. The current line-up of Billingslea, Potts, Arthur Hinson, Charles Davis and Darrel Nunlee issued *Running In Circles* on Ian Levine's Motor City label in 1990. The former lead vocalist Joe Stubbs also recorded *Round And Round* for the same label.
● ALBUMS: *Do You Love Me* (Gordy 1962) ★★★, *Running In Circles* (Motor City 1990) ★★.
● COMPILATIONS: *Baby Hit And Run* (1974) ★★★, *The Very Best* (Essential Gold 1996) ★★★, *The Very Best Of The Countours* (Motown 1999) ★★★★.

COOKE, SAM
b. Sam Cook, 22 January 1931, Clarksdale, Mississippi, USA, d. 11 December 1964, Los Angeles, California, USA. Reverend Charles Cook and his wife Annie May relocated their family to Chicago during the 30s. The devout young Sam Cook first performed publicly with his brother and two sisters in their Baptist quartet, the Soul Children. As a teenager he joined the Highway QCs, before replacing Rebert 'R.H.' Harris in the Soul Stirrers. Between 1951 and 1956 Cook (now with an 'e') sang lead with this innovative gospel group after being coached by another member, R.B. Robinson. Cooke's distinctive florid vocal style was soon

obvious on 'Touch The Hem Of His Garment' and 'Nearer To Thee'. The Soul Stirrers recorded for the Specialty Records label, where the singer's popularity encouraged producer Robert 'Bumps' Blackwell to provide Cooke with pop material. 'Loveable'/'Forever' was issued as a single in 1957, disguised under the pseudonym 'Dale Cook' to avoid offending the gospel audience. Initially content, the label's owner, Art Rupe, then objected to the sweetening choir on a follow-up recording, 'You Send Me', and offered Cooke a release from his contract in return for outstanding royalties. The song was then passed to the Keen label, where it became a smash hit and sold in excess of two million copies and topped the US singles chart for three weeks.

Further hits, including 'Only Sixteen' and 'Wonderful World', followed, and Cooke also had the foresight to set up his own publishing company, Kags Music, with J.W. Alexander in 1958. Cooke left Keen for RCA Records where original compositions such as 'Chain Gang' (1960), 'Cupid' (1961) and 'Twistin' The Night Away' (1962), displayed a pop craft later offset by such grittier offerings as 'Bring It On Home To Me' and Willie Dixon's 'Little Red Rooster'. Other magnificent offerings were to follow as Cooke just seemed to get better and better. 'Nothing Can Change This Love', 'Having A Party', 'Mean Old World' and 'Somebody Have Mercy' were all first class songs. Although RCA attempted to market him as a supper-club performer in the tradition of Sammy Davis Jnr. and Nat 'King' Cole, Cooke was effectively creating a new style of music; soul, by reworking the gospel anthems that remained at the heart of his music. To promote this new music, Cooke and Alexander founded the SAR and Derby labels, on which the Simms Twins' 'Soothe Me' and the Valentinos' 'It's All Over Now' were issued. Cooke also enlisted Allen Klein to become his business manager in 1963 and handle his other interests. Cooke's singing career was in the ascendant at the time of his tragic death. He had just released the superb Ain't That Good News, but the purity of the music on the album made his tawdry fate all the more perplexing. Already he had already experienced the death of his first wife and the tragic drowning of his son Vincent in a swimming pool in June 1963. On 11 December 1964, according to the Los Angles police department, Cooke was involved in an altercation at a downmarket Los Angeles motel with Lisa Boyer, a woman he had allegedly picked up that night. The singer was fatally shot by the manager of the motel, Bertha Franklin, and although subsequent investigations have disputed this outcome no definitive version has been forthcoming.

Sadly, the ebullient 'Shake' became a posthumous hit, but its serene coupling, 'A Change Is Gonna Come', was a more melancholic and powerful epitaph. Arguably his finest composition, its title suggested a metaphor for the concurrent Civil Rights movement. Cooke's legacy continued through his various disciples – Johnnie Taylor, who had replaced Cooke in the Soul Stirrers, bore an obvious debt, as did Bobby Womack of the Valentinos. Cooke's songs were interpreted by acts as diverse as Rod Stewart, the Animals and Cat Stevens, while the Rolling Stones' cover version of 'Little Red Rooster' echoed Cooke's reading rather than that of Howlin' Wolf. Otis Redding, Aretha Franklin, Smokey Robinson – the list of those acknowledging Cooke's skill is a testimony in itself. The 1986 compilation The Man And His Music provides an excellent overview of the singer's career. Cooke was a seminal influence on all soul music and R&B. His effortless and smooth delivery demonstrated an incredible natural singing voice that has rarely been surpassed.

● ALBUMS: Sam Cooke i (Keen 1958) ★★★, Encore (Keen 1959) ★★★, Tribute To The Lady (Keen 1959) ★★★, Hit Kit (Keen 1960) ★★★, I Thank God (Keen 1960) ★★★, The Wonderful World Of Sam Cooke (Keen 1960) ★★★, Cooke's Tour (RCA Victor 1960) ★★★, Hits Of The 50's (RCA Victor 1960) ★★★, Swing Low (RCA Victor 1960) ★★★, My Kind Of Blues (RCA Victor 1961) ★★★★, Twistin' The Night Away (RCA Victor 1962) ★★★★, Mr. Soul (RCA Victor 1963) ★★★★, Night Beat (RCA Victor 1963) ★★★, Ain't That Good News (RCA Victor 1964) ★★★★, Sam Cooke At The Copa (RCA Victor 1964) ★★★★, Shake (RCA Victor 1965) ★★★, Try A Little Love (RCA Victor 1965) ★★★, Sam Cooke Sings Billie Holiday (RCA 1976) ★★★, Sam Cooke Live At The Harlem Square Club, 1963 (RCA 1985) ★★★.

● COMPILATIONS: The Best Of Sam Cooke (RCA Victor 1962) ★★★★, The Best Of Sam Cooke, Volume 2 (RCA Victor 1965) ★★★★, The Unforgettable Sam Cooke (RCA Victor 1966) ★★★, The Man Who Invented Soul (RCA Victor 1968) ★★★, The Gospel Soul Of Sam Cooke With The Soul Stirrers, Volume 1 (Specialty 1969) ★★★★, The Gospel Soul Of Sam Cooke With The Soul Stirrers, Volume 2 (Specialty 1970) ★★★★, The Two Sides Of Sam Cooke (Specialty 1970) ★★★, This Is Sam Cooke (RCA 1971) ★★★, That's Heaven To Me: Sam Cooke With The Soul Stirrers (Specialty 1972) ★★★★, The Golden Age Of Sam Cooke (RCA 1976) ★★★, The Man And His Music (RCA 1986) ★★★★★, Forever (Specialty 1986) ★★★, Sam Cooke ii (Déjà Vu 1987) ★★★, You Send Me (Topline/Charly 1987) ★★★, 20 Greatest Hits (Compact Collection 1987) ★★★★, Wonderful World (Fame 1988) ★★★★, The World Of Sam Cooke (Instant 1989) ★★★★, Legend (EMS 1990) ★★★, The Magic Of Sam Cooke (Music Club 1991) ★★★, Sam Cooke With The Soul Stirrers (Specialty 1991) ★★★★, Sam Cooke's Sar Records Story (ABKCO 1994) ★★★, Hits! (RCA 2000) ★★★★, The Man Who

Invented Soul 4-CD box set (RCA 2000) ★★★★★.
● FURTHER READING: *Sam Cooke: The Man Who Invented Soul: A Biography In Words & Pictures*, Joe McEwen. *You Send Me: The Life And Times Of Sam Cooke*, S.R. Crain, Clifton White and G. David Tenenbaum.

COOKIES
This US vocal group trio was formed in the early 50s by Doretta (Dorothy) Jones (b. South Carolina, USA). Early members included Pat Lyles, Ethel 'Dolly' McCrae and Margorie Hendrickse. They were signed by Atlantic Records in 1956 where they recorded four singles, of which 'In Paradise' reached the R&B Top 10. However, the group was better known for session work, and can be heard on successful releases by Joe Turner ('Lipstick, Powder And Paint') and Chuck Willis ('It's Too Late'). The Cookies also backed Ray Charles on several occasions and Hendrickse, now known as Margie Hendrix, left to form Charles' own singing ensemble, the Raelettes. Her erstwhile colleagues continued their career as contract singers with newcomer Margaret Ross. Work with Neil Sedaka resulted in their meeting songwriter Carole King, who in turn brought the trio to the Dimension label. Here they enjoyed two US Top 20 hits with the effervescent 'Chains' (later covered by the Beatles) and 'Don't Say Nothin' Bad (About My Baby)', while their voices also appeared on various releases by Little Eva, herself an auxiliary member of the group. The Cookies later moved to Warner Brothers Records following Dimension's collapse. Altogether the trio recorded seven singles, all of which are excellent examples of the girl-group genre. Jones and McCrae also recorded in their own right, the latter under the name Earl-Jean.
● COMPILATIONS: *The Complete Cookies* (Sequel 1994) ★★★.

CORDET, LOUISE
b. Louise Boisot, 1946, Buckinghamshire, England. The daughter of cabaret and television actress Helene Cordet – and god-daughter of HRH Prince Phillip – Louise assumed her mother's stage-surname upon signing with Decca Records in 1962. Her first single for the label, 'I'm Just A Baby', was written by Jerry Lordan and recorded under the aegis of former Shadows drummer Tony Meehan; her perky delivery was rewarded with a UK number 13 hit. Later releases included her original rendition of 'Don't Let The Sun Catch You Crying', specifically written for Cordet by Gerry Marsden and later recorded, more successfully, by his group, Gerry And The Pacemakers. Despite appearances in the lightweight pop films *Just For Fun* and *Just For You*, Cordet was unable to sustain her performing career and by 1965 was described as a 'former singer' when the *New Musical Express* announced her intention to help publicize Marianne Faithfull.

CORNELL, LYNN
b. Liverpool, England. Cornell had been a prominent member of the Vernons Girls when she married drummer Andy White and subsequently recorded solo for Decca Records when the original troupe was nearing its 1961 disbandment. She is remembered chiefly for the much-covered, Greek-flavoured film title theme to 1960's *Never On Sunday* (her only UK Top 30 entry) and an ebullient 'African Waltz', which paled in the shadow of the bigger-selling Johnny Dankworth instrumental. Its b-side, an arrangement of the Jon Hendricks jazz standard 'Moanin'', illustrated that, beyond mere pop, Cornell could unfurl a suppleness of vocal gesture that was denied to luckier but less stylistically adventurous contemporaries. In more light-hearted vein was Jack Good's eccentric production of her 1962 duplication of the Blue-Belles' US hit, 'I Sold My Heart To The Junkman', but despite airplay on the BBC Light Programme, this, too, could not supersede even the chart honours gained by 'Never On Sunday'.

CORSAIRS
A family vocal group from La Grange, North Carolina, USA, this quartet comprised three brothers – lead Jay 'Bird' Uzzell (b. 13 July 1942), James Uzzell (b. 1 December 1940), and Moses 'King Moe' Uzzell (b. 13 September 1939) – and a cousin, George Wooten (b. 16 January 1940). Their songs had a standard mid-tempo pop feel, yet with an edge provided by Jay Uzzell's wailing lead, burbling bass and strong chorusing. The Corsairs found their opportunity by moving from their native North Carolina to New Jersey in 1961 to be nearer to the New York recording business. The quartet was discovered in a New Jersey club by independent producer Abner Spector, who released their records on his Tuff Records label. In 1962, they reached the charts twice, with 'Smoky Places' (number 10 R&B, number 12 pop) and 'I'll Take You Home' (number 26 R&B, number 68 pop). One unrecognized classic in their repertoire was 'Stormy' (their 1963 remake of a 1956 hit by Illinois act the Prophets). The Corsairs ideally evoke that fuzzy, intermediate era when the shuffle beats and doo-wop harmonies of the 50s were fast fading and had yet to be superseded by gospelized soul stylings. By 1965 Spector's well had run dry and the Corsairs' recording career was finished.

CORTEZ, DAVE 'BABY'
b. David Cortez Clowney, 13 August 1938, Detroit, Michigan, USA. Cortez played piano in church as a boy and progressed from there to Hammond organ, performing on the chitlin' (southern fried) circuit through the Midwest and California in the late 50s. From 1955-57 he performed with vocal group the Pearls and in 1956-57 also worked with the Valentines. In 1956 he made his first recording (under the

name of Dave Clooney) for the Ember label. He recorded for RCA-Victor in September 1959 and had a hit with Clock Records ('Happy Organ') in the same year. In 1962 he hit again with 'Rinky Dink', a crude 'Louie Louie'-type instrumental that could define 60s teen rock naïvety. He recorded an album for Chess Records in 1963 called, predictably, *Rinky Dink* and then signed with Roulette Records, who issued 'Shindig', 'Tweetie Pie' and 'In Orbit'. In February 1966 *The Fabulous Dave 'Baby' Cortez* appeared on Metro. In 1972 All Platinum released *Soul Vibration* with Frank Prescod (bass) and Bunky Smith (drums). Producer Joe Richardson gave the bass a funk depth comparable to reggae dub experiments. The hilarious dialogue of 'Tongue Kissing', plus liner notes by the organist's mum, make the album a gem. Signed to the T-Neck label – a Buddha Records subsidiary – he worked with the Isley Brothers to produce *The Isley Brothers Go All The Way*.
● ALBUMS: *Dave 'Baby' Cortez And His Happy Organ* (RCA Victor 1959) ★★★★, *Dave 'Baby' Cortez* (Clock 1960) ★★★, *Rinky Dink* (Chess 1962) ★★★, *Organ Shindig* (Roulette 1965) ★★★, *Tweety Pie* (Roulette 1966) ★★★, *In Orbit With Dave 'Baby' Cortez* (Roulette 1966) ★★★, *The Fabulous Dave 'Baby' Cortez* (Metro 1966) ★★★, *Soul Vibration* (All Platinum 1972) ★★★.
● COMPILATIONS: *Happy Organs, Wild Guitars And Piano Shuffles* (Ace 1993) ★★★★, *Happy Organ* (Collectables 1999) ★★★★.

CORVETTES

This Los Angeles, USA, country rock band was founded in 1968 by Chris Darrow (guitar/vocals) and Jeff Hanna (guitar/vocals), both ex-members of the Nitty Gritty Dirt Band. John London (bass) and John Ware (drums) completed the line-up featured on the act's two singles, 'Back Home Girl'/'Beware Of Time' and 'Level With Your Senses'/'Lion In Your Heart', but this promising quartet was unable to find commercial success. In January 1969 they became the backing group for Linda Ronstadt, touring with the singer as she promoted *Home Grown*. Bernie Leadon replaced Hanna in May when the latter rejoined the Dirt Band, but by September the Corvettes had disbanded. Darrow then pursued a solo career, Leadon switched to the Flying Burrito Brothers, while Ware and London became founder members of Mike Nesmith's First National Band.

COUGARS

Formed in 1961 in Bristol, England, the Cougars consisted of Keith 'Rod' Owen (guitar/arranger), Dave Tanner (rhythm guitar), Adrian Morgan (bass) and Dave Hack (drums). An instrumental group in the mould of the Shadows, the quartet was signed to EMI by A&R manager Norrie Paramor following a talent contest. Their debut single, 'Saturday Night At The Duck Pond', a frenetic reworking

of Tchaikovsky's 'Swan Lake', incurred a BBC ban on the grounds that it 'defaced a classical melody', but nonetheless reached the number 33 spot in 1963. The same composer was the inspiration for several ensuing releases, including 'Red Square' and 'Caviare And Chips', but the group was unable to repeat its initial success.

COULTER, PHIL

b. 19 February 1942, Derry, Northern Ireland. One of the most eclectic and accomplished arranger/musicians to emerge from Ireland during the 60s, Coulter first began as songwriter, composing the hit 'Foolin' Time' for the Capitol showband. At the time, Coulter was studying at Queens University, Dublin, but his talents were swiftly captured by leading entrepreneur Phil Solomon. Initially working with such showbands as the Cadets and Pacific, he continued to compose for the Capitol and even penned their 1965 Eurovision Song Contest entry, 'Walking The Streets In The Rain'. In the meantime, he worked on Solomon's other acts, including Twinkle, who enjoyed a major UK hit with the Coulter-arranged 'Terry'. Coulter also contributed to Them's song catalogue, with the driving 'I Can Only Give You Everything'. After leaving the Solomon stable in 1967, Coulter, now based in London, formed a partnership with Bill Martin, which became one of the most successful of its era. The duo were particularly known for their ability to produce instantly memorable pop hits, and achieved international fame after penning Sandie Shaw's 1967 Eurovision winner, 'Puppet On A String'. They barely missed repeating that feat the following year with Cliff Richard's stomping 'Congratulations'.
Coulter subsequently led his own country to victory in the contest by arranging Dana's 1970 winner, 'All Kinds Of Everything'. That same year, Coulter/Martin were commissioned to write 'Back Home', the official song for the England World Cup Squad, which proved a lengthy UK number 1. As well as his pop outings, which included writing 'My Boy' and an album's worth of material for Richard Harris, Coulter maintained his connection with the Irish folk scene, via his work with another of Solomon's acts, the Dubliners. He also produced three albums for the groundbreaking Planxty and worked with the Fureys. During the mid-70s, Coulter and Martin were called in to assist the Bay City Rollers, and subsequently composed a string of hits for the Scottish teenyboppers, including 'Remember (Sha-La-La)', 'Shang-A-Lang', 'Summerlove Sensation', 'Saturday Night', and 'All Of Me Loves All Of You'. During the same period, they enjoyed three Top 10 hits with Kenny and reached the top again in 1976 with Slik's 'Forever And Ever'. Coulter also produced several records by comedian Billy Connolly, including 1975's UK

umber 1 'D.I.V.O.R.C.E.'. After his partnership with Martin ended in the late 70s, Coulter specialized in orchestral recordings, which proved hugely successful in Irish communities. lbums such as *Classic Tranquillity* and *Sea Of Tranquillity* (both 1984), *Words And Music* (1989), *American Tranquillity* (1994), *Celtic Horizons* (1996), and collaborations with flautist James Galway and Roma Downey, have also enjoyed major international success, and Coulter is a regular fixture in the upper regions of the US New Age album chart.

Despite his successes, Coulter has suffered several family tragedies. His son was born with own's syndrome and died at the age of three; the song 'Scorn Not His Simplicity' was written in his memory. Coulter's brother also died tragically in a drowning incident in Ireland, which briefly caused him to retreat from the music business. He recorded the anthemic Home From The Sea' with the Lifeboat Chorus as a tribute. Coulter's production credits during the 90s have included work for Sinead O'Connor and Boyzone. His lengthy career, as producer, arranger, songwriter and performer, is all the more remarkable for encompassing such contrasting musical areas from folk and orchestral to straightforward Tin Pan Alley pop.

● ALBUMS: *Classic Tranquillity* (K-Tel 1984) ★★, *Sea Of Tranquillity* (K-Tel 1984) ★★★, *Peace And Tranquillity* (K-Tel 1985) ★★★, *Serenity* (K-Tel 1986) ★★, *The Christmas Collection* (K-Tel 1987) ★★, *Forgotten Dreams* (K-Tel 1988) ★★★, *Words And Music* (K-Tel 1989) ★★, *Local Heroes* (K-Tel 1990) ★★★, *American Tranquillity* (K-Tel 1994) ★★★, *The Live Experience* (K-Tel 1994) ★★★, *Celtic Anpipes* (K-Tel 1995) ★★★, *Celtic Horizons* (K-Tel 1996) ★★★, *Celtic Collections* (K-Tel 1996) ★★, with James Galway *Legends* (RCA 1997) ★★, with Galway *Winter's Crossing* (RCA 1998) ★★★, with Roma Downey *Healing Angel* (RCA 1999) ★★★, *Highland Cathedral* (RCA Victor 2000) ★★★.

COMPILATIONS: *The Essential Collection* (K-Tel 1994) ★★★, *Tranquillity Gold: The Very Best of Phil Coulter* (K-Tel 1999) ★★★★.

VIDEOS: *A Touch Of Tranquillity* (Shanachie 1995), *The Live Experience* (Shanachie 1996).

COUNT FIVE

Formed in 1964 in San Jose, California, USA. The Count Five were a classic one-hit-wonder whose Yardbirds-inspired psychedelic-punk hit 'Psychotic Reaction', reached the US Top 5 in 1966. The band's line-up consisted of Ken Ellner (b. 1948, Brooklyn, New York, USA; vocals/harmonica), Sean Byrne (b. 1947, Dublin, Eire; guitar/vocals), John Michalski (b. 1949, Cleveland, Ohio, USA; lead guitar), Roy Chaney (b. 1948, Indianapolis, Indiana, USA; bass) and Craig Atkinson (b. 1947, Springfield, Missouri, USA; drums). They first drew attention by wearing Dracula-style capes to

their gigs. After recording one album, also titled *Psychotic Reaction*, they continued to release singles into 1968 before disbanding. Byrne returned to Eire and featured on one album in 1973 as a member of Public Foot The Roman and in 1978 he turned up yet again for the group Legover on their album *Wait Till Nightime*.

● ALBUMS: *Psychotic Reaction* (Double Shot 1966) ★★★.

COUNTRY JOE AND THE FISH

Formed in Berkeley, California, USA, in 1965, this imaginative quintet began life as the Instant Action Jug Band. Former folk singer Country Joe McDonald (b. 1 January 1942, El Monte, California, USA) established the group with guitarist Barry Melton (b. 1947, Brooklyn, New York, USA), the only musicians to remain in the line-up throughout its turbulent history. Part of a politically active family, McDonald immersed himself in the activism centred on Berkeley, and his group's earliest recording, 'I Feel Like I'm Fixin' To Die Rag' (1965), was a virulent attack on the Vietnam war. The following year an expanded line-up, McDonald, Melton, David Cohen (guitar/keyboards), Paul Armstrong (bass) and John Francis Gunning (drums) embraced electricity with a privately pressed EP. By 1967 Armstrong and Gunning had been replaced, respectively, by Bruce Barthol and Gary 'Chicken' Hirsh. This reshaped quintet was responsible for *Electric Music For The Mind And Body*, one of the 60s 'west coast' era's most striking releases.

Although politics were still prevalent on 'Superbird', this excellent collection also included shimmering instrumentals ('Section 43'), drug songs ('Bass Strings') and unflinching romanticism ('Porpoise Mouth'). It was followed by *I-Feel-Like-I'm-Fixin'-To-Die*, which not only featured a new version of that early composition, but also contained a poignant tribute to singer Janis Joplin. The controversial and outspoken McDonald instigated the famous 'fish cheer' which, more often than not, resulted in thousands of deliriously stoned fans spelling out not F.I.S.H. but F.U.C.K. with carefree abandon. Beset by internal problems, the group's disappointing third album, *Together*, marked the end of this innovative line-up. *Here We Are Again* was completed by various musicians, including Peter Albin and Dave Getz from Big Brother And The Holding Company, and although piecemeal, included the haunting country-tinged 'Here I Go Again' (later a hit for the 60s model, Twiggy). Mark Kapner (keyboards), Doug Metzner (bass) and Greg Dewey (drums – formerly of Mad River), joined McDonald and Melton in the summer of 1969. The new line-up was responsible for the group's final album, *C.J. Fish*, on which glimpses of the former fire were present. The 'classic' line-up, which appeared on the group's first three albums, was briefly reunited between 1976 and 1977 but the resultant release, *Reunion*, was a disappointment. McDonald aside, Barry Melton has enjoyed the highest profile, recording several albums under his own name and performing with the San Francisco 'supergroup', the Dinosaurs. McDonald continues to delight old folkies and hippies and is always a popular attraction at outdoor festivals.

● ALBUMS: *Electric Music For The Mind And Body* (Vanguard 1967) ★★★★, *I-Feel-Like-I'm-Fixin'-To-Die* (Vanguard 1967) ★★★, *Together* (Vanguard 1968) ★★, *Here We Are Again* (Vanguard 1969) ★★★, *C.J. Fish* (Vanguard 1970) ★★, *Reunion* (Fantasy 1977) ★, *Live! Fillmore West 1969* (Vanguard 1994) ★★★.

● COMPILATIONS: *Greatest Hits* (Vanguard 1969) ★★★, *The Life And Times Of Country Joe And The Fish From Haight-Ashbury To Woodstock* (Vanguard 1971) ★★★, *Collectors' Items - The First Three EPs* (Rag Baby 1980) ★★★, *The Collected Country Joe And The Fish* (Vanguard 1987) ★★★.

● FILMS: *Gas! Or It Became Necessary ...* (1970).

COUNTRYMEN

Formed in Hull, Yorkshire, England, in the early 60s, singing guitarists Alan Beach, David Kelsey and David Waite sported uniform waistcoats and embroidered shirts while performing commercial folk – 'I Know Where I'm Going' reached the lower reaches of the UK Top 50 in spring 1962. They were also noted as the first UK act to cover a Paul Simon opus when 'Carlos Dominguez' was issued in Britain a month prior to the version by the composer (as 'Jerry Landis') in May 1964. They had the advantage, too, of a virtual residency on UK television's *Five O'Clock Club*, before being lost to the archives of oblivion when this ITV children's series ended.

● ALBUMS: *The Countrymen* (Piccadilly 1963) ★★.

COVAY, DON

b. Donald Randolph, 24 March 1938, Orangeburg, South Carolina, USA. Covay resettled in Washington during the early 50s and initially sang in the Cherry Keys, his family's gospel quartet. He crossed over to secular music with the Rainbows, a formative vocal group that also included Marvin Gaye and Billy Stewart. Covay's solo career began in 1957 as part of the Little Richard revue. The most tangible result of this liaison was a single, 'Bip Bop Bip', on which Covay was billed as 'Pretty Boy'. Released on Atlantic Records, it was produced by Richard and featured the weight of his backing band, the Upsetters. Over the next few years Covay drifted from label to label. His original version of 'Pony Time' (credited to the Goodtimers) lost out to Chubby Checker's cover version, but a further dance-oriented offering, 'The Popeye Waddle', was a hit in 1962. Covay,

meanwhile, honed his songwriting skills and formed partnerships with several associate including Horace Ott and Ronnie Miller. Such work provided Solomon Burke with 'I'r Hanging Up My Heart For You' while Glady Knight And The Pips reached the US Top 2 with 'Letter Full Of Tears'.

Covay's singing career continued to falter unt 1964 when he signed with New York's Roseman label. Still accompanied by the Goodtimers (Ac Hall, Harry Tiffen and George Clane), his debu single there, the vibrant 'Mercy Mercy' established his effortless, bluesy style. Atlanti subsequently bought his contract but whil several R&B hits followed, it was a year befor Covay returned to the pop chart. 'See Saw', cc written with Steve Cropper and recorded at Sta Records, paved the way for other exceptiona singles, including 'Sookie Sookie' and 'Iron Ou The Rough Spots' (both 1966). Covay's late 6C output proved less fertile, while the ill-founde Soul Clan (with Solomon Burke, Arthur Conley Wilson Pickett, Joe Tex and Ben E. King) ende after one single ('Soul Meeting'). Covay's song still remained successful, Aretha Franklin wo a Grammy for her performance of hi composition 'Chain Of Fools'. Covay switched t Janus in 1971, and from there moved t Mercury Records where he combined recordin with A&R duties. *Superdude 1*, a critic favourite, reunited the singer with Horace Ot Further releases appeared on Philadelphi International Records (1976), U-Von Record (1977) and Newman Records (1980), but whil Randy Crawford and Bonnie Raitt resurrecte his songs, Covay's own career continued to slid downhill. In 1993, the Rhythm & Blue Foundation honoured the singer-songwrite with one of its prestigious Pioneer Award Covay, unfortunately, was by then suffering th after-effects of a stroke. A tribute album, *Bac To The Streets: Celebrating The Music Of Dc Covay*, recorded by many first-rate artist including Chuck Jackson, Ben E. King, Bobb Womack, Robert Cray and Todd Rundgren, wa released by Shanachie in 1994. The same yea the Razor & Tie label released a fine 23-trac retrospective of his best work, compiled an annotated by soul archivist and producer Bil Vera. Covay returned to the studio at the end c the decade to record his first new album in ove 25 years.

● ALBUMS: *Mercy!* (Atlantic 1965) ★★★, *Se Saw* (Atlantic 1966) ★★★★, with the Jeffersc Lemon Blues Band *The House Of Blue Ligh* (Atlantic 1969) ★★★, *Different Strokes* (Atlant 1970) ★★, *Superdude 1* (Mercury 1973) ★★∙ *Hot Blood* (Mercury 1975) ★★, *Travellin' ∙ Heavy Traffic* (Philadelphia International 197∙ ★★, *Ad Lib* (Cannonball 2000) ★★.

● COMPILATIONS: *Sweet Thang* (Topline 198∙ ★★★, *Checkin' In With Don Covay* (Mercur 1989) ★★★, *Mercy Mercy: The Definitive Dc Covay* (Razor & Tie 1994) ★★★★.

COWSILLS

Billed as 'America's First Family Of Music', the Cowsills were all born in Newport, Rhode Island, USA. The group featured Bill (b. 9 January 1948; guitar/vocals), Bob (b. 26 August 1949; guitar/vocals), Paul (b. 11 November 1952; keyboards/vocals), Barry (b. 14 September 1954; bass/vocals), John (b. 2 March 1956; drums) and Susan (b. 20 May 1960; vocals). Occasionally augmented by their mother Barbara (b. 1928; vocals), they came to the attention of writer/producer Artie Kornfeld who co-wrote and produced their debut single 'The Rain, The Park And Other Things' which reached number 2 in the US charts in December 1967. Featuring lyrics by Bill, their happy, bouncy harmonies were evident on the subsequent singles 'We Can Fly', 'In Need Of A Friend' and the 1968 Top 10 hit 'Indian Lake'. Their energetic interpretation of the title song from the rock musical *Hair* reached number 2 in May 1969 and proved to be their swansong. Shortly afterwards Bill left to pursue a career in composing. Before they split up in 1972, they became the inspiration for the NBC US television series *The Partridge Family*, starring David Cassidy, in 1970. In January 1985 Barbara died of emphysema, aged 56, in Tempe, Arizona, USA.

● ALBUMS: *The Cowsills* (MGM 1967) ★★★, *We Can Fly* (1968) ★★★, *Captain Sad And His Ship Of Fools* (1968) ★★, *The Cowsills In Concert* (1969) ★★, *On My Side* (London 1971) ★★.
● COMPILATIONS: *The Best Of The Cowsills* (1968) ★★★, *The Best Of The Cowsills* (Rebound 1994) ★★★, *20th Century Masters: The Best Of The Cowsills, The Millennium Collection* (Polydor 2001) ★★★.

COX, MICHAEL

b. Michael James Cox, Liverpool, England. After his sisters wrote to producer Jack Good demanding an audition, Cox found himself transformed into a television singing star. Fellow pop singer Marty Wilde kindly presented him with a demo of John D. Loudermilk's 'Angela Jones', which brought Cox a UK Top 10 hit in 1960. Only one minor success followed, Along Came Caroline', but the singer enjoyed considerable success in Scandinavia where he toured with the Outlaws, featuring Ritchie Blackmore. Several continental jaunts kept Cox in regular work during the mid-60s and beyond. Following a bizarre experience with a ouija board, he decided to abandon his surname and call himself simply Michael James. Today he still plays the cabaret circuit and has also acted in several minor film productions.

COXSONE, LLOYD

b. Lloyd Blackwood. An influential figure in the growth of the UK reggae scene, Lloyd Coxsone left his home in Morant Bay, Jamaica, and arrived in the UK in 1962, settling in south-west London and setting up his first sound system, Lloyd The Matador. This venture floundered due to inexperience and Coxsone joined the UK-based Duke Reid sound, but he eventually left in 1969, taking some of that operation's personnel with him. He went on to form his own sound system, adopting the name of the biggest sound in Jamaica at the time, and also, pointedly, the main rival to Jamaica's Duke Reid, Sir Coxsone. Coxsone sound soon gained a strong following that eventually led to his residency at the famous London nightclub the Roaring Twenties, in Carnaby Street. Throughout the 70s Sir Coxsone Sound's success lay with maintaining the sound to rigorous standards, playing the most exclusive dub plates direct from Jamaica, and keeping abreast of trends within the music. Rather than specializing in one particular style, Coxsone Sound offered music for all tastes.

Coxsone, like other sound men, also expanded into the record business, licensing music from Jamaica at first, then trying his hand at his own productions using local UK artists. In 1975 he enjoyed huge success, and kickstarted the UK lovers rock phenomenon in the process, with his production of 'Caught You In A Lie' – originally a US soul hit by Robert Parker – featuring the vocal talents of 14-year-old south London schoolgirl Louisa Mark. That same year he issued one of the best dub albums of the era, King Of The Dub Rock, which featured dubwise versions of his own productions and those of Gussie Clarke, mixed in part at King Tubby's. Other notable records appeared on his Tribesman and Lloyd Coxsone Outernational labels and elsewhere during the late 70s and early 80s, including Fabian's Jack Ruby-produced 'Prophecy', 'Love And Only Love' and 'Voice Of The Poor' by Fred Locks. Others included 'Stormy Night' and 'Homeward Bound' by the Creation Steppers, a version of the Commodores' 'Easy' by Jimmy Lindsay (many of which are available on 12 The Hard Way) and many more. During the mid-80s Coxsone handed control of his sound over to the younger elements in his team, notably Blacker Dread, and a new breed of DJs. Blacker released his own productions by the likes of Fred Locks, Frankie Paul, Mikey General, Sugar Minott, Michael Palmer, Don Carlos, Earl Sixteen and Coxsone DJ, Jah Screechy. Recently, as interest in the roots music of the 70s has increased, Coxsone has emerged from his semi-retirement to stand again at the controls of his sound.

● ALBUMS: *King Of The Dub Rock* (Safari 1975) ★★★★, *King Of The Dub Rock Part 2* (Tribesman 1982) ★★★, *12 The Hard Way* (Tribesman 1989) ★★★.

CRAMER, FLOYD

b . 27 October 1933, Shreveport, Louisiana, USA, d. 31 December 1997. The style and sound of Cramer's piano-playing was arguably one of the biggest influences on post-50s country music. His delicate rock 'n' roll sound was achieved by accentuating the discord in rolling from the main note to a sharp or flat, known as 'slip note'. This is perfectly highlighted in his first major hit, 'Last Date', in 1960. He was already a vastly experienced Nashville session player, playing on countless records during the 50s. He can be heard on many Jim Reeves and Elvis Presley records (one of his first sessions was 'Heartbreak Hotel'), often with his long-time friend Chet Atkins, and also recorded with Patsy Cline, Roy Orbison and Kitty Lester. During the early 60s he regularly entered the US charts. Two notable hits were the superb 'On The Rebound', which still sounds fresh and lively more than 30 years later, and his sombre reading of Bob Wills' 'New San Antonio Rose'. After dozens of albums Cramer was still making commercially successful recordings into the 80s, having a further hit in 1980 with the theme from the television soap opera Dallas. With Atkins, Cramer remained Nashville's most prolific musician until his death from cancer in 1997.

● ALBUMS: *That Honky Tonk Piano* reissued as *Floyd Cramer Goes Honky Tonkin'* (MGM 1957) ★★★, *Hello Blues* (RCA 1960) ★★★, *Last Date* (RCA 1961) ★★★★, *On The Rebound* (RCA 1961) ★★★★, *America's Biggest Selling Pianist* (RCA 1961) ★★★, *Floyd Cramer Get Organ-ized* (RCA 1962) ★★, *I Remember Hank Williams* (RCA 1962) ★★★, *Swing Along With Floyd Cramer* (RCA 1963) ★★★, *Comin' On* (RCA 1963) ★★★, *Country Piano - City Strings* (RCA 1964) ★★★, *Cramer At The Console* (RCA 1964) ★★★, *Hits From The Country Hall Of Fame* (RCA 1965) ★★★, *The Magic Touch Of Floyd Cramer* (RCA 1965) ★★★, *Class Of '65* (RCA 1965) ★★★, *The Distinctive Piano Styling Of Floyd Cramer* (RCA 1966) ★★★, *The Big Ones* (RCA 1966) ★★★, *Class Of '66* (RCA 1966) ★★★, *Here's What's Happening* (RCA 1967) ★★★, *Floyd Cramer Plays The Monkees* (RCA 1967) ★★★, *Class Of '67* (RCA 1967) ★★★, *Floyd Cramer Plays Country Classics* (RCA 1968) ★★★, *Class Of '68* (RCA 1968) ★★★, *Floyd Cramer Plays MacArthur Park* (RCA 1968) ★★, *Class Of '69* (RCA 1969) ★★★★, *More Country Classics* (RCA 1969) ★★★, *Looking For Mr. Goodbar* (RCA 1968) ★★★, *The Big Ones - Volume 2* (RCA 1970) ★★★, *Floyd Cramer With The Music City Pops* (RCA 1970) ★★★, *Class Of '70* (RCA 1970) ★★, *Sounds Of Sunday* (RCA 1971) ★★, with Chet Atkins, 'Boots' Randolph *Chet, Floyd, Boots* (RCA Camden 1971) ★★★, *Class Of '71* (RCA 1971) ★★★, *Floyd Cramer Detours* (RCA 1972) ★★★, *Class Of '72* (RCA 1972) ★★★, *Super Country Hits Featuring Crystal Chandelier And Battle Of New Orleans* (RCA 1973) ★★, *Class Of '73* (RCA 1973) ★★, *The Young And The Restless* (RCA 1974) ★★, *Floyd Cramer In Concert* (RCA 1974) ★★, *Class Of '74 And '75* (RCA 1975) ★★, *Floyd Cramer Country* (RCA 1976) ★★, with Chet Atkins, Danny Davis *Chet, Floyd & Danny* (RCA Victor 1977) ★★★★, *Floyd Cramer And The*

Keyboard Kick Band (RCA 1977) ★★★, *Superhits* (RCA 1979) ★★, *Dallas* (RCA 1980) ★★, *The Best Of The West* (RCA 1981) ★★, *Country Gold* (RCA 1988) ★★, *Just Me And My Piano!* (RCA 1988) ★★★, *Special Songs Of Love* (RCA 1988) ★★, *Originals* (RCA 1991) ★★★, *Classics* (RCA 1992) ★★★.

● COMPILATIONS: *The Best Of Floyd Cramer* (RCA 1964) ★★★★, *The Best Of Floyd Cramer - Volume 2* (RCA 1968) ★★★, *This Is Floyd Cramer* (RCA 1970) ★★★★, *Plays The Big Hits* (Camden 1973) ★★★, *Best Of The Class Of* (RCA 1973) ★★★, *Spotlight On Floyd Cramer* (1974) ★★★, *Piano Masterpieces 1900-1975* (RCA 1975) ★★, *All My Best* (RCA 1980) ★★★, *Great Country Hits* (RCA 1981) ★★★, *Treasury Of Favourites* (1984) ★★★, *Country Classics* (1984) ★★★★, *20 Of The Best: Floyd Cramer* (RCA 1986) ★★★, *Our Class Reunion* (1987) ★★★, *Easy Listening Favorites* (1991) ★★★, *Favorite Country Hits* (Ranwood 1995) ★★★, *King Of Country Piano* (Pickwick 1995) ★★★, *Collector's Series* (RCA 1995) ★★★, *The Essential Floyd Cramer* (RCA 1996) ★★★★.

CREAM

Arguably the most famous trio in rock music, Cream comprised Jack Bruce (b. John Symon Asher, 14 May 1943, Glasgow, Lanarkshire, Scotland; bass, vocals), Eric Clapton (b. Eric Patrick Clapp, 30 March 1945, Ripley, Surrey, England; guitar) and Ginger Baker (b. Peter Baker, 19 August 1939, Lewisham, London, England; drums). In their two and a half years together, Cream made such an impression on fans, critics and musicians as to make them one of the most influential bands since the Beatles. They formed in the height of swinging London during the 60s and were soon thrust into a non-stop turbulent arena, hungry for new and interesting music after the Merseybeat boom had quelled. Cream were promoted in the music press as a pop group, with Clapton from John Mayall's Bluesbreakers, Bruce from Graham Bond and briefly Manfred Mann, and Baker from the Graham Bond Organisation via Alexis Korner's Blues Incorporated. Baker and Bruce had originally played together in the Johnny Burch Octet in 1962. Cream's debut single, 'Wrapping Paper', was a comparatively weird pop song, and made the lower reaches of the charts on the strength of its insistent appeal. This was a paradox to their great strength of jamming and improvisation; each member was already a proven master of their chosen instrument.Their follow-up single, 'I Feel Free', unleashed such energy that it could only be matched by Jimi Hendrix. The debut album *Fresh Cream* confirmed the promise: this band were not what they seemed, another colourful pop group singing songs of tangerine bicycles. With a mixture of blues standards and exciting originals, the album became a record that every credible music fan should own. It reached number 6 in the UK charts. The following year,

)israeli Gears, with its distinctive dayglo cover, vent even higher, and firmly established Cream n the USA, where they spent most of their)uring life. This superb album showed a marked progression from their first, in particular, in the 1igh standard of songwriting from Jack Bruce nd his lyricist partner, former beat poet Pete 3rown. Landmark songs such as 'Sunshine Of 'our Love', 'Strange Brew' and 'SWLABR' (She Vas Like A Bearded Rainbow) were performed vith precision.Already rumours of a split revailed as news filtered back from America of ights and arguments between Baker and Bruce. 1eanwhile, their live performances did not eflect the music already released from studio essions. The long improvisational pieces, based round fairly simple blues structures, were often wesome. Each member had a least one party iece during concerts, Bruce with his frantic armonica solo on 'Traintime', Baker with his rademark drum solo on 'Toad', and Clapton with .is strident vocal and fantastic guitar solo on 3rossroads'. One disc of the magnificent two-ecord set, Wheels Of Fire, captured Cream live, t their inventive and exploratory best. Just a 1onth after its release, while it sat on top of the /S charts, they announced they would disband t the end of the year following two final oncerts. The famous Royal Albert Hall farewell oncerts were captured on film; the posthumous roodbye reached number 1 in the UK charts and umber 2 in the USA, while even some later live crapings from the bottom of the barrel enjoyed hart success.The three members came together 1 1993 for an emotional one-off performance at 1e Rock And Roll Hall Of Fame awards in New ork, before the CD age finally recognized their ontribution in 1997, with the release of an xcellent 4-CD box set, Those Were The Days. Two Ds from the studio and two from the stage wrap p this brief career, with no stone left unturned. 1 addition to all of their previously issued 1aterial there is the unreleased 'Lawdy Mama', hich Bruce claims features the wrongly ecorded original bass line of 'Strange Brew'. nother gem is a demo of the Bruce/Brown iamond, 'The Weird Of Hermiston', which later ppeared on Bruce's debut solo album, Songs For Tailor. This collection reaffirms their reatness, as three extraordinary musicians ising their musical personalities together as a nit. Cream came and went almost in the blink f an eye, but left an indelible mark on rock 1usic.

ALBUMS: Fresh Cream (Polydor 1966) ★★★★, israeli Gears (Polydor 1967) ★★★★★, Wheels f Fire (Polydor 1968) ★★★★, Goodbye (Polydor)69) ★★★, Live Cream (Polydor 1970) ★★★, ive Cream, Volume 2 (Polydor 1972) ★★★.

COMPILATIONS: The Best Of Cream (Polydor)69) ★★★★, Heavy Cream (Polydor 1973) ★★, Strange Brew - The Very Best Of Cream 'olydor 1986) ★★★★, Those Were The Days 4-D box set (Polydor 1997) ★★★★★.

● VIDEOS: Farewell Concert (Polygram Music Video 1986), Strange Brew (Warner Music Video 1992), Fresh Live Cream (PolyGram Music Video 1994).
● FURTHER READING: Cream In Gear (Limited Edition), Gered Mankowitz and Robert Whitaker (Photographers). Strange Brew, Chris Welch. Cream, Chris Welch.

CREATION

Still revered as one of the UK's most inventive mod/pop-art acts, the Creation evolved out of the Enfield, Middlesex, England, beat group, the Mark Four. Kenny Pickett (b. 1942, Middlesex, England, d. 10 January 1997; vocals), Eddie Phillips (lead guitar), Mick Thompson (rhythm guitar), John Dalton (bass) and Jack Jones (drums) completed four singles before Dalton left to join the Kinks and Thompson abandoned music altogether. The remaining trio added Bob Garner, formerly of the Merseybeats, and Tony Sheridan, and changed their name in 1966 upon securing a deal with producer Shel Talmy. The Creation's early singles, 'Making Time' and 'Painter Man', offered the same propulsive power as the Who, while Phillips' distinctive bowed guitar sound was later popularized by Jimmy Page. Although both releases were only minor hits in the UK, they proved highly successful on the Continent, but the group's undoubted promise was undermined by personality clashes between Pickett and Garner. The singer left the group in June 1967 and although several strong singles for Polydor Records followed, they lacked the impact of earlier recordings. The group broke up in February 1968, but re-formed the following month around Pickett, Jones, Kim Gardner (b. 27 January 1946, Dulwich, London, England; bass) and ex-Birds member, Ron Wood (guitar). This realignment proved temporary and, impromptu reunions apart, the Creation broke up in June 1968. However, after 25 years, the band re-formed and made a live album, Lay The Ghost, in 1993. A disappointing all-new album was issued on Alan McGee's Creation label in 1996. Pickett died in 1997 and the best compilation to date, Our Music Is Red, With Purple Flashes appeared on Demon Records in 1998. No band has ever made a guitar played with a violin bow, sound exactly like a guitar played with a tenon saw, other than the Creation.
● ALBUMS: We Are Paintermen (Hi-Ton 1967) ★★★, Lay The Ghost (1993) ★★, The Creation (Creation 1996) ★★, Power Surge (Creation 1996) ★★.
● COMPILATIONS: The Best Of Creation (Pop Schallplatten 1968) ★★★, The Creation 66-67 (Charisma 1973) ★★★, How Does It Feel To Feel? (Edsel 1982) ★★★, Recreation (1984) ★★, Our Music Is Red, With Purple Flashes (DiAblo/ Demon 1998) ★★★★, Making Time: Volume 1 (Retroactive 1998), Biff Bang Pow! Volume 2 (Retroactive 1998).

CREEDENCE CLEARWATER REVIVAL

Although generally bracketed with the post-psychedelic wave of San Franciscan groups, Creedence Clearwater Revival boasted one of the region's longest pedigrees. John Fogerty (b. 28 May 1945, Berkeley, California, USA; lead guitar/vocals), Tom Fogerty (b. 9 November 1941, Berkeley, California, USA, d. 6 September 1990, Scottsdale, Arizona, USA; rhythm guitar/vocals), Stu Cook (b. 25 April 1945, Oakland, California, USA; bass) and Doug Clifford (b. 24 April 1945, Palo Alto, California, USA; drums) began performing together in 1959 while attending high school. Initially known as the Blue Velvets, then Tommy Fogerty And The Blue Velvets, the quartet became a popular attraction in the Bay Area suburb of El Cerrito and as such completed a single, 'Bonita', for the local independent Orchestra. In 1964 they auditioned for the more prestigious Fantasy Records, who signed them on the understanding that they change their name to the more topical Golliwogs to monopolize on the concurrent 'British Invasion'. Between 1965 and 1967, the re christened group recorded seven singles, ranging from the Beatles-influenced 'Don't Tell Me No More Lies' to the compulsive 'Fight Fire' and 'Walk Upon The Water', two superb garage band classics. The quartet turned fully professional in December 1967 and in doing so became known as Creedence Clearwater Revival.Their debut album reflected a musical crossroads. Revamped Golliwogs tracks and new John Fogerty originals slotted alongside several rock 'n' roll standards, including 'Suzie-Q' and 'I Put A Spell On You', the former reaching number 11 in the US charts. *Bayou Country*, issued within a matter of months, was a more substantial affair, establishing Fogerty as a perceptive composer, and the group as America's consummate purveyors of late 60s pop. 'Proud Mary' reached the Top 10 in both the US and UK and in the process become the quartet's first gold disc. More importantly, it introduced the mixture of Southern Creole styles, R&B and rockabilly through which the best of the group's work was filtered. *Green River* consolidated the group's new-found status and contained two highly successful singles, 'Green River' and 'Bad Moon Rising', the latter of which topped the UK charts. The set confirmed Fogerty's increasingly fertile lyricism which ranged from personal melancholia ('Lodi') to a plea for mutual understanding ('Wrote A Song For Everyone'). This social perspective flourished on the 'Fortunate Son', an acerbic attack on a privileged class sending others out to war, one of several highlights captured on *Willie And The Poor Boys*. By this point the group was indisputably America's leading attraction, marrying commercial success with critical approbation. 'Down On The Corner', a euphoric tribute to popular music, became their fifth US Top 10 single and confirmed a transformation from gutsy bar band to international luminaries. CCR reached a peak with *Cosmo's Factory*. It included three gold singles, 'Travelin' Band', 'Up Around The Bend' and 'Looking Out My Back Door', as well as an elongated reading of the Tamla/Motown Records classic 'I Heard I Through The Grapevine'. The album defined the consummate Creedence Clearwater Revival sound: tight, economical and reliant on an implicit mutual understanding, and deservedly became 1970's best-selling set. However relationships between the Fogerty brothers grew increasingly strained, reflected in the standard of the disappointing *Pendulum*. Although it featured their eighth gold single in 'Have You Ever Seen The Rain', the set lacked the overall intensity of its immediate predecessors, a sparkle only occasionally rekindled in 'Pagan Baby' and 'Molina'. Tom Fogerty left for a solo career in February 1971, but although the remaining members continued to work as a trio, the band had lost much of its impetus. Major tours of the USA, Europe, Australia and Japan did ensue, but a seventh collection, *Mardi Gras*, revealed an artistic impasse. Cook and Clifford were granted democratic rights, but their uninspired compositions only proved how much the group owed to John Fogerty's vision. Creedence Clearwater Revival was officially disbanded in July 1972. It was a dispiriting close to one of the era's most compulsive and successful groups, combination rarely found.The rhythm section followed low-key pursuits both independently and together, with Cook enjoying most success in the late 80s as a member of Southern Pacific. Their erstwhile leader began an erratic path dogged by legal and contractual disputes although he deservedly re-emerged in 1985 with the American chart-topper *Centrefield*. Tom Fogerty left the music business in the early 80 to work in real estate, but died in 1990 from tuberculosis. In 1993 the band were inducted into the Rock And Roll Hall Of Fame, although the animosity between Fogerty, Clifford and Cook was clearly evident. The dispute flared up again in 1998 when Clifford and Cook began touring as Creedence Clearwater Revisited, with former Cars guitarist Elliot Easton and vocalist John Tristano included in the line-up. A live album was issued as John Fogerty attempted to stop Clifford and Cook from using the Creedence name.

● ALBUMS: *Creedence Clearwater Revival* (Fantasy 1968) ★★★, *Bayou Country* (Fantasy 1969) ★★★★, *Green River* (Fantasy 1969) ★★★★, *Willie And The Poor Boys* (Fantasy 1969) ★★★★, *Cosmo's Factory* (Fantasy 1970) ★★★★, *Pendulum* (Fantasy 1970) ★★★, *Mardi Gras* (Fantasy 1972) ★★, *Live In Europe* (Fantasy 1973) ★★, *Live At The Royal Albert Hall* aka *The Concert* (Fantasy 1980) ★★, as Creedence Clearwater Revisited *Recollection* (SPV 1998) ★★★.

● COMPILATIONS: *Creedence Gold* (Fantasy 1972) ★★★★, *More Creedence Gold* (Fantasy

1973) ★★★★, *Chronicle: The 20 Greatest Hits* (Fantasy 1976) ★★★★, *Greatest Hits* (Fantasy 1979) ★★★, *Creedence Country* (Fantasy 1981) ★★★, *Creedence Clearwater Revival Hits Album* (Fantasy 1982) ★★★★, *The Creedence Collection* (Impression 1985) ★★★, *Chronicle II* (Fantasy 1986) ★★★★, *Best Of Volume 1* (Fantasy 1988) ★★★★, *Best Of Volume 2* (Fantasy 1988) ★★★★, *At The Movies* (Fantasy 2000) ★★★, *Creedence Clearwater Revival* 6-CD box set (Fantasy 2001) ★★★★.
● FURTHER READING: *Inside Creedence*, John Hallowell.

CREWE, BOB

b. Stanley Robert Crewe, 12 November 1931, Newark, New Jersey, USA. Bob Crewe was an important songwriter and record producer during the 60s, best known for his work with the Four Seasons. Among the classic pop songs with which he had a hand in writing were the Four Seasons' 'Big Girls Don't Cry', 'Rag Doll', 'Bye Bye Baby', 'Let's Hang On' and 'Walk Like A Man', Frankie Valli's solo hits 'My Eyes Adored You', 'Can't Take My Eyes Off You' and 'Swearin' To God', Mitch Ryder's 'Sock It To Me, Baby' Freddy Cannon's 'Tallahassee Lassie', the Rays' 'Silhouettes', the Walker Brothers' 'The Sun Ain't Gonna Shine Anymore' and Diane Renay's 'Navy Blue'. Later, in the 70s he worked on Disco Tex And The Sex-O-Lettes' 'Get Dancin'' and LaBelle's 'Lady Marmalade'. Crewe also owned the Dyno-Voice and Crewe record labels, production companies and music publishing firms. His first music industry experience was as an aspiring vocalist in Detroit in the 50s. Unsuccessful, he moved to Philadelphia and co-ran XYZ Records, whose major hit was a song he co-wrote, the Rays' 'Silhouettes'.In the early 60s he began working with the Four Seasons as writer and producer, helping to turn them into one of the most successful American groups of the decade. Although Crewe was not primarily a recording artist under his own name, he did chart with four singles. The first was a 1960 version of 'The Whiffenpoof Song', the theme song of the Yale University Glee Club. His biggest chart hit under his own name was a 1967 instrumental, 'Music To Watch Girls By', originally used in a Pepsi Cola commercial. Released on Crewe's Dyno-Voice label by the Bob Crewe Generation, it reached the US Top 20. He had one more minor chart single in 1967 and then rebounded in 1976 with 'Street Talk', released on 20th Century Fox Records under the name of BCG. It was during this period that Crewe enjoyed his last major impact on the popular music scene, writing and producing hits for LaBelle, Disco Tex And The Sex-O-Lettes, Eleventh Hour and others.
● ALBUMS: *Kicks* (Warwick 1960) ★★★, *Crazy In The Heart* (Warwick 1961) ★★, *All The Song Hits Of The Four Seasons* (Philips 1964) ★★★, *Bob Crew Plays The Four Seasons' Hits* (Philips

1967) ★★★, *Music To Watch Girls By* (1967) ★★, *Motivation* (20th Century Fox 1977) ★★.

CRICKETS

The Crickets have continued occasionally to record and tour as a group ever since Buddy Holly's death in 1959. In addition to Holly, the members were drummer Jerry Allison (b. 31 August 1939, Hillsboro, Texas, USA), bassist Joe B. Mauldin and guitarist Niki Sullivan. When Holly was signed to Decca Records in 1957, it was decided that these Nashville-produced tracks produced by Norman Petty should be released under two names, as Holly solo items (on Coral Records) and as the Crickets (on Brunswick Records). It was 'That'll Be The Day', credited to the Crickets' which was the first number 1 hit. Other Crickets' successes with Holly on lead vocals included 'Oh Boy', 'Maybe Baby' and 'Think It Over'. However, by the end of 1958, Holly had moved to New York to concentrate on his solo career and the Crickets did not accompany him on his final tour. Petty and Allison had already begun recording independently of Holly, issuing 'Love's Made A Fool Of You' with Earl Sinks on lead vocals. On the later singles 'Peggy Sue Got Married' and 'More Than I Can Say' Sinks was replaced by Sonny Curtis (b. 9 May 1937, Meadow, Texas, USA; guitar/vocals), who was an early Texas associate of Holly and Allison. Written by Curtis and Allison, 'More Than I Can Say' was a hit for Bobby Vee, and in 1961 the Crickets moved to Vee's label, Liberty Records and recorded an album of Holly numbers with the singer the following year. Glen D. Hardin (b. 18 April 1939, Wellington, Texas, USA; piano) joined at this point. The group also released a series of singles between 1962 and 1965. These made little impact in the USA but 'Please Don't Ever Change' (a Carole King/Gerry Goffin number) and 'My Little Girl' were Top 20 hits in the UK, where the group continued to tour. There followed a five-year hiatus in the group's career as Curtis and Allison worked as songwriters and session musicians. They were persuaded to re-form the Crickets in 1970, to record a rock revival album for the Barnaby label. This led to a contract with Mercury and two albums containing mostly original country rock style songs, such as Allison's powerfully nostalgic 'My Rockin' Days'. The producer was Bob Montgomery who had been Holly's earliest songwriting partner. The group now included singer/writer Steve Krikorian and two English musicians: guitarist Albert Lee and ex-Family and Blind Faith bassist Ric Grech.The most recent phase of the Crickets' career was stimulated by the purchase from Paul McCartney's publishing company of Petty's share of the Holly/Allison song catalogue. During the 80s, Allison led the band for revival tours and he returned to recording in 1987 with original bassist Mauldin and newcomer Gordon

Payne on guitar and vocals. They released *Three-Piece* on Allison's own Rollercoaster label, which became *T-Shirt* on CBS Records with the addition of the title track, the winner of a UK songwriting competition organized by McCartney's company MPL.

● ALBUMS: *The Chirpin' Crickets* (Brunswick 1957) ★★★★, *In Style With The Crickets* (Coral 1960) ★★★★, *Bobby Vee Meets The Crickets* (Liberty 1962) ★★★, *Something Old, Something New, Something Borrowed, Something Else* (Liberty 1963) ★★★★, *California Sun* (Liberty 1964) ★★★, *Rockin' 50s Rock 'N' Roll* (Barnaby 1970) ★★★, *Bubblegum, Bop, Ballads And Boogies* (Mercury 1973) ★★, *A Long Way From Lubbock* (Mercury 1975) ★★, *Three-Piece* (Rollercoaster 1988) ★★, *T-Shirt* (Columbia 1989) ★★, *Too Much Monday Morning* (Carlton 1997) ★★.

● COMPILATIONS: *The Singles Collection 1957-1961* (Pickwick 1994) ★★★, *25 Greatest Hits* (MFP 1998) ★★★.

● VIDEOS: *My Love Is Bigger Than A Cadillac* (Hendring Music Video 1990).

● FILMS: *Girls On The Beach* (1965).

CRITTERS

This US group was founded in 1964 by guitarists Jim Ryan and Don Ciconne. Kenny Gorka (bass), Chris Darway (organ) and Jack Decker (drums) then completed the line-up, which was initially based in Plainfield, New Jersey, USA. 'Children And Flowers', a Jackie DeShannon song, was their first release on Kapp Records, but it was a follow-up single, 'Younger Girl', that gave the Critters their first hit, reaching number 42 in May 1966. This harmonious reading of the John Sebastian (Lovin' Spoonful) song established the quintet as a leading folk rock ensemble while later releases, 'Mr. Dieingly Sad' (number 17, August 1966), 'Bad Misunderstanding' (number 55, December 1966) and 'Don't Let The Rain Fall Down On Me' (number 39, July 1967), embellished this facet with classic New York-styled productions. Ciconne, who also enjoyed a brief, but fruitful partnership with songwriters Anders And Poncia, left the line-up on his induction into the army. Jeff Pelosi (drums) and Bob Spinella (keyboards), joined the group in late 1967, but despite several further releases, the Critters were unable to recapture the magic of that original quintet. Ryan became a session musician following the band's final collapse, while Ciconne returned to the limelight in 1974 on replacing Clay Jordan in the Four Seasons.

● ALBUMS: *Younger Girl* (Kapp 1966) ★★★, *Touch 'N Go With The Critters* (Project 3 1967) ★★, *The Critters* (Project 3 1968) ★★.

● COMPILATIONS: *New York Bound* (1968) ★★★, *Anthology: The Complete Kapp Recordings: 1965-1967* (Taragon 1995) ★★★.

CROME CYRCUS

Lee Graham (vocals/bass/flute); John Garborit (lead guitar), Ted Sheffler (keyboards), Dick Powell (harmonica) and Rod Pilloud (drums) made up this enigmatic 'progressive' San Francisco group. Their lone album, *The Love Cycle*, featured an ambitious, extended title-track in which the musicians attempted to compress much of the city's experimental musical styles. Although not wholly convincing, Crome Cyrcus were applauded for their ambition and in 1969 won a Bay Area songwriting award. However, the group dissolved soon afterwards.

● ALBUMS: *The Love Cycle* (Command 1968) ★★.

CROPPER, STEVE

b. 21 October 1942, Willow Spring, Missouri, USA. This economical but effective guitarist was a founder-member of the Mar-Keys, a high school band whose instrumental single, 'Last Night', provided a cornerstone for the emerging Stax Records label in 1961. Cropper worked with several groups constructed around the company's house musicians, the most successful of which was Booker T. And The MGs. The latter group not only had several hits under its own identity, but over the next few years was the muscle behind almost every performance released via the Stax studio. However, Cropper's prowess was not only confined to playing. His songwriting and arranging skills were prevalent on many of these performances, including 'Knock On Wood' (Eddie Floyd), 'Sookie Sookie' (Don Covay), 'In The Midnight Hour' (Wilson Pickett) and 'Mr. Pitiful' and '(Sittin' On) The Dock Of The Bay' (Otis Redding). The MGs continued to record until the end of the decade, but they broke up when organist Booker T. Jones moved to California. Cropper preferred to maintain a low-key profile and although he recorded a pleasant solo album, *With A Little Help From My Friends*, he chose to concentrate on running his Memphis-based studio, TMI, rather than embrace the public acclaim he richly deserved. TMI subsequently folded and Cropper resettled in Los Angeles, returning to session work and production.

He featured prominently on Rod Stewart's chart-topping 1975 album, *Atlantic Crossing*. The surviving MGs were reunited following the death of drummer Al Jackson, and the group has since pursued this erratic existence. Cropper was also a member of the Blues Brothers, a band formed by comedians John Belushi and Dan Aykroyd that led to the successful movie of the same name. The group recorded three albums, following which Cropper released his second solo collection, *Playing My Thang*. Cropper continued a low-key approach to his art during the 80s although he made several live appearances in the UK in the early 90s, particularly in the wake of a revived interest in

he Blues Brothers. His distinctive sparse,
ipped, high treble sound with his Fender
elecaster has been heard on many hundreds of
ngles and albums. His reluctance to hog the
melight cannot disguise the fact that he is one
f the major figures in vintage soul music, both
s a composer and guitarist. All the more
emarkable in that he is an 'all-American white
oy'. In the late 90s, the UK's Mojo magazine put
ropper just one place behind Jimi Hendrix as
he greatest ever guitarist, an accolade Cropper
ad difficulty coming to terms with.
ALBUMS: with Albert King, 'Pops' Staples
ammed Together (Stax 1969) ★★★, With A Little
elp From My Friends (Stax 1971) ★★, Playing
y Thang (1980) ★★.
FILMS: The Blues Brothers (1980), Blues
rothers 2000 (1999).

ROSBY, STILLS AND NASH
avid Crosby (b. 14 August 1941, Los Angeles,
aliforna, USA), Stephen Stills (b. 3 January
945, Dallas, Texas, USA) and Graham Nash (b.
February 1942, Blackpool, Lancashire,
ngland) joined forces in 1969 after parting
ith their previous groups, the Byrds, Buffalo
pringfield and the Hollies, respectively.
nevitably, they attracted considerable media
ttention as a 'supergroup' but unlike similar
ggregations of their era, they were a genuine
am who respected each other's work and
ecognized the importance of their contribution
o American popular music. Their self-titled
ebut album was a superlative achievement
ontaining several of the finest songs that they
ave ever written: 'Long Time Gone', 'Suite:
udy Blue Eyes', (with possibly the most joyous
imax ever recorded), 'Lady Of The Island' and
he powerfully thought-provoking 'Wooden
hips'. Strong lyrics, solid acoustic musicianship
nd staggeringly faultless three-part harmonies
as the mixture that they concocted and it
as enough to influence a new generation of
merican performers for the next decade. The
eed to perform live convinced them to extend
eir ranks and with the induction of Neil
oung they reached an even bigger
ternational audience as Crosby, Stills, Nash
nd Young.
ternal bickering and policy differences split
e group at its peak and although Crosby And
ash proved a successful offshoot, the power of
e original trio was never forgotten and only
ccasionally matched by its descendants. It was
ot until 1977 that the CS&N permutation
eunited for CSN, a strong comeback album
ith such highlights as 'Shadow Captain', 'Dark
tar' and 'Cathedral'. The trio toured the USA
nd seemed more united than at any time since
s inception, but subsequent recording sessions
roved unsatisfactory and the individuals once
ore drifted apart. A further five years passed,
uring which Crosby's drug abuse gradually
ienated him from his colleagues. In a

previously untried combination, Stills and Nash
set about recording an album, but were
eventually persuaded by Atlantic Records'
founder Ahmet Ertegun to bring back Crosby to
the fold. He returned late in the sessions and
although his contribution was not major, he did
proffer one of the strongest tracks, 'Delta'.
The resulting album, Daylight Again, was
disproportionately balanced as a result of
Crosby's late arrival, but the songs were
nevertheless good. The title track from Stills
was one of his best, borrowed from the
memorable live set of his 1973 group, Manassas.
Nash's offerings included the US Top 10 hit
'Wasted On The Way' and provided the
commercial clout to sustain CS&N as one of the
major concert attractions of the day.
Following a tour of Europe, the trio again
splintered and with Crosby incapacitated by
cocaine addiction it seemed that their zigzag
story had finally ended. Fortunately,
imprisonment reached Crosby before the Grim
Reaper and upon his release he reunited
CSN&Y for an album and took CS&N on the
road. Live It Up, their first recording as a trio in
10 years, boasted a tasteless sleeve of hot dogs
on the moon, while the material lacked the
edge of their best work. Now the doyens of the
70s rock circuit, their concerts still show flashes
of the old brilliance while overly relying on
former classics that occasionally come
dangerously close to nostalgia at the expense of
their finest quality: innovation.
A magnificent CD box set was put together
by Nash in 1991. This collection included
unreleased tracks and alternative versions and
led to a critical reappraisal that year. Recent live
concerts (in the late 90s) indicate that the trio
are singing with more passion and confidence
than ever, although their recent studio
recordings have suffered from a lack of strong
songs. This was highlighted on After The Storm,
a disappointing collection to which the public
reacted with indifference. They reunited with
Neil Young in the late 90s for a tour and album.
Nash had a serious boating accident in
September 1999, resulting in two broken legs.
● ALBUMS: Crosby, Stills And Nash (Atlantic
1969) ★★★★★, CSN (Atlantic 1977) ★★★★,
Daylight Again (Atlantic 1982) ★★★, Allies
(Atlantic 1983) ★★★, Live It Up (Atlantic 1990)
★★, After The Storm (Atlantic 1994) ★★.
● COMPILATIONS: Replay (Atlantic 1980)
★★★★, CSN 4-CD box set (Atlantic 1991)
★★★★★.
● VIDEOS: Daylight Again (CIC 1983), Acoustic
(Warner Music Vision 1991), Crosby, Stills And
Nash: Long Time Comin' (Wienerworld 1994).
● FURTHER READING: Crosby, Stills & Nash:
The Authorized Biography, Dave Zimmer and
Henry Diltz. Prisoner Of Woodstock, Dallas
Taylor. Crosby, Stills, Nash & Young: The Visual
Documentary, Johnny Rogan.

CRYAN' SHAMES

Two 60s groups claimed the above name , although a misspelling differentiated the British and American bands. Formed in Hinsdale, Illinois, USA in 1965, the Cryan' Shames – Tom 'Toad' Doody (vocals), J.C. Hooke (b. Jim Pilster; percussion, vocals), Jim Fairs (guitar, bass, flute, vocals), Gerry 'Stonehenge' Stone (rhythm guitar), Dave 'Grape' Purple (guitar, vocals) and Dennis Conroy (drums, vocals) – made their debut on the Destination label with a version of 'Sugar And Spice', previously a hit for the Searchers. Although the single only rose to number 49 in the US charts in July 1966, interest in the band proved sufficient to warrant an album. *Sugar & Spice* was a hurried affair, indebted to the Byrds and British beat. Purple and Stone were replaced by Isaac Guillory (b. 27 February 1947, US Navy Base, Guantanamo Bay, Cuba, d. 31 December 2000, England; guitar, bass, keyboards) and Lenny Kerley (guitar, bass, vocals) later in the year. The band asserted a greater individuality on a second selection, *A Scratch In The Sky*. Here they showed an understanding of harmony pop akin to that of the Association, while the band's final album, *Synthesis*, with Dave Carter and Alan Dawson replacing Fairs and Conroy in the line-up, blended such talent with some truly lavish instrumentation. By 1970 they had broken up; Guillory embarked on a solo career, Kerley and Conroy formed the Possum River Band, and the brief career of the Cryan' Shames was ended. The band continued to perform in various reunion shows, however, and in 1986 Doody and Pilster revived the Cryan' Shames name for touring purposes.

● ALBUMS: *Sugar & Spice* (Columbia 1966) ★★, *A Scratch In The Sky* (Columbia 1967) ★★★, *Synthesis* (Columbia 1969) ★★★★.
● COMPILATIONS: *The Best Of The Cryan' Shames* (CBS 1985) ★★★, *Sugar & Spice: A Collection* (Sony 1992) ★★★.

CRYSTALS

This highly influential 60s US female vocal group were the product of Phil Spector, for his pioneering Philles record label. They, along with the Ronettes, were one of the definitive 'wall of sound' groups of the 60s. They came together after meeting in the legendary Brill Building where the group were preparing demos for the Aberbach's famous publishing company Hill and Range. The line-up comprised Dee Dee Kennibrew (b. Dolores Henry, 1945, Brooklyn, New York, USA), La La Brooks (b. 1946, Brooklyn, New York, USA), Pat Wright (b. 1945, Brooklyn, New York, USA), Mary Thomas (b. 1946, Brooklyn, New York, USA) and Barbara Alston, who was their manager's niece. Spector was impressed and produced the debut 'There's No Other (Like My Baby)' in 1961. At this time Spector was developing his unique sound by mixing numerous layers of vocals and instruments onto one mono track. The blurred result was demonstrated on 'Uptown' but it was taken to its glorious extreme on Gene Pitney's song 'He's A Rebel'. The latter featured the lead vocals of Darlene Wright (Love), and, as Spector owned the name, he could use whoever he wanted as the Crystals. It became a number 1 single in the USA (UK number 19). La La Brooks returned to the lead vocal on two further hits that have since become timeless classics, 'Da Doo Ron Ron' and 'Then He Kissed Me', both major hits in 1963. The Beach Boys attempted a Spector-like production with their own version 'Then I Kissed Her', in 1967. The Crystals were soon overtaken when their mentor devoted more time to the Ronettes, and consequently their career faltered. New members passed through, including Frances Collins, and the band were prematurely banished to the nostalgia circuit.

● ALBUMS: *Twist Uptown* (Philles 1962) ★★, *He's A Rebel* (Philles 1963) ★★★.
● COMPILATIONS: *The Crystals Sing Their Greatest Hits* (Philles 1963) ★★★, *Uptown* (Spectrum 1988) ★★★, *The Best Of* (ABKCO 1992) ★★★, *Greatest Hits* (Classic World 2000) ★★★.

CUFF LINKS

The brainchild of Pat Rizzo (formerly of Joey Dee And The Starliters), the Cuff Links were a studio group featuring Ron Dante, lead singer of the Archies. Rizzo had recruited songwriters Paul Vance and Lee Pockriss who had previously composed hits for Perry Como ('Catch A Falling Star') and Brian Hyland ('Itsy Bitsy Teenie Weenie Yellow Polkadot Bikini'). The songwriting duo came up with the catchy bubblegum singalong 'Tracy', which became an international hit. Dante was the sole multi voiced singer on the original recording but once the song charted, a group was specially created comprising Pat Rizzo (vocals), Rick Dimino (keyboards), Bob Gill (trumpet/flugelhorn/ flute), Dave Loxender (guitar), Andrew 'Junior' Deno (bass), Joe Cord (vocals) and Davy Valentine (drums). The group recorded a handful of further singles and two albums before disbanding in the early 70s.

● ALBUMS: *Tracy* (MCA 1969) ★★★, *The Cuff Links* (1970) ★★.

CUPID'S INSPIRATION

Based in Stamford, Lincolnshire, England, and initially known as the Ends, this pop attraction secured a recording deal with NEMS on the strength of vocalist T. (Terry) Rice-Milton (b. 5 June 1946). The line-up was completed by Wyndham George (b. 20 February 1947; guitar), Laughton James (b. 21 December 1946; bass) and Roger Gray (b. 29 April 1949) and featured on 'Yesterday Has Gone' (1968), a song originally recorded by Little Anthony And The Imperials. Cupid's cover version rose to number 4 in the

UK chart, during which time pianist Garfield Tonkin (b. 28 September 1946) was added to the group. However, despite enjoying a subsequent minor hit with 'My World', the quintet was unable to repeat the success of their powerful and catchy debut single. The line-up was disbanded at the end of the year, but within weeks Rice-Milton and Gray re-emerged alongside newcomers Bernie Lee (guitar) and Gordon Haskell (b. 27 April 1946, Bournemouth, Dorset, England; bass). A new-found, more 'progressive' style failed to reverse declining fortunes and the group disintegrated. Its vocalist began a short-lived solo career in 1970 with a revival of Cilla Black's 'You're My World', while Haskell, formerly of Fleur De Lys, later found fame with King Crimson and in 2001 he almost hit the top of the UK chart with 'How Wonderful You Are'. This was followed by the hit album *Harry's Bar* in January 2002.
● ALBUMS: *Yesterday Has Gone* (NEMS 1968) ★★.

CURTIS, LEE, AND THE ALL-STARS
Lee Curtis And The All Stars was one of many aspiring beat combos active in Liverpool, England during the early 60s. Curtis (b. Peter Flannery) was a pop vocalist indebted to the pop style of the late 50s, but in September 1962 his career was given a considerable fillip when former Beatles drummer Pete Best joined his group. Frank Bowen (lead guitar), Tony Waddington (rhythm guitar) and Wayne Bickerton (bass) completed the line-up, although Bowen was later replaced by Tommy McGurk. Best's arrival boosted the All-Stars' popularity and they came second only to the Beatles in a *Mersey Beat* readers' poll in 1963. However, the group was rather staid onstage, lacking the passion of many contemporaries. Decca Records signed Curtis as a solo artist in 1963 – much to the chagrin of his 'backing' group – and his debut, 'Little Girl', was recorded with session musicians. The All-Stars appeared on the follow-up, 'Let's Stomp' (1963), but the results were poor and the singer and band then parted company. Curtis formed a new All-Stars and continued his recording career with 'What About Me' (1964) and 'Ecstacy' (1965). Two live performances, 'Skinny Minnie' and 'Jezebel', are enshrined on the various artists' compilation, *At The Cavern*. Meanwhile, his erstwhile colleagues regrouped as the Pete Best Four.

CYMBAL, JOHNNY
b. 3 February 1945, Ochiltree, Clyde, Scotland. Cymbal's family moved to Canada while he was a child. He became infatuated with music in his teens and in 1960 the singer, then living in Cleveland, Ohio, USA, secured a recording deal with MGM Records. His early releases included 'The Water Is Red', a macabre 'death disc' in which Cymbal's girlfriend was eaten by a shark. In 1963 the artist switched outlets to Kapp Records for whom he recorded 'Mr. Bass Man', a humorous paean to the vocalist carrying the bottom line in a harmony group, in this case one Ronnie Bright. The single, evocative of a passing singing style, reached number 16 in the US and number 24 in the UK, and has since become one of the most memorable novelty songs of the pre-Beatles era. However, despite a succession of subsequent releases, Cymbal was unable to secure another hit and instead forged a new career in songwriting. He penned 'Mary In The Morning', a US hit for Al Martino in 1967 and later produced several records for David Cassidy and Gene Pitney. Domiciled in Nashville since 1980, Cymbal now concentrates on country material.
● ALBUMS: *Mr. Bass Man* (Kapp 1963) ★★.

CYRKLE
Founder members of this harmony pop act, Don Dannemann (b. Albany, New York, USA; guitar/vocals) and Tom Dawes (b. Brooklyn, New York, USA; guitar/vocals) met while studying at Lafayette College. Together they formed a 'frat' band, the Rhondells, with Earl Pickens (keyboards) and Marty Fried (drums) which honed a set drawn from songs by the Beach Boys and Four Seasons. They were 'discovered' playing at New Jersey's Alibi Lounge by New York attorney Nat Weiss, who introduced the group to Beatles manager Brian Epstein. He signed the Rhondells to his NEMS roster; John Lennon reportedly suggested their new name, the Cyrkle. The incipient act then broke up temporarily, leaving Dawes free to tour with Simon And Garfunkel. Paul Simon offered the bassist 'Red Rubber Ball', a song he co-wrote with Bruce Woodley of the Seekers which gave the reconvened Cyrkle a number 2 US hit in May 1966. The group supported the Beatles on the latter's final tour but having passed on another Simon composition, '59th Street Bridge Song (Feeling Groovy)', later a hit for Harpers Bizarre, the Cyrkle enjoyed their only other Top 20 entry with 'Turn Down Day' (number 16, August 1966), which featured Dawes' memorable sitar line. Pickens was replaced by Mike Losecamp for *Neon*, but the death of Epstein in 1967 virtually ended the Cyrkle's career. They broke up in January 1968 when Dawes and Losecamp quit the line-up. The former later found success penning advertising jingles, a career Dannemann also followed.
● ALBUMS: *Red Rubber Ball* (Columbia 1966) ★★, *Neon* (Columbia 1967) ★★.
● COMPILATIONS: *Red Rubber Ball (A Collection)* (Columbia Legacy 1991) ★★.

D

D'ABO, MICHAEL
b. 1 March 1944, Betchworth, Surrey, England. Vocalist/songwriter D'Abo was a founder member of beat group A Band Of Angels, formed at Harrow Public School. A highly competent songwriter, he penned the last of the group's four singles, 'Invitation', before replacing Paul Jones in Manfred Mann in 1966. D'Abo proved a worthy successor, and was featured on many of their best-known releases, including 'Semi-Detached Suburban Mr. Jones' (1966), 'Ha! Ha! Said The Clown' (1967) and 'Mighty Quinn' (1968). D'Abo also won plaudits for his much-covered composition (including Rod Stewart and Stereophonics), 'Handbags And Gladrags', while 'Build Me Up Buttercup', a collaboration with Tony Macauley, was a million-selling hit for the Foundations. D'Abo left Manfred Mann in 1969 when they embraced a 'progressive rock' style, and subsequently unveiled his affection for crafted pop. The ambitious pop opera *Gulliver's Travels* was a brave solo debut which was performed at the Mermaid Theatre in London. The album sunk without a trace (although it was masterfully remastered and reissued in 2001). *Broken Rainbows* featured a stellar cast, including Graham Nash and Mike Bloomfield, but the singer was unable to achieve commercial success. In 1976, he joined Mike Smith, ex-Dave Clark Five, in a performing/songwriting partnership, Smith And D'Abo. Once again widespread acclaim proved elusive, and the artist has since pursued a less public, yet still productive, career. D'Abo composed several advertising jingles, including television's long-running 'finger of fudge' for Cadbury's chocolate. In the 90s he was back with the Manfreds, together with Paul Jones and most of the original band.
● ALBUMS: *Gulliver's Travels* (Instant 1968) ★★★, *D'Abo* (MCA 1970) ★★★, *Down At Rachel's Place* (A&M 1972) ★★, *Broken Rainbows* (A&M 1974) ★★, with Mike Smith *Smith & D'Abo* (1976) ★★★, *Indestructible* (1987) ★★, *Tomorrow's Troubadour* (1988) ★★.

DAILY FLASH
Formed in Seattle, Washington, USA, in 1965, the Daily Flash was the confluence of former bluegrass veteran Don MacAllister (bass), ex-folk singer Steve Lalor (guitar), jazz drummer Jon Keliehor and lead guitarist Doug Hastings (b. 21 June 1946, Seattle, Washington, USA). The unit boasted a repertoire drawn from all these sources and was quickly established as the city's leading 'alternative' attraction. Their debut single, 'Jack Of Diamonds'/Bob Dylan's 'Queen Jane Approximately', was released in 1965 and preceded a successful series of concerts in San Francisco and Los Angeles the following year. Despite an acclaimed second single, 'The French Girl'/'Green Rocky Road', and a bizarre appearance in television's The Girl From UNCLE, the group did not achieve commercial success and the line-up then fragmented. Keliehor left in May 1967, while Hastings briefly replaced Neil Young in Buffalo Springfield before becoming a founder member of Rhinoceros. Craig Tarwater (guitar) and Tony Dey (drums) subsequently joined Daily Flash, but the group broke up the following year. MacAllister became immersed in the blues circuit prior to his premature death in 1969, while Keliehor and Lalor pursued several projects both together and individually. The most notable of those was *1 Flash Daily*, a collection of previously issued and archive selections, which featured a lengthy live rendition of Herbie Hancock's 'Canteloupe Island'.
● ALBUMS: *1 Flash Daily* (Psycho 1984) ★★.

DAKOTAS
Originally formed in Manchester, England, the Dakotas – Mike Maxfield (b. 23 February 1944, Manchester, England; guitar), Robin McDonald (b. 18 July 1943, Nairn, Scotland; guitar), Ray Jones (b. 22 October 1939, Oldham, Lancashire, England, d. 20 January 2000; bass) and Tony Mansfield (b. Anthony Bookbinder, 28 May 1943, Salford, Lancashire, England; drums) – achieved fame as the backing group to Liverpudlian singer Billy J. Kramer. His success inspired the quartet's own recording career which enjoyed a promising beginning when their debut single, 'The Cruel Sea', reached the UK Top 20 in July 1963. This surf-influenced instrumental was succeeded by 'Magic Carpet', but this release failed to achieve a similar profile. When Jones left the line-up in July 1964, McDonald switched to bass in order to accommodate former Pirates guitarist Mick Green. Tony Mansfield was the older brother of singer Elkie Brooks. The Dakotas continued to support Kramer, and over the next four years they recorded three further singles in their own right. The group was reduced to a trio in 1965 when Maxfield left to concentrate on songwriting. Another ex-Pirate, drummer Frank Farley, replaced Mansfield in 1966. He, Green and MacDonald later joined singer Cliff Bennett following the Dakotas' demise in 1968.

DALE AND GRACE
This pop vocal duo comprised Dale Houston (b. Baton Rouge, Louisiana, USA), and Grace Broussard (b. Prairieville, Louisiana, USA). Both singers had sung solo and Grace had also sung with her brother Van (later of soul duo Van And Titus) before they teamed up at a recording

ession for the local Montel label in 1963. Their first recording, a revival of Don And Dewey's ballad 'I'm Leaving It Up To You', found success in the south and soon went to number 1 in the US charts and narrowly missed the UK Top 40. The duo also put their follow-up 'Stop And Think It Over' into the US Top 10 and had a minor hit with 'The Loneliest Night'. Their debut album also made the US Top 100. This distinctive R&B-orientated pop duo later had unsuccessful releases on Guyden and Hanna-Barbera. Their biggest hit song became a transatlantic Top 10 record in 1974 for Donny and Marie Osmond.

● ALBUMS: *I'm Leaving It Up To You* (Montel 1964) ★★.

DALE, DICK

b. Richard Monsour, 4 May 1937, Boston, Massachusetts, USA. (Note: Dale himself has been quoted in interviews as saying he was born in Beirut, Lebanon, and that his family emigrated to Quincy, Massachusetts, when he was a child. Now, however Dale denies that story and claims to have been born in Boston.) Dale is usually credited as the inventor of the instrumental surf music style and the major influence on surf guitar. With his band the Del-Tones, Dale's early 60s records sparked the surf music craze on the US west coast, and his guitar-playing influenced hundreds of other musicians.

Dale started out as a pianist at the age of nine, and also played trumpet and harmonica, before switching to the ukulele and then finally guitar. His first musical interest was country music and his idol was Hank Williams. Dale's family moved to El Segundo, California in 1954 and he took a job at an aircraft company after graduating from high school. Having learned country guitar, he entered talent contests, still performing under his real name. The name Dick Dale was suggested to him by a Texas disc jockey named T. Texas Tiny. Dale gained popularity as a local country singer and also appeared in concerts with rhythm and blues artists. He also gained a small role in a Marilyn Monroe movie, *Let's Make Love*.

Dale's first record was 'Ooh-Whee-Marie' on the Deltone label, which his father owned. He eventually recorded nine singles for Del-Tone between 1959 and 1962, and also recorded for the Cupid label. One of those Del-Tone singles, 'Let's Go Trippin'', released in 1961, is generally considered to be the first instrumental surf record. According to Dale, he and his cousin were riding motorcycles to the beach on the Balboa Peninsula in southern California, where Dale befriended the local surfers. There he also began playing with a band at a club called the Rinky Dink. Another guitar player showed him how to make certain adjustments to the pickup settings on his Stratocaster guitar to create different sounds, and that sound, aided by other

sonic developments and featuring Dale's staccato attack, became his trademark. Although he was still playing country music, he moved closer to the beach and began surfing during the day and playing music at night, adding rock 'n' roll to his repertoire.

By then Dale had formed his own band, the Del-Tones, including piano, guitars, bass, drums and saxophone, and shifted his home base to the Rendezvous Ballroom down the beach from the Rinky Dink. The band, like most others, performed vocal compositions, until one patron asked Dale if they could play an instrumental song. Inspired by his surfing hobby, Dale composed a tune that he felt captured the feeling of riding the waves and the power of the ocean. Once the band began adding more instrumental songs in this style to its repertoire, the crowd grew in size until the Rendezvous was packed to capacity. At one point city officials tried to run Dale out of town, believing that his music was having a negative effect on the local youth. Playing left-handed without reversing the strings, Dale started to fine-tune the surf guitar style. He met with Leo Fender, the inventor of the Fender guitar and amplifier line, and worked with him on designing equipment that would be more suited to that style of music (Dale helped to develop the popular Showman amp). Along with other innovations, such as the first outboard reverb unit, which helped define the surf sound, the JBL speaker and the Rhodes piano, Dale was able virtually to reinvent this new style of rock 'n' roll as he went along. 'Let's Go Trippin'' was the first instrumental recording by Dale, and one of only two singles to make the US national charts (at number 60, based entirely on local sales in California), with 'Shake 'N' Stomp' and 'Misirlou' also popular early Dale singles on Deltone.

Dale released his first album, *Surfer's Choice*, also on Deltone, in 1962. Recorded live, it was one of the first albums to feature a surfer (Dale) on the cover. (At the same time, vocal surf music, as pioneered by the Beach Boys, began to take off, but the two styles had little in common musically. Moreover Dale's first recording preceded theirs by two months.) The instrumental surf music craze was initially largely confined to the Orange County area, but its popularity there became so overwhelming that Los Angeles radio stations began playing the music of Dale and the other new surf bands. In 1963, after *Surfers' Choice* made the national album charts (number 59), Capitol Records signed Dale to a seven-album contract (only five were released). One of Dale's singles for Capitol, 'The Scavenger', made the US charts, as did the *Checkered Flag* album that year, but Dale never charted again, remaining almost entirely a local phenomenon while becoming a major influence on other musicians. Dale appeared on the *Ed Sullivan Show* on US television and received national press coverage, but his reluctance to travel, combined with the brief popularity of surf music, hindered his career advancement. He appeared in the 1964 movie *Muscle Beach Party* but that same year, with the arrival of the British beat bands, Capitol had shifted its priorities and Dale was dropped from the label less than two years after signing to it.

Dale continued to record sporadically throughout the rest of the 60s and 70s for numerous labels but a cancer scare, which he overcame, effectively sidelined his career. His music was rediscovered in the 80s, and he recorded a scorching duet with Stevie Ray Vaughan of the old Chantays surf instrumental 'Pipeline' in 1987 for the movie *Back To The Beach*. In 1989, Rhino Records released a compilation of Dale's best recordings, and in the early 90s Dale signed with the US label Hightone Records. His 1993 album *Tribal Thunder* and the 1994 follow-up, *Unknown Territory*, as well as numerous live gigs across the USA, have showed that Dale's influence remains strong and that his powers as a musician, although limited, are undiminished. In 1994, his recording of 'Misirlou' was prominently featured in the Quentin Tarantino movie *Pulp Fiction*, bringing Dale new recognition to a much younger audience. This resulted in Dale being able to trade on the word 'legendary' wherever he went and launching a revitalized recording career.

● ALBUMS: *Surfers' Choice* (Deltone 1962) ★★★, *King Of The Surf Guitar* (Capitol 1963) ★★★, *Checkered Flag* (Capitol 1963) ★★★, *Mr. Eliminator* (Capitol 1964) ★★★, *Summer Surf* (Capitol 1964) ★★★, *Rock Out With Dick Dale And His Del-Tones – Live At Ciro's* (Capitol 1965) ★★, *The Tiger's Loose* (Balboa 1983) ★★, *Tribal Thunder* (Hightone 1993) ★★, *Unknown Territory* (Hightone 1994) ★★★, *Calling Up Spirits* (Beggars Banquet 1996) ★★, *Spacial Disorientation* (Sin-Drome 2002) ★★★.

● COMPILATIONS: *Dick Dale's Greatest Hits* (GNP Crescendo 1975) ★★★, *King Of The Surf Guitar: The Best Of Dick Dale And His Del-Tones* (Rhino 1986) ★★★★, *Better Shred Than Dead: The Dick Dale Anthology* (Rhino 1997) ★★★★.

● FURTHER READING: *Surf Beat: The Dick Dale Story*, Stephen J. McParland.

● FILMS: *Let's Make Love* (1960), *A Swingin' Affair* (1963), *Beach Party* (1963), *Muscle Beach Party* (1964), *Back To The Beach* (1987), *Treasure* (1990), *Liquid Stage: The Lure Of Surfing* television (1994).

DALE, JIM

b. Jim Smith, 15 August 1935, Kettering, Northamptonshire, England. Dale, a failed impressionist, who wanted to be an all-round entertainer, had a two-year stint with Carrol Levis' touring show as part of a comedy tumbling act. He then became a solo comedian and only turned to singing when he found people preferred his finale song to his tame

comedy. He joined the BBC Television series *6.5 Special* in April 1957, and shortly afterwards signed to Parlophone Records, where he was produced by George Martin. His only Top 20 hit came with his second single, a cover version of Johnny Madara's 'Be My Girl', which reached number 2 in late 1957. He had three more UK Top 40 entries, the last being a version of the McGuire Sisters' US hit 'Sugartime' in 1958. In the 60s Dale pursued his acting career, and appeared in a string of successful *Carry On* films, and others, such as *Lock Up Your Daughters*. He made his West End debut in a musical, *The Wayward Way*, and appeared at the Edinburgh Festival in a pop version of *The Winter's Tale*. He also co-wrote the Seekers' smash hit 'Georgy Girl', for which he was nominated for an Academy Award, and contributed to the music for movies such as *Shalako* and *Lola*. In the late 60s and early 70s, as member of the National Theatre Company, he appeared in several productions at the Old Vic and the Young Vic. He also made more films, including *Adolf Hitler – My Part In His Downfall* and *Digby, The Biggest Dog In The World*. In 1973, Dale played for six months at the Queen's Theatre, London, in the musical *The Card*, and around the same time, hosted the popular television show, *Sunday Night At The London Palladium*. In 1974 he went to the USA with the National Theatre Company and created a stir with his performance as an 'ingratiating scamp' in the Molière farce *Scapino*, which brought him Drama Desk and Outer Critics Circle Awards, and a Tony Award nomination. During the late 70s, by now domiciled in the USA, he appeared in stage productions of *Comedians* and *Privates On Parade*, as well as making several other movies, three of them for the Disney Studio. In 1980 Dale found the ideal vehicle for his talents in *Barnum*, a musical about the life of the famed US showman, which involved juggling, trampolining and tightrope walking, among other skills. He won a Tony Award for his performance and stayed with the show for over a year, following ecstatic opening reviews. In the 80s he made more films, and appeared on the New York stage in productions as diverse as Peter Nichol's *Joe Egg* (1985), *Me And My Girl* (1987), and a revival of *Privates On Parade* (1989). During the 90s, as well as appearing on the American stage and in television movies such as *The American Clock* (1993) and *The Hunchback* (1997), he returned to the UK on occasions, playing the title role in the film *Carry On Columbus*, Professor Harold Hill in a BBC Radio 2 recording of *The Music Man* (1995), and Fagin in Cameron Mackintosh's record-breaking revival of *Oliver!* at the London Palladium (1995 and 1997). He was also nominated for the best leading actor in a musical Tony Award for his performance on Broadway in *Candide* (1997).

● ALBUMS: *Jim!* (Parlophone 1958) ★★, *This Is*

Me (Pye 1973) ★★★, and cast recordings.
● FILMS: *6.5 Special* (1958), *Raising The Wind* (1961), *Nurse On Wheels* (1963), *Carry On Cabby* (1963), *Carry On Spying* (1964), *Carry On Jack* (1964), *Carry On Cleo* (1964), *Carry On Cowboy* (1965), *The Big Job* (1965), *Carry On Screaming!* (1966), *The Plank* (1967), *Follow That Camel* (1967), *Don't Lose Your Head* (1967), *The Winter's Tale* (1968), *Carry On Doctor* (1968), *Lock Up Your Daughters!* (1969), *Carry On Again, Doctor* (1969), *Adolf Hitler – My Part In His Downfall* (1972), *The National Health* (1973), *Digby – The Biggest Dog In The World* (1973), *Joseph Andrews* (1977), *Pete's Dragon* (1977), *Hot Lead And Cold Feet* (1978), *Unidentified Flying Oddball* (1979), *Scandalous* (1984), *Adventures Of Huckleberry Finn* television (1985), *Carry On Columbus* (1992), *Lincoln* television (1992), *The American Clock* television (1993), *The Hunchback* television (1997).

DANA, VIC

b. 26 August 1942, Buffalo, New York, USA. As a young boy, Dana trained as a dancer, and at the age of 11 was spotted, performing in Buffalo, by Sammy Davis Jnr. Influenced by Davis, the Dana family moved to California, where young Dana worked on his dancing and also studied singing. In 1960, he toured as a solo act, appearing on the same bill as the Fleetwoods, and then signed for the same record company, Dolton. In the early 60s he had some success with 'Little Altar Boy', 'I Will' and 'More', before making the US Top 30 with 'Shangri-La' in 1964. The Top 10 hit 'Red Roses For A Blue Lady' followed in 1965, and 'I Love You Drops' in 1966. He also had a Top 20 album with *Red Roses For A Blue Lady*. In 1970 he switched to Liberty Records for 'If I Never Knew Your Name' and Red Red Wine'.
● ALBUMS: *This Is Vic Dana* (Dolton 1961) ★★★, *Warm And Wild* (Dolton 1962) ★★, *More* (Dolton 1964) ★★★, *Shangri-La* (Dolton 1964) ★★★, *Red Roses For A Blue Lady* (Dolton 1965) ★★★, *Crystal Chandelier* (Dolton 1966) ★★, *Now!* (Dolton 1966) ★★★, *Young, Warm And Wonderful* (Dolton 1966) ★★, *Foreign Affairs* (Dolton 1967) ★★, *Viva!* (Dolton 1967) ★★, *On The Country Side* (Dolton 1967) ★★, *Town And Country* (Dolton 1968) ★★.
● COMPILATIONS: *Golden Greats* (Dolton 1966) ★★★, *Complete Hits Of Vic Dana* (Eric 2000) ★★★.
● FILMS: *Don't Knock The Twist* (1962).

DANTALIAN'S CHARIOT

Formed in London, England, in 1967, Dantalian's Chariot comprised three ex-members of Zoot Money's Big Roll Band; Zoot Money (vocals/keyboards), Andy Somers (guitar), Colin Allen (drums), with Pat Donaldson added on bass. The new act eschewed the R&B style of its predecessor in favour of the prevailing 'flower power' trend.

Indeed, Dantalian's Chariot boasted one of the most innovative light shows of the era. The group issued one single during its short life span. 'Madman Running Through The Fields/Sun Came Bursting Through My Cloud' is a quintessential slice of English psychedelia, replete with sound effects, backward-running tapes and escapist lyrics. Other tracks, recorded at the same time for CBS offshoot Direction, remained unissued, although some were resurrected for Money's 'solo' release *Transition* (1968). He and Somers subsequently joined Eric Burdon And The New Animals. Donaldson was later a member of Fotheringay, while Allen played with John Mayall and Stone The Crows. Money has remained a popular attraction both as a singer and actor, while Somers, as Andy Summers, found fame in the Police.
● ALBUMS: *Chariot Rising* (Wooden Hill 1997) ★★★.

DARIN, BOBBY

b. Walden Robert Cassotto, 14 May 1936, New York, USA, d. 20 December 1973, Los Angeles, California, USA. Darin's entry to the music business occurred during the mid-50s following a period playing in New York coffee-houses. His friendship with co-writer/entrepreneur Don Kirshner resulted in his first single, 'My First Love'. A meeting with Connie Francis' manager George Scheck led to a prestigious television appearance on the Tommy Dorsey television show and a contract with Decca Records. An unsuccessful attempt at a hit with a cover version of Lonnie Donegan's 'Rock Island Line' was followed by a move towards pop novelty with 'Splish Splash'. Darin's quirky vocal ensured that his song was a worldwide hit, although he was outsold in Britain by a rival version from comedian Charlie Drake. During this period, Darin also recorded in a band called the Ding Dongs, which prompted a dispute between Atco Records and Brunswick Records, culminating in the creation of a new outfit, the Rinky Dinks, who were credited as the backing artists on his next single, 'Early In The Morning'.
Neither that, nor its successor, 'Mighty Mighty', proved commercially viable, but the intervening Darin solo release, 'Queen Of The Hop', sold a million. The period charm of 'Plain Jane' presaged one of Darin's finest moments – the exceptional 'Dream Lover'. An enticing vocal performance allied to strong production took the song to number 1 in the UK and number 2 in the USA. Already assured of considerable status as a pop artist, Darin dramatically changed direction with his next recording and emerged as a finger-clicking master of the supper club circuit. 'Mack The Knife', composed by Bertolt Brecht and Kurt Weill for the celebrated musical *The Threepenny Opera*, proved a million-seller and effectively raised Darin to new status as a 'serious singer' – he even compared himself favourably with Frank Sinatra, in what was a classic example of

pop hubris. Darin's hit treatments of 'La Mer' (as 'Beyond The Sea'), 'Clementine', 'Won't You Come Home Bill Bailey?' and 'You Must Have Been A Beautiful Baby' revealed his ability to tackle variety material and transform it to his own ends.

In 1960, Darin adeptly moved into the movies and was highly praised for his roles in *Come September* (whose star Sandra Dee he later married), *Too Late Blues*, *Pressure Point*, *If A Man Answers*, *State Fair*, *Hell Is For Heroes* and *Captain Newman, M.D.* He returned to form as a pop performer with the lyrically witty 'Multiplication' and the equally clever 'Things'. In the meantime, he had recorded an album of Ray Charles' songs, including the standard 'What'd I Say'. During the beat boom era Darin briefly reverted to show tunes such as 'Baby Face' and 'Hello Dolly', but a further change of style beckoned with the folk rock boom of 1965. Suddenly, Darin was a protest singer, summing up the woes of a generation with the surly 'We Didn't Ask To Be Brought Here'. Successful readings of Tim Hardin songs, including 'If I Were A Carpenter' and 'The Lady Came From Baltimore', and John Sebastian's 'Lovin' You' and 'Darling Be Home Soon' demonstrated his potential as a cover artist of seemingly limitless range. A more contemporary poetic and political direction was evident on the album *Born Walden Robert Cassotto*, and its serious follow-up *Commitment*.

As the 60s ended Darin was more actively involved in related business interests, although he still appeared regularly on television. One of the great vocal chameleons of pop music, Darin suffered from a weak heart and after several operations, time finally caught up with the singer at Hollywood's Cedars of Lebanon Hospital in December 1973. Since his death, Darin's reputation as a vocalist has continued to grow, and in 1990 he was inducted into the Rock And Roll Hall Of Fame. The box set *As Long As I'm Singing* received universally excellent reviews and helped introduce his work to a much younger audience. In June 1999, he was posthumously inducted into the Songwriters' Hall Of Fame, having composed/co-composed numbers such as 'Come September', 'Dream Lover', 'Early In The Morning', 'Eighteen Yellow Roses', 'I'll Be There', 'If A Man Answers', 'Multiplication', 'Queen Of The Hop', 'Splish Splash', 'This Little Girl's Gone Rockin'', and 'You're The Reason I'm Living'.

● ALBUMS: *Bobby Darin* (Atco 1958) ★★★★, *That's All* (Atco 1959) ★★★, *This Is Darin* (Atco 1960) ★★★, *Darin At The Copa* (Atco 1960) ★★★, *For Teenagers Only* (Atco 1960) ★★★, *The 25th Day Of December* (Atco 1960) ★★★, with Johnny Mercer *Two Of A Kind* (Atco 1961) ★★★, *Love Swings* (Atco 1961) ★★★, *Twist With Bobby Darin* (Atco 1962) ★★★, *Bobby Darin Sings Ray Charles* (Atco 1962) ★★★, *Things & Other Things* (Atco 1962) ★★★, *Oh! Look At Me Now* (Capitol

1962) ★★★, *You're The Reason I'm Living* (Capitol 1963) ★★★, *It's You Or No One* 1960 recording (Atco 1963) ★★★, *18 Yellow Roses & 11 Other Hits* (Capitol 1963) ★★★, *Earthy!* (Capitol 1963) ★★★, *Golden Folk Hits* (Capitol 1963) ★★★, *Winners* (Atco 1964) ★★★, *From Hello Dolly To Goodbye Charlie* (Capitol 1964) ★★, *Venice Blue* (Capitol 1965) ★★, *Bobby Darin Sings The Shadow Of Your Smile* (Atlantic 1966) ★★, *In A Broadway Bag* (Atlantic 1966) ★★, *If I Were A Carpenter* (Atlantic 1966) ★★★★, *Inside Out* (Atlantic 1967) ★★★, *Bobby Darin Sings Doctor Dolittle* (Atlantic 1967) ★, *Born Walden Robert Cassotto* (Direction 1968) ★★★, *Commitment* (Direction 1969) ★★★, *Bobby Darin* (Motown 1972) ★★.

● COMPILATIONS: *The Bobby Darin Story* (Atco 1961) ★★★★, *Clementine* (Clarion 1964) ★★★★, *The Best Of Bobby Darin* (Capitol 1965) ★★★, *Something Special* television soundtrack (Atlantic 1967) ★★★, *The Legendary Bobby Darin* (Candlelite 1976) ★★★, *The Versatile Bobby Darin* (Capitol 1985) ★★★, *The Legend Of Bobby Darin* (Stylus 1985) ★★★, *His Greatest Hits* (Capitol 1985) ★★★, *Bobby Darin: Collectors Series* (Capitol 1989) ★★★, *Splish Splash: The Best Of Bobby Darin Volume One* (Atco 1991) ★★★, *Mack The Knife: The Best Of Bobby Darin Volume 2* (Atco 1991) ★★★, *From Sea To Sea: Recorded Live From 1959 To 1967* (Live Gold 1992) ★★★, *Spotlight On Bobby Darin* (Capitol 1995) ★★★, *As Long As I'm Singing: The Bobby Darin Collection* 4-CD box set (Rhino 1995) ★★★★, *Roberto Cassotto: Rare, Rockin' & Unreleased* (Ring Of Stars 1997) ★★★, *A&E Biography* (Capitol 1998) ★★★, *Mood Swings: The Best Of The Atlantic Years 1965-1967* (Edsel 1999) ★★★★, *The Capitol Years* 3-CD box set (EMI 1999) ★★★, *Swingin' The Standards* (Varèse Sarabande 1999) ★★★, *Wild, Cool & Swingin'* (Capitol 1999) ★★★, *The Unreleased Capitol Sides* (Collector's Choice 1999) ★★★, *The Very Best Of Bobby Darin 1966-1969: If I Were A Carpenter* (Varèse Sarabande 1999) ★★★★.

● VIDEOS: *Bobby Darin – Live!* (Legends Of Entertainment 1999).

● FURTHER READING: *Borrowed Time: The 37 Years Of Bobby Darin*, Al Diorio. *That's All: Bobby Darin On Record, Stage And Screen*, Jeff Bleiel. *Dream Lovers*, Dodd Darin.

● FILMS: *Pepe* (1960), *Too Late Blues* (1961), *Come September* (1961), *Pressure Point* (1962), *If A Man Answers* (1962), *State Fair* (1962), *Hell Is For Heroes* (1962), *Captain Newman, M.D.* (1963), *That Funny Feeling* (1965), *Cop-Out* aka *Stranger In The House* (1967), *Gunfight In Abilene* (1967), *Happy Mother's Day, Love George* aka *Run, Stranger, Run* (1973).

DARREN, JAMES

b. James William Ercolani, 8 June 1936, Philadelphia, Pennsylvania, USA. This photogenic actor/singer was signed to Columbia Pictures in the mid-50s, his first movie being *umble On The Docks* in 1956. He first sang in *idget* in 1959, from which the title song made ie US chart. Other notable starring roles include *Because They're Young* in 1960 and the epic *The Guns Of Navarone* in 1961. In 1962 he reached the US Top 5 with his lucky 13th single 'Goodbye Cruel World' and followed it with two more transatlantic hits 'Her Royal Majesty', a Carole King song, and 'Conscience', written by Barry Mann. Darren later recorded with little success on Warner Brothers Records in 1965, Kirshner in 1969, Buddah Records in 1970, MGM Records in 1973, Private Stock in 1975 (where he returned briefly to the US Top 100 in 1977 with 'You Take My Heart Away', from the hit movie *Rocky*) and RCA Records in 1978. Darren is now best known for his television roles, playing the role of Dr. Tony Newman in the popular and often re-run 60s television series *The Time Tunnel*, Officer James Corrigan in *T.J. Hooker*, the singing hologram Vic Fontaine in *Star Trek: Deep Space Nine* and Tony Marlin in *Melrose Place*. During the 90s he established himself as an in-demand television director. The memorable fairground atmosphere of 'Goodbye Cruel World' remains his finest moment on record, although he made a welcome return to recording in 1999 with an album of jazz standards for Concord.

ALBUMS: *James Darren Volume 1* (Colpix 1960) ★, *Gidget Goes Hawaiian (James Darren Sings The Movies)* (Colpix 1961) ★★, *James Darren Sings For All Sizes* (Colpix 1962) ★★★, *Love Among The Young* (Colpix 1962) ★★, *Bye Bye Birdie* (Colpix 1963) ★★, with Shelley Fabares, Paul Petersen *Teenage Triangle* (Colpix 1963) ★, *The Lively Set* film soundtrack (Decca 1964) , with Fabares, Petersen *More Teenage Triangle* (Colpix 1964) ★, *All* (Warners 1967) ★, *This One's From The Heart* (Concord Jazz 1999) ★★★.

COMPILATIONS: *The Best Of James Darren* (Rhino/Sequel 1994) ★★★, *Teenage Tears: 32 Original Colpix Recordings 1959-1964* (Raven 1996) ★★★.

FILMS: *Rumble On The Docks* (1956), *Operation Mad Ball* (1957), *The Tijuana Story* (1957), *The Brothers Rico* (1957), *Gunman's Walk* (1958), *Gidget* (1959), *The Gene Krupa Story* aka *Drum Crazy* (1959), *Because They're Young* (1960), *All The Young Men* (1960), *Let No Man Write My Epitaph* (1960), *The Guns Of Navarone* (1961), *Gidget Goes Hawaiian* (1961), *Diamond Head* (1962), *Gidget Goes To Rome* (1963), *The Lively Set* (1964), *Hey There, It's Yogi Bear* (1964), *For Those Who Think Young* (1964), *Paroxismus* aka *Black Angel* (1969), *The Boss' Son* (1978).

DAVE DEE, DOZY, BEAKY, MICK AND TICH

Formed in 1961 as Dave Dee And The Bostons, this zany pop quintet found a settled hit line-up as Dave Dee (b. David Harman, 17 December 1943, Salisbury, Wiltshire, England; vocals), Dozy (b. Trevor Davies, 27 November 1944,

Enford, Wiltshire, England; bass), Beaky (b. John Dymond, 10 July 1944, Salisbury, Wiltshire, England; guitar), Mick (b. Michael Wilson, 4 March 1944, Amesbury, Wiltshire, England; lead guitar) and Tich (Ian Amey, 15 May 1944, Salisbury, Wiltshire, England). The band established their power as live performers during residencies at various Hamburg clubs in 1962. Their act featured rock 'n' roll spiced with comedy routines and an element of risqué patter from their engaging frontman. While supporting the Honeycombs on a 1964 UK tour, they came to the attention of managers Howard And Blaikley (Ken Howard and Alan Blaikley) and were subsequently signed to Fontana Records by Jack Baverstock and assigned to producer Steve Rowland. After two unsuccessful singles, 'No Time' and 'All I Want', they hit the UK chart with the upbeat 'You Make It Move'. Thereafter, they had an incredible run of a dozen strong chart hits, all executed with a camp flair and costume-loving theatricalism that proved irresistible. With songs provided by Howard And Blaikley, they presented a veritable travelogue of pop, filled with melodramatic scenarios. 'Bend It' was their 'Greek' phase, and allowed Dave Dee to wiggle his little finger while uttering the curiously suggestive lyric; 'Zabadak' was an exotic arrangement sung in unknown language; 'The Legend Of Xanadu' was a ripping yarn, which allowed Dee to brandish a bullwhip in live performance; 'Last Night In Soho' was a leather-boy motorbike saga portraying lost innocence in London's most notorious square mile. The sheer diversity of the hits maintained the band's appeal but they lost ground at the end of the 60s and Dave Dee left for an unsuccessful solo career before venturing into television presenting and A&R. The others continued as a quartet, but after one minor hit, 'Mr President', and an album, *Fresh Ear*, they broke up. A couple of brief nostalgic reunions later occurred, but not enough to encourage a serious relaunch. *Zabadak*, a fascinating fanzine, is published in France for those fans who wish to monitor their every move.

● ALBUMS: *Dave Dee, Dozy, Beaky, Mick And Tich* (Fontana 1966) ★★★, *If Music Be The Food Of Love* (Fontana 1967) ★★★, *If No One Sang* (Fontana 1968) ★★★, *The Legend Of Dave Dee, Dozy, Beaky, Mick And Tich* (Fontana 1969) ★★, *Together* (Fontana 1969) ★★.

● COMPILATIONS: *Greatest Hits* (Fontana 1968) ★★★, *Hold Tight! The Best Of The Fontana Years* (Collectables 1995) ★★★, *The Best Of Dave Dee, Dozy, Beaky, Mick And Tich* (Spectrum 1996) ★★★, *The Complete Collection* (Mercury 1997) ★★★, *Boxed* 4-CD box set (BR 1999) ★★★, *The Singles* (BR 1999) ★★★.

DAVID AND JONATHAN

Songwriting duo Roger Greenaway ('David') and Roger Cook ('Jonathan') began their partnership in 1965 after the demise of the former's beat group, the Kestrels, and enjoyed instant success when an early collaboration, 'You've Got Your Troubles', was a number 2 hit for the Fortunes. The pair began a performing/recording career at the end of the year, but paradoxically scored their first chart entry with a version of the Beatles' 'Michelle'. Although the Overlanders enjoyed a concurrent UK chart topper with the same song, David And Jonathan reached a respectable number 11, before securing a Top 10 slot with their self-penned follow-up, 'Lovers Of The World Unite'. Although the duo continued to record under their adopted appellation, they found much greater commercial success with a series of crafted compositions including 'Gasoline Alley Bred' (the Hollies), 'Home Lovin' Man' (Andy Williams), 'I'd Like To Teach The World To Sing' (the New Seekers) and 'Something Tells Me (Something Is Gonna Happen Tonight)' (Cilla Black). Such work was often undertaken with other songwriters, including Tony Macauley and Albert Hammond, but were copyrighted to the duo's Cookaway publishing company. Their commercial touch was maintained into the 70s with Blue Mink, a group comprising session musicians fronted by Cook and Madeline Bell, and they remain one of the most efficacious pop songwriting teams the UK ever produced.

● ALBUMS: *David And Jonathan* (Columbia 1966) ★★★.
● COMPILATIONS: *Lovers Of The World Unite* aka *The Very Best Of David And Jonathan* (See For Miles 1984) ★★★.

DAVID, HAL

b. 25 May 1921, Brooklyn, New York, USA. David began writing lyrics during his service in the US Army. Following his discharge he collaborated with Don Rodney on the 1949 Sammy Kaye hit 'Four Winds And Seven Seas'. Other notable David hit songs from the pre-rock 'n' roll era included Frank Sinatra's 'American Beauty Rose', and Teresa Brewer's 'Broken Hearted Melody'. It was in 1959 that David found the perfect musical companion in Burt Bacharach. Their collaboration continued through the 60s and resulted in some of the finest and enduring songs in popular music history. Artists as accomplished as Gene Pitney, Dionne Warwick, Cilla Black, Dusty Springfield, Sandie Shaw, Aretha Franklin, the Walker Brothers, Tom Jones, Jackie DeShannon, Herb Alpert and B.J. Thomas; all enjoyed crucial chart hits, courtesy of the Bacharach/David pen. While Burt was the melodic genius, Hal provided lyrics that brought a fresh vocabulary to the love song. Many of the songs dealt dramatically with the emotional and psychological problems produced by intense relationships.

The wish-fulfilling 'Tower Of Strength' presents an imaginary scenario in which the lover rejects and berates his beloved, even forcing her down on her knees, before finally admitting that he lacks the courage to leave the relationship ('for tower of strength is something I'll never be'). In 'Twenty Four Hours From Tulsa', the narrator is haunted not merely by his own infidelity, but the fact that it occurred a mere 24 hours before he was to be reunited with his lover. That same niggling neuroticism can be observed in '(There's) Always Something There To Remind Me', in which the very streets the singer walks provide haunting memories of a lost love. 'Anyone Who Had A Heart' communicates callousness of such unfathomable proportions ('couldn't be another heart that hurt me like you hurt me . . . what am I to do?') that the spurned lover is left to consider that literally anyone who had a heart would not fail to offer her love. The extraordinary 'Make It Easy On Yourself' is presented in the form of an inner debate in which the defeated lover's nobility is so intense that it borders on masochism ('Don't try to spare my feelings/Just tell me that we're through'). In 'Say A Little Prayer' the woman is so obsessed with her object of devotion that she is incapable of putting on her make-up or enduring a second of her coffee break without the constant need to offer up a prayer in his honour. This is a lyric of simple love but written from a woman's perspective; a remarkable achievement by a man.

David's romantic intensity probably reached its peak on the last major hit provided by the collaboration 'Close To You'. In this song, the central character is a lover of ultimate perfection, fashioned by angels using a peculiar alchemy of moondust and golden starlight to create a particular hair and eye colour. The very opening line invokes a being so attractive as to appear literally otherworldly ('Why do birds suddenly appear every time you are near? Just like me they long to be close to you'). In spite of the inherent drama in these lyrics, the songs seldom, if ever, take the form of doomed maudlin dirges. On the contrary, many of the arrangements are breezy and it was Bacharach' neat handling of suitably contrasting melody lines that made the partnership so appealing. Sadly, the team separated acrimoniously in 197 and each partner suffered commercially. David later became president of ASCAP and subsequently later enjoyed chart success with Albert Hammond with whom he wrote 'To All The Girls I've Loved Before' (a 1984 hit for Julio Iglesias and Willie Nelson). Although occasionally overshadowed by Bacharach David's lyrics made the partnership work, a fact borne out by Bacharach's failure to register single chart entry during the 70s. In 1992, David and Bacharach finally got together again to write some songs, including 'Sunny Weather Lover' for Dionne Warwick's new album. Warwick also sang one of the collaborators' numbers in the 1999 Bette Midler movie *Isn't She Great?*. In the same year, David received a Special International Ivor Novello Award.

DAVIES, CYRIL

b. 1932, Buckinghamshire, England, d. 7 January 1964. Along with Alexis Korner and Graham Bond, the uncompromising Davies was a seminal influence in the development of British R&B during the beat boom of the early 60s. His superb wailing and distorted harmonica shook the walls of many clubs up and down the UK. Initially he played with Alexis Korner's Blues Incorporated and then formed his own band, the All-Stars, featuring Long John Baldry, renowned session pianist Nicky Hopkins and drummer Mickey Waller. Their Chicago-based blues was raw, loud and exciting. Davies was a key figure in creating an interest in both pre-war and post-war American blues and giving it a platform in the pop-drenched British Isles. Like Bond, he died at a tragically young age, after losing his battle with leukemia.
● ALBUMS: *The Legendary Cyril Davies* (Folklore 1970) ★★★.

DAVIS, BILLIE

b. Carol Hedges, 1945, Woking, Surrey, England. Discovered by entrepreneur Robert Stigwood, this blue-eyed soul singer first came to chart prominence in 1962, duetting with Mike Sarne on the novelty hit, 'Will I What?' The following year, she emerged in her own right with a upbeat rendition of the Exciters' 'Tell Him'. Although well poised to take advantage of the beat boom, Davis' strong voice proved insufficient to take the follow-up, 'He's The One', into the Top 30. Her romantic entanglement with former Shadows guitarist Jet Harris gained considerable publicity, especially when both were involved in a car crash. With singles, however, further success proved elusive, although 'I Want You To Be My Baby' scraped into the lower chart regions in 1968. Thereafter, Davis concentrated on the European market, particularly Spain, where she retained a healthy following.
● ALBUMS: *Billie Davis* (Decca 1970) ★★.

DAVIS, MILES

b. Miles Dewy Davis, 25 May 1926, Alton, Illinois, USA, d. 28 September 1991, Santa Monica, California, USA. Davis was born into a comparatively wealthy middle-class family and both his mother and sister were capable musicians. He was given a trumpet for his thirteenth birthday by his dentist father, who could not have conceived that his gift would set his son on the road to becoming a giant figure in the development of jazz. Notwithstanding his outstanding talent as master of the trumpet, Davis' versatility encompassed flügelhorn and keyboards together with a considerable gift as a composer. This extraordinary list of talents earned Davis an unassailable reputation as the greatest leader/catalyst in the history of jazz. Such accolades were not used lightly, and he can justifiably be termed a 'musical genius'. Davis

quickly progressed from his high school band into Eddie Randall's band in 1941, after his family had moved to St. Louis. He studied at the Juilliard School of Music in New York in 1945 before joining Charlie 'Bird' Parker, with whom he had previously played in the Billy Eckstine band.
In 1947 Davis had topped a *Down Beat* poll and by 1948 he had already played or recorded with many jazz giants, most notably Coleman Hawkins, Dizzy Gillespie, Benny Carter, Max Roach, George Russell, John Lewis, Illinois Jacquet and Gerry Mulligan. The following year was to be a landmark for jazz; Davis, in collaboration with arranger Gil Evans, whose basement apartment Davis rehearsed in, made a series of 78s for Capitol Records that were eventually released as one long-player in 1954, the highly influential *Birth Of The Cool*. Davis had now refined his innovative style of playing, which was based upon understatement rather than the hurried action of the great bebop players. Sparse and simple, instead of frantic and complicated, it was becoming 'cool'. The *Birth Of The Cool* sessions between January 1949 and March 1950 featured a stellar cast, mostly playing and recording as a nonet, including Lee Konitz (saxophone), Kenny Clarke (drums), Mulligan (baritone saxophone), Kai Winding (trombone), Roach (drums). Davis was on such a creative roll that he could even pass by an invitation to join Duke Ellington! During the early 50s Davis became dependent on heroin and his career was effectively put on hold for a lengthy period. This spell of drug dependency lasted until as late as 1954, although he did record a few sessions for Prestige during this time. The following year his seminal quintet/sextets included, variously, Red Garland, John Coltrane, Percy Heath, Thelonious Monk, Milt Jackson, Paul Chambers, Philly Joe Jones, Horace Silver, J.J. Johnson, Lucky Thompson, Cannonball Adderley, Bill Evans and Sonny Rollins. Among their output was the acclaimed series of collections released on the Prestige label, *Walkin'*, *Cookin'*, *Relaxin'*, *Workin'* and *Steamin'*. During this time Davis was consistently voted the number 1 artist in all the major jazz polls. No longer totally dependent on drugs by this time, he set about collaborating with Gil Evans once again, now that he had signed with the prestigious Columbia Records. The orchestral albums made with Evans between 1957 and 1960 have all become classics: *Miles Ahead*, (featuring pianist Wynton Kelly and drummer Art Taylor), *Porgy And Bess* and the sparsely beautiful *Sketches Of Spain* (influenced by composer Joaquin Rodrigo). Evans was able to blend lush and full orchestration with Davis' trumpet, allowing it the space and clarity it richly deserved. Davis went on further.By 1957 he had assembled a seminal sextet featuring a spectacular line-up, including Coltrane, Chambers, Bill Evans, Jimmy Cobb and Cannonball Adderley. Two further landmark

albums during this fertile period (1957-1959), were the aptly titled *Milestones*, followed in 1959 by the utterly fabulous *Kind Of Blue*. The latter album is cited by most critics as the finest in jazz history. More than 40 years later all his albums are still available, and form an essential part of any jazz record collection, but *Kind Of Blue* is at the top of the list. 'So What', the opening track, has been covered by dozens of artists, with recent offerings from guitarist Ronny Jordan, Larry Carlton, saxophonist Candy Dulfer and reggae star Smiley Culture, who added his own lyrics and performed it in the movie *Absolute Beginners*. Ian Carr, Davis' leading biographer, perceptively stated of *Kind Of Blue* in 1982: 'The more it is listened to, the more it reveals new delights and fresh depths'. Davis was finding that as Coltrane grew as a musician their egos would clash. Davis would always play simple and sparingly, Coltrane began to play faster and more complicated pieces that soloed for far too long. Shortly before their inevitable final split, an incident occurred which has been passed down and repeated by musicians and biographers. Davis, who had a dry sense of humour and did not tolerate fools, had chastised Coltrane for playing too long a solo. Coltrane replied apologetically that; 'Sorry Miles, I just get carried away, I get these ideas in my head which just keep coming and coming and sometimes I just can't stop'. Davis laconically replied; 'Try taking the motherfucker out of yo' mouth'. Another repeated anecdote (this time from Adderley); Miles; 'Why did you play so long, man?', Coltrane; 'It took that long to get it all in'.In 1959, following an incident outside a New York club during which Davis was provoked and arrested for loitering, he was taken to the police headquarters and arrived covered in blood from a large cut in his head. Davis took out a lawsuit against the New York Police, which he subsequently and wisely dropped after they had accepted he was wrongfully arrested. This incident deeply upset Davis. However, he entered the 60s comfortably as the leading innovator in jazz, and shrugged off attempts from John Coltrane to dethrone him in the jazz polls. Davis chose to keep to his sparse style, allowing his musicians air and range. In 1964, while the world experienced Beatlemania, Davis created another musical landmark when he assembled a line-up to match the classic sextet. The combination of Herbie Hancock, Wayne Shorter, Ron Carter and Tony Williams delivered the monumental *E.S.P.* in 1965. He continued with this acoustic line-up through another three recordings, including *Miles Smiles* and ending with *Nefertiti*. By the time of *Filles De Kilimanjaro*, Davis had gradually electrified his various groups and taken bold steps towards rock music, integrating multiple electric keyboards and utilizing a wah-wah pedal connected to his electrified trumpet. Additionally, his own fascination with the possibilities of electric guitar, as demonstrated by Jimi Hendrix, assumed an increasing prominence in his music. Young US west coast rock musicians had begun to produce a form of music based upon improvisation (mostly through the use of hallucinogenics). This clearly interested Davis, who recognized the potential of blending traditional rock rhythms with jazz, although he was often contemptuous of some white rock musicians at this time. The decade closed with his band being accepted by rock fans. Davis appeared at major festivals with deliriously stoned audiences appreciating his line-up, which now featured the brilliant electric guitarist John McLaughlin, of whom Davis stated in deference to black musicians: 'Show me a black who can play like him, and I'd have him instead'.Other outstanding musicians Davis employed included Keith Jarrett, Airto Moreira, Chick Corea, Dave Holland, Joe Zawinul, Billy Cobham and Jack DeJohnette. Two major albums from this period were *In A Silent Way* and *Bitches Brew*, which unconsciously invented jazz rock and what was later to be called fusion. These records were marketed as rock albums, and consequently appeared in the regular charts.By the early 70s Davis had alienated himself from the mainstream jazz purists by continuing to flirt with rock music. In 1975, after a succession of personal upheavals including a car crash, further drug problems, a shooting incident, more police harassment and eventual arrest, Davis, not surprisingly, retired. During this time he became seriously ill, and it was generally felt that he would never play again, but, unpredictable as ever, Davis returned healthy and fit six years later with the comeback album, *The Man With The Horn*. He assembled a new band and received favourable reviews for live performances. Among the personnel were guitarist John Scofield and the young saxophonist Bill Evans. On the predominantly funk-based *You're Under Arrest*, he tackled pure pop songs, and although unambitious by jazz standards, tracks such as Cyndi Lauper's 'Time After Time' and Michael Jackson's 'Human Nature' were given Davis' brilliant master touch. The aggressive disco album *Tutu* followed, featuring his trumpet played through a synthesizer. A soundtrack recording for the Dennis Hopper movie *The Hot Spot* found Davis playing the blues alongside Taj Mahal, John Lee Hooker, Tim Drummond and slide guitarist Roy Rogers.During his final years Davis settled into a comfortable pattern of touring the world and recording, able to dictate the pace of his life with the knowledge that ecstatic audiences were waiting for him everywhere. Following further bouts of ill health, during which times he took to painting, Davis was admitted to hospital in California and died in September 1991. The worldwide obituaries were neither sycophantic nor morose; great things had already been said about Davis for many years. Django Bates stated that his own favourite Davis recordings were those between 1926 and mid-1991. Ian Carr added, in his impressive obituary, with regard to Davis' music: 'unflagging intelligence, great courage, integrity, honesty and a sustained spirit of enquiry always in the pursuit of art – never mere experimentation for its own sake'. Miles Davis' influence on rock music is considerable; his continuing influence on jazz is inestimable.

● ALBUMS: *Bopping The Blues* 1946 recording (Black Lion) ★★, *Cool Boppin'* 1948-1949 recordings (Fresh Sounds) ★★★, *Young Man With A Horn* 10-inch album (Blue Note 1952) ★★★, *The New Sounds Of Miles Davis* 10-inch album (Prestige 1952) ★★★★, *Blue Period* 10-inch album (Prestige 1953) ★★★, *Miles Davis Plays Al Cohn Compositions* 10-inch album (Prestige 1953) ★★★, *Miles Davis Quintet* 10-inch album (Prestige 1953) ★★★★, *Miles Davis Quintet Featuring Sonny Rollins* 10-inch album (Prestige 1953) ★★★, *Miles Davis Volume 3* 10-inch album (Blue Note 1954) ★★★, *Miles Davis Sextet* 10-inch album (reissued as *Walkin'*) (Prestige 1954) ★★★★, *Jeru* 10-inch album (Capitol 1954) ★★★★★, *Birth Of The Cool* 1949-50 recordings (Capitol 1954) ★★★★★, *Miles Davis All Stars Volume 1* 10-inch album (Prestige 1955) ★★★★, *Miles Davis All Stars Volume 2* 10-inch album (Prestige 1955) ★★★★, *Miles Davis Volume 1* (Blue Note 1955) ★★★, *Miles Davis Volume 2* (Blue Note 1955) ★★★★, *Hi-Hat All Stars* 1955 recording (Fresh Sound) ★, *Blue Moods* (Debut 1955) ★★★, *Musings Of Miles* reissued as *The Beginning* (Prestige 1955) ★★★, with Sonny Rollins *Dig Miles Davis/Sonny Rollins* reissued as *Diggin'* (Prestige 1956) ★★★, *Collectors Item* (Prestige 1956) ★★★, *Miles – The New Miles Davis Quintet* reissued as *The Original Quintet* (Prestige 1956) ★★★, *Blue Haze* 1953-54 recordings (Prestige 1956) ★★★, *Miles Davis And Horns* reissued as *Early Miles* (Prestige 1956) ★★★, *Miles Davis And Milt Jackson Quintet/Sextet* reissued as *Odyssey* (Prestige 1956) ★★★, *Cookin' With The Miles Davis Quintet* (Prestige 1957) ★★★★, *Relaxin' With The Miles Davis Quintet* (Prestige 1957) ★★★★, *Bags Groove* 1954 recording (Prestige 1957) ★★★★, *Round About Midnight* 1955-56 recordings (Columbia 1957) ★★★★, *Miles Ahead* (Columbia 1957) ★★★★★, *Miles Davis And The Modern Jazz Giants* 1954-56 recordings (Prestige 1958) ★★★, with John Coltrane *Miles And Coltrane* 1955-58 recordings (Columbia 1958) ★★★, *Milestones* (Columbia 1958) ★★★★, *Porgy And Bess* (Columbia 1958) ★★★★★, *'58 Miles* (Columbia 1958) ★★★★, *Jazz Track (Ascenseur Pour L'Échafaud)* soundtrack (Fontana 1958) ★★★, *Mostly Miles* 1958 recording (Phontastic) ★★, *Workin' With The Miles Davis Quintet* (Prestige 1959) ★★★★, *Kind Of Blue* (Columbia 1959) ★★★★★, *Sketches Of Spain* (Columbia 1960) ★★★★, *On Green Dolphin Street* 1960 recording (Jazz Door 1960) ★★★, *Jazz At The Plaza* (Columbia 1960) ★★, *Live In Zurich* (Jazz

Unlimited 1960) ★★★, *Live In Stockholm 1960* reissued as *Miles Davis In Stockholm Complete* (Royal Jazz 1960) ★★★, *Steamin' With The Miles Davis Quintet* (Prestige 1961) ★★★★, *Friday Night At The Blackhawk Vol 1* (Columbia 1961) ★★★★, *Saturday Night At The Blackhawk Volume 2* (Columbia 1961) ★★★★, *Someday My Prince Will Come* (Columbia 1961) ★★★★, with Teddy Charles, Lee Konitz *Ezz-Thetic* (New Jazz 1962) ★★★, with Dizzy Gillespie, Fats Navarro *Trumpet Giants* (New Jazz 1962) ★★★★, *Miles Davis At Carnegie Hall* (Columbia 1962) ★★★★, *Seven Steps To Heaven* (Columbia 1963) ★★★, *Quiet Nights* (Columbia 1963) ★★, with Thelonious Monk *Miles And Monk At Newport* 1958 And 1963 (Columbia 1964) ★★★, *Miles Davis In Europe* (Columbia 1964) ★★★, *My Funny Valentine: Miles Davis In Concert* (Columbia 1965) ★★★★, *E.S.P.* (Columbia 1965) ★★★★, *Miles Davis Plays For Lovers* (Prestige 1965) ★★★, *Jazz Classics* (Prestige 1965) ★★★, *'Four' And More – Recorded Live In Concert* (Columbia 1966) ★★★, *Miles In Antibes* (Columbia 1966) ★★★, *Miles Smiles* (Columbia 1966) ★★★, *Sorcerer* (Columbia 1967) ★★★, *Nefertiti* (Columbia 1968) ★★★, *Miles In The Sky* (Columbia 1968) ★★★, *Miles Orbits* (Columbia Record Club 1968) ★★★, *In A Silent Way* (Columbia 1969) ★★★★★, *Double Image* (Moon 1969) ★★★, *Filles De Kilimanjaro* (Columbia 1969) ★★★★, *Paraphernalia* (JMY 1969) ★★★, *Bitches Brew* (Columbia 1970) ★★★★★, *Miles Davis At The Fillmore* (Columbia 1970) ★★★★, *A Tribute To Jack Johnson* (Columbia 1971) ★★★★, *What I Say? Volumes 1 & 2* (JMY 1971) ★★★, *Live-Evil* (Columbia 1971) ★★★, *On The Corner* (Columbia 1972) ★★★, *In Concert* (Columbia 1972) ★★★, *Tallest Trees* (Prestige 1973) ★★★, *Black Beauty* 1970 recording (Columbia 1974) ★★★★, *Big Fun* 1969-70-72 recordings (Columbia 1974) ★★★, *Get Up With It* 1970-74 recordings (Columbia 1974) ★★★, *Jazz At The Plaza Volume 1* (1974) ★★★, *Agharta* (Columbia 1976) ★★★★, *Pangaea* (Columbia 1976) ★★★, *Live At The Plugged Nickel* 1965 recording (Columbia 1976) ★★★★, *Water Babies* (Columbia 1977) ★★★, *The Man With The Horn* (Columbia 1981) ★★★, *A Night In Tunisia* (Star Jazz 1981) ★★★, *We Want Miles* (Columbia 1982) ★★★, *Star People* (Columbia 1983) ★★★, *Blue Christmas* (Columbia 1983) ★★★, *Heard 'Round the World* 1964 concert recordings (Columbia 1983) ★★★, *At Last! Miles Davis And The Lighthouse All Stars* 1953 recording (Boplicity 1985) ★★★, *Decoy* (Columbia 1984) ★★★, *You're Under Arrest* (Columbia 1985) ★★★★, *Tutu* (Warners 1986) ★★★★, *Music From Siesta '88* (Warners 1988) ★★★★, *Amandla* (Warners 1989) ★★★, *Aura* 1985 recording (Columbia 1989) ★★★★, *The Hot Spot* (Antilles 1990) ★★★, with Michel Legrand *Dingo* (Warners 1991) ★★★, *Doo-Bop* (Warners 1992) ★★★, *The Complete Concert 1964: My Funny Valentine And 'Four' And More* (Columbia 1992) ★★★★, with Quincy

Jones *Miles And Quincy Jones Live At Montreux* 1991 recording (Reprise 1993) ★★★★, *Live Around The World* (Warners 1996) ★★★, *Miles Davis Live And Electric: Live Evil* (Columbia/Legacy 1997) ★★★★, *Miles Davis Live And Electric: Miles Davis At The Fillmore East* (Columbia/Legacy 1997) ★★★★, *Miles Davis Live And Electric: Black Beauty, Miles Davis Live At The Fillmore West* (Columbia/Legacy 1997) ★★★★, *Miles Davis Live And Electric: Dark Magus, Live At Carnegie Hall* 1974 recording (Columbia/Legacy 1997) ★★★★, *Miles Davis Live And Electric: Miles Davis In Concert, Live At The Philharmonic Hall* (Columbia/Legacy 1997) ★★★★, *The Complete Birth Of The Cool* (Capitol 1998) ★★★★★, *The Complete Bitches Brew Sessions* 4-CD box set (Columbia/Legacy 1998) ★★★★★, *Miles Davis At Carnegie Hall: The Complete Concert 1961* recording (Columbia/Legacy 1998) ★★★★, *At Fillmore East (March 7 1970): It's About That Time* (Columbia/Legacy 2001) ★★★, *Jazz At The Plaza* 1958 recording (Columbia 2001) ★★.
● COMPILATIONS: *Miles Davis' Greatest Hits* (Prestige 1957) ★★★★, *Greatest Hits* (Columbia 1969) ★★★★, *Basic Miles – The Classic Performances Of Miles Davis* 1955-1958 recordings (Columbia 1973) ★★★★, *Circle In The Round* 1955-1970 recordings (Columbia 1979) ★★★, *Directions* unreleased recordings 1960-1970 (Columbia 1981) ★★★, *Chronicle: The Complete Prestige Recordings* (Prestige 1987) ★★★★, *The Columbia Years 1955-1985* (Columbia 1988) ★★★★, *Ballads* 1961-1963 recordings (Columbia 1988) ★★★★, *Mellow Miles* 1961-1963 recordings (Columbia 1989) ★★★, *First Miles* (Savoy 1989) ★★★, *The Essence Of Miles Davis* (Columbia 1991) ★★★★, *Collection* (Castle 1992) ★★★★, *The Complete Live At The Plugged Nickel 1965* 8-CD box set (Columbia 1995) ★★★★★, *Highlights From The Plugged Nickel 1965* (Columbia 1995) ★★★★, *Ballads And Blues* (Blue Note 1996) ★★★★, *Miles Davis Acoustic: This Is Jazz No. 8* (Legacy 1996) ★★★, with Gil Evans *Miles Davis/Gil Evans: The Complete Columbia Studio Recordings* 6-CD/11-LP box set (Columbia/Mosaic 1996) ★★★★★, *Miles Davis Plays Ballads; This Is Jazz No. 22* (Legacy 1997) ★★★★, *The Complete Studio Recordings Of The Miles Davis Quintet 1965-June 1968* 7-CD/10-LP box set (Columbia/Mosaic 1998) ★★★★, *Love Songs* (Columbia 1999) ★★★, with John Coltrane *The Complete Columbia Recordings 1955-1961* (Columbia/Legacy 2000) ★★★★, *Blue Miles* (Columbia 2000) ★★★★, *Young Miles* 4-CD box set (Proper 2001) ★★★★, *The Essential Miles Davis* (Columbia 2001) ★★★★★, *Complete In A Silent Way Sessions* 3-CD box set (Columbia 2001) ★★★★.
● VIDEOS: *Miles Davis And Jazz Hoofer* (Kay Jazz 1988), *Miles In Paris* (Warner Music Video 1990), *Miles Davis And Quincy Jones: Live At Montreux* (Warner Music Video 1993).
● FURTHER READING: *Milestones: 1. Miles Davis, 1945-60*, Jack Chambers. *Milestones: 2.*

Miles Davis Since 1960, Jack Chambers. *Miles: The Autobiography*, Miles Davis with Quincy Troupe. *Miles Davis*, Barry McRae. *Miles Davis: A Critical Biography*, Ian Carr. *Miles Davis For Beginners*, Daryl Long. *The Man In The Green Shirt: Miles Davis*, Richard Williams. *Miles Davis: The Early Years*, Bill Cole. *'Round About Midnight: A Portrait Of Miles Davis*, Eric Nisenson. *The Miles Davis Companion*, Gary Carner (ed.). *Milestones: The Music And Times Of Miles Davis*, Jack Chambers. *A Miles Davis Reader*, Bill Kirchner (ed.). *Kind Of Blue: The Making Of The Miles Davis Masterpiece*, Ashley Kahn. *The Making Of Kind Of Blue: Miles Davis And His Masterpiece*, Eric Nisenson. *Miles And Me*, Quincey Troupe. *Miles Davis: Complete Discography*, Nasuki Nakayama. *Miles Beyond: The Electric Explorations Of Miles Davis 1967-1999*, Paul Tingen. *Miles Davis And American Culture*, Gerald Early (ed.).
● FILMS: *Dingo* (1991).

DAVIS, SAMMY, JNR.

b. 8 December 1925, Harlem, New York, USA, d. 16 May 1990, Los Angeles, California, USA. A dynamic and versatile all-round entertainer, Davis was a trouper in the old-fashioned tradition. The only son of two dancers in a black vaudeville troupe, called Will Mastin's Holiday In Dixieland, Davis made his professional debut with the group at the age of three, as 'Silent Sam, The Dancing Midget'. While still young he was coached by the legendary tap-dancer Bill 'Bojangles' Robinson. Davis left the group in 1943 to serve in the US Army, where he encountered severe racial prejudice for the first, but not the last, time. After the war he rejoined his father and adopted uncle in the Will Mastin Trio. By 1950 the Trio were headlining at venues such as the Capitol in New York and Ciro's in Hollywood with stars including Jack Benny and Bob Hope, but it was Davis who was receiving the standing ovations for his singing, dancing, drumming, comedy and apparently inexhaustible energy.

In 1954 he signed for Decca Records, and released two albums, *Starring Sammy Davis Jr.* (number 1 in the US chart), featuring his impressions of stars such as Dean Martin, Jerry Lewis, Johnnie Ray and Jimmy Durante, and *Just For Lovers*. He also made the US singles chart with 'Hey There' from *The Pajama Game*, and in the same year he lost his left eye in a road accident. When he returned to performing in January 1955 wearing an eye patch, he was greeted even more enthusiastically than before. During that year he reached the US Top 20 with 'Something's Gotta Give', 'Love Me Or Leave Me' and 'That Old Black Magic'. In 1956 he made his Broadway debut in the musical *Mr Wonderful*, with music and lyrics by Jerry Bock, Larry Holofcener and George Weiss. Also in the show were the rest of the Will Mastin Trio, Sammy's uncle and Davis Snr. The show ran for nearly 400 performances and produced two hits, 'Too lose For Comfort', and the title song, which was ery successful for Peggy Lee. Although enerally regarded as the first popular American lack performer to become acceptable to both lack and white audiences, Davis attracted eavy criticism in 1956 over his conversion to udaism, and later for his marriage to Swedish ctress Mai Britt. He described himself as a 'one-yed Jewish nigger'.

part from a few brief appearances when he was ery young, Davis started his film career in 1958 ith *Anna Lucasta*, and was critically acclaimed he following year for his performance as porting Life in *Porgy And Bess*. By this time)avis was a leading member of Frank Sinatra's nner circle', called, variously, the 'Clan' or the Rat Pack'. He appeared with Sinatra in three novies, *Ocean's Eleven* (1960), *Sergeants 3* (1962), nd *Robin And The 7 Hoods* (1964), but made, erhaps, a greater impact when he co-starred ith another member of the 'Clan', Shirley MacLaine, in the Cy Coleman and Dorothy ields film musical *Sweet Charity*. The 60s were ood times for Davis, who was enormously opular on records and television, but especially ive', at Las Vegas and in concert. In 1962 he nade the US chart with the Anthony Iewley/Leslie Bricusse number 'What Kind Of ool Am I?', and thereafter featured several of heir songs in his act. He sang Bricusse's ominated song, 'Talk To The Animals', at the 967 Academy Awards ceremony, and collected ne Oscar on behalf of the songwriter when it on. In 1972, he had a million-selling hit record ith another Newley/Bricusse song, 'The Candy Ian', from the film *Willy Wonka And The hocolate Factory*.

Ie appeared again on Broadway in 1964 in *olden Boy*, Charles Strouse and Lee Adams' usical adaptation of Clifford Odet's 1937 drama f a young man torn between the boxing ring nd his violin. Also in the cast was Billy Daniels. he show ran for 569 performances in New ork, and went to London in 1968. During the)s Davis worked less, suffering, allegedly, as a esult of previous alcohol and drug abuse. In ntertained US troops in the Lebanon in 1983, nd five years later undertook an arduous omeback tour of the USA and Canada with inatra and Dean Martin. In 1989 he travelled urther, touring Europe with the show *The ltimate Event*, along with Liza Minnelli and inatra. While he was giving everything to areer favourites such as 'Birth Of The Blues', Ir Bojangles' and 'That Old Black Magic', he as already ill, although it was not apparent to udiences. After his death in 1990 it was evealed that his estate was almost worthless. In)92, an all-star tribute, led by Liza Minnelli, as mounted at the Royal Albert Hall in ondon, the city that had always welcomed him. roceeds from the concert went to the Royal Iarsden Cancer Appeal. Few all-round ntertainers in the history of popular song and

showbusiness have retained such a long-standing appeal.

● ALBUMS: *Starring Sammy Davis Jr.* (Decca 1955) ★★★, *Just For Lovers* (Decca 1955) ★★★, *Mr. Wonderful* film soundtrack (Decca 1956) ★★, *Here's Looking At You* (Decca 1956) ★★★, with Carmen McRae *Boy Meets Girl* (Epic 1957) ★★★, *Sammy Swings* (Decca 1957) ★★★★, *It's All Over But The Swingin'* (Decca 1957) ★★★★, *Mood To Be Wooed* (Decca 1958) ★★★, *All The Way And Then Some* (Decca 1958) ★★★★, *Sammy Davis Jr. At Town Hall* (Decca 1959) ★★★★, *Porgy And Bess* (Decca 1959) ★★★, *I Got A Right To Swing* (Decca 1960) ★★★★, *Sammy Awards* (Decca 1960) ★★★, *What Kind Of Fool Am I And Other Show-Stoppers* (Reprise 1962) ★★★★, *Sammy Davis Jr. At The Cocoanut Grove* (Reprise 1963) ★★★★, *Johnny Cool* film soundtrack (United Artists 1963) ★★★, *As Long As She Needs Me* (Reprise 1963) ★★★, *Sammy Davis Jr. Salutes The Stars Of The London Palladium* (Reprise 1964) ★★★, *The Shelter Of Your Arms* (Reprise 1964) ★★★, *Golden Boy* film soundtrack (Capitol 1964) ★★, with Count Basie *Our Shining Hour* (Verve 1965) ★★★, *That's All!* (Reprise 1965) ★★★, *A Man Called Adam* film soundtrack (Reprise 1966) ★★, *I've Gotta Be Me* (Reprise 1969) ★★★, *Sammy Davis Jr. Now* (MGM 1972) ★★★, *Portrait Of Sammy Davis Jr.* (MGM 1972) ★★★, *It's A Musical World* (MGM 1976) ★★★, *The Song And Dance Man* (20th Century 1977) ★★★★, *Sammy Davis Jr. In Person 1977* (RCA 1983) ★★★, *Closest Of Friends* (Vogue 1984) ★★★.

● COMPILATIONS: *The Best Of Sammy Davis Jr.* (MCA 1982) ★★★, *Collection* (Castle 1989) ★★★, *The Great Sammy Davis Jr.* (MFP 1989) ★★★, *Capitol Collectors Series* (Capitol 1990) ★★★, *The Decca Years* (MCA 1990) ★★★★, *The Wham Of Sam* (Warners 1995) ★★★, *That Old Black Magic* (MCA 1995) ★★★, *I've Gotta Be Me: The Best Of Sammy Davis Jr. On Reprise* (Reprise 1996) ★★★★, *Yes I Can!* 4-CD box set (Reprise/Rhino 2000) ★★★.

● VIDEOS: with Liza Minnelli, Frank Sinatra *The Ultimate Event!* (Video Collection 1989), *Mr Bojangles* (Decca/PolyGram Music Video 1991).

● FURTHER READING: *Yes I Can: The Story Of Sammy Davis Jr.*, Sammy Davis Jnr. *Hollywood In A Suitcase*, Sammy Davis Jnr. *Why Me: The Autobiography Of Sammy Davis Jr.*, Sammy Davis Jnr. with Burt Boyar.

● FILMS: *The Benny Goodman Story* (1956), *Anna Lucasta* (1958), *Porgy And Bess* (1959), *Pepe* (1960), *Ocean's Eleven* (1960), *The Threepenny Opera* (1962), *Convicts Four* (1962), *Sergeants 3* (1962), *Johnny Cool* (1963), *Robin And The 7 Hoods* (1964), *A Man Called Adam* (1966), *Movin' With Nancy* (1968), *Salt And Pepper* (1968), *Sweet Charity* (1969), *One More Time* (1970), *Save The Children* concert film (1973), *James Dean, The First American Teenager* (1975), *Gone With The West* (1975), *Sammy Stops The World* (1978), *The Cannonball Run* (1981), *Heidi's Song* (1982),

Cracking Up (1983), Cannonball Run II (1984), That's Dancing! (1985), Moon Over Parador (1988), Tap (1989).

DAVIS, SKEETER

b. Mary Frances Penick, 30 December 1931, Dry Ridge, Kentucky, USA. Penick was raised on a farm and as a child knew that she wanted to be a country singer. She acquired the nickname of 'Skeeter' (a local term for a mosquito) from her grandfather because she was always active and buzzing around like the insect. In her mid-teens, she formed a duo with schoolfriend Betty Jack Davis (b. 3 March 1932, Corbin Kentucky, USA, d. August 1953) and together they began to sing in the Lexington area. In 1949, they appeared on local radio WLAX and later were featured on radio and television in Detroit, Cincinnati, and eventually on the WWVA Wheeling Jamboree in West Virginia. They first recorded for Fortune in 1952 but the following year they successfully auditioned for RCA Records and their recording of 'I Forgot More Than You'll Ever Know' quickly became a number 1 US country and number 18 US pop hit.

On 23 August 1953, the singers' car was involved in a collision with another vehicle, resulting in the death of Betty Jack and leaving Davis critically injured. It was over a year before Davis recovered physically and mentally from the crash, and it was only with great difficulty that she was persuaded to resume her career. Eventually she briefly teamed up with Betty Jack's sister, Georgia Davis, and returned to singing. In 1955, she went solo and for a time worked with RCA's touring Caravan Of Stars as well as with Eddy Arnold and Elvis Presley. Her recording career, under the guidance of Chet Atkins, progressed and she gained her first solo US country chart hit in 1958 with 'Lost To A Geisha Girl', the female answer to the Hank Locklin hit 'Geisha Girl'. The following year, her co-written song 'Set Him Free' became her first country Top 10 hit. She fulfilled one of her greatest ambitions in 1959, when she moved to Nashville and became a regular member of the Grand Ole Opry. During the 60s, she became one of RCA's most successful country artists, registering 26 US country hits, 12 of them achieving crossover US pop chart success. The most popular included another 'answer' song in '(I Can't Help You) I'm Falling Too' (the reply to Hank Locklin's 'Please Help Me, I'm Falling'), and 'My Last Date'. She co-wrote the latter with Boudleaux Bryant and pianist Floyd Cramer, whose instrumental version had been a million-seller in 1960. In 1963, she achieved a million-selling record herself with 'The End Of The World', which peaked at number 2 in both the US country and pop charts. It also gave Davis her only UK pop chart entry, reaching number 18 in a 13-week chart life in 1963 (the song also became a UK pop hit for Sonia in 1990). Davis also had successful recordings with Bobby Bare

('A Dear John Letter') and Don Bowman (a novelty number, 'For Loving You').

Davis toured extensively in the 60s and 70s, not only throughout the USA and Canada but also to Europe and the Far East, where she is very popular. She played all the major US television network shows, including regular appearances with Duke Ellington and also appeared on a Rolling Stones tour. Her recording career slowed down in the 70s but her hits included 'I'm A Lover Not A Fighter', 'Bus Fare To Kentucky' and 'One Tin Soldier'. She also made the charts with Bobby Bare on 'Your Husband, My Wife' and with George Hamilton IV on 'Let's Get Together' (a US pop hit for the Youngbloods in 1969). In 1973, she had a minor hit with the Bee Gees' 'Don't Forget To Remember' and a Top 20 country and minor pop hit with 'I Can't Believe That It's All Over'. It was to prove a slightly prophetic title, since only two more chart hits followed, the last being 'I Love Us' on Mercury Records in 1976 (Davis having left RCA two years earlier). She has recorded several tribute albums, including one to Buddy Holly, which featured Waylon Jennings on guitar and also one to her friend Dolly Parton. She also re-recorded 'May You Never Be Alone', a Davis Sisters success, with NRBQ in 1985. From 1960-64, she was married to well-known WSM radio and television personality Ralph Emery, but she subsequently received heavy criticism in Emery's autobiography.

She later married Joey Spampinato of NRBQ. She became something of a rebel after the break up of her second marriage. She settled in colonial-style mansion set in several hundred acres in Brentwood, Tennessee, and surrounded herself with dogs, Siamese cats, a dove in a gilded cage and even an ocelot named Fred. Her extreme religious beliefs saw her refusing to appear in places that sold intoxicating drinks. She even stopped growing tobacco on her farm, giving the reason for both actions: 'As a Christian, I think it's harmful to my body'. In 1973, her strong criticisms of the Nashville Police Department during her act at the Grand Ole Opry caused her to be dropped from the roster. She was later reinstated and still sings religious or gospel songs on her regular appearances.

● ALBUMS: with the Davis Sisters Hits (Fortune 1952) ★★, with the Davis Sisters Jealous Love (Fortune 1952) ★★★, I'll Sing You A Song And Harmonize Too (RCA Victor 1960) ★★, Here's The Answer (RCA Victor 1961) ★★★, The End Of The World (RCA Victor 1962) ★★★★, with Porter Wagoner Porter Wagoner And Skeeter Davis Sing Duets (RCA Victor 1962) ★★, Cloudy With Occasional Tears (RCA Victor 1963) ★★★, Forgot More Than You'll Ever Know (RCA Victor 1964) ★★★, Let Me Get Close To You reissued as Easy To Love (RCA Victor 1964) ★★★, Authentic Southern Style Gospel (RCA Victor 1964) ★★, Blueberry Hill (& Other Favorites) (RCA Victor

65) ★★★, *Sings Standards* (RCA Victor 1965)
★★, *Written By The Stars* (RCA Victor 1965)
★★, with Bobby Bare *Tunes For Two* (RCA
ctor 1965) ★★★, *My Heart's In The Country*
CA Victor 1966) ★★★, *Singing In The Summer*
n (RCA Victor 1966) ★★★, *Hand In Hand With*
us (RCA Victor 1967) ★★, *What Does It Take*
 Keep A Man Like You Satisfied) (RCA Victor
67) ★★★, *Skeeter Davis Sings Buddy Holly*
CA Victor 1967) ★★, *Why So Lonely* (RCA
ctor 1968) ★★★, *I Love Flatt & Scruggs* (RCA
ctor 1968) ★★, with Don Bowman *Funny Folk*
ps (RCA Victor 1968) ★★, *The Closest Thing*
 Love (RCA Victor 1969) ★★★, *Mary Frances*
CA Victor 1969) ★★★, *A Place In The Country*
CA Victor 1970) ★★, *It's Hard To Be A Woman*
CA Victor 1970) ★★★, with Bare *Your*
sband, *My Wife* reissued as *More Tunes For*
o (RCA Victor 1970) ★★★, with George
milton IV *Down Home In The Country* (RCA
ctor 1970) ★★★, *Skeeter* (RCA Victor 1971)
★★, *Love Takes A Lot Of My Time* (RCA Victor
71) ★★★, *Foggy Mountain Top* (RCA Victor
71) ★★, *Sings Dolly* (RCA Victor 1972) ★★★,
ng It On Home (RCA Victor 1972) ★★★, *I*
n't Believe That It's All Over (RCA Victor 1973)
★★★, *The Hillbilly Singer* (RCA Victor 1973)
★★, *He Wakes Me With A Kiss Every Morning*
CA Victor 1974) ★★★, *Heart Strings* (Tudor
83) ★★★, with NRBQ *She Sings, They Play*
under 1985) ★★★.
COMPILATIONS: the Davis Sisters *Memories*
CD set (Bear Family 1993) ★★★★, *The Best Of*
eter Davis (RCA Victor 1965) ★★★, *The Best*
 Skeeter Davis Volume 2 (RCA Victor 1973)
★★, *20 Of The Best: Skeeter Davis* (RCA 1985)
★★, *The Essential Skeeter Davis* (RCA 1995)
★★★, *RCA Country Legends: Skeeter Davis*
uddah 2001) ★★★★.
FURTHER READING: *Bus Fare To Kentucky:*
 e Autobiography Of Skeeter Davis, Skeeter
vis.

AVIS, SPENCER, GROUP

rmed in Birmingham, England, in 1962 as the
ythm And Blues Quartet, the band featured
encer Davis (b. 17 July 1941, Swansea, South
les; guitar/vocals), Steve Winwood (b. 12 May
48, Birmingham, England; guitar/organ/
cals), Muff Winwood (b. Mervyn Winwood, 15
ne 1943, Birmingham, England; bass) and Pete
rk (b. 15 August 1942, Middlesborough,
eveland, England; drums). School teacher
vis, the elder Winwood brother and drummer
rk were already experienced performers with
ckgrounds in modern and traditional jazz,
es, and skiffle. The band were gradually
arfed by the younger Winwood's immense
tural musical talent. While they were much in
mand on the fast-growing club scene as
rformers, their bluesy/pop records failed to
l, until they made a breakthrough in 1965 with
ep On Running', which reached number 1 in
 UK. This was followed in quick succession by

another chart-topper, 'Somebody Help Me', and
three more notable hits, 'When I Come Home',
'Gimme Some Lovin', and 'I'm A Man'.
In keeping with 60s pop tradition they also
appeared in a low-budget UK film, *The Ghost
Goes Gear*. Throughout their career they were
managed by Chris Blackwell, founder of Island
Records. Amid press reports and months of
speculation, Steve Winwood finally left to form
Traffic in 1967. A soundtrack album, *Here We Go
Round The Mulberry Bush*, released that year,
ironically had both Traffic and the Spencer Davis
Group sharing the billing. Muff Winwood also
left, joining Island as head of A&R. Davis
soldiered on with the addition of Phil Sawyer,
who was later replaced by guitarist Ray Fenwick
from After Tea and Eddie Hardin (keyboards).
The latter had an uncannily similar voice to
Steve Winwood. They were unable to maintain
their previous success but had two further minor
hits, 'Mr Second Class' and the richly
psychedelia-phased 'Time Seller'. After a number
of line-up changes including Dee Murray and
Nigel Olsson, Hardin And York departed to form
their own band, and enjoyed some success
mainly on the continent during the progressive
boom of 1969-70. Davis eventually went to live in
America where he became involved in the
business side of music, working in A&R for
various major record companies.
The Davis/York/Hardin/Fenwick team re-
formed briefly in 1973 with the addition of
Charlie McCracken (ex-Taste) on bass and made
a further two albums. The infectious single
'Catch Me On The Rebop' almost became a
belated hit. Today, York can still be found
playing in various jazz-style bands; his
acknowledged talent as a drummer being
regularly in demand. Spencer Davis is still
making the occasional album from his base on
the west coast of America. Muff Winwood went
on to become head of Artist Development at CBS
Records, with signings including Shakin'
Stevens, Bros, Paul Young and Terence Trent
D'Arby. Steve Winwood, after progressing
through Blind Faith and Airforce, became a
highly successful solo artist. In 1997 Davis was
touting a new version of the band, which
included the original drummer York together
with ex-Keef Hartley Band vocalist/guitarist
Miller Anderson.
● ALBUMS: *The First Album* (Fontana 1965)
★★★, *The Second Album* (Fontana 1966) ★★★,
Autumn '66 (Fontana 1966) ★★★★, *Here We Go
Round The Mulberry Bush* film soundtrack
(United Artists 1967) ★★★, *Gimme Some Lovin'*
(United Artists 1967) ★★★, *I'm A Man* (United
Artists 1967) ★★★★, *With Their New Face On*
(United Artists 1968) ★★, *Heavies* (United
Artists 1969) ★★, *Funky* recorded 1969
(Columbia 1971) ★★, *Gluggo* (Vertigo 1973)
★★★, *Living In The Back Street* (Vertigo 1974)
★★, *Catch You On The Rebop: Live In Europe*
(RPM 1995) ★★★★.

● COMPILATIONS: *The Best Of The Spencer Davis Group* (Island 1968) ★★★★, *The Best Of Spencer Davis Group* (EMI America 1987) ★★★, *Keep On Running* (Royal Collection 1991) ★★★, *Taking Out Time 1967-69* (RPM 1994) ★★, *Spotlight On Spencer Davis* (Javelin 1994) ★★, *Live Together* 1988 recordings (In Akustik 1995) ★, *24 Hours Live In Germany* 1988 recordings (In Akustik 1995) ★, *Eight Gigs A Week: The Steve Winwood Years* (Island/Chronicles 1996) ★★★★, *Mulberry Bush* (RPM 1999) ★★★, *Mojo Rhythms & Midnight Blues Vol. 1: Sessions 1965-1968* (RPM 2000) ★★★★, *Mojo Rhythms & Midnight Blues Vol. 2: Shows 1965-1968* (RPM 2000) ★★★★, *Live Anthology* (Varèse Sarabande 2001) ★★★★.

● FURTHER READING: *Keep On Running: The Steve Winwood Story*, Chris Welch. *Back In The High Life: A Biography Of Steve Winwood*, Alan Clayson.

DEE, JOEY, AND THE STARLITERS

This US group helped make the twist a national craze. Joey Dee (b. Joseph DiNicola, 11 June 1940, Passaic, New Jersey, USA; vocals) formed his first group, the Thunder Trio, while still at high school. Various members passed through the group before Dee recorded the ballad 'Lorraine' for the independent Little label. Lead singer Rogers Freeman was replaced by David Brigati, following which the group recorded several tracks for Scepter Records. The most famous line-up of the group, comprising Dee, Brigati, Carlton Lattimore (keyboards), Willie Davis (drums) and Larry Vernieri (backing vocals), took up residency at New York's famed Peppermint Lounge club in 1960. In late 1961, a year after Chubby Checker's 'The Twist' topped the US chart, the wealthy socialites who frequented the club belatedly discovered the dance. Dee incorporated it into his act and even wrote a special club song, 'Peppermint Twist'. The memorable, uplifting single shot to the top of the charts and *Doin' The Twist At The Peppermint Lounge*, on new label Roulette Records, reached number 2.

In 1962 the group, which now included a 10-piece dance team incorporating the original line-up of the Ronettes, starred in the low-budget movie *Hey, Let's Twist* with the soundtrack album and title track both reaching the US Top 20. They followed this with a breakneck version of the Isley Brothers' 'Shout', which reached number 6. Dee appeared in the movie *Two Tickets To Paris* and his solo version of Johnny Nash's 'What Kind Of Love is This?', taken from it, became his fourth and final Top 20 entry in 1962. In all, this distinctive group notched up nine US chart singles and three albums between 1961 and 1963. Dee embarked on an abortive solo career, and opened his own club, The Starliter, in New York in 1964. That year he formed a new band which included Gene Cornish, Felix Cavaliere and Eddie Brigati, who became the very successful Young Rascals and a couple of years later he

hired guitarist Jimi Hendrix to play with the group. Dee recorded an album for Jubilee 1966, and later recordings appeared on the obscure Tonsil and Sunburst labels. He is now the spokesman of The National Music Foundation, an association representing American 'oldie' acts.

● ALBUMS: *Joey Dee And The Starliters* (Scepter 1960) ★★★, *Doin' The Twist At The Peppermint Lounge* (Roulette 1961) ★★★, *The Peppermint Twist* (Scepter 1961) ★★★, *Hey, Let's Twist* film soundtrack (Roulette 1962) ★★, *Back At The Peppermint Lounge* (Roulette 1962) ★★★, *All The World Is Twistin'* (Roulette 1962) ★★★, *Two Tickets To Paris* film soundtrack (Roulette 1962) ★★, *Joey Dee* (Roulette 1963) ★★★, *Dance, Dance, Dance* (Roulette 1963) ★★, *Hitsville* (Jubilee 1966) ★★.

● COMPILATIONS: *Hey Let's Twist! The Best Of Joey Dee And The Starliters* (Rhino 1990) ★★, *Starbright* (Westside 1999) ★★★, *Joey Dee Hollywood* (Soundies 1999) ★★★★.

● FILMS: *Hey, Let's Twist* (1961), *Two Tickets To Paris* (1962), *Twist* (1992).

DEENE, CAROL

b. 1944, Thurnscoe, Yorkshire, England. The daughter of a singing miner, the clean-cut pop singer moved to London at the age of 16, and after appearing on the Joan Regan television show in 1961, was snapped up by HMV. Deene had four UK Top 50 entries in a 12 month period, all with cover versions, but none made the Top 20. The songs were 'Sad Movies (Make Me Cry)' and the irritating 'Norman' (which were both John D. Loudermilk songs that had been US hits for Sue Thompson), 'Johnny Get Angry' (a US hit for Joanie Sommers) and 'Some People', which was originally performed by UK act Valerie Mountain And The Eagles in the film of the same name. In 1962 she had her own series as a disc jockey on Radio Luxembourg and was seen in the Acker Bilk film *Band Of Thieves*. She later had unsuccessful releases on Columbia Records in 1966, CBS Records in 1968, Conquest in 1969, Pye Records in 1970; and reappeared in the late 70s on the Koala and Rim labels.

● ALBUMS: *A Love Affair* (World Records 1970) ★★.

● FILMS: *It's All Happening* (1963).

DEKKER, DESMOND

b. Desmond Dacres, 16 July 1942, Kingston, Jamaica, West Indies. Dacres spent much of his orphaned childhood near Seaforth in St. Thomas before returning to Kingston, where he worked as a welder. His workmates encouraged him to seek a recording audition and, after receiving rejections from leading producers Clement Dodd and Duke Reid, he found a mentor in the influential Leslie Kong. In 1963, the newly named Dekker released his first single, 'Honour Your Father And Mother', which was also issued in the UK courtesy of Island Records. During the same period, Dekker teamed up with his backing group, the Aces. Together, they enjoyed enormous success in Jamaica during the mid- to late 60s with a formidable run of 20 number 1 hits to their credit. The emergence of rocksteady in the latter half of 1966 propelled his *James Bond*-inspired '007' into the UK charts the following year. A catchy, rhythmically infectious articulation of the 'rude boy' street gang shenanigans, the single presaged Dekker's emergence as an internationally famous artist. In 1967, Dekker came second in the Jamaican Song Festival with 'Unity' and continued his chart-topping run in his home country with such titles as 'Hey Grandma', 'Music Like Dirt', 'Rudie Got Soul', 'Rude Boy Train' and 'Sabotage'.

In 1969 Dekker achieved his greatest international success. 'Get up in the morning, slaving for bread, sir, so that every mouth can be fed', was a patois-sung opening line that entranced and confused pop listeners on both sides of the Atlantic. The intriguing 'Israelites' had been a club hit the previous year, and by the spring of 1969 had become the first reggae song to top the UK charts, a considerable achievement for the period. Even more astonishing was its Top 10 success in the USA, a country that had previously proved commercially out of bounds to Jamaican performers. Back in Britain, Dekker's follow-up was the Top 10 hit 'It Mek'. It was originally recorded the previous year under the title 'A It Mek', which roughly translates as 'That's Why It Happened'. 'It Mek' was inspired by Desmond's sister Elaine, who fell off a wall at her home and cried 'like ice water'. Dekker enjoyed translating everyday observations into sharp, incisive lines. 'Israelites' similarly articulated the plight of the downtrodden working man, while 'Problems' was a rousing protest number featuring the refrain '*everyday* is problems'. Dekker's success in the UK, buoyed by consistent touring, spearheaded the arrival of a number of Jamaican chart singles by such artists as the Harry J's All Stars, the Upsetters and the Pioneers. Until the arrival of Bob Marley, Dekker remained the most famous reggae artist on the international scene.

Dekker took up residence in the UK in 1969, where he was a regular club performer and continued to lay down his vocals over rhythm tracks recorded in Jamaica. A further minor success with 'Pickney Gal' was followed by a massive number 2 hit with the Jimmy Cliff composition 'You Can Get It If You Really Want', from the film *The Harder They Come*. When Dekker's long-term manager/producer Kong died from heart failure in 1971, the artist joined the Cactus label. A reissue of 'Israelites' restored him to the UK Top 10 in 1975 and was followed by the pop/reggae 'Sing A Little Song', which reached number 16. During the 2-Tone ska/mod revival in 1980, Dekker recorded *Black And Dekker* with Graham Parker's Rumour, but the experiment was not commercially successful. A follow-up,

also on Stiff Records, *Compass Point*, was his last major attempt at chart action, though he remained a perennial performer of old hit material and has frequently been featured on compilation albums. In 1984 he was found bankrupt by a British court, and publicly complained that he had failed to receive funds from his former manager. It was a sad moment for one of reggae's best-known personalities. In 1993, during another 2-Tone revival, Dekker released *King Of Kings* with four original members of the Specials followed by a disappointing new album *Halfway To Paradise*. His unmistakable falsetto vocal remains one of reggae's most memorable, while his pioneering importance as the first major reggae artist to achieve international success deserves wider acknowledgement.

● ALBUMS: *007 (Shanty Town)* (Beverley's 1967) ★★★★, *Action!* (Beverley's 1968) ★★★, *The Israelites* (Beverley's 1969) ★★★★, *This Is Desmond Dekker* (Trojan 1969) ★★★★, *You Can Get It If You Really Want* (Trojan 1970) ★★★★, *Black And Dekker* (Stiff 1980) ★★★, *Compass Point* (Stiff 1981) ★★★, *Officially Live And Rare* (Trojan 1987) ★★, *Music Like Dirt* (Trojan 1992) ★★★, with the Specials *King Of Kings* (Trojan 1993) ★★★, *Halfway To Paradise* (Trojan 1999) ★★.

● COMPILATIONS: *Double Dekker* (Trojan 1974) ★★★★, *Sweet 16 Hits* (Trojan 1978) ★★★★, *The Original Reggae Hitsound* (Trojan 1985) ★★★★, *20 Golden Pieces* (Bulldog 1987) ★★★★, *Best Of And The Rest Of* (Action Replay/Trojan 1989) ★★★, *King Of Ska* (Trojan 1991) ★★★★, *20 Greatest Hits* (Point 2 1992) ★★★★, *Crucial Cuts – The Best Of Desmond Dekker* (1993) ★★★★, *First Time For Long Time* (Trojan 1997) ★★★, *The Writing On The Wall* (Trojan 1998) ★★★, *Israelites: Anthology 1963-1999* (Trojan 2001) ★★★★.

DENNISONS

One of the youngest Liverpool beat groups, the Dennisons – Eddie Parry (d. 1995; vocals), Steve McLaren (guitar), Clive Hornsby (drums), Alan Willis and Ray Scragge – made their debut at the Cavern Club in May 1962. The following year the quintet came third in the prestigious *Mersey Beat* poll, trailing behind only the Beatles and Gerry And The Pacemakers, and released their first single, the lightweight 'Come On Be My Girl'. Willis was later replaced by Terry Carson as the Dennisons continued their recording career with enthusiastic versions of 'Walking The Dog' and 'Lucy (You Sure Did It This Time)', the latter produced by Shel Talmy. The group was sadly unable to convert regional popularity into national prominence and split up in 1965. Hornsby is now better known as Jack Sugden in UK soap opera *Emmerdale*.

DENNY, MARTIN

b. 10 April 1911, New York, USA. A pianist, composer, arranger, and conductor, Denny trained as a classical pianist and toured with various bands before moving to Hawaii in 1954. The story goes that while playing in the Shell Bar of the alfresco Hawaiian Village nightclub in Honolulu, he began to incorporate the sounds of the frogs, birds, and various other nocturnal creatures into his music. He also used unusual (some say, weird) instruments to create a kind of Latin/Hawaiian 'exotic fruit cocktail'. The recipe was a tremendous success, and the Exotic Sounds Of Martin Denny had a US number 1 album in 1959 with *Exotica*. One of the tracks, 'Quiet Village', a 1951 Les Baxter composition, also made the Top 5. The group, which initially consisted of Denny (piano), John Kramer (bass), August Colon (bongos), and Arthur Lyman (vibes), later featured Julius Wechter (vibes and marimba), who went on to form the Baja Marimba Band. There followed a series of phenomenally successful albums as Denny's music permeated into the most unexpected areas. In the late 70s, Genesis P-Orridge of Throbbing Gristle was an enthusiastic fan. After touring throughout America in his heyday, Denny eventually opted for semi-retirement in Honolulu. He emerged in 1995 to take part in *Without Walls: The Air-Conditioned Eden*, a UK Channel 4 television documentary which reflected post-war America's obsession with the 'tiki' culture. His catalogue was revived following the rediscovery of people like Esquivel! and a vogue for 'space age bachelor pad music' in the mid-90s.

● ALBUMS: *Exotica* (Liberty 1957) ★★★★, *Exotica Volume II* (Liberty 1957) ★★★★, *Primitiva* (Liberty 1958) ★★★, *Forbidden Island* (Liberty 1958) ★★★★, *Exotica Volume III* (Liberty 1959) ★★★, *Hypnotique* (Liberty 1959) ★★★, *Afro-Desia* (Liberty 1959) ★★★, *Quiet Village* (Liberty 1959) ★★★, *Exotic Sounds From The Silver Screen* (Liberty 1960) ★★★, *Exotic Sounds Visits Broadway* (Liberty 1960) ★★★, *Enchanted Sea* (Liberty 1960) ★★★, *Romantica* (Liberty 1961) ★★★, *Exotic Percussion* (Liberty 1961) ★★★, *In Person* (Liberty 1962) ★★★, *A Taste Of Honey* (Liberty 1962) ★★★, *Exotica Suite* (Liberty 1962) ★★★, *Versatile* (Liberty 1963) ★★★, *Latin Village* (Liberty 1964) ★★★, *Golden Hawaiian Hits* (Liberty 1965) ★★★, *Golden Greats* (Liberty 1966) ★★★, *Hawaii Tattoo* (Liberty 1966) ★★★, *Paradise Moods* (Sunset 1966) ★★★★, *Hawaiian A Go-Go* (Liberty 1966) ★★★, *Hawaii* (Liberty 1967) ★★★, *Exotica Classica* (Liberty 1967) ★★★, *Sayonara* (Sunset 1967) ★★★, *Exotica Today* (Liberty 1969) ★★★, *Exotic Moog* (Liberty 1969) ★★★.

● COMPILATIONS: *Best Of* (Liberty 1962) ★★★, *The Best Of Martin Denny* (Rhino 1995) ★★★★, *The Exotic Sounds Of Martin Denny* (Capitol 1996) ★★★★.

DENVER, KARL
b. Angus McKenzie, 16 December 1931, Glasgow, Scotland, d. 21 December 1998. Denver was raised in Glasgow, but left school at 15 to join the

Norwegian merchant navy. He enlisted in the Argyll and Sutherland Highlanders in 1951, and fought in the Korean war. Rejoining the navy after he was discharged, Denver jumped ship in America and ended up in Nashville. Adopting his new stage name, he appeared on radio and television and played the *Grand Ole Opry* before being deported in 1959. In England he teamed up with Gerry Cottrell and Kevin Neil to form the Karl Denver Trio. They were discovered by impresario Jack Good, who featured the trio on his television series *Wham!* and placed them on a national tour with Billy Fury and Jess Conrad. During his travels Denver had developed a love of contrasting folk forms and his repertoire consisted of traditional material from the Middle East, Africa and China.

His flexible voice spanned several octaves and his unusual inflections brought much contemporary comment. He enjoyed four UK Top 10 hits during 1961/2, including 'Marcheta' (number 8, June 1961), 'Mexicali Rose' (number 8, October 1961), 'Never Goodbye' (number 9, February 1962) and 'Wimoweh'. The latter, a Zulu folk song already covered by the Weavers and re-recorded by the Tokens as 'The Lion Sleeps Tonight', reached number 4 in January 1962. Denver continued to enjoy minor chart success over the next two years, with 'A Little Love A Little Kiss' and 'Still' both reaching the Top 20. Denver also hosted the BBC Light Programme radio show *Side By Side*, which featured the Beatles as regular guests. With the advent of beat groups, though, he progressively turned to cabaret work. By his own admission he began to depend on alcohol, and this hampered his career. He based himself in Manchester, which in part explained 'Lazyitis (One Armed Boxer)', his 1989 collaboration with the city's neo-psychedelic favourites, the Happy Mondays, which reached UK number 46 the following June. He also released an updated version of 'Wimoweh' on Factory Records. He was recording new material shortly before his death in 1998.

● ALBUMS: *Wimoweh* (Decca 1961) ★★★, *Karl Denver* (Decca 1962) ★★★, *Karl Denver At The Yew Tree* (Decca 1962) ★★, *With Love* (Decca 1964) ★★★, *Karl Denver* (Narvis 1972) ★★, *Just Loving You* (Plaza 1993) ★★★.

● COMPILATIONS: *The Best Of* (Spectrum 1999) ★★★★, *The Best Of Karl Denver* (Prism 2001) ★★★.

DeSANTO, SUGAR PIE
b. Umpeylia Marsema Balinton, 16 October 1935, Brooklyn, New York, USA. Raised in San Francisco, DeSanto was discovered at a talent show by Johnny Otis, who later dubbed her 'Little Miss Sugar Pie'. She recorded for Federal and Aladdin Records before 'I Want To Know' (1960) on Veltone reached the R&B charts. Signed to Checker Records in 1961, her first releases made little impact and for two years she toured as part of the James Brown Revue. 'Slip

In Mules' (1964), an amusing 'answer' to Tommy Tucker's 'Hi-Heel Sneakers', regained her chart position. It was followed by the sassy 'Soulful Dress', while an inspired pairing with Etta James produced 'Do I Make Myself Clear' (1965) and 'In The Basement' (1966). Although her recording career at Checker was drawing to a close, DeSanto's songs were recorded by such acts as Billy Stewart, Little Milton and Fontella Bass. DeSanto returned to San Francisco during the 70s where she continues to perform and record today.

● ALBUMS: *Sugar Pie* (Checker 1961) ★★★, *Hello San Francisco* (1984) ★★, *Classic Sugar Pie: The Last Of The Red Hot Mamas* (Jasman 1998) ★★, *A Slice Of Pie* (Jasman 2000) ★★.

● COMPILATIONS: *Loving Touch* (Diving Duck 1987) ★★★, *Down In The Basement – The Chess Years* (Chess 1988) ★★★★, *Sisters Of Soul* 12 tracks Sugar Pie DeSanto/14 tracks Fontella Bass (Roots 1990) ★★★.

DE SHANNON, JACKIE

b. Sharon Lee Myers, 21 August 1944, Hazel, Kentucky, USA. This highly talented singer and songwriter was introduced to gospel, country and blues styles while still a child. She was actively performing by the age of 15 and, having travelled to Los Angeles, commenced a recording career in 1960 with a series of releases on minor labels. De Shannon's collaborations with Sharon Sheeley resulted in several superior pop songs including 'Dum Dum' and 'Heart In Hand' for Brenda Lee and 'Trouble' for the Kalin Twins. De Shannon then forged equally fruitful partnerships with Jack Nitzsche and Randy Newman, the former of which spawned 'When You Walk In The Room', a 1964 smash for the Searchers. Resultant interest in the UK inspired several television appearances and De Shannon's London sojourn was also marked by songwriting collaborations with Jimmy Page.

Despite a succession of excellent singles, De Shannon's own recording career failed to achieve similar heights, although her work continued to be covered by Helen Shapiro, Marianne Faithfull, the Byrds and the Critters. De Shannon enjoyed a US Top 10 single with the Burt Bacharach/Hal David-penned 'What The World Needs Now Is Love' (1965), but her biggest hit came four years later when 'Put A Little Love In Your Heart' reached number 4 in the same chart. Although she continued to write and record superior pop, as evinced on *Jackie* and *Your Baby Is A Lady*, De Shannon was unable to sustain the same profile during the 70s and 80s. Her songs, however, continued to provide hits for others, notably 'Bette Davis Eyes' (Kim Carnes in 1981), 'Breakaway' (Tracey Ullman in 1983) and 'Put A Little Love In Your Heart' (Annie Lennox and Al Green in 1988). In September 2000 De Shannon released the anodyne *You Know Me*, her first new recording

in over 20 years. Her position as one of the 60s leading pop composers remains undiminished, however.

● ALBUMS: *Jackie De Shannon* (Liberty 1963) ★★, *Breakin' It Up On The Beatles Tour!* (Liberty 1964) ★★, *This Is Jackie De Shannon* (Imperial 1965) ★★★, *In The Wind* (Imperial 1965) ★★★, *Are You Ready For This?* (Imperial 1966) ★★★, *New Image* (Imperial 1967) ★★, *For You* (Imperial 1967) ★★, *Me About You* (Imperial 1968) ★★, *What The World Needs Now Is Love* (Imperial 1968) ★★★, *Laurel Canyon* (Imperial 1968) ★★★, *Put A Little Love In Your Heart* (Imperial 1969) ★★, *To Be Free* (Imperial 1970) ★★, *Songs* (Capitol 1971) ★★★, *Jackie* (Atlantic 1972) ★★, *Your Baby Is A Lady* (Atlantic 1974) ★★★, *New Arrangement* (Columbia 1975) ★★, *You're The Only Dancer* (Amherst 1977) ★★, *Quick Touches* (Amherst 1978) ★★, *You Know Me* (Varèse Sarabande 2000) ★★.

● COMPILATIONS: *You Won't Forget Me* (Imperial 1965) ★★★, *Lonely Girl* (Sunset 1968) ★★, *The Very Best Of Jackie De Shannon* (United Artists 1975) ★★★, *Good As Gold!* (Pair 1990) ★★★, *The Best Of Jackie De Shannon* (Rhino 1991) ★★★★, *What The World Needs Now Is Jackie De Shannon: The Definitive Collection* (EMI 1993) ★★★★, *The Early Years* (Missing 1998) ★★, *Best Of ... 1958-1980: Come And Get Me* (Raven 2000) ★★★★.

● FILMS: *Surf Party* (1964), *Intimacy* aka *The Deceivers* (1966), *C'mon, Let's Live A Little* (1967).

DETERGENTS

Formed in the New York City area, the Detergents were a trio consisting of Ron Dante, Danny Jordan and Tommy Wynn. Dante had been a songwriter and demo singer at New York's Brill Building, where his compositions had been placed with such artists as Johnny Mathis, Bobby Vee and Gene Pitney. In 1964, Dante hooked up with Jordan and Wynn and recorded a parody of the hit song by the Shangri-Las, 'Leader Of The Pack'. Entitled 'Leader Of The Laundromat' it was composed not by Dante, but by Paul Vance and Lee Pockriss, earlier responsible for such hits as 'Itsy Bitsy Teenie Weenie Yellow Polkadot Bikini' and 'Catch A Falling Star'. The song was released on the Roulette label and eventually climbed to number 19 in the US singles chart. By the time the follow-up single was released, Jordan and Wynn were replaced by Phil Patrick and Tony Favio. The single, 'Double-O-Seven', made the lower regions of the US charts in 1965 and the group released one album. Dante went on to become the vocalist behind the hits by the Archies in the late 60s and produced some of the earliest recordings by Barry Manilow for Bell Records. Jordan later produced the 1972 novelty hit 'Popcorn' by Hot Butter.

● ALBUMS: *The Many Faces Of The Detergents* (Roulette 1965) ★★.

DEVIANTS

Originally known as the Social Deviants, this pioneering British underground band merged R&B, pseudo-politics and an amateurism inspired by New York radicals, the Fugs. The 'Social' prefix was dropped in 1967 with the departure of Clive Muldoon and Pete Munroe, while the remaining core, Mick Farren (b. Cheltenham, Gloucester, England; vocals), Sid Bishop (guitar), Cord Rees (bass) and Russell Hunter (drums) began work on the Deviants' debut album, *Ptooff!* This characteristically rabblehouse collection was initially issued on the band's own label and distributed through the network purveying the era's alternative publications, *International Times* and *Oz*. Rees was replaced by Duncan Sanderson for *Disposable*, memorable for Farren's call-to-arms composition, 'Let's Loot The Supermarket'. Canadian guitarist Paul Rudolph joined the band on Bishop's departure and the reconstituted quartet completed *Deviants* prior to embarking for America. Farren was fired during the tour and on their return his former colleagues dropped their erstwhile name and became the Pink Fairies upon the addition of former Pretty Things drummer Twink. Farren, who pursued a multi-faceted career as a novelist, rock journalist and sometime musician, later re-established the Deviants' appellation for an EP, *Screwed Up* (1977) and an informal live performance captured on the *Human Garbage* album.
● ALBUMS: *Ptooff!* (Underground Impresarios 1967) ★★★, *Disposable* (Stable 1968) ★★, *Deviants* (Transatlantic 1969) ★★, *Human Garbage* (Psycho 1984) ★★, *Eating Jello With A Heated Fork* (Alive 1996) ★★.
● COMPILATIONS: with Mick Farren *3/Mona The Carnivorous Circus* (Essential 1999) ★★★, with the Deviants *On Your Knees Earthlings!!* (Total Energy 2001) ★★★.
● FURTHER READING: *Give The Anarchist A Cigarette*, Mick Farren.

DEVOTIONS

Formed in 1960 in Astoria, New York, USA, the Devotions were a doo-wop group best known for their 1964 novelty recording 'Rip Van Winkle'. The group included Ray Sanchez, who sang bass-lead, Bob Weisbrod, Bob Hovorka and brothers Frank and Joe Pardo. With their manager, the group auditioned in 1960 for a small record label, Delta, whose owner, Bernie Zimming, was not impressed with their sound. The group wrote 'Rip Van Winkle' that day and Zimming liked it. However, it did not sell, but two years later, when the larger Roulette Records acquired Delta, it was released again. It still did not reach the charts, and the group disbanded. In 1964, however, Roulette included the song as part of a *Golden Goodies* album series and it attracted more attention. Roulette issued the single for a third time and this time it made the US Top 40. A new Devotions group was assembled including three original members, but when further singles flopped, they disbanded in 1965.

DICK AND DEE DEE

This American boy/girl vocal duo was formed in 1961 by Dick St John Gostine (b. 1944, Santa Monica, California, USA) and Dee Dee Sperling (b. 1945, Santa Monica, California, USA) while they were at a local high school. The Gostine-written 'The Mountain's High' was originally released on the small local label Lama, but was picked up by Liberty and became a US hit. Gostine had already made some solo recordings for the label. The fact that they were still at college while this happened precluded touring, however. Visually, the duo dressed as high school kids for an end of term 'prom', and remained highly popular in the US for several years. They switched to Warner Brothers in 1962, and had several more hits before fading out of fashion in the mid-60s. Afterwards they retired from pop music.
● ALBUMS: *Tell Me/The Mountain's High* (Liberty 1962) ★★★, *Young And In Love* (Warners 1963) ★★★, *Turn Around* (Warners 1964) ★★★, *Thou Shalt Not Steal* (Warners 1965) ★★★, *Songs We've Sung On Shindig* (Warners 1966) ★★.
● COMPILATIONS: *The Best Of ...* (Varèse Sarabande 1996) ★★★.

DIDDLEY, BO

b. Otha Ellas Bates (later known as Ellas McDaniel), 28 December 1928, McComb, Mississippi, USA. After beginning his career as a boxer, where he received the sobriquet 'Bo Diddley', the singer worked the blues clubs of Chicago with a repertoire influenced by Louis Jordan, John Lee Hooker and Muddy Waters. In late 1954, he teamed up with Billy Boy Arnold and recorded demos of 'I'm A Man' and 'Bo Diddley'. Re-recorded at Chess Studios with a backing ensemble comprising Otis Spann (piano), Lester Davenport (harmonica), Frank Kirkland (drums) and Jerome Green (maracas), the a-side, 'Bo Diddley', became an R&B hit in 1955. Before long, Diddley's distorted, amplified, custom-made guitar, with its rectangular shape and pumping rhythm style became a familiar, much-imitated trademark, as did his self-referential songs with such titles as 'Bo Diddley's A Gunslinger', 'Diddley Daddy' and 'Bo's A Lumberjack'. His jive-talking routine with 'Say Man' (a US Top 20 hit in 1959) continued on 'Pretty Thing' and 'Hey Good Lookin'', which reached the lower regions of the UK charts in 1963. By then, Diddley was regarded as something of an R&B legend and found a new lease of life courtesy of the UK beat boom. The Pretty Things named themselves after one of his songs, while his work was covered by such artists as the Rolling Stones

Animals, Manfred Mann, Kinks, Yardbirds, Downliner's Sect and the Zephyrs. Diddley subsequently jammed on albums by Chuck Berry and Muddy Waters and appeared infrequently at rock festivals. His classic version of 'Who Do You Love' became a staple cover for a new generation of US acts ranging from Quicksilver Messenger Service to the Doors, Tom Rush and Bob Seger, while the UK's Juicy Lucy took the song into the UK Top 20. Like many of his generation, Diddley attempted to update his image and in the mid-70s released *The Black Gladiator* in the uncomfortable guise of an ageing funkster. *Where It All Begins*, produced by Johnny Otis (whose hit 'Willie And The Hand Jive' owed much to Diddley's style), was probably the most interesting of his post-50s albums. In 1979, Diddley toured with the Clash and in 1984 took a cameo role in the film *Trading Places*. A familiar face on the revival circuit, Diddley is rightly regarded as a seminal figure in the history of rock 'n' roll. His continued appeal to younger performers was emphasized by Craig McLachlan's hit recording of 'Mona' in 1990. Diddley's sound and 'chunk-a-chunka-cha' rhythm continues to remain an enormous influence on pop and rock, both consciously and unconsciously. It was announced in 1995, after many years of relative recording inactivity, that Diddley had signed for Mike Vernon's Code Blue record label; the result was *A Man Amongst Men*. Even with the assistance of Richie Sambora, Jimmie Vaughan, Ronnie Wood, Keith Richards, Billy Boy Arnold, Johnny 'Guitar' Watson and the Shirelles, the anticipation was greater than the result.

● ALBUMS: *Bo Diddley* (Checker 1957) ★★★, *Go Bo Diddley* (Checker 1958) ★★★, *Have Guitar Will Travel* (Checker 1959) ★★★, *Bo Diddley In The Spotlight* (Checker 1960) ★★★, *Bo Diddley Is A Gunslinger* (Checker 1961) ★★★, *Bo Diddley Is A Lover* (Checker 1961) ★★★, *Bo Diddley* (Checker 1962) ★★★, *Bo Diddley Is A Twister* (Checker 1962) ★★★, *Hey Bo Diddley* (Checker 1963) ★★★, *Bo Diddley And Company* (Checker 1963) ★★★, *Bo Diddley Rides Again* (Checker 1963) ★★★, *Bo Diddley's Beach Party* (Checker 1963) ★★★, *Bo Diddley Goes Surfing* aka *Surfin' With Bo Diddley* (Checker 1963) ★★★, *Hey Good Looking* (Checker 1964) ★★★, with Chuck Berry *Two Great Guitars* (Checker 1964) ★★★, *500% More Man* (Checker 1965) ★★★, *Let Me Pass* (Checker 1965) ★★★, *The Originator* (Checker 1966) ★★★, *Boss Man* (Checker 1967) ★★★, *Superblues* (Checker 1968) ★★★, *The Super Super Blues Band* (Checker 1968) ★★★, *The Black Gladiator* (Checker 1969) ★★, *Another Dimension* (Chess 1971) ★★★, *Where It All Begins* (Chess 1972) ★★, *The Bo Diddley London Sessions* (Chess 1973) ★★, *Big Bad Bo* (Chess 1974) ★★★, *Got My Own Bag Of Tricks* (Chess 1974) ★★★, *The 20th Anniversary Of Rock 'N' Roll* (1976) ★★, *I'm A Man* (1977) ★★, *Signifying*

Blues (1993) ★★★, *Bo's Blues* (1993) ★★, *A Man Amongst Men* (Code Blue 1996) ★★.

● COMPILATIONS: *Chess Master* (Chess 1988) ★★★, *EP Collection* (See For Miles 1991) ★★★★, *Bo Diddley: The Chess Years* 12-CD box set (Charly 1993) ★★★★★, *Bo Diddley Is A Lover ... Plus* (See For Miles 1994) ★★★, *Let Me Pass ... Plus* (See For Miles 1994) ★★★, *His Best: The Chess 50th Anniversary Collection* (Chess 1997) ★★★★.

● VIDEOS: *I Don't Sound Like Nobody* (Hendring Video 1990).

● FURTHER READING: *Where Are You Now Bo Diddley?*, Edward Kiersh. *The Complete Bo Diddley Sessions*, George White (ed.). *Bo Diddley: Living Legend*, George White.

DILLARD AND CLARK

Refugees from the Dillards and the Byrds, respectively, Doug Dillard (b. 6 March 1937, East St. Louis, Illinois, USA) and Gene Clark (b. Harold Eugene Clark, 17 November 1941, Tipton, Missouri, USA, d. 24 May 1991) joined forces in 1968 to form one of the first country rock groups. Backed by the Expedition, featuring Bernie Leadon (banjo, guitar), Don Beck (dobro, mandolin) and David Jackson (string bass), they recorded two albums for A&M Records, which confirmed their standing among the best of the early country rock exponents. *The Fantastic Expedition Of Dillard And Clark* featured several strong compositions by Clark and Leadon including 'The Radio Song', 'Out On The Side', 'Something's Wrong' and 'Train Leaves Here This Mornin''. Leadon later took the latter to his next band, the Eagles, who included the song on their debut album. By the time of their second album, Dillard and Clark displayed a stronger country influence with the induction of Flying Burrito Brothers drummer Jon Corneal, champion fiddle player Byron Berline and additional vocalist Donna Washburn. *Through The Morning, Through The Night* combined country standards with Clark originals and featured some sumptuous duets between Clark and Washburn that pre-empted the work of Gram Parsons and Emmylou Harris. Although the Expedition experiment showed considerable promise, the group scattered in various directions at the end of the 60s, with Clark reverting to a solo career. Both albums were issued together on one CD in 1999.

● ALBUMS: *The Fantastic Expedition Of Dillard And Clark* (A&M 1968) ★★★★, *Through The Morning, Through The Night* (A&M 1969) ★★★★.

● FURTHER READING: *The Byrds: Timeless Flight Revisited*, Johnny Rogan.

DILLARDS

Brothers Rodney (b. 18 May 1942, East St. Louis, Illinois, USA; guitar, vocals) and Doug Dillard (b. 6 March 1937, East St. Louis, Illinois, USA;

banjo, vocals) formed this seminal bluegrass group in Salem, Missouri, USA. Roy Dean Webb (b. 28 March 1937, Independence, Missouri, USA; mandolin, vocals) and former radio announcer Mitch Jayne (b. 7 May 1930, Hammond, Indiana, USA; bass) completed the original line-up which, having enjoyed popularity throughout their home state, travelled to Los Angeles in 1962 where they secured a recording contract with the renowned Elektra Records label. *Back Porch Bluegrass* and *The Dillards Live! Almost!* established the unit as one of America's leading traditional acts, although purists denigrated the band's sometimes irreverent attitude. *Pickin' & Fiddlin'*, a collaboration with violinist Byron Berline, was recorded to placate such critics. The Dillards shared management with the Byrds and, whereas their distinctive harmonies proved influential to the latter band's development, the former act then began embracing a pop-based perspective. Dewey Martin (b. 30 September 1942, Chesterville, Ontario, Canada), later of Buffalo Springfield, added drums on a folk rock demo that in turn led to a brace of singles recorded for the Capitol Records label.

Doug Dillard was unhappy with this new direction and left to form a duo with ex-Byrd Gene Clark. Herb Peterson joined the Dillards in 1968 and, having resigned from Elektra, the reshaped quartet completed two exceptional country rock sets, *Wheatstraw Suite* and *Copperfields*. The newcomer was in turn replaced by Billy Rae Latham for *Roots And Branches*, on which the unit's transformation to full-scale electric instruments was complete. A full-time drummer, Paul York, was now featured in the line-up, but further changes were wrought when founder-member Jayne dropped out following *Tribute To The American Duck*. Rodney Dillard has since remained at the helm of a capricious act, which by the end of the 70s, returned to the traditional music circuit through the auspices of the respected Flying Fish Records label. He was also reunited with his prodigal brother in Dillard-Hartford-Dillard, an occasional sideline, which also featured the wonderfully talented multi-instrumentalist John Hartford.

● ALBUMS: *Back Porch Bluegrass* (Elektra 1963) ★★★, *The Dillards Live! Almost!* (Elektra 1964) ★★★, with Byron Berline *Pickin' & Fiddlin'* (Elektra 1965) ★★★, *Wheatstraw Suite* (Elektra 1968) ★★★★, *Copperfields* (Elektra 1970) ★★★, *Roots And Branches* (Anthem 1972) ★★, *Tribute To The American Duck* (Poppy 1973) ★★★★, *The Dillards Versus The Incredible LA Time Machine* (Sonet 1977) ★★, *Glitter-Grass From The Nashwood Hollyville Strings* (1977) ★★★, *Decade Waltz* (Flying Fish 1979) ★★, *Homecoming & Family Reunion* (Flying Fish 1980) ★★★, *Mountain Rock* (Flying Fish 1980) ★★★, *Let It Fly* (Vanguard 1990) ★★★, *A Long Time Ago: The First Time Live!* (Varèse

Sarabande 1999) ★★★.
● COMPILATIONS: *Country Tracks* (Elektra 1974) ★★★, *I'll Fly Away* (Edsel 1988) ★★★, *There Is A Time (1963-1970)* (Vanguard 1991) ★★★★.
● VIDEOS: *A Night In The Ozarks* (Hendring Music Video 1991).
● FURTHER READING: *Everybody On The Truck*, Lee Grant.

DINO, DESI AND BILLY

The trio comprised the son of actor/singer Dean Martin, Dino (b. Dean Paul Anthony Martin Jnr., 12 November 1951, Los Angeles, California, USA, d. 21 March 1987), the son of actors Desi Arnaz and Lucille Ball, Desi (b. Desiderio Alberto Arnaz IV, 19 January 1953, Los Angeles, California, USA) and Billy (b. William Ernest Joseph Hinsche, 29 June 1951, Manilla, The Philippines), a friend from school. The trio met while playing Little League baseball in Beverly Hills in 1965 and decided to form a pop group. With their connections, they were easily signed to Frank Sinatra's Reprise label. Their first single, the easy listening 'I'm A Fool', was their biggest hit, reaching number 17 in the summer of 1965, and they placed five other singles and two albums on the charts before breaking up in 1970. Although Martin and Arnaz joined a blues band in the 70s, Hinsche kept the highest musical profile, as a session musician and briefly a member of the Beach Boys' stage back-up band. Martin was killed in 1987 when his Air National Guard jet crashed.
● ALBUMS: *I'm A Fool* (Reprise 1965) ★★★, *Our Times Are Coming* (Reprise 1966) ★★, *Memories Are Made Of This* (Reprise 1966) ★★, *Souvenir* (Reprise 1966) ★★★, *Follow Me* (1969) ★★.
● COMPILATIONS: *The Rebel Kind* (Sundazed 1996) ★★★.

DION

During his peak, from 1958-63, Dion (b. Dion DiMucci, 18 July 1939, Bronx, New York, USA) was the quintessential Italian-American New York City rocker and was, perhaps, the first major white rock singer who was not from a southern city. The career of one of America's legendary artists has spanned six decades, during which time he has made numerous musical style changes. Between 1958 and 1960 Dion And The Belmonts were one of the leading doo-wop groups. The Belmonts comprised Angelo D'Aleo (b. 3 February 1940, Bronx, New York, USA), Carlo Mastrangelo (b. 5 October 1938, Bronx, New York, USA), and Freddie Milano (b. 22 August 1939, Bronx, New York USA). The slick besuited Italian look rivalled the black harmony groups that dominated the era. They had nine hits in two years, including two of the all-time great examples of white doo-wop 'I Wonder Why' and 'No One Knows'. Their classic reading of the Doc Pomus and Mort Shuman song 'A Teenager In Love' with the

emorable line of teenage despair 'each night I
k, the stars up above, (bom, bom, bom, bom),
ny must I be a teenager in love?' poignantly
ticulated growing pains in an era when
nservative values were being challenged by a
w moral climate. In 1960 they attempted a
rsion of 'When You Wish Upon A Star' from
alt Disney's *Pinocchio* and followed with a
orthy, but slushy cover of Cole Porter's 'In
ie Still Of The Night'.
on left for a solo career in 1960 and had
imediate success in the USA with 'Lonely
enager'. The following year he had two
nsecutive hits that made him one of
nerica's biggest artists. Both 'Runaround Sue'
d 'The Wanderer' are rock classics; the
rmer, warning everybody to keep away from
e, while the latter warns Flo, Jane and Mary
steer clear of the wanderer. The similarity of
e theme can be forgiven as they are both
onderfully uplifting songs, great dance
cords and two of the finest of the era. Dion
stained an incredible output of hits, including
other classic 'Lovers Who Wander'. In 1963
th seven major singles he was in the US
arts for the entire year. The following year
on disappeared from the scene to fight a
rious addiction to heroin, a drug to which he
d fallen victim in 1960. Although he and the
lmonts reunited briefly in 1967, little was
ard of him until December 1968. He returned
ring a turbulent year in American history;
e escalation of the Vietnam War had received
ong opposition, particularly from the music
orld, and the assassinations of Robert
nnedy and Martin Luther King were fresh in
ople's minds. The emotional Dick Holler
ng, 'Abraham, Martin And John' was a
rfectly timed stroke of genius. This lilting
ksy ballad barely left a dry eye as it climbed
number 4 in the US charts. The following
ar a heroin-free Dion delighted festival and
ncert audiences with a striking solo act,
companied on acoustic guitar. That same
ar the excellent *Dion* was released, including
isitive covers of songs by Bob Dylan, Joni
tchell, Leonard Cohen, and a brave attempt
Jimi Hendrix's 'Purple Haze'.
on's critical ranking was high but his
mmercial standing dwindled, and two
oustic-based albums were commercial
iasters. Wily entrepreneurs encouraged
other reunion with the Belmonts in 1973, and
1975 Phil Spector produced 'Born To Be With
u'. An excellent album of the same name (on
ector's own label) failed, and another
nderrated album, *The Return Of The Wanderer*,
peared in 1978 on Lifesong Records. For the
xt few years Dion was a devout born-again
ristian and recorded sporadically, releasing
ristian albums including *Inside Job* and
igdom Of The Street*. He returned to rock 'n'
l in 1988 playing with Bruce Springsteen and
eased the Dave Edmunds-produced *Yo*

Frankie; and toured the UK where he has always
found an enthusiastic cult following. Dion is
one of the few survivors from a school of
American vocalists who had genuine talent,
and he should be credited for a series of
uplifting songs that still sound remarkably
fresh. He was elected to the Rock And Roll Hall
Of Fame in 1989. A surprisingly fresh new
album was released in 2000
● ALBUMS: with the Belmonts *Presenting Dion
And The Belmonts* (Laurie 1959) ★★★, with the
Belmonts *Wish Upon A Star* (Laurie 1960) ★★,
Alone With Dion (Laurie 1961) ★★★, *Runaround
Sue* (Laurie 1961) ★★★, *Lovers Who Wander*
(Laurie 1962) ★★★★, *Dion Sings His Greatest
Hits* (Laurie 1962) ★★★, *Love Came To Me*
(Laurie 1963) ★★★, *Ruby Baby* (Columbia
1963) ★★★, *Dion Sings The 15 Million Sellers*
(Laurie 1963) ★★★★, *Donna The Prima Donna*
(Columbia 1963) ★★★★, *Dion Sings To Sandy*
(Laurie 1963) ★★★, with the Belmonts *Together*
(Laurie 1963) ★★★, with the Belmonts *Together
Again* (ABC 1967) ★★★, *Dion* (Laurie 1968)
★★★★, *Sit Down Old Friend* (Warners 1969)
★★★, *You're Not Alone* (Warners 1971) ★★★,
Sanctuary (Warners 1971) ★★★, *Suite For Late
Summer* (Warners 1972) ★★★, with the
Belmonts *Reunion: Live 1972* (Reprise 1973) ★★,
Born To Be With You (Spector 1975) ★★★★,
Streetheart (Warners 1976) ★★★, *The Return Of
The Wanderer* (Lifesong 1978) ★★★, *Inside Job*
(Dayspring 1980) ★★, *Only Jesus* (Dayspring
1981) ★★, *I Put Away My Idols* (Dayspring 1983)
★★★, *Seasons* (Dayspring 1984) ★★★, *Kingdom
In The Streets* (Myrrh 1985) ★★, *Velvet And Steel*
(Dayspring 1986) ★★★, *Yo Frankie!* (Arista
1989) ★★★, *Dream On Fire* (Vision 1992) ★★★,
Déjà Nu (Collectables 2000) ★★★★.
● COMPILATIONS: *Dion's Greatest Hits*
(Columbia 1973) ★★★, *20 Golden Greats* (K-Tel
1980) ★★★★, *24 Original Classics* (Arista 1984)
★★★★, *So Why Didn't You Do That The First
Time?* (Ace 1985) ★★★★, *Runaround Sue: The
Best Of The Rest* (Ace 1988) ★★★, *Bronx Blues:
The Columbia Recordings (1962-1965)* (Columbia
1990) ★★★★, *The Road I'm On: A Retrospective*
(Columbia Legacy 1997) ★★★, *The Best Of The
Gospel Years* (Ace 1997) ★★★, *Bronx Blues: The
Columbia Recordings (1962-1965)* (Columbia
1999) ★★★, *King Of The New York Streets* 3-CD
box set (The Right Stuff 2000) ★★★★, *Dion: The
EP Collection* (See For Miles 2001) ★★★.
● FURTHER READING: *The Wanderer*, Dion
DiMucci with Davin Seay.

DIXIE CUPS

Formed in New Orleans, Louisiana, USA, in
1963, the Dixie Cups were a female trio best
known for the original recording of the hit
'Chapel Of Love' in the early 60s. The group
consisted of sisters Barbara Ann Hawkins (b. 23
October 1943) and Rosa Lee Hawkins (b. 24
September 1944) and their cousin Joan Marie
Johnson (b. January 1945, New Orleans,

Louisiana, USA). Having sung together in church and at school, the girls formed a group called the Meltones for a high school talent contest in 1963. There they were discovered by Joe Jones, a New Orleans singer who had secured a hit himself with 'You Talk Too Much' in 1960. He became their manager and signed the trio with producers/songwriters Jerry Leiber and Mike Stoller, who were then starting their own record label, Red Bird, with industry veteran George Goldner.

The Dixie Cups recorded Jeff Barry and Ellie Greenwich's 'Chapel Of Love' despite the fact that both the Ronettes and the Crystals had failed to have hits with the song, which was described by co-producer Mike Leiber as 'a record I hated with a passion'. Released as the debut Red Bird single, the trio's first single reached number 1 in the USA during the summer of 1964 (the trio later claimed that they received only a few hundred dollars for their part in the recording). Following that hit, the Dixie Cups toured the USA and released a number of follow-up singles for Red Bird, four of which charted. 'People Say', the second, made number 12 and the last, 'Iko Iko', a traditional New Orleans chant, reached number 20. The song was subsequently used in soundtracks for a number of films, in common with 'Chapel Of Love'. After Red Bird closed down in 1966, the Dixie Cups signed with ABC-Paramount Records. No hits resulted from the association, and the trio have not recorded since, although they continue to perform (the two sisters are the only originals still in the act).

● ALBUMS: *Chapel Of Love* reissued as *Iko Iko* (Red Bird 1964) ★★★, *Ridin' High* (ABC/Paramount 1965) ★★.
● COMPILATIONS: *The Best Of The Dixie Cups* (Delta 1997) ★★★, *Chapel Of Love: The Very Best Of The Dixie Cups* (Collectables 1999) ★★★,

DOCTOR WEST'S MEDICINE SHOW AND JUG BAND

Founded in Los Angeles, California, USA, Doctor West's Medicine Show And Jug Band were led by former Boston-based folk singer, Norman Greenbaum. Bonnie Wallach (guitar/vocals), Jack Carrington (guitar/vocals/percussion) and Evan Engber (percussion) completed the original line-up. The group played a mixture of jug and goodtime music similar to Sopwith Camel. They enjoyed a minor US hit in 1967 with the novelty song, 'The Eggplant That Ate Chicago' and attracted attention for the title of its follow-up, 'Gondoliers, Overseers, Playboys And Bums'. They broke up at the end of that year after which Greenbaum formed several low-key acts before teaming with producer Erik Jacobsen and scoring international success with 'Spirit In The Sky'.

● ALBUMS: *The Eggplant That Ate Chicago* (Go Go 1967) ★★.

DODD, KEN

b. 8 November 1927, Liverpool, England. Primarily one of Britain's all-time great stand-up comedians, Dodd has also had a successful recording career singing romantic ballads in a warm mezzo-tenor voice. His only comedy record – as the Diddy Men in 1965 – was a flop. He grew up in Liverpool and sang in a church choir before developing a comedy act as Professor Yaffle Chuckabutty, Operatic Tenor and Sausage Knotter, in which he sang comic versions of well-known songs. Dodd worked in sales before becoming a professional comic in 1954, playing theatres and summer shows. Blackpool's Central Pier, where he topped the bill in 1958. This led to appearances at the London Palladium and a television series in the 60s. Like other comedians of his generation, Dodd was a competent singer and frequently closed his shows with a romantic ballad. In 1960 he signed to Decca and recorded 'Love Is Like A Violin', a 20s ballad which became a Top 10 hit. This was followed by 'Once In Every Lifetime' (1961) and 'Pianissimo' (1962). He next switched to EMI's Columbia label, where Geoff Love was the musical director for the minor hits 'Still' (1963) and the exuberant 'Happiness' (1964). But the biggest hit of his career was the contrasting 'Tears' (1965), a weepie of a ballad produced by Norman Newell. After five weeks at number 1 in the UK, it was displaced by the Rolling Stones' 'Get Off Of My Cloud'. A hit for Rudy Vallee in 1931, 'Tears' sold nearly two million copies for Dodd and led to six more Top 20 singles in the next few years. Among these were translations of three Italian Ken Dodd hits ('The River', 'Broken Hearted' and 'When Love Comes Round Again') and 'Promises', based on Beethoven's *Pathetique Sonata*. During the 80s, Dodd had modest success with 'Hold My Hand' (1981). In 1990 he hit the headlines following a controversial High Court action brought by the Inland Revenue, which he won. Four years later he began a six-part BBC Radio 2 series, *Ken Dodd's Comedy Club*, explaining: 'I'm an intellectual entertainer; at one time there was only me and Noël Coward doing this sort of stuff.'

● ALBUMS: *Tears Of Happiness* (Columbia 1965) ★★★, *Hits For Now And Always* (Columbia 1965) ★★★, *For Someone Special* (Columbia 1966) ★★★, *Now And Forever* (VIP 1983) ★★.
● COMPILATIONS: *Ken Dodd Collection* (One Up/EMI 1975) ★★★, *20 Golden Greats* (Warwick 1980) ★★, *More Than Ever* (MFP/EMI 1981) ★★, *The Very Best Of Ken Dodd* (MFP/EMI 1985) ★★★, *Greatest Hits* (Hour Of Pleasure/EMI 1986) ★★★, *Happiness: The Very Best Of Ken Dodd* (EMI 2001) ★★★.

DOLBY, RAY, DR.

Through his eponymous noise-reduction unit, Dolby made the most important technical contribution to the success of the tape cassette

From 1949 he was employed by Ampex on noise reduction programmes and then studied physics in London, England. After working in India for some years, Dolby opened a laboratory in London in 1965, selling his initial A-type system, designed for recording studios, to Decca Records and others. His research on reducing tape hiss for the 8-track cartridge and the cassette resulted in the B-type system in 1971. Within 12 months almost every major cassette manufacturer was using this system, although Philips Records held out for a few years before converting. In 1978, Dolby's invention was adapted for the cinema and *Star Wars* was the first movie to have its soundtrack enhanced by the noise-reduction method. This system was upgraded for digital sound in 1991. So jealously guarded was the Dolby name that in 1987 Dolby Laboratories sued the musician/producer Thomas Dolby (b. Thomas Morgan Robertson) for copyright infringement. Robertson agreed to 'license' the name from Ray Dolby's company.

DONNER, RAL

b. Ralph Stuart Donner, 10 February 1943, Chicago, Illinois, USA, d. 6 April 1984, Chicago, Illinois, USA. Donner had a short string of US chart singles in the early 60s, most notably the number 4 'You Don't Know What You've Got (Until You Lose It)'. He began singing in church in his teens and formed his first band at the age of 13, and began touring two years later. Building a reputation for a singing voice uncannily similar to that of Elvis Presley, Donner chose a Presley album track, 'Girl Of My Best Friend', for his attempt to break through. After recording it in Florida, Donner leased the track to Gone Records and it ultimately climbed to number 19 in the US charts. His second single was his only Top 10 hit (number 25 in the UK) and Donner subsequently placed three other singles in the US chart, with 'She's Everything (I Wanted You To Be)' the most successful at number 18. His debut, *Takin' Care Of Business*, was also released on Gone in 1961, and has, in subsequent years, increased in value as a collectors' item. Donner continued to record after leaving Gone, for labels such as Reprise Records and several small independents. Although his commercial popularity was in the early 60s, Donner gained recognition among fans and collectors of Presley-styled rock 'n' roll and he continued to capitalize on that association. In 1981, Donner provided the narration for the movie *This Is Elvis*, mimicking the late Presley's speaking voice with the same expertize he had applied to the sound-alike singing. Donner died of lung cancer at the age of 41.

● ALBUMS: *Takin' Care Of Business* (Gone 1961) ★★★, with Ray Smith And Bobby Dale *Ral Donner, with Ray Smith And Bobby Dale* (Crown 1963) ★★, *The Elvis Presley Sound Of Ral Donner* (Treasure 1986) ★★★, *Loneliness Of A Star* (1986) ★★★.

● COMPILATIONS: *The Complete Ral Donner* (Sequel 1991) ★★★, *You Don't Know What You've Got Until You Lose It* (Collectables 1995) ★★★, *You Don't Know What You've Got: The Anthology* (Castle 2001) ★★★.

DONOVAN

b. Donovan Leitch, 10 May 1946, Maryhill, Glasgow, Scotland. Uncomfortably labelled 'Britain's answer to Bob Dylan' Donovan did not fit in well with the folk establishment. Instead, it was the pioneering UK television show *Ready Steady Go* that adopted him, and from then on success was assured. His first single, 'Catch The Wind', launched a career that lasted through the 60s with numerous hits, developing as fashions changed. The expressive 'Colours' and 'Turquoise' continued his hit folk image, although hints of other influences began to creep into his music. Donovan's finest work, however, was as an ambassador of 'flower power' with memorable singles like 1966's 'Sunshine Superman' (UK number 2/US number 1) and 'Mellow Yellow' (UK number 8/US number 2). His subtle drug references endeared him to the hippie movement, although some critics felt his stance was too fey and insipid. He enjoyed several hits with lighter material such as the calypso influenced 'There Is A Mountain' and 'Jennifer Juniper' (written for Jenny Boyd during a much publicized sojourn with the guru, Maharishi Mahesh Yogi).

A number of the tracks on his ambitious 1967 boxed set, *A Gift From A Flower To A Garden*, displayed a jazzier feel, a style he had previously flirted with on excellent b-sides such as 'Sunny Goodge Street' and 'Preachin' Love'. Meanwhile, his drug/fairy tale imagery reached its apotheosis in 1968 with the Lewis Carroll-influenced 'Hurdy Gurdy Man' (UK number 4/US number 5). As the 60s closed, however, he fell from commercial grace, despite adopting a more gutsy approach for his collaboration with Jeff Beck on 'Goo Goo Barabajagal (Love Is Hot)'. Undeterred, Donovan found greater success in the USA, and many of his later records were issued only in America. *Cosmic Wheels* (1973) was an artistic and commercial success, and contained the witty 'Intergalactic Laxative'. Anticipating continued success, Donovan then released the bitterly disappointing *Essence To Essence*, and thereafter ceased to be a major concert attraction although he continued to release low-key studio albums on a variety of labels. In 1990, after many inactive years, the Happy Mondays bought him back into favour by praising his work and invited him on tour in 1991.

Their irreverent tribute 'Donovan' underlined this new-found favouritism. He also appeared on UK television as part of a humorous remake of 'Jennifer Juniper' with comedians Trevor and Simon. A flood of reissues arrived as Donovan was deemed hip again, and he undertook a major UK tour in 1992. *Troubadour*, an excellent CD box set was issued in 1992 covering vital material from his career. The highest profile he has received in the recent past is becoming ex-Happy Monday/Black Grape vocalist Shaun Ryder's father-in-law. *Sutras* was released to a considerable amount of press coverage but achieved little in terms of sales. On this album he revisited whimsical and 'cosmic' territory. Instead of catchy folk songs (early period) and acid-soaked rockers (late period), he opted for cloying, though sincere, material.

● ALBUMS: *What's Bin Did And What's Bin Hid* (UK) *Catch The Wind* (US) (Pye/Hickory 1965) ★★★★, *Fairytale* (Pye/Hickory 1965) ★★★★, *Sunshine Superman* US only (Epic 1966) ★★★★, *Mellow Yellow* US only (Epic 1967) ★★★★, *A Gift From A Flower To A Garden* (Epic 1967) ★★★, *Wear Your Love Like Heaven* US only (Epic 1967) ★★★, *For Little Ones* US only (Epic 1967) ★★★, *Donovan In Concert* (Epic/Pye 1968) ★★★, *The Hurdy Gurdy Man* US only (Epic 1968) ★★★★, *Barabajagal* (Epic 1969) ★★★★, *Open Road* (Dawn/Epic 1970) ★★★, *HMS Donovan* (Dawn 1971) ★★★, *Brother Sun, Sister Moon* film soundtrack (EMI 1972) ★★, *Colours* (Hallmark 1972) ★★★, *Cosmic Wheels* (Epic 1973) ★★★, *Live In Japan* (Sony 1973) ★★★, *Essence To Essence* (Epic 1973) ★★, *7-Tease* (Epic 1974) ★★★, *Slow Down World* (Epic 1976) ★★, *Donovan* (RAK/Arista 1977) ★★, *Neutronica* (Barclay/RCA 1980) ★★, *Love Is Only Feeling* (RCA 1981) ★★, *Lady Of The Stars* (RCA/Allegiance 1984) ★★, *Donovan Rising* (UK) *The Classics Live* (US) (Permanent/Great Northern Arts 1993) ★★★, *Sutras* (American Recordings 1996) ★★★, *Greatest Hits Live: Vancouver 1986* (Varèse Vintage 2001) ★★★.

● COMPILATIONS: *The Real Donovan* US only (Hickory 1966) ★★★, *Sunshine Superman* UK only (Pye 1967) ★★★★, *Universal Soldier* (Marble Arch 1967) ★★★★, *Like It Is, Was, And Evermore Shall Be* (Hickory 1968) ★★★, *The Best Of Donovan* (Epic/Pye 1969) ★★★★, *The Best Of Donovan* (Hickory 1969) ★★★, *The World Of Donovan* (Marble Arch 1969) ★★★, *Donovan P. Leitch* US only (Janus 1970) ★★★, *Catch The Wind* (Hallmark 1971) ★★★, *Golden Hour Of Donovan* (Golden Hour 1971) ★★★★, *Colours* (Hallmark 1972) ★★★, *The World Of Donovan* US only (Epic 1972) ★★★, *Early Treasures* US only (Bell 1973) ★★★, *Four Shades* 4-LP box set (Pye 1973) ★★★, *Hear Me Now* (Janus 1974) ★★★, *The Pye History Of British Pop Music: Donovan* US only (Pye 1975) ★★★, *The Pye History Of British Pop Music: Donovan, Vol. 2* US only (Pye 1976) ★★★, *The Donovan File* (Pye 1977) ★★★, *Spotlight On Donovan* (PRT 1981) ★★★★, *Universal Soldier* (Spot 1983) ★★★, *Catch The Wind* (Showcase 1986) ★★★, *Colours* (PRT 1987) ★★★, *Catch The Wind* US only (Garland 1988) ★★★, *Greatest Hits ... And More* (EMI 1989) ★★★★, *The EP Collection* (See For Miles 1990) ★★★★, *The Collection* (Castle 1991)

★★★, *The Trip* (EMI 1991) ★★★★, *Colours* (Del Rack 1991) ★★★★, *Troubadour: The Definitive Collection 1964-1976* 2-CD box set (Epic/Legacy 1992) ★★★★, *The Early Years* (Dojo 1993) ★★★, *Sunshine Superman – 18 Songs Of Love And Freedom* (Remember 1993) ★★★, *Gold* (Disky 1993) ★★★, *Josie* (Castle 1994) ★★★, *Universal Soldier* (Spectrum 1995) ★★★★, *Peace And Love Songs* (Sony 1995) ★★★, *Catch The Wind: The Best Of Donovan* (Pulse 1996) ★★★, *Sunshine Troubadour* (Hallmark 1996) ★★★, *Love Is Hot, Truth Is Molten: Original Essential Recordings 1965-1973* (HMV 1998) ★★★, *Mellow* (Snapper 1997) ★★★, *Catch The Wind* (Laserlight 1998) ★★★, *Fairytales And Colours* (Select 1998) ★★★, *Summer Day Reflection Songs* (Castle 2000) ★★★★.

● FURTHER READING: *Dry Songs And Scribbles*, Donovan. *She*, Donovan.

DOONICAN, VAL

b. Michael Valentine Doonican, 3 February 1928, Waterford, Eire. Doonican learned to play the mandolin and guitar as a boy, and later toured northern and southern Ireland in various bands before travelling to England in 1951 to join an Irish vocal quartet, the Four Ramblers. He wrote the group's vocal arrangements as well as singing and playing guitar in their BBC radio series *Riders Of The Range*. In the late 50s, on the advice of Anthony Newley, he went solo, and appeared on television in *Beauty Box*, and on radio in *Dreamy Afternoon*, later retitled, *A Date With Val*. In 1963 he was recommended to impresario Val Parnell by comedian Dickie Henderson, and gained a spot on ITV's top-rated television show *Sunday Night At The London Palladium*. He made an immediate impact with his friendly, easy-going style and in 1964 commenced an annual series for BBC television, which ran until the 80s. He soon became one of the most popular entertainers in the UK, and was voted Television Personality Of The Year three times.

The closing sequence of his television show, in which he sang a song while seated in a rocking chair, was especially effective. The idea was later used as a self-deprecating album title, *Val Doonican Rocks, But Gently*. Later, in the age of video tape, he still preferred his shows to be transmitted 'live'. His first record hit, 'Walk Tall', in 1964, was followed by a string of chart entries through to the early 70s, including 'The Special Years', 'Elusive Butterfly', 'What Would I Be?', 'Memories Are Made Of This', 'If The Whole World Stopped Loving', 'If I Knew Then What I Know Now' and 'Morning'. Equally popular, but not chart entries, were a number of novelty songs such as 'O'Rafferty's Motor Car', 'Delaney's Donkey' and 'Paddy McGinty's Goat', written by the prolific English team of Bob Weston and Bert Lee. By the early 90s Doonican was semi-retired – performing 'laps of honour', as he put it. In 1993 he released a video, 'a ibute to his favourite artists', entitled *Thank ou For The Music*.

ALBUMS: *Lucky 13 Shades Of Val Doonican* Decca 1964) ★★★, *Gentle Shades Of Val Doonican* (Decca 1966) ★★★, *Val Doonican ocks, But Gently* (Pye 1967) ★★★, *Val* (Pye 968) ★★★, *Sounds Gentle* (Pye 1969) ★★★, *The Magic Of Val Doonican* (Philips 1970) ★★★, *This Val Doonican* (Philips 1971) ★★★, *Morning as Broken* (Philips 1973) ★★, *Song Sung Blue* Philips 1974) ★★★, *I Love Country Music* Philips 1975) ★★, *Life Can Be Beautiful* (Philips 976) ★★★, *Some Of My Best Friends Are Songs* Philips 1977) ★★★, *Quiet Moments* (RCA 1981) ★★, *Val Sings Bing* (RCA 1982) ★★★, *The Val oonican Music Show* (BBC 1984) ★★, *By Request* MFP/EMI 1987) ★★★, *Portrait Of My Love* (CRC 989) ★★★, *Songs From My Sketch Book* Parkfield 1990) ★★★, *Christmas With Val oonican* (Castle 1999) ★★.

COMPILATIONS: *The World Of Val Doonican* Decca 1969) ★★★★, *The World Of Val Doonican, olume Two* (Decca 1969) ★★★★, *The World Of al Doonican, Volume Three* (Decca 1970) ★★★, he World Of Val Doonican, Volume Four* (Decca 971) ★★★, *The World Of Val Doonican, Volume ive* (Decca 1972) ★★★, *Spotlight On Val oonican* (1974) ★★★, *Focus On Val Doonican* Decca 1976) ★★★, *Mr Music Man* (Hallmark 988) ★★★, *Memories Are Made Of This* lite/Decca 1981) ★★★, *Forty Shades Of Green* MFP/EMI 1983) ★★★, *The Very Best Of Val oonican* (MFP/EMI 1984) ★★★★, *Twenty ersonal Favourites For You* (Warwick 1986) ★★, *It's Good To See You* (K-Tel 1988) ★★★, *The ery Best Of Val Doonican* (Music Club 1998) ★★, *His Special Years: The Very Best Of olygram* 1999) ★★★★, *Walk Tall* (Amou 2001) ★★.

VIDEOS: *Songs From My Sketch Book* (Parkfield 990), *Thank You For The Music* (1993).

FURTHER READING: *The Special Years: An utobiography*, Val Doonican.

OORS

f the doors of perception were cleansed, verything would appear to man as it is, infinite.' his quote from poet William Blake, via Aldous uxley, was an inspiration to Jim Morrison (b. mes Douglas Morrison, 8 December 1943, elbourne, Florida, USA, d. 3 July 1971, Paris, rance), a student of theatre arts at the niversity of California and an aspiring usician. His dream of a rock band entitled 'the oors' was fulfilled in 1965, when he sang a dimentary composition, 'Moonlight Drive', to llow scholar Ray Manzarek (b. Raymond aniel Manzarek, 12 February 1939, Chicago, linois, USA; keyboards). Impressed, he invited orrison to join his campus R&B band, Rick nd The Ravens, which also included the ganist's two brothers. Ray then recruited rummer John Densmore (b. 1 December 1944, nta Monica, California, USA), and the

reshaped outfit recorded six Morrison songs at the famed World Pacific studios. The session featured several compositions that the band subsequently re-recorded, including 'Summer's Almost Gone' and 'End Of The Night'. Manzarek's brothers disliked the new material and later dropped out. They were replaced by Robbie Krieger (b. Robert Alan Krieger, 8 January 1946, Los Angeles, California, USA), an inventive guitarist, whom Densmore met at a meditation centre. Morrison was now established as the vocalist and the quartet began rehearsing in earnest.

The Doors' first residency was at the London Fog on Sunset Strip, but they later found favour at the prestigious Whisky-A-Go-Go. They were, however, fired from the latter establishment, following a performance of 'The End', Morrison's chilling, oedipal composition. Improvised and partly spoken over a raga/rock framework, it proved too controversial for timid club owners, but the band's standing within the music fraternity grew. Local rivals Love, already signed to Elektra Records, recommended the Doors to the label's managing director, Jac Holzman who, despite initial caution, signed them in July 1966. *The Doors*, released the following year, unveiled many contrasting influences. Manzarek's thin sounding organ (he also performed the part of bassist with the aid of a separate bass keyboard) recalled the garage-band style omnipresent several months earlier, but Krieger's liquid guitar playing and Densmore's imaginative drumming were already clearly evident. Morrison's striking, dramatic voice added power to the exceptional compositions, which included the pulsating 'Break On Through' and an 11-minute version of 'The End'. Cover versions of material, including Willie Dixon's 'Back Door Man' and Bertolt Brecht/Kurt Weill's 'Alabama Song (Whiskey Bar)', exemplified the band's disparate influences.

The best-known track, however, was 'Light My Fire', which, when trimmed down from its original seven minutes, became a number 1 single in the USA. Its fiery imagery combined eroticism with death, and the song has since become a standard. Its success created new problems and the Doors, perceived by some as underground heroes, were tarred as teenybop fodder by others. This dichotomy weighed heavily on Morrison who wished to be accepted as a serious artist. A second album, *Strange Days*, showcased 'When The Music's Over', another extended piece destined to become a *tour de force* within the band's canon. The quartet enjoyed further chart success when 'People Are Strange' broached the US Top 20, but it was 1968 before they secured another number 1 single with the infectious 'Hello I Love You'. The song was also the band's first major UK hit, although some of this lustre was lost following legal action by Ray Davies of the Kinks, who claimed infringement of his own composition, 'All Day And All Of The Night'. The action coincided with the Doors' first European tour. A major television documentary, *The Doors Are Open*, was devoted to the visit and centred on their powerful performance at London's Chalk Farm Roundhouse. The band showcased several tracks from their third collection, *Waiting For The Sun*, including the declamatory 'Five To One', and a fierce protest song, 'The Unknown Soldier', for which they also completed an uncompromising promotional film. However, the follow-up album, *The Soft Parade*, on which a horn section masked several unremarkable songs, was a major disappointment, although the tongue-in-cheek 'Touch Me' became a US Top 3 single and 'Wishful Sinful' was a Top 50 hit.

Continued commercial success exacted further pressure on Morrison, whose frustration with his role as a pop idol grew more pronounced. His anti-authoritarian persona combined with a brazen sexuality and notorious alcohol and narcotics consumption to create a character bedevilled by doubt and cynicism. His confrontations with middle America reached an apogee on 1 March 1969 when, following a concert at Miami's Dinner Key auditorium, the singer was indicted for indecent exposure, public intoxication and profane, lewd and lascivious conduct. Although Morrison was later acquitted of all but the minor charges, the incident clouded the band's career when live dates for the next few months were cancelled. Paradoxically, this furore re-awoke the Doors' creativity. *Morrison Hotel*, a tough R&B-based collection, matched the best of their early releases and featured seminal performances in 'Roadhouse Blues' and 'You Make Me Real'. *Absolutely Live*, an in-concert set edited from a variety of sources, gave the impression of a single performance and exhibited the band's power and authority. However, Morrison, whose poetry had been published in two volumes, *The Lords* and *The New Creatures*, now drew greater pleasure from this more personal art form. Having completed more sessions at the band's workshop for a new album, the last owed to Elektra, the singer escaped to Paris where he hoped to follow a literary career and abandon music altogether. Tragically, years of hedonistic excess had taken its toll and on 3 July 1971, Jim Morrison was found dead in his bathtub, his passing recorded officially as a heart attack. He was buried in Paris' Père Lachaise cemetery in the esteemed company of Oscar Wilde, Marcel Proust, and Honore de Balzac.

L.A. Woman, his final recording with the Doors, is one of the band's finest achievements. It was also their first album recorded without producer Paul A. Rothchild, with engineer Bruce Botnick tackling co-production duties. The album's simple intimacy resulted in some superb performances, including 'Riders On The Storm', whose haunting imagery and stealthy accompaniment created a timeless classic. Th survivors continued to work as the Doors, bu while *Other Voices* showed some promise, *Fu Circle* was severely flawed and the band soo dissolved. Densmore and Krieger formed th Butts Band, with whom they recorded tw albums before splitting to pursue different path: Manzarek undertook several projects as eithe artist, producer or manager, but the spectre c the Doors refused to die. Interest in the ban flourished throughout the decade and in 197 the remaining trio supplied newly recorde music to a series of poetry recitations, whic Morrison had taped during the *L.A. Woma* sessions. The resultant album, *An America Prayer*, was a major success and prompted suc archive excursions as *Alive, She Cried*, compendium of several concert performance and *Live At The Hollywood Bowl*. The evocativ use of 'The End' in Francis Ford Coppola's 197 Vietnam war movie, *Apocalypse Now*, als generated renewed interest in the Door's legac and indeed, it is on those first recordings tha the Doors' considerable reputation, an influence, rest. Since then their catalogue ha never been out of print, and future generation of rock fans will almost certainly use them as major role model. Director Oliver Stone's 199 movie biography *The Doors*, starring Val Kilme helped confirm Morrison as one of the 60s' grea cultural icons.

● ALBUMS: *The Doors* (Elektra 1967) ★★★★
Strange Days (Elektra 1967) ★★★★, *Waiting F The Sun* (Elektra 1968) ★★★, *The Soft Parac* (Elektra 1969) ★★, *Morrison Hotel* (Elektra 197(★★★★, *Absolutely Live* (Elektra 1970) ★★, *L.A Woman* (Elektra 1971) ★★★★, *Other Voice* (Elektra 1971) ★★, *Full Circle* (Elektra 1972) ★ *An American Prayer* (Elektra 1978) ★★, *Aliv She Cried* (Elektra 1983) ★★, *Live At Th Hollywood Bowl* 1968 recording (Elektra 1987 ★★, *The Doors* film soundtrack (Elektra 199] ★★★, *Bright Midnight: Live In Americ* 1969/1970 recordings (Elektra 2001) ★★★.

● COMPILATIONS: *13* (Elektra 1970) ★★★★
Weird Scenes Inside The Goldmine (Elektra 197: ★★★, *The Best Of The Doors* (Elektra 197: ★★★, *Greatest Hits* (Elektra 1980) ★★★★
Classics (Elektra 1985) ★★★★, *The Best Of Tt Doors* (Elektra 1985) ★★★★, *In Concert* (Elektr 1991) ★★★, *Greatest Hits* enhanced CD (Elektr 1996) ★★★★, *The Doors Box Set* 4-CD box se (Elektra 1997) ★★★, *Box Set Part One* (Elektr 1998) ★★★, *Box Set Part Two* (Elektra 1998 ★★★, *The Complete Studio Recordings* 7-CD bc set (Elektra 1999) ★★★, *Essential Rariti* (Elektra 2000) ★★★.

● VIDEOS: *Dance On Fire: Classic Performanc & Greatest Hits* (Pioneer 1985), *Live At Tt Hollywood Bowl* (Elektra 1987), *A Tribute To Ji Morrison* (Warner Home Video 1988), *Live l Europe 1968* (Atlantic 1989), *The Soft Parade: Retrospective* (MCA 1991), *The Doors Are Ope* (Warner Home Video 1992), *The Best Of Tt*

Doors (Universal 1997), *The Doors: 30 Years Commemorative Edition* (Universal 2001), *VH1 Storytellers – The Doors: A Celebration* (Aviva International 2001).
● FURTHER READING: *Jim Morrison And The Doors: An Unauthorized Book*, Mike Jahn. *An American Prayer*, Jim Morrison. *The Lords & The New Creatures*, Jim Morrison. *Jim Morrison Au Dela Des Doors*, Herve Muller. *No One Here Gets Out Alive*, Jerry Hopkins and Danny Sugerman. *Burn Down The Night*, Craig Kee Strete. *Jim Morrison: The Story Of The Doors In Words And Pictures*, Jim Morrison. *Jim Morrison: An Hour For Magic*, Frank Lisciandro. *The Doors: The Illustrated History*, Danny Sugerman. *The Doors*, John Tobler and Andrew Doe. *Jim Morrison: Dark Star*, Dylan Jones. *Images Of Jim Morrison*, Edward Wincentsen. *The End: The Death Of Jim Morrison*, Bob Seymore. *The American Night: The Writings Of Jim Morrison*, Jim Morrison. *The American Night Volume 2*, Jim Morrison. *Morrison: A Feast Of Friends*, Frank Lisciandro. *Light My Fire*, John Densmore. *Riders On The Storm: My Life With Jim Morrison And The Doors*, John Densmore. *The Doors Complete Illustrated Lyrics*, Danny Sugerman (ed.). *Break On Through: The Life And Death Of Jim Morrison*, James Riordan & Jerry Prochnicky. *The Doors: Lyrics, 1965-71*, no author. *The Lizard King: The Essential Jim Morrison*, Jerry Hopkins. *The Doors: Dance On Fire*, Ross Clarke. *The Complete Guide To The Music Of The Doors*, Peter K. Hogan. *The Doors: Moonlight Drive*, Chuck Crisafulli. *Wild Child: Life With Jim Morrison*, Linda Ashcroft. *The Tragic Romance Of Pamela & Jim Morrison*, Patricia Butler. *Light My Fire: My Life With The Doors*, Ray Manzarek.
● FILMS: *American Pop* (1981), *The Doors* (1991).

DORSEY, LEE

b. Irving Lee Dorsey, 24 December 1926, New Orleans, Louisiana, USA, d. 1 December 1986. An ex-boxer (nicknamed 'Kid Chocolate') turned singer, Dorsey first recorded for Joe Banashak's Instant label. One song, 'Lottie Mo', became a regional hit and led to a contract with Fury. The infectious 'Ya Ya' (1961) was a number 1 US R&B and pop Top 10 single. A year later a version by Petula Clark, retitled 'Ya Ya Twist', made the US Top 10 and reached the UK Top 20. Dorsey's next release 'Do-Re-Mi' (regularly performed by Georgie Fame and Dusty Springfield) was also a hit, although this time reaching no higher than 27 in the *Billboard* pop chart, and subsequent releases on Fury Records were less successful. His career stalled temporarily when Fury collapsed, but Dorsey re-emerged in 1965 with the classic 'Ride Your Pony' on the Amy label. Written by Allen Toussaint and produced by Marshall Sehorn, this combination created a series of impeccable singles that blended crisp arrangements with the singer's easy delivery. In 1966 he reached the peak of his success by

gaining four Top 40 hits in the UK, including two Top 10 singles with 'Working In The Coalmine', featuring a wonderful bass riff, and 'Holy Cow', with a mix that enhances Dorsey's melancholic vocals. Both songs reached the US R&B and pop charts. The sweetly doom-laden 'Get Out Of My Life, Woman' was another excellent song that deserved a better commercial fate. 'Everything I Do Gohn Be Funky (From Now On)' became Dorsey's last substantial hit in 1969, although the title track to his 'concept' album, 'Yes We Can', did reach the US R&B Top 50. Dorsey continued to record for Polydor Records and ABC Records and remained a popular figure, so much so that he guested on the 1976 debut album by Southside Johnny And The Asbury Dukes and supported the Clash on their 1980 tour of North America. Sadly, he died of emphysema in December 1986 and deserves to be remembered for the outstanding examples of melodic soul he recorded.
● ALBUMS: *Ya Ya* (Fury 1962) ★★★, *Ride Your Pony* (Amy/Stateside 1966) ★★★, *The New Lee Dorsey* (Amy/Stateside 1966) ★★★★, *Yes We Can* (Polydor 1970) ★★, *Night People* (ABC 1978) ★★.
● COMPILATIONS: *The Best Of Lee Dorsey* (Sue 1965) ★★, *All Ways Funky* (Charly 1982) ★★★, *Gohn Be Funky* (Charly 1985) ★★★, *Holy Cow! The Best Of Lee Dorsey* (1985) ★★★★, *Am I That Easy To Forget?* (Charly 1987) ★★★, *Can You Hear Me* (Charly 1987) ★★★, *Ya Ya* (Relic 1992) ★★★, *Freedom For The Funk* (Charly 1994) ★★★, *Wheelin' & Dealin': The Definitive Collection* (Arista 1998) ★★★★, *Working In A Coalmine: The Very Best Of* (Music Club 2001) ★★★.

DOUGLAS, CRAIG

b. Terence Perkins, 12 August 1941, Newport, Isle Of Wight, England. After moving to London in the mid-50s, Douglas came under the wing of agent Bunny Lewis, appeared on the television show *6.5 Special*, and won a record contract with Decca Records before moving to Dick Rowe's label, Top Rank. Covering American hits was the classic route to chart success, and in 1959 Douglas scored with Dion's 'A Teenager In Love' and reached number 1 with Sam Cooke's 'Only Sixteen'. He co-starred with Helen Shapiro in the film *It's Trad Dad* (1962). Several more hits followed but after four consecutive number 9s with 'A Hundred Pounds Of Clay', 'Time', 'When My Little Girl Is Smiling' and 'Our Favourite Melodies', Douglas felt the sting of the approaching beat boom. He then travelled the world, returning for a career in cabaret in the UK, where he still resides. In 1992 he joined other 60s survivors, including Helen Shapiro, on the Walkin' Back To Happiness Tour. Douglas possesses a good singing voice that should have moved into the classic pop song. His recycled past hits now sound trite and tired, although the voice is still intact.
● ALBUMS: *Craig Douglas* (Top Rank 1960)

★★★, *Bandwagon Ball* (Top Rank 1961) ★★★, *Our Favourite Melodies* (Columbia 1962) ★★★, *Oh Lonesome Me* (Jackson 1981) ★★.
● COMPILATIONS: *The Best Of The EMI Years* (EMI 1993) ★★★, *Only Sixteen* (SFM 1990) ★★★.
● FILMS: *It's Trad, Dad* aka *Ring-A-Ding Rhythm* (1962).

DOVELLS

Originally called the Brooktones, this Philadelphia-based R&B vocal group comprised Len Barry (b. Leonard Borisoff, 6 December 1942, Philadelphia, Pennsylvania, USA), Jerry Summers (b. Jerry Gross), Mike Dennis (b. Michael Freda) and Danny Brooks (b. Jim Meeley). Signed to the Parkway Records label, the group had a US number 2 hit in 1961 with 'Bristol Stomp', succeeded the following year by the Top 40 hits 'Do The Continental', 'Bristol Twistin' Annie' and 'Hully Gully Baby', all of which became dance favourites of the era. Len Barry was responsible for introducing their contemporaneous friends, the Orlons, to Cameo Records, and after the departure of Brooks in 1962, the Dovells achieved another major US hit with a cover of the Phil Upchurch Combo hit 'You Can't Sit Down'. Barry departed from the group later that year and they continued as a trio. The Dovells recorded for MGM Records in the late 60s under the name of the Magistrates, but met with little success.
● ALBUMS: *The Bristol Stomp* (Parkway 1961) ★★★, *All The Hits Of The Teen Groups* (Parkway 1962) ★★★, *Don't Knock The Twist* film soundtrack (Parkway 1962) ★★, *For Your Hully Gully Party* (Parkway 1963) ★★, *You Can't Sit Down* (Parkway 1963) ★★★, with Len Barry *Len Barry Sings With The Dovells* (Cameo 1964) ★★★, *Discotheque* (1965) ★★.
● COMPILATIONS: *Golden Hits Of The Orlons And The Dovells* (1963) ★★★, *The Dovells' Biggest Hits* (Parkway 1965) ★★★, *Cameo/Parkway Sessions* (London 1979) ★★★, *All Their Hits & Much More* (Campary 1996) ★★★.
● FILMS: *Don't Knock The Twist* (1962).

DOWD, TOM

b. *c.*1930. This much-respected engineer began his career in 1947 at New York's Ampex Studio. Here he became acquainted with Ahmet Ertegun, co-founder of Atlantic Records, who invited Dowd, then still a teenager, to join the label. His early sessions included releases by Joe Turner, Ray Charles and Ruth Brown, to whom he brought a clarity hitherto unheard in R&B recordings. Always striving for new techniques, Dowd engineered the first stereo album, by the Wilbur De Paris Dixieland Band, which required customized equipment, including two needles, to play it. His collaborations with producers Leiber And Stoller brought commercial success to the Coasters and Drifters, while in the 60s Dowd engineered

Atlantic's sessions at the Stax Records and Fame studios. His first work with Otis Redding, *Otis Blue*, is generally regarded as the singer's finest album and was responsible for taking the artist into the pop market. Dowd also enjoyed commercially fruitful recordings with the (Young) Rascals, Dusty Springfield and Aretha Franklin and later helped create the label's custom-built studio, Criteria, in Miami. Dowd later became a fully-fledged producer, and during the 70s left the Atlantic staff to pursue freelance work, notably with Eric Clapton on *461 Ocean Boulevard* (1974), *E.C. Was Here* and *There's One In Every Crowd* (both 1975), the Allman Brothers on *Live At Fillmore East* (1971), and Rod Stewart on *Atlantic Crossing* (1975) and *A Night On The Town* (1976).

DOWNLINERS SECT

Formed in 1962, this enduring UK act was initially known as the Downliners, but the original line-up fell apart following a brief tour of US air bases. Founder members Don Craine (b. Michael O'Donnel: vocals/rhythm guitar) and Johnny Sutton (drums) then reshaped the group around Keith Grant (b. Keith Evans: bass) and Terry Gibson (b. Terry Clemson: lead guitar) and, having added the 'Sect' suffix, the quartet secured a residency at London's Studio 51 club. A privately pressed EP, *A Nite In Great Newport Street*, captured their brash interpretation of Chicago R&B, and was a contributory factor to a subsequent recording deal with EMI Records. A version of Jimmy Reed's 'Baby What's Wrong' became the group's first single in June 1964, by which time Ray Sone (harmonica) had been added to the line-up. The Sect's brazen musical approach, redolent of the contemporaneous Pretty Things, was showcased on their debut album, but not only did its irreverence anger purists, Craine's ever present deerstalker hat and autoharp also did little to attract a younger, more fashion-conscious audience. The group, however, seemed unmoved by such considerations and in 1965 further confused any prospective audience with *The Country Sect*, an album of folk and country material, and *The Sect Sing Sick Songs* EP, which included the ghoulish 'I Want My Baby Back', and 'Leader Of The Sect', a riposte to the Shangri-Las' death-disc, 'Leader Of The Pack'. Sone left the group prior to recording *The Rock Sect's In*, which neatly combined almost all of the group's diverse styles. It is now notable for the inclusion of 'Why Don't You Smile Now', which was part-composed by Lou Reed and John Cale prior to their founding the Velvet Underground. The Sect, however, were still struggling to find commercial success and the line-up disintegrated when two pop-oriented singles, 'Glendora' and the Graham Gouldman-penned 'Cost Of Living', failed to chart. Gibson and Sutton were replaced, respectively, by Bob Taylor and Kevin Flanagan, while pianist

Matthew Fisher, later of Procol Harum, was also briefly a member. Craine abandoned his creation following the release of 'I Can't Get Away From You', after which Grant and the prodigal Sutton took the group to Sweden, where they recorded a handful of tracks before disbanding altogether. Craine and Grant revived Sect in 1976 with ex-Black Cat Bones singer Paul Miller and Paul Holm (drums) joining in 1977, in the wake of the pub rock/R&B phenomenon, and the resultant *Showbiz* invoked the gutsy styles of Dr. Feelgood or Count Bishops. With further line-up changes (Holm had now departed, they continued throughout the 80s, and they are also an integral part of the British Invasion All-Stars with former members of the Yardbirds, Creation and Nashville Teens. However, it is their 60s recordings which afford the Sect their cult-based appeal, although they continue to pack out small blues clubs with tried and tested versions of 'Got My Mojo Workin'' and 'Route 66'.

● ALBUMS: *The Sect* (Columbia 1964) ★★★, *The Country Sect* (Columbia 1965) ★★, *The Rock Sect's In* (Columbia 1966) ★★, *Showbiz* (Raw 1979) ★★★, *Sect Appeal* (Indigo 2000) ★★.
● COMPILATIONS: *I Want My Baby Back* (Charly 1978) ★★★, *Be A Sect Maniac* (Out Line 1983) ★★, *Savage Return* (1991) ★★, *The Definitive Downliners Sect – Singles A's & B's* (See For Miles 1994) ★★★.

DR. STRANGELY STRANGE

This Irish folk group – Ivan Pawle (vocals/bass), Tim Booth (vocals/guitar) and Tim Goulding (vocals/keyboards) – made its recording debut in 1969. Although *Kip Of The Serenes* betrayed an obvious debt to the Incredible String Band (both groups were produced by Joe Boyd), the album nonetheless offered a whimsical charm. The trio then embraced a rock-based style on *Heavy Petting*, despite the assistance of traditional musicians Andy Irvine and Johnny Moynahan. Guitarist Gary Moore guested on four of the tracks, including the catchy yet subtly humorous 'I Gave My Love An Apple', but this electric album lacked the purpose of its predecessor. Dr. Strangely Strange disbanded in 1971 following their appearance on Mike Heron's all-star solo album, *Smiling Men With Reputations*. In a strange development, the band regrouped 25 years later for 1997's *Alternative Medicine*.

● ALBUMS: *Kip Of The Serenes* (Island 1969) ★★, *Heavy Petting* (Vertigo 1970) ★★★, *Alternative Medicine* (Big Beat 1997) ★★.

DREAMERS

R&B/doo-wop group the Dreamers formed in 1958 at a family wedding, attended by cousins Frank Cammarata (lead and tenor), Bob Malara (tenor), Luke 'Babe' Beradis (tenor and baritone) and Dominic Canzano (baritone and bass), with the only non-cousin John 'Buddy'

Trancynger (baritone and bass). End Records promptly signed the band to its new offshoot, Goldisc. The sentimental ballad 'Teenagers Vow Of Love' proved popular in the New York area during 1960, when it was released as their debut recording. Afterwards Berardis and Canzano were replaced by Frank Nicholas (from the Meridians) and Frank DiGilio as the group found a new home at Cousins Records. Their first release there was a highly idiosyncratic version of Tony Bennett's 'Because Of You', but when it transferred mid-release to Cousins' May Records subsidiary, the momentum was lost, and with it the chance of an extended musical career. Afterwards, their opportunities to record disappeared as they concentrated on a stage show that proved particularly popular at service bases. They broke up in 1963, but re-formed briefly in the mid-80s.

● ALBUMS: *Yesterday Once More* (Dream 1987) ★★★.

DREAMLOVERS

Formed as the Romances in Philadelphia, Pennsylvania, USA, in 1956, the Dreamlovers notched up two claims to fame: their own US Top 10 doo-wop ballad, 1961's 'When We Get Married', and their role as Chubby Checker's back-up group on his top-selling dance hit 'The Twist'. The quintet initially consisted of lead vocalist William Johnson, tenor Tommy Ricks, tenor Cleveland Hammock Jnr., baritone Conrad Dunn and bass James Ray Dunn. After Johnson was killed in a street fight, Morris Gardner was brought in as his replacement, and a new name, the Dreamlovers, was taken. In 1960, they recorded their first tracks for the Len and V-Tone labels, which failed to sell, but that same year Cameo-Parkway Records hired the group to provide vocals behind Chubby Checker on his future hit, as well as subsequent Cameo label tracks by Checker, Dee Dee Sharp, and the Dovells. The Dreamlovers made their mark in the pop history books with 'When We Get Married', written by Don Hogan, a part-time member of the group. One single for End Records also charted and in 1973, after making a single under the name A Brother's Guiding Light, the group disbanded. Some of the members formed a new Dreamlovers in 1980 and were still performing in the early 90s.

● ALBUMS: *The Bird And Other Golden Dancing Grooves* (Columbia 1963) ★★★.
● COMPILATIONS: *Best Of ...* (Collectables 1990) ★★★, *Best Of ... Volume 2* (Collectables 1990) ★★, *The Best Of ...* (Sequel 1994) ★★★, *The Heritage Masters Plus ...* (Sequel 1997) ★★★.

DRIFTERS

Formed in 1953 in New York, USA, at the behest of Atlantic Records, this influential R&B vocal group was initially envisaged as a vehicle for ex-Dominoes singer Clyde McPhatter (b. Clyde Lensley McPhatter, 15 November 1932,

Durham, North Carolina, USA, d. 13 June 1972, New York City, New York, USA). Gerhart Thrasher, Andrew Thrasher and Bill Pinkney (b. 15 August 1925, Sumter, North Carolina, USA) completed the new quartet which, as Clyde McPhatter and the Drifters, achieved a million-selling number 1 R&B hit with their debut single, 'Money Honey'. Follow-up releases, including 'Such A Night' (number 5 R&B), 'Lucille' (number 7 R&B) and 'Honey Love' (a second chart-topper), also proved highly successful, while the juxtaposition of McPhatter's soaring tenor against the frenzied support of the other members provided a link between gospel and rock 'n' roll styles. The leader's interplay with bassist Pinkney was revelatory, but McPhatter's induction into the armed forces in 1954 was a blow that the Drifters struggled to withstand.

The vocalist opted for a solo career upon leaving the services, and although his former group did enjoy success with 'Adorable' (number 1 R&B 1955), 'Steamboat' (1955), 'Ruby Baby' (1956) and 'Fools Fall In Love' (1957), such recordings featured a variety of lead singers, most notably Johnny Moore (b. 1934, Selma, Alabama, USA, d. 30 December 1998, London, England). Other new members included Charlie Hughes, Bobby Hendricks (who came in as lead tenor when Moore was drafted in 1957), Jimmy Millender and Tommy Evans. A greater emphasis on pop material ensued, but tension between the group and their manager, George Treadwell, resulted in an irrevocable split. Having fired the extant line-up in 1958, Treadwell, who owned the copyright to the Drifters' name, invited another act, the Five Crowns, to adopt the appellation. Charlie Thomas (tenor), Doc Green Jnr. (d. 10 March 1989; bass/baritone) and lead singer Ellsbury Hobbs (b. c.1936, d. 31 May 1996, New York, USA; bass), plus guitarist Reggie Kimber, duly became 'the Drifters'. Hobbs was drafted and replaced by Ben E. King (b. Benjamin Earl Nelson, 28 September 1938, Henderson, North Carolina, USA). The new line-up declared themselves with 'There Goes My Baby'. Written and produced by Leiber And Stoller, this pioneering release featured a Latin rhythm and string section, the first time such embellishments had appeared on an R&B recording. The single not only topped the R&B chart, it also reached number 2 on the US pop listings, and anticipated the 'symphonic' style later developed by Phil Spector.

Further excellent releases followed, notably 'Dance With Me' (1959), 'This Magic Moment' (1960) and 'Save The Last Dance For Me', the latter a million seller which topped the US pop chart and reached number 2 in the UK. However, King left for a solo career following 'I Count The Tears' (1960), and was replaced by Rudy Lewis (b. 27 May 1935, Chicago, Illinois, USA) who fronted the group until his premature death from drug-induced asphyxiation in 1964.

The Drifters continued to enjoy hits during thi period and songs such as 'Sweets For My Sweet' 'When My Little Girl Is Smiling', 'Up On The Roof' and 'On Broadway' were not onl entertaining in their own right, but als provided inspiration, and material, for man emergent British acts, notably the Searchers who took the first-named song to the top of the UK chart. Johnny Moore, who had returned t the line-up in 1963, took over the lead vocal slo from Lewis. 'Under The Boardwalk', recorde the day after the latter's passing, was the Drifters' last US Top 10 pop hit, although th group remained a popular attraction. Bert Bern had taken over production from Leiber an Stoller, and in doing so brought a soul-base urgency to their work, as evinced by 'One Wa Love' and 'Saturday Night At The Movies' (1964) When he left Atlantic to found the Bang labe the Drifters found themselves increasingl overshadowed by newer, more contemporar artists and, bedevilled by lesser material an frequent changes in personnel, the group bega to slip from prominence. However, their caree was revitalized in 1972 when two re-release singles, 'At The Club' and 'Come On Over To M Place', reached the UK Top 10. A new recordin contract with Bell was then secured and Britis songwriters/producers Tony Macauley, Roge Cook and Roger Greenaway fashioned a series o singles redolent of the Drifters' 'classic' era Purists poured scorn on their efforts, but between 1973 and 1975, the group, still led b Moore, enjoyed several UK Top 10 hits including 'Like Sister And Brother', 'Kissin' I The Back Row Of The Movies', 'Down On The Beach Tonight', 'There Goes My First Love' an 'Can I Take You Home Little Girl'. This succes ultimately waned as the decade progressed, an in 1982 their stalwart lead singer Moore briefl left the line-up. He was replaced, paradoxically by Ben E. King, who in turn brought the Drifter back to Atlantic. However, despite completin some new recordings, the group found i impossible to escape its heritage, as evince by the numerous 'hits' repackages and corresponding live appearances on the cabare and nostalgia circuits. They were inducted int the Rock And Roll Hall Of Fame in 1988, a yea after McPhatter's posthumous award.

● ALBUMS: *Save The Last Dance For M* (Atlantic 1961) ★★★★, *The Good Life With Th Drifters* (Atlantic 1964) ★★★★, *The Drifter* (Clarion 1964) ★★, *I'll Take You Where Th Music's Playing* (Atlantic 1965) ★★★, *Souvenir* (Bell 1974) ★★★, *Love Games* (Bell 1975) ★★★ *There Goes My First Love* (Bell 1975) ★★★, *Ever Night's A Saturday Night* (Bell 1976) ★★★ *Greatest Hits Live* (Astan 1984) ★★, *Live A Harvard University* (Showcase 1986) ★★, *Too Ho* (Columbia 1989) ★★.

● COMPILATIONS: *Up On The Roof – The Best O The Drifters* (Atlantic 1963) ★★★★, *Under Th Boardwalk* (Atlantic 1964) ★★★★, *The Drifters*

Golden Hits (Atlantic 1968) ★★★, 24 Original Hits (Atlantic 1975) ★★★★, The Collection (Castle 1987) ★★★, Diamond Series: The Drifters (RCA 1988) ★★★, Best Of The Drifters (Pickwick 1990) ★★★, Let The Boogie Woogie Roll – Greatest Hits (1953-58) (Atlantic 1993) ★★★, All Time Greatest Hits And More (1959-65) (Atlantic 1993) ★★★★, Up On The Roof, On Broadway & Under The Boardwalk (Rhino/Pickwick 1995) ★★★★, Rockin' And Driftin': The Drifters Box 3-CD box set (Rhino 1996) ★★★★, Anthology One: Clyde & The Drifters (Sequel 1996) ★★★★, Anthology Two: Rockin' & Driftin' (Sequel 1996) ★★★, Anthology Three: Save The Last Dance For Me (Sequel 1996) ★★★★, Anthology Four: Up On The Roof (Sequel 1996) ★★★★, Anthology Five: Under The Boardwalk (Sequel 1997) ★★★★, Anthology Six: The Good Life With The Drifters (Sequel 1997) ★★★, Anthology Seven: I'll Take You Where The Music's Playing (Sequel 1997) ★★★★.

● FURTHER READING: The Drifters: The Rise And Fall Of The Black Vocal Group, Bill Millar. Save The Last Dance For Me: The Musical Legacy 1953-92, Tony Allan and Faye Treadwell.

DRISCOLL, JULIE

b. 8 June 1947, London, England. Driscoll was employed by producer/manager Giorgio Gomelsky as administrator of the Yardbirds' fan club when the former suggested a singing career. Her singles included a version of the Lovin' Spoonful's 'Didn't Want To Have To Do It' (1965) and an early Randy Newman composition 'If You Should Ever Leave Me' (1967), but this period is better recalled for Driscoll's membership of Steam Packet, an R&B-styled revue which also featured Long John Baldry, Rod Stewart and the Brian Auger Trinity. Driscoll remained with the last-named act when the larger group folded, and in 1968 had a number 5 hit with Bob Dylan's 'This Wheel's On Fire'. Her striking appearance engendered much publicity, and a cool, almost disinterested vocal style formed the ideal counterpoint to Auger's jazz-based ambitions. 'Jools' left the group following the release of Streetnoise in order to pursue a more radical direction. She contributed to B.B. Blunder's Workers Playtime, and released the excellent 1969, which featured support from members of the Soft Machine, Nucleus and Blossom Toes as well as pianist Keith Tippett, whom the singer later married. She has since appeared on many of her husband's avant garde jazz creations, notably Centipede's Septober Energy (1971) and Ark's expansive Frames (Music For An Imaginary Film) (1978), as well appearing and recording with Maggie Nicols and the experimental vocal quartet Voice. Her first album in over 20 years, Shadow Puppeteer, was released at the end of 1999. Although challenging, it is an interesting suite of avant garde vocal experimentation.

● ALBUMS: with Brian Auger Trinity Open (Marmalade/Atco 1967) ★★★, with Auger Streetnoise (Polydor/Atco 1968) ★★★, 1969 (Polydor 1969) ★★, Keith Tippett, Julie Tippetts, Harry Miller, Frank Perry (Ogun 1975) ★★★, as Julie Tippetts Sunset Glow (Utopia 1976) ★★★, with Keith Tippett, Maggie Nicols Mr Invisible And The Drunken Sheilas (FMP 1986) ★★★, with Keith Tippett Couple In Spirit (Editions EG 1987) ★★★, with Keith Tippett, Willi Kellers Twilight Etchings (FMP 1993) ★★★, with Keith Tippett Couple In Spirit II: Live At The Stadtgarten, Cologne (ASC 1996) ★★★, as Julie Tippetts Shadow Puppeteer (Voiceprint 1999) ★★★.

● COMPILATIONS: with Brian Auger Trinity Jools/Brian (EMI 1968) ★★★, with Auger London 1964-1967 (Charly 1977) ★★★, The Best Of Julie Driscoll (Charly 1982) ★★★, with Auger The Road To Vauxhall 1967-1969 (Charly 1989) ★★★.

DUBLINERS

The Dubliners originally comprised Barney MacKenna (b. 16 December 1939, Donnycarney, Dublin, Eire), Luke Kelly (b. 16 November 1940), Ciaran Bourke (b. 18 February 1936, Dublin, Eire) and former teacher Ronnie Drew (b. 18 September 1935, Dun Laoghaire, Co. Dublin, Eire). They formed in 1962, in the back of O'Donoghue's bar in Merion Row, Dublin, Eire, and were originally named the Ronnie Drew Group. The members were known faces in the city's post-skiffle folk haunts before pooling their assorted singing and fretboard skills in 1962. In 1964 Kelly left the group and went to England where he continued to play on the folk scene. Two other members joined shortly after Kelly had left: Bob Lynch (b. Dublin, Eire) and ex-draughtsman John Shehan (b. 19 May 1939, Dublin, Eire). Dubliners In Concert was the result of a live recording on 4 December 1964 in the concert hall at Cecil Sharp House in London. The band played various theatre bars, made several albums for Transatlantic and gained a strong following on the Irish folk circuit. After an introduction by Dominic Behan, they were signed by manager Phil Solomon and placed on his label, Major Minor. In 1965, the group took the decision to turn professional, and Kelly wanted to return. He replaced Lynch who had wished to stay semi-professional.

Throughout their collective career, each member pursued outside projects – among them Kelly's stints as an actor and MacKenna's 'The Great Comic Genius', a solo single issued after the Irishmen transferred from Transatlantic to the Major Minor label in 1966. During this time they received incessant plugging on the Radio Caroline pirate radio station. Bigoted folk purists were unable to regard them with the same respect as the similarly motivated Clancy Brothers and Tommy Makem after the Dubliners were seen on Top Of The Pops promoting 1967's censored

'Seven Drunken Nights' and, next, 'Black Velvet Band'. 'Never Wed An Old Man' was only a minor hit, but high placings for *A Drop Of The Hard Stuff* and three of its successors in the album list were a firm foundation for the outfit's standing as a thoroughly diverting international concert attraction. A brain haemorrhage forced Bourke's retirement in 1974, and Drew's return to the ranks – after a brief replacement by Jim McCann (b. 26 October 1944, Dublin, Eire) – was delayed by injuries sustained in a road accident. Nevertheless, Drew's trademark vocal, 'like coke being crushed under a door', was heard on the group's 25th anniversary single, 'The Irish Rover', a merger with the Pogues that signalled another sojourn in the Top 10.

● ALBUMS: *Dubliners In Concert* (1965) ★★★, *Finnegan Wakes* (Transatlantic 1966) ★★★★, *A Drop Of The Hard Stuff* (Major Minor 1967) ★★★★, *More Of The Hard Stuff* (Major Minor 1967) ★★★, *The Dubliners* (Major Minor 1968) ★★★★, *Drinkin' And Courtin'* (Major Minor 1968) ★★★, *At It Again* (Major Minor 1968) ★★★, *A Drop Of The Dubliners* (1969) ★★★★, *Live At The Albert Hall* (1969) ★★★, *At Home With The Dubliners* (Columbia 1969) ★★★, *Revolution* (Columbia 1970) ★★★, *Hometown!* (1972) ★★★, *Double Dubliners* (1973) ★★★, *Plain And Simple* (Polydor 1973) ★★★, *The Dubliners Live* (1974) ★★★, *Dubliners Now* (1975) ★★★, *A Parcel Of Rogues* (1976) ★★★, *The Dubliners – Fifteen Years On* (1977) ★★★, *Prodigal Sons* (1983) ★★★, *The Dubliners 25 Years Celebration* (Stylus 1987) ★★★, *The Dubliners Ireland* (1992) ★★★, *Thirty Years A-Greying* (1992) ★★★, *The Original Dubliners* (1993) ★★★, *Milestones* (Transatlantic 1995) ★★★, *Further Along* (Transatlantic 1996) ★★★, *Irish Rover & Other Favorites* (Celtic Pride 1999) ★★★.

● COMPILATIONS: *Best Of The Dubliners* (Transatlantic 1967) ★★★, *Very Best Of The Dubliners* (EMI 1975) ★★★★, *Collection* (Castle 1987) ★★★, *20 Original Greatest Hits* (Chyme 1988) ★★★, *20 Greatest Hits: Dubliners* (Sound 1989) ★★★★, *20 Original Greatest Hits Volume 2* (Chyme 1989) ★★★, *Collection Volume 2* (Castle 1990) ★★★, *The Best Of ...* (Wooden Hill 1996) ★★★, *The Definitive Transatlantic Collection* (Transatlantic 1997) ★★★★, *The Collection* (Camden 1999) ★★★.

● VIDEOS: *Dublin* (Hendring Music Video 1990).

● FURTHER READING: *The Dubliners Scrapbook*, Mary Hardy.

DUMMER, JOHN, BLUES BAND

This UK band came into being in 1965, evolving from the Muskrats and the Grebbells, and lasted until the early 70s, surviving numerous personnel changes. The line-up included prominent British blues artists such as pianist Bob Hall, guitarist Dave Kelly and his sister Jo Ann Kelly, Mike Cooper, and Tony McPhee. The band backed touring American artists John Lee Hooker and Howlin' Wolf, and recorded albums for Mercury and Vertigo between 1969 and 1973. Drummer John Dummer went on to work with English pop vocal group Darts in the mid-70s. In recent years all Dummer's albums have become much sought after items in the collectors' market and currently carry very high prices.

● ALBUMS: *Cabal* (Mercury 1969) ★★★, *John Dummer's Blues Band* (Mercury 1969) ★★★★, *Famous Music Band* (Philips 1970) ★★, *This Is John Dummer* (Philips 1972) ★★★, *Volume II, Try Me One More Time* (Philips 1973) ★★, *Blue* (Vertigo 1973) ★★, *Oobleedooblee Jubilee* (Vertigo 1973) ★★.

DUNBAR, AYNSLEY, RETALIATION

This unit was formed in 1967 by ex-John Mayall drummer Aynsley Dunbar (b. 10 January 1946, Liverpool, England). Having recorded an informal version of Buddy Guy's 'Stone Crazy' with an embryonic line-up of Rod Stewart (vocals), Peter Green (guitar) and Jack Bruce (bass), Dunbar created a permanent Retaliation around ex-Johnny Kidd And The Pirates and Shotgun Express guitarist, John Moorshead, Keith Tillman (bass) and ex-Alexis Korner vocalist, Victor Brox. This line-up completed a solitary single, 'Warning'/'Cobwebs', for the Blue Horizon Records label before Tillman was replaced by Alex Dmochowski (ex-Neil Christian's Crusaders). *The Aynsley Dunbar Retaliation* showcased this superior blues act's self-assurance, with one side devoted to concise performances and the other to freer, instrumentally based workouts. Although it lacked the overall strength of its predecessor, *Doctor Dunbar's Prescription* was another worthwhile album that offered strong original songs and several judicious cover versions. However, the group is best recalled for *Retaliation* aka *To Mum From Aynsley And The Boys*, which was produced by John Mayall. Former Grease Band keyboard player Tommy Eyre was added for this powerful, moody collection on which the unit created some of its finest recordings, including 'Don't Take The Power Away' and 'Journey's End'. In November 1969 Dunbar and Eyre left the group to form Aynsley Dunbar's Blue Whale. A fourth set, *Remains To Be Heard*, was culled from remaining masters and newer recordings by the extant trio with singer Annette Brox, but the Retaliation broke up soon after its completion.

● ALBUMS: *The Aynsley Dunbar Retaliation* (Liberty 1968) ★★★, *Doctor Dunbar's Prescription* (Liberty 1969) ★★★, *Retaliation* aka *To Mum From Aynsley And The Boys* (Liberty 1969) ★★★, *Remains To Be Heard* (Liberty 1970) ★★.

DUPREE, SIMON, AND THE BIG SOUND

Formed in Portsmouth, England, by the Shulman brothers, Derek (b. 11 February 1947,

Glasgow, Scotland; lead vocals), Ray (b. 3 December 1949, Portsmouth, Hampshire, England; lead guitar) and Phil (b. 27 August 1937, Glasgow, Scotland; saxophone, trumpet). The siblings had led several local groups, including the Howlin' Wolves and Roadrunners, before a newly acquired manager suggested the above appellation in 1966. Eric Hine (keyboards), Pete O'Flaherty (bass) and Tony Ransley (drums) completed the line-up which then became a regular attraction in London's soul and R&B clubs. 'I See The Light', 'Reservations' and 'Daytime Nightime' (penned by Manfred Mann drummer Mike Hugg) were all radio hits and a *de rigueur* compendium of dance-floor favourites, *Without Reservations*, preceded the sextet's switch to flower-power with 'Kites'. The group disliked the song's overt trappings – gongs, finger cymbals and Jackie Chan's Chinese narration – but it became their biggest hit, rising to number 9 in 1967. Subsequent singles failed to emulate this success, but the band achieved a measure of notoriety the following year when their psychoactive single, 'We Are The Moles', credited pseudonymously to the Moles, was assumed to be the Beatles in disguise. The unit was disbanded in 1969 when Derek Shulman, tired of being 'Simon Dupree', suffered a nervous breakdown. Upon recovery he joined his brothers in Gentle Giant.

● ALBUMS: *Without Reservations* (Parlophone 1967) ★★.

● COMPILATIONS: *Amen* (EMI 1982) ★★, *Kites* (See For Miles 1987) ★★.

DUPREES

A rock 'n' roll vocal group from Jersey City, New Jersey, USA. One of the most pop-sounding of the Italian-American groups that were in abundance during the late 50s and early 60s, the Duprees specialized in recording updated versions of old pop hits in a smooth style with a slight rock 'n' roll feel. The group comprised lead vocalist Joseph (Joey Vann) Canzano (d. 28 February 1984), Mike Arnone, Tom Bialablow, John Salvato, and Joe Santollo (d. 3 June 1981). The Duprees signed with Coed, who with their other acts, notably the Rivieras, revived old pop hits using teenage vocal harmony groups to convey them to the new rock 'n' roll audience. The Duprees' biggest hit was their 1962 remake of the old Jo Stafford hit, 'You Belong To Me' (number 7 pop). The best of their other seven chart entries were 'My Own True Love' (number 13 pop, a vocal version of 'Tara's Theme') and 'Have You Heard?' (number 18 pop), a remake of the decade-old Joni James hit. The Duprees' last national hit record was in 1965. Recording for Jerry Ross's Heritage/Colossus label complex during 1968/9, the Duprees failed to chart with the same formula of updating old pop hits, such as Bobby Helms' 'My Special Angel' and Don Rondo's 'Two Different Worlds'. The group's last recording was 'Delicious', a disco song for RCA in

1975. Santollo died in 1981 and Canzano in 1984, but remnants of the Duprees have subsequently built a successful career playing the oldies doo-wop circuit in the New York and New Jersey area.

● ALBUMS: *You Belong To Me* (Coed 1962) ★★★, *Have You Heard* (Coed 1963) ★★★, *Total Recall* (Heritage 1968) ★★, *Take Me As I Am* (1st Choice 1984) ★★, *Silver Anniversary* (1987) ★★.

● COMPILATIONS: *The Best Of The Duprees* (Rhino 1990) ★★★, *The Best Of The Duprees* (Collectables 1990) ★★★, *The Best Of The Duprees* (Sequel 1993) ★★★, *Delicious: The Heritage Years* (Sequel 1994) ★★★, *The Complete Coed Masters* (Ace 1996) ★★★.

DYLAN, BOB

b. Robert Allen Zimmerman, 24 May 1941, Duluth, Minnesota, USA. Bob Dylan is unquestionably one of the most influential figures in the history of popular music. He is the writer of scores of classic songs and is generally regarded as the man who brought literacy to rock lyrics. The son of the middle-class proprietor of an electrical and furniture store, as a teenager, living in Hibbing, Minnesota, he was always intrigued by the romanticism of the outsider. He loved James Dean movies, liked riding motorcycles and wearing biker gear, and listened to R&B music on radio stations transmitting from the south. A keen fan of folk singer Odetta and country legend Hank Williams, he was also captivated by early rock 'n' roll. When he began playing music himself, with schoolfriends in bands such as the Golden Chords and Elston Gunn And The Rock Boppers, it was as a clumsy but enthusiastic piano player, and it was at this time that he declared his ambition in a high school yearbook 'to join Little Richard'. In 1959, he began visiting Minneapolis at weekends and on his graduation from high school, enrolled at the University of Minnesota there, although he spent most of his time hanging around with local musicians in the beatnik coffee-houses of the Dinkytown area. It was in Minneapolis that he first discovered blues music, and he began to incorporate occasional blues tunes into the primarily traditional material that made up his repertoire as an apprentice folk singer.

Zimmerman, who by this time had changed his name to Dylan, played occasionally at local clubs but was, by most accounts, a confident but, at best, unremarkable performer. In the summer of 1960, however, Dylan spent some time in Denver, and developed as an artist in several extraordinary and important ways. First, he adopted a persona based upon the Woody Guthrie romantic hobo figure in the movie *Bound For Glory*. Dylan had learned about Guthrie in Minnesota and had quickly devoured and memorised as many Guthrie songs as he could. In Denver, he assumed a new voice, began speaking with an Okie twang, and adopted a new 'hard travellin'' appearance. Second, in Denver Dylan had met Jesse Fuller, a blues performer who played guitar and harmonica simultaneously by using a harp rack. Dylan was intrigued and soon afterwards began to teach himself to do the same. By the time he returned to Minneapolis, he had developed remarkably as a performer. By now sure that he intended to make a living as a professional musician, he returned briefly to Hibbing, then set out, via Madison and Chicago, for New York, where he arrived on 24 January 1961.

For a completely unknown and still very raw performer, Dylan's impact on the folk scene of Greenwich Village was immediate and enormous. He captivated anyone who saw him with his energy, his charisma and his rough-edged authenticity. He spun stories about his background and family history, weaving a tangled web of tall tales and myths about who he was and where he was from. He played in the coffeehouses of the Village, including Cafe Wha?, The Commons, The Gaslight and, most importantly, Gerde's Folk City, where he made his first professional appearance, supporting John Lee Hooker, in April 1961. He was also paid for playing harmonica on records by Harry Belafonte and Carolyn Hester, as a result of which he came the attention of producer John Hammond, who signed him to Columbia Records in Autumn 1961. At the same time, a gig at Gerde's was reviewed favourably in the *New York Times* by Robert Shelton, who declared that Bob Dylan was clearly destined for fortune and fame. His first album, called simply *Bob Dylan*, was released in March 1962. It presented a collection of folk and blues standards, often about death and sorrows and the trials of life, songs that had been included in Dylan's repertoire over the past year or so, performed with gusto and an impressive degree of sensitivity for a 20-year-old. But it was the inclusion of two of his own compositions, most notably the mature and affectionate tribute, 'Song To Woody', that pointed the way forward. Over the next few months, Dylan wrote dozens of songs, many of them 'topical' songs. Encouraged by his girlfriend, Suze Rotolo, Dylan became interested in, and was subsequently adopted by, the Civil Rights movement. His song 'Blowin' In The Wind', written in April 1962, was to be the most famous of his protest songs and was included on his second album, *The Freewheelin' Bob Dylan*, released in May 1963. In the meantime, Dylan had written and recorded several other noteworthy early political songs, including 'Masters Of War' and 'A Hard Rain's A-Gonna Fall', and, during a nine-month separation from Suze, one of his greatest early love songs, 'Don't Think Twice, It's All Right'.

At the end of 1962, he recorded a single, a rock 'n' roll song called 'Mixed Up Confusion', with backing musicians. The record was quickly deleted, apparently because Dylan's manager,

Albert Grossman, saw that the way forward for his charge was not as a rocker, but as an earnest acoustic folky. Similarly, tracks that had been recorded for Dylan's second album with backing musicians were scrapped, although the liner notes which commented on them and identified the players remained carelessly unrevised. The *Freewheelin'* record was so long in coming that four original song choices were substituted at the last moment by other, more newly composed songs. One of the tracks omitted was 'Talking John Birch Society Blues', which Dylan had been controversially banned from singing on the *Ed Sullivan Show* in May 1963. The attendant publicity did no harm whatsoever to Dylan's stature as a radical new 'anti-establishment' voice. At the same time, Grossman's shrewd decision to have a somewhat saccharine version of 'Blowin' In The Wind' recorded by Peter, Paul And Mary also paid off, the record becoming a huge hit in the USA, and bringing Dylan's name to national, and indeed international, attention for the first time.

At the end of 1962, Dylan flew to London to appear in the long-lost BBC Television play, *The Madhouse On Castle Street*. The experience did little to further his career as an actor, but while he was in London, he learned many English folk songs, particularly from musician Martin Carthy, whose tunes he subsequently 'adapted'. Thus, 'Scarborough Fair' was reworked as 'Girl From The North Country', 'Lord Franklin' as 'Bob Dylan's 'Dream', and 'Nottamun Town' as 'Masters Of War'. The songs continued to pour out and singers began to queue up to record them. It was at this time that Joan Baez first began to play a prominent part in Dylan's life. Already a successful folk-singer, Baez covered Dylan songs at a rapid rate, and proclaimed his genius at every opportunity. Soon she was introducing him to her audience and the two became lovers, the King and Queen of folk music. Dylan's songwriting became more astute and wordy as the months passed. Biblical and other literary imagery began to be pressed into service in songs like 'When The Ship Comes In' and the anthemic 'Times They Are A-Changin'', this last written a day or two after Dylan had sung 'Only A Pawn In Their Game' in front of 400,000 people at the March On Washington, 28 August 1963. Indeed, the very next day, Dylan read in the local newspaper of the murder of black waitress Hattie Carroll, which inspired his best, and arguably the last, of his protest songs, 'The Lonesome Death Of Hattie Carroll', included on his third album, *The Times They Are A-Changin'*, released in January 1964.

Dylan's songwriting perspectives underwent a huge change in 1964. Now finally separated from Suze Rotolo, disenchanted with much of the petty politics of the Village, and becoming increasingly frustrated with the 'spokesman of a generation' tag that had been hung around his neck, the ever-restless Dylan sloughed off the expectations of the old folky crowd, and, influenced by his reading the poetry of John Keats and French symbolist Arthur Rimbaud, began to expand his own poetic consciousness. He then wrote the songs that made up his fourth record, *Another Side Of Bob Dylan* – including the disavowal of his past, 'My Back Pages', and the Illuminations-inspired 'Chimes Of Freedom' – while yet newer songs such as 'Mr Tambourine Man' (which he recorded for but did not include on *Another Side*), 'Gates Of Eden' and 'It's Alright Ma, I'm Only Bleeding', which he began to include in concert performances over the next few weeks, dazzled with their lyrical complexity and literary sophistication.

Here, then, was Dylan the poet, and here the arguments about the relative merits of high art and popular art began. The years 1964-66 were, inarguably, Dylan's greatest as a writer and as a performer; they were also his most influential years and many artists today still cite the three albums that followed, *Bringing It All Back Home* and *Highway 61 Revisited* from 1965 and 1966's double album *Blonde On Blonde* as being seminal in their own musical development.

Another Side Of Bob Dylan was to be Dylan's last solo acoustic album for almost 30 years. Intrigued by what the Beatles were doing – he had visited London again to play one concert at the Royal Festival Hall in May 1964 – and particularly excited by the Animals' 'folk-rock' cover version of 'House Of The Rising Sun', a track Dylan himself had included on his debut album, he and producer Tom Wilson fleshed out some of the *Bringing It All Back Home* songs with rock 'n' roll backings – the proto-rap 'Subterranean Homesick Blues' and 'Maggie's Farm', for instance. However, the song that was perhaps Dylan's most important mid-60s composition, 'Like A Rolling Stone', was written immediately after the final series of acoustic concerts played in the UK in April and May 1965, and commemorated in D.A. Pennebaker's famous documentary film, *Don't Look Back*. Dylan said that he began to write 'Like A Rolling Stone' having decided to 'quit' singing and playing. The lyrics to the song emerged from six pages of stream-of-consciousness 'vomit'; the sound of the single emerged from the immortal combination of Chicago blues guitarist Michael Bloomfield, bass man Harvey Brooks and fledgling organ-player Al Kooper. 'Like A Rolling Stone' was producer Tom Wilson's last, and greatest, Dylan track. At six minutes, it destroyed the formula of the sub-three-minute single forever. It was a huge hit and was played, alongside the Byrds' equally momentous version of 'Mr Tambourine Man', all over the radio in the summer of 1965.

Consequently, it should have come as no surprise to those who went to see Dylan at the Newport Folk Festival on 25 July that he was now a fully fledged folk rocker; but, apparently, it did. Backed by the Paul Butterfield Blues Band,

Dylan's supposedly 'new sound' – although admittedly it was his first concert with supporting musicians – was met with a storm of bewilderment and hostility. Stories vary as to how much Dylan was booed that night, and why, but Dylan seemed to find the experience both exhilarating and liberating. If, after the UK tour, he had felt ready to quit, now he was ready to start again, to tour the world with a band and to take his music, and himself, to the farthest reaches of experience, just like Rimbaud. Dylan's discovery of the Hawks, a Canadian group who had been playing roadhouses and funky bars until introductions were made via John Hammond Jnr. and Albert Grossman's secretary Mary Martin, was one of those pieces of alchemical magic that happen hermetically. The Hawks, later to become the Band, comprised Robbie Robertson, Richard Manuel, Garth Hudson, Rick Danko and Levon Helm. Dylan's songs and the Hawks' sound were made for each other. After a couple of stormy warm-up gigs, they took to the road in the autumn of 1965 and travelled through the USA, then, via Hawaii, to Australia, on to Scandinavia and finally to Britain, with a hop over to Paris for a birthday show, in May 1966. Dylan was deranged and dynamic, the group wild and mercurial. Their set, the second half of a show that opened with Dylan playing acoustically to a reverentially silent house, was provocative and perplexing for many. It was certainly the loudest thing anyone had ever heard, and, almost inevitably, the electric set was greeted with mayhem and dismay. Drummer Levon Helm was so disheartened by the ferocity of the booing that he quit before the turn of the year – drummers Sandy Konikoff and Mickey Jones completed the tour.

Offstage, Dylan was spinning out of control, not sleeping, not eating, looking wasted and apparently heading rapidly for rock 'n' roll oblivion. Pennebaker again filmed the tour, this time in Dylan's employ. The 'official' record of the tour was the rarely seen *Eat The Document*, a film originally commissioned by ABC TV. The unofficial version compiled by Pennebaker himself was *You Know Something Is Happening*. 'What was happening,' says Pennebaker, 'was drugs . . .'

Dylan was physically exhausted when he returned to America in June 1966, but had to complete the film and finish *Tarantula*, the book that was overdue for Macmillan. He owed Columbia two more albums before his contract expired, and was booked to play a series of concerts right up to the end of the year in increasingly bigger venues, including Shea Stadium. Then, on 29 July 1966, Dylan was injured in a motorcycle accident near his home in Bearsville, near Woodstock, upper New York State.

Was there really a motorcycle accident? Dylan still claims there was. He hurt his neck and had treatment. More importantly, the accident allowed him to shrug off the responsibilities that had been lined up on his behalf by manager Grossman. By now, the relationship between Dylan and Grossman was less than cordial and litigation between the two of them was ongoing until Grossman's death almost 20 years later. Dylan was nursed through his convalescence by his wife, Sara – they had been married privately in November 1965 – and was visited only rarely. Rumours spread that Dylan would never perform again. Journalists began to prowl around the estate, looking for some answers but finding no-one to ask.

After several months of doing little but feeding cats, bringing up young children, and cutting off his hair, Dylan was joined in the Bearsville area by the Hawks, who rented a house called Big Pink in West Saugerties. Every day they met and played music. It was the final therapy that Dylan needed. A huge amount of material was recorded in the basement of Big Pink – old folk songs, old pop songs, old country songs – and, eventually, from these sessions came a clutch of new compositions, which came to be known generically as *The Basement Tapes*. Some of the songs were surreally comic – 'Please Mrs Henry', 'Quinn The Eskimo', 'Million Dollar Bash'; others were soul-searchingly introspective musings on fame, guilt, responsibility and redemption – 'Tears Of Rage', 'Too Much Of Nothing', 'I Shall Be Released'. Distributed by Dylan's music publisher on what became a widely bootlegged tape, many of these songs were covered by, and became hits for, other artists and groups. Dylan's own recordings of some of the songs were not issued until 1975.

In January 1968, Dylan appeared with the Hawks, at this time renamed the Crackers, at the Woody Guthrie Memorial Concert at Carnegie Hall in New York. The following month *John Wesley Harding* was released, a stark, heavily moralistic collection of deceptively simple songs such as 'All Along The Watchtower', 'The Ballad Of Frankie Lee And Judas Priest', 'Dear Landlord' and 'Drifter's Escape', many of which can be heard as allegorical reflections on the events of the previous couple of years. The record's final song, however, 'I'll Be Your Baby Tonight', was unambivalently simple and presaged the warmer love songs of the frustratingly brief *Nashville Skyline*, released in April 1969. After the chilly monochrome of *John Wesley Harding*, here was Dylan in full colour, smiling, apparently at ease at last, and singing in a deep, rich voice, which, oddly, some of his oldest acquaintances maintained was how 'Bobby' used to sound back in Minnesota when he was first learning how to sing. 'Lay Lady Lay', 'Tonight I'll Be Staying Here With You', a duet with Johnny Cash on 'Girl From The North Country' – it was all easy on the ear, lyrically unsophisticated and, for some, far too twee. Nevertheless, *Nashville Skyline* was an

extraordinarily influential record. It brought a new hipness to the hopelessly out-of-fashion Nashville (where, incidentally and incongruously, *Blonde On Blonde* had also been recorded) and it heralded a new genre of music – country rock – and a new movement that coincided with, or perhaps helped to spawn, the Woodstock Festival of the same summer. A return to simplicity and a love that was in truth only a distant relation of that psychedelically celebrated by the hippies in San Francisco a couple of years earlier, to whom Dylan paid no heed whatsoever. There are, therefore, no photographs of Bob Dylan in kaftan, beads and flowers or paisley bell-bottoms.

Dylan chose to avoid the Woodstock Festival (though the Band – the newly rechristened Crackers, who by now had two of their own albums, *Music From Big Pink* and *The Band*, to their credit – did play there), but he did play at the Isle Of Wight Festival on 31 August 1969. In a baggy Hank Williams-style white suit, it was a completely different Bob Dylan from the fright-haired, rabbit-suited marionette who had howled and screamed in the face of audience hostility at the Albert Hall more than three years earlier. This newly humble Dylan cooed and crooned an ever-so-polite, if ever-so-unexciting, set of songs and in doing so left the audience just as bewildered as those who had booed back in 1966. But that bewilderment was as nothing compared with the puzzlement that greeted the release, in June 1970, of *Self Portrait*. This new record most closely resembled the Dylan album that preceded it – the bootleg collection *Great White Wonder*. Both were double albums; both offered mish-mash mix-ups of undistinguished live tracks, alternate takes, odd cover versions, botched beginnings and endings. Some even heard *Self Portrait*'s opening track, 'All The Tired Horses', as a caustic comment on the bootleggers' exploitation of ages-old material – was Dylan complaining 'How'm I supposed to get any ridin' done?' or 'writin' done?' There was little new material on *Self Portrait*, but there was 'Blue Moon'. The critics howled. Old fans were (yes, once again) dismayed. *Rolling Stone* magazine was vicious: 'What is this shit?', the review by Greil Marcus began.

'We've Got Dylan Back Again', wrote Ralph Gleason in the same magazine just four months later, heralding the hastily released *New Morning* as a 'return to form'. There was Al Kooper; there was the Dylan drawl; there were some slightly surreal lyrics; there was a bunch of new songs; but these were restless times for Dylan. He had left Woodstock and returned to New York, to the heart of Greenwich Village, having bought a townhouse on MacDougal Street. It was, he later realized, an error, especially when A.J. Weberman, the world's first Dylanologist, turned up on his doorstep to rifle through his garbage in search of clues to unlocking the secret code of his poetry and (unintentionally) scaring his kids.

Leberman saw it as his duty to shake Dylan out of his mid-life lethargy and reanimate him into embracing political and moral causes, and remarkably, met with some success. On 1 August 1971, Dylan appeared at the Concert For Bangladesh benefit, his only live performance between 1970 and 1974, and in November of the same year released 'George Jackson', a stridently powerful protest song, as a single. Little else happened for some time. Dylan cropped up so frequently as a guest on other people's albums that it ceased to be seen as a coup. He began to explore his Jewishness and was famously pictured at the Wailing Wall in Jerusalem. In 1973 he played, with some aplomb, the enigmatic Alias in Sam Peckinpah's brilliant *Pat Garrett & Billy The Kid*, for which movie he also supplied the soundtrack music, including the hit single 'Knockin' On Heaven's Door'.

Also in 1973, in a move that confounded industry-watchers, Dylan left Columbia Records, having been persuaded by David Geffen of the advantages of signing to his Asylum Records label. The disadvantage, some might say, was the cruelly spurned Columbia's misguided desire to exact a kind of revenge. They put out the shambolic *Dylan*, an album of out-takes and warm-ups, presumably intending either to embarrass Dylan beyond endurance or to steal some of the thunder from his first Asylum album, *Planet Waves*, newly recorded with the Band. In terms of the records' merits, there was no contest, although a few of the *Dylan* tracks were actually quite interesting, and the only embarrassment suffered was by Columbia, who were widely condemned for their petty-minded peevishness.

US tour followed. Tickets were sold by post and attracted six million applications. Everybody who went to the shows agreed that Dylan and the Band were fantastic. The recorded evidence, *Before The Flood*, also released by Asylum, certainly oozes energy, but lacks subtlety: Dylan seemed to be trying too hard, pushing everything too fast. It is good, but not that good.

That is *that* good, unarguably and incontestably, is *Blood On The Tracks*. Originally recorded (for Columbia, no hard feelings, etc.) in late 1974, Dylan substituted some of the songs with versions reworked in Minnesota over the Christmas period. They were his finest compositions since the *Blonde On Blonde* material. 'Tangled Up In Blue', 'Idiot Wind', 'If You See Her Say Hello', 'Shelter From The Storm', 'Simple Twist Of Fate', 'You're A Big Girl Now' . . . one masterpiece followed another. It was not so much a divorce album as a separation album (Dylan's divorce from Sara wasn't completed until 1977), but it was certainly a diary of despair. 'Pain sure brings out the best in people, doesn't it?' Dylan sang in 1966's 'She's Your Lover Now'; *Blood On The Tracks* gave the lie to all those who had argued that Dylan was a spent force.

If Dylan the writer was reborn with *Blood On The Tracks*, Dylan the performer re-emerged on the Rolling Thunder Revue. A travelling medicine show, moving from small town to small town, playing just about unannounced, the line-up extensive and variable, but basically consisting of Dylan, Joan Baez, Roger McGuinn, Rambling Jack Elliott, Allen Ginsberg, Mick Ronson, Bobby Neuwirth and Ronee Blakely, the Revue was conceived in the Village in the summer of 1975 and hit the road in New England, in Plymouth, Massachusetts, on 31 October. It was a long wished-for dream, and Dylan, face painted white, hat festooned with flowers, was inspired, delirious, imbued with a new vitality and singing like a demon. Some of those great performances are preserved in the four-hour movie *Renaldo And Clara*, the self-examination through charade and music that Dylan edited through 1977 and defended staunchly and passionately on its release to the almost inevitable uncomprehending or downright hostile barrage of criticism that greeted it. The Revue reconvened for a 1976 tour of the south, musical glimpses of its excitement being issued on the live album *Hard Rain*. A focal point of the Revue had been the case of wrongly imprisoned boxer Hurricane Carter, to whose cause Dylan had been recruited after having read his book, *The Sixteenth Round*. Dylan's song 'Hurricane' was included just about every night in the 1975 Revue, and also on the follow-up album to *Blood On the Tracks*, *Desire*, which also offered several songs co-written with Jacques Levy. *Desire* was an understandably popular record; 'Isis', 'Black Diamond Bay', 'Romance In Durango' represented some of Dylan's strongest narrative ballads.

This was further borne out by the songs on *Street Legal*, the 1978 album that was released in the middle of a year-long stint with the biggest touring band with which Dylan ever played. Some critics dubbed it the alimony tour, but considerably more funds could have been generated if Dylan had gone out with a four-piece. Many of the old songs were imaginatively reworked in dramatic new arrangements, although the recording is of poor quality. *At Budokan*, released in 1979, documents the tour at its outset; the Earl's Court and Blackbushe concerts caught it memorably mid-stream; while an exhausting trip around the USA in the latter part of the year seemed to bring equal amounts of acclaim and disapproval. 'Dylan's gone Vegas', some reviewers moaned. True, he wore trousers with lightening flashes while behind him flutes and bongos competed for attention with synthesizers and keyboards, but some of the performances were quite wonderful and the new songs, 'Senor (Tales Of Yankee Power)', 'Changing Of The Guard', 'Where Are You Tonight? (Journey Through Dark Heat)', 'True Love Tends To Forget', sounded terrific.

In 1979, Dylan became a born-again Christian

and released an album of fervently evangelical songs, *Slow Train Coming*, recorded in Muscle Shoals, Alabama, with Jerry Wexler and Barry Beckett, and featuring Mark Knopfler and Pick Withers from Dire Straits, and in November and December played a series of powerful concerts featuring nothing but his new Christian material. Cries of disbelief? Howls of protest? Well, naturally; but the record was crisp and contemporary-sounding, the songs strong, the performances admirable (Dylan was to win a Grammy for best rock vocal performance on 'Gotta Serve Somebody'), and the concerts, which continued in 1980, among the most powerful and spine-tingling as any in his entire career. The second Christian album, *Saved*, was less impressive, however, and the fervour of the earlier months was more muted by the end of the year. Gradually, old songs began to be reworked into the live set and by the time of 1981's *Shot Of Love*, it was no longer clear whether or not – or to what extent – Dylan's faith remained firm. The sarcastic 'Property Of Jesus' and the thumping 'Dead Man, Dead Man' suggested that not much had changed, but the retrospective 'In The Summertime' and the prevaricating 'Every Grain Of Sand' hinted otherwise.

After three turbulent years, it was hardly surprising that Dylan dropped from sight for most of 1982, but the following year he was back in the studio, again with Mark Knopfler, having, it was subsequently established, written a prolific amount of new material. The album that resulted, *Infidels*, released in October 1983, received a mixed reception. Some songs were strong – 'I&I' 'Jokerman' among them – others relatively unimpressive. Dylan entered the video age by making promos for 'Sweetheart Like You' and 'Jokerman', but did not seem too excited about it. Rumours persisted about his having abandoned Christianity and re-embraced the Jewish faith. His name began to be linked with the ultra-orthodox Lubavitcher sect: the inner sleeve of *Infidels* pictured him touching the soil of a hill above Jerusalem, while 'Neighbourhood Bully' was a fairly transparent defence of Israel's policies towards its neighbours. Dylan, as ever, refused to confirm or deny his state of spiritual health.

In 1984, he appeared live on the David Letterman television show, giving one of his most extraordinary and thrilling performances, backed by a ragged and raw Los Angeles trio, the Cruzados. However, when, a few weeks later, he played his first concert tour for three years, visiting Europe on a package with Santana put together by impresario Bill Graham, Dylan's band was disappointingly longer in the tooth (with Mick Taylor on guitar and Ian McLagan on organ). An unimpressive souvenir album, *Real Live*, released in December, was most notable for its inclusion of a substantially rewritten version of 'Tangled Up In Blue'.

The following year opened with Dyla[n] contributing to the 'We Are The World' USA Fo[r] Africa single, and in summer, after the release o[f] *Empire Burlesque*, a patchy record somewha[t] over-produced by remix specialist Arthur Bake[r] but boasting the beautiful acoustic closer 'Dar[k] Eyes', he was the top-of-the-bill act at Live Aid. Initially, Dylan had been supposed to play wit[h] a band, but then was asked to perform solo, t[o] aid the logistics of the grande finale. In th[e] event, he recruited Ron Wood and Keit[h] Richards from the Rolling Stones to help hi[m] out. The results were disastrous. Hopelessl[y] under-rehearsed and hampered both by the lac[k] of monitors and the racket of the stage being se[t] up behind the curtain in front of which the[y] were performing, the trio were a shambles[.] Dylan, it was muttered later, must have been th[e] only artist to appear in front of a billio[n] television viewers worldwide and end up wit[h] fewer fans than he had when he started. Matter[s] were redeemed a little, however, at the Farm Ai[d] concert in September, an event set up as a resu[lt] of Dylan's somewhat gauche onstage 'charit[y] begins at home' appeal at Live Aid. Backed b[y] Tom Petty And The Heartbreakers, it wa[s] immediately apparent that Dylan had found hi[s] most sympathetic and adaptable backing ban[d] since the Hawks. The year ended positively, to[o] with the release of the five album (3-CD[)] retrospective feast, *Biograph*, featuring man[y] previously unreleased tracks.

The collaboration with Tom Petty having gon[e] so well, it was decided that the partnershi[p] should continue, and a tour was announced t[o] begin in New Zealand, Australia and Japan wit[h] more shows to follow in the USA. It was th[e] summer's hottest ticket and the Petty/Dyla[n] partnership thrived for a further year with [a] European tour, the first shows of which saw[e] Dylan appearing in Israel for the very first tim[e] Unfortunately, the opening show in Tel Aviv wa[s] not well received either by the audience or b[y] the press, whose reviews were vitriolic. Th[e] second show in Jerusalem was altogether mor[e] enjoyable, until the explosion of the PA syste[m] brought the concert to an abrupt end.

Between the two tours, Dylan appeared in hi[s] second feature, the Richard Marquand-directe[d] *Hearts Of Fire*, made in England and Canada an[d] co-starring Rupert Everett and Fiona Flanaga[n] Dylan played Billy Parker, a washed-up one-tim[e] mega-star who in all but one respect (th[e] washed-up bit) bore an uncanny resemblance t[o] Dylan himself. Despite Dylan's best efforts – an[d] he was arguably the best thing in the movie [–] the film was a clunker. Hoots of derision marre[d] the premiere in October 1987 and its theatrica[l] release was limited to one week in the UK. Th[e] poor movie was preceded by a poor albu[m] *Knocked Out Loaded*, which only had the epi[c] song 'Brownsville Girl', co-written wit[h] playwright Sam Shepard, to recommend it.

Increasingly, it appeared that Dylan's bes[t]

attentions were being devoted to his concerts. The shows with Tom Petty had been triumphant. Dylan also shared the bill with the Grateful Dead at several stadium venues, and learned from the experience. He envied their ability to keep on playing shows year in, year out, commanding a following wherever and whenever they played. He liked their two drummers and also admired the way they varied their set each night, playing different songs as and when they felt like it. These peculiarly Deadian aspects of live performance were soon incorporated into Dylan's own concert philosophy.

Down In The Groove, an album of mostly cover versions of old songs, was released in the same month, June 1988, as Dylan played the first shows of what was to become known as the Never-Ending Tour. Backed by a three-piece band led by G.E. Smith, Dylan had stripped down his sound and his songs and was, once again, seemingly re-energized. His appetite for work had never been greater, and this same year he found himself in the unlikely company of George Harrison, Jeff Lynne, Tom Petty and Roy Orbison as one of the Traveling Wilburys, a jokey rock band assembled on a whim in the spring. Their album, *Volume 1*, on which Dylan's voice was as prominent as anyone's, was, unexpectedly, a huge commercial success.

His Wilbury star in the ascendancy, Dylan's next album emerged as his best of the 80s. *Oh Mercy*, recorded informally in New Orleans and idiosyncratically produced by Daniel Lanois, sounded fresh and good, and the songs were as strong a bunch as Dylan had come up with in a long time. However, for reasons best known only to himself, it transpired from bootleg tapes that Dylan had been excluding many excellent songs from the albums he had been releasing in the 80s, most notably the masterpiece 'Blind Willie McTell', which was recorded for, but not included on, *Infidels*. Indeed, despite the evident quality of the songs on *Oh Mercy* – 'Shooting Star' and 'Most Of The Time' were, for once, both songs of experience, evidence of a maturity that many fans had long been wishing for in Dylan's songwriting – it turned out that Dylan was still holding back. The crashing, turbulent 'Series Of Dreams' and the powerful 'Dignity' were products of the Lanois sessions, but were not used on *Oh Mercy*. Instead, both later appeared on compilation albums.

Not without its merits (the title track and 'God Knows' are still live staples, while 'Born In Time' is a particularly emotional love song), the nursery-rhyme-style *Under The Red Sky*, released in September 1990, was for most a relative, probably inevitable, disappointment, as was the Roy-Orbison-bereft Wilburys follow-up, *Volume 3*. However, the touring continued, with Dylan's performances becoming increasingly erratic – sometimes splendid, often shambolic. It was one thing being spontaneous and improvisatory, but it was quite another being

slapdash and incompetent. Dylan could be either, and was sometimes both. His audiences began to dwindle, his reputation started to suffer. The three-volume collection of out-takes and rarities, *The Bootleg Series, Volumes 1-3 (Rare And Unreleased) 1961-1991*, redeemed him somewhat, as did the 30th Anniversary Celebration concert in Madison Square Garden in 1992, in which some of rock music's greats and not-so-greats paid tribute to Dylan's past achievements as a songwriter.

There was, however, precious little present songwriting to celebrate. Both *Good As I Been To You* (1992) and *World Gone Wrong* (1993), although admirable, were collections of old folk and blues material, performed, for the first time since 1964, solo and acoustically. *Greatest Hits Volume 3* (1994) threw together a clump of old non-hits and *Unplugged* (1995) saw Dylan revisiting a set of predominantly 60s songs in desultory fashion. Even the most ambitious CD-ROM so far, *Highway 61 Interactive*, while seemingly pointing to a Dylan-full future, wallowed nostalgically in, and was marketed on the strength of, past glories. Although Dylan's live performances became more coherent and controlled, his choice of material grew less imaginative through 1994, while many shows in 1995, which saw continued improvement in form, consisted almost entirely of songs written some 30 years earlier.

In 1997 it was rumoured that Dylan was knocking on heaven's door. Although he had suffered a serious inflammation of the heart muscles he was discharged from hospital after a short time, eliciting his priceless quote to the press: 'I really thought I'd be seeing Elvis soon'. It was time, perhaps, for doubters to begin to consign Dylan to the pages of history. However, as time has often proved, you can never write off Bob Dylan. He is a devil for hopping out of the hearse on the way to the cemetery. The Lanois-produced *Time Out Of Mind* was a dark and sombre recording, with Dylan reflecting over lost love and hints of death. It was his best work for many years, and although his voice continues to decline, the strength of melody and lyric were remarkable. One outstanding example of Dylan's continuing ability to write a tender love song was 'To Make You Feel My Love'. Both Garth Brooks and Trisha Yearwood recorded excellent versions for the movie soundtrack *Hope Floats* in 1998 (Brooks took it to number 1 on the US country chart). That same year, the official release of the legendary bootleg, recorded at the Manchester Free Trade Hall in 1966, received a staggering amount of praise from the press. This was completely justified because the concert of familiar songs reminded and confirmed his towering importance as a songwriter. Dylan's first recording of the new millennium was 'Things Have Changed', the Grammy-award winning main and end-title theme for Curtis Hanson's movie *Wonder Boys*.

Love And Theft received generous praise, far in excess of its overall quality. Only 'Mississippi' could be classed as a great Dylan song. Whatever quality his musical output is in the future he is unquestionably the greatest musical poet of the 20th century.

● ALBUMS: *Bob Dylan* (Columbia 1962) ★★★, *The Freewheelin' Bob Dylan* (Columbia 1963) ★★★★, *The Times They Are A-Changin'* (Columbia 1964) ★★★★, *Another Side Of Bob Dylan* (Columbia 1964) ★★★★, *Bringing It All Back Home* (Columbia 1965) ★★★★★, *Highway 61 Revisited* (Columbia 1965) ★★★★★, *Blonde On Blonde* (Columbia 1966) ★★★★★, *John Wesley Harding* (Columbia 1968) ★★★★, *Nashville Skyline* (Columbia 1969) ★★★, *Self Portrait* (Columbia 1970) ★★, *New Morning* (Columbia 1970) ★★★, *Pat Garrett & Billy The Kid* (Columbia 1973) ★★★, *Dylan (A Fool Such As I)* (Columbia 1973) ★, *Planet Waves* (Island 1974) ★★★★, with The Band *Before The Flood* (Asylum 1974) ★★★, *Blood On The Tracks* (Columbia 1975) ★★★★★, with The Band *The Basement Tapes* (Columbia 1975) ★★★, *Desire* (Columbia 1976) ★★★★★, *Hard Rain* (Columbia 1976) ★★, *Street Legal* (Columbia 1978) ★★★, *Slow Train Coming* (Columbia 1979) ★★★, *At Budokan* (Columbia 1979) ★★★, *Saved* (Columbia 1980) ★, *Shot Of Love* (Columbia 1981) ★★, *Infidels* (Columbia 1983) ★★★, *Real Live* (Columbia 1984) ★, *Empire Burlesque* (Columbia 1985) ★★, *Knocked Out Loaded* (Columbia 1986) ★★, *Down In The Groove* (Columbia 1988) ★, with the Grateful Dead *Dylan And The Dead* (Columbia 1989) ★, *Oh Mercy* (Columbia 1989) ★★★★, *Under The Red Sky* (Columbia 1990) ★★★, *Good As I Been To You* (Columbia 1992) ★★★, *World Gone Wrong* (Columbia 1993) ★★, *The 30th Anniversary Concert Celebration* (Columbia 1993) ★★★★, *MTV Unplugged* (Columbia 1995) ★★, *Time Out Of Mind* (Columbia 1997) ★★★★, *The Bootleg Series Vol. 4: Bob Dylan Live 1966: The "Royal Albert Hall" Concert* (Columbia/Legacy 1998) ★★★★★, *Live 1961/2000* (Columbia 2001) ★★★, *Love And Theft* (Columbia 2001) ★★★.

● COMPILATIONS: *Bob Dylan's Greatest Hits* (Columbia 1967) ★★★★★, *More Bob Dylan Greatest Hits* (Columbia 1972) ★★★★, *Biograph* 5-LP box set (Columbia 1985) ★★★★, *The Bootleg Series, Volumes 1-3, Rare And Unreleased 1961-1991* 3-LP box set (Columbia/Legacy 1991) ★★★★★, *Greatest Hits Volume 3* (Columbia 1994) ★★★, *The Best Of Bob Dylan Volume 2* (Columbia 2000) ★★★, *The Essential Bob Dylan* (Columbia 2000) ★★★★.

● VIDEOS: *Hard To Handle* (Virgin Vision 1987), *Don't Look Back* (Virgin Vision 1988), *30th Anniversary Concert Celebration* (1993), *MTV Unplugged* (1995).

● FURTHER READING: Like all major artists there are many books available. The editor's recommendation would contain three essential works: *No Direction Home*, Robert Shelton. *Song*

& Dance Man III, Michael Gray. *Wanted Man: In Search Of Bob Dylan*, John Bauldie. Others: *Bob Dylan In His Own Write*, Bob Dylan. *Eleven Outlined Epitaphs & Off The Top Of My Head*, Bob Dylan. *Folk-Rock: The Bob Dylan Story*, Sy and Barbra Ribakove. *Don't Look Back*, D.A. Pennebaker. *Bob Dylan: An Intimate Biography*, Anthony Scaduto. *Positively Main Street: An Unorthodox View Of Bob Dylan*, Toby Thompson. *Bob Dylan: A Retrospective*, Craig McGregor. *Song And Dance Man: The Art Of Bob Dylan*, Michael Gray. *Bob Dylan: Writings And Drawings*, Bob Dylan. *Knocking On Dylan's Door*, Rolling Stone editors. *Rolling Thunder Logbook*, Sam Shepard. *On The Road With Bob Dylan: Rolling With The Thunder*, Larry Sloman. *Bob Dylan: The Illustrated Record*, Alan Rinzler. *Bob Dylan In His Own Words*, Miles. *Bob Dylan: An Illustrated Discography*, Stuart Hoggard and Jim Shields. *Bob Dylan: An Illustrated History*, Michael Gross. *Bob Dylan: His Unreleased Recordings*, Paul Cable. *Dylan: What Happened?*, Paul Williams. *Conclusions On The Wall: New Essays On Bob Dylan*, Liz Thomson. *Twenty Years Of Recording: The Bob Dylan Reference Book*, Michael Krogsgaard. *Voice Without Restraint: A Study Of Bob Dylan's Lyrics And Their Background*, John Herdman. *Bob Dylan: From A Hard Rain To A Slow Train*, Tim Dowley and Barry Dunnage. *No Direction Home: The Life And Music Of Bob Dylan*, Robert Shelton. *Bringing It All Back Home*, Robbie Wolliver. *All Across The Telegraph: A Bob Dylan Handbook*, Michael Gray and John Bauldie (eds.). *Raging Glory*, Dennis R. Liff. *Bob Dylan: Stolen Moments*, Clinton Heylin. *Jokerman: Reading The Lyrics Of Bob Dylan*, Aidan Day. *Dylan: A Biography*, Bob Spitz. *Performing Artist: The Music Of Bob Dylan Volume 1, 1960-1973*, Paul Williams. *Dylan Companion*, Elizabeth M. Thomson and David Gutman. *Lyrics: 1962-1985*, Bob Dylan. *Bob Dylan: Performing Artist*, Paul Williams. *Oh No! Not Another Bob Dylan Book*, Patrick Humphries and John Bauldie. *Absolutely Dylan*, Patrick Humphries and John Bauldie. *Dylan: Behind The Shades*, Clinton Heylin. *Bob Dylan: A Portrait Of The Artist's Early Years*, Daniel Kramer. *Wanted Man: In Search Of Bob Dylan*, John Bauldie (ed.). *Bob Dylan: In His Own Words*, Chris Williams. *Tangled Up In Tapes*, Glen Dundas. *Hard Rain: A Dylan Commentary*, Tim Riley. *Complete Guide To The Music Of Bob Dylan*, Patrick Humphries. *Bob Dylan Drawn Blank* (Folio of drawings), Bob Dylan. *Watching The River Flow (1966-1995)*, Paul Williams. *Like The Night: Bob Dylan And The Road To The Manchester Free Trade Hall*, C.P. Lee. *Classic Bob Dylan 1962-69*, Andy Gill. *Touched By The Hand Of Bob: Epiphanal Bob Dylan Experiences From A Buick Six*, Dave Henderson. *Song & Dance Man III: The Art Of Bob Dylan*, Michael Gray. *Like A Bullet Of Light: The Films Of Bob Dylan*, C.P. Lee. *Encounters With Bob Dylan: If You See Him, Say Hello*, Tracy Johnson (ed.). *The Bob Dylan Companion: Four Decades Of Commentary*, Carl

Benson (ed.). *Down The Highway: The Life Of Bob Dylan*, Howard Sounes. *Razor's Edge: Bob Dylan And The Never Ending Tour*, Andrew Muir. *Positively 4th Street: The Lives And Times Of Joan Baez, Bob Dylan, Mimi Baez Fariña And Richard Fariña*, David Hadju. *The Nightingale's Code: A Poetic Study Of Bob Dylan*, John Gibbens. *Isis: A Bob Dylan Anthology*, Derek Barker (ed.).
● FILMS: *Don't Look Back* (1966), *Eat The Document* (1971), *Pat Garrett & Billy The Kid* (1973), *Renaldo And Clara* (1978), *Hearts Of Fire* (1987).

EARLS

Although 'Remember Then' was their only hit, the Earls were one of the most accomplished white doo-wop groups of the early 60s. The lead singer Larry Chance (b. Larry Figueiredo, 19 October 1940, Philadelphia, Pennsylvania, USA) formed the group in New York's Bronx area in the late 50s. The other members were first tenor Robert Del Din (b. 1942), second tenor Eddie Harder (b. 1942), baritone Larry Palumbo (b. 1941) and bass John Wray (b. 1939). For their first single, the group revived the Harptones' 1954 R&B hit 'Life Is But A Dream', released by the local Rome label in 1961. The following year, the group moved to another New York label, Old Town, and made 'Remember Then' which reached the Top 30. The Earls continued to release singles on Old Town until 1965, but the only record to make an impact was a maudlin version of 'I Believe', dedicated to Palumbo, who had died in a parachute accident. With various personnel changes, including the addition of Hank DiScuillo on guitar, Chance continued to lead the group on occasional records for Mr G and ABC Records. With their big hit on numerous oldies compilations during the 70s, the Earls appeared on rock revival shows. 'Remember Then' was a UK Top 20 hit in 1979 for revivalist band Showaddywaddy.
● ALBUMS: *Remember Me Baby* (Old Town 1963) ★★★.
● COMPILATIONS: *Remember Rome: The Early Years* (Crystal Ball 1982) ★★, *Remember Then! The Best Of The Earls* (Ace 1992) ★★★, *Remember Me Baby: The Golden Classic Edition* (Collectables 1992) ★★, *Remember Then!* (Collectables 1999) ★★★.

EARTH OPERA

Formed in Boston, New England, USA, in 1967, Earth Opera revolved around Peter Rowan (b. 4 July 1942, Boston, Massachusetts, USA; vocals, guitar) and David Grisman (b. 1945, Hackensack, New Jersey, USA; mandocello, mandolin). Both were veterans of the bluegrass and old-time circuit; Rowan with Bill Monroe's Blue Grass Boys and the Mother State Bay Entertainers, and Grisman as leader of the New York Ramblers and a member of the Even Dozen Jug Band. The two musicians worked as a duo, performing Rowan's original songs, before adding John Nagy (bass) and Bill Stevenson (keyboards, vibes). *Earth Opera* was produced by fellow folk music associate Peter Siegel, who shared an unerring empathy with the material. Rowan's lyrical, highly visual compositions were enhanced by his unusual, expressive tenor, particularly on the graphic 'Death By Fire' and 'The Child Bride'. Elsewhere the material reflected the questioning rootlessness prevalent in the immediate post-1967 era. Drummer Paul Dillon was then added to the line-up, but Bill Stevenson left the group prior to recording a second album.

Although worthy, *The Great American Eagle Tragedy* featured a roughshod horn section which altered the tone of several songs, with only one track, 'Mad Lydia's Waltz', retaining the delicacy of the previous set. The collection was marked by its uncompromising title-track, a lengthy impassioned attack on the Vietnam War. A compulsive example of the genre, replete with images of terror and madness, this accomplished piece overshadowed much of the remaining content, although Rowan's talent was equally obvious on 'Home To You' and 'Sanctuary From The Law'. The former contained the memorably quirky lyric, 'It's tired and I'm getting late'. Earth Opera broke up soon after the set was issued. Rowan later joined Sea Train, before enjoying a successful solo career, while Grisman became a leading figure in traditional music circles.
● ALBUMS: *Earth Opera* (Elektra 1968) ★★, *The Great American Eagle Tragedy* (Elektra 1969) ★★★.

EAST OF EDEN

Formed in 1968, this versatile UK outfit best known line-up comprised Dave Arbus (violin), Ron Caines (alto saxophone), Geoff Nicholson (lead guitar), Andy Sneddon (bass) and Geoff Britton (drums). Their debut, *Mercator Projected*, offered an imaginative brew of progressive rock, jazz and neo-eastern predilections, but this robust, *avant garde* direction contrasted with the novelty tag placed on the band in the wake of their surprise hit single, 'Jig A Jig'. This lightweight, fiddle-based instrumental reached number 7 in the UK in April 1971, and in the process confused prospective audiences. East Of Eden was plagued by personnel problems and by 1972 had shed every original member. Joe O'Donnell (violin), Martin Fisher (bass) and Jeff Allen (drums, ex-Beatstalkers) then maintained the band's name in Europe before their demise later in the decade. Meanwhile, Arbus gained further acclaim for his contributions to the Who's *Who's Next* while Geoff Britton later joined Wings.
● ALBUMS: *Mercator Projected* (Deram 1969) ★★★★, *Snafu* (Deram 1970) ★★★, *East Of Eden* (Harvest 1971) ★★★, *New Leaf* (Harvest 1971) ★★, *Another Eden* (1975) ★★, *Here We Go Again* (1976) ★★ *It's The Climate* (1976) ★★, *Silver Park* (1978) ★★.
● COMPILATIONS: *The World Of East Of Eden* (Deram 1971) ★★★, *Masters Of Rock* (EMI 1975) ★★★, *Things* (1976) ★★★, *Kalipse* (Castle 2000) ★★.

EASYBEATS

Formed in Sydney, Australia, in 1964, this beat group comprised Harry Vanda (b. Harry Vandenberg, 22 March 1947, The Hague, The Netherlands; guitar), Dick Diamonde (b. Dingeman Van Der Sluys, 28 December 1947, Hilversum, The Netherlands; bass), Steve Wright (b. 20 December 1948, Leeds, Yorkshire, England; vocals), George Young (b. 6 November 1947, Glasgow, Scotland; guitar) and Gordon 'Snowy' Fleet (b. 16 August 1946, Bootle, Lancashire, England; drums). Originally known as the Starfighters, they changed their name after the arrival of Fleet, who modelled their new style on that of the Liverpool beat groups of the period. After a series of hits in their homeland, including six number 1 singles, the group relocated to England in the summer of 1966 and were offered the opportunity to work with top pop producer Shel Talmy. The combination resulted in one of the all-time great beat group singles of the 60s: 'Friday On My Mind'. Strident guitars, clever counter-harmonies and a super-strong beat were the ingredients that provided the disc with its power. Following a solid push on pirate radio, it peaked at number 6 in the UK. Unfortunately, the group found it difficult to follow up their hit and their prospects were not helped after splitting with Talmy during the recording of their first UK-released album. When they finally returned to the UK charts in 1968, it was with the ballad 'Hello, How Are You', the mood of which contrasted sharply with that of their first hit. Lack of morale and gradual line-up changes, including new drummer Tony Cahil, subtly transformed the group into a vehicle for key members Vanda and Young, who were already writing material for other artists. In 1969, after an Australian tour, the Easybeats split up. Ironically, they enjoyed a US hit some months later with 'St. Louis'.

In the wake of their demise, Vanda/Young went into production, released records under a variety of pseudonyms and were largely responsible for the Australian success of such artists as John Paul Jones and William Shakespeare. George Young and his two brothers, Angus and Malcolm were part of the original line-up of AC/DC, while Vanda/Young found success in their own right during the early 80s as Flash In The Pan. Wright enjoyed brief solo success in Australia with tracks such as Vanda and Young's 'Evie', but his career was blighted by addiction. The Easybeats undertook a national reunion tour in 1986, the flavour of which can be sampled on the final five tracks of 1995's *Live Studio And Stage* release.
● ALBUMS: *Easy* (Parlophone 1965) ★★, *It's 2 Easy* (Parlophone 1966) ★★, *Volume 3* (Parlophone 1966) ★★★, *Good Friday* (United Artists 1967) ★★★, *Vigil* (United Artists 1968) ★★, *Friends* (Polydor 1969) ★★, *Live Studio And Stage* (Raven 1995) ★★.

● COMPILATIONS: *The Shame Just Drained* Alberts 1977), *Absolute Anthology* (Alberts 1980) ★★★, *Best Of The Easybeats* (Rhino 1986) ★★★, *The Best Of The Easybeats* (Repertoire 1995) ★★, *Aussie Beat That Shook The World* Repertoire 1996) ★★★, *Gonna Have A Good Time* (Sin-Drome 1999) ★★★, *The Definitive Anthology* (Repertoire 2000) ★★★.

ECLECTION

Formed in London, England, in 1967, Eclection took their name from the contrasting backgrounds of its original line-up. Although Mike Rosen (guitar), Kerilee Male (vocals), Georg Hultgren (bass) and Gerry Conway (b. 11 September 1947, Kings Lynn, Norfolk, England; drums) were not well-known figures, guitarist Trevor Lucas (b. 25 December 1943, Bungaree, Victoria, Australia, d. 4 February 1989, Sydney, Australia) had established himself on the folk circuit following his arrival from Australia. The quintet used his undoubted talent to forge an imaginative folk rock style which used influences from both British and American sources. Male left the group in October 1968, following the release of Eclection's debut album. Her replacement was Dorris Henderson, a black American singer who had previously recorded two folk-influenced collections with guitarist John Renbourn. A further change occurred when John 'Poli' Palmer succeeded Rosen, but the group was sadly unable to fulfil its obvious potential. In October 1969 Palmer left to join Family, and Eclection simply folded. Lucas and Conway soon resurfaced in Fotheringay, while Hultgren later changed his surname to Kajanus and found fame with the pop group Sailor. Rosen joined the early line-up of the Average White Band. In the 70s Henderson attempted to revive Eclection with different musicians, but she was largely unsuccessful.

ALBUMS: *Eclection* (Elektra 1968) ★★★.

EDDY, DUANE

26 April 1938, Corning, New York, USA. The legendary simple 'twangy' guitar sound of Duane Eddy has made him one of rock 'n' roll's most famous instrumental artists. The sound was created after hearing Bill Justis' famous 'Raunchy' (the song that George Harrison first learned to play). Together with producer Lee Hazlewood, Eddy co-wrote a deluge of hits mixed with versions of standards, using the bass strings of his Gretsch guitar recorded through an echo chamber. The debut 'Movin' 'N' Groovin' made the lower end of the US chart, and for the next six years Eddy repeated this formula with greater success. His backing group, the Rebel Rousers was a tight, experienced band with a prominent saxophone sound played by Jim Horn and Steve Douglas, completed by pianist Larry Knechtel. Among their greatest hits were 'Rebel-Rouser', 'Shazam', 'Peter Gunn', 'Ballad Of Paladin' and 'Theme From Dixie'. The latter was a variation

on the Civil War standard written in 1860. One of Eddy's most memorable hits was the superlative theme music for the film *Because They're Young*, brilliantly combining his bass notes with evocative strings. The song has been used by UK disc jockey Johnny Walker as his theme music for over 25 years and this classic still sounds fresh. Eddy's '(Dance With The) Guitar Man' was another major hit, which was unusual for the fact that the song had lyrics, sung by a female group. Eddy's albums played heavily on the use of 'twang' in the title, but that was exactly what the fans wanted.

The hits dried up in 1964 at the dawn of the Beatles' invasion, and for many years his sound was out of fashion. An attempt in the contemporary market was lambasted with *Duane Goes Dylan*. Apart from producing Phil Everly's excellent *Star Spangled Springer* in 1973, Eddy travelled the revival circuit, always finding a small but loyal audience in the UK. Tony Macauley wrote 'Play Me Like You Play Your Guitar' for him in 1975, and after more than a decade he was back in the UK Top 10. He slipped back into relative obscurity but returned to the charts in 1986 when he was flattered to be asked to play with the electro-synthesizer band Art Of Noise, all the more complimentary was that it was his song, 'Peter Gunn'. The following year Jeff Lynne produced his first album for many years, being joined by Paul McCartney, George Harrison and Ry Cooder, all paying tribute to the man who should have legal copyright on the word 'twang'.

● ALBUMS: *Have 'Twangy' Guitar Will Travel* (Jamie 1958) ★★★, *Especially For You* (Jamie 1958) ★★★★, *The 'Twang's The 'Thang'* (Jamie 1959) ★★★★, *Songs Of Our Heritage* (Jamie 1960) ★★★, *$1,000,000 Worth Of Twang* (Jamie 1960) ★★★★, *Girls! Girls! Girls!* (Jamie 1961) ★★★, *$1,000,000 Worth Of Twang, Volume 2* (Jamie 1962) ★★★, *Twistin' And Twangin'* (RCA-Victor 1962) ★★★★, *Twisting With Duane Eddy* (Jamie 1962) ★★★, *Twangy Guitar-Silky Strings* (RCA-Victor 1962) ★★★★, *Dance With The Guitar Man* (RCA-Victor 1963) ★★★★, *Duane Eddy & The Rebels In Person* (Jamie 1963) ★★★, *Surfin' With Duane Eddy* (Jamie 1963) ★★★, *Twang A Country Song* (RCA-Victor 1963) ★★, *Twanging Up A Storm!* (RCA-Victor 1963) ★★★, *Lonely Guitar* (RCA-Victor 1964) ★★★, *Water Skiing* (RCA-Victor 1964) ★★, *Twangsville* (RCA-Victor 1965) ★★, *Twangin' The Golden Hits* (RCA-Victor 1965) ★★★, *Duane Goes Bob Dylan* (RCA-Victor 1965) ★★, *Duane A Go Go* (RCA-Victor 1965) ★★, *Biggest Twang Of Them All* (RCA-Victor 1966) ★★, *Roaring Twangies* (RCA-Victor 1967) ★★, *Twangy Guitar* (1970) ★★★, *Duane Eddy* (1987) ★★★.
● COMPILATIONS: *16 Greatest Hits* (Jamie 1964) ★★★★, *The Best Of Duane Eddy* (RCA-Victor 1966) ★★★★, *The Vintage Years* (Sire 1975) ★★★, *Legends Of Rock* (Deram 1975) ★★★, *Twenty Terrific Twangies* (RCA 1981) ★★★, *Greatest Hits* (1991) ★★★★, *Twang Thang: The*

Duane Eddy Anthology (1993) ★★★★, *That Classic Twang* 2-CD set (Bear Family 1994) ★★★★, *Twangin' From Phoenix To L.A. – The Jamie Years* 5-CD box set (Bear Family 1995) ★★★★★, *Rebel Rouser* (Sony 1995) ★★★, *Boss Guitar* (Camden 1997) ★★★, *Deep In The Heart Of Twangsville: The Complete RCA Victor Recordings* 6-CD box set (Bear Family 1999) ★★★.
● FILMS: *Because They're Young* (1960).

EDSELS

This R&B vocal ensemble from Campbell, Ohio, USA, led by George Jones Jnr. (lead vocal), also included Marshall Sewell, James Reynolds, and brothers Harry and Larry Greene. They were named after the popular make of car. In 1959, they auditioned for a local music publisher who helped them secure a recording contract. Their debut single was the fast doo-wop outing 'Rama Lama Ding Dong' (written by Jones), originally released under the incorrect title of 'Lama Rama Ding Dong'. It was a local hit but flopped nationally. Two years later, when Marcels had a big hit with the similar-sounding doo-wop version of 'Blue Moon', a disc jockey was reminded of 'Rama Lama Ding Dong' and started playing it. Demand grew and it was re-released under its correct title and became a hit in the USA. By this time the Edsels had moved on and could not capitalize on their success. Although the original failed in the UK the song was a hit in 1978 when it was covered by Rocky Sharpe And The Replays.
● COMPILATIONS: *Rama Lama Ding Dong* (Relic 1993) ★★.

EDWARDS, JACKIE

b. Wilfred Edwards, 1938, Jamaica, West Indies, d. 15 August 1992. The honeyed tones of Jackie Edwards graced hundreds of ska, R&B, soul, rocksteady, reggae and ballad recordings since he composed and sang 'Your Eyes Are Dreaming', a sentimental ballad, and the gentle Latin-beat 'Tell Me Darling', for future Island Records owner Chris Blackwell in 1959. Probably the most accomplished romantic singer and songwriter that Jamaica ever produced, he always had enough soul in his voice to escape the descent into schmaltz. In 1962, when Blackwell set up Island Records in London, Edwards made the trip to Britain with him. At Island in the early years, his duties included not only singing and songwriting, but also delivering boxes of ska records by bus to the capital's suburban shops. His persistence paid off when, in 1966, the Spencer Davis Group enjoyed two consecutive UK number 1 pop hits with his now classic compositions, 'Keep On Running' and 'Somebody Help Me'. In more recent years he continued to issue records whose standards of production were variable, but on which his crooning justified his sobriquet of 'the original cool ruler'.

● ALBUMS: *The Most Of ...* (Island 1963) ★★★ *Stand Up For Jesus* (Island 1964) ★★★, *Come Or Home* (Island 1966) ★★★★, *By Demand* (Island 1967) ★★★, *Premature Golden Sands* (Island 1967) ★★★, with Millie Small *Pledging My Love* (1967) ★★★, *I Do Love You* (Trojan 1973) ★★★ with Hortense Ellis *Let It Be Me* (Jamaica Sound 1978) ★★★, *Sincerely* (Trojan 1978) ★★, *King Of The Ghetto* (Black Music 1983) ★★, *Original Cool Ruler* (Vista Sounds 1983) ★★, *Christmas Feeling* (TP Records 2001) ★★.
● COMPILATIONS: *The Best Of* (Island 1966 ★★★, with Millie Small *The Best Of Jackie & Millie* (1968) ★★★, *20 Super Hits* (Sonic Sounds 1994) ★★★, *Do It Sweet* (House Of Reggae 1996 ★★★, *Escape* (Jamaican Authentic Classics 1998) ★★.

EIRE APPARENT

Originally known as the People, this Irish quartet – Mike Cox (lead guitar), Ernie Graham (vocals, guitar), Chris Stewart (bass) and Dave Lutton (drums) – came to prominence in 1967 when they were signed by the Mike Jeffery/Chas Chandler management team which they shared with Jimi Hendrix and the Soft Machine. Hendrix produced and guested on the group's sole album, *Sunrise*. A crafted blend of pop and neo-psychedelia, this underrated collection featured several excellent performances, including the vibrant 'Yes I Need Someone'. Eire Apparent supported Hendrix on a gruelling US tour, but split up after its completion. Ernie Graham later joined Help Yourself, before recording a solo album on which he was backed by Brinsley Schwarz Although he did not record with them, Henry McCullough was another former member of Eire Apparent. This respected guitarist subsequently featured in the Grease Band and Wings.
● ALBUMS: *Sunrise* (Buddah 1969) ★★★.

ELBERT, DONNIE

b. 25 May 1936, New Orleans, Louisiana, USA, d 31 January 1989. Elbert's prolific career began in the 50s as a member of the Vibraharps. His first solo hit, 'What Can I Do?', was released in 1957, but the singer's career was interrupted by a spell in the US Army. Discharged in 1961 recordings for Parkway Records and Checker then followed, before Elbert joined the labels Gateway/ Upstate, co-founded by Robert Schachner in 1964. His reputation was secured by 'Run Little Girl' and 'A Little Piece Of Leather', compulsive performances highlighting Elbert's irrepressible falsetto. The latter single became a standard in UK soul clubs when it was released on the Sue label and on the strength of this popularity Elbert went to the UK where he married and settled. The singer pursued his career with several releases, including an album of Otis Redding cover versions, *Tribute To A King*. Elbert returned to the USA in 197

iough his pounding version of the Supremes'
iere Did Our Love Go?' (1972) was recorded
London. A hit on both sides of the Atlantic, it
s followed in 1972 by 'I Can't Help Myself',
ther reworking of a Tamla/Motown classic.
ert's last UK chart entry came with a new,
inferior, version of 'A Little Bit Of Leather'
72), although he continued to appear in the
R&B listings up until 1977. Elbert later
ved to Canada where he became an A&R
ctor with PolyGram Records.
LBUMS: *The Sensational Donnie Elbert Sings*
ng 1959) ★★★, *Tribute To A King* (Gateway
8) ★★, *Where Did Our Love Go?* (All
tinum 1971) ★★, *Have I Sinned?* (1971) ★★,
> *In The Name Of Love* (Avco 1972) ★★, *A*
le Bit Of Leather (1972) ★★, *Dancin' The*
ht Away (1977) ★★.
COMPILATIONS: *The Roots Of Donnie Elbert*
ber 1973) ★★★★, *Greatest Hits Of Donnie*
ert (Collectables 1996) ★★★★.

ECTRIC FLAG
 brief career of the much-vaunted Electric
g was begun in 1967 by Mike Bloomfield (b.
hael Bernard Bloomfield, 28 July 1944,
cago, Illinois, USA, d. 15 February 1981, San
ncisco, California, USA), following his
arture from the influential Paul Butterfield
es Band. The original band comprised
omfield, Buddy Miles (b. George Miles, 5
tember 1945, Omaha, Nebraska, USA;
ms, vocals), Nick Gravenites (b. Chicago,
nois, USA; vocals), Barry Goldberg (b.
cago, Illinois, USA; keyboards), Harvey
oks (b. Harvey Goldstein, USA; bass), Peter
zza (tenor saxophone), Marcus Doubleday
mpet) and Herbie Rich (baritone
phone). All members were well-seasoned
fessionals coming from a variety of musical
kgrounds. The group recorded the
ndtrack for the 1967 movie *The Trip* before
king a noble live debut at the same year's
nterey Pop Festival. Their excellent *A Long*
e Comin' was released in 1968 with
itional members Stemziel (Stemsy) Hunter
 Mike Fonfara, and was a significant hit in
 USA. The tight, brassy-tinged blues
nbers were laced with Bloomfield's sparse
 bitingly crisp Fender Stratocaster guitar.
ir cover version of 'Killing Floor' was a fine
mple of the sound that Bloomfield was
ing to achieve, but the band was unable to
ow this release and immediately began to
olve, with Goldberg and Bloomfield the first
go. Miles attempted to hold the band
ether but the second album was a pale
dow of their debut, with only 'See To Your
ghbour' showing signs of a unified
formance. Miles then left to form the Buddy
es Express, while Gravenites became a
gwriting legend in San Francisco. Brooks,
owing years of session work that included
 Bloomfield/Al Kooper/Stephen Stills *Super*

Session, reappeared as a member of Sky. An
abortive Electric Flag reunion produced the
lacklustre and inappropriately titled *The Band*
Kept Playing.
● ALBUMS: *The Trip* film soundtrack (Sidewalk
1967) ★★, *A Long Time Comin'* (Columbia 1968)
★★★★, *The Electric Flag* (Columbia 1969) ★★,
The Band Kept Playing (Atlantic 1974) ★, *Small*
Town Blues (Columbia River 2000) ★★.
● COMPILATIONS: *The Best Of The Electric Flag*
(Columbia 1971) ★★★, *Old Glory: The Best Of*
Electric Flag - An American Music Band
(Columbia/Legacy 1995) ★★★★.

ELECTRIC PRUNES
Formed in Los Angeles, California, USA in 1965,
the Electric Prunes originally consisted of Jim
Lowe (b. San Luis Obispo, California, USA;
vocals, guitar, autoharp), Ken Williams (b. Long
Beach, California, USA; lead guitar), James
'Weasel' Spagnola (b. Cleveland, Ohio, USA;
guitar), Mark Tulin (b. Philadelphia,
Pennsylvania, USA; bass) and Michael Weakley
aka Quint (drums), although the latter was
quickly replaced by Preston Ritter (b. Stockton,
California, USA). The quintet made its debut
with the low-key 'Ain't It Hard', before
achieving two US Top 20 hits with 'I Had Too
Much To Dream (Last Night)' and 'Get Me To
The World On Time'. These exciting singles
blended the drive of garage/punk rock, the
rhythmic pulse of the Rolling Stones and the
experimentalism of the emerging psychedelic
movement. Such performances were enhanced
by Dave Hassinger's accomplished production.
The Prunes' debut album was hampered by
indifferent material, but the excellent follow-
up, *Underground*, featured three of the group's
finest achievements, 'Hideaway', 'The Great
Banana Hoax' and 'Long Day's Flight'. However,
the Prunes were sadly unable to sustain their
hit profile and grew increasingly unhappy with
the artistic restrictions placed on them by
management and producer.
Ritter was replaced by the prodigal Quint before
the remaining original members dropped out
during sessions for *Mass In F Minor*. This
acclaimed combination of Gregorian styles and
acid rock was composed and arranged by David
Axelrod, who fulfilled the same role on a follow-
up set, *Release Of An Oath*. An entirely new
line-up – Ron Morgan (guitar), Mark Kincaid (b.
Topeka, Kansas, USA; guitar), Brett Wade (b.
Vancouver, British Columbia, Canada; bass) and
Richard Whetstone (b. Hutchinson, Kansas,
USA; drums) – completed the lacklustre *Just*
Good Old Rock 'N' Roll, which bore no trace of
the founding line-up's sense of adventure. The
Electric Prunes' name was then abandoned.
● ALBUMS: *The Electric Prunes (I Had Too Much*
To Dream Last Night) (Reprise 1967) ★★★,
Underground (Reprise 1967) ★★★, *Mass In F*
Minor (Reprise 1967) ★★, *Release Of An Oath*
(Reprise 1968) ★★, *Just Good Old Rock 'N' Roll*

(Reprise 1969) ★, *Stockholm 67* (Heartbeat 1997) ★★.
● COMPILATIONS: *Long Day's Flight* (Demon 1986) ★★★, *Lost Dreams* (Birdman 2001) ★★★★.

ELEKTRA RECORDS

Founded in New York, USA, in 1950 by student and traditional music enthusiast Jac Holzman, this much respected label initially showcased recordings drawn from America's rich heritage. Early releases included Jean Ritchie's *Songs Of Her Kentucky Mountain Family* and Ed McCurdy's *Songs Of The Old West*, but the catalogue also boasted collections encompassing material from international sources. Elektra also made several notable jazz and blues recordings but, as the 50s progressed, became renowned for its interest in contemporary folk. It thus attracted many of the performers from the Greenwich Village and New England enclaves, notably Judy Collins, Tom Paxton, Koerner, Ray And Glover, Fred Neil and Phil Ochs, before embracing electric styles in 1966 with the Paul Butterfield Blues Band and Love. Elektra then became established on America's west coast and its transformation from folk to rock was confirmed the following year with the Doors. Subsequent signings included the MC5, Rhinoceros, the Stooges and Earth Opera, while the label achieved concurrent commercial success with Bread. Elektra also became an important outlet for many singer-songwriters, and its catalogue included superior releases by David Ackles, Tom Rush, Tim Buckley, Harry Chapin, Incredible String Band and Carly Simon.

In 1971 Elektra was absorbed into the WEA Records conglomerate and incongruous releases by the New Seekers and Queen robbed the company of its individuality. Two years later, and with the departure of Holzman, the label was amalgamated with Asylum Records and for much of the decade remained the junior partner. Television's *Marquee Moon* rekindled memories of the outlet's classic era, while during the 80s Elektra was responsible for releases by 10,000 Maniacs, the Screaming Blue Messiahs and the Pixies (the latter US only). The label was unwilling, or unable, to shake off its early heritage which was commemorated in a series of boxed sets under the umbrella title *The Jac Holzman Years*. Elektra's 40th anniversary was celebrated with *Rubaiyat*, in which representatives from the current roster performed songs drawn from the 'classic' era. A worthy reissue programme of forgotten gems was initiated in 2001 by Stuart Batsford of Warners, releasing numerous albums as bargain double CD packages including those by Judy Henske, Tom Rush, David Blue, Tim Buckley and Fred Neil.
● COMPILATIONS: *What's Shakin'* (Elektra 1966) ★★★★, *Select Elektra* (Elektra 1967) ★★★★, *Begin Here* (Elektra 1969) ★★★★, *Love Is Teasing: Anglo-American Mounta Balladry* (Elektra 1983) ★★★, *Bleecker MacDougal: The Folk Scene Of The 60s* (Elekt 1983) ★★★, *Crossroads: White Blues In The 6* (Elektra 1985) ★★★, *Elektrock: The Sixt* (Elektra 1985) ★★★.
● FURTHER READING: *Follow The Music: T Life And High Times Of Elektra Records*, J Holzman and Gavan Daws.

ELGINS

US-born Johnny Dawson, Cleo Miller a Robert Fleming, later replaced by Norbe McClean, sang together in three Detroit vo(groups in the late 50s, the Sensations, the Fi Emeralds and the Downbeats. Under the last these names, they recorded two singles **1** Motown Records in 1959 and 1962. Also in 19(Saundra Mallett (later Saundra Mallett Edwar(issued 'Camel Walk' for Tamla, backed by t Vandellas. Motown suggested that she jc forces with the Downbeats, and the new gro was named the Elgins after the title origina used by the Temptations when they first sign with Motown. In the fiercely competiti climate of Motown in the mid-60s, the Elgi were forced to wait three years before th could issue a single, but 'Darling Baby' – writt and produced by Holland/Dozier/Holland reached the US R&B Top 10 early in 19('Heaven Must Have Sent You', which a| exhibited the traditional Motown sound of t period, matched that success, but after o further hit in 1967, the group broke up. In 19* the group enjoyed two unexpected UK Top hits when Motown reissued 'Heaven Must Ha Sent You' and the former b-side 'Put Yourself My Place'. The Elgins re-formed to tour Brita with Yvonne Allen (a former session vocali taking the place of Saundra Mallett, but pla for the revitalized group to renew th(recording career foundered. In 1989 Yvon Allen, Johnny Dawson, Norman McLean a Jimmy Charles recorded a new arrangement 'Heaven Must Have Sent You' for producer I Levine. They continued working for his Mo City label in the 90s, releasing *Take The Tr* and *Sensational*. The original lead vocalist on their Motown material, Saundra Edwards, w also recording for the same label.
● ALBUMS: *Darling Baby* (VIP 1966) ★★★, *T* *The Train* (Motor City 1990) ★★, *Sensatio* (Motor City 1991) ★★.

ELLIOT, 'MAMA' CASS

b. Ellen Naomi Cohen, 19 September 19 Baltimore, Maryland, USA, d. 29 July 19 London, England. Elliot's professional singi career began in the early 60s as a member of **i** Triumvirate with Tim Rose and John Brov This evolved into the Big Three, a pivotal f(group comprising Rose, Elliot and her fi husband, James Hendricks. When R(

embarked on a solo career, the remaining duo founded the Mugwumps with Denny Doherty and Zalman 'Zally' Yanovsky. Elliot later joined the former in the Mamas And The Papas, one of the most enduring folk rock attractions of the 60s. Her assured, soaring voice proved ideal for songwriter John Phillips' optimistic compositions, but internal disputes robbed the band of its momentum. In 1968, Elliot began an independent career with *Dream A Little Dream*, the title track from which reached the US and UK Top 20s (credited to Mama Cass with the Mamas And The Papas). 'It's Getting Better' from *Bubblegum, Lemonade And ... Something For Mama* fared better still, climbing to number 8 in the UK despite competition from Paul Jones' cover version. Elliot's third set, *Make Your Own Kind Of Music*, preceded a temporary Mamas And The Papas reunion, after which she forged an equally short-lived partnership with ex-Traffic singer/guitarist Dave Mason. Tiring of her erstwhile image, Elliot began courting a wider MOR audience with appearances on prime time American television, but later recordings lacked the naive charm of their predecessors. Elliot nonetheless remained a popular figure and her death from a heart attack in July 1974 (apocryphally reported as the result of choking on a ham sandwich), robbed pop of one of its most endearing characters.

● ALBUMS: *Dream A Little Dream* (Dunhill 1968) ★★★, *Bubblegum, Lemonade And ... Something For Mama* (Dunhill 1969) ★★★, *Make Your Own Kind Of Music* (Dunhill 1969) ★★, with Dave Mason *Dave Mason And Mama Cass* (Blue Thumb 1971) ★★, *Cass Elliot* (RCA 1972) ★★, *The Road Is No Place For A Lady* (RCA 1972) ★★, *Don't Call Me Mama Anymore* (RCA 1973) ★★.

● COMPILATIONS: *Mama's Big Ones: The Best Of Mama Cass* (Dunhill 1970) ★★★, *Dream A Little Dream: The Cass Elliot Collection* (MCA 1997) ★★★.

● FILMS: *Pufnstuf* (1970).

ELLIOTT, BERN, AND THE FENMEN

Formed in Erith, Kent, England, in 1961, Bern Elliott And The Fenmen spent many of their early years playing in German clubs. Signed to Decca Records in 1963, they had a UK Top 20 hit with their debut single, 'Money', arguably the finest cover version of this recurrent beat group favourite. A rendition of 'New Orleans' provided another chart entry, but the singer and backing group broke up following the release of 'Good Times'. While the Fenmen: Alan Judge (guitar), Wally Allen (guitar), Eric Willmer (bass) and Jon Povey (drums) – continued to record in an engaging, close-harmony style, Elliott formed a new group, the Klan, around Dave Cameron (organ), Tim Hamilton (guitar), John Silby-Pearce (bass) and Pete Adams (drums). Despite several excellent singles, including 'Voodoo Woman' (1965), the vocalist was unable to regain

their initial success. Former colleagues Allen and Povey later found fame in the Pretty Things.

● COMPILATIONS: *The Beat Years* (1988) ★★.

ELLIOTT, RAMBLIN' JACK

b. Elliott Charles Adnopoz, 1 August 1931, Brooklyn, New York City, New York, USA. The son of an eminent doctor, Elliott forsook his middle-class upbringing as a teenager to join a travelling rodeo. Embarrassed by his family name, he dubbed himself Buck Elliott, before adopting the less-mannered Jack. In 1949 he met and befriended Woody Guthrie, who in turn became his mentor and prime influence. Elliott travelled and sang with Guthrie whenever possible, before emerging as a talent in his own right. He spent a portion of the 50s in Europe, introducing America's folk heritage to a new and eager audience and recording material for Topic Records, often in partnership with Derroll Adams. By the early 60s he had resettled in New York where he became an inspirational figure to a new generation of performers, including Bob Dylan. *Ramblin' Jack Elliott* was an important release which saw the singer shaking off the imitator tag by embracing a diverse selection of material, including songs drawn from the American tradition, the Scottish music hall and Ray Charles. Further releases included the Vanguard Records release *Jack Elliott*, which featured Dylan playing harmonica under the pseudonym Tedham Porterhouse, and *Young Brigham* in 1967, which offered songs by Tim Hardin and the Rolling Stones as well as an adventurous use of dobros, autoharps, fiddles and tablas.

The singer also guested on albums by Tom Rush, Phil Ochs and Johnny Cash. In 1975 Elliott was joined by Dylan during an appearance at the New York, Greenwich Village club, The Other End, and he then became a natural choice for Dylan's nostalgic carnival tour, the Rolling Thunder Revue. Elliott later continued his erratic, but intriguing, path, and an excellent early 80s release, *Kerouac's Last Dream*, showed his power undiminished. He was relatively prolific in the 90s. *Friends Of Mine* featured 'Bleecker Street Blues', written when Dylan fell seriously ill in 1997, and a host of celebratory guest singers including Tom Waits, Emmylou Harris, Arlo Guthrie and Nanci Griffith. In 2000, his daughter directed the documentary film *The Ballad Of Ramblin' Jack*. The accompanying soundtrack album serves as a useful career retrospective.

● ALBUMS: *Woody Guthrie's Blues* (Topic 1957) ★★★, with Derroll Adams *The Rambling Boys* 10-inch album (Topic 1957) ★★★, *Jack Takes The Floor* 10-inch album (Topic 1958) ★★★, *In London* (UK) *Monitor Presents Jack Elliott: Ramblin' Cowboy* (US) (Columbia/Monitor 1959) ★★★, *Sings Songs By Woody Guthrie And Jimmy Rogers* (Columbia/Monitor 1960) ★★★, *Sings The Songs Of Woody Guthrie* (Stateside/Prestige

1961) ★★★, *Songs To Grow On By Woody Guthrie, Sung By Jack Elliott* (Folkways 1961) ★★★, *Ramblin' Jack Elliott* (Prestige 1961) ★★★★, *Jack Elliott At The Second Fret* aka *Hootenanny With Jack Elliott* (Prestige 1962) ★★★, *Country Style* (Prestige 1962) ★★★, *Talking Woody Guthrie* (Topic 1963) ★★★, with Adams *Roll On Buddy* (Topic 1963) ★★★, *Muleskinner* (Topic/Delmark 1964) ★★★, *Jack Elliott i* (Everest Archive 1964) ★★★, *Jack Elliott ii* (Vanguard/Fontana 1964) ★★★, *Young Brigham* (Reprise 1967) ★★★, *Bill Durham Sacks & Railroad Tracks* (Reprise 1967) ★★★, with Adams *Folkland Songs* aka *America: Folk Songs-West-Ballads* 1955-1961 recordings (Joker 1969) ★★★, *Kerouac's Last Dream* (Folk Freak 1981) ★★★, with Spider John Koerner, U. Utah Phillips *Legends Of Folk* (Red House 1992) ★★★, *South Coast* (Red House 1995) ★★★, *Friends Of Mine* (Hightone 1998) ★★★, *Live In Japan* 1974 recording (Vivid/Bellwood 1998) ★★★, *The Long Ride* (Hightone 1999) ★★★, *The Ballad Of Ramblin' Jack* film soundtrack (Vanguard 2000) ★★★.

● COMPILATIONS: *The Essential Ramblin' Jack Elliott* (Vanguard 1976) ★★★, *Hard Travelin': Songs By Woody Guthrie And Others* (Fantasy/Big Beat 1989) ★★★★, *Talking Dust Bowl: The Best Of Ramblin' Jack Elliott* (Big Beat 1989) ★★★★, *Sings Woody Guthrie And Jimmie Rodgers & Cowboy Songs* (Monitor 1994) ★★★, *Me & Bobby McGee* (Rounder 1995) ★★★, *Ramblin' Jack: The Legendary Topic Masters* (Topic 1995) ★★★, *Country Style/Live* (Fantasy 1999) ★★★, *The Best Of The Vanguard Years* (Vanguard 2000) ★★★★.

● FILMS: *The Ballad Of Ramblin' Jack* (2000).

ELLIS, SHIRLEY
b. New York City, New York, USA. Before striking out on a solo career in 1963, Ellis served an apprenticeship singing with an unsuccessful vocal group, the Metronones. Her strong voice was used to good effect on dance-floor ravers 'The Nitty Gritty' (number 4 R&B and number 8 pop in 1963) and '(That's) What The Nitty Gritty Is' (number 14 R&B 1964), and her future looked bright. Ellis, however, soon found herself in novelty song territory with catchy ditties written by her manager Lincoln Chase, namely, 'The Name Game' (number 4 R&B and number 3 pop in 1965) and 'The Clapping Song (Clap Pat Clap Slap)' (number 16 R&B and number 8 pop in 1965). The latter was the only UK success for Ellis, amazingly hitting twice, in 1965, when it reached number 6, and on an EP in 1978. The Belle Stars successfully revived 'The Clapping Song' in 1982.

● ALBUMS: *In Action* (Congress 1964) ★★, *The Name Game* (Congress 1965) ★★★, *Sugar, Let's Shing A Ling* (Columbia 1967) ★★.

● COMPILATIONS: *The Very Best Of ...* (Taragon 1995) ★★★, *The Complete Congress Recordings* (Connoisseur 2001) ★★★.

ELLISON, LORRAINE
b. 1943, Philadelphia, Pennsylvania, USA, d. 17 August 1985. Although only associated with a few minor hits in the history of R&B, Ellison's intense, dramatic and highly gospelized vocal delivery helped to define deep soul as a particular style. Ellison recorded with two gospel groups, the Ellison Singers and the Golden Chords, but left the latter in 1964 to pursue a solo career in R&B music. 'I Dig You Baby' (number 22 R&B) in 1965 was her first chart entry, but it was the powerful 'Stay With Me' (number 11 R&B, number 64 pop) in 1966 that established her reputation. Written and produced by Jerry Ragovoy, the song, featuring Ellison's awe-inspiring vocal pleas, ultimately proved to be a spectacular one-off performance. Nothing in her subsequent recordings emulated its naked emotion, and even the excellent 'Heart Be Still' (number 43 R&B, number 89 pop) from 1967, was something of an anti-climax. Ellison never charted again, not even with the original version of 'Try Just A Little Bit Harder' (1968), which rock singer Janis Joplin later remade with great success. Ellison's compositions, on which she often collaborated with her manager, Sam Bell (of Garnet Mimms And The Enchanters fame), were recorded by Howard Tate and Garnet Mimms.

● ALBUMS: *Heart And Soul* (Warners 1966) ★★, *Stay With Me* (Warners 1970) ★★★, *Lorraine Ellison* (Warners 1974) ★★.

● COMPILATIONS: *The Best Of Philadelphia's Queen* (Warners 1976) ★★★, *Stay With Me* (Ichiban 1995) ★★★★.

EPISODE SIX
This respected beat group evolved in 1964 when two amateur groups amalgamated. Roger Glover (b. 30 November 1945, Brecon, Wales; bass), Harvey Shields (drums) and Tony Lander (guitar) were former members of the Madisons; Sheila Carter-Dimmock (organ), her brother Graham (rhythm guitar) and Andy Ross (vocals) were from the Lightnings. Ross, who quickly tired of touring, left in May 1965, and was replaced by Ian Gillan (b. 19 August 1945, Hounslow, Middlesex, England). The sextet had already secured a recording deal with Pye Records; 'Put Yourself In My Place', written by the Hollies' team, Clarke/Hicks/Nash, duly became their debut single the following January. Episode Six specialized in releasing cover versions, bringing strong harmony work to the Beatles' 'Here, There And Everywhere', the Tokens' 'I Hear Trumpets Blow' and Tim Rose's 'Morning Dew'. Lack of direction doubtlessly doomed their commercial prospects, but despite this, two solo singles, by Sheila Carter-Dimmock and Graham Carter-Dimmock, were also issued. The latter's release, credited to 'Neo Maya', was a cover version of 'I Won't Hurt You', originally recorded by the West Coast Pop Art Experimental Band. Shields was replaced by

ormer Pirates drummer John Kerrison in 1967. The following year the sextet switched to MGM, dropping the 'Six' suffix for one single, 'Little One'. Mick Underwood (ex-Outlaws) then joined in place of a disenchanted Kerrison, after which the group joined the Chapter One label for two more singles. Their final release, 'Mozart Versus The Rest', was a brazen pop/classical workout. Plans for an album, *The Story So Far*, were mooted, but in July 1969 Ian Gillan was invited to join Deep Purple. Within weeks he was joined by Roger Glover, although Underwood kept Episode Six alive with the addition of John Gustafson (bass, ex-Big Three) and Peter Robinson (keyboards). In 1969 the three broke away to found progressive act Quatermass, effectively ending the career of Episode Six.
● COMPILATIONS: *Put Yourself In My Place* (1987) ★★★, *The Roots Of Deep Purple: The Complete Episode Six* (1992) ★★★, *Cornflakes and Crazyfoam* (RPM 1997) ★★.

EPSTEIN, BRIAN

. Brian Samuel Epstein, 19 September 1934, Liverpool, England, d. 27 August 1967, London, England. One of the most famous pop managers in music business history, Epstein began his working life in the family business as a provincial shopkeeper, overseeing the North End Road Music Stores (NEMS) in central Liverpool. His life took a new direction on Saturday 28 October 1961 when a customer requested a record entitled 'My Bonnie' by a group called the Beatles. When Epstein subsequently attended one of their gigs at the Cavern in Mathew Street he was drawn into the alien netherworld of leather-clad beat groups and, against the advice of his friends, became a pop manager. His early efforts at promoting the Beatles proved haphazard, but using his influence with record companies he secured a number of interviews with important A&R representatives. A slew of rejections followed, but Decca Records at least offered the Beatles an audition before finally turning them down. Epstein took his revenge by crediting the unfortunate Dick Rowe with the immortal words: 'Groups of guitarists are on the way out'. Epstein's tardiness in securing a record deal did not diminish his abilities in other areas.
He transformed the Beatles into a more professional outfit, banned them from swearing or eating on stage and even encouraged the establishment of a rehearsed repertoire. Perhaps his most lasting contribution at this point was persuading them to replace their menacing black leather garb with smart, grey lounge suits, with eye-catching matching collars. By the spring of 1962, Epstein at last won a record deal thanks to the intuitive intervention of producer George Martin. A near-crisis followed shortly afterwards when Epstein had to oversee the dismissal of drummer Pete Best, who was replaced by Ringo Starr. During October 1962, a

management contract was belatedly finalized with the Beatles by which Epstein received 25 per cent of their earnings, a figure he maintained for all future signings. Weeks later, he struck a deal with music publisher Dick James, which culminated in the formation of Northern Songs, a company dealing exclusively with compositions by John Lennon and Paul McCartney. In an extremely clever and unusual deal for the period, the powers agreed on a 50/50 split: half to Dick James and his partner Charles Emmanuel Silver; 20 per cent each to Lennon and McCartney; and 10 per cent to Epstein.
Long before the Beatles became the most successful entertainers in music history, Epstein had signed his second group, Gerry And The Pacemakers. Scouring the Cavern for further talent he soon added Tommy Quickly, the Fourmost, Billy J. Kramer And The Dakotas, the Big Three and Cilla Black. The spree of NEMS signings during 1963 was the most spectacular managerial coup since Larry Parnes' celebrated discoveries during the late 50s. More importantly, the artists dominated the UK charts throughout the year, logging an incredible nine number 1 hits spanning 32 weeks at the top. By early 1964, Beatlemania had crossed from Britain to America and NEMS had transformed from a small family business into a multi-million-pound organization. The strength of the company ensured that the Beatles had few administrative problems during the Epstein era. Scrupulously fair, he even allowed his charges a 10 per cent interest in NEMS. One area where Epstein was deemed fallible was in the merchandising agreements that he concluded on behalf of the Beatles. Ironically, it was the result of delegating the matter to the inexperienced solicitor David Jacobs that the group found themselves receiving a mere 10 per cent of the sums received by the company set up to merchandise goods in their name.
By the mid-60s, licences had been granted for every product that the American merchandising mentality could conceive. This meant not only badges, dolls and toys, but even cans of Beatle breath. The lost revenue that Epstein had allowed to slip through his fingers was gruesomely revealed in the pages of the *Wall Street Journal*. According to their figures, Americans spent approximately $50 million on Beatles goods up to the end of 1964, while the world market was estimated at roughly £40 million. Although Epstein attempted to rectify the poor merchandising deal through litigation and even contributed massive legal expenses from his own pocket, the stigma of the unfortunate deal remained. Few pointed out that it was less Epstein's error than that of the inexperienced Jacobs, who had agreed to the arrangement without consulting his client. The merchandising dispute has all too often eclipsed Epstein's achievements in other areas. It

deserves to be remembered that the Liverpudlian effectively ushered in the era of stadium rock with the Beatles' Hollywood Bowl concert, an event that changed rock economics for ever. Even while the Beatles were conquering the New World, Epstein was expanding his empire. Although he signed a couple of unsuccessful artists, most of the NEMS stable enjoyed tremendous success. The career of Cilla Black was a tribute to Epstein's creative management. He helped her adapt to the rigours of showbusiness success with a feminine solicitude typical of a would-be dress designer. More importantly, however, he immediately recognized her lasting charm as the gauche, unpretentious girl-next-door, an image that another manager might have suppressed. Epstein's expert exploitation of her appeal paved the way for her eventual acceptance and remarkable success as a television host. When the Beatles ceased touring after the summer of 1966, Epstein's role in their day-to-day lives was minimal. For a time, he attempted to find satisfaction in other areas, purchasing the Savile Theatre in London's Shaftesbury Avenue and alternating serious drama with Sunday pop shows. Ever-puzzling, Epstein even sponsored an Anglo-Spanish bullfighter named Henry Higgins and astonished his colleagues by attempting to persuade the perpetually nervous Billy J. Kramer to pursue an acting career. NEMS, meanwhile, ceased to inspire the entrepreneur and he inexplicably offered a 51 per cent controlling interest to the Australian adventurer Robert Stigwood. By 1967, Epstein was losing control. Drug dependence and homosexual guilt brought him to the verge of a nervous breakdown and attempted suicide. He suffered at the hands of the press for advocating the use of the drug LSD. On August Bank Holiday 1967 the Beatles were in north Wales attending a course in transcendental meditation with their new mentor, the Maharishi Mahesh Yogi. Epstein, meanwhile, was lying dead at his London home in Chapel Street, Mayfair. The inquest subsequently established that he had died from a cumulative overdose of the sleep-inducing drug Carbatrol. Although suicide was suspected and some fanciful conspiracy theories have suggested the remote possibility of foul play, the coroner concluded with a prosaic verdict of accidental death from 'incautious self-overdoses'. In spite of his foibles, Epstein is rightly regarded as a great manager, possibly the greatest in British pop history. Judged in the context of his era, his achievements were remarkable. Although it is often claimed that he did not exploit the Beatles' earning power to its maximum degree, he most certainly valued their reputation above all else. During his tenure as manager, he insulated them from corporate avarice and negotiated contracts that prevented EMI Records from marketing cheap reissues or unauthorized compilations. In this sense, he was

the complete antithesis of Elvis Presley's manager, Colonel Tom Parker, who allowed his artist to atrophy through a decade of bad movies. As the custodian of the Beatles' international reputation, Epstein's handling of their career was exemplary. For Epstein, honour meant more than profit and he brought an integrity to pop management that few of his successors have matched.
● FURTHER READING: A Cellarful Of Noise, Brian Epstein. Brian Epstein: The Man Who Made The Beatles, Ray Coleman. The Brian Epstein Story, Deborah Geller.

EQUALS

Twins Derv and Lincoln Gordon (b. 29 June 1948, Jamaica; vocals and rhythm guitar, respectively), Eddy Grant (b. Edmond Montague Grant, 5 March 1948, Plaisance, Guyana, West Indies; lead guitar), Patrick Lloyd (b. 17 March 1948, Holloway, London, England; rhythm guitar) and John Hall (b. 25 October 1947, Holloway, London, England; drums) began playing together in 1965 on a council estate in Hornsey Rise, north London. Their best-remembered single 'Baby Come Back', was recorded the following year as a b-side, but the quintet's early release made little impression. Over the ensuing months the band became highly regarded on the continent, where they toured extensively. 'Baby Come Back' became a major hit in Germany during 1967 and later topped the charts in Holland and Belgium. This propulsive, infectious song was then reissued in Britain where it eventually rose to number 1. Although the Equals enjoyed other hits, only 'Viva Bobby Joe' (1969) and 'Black Skinned Blue-Eyed Boys' (1970) reached the Top 10 as their reliance on a tested formula wore thin. Chief songwriter Grant left for a solo career in 1971, after which the band underwent several changes in personnel before finding security on the cabaret circuit. However, their career was resurrected in 1978 when Grant, by then a self-sufficient artist and entrepreneur, signed them to his Ice label for Mystic Synster.
● ALBUMS: Unequalled Equals (President 1967) ★★★, Equals Explosion aka Equal Sensation/Equals (President 1968) ★★★, Equals Supreme (President 1968) ★★★, Baby Come Back (1968) ★★★★, Equals Strike Back (President 1969) ★★, Equals At The Top (President 1970) ★★, Equal Rock Around The Clock (1974) ★★, Doin' The 45 (1975) ★★★, Born Ya (Mercury 1976) ★★, Mystic Synster (Ice 1978) ★★.
● COMPILATIONS: The Best Of The Equals (President 1969) ★★★, Greatest Hits (1974) ★★★★, The Very Best Of The Equals (See For Miles 1996) ★★★, Viva Equals! The Very Best Of The Equals (Music Club 1999) ★★★.

ESCORTS

Terry Sylvester (vocals, guitar), John Kinrade (lead guitar) and Mike Gregory (b. 1947; vocals, bass) formed the Escorts at Liverpool's Ros-

Lane school in 1962. They were originally augmented by drummer John Foster, aka Johnny Sticks, a cousin of Ringo Starr, replaced by Pete Clark (b. 1947) in 1963. The quartet made their debut in April 1964 with a powerful interpretation of 'Dizzie Miss Lizzie', before scoring a minor hit two months later with 'The One To Cry'. Their next release, 'I Don't Want To Go On Without You', was also recorded by the Moody Blues, who secured the chart entry. This undermined the Escorts' confidence, and subsequent releases, although carefully crafted, proved unsuccessful. The group's line-up was also unstable. Sylvester left for the Swinging Blue Jeans, from where he later replaced Graham Nash in the Hollies and by mid-1966, Kinrade and Gregory were the sole original members. Paddy Chambers (guitar, ex-Big Three; Paddy, Klaus And Gibson) and Paul Comerford (drums, ex-Cryin' Shames) completed the group featured on 'From Head To Toe', the Escorts' final single. This accomplished performance featured Paul McCartney on tambourine, but the quartet split up within weeks of its release.
● COMPILATIONS: *From The Blue Angel* (1982) ★★.

ESQUIRES
Formed in Milwaukee, USA, in 1957 with a line-up featuring Gilbert Moorer, Alvis Moorer and Betty Moorer. Originally conceived as a doo-wop group, the Esquires were briefly augmented by Harvey Scales before Sam Pace joined in 1961. In 1965 Betty Moorer was replaced by Shawn Taylor. The group then moved to Chicago where they signed to the Bunky label. An original song, 'Get On Up', was recorded with the help of Millard Edwards, who sang its distinctive bass line. Edwards became a permanent member when this infectious single was an R&B hit in 1967. Shawn Taylor left before a similar-sounding follow-up, 'And Get Away', was issued, but rejoined in 1971. That same year, 'Girls In The City', featuring Taylor as lead, was a Top 20 US R&B hit. The opportunistic 'Get Up '76' was the Esquires' most recent hit; by the early 80s only Gilbert and Alvis Moorer remained from the group's heyday.
● ALBUMS: *Get On Up And Get Away* (Bunky 1967) ★★★, with the Marvelows *Chi-Town Showdown* (1982) ★★★.

ESQUIVEL!
b. Juan Garcia Esquivel, 20 January 1918, Tampico, Mexico, d. 3 January 2002, Jiutepec, Morelos, Mexico. Although he was a huge inspiration for the revival of 'lounge' or 'easy listening' music in the 90s, Esquivel in fact began recording his heavily orchestrated pop muzak four decades earlier. Although none of his recordings from this period charted, he was widely recognized as an influence on Californian music of the time with his swinging

pop arrangements. Indeed, in the 70s Steely Dan acknowledged Esquivel as the reason they introduced marimba, vibes and percussion into the recording of *Pretzel Logic*.
Esquivel's intention was to realize the possibilities allowed by the development of stereo technology, and his records were thus infused with all manner of diverting intrusions, such as whistling and pinball percussion, that adorned big band Latin pop. He had been brought to America in 1957 by the RCA Records executive Herman Diaz Jnr. and became a prolific bandleader, overseeing singers including Yvonne DeBourbon and Randy Van Horne. As 'The Sights And Sounds Of Esquivel' they toured widely in the USA, appearing in New York, Hollywood and Las Vegas. A visual as well as aural perfectionist, one anecdote from these times concerns Esquivel's development of a special 'walk' so as not to crease his shoes. The women in his band were severely and outrageously disciplined. Forced to step on scales before each performance, they would be summarily fined $5 for each pound of weight gained. By the artist's own reckoning, his music has been used in over 200 television shows, including *Baywatch*.
In the 90s, now retired, Esquivel was widely celebrated as 'the father of Lounge Music' and 'space age bachelor pad music' with the release of compilation albums on Bar/None Records which became staples of US college radio. Contemporary groups including Combustible Edison, Stereolab and Black Velvet Flag appropriated his style, while Chicago's Vinyl Dance nightclub dedicated itself to his music. Despite being bed-ridden after a fall, he relished this new wave of attention. 'Perhaps I was too far ahead of my time,' he told *Rolling Stone* in 1995. He died of a stroke in 2002.
● ALBUMS: *Las Tandas De Juan Garcia Esquivel* (RCA Victor Mexicana 1956), *To Love Again* (RCA Victor Mexicana 1957) ★★★, *Other Worlds, Other Sounds* (RCA Victor 1958) ★★★★, *4 Corners Of The World* (RCA Victor 1958), *Exploring New Sounds In Hi-Fi* (RCA Victor 1959) ★★★, *Strings Aflame* (RCE Victor 1959) ★★★ , *Infinity In Sound* (RCA Victor 1960), *Infinity In Sound Volume 2* (RCA Victor 1961) ★★★★, *More Of Other Worlds, Other Sounds* (Reprise 1962) ★★★, *Latin-Esque* (RCA Victor 1962) ★★★★, *Esquivel 68* (RCA Victor Mexicana 1968) ★★★.
● COMPILATIONS: *Esquivel!* (Bar/None 1994) ★★★★, *Space Age Bachelor Pad Music* (Bar/None 1994) ★★★★, *Music From A Sparkling Planet* (Bar/None 1995) ★★★★, *Merry Xmas* (Bar/None 1996) ★★, *Loungecore* (Camden 1998) ★★★.

ESSEX
A rock 'n' roll vocal group formed in the early 60s by members of the US Marine Corps at Camp LeJeune, North Carolina, USA. Members were lead Anita Humes, Walter Vickers, Rodney

Taylor, Rudolph Johnson, and Billie Hill. The group exploded on the scene in 1963 with three singles, 'Easier Said Than Done' (number 1 R&B and pop), 'A Walkin' Miracle' (number 11 R&B, number 12 pop), and 'She's Got Everything' (number 56 pop). The vocal sound of the group, unlike many African-American groups of the day, featured meagre vocal harmony and concentrated on the warm engaging voice of Humes, and the group never sang R&B. After the initial hits, their company, Roulette, focused on Humes, and on their final album put only her picture on the cover, calling the artist Anita Humes With The Essex. The Essex's later soul-styled recordings, although thoroughly appealing, never found a market. In 1966 the group recorded a final single for Bang Records before disbanding.
● ALBUMS: *Easier Said Than Done* (Roulette 1963) ★★, *A Walkin' Miracle* (Roulette 1963) ★★, *Young And Lively* (Roulette 1964) ★★.
● COMPILATIONS: *The Best Of The Essex* (Sequel 1994) ★★.

EVANS, MAUREEN
b. 1940, Cardiff, Wales. Evans began her singing career on the Embassy label, which made budget-priced recordings of contemporary hits for the UK's Woolworths chain-store. She later enjoyed chart success in her own right, beginning in 1960 with 'The Big Hurt', and peaking two years later with 'Like I Do'. This perky offering, more teen-orientated than Evans' normal fare, reached the UK Top 3, but later releases failed to emulate its success. Her rather dated style was quickly surpassed by younger-minded artists, although 'Never Let Him Go', one of the singer's final releases, was an excellent interpretation of a David Gates song.
● ALBUMS: *Like I Do* (Oriole 1963) ★★.

EVERETT, BETTY
b. 23 November 1939, Greenwood, Mississippi, USA, d. 19 August 2001, Beloit, Wisconsin, USA. Having moved to Chicago in the late 50s, R&B/soul singer Everett recorded unsuccessfully for several local labels, including Cobra, C.J. and One-derful, and briefly sang lead with the all-male group the Daylighters. Her hits came on signing to Vee Jay Records where 'You're No Good' (1963) and 'The Shoop Shoop Song (It's In His Kiss)' (1964) established her pop/soul style. A duet with Jerry Butler, 'Let It Be Me' (1964), consolidated this position, but her finest moment came with 'Getting Mighty Crowded', a punchy Van McCoy song. Her career faltered on Vee Jay's collapse in 1966, and an ensuing interlude at ABC Records was unproductive, despite producing classic tracks such as 'Love Comes Tumbling Down'. However, in 1969, 'There'll Come A Time' reached number 2 in the R&B charts, a momentum that continued into the early 70s with further

releases on Uni and Fantasy Records. Everett's last chart entry was in 1978 with 'True Love (You Took My Heart)', on the United Artists Records label. Cher took her version of 'The Shoop Shoop Song (It's In His Kiss)' to the top of the UK chart in 1991.
● ALBUMS: *You're No Good* (Vee Jay 1964) ★★★, *It's In His Kiss* (Vee Jay/Fontana 1964) ★★★, with Jerry Butler *Delicious Together* (Vee Jay 1964) ★★★★, *There'll Come A Time* (Uni 1969) ★★, *Love Rhymes* (Fantasy 1974) ★★, *Black Girl* (Fantasy 1974) ★★, *Happy Endings* (Fantasy 1975) ★★.
● COMPILATIONS: *The Very Best Of Betty Everett* (Vee Jay 1965) ★★★, *Getting Mighty Crowded* (Charly 1980) ★★★★, *Hot To Hold* (Charly 1982) ★★★, *The Real Thing* (Charly 1987) ★★★★, *The Fantasy Years* (Fantasy 1995) ★★★, *The Best Of Betty Everett: Let It Be Me* (Aim 1998) ★★★★, *The Shoop Shoop Song: 20 Greatest Hits* (Collectables 2000) ★★★.

EVERLY BROTHERS
Don (b. Isaac Donald Everly, 1 February 1937, Brownie, Kentucky, USA) and Phil (b. Phillip Everly, 19 January 1939, Chicago, Illinois, USA), the world's most famous rock 'n' roll duo, had already experienced a full career before their first record, 'Bye Bye Love', was released. As sons of popular country artists Ike and Margaret, they were pushed into the limelight from an early age. They regularly appeared on their parents' radio shows throughout the 40s and accompanied them on many tours. In the mid-50s, as rockabilly was evolving into rock 'n' roll, the boys moved to Nashville, the mecca for such music. Don had a minor hit when Kitty Wells recorded his composition 'Thou Shalt Not Steal' in 1954. In 1957 they were given a Felice and Boudleaux Bryant song that was finding difficulty being placed. They took 'Bye Bye Love' and made it their own; it narrowly missed the US number 1 position and reached number 6 in the UK. The brothers then embarked on a career that made them second only to Elvis Presley in the rock 'n' roll popularity stakes. Their blend of country and folk did much to sanitize and make respectable a phenomenon towards which many parents still showed hostility. America, then a racially segregated country, was not ready for its white teenagers to listen to black-based rock music. The brothers' clean looks and even cleaner harmonies did much to change people's attitudes.
They quickly followed this initial success with more irresistible Bryant songs, 'Wake Up Little Susie', 'All I Have To Do Is Dream', 'Bird Dog', 'Problems', 'So Sad' and the beautiful 'Devoted To You'. The brothers were supremely confident live performers, both with their trademark Gibson Dove and later, black J50 guitars. By the end of the 50s they were the world's number 1 vocal group. Amazingly, their career gained further momentum when, after signing with the

newly formed Warner Brothers Records for $1 million, they delivered a song that was catalogued WB1. This historical debut was the superlative 'Cathy's Clown', written by Don. No Everly record had sounded like this before; the echo-laden production and the treble-loaded harmonies ensured that it stayed at number 1 in the USA for five weeks. In the UK it stayed on top for over two months, selling several million and making it one of the most successful records of all time. The brothers continued to release immaculate records; many of them reached the US Top 10, although in England their success was even greater, with two further number 1 hits during 1961. Again the echo and treble dominated in two more classics, 'Walk Right Back' and a fast-paced reworking of the former Bing Crosby hit 'Temptation'. At the end of 1961 they were drafted into the US Marines, albeit for only six months, and resumed by embarking on a European tour. Don became dependent on drugs, and the pressures from constant touring and recording began to show; during one historic night at London's East Ham Granada, England, a nervous Phil performed solo. The standard 'food poisoning/exhaustion' excuse was used. What was not known by the doting fans was that Don had attempted a suicidal drug overdose twice in 48 hours. Phil completed the tour solo. Don's addiction continued for another three years, although they were able to work during part of this time.

The advent of the beat boom pushed the brothers out of the spotlight and while they continued to make hit records, none approached their previous achievements. The decline was briefly halted in 1965 with two excellent major UK hits, 'The Price Of Love' and 'Love Is Strange'. The former, a striking chart-topper, recalled their early Warner sound, while the latter harked back even earlier, with a naïve but infectious call-and-answer spoken segment. In 1966 they released Two Yanks In England, a strong album that contained eight songs by Nash/Clarke/Hicks of the Hollies; surprisingly, the album failed to chart. The duo were recognized only for their superb singles, and many of their albums were less well-received. Stories We Could Tell, recorded with an array of guest players, threatened to extend their market into the rock mainstream, but it was not to be. After a few years of declining fortunes and arrival at the supper-club circuit, the brothers parted acrimoniously. Following a show at Knotts Berry Farm, California, in 1973, during which a drunken Don had insulted Phil, the latter walked off, smashed one of his beloved Gibsons and vowed, 'I will never get on a stage with that man again'. The only time they met over the next 10 years was at their father's funeral.

Both embarked on solo careers with varying degrees of accomplishment. Their country-flavoured albums found more favour with the Nashville audience of their roots. Don and his

band, the Dead Cowboys, regularly played in Nashville, while Phil released the critically acclaimed Star Spangled Springer. Inexplicably, the album was a relatively poor seller, as were several follow-ups. Phil made a cameo appearance in the movie Every Which Way But Lose, performing with actress Sondra Locke. While Don maintained a steady career, playing with ex-Heads, Hands And Feet maestro Albert Lee, Phil concentrated on writing songs. 'She Means Nothing To Me' was a striking duet with Cliff Richard which put the Everly name back in the UK Top 10. Rumours began to circulate of a reunion, which was further fuelled by an UK television advertisement for an Everly Brothers compilation. In June 1983 they hugged and made up and their emotional reconciliation was made before an ecstatic, wet-eyed audience at London's Royal Albert Hall. The following year EB84 was released and gave them another major hit with Paul McCartney's 'Wings Of A Nightingale'. In 1986 they were inducted into the Rock And Roll Hall Of Fame and the following year Phil gave Don a pound of gold and a handmade guitar for his 50th birthday. They now perform regularly together, with no pressure from record companies. Don lives quietly in Nashville and tours with his brother for a few months every year. A major reissue programme, with alternative takes was undertaken by Warners in 2001. The Everly Brothers' influence on a generation of pop and rock artists is inestimable; they set a standard for close harmony singing that has rarely been bettered and is still used as a blueprint for many of today's harmony vocalists.

● ALBUMS: The Everly Brothers (Cadence 1958) ★★★★, Songs Our Daddy Taught Us (Cadence 1959) ★★★★, The Everly Brothers' Best (Cadence 1959) ★★★, It's Everly Time (Warners 1960) ★★★, The Fabulous Style Of The Everly Brothers (Cadence 1960) ★★★★, A Date With The Everly Brothers (Warners 1960) ★★★★, Both Sides Of An Evening (Warners 1961) ★★★, Folk Songs Of the Everly Brothers (Cadence 1962) ★★★, Instant Party (Warners 1962) ★★★, Christmas With The Everly Brothers And The Boys Town Choir (Warners 1962) ★★, The Everly Brothers Sing Great Country Hits (Warners 1963) ★★★, Gone Gone Gone (Warners 1965) ★★★★, Rock 'N' Soul (Warners 1965) ★★★, Beat 'N' Soul (Warners 1965) ★★★, In Our Image (Warners 1966) ★★★, Two Yanks In England (Warners 1966) ★★★, The Hit Sound Of The Everly Brothers (Warners 1967) ★★★, The Everly Brothers Sing (Warners 1967) ★★★, Roots (Warners 1968) ★★★★, The Everly Brothers Show (Warners 1970) ★★★, End Of An Era (Barnaby/Columbia 1971) ★★★, Stories We Could Tell (RCA-Victor 1972) ★★★, Pass The Chicken And Listen (RCA-Victor 1973) ★★, The Exciting Everly Brothers (RCA 1975) ★★★, Living Legends (Warwick 1977) ★★★, The New Album previously unissued Warners material (Warners 1977) ★★★, The Everly Brothers Reunion Concert

(Impression 1983) ★★★★, *Nice Guys* previously unissued Warners material (Magnum Force 1984) ★★, *EB84* (Mercury 1984) ★★★, *In The Studio* previously unissued Cadence material (Ace 1985) ★★★, *Born Yesterday* (Mercury 1985) ★★★, *Some Hearts* (Mercury 1988) ★★★, *Live In Paris* 1963 recording (Big Beat 1997) ★★★, *Live At The Olympia* 10-inch album (Big Beat 1997) ★★★.

Solo: Don Everly *Don Everly* (A&M 1971) ★★, *Sunset Towers* (Ode 1974) ★★, *Brother Juke Box* (Hickory 1976) ★★★. Phil Everly *Star Spangled Springer* (RCA 1973) ★★★, *Phil's Diner (There's Nothing Too Good For My Baby)* (Pye 1974) ★★, *Mystic Line* (Pye 1975) ★★, *Living Alone* (Elektra 1979) ★★, *Phil Everly* (Capitol 1983) ★★.

● COMPILATIONS: *The Golden Hits Of The Everly Brothers* (Warners 1962) ★★★★, *15 Everly Hits* (Cadence 1963) ★★★, *The Very Best Of The Everly Brothers* (Warners 1964) ★★★★, *The Everly Brothers' Original Greatest Hits* (Columbia 1970) ★★★★★, *The Most Beautiful Songs Of The Everly Brothers* (Warners 1973) ★★★, *Don's And Phil's Fabulous Fifties Treasury* (Janus 1974) ★★★, *Walk Right Back With The Everlys* (Warners 1975) ★★★★, *The Everly Brothers Greatest Hits Collection* (Pickwick 1979) ★★★, *The Sensational Everly Brothers* (Reader Digest 1979) ★★, *Cathy's Clown* (Pickwick 1980) ★★★, *The Very Best Of The Everly Brothers* (Marks & Spencer 1980) ★★, *The Everly Brothers* (Warners 1981) ★★★, *Rock 'N' Roll Forever* (Warners 1981) ★★★, *Love Hurts* (K-Tel 1982) ★★, *Rip It Up* (Ace 1983) ★★★, *Cadence Classics (Their 20 Greatest Hits)* (Rhino 1985) ★★★★, *The Best Of The Everly Brothers* (Rhino 1985) ★★★, *All They Had To Do Is Dream* US only (Rhino 1985) ★★★, *Great Recordings* (Ace 1986) ★★★, *The Everly Brothers Collection* (Castle 1988) ★★★, *The Very Best Of The Everly Brothers* (Pickwick 1988) ★★★, *Hidden Gems* Warners material (Ace 1989) ★★★, *The Very Best Of The Everly Brothers Volume 2* (Pickwick 1990) ★★, *Perfect Harmony* box set (Knight 1990) ★★★, *Classic Everly Brothers* 3-CD box set (Bear Family 1992) ★★★★, *The Golden Years Of The Everly Brothers* (Warners 1993) ★★★★, *Heartaches And Harmonies* 4-CD box set (Rhino 1995) ★★★★★, *Walk Right Back: On Warner Bros. 1960 To 1969* 2-CD set (Warners 1996) ★★★★, *All I Have To Do Is Dream* (Carlton 1997) ★★★, *The EP Collection* (See For Miles 1998) ★★★, *The Masters* (Eagle 1998) ★★★, *The Very Best Of The Cadence Era* (Repertoire 1999) ★★★, *Devoted To You: Love Songs* (Varèse Sarabande 2000) ★★★★, *The Complete Cadence Recordings: 1957-1960* (Varèse Sarabande 2001) ★★★★.

● VIDEOS: *Rock 'N' Roll Odyssey* (MGM 1984).

● FURTHER READING: *Everly Brothers: An Illustrated Discography*, John Hosum. *The Everly Brothers: Walk Right Back*, Roger White. *Ike's Boys*, Phyllis Karpp. *The Everly Brothers: Ladies Love Outlaws*, Consuelo Dodge. *For-Everly Yours*, Peter Aarts and Martin Alberts.

EXCITERS

Formed in the Jamaica district of Queens, Ne[w] York City, this aptly named group, whic[h] included sole male Herb Rooney (b. New Yor[k] City, New York, USA) alongside Brenda Rei[d] Carol Johnson and Lillian Walker, first came [to] prominence with the vibrant 'Tell Him', a U[S] Top 5 hit in 1962 (also a hit in the UK for Billi[e] Davis in 1963). Produced by Leiber And Stoll[er], and written by Bert Berns (under h[is] pseudonym Bert Russell), the single's energ[y] established the pattern for subsequent release[s] 'Do Wah Diddy Diddy' (later a hit by Manfre[d] Mann) and 'He's Got The Power' took elemen[ts] from both uptown soul and the all-female grou[p] genre, but later singles failed fully to exploit th[e] powerful combination. The group had lesse[r] hits with 'I Want You To Be My Boy' (1965), [a] revival of 'A Little Bit Of Soap' (1966) and 'Yo[u] Don't Know What You're Missing (Till It's Gone[)] (1969), but failed to recapture the verve of thos[e] first releases. They re-entered the UK charts [in] 1975 with 'Reaching For The Best'. Ronnie Pa[ce] and Skip McPhee later replaced Johnson an[d] Walker, while Rooney and Reid (his wife) had [a] minor 1978 hit as Brenda And Herb, releasi[ng] one album in 1979, *In Heat Again*.

● ALBUMS: *Tell Him* (United Artists 196[2]) ★★★, *The Exciters* (Roulette 1965) ★★★, *Cavi[ar] And Chitlins* (RCA Victor 1969) ★★, *Black Beau[ty]* (Today 1971) ★★, *Heaven Is Wherever You A[re]* (20th Century 1976) ★★.

● COMPILATIONS: *Tell Him* (EMI 1991) ★★[★] *Reaching For The Best* (Hot 1995) ★★[★] *Something To Shout About* (Sequel 1995) ★★★.

● FILMS: *Bikini Beach* (1964).

EYES

Formed in Ealing, London, England in 1965, t[he] Eyes were one of the era's most exciting 'pop-a[rt]' acts. Founders Terry Nolder (vocals), Chr[is] Lovegrove (guitar), Phil Heatly (guitar) a[nd] Barry Allchin (bass) were all previous[ly] members of aspiring beat groups Dave Russe[ll] And The Renegades and Gerry Hart And T[he] Hartbeats. They forged the Eyes upon securi[ng] drummer Bryan Corcoran and were signed [by] Mercury Records soon afterwards. Released [in] November 1965, 'When The Night Falls' is [a] doomy, atmospheric single marked by a slo[w] tempo, unorthodox, 'scratchy' guitar breaks a[nd] Holder's semi-spoken vocal. It was succeeded [by] 'My Immediate Pleasure', a brash compositi[on] encapsulating the concurrent Mod ethos. The[se] singles were later combined on a much-priz[ed] EP, *The Arrival Of The Eyes*. Having failed [to] chart with original material, the Eyes opted [to] record cover versions for later release[s]. Meritorious interpretations of the Ever[ly] Brothers' 'Man With Money' and the Beatle[s'] 'Good Day Sunshine' (both 1966) followed, b[ut] they lacked the innovative features of the[ir] predecessors. The Eyes were then persuaded [to] record *A Tribute To The Rolling Stones*, collection of Mick Jagger/Keith Richards' songs and associated material issued on a budget-priced imprint and credited to the Pupils. By this point Heatly had been replaced by Steve Valentine but, sensing their career was over, the Eyes split up in 1967. Nolder then formed the Entire Sioux Nation with future Pink Fairies/Motörhead guitarist Larry Wallis.

● ALBUMS: as the Pupils *A Tribute To The Rolling Stones* (Wing 1967) ★★.

● COMPILATIONS: *The Eyes: Blink* (Bam Caruso 1983) ★★★, *Scene But Not Heard* (Bam Caruso 1985) ★★★.

EYES OF BLUE

Founded in Neath, Wales, by Ritchie Francis (bass, vocals), Gary Pickford Hopkins (vocals, guitar), Phil Ryan (keyboards), Ray Williams (guitar) and Wyndham Rees (drums), Eyes Of Blue started out as a soul revival band before gradually attuning their musical sensibilities to the emergent US west coast rock scene. They initially recorded two singles for Deram Records, 'Heart Trouble' and 'Supermarket Full Of Cans', in 1966 and 1967, but for their debut album moved to Mercury Records. The band covered two Graham Bond songs on the album and he also wrote the sleevenotes. *The Crossroads Of Time* was a satisfying mix of diverse musical influences, ranging from psychedelic and ethnic instrumentation to jazz and classical styles. However, their own songwriting suffered in comparison to Bond's songs and their cover version of the Beatles' 'Yesterday'. For their second album, 1969's reincarnation-themed *In Fields Of Ardath*, they replaced their original drummer with John 'Pugwash' Weathers (b. 2 February 1947, Carmarthen, Glamorganshire, Wales; drums). The album featured their collaboration with Quincy Jones, 'Merry Go Round', which was included on the soundtrack to Jones' *Toy Grabbers* movie score, and the band itself was later seen on film in *Connecting Rooms*. Other tracks revealed a debt to the UK progressive rock movement, although another Bond cover, 'Spanish Blues', was present as continuity. It was the band's final release, although they did also record 1971's *Bluebell Wood* under the moniker Big Sleep. After their eventual demise, the band members scattered. Ryan joined Man, Weathers worked with Pete Brown and Gentle Giant, while Francis recorded a solo album.

● ALBUMS: *The Crossroads Of Time* (Mercury 1968) ★★★, *In Fields Of Ardath* (Mercury 1969) ★★.

FABARES, SHELLEY

b. Michelle Fabares, 19 January 1944, Santa Monica, California, USA. Fabares, whose music career was highlighted by the 1962 US number 1 song 'Johnny Angel', was the niece of actress Nanette Fabray. Turning to acting herself, Fabares debuted as Trudy in the television series Annie Oakley. She subsequently landed roles in such 50s movies as *Never Say Goodbye*, *Rock, Pretty Baby* and *Summer Love*, before being offered the part of Mary Stone in the US television situation comedy *The Donna Reed Show* in 1958. As the show's popularity rose, both she and series co-star Paul Petersen signed recording contracts with Colpix Records. Fabares was given the ballad 'Johnny Angel', written by Lee Pockriss and Lyn Duddy, and after its debut on the television show, the single quickly rose to number 1. Three follow-up singles did not fare nearly as well, and neither did the two albums she recorded for Colpix. In 1964 Fabares married record producer Lou Adler, who arranged a record deal for Fabares with Vee Jay Records. There were no hits and Fabares then became the first artist signed to his new Dunhill Records label. Again there were no hits and Fabares returned to acting, working with Herman's Hermits in their movie *Hold On!* and with Elvis Presley in *Girl Happy*, *Spinout* and *Clambake*. She divorced Adler in 1967 and continued to work in film and television. In the early 80s, she appeared in the series *One Day At A Time* as Francine Webster. She married actor Mike Farrell in 1984, and in the late 80s and early 90s was a member of the cast of *Coach*, a popular US television situation comedy. Her work rate slowed in the latter part of the decade, and in October 2000 she underwent a liver transplant.

● ALBUMS: *Shelley!* (Colpix 1962) ★★, *The Things We Did Last Summer* (Colpix 1962) ★★, with James Darren, Paul Petersen *Teenage Triangle* (Colpix 1963) ★★, with Darren, Petersen *More Teenage Triangle* (Colpix 1964) ★, *A Time To Sing* (MGM 1968) ★★.

● COMPILATIONS: *The Best Of Shelley Fabares* (Rhino/Sequel 1994) ★★★.

● FILMS: *The Girl Rush* (1965), *Never Say Goodbye* (1956), *Rock, Pretty Baby* (1956), *The Bad Seed* (1956), *Summer Love* (1958), *Marjorie Morningstar* (1958), *Annette* (1958), *Ride The Wild Surf* (1964), *Girl Happy* (1965), *Spinout* aka *California Holiday* (1966), *Hold On!* aka *There's No Place Like Space* (1966), *Clambake* (1967), *A Time To Sing* (1968), *Hot Pursuit* (1987), *Love Or Money* (1990).

FACTORY (USA 60s)

Formed in Los Angeles, California in 1965, the Factory were one of countless acts evolving in the wake of the Byrds and the Turtles. Lead guitarist Lowell George, Warren Klein (rhythm guitar) and Martin Kibbee (bass) were initially joined by drummer Dallas Taylor, but the last-named was quickly replaced by Richie Hayward. Taylor later resurfaced in Clear Light, Crosby, Stills And Nash and Manassas. The Factory reportedly played 'Hey Joe' louder than any local rivals, although contemporaneous releases; 'Smile, Let Your Life Begin' and 'No Place I'd Rather Be', show a group combining adventurism with melody. Former Teddy Bears member Marshall Leib produced these sessions, but following a support slot with the Mothers Of Invention, the Factory fell under the sway of the former's leader, Frank Zappa. He allowed the quartet an artistic freedom which ranged from the Captain Beefheart-influenced 'Lightning-Rod Man' to the fuzz-guitar folk/rock of 'The Loved One'. These recordings remained unreleased for 25 years. The Factory split up in 1967; George spent several weeks in the Standells, before replacing Ray Collins in the Mothers, while Klein, Kibbee and Hayward formed the Fraternity Of Man. George and Hayward were subsequently reunited in Little Feat.
● COMPILATIONS: *Lightning-Rod Man* (1994) ★★★.

FAHEY, JOHN

b. John Aloysius Fahey, 28 February 1939, Takoma Park, Maryland, USA, d. 22 February 2001, Salem, Oregon, USA. Fahey learned to play country-style guitar in the footsteps of Hank Williams and Eddy Arnold at the age of 14, inspired by the recordings of 'Blind' Willie Johnson, and other blues greats. He toured during his teens with Henry Vestine (later of Canned Heat), and studied for several years at the American University in Washington to gain a BA in Philosophy and Religion. In 1963, he briefly attended the University Of California at Berkeley before transferring to UCLA to study folklore and write his thesis on Charley Patton. Fahey announced himself with a style based on an original folk blues theme, encompassing blues, jazz, country and gospel music, and at times incorporating classical pieces, although retaining an almost traditional edge to his arrangements. His 12-string work, featuring intricate fingerpicking and open tunings, became a major influence on other American acoustic guitarists. Fahey was also quick to spot other talent. He persuaded Bukka White and Skip James to return to music, and was the first to record Leo Kottke.

Fahey's early recordings appeared under the Blind Thomas moniker on the obscure Fonotone label. These 1958 recordings, pressed up as 78s and catalogued as 'authentic Negro folk music', were an elaborate joke at the expense of folk purists, but also demonstrated Fahey's mastery of the blues idiom. He released only a hundred copies of his 1959 debut, *Blind Joe Death*, financing the pressing with $300 raised from his job at a gas station. His satirical humour was again in evidence, with one side of the album credited to an obscure bluesman called Blind Joe Death who Fahey alleged to have discovered on a field trip to the south. Fahey re-recorded the album in 1964 and 1967 (*The Legend Of Blind Joe Death*, released in 1996, is a mix of all three albums), and by the late 60s it had become a cult record, one with which to be seen, rather than actually play. Fahey's early recordings appeared on his own Takoma Records imprint, with his second and third albums also being re-recorded for reissue in 1967.

The masterful *The Transfiguration Of Blind Joe Death*, arguably his greatest album, was originally released on the River Boat label in 1965. Fahey signed with Vanguard Records in 1967, although he only recorded two albums for the company, including the *musique concrete* album *Requia And Other Compositions For Guitar Solo*. Later still, after a brief sojourn with Reprise Records during which he recorded two albums with an orchestra of Dixieland musicians, he was dropped due to insufficient sales. Fahey's work was heard in the counter-culture classic *Zabriskie Point*, but generally, his influence was greater than his own success. The ambitious *America*, which was restored to its intended double album length when reissued in the late 90s, didn't sell as well as its predecessors and Takoma suffered in the general recession which hit the music industry in the 70s. The label was eventually sold to Chrysalis Records.

Fahey's personal problems intensified in the 80s as, suffering from diabetes and chronic fatigue caused by the Epstein Barr virus, he fell upon hunting down and selling collectable records to earn money. He retained his cult following, however, and continued to release the occasional album. Fahey affiliated himself with the alternative rock community in the 90s, concentrating on the electric guitar and *musique concrete* instead of the acoustic blues/folk of his earlier albums. He co-founded the influential Revenant label, while his intent to disown his past was signalled by the dissonant soundscape of 'On The Death And Disembowelment Of The New Age', the key track on his comeback release *City Of Refuge*. The album, which included a dedication of the song 'Hope Slumbers Eternal' to Mazzy Star's vocalist Hope Sandoval, received a good reception in the alternative press. In 1997, Fahey recorded an album with the *avant garde*'s figurehead Jim O'Rourke, and teamed up with Boston-based post rock outfit Cul De Sac on *The Epiphany Of Glenn Jones*. The following year he recorded his first solo electric guitar album, *Georgia Stomps, Atlanta Struts, And Other Contemporary Dance*

Favorites. Fahey's creative renaissance was sadly cut short by his death in February 2001, two days after undergoing coronary bypass surgery.
● ALBUMS: *Blind Joe Death* i (Takoma 1959) ★★★★, *Death Chants, Break Downs & Military Waltzes* i (Takoma 1963) ★★★★, *Blind Joe Death* ii (Takoma 1964) ★★★★, *Dance Of Death & Other Plantation Favorites: John Fahey Vol 3* i (Takoma 1964) ★★★, *The Transfiguration Of Blind Joe Death* (River Boat/Takoma 1965) ★★★★, *Guitar: John Fahey Vol. 4* aka *The Great San Bernardino Birthday Party And Other Excursions* (Takoma 1966) ★★★, *Volume 1: Blind Joe Death* iii (Takoma 1967) ★★★★, *Volume 2: Death Chants, Breakdowns, & Military Waltzes* ii (Takoma 1967) ★★★★, *Volume 3: The Dance Of Death & Other Plantation Favorites* ii (Takoma 1967) ★★★★, *Volume 6: Days Have Gone By* (Takoma 1967) ★★★, *Requia And Other Compositions For Guitar Solo* (Vanguard 1968) ★★★, *The Voice Of The Turtle* (Takoma 1968) ★★★★, *The New Possibility: John Fahey's Guitar Solo Christmas Album* (Takoma 1969) ★★★, *The Yellow Princess* (Vanguard 1969) ★★★★, *America* (Takoma 1971) ★★★, *Of Rivers And Religion* (Reprise 1972) ★★★★, *After The Ball* (Reprise 1973) ★★★, *Fare Forward Voyagers (Soldier's Choice)* (Takoma 1973) ★★★★, *John Fahey, Leo Kottke, Peter Lang* (Takoma 1974) ★★★, *Old Fashioned Love* (Takoma 1975) ★★★, *Christmas With John Fahey Vol II* (Takoma 1975) ★★, *Visits Washington, D.C.* (Takoma/Chrysalis 1979) ★★★, *Yes! Jesus Loves Me: Guitar Hymns* (Takoma/Chrysalis 1980) ★★★, *Live In Tasmania* (Takoma/Chrysalis 1981) ★★★, *Christmas Guitar: Volume One* (Varrick 1982) ★★★, with Terry Robb *Popular Songs Of Christmas & New Year's* (Varrick 1983) ★★★, *Railroad I* (Takoma 1983) ★★★★, *Let Go* (Varrick 1984) ★★★, *Rain Forests, Oceans, And Other Themes* (Varrick 1985) ★★★, *I Remember Blind Joe Death* (Varrick 1987) ★★★, *God, Time And Causality* (Shanachie 1989) ★★★, *Old Girlfriends And Other Horrible Memories* (Varrick 1992) ★★★, *City Of Refuge* (Tim/Kerr 1996) ★★★, *Womblife* (Table Of The Elements 1997) ★★★, with Cul De Sac *The Epiphany Of Glenn Jones* (Thirsty Ear 1997) ★★★, *Georgia Stomps, Atlanta Struts, And Other Contemporary Dance Favorites* (Table Of The Elements 1998) ★★★, *Hitomi* (LivHouse 2000) ★★★.
COMPILATIONS: *The Early Sessions* (Takoma) ★★★, *The Essential John Fahey* (Vanguard 1974) ★★, *The Best Of John Fahey 1959-1977* (Takoma/Sonet 1977) ★★★★, *Return Of The Repressed: The John Fahey Anthology* (Rhino 1994) ★★★★, *The Legend Of Blind Joe Death* (Fantasy 1996) ★★★★, *Best Of The Vanguard Years* (Vanguard 1999) ★★★.
VIDEOS: *In Concert* (Vestapol Video 1996).
FURTHER READING: *How Bluegrass Music Destroyed My Life: Stories By John Fahey*, John Fahey.

FAIRIES
Formed in Colchester, Essex, England, in 1963 as Dane Stephens And The Deepbeats, this vibrant R&B group consisted of Dane Stephens (vocals), Fred Gandy (guitar), John Acutt (guitar), Mick 'Wimp' Weaver (bass) and John 'Twink' Alder (drums). In 1964 they secured a 'one-off' deal with Decca Records. Having opted for the more contemporary-sounding Fairies, the group completed a hurried version of Bob Dylan's 'Don't Think Twice It's All Right'. Stephens left the line-up soon after its release and was replaced by Nick Wymer. Wymer had previously led another local act, Nick And The Nomads aka Nix-Nomads who had already recorded a single for HMV Records. 'You're Nobody ('Til Somebody Loves You)' was pedestrian, but its b-side, 'She'll Be Sweeter Than You', is an English R&B/punk classic. The Fairies were signed to HMV through Wymer's association. Having passed on an option to record 'Don't Bring Me Down', later a hit for the Pretty Things, the Fairies recorded 'Get Yourself Home', which the Pretty Things themselves had rejected. The result was another impressive slice of rhythmic R&B and, although not a hit, was one of the finest UK discs of 1965. Sadly, the Fairies were forced to tame their image for their last release, the disappointing 'Don't Mind'. A chastened Wymer left the line-up and dropped out of professional music when plans for a projected group with Them's Billy Harrison fell through. The Fairies split up soon after his departure. Twink joined the In Crowd and was later a member of a host of groups including Tomorrow, the Pretty Things and Pink Fairies.

FAITH, ADAM
b. Terence Nelhams, 23 June 1940, Acton, London, England. During the British 'coffee bar' pop music phenomenon of the late 50s two artists reigned supreme: Cliff Richard and Adam Faith. While the former has shown astonishing staying power the young Faith had a remarkable run of hit records during the comparatively short time before he retired from singing. In seven years between 1959 and 1966 he made the UK chart 24 times. Both his UK chart-toppers, 'What Do You Want?' and 'Poor Me' lasted barely two minutes; both featured the infectious pizzicato strings of John Barry's orchestra, both were written by Les Vandyke (alias Johnny Worth) and both featured the hiccuping delivery with the word, 'baby' pronounced 'bybeee'. 'Poor Me' is also notable because of the Barry arrangement contains an early glimmer of the 'James Bond Theme'. This became Faith's early 'gimmick'. Faith's continued success rivalled that of Richard's, when in a short period of time he appeared in three films: *Beat Girl*, *Never Let Go* and *What A Whopper!*, and made a surprisingly confident appearance, being interviewed by John Freeman in a serious BBC television programme, *Face To Face*. Adults were shocked

to find that during this conversation, this lucid teenager admitted to pre-marital sex and owned up to listening to Sibelius.

The following year, still enjoying chart hits, he appeared in the film *Mix Me A Person*. His career continued until the dawn of the Beatles, then Faith was assigned the Roulettes (featuring a young Russ Ballard). Songwriter Chris Andrews proceeded to feed Adam with a brief second wave of infectious beat-group hits most notably 'The First Time'. In the mid-60s he gave up singing and went into repertory theatre and in 1971 became an acting star in the UK television series *Budgie*. Additionally Faith has produced records for Roger Daltrey and Lonnie Donegan and managed Leo Sayer. His two supporting actor roles in *Stardust* and *McVicar* bought him critical success in addition to appearing in *Yesterday's Hero*. For a number of years he has been a wealthy financial consultant, although in the 90s he returned to the stage with *Budgie* and *Alfie*, and to UK television as Frank Carver in *Love Hurts*. Faith still works on the perimeter of the musical world, and released a new album in 1993. While he will readily admit that his vocal range was limited, his contribution to popular music was significant insofar as he was the first British teenager to confront a hostile world of respectable parents and adults, and demonstrate that pop singers were not all mindless 'layabouts and boneheads'.

● ALBUMS: *Adam* (Parlophone 1960) ★★★, *Beat Girl* film soundtrack (Columbia 1961) ★★★, *Adam Faith* (Parlophone 1962) ★★★, *From Adam With Love* (Parlophone 1963) ★★★, *For You* (Parlophone 1963) ★★★, *On The Move* (Parlophone 1964) ★★★, *Faith Alive* (Parlophone 1965) ★★, *I Survive* (Warners 1974) ★★, *Midnight Postcards* (PolyGram 1993) ★★.
● COMPILATIONS: *Best Of Adam Faith* (Starline 1974) ★★★, *The Two Best Sides Of Adam Faith* (EMI 1978) ★★★, *20 Golden Greats* (Warwick 1981) ★★★, *Not Just A Memory* (See For Miles 1983) ★★★★, *The Best Of Adam Faith* (MFP 1985) ★★★★, *The Adam Faith Singles Collection: His Greatest Hits* (EMI 1990) ★★★, *The EP Collection* (See For Miles 1991) ★★★★, *The Best Of The EMI Years* (EMI 1994) ★★★★, *The Very Best Of Adam Faith* (EMI Gold 1997) ★★★★.
● FURTHER READING: *Adam, His Fabulous Year*, Adam Faith. *Poor Me*, Adam Faith. *Acts Of Faith*, Adam Faith.
● FILMS: *Beat Girl* aka *Wild For Kicks* (1960), *Never Let Go* (1960), *What A Whopper!* (1961), *What A Carve Up!* aka *No Place Like Homicide* (1962), *Mix Me A Person* (1962), *Stardust* (1974), *Yesterday's Hero* (1979), *Foxes* (1980), *McVicar* (1980).

FAITHFULL, MARIANNE
b. 29 December 1946, Hampstead, London, England. Ex-convent schoolgirl Faithfull began her singing career upon meeting producer

Andrew Loog Oldham at a London party. She was thus introduced into the Rolling Stones circle and a plaintive Mick Jagger/Keith Richard song, 'As Tears Go By', became her debut single in 1964. This folksy offering reached number 9, the first of four UK Top 10 hits, which also included 'Come And Stay With Me' (penned by Jackie DeShannon) and the pounding 'Summer Nights'. Her album reflected an impressive balance between folk and rock, featuring material by Donovan, Bert Jansch and Tim Hardin, but her doomed relationship with Jagger undermined ambition as a performer. Faithfull also pursued her thespian aspirations, appearing on stage in Chekhov's *Three Sisters* and on celluloid in the title role of *Girl On A Motorcycle*, but withdrew from the public eye following a failed suicide attempt upon her break with Jagger. Drug problems bedevilled her recovery, but Faithfull re-emerged in 1976 with *Dreamin' My Dreams*, mild country set on which she was backed by the Grease Band.

A further period of seclusion followed but the singer rekindled her career three years later with the impressive *Broken English*. The once virginal voice was now replaced by a husky drawl, particularly effective on the atmospheric title track and her version of Shel Silverstein's 'The Ballad Of Lucy Jordan' reached number 4 in the UK charts. Faithfull's later releases followed a similar pattern, but nowhere was the trauma of her personal life more evident than on *Blazing Away*, a live album on which the singer reclaimed songs from her past. Recorded live in Brooklyn's St. Ann's Cathedral, her weary intonation, although artistically effective, contravened the optimism of those early recordings. *A Secret Life* was a return to the brooding atmosphere of *Broken English*, but although her voice was still captivating, the songs were generally uninspiring. *20th Century Blues* was a an ill-chosen live album from a Paris concert featuring songs by Kurt Weill, Noël Coward and, in Marlene Dietrich pose, 'Falling In Love Again'. More suitable was Faithfull's dramatic interpretation of the Bertolt Brecht/Kurt Weill piece, *The Seven Deadly Sins*, recorded live in Vienna. Her autobiography was a revealing and fascinating insight into a true survivor of the 60s and all that followed.

● ALBUMS: *Come My Way* (Decca 1965) ★★★, *Marianne Faithfull* (Decca 1965) ★★★★, *Go Away From My World* (Decca 1965) ★★★, *Faithfull Forever* (Decca 1966) ★★★, *North Country Maid* (Decca 1966) ★★, *Loveinamist* (Decca 1967) ★★, *Dreamin' My Dreams* (Nems 1976) ★★, *Faithless* (Immediate 1977) ★★, *Broken English* (Island 1979) ★★★★, *Dangerous Acquaintances* (Island 1981) ★★★, *A Child's Adventure* (Island 1983) ★★★, *Strange Weather* (Island 1987) ★★★, *Blazing Away* (Island 1990) ★★★, *A Secret Life* (Island 1995) ★★, *20th Century Blues* (RCA 1996) ★★, *The Seven Deadly*

Sins (RCA 1998) ★★★, *Vagabond Ways* (It Records 1999) ★★★★.

● COMPILATIONS: *The World Of Marianne Faithfull* (Decca 1969) ★★★★, *Marianne Faithfull's Greatest Hits* (Abkco 1969) ★★★, *As Tears Go By* (Decca 1981) ★★★★, *Summer Nights* (Rock Echoes 1984) ★★★, *Rich Kid Blues* Castle 1985) ★★★, *The Very Best Of Marianne Faithfull* (London 1987) ★★★, *Faithfull: A Collection Of Her Best Recordings* (Island 1994) ★★★, *A Perfect Stranger: The Island Anthology* Island 1998) ★★★★, *A Stranger On Earth: An Introduction To Marianne Faithfull* (Decca 2001) ★★★★.

● FURTHER READING: *Marianne Faithfull: As Tears Go By*, Mark Hodkinson. *Faithfull*, Marianne Faithfull and David Dalton.

FALCONS

This R&B vocal group from Detroit, Michigan, USA, helped define soul music in the early 60s. The great legacy of music left by the Falcons has unfortunately been obscured by the group's reputation as the genesis of so many great talents. The group has at one time claimed as members Eddie Floyd (b. 25 June 1935, Montgomery, Alabama, USA), Wilson Pickett (b. 18 March 1941, Prattville, Alabama, USA), Joe Stubbs (b. Joe Stubbles), brother of the Four Tops' Levi Stubbs and later a member of the Contours and then the Originals, Mack Rice, the original singer of 'Mustang Sally', and guitarists Lance Finnie and Robert Ward successively, whose bluesy guitar work helped immeasurably to raise the reputation of the group. The Falcons' chart success was surprisingly slim, with only five releases making the chart, the best-known being 'You're So Fine', a proto-soul number led by Stubbs that went to number 2 R&B (number 17 pop) in 1959, and 'I Found A Love', the incredibly torrid secular gospel number led by Wilson Pickett that went to number 6 R&B (number 75 pop) in 1962.

The original Falcons formed in 1955 and comprised lead Eddie Floyd, Bob Manardo, Arnett Robinson, Tom Shetler, and Willie Schofield. In 1956 they met Detroit producer Robert West and for the next three years issued releases by the Falcons on several labels, including his own Flick label, but without achieving any national success. After Joe Stubbs and Mack Rice replaced Shetler, Manardo and Robinson in 1957, and guitarist Lance Finnie joined the group, the classic group of Falcons were together, blending gospel fervour to rhythm and blues harmony, as reflected in their 'You're So Fine' hit of 1959. They managed two more hits with Stubbs as lead with 'Just For Your Love' (number 26 R&B 1959) and 'The Teacher' (number 18 R&B 1960), before Wilson Pickett replaced Stubbs in 1960. The memorable 'I Found A Love', and several other Falcons records, featured as backing the Dayton group the Ohio Untouchables, centred

on the great guitar of Robert Ward. In the 70s the Ohio Untouchables had emerged as the premier funk group the Ohio Players, and Ward re-emerged from 25 years' retirement in 1991 to release a well-received blues album. The Falcons disbanded in 1963, but the name continued with another Detroit ensemble, consisting of Carlis 'Sonny' Monroe, James Gibson, Johnny Alvin and Alton Hollowell. This group made the R&B chart in 1966 with 'Standing On Guard'.

● COMPILATIONS: *You're So Fine* (Relic 1985) ★★★, *I Found A Love* (Relic 1985) ★★★.

FAME, GEORGIE

b. Clive Powell, 26 June 1943, Leigh, Lancashire, England. Entrepreneur Larry Parnes gave the name to this talented organist during the early 60s following a recommendation from songwriter Lionel Bart. Parnes already had a Power, a Wilde, an Eager and a Fury. All he now needed was Fame. It took a number of years before Fame and his band the Blue Flames had commercial success, although he was a major force in the popularizing of early R&B, bluebeat and ska at London's famous Flamingo club. The seminal *Rhythm And Blues At The Flamingo* was released in January 1964. Chart success came later that year with a UK number 1, 'Yeh, Yeh'. Fame's jazzy nasal delivery, reminiscent of Mose Allison, made this record one of the decade's classic songs. He continued with another 11 hits, including two further UK chart toppers, 'Getaway' and 'The Ballad Of Bonnie And Clyde', the latter of which was his only US Top 10 single in 1968. The former maintained his jazz feel, which continued on such striking mood pieces as 'Sunny' and 'Sitting In The Park'. Thereafter, he veered towards straight pop. His recent change of record labels (from Columbia Records to CBS Records) had attempted to re-market him and at one stage teamed him with the Harry South Big Band. While his albums showed a more progressive style his singles became lightweight, the nadir being when he teamed up with Alan Price to produce some catchy pop songs. Fame has also played straight jazz at Ronnie Scott's club, performed a tribute to Hoagy Carmichael with singer Annie Ross, and has sung over Esso advertisements. In recent times Fame has been content touring with Van Morrison as keyboard player, given a brief cameo to perform the occasional hit. During the renaissance of the Hammond B3 organ (an instrument that Fame had originally pioneered in the London clubs) during another jazz boom of the early 90s it was announced that Fame had recorded a new album *Cool Cat Blues*; and its subsequent release to favourable reviews and regular concert appearances indicated a new phase. The album was recorded to the highest standards and featured smooth contributions from Steve Gadd, Robben Ford,

Richard Tee, Jon Hendricks and Boz Scaggs. A reggae reworking of 'Yeh, Yeh' and a graceful version of Carmichael's 'Georgia' were two outstanding tracks. Morrison joined Fame on the former's classic 'Moondance'.

Fame followed up with *The Blues And Me*, an album of a similar high standard. Tragedy struck Fame in 1994 when his wife committed suicide. Since then he has continued to work and record with Morrison and Bill Wyman as well as gigging with his latter-day version of the Blue Flames, which features two of his sons. Tristan Powell (guitar) and James Powell (drums) are both excellent young musicians, moulding well into their father's warm musical niche. Fame has reached a stage in his career where he can play what he chooses; now he has reverted to his first love, jazz. He is an exemplary musician whose early and latest work is necessary for any discerning record collection.

● ALBUMS: *Rhythm And Blues At The Flamingo* (Columbia 1964) ★★★★, *Fame At Last* (Columbia 1964) ★★★★, *Sweet Things* (Columbia 1966) ★★★, *Sound Venture* (Columbia 1966) ★★★★, *Two Faces Of Fame* (CBS 1967) ★★★, *The Third Face Of Fame* (CBS 1968) ★★★, *Seventh Son* (CBS 1969) ★★, *Georgie Does His Thing With Strings* (CBS 1970) ★★, *Goin' Home* (CBS 1971) ★★, with Alan Price *Fame And Price, Price And Fame Together* (CBS 1971) ★★★, *All Me Own Work* (Reprise 1972) ★★, *Georgie Fame* (Island 1974) ★★, *Right Now!* (Pye 1979) ★★★, *That's What Friends Are For* (Pye 1979) ★★★, *Closing The Gap* (Piccadilly 1980) ★★, with Annie Ross *In Hoagland '81* (Bald Eagle 1981) ★★★★, *No Worries* (4 Leaf Clover 1988) ★★, *Cool Cat Blues* (Go Jazz 1991) ★★★★, *The Blues And Me* (Go Jazz 1994) ★★★, with Van Morrison *How Long Has This Been Going On* (Verve 1995) ★★★★, with Morrison, Ben Sidran, Mose Allison *Tell Me Something: The Songs Of Mose Allison* (Verve 1996) ★★, *Name Droppin': Live At Ronnie Scott's* (Go Jazz 1999) ★★★, *Poet In New York* (Go Jazz 2000) ★★★, *Walking Wounded: Live At Ronnie Scott's* (Go Jazz 2000) ★★★★, *Relationships* (Three Line Whip 2001) ★★★★.

● COMPILATIONS: *Hall Of Fame* (Columbia 1967) ★★★★, *Georgie Fame* (Starline 1969) ★★★★, *Fame Again* (Starline 1972) ★★★★, *20 Beat Classics* (Polydor 1982) ★★★★, *The First 30 Years* (Connoisseur 1989) ★★★, *The Very Best Of Georgie Fame And The Blue Flames* (Spectrum 1998) ★★★★, *Funny How Time Slips Away* (Castle 2001) ★★★.

FAMILY DOGG

Formed in the UK in 1969, the original line-up comprised Steve Rowland, Albert Hammond, Mike Hazelwood, Doreen De Veuve and Zooey. Rowland already had a chequered history as a film-maker, actor and continental recording artist before forming the Double R production company with Ronnie Oppenheimer. With the backing of Fontana A&R head Jack Baverstock, Rowland produced a string of hits for Dave Dee, Dozy, Beaky, Mick And Tich and the Herd, while his company also recorded such artists as P.J. Proby, the Magic Lanterns and Amory Kane. After assembling a talented back-up crew, Rowland launched Family Dogg and soon scaled the charts with 'A Way Of Life', written by Roger Cook and Roger Greenaway. Specializing in high harmony and classy covers, the Dogg followed up unsuccessfully with Paul Simon's 'Save The Life Of My Child' and recorded an album of hit standards with backing by several members of the newly formed Led Zeppelin. Although the Dogg had considerable commercial potential they were clearly a studio group with a tendency to lose members at short notice. In July 1969, De Veuve was replaced by the glamorous ex-*Charlie Girl* star Christine Holmes, and several months later Ireen Scheer took over Zooey's role. With Hammond and Hazelwood busy writing the 13-piece suite *Oliver In The Overworld* for Freddie And The Dreamers, Rowland was forced to explain that his group was a concept that only came together occasionally before dissipating into individual projects. The UK music press, unconvinced by such rhetoric, made sarcastic news item remarks such as 'No change in Family Dogg line-up this week'. Nobody was too surprised when the Dogg ceased operations early in the new decade.

● ALBUMS: *A Way Of Life* (Bell 1969) ★★, *The View From Rowland's Head* (Polydor 1972) ★.

FAMILY TREE

Bob Segarini (guitar/vocals), Mike Olsen (keyboards), Bill Whittington (bass) and Newman Davis (drums) formed Family Tree in 1965. This San Franciscan rock group was bedevilled by internal unrest, and by the time their debut album was released, Segarini was the only remaining original member. *Miss Butters* unveiled the anglophile persuasion that marked his subsequent music, but was deemed out of step with the prevailing musical trend. Mike Dure (guitar), Jim De Cocq (keyboards), Bill 'Kootch' Troachim (bass) and Vann Slatter (drums) completed the band's final line-up, which broke apart in 1970. Segarini and De Cocq formed Roxy, while founder-member Olsen found fame as virtuoso Lee Michaels.

● ALBUMS: *Miss Butters* (RCA 1968) ★★.

FANTASTIC BAGGYS

The Fantastic Baggys was a recording outlet for songwriting team P.F. Sloan (herein known as 'Flip') and Steve Barri. The duo supplied surfing act Jan And Dean with several compositions, notably 'Summer Means Fun' and 'From All Over The World', and added backing harmonies on several sessions, factors which in turn inspired this concurrent career. Bob Myman (drums) and Jerry Cargman completed the ominal Baggys line-up, but the venture was, in essence, studio-based. The Sloan/Barri team wrote arranged and produced every track on *Tell 'Em I'm Surfin'*, but the duo quickly tired of their creation and ceased using the name following the release of the Gary Paxton-penned 'It Was I' (1965). However, the Fantastic Baggys had proved highly popular in South Africa and a second album, *Ride The Wild Surf*, was compiled the following year. Although five tracks, drawn from singles and out-takes, did feature Sloan and Barri, more than half the set featured anonymous musicians imitating the original group. By the release of *Surfer's Paradise*, the ruse had run its course. Here any connection was even more tenuous and the sole Sloan/Barri performance, 'Only When You're Lonely', was mistakenly drawn from another studio project, the Grass Roots. When the album proved commercially moribund, the Baggy's appellation was mercifully abandoned.

● ALBUMS: *Tell 'Em I'm Surfin'* (Imperial 1964) ★★, *Ride The Wild Surf* (1964) ★★, *Surfer's Paradise* (1967) ★.

● COMPILATIONS: *Surfin' Craze* (1983) ★★★, *Anywhere The Girls Are! The Best Of Fantastic Baggys* (Sundazed 2000) ★★★.

ARDON, DON

Don Maughn, *c.*1943, Coventry, West Midlands, England. As the vocalist with the Sorrows, Maughn was featured on this cult group's most durable release, the pulsating 'Take A Heart'. A number 21 hit in September 1965, its hypnotic, throbbing beat was maintained on subsequent releases, several of which the singer co-composed. Here, however, he preferred to use an alternative surname, Ardon, which was then retained for the artist's solo career. His version of John D. Loudermilk's 'Indian Reservation (The Lament Of The Cherokee Reservation Indian)' gave him his first and only US hit single in 1968, reaching the Top 20. He broke into the UK charts in 1970 with 'Belfast Boy', a homage to the talented, but troubled footballer, George Best. This success paved the way for the re-issue of 'Indian Reservation' which, when resurrected, climbed to a respectable number 3 and became one of that year's most distinctive chart entries. Yet despite several further releases, some of which were remakes of former Sorrows material, Ardon was unable to secure consistent success.

● ALBUMS: *I've Paid My Dues* (Young Blood 1970) ★★, *Released* (Young Blood 1970) ★★.

● COMPILATIONS: *Indian Reservation: The Best Of* (See For Miles 1996) ★★.

ARIÑA, MIMI

Mimi Margharita Baez, 30 April 1945, Palo Alto, California, USA, d. 18 July 2001, Mt. Tamalpais, California, USA. The younger sister of folk singer Joan Baez, Mimi was pursuing a solo career when she met and married Richard

Fariña. The couple began performing together in 1964 and completed two exceptional albums, *Celebrations For A Grey Day* and *Reflections In A Crystal Wind*, before Richard was killed in a motorcycle accident on 30 April 1966. Two years later Mimi helped to compile the commemorative *Memories*, as well as *Long Time Coming And A Long Time Gone*, a collection of her husband's lyrics, poetry and short stories. Unsure of direction, she later joined the Committee, a satirical theatre group, where she worked as an improvisational actor before returning to singing. Having forged a short-lived partnership with Tom Jans, which resulted in one low-key album, she resumed her solo career. The consuming passion of Fariña's later years was Bread And Roses, an organization which brought live music into convalescent homes, psychiatric wards and drug rehabilitation centres.

● ALBUMS: with Richard Fariña *Celebrations For A Grey Day* (Vanguard 1965) ★★★, with Fariña *Reflections In A Crystal Wind* (Vanguard 1966) ★★★, with Tom Jans *Take Heart* (A&M 1971) ★★★, *Solo* (Philo 1985) ★★★.

● COMPILATIONS: with Fariña *Memories* (Vanguard 1968) ★★, *The Best Of Mimi And Richard Fariña* (Vanguard 1970) ★★★, with Fariña *Pack Up Your Sorrows: Best Of The Vanguard Years* (Vanguard 2000) ★★★.

● FURTHER READING: *Positively 4th Street: The Lives And Times Of Joan Baez, Bob Dylan, Mimi Baez Fariña And Richard Fariña*, David Hadju.

● FILMS: *Festival* (1967), *Fools* (1970), *Celebration At Big Sur* (1971), *Sing Sing Thanksgiving* (1974), *Massive Retaliation* (1984).

FARIÑA, RICHARD

b. 1937, Brooklyn, New York City, New York, USA, d. 30 April 1966, Carmel, California, USA. A songwriter, novelist and political activist, Fariña was drawn into folk music following his marriage to singer Carolyn Hester. Their ill-starred relationship ended in 1961 when, following a European tour, Richard decided to remain 'in exile' to work on his first novel *Been Down So Long It Looks Like Up To Me*. It was during this time that Fariña's first recordings were made. *Dick Fariña & Eric Von Schmidt*, the product of a two-day session in the cellar of London's Dobell's Jazz Shop, also featured an impromptu appearance by Bob Dylan, masquerading under his celebrated pseudonym, Blind Boy Grunt. Fariña returned to America in 1963 where he married Mimi Baez, the sister of folk singer Joan Baez. The couple began performing together and were latterly signed to Vanguard Records. Their two superb albums were released in the mid-60s, the first of which, *Celebrations For A Grey Day*, included Richard's classic song, 'Pack Up Your Sorrows'. His novel was published in 1966, but its author was killed in a motorbike crash during a celebratory party. Fariña's death robbed a generation of an excellent writer and gifted musician.

● ALBUMS: *Dick Fariña & Eric Von Schmidt* (1964) ★★★, with Mimi Fariña *Celebrations For A Grey Day* (Vanguard 1965) ★★★, with Fariña *Reflections In A Crystal Wind* (Vanguard 1966) ★★★.

● COMPILATIONS: *Memories* (Vanguard 1968) ★★, *The Best Of Mimi And Richard Fariña* (Vanguard 1970) ★★★, with Fariña *Pack Up Your Sorrows: Best Of The Vanguard Years* (Vanguard 2000) ★★★.

● FURTHER READING: *Been Down So Long It Looks Like Up To Me*, Richard Fariña. *Positively 4th Street: The Lives And Times Of Joan Baez, Bob Dylan, Mimi Baez Fariña And Richard Fariña*, David Hajdu.

FARINAS
Formed at Leicester Art College, Leicestershire, England, in 1962, the Farinas originally comprised Jim King (saxophone), Harry Overnall (drums), Charlie Whitney (guitar/vocals) and Tim Kirchin (bass). Their primary influence was the Chess Records catalogue of the 50s, and blues rock 'n' rollers such as Chuck Berry in particular. The group recorded its solitary single, 'You'd Better Stop' backed by a cover version of Chris Kenner's 'I Like It Like That', for Fontana Records in 1964. A year later Ric Grech replaced Kirchin, while Roger Chapman came in to take over lead vocals in 1966. Shortly thereafter they abandoned the name Farinas and became first the Roaring Sixties then Family at the suggestion of Kim Fowley.

FARLOWE, CHRIS
b. John Henry Deighton, 13 October 1940, Essex, England. Farlowe's long career began during the 50s skiffle boom when the John Henry Skiffle Group won the all-England championship. He then formed the original Thunderbirds, which remained semi-professional until 1962 when they embarked on a month's engagement in Frankfurt, Germany. Farlowe then met Rik Gunnell, owner of London's Ram Jam and Flamingo clubs, and the singer quickly became a stalwart of the city's R&B circuit. He made his recording debut that year with the pop-orientated 'Air Travel', but failed to secure commercial success until 1966 when his version of the Rolling Stones' song, 'Out Of Time', produced by Mick Jagger, soared to the top of the UK charts. Several minor hits, including 'Ride On Baby' (1966) and 'Handbags And Gladrags' (1967), followed, as well as a brace of pop/soul albums, but Farlowe's intonation proved too craggy for popular consumption. He and the Thunderbirds – which between 1964 and 1967 featured Albert Lee (guitar), Dave Greenslade (organ), Bugs Waddell (bass), Ian Hague (drums) and Jerry Temple (congas) – remained one of the country's most

impressive R&B acts, although sessio musicians were increasingly employed fc recording purposes. By 1968 the group had bee reduced to a line-up of Farlowe, Lee, Pete Solle (keyboards) and Carl Palmer (drums), but tw years later the singer founded an all-new grou; the Hill. The venture's sole album, *From Here 'Mama Rosa*, was not a commercial success an Farlowe joined ex-colleague Greenslade i Colosseum. This powerful jazz-rock grou; disbanded in 1971, and having briefly switche allegiances to Atomic Rooster, Farlowe retire from rock to pursue an interest in military an Nazi memorabilia.

He re-emerged in 1975 with *Live!*, but durir the rest of the decade conspicuously failed find a satisfactory niche for his powerful, gritt voice. Cameo appearances during the 80s o sessions for Jimmy Page engendered the widel acclaimed *Out Of The Blue* and *Born Agai* which together served notice that the singer feeling for the blues remained intact. Althoug he gigs infrequently he can still be see performing as a support act, and he can sti cause goosebumps with his sensational versio of 'Stormy Monday Blues'. He rejoined h colleagues in Colosseum in 1996 for a reunio tour and album, before resuming his solo caree Farlowe is blessed with a magnificent voice b has never been rewarded with the kind c commercial breakthrough achieved by To; Jones.

● ALBUMS: *Chris Farlowe & The Thunderbirc* aka *Stormy Monday* (Columbia 1966) ★★★, *Things To Think About* (Immediate 1966) ★★★ *The Art Of Chris Farlowe* (Immediate 196(★★★, *The Last Goodbye* (Immediate 1969) ★★ as Chris Farlowe And The Hill *From Here 'Mama Rosa* (Polydor 1970) ★★, *Live!* (Polydc 1975) ★★★, *Out Of The Blue* (Brand New 198! ★★★, *Born Again* (Brand New 1986) ★★★ *Farlowe* aka *Waiting In The Wings* (Barsa/Lin 1991) ★★★, with Roy Herrington *Live In Berli* (Backyard 1991) ★★★, *Lonesome Road* (Indig 1995) ★★★, *As Time Goes By* (KEG 1995) ★★ *BBC In Concert* 1969, 1976 recordings (Windson 1996) ★★★, *The Voice* (Citadel 1998) ★★★ *Glory Bound* (Out Of Time 2001) ★★★.

● COMPILATIONS: *The Best Of Chris Farlou Volume 1* (Immediate 1967) ★★★, *Out Of Tim* (Immediate 1975) ★★★★, *Out Of Time – Paint Black* (Charly 1978) ★★★, *Greatest Hi* (Immediate 1978) ★★★★, *Mr. Soulful* (Castl 1986) ★★★, *Buzz With The Fuzz* (Decal 198; ★★★, *I'm The Greatest* (See For Miles 199(★★★★, *Hits* (Repertoire 1999) ★★★, *Dig Tl Buzz: First Recordings '62-'65* (RPM 2001) ★★★.

FARON'S FLAMINGOS
Formed in Liverpool, England, in 1961, Faron Flamingos were one of the pivotal acts of th Merseybeat era who completely missed th ferry (sic) with no commercial succes whatsoever. Founding members Nicky Crouc

(guitar/vocals), Billy Jones (guitar/vocals), Eric London (bass) and Trevor Morias (b. 16 October 1943, Liverpool, England; drums) had worked together since 1959 as the Ravens, before adding vocalist Faron (b. Bill Roughley). Cavern Club DJ Bob Wooler suggested the name Faron's Flamingos. In 1962 London and Jones left the group which continued as a four-piece with ex-Undertakers bassist Mushy Cooper. Following a tour of France, Paddy Chambers (b. Patrick John Chambers, 30 April 1944, Liverpool, England, d. 28 September 2000; guitar/vocals) was added to the line-up and when Cooper left for Lee Curtis in 1963, Faron took over on bass. This version of Faron's Flamingos recorded four tracks for *This Is Merseybeat*, before securing a deal with Oriole Records. Sadly, their rousing version of 'Do You Love Me' was eclipsed by Brian Poole And The Tremeloes' inferior reading and an equally ebullient 'Shake Sherry' made little impression. The disillusioned group broke up in November 1963. Faron and Chambers joined the Big Three, while Morias later found success in the Peddlers.

FARR, GARY

Gary Farr began his music career playing folk and blues in English south coast pubs and clubs. He was persuaded to form an R&B band which, having adopted the name the T-Bones, secured the resident slot at London's Crawdaddy club, previously the home of the Rolling Stones and the Yardbirds. Farr led several versions of the T-Bones before dissolving the group in 1967. He joined former Blossom Toes drummer Kevin Westlake in a short-lived duo, the Lion and the Fish, before recording his debut solo album, *Take Something With You*. This excellent set featured contributions from members of Mighty Baby and the aforementioned Blossom Toes, while a similar line-up was responsible for the singer's second collection, *Strange Fruit*, which also featured guitarist Richard Thompson. In 1972 Farr moved to America where he completed a third album at the famed Muscle Shoals studio. He subsequently became resident in Los Angeles, but despite continuing to write material, the singer has made no subsequent recordings.
● ALBUMS: *Take Something With You* (1969) ★★★★, *Strange Fruit* (1971) ★★★, *Addressed To The Censors Of Love* (1972) ★★.
● COMPILATIONS: *London 1964/65* (1977) ★★★.

FARRELL, WES

b. 21 December 1940, New York, USA, d. 29 February 1996, Fisher Island, Florida, USA. One of pop's most successful entrepreneurs, Farrell rose to prominence in the early 60s as an associate of Luther Dixon. He co-wrote several songs for the Shirelles, including the frenetic R&B song 'Boys', later covered by the Beatles, before joining Roosevelt Music in an A&R capacity. Farrell signed Neil Diamond and the

Feldman/Gottehrer/Goldstein team, and showed a flair for unashamed pop through his association with Jay And The Americans. The artist co-wrote two of their best-known singles, 'Come A Little Bit Closer' and 'Let's Lock The Door (And Throw Away The Key)', and these major US hits were the prelude to a highly lucrative period. His Picturetone publishing company became a feature of the 'teenybop' market while Farrell enjoyed success as a producer with the Cowsills and Every Mother's Son, both of which he leased to MGM Records. He dabbled with underground rock through an association with Boston group the Beacon Street Union, before returning to 'bubblegum' styles with the immensely popular Partridge Family and continued successfully with Tony Orlando And Dawn. An attendant television series helped this group secure five US Top 20 hits during 1970/1. Farrell later founded the Chelsea label, which became one of the leading labels of the disco era. He died from cancer in 1996.

FASCINATIONS

Formed in 1960 in Detroit, Michigan, USA, the Fascinations were a female vocal quartet who were produced by Curtis Mayfield. The group was originally called the Sabre-ettes, and included lead singer Shirley Walker and Martha Reeves (b. 18 July 1941, Alabama, USA), who went on to lead Martha And The Vandellas. After several personnel changes, the group comprised Walker, new lead vocalist Bernadine Boswell Smith, her sister Joanne Boswell Levell, and Fern Bledsoe. They moved to Chicago and were discovered there by members of the Impressions, who brought them to Mayfield's attention. Their first two singles were recorded for the ABC-Paramount label in 1962-63, and did not sell well. That label dropped them, but Mayfield did not forget the group and in 1966, when he started his own Mayfield label, he signed the Fascinations, eventually releasing five singles by the group. Of those, three made the US R&B charts, with the second of those, 'Girls Are Out To Get You', rising to number 13 (it also made number 92 on the pop chart). When the Fascinations' contract came up for renewal in 1969, Mayfield did not sign them again, and the Fascinations disbanded. In 1971, they reunited for a tour of England but split permanently after that tour.
● COMPILATIONS: *Out To Getcha!* (Sequel 1997) ★★★★.

FAT MATTRESS

Formed in 1969 by Noel Redding (b. David Redding, 25 December 1945, Folkestone, Kent, England), the disaffected bassist from the Jimi Hendrix Experience. A frustrated guitarist and songwriter, Redding established this outfit to run concurrently as an outlet for his talents. He was joined by ex-Cheetahs vocalist Neil Landon, a previous colleague from beat group the Loving

Kind and latterly a member of the Flowerpot Men, and two long-standing friends, ex-Big Beats, Jim Leverton (keyboards/bass) and Eric Dillon (drums). Fat Mattress secured a large advance, but although their debut was an enjoyable, melodic set, in the English pop vein of the Move and Small Faces, it lacked a sense of identity. The quartet made its live debut in February 1969, but prestigious slots on Hendrix tours failed to generate public interest. Three singles were released of which 'Naturally' was the strongest, but none failed to sell in sufficient quantity. The final ignominy came when Redding was fired by the rest of the band and replaced by guitarist Steve Hammond and Mick Weaver. This reshaped line-up completed *Fat Mattress II* before breaking up.
● ALBUMS: *Fat Mattress* (Polydor 1969) ★★★, *Fat Mattress II* (Polydor 1970) ★★.
● COMPILATIONS: *The Black Sheep Of The Family: The Anthology* (Essential 2000) ★★★.

FELIX, JULIE

b. 14 June 1938, Santa Barbara, California, USA. Felix arrived in the UK during the early 60s at a time when several US folk singers, including Paul Simon and Jackson C. Frank, had also relocated to London. Her early recordings revealed a commercial, rather than innovative talent, a fact emphasized by weekly appearances on UK television's *The Frost Report* (1967/68). She followed the liberal tradition of Tom Paxton or Pete Seeger, rather than that of the radical left, although she was an early champion of the folk-styled singer/songwriter movement, notably Leonard Cohen, and was proclaimed as 'Britain's Leading Lady of Folk'. Her humanitarian beliefs had, however, been put to practical use by the singer's tour of the African states of Kenya and Uganda, working for the Christian Aid and Freedom From Hunger charities. Felix enjoyed two successful British television series in her own right, *Once More With Felix* (1969/70) and *The Julie Felix Show* (1971), and enjoyed a UK Top 20 hit in 1970 with a version of 'El Condor Pasa', produced by pop svengali Mickie Most. The singer's 'wholesome' image was tarred by a conviction for possession of marijuana, but she continued a prolific recording career, albeit to less publicity, into the 80s, as well as performing for Women's Rights, Green and environmental benefits, and founding Britain's first 'New Age Folk Club'.
● ALBUMS: *Julie Felix* (Decca 1964) ★★★, *2nd Album* (Decca 1965) ★★★, *3rd Album* (Decca 1966) ★★★, *Julie Felix Sings Dylan And Guthrie* (Decca 1966) ★★★, *Changes* (Fontana 1966) ★★★, *Julie Felix In Concert* (Fontana 1967) ★★★, *Flowers* (Fontana 1968) ★★, *This World Goes Round And Round* (Fontana 1969) ★★★, *Going To The Zoo* (Fontana 1969) ★★★, *Clotho's Web* (1971) ★★, *Lightning* (1974) ★★★, *London Palladium* (1974) ★★★, *Hota Chocolata* (1977)

★★, *Blowing In The Wind* (1982) ★★★, *Bright Shadows* (1989) ★★★.
● COMPILATIONS: *The World Of Julie Felix* (Decca 1969) ★★★, *The World Of Julie Felix Volume 2* (Decca 1970) ★★★, *This Is Julie Felix* (1970) ★★★, *The Most Collection* (1972) ★★★, *This Is Julie Felix Volume 2* (1974) ★★★, *Amazing Grace* (1987) ★★★, *El Condor Pasa* (Start 1995) ★★★.

FENDERMEN

Formed in 1959 in Milwaukee, Wisconsin, USA, the Fendermen were a trio best known for the 1960 US chart Top 5 rock 'n' roll adaptation of the Jimmie Rodgers country standard 'Muleskinner Blues'. The group consisted of guitarists Jim Sundquist and Phil Humphrey (both b. 26 November 1937, Sundquist in Niagara, Wisconsin, USA, and Humphrey in Stoughton, Wisconsin, USA) and drummer John Howard, of LaCrosse, Wisconsin, USA. The two guitarists, who preferred the Fender brand of electric guitar, hence the name of the group, recorded 'Muleskinner Blues' initially for the small Cuca label. It was picked up by the somewhat larger Minnesota-based Soma label and became a hit in May 1960. (Howard was added at that time, for live appearances.) The group recorded one album for Soma, now a valued rarity in the USA, and continued together until 1966, with no other chart successes.
● ALBUMS: *Mule Skinner Blues* (Soma 1960) ★★.

FENTON, SHANE

b. Bernard William Jewry, 27 September 1942, London, England. Fenton achieved his first notable success after securing a spot on *Saturday Club*, BBC Radio's influential show. Backed by the Fentones and sporting a distinctive silver lamé suit, the singer quickly became a part of Britain's pre-beat enclave, beside other home-grown talent including Cliff Richard, Marty Wilde, Duffy Power and Billy Fury. Fenton had a UK Top 30 hit in 1961 with the mythologizing 'I'm A Moody Guy', but despite several similarly structured releases, only 'Cindy's Birthday' (1962) broached the UK Top 20. Deemed passé on the rise of the Beatles, Fenton eked out a living from the rock 'n' roll/cabaret circuit until revitalizing his career in the 70s under a new guise, Alvin Stardust.
● ALBUMS: *Good Rockin' Tonight* (Contour 1974) ★★.
● FILMS: *It's All Happening* (1963).

FENTONES

Jerry Wilcox (b. 1940; lead guitar), Mickey Eyre (b. 1942; rhythm guitar), William Walter Edward 'Bonney' Oliver (bass) and Tony Hinchcliffe (b. 1940; drums) provided the backing to singer Shane Fenton. They became a popular attraction in their own right, recording several instrumental singles, including 'The Mexican' and 'The Breeze And I', both of which reached ıe UK Top 50 in 1962. Briefly touted as possible ıvals to the Shadows, such aspirations proved ver-ambitious and in keeping with many pre-eat contemporaries, the Fentones were later clipsed by the Beatles and the new generation ıllowing in their wake.

● FILMS: *It's All Happening* (1963).

ʹEVER TREE

ılthough a Texas group, Fever Tree made its ıark with a tribute to the Summer of Love's ıost city with their 1968 anthem 'San Francisco ɨirls (Return Of The Native)'. Comprising Rob ıandes (keyboards), Dennis Keller (vocals), ı.E. Wolfe (bass), John Tuttle (drums) and ʹichael Knust (guitar), the psychedelic group ırmed in Houston, Texas, in the mid-60s as ıostwick Vine. The name change came in 1967 ınd the group subsequently signed with ɔhicago-based Mainstream Records. Two ınsuccessful singles were recorded, and the ıroup then signed to Uni Records, and recorded ıeir self-titled debut album in 1968. 'San ʹrancisco Girls (Return Of The Native)' was ıenned by Vivian Holtzman, one of the group's ɔroducers. Although only a minor chart hit, it ıeceived much airplay on the new USA FM rock ıtations and on John Peel's *Top Gear* radio ɔrogramme in the UK. The group recorded four ılbums, three of which charted in the USA, ıefore splitting up in 1970. Interest in the group ʹas renewed in the mid-80s psychedelic revival, ınd compilation albums were issued in both the ʹSA and UK.

● ALBUMS: *The Fever Tree* (Uni 1968) ★★★, ınother *Time, Another Place* (Uni 1968) ★★, ɔreation (Uni 1969) ★★, *Angels Die Hard* film ɔundtrack (Uni 1970) ★, *For Sale* (Ampex 1970) ★★, *Live At Lake Charles 1978* (Shroom 1998) ★★.

COMPILATIONS: *Best Of Fever Tree* (1985) ★★★, *San Francisco Girls: The Best Of Fever Tree Era* 1986) ★★★.

ɔTH DIMENSION

ɔriginally known as the Versatiles and later as ıe Vocals, Marilyn McCoo (b. 30 September ɔ943, Jersey City, New Jersey, USA), Florence ıaRue (b. 4 February 1944, Philadelphia, ʹennsylvania, USA), Billy Davis Jnr. (b. 26 June ɔ940, St. Louis, Missouri, USA), Lamont ʹcLemore (b. 17 September 1940, St. Louis, ʹissouri, USA) and Ron Townson (b. 20 January ɔ933, St. Louis, Missouri, USA, d. 3 August 2001, ıas Vegas, USA) were a soul-influenced harmony ıroup, based in Los Angeles, and signed to ɔohnny Rivers' fledgling Soul City label. They ıprang to fame in 1967 as an outlet for the then ınknown talents of songwriter Jimmy Webb. ʹbullient singles on the pop charts, including ɔo Where You Wanna', 'Up, Up And Away' and ɔarpet Man', established their fresh voices, ʹhich wrapped themselves around producer ıones Howe's dizzy arrangements.

Having completed two albums containing a number of Webb originals, the group then took to another composer, Laura Nyro, whose beautiful soul-styled songs 'Stoned Soul Picnic', 'Sweet Blindness' (both 1968), 'Wedding Bell Blues' (1969) and 'Save The Country' (1970) continued the 5th Dimension's success and introduced the group to the R&B charts. These popular recordings were punctuated by 'Aquarius/Let The Sunshine In', a medley of songs from the rock musical *Hair*, which topped the US chart in 1969 and reached number 11 in Britain that same year. In 1971 the group reached number 2 in the USA with the haunting 'One Less Bell To Answer'. From then on, however, the MOR elements within their style began to take precedence and the quintet's releases grew increasingly bland. In 1976 McCoo and Davis (who were now married) left for a successful career both as a duo and as solo artists. They had a US number 1 hit together in 1976 with 'You Don't Have To Be A Star', which was followed up in 1977 by their last Top 20 hit, 'Your Love'. McCoo went on to host the US television show *Solid Gold* for much of the early 80s. Townson, McLemore and LaRue carried on with new members, recording two albums for Motown Records before establishing themselves on the nightclub circuit. The original quintet briefly reunited in the early 90s for a series of concerts, touring as the Original 5th Dimension. Townson retired from the group in 1997 due to ill health, and passed away four years later.

● ALBUMS: *Up Up And Away* (Soul City 1967) ★★★, *The Magic Garden* (Soul City 1967) ★★★, *Stoned Soul Picnic* (Soul City 1968) ★★★, *The Age Of Aquarius* (Soul City 1969) ★★★, *Portrait* (Bell 1970) ★★, *Love's Lines, Angles & Rhymes* (Bell 1971) ★★★, *Live!* (Bell 1971) ★★, *Individually & Collectively* (Bell 1972) ★★, *Living Together, Growing Together* (Bell 1973) ★★, *Soul & Inspiration* (Bell 1974) ★★, *Earthbound* (ABC 1975) ★★, *Star Dancing* (Motown 1978) ★★, *High On Sunshine* (Motown 1978) ★★, *In The House* (Click 1995) ★★.

● COMPILATIONS: *The Greatest Hits* (Soul City 1969) ★★★, *The July 5th Album* (Soul City 1969) ★★★, *Reflections* (Bell 1971) ★★★, *Greatest Hits On Earth* (Bell 1972) ★★★, *Anthology* (Rhino 1986) ★★★, *The Definitive Collection* (Arista 1997) ★★★, *The Very Best Of 5th Dimension* (Camden 1999) ★★★★.

FIREBALLS

Formed in the autumn of 1957 in Raton, New Mexico, USA, the Fireballs originally comprised George Tomsco (b. 24 April 1940, Raton, New Mexico, USA; guitar, vocals), Chuck Tharp (b. 3 February 1941; lead vocals), Danny Trammell (b. 14 July 1940; rhythm guitar), Stan Lark (b. 27 July 1940; bass, vocals) and Eric Budd (b. 23 October 1938; drums). Their Tex-Mex instrumental rock 'n' roll was driven by Tomsco's clear and concise guitar sound, which helped the group place 11 singles in the US charts between 1959 and 1969, although they achieved their greatest success when they hooked up with singer Jimmy Gilmer. The Fireballs also attracted controversy in the 60s, when they were used to overdub music behind unfinished tapes recorded by Buddy Holly before his death in 1959.

Founder members Tomsco and Tharp met at Raton High School in New Mexico. After the others came in, they rehearsed and won a talent contest in January 1958 with a performance of 'Great Balls Of Fire', from which they took their name. After a shaky start that found members leaving for college and then returning, they recorded at Norman Petty's studio in Clovis, New Mexico, in August 1958. Their debut single on Kapp Records was the instrumental 'Fireball', b/w a vocal performance by Tharp, 'I Don't Know'. A contract with the Top Rank label led to the breakthrough instrumental 'Torquay', which scraped into the US Top 40 in September 1959 and saw the band appearing on Dick Clark's *American Bandstand*. Another Top Rank single, 'Bulldog', reached number 24 in January 1960 and one on Warwick, 'Quite A Party', reached number 27 the following June. Several non-charting singles also appeared on the Jaro and Hamilton labels. Tharp left the group and was replaced by Jimmy Gilmer (b. 15 September 1940, LaGrange, Illinois, USA). During 1962 the Fireballs were signed to Dot Records, where they recorded *Torquay*, after which Budd entered the army and was replaced by Doug Roberts (d. 18 November 1981). In early 1963, now billed as Jimmy Gilmer And The Fireballs, they recorded 'Sugar Shack', using an unusual keyboard called a Solovox to give the record a distinctive sound. The result was one of the bestselling hits of 1963 – 'Sugar Shack' stayed at number 1 for five weeks late in the year. An album of the same title also charted. Although several other singles and albums were released, the group was unable to capitalize on that success, although 'Daisy Petal Pickin'' made number 15 in December. Such efforts as *Folk Beat*, a 1965 album crediting only Gilmer, were unsuccessful. By the following year, Dot was sold and in 1967 the Fireballs, minus Gilmer, signed to Atco Records. Before Christmas that year they recorded a Tom Paxton song, 'Bottle Of Wine', which reached number 9 in late December 1967. Three other minor chart singles followed before the end of 1969, including the politically charged 'Come On, React!'. Although the latter marked the end of their chart success, the Fireballs continue as a popular live unit with a line-up now comprising Lark, Tomsco, Ron Cardenas (vocals, keyboards, guitar) and Daniel Aguilar (drums).

● ALBUMS: *The Fireballs* (Top Rank 1960) ★★★, *Vaquero* (Top Rank 1960) ★★★, *Here Are The Fireballs* (Warwick 1961) ★★★, *Torquay*

(Dot 1963) ★★★, as Jimmy Gilmer And The Fireballs *Sugar Shack* (Dot 1963) ★★★, *The Sugar Shackers* (Crown 1963) ★★★, *Sensationa* (Crown 1963) ★★★, as Jimmy Gilmer And The Fireballs *Buddy's Buddy* (Dot 1964) ★★★, as Jimmy Gilmer *Lucky 'Leven* (Dot 1965) ★★, as Jimmy Gilmer *Folk Beat* (Dot 1965) ★★ *Campusology* (Dot 1966) ★★, *Firewater* (Do' 1968) ★★, *Bottle Of Wine* (Atco 1968) ★★★ *Come On, React!* (Atco 1969) ★★.

● COMPILATIONS: *The Best Of The Fireball. (The Original Norman Petty Masters)* (Ace 1992 ★★★★, *Blue Fire & Rarities* (Ace 1993) ★★★ *The Best Of The Fireballs Vocals* (Ace 1994 ★★★, *The Fireballs/Fireball Country* (Calf Creek 1995) ★★★, *Sugar Shack: The Best Of Jimmy Gilmer And The Fireballs* (Varèse Sarabande 1996) ★★★, *The Tex-Mex Fireball* George Tomsco retrospective (Ace 1998) ★★★.

FLAMING YOUTH

This short-lived UK act comprised Gordon Smith (guitar), Brian Chatton (keyboards), Ronnie Caryl (bass) and Phil Collins (drums). Their sole recording, *Ark 2*, was an ambitiously packaged concept album, written and arranged by Ker Howard/Alan Blakely, a team better known for creating the unashamed pop of the Herd and Dave Dee, Dozy, Beaky, Mick And Tich. The project was the subject of considerable hype, bu' its new musical departure proved unconvincing and prematurely doomed Flaming Youth's career. The group was effectively disbanded when Collins successfully auditioned for Genesis in 1970.

● ALBUMS: *Ark 2* (Fontana 1969) ★★★.

FLEE-REKKERS

Originally known as the Ramblers, then Statesiders, this primarily instrumental unit based in the UK was led by Peter Fleerackers, a Dutch-born tenor saxophonist. Elmy Durran (tenor saxophone), Dave 'Tex' Cameron (lead guitar), Ronald Marion (rhythm guitar), Derek Skinner (bass) and Phil Curtis (drums' completed the line-up signed by producer Joe Meek in 1960. 'Green Jeans', a raucous version of the traditional 'Greensleeves', reached number 23 that year, but despite a series of competent singles reminiscent of Johnny And The Hurricanes, this was the group's only chart entry. 'Fireball', arranged by Tony Hatch became the unit's final release in 1963, by which time Alan Monger and Mickey Waller had replaced Marion and Curtis. Cameron, Durran and Monger later enjoyed success in Germany with the Giants, but Fleerackers failed to pursue a high profile career in music. Although Skinner joined the popular Spotniks, it was left to newcomer Waller to achieve greater fame with Jeff Beck and Rod Stewart.

● ALBUMS: *Joe Meek's Fabulous Flee-Rekkers* (Sequel 1991) ★★★★.

FLIRTATIONS

A British-based R&B female group, who originally came from New York City, New York, USA. The Supremes were extremely popular during the late 60s, and record companies were keen to record any female groups who sounded like them. The Flirtations were the beneficiaries of this phenomenon. The members were sisters Shirley and Earnestine Pearce and Viola Billups. The Pearce sisters had earlier been in the Gypsies, but after minor success the group broke up. Recording in England for Deram Records, the Flirtations had a notable US hit in 1969 with a Supremes-styled number, 'Nothing But A Heartache' (number 34 pop), which sounded rather retrograde in the soul market, where it did not chart. The track later became a favourite in Northern Soul clubs.
● ALBUMS: *Love Makes The World Go Round* (Deram 1969) ★★.

FLOATING BRIDGE

The line-up of this US Seattle-based rock group included Rich Dangel, Joe Johansen, Joe Johnson and Michael Marinelli. Their sole album, released in 1969, showcased an exciting twin-lead guitar assault and mixed exciting original material with rearranged cover versions, including a rousing rendition of the Beatles' 'Hey Jude' and a compulsive medley of the Byrds' 'Eight Miles High' and the Rolling Stones' 'Paint It, Black'. However, despite their undoubted skills, and the approbation of then-influential English disc jockey, Simon Stable, who penned enthusiastic liner notes on the UK release, Floating Bridge made little commercial headway.
● ALBUMS: *Floating Bridge* (Liberty 1969) ★★★.

FLOCK

Although they were formed in 1966 (Chicago, Illinois, USA) it was not until 1969 that Flock burst upon a most receptive market. CBS Records had successfully taken the lion's share of the progressive boom and for a short time Flock became one of their leading products. The original band comprised Jerry Goodman (violin), Fred Glickstein (guitar, vocals), Tom Webb and Rick Canoff (saxophones), Ron Karpman (drums), Jerry Smith (bass) and Frank Posa (trumpet). Their blend of jazz and rock improvisations soon exhausted audiences as the solos became longer and longer. Jerry Goodman was the outstanding musician, stunning fans with his furious and brilliant electric violin playing. Their version of the Kinks' 'Tired Of Waiting For You' was memorable if only for the fact that they managed to turn a three-minute pop song into a magnum opus lasting, on occasions, over 10 minutes. Goodman left in 1971 to team up with John McLaughlin in the Mahavishnu Orchestra.
● ALBUMS: *The Flock* (Columbia 1969) ★★★, *Dinosaur Swamps* (Columbia 1970) ★, *Inside Out*

(Mercury 1975) ★.
● COMPILATIONS: *Flock Rock: The Best Of The Flock* (Columbia 1993) ★★★.

FLOWERPOT MEN

This UK outfit was formed in 1967 by the Carter And Lewis songwriting team John Carter (b. John Shakespeare, 20 October 1942, Birmingham, England) and Ken Lewis (b. Kenneth James Hawker, 3 December 1942, Birmingham, England). They magnificently exploited the concurrent flower-power boom. The ensuing single, 'Let's Go To San Francisco', became a UK Top 5 hit and a quartet of session vocalists – Tony Burrows, Robin Shaw, Pete Nelson and Neil Landon – then assumed the name. Burrows, Shaw and Landon went on to complete several well-sculpted releases, notably 'A Walk In The Sky'. An instrumental section, comprising Ged Peck (guitar), Jon Lord (b. 9 June 1941, Leicester, Leicestershire, England; organ), Nick Simper (b. 3 November 1945, Norwood Green, Southall, Middlesex, England; bass) and Carlo Little (drums), accompanied the singers on tour, but this line-up was dissolved when Lord and Simper founded Deep Purple. The three singers changed their name to Friends in late 1968, but were unable to revive their fortunes. In 1970, Burrows enjoyed great success as a vocalist for hire with Edison Lighthouse, the Brotherhood Of Man and White Plains. Landon resurfaced in Fat Mattress, while Shaw and Nelson played alongside Burrows in White Plains.
● COMPILATIONS: *Let's Go To San Francisco* (C5 1988) ★★★, *A Walk In The Sky* (RPM 2001) ★★★.

FLOYD, EDDIE

b. 25 June 1935, Montgomery, Alabama, USA. A founder-member of the Detroit-based Falcons, Floyd was present on both their major hits, 'You're So Fine' (1959) and 'I Found A Love' (1962). He then recorded solo for Lupine in Detroit and Safice in Washington, DC, before moving to Memphis in 1965 to join the Stax Records organization. He first made his mark there as a composer, penning Wilson Pickett's '634-5789', among others. During Floyd's recording tenure at Stax, he enjoyed the use of the session bands Booker T. And The MGs and the Mar-Keys. He opened his account with 'Things Get Better' (1965), followed by the anthem-like 'Knock On Wood' (1966), one of soul's enduring moments, and probably the only time 'lightning' and 'frightening' have been coupled without sounding trite. Although subsequent releases failed to match its success, a series of powerful singles, including 'Love Is A Doggone Good Thing' (1967) and 'Big Bird' (1968), confirmed Floyd's stature both as a performer and songwriter. Although his compositions were recorded by several acts, his next US Top 20 pop hit came with Sam Cooke's 'Bring It On Home To Me' in 1968. Floyd stayed with Stax until its bankruptcy in 1975, whereupon he moved to Malaco Records. His spell there was thwarted by commercial indifference and he left the label for Mercury Records in 1977, but met with no better results. Briefly relocated to London, he recorded under the aegis of Mod resurrectionists Secret Affair. In 1988, Floyd linked up with William Bell's Wilbe venture to release the *Flashback* album. In 1990 Floyd appeared live with a re-formed Booker T. And The MGs and continues to gig consistently up to the present day, although new recordings are rare.

● ALBUMS: *Knock On Wood* (Stax 1967) ★★★, *I've Never Found A Girl* (Stax 1968) ★★★, *You've Got To Have Eddie* (Stax 1969) ★★★, *California Girl* (Stax 1970) ★★, *Down To Earth* (Stax 1971) ★★, *Baby Lay Your Head Down* (Stax 1973) ★★, *Soul Street* (Stax 1974) ★★, *Experience* (Malaco 1977) ★★, *Flashback* (Wilbe 1988) ★★, *Rare Stamps* (Stax 1993) ★★.

● COMPILATIONS: *Rare Stamps* (Stax 1968) ★★★, *Chronicle* (Stax 1979) ★★★, *Knock On Wood: The Best Of Eddie Floyd* (Atlantic 1988) ★★★★.

FOLKES BROTHERS

The three brothers Folkes, Michael, John and Eric together with Count Ossie and his drummers, Owen Gray (piano) and extra vocalist Skitter went to Prince Buster's studio and recorded a classic of Jamaican music. To be labelled a one-hit-wonder is generally something of an insult, but to be a one-record-wonder is an accolade. The Jamaican artists who have made one perfect recording and then vanished, leaving a reputation forever untarnished by later lapses, could be counted on the fingers of one hand. The Folkes Brothers are among that number: in 1961 or early 1962 they recorded 'Oh Carolina', a unique and perfect single, and never appeared again. The record has Count Ossie's Rastafarian drummers thundering out complex African cross-rhythms, Gray's contrastingly American-styled on piano, and the Brothers, with a soulful lead singer Skitter and two lighter-voiced male accompanists, delivering the song. In 1993 an updated version of 'Oh Carolina' reached number 1 in the UK charts for ragga singer Shaggy.

FONTANA, WAYNE

b. Glyn Ellis, 28 October 1945, Manchester, England. After changing his name in honour of Elvis Presley's drummer D.J. Fontana, Wayne was signed to the appropriately named Fontana Records by A&R head Jack Baverstock. Wayne's backing group, the Mindbenders from the horror film of the same name, were as accomplished as their leader and provided a gritty accompaniment. Their first minor hit was with the unremarkable 'Hello Josephine' in 1963. Specializing in mild R&B covers, the group finally broke through with their fifth release, the Major Lance cover 'Um, Um, Um, Um, Um, Um',

which reached number 5 in the UK. The 1965 follow-up, 'The Game Of Love', hit number 2 and spearheaded a Kennedy Street Enterprises Manchester invasion of the USA which lifted the group to number 1. Thereafter, the group struggled, with 'Just A Little Bit Too Late' and the below par 'She Needs Love' being their only further hits. In October 1965, Wayne decided to pursue a solo career, first recording the Bert Berns and Jerry Ragovoy ballad 'It Was Easier To Hurt Her' before finding success with Jackie Edwards' catchy 'Come On Home'. Erratic progress followed, with only the Graham Gouldman composition 'Pamela Pamela' breaking a run of misses. After giving up music during the early 70s, Fontana joined the revivalist circuit, although his progress was frequently dogged by personal problems.

● ALBUMS: *Wayne Fontana And The Mindbenders* (Fontana 1965) ★★★, *The Game Of Love* (Fontana 1965) ★★★, *Eric, Rick Wayne And Bob* (Fontana 1966) ★★★, *Wayne One* (Fontana 1966) ★★, *Wayne Fontana* (MGM 1967) ★★.

● COMPILATIONS: *The Best Of Wayne Fontana & The Mindbenders* (PolyGram 1994) ★★★, *The Very Best Of* (Spectrum 1996) ★★★, *World Of Wayne Fontana & The Mindbenders* (Musicrama 1997) ★★★.

FORD, CLINTON

b. Ian George Stopford-Harrison, 4 November 1931, Salford, Lancashire, England. A popular singer in the UK during the late 50s and 60s, perhaps best known for his novelty songs, such as 'Fanlight Fanny' and 'Madame Moscovitch', but equally at home with a romantic ballad like 'A Little White Gardenia'. Ford entered showbusiness at the age of 24, and made his first public appearance at the Halifax Palace, Yorkshire. After the inevitable grind of small halls and theatres, his rise coincided with the beginning of the UK's 'trad jazz' boom, which suited his breezy, ebullient style. Ironically, his first hit, for Oriole Records in 1959, was exactly the opposite of that style – the somewhat maudlin 'Old Shep'. However, soon after its release, he was in great demand for concerts and radio broadcasts, and made his first television appearance on the top-rated *Ken Dodd Show*. In January 1961 he attracted great attention by singing a 20s number, 'Oh! By Jingo! Oh! By Gee!', on BBC Television's top pop music programme *Easy Beat*, and he subsequently made the UK chart with 'Too Many Beautiful Girls' (1961), 'Fanlight Fanny' (1962) and 'Run To The Door' (1967). One of his most appealing albums was *The Melody Man*, which consisted of a mixture of uptempo numbers such as 'Wild, Wild Women' and 'I Never See Maggie Alone', and the ballads 'By The Fireside' and 'A Beggar In Love'. His own compositions have included 'Crazy Horse' and 'Dream City Lullaby'. With his showbusiness flair and a reputed repertoire of several hundred songs, including perennial

ꞁvourites such as 'What A Little Moonlight Can
o' and 'Everything Is Peaches Down In
ꞁeorgia', Ford was well equipped to survive
hen the hit records dried up. Since then, he has
ꞁntinued to work in various aspects of the
ꞁusiness, including variety and nostalgic re-
ꞁreations of the good old days of music hall. In
ꞁore recent years he is reported to have spent
ꞁuch of his time as an hotelier in Douglas on the
ꞁle Of Man, although he hosted his own series of
ꞁadio 2 programmes in the early 90s.

● ALBUMS: *Clinton Ford* (Time-Oriole 1962)
★★, *The Melody Man* (Columbia 1963) ★★★★,
ꞁh! By Jingo! (Realm-Oriole 1964) ★★★, *Country*
ꞁyle-Ancient And Modern (Time-Oriole 1964)
★★, *Listen With Us* (Columbia 1965) ★★★★,
ꞁandy (Pye 1966) ★★★★, *Big Willy Broke Jail*
ꞁnight (Pye 1966), *Give A Little-Take A Little* (Pye
ꞁ967) ★★★, *Clinton Ford Sings Fanlight Fanny*
ꞁallmark 1967) ★★, *Clinton The Clown* (Pye
ꞁ968) ★★, *Songs For Children Aged One To A*
ꞁundred (Bell 1969) ★, *30 Smash Hits Of The War*
ꞁears Volumes 1 & 2 (70s) ★★, *Let Me Sing A*
ꞁlson Song (Chevron 1979) ★★★, with Alan
ꞁsdon *Clinton Sings Alan Swings* (Lake 2001)
ꞁ★★.

ꞁORD, DEAN, AND THE GAYLORDS

ꞁormed in 1960 in Glasgow, Scotland, Dean Ford
ꞁnd The Gaylords were a musically
ꞁccomplished act before the dawning of the Beat
ꞁge. Junior Campbell (b. William Campbell, 31
ꞁ1ay 1947, Glasgow, Scotland; lead guitar), Pat
ꞁairley (b. 14 April 1946, Glasgow, Scotland;
ꞁhythm guitar), Bill Irving (bass) and Raymond
ꞁuffy (drums) had been fronted
ꞁy various vocalists prior to the arrival of
ꞁhomas MacAleese (b. 5 September 1946,
ꞁoatbridge, Glasgow) in 1963, who assumed the
ꞁean Ford name. The group was signed to
ꞁolumbia Records by Norrie Paramor following
ꞁn audition in Glasgow's Locarno Ballroom.
ꞁean Ford And The Gaylords first single,
ꞁeleased in 1964, was a breezy version of Chubby
ꞁhecker's 'Twenty Miles'. It was succeeded by
ꞁe less distinguished 'Mr. Heartbreak's Here
ꞁnstead', which in turn was followed by a
ꞁowerhouse reading of Shirley Ellis' 'The Name
ꞁame'. In 1965 Graham Knight (b. 8 December
ꞁ946, Glasgow, Scotland) replaced Bill Irving as
ꞁe group made plans to relocate in London,
ꞁngland. Upon their arrival in 1966 they dropped
ꞁe Dean Ford prefix and, as the Gaylords,
ꞁeleased their strongest single to date, 'He's A
ꞁood Face (But He's Down And Out)'. Despite its
ꞁod connotations, the song was written by US
ꞁeam Al Kooper and Irwin Levine. Although not
ꞁ chart hit, the single was often played on pirate
ꞁadio and helped solidify the Gaylords' career.
ꞁomewhat bravely they then decided to change
ꞁeir name completely, rechristening
ꞁemselves the Marmalade, who went on to top
ꞁe UK charts in December 1968 with a cover
ꞁersion of the Beatles' 'Ob-La-Di, Ob-La-Da'.

FORD, EMILE, AND THE CHECKMATES

b. 16 October 1937, Castries, St. Lucia, West
Indies. Having arrived in Britain to study at
technical college, Ford later began singing
professionally in London's dancehalls and coffee
bars. In 1958 he formed the Checkmates with
step-brothers George and Dave Sweetman (bass
and saxophone, respectively), Ken Street
(guitar), Les Hart (saxophone), Peter Carter
(guitar), Alan Hawkshaw (piano) and John
Cuffley (drums) and the following year secured
a recording deal as first prize in a Soho talent
contest. The group's debut single, 'What Do You
Want To Make Those Eyes At Me For?', topped
the charts that year and this Caribbean-
influenced rendition of a popular standard
remains their best-known release. The octet
enjoyed further success with the similarly styled
'Slow Boat To China', 'Them There Eyes'
(credited solely to Ford) and 'Counting
Teardrops'. A concurrent album featured
material drawn from Elvis Presley, Lloyd Price
and Les Paul and Mary Ford, but Ford's novelty
aspect quickly faltered. Having parted from the
Checkmates, who later accompanied P.J. Proby,
the singer spent many years performing in UK
clubs before emigrating to Los Angeles,
California.

● ALBUMS: *New Tracks With Emile* (Pye 1960)
★★★, *Emile* (Piccadilly 1961) ★★★, *Emile Ford*
(1972) ★★★.

● COMPILATIONS: *Under The Midnight Sun*
(Pye Golden Guinea 1965) ★★★, *The Best Of*
Emile Ford And The Checkmates (1991) ★★★,
Greatest Hits (1993) ★★★, *The Very Best Of ...*
(Sound Waves 1994) ★★★, *Counting Teardrops:*
The Pye/Piccadilly Anthology (Sequel 2000)
★★★★.

FOREST

Originally known as the Foresters Of Walesby,
this Birmingham group consisted of brothers
Martin and Hadrian Welham (guitars, vocals)
and Derek Allensby (mandolin, pipes,
harmonium). Formed in 1968, they enjoyed the
patronage of pioneering disc jockey John Peel,
who introduced the trio to the influential
Blackhill agency and penned the liner notes to
their debut album. *Forest* revealed a brand of
underground, 'hippie folk', popularized by the
Incredible String Band and Dr. Strangely
Strange, but the set failed to reap a similar
commercial success. *Full Circle* was a more
professional and accomplished collection, but it
also failed to rise above cult status and Forest
split up soon after its release.

● ALBUMS: *Forest* (Harvest 1969) ★★, *Full Circle*
(Harvest 1970) ★★★.

FORTUNES

Originally formed in March 1963 as a trio, this
UK beat group comprised Glen Dale (b. Richard
Garforth, 24 April 1943, Deal, Kent, England;
guitar); Rod Allen (b. Rodney Bainbridge, 31

March 1944, Leicester, England; bass) and Barry Pritchard (b. 3 April 1944, Birmingham, England, d. 11 January 1999, Swindon, Wiltshire, England; guitar). The group had come together at Clifton Hall, the pop academy in the Midlands masterminded by their manager Reg Calvert. After perfecting their harmonic blend, the group recruited David Carr (b. 4 August 1943, Leyton, Essex, England; keyboards) and Andy Brown (b. 7 July 1946, Birmingham, England; drums) and toured consistently in the Midlands. Their debut single, 'Summertime Summertime' passed without notice, but the follow-up 'Caroline' was taken up as the theme song for the pirate radio station of the same name. By 1965 the group had broken into the UK and US Top 10 with 'You've Got Your Troubles' and modestly stated their ambition of recording pop ballads and harmonious standards. 'Here It Comes Again' and 'This Golden Ring' displayed their easy listening appeal and suggested the possibility of a long-term showbusiness career. Unfortunately, the group was hampered by the departure of vocalist Glen Dale who went on to pursue an unsuccessful solo career. To make matters worse, their manager was shot dead in a dispute over the ownership of the UK pirate station Radio City. The group continued and after switching record labels scored an unexpectedly belated US hit with 'Here Comes That Rainy Day Feeling Again' in 1971. Back in the UK, they also enjoyed their first hits in over five years with 'Freedom Come Freedom Go' and 'Storm In A Teacup' and have since sustained their career, albeit with changing personnel, on the cabaret circuit.
● ALBUMS: *The Fortunes* i (Decca 1965) ★★★, *That Same Old Feeling* (World Pacific 1969) ★★★, *The Fortunes* ii (Capitol 1971) ★★★, *Here Comes That Rainy Day Feeling Again* (Capitol 1971) ★★★, *Storm In A Teacup* (Capitol 1972) ★★★.
● COMPILATIONS: *Remembering* (Decca 1977) ★★★, *Best Of The Fortunes* (EMI 1983) ★★★, *Music For The Millions* (Decca 1984) ★★★, *Greatest Hits* (BR 1985) ★★★, *Here It Comes Again* (Deram 1996) ★★★, *The Singles* (BR 1999) ★★★.

FOUNDATIONS

Formed in January 1967, the Foundations were discovered by London record dealer Barry Class as they rehearsed in the Butterfly, a club situated in a basement below his office. He introduced the group to songwriters Tony Macauley and John MacLeod, whose composition 'Baby, Now That I've Found You' became the group's debut release. An engaging slice of commercial pop/soul, the single soared to the top of the UK charts and by February 1968 had reached number 9 in the USA, with global sales eventually exceeding three million. The group's multiracial line-up included Clem Curtis (b. 28 November 1940, Trinidad, West Indies; vocals), Alan Warner (b. 21 April 1947, London,

England; guitar), Tony Gomez (b. 13 Decembe 1948, Colombo, Sri Lanka; organ), Pat Burke (9 October 1937, Jamaica, West Indies; teno saxophone, flute), Mike Elliot (b. 6 August 192! Jamaica, West Indies; tenor saxophone), Eri Allandale (b. 4 March 1936, Dominica, We: Indies, d. September 2001; trombone), Pete Macbeth (b. 2 February 1943, London, Englanc bass) and Tim Harris (b. 14 January 194! London, England; drums). Allandale was former member of the Terry Lightfoot and Ale Welsh jazz bands, while Elliot had backed Coli Hicks, brother of British rock 'n' roll singe Tommy Steele. This mixture of youth an experience drew much contemporary commen The Foundations scored a second multi-millior seller in 1968 with 'Build Me Up Buttercu Written by Macauley in partnership wit Manfred Mann's Michael D'Abo, this compulsiv song reached number 2 in Britain before toppin the US chart for two weeks. The group enjoye further success with several similarly style releases, including 'Back On My Feet Again' an 'Any Old Time' (both 1968), but thei momentum faltered when Curtis embarked o an ill-starred solo career. He was replaced b Colin Young (b. 12 September 1944, Barbado: West Indies), but the departure of Ellic signalled internal dissatisfaction. 'In The Ba Bad Old Days' (1969) returned the group to th UK Top 10, but that year's minor hit, 'Born T Live And Born To Die', was their last chart entry The septet split up in 1970 when the rhythr section broke away to form the progressiv group Pluto. A completely new line-up late resurrected the Foundations' name with littl success.
● ALBUMS: *From The Foundations* (Pye 1967 ★★, *Rocking The Foundations* (Pye 1968) ★★ *Digging The Foundations* (Pye 1969) ★★.
● COMPILATIONS: *Back To The Beat* (PRT 1983 ★★, *The Best Of The Foundations* (PRT 1987 ★★★, *Foundations Greatest Hits* (Knight 199(★★★, *Strong Foundations: The Singles And Mor* (Music Club 1997) ★★★★, *Baby Now That I'u Found You* (Sequel 1999) ★★★.
● FILMS: *The Cool Ones* (1967).

FOUR PENNIES

This Blackburn, Lancaster beat group comprise Lionel Morton (14 August 1942, Blackburr Lancashire, England; vocals/rhythm guitar Fritz Fryer (b. David Roderick Carnie Fryer, December 1944, Oldham, England; lead guitar Mike Wilsh (b. 21 July 1945, Stoke-on-Tren England; bass) and Alan Buck (b. 7 April 194: Brierfield, Lancashire, England; drums). The scored a notable UK number 1 hit in 1964 wit 'Juliet' – a Morton-penned ballad that wa originally the b-side of the less immediate 'Te Me Girl', which had a stark simplicity tha enhanced its plaintive qualities. The quarte enjoyed three further Top 20 entries with ' Found Out The Hard Way', 'Black Girl' (bot

1964) and 'Until It's Time For You To Go' (1965), but were unable to sustain a long career. Fryer, having briefly fronted a new act, Fritz, Mike and Mo, later became a successful record producer, while Morton, who married actress Julia Foster, made frequent appearances in children's television programmes.

● ALBUMS: *2 Sides Of The 4 Pennies* (Philips 1964) ★★★, *Mixed Bag* (Philips 1966) ★★★.
● COMPILATIONS: *Juliet* (Wing 1967) ★★★.

FOUR SEASONS

This highly acclaimed New Jersey, USA vocal group first came together in the mid-50s with a line-up comprising vocalists Frankie Valli (b. Francis Castelluccio, 3 May 1937, Newark, New Jersey, USA), brothers Nick and Tommy DeVito (b. 19 June 1936, Bellville, New Jersey, USA) and Hank Majewski. Initially known as the Variatones, then the Four Lovers, they enjoyed a minor US hit in 1956 with 'You're The Apple Of My Eye', composed by Otis Blackwell. After being dropped by RCA Records, they recorded a single for Epic, following which Valli departed in 1958. As a soloist he released 'I Go Ape', composed by singer Bob Crewe. Meanwhile, the Four Lovers released several records under pseudonymous names, during which Nick DeVito and Majewski departed to be replaced by Nick Massi (b. Nicholas Macioci, 19 September 1935, Newark, New Jersey, USA, d. 24 December 2000, Newark, New Jersey, USA) and Bob Gaudio (b. 17 December 1942, the Bronx, New York, USA), a former member of the Royal Teens. After combining with Crewe and Gaudio, the group evolved into the Four Seasons, recording the single 'Bermuda'/'Spanish Lace' for the End label, before signing with Vee Jay Records.

There, they released 'Sherry', which reached number 1 in the USA in September 1962. A brilliant example of falsetto, harmony pop, the track established the group as one of America's most popular. Two months later, they were back at the top with the powerful 'Big Girls Don't Cry' and achieved the same feat the following March with the equally powerful 'Walk Like A Man'. All these hits were underpinned by lustrous, soaring harmonies and thick up-front production, which gave the Seasons a sound that was totally unique in pop at that time. Their international fame continued throughout 1964 when they met fierce competition from the Beatles. A sign of their standing was evinced by Vee Jay's release of a battle of the bands album featuring the Seasons and the Beatles. Significantly, when the Fab Four held four of the Top 5 positions in the *Billboard* chart during early 1964, the Four Seasons represented the solitary competition with 'Dawn (Go Away)' at number 3. The sublime 'Rag Doll' brought them back to the top in the summer of 1964. Nick Massi left the group the following year and was replaced by Charles Calello and then Joe Long.

It was during this period that they playfully released a version of Bob Dylan's 'Don't Think Twice, It's All Right' under the pseudonym the Wonder Who?.

Valli, meanwhile, was continuing to enjoy solo hits including the US number 2 single 'Can't Take My Eyes Off You'. By the end of the 60s, the group reflected the changing times by attempting to establish themselves as a more serious act with *Genuine Imitation Life Gazette*. The album was poorly received, however, and following its release Gaudio replaced Crewe as producer. When Tommy DeVito left in 1970, the lucrative Four Seasons back catalogue and rights to the group name rested with Valli and Gaudio. A brief tie-up with Berry Gordy's Motown Records label saw the release of *Chameleon*, which despite favourable reviews sold poorly. Meanwhile, Valli was receiving unexpected success in the UK thanks to a northern soul dancefloor revival of 'You're Ready Now', which reached number 11 in 1971.

Throughout the early 70s, membership of the Four Seasons was erratic, and Gaudio retired from performing to concentrate on producing. Despite impending deafness, Valli was back at number 1 in 1975 with 'My Eyes Adored You'. With an old track from *Chameleon*, 'The Night', adding to the glory and the latest group line-up reaching the US Top 3 with 'Who Loves You', it was evident that the Four Seasons were as popular as ever. Immense success followed as the group became part of the disco boom sweeping America. The nostalgic 'December 1963 (Oh What A Night)' was a formidable transatlantic number 1 in 1976, but the following year, Valli left the group to concentrate on his solo career. While he again hit number 1 in the USA with the Barry Gibb movie theme, *Grease*, the Four Seasons continued with drummer Gerry Polci taking on lead vocals. Valli returned to the group for a double album recorded live at Madison Square Garden. A team-up with the Beach Boys on the single 'East Meets West' in 1984 was followed by a studio album, *Streetfighter*, which featured Valli. In 1990, the group was inducted into the Rock And Roll Hall Of Fame. Still going strong, Frankie Valli and the Four Seasons have become an institution whose illustrious history spans several musical eras, from the barber shop harmonies of the 50s to the disco beat of the 70s and beyond. It is however the timeless hit singles of the 60s to which the group are indelibly linked.

● ALBUMS: *Sherry And 11 Others* (Vee Jay 1962) ★★★★, *Ain't That A Shame And 11 Others* (Vee Jay 1963) ★★★, *The 4 Seasons Greetings* (Vee Jay 1963) ★★★, *Big Girls Don't Cry* (Vee Jay 1963) ★★★, *Folk-Nanny* (Vee Jay 1963) ★★★, *Born To Wander* (Philips 1964) ★★★, *Dawn And 11 Other Great Songs* (Philips 1964) ★★★★, *Stay And Other Great Hits* (Vee Jay 1964) ★★★, *Rag Doll* (Philips 1964) ★★★★, *We Love Girls* (Vee Jay 1965) ★★★, *The Four Seasons Entertain You*

(Philips 1965) ★★★, *Recorded Live On Stage* (Vee Jay 1965) ★★, *The Four Seasons Sing Big Hits By Bacharach, David And Dylan* (Philips 1965) ★★, *Working My Way Back To You* (Philips 1966) ★★★, *Lookin' Back* (Philips 1966) ★★★, *Christmas Album* (Philips 1967) ★★★, *Genuine Imitation Life Gazette* (Philips 1969) ★★★, *Edizione D'Oro* (Philips 1969) ★★★★, *Chameleon* (Mowest 1972) ★★★, *Who Loves You* (Warners 1976) ★★★, *Helicon* (Warners 1977) ★★★, *Reunited Live* (Sweet Thunder 1981) ★★, *Streetfighter* (Curb 1985) ★★★, *Hope/Glory* (Curb 1992) ★★★.
● COMPILATIONS: *Golden Hits Of The Four Seasons* (Vee Jay 1963) ★★★★, *More Golden Hits By The Four Seasons* (Vee Jay 1964) ★★★★, *Gold Vault Of Hits* (Philips 1965) ★★★★, *Second Vault Of Golden Hits* (Philips 1967) ★★★★, *Seasoned Hits* (Fontana 1968) ★★★★, *The Big Ones* (Philips 1971) ★★★★, *The Four Seasons Story* (Private Stock 1976) ★★★★, *Greatest Hits* (K-Tel 1976) ★★★, *The Collection* (Telstar 1988) ★★★★, *Anthology* (Rhino 1988) ★★★★, *Rarities Volume 1* (Rhino 1990) ★★★, *Rarities Volume 2* (Rhino 1990) ★★★, *The Very Best Of Frankie Valli And The Four Seasons* (PolyGram 1992) ★★★★, *In Season: Frankie Valli And The Four Seasons Anthology* (Rhino 2001) ★★★★, *Off Season: Criminally Ignored Sides From Frankie Valli & The 4 Seasons* (Rhino 2001) ★★★★, *The Definitive Frankie Valli & The Four Seasons* (Warners 2001) ★★★★.
● FILMS: *Beach Ball* (1965).

FOUR TOPS

Levi Stubbs (b. 6 June 1936, Detroit, Michigan, USA), Renaldo 'Obie' Benson (b. 14 June 1936, Detroit, Michigan, USA), Lawrence Peyton (b. 1938, Detroit, Michigan, USA, d. 10 June 1997, USA) and Abdul 'Duke' Fakir (b. 26 December 1935, Detroit, Michigan, USA), first sang together at a party in Detroit in 1954. Calling themselves the Four Aims, they began performing at supper clubs in the city, with a repertoire of jazz songs and standards. In 1956, they changed their name to the Four Tops to avoid confusion with the popular singing group the Ames Brothers, and recorded a one-off single for the R&B label Chess Records. Further unsuccessful recordings appeared on Red Top, Columbia Records and Riverside between 1958 and 1962, before the Four Tops were signed to the Motown Records jazz subsidiary Workshop, in 1963. Motown boss Berry Gordy elected not to release their initial album, *Breaking Through*, in 1964, and suggested that they record with the label's Holland/Dozier/Holland writing and production team. The initial release from this liaison was 'Baby I Need Your Lovin'', which showcased the group's strong harmonies and the gruff, soulful lead vocals of Levi Stubbs; it reached the US Top 20. The following year, another Holland/Dozier/Holland song, 'I Can't Help Myself', topped the charts, and established the Four Tops as one of Motown's most successful groups. Holland/Dozier/Holland continued to write and produce for the Four Tops until 1967.

The peak of this collaboration was 'Reach Out, I'll Be There', a transatlantic hit in 1966. This represented the pinnacle of the traditional Motown style, bringing an almost symphonic arrangement to an R&B love song; producer Phil Spector described the record as 'black [Bob] Dylan'. Other major hits such as 'It's The Same Old Song' and 'Bernadette' were not as ambitious, although they are still regarded as Motown classics today. In 1967, the Four Tops began to widen their appeal with soul-tinged versions of pop hits, such as the Left Banke's 'Walk Away Renee' and Tim Hardin's 'If I Were A Carpenter'. The departure of Holland, Dozier and Holland from Motown later that year brought a temporary halt to the group's progress, and it was only in 1970, under the aegis of producer/writers like Frank Wilson and Smokey Robinson, that the Four Tops regained their hit status with a revival of the Tommy Edwards hit 'It's All In The Game', and the socially aware ballad 'Still Water (Love)'. That same year, they teamed up with the Supremes for the first of three albums of collaborations. Another revival, Richard Harris' hit 'MacArthur Park', brought them success in 1971, while Renaldo Benson also co-wrote Marvin Gaye's hit single 'What's Going On'. However, after working with the Moody Blues on 'A Simple Game' in 1972, the Four Tops elected to leave Motown when the corporation relocated its head office from Detroit to California.

They signed a contract with Dunhill Records, and immediately restored their chart success with records that marked a return to their mid-60s style, notably the theme song to the 'blaxploitation' movie *Shaft In Africa*, 'Are You Man Enough'. Subsequent releases were less dynamic, and for the remainder of the 70s the Four Tops enjoyed only sporadic chart success, although they continued touring and performing their Motown hits. After two years of inactivity at the end of the decade, they joined Casablanca Records, and immediately secured a number 1 soul hit with 'When She Was My Girl', which revived their familiar style. Subsequent releases in a similar vein also charted in Britain and America.

In 1983, the group performed a storming medley 'duel' of their 60s hits with the Temptations during the Motown 25th Anniversary television special. They re-signed to the label for the aptly titled *Back Where I Belong*, one side of which was produced by Holland/Dozier/Holland. However, disappointing sales and disputes about the group's musical direction led them to leave Motown once again for Arista Records, where they found immediate success in 1988 with the singles 'Indestructible' and 'Loco In Acapulco', the latter taken from the soundtrack to the movie *Buster*. The Four Tops retained a constant line-up from their inception up until Peyton's death in June 1997. Their immaculate choreography and harmonies built around the sensational voice of Stubbs, has ensured them ongoing success as a live act from the mid-60s to the present day – notably in the UK and Europe, where they have always been held in higher regard than in their homeland.

● ALBUMS: *Four Tops* (Motown 1965) ★★★, *Four Tops No. 2* (Motown 1965) ★★★★, *Four Tops On Top* (Motown 1966) ★★★★, *Four Tops Live!* (Motown 1966) ★★★★, *Four Tops On Broadway* (Motown 1967) ★★★, *Four Tops Reach Out* (Motown 1967) ★★★★, *Yesterday's Dreams* (Motown 1968) ★★★, *Four Tops Now!* (Motown 1969) ★★★, *Soul Spin* (Motown 1969) ★★★, *Still Waters Run Deep* (Motown 1970) ★★★, *Changing Times* (Motown 1970) ★★★, with the Supremes *The Magnificent Seven* (Motown 1970) ★★★★, with the Supremes *The Return Of The Magnificent Seven* (Motown 1971) ★★, with the Supremes *Dynamite* (Motown 1972) ★★★, *Nature Planned It* (Motown 1972) ★★★, *Keeper Of The Castle* (Dunhill 1972) ★★★, *Shaft In Africa* film soundtrack (Dunhill 1973) ★★, *Main Street People* (Dunhill 1973) ★★, *Meeting Of The Minds* (Dunhill 1974) ★★, *Live And In Concert* (Dunhill 1974) ★★, *Night Lights Harmony* (ABC 1975) ★★, *Catfish* (ABC 1976) ★★, *The Show Must Go On* (ABC 1977) ★★, *At The Top* (MCA 1978) ★★, *The Four Tops Tonight!* (Casablanca 1981) ★★, *One More Mountain* (Casablanca 1982) ★★, *Back Where I Belong* (Motown 1983) ★★, *Magic* (Motown 1985) ★★, *Hot Nights* (Motown 1986) ★★, *Indestructible* (Arista 1988) ★★.

● COMPILATIONS: *Four Tops Greatest Hits* (Motown 1967) ★★★★★, *Four Tops Greatest Hits, Volume 2* (Motown 1971) ★★★★, *Four Tops Story* (Motown 1973) ★★★★, *Four Tops Anthology* (Motown 1974) ★★★★★, *Best Of The Four Tops* (K-Tel 1982) ★★★, *Collection: Four Tops* (Castle 1992) ★★★, *Early Classics* (Spectrum 1996) ★★★ , *The Best Of The ABC Years 1972-77* (Music Club 1998) ★★★, *The Ultimate Collection* (Motown 1998) ★★★★, *Breaking Through* (Motown 1999) ★★★, *The Best Of The Four Tops: The Millennium Collection* (Polydor 1999) ★★★★, *Fourever* 4-CD box set (Hip-O 2001) ★★★★.

FOURMOST

Originally known as the Blue Jays, then the Four Jays, then the Four Mosts, this Merseybeat group comprising Brian O'Hara (b. 12 March 1942, Liverpool, England, d. 27 June 1999, Liverpool, England; lead guitar/vocals), Mike Millward (b. 9 May 1942, Bromborough, Cheshire, England, d. March 1966; rhythm guitar/vocals), Billy Hatton (b. 9 June 1941, Liverpool, England; bass) and Dave Lovelady (b. 16 October 1942, Liverpool, England; drums) achieved momentary fame under the management wing of Brian Epstein. The unit had already been part of the boom of beat music in Liverpool, and played the famous Cavern Club in 1961, long before the Beatles had made their debut. After being auditioned by George Martin they were signed to Parlophone Records, the same label as the Beatles. Two commercial John Lennon and Paul McCartney songs, 'Hello Little Girl' and 'I'm In Love', served as their initial a-sides, but the unflinchingly chirpy 'A Little Lovin'' became the quartet's biggest hit on reaching number 6 in April 1964.

An archetypal Merseybeat group, the Fourmost's later releases veered from Motown Records with an excellent version of the Four Tops' 'Baby I Need Your Lovin'' to the music hall humour of George Formby ('Aunt Maggie's Remedy') and their unswerving 'showbusiness' professionalism was deemed anachronistic in the wake of the R&B boom. Millward developed leukemia and recovered from the chemotherapy but he then died in March 1966. Some reports stated that he died of throat cancer. This tragedy undermined the group's confidence, and despite McCartney's continued patronage – he produced their 1969 rendition of 'Rosetta' – the Fourmost were later consigned to the cabaret circuit and variety engagements. The Fourmost were one of the better outfits to come from the Merseybeat era. Their vocal prowess was powerful and their instrumental delivery always crisp and punchy. Brian O'Hara continued the name until the early 80s before moving onto become a second-hand car dealer. He committed suicide in 1999.

● ALBUMS: *First And Fourmost* (Parlophone 1965) ★★★.

● COMPILATIONS: *The Most Of The Fourmost* (Parlophone 1982) ★★★.

● FILMS: *Pop Gear* (1964), *Ferry Cross The Mersey* (1964).

FOWLEY, KIM

b. 27 July 1942, Los Angeles, California, USA. A prodigious talent, Fowley's role as a producer, songwriter, recording artist and catalyst proved important to 60s and 70s pop. He recorded with drummer Sandy Nelson during the late 50s and later worked with several short-lived hit groups including the Paradons ('Diamonds And Pearls') and the Innocents ('Honest I Do'). Durable success came from his collaborations with schoolfriends Gary S. Paxton and Skip Battin, who performed as Skip And Flip. Fowley produced 'Cherry Pie' (1960), their US Top 20 entry and and, with Paxton, created the Hollywood Argyles whose novelty smash, 'Alley Oop' (1960) topped the US charts. The pair were also responsible for shaping Paul Revere And The Raiders' debut hit, 'Like Long Hair' and in 1962 they assembled the Rivingtons, whose gloriously nonsensical single, 'Papa-Oom-Mow-Mow', was a minor success. That same year Fowley produced 'Nut Rocker' for B. Bumble

And The Stingers, which was a hit on both sides of the Atlantic and a UK number 1. In 1964 Fowley undertook promotional work for singer P.J. Proby and the following year began embracing the Los Angeles counter-culture through his association with scene guru Vito and Frank Zappa's nascent Mothers Of Invention.

Fowley came to Britain on several occasions. The Rockin' Berries recorded 'Poor Man's Son' at his suggestion, he composed 'Portobello Road' with Cat Stevens, and produced sessions for Deep Feeling (which included Dave Mason and Jim Capaldi, later of Traffic), the Farinas (who evolved into Family), the Belfast Gypsies and the Soft Machine. Fowley also recorded in his own right, completing a cover version of the Napoleon XIV hit, 'They're Coming To Take Me Away, Ha-Haaa!', and 'The Trip', a hypnotic paean to underground predilections. He became closely associated with flower power, recording *Love Is Alive And Well* in 1967. This debut album was the first of a prolific output which, although of undoubted interest and merit, failed to match the artist's intuitive grasp of current trends for other acts. He produced material for the Seeds, A.B. Skhy, Warren Zevon and Gene Vincent, while maintaining his links with Europe through Finnish progressive act Wigwam.

Skip Battin joined the Byrds in 1970 and several collaborations with Fowley became a part of the group's late period repertoire, although long-time fans baulked at such ill-fitting material as 'Citizen Kane' and 'America's Great National Pastime'. Battin's first solo album, *Skip*, consisted of songs written with Fowley, while their partnership continued when the bass player joined the New Riders Of The Purple Sage. Fowley's role as a pop svengali continued unabated and he was responsible for piecing together the Runaways, an all-female group whose average age was 16. They quickly outgrew the initial hype and abandoned their mentor, who in turn formed a new vehicle, Venus And The Razorblades. The advent of punk provided scope for further exploitation, but as the 80s progressed Fowley's once-sure touch seemed to desert him. He remains a cult name, however, and as such can still release challenging records. *Let The Madness In* was idiosyncratic and unfunny, while *The Trip Of A Lifetime* saw Fowley attempting to record a dance music album.

● ALBUMS: *Love Is Alive And Well* (Tower 1967) ★★★, *Born To Be Wild* (Imperial 1968) ★★, *Outrageous* (Imperial 1968) ★★, *Good Clean Fun* (Imperial 1969) ★★, *The Day The Earth Stood Still* (MNW 1970) ★★, *I'm Bad* (Capitol 1972) ★★, *International Heroes* (Capitol 1973) ★★, *Visions Of The Future* (Capitol 1974) ★★, *Animal God Of The Street* (Capitol 1975) ★★★, *Living In The Streets* (Sonet 1978) ★★, *Sunset Boulevard* (PVC 1978) ★★, *Snake Document Masquerade*

(Antilles 1979) ★★, *Hollywood Confidential* (GNP 1980) ★★, *Frankenstein & Monster Band* (Sonet 1984) ★★, *Hotel Insomnia* (Maria 1993) ★★, *White Negroes In Deutschland* (Marilyn 1994) ★★, *Bad News From The Underworld* (Marilyn 1994) ★★, with Ben Vaughn *Kings Of Saturday Night* (Sector Two 1995) ★★, *Let The Madness In* (Receiver 1995) ★, *Mondo Hollywood: The Phantom Jukebox Collection* (Rev-Ola 1996) ★★, *Hidden Agenda* (Receiver 1997) ★★, *The Trip Of A Lifetime* (Resurgence 1998) ★★, *Sex Cars & God* (Koch 1999) ★★★.
● COMPILATIONS *Legendary Dog Duke Sessions* (BFD 1979) ★★, *Underground Animal* (Dionysuc/Bacchus Archives 1999) ★★★.

FOXX, INEZ AND CHARLIE

Inez Foxx (b. 9 September 1942, Greensboro, North Carolina, USA) and Charlie Foxx (b. 29 October 1939, Greensboro, North Carolina, USA, d. 18 September 1998, Mobile, Alabama, USA). A brother and sister duo, Inez was a former member of the Gospel Tide Chorus. Her first solo single, 'A Feeling', was issued on Brunswick Records, credited to 'Inez Johnston'. Charlie was, meanwhile, a budding songwriter and his reworking of a nursery rhyme, 'Mockingbird', became their first single together. Released on Sue Records' subsidiary Symbol, it was a US Top 10 hit in 1963, although it was not until 1969 that the song charted in the UK Top 40. Their immediate releases followed the same contrived pattern, but later recordings for Musicor/Dynamo, in particular 'I Stand Accused', were more adventurous. However, their final hit together, '(1-2-3-4-5-6-7) Count The Days' (1967), was modelled closely on that early style. Solo again, Inez continued to record for Dynamo before signing with Stax Records in 1972. Although apparently uncomfortable with their recording methods, the results, including the *Inez Foxx In Memphis* album, were excellent.
● ALBUMS: *Mockingbird* (Sue 1963) ★★★, *Inez And Charlie Foxx* (Sue 1964) ★★★, *Come By Here* (Musicor/Dynamo 1965) ★★★.
Solo: Inez Foxx *Inez Foxx In Memphis* (Volt 1972) ★★★★, *At Memphis And More* (Ace 1990) ★★★. Charlie Foxx *Foxx/Hill* (Foxx/Hill 1982) ★★★.
● COMPILATIONS: *The Best Of Charlie And Inez Foxx* (Stateside 1986) ★★★, *Count The Days* (Charly 1995) ★★★, *Greatest Hits* (Musicor/Dynamo 1996) ★★★★, *The Dynamic Duo* (Kent 2001) ★★★, *Mockingbird – Phase 1: The Complete Sue Recordings* (Connoisseur 2001) ★★★★.

FRANKLIN, ARETHA

b. 25 March 1942, Memphis, Tennessee, USA. Aretha Franklin's music is steeped in the traditions of the church. Her father, Rev. C.L. Franklin, was a Baptist preacher who, once he had moved his family to Detroit, became famous throughout black America for his fiery sermons and magnetic public appearances. He knew the major gospel stars Mahalia Jackson and Clara Ward, who in turn gave his daughter valuable tutelage, along with two other sisters Erma and Carolyn. At the age of 12, Aretha was promoted from the choir to become a featured soloist. Two years later she began recording for JVB and Checker. Between 1956 and 1960, her output consisted solely of devotional material, but the secular success of Sam Cooke encouraged a change of emphasis. Franklin auditioned for John Hammond Jnr., who signed her to Columbia Records. Sadly, the company was indecisive on how best to showcase her remarkable talent. They tried blues, cocktail jazz, standards, pop songs and contemporary soul hits, each of which wasted the singer's natural improvisational instincts. There were some occasional bright spots – 'Runnin' Out Of Fools' (1964) and 'Cry Like A Baby' (1966) – but in both cases content succeeded over style. After a dozen albums, a disillusioned Franklin joined Atlantic Records in 1966, where the magnificent 'I Never Loved A Man (The Way I Loved You)', recorded in January 1967 in New York, declared her liberation. An album was scheduled to be made in Muscle Shoals, but Franklin's husband Ted White had an argument with the owner of Fame Studios, Rick Hall. At short notice Jerry Wexler flew the musicians to New York. The single soared into the US Top 10 and, coupled with the expressive 'Do Right Woman – Do Right Man', only the backing track of which was recorded in Alabama, it announced the arrival of a major artist. The releases that followed – 'Respect', 'Baby I Love You', '(You Make Me Feel Like) A Natural Woman', 'Chain Of Fools' and '(Sweet Sweet Baby) Since You've Been Gone' – many of which featured the Fame rhythm section 'borrowed' by Wexler for sessions in New York, confirmed her authority and claim to being the 'Queen Of Soul'. The conditions and atmosphere created by Wexler and the outstanding musicians gave Franklin such confidence that her voice gained amazing power and control.

Despite Franklin's professional success, her personal life grew confused. Her relationship with husband and manager White disintegrated, and while excellent singles such as 'Think' still appeared, others betrayed a discernible lethargy. She followed 'Think' with a sublime cover version of Hal David and Burt Bacharach's 'I Say A Little Prayer', giving power and authority to simple yet delightful lyrics: 'the moment I wake up, before I put on my make-up, I say a little prayer for you'. Following a slight dip in her fortunes during the late 60s, she had regained her powers in 1970 as 'Call Me', 'Spirit In The Dark' and 'Don't Play That Song' ably testified. *Aretha Live At Fillmore West* (1971), meanwhile, restated her in-concert power. The following year, another live appearance resulted in *Amazing Grace*, a double gospel set recorded with James Cleveland and the Southern California Community Choir. Its passion encapsulated her career to date. Franklin continued to record strong material throughout the early 70s and enjoyed three R&B chart-toppers, 'Angel', 'Until You Come Back To Me (That's What I'm Gonna Do)' and 'I'm In Love'. Sadly, the rest of the decade was marred by recordings that were at best predictable, at worst dull. It was never the fault of Franklin's voice, merely that the material was often poor and indifferent. Her cameo role in the movie *The Blues Brothers*, however, rekindled her flagging career.

Franklin moved to Arista Records in 1980 and she immediately regained a commercial momentum with 'United Together' and two confident albums, *Aretha* and *Love All The Hurt Away*. 'Jump To It' and 'Get It Right', both written and produced by Luther Vandross, and *Who's Zoomin' Who?*, continued her rejuvenation. From the album, produced by Narada Michael Walden, Franklin had hit singles with 'Freeway Of Love', 'Another Night' and the superb title track. In the mid-80s, she made the charts again, in company with Annie Lennox ('Sisters Are Doin' It For Themselves') and George Michael ('I Knew You Were Waiting (For Me)'), which went to number 1 in the USA and UK in 1987. Though by now lacking the instinct of her classic Atlantic recordings, Franklin's 'return to gospel' *One Lord One Faith One Baptism* proved she was still a commanding singer. *Through The Storm*, from 1989, contained more powerful duets, this time with Elton John on the title track, James Brown ('Gimme Some Lovin'', remixed by Prince for 12-inch), and Whitney Houston ('It Isn't, It Wasn't, It Ain't Never Gonna Be'). The album also included a remake of her 1968 US Top 10 title, 'Think'. *What You See Is What You Sweat*, her first album of the 90s, was criticised for its cornucopia of different styles: a couple of tracks by Burt Bacharach and Carole Bayer Sager; a collaboration with Luther Vandross; a fairly thin title ballad; and the highlight, 'Everyday People', a mainstream disco number, written by Sly Stone and brilliantly produced by Narada Michael Walden. Another lengthy hiatus ensued before the release of the impressive *A Rose Is Still A Rose*, on which Franklin co-opted the songwriting and production talents of the cream of contemporary urban music.

Franklin possesses an astonishing voice that has often been wasted on a poor choice of material, but she is rightfully heralded as the Queen of Soul, even though that reputation was gained in the 60s. There are certain musical notes that can be played on a saxophone that are chilling; similarly, there are sounds above the twelfth fret on a guitar that are orgasmic – Aretha Franklin is better than any instrument, as she can hit notes that do not exist in instrumental terms. The superlative 4-CD box set *Queen Of Soul*, highlighting the best of her Atlantic recordings, confirmed her position as one of the greatest voices in recording history.

● ALBUMS: *Aretha* (Columbia 1961) ★★, *The Electrifying Aretha Franklin* (Columbia 1962) ★★, *The Tender, The Moving, The Swinging Aretha Franklin* (Columbia 1962) ★★, *Laughing On The Outside* (Columbia 1963) ★★, *Unforgettable* (Columbia 1964) ★★, *Songs Of Faith* (Checker 1964) ★★, *Runnin' Out Of Fools* (Columbia 1964) ★★, *Yeah!!!* (Columbia 1965) ★★, *Soul Sister* (Columbia 1966) ★★★, *Take It Like You Give It* (Columbia 1967) ★★★, *I Never Loved A Man The Way That I Love You* (Atlantic 1967) ★★★★★, *Aretha Arrives* (Atlantic 1967) ★★★★, *Take A Look* early recordings (Columbia 1967) ★★★, *Aretha: Lady Soul* (Atlantic 1968) ★★★★★, *Aretha Now* (Atlantic 1968) ★★★★, *Aretha In Paris* (Atlantic 1968) ★★, *Aretha Franklin: Soul '69* (Atlantic 1969) ★★★★, *Today I Sing The Blues* (Columbia 1969) ★★★★, *Soft And Beautiful* (Columbia 1969) ★★★, *This Girl's In Love With You* (Atlantic 1970) ★★★, *Spirit In The Dark* (Atlantic 1970) ★★★, *Aretha Live At Fillmore West* (Atlantic 1971) ★★★★, *Young, Gifted And Black* (Atlantic 1972) ★★★, *Amazing Grace* (Atlantic 1972) ★★★★, *Hey Now Hey (The Other Side Of The Sky)* (Atlantic 1973) ★★, *Let Me Into Your Life* (Atlantic 1974) ★★★★, *With Everything I Feel In Me* (Atlantic 1974) ★★★, *You* (Atlantic 1975) ★★, *Sparkle* film soundtrack (Atlantic 1976) ★★, *Sweet Passion* (Atlantic 1977) ★★, *Almighty Fire* (Atlantic 1978) ★★, *La Diva* (Atlantic 1979) ★★, *Aretha* (Arista 1980) ★★★, *Love All The Hurt Away* (Arista 1981) ★★, *Jump To It* (Arista 1982) ★★, *Get It Right* (Arista 1983) ★★, *Who's Zoomin' Who?* (Arista 1985) ★★, *Aretha* (Arista 1986) ★★★, *One Lord, One Faith, One Baptism* (Arista 1987) ★★★, *Through The Storm* (Arista 1989) ★★, *What You See Is What You Sweat* (Arista 1991) ★★, *A Rose Is Still A Rose* (Arista 1998) ★★★, with Mariah Carey, Celine Dion, Gloria Estefan, Shania Twain *Divas Live* (Epic 1998) ★★.

● COMPILATIONS: *Aretha Franklin's Greatest Hits* Columbia recordings 1961-66 (Columbia 1967) ★★★, *Aretha's Gold* (Atlantic 1969) ★★★★, *Aretha's Greatest Hits* (Atlantic 1971) ★★★★, *In The Beginning /The World Of Aretha Franklin 1960-1967* (Columbia 1972) ★★★, *The Great Aretha Franklin: The First 12 Sides* (Columbia 1973) ★★★, *Ten Years Of Gold* (Atlantic 1976) ★★★★, *Legendary Queen Of Soul* (Columbia 1983) ★★★★, *Aretha's Jazz* (Atlantic 1984) ★★★, *Aretha Sings The Blues* (Columbia 1985) ★★★, *The Collection* (Castle 1986) ★★★★, *Never Grow Old* (Chess 1987) ★★★, *20 Greatest Hits* (Warners 1987) ★★★★, *Aretha Franklin's Greatest Hits 1960-1965* (Columbia 1987) ★★★★, *Queen Of Soul: The Atlantic Recordings* 4-CD box set (Rhino/Atlantic 1992) ★★★★★, *Aretha's Jazz* (Atlantic 1993) ★★★, *Greatest Hits 1980-1994* (Arista 1994) ★★★, *Love Songs* (Rhino/Atlantic 1997) ★★★, *This Is Jazz* (Columbia Legacy 1998)

★★★, *Greatest Hits* (Global/Warners 1998) ★★★★, *Amazing Grace: The Complete Recordings* (Rhino 1999) ★★★★, *Aretha's Best* (Rhino 2001) ★★★★.

● VIDEOS: *Queen Of Soul* (Music Club 1988), *Live At Park West* (PVE 1995), with Mariah Carey, Celine Dion, Gloria Estefan, Shania Twain *Divas Live* (Sony Music Video 1998).

● FURTHER READING: *Aretha Franklin*, Mark Bego. *Aretha: From These Roots*, Aretha Franklin and David Ritz.

● FILMS: *The Blues Brothers* (1980).

FRANKLIN, ERMA

b. 1943, Memphis, Tennessee, USA. The younger sister of Aretha Franklin, this excellent singer's career has been overshadowed by that of her illustrious sibling. Erma's most celebrated moment came in 1967 with 'Piece Of My Heart', an intense uptown soul ballad co-written and produced by Bert Berns. The song was adopted by Janis Joplin, but Franklin's own progress faltered with the collapse of her record label. Although she did secure a minor 1969 hit with 'Gotta Find Me A Lover (24 Hours A Day)', her later work failed to match that early promise. During the past three decades much of her time has been spent running Boysville, a childcare charity in Detroit. In 1992 Levi's chose 'Piece Of My Heart' for one of their television advertisements, and in predictable fashion it scaled the charts and gave Aretha's often overlooked sister her true moment of (belated) glory.

● ALBUMS: *Her Name Is Erma* (Epic 1962) ★★★, *Soul Sister* (Brunswick 1969) ★★★.

● COMPILATIONS: *Piece Of My Heart – The Best Of* (Epic 1992) ★★★, *Golden Classics* (Collectables 1993) ★★★.

FRATERNITY OF MAN

This US outfit was formed in Los Angeles, California, USA in 1967 when Elliot Ingber (guitar, ex-the Mothers Of Invention) joined forces with three members of struggling aspirants the Factory: Warren Klein (guitar/sitar), Martin Kibbee (bass) and Richard Hayward (drums). Lawrence 'Stash' Wagner (lead vocals/guitar) completed the line-up featured on *Fraternity Of Man*, a musically disparate selection ranging from melodic flower-power ('Wispy Paisley Skies') to rhetorical politics ('Just Doin' Our Job'). The album also featured a version of Frank Zappa's 'Oh No I Don't Believe It', but is best recalled for the 'dopers' anthem 'Don't Bogart Me', later immortalized in the movie *Easy Rider*. The blues-influenced *Get It On* lacked the charm of its predecessor, but featured contributions from pianist Bill Payne and former Factory guitarist Lowell George, both of whom resurfaced, with Hayward, in Little Feat. Ingber was also involved with the last-named act during its embryonic stages, but left to join Captain

efheart, where he was rechristened Winged
l Fingerling. In later years he emerged
a member of the Mothers' offshoot,
andmothers.
ALBUMS: *Fraternity Of Man* (ABC 1968) ★★★,
t It On (Dot 1969) ★★.

RED, JOHN, AND HIS PLAYBOY BAND

hn Fred (b. John Fred Gourrier, 8 May 1941,
ton Rouge, Louisiana, USA) was a 6 foot 5
ch, blue-eyed soul singer who originally
rmed John Fred And The Playboys in 1956.
is unit cut their first record ('Shirley') two
ars later with Fats Domino's backing group.
ıring the early 60s various versions of the
ıyboys recorded for small independent record
ıels such as Jewel and N-Joy, and eventually
came known as John Fred And His Playboy
nd. It was not until the end of 1967 that
ccess finally came with the international hit,
ıdy In Disguise (With Glasses)'. An amusing
tire on the Beatles' 'Lucy In The Sky With
amonds', the single beat off a rival version by
nboy Dukes. Unfortunately this meant the
ıyboy Band were unfairly perceived as a
velty group, when in fact they were a tight,
ell organized and long-serving unit. Fred's
ıe-eyed soul vocals were most evident on
nes English, which included a rasping version
'She Shot A Hole In My Soul'. By the end of
e 60s the band had split-up, with Fred going on
record with a new group and work as a
oducer for RCS in Baton Rouge.
ALBUMS: *John Fred And His Playboys* (Paula
55) ★★★, *34:40 Of John Fred And His Playboys*
ıula 1966) ★★★, *Agnes English* aka *Judy In
sguise* (Paula 1967) ★★★, *Permanently Stated*
ıula 1968) ★★★, *Love My Soul* (Universal City
69) ★★★.
COMPILATIONS: *With Glasses: The Very Best*
John Fred And His Playboy Band (Westside
01) ★★★★.

REDDIE AND THE DREAMERS

is Manchester, England-based 60s beat group,
nprising Freddie Garrity (b. 14 November
40, Manchester, England; vocals), Roy
ewsdon (b. 29 May 1941; guitar), Derek Quinn
24 May 1942; guitar), Pete Birrell (b. 9 May
41; bass) and Bernie Dwyer (b. 11 September
40; drums), was briefly renowned for its
xture of beat music and comedy. Garrity
rmed the group in 1959 and it remained semi-
ofessional until passing a BBC audition in
33. Although their debut, 'If You Gotta Make A
ol Of Somebody', was an R&B favourite
mes Ray and Maxine Brown), subsequent
eases were tailored to the quintet's
ervescent insouciant image. 'I'm Telling You
w' and 'You Were Made For Me' also reached
e UK Top 3, establishing the group at the
ight of the beat boom. Although Garrity
played his songwriting skill with strong
ıads such as 'Send A Letter To Me', his work

was not used for a-side recordings. Further hits
followed in 1964 with 'Over You', 'I Love You
Baby', 'Just For You', and the seasonal favourite
'I Understand'.
The group's appeal declined in the UK but early
in 1965, they made a startling breakthrough in
America where 'I'm Telling You Now' topped the
charts. American audiences were entranced by
Garrity's zany stage antics (which resulted in
frequent twisted ankles) and eagerly demanded
the name of his unusual dance routine. 'It's
called the Freddie', he innocently replied. A US
Top 20 hit rapidly followed with 'Do The
Freddie'. Although the group appeared in a
couple of movies, *Just For You* And *Cuckoo Patrol*,
their main audience was in pantomime and
cabaret. They broke up at the end of the decade,
but Garrity and Birtles remained together in the
children's show *Little Big Time*. Garrity revived
the group during the mid-70s, with new
personnel, for revival concerts at home and
abroad. By the late 80s Garrity was attempting to
establish an acting career, but has since returned
to the cabaret circuit with a new line-up of the
Dreamers.
● ALBUMS: *Freddie And The Dreamers*
(Columbia 1963) ★★★, *You Were Made For Me*
(Columbia 1964) ★★★, *Freddie And The
Dreamers* (Mercury 1965) ★★★, *Sing-Along Party*
(Columbia 1965) ★★, *Do The Freddie* (Mercury
1965) ★★, *Seaside Swingers* aka *Everyday's A
Holiday* film soundtrack (Mercury 1965) ★★,
Frantic Freddie (Mercury 1965) ★★, *Freddie And
The Dreamers In Disneyland* (Columbia 1966) ★,
Fun Lovin' Freddie (Mercury 1966) ★★, *King
Freddie And His Dreaming Knights* (Columbia
1967) ★★, *Oliver In The Underworld* (Starline
1970) ★★.
● COMPILATIONS: *The Best Of Freddie And The
Dreamers* (EMI 1982) ★★★, *The Hits Of Freddie
And The Dreamers* (EMI 1988) ★★★, *The Best Of
Freddie And The Dreamers: The Definitive
Collection* (EMI 1992) ★★★, *The Very Best Of
Freddie And The Dreamers* (MFP 2001) ★★★.
● FILMS: *What A Crazy World* (1963), *Cuckoo
Patrol* (1965).

FRIENDS OF DISTINCTION

Formed in 1968 by Floyd Butler (b. 5 June 1941,
San Diego, California, USA), Harry Elston (b. 4
November 1938, Dallas, Texas, USA), Jessica
Cleaves (b. 10 December 1948, Los Angeles,
California, USA) and Barbara Jean Love (b. 24
July 1941, Los Angeles, California, USA). This
smooth vocal quartet began working together in
the Ray Charles' revue. Stylistically similar to
the 5th Dimension, the Friends scored a million-
selling hit with a vocal version of Hugh
Masekela's 'Grazing In The Grass' (1969). Two
further releases, 'Going In Circles' and 'Love Or
Let Me Be Lonely', were also substantial hits,
before their sweet-harmony, MOR soul
established them as an attraction on the cabaret
circuit.

● ALBUMS: *Grazin'* (RCA 1969) ★★★, *Friends And People* (RCA 1971) ★★★, *Highly Distinct* (RCA 1969) ★★★, *Real Friends* (RCA 1970) ★★, *Whatever* (RCA 1970) ★★, *Friends And People* (RCA 1971) ★★.
● COMPILATIONS: *Best Of Friends Of Distinction* (RCA 1996) ★★★.

FRUMIOUS BANDERSNATCH

This highly promising quintet was based in Berkeley, California, USA in the late 60s. They completed an album for Fantasy Records that was never issued and consequently, their sole recorded legacy lies in a privately pressed EP. The group – Jimmy Warner (solo guitar/vocals), David Denny (b. 5 February 1948, Berkeley, California, USA; lead guitar/vocals), Bob Winkelman (rhythm guitar/vocals), Ross Vallory (b. 2 February 1949, San Francisco, California, USA; bass/vocals) and Jackson King (drums/vocals) – were highly accomplished musicians and the opening track, 'Hearts To Cry', offered some exciting, *de rigueur*, acid-rock. Denny was later replaced by George Tickner, but the band subsequently folded in the face of corporate disinterest. Winkelman, Warner, King and Vallory all appeared at various times as members of the Steve Miller Band. Vallory then found greater success with Tickner as members of Journey.
● COMPILATIONS: *A Young Man's Song* (Big Beat 1996) ★★.

FUGS

Formed in 1965 in the USA, the Fugs combined the bohemian poetry of New York's Lower East Side with an engaging musical naïvety and the shock tactic of outrage. Writers Ed Sanders, Tuli Kupferberg and Ken Weaver made their recording debut on the Broadside label, which viewed the group's work as 'ballads of contemporary protest'. The set included poetry by William Blake alongside such irreverent offerings as 'I Couldn't Get High' and 'Slum Goddess', while the original trio was supported by several musicians, including Peter Stampfel and Steve Weber from fellow cultural dissidents the Holy Modal Rounders. The Fugs' album was subsequently issued by ESP, a notorious outlet for the *avant garde*. A projected second collection was withheld when the company deemed it 'too obscene', and a feverish rock album, entitled *The Fugs*, was issued instead. This excellent collection featured Kupferberg's satirical 'Kill For Peace' and the almost lyrical 'Morning Morning'. The disputed second album was then released as *Virgin Fugs*. In 1967 the group switched outlets to Reprise Records. Although *Tenderness Junction* featured a more proficient backing group, including Danny Kootch (b. Dan Kortchmar; guitar) and Charles Larkey (bass), the subject matter – hippie-politics and sex – remained as before. *It Crawled Into My Hand, Honest*, released the following

year, was another idiomatic record, bu subsequent releases undermined the balanc between literary and carnal pursuits, erring i favour of the latter. They disbanded to avoid th dangers of self-parody, although Ed Sande continued his musical pursuits with tw country-influenced selections and wrote a acclaimed book, *The Family*, about the hippi cult leader Charles Manson. *The Fugs Rounders Score*, in 1975, contained unrelease Holy Modal Rounders material. Sanders and Kupferberg resumed work as th Fugs during the 80s. Contemporary release invoked a world-consciousness portrayed in th group's earlier political work, and they retaine the same idealistic optimism. During the 9(Sanders and Kupferberg retrieved the rights their ESP recordings. The material was the licensed to Ace Records on the recommendatio of the Grateful Dead. Subsequent repackage have been augmented by archive photograph and previously unissued recordings. Sande and Kupferberg attempted to hold a riv Woodstock anniversary festival in 1994. Th results were issued on a double CD in 1995, b the duo's satire and humour was now sad dated.
● ALBUMS: *The Village Fugs* aka *The Fugs Fir Album* (ESP 1965) ★★★★, *The Fugs* (ESP 196(★★★★, *Virgin Fugs* (ESP 1966) ★★★★ *Tenderness Junction* (Reprise 1967) ★★★, *Crawled Into My Hand, Honest* (Reprise 196{ ★★★, *The Belle Of Avenue A* (Reprise 1969) ★ *No More Slavery* (New Rose 1986) ★★★, *St Peace* (New Rose 1987) ★★, *The Real Woodstoc Festival* (Fugs 1995) ★★.
● COMPILATIONS: *Golden Filth* (Reprise 196(★★★★, *The Fugs 4, Rounders Score* (ESP 197{ ★★★, *Refuse To Be Burnt Out: Live In The 196((New Rose 1985) ★★, *Live From The 60s* (Fu{ 1994) ★★.

FULLER, BOBBY

b. 22 October 1943, Baytown, Texas, USA, d. 1 July 1966, Los Angeles, California, USA. A inventive and compulsive musician, Bobl Fuller made his recording debut in 1961. 'You' In Love' was the first of several outings for loc independent labels, but the artist's developme was more apparent on the many dem completed in his home-based studio. Fuller late moved to Los Angeles where his group, th Bobby Fuller Four – Randy Fuller (bass), Ji Reese (rhythm guitar) and DeWayne Quiric (drums) – became a leading attraction, infusir Buddy Holly-styled rockabilly with the emerge British beat. Their early releases were region hits; nevertheless, in January 1966 the grou reached the US Top 10 with an ebullient readi of the Crickets' 'I Fought The Law'. This po classic, later memorably covered by UK pur rockers Clash, was followed up by a Top 30 h 'Love's Made A Fool Of You'. The singer's statu now seemed assured, but on 18 July that san year any hope for a bright future was cut short when Fuller's badly beaten body was discovered in a parked car in Los Angeles. His death was attributed to asphyxia through the forced inhalation of gasoline, but further investigations as to the perpetrators of this deed remain unresolved.

● ALBUMS: *KRLA King Of The Wheels* (Mustang 1965) ★★★, *I Fought The Law* aka *Memorial Album* (Mustang 1966) ★★★★, *Live Again* (Eva 1984) ★★.

● COMPILATIONS: *The Best Of The Bobby Fuller Four* (Rhino 1981) ★★★★, *The Bobby Fuller Tapes, Volume 1* (Voxx 1983) ★★★, *Bobby Fuller Tapes Volume 2* (Voxx 1984) ★★, *The Bobby Fuller Instrumental Album* (Rockhouse 1985) ★★, *Never To Be Forgotten* 3-CD box set (Mustang 1998) ★★★.

FURY, BILLY

b. Ronald Wycherley, 17 April 1940, Dingle, Liverpool, England, d. 28 January 1983. An impromptu audition in a Birkenhead dressing room resulted in Wycherley joining Larry Parnes' management stable. The entrepreneur provided the suitably enigmatic stage name, and added the aspirant to the bill of a current package tour. Fury enjoyed a UK Top 20 hit with his debut single, 'Maybe Tomorrow', in 1959 and the following year completed *The Sound Of Fury*, which consisted entirely of the artist's own songs. Arguably Britain's finest example of the rockabilly genre, it owed much of its authenticity to sterling support from guitarist Joe Brown, while the Four Jays provided backing vocals. However, Fury found his greatest success with a series of dramatic ballads which, in suggesting a vulnerability, enhanced the singer's undoubted sex appeal. His stylish good looks complimented a vocal prowess blossoming in 1961 with a cover version of Tony Orlando's 'Halfway To Paradise'. This superior single, arranged and scored by Ivor Raymonde, established a pattern that provided Fury with 16 further UK Top 30 hits, including 'Jealousy' (1961), 'Last Night Was Made For Love' (1962), 'Like I've Never Been Gone' (1963), 'It's Only Make Believe' (1964), and 'In Thoughts Of You' (1965). Fury also completed two exploitative pop movies, *Play It Cool* (1962) and *I've Gotta Horse* (1965) and remained one of Britain's leading in-concert attractions throughout the early 60s. Supported initially by the Tornados, then the Gamblers, the singer showed a wider repertoire live than his label would allow on record. Bedevilled by ill health and overtaken by changing musical fashions, Fury's final hit came in 1965 with 'Give Me Your Word'. The following year he left Decca for Parlophone, debuting with a Peter And Gordon song, 'Hurtin' Is Lovin'. Subsequent recordings included David Bowie's 'Silly Boy Blue', the Bee Gees' 'One Minute Woman' (both 1968) and Carole King's 'Why Are You Leaving?' (1970), but the singer was unable to regain his erstwhile success. In 1971 he underwent open-heart surgery, but recovered to record 'Will The Real Man Stand Up?' on his own Fury label, and played the part of 'Stormy Tempest' in the film *That'll Be The Day* (1973). A second major operation in 1976 forced Billy to retire again, but he re-emerged at the end of the decade with new recordings of his best-known songs, and several live and television appearances. In 1981 Fury struck a new deal with Polydor, but his health was rapidly deteriorating and on 28 January 1983 he succumbed to a fatal heart attack. Unlike many of his pre-Beatles contemporaries, the artist's reputation has grown over the years, and Billy Fury is now rightly regarded as one of the finest rock 'n' roll singers Britain ever produced.

● ALBUMS: *Sound Of Fury* 10-inch album (Decca 1960) ★★★★, *Billy Fury* (Ace Of Clubs 1960) ★★★, *Halfway To Paradise* (Ace Of Clubs 1961) ★★★, *Billy* (Decca 1963) ★★★, *We Want Billy* (Decca 1963) ★★, *I've Got A Horse* (Decca 1965) ★★★, *The One And Only* (Polydor 1983) ★★★.

● COMPILATIONS: *The Best Of Billy Fury* (Ace Of Clubs 1967) ★★★★, *The World Of Billy Fury* (Decca 1972) ★★★★, *The Billy Fury Story* (Decca 1977) ★★★, *The World Of Billy Fury, Volume 2* (Decca 1980) ★★★, *The Missing Years 1967-1980* (Red Bus 1983) ★★★, *The Billy Fury Hit Parade* (Rock Echoes 1983) ★★★, *The Other Side Of Fury* (See For Miles 1984) ★★★★, *Loving You* (Magnum Force 1984) ★★★, *Stick 'N' Stones* (Magnum Force 1985) ★★★, *The EP Collection* (See For Miles 1985) ★★★★, *The Collection* (Castle 1987) ★★★, *The Best Of Billy Fury* (K-Tel 1988) ★★★, *The Sound Of Fury + 10* (Decca 1988) ★★★, *Am I Blue?* (Decca 1993) ★★★, *The 40th Anniversary Anthology* (Deram 1998) ★★★★.

● FILMS: *Play It Cool* (1962), *I've Gotta Horse* (1965), *That'll Be The Day* (1973).

G

GAINSBOURG, SERGE

b. Lucien Ginsburg, 2 April 1928, Paris, France, d. 2 March 1991, Paris, France. Gainsbourg was a frustrated painter who eked a living as a bar pianist before joining the band hired for the musical *Milord L'Arsouville* starring Michèle Arnaud. Eventually given a reluctant singing role, his stage fright was interpreted by the audience as part of the act. His subsequent self-penned hit parade successes included 'Le Poinçonneur Des Lilas', 'La Chanson De Prévert' (a homage to the renowned French poet) and 'La Javanaise' but, an unlikely looking pop star with his heavy-lidded homeliness, he preferred to compose for others. More prestigious than his soundtrack work and songs for Régine, Valérie Lagrange and Dominique Walter were those commissioned by such as Juliette Gréco, France Gall, Sacha Distel, Johnny Hallyday, Claude Francois and also English language vocalists, Petula Clark and Dionne Warwick. 'Je T'Aime ... Moi Non Plus' was written for Brigitte Bardot, with whom Gainsbourg was having an affair, but her management were unwilling to risk releasing a record that famously simulated the sounds of sexual congress.

Instead, Gainsbourg recorded it himself as an album track with English actress Jane Birkin, the 'constant companion' he had met on the set of the movie *Slogan*. Issued as a single in 1969, publicity earned via a BBC ban caused its abrupt deletion by Fontana Records but, unworried by moral opprobrium, other labels seized the opportunity to take up the slack as it swept to number 1 all over Europe and hovered around the middle of the US Hot 100. It would enjoy a further few weeks in the UK Top 40 when reissued in 1974. Other Gainsbourg records were confined to home charts, with his pop genius managing to encompass subjects as diverse and shocking as Nazi death camps, incest, underage sex, farting and cabbages. The 1979 reggae outing *Aux Armes Et Caetera* earned particular notoriety for its Jamaican reworking of 'La Marseillaise'. The artist's occasional outrages on Gallic chat-shows, including one memorable live moment where he asked Whitney Houston if she would sleep with him, were thought newsworthy in those areas that remembered his erotic duet. The whole of France went into mourning when Gainsbourg, one of the country's national sons, suffered a fatal heart attack in March 1991. His work as a singer, songwriter, composer, actor, novelist, artist, photographer and screenwriter

continues to influence.

● ALBUMS: *Du Chant À La Une!* 10-inch album (Philips 1958) ★★★, *No. 2* 10-inch album (Philips 1959) ★★★, *L'Étonnant Serge Gainsbourg* 10-inch album (Philips 1961) ★★★, *No. 4* 10-inch album (Philips 1962) ★★★, *Gainsbourg Confidentiel* (Philips 1964) ★★★, *Gainsbourg Percussions* (Philips 1964) ★★★, *Anna* film soundtrack (Philips 1967) ★★★, with Brigitte Bardot *Bonnie And Clyde* (Fontana 1968) ★★★, *Initials B.B.* (Philips 1968) ★★★, *Mister Freedom* film soundtrack (Barclay 1969) ★★★, with Jane Birkin *Jane Birkin/Serge Gainsbourg* (Fontana 1969) ★★★, *Cannabis* film soundtrack (Philips 1970) ★★★, *Histoire De Melody Nelson* (Philips 1971) ★★★★, *Vu De L'Extérieur* (Philips 1973) ★★★, *Rock Around The Bunker* (Philips 1975) ★★★, *L'Homme À Tête De Chou* (Philips 1976) ★★★★, *Je T'Aime ... Moi Non Plus* film soundtrack (Philips 1976) ★★, *Madame Claude* film soundtrack (Philips 1977) ★★★, *Aux Armes Et Caetera* (Philips 1979) ★★★, *Enregistrement Public Au Théâtre Le Palace* (Philips 1980) ★★★, *Je Vous Aime* film soundtrack (Philips 1980) ★★★, *Mauvaises Nouvelles Des Étoiles* (Philips 1981) ★★★, *Love On The Beat* (Philips 1984) ★★★, *Live* (Philips 1986) ★★★, *Tenue De Soirée* film soundtrack (Apache/WEA 1986) ★★★, *You're Under Arrest* (Philips 1987) ★★★, *Le Zénith De Gainsbourg* (Philips 1989) ★★★.

● COMPILATIONS: *De Gainsbourg À Gainsbarre* 3-CD set (Philips 1989) ★★★, *De Gainsbourg À Gainsbarre* 9-CD box set (Philips 1989) ★★★, *Chansons Et Musiques De Film* (Hortensia 1990) ★★★, *Master Serie: Vol. 1* (Philips 1991) ★★★★, *Master Serie: Vol. 2* (Philips 1991) ★★★, *Master Serie: Vol. 3* (Philips 1991) ★★★, *Forever 1958-1987* 18-CD box set (Mercury 1998) ★★★, *Jane Birkin & Serge Gainsbourg* (Mercury 1998) ★★★.

● FURTHER READING: *Evguénie Sokolov*, Serge Gainsbourg. *Gainsbourg*, Micheline de Pierrefeu, Jean-Claude Maillard. *Gainsbourg Sans Filtre*, Marie-Dominique Lelièvre. *Gainsbourg Ou La Provocation Permanante*, Yves Salgues. *Gainsbourg: Le Livre Du Souvenir*, Bernard Pascuito. *Gainsbourg*, Gilles Verlant. *Gainsbourg Et Caetera*, Isabelle Salmon, Gilles Verlant. *Dernières Nouvelles Des Étoiles: L'Intégrale*, Serge Gainsbourg. *Serge Gainsbourg: Viewed From The Exterior*, Allan Clayson. *Serge Gainsbourg: A Fistful Of Gitanes*, Sylvie Simmons.

● FILMS: *Voulez-Vous Danser Avec Moi?* aka *Come Dance With Me* (1959), *La Rivolta Degli Schiavi* aka *The Revolt Of The Slaves* (1961), *La Furia Di Ercole* aka *The Fury Of Hercules* (1961), *L'Inconnue De Hong Kong* (1963), *Le Jardinier D'Argenteuil* (1965), *Anna* (1965), *Estouffade À La Caraibe* aka *The Looters* (1966), *Vivre La Nuit* (1967), *Toutes Folles De Lui* (1967), *Le Pacha* (1967), *L'Inconnu De Shandigor* (1967), *Ce Sacré Grand-Père* aka *The Marriage Came Tumbling Down* (1967), *Paris N'Existe Pas* (1968), *Erotissimo* (1968), *Mister Freedom* (1969), *Slogan* (1969), *Les Chemins De Katmandou* aka *The Road To Katmandu* (1969),

Cannabis aka *The Mafia Wants Your Blood* (1969), *Romance Of A Horsethief* (1971), *19 Djevojaka i Mornar* (1971), *Trop Jolies Pour Être Honnêtes* aka *Too Pretty To Be Honest* (1972), *Le Sex Shop* (1973), *La Morte Negli Occhi Del Gatto* aka *Seven Deaths In The Cat's Eye* (1973), *Sérieux Comme Le Plaisir* aka *Serious As Pleasure* (1974), *Je Vous Aime* aka *I Love You All* (1980), *Le Grand Pardon* (1981), *Charlotte For Ever* (1986).

GARRICK, DAVID

b. 1946, Liverpool, England. Opera-trained Garrick began his career at the famed Cavern club, where he performed as a member of the Dions, before moving to London on securing a deal with the Piccadilly label as a solo artist. Two unsuccessful singles were released before the singer scored a UK Top 30 hit with 'Lady Jane', originally recorded by the Rolling Stones, in June 1966. Garrick enjoyed a second chart entry with 'Dear Mrs Applebee', a boyish performance redolent of Herman's Hermits, which sold a million copies in Germany. Despite sharing management with the Kinks and enjoying a front page advertisement for 'I Found A Love', further chart success proved elusive.
● ALBUMS: *A Boy Called David* (Piccadilly 1966) ★★★, *Don't Go Out Into The Rain Sugar* (Piccadilly 1968) ★★.
● COMPILATIONS: *David Garrick (The Pye Anthology)* (Sequel 1998) ★★★.

GAYE, MARVIN

b. Marvin Pentz Gay Jnr., 2 April 1939, Washington, DC, USA, d. 1 April 1984, Los Angeles, California, USA. Gaye was named after his father, a minister in the Apostolic Church. The spiritual influence of his early years played a formative role in his musical career, particularly from the 70s onwards, when his songwriting shifted back and forth between secular and religious topics. He abandoned a place in his father's church choir to team up with Don Covay and Billy Stewart in the R&B vocal group the Rainbows. In 1957, he joined the Marquees, who recorded for Chess Records under the guidance of Bo Diddley. The following year the group was taken under the wing of producer and singer Harvey Fuqua, who used them to re-form his doo-wop outfit the Moonglows. When Fuqua moved to Detroit in 1960, Gay went with him: Fuqua soon joined forces with Berry Gordy at Motown Records, and Gay became a session drummer and vocalist for the label.

In 1961, he married Gordy's sister, Anna, and was offered a solo recording contract. Renamed Marvin Gaye, he began his career as a jazz balladeer, but in 1962 he was persuaded to record R&B, and notched up his first hit single with the confident 'Stubborn Kind Of Fellow', a Top 10 R&B hit. This record set the style for the next three years, as Gaye enjoyed hits with a series of joyous, dance-flavoured songs that cast him as a smooth, macho, Don Juan figure. He also continued to work behind the scenes at Motown, co-writing Martha And The Vandellas' hit 'Dancing In The Street', and playing drums on several early recordings by Little Stevie Wonder. In 1965, Gaye dropped the call-and-response vocal arrangements of his earlier hits and began to record in a more sophisticated style. The striking 'How Sweet It Is (To Be Loved By You)' epitomized his new direction, and it was followed by two successive R&B number 1 hits, 'I'll Be Doggone' and 'Ain't That Peculiar'. His status as Motown's bestselling male vocalist left him free to pursue more esoteric avenues on his albums, which in 1965 included a tribute to the late Nat 'King' Cole and a misguided collection of Broadway standards.

To capitalize on his image as a ladies' man, Motown teamed Gaye with his leading female vocalist, Mary Wells, for some romantic duets. When Wells left Motown in 1964, Gaye recorded with Kim Weston until 1967, when she was succeeded by Tammi Terrell. The Gaye/Terrell partnership represented the apogee of the soul duet, as their voices blended sensually on a string of hits written specifically for the duo by Ashford And Simpson. Terrell developed a brain tumour in 1968, and collapsed onstage in Gaye's arms. Records continued to be issued under the duo's name, although Simpson allegedly took Terrell's place on some recordings. Through the mid-60s, Gaye allowed his duet recordings to take precedence over his solo work, but in 1968 he issued the epochal 'I Heard It Through The Grapevine' (written by Whitfield/Strong), a song originally released on Motown by Gladys Knight And The Pips, although Gaye's version had actually been recorded first. With its tense, ominous rhythm arrangement, and Gaye's typically fluent and emotional vocal, the record represented a landmark in Motown's history – not least because it became the label's biggest-selling record to date. Gaye followed up with another number 1 R&B hit, 'Too Busy Thinking 'Bout My Baby', but his career was derailed by the insidious illness and eventual death of Terrell in March 1970.

Devastated by the loss of his close friend and partner, Gaye spent most of 1970 in seclusion. The following year, he emerged with a set of recordings that Motown at first refused to release, but which eventually formed his most successful solo album. On 'What's Going On', a number 1 hit in 1971, and its two chart-topping follow-ups, 'Mercy Mercy Me (The Ecology)' and 'Inner City Blues', Gaye combined his spiritual beliefs with his increasing concern about poverty, discrimination and political corruption in American society. To match the shift in subject matter, Gaye evolved a new musical style that influenced a generation of black performers. Built on a heavily percussive base, Gaye's arrangements mingled jazz and classical influences into his soul roots, creating a fluid instrumental backdrop for his sensual, almost despairing vocals. The three singles were all contained on *What's Going On*, a conceptual masterpiece on which every track contributed to the spiritual yearning suggested by its title. After making a sly comment on the 1972 US presidential election campaign with the single 'You're The Man', Gaye composed the soundtrack to the 'blaxploitation' thriller *Trouble Man*. His primarily instrumental score highlighted his interest in jazz, while the title song provided him with another hit single.

Gaye's next project saw him shifting his attention from the spiritual to the sexual with *Let's Get It On*, which included a quote from T.S. Eliot on the sleeve and devoted itself to the art of talking a woman into bed. Its explicit sexuality marked a sea-change in Gaye's career; as he began to use cocaine more and more regularly, he became obsessed with his personal life, and rarely let the outside world figure in his work. Paradoxically, he continued to let Motown market him in a traditional fashion by agreeing to collaborate with Diana Ross on a sensuous album of duets in 1973 – although the two singers allegedly did not actually meet during the recording of the project. The break-up of his marriage to Anna Gordy in 1975 delayed work on his next album. *I Want You* was merely a pleasant reworking of the *Let's Get It On* set, albeit cast in slightly more contemporary mode. The title track was another number 1 hit on the soul charts, however, as was his 1977 disco extravaganza, 'Got To Give It Up'. Drug problems and tax demands interrupted his career, and in 1978 he fled the US mainland to Hawaii in a vain attempt to salvage his second marriage. Gaye devoted the next year to the *Here, My Dear* double album, which provided a bitter commentary on his relationship with his first wife. Its title was ironic: he had been ordered to give all royalties from the project to Anna as part of their divorce settlement.

With this catharsis behind him, Gaye began work on an album to be called *Lover Man*, but he cancelled its release after the lukewarm sales of its initial single, the sharply self-mocking 'Ego Tripping Out', which he had presented as a duet between the warring sides of his nature. In 1980, under increasing pressure from the Internal Revenue Service, Gaye moved to Europe where he began work on an ambitious concept album, *In My Lifetime*. When it emerged in 1981, Gaye accused Motown of remixing and editing the album without his consent, of removing a vital question mark from the title, and of parodying his original cover artwork. The relationship between artist and record company had been shattered, and Gaye left Motown for Columbia Records in 1982. Persistent reports of his erratic personal conduct and reliance on cocaine fuelled pessimism about his future career, but instead he re-emerged in 1982 with a startling single, 'Sexual Healing', which combined his passionate

soul vocals with a contemporary electro-disco backing. The subsequent album, *Midnight Love*, offered no equal surprises, but the success of the single seemed to herald a new era in Gaye's music. He returned to the USA, where he took up residence at his parents' home. The intensity of his cocaine addiction made it impossible for him to work on another album, and he fell into a prolonged bout of depression. He repeatedly announced his wish to commit suicide in the early weeks of 1984, and his abrupt shifts of mood brought him into heated conflict with his father, rekindling animosity that had festered since Gaye's adolescence. On 1 April 1984, another violent disagreement provoked Marvin Gay Snr. to shoot his son dead, a tawdry end to the life of one of soul music's premier performers.

Motown and Columbia collaborated to produce two albums based on Gaye's unfinished recordings. *Dream Of A Lifetime* mixed spiritual ballads from the early 70s with sexually explicit funk songs from a decade later, while *Romantically Yours* offered a travesty of Gaye's original intentions in 1979 to record an album of big-band ballads. Although Gaye's weighty canon is often reduced to a quartet of 'I Heard It Through The Grapevine', 'Sexual Healing', *What's Going On* and *Let's Get It On*, his entire recorded output signifies the development of black music from raw rhythm and blues, through sophisticated soul to the political awareness of the early 70s, and the increased concentration on personal and sexual politics thereafter. Gaye's remarkable vocal range and fluency remains a touchstone for all subsequent soul vocalists, and his lover man stance has been frequently copied as well as parodied.

● ALBUMS: *The Soulful Moods Of Marvin Gaye* (Tamla 1961) ★★★, *That Stubborn Kind Of Fella* (Tamla 1963) ★★★★, *Recorded Live: On Stage* (Tamla 1964) ★★★, *When I'm Alone I Cry* (Tamla 1964) ★★★, with Mary Wells *Together* (Motown 1964) ★★★, *Hello Broadway This Is Marvin* (Tamla 1965) ★★★, *How Sweet It Is To Be Loved By You* (Tamla 1965) ★★★, *A Tribute To The Great Nat King Cole* (Tamla 1965) ★★★, *Moods Of Marvin Gaye* (Tamla 1966) ★★★, with Kim Weston *Take Two* (Tamla 1966) ★★★, with Tammi Terrell *United* (Tamla 1967) ★★★, *In The Groove* (Tamla 1968) ★★★, with Terrell *You're All I Need* (Tamla 1968) ★★★, with Terrell, Weston, Mary Wells *Marvin Gaye And His Girls* (Tamla 1969) ★★★, with Terrell *Easy* (Tamla 1969) ★★★, *M.P.G.* (Tamla 1969) ★★★, *That's The Way Love Is* (Tamla 1970) ★★★, *What's Going On* (Tamla 1971) ★★★★★, *Trouble Man* film soundtrack (Tamla 1972) ★★★, *Let's Get It On* (Tamla 1973) ★★★★★, with Diana Ross *Diana And Marvin* (Motown 1973) ★★★, *Marvin Gaye Live!* (Tamla 1974) ★★, *I Want You* (Tamla 1976) ★★★★, *Marvin Gaye Live At The London Palladium* (Tamla 1977) ★★★, *Here, My Dear* (Tamla 1978) ★★★★, *In Our Lifetime* (Tamla

1981) ★★★, *Midnight Love* (Columbia 1982) ★★★★, *Romantically Yours* (Columbia 1985) ★★★, *The Last Concert Tour* (Giant 1991) ★★, *Vulnerable* (Motown 1997) ★★★, *Midnight Love & The Sexual Healing Sessions* (Columbia/Legacy 1998) ★★★, *The Final Concert* 1983 recording Capitol 2000) ★★★.

● COMPILATIONS: *Marvin Gaye's Greatest Hits* Tamla 1964) ★★★★, *Marvin Gaye's Greatest Hits Vol. 2* (Tamla 1967) ★★★, *Marvin Gaye & Tammi Terrell: Greatest Hits* (Tamla 1970) ★★★, *Super Hits* (Tamla 1970) ★★★, *Anthology* (Motown 1974) ★★★, *Marvin Gaye's Greatest Hits* (Tamla 1976) ★★★★, *Every Great Motown Hit Of Marvin Gaye* (Motown 1983) ★★★★, *Dream Of A Lifetime* (Columbia 1985) ★★★, *Motown Remembers Marvin Gaye* (Tamla 1986) ★★★, *18 Greatest Hits* (Motown 1988) ★★★★, *Love Songs* (Telstar 1990) ★★★★, *The Marvin Gaye Collection* 4-CD box set (Tamla/Motown 1990) ★★★★★, *Seek And You Shall Find: More Of The Best (1963-1981)* (Rhino 1993) ★★★, *Love Starved Heart* (Motown 1994) ★★★, *The Master: 1961-1984* 4-CD box set (Motown 1995) ★★★★, *Early Classics* (Spectrum 1996) ★★★, *The Love Songs* Motown 2000) ★★★★.

● FURTHER READING: *Divided Soul: The Life Of Marvin Gaye*, David Ritz. *I Heard It Through The Grapevine: Marvin Gaye, The Biography*, Sharon Davis. *Trouble Man: The Life And Death Of Marvin Gaye*, Steve Turner. *What's Going On And The Last Days Of The Motown Sound*, Ben Edmunds.

GENTRY, BOBBIE

b. Roberta Lee Streeter, 27 July 1944, Chickasaw County, Mississippi, USA. Gentry, of Portuguese descent, was raised on a poverty-stricken farm in Greenwood, Mississippi, and was interested in music from an early age. She wrote her first song at the age of seven ('My Dog Sergeant Is A Good Dog') and learned piano – black keys only! – guitar, banjo and vibes. By her teens, she was performing regularly and took her stage name from the movie *Ruby Gentry*. After studying both philosophy and music, she was signed to Capitol Records and recorded 'Mississippi Delta' for an a-side. To her own guitar accompaniment, Gentry recorded for the b-side one of her own songs, 'Ode To Billie Joe', in 30 minutes. Violins and cellos were added, the song was reduced from its original seven minutes, and, as a result of disc jockeys' reactions, it became the a-side. Despite competition from Lee Hazlewood, Gentry's version topped the US charts for four weeks and reached number 13 in the UK. Capitol's truncated version added to the song's mystery: what did Billie Joe and his girlfriend throw off the Tallahatchie Bridge and why did Billie Joe commit suicide? The song's main thrust, however, was the callousness of the girl's family regarding the event, and it can be twinned with Jeannie C. Riley's subsequent story song, 'Harper Valley PTA'.

Gentry became a regular headliner in Las Vegas and she married Bill Harrah, the manager of the Desert Inn Hotel (Gentry's second marriage, in 1978, was to singer-songwriter Jim Stafford). Gentry made an easy listening album with Glen Campbell, which included successful revivals of the Everly Brothers hits 'Let It Be Me' (US Top 40) and 'All I Have To Do Is Dream' (US Top 30/UK number 3). Gentry, with good looks similar to Priscilla Presley, was given her own UK television series, *The Bobbie Gentry Show*, which helped her to top the charts in 1969 with the Burt Bacharach and Hal David song from *Promises, Promises*, 'I'll Never Fall In Love Again'. The 1976 movie *Ode To Billy Joe* (sic), starred Robby Benson and Glynnis O'Connor, and had Billy Joe throw his girlfriend's ragdoll over the bridge and commit suicide because of a homosexual affair. Gentry herself retired from performing to devote time to her business interests.

● ALBUMS: *Ode To Billie Joe* (Capitol 1967) ★★★, *Delta Sweetie* (Columbia 1968) ★★★, *Bobbie Gentry And Glen Campbell* (Capitol 1968) ★★★, *Local Gentry* (1968) ★★, *Touch 'Em With Love* (Capitol 1969) ★★★, *I'll Never Fall In Love Again* (Capitol 1970) ★★★, *Fancy* (Capitol 1970) ★★, *Patchwork* (Capitol 1971) ★★★, *Sittin' Pretty/Tobacco Road* (Capitol 1971) ★★.

● COMPILATIONS: *Bobby Gentry's Greatest* (Capitol 1969) ★★★, *Greatest Hits* (Curb 1990) ★★★, *The Best Of* (Music For Pleasure 1994) ★★★, *Ode To Bobbie Gentry: The Capitol Years* (Capitol 2000) ★★★.

GENTRYS

Formed in 1963 in Memphis, Tennessee, USA, the Gentrys forged their early reputation playing high school dances. The group – Larry Raspberry (vocals, guitar), Bruce Bowles (vocals), Jimmy Hart (vocals), Bobby Fisher (tenor saxophone, piano, guitar), Jimmy Johnson (trumpet, organ), Pat Neal (bass) and Larry Wall (drums) – later won the city's 'Battle Of The Bands' contest and within months had secured a recording contract with the independent Youngstown label. Their first release, 'Sometimes', was coupled with the infectious 'Keep On Dancing', an R&B track that attracted more interest than the a-side. The major label MGM Records picked up the national distribution rights to the single, resulting in the single reaching number 4 in the US charts, subsequently selling in excess of one million copies. The song was later covered by the Bay City Rollers, giving them their first chart hit in 1971. The Gentrys were unable to repeat their early success, but remained a popular live attraction throughout America's southern states. After the break-up of the group in 1970, Jimmy Hart resuscitated the Gentrys' name by forming a new line-up with Steve Speer (bass), Dave Beaver (keyboards), Jimmy Tarbutton (guitar) and Mike Gardner (drums). This incarnation achieved some success with minor placings in

the singles chart. Late-period member Rick Allen resurfaced in the Box Tops, while Raspberry later embarked on a solo career, leading a new group, the High-Steppers.
● ALBUMS: *Keep On Dancing* (MGM 1965) ★★★, *Time* (MGM 1966) ★★★, *The Gentrys* (Sun 1970) ★★.
● COMPILATIONS: *Gentrys* (MGM 1966) ★★★.
● FILMS: *It's A Bikini World* (1967).

GERRY AND THE PACEMAKERS
Gerry Marsden (b. Gerard Marsden, 24 September 1942, Liverpool, Lancashire; guitar/vocals), Freddie Marsden (b. 23 October 1940, Liverpool, Lancashire; drums) and John 'Les' Chadwick (b. 11 May 1943, Liverpool, Lancashire; bass) formed the original Pacemakers in 1959. Two years later they were joined by Les Maguire (b. 27 December 1941, Wallasey, Cheshire; piano) and having completed highly successful spells in German beat clubs, became the second group signed to Brian Epstein's management stable. The effervescent 'How Do You Do It', rejected as unsuitable by the Beatles, gave the more pliant Pacemakers a number 1 hit. Further chart-toppers 'I Like It' and 'You'll Never Walk Alone' (both 1963) followed in quick succession, earning the group the distinction of becoming the first act to have their first three releases reach number 1. The latter song, taken from the musical *Carousel*, was later adopted as the anthem of Liverpool Football Club.
Although the group's sole UK album revealed a penchant for R&B, their singles often emphasized Gerry Marsden's cheeky persona. The exceptions included two excellent in-house compositions 'Don't Let The Sun Catch You Crying' (1964) and 'Ferry Cross The Mersey' (1965), the theme song to the Pacemakers' starring film. A follow-up release, 'I'll Be There', was the quartet's final Top 20 entry and in 1967 Gerry embarked on a solo career. He remained a popular figure in television and on the cabaret circuit, but regained the national spotlight in 1985 following the Bradford City Football Club fire tragedy, when a charity recording, credited to the Crowd and featuring an all-star cast, took a new version of 'You'll Never Walk Alone' to the top of the UK chart for the second time. Another re-recording of an earlier hit for charity, 'Ferry Cross The Mersey', this time for the victims of the Hillsborough crowd disaster, involving supporters of Liverpool FC in 1989, reached number 1. Marsden is still very active gigging with various versions of the Pacemakers.
● ALBUMS: *How Do You Like It* (Columbia 1963) ★★★★, *Don't Let The Sun Catch You Crying* US only (Laurie 1964) ★★★, *Second Album* US only (Laurie 1964) ★★★, *I'll Be There* US only (Laurie 1964) ★★★, *Ferry Cross The Mersey* film soundtrack (Columbia/United Artists 1965) ★★★★, *Girl On A Swing* (Laurie 1966) ★★★, *20 Year Anniversary Album* (Deb 1982) ★★.

Solo: Gerry Marsden *Much Missed Man* (Ozit 2001) ★.
● COMPILATIONS: *Gerry And The Pacemakers' Greatest Hits* (Laurie 1965) ★★★★, *The Best Of Gerry And The Pacemakers* (Capitol 1977) ★★★★, *The Very Best Of Gerry And The Pacemakers* (MFP 1984) ★★★★, *Hit Singles Album* (EMI 1986) ★★★★, *The EP Collection* (See For Miles 1987) ★★★★, *The Singles Plus* (EMI 1987) ★★★★, *All The Hits Of Gerry And The Pacemakers* (Razor & Tie 1995) ★★★★, *Ferry Cross The Mersey* (Castle 1999) ★★★★.
● VIDEOS: *In Concert* (Legend 1990).
● FURTHER READING: *I'll Never Walk Alone*, Gerry Marsden with Ray Coleman.
● FILMS: *Ferry Cross The Mersey* (1965).

GIBSON, BOB
b. 16 November 1931, New York City, New York, USA. Although commercial success proved illusive, Gibson was one of folk music's most influential figures. His songs were recorded by the Kingston Trio and Peter, Paul And Mary and he was responsible for launching and/or furthering the careers of Bob Camp, Judy Collins and Joan Baez. Having recorded his debut single, 'I'm Never To Marry', in 1956, Gibson embarked on a series of excellent albums including *Offbeat Folksongs* and *Carnegie Concert*. Indifferent to marketplace pressure, his novelty collection, *Ski Songs*, was issued at the height of the hootenanny boom while *Yes I See*, arguably the nadir of his recording career, appeared as Bob Dylan began to attract peer group acclaim. These disappointing releases were followed by a duet with Bob (Hamilton) Camp, *At The Gate Of Horn*, paradoxically one of American folk's definitive works. Gibson was absent from music for much of the 60s, but he re-emerged early in the 70s with a melodic album which featured Roger McGuinn, Spanky McFarland and Cyrus Faryar. This respected artist has since pursued a more public path. During the 80s he toured with Tom Paxton and was a frequent performer at international folk festivals.
● ALBUMS: *Folksongs Of Ohio* (Stateside 1956) ★★★, *Offbeat Folksongs* (Riverside 1956) ★★★, *I Come For To Sing* (Riverside 1957) ★★★★, *Carnegie Concert* (Riverside 1957) ★★★★, *There's A Meeting Here Tonight* (Riverside 1959) ★★★, *Ski Songs* (Elektra 1959) ★★★, *Yes I See* (Elektra 1961) ★★★, with Bob 'Hamilton' Camp *At The Gate Of Horn* (1961) ★★, *Hootenanny At Carnegie* (Riverside 1963) ★★★★, *Where I'm Bound* (Elektra 1963) ★★★, *Bob Gibson* (70s) ★★★, *Funky In The Country* (1974) ★★, with Camp *Homemade Music* (1978) ★★★.

GILBERTO, ASTRUD
b. 1940, Bahia, Brazil. Gilberto's career began by accident in March 1963 during a recording session featuring her husband, guitarist João Gilberto, and saxophonist Stan Getz. A projected track, 'The Girl From Ipanema', required a

nger conversant with English and although ictly a non-professional, Astrud was coaxed to performing the soft, *sang-froid* vocal. er contribution was considered relatively nimportant – early pressings of the resultant *an Getz/João Gilberto* did not credit the singer – en when the track was issued as a single the llowing year. 'The Girl From Ipanema' 'entually reached the US Top 5 and UK Top 20, rnering sales in excess of one million and rever binding the artist to the subject of the ng. Astrud later toured with Getz; their llaboration was chronicled on *Getz A-Go-Go*, t she later pursued an independent career, inging her distinctive, if limited, style to a riety of material, including standards, azilian samba/bossa nova and contemporary ngs from Tim Hardin, Jimmy Webb and the oors. Gilberto was the subject of renewed tention when 'The Girl From Ipanema' re-tered the UK charts in 1984 as a result of the K bossa nova/jazz revival perpetrated by tists such as Everything But The Girl, the Style ouncil, Weekend and Sade.

ALBUMS: *The Astrud Gilberto Album* (Verve 65) ★★★★, *The Shadow Of Your Smile* (Verve 65) ★★★, *Look To The Rainbow* (Verve 1965) ★★, *A Certain Smile, A Certain Sadness* (Verve 66) ★★★, *Beach Samba* (Verve 1967) ★★★★, *ndy* (Verve 1968) ★★, *I Haven't Got Anything tter To Do* (Verve 1969) ★★★, *September 17 69* (Verve 1969) ★★, *Astrud Gilberto With nley Turrentine* (Columbia 1971) ★★★, *Astrud lberto Plus James Last* Orchestra (Verve 1987) ★★.

COMPILATIONS: *Once Upon A Summertime* erve 1971) ★★★, *That Girl From Ipanema* erve 1977) ★★★★, *The Best Of Astrud Gilberto* erve 1982) ★★★★, *The Essential Astrud lberto* (Verve 1984) ★★★★ *Compact Jazz* erve 1987) ★★★★, *Talkin' Verve* (Verve 1998) ★★, *Astrud Gilberto's Finest Hour* (Verve 2001) ★★.

LMER, JIMMY, AND THE FIREBALLS
e Fireballs)

LASS MENAGERIE
ter moving from their native Lancashire to ek commercial success in London, England, is psych-pop quartet released a series of gles for Pye Records and Polydor Records thout ever completing an album. Comprising l Atkinson (drums), John Medley (bass), Alan ndall (guitar) and Lou Stonebridge ocals/harmonica), the group made their debut 1968 with the typically floral 'She's A inbow'. Two further singles followed for Pye in e same year, 'You Don't Have To Be So Nice' d 'Frederick Jordan', but neither reached the arts. Transferring to Polydor in 1969, 'Have u Forgotten Who You Are' and 'Do My Thing yself' failed to rectify their commercial sfortune. By now the group had adopted a

heavier, progressive rock-styled sound, which might have been better sampled on a full album release. However, despite the existence of an album acetate, Polydor declined to release it officially and the group broke up. Kendall subsequently joined Toe Fat, while Stonebridge worked with Paladin and McGuinness Flint.

GODS
Formed in 1965 in Hatfield, England, the first incarnation of the Gods consisted of Mick Taylor (b. Michael Kevin Taylor, 17 January 1948, Welwyn Garden City, Hertfordshire, England; guitar), Ken Hensley (keyboards/vocals), John Glascock (bass/vocals) and Brian Glascock (drums). They remained active until 1967, but broke up when Taylor joined John Mayall's Bluesbreakers. Within months Hensley had reconstituted the band around Joe Konas (guitar/vocals), Paul Newton (bass) and Lee Kerslake (drums). Greg Lake (b. 10 November 1948, Bournemouth, Dorset, England) then replaced Newton, but the newcomer left to help found King Crimson in 1968. John Glascock returned to the fold as the Gods secured a recording deal with Columbia Records. *Genesis* was an ambitious concept album, brimming with late 60s naïve pretension, but it was not a commercial success. The Gods did create a minor stir with their reading of the Beatles' 'Hey Bulldog', but they disbanded in February 1969. *To Samuel A Son* was issued posthumously when various ex-members had achieved a higher profile elsewhere. Hensley, Kerslake and both Glascock brothers were all members of Toe Fat, before Hensley, Kerslake and Paul Newton found fame at various different points in Uriah Heep.
● ALBUMS: *Genesis* (Columbia 1968) ★★★, *To Samuel A Son* (Columbia 1970) ★★, *Gods* (Harvest 1976) ★★.
● COMPILATIONS: *The Gods: Featuring Ken Hensley* (Harvest Heritage 1976) ★★★.

GOFFIN, GERRY
b. 11 February 1939, New York City, New York, USA. Goffin was a chemistry major at New York's Queens College when he met fellow student Carole King. Both harboured songwriting ambitions and pooled resources when the former's lyrical gifts gelled with the latter's musical talent. The now-married couple were introduced to publisher Don Kirshner in 1960 following the release of 'Oh! Neil', King's answer disc to Neil Sedaka's 'Oh! Carol'. They joined the staff of the magnate's Aldon company where their early compositions included 'Will You Still Love Me Tomorrow?' (the Shirelles), 'Take Good Care Of My Baby' (Bobby Vee), 'Go Away Little Girl' (Steve Lawrence) and 'Up On The Roof' (the Drifters). Goffin also enjoyed success with Jack Keller and Barry Mann, but the compositions he produced with his wife ultimately proved the most memorable.

Together they wrote 'The Loco-Motion' (Little Eva), 'One Fine Day' (the Chiffons), 'I'm Into Something Good' (Earl-Jean/Herman's Hermits), 'Just Once In My Life' (the Righteous Brothers) and 'Oh No Not My Baby' (Maxine Brown/Manfred Mann), and as the 60s developed so Goffin's lyrics developed from the mundane to the meaningful.

'Don't Bring Me Down', a 1966 hit for the Animals, established a personal perspective, while the images evoked in Aretha Franklin's 'A Natural Woman' – 'when my soul was in the lost and found, you came along to claim it' – verged on the poetic. His ability to assume a feminine perspective emphasized a now incontrovertible skill, consolidated in the introspection of 'Goin' Back' (Dusty Springfield/the Byrds) and the anti-suburbia protest of 'Pleasant Valley Sunday' (the Monkees). However, pressure both professional and personal undermined the couple's relationship and their marriage ended in 1967. Whereas King forged a second successful career during the 70s singer/songwriter boom, Goffin enjoyed a less public profile. Bereft of a melodious partner and out of place in an era where musicians both composed and performed, he remained in the public eye due to the enduring popularity of his early compositions. Blood, Sweat And Tears recorded 'Hi De Hi', Grand Funk Railroad covered 'The Loco-Motion', while his ex-wife later paid tribute to their partnership with *Pearls*, a selection of their 60s collaborations. During the 70s Goffin worked as a producer for several artists, including Diana Ross. He did record a solo album, *It Ain't Exactly Entertainment*, in 1973, but it failed to emulate the popularity of his former partner. Goffin's contribution to popular music is considerable and many of former hits are now classics. Always literate and melodic, his work remains timeless. He had a second attempt at fame as a recording artist in 1996.
● ALBUMS: *It Ain't Exactly Entertainment* (Adelphi 1973) ★★, *Back Room Blood* (Adelphi 1996) ★★.
● COMPILATIONS: *The Goffin And King Songbook* various artists interpretations of Goffin And King compositions (Columbia 1989) ★★★.

GOINS, HERBIE

Goins, like Geno Washington, was a former US serviceman who remained in the UK when his military service ended. In 1963 he joined Alexis Korner's Blues Incorporated and was featured vocalist on several of this seminal band's releases, including *Red Hot From Alex* and *At The Cavern*. In 1965 he left to lead Herbie Goins And The Night Timers, which became a highly popular attraction in London's clubs. The group was signed to Parlophone Records, for whom they recorded several excellent dance-orientated soul singles, including 'The Music Played On' (1965), 'Number One In Your Heart' and 'Incredible Miss Brown' (both 1966). In 1967 the

Night Timers recorded their only album *Number One In Your Heart* is an exciting set, with swinging versions of such club standards as 'Pucker Up Buttercup', 'Knock On Wood' and 'Look At Granny Run, Run', but it was deemed anachronistic when compared with the contemporary psychedelic trends. The group broke up in 1968.
● ALBUMS: *Number One In Your Heart* (Parlophone 1967) ★★★.

GOLDBERG, BARRY

b. 1941, Chicago, Illinois, USA. Goldberg was one of several white aspirants frequenting Chicago blues clubs during the early 60s. He befriended guitarist Michael Bloomfield prior to forming the Goldberg-Miller Blues Band with itinerant Texan Steve Miller. Goldberg assumed the group leadership on his partner's departure, and the resultant album is a fine example of pop-influenced R&B. An accomplished keyboard player, Goldberg was part of the back-up band supporting Bob Dylan on his controversial appearance at 1965's Newport Folk Festival. Sessions supporting Mitch Ryder preceded a brief spell with Chicago Loop before Goldberg joined the Electric Flag. The artist resumed his own career in 1968 with the Barry Goldberg Reunion. Several erratic albums followed including *Two Jews Blues*, which featured contributions from Bloomfield and Duane Allman, and a collaboration with Neil Merryweather and Charlie Musselwhite, *Ivar Avenue Reunion*. Goldberg also continued his session work and produced albums for Musselwhite and the Rockets, but has been unable to translate his status as a sideman into coherent solo path.
● ALBUMS: *Blowing My Mind* (Epic 1966) ★★, *The Barry Goldberg Reunion* (Buddah 1968) ★★★, with Mike Bloomfield *Two Jews Blues* (Buddah 1969) ★★, *Barry Goldberg And Friends* (Record Man 1969) ★★, *Streetman* (1970) ★★, with Neil Merryweather, Charlie Musselwhite *Ivar Avenue Reunion* (1970) ★★★, *Blasts From My Past* (Buddah 1971) ★★★, *Barry Goldberg* (1974) ★★, *Barry Goldberg And Friends Recorded Live* (Buddah 1976) ★★★.

GOLDIE AND THE GINGERBREADS

Formed in Brooklyn, New York, USA, in 1962, Goldie And The Gingerbreads made their debut at the city's famed Peppermint Lounge. They were discovered by British group the Animals who, impressed by the quartet's musical abilities, suggested they move to the UK. Goldie (b. Genya Zelkowitz, 1943, Poland; vocals), Carol MacDonald (b. 1944, Wilmington, Delaware, USA; guitar), Margo Crocitto (b. 1943, Brooklyn, New York, USA; organ) and Ginger Panebianco (b. 1945, Long Island, New York, USA; drums) arrived in London in November 1964 and their debut single was issued the following year in the wake of successful appearances at the Crazy

Elephant and Flamingo clubs. Animals keyboard player Alan Price produced the excellent 'Can't You Hear My Heart Beat?', a UK Top 30 entry, but two further singles failed to achieve similar success. The group toured with the Rolling Stones and Kinks, but despite their undoubted dexterity – Crocitto made several session appearances – they were unfairly perceived as a novelty. The quartet split up in October 1965 when Goldie embarked on a solo career, but the remaining trio maintained contact and the group continued to record upon returning to New York, releasing 'Song To The Moon'/'Walking In Different Circles' in 1967. They later re-emerged during the 70s as part of Isis, an all-female group.

GOLLIWOGS

Formed in El Cerrito, California, USA, this accomplished quartet – John Fogerty (b. 28 May 1945, Berkeley, California, USA; guitar/vocals), Tom Fogerty (b. 9 November 1941, Berkeley, California, USA, d. 6 September 1990, Scottsdale, Arizona, USA; guitar/vocals), Stu Cook (b. 25 April 1945, Oakland, California, USA; bass) and Doug Clifford (b. 24 April 1945, Palo Alto, California, USA; drums) – were initially known as the Blue Velvets, but took the Golliwogs' name as a precondition to their recording deal with Fantasy Records. The group was never happy with the appellation, nor the blond wigs they were sometimes required to wear, but between 1964 and 1967 they completed a series of excellent singles. Tom Fogerty dominated early releases, but by 1966 his younger brother was wresting control of the group. 'Walk On The Water' and 'Fight Fire' showed the unit developing a defined, original sound. Having turned fully professional in December 1967, they evolved into Creedence Clearwater Revival.

● COMPILATIONS: *The Golliwogs* (Fantasy 1975) ★★★.

GOMELSKY, GIORGIO

b. 28 February 1934, Georgia, formerly USSR. Exiled to Switzerland and educated in Italy, Gomelsky later settled in Britain where he became a leading figure of London's jazz scene during the 50s. He organized the first Richmond Jazz Festival and was later responsible for bringing bluesman Sonny Boy 'Rice Miller' Williamson to Europe. Giorgio's first club was the Piccadilly, but in 1963 he established the famed Crawdaddy Club in Richmond's Station Hotel, which quickly became one of the country's leading venues for rhythm and blues. The Rolling Stones enjoyed a successful residency there prior to recording and Gomelsky initially acted as the group's manager before being supplanted by Andrew Loog Oldham. However, the impresario fared better with their successors, the Yardbirds, whom he guided and produced between 1964 and 1966.

Gomelsky subsequently managed the T-Bones and the Steampacket before founding the Marmalade label in 1967. He enjoyed a modicum of success with Blossom Toes, before securing international hits with protégés Julie Driscoll and Brian Auger And The Trinity. The company, however, proved short-lived and Giorgio subsequently left England for Paris where he established an alternative music circuit for radical groups Magma, whom he also managed, and Gong. Gomelsky also enjoyed a fruitful relationship with BYG Records, who issued several albums culled from tapes he had recorded during the 60s. Having founded a new label, Utopia, in 1975, he then moved to New York, where he continues to supervise releases drawn from his considerable archive.

GOOD RATS

This US group was formed while the members were at college in 1964 by Peppi and Mickey Marchello, both from Long Island, New York, USA. Their debut was a mixture of rock 'n' roll and progressive rock. A succession of poor-selling albums coupled with regular changes of record labels hampered their commercial prospects. They broke up for three years during 1969-72. By the time of their fourth and best album – *From Rats To Riches* – (which was later issued on Radar in the UK), the line-up was the gruff-voiced Peppi, Mickey (guitar), John 'the Cat' Gatto (guitar), Lenny Kotke (bass) and Joe Franco (drums). This album was recorded on Long Island in late 1977 with Flo And Eddie (Mark Volman and Howard Kaylan) producing. Although their place in the market was never clear they were essentially a good old-fashioned, basic US rock 'n' roll band.

● ALBUMS: *The Good Rats* (Kapp 1968) ★★★, *Tasty* (Rat City 1974) ★★, *Rat City In Blue* (Rat City 1976) ★★, *From Rats To Riches* (Passport/Radar 1978) ★★★, *Rats The Way You Like It – Live* (Passport 1978) ★★, *Birth Comes To Us All* (Passport 1978) ★★, *Live At Last* (Rat City 1980) ★★, *Great American Music* (Great American/Passport 1981) ★★, *Cover Of Night* (Frontier 2000) ★★.

● COMPILATIONS: *Tasty Seconds* (Uncle Rat Music 1997) ★★★.

GOOD, JACK

b. 1931, London, England, this founder of British pop television was president of Oxford University Drama Society and then a stand-up comedian before enrolling on a BBC training course. His final test film was centred on Freddie Mills. The late boxer was also an interlocutor on 1957's *6.5 Special*, a magazine series for teenagers produced by Good and Josephine Douglas. While he became evangelical about rock 'n' roll, Good's staid superiors obliged him to balance the pop with comedy sketches, string quartets and features on sport and hobbies. He was fired for flaunting

Corporation dictates by presenting a stage version of the show. Snapped up by ITV, he broke ground with *Oh Boy!* which introduced Cliff Richard, Marty Wilde and other homegrown rockers to the nation. So swiftly did its atmospheric parade of idols – mostly male – pass before the cameras that the screaming studio audience, urged on by Good, scarcely had pause to draw breath. While overseeing the less exciting *Boy Meets Girls* and *Wham!*, Good branched out into publishing and record production, such as Billy Fury's *The Sound Of Fury*.

In 1962 Good was in North America where he worked intermittently as an actor – notably on Broadway in C.P. Snow's *The Affair* and, in 1967, as a hotelier in *Clambake*, an Elvis Presley vehicle. His self-financed pilot programme, *Young America Swings The World*, fell on stony ground but, after Brian Epstein commissioned him for *Around The Beatles*, he superintended the nationally broadcast pop showcase *Shindig* which, as well as making 'discoveries' such as the Righteous Brothers and Sonny And Cher, represented a media breakthrough for diverse black artists from Howlin' Wolf to the Chambers Brothers – and held its own in a ratings war against *The Beverly Hillbillies* on a main rival channel. Leaving *Shindig* to fend for itself, his most interesting career tangent of the later 60s was *Catch My Soul*, 1968's rock adaptation in a Los Angeles theatre of Shakespeare's *Othello* with Jerry Lee Lewis as Iago. For a season in London, P.J. Proby assumed the Lewis role with Good himself as the Moor. Back in the USA, he ticked over with one-shot television specials concerning, among others, Andy Williams, the Monkees and 1970's Emmy award-winning classical/pop hybrid of Ray Charles, Jethro Tull, the Nice and the LA Philharmonic.

On an extended visit to England from his Santa Fe home, Good put on *Elvis*, a biographical musical starring, initially, Proby and Shakin' Stevens before daring an updated reconstruction of *Oh Boy!* (later transferred to television) at the same London West End theatre. By the 80s, income from the inspired Good's less frequent television and stage ventures underwrote another vocational episode – as a painter. In the 90s it was reported that Good was training to become a monk, but, while he was contemplating it, he travelled to London to oversee the West End launch of his own autobiographical musical, *Good Rockin' Tonite*, which had them dancing in the aisles – just like the old days.

GORDY, BERRY

b. Berry Gordy Jnr., 28 November 1929, Detroit, Michigan, USA. Gordy took his first tentative steps into the music business in 1955, when he opened a jazz record store in Detroit. When it folded, he returned to the automobile assembly lines until he met the manager of young R&B singer Jackie Wilson. Gordy wrote Wilson's first major hit, the novelty and now classic 'Reet Petite', and joined the singer's entourage, composing four further chart successes over the next two years. In 1958, Gordy set himself up as an independent producer, working with young unknowns such as the Miracles, Marv Johnson and Eddie Holland. That year he formed the Jobete Music company to handle songs by himself and his associates. At the suggestion of the Miracles' vocalist Smokey Robinson, Gordy went a stage further in 1959 by launching his own record company, Tamla Records. This was merely the first of a succession of labels gathered under his Motown Records umbrella, which rapidly became one of America's most important independent concerns.

Gordy masterminded Motown from the outside, choosing the artist-roster, writing and producing many of the early releases, and chairing weekly meetings that determined every aspect of the company's artistic direction. Having co-produced and co-written Motown's first major hit, the Miracles' 'Shop Around' in 1960, Gordy was also responsible for hits such as 'Do You Love Me' and 'Shake Sherry' by the Contours, 'Fingertips (Part 2)' by Stevie Wonder, 'Try It Baby' by Marvin Gaye and 'Shotgun' by Junior Walker And The All Stars. As Motown's influence and reputation grew, Gordy groomed a school of producers and writers to create the style that he dubbed 'The Sound of Young America'. Gradually his own artistic input lessened, although he continued to collaborate on Supremes hits such as 'Love Child' and 'No Matter What Sign You Are' until the end of the decade. His time was primarily devoted to increasing Motown's market share, and to dealing with a series of bitter clashes between artists and company, which threatened to halt the label's progress by the early 70s. Anxious to secure new power bases, Gordy shifted Motown's main offices from Detroit to California, and inaugurated a new films division with the highly acclaimed *Lady Sings The Blues*. This movie on the life of Billie Holiday starred former Supreme Diana Ross, with whom Gordy had long been rumoured to be enjoying a romantic liaison. Their relationship was part of the company's backbone, and her eventual decision to leave Motown in the early 80s was read as an indicator of the label's declining fortunes.

Having lost many of its major creative talents, Motown subsisted through the 70s and early 80s on the backs of several unique individuals, notably Stevie Wonder and Lionel Richie. Gordy was no longer finding significant new talent, however. Ironically, one of his company's most successful newcomers of the 80s was his own son, Rockwell. Gordy's personal career has long since been synonymous with the fortunes of his company, and he surprised the industry when he sold Motown Records to MCA in 1988 – just weeks after he had been inducted into the Rock And Roll Hall Of Fame in recognition of his pioneering talents as a major songwriter, impresario and executive. In the 90s, new label head Andre Harrell attempted to reassert the label as a leading force in black music, achieving notable success with acts such as Johnny Gill, Boyz II Men and Queen Latifah. In 1997 Gordy sold 50% of his Jobete music publishing to EMI. This catalogue of the golden age of Motown contains many of the finest songs of the era, and is unquestionably worth the purchase price of $135 million.

FURTHER READING: *Movin' Up*, Berry Gordy. *To Be Loved: The Music, The Magic, The Memories Of Motown* Berry Gordy. *Where Did Our Love Go?*, Nelson George.

GORE, LESLEY

b. Lesley Goldstein, 2 May 1946, New York City, USA, and raised in Tenafly, New Jersey. Having secured a recording contract with Mercury Records on the basis of a privately financed demonstration disc, Gore enjoyed a sensational debut when 'It's My Party' topped the US chart in May 1963, reached number 9 in the UK and grossed sales in excess of one million. This tale of adolescent trauma has retained its timeless appeal – the singer's birthday celebrations are irrevocably marred on losing boyfriend Johnny to Judy – and it remains one of the era's most memorable releases. The vengeful follow-up, 'Judy's Turn To Cry', reached US number 5 and earned another gold disc, but successive releases, including 'She's A Fool' (US number 5), 'You Don't Own Me' (US number 2), a powerful call for independence, 'That's The Way Boys Are' (US number 12) and 'Maybe I Know' (US number 14), confirmed that the singer was not simply a novelty act. Gore made several appearances in teen-oriented movies including *The Girls On The Beach* and *Ski Party*, and television shows including *Batman*, but her career was marred by periods of inactivity. After a few singles on the Crew label she re-merged in 1972 with *Someplace Else Now*, released on Motown Records' MoWest subsidiary. Three years later she was briefly reunited with producer/songwriter Quincy Jones, who had produced her early Mercury recordings, on the exceptional A&M Records single, 'Immortality'. Gore established herself as a songwriter of note with her contribution to the *Fame* soundtrack, earning an Oscar nomination for 'Out Here On My Own', which was co-written with her songwriter brother Michael. Her own recordings have been few and far between, with only an album for the short-lived 51 West label in 1981, and a single five years later on the Manhattan label. She has continued to tour to packed audiences on the cabaret circuit, while her acting career includes highlights such as 1999's appearance on Broadway in *Smokey Joe's Cafe*. Despite the frailty exhibited on her debut single, Lesley Gore is now viewed by commentators as an early champion of women's rights, despite the fact that the songs which made her famous were penned by a male writing team.

● ALBUMS: *I'll Cry If I Want To* (Mercury 1963) ★★★★, *Lesley Gore Sings Of Mixed-Up Hearts* (Mercury 1963) ★★★★, *Boys, Boys, Boys* (Mercury 1964) ★★★, *Girl Talk* (Mercury 1964) ★★★, *My Town, My Guy & Me* (Mercury 1965) ★★★, *Lesley Gore Sings All About Love* aka *Love Love* (Mercury 1966) ★★★, *California Nights* (Mercury 1967) ★★, *Someplace Else Now* (MoWest 1972) ★★, *Love Me By Name* (A&M 1976) ★★★, *The Canvas Can Do Miracles* (51 West 1982) ★★★.

● COMPILATIONS: *The Golden Hits Of Lesley Gore* (Mercury 1965) ★★★★, *Golden Hits Vol. 2* (Mercury 1968) ★★★, *The Sound Of Young Love* (Wing 1969) ★★★, *The Lesley Gore Anthology* (Rhino 1986) ★★★, *It's My Party* (Mercury 1991) ★★★, *Start The Party Again* (Raven 1993) ★★★, *It's My Party!* 5-CD box set (Bear Family 1994) ★★★, *It's My Party: The Mercury Anthology* (PolyGram 1996) ★★★, *Sunshine, Lollipops & Rainbows: The Best Of Lesley Gore* (Rhino 1998) ★★★★, *Lesley Gore: The Essential Collection* (Spectrum 1999) ★★★.

● FILMS: *The T.A.M.I. Show* (1964), *Ski Party* (1965), *The Girls On The Beach* aka *Summer Of '64* (1965),

GOULET, ROBERT

b. 26 November 1933, Lawrence, Massachusetts, USA. An actor and singer, Goulet made his first professional appearance in 1951 with the Edmonton Summer Pops. He also played in *Thunder Rock* and *Visit To A Small Planet*. After appearing in Canadian productions of *South Pacific*, *Finian's Rainbow*, and *Gentlemen Prefer Blondes*, he moved to the USA, and made his Broadway debut in 1960, when he played Sir Lancelot in the musical *Camelot*, introducing the poignant 'If Ever I Would Leave You'. He also began launching his singing career during this time, and appeared on the Ed Sullivan television variety programme as well as others of that kind. Goulet signed with Columbia Records in 1962 and had his first chart entry with 'What Kind Of Fool Am I?' from the musical *Stop The World – I Want To Get Off*. He won the Grammy Award for Best New Artist in 1962, and his greatest singles success came in 1965 with the operatic 'My Love Forgive Me (Amore, Scusami)'. By then he had already proven that his strength was in album sales, as was often the case with middle of the road performers at that time. His 1962 Columbia debut, *Always You*, had charted, but it was the following year's *Sincerely Yours ...* and 1964's *My Love Forgive Me* that became Goulet's top-performing albums. In 1968, he returned to the Broadway musical theatre in *The Happy Time*, and won a Tony Award for his portrayal of the French-Canadian man-about-the-world Uncle

Jacques. In the 70s and 80s he toured in several musical revivals and appeared extensively in concerts, cabaret (with his wife Carol Lawrence), and on his own television series. In 1993, after taking a new production of *Camelot* around the USA (in which, more than 30 years on, he played King Arthur instead of Lancelot), Goulet took the show to New York where it was greeted without enthusiasm. The same year he was diagnosed with prostate cancer.

● ALBUMS: *Always You* (Columbia 1962) ★★★, *Two Of Us* (Columbia 1962) ★★★, *Sincerely Yours* ... (Columbia 1963) ★★★★, *The Wonderful World Of Love* (Columbia 1963) ★★★, *Robert Goulet In Person* (Columbia 1963) ★★★, *Manhattan Tower/The Man Who Loves Manhattan* (Columbia 1964) ★★★, *Without You* (Columbia 1964) ★★★, *My Love Forgive Me* (Columbia 1964) ★★★★, *Begin To Love* (Columbia 1965) ★★★, *Summer Sounds* (Columbia 1965) ★★★, *Robert Goulet On Broadway* (Columbia 1965) ★★★, *Traveling On* (Columbia 1966) ★★★, *I Remember You* (Columbia 1966) ★★★, *Robert Goulet On Broadway, Volume 2* (Columbia 1967) ★★★, *Woman, Woman* (Columbia 1968) ★★★★, *Hollywood Mon Amour – Great Love Songs From The Movies* (Columbia 1968) ★★★, *Both Sides Now* (Columbia 1969) ★★, *Souvenir D'Italie* (Columbia 1969) ★★★, *Greatest Hits* (Columbia 1969) ★★★★, *I Wish You Love* (Columbia 1970) ★★, *Close To You* (Columbia 1992) ★★.

● COMPILATIONS: *The Best Of Robert Goulet* (Atlantic 1990) ★★★, *Golden Classics Edition* (Collectables 1997) ★★★.

GRAHAM, BILL

b. Wolfgang Wolodia Grajonca, 8 January 1931, Berlin, Germany, d. 25 October 1991, Concord, California, USA. Born into a Russian-Jewish family, Graham arrived in New York during 1941, a refugee from Nazi persecution. After earning a degree in business administration, he moved to the west coast. By 1965 he was managing the San Francisco Mime Troupe, organizing the requisite benefit gigs to keep the revue afloat. Such work brought him into contact with the nascent rock fraternity and Graham began promoting concerts at the city's Fillmore Auditorium. The venue became the leading showcase for the 'San Francisco Sound', exemplified by Jefferson Airplane, Quicksilver Messenger Service, the Grateful Dead and Big Brother And The Holding Company. Graham, in turn, became a leading impresario, and by 1968 had bought the larger Carousel Ballroom, renaming it the Fillmore West. Within weeks he had opened a corresponding Fillmore East in a vacant cinema on New York's Second Avenue. As a hard headed entrepreneur, he often came into conflict with the free-loading hippie idealism inherent in running a music venue. Yet Graham often confounded his critics by contributing to local organizations in the form of benefits. In addition, the presentation of concerts at his venues paved the way for future promoters by way of introducing light shows showing films between acts, free apples and taking a personal interest in the musicians giving a professional performance. He was also instrumental in efforts to integrate black artists on billings, so introducing many musicians to a predominantly white audience. These artists included B.B. King, Leon Thomas, Raahsar, Roland Kirk, Miles Davis, Muddy Waters and Ravi Shankar.

By the end of 1971, Graham had closed down both halls and was determined to retire from a business for which he was losing respect. The final performances at the Fillmore West were captured on the film and accompanying album box set, *Fillmore – The Last Days* (1972). The sabbatical was brief and during the next decade he was involved in national tours by Bob Dylan and Crosby, Stills, Nash And Young, as well as major one-off events. Such work culminated on 13 July 1985 when Graham organized the American segment of the Live Aid concert for famine relief. A controversial and outspoken character, he also pursued a successful career in management, guiding, at different times, the paths of Jefferson Airplane, Santana, Van Morrison and Dylan. Graham's tragic death in a helicopter crash occurred while returning from a Huey Lewis And The News concert he had promoted in South County, California. It robbed the rock music business of one its most legendary characters and greatest promoters. His funeral service was attended by members of the Grateful Dead, Santana and Quicksilver Messenger Service who offered musical tributes.

● FURTHER READING: *Bill Graham Presents* Bill Graham and Robert Greenfield.

GRANT, JULIE

b. *c.*1945, England. A product of early 60s vintage UK pop, Grant found some success with a string of singles for Pye Records. Her half-beehive hairstyle and angular eye make-up was seen regularly on package tours and UK television. Her manager was Eric Easton, who briefly managed the Rolling Stones, with whom she shared the bill on their first major package tour. Her 1962 cover of the Drifters' 'Up On The Roof' made the UK hit parade but was overtaken by Kenny Lynch's version. Nevertheless, she bounced back with 'Count On Me', reaching number 24 – her highest (and penultimate) chart placing. However, after 1964's 'Come To Me', a tempestuous ballad that was frequently played on the BBC Light Programme, and consequently wended its way to the edge of the Top 30, Grant's fortunes on record declined irrecoverably.

GRAPEFRUIT

Formed in Britain during 1967, Grapefruit was originally comprised of three former member of harmony group Tony Rivers And The

Castaways – John Perry (b. 16 July 1949, London, England; lead guitar/vocals), Pete Sweetenham (b. 24 April 1949, London, England; rhythm guitar/vocals) and Geoff Sweetenham (b. 8 March 1948, London, England; drums), and songwriter George Alexander (b. 28 December 1946; Glasgow, Scotland; bass/vocals). The quartet, named by John Lennon, (after the title of a book written by Yoko Ono)was the first act signed to the Beatles' Apple publishing company, whose faith was confirmed when Grapefruit's debut single, 'Dear Delilah', became a UK Top 30 hit. Alexander's penchant for high-quality British pop was matched by Terry Melcher's sympathetic production, but despite several equally excellent follow-up releases, the group's only other chart entry was 'C'mon Marianne', originally recorded by the Four Seasons. By 1969 Mick Fowler (keyboards) had been added to the line-up while Geoff Sweetenham was later replaced by Bobby Ware. *Deep Water* revealed an unsatisfactory soul/rock perspective and Alexander subsequently dissolved the band. He joined former Easybeats members George Young and Harry Vanda (Young and Alexander were brothers) for a variety of projects issued under different names. The Grapefruit appellation was briefly revived in 1971 for 'Universal Party', a melodic pop song redolent of the act's initial releases, although it failed to make a similar impact on the singles chart.

● ALBUMS: *Around Grapefruit* (Dunhill 1968) ★★★, *Deep Water* (RCA Victor 1969) ★★.

GRASS ROOTS

Although several Californian groups claimed this sobriquet, including the embryonic Love, it was appropriated by songwriters P.F. Sloan and Steve Barri, who employed the name pseudonymously on several folk rock performances. When 'Where Were You When I Needed You?' reached the US Top 30 in 1966, the need for a permanent line-up arose and the duo enticed Warren Entner (b. 7 July 1944, Boston, Massachusetts, USA; vocals/guitar), Creed Bratton (b. 8 February 1943, Sacramento, California, USA; guitar), Rob Grill (b. 30 November 1944, Los Angeles, California, USA; vocals/bass) and Rick Coonce (b. Erik Michael Coonce, 1 August 1947, Los Angeles, California, USA; drums) to adopt the Grass Roots name. The new group enjoyed immediate success with 'Let's Live For Today', a remake of an Italian hit. This distanced the quartet from their mentors, but although Sloan's input decreased dramatically, Barri retained his role as producer. The Grass Roots then became one of America's leading commercial attractions with a series of confident, if undemanding, performances, including 'Midnight Confessions' (1968), 'Bella Linda' (1968), 'I'd Wait A Million Years' (1969) and 'Sooner Or Later' (1971). The group remained a popular attraction into the 80s,

although the verve of their early work had, by then, evaporated.

● ALBUMS: *Where Were You When I Needed You* (Dunhill 1966) ★★★, *Let's Live For Today* (Dunhill 1967) ★★★, *Feelings* (Dunhill 1968) ★★★, *Lovin' Things* (Dunhill 1969) ★★★, *Leaving It All Behind* (Dunhill 1969) ★★★, *Move Along* (Dunhill 1972) ★★, *A Lotta' Mileage* (1973) ★★.

● COMPILATIONS: *Golden Grass (Their Greatest Hits)* (Stateside 1968) ★★★, *More Golden Grass* (1970) ★★, *Their Sixteen Greatest Hits* (Dunhill 1974) ★★★, *Anthology 1965-1975* (Rhino 1991) ★★★, *Symphonic Hits* (Cleopatra 2001) ★★★.

GRATEFUL DEAD

The enigmatic, erratic and mercurial (cliché, but absolutely true) Grateful Dead evolved from Mother McCree's Uptown Jug Champions to become the Warlocks in 1965. A number of conflicting reasons for the choice of name have arisen over the years. The most popular one is that the name was chosen from a randomly opened copy of the *Oxford Companion To Classical Music* (others say a Funk & Wagnells dictionary) the juxtaposition of words evidently immediately appealing to Garcia and his chums, who at the time were somewhat chemically stimulated on DMT. The theory that it came from the *Egyptian Book Of The Dead* has been denied by each member of the band. The original line-up comprised Jerry Garcia (b. Jerome John Garcia, 1 August 1942, San Francisco, California, USA, d. 9 August 1995, Forest Knolls, California, USA; lead guitar), Bob Weir (b. Robert Hall, 16 October 1947, San Francisco, California, USA; rhythm guitar), Phil Lesh (b. Philip Chapman, 15 March 1940, Berkeley, California, USA; bass), Ron 'Pigpen' McKernan (b. 8 September 1945, San Bruno, California, USA. d. 8 March 1973; keyboards) and Bill Kreutzmann (b. 7 April 1946, Palo Alto, California, USA; drums). The Grateful Dead have been synonymous with the San Francisco/Acid Rock scene since its inception in 1965 when they took part in Ken Kesey's Acid Tests. Stanley Owsley manufactured the then legal LSD and plied the band and their friends with copious amounts. This hallucinogenic opus was duly recorded onto tape over a six-month period, and documented in Tom Wolfe's book *The Electric Kool-Aid Acid Test*. Wolfe stated that 'They were not to be psychedelic dabblers, painting pretty pictures, but true explorers.'

Their music, which started out as straight-forward rock, blues and R&B, germinated into a hybrid of styles, but has the distinction of being long, wandering and improvisational. By the time their first album was released in 1967 they were already a huge local cult band. *Grateful Dead* sounds raw in the light of 90s record production, but it was a brave, early attempt to capture a live concert sound on a studio album. 'Cold Rain And Snow' and 'The Golden Road To

Unlimited Devotion' are short compositions that could have been successful pop singles, had Warner Brothers known how to market the band. The follow-up *Anthem Of The Sun* was much more satisfying. On this alleged 'live' record, 17 different concerts and four different live studios were used. The non-stop suite of ambitious segments with tantalizing titles such as 'The Faster We Go, The Rounder We Get' and 'Quadlibet For Tenderfeet' was an artistic success. Their innovative and colourful album covers were among the finest examples of San Franciscan art, utilizing the talents of Kelley Mouse Studios (Alton Kelley and Stanley Mouse). The third album contained structured songs and was not as inaccessible as the palindrome title *Aoxomoxoa* suggested. Hints of a mellowing Grateful Dead surfaced on 'China Cat Sunflower' and the sublime 'Mountains Of The Moon', complete with medieval-sounding harpsichord. It was with this album that their lyrics came under close scrutiny as being something special. In particular those by Robert Hunter, who wrote mysterious tales of intrigue. In concert, the band were playing longer and longer sets, sometimes lasting six hours with only as many songs. Their legion of fans, now known as 'Deadheads' relished the possibility of a marathon concert. It was never ascertained who imbibed more psychedelic chemicals, the audience or the band. Nevertheless, the sounds produced sometimes took them to breathtaking heights of musical achievement. The interplay between Garcia's shrill, flowing solos and Lesh's meandering bass lines complemented the adventurous jazzy chords of Weir's rhythm guitar. The band had now added a second drummer, Mickey Hart (b. 11 September 1943, New York, USA), and a second keyboard player, Tom Constanten, to accompany the unstable McKernan, who had, by now, a severe drinking problem. It was this line-up that produced the seminal double album *Live/Dead* in 1970. Their peak of improvisation is best demonstrated on the track 'Dark Star'. During its 23 minutes of recorded life, the music simmers, builds and explodes four times, each with a crescendo of superb playing from Garcia and his colleagues. For many, this one song was the epitome of what the band were all about.

On the two following records *Workingman's Dead* and *American Beauty*, a strong Crosby, Stills And Nash harmony influence prevailed. The short, country-feel songs brought Garcia's pedal steel guitar to the fore (he had recently guested on Crosby, Stills, Nash And Young's *Déjà Vu*). Uplifting songs such as 'Uncle John's Band', 'Ripple' and 'Till The Morning Come' were shared with powerful yet sentimental ballads such as 'Attics Of My Life', 'Brokendown Palace' and 'High Time'. These two outstanding albums were like sister and brother, and broke the band to a much wider audience. Paradoxically, the 'Dead' reverted to releasing live sets by issuing a

second, self-titled double album (originally to be named *Skullfuck*), closely followed by the triple, *Europe '72*. After years of ill health through alcohol abuse, McKernan died in 1973. He was replaced by Keith Godchaux from Dave Mason's band, who, together with his wife Donna on vocals, compensated for the tragic loss of Pigpen. *Wake Of The Flood* in 1973 showed a delicate jazz influence and proved to be their most commercially successful album to date. With this and subsequent studio albums the band produced a more mellow sound. It was not until *Terrapin Station* in 1977 that their gradual move towards beautiful lethargy was averted. Producer Keith Olsen expertly introduced a fuller, more orchestrated sound, and forced them to be more musically disciplined in the studio.

As a touring band the Grateful Dead continued to prosper, but their studio albums began to lose direction. For their funky but disappointing *Shakedown Street* they enlisted Little Feat's Lowell George as producer. Although they had been with the band for some years, Keith and Donna Godchaux had never truly fitted in. Donna often had trouble with her vocal pitch, resulting in some excruciating performances, while Keith began to use hard drugs. They were asked to leave at the end of 1979 and on 21 July 1980, Keith was killed in a car crash. *Go To Heaven* (1980) with new keyboard player Brent Mydland betrayed a hint of disco-pop. The album sleeve showed the band posing in white suits which prompted 'Deadheads' to demand: 'Have they gone soft?' Ironically, it was this disappointing record that spawned their first, albeit minor, success in the US singles chart with 'Alabama Getaway'. All of the band had seriously experimented with drugs for many years and, unlike many of their contemporaries, had survived. Garcia, however, succumbed to heroin addiction in 1982. This retrospectively explained his somnolent playing and gradual decline as a guitarist over recent years, together with his often weak and shaky vocals. By the mid-80s, the band had become amorphous but still commanded a massive following. Garcia eventually collapsed and came close to death when he went into a diabetic coma in 1986.

The joy and relief of his survival showed in their first studio album in seven years, *In The Dark*. It was a stunning return to form, resulting in a worldwide hit single 'Touch Of Grey', with Garcia singing his long-time co-songwriter Robert Hunter's simplistic yet honest lyric: 'Oh well a touch of grey, kinda suits you anyway, that's all I've got to say, it's alright'. The band joined in for a joyous repeated chorus of 'I will survive' followed by 'We will survive'. They were even persuaded to make a video and the resulting exposure on MTV introduced them to a whole new generation of younger fans. The laconic Garcia humorously stated that he was 'appalled' to find they had a smash hit on their ands. Garcia attempted to get fit and to shake ff years of drug abuse. While *Built To Last* 1989) was a dull affair, they continued to play to ast audiences. They have since received the ccolade of being the largest grossing band in nusical history. In August 1990 Mydland died rom a lethal combination of cocaine and norphine. Remarkably, this was the third eyboard player to die in the band. Mydland's emporary replacement was Bruce Hornsby ntil Vince Welnick was recruited full-time. In 990, the band's live album catalogue was ncreased with the release of the erratic *Without Net* and the poor *Dylan And The Dead.*

'he transcendental Grateful Dead have ndured, throughout the many difficult stages in heir long career. Their progress was again alted when Garcia became seriously ill with a ung infection. After a long spell in hospital jarcia returned, this time promising to listen to octors' advice. They continued to tour hroughout 1993 and 1994, after which they egan to record a new studio album. However, n 9 August 1995, Garcia suffered a fatal heart ttack, ironically while staying in Serenity nolls, a drug treatment centre in Marin ounty. It was alleged he was found curled on is bed clutching an apple with a smile on his ace. The reaction from the world press was urprisingly significant: Garcia would have had a vry grin at having finally achieved this kind of espectability all over the planet. The press were argely in agreement, concurring that a major alent in the world of music had passed on either that or all the news editors on daily iewspapers were all 40-something ex-hippies). n the USA the reaction was comparable to the eath of President Kennedy, Martin Luther ing, Elvis Presley and John Lennon. Within iours over 10,000 postings were made on the nternet, an all night vigil took place in San rancisco and the president of the USA Bill linton gave him high praise and called him a enius. The mayor of San Francisco called for lags to be flown at half-mast and, appropriately, lew a tie dyed flag from city hall. Bob Dylan aid that there was no way to measure his reatness or magnitude.

jarcia's high standing in the USA is undisputed, ut it is hoped that he will be remembered lsewhere in the world not just as the man who layed the familiar opening pedal steel guitar olo on Crosby, Stills And Nash's 'Teach Your Children'. Garcia was a giant who remained hip, umorous, philosophical, humble and credible ight up to his untimely death. At a press onference in December 1995 the remaining and members announced that they would bury he band name along with Garcia. With no inancial worries, all of the members except for reutzmann have a number of forthcoming solo rojects that will see them well into the twenty-irst century, which is precisely where many of heir fans believed that they always belonged. In

1998, Lesh was hospitalized with hepatitis which briefly curtailed his activity with Bob Weir in their new project, the Other Ones.

The Grateful Dead felt all the emotions of folk, soul, blues and country music, and they played it always from the heart. The resulting sound was a hybrid that was unique to them. Sometimes they were ragged and occasionally they were lacklustre, but mostly they were outstanding in their ability to interact and improvise. Love or hate, black or white, it is impossible to be indifferent about the Grateful Dead's music. Quite simply, you either get it or you don't.

● ALBUMS: *The Grateful Dead* (Warners 1967) ★★★, *Anthem Of The Sun* (Warners 1968) ★★★★, *Aoxomoxoa* (Warners 1969) ★★★★, *Live/Dead* (Warners 1970) ★★★★, *Workingman's Dead* (Warners 1970) ★★★★★, *Vintage Dead* (Sunflower 1970) ★, *American Beauty* (Warners 1970) ★★★★★, *Historic Dead* (Sunflower 1971) ★, *Grateful Dead* (Warners 1971) ★★★★, *Europe '72* (Warners 1972) ★★★, *History Of The Grateful Dead, Vol. 1 (Bear's Choice)* (Warners 1973) ★★★, *Wake Of The Flood* (Grateful Dead 1973) ★★★★, *From The Mars Hotel* (Grateful Dead 1974) ★★★★, *Blues For Allah* (Grateful Dead 1975) ★★, *Steal Your Face* (Grateful Dead 1976) ★★, *Terrapin Station* (Arista 1977) ★★★★, *Shakedown Street* (Arista 1978) ★★, *Go To Heaven* (Arista 1980) ★, *Reckoning* (Arista 1981) ★★★, *Dead Set* (Arista 1981) ★★, *In The Dark* (Arista 1987) ★★★★, *Built To Last* (Arista 1989) ★★, with Bob Dylan *Dylan And The Dead* (Columbia 1990) ★, *Without A Net* (Arista 1990) ★★, *One From The Vault* (Grateful Dead 1991) ★★★, *Infrared Roses* (Grateful Dead 1991) ★★, *Two From The Vault* (Grateful Dead 1992) ★★★, *Dick's Picks, Volume One: Tampa, Florida December 19 1973* (Grateful Dead 1993) ★★★, *Dick's Picks, Volume Two: Columbus, Ohio October 31 1971* (Grateful Dead 1995) ★★★, *Hundred Year Hall* (Arista 1995) ★★★★, *Dick's Picks, Volume Three: Pembroke Pines, Florida May 22 1977* (Grateful Dead 1995) ★★★, *Dick's Picks, Volume Four: Fillmore East, New York 13/14 February 1970* (Grateful Dead 1996) ★★★★, *Dick's Picks, Volume Five: Oakland Auditorium Arena, California December 26 1979* (Grateful Dead 1996) ★★★, *Dozin' At The Knick* (Grateful Dead/Arista 1996) ★★★★, *Dick's Picks, Volume Six: Hartford Civic Center October 14 1983* (Grateful Dead 1996) ★★★★, *Dick's Picks, Volume Seven: Alexandra Palace, London, England, September 1974* (Grateful Dead 1997) ★★, *Dick's Picks, Volume Eight: Harpur College, Binghamton, NY, May 2 1970* (Grateful Dead 1997) ★★★, *Fallout From The Phil Zone* (Grateful Dead/Arista 1997) ★★★★★, *Dick's Picks, Volume Nine: Madison Square Garden, September 16 1990* (Grateful Dead 1997) ★★★, *Fillmore East 2-11-69* (Grateful Dead 1997) ★★★★, *Dick's Picks, Volume Ten: Winterland Arena, December 29 1977* (Grateful Dead 1998) ★★★★, *Dick's Picks, Volume Eleven: Stanley Theater, Jersey City,*

September 27 1972 (Grateful Dead 1998) ★★★, *Dick's Picks, Volume Twelve: Providence Civic, June 26 1974, Boston Garden June 28 1974* (Grateful Dead 1998) ★★★, *Trouble Ahead, Trouble Behind: The Dead Live In Concert 1971* (Pinnacle 1999) ★★, *Dick's Picks, Volume Thirteen: Nassau Coliseum, New York May 6 1981* (Grateful Dead 1999) ★★★★, *Dick's Picks, Volume Fourteen* (Grateful Dead 1999) ★★★★, *Dick's Picks, Volume Fifteen: Englishtown, New Jersey, September 3 1977* (Grateful Dead 1999) ★★★, *Dick's Picks, Volume Sixteen: Fillmore Auditorium, San Francisco November 8 1969* (Grateful Dead 2000) ★★★, *Dick's Picks, Volume Seventeen: Boston Garden September 25 1991* (Grateful Dead 2000) ★★★★, *View From The Vault Soundtrack* 1990 live recording (Grateful Dead 2000) ★★★, *Dick's Picks, Volume Eighteen: Dane County Coliseum February 3 1978, Uni-Dome, University Of North Iowa February 5 1978* (Grateful Dead 2000) ★★★, *Ladies And Gentlemen ... Fillmore East: New York City, April 1971* 4-CD set (Arista 2000) ★★★★, *Dick's Picks, Volume Nineteen: Fairgrounds Arene, Oklahoma City, OK October 19 1973* (Grateful Dead 2000) ★★★, *Dick's Picks, Volume Twenty* 1976 Capital Centre/Onondaga County War Memorial (Grateful Dead 2001) ★★★, *Dick's Picks, Volume Twenty-One* (Grateful Dead 2001) ★★★, *Dick's Picks, Volume Twenty-Two* 1968 live recording (Grateful Dead 2001) ★★★★, *View From The Vault II Soundtrack* 1990/1991 live recordings (Grateful Dead 2001) ★★★, *Nightfall Of Diamonds* (Arista 2001) ★★★★, *Dick's Picks, Volume Twenty-Three* live recording (Grateful Dead 2001) ★★★.
● COMPILATIONS: *The Best Of: Skeletons From The Closet* (Warners 1974) ★★★★, *What A Long Strange Trip It's Been: The Best Of The Grateful Dead* (Warners 1977) ★★★★, *The Arista Years* (Arista 1996) ★★★, *So Many Roads (1965-1995)* 5-CD box set (Grateful Dead/Arista 1999) ★★★★, *The Golden Road (1965-1973)* 12-CD box set (Rhino 2001) ★★★★★.
● VIDEOS: *Grateful Dead In Concert* (RCA Video 1984), *So Far* (Virgin Vision 1988), *The Grateful Dead Movie* (Palace Premiere 1990), *Infrared Sightings* (Trigon 1995), *Dead Ahead* (Monterey 1995), *Backstage Pass: Access All Areas* (Pearson 1995), *Ticket To New Year's* (Monterey Home Video 1996), *Tie Died: Rock 'n' Roll's Most Dedicated Fans* (BMG Video 1996), *Downhill From Here* (Monterey 1997), *Anthem To Beauty* (Rhino Home Video 1998), *View From The Vault II* (Monterey Home Video 2001).
● FURTHER READING: *The Dead Book: A Social History Of The Grateful Dead*, Hank Harrison. *The Grateful Dead*, Hank Harrison. *Grateful Dead: The Official Book Of The Deadheads*, Paul Grushkin, Jonas Grushkin and Cynthia Bassett. *History Of The Grateful Dead*, William Ruhlmann. *Built To Last: Twenty-Five Years Of The Grateful Dead*, Jamie Jensen. *Drumming At The Edge Of Magic*, Mickey Hart. *Grateful Dead Family Album*, Jerilyn Lee Brandelius. *Sunshine Daydreams:*

Grateful Dead Journal, Herb Greene. *Aesthetics Of The Grateful Dead*, David Womack. *One Mor Saturday Night: Reflections With The Grateful Dead*, Sandy Troy. *Drumming At the Edge O Magic*, Mickey Hart and Jay Stevens. *Plane Drum*, Mickey Hart and Fredric Lieberman. *Boo Of The Dead: Celebrating 25 Years With Th Grateful Dead*, Herb Greene. *Conversations Wit The Grateful Dead*, David Gans. *Story Of Th Grateful Dead*, Adrian Hall. *Dead Base IX Complete Guide To Grateful Dead Song Lists*, Nixo and Scot Dolgushkin. *Living With The Dead*, Roc Scully with David Dalton. *Box Of Rain*, Rober Hunter. *Dead To The Core: A Grateful Dea Almanack*, Eric F. Wybenga. *The Music Neve Stopped*, Blair Jackson. *Captain Trips: Biography Of Jerry Garcia*, Sandy Troy. *Swee Chaos: The Grateful Dead's American Adventure* Carol Brightman. *Dark Star: An Oral Biograph Of Jerry Garcia*, Robert Greenfield. *What A Lon Strange Trip: The Stories Behind Every Gratefu Dead Song 1965-1995*, Stephen Peters. *Garcia: A American Life*, Blair Jackson.

GRAY, DOBIE

b. 26 July 1940, Simonton, Texas, USA. Gra moved from Texas to California in the early 60s where he began recording for local labels. Hi seventh single 'Look At Me' was a minor hit fo the Cordak label in January 1963. Th compulsive, if boastful, single 'The "In" Crowd (written by Billy Page) was his majo breakthrough in 1965, spending several month in the *Billboard* pop charts and peaking a number 13. It was followed by 'See You At Th "Go Go"', which featured leading session player Hal Blaine, Carol Kaye and Larry Knechtal a backing musicians. It was eight years before th singer secured another chart entry. In th intervening period, Gray worked as an acto appearing in productions of *Hair* and th controversial play *The Beard*. He als contributed to the soundtracks for the movie *Out Of Sight*, *Uptown Saturday Night* and *Th Commitment*. In the early 70s Gray sang severa lead vocals for a hard rock group, Pollution; the recorded two albums for the Prophecy label tha were well received, but were commercia failures. He also recorded several demos fo songwriter Paul Williams, whose brothe Mentor, a producer, was responsible fo relaunching Dobie's singing career. Th superbly crafted 'Drift Away' (a US Top 5 hit i February 1973), provided an artistic an commercial success that the singer followe with further examples of progressive souther rock/soul, including Tom Jans' oft-covere 'Loving Arms'. Relocating to Nashville Tennessee to concentrate on his songwriting Gray remained a popular concert dra throughout the world, including South Afric where he played to integrated audiences i defiance of the apartheid government. Mino chart successes for the Capricorn and Infinit labels followed in the late 70s, after which Gray remained quiet for several years. He resurfaced on Capitol/EMI America, recording with Nashville producer Harold Shedd and enjoyed country chart hits with 'That's One To Grow On', 'The Dark Side Of Town' and 'From Where I Stand'. He also made several appearances at Charlie Daniels' hugely popular Volunteer Jam concerts. Gray's songs have been performed by artists of the calibre of Ray Charles, Johnny Mathis, Julio Iglesias, Nina Simone, Tammy Wynette and Charly Pride. He returned to the studio in the mid-90s, releasing *The Diamond Cuts*, which featured reworkings of his old classics alongside new material.

● ALBUMS: *Look!* (Stripe 1963) ★★★, *Dobie Gray Sings For 'In' Crowders That Go 'Go Go'* (Charger 1965) ★★★, *Drift Away* (Decca 1973) ★★★, *Loving Arms* (MCA 1974) ★★★, *Hey Dixie* (MCA 1974) ★★★, *New Ray Of Sunshine* (Capricorn 1975) ★★, *Let Go* (Capricorn 1977) ★★, *Midnight Diamond* (Infinity 1978) ★★★, *Dobie Gray* (Infinity 1979) ★★★, *From Where I Stand* (Capitol/EMI America 1986) ★★★★, *Love's Talkin'* (Capitol/EMI America 1987) ★★★, *The Diamond Cuts* (Dobie Gray 1997) ★★★.

● COMPILATIONS: *Best Of Dobie Gray* (MCA 1973) ★★★★, *Drift Away: His Very Best* (Razor & Tie 1996) ★★★★, *The Soulful Sound Of* (Half Moon 1998) ★★★, *Out On The Floor With The In Crowd* (Music Club 1999) ★★★.

GREAT AWAKENING

This little-known band made a brief impression in 1969 with an outstanding instrumental version of 'Amazing Grace', long before Judy Collins popularized the song. The mantra-like fuzz guitar added a spiritual quality that was missing from later versions. So little was known of the group that they were often referred to as Amazing Grace, and the song as 'The Great Awakening'! For years it was thought that the man responsible was guitarist David Cohen from Country Joe And The Fish; others suggested it was by members of the Band. Later it was discovered that it was a different David Cohen, helped out by Joe Osborn (bass) and Jimmy Gordon (drums). The latter Cohen has worked as session guitarist for Bobby Darin, Tim Hardin and Frank Sinatra.

GREAT SOCIETY

The Great Society was formed in August 1965 by Grace Slick (b. Grace Barnett Wing, 30 October 1939, Evanston, Illinois, USA; vocals, piano, recorder, guitar), her husband Jerry (drums) and his brother Darby Slick (lead guitar). David Minor (rhythm guitar) and Bard DuPont (bass) completed the original line-up, although the latter was replaced by Peter Vandergelder, who also doubled on saxophone. One of the first San Franciscan rock groups, the quintet was active for 13 months, during which they issued one single, 'Someone To Love' (later known as

'Somebody To Love') on Tom Donahue's Autumn Records/Northbeach label. This intriguing Darby Slick composition achieved fame when it was adopted by Jefferson Airplane, the group Grace joined in October 1966. The Great Society broke up on her departure, but two live collections, released solely in the wake of the singer's subsequent fame, show a group of rare imagination. The first album features 'White Rabbit', another composition Grace introduced to her new-found companions, which is preceded by a lengthy instrumental passage performed in a raga style that typified the Great Society's approach to many of their songs. Indeed, on the dissolution of the group, Darby Slick, Vandergelder and Minor went to study music in India, while Jerry was briefly a member of Final Solution before returning to film work.

● ALBUMS: *Conspicuous Only In Its Absence* (Columbia 1968) ★★★, *How It Was* (Columbia 1968) ★★.

● COMPILATIONS: *Live At The Matrix* (Sundazed 1989) ★★, *Born To Be Burned* (Sundazed 1996) ★★★.

● FURTHER READING: *The Jefferson Airplane And The San Francisco Sound*, Ralph J. Gleeson. *Grace Slick – The Biography*, Barbara Rowe. *Don't You Want Somebody To Love*, Darby Slick.

GREENWICH, ELLIE

b. 23 October 1940, Brooklyn, New York, USA. Greenwich's singing career began in 1958 with 'Cha-Cha-Charming', released under the name Ellie Gaye. Two years later she met budding songwriter Jeff Barry and, following a release as Ellie Gee And The Jets, the couple formed the Raindrops in 1963. The group enjoyed a US Top 20 hit with 'The Kind Of Boy You Can't Forget', but increased demand on the now-married duo's compositional skills led to the band's demise. Having abandoned respective partnerships with Toni Powers and Art Resnick, Greenwich and Barry enjoyed a sustained period of success with a series of notable compositions, including 'Do Wah Diddy Diddy' (the Exciters/Manfred Mann), 'I Wanna Love Him So Bad' (the Jelly Beans) and 'Hanky Panky' (Tommy James And The Shondells). Collaborations with Phil Spector generated hits for the Crystals ('Da Doo Ron Ron' and 'Then He Kissed Me'), the Ronettes ('Be My Baby' and 'Baby, I Love You') and Ike And Tina Turner ('River Deep – Mountain High') while work with Shadow Morton reaped commercial success for the Shangri-Las, notably 'Leader Of The Pack'. Ellie also rekindled her solo career with 'You Don't Know', but her divorce from Barry in 1965 put an intolerable strain on their working relationship. Together they produced Neil Diamond's early recordings, but in 1967 she severed their partnership and made an exclusive songwriting deal with Unart Music.

Ellie Greenwich Composes, Produces, Sings

combined original songs with current favourites, but was a commercial failure, while her subsequent Pineywood Productions company was similarly ill-starred in the wake of changing musical tastes. 'I couldn't understand what (acid rock) was all about', she later stated, and instead switched to writing jingles. She re-emerged during the singer/songwriter boom with *Let It Be Written, Let It Be Sung*, but this excellent album failed to rekindle her career when stage fright blighted an attendant tour. Ellie remained in seclusion for most of the ensuing decade but re-emerged in the 80s as a performer in the acclaimed biographical revue *Leader Of The Pack*. A new generation of acts, including Nona Hendryx, Cyndi Lauper and Ellen Foley, recorded her songs, ensuring Greenwich's position as one of pop's finest composers.
● ALBUMS: *Ellie Greenwich Composes, Produces And Sings* (United Artists 1968) ★★★, *Let It Be Written, Let It Be Sung* (Verve 1973) ★★★.
● COMPILATIONS: *I Can Hear Music: The Ellie Greenwich Collection* (Razor & Tie 1999) ★★★.

GTOs

An acronym for Girls Together Outrageously, this all-female group was lauded in 1969 as part of Frank Zappa's Straight label roster. Initially known as the Laurel Canyon Ballet Company, they were, alongside the notorious Plaster Casters, the best-known members of the 60s groupie sub-culture. After meeting the overtly polite Tiny Tim, each member abandoned her respective surname and became Miss Lucy, Miss Pamela, Miss Christine (d. 5 November 1972), Miss Sparky, Miss Mercy, Miss Sandra and Miss Cynderella. The septet decamped to Zappa's home when Miss Christine became governess to his daughter Moon, and they occasionally performed live with his group, the Mothers Of Invention. Zappa produced the bulk of the GTOs, audio-vérité *Permanent Damage*, while future Little Feat guitarist Lowell George took charge of two tracks – his distinctive slide style is apparent on 'I Have A Paintbrush In My Hand To Colour A Triangle'. Members of the Mothers and the Jeff Beck Group also made several contributions, but the album's release was almost cancelled when Misses Mercy, Cynderella and Sparky were arrested on drugs charges. The GTOs split into two camps, and the final recordings were made solely by Pamela and Sparky. Each member then went her separate way, but their collective flirtation with the rock élite continued. Miss Christine was pictured emerging from a tomb on the cover of Zappa's *Hot Rats* and on the inner sleeve of Todd Rundgren's *Runt*. She was also the subject of the Flying Burrito Brothers' song 'Christine's Tune', but this title was later amended to 'She's The Devil In Disguise' following her death in 1972. Miss Mercy and Miss Pamela joined the chorus on the same group's 'Hippie Boy' and Miss

Cynderella was briefly married to John Cale. Pamela later sang on tour with the Pink Fairies, married former Silverhead vocalist Michael Des Barres and in 1989 penned a kiss-and-tell autobiography, *I'm With The Band*.
● ALBUMS: *Permanent Damage* (Straight 1969) ★★.

GUARALDI, VINCE

b. 17 July 1928, San Francisco, California, USA, d. 6 February 1976, Menlo Park, California, USA. Jazz pianist and latter-day easy listening jazz composer Guaraldi played with Cal Tjader in the early 50s before moving through Bill Harris' combo, and worked with Sonny Criss and George Auld. He also served as part of Woody Herman's touring band in the late 50s. It was in the 60s, however, that Guaraldi made a name for himself as a composer of light romantic jazz-influenced songs. His most famous and deservedly long-lasting classic is 'Cast Your Fate To The Wind', which was a hit for his trio in 1962 and subsequently won him a Grammy award. A cover version surprisingly appeared high in the UK charts at the end of 1964 by a studio-only group Sounds Orchestral. In recent years the song has been covered many times, one of the better interpretations being by David Benoit from his 1989 album *Waiting For Spring*. Less creditable although also widely known is his soundtrack theme music for the Charlie Brown *Peanuts* cartoon television series. He also recorded with Conte Candoli and Frank Rosolino in the 60s. His music received an unexpected boost in the mid-90s when some of his work was reappraised during the 'space age bachelor pad music' cult boom.
● ALBUMS: *Modern Music From San Francisco* (Fantasy 1956) ★★★, *Vince Guaraldi Trio* (Fantasy 1956) ★★★, *A Flower Is A Lovesome Thing* (Fantasy 1958) ★★★, *Cast Your Fate To The Wind; Jazz Impressions Of Black Orpheus* (Fantasy 1962) ★★★, *Vince Guaraldi In Person* (Fantasy 1963) ★★★, with Frank Rosolino *Vince Guaraldi/Frank Rosolino Quintet* (Premier 1963) ★★★, with Conte Candoli *Vince Guaraldi/Conte Candoli Quartet* (Premier 1963) ★★★, *Vince Guaraldi, Bola Sete And Friends* (Fantasy 1963) ★★★, *Tour De Force* (Fantasy 1963) ★★★, *Jazz Impressions Of Charlie Brown* (Fantasy 1964) ★★★, *Jazz Impressions* (Fantasy 1964) ★★★★, *A Boy Named Charlie Brown* (Fantasy 1964) ★★, *A Charlie Brown Christmas* (Fantasy 1964) ★★★, *The Latin Side Of Vince Guaraldi* (Fantasy 1964) ★★★, *Vince Guaraldi At Grace Cathedral* (Fantasy 1965) ★★★, *From All Sides* (Fantasy 1965) ★★★, *Live At The El Matador* (Fantasy 1966) ★★★, *Oh Good Grief!* (Warners 1968) ★★★, *Charlie Brown's Holiday Hits* (Fantasy 1998) ★★★★.
● COMPILATIONS: *Greatest Hits* (Fantasy 1989) ★★★★.

GUN (60s)

This late 60s high-powered UK trio had an interesting ancestry, as two of their number were the offspring of the Kinks' irreverent and exuberant road manager Sam Curtis. Paul Curtis (b. Paul Gurvitz, 6 July 1947) and Adrian Curtis (b. Adrian Gurvitz, 26 June 1949, London, England) joined drummer Louie Farrell (b. Brian Farrell, 12 December 1947) at a time when the boundaries between pop and progressive music were still a matter of hot debate. Gun were featured on John Peel's influential BBC Radio show, *Top Gear*, and enjoyed a strong chart hit with the driving, riff-laden 'Race With The Devil' in 1968, which was uncannily similar to Moby Grape's 'Can't Be So Bad'. Uncertain of their appeal in the pop market, they came unstuck with their follow-up, the frantic 'Drives You Mad', and when 'Hobo' also flopped, it was clear that their chart days were over. Their record label attempted to market them as counter-culture heroes with advertisements proclaiming 'the revolutionaries are on CBS', but the band failed to establish themselves as album artists. After dissolving the band in the early 70s, Adrian Gurvitz teamed up with Ginger Baker to form the Baker Gurvitz Army, and later achieved a hit single, 'Classic', as a soloist in 1982.

● ALBUMS: *Gun* (CBS 1969) ★★★, *Gun Sight* (CBS 1969) ★★.

H.P. LOVECRAFT

This imaginative group was formed in Chicago, Illinois, USA, by George Edwards (guitar, vocals) and David Michaels (keyboards, woodwind, vocals). They made their debut in 1967 with a folk rock reading of 'Anyway That You Want Me', a Chip Taylor composition successfully revived by the Troggs. The duo was initially backed by a local outfit, the Rovin' Kind, until Tony Cavallari (lead guitar), Jerry McGeorge (bass, ex-Shadows Of Knight) and Michael Tegza (drums) completed the new venture's line-up. Their debut album, *H.P. Lovecraft*, fused haunting, folk-based material with graphic contemporary compositions. It featured stirring renditions of 'Wayfaring Stranger' and 'Let's Get Together', but the highlight was 'The White Ship', a mesmerizing adaptation of a short story penned by the author from whom the quintet took its name. McGeorge was replaced by Jeffrey Boyan for *H.P. Lovecraft II*. This enthralling set included 'At The Mountains Of Madness', in which the group's distinctive harmonies cultivated an eerie, chilling atmosphere. Commercial indifference sadly doomed their progress and the quintet disintegrated, although Tegza re-emerged in 1970 with three new musicians, Jim Dolinger (guitar), Michael Been (bass) and Marty Grebb (keyboards). Now dubbed simply Lovecraft, the group completed *Valley Of The Moon*, a set that bore little resemblance to those of its pioneering predecessor. In 1975 the drummer employed a completely new line-up for *We Love You Whoever You Are*, before finally laying the name to rest.

● ALBUMS: *H.P. Lovecraft* (Philips 1967) ★★★, *H.P. Lovecraft II* (Philips 1968) ★★★, as Lovecraft *Valley Of The Moon* (Reprise 1970) ★★, as Lovecraft *We Love You Whoever You Are* (Mercury 1975) ★★, as H.P. Lovecraft *Live – May 11, 1968* (Sundazed 1992) ★★.

● COMPILATIONS: *At The Mountains Of Madness* (Edsel 1988) ★★★★.

HALLYDAY, JOHNNY

b. Jean-Philippe Smet, 15 June 1943, Paris, France. After his Belgian father's desertion, Smet was adopted by his aunt Helene Mar, wife of North American song-and-dance man Lee Hallyday, from whom the child later derived his stage surname. His aptitude for the performing arts earned him a role in his uncle's act, and he developed a passable mastery of the guitar after giving up violin lessons. By the late 50s, he had become an incorrigible *ye-ye* – a Parisian species of rock 'n' roller that trod warily amid official disapproval. His stamping ground was Le Golf Drouot club with its jukebox of US discs. Singing in public was second nature to him, and he sounded so much like the genuine American article during his 1960 radio debut that, via the brother who managed him, Vogue contracted Hallyday for an immediate single, 'T'Ai Mer Follement'. However, it was a million-selling bilingual cover of Chubby Checker's 'Let's Twist Again' on Philips in 1961, a film part (in *Les Parisiennes*) that same year, and, crucially, the intensity of his recitals that convinced most that this svelte, blond youth was to France what Elvis Presley was to the USA.

The title of 1962's *Johnny Hallyday Sings America's Rockin' Hits* was a reliable indicator of future direction. The preponderance of English language material in his concert sets was commensurate with recorded interpretations of songs such as 'The House Of The Rising Sun', 'Black Is Black', 'In The Midnight Hour', 'Hey Joe' and in the 70s and 80s' 'Delta Lady' and – in a remarkable 1985 duet with Emmylou Harris – 'If I Were A Carpenter'. An appearance in 1964 on *Ready Steady Go* had been well received but he was unable to duplicate even Richard Anthony's modest triumphs in the UK chart. If neither made much headway in the USA, Johnny eclipsed his rival in Africa and South America, where a 25,000 attendance at a Hallyday show in Argentina was not atypical. Several degrees from blatant bandwagon-jumping, Hallyday continued to thrive on a certain hip sensibility, manifested in his block-bookings of fashionable studios in Britain and the USA, and employment of top session musicians like Bobby Keyes, Jim Price and Gary Wright – all prominent on *Flagrant Delit* which, like most of his albums, contained a few Hallyday originals. Details of his stormy marriage to Sylvie Vartan and a more recent hip operation attracted headlines as he entered middle age. Yet Hallyday maintained a jocular bonhomie in interview, and on stage he remained as melodramatic as ever, evolving less as France's Presley, more its 'answer' to Cliff Richard, as he is still one of the few European stars in direct artistic debt to US pop to be regarded with anything approaching strong interest beyond his country's borders. Dozens of albums have been released, but mainly in France and Canada, and an extraordinary box set containing 42 CDs was issued for his 50th birthday. In 1997 he provoked outrage in his home country when he admitted to taking cocaine 'morning, noon and night.'

● ALBUMS: *Johnny Hallyday Sings America's Rockin' Hits* (Philips 1961) ★★★, *Johnny A Nashville – La Fantastique Epopee Du Rock* (Philips 1962) ★★★, *Generation Perdue* (Philips 1966) ★★, *Olympia 1967* (Philips 1967) ★★★, *Que Je T'Aime* (Philips 1969) ★★, *Je Suis Ne Dans La Rue* (Philips 1969) ★★★, *Vie* (Philips 1970)

★★★, *Flagrant Delit* (Philips 1971) ★★★, *Country Folk Rock* (Philips 1972) ★★★, *Insolitude* (Philips 1973) ★★★, *Derriere L'Amour* (Philips 1976) ★★★, *C'Est La Vie* (Philips 1977) ★★★, *Solitudes A Deux* (Philips 1978) ★★★, *Hollywood* (Philips 1979) ★★★, *Drôle De Métier* (Philips 1984) ★★★, *Rock 'N' Roll Attitude* (Philips 1985) ★★★, *Gang* (Philips 1986) ★★★, *Trift De Rattles* (Philips 1986) ★★★★, *Les Grands Success De Johnny Hallyday* (Philips 1988) ★★★, *La Peur* (Philips 1988) ★★★, *Cadillac* (Philips 1989) ★★★, *Ça Ne Change Pas Un Homme* (Philips 1991) ★★★, *Parc Des Princes 1993* (Philips 1993) ★★, *Lorada* (Philips 1995) ★★★, *Ce Que Je Sais* (Mercury 1998) ★★★, *Sang Pour Sang* (Mercury 1999) ★★★, *Tour Eiffel* (Mercury 2000) ★★.

● COMPILATIONS: *La Nuit Johnny* 42-CD box set (Philips 1993) ★★★, *Ballades* (Mercury 1999) ★★★.

● FILMS: *Les Diaboliques* aka *The Fiends* (1955), *Dossier 1413* aka *Secret File 1413* (1961), *Les Parisiennes* aka *Tales Of Paris* (1962), *Cherchez L'Idole* aka *The Chase* (1963), *D'Où Viens-Tu L'Idole* (1964), *À Tout Casser* aka *Breaking It Up* (1967), *Les Poneyttes* (1967), *Visa De Censure* (1968), *Gli Specialisti* aka *Drop Them Or I'll Shoot* (1969), *Point De Chute* (1970), *Malpertuis: Histoire D'Une Maison Maudite* (1971), *L'Aventure, C'Est Aventure* aka *Money Money Money* (1972), *J'Ai Tout Donné* (1972), *L'Animal* aka *The Animal* (1977), *Le Jour Se Lève Et Les Conneries Commencement* (1981), *Détective* (1985), *Terminus* (1986), *Le Conseil De Famille* aka *Family Business* (1986), *The Iron Triangle* (1989), *La Gamine* (1991), *Paparazzi* (1998), *Porquoi Pas Moi?* (1999), *Love Me* (2000), *Eau Et Gaz À Tous Les Étages* (2000).

HAPPENINGS

The Happenings were a vocal harmony group from Paterson, New Jersey, USA that specialized in reviving classic songs. They comprised Bob Miranda (lead), Ralph DiVito (baritone; replaced by Bernie LaPorta in 1968), David Libert (bass) and Thomas Giuliano (tenor). They met while in military service at Fort Dix, New Jersey, and after leaving formed the Four Graduates. In addition to their roles as session singers, the quartet recorded a couple of singles for Crystal Ball Records and Rust, the latter being produced in 1963 by members of the successful group the Tokens. When the Tokens formed their own B.T. Puppy label in 1965 they signed the group, now called the Happenings, and their second release, a revival of the Tempos' 1959 hit, 'See You In September', reached US number 3 in July 1966. Despite the fact that their distinctively dated yet somehow contemporary style seemed out of place with other 60s groups, they strung together an enviable nine US chart entries between 1966 and 1969. The biggest of these were their revivals of Steve Lawrence's 'Go Away Little Girl' (number 12, October 1966), George Gershwin's 'I Got Rhythm' (number 3,

April 1967) and Al Jolson's 'My Mammy' number 13, July 1967). They later recorded for Jubilee, Big Tree and Midland International, and in the 80s Miranda and Giuliano were fronting a new line-up of the group on oldies shows.

● ALBUMS: *The Happenings* (BT Puppy 1966) ★★★, *Psycle* (BT Puppy 1967) ★★★, *Piece Of Mind* (Jubilee 1969) ★★, *Still Going Strong* (2001) ★★★.

● COMPILATIONS: *Happenings Golden Hits* (BT Puppy 1968) ★★★, *The Happening's Greatest Hits* (Jubilee 1969) ★★★, *The Best Of Happenings Sequel 1995) ★★★.

HAPSHASH AND THE COLOURED COAT

Hapshash And The Coloured Coat was the name adopted by graphic artists Michael English and Nigel Weymouth. They met in London, England, in 1966, collaborating on the Love Festival poster that showed the joint influence of Man Ray and US pop artist Tom Wesselman. Their work defined the romanticism of the English Underground movement and included posters promoting the Soft Machine, Tomorrow, Jimi Hendrix and Arthur Brown, as well as concerts held at the UFO Club and Brian Epstein's Saville Theatre, both located in London. Having become acquainted with producer/svengali Guy Stevens, English and Weymouth recorded their debut album. *Hapshash And The Coloured Coat* featured lengthy, semi-improvised pieces fused to hard, repetitive riffs and chanted vocals. The accompaniment was supplied by Stevens' protégés Art. Housed in a *de rigeur* psychedelic sleeve and pressed on red vinyl, the album became a lynchpin release of the English 'underground' movement. However, with Stevens now in absentia and English preferring art to music, it was largely left to Weymouth to record *Western Flyer*. Groundhogs' guitarist Tony McPhee and future Wombles producer/ songwriter Mike Batt assisted on a set encompassing pop, progressive and cajun styles, all delivered in a suitably quirky manner. English and Weymouth sundered their partnership soon afterwards.

● ALBUMS: *Hapshash And The Coloured Coat Featuring The Human Host And The Heavy Metal Kids* (Minit 1967) ★★, *Western Flyer* (Liberty 1969) ★.

HARD MEAT

Taking its cue from Traffic, this trio were among many outfits who, in the late 60s, 'got it together in the country' – in their case, the wilds of Cornwall. To make ends meet, guitarist Michael Dolan, his bass-plucking brother Steve – with whom he shared both vocals and a Birmingham upbringing – and drummer Mick Carless took on a summer residency as the Ebony Combo at Bude's Headland Pavilion before assuming their genital moniker in 1969. By then, they had cultivated a faintly sinister 'stoned hippie' image, and their repertoire hinged on originals

of 'progressive' rock plus reinventions of works by Bob Dylan ('Most Likely You Go Your Way (And I'll Go Mine)') and Richie Havens. After amassing an extensive work schedule they were signed to Warner Brothers Records for whom they recorded two unremarkable albums and a single – an arrangement of the Beatles' 'Rain' – before disbanding in 1971. Two years later, Steve Dolan was among the cast on Pete Sinfield's *Under The Sky*.

● ALBUMS: *Hard Meat* (Warners 1970) ★★, *Through A Window* (Warners 1970) ★★.

HARDIN, TIM

b. 23 December 1941, Eugene, Oregon, USA, d. 29 December 1980, Hollywood, California, USA. Hardin arrived in New York following a tour of duty with the US Marines. He initially studied acting, but dropped out of classes to develop his singing and songwriting talent. By 1964 he was appearing regularly in New York's Greenwich Village cafés, where he forged a unique blend of poetic folk/blues. Hardin's first recordings were made in 1964 although the results of this traditional-based session were shelved for several years and were only issued, as *This Is Tim Hardin*, in the wake of the singer's commercial success. His debut album, *Tim Hardin 1*, was a deeply poignant affair, wherein Tim's frail, weary intonation added intrigue to several magnificent compositions, including 'Don't Make Promises', 'Misty Roses' (sensitively covered by Colin Blunstone) and 'Hang On To A Dream' (which became a regular part of the Nice's live performances) as well as the much-covered 'Reason To Believe'. *Tim Hardin 2*, featured his original version of 'If I Were A Carpenter', an international hit in the hands of Bobby Darin and the Four Tops, which confirmed Hardin's position as a writer of note. However, the artist was deeply disappointed with these releases and reportedly broke down upon hearing the finished master to his first selection.

Hardin's career then faltered on private and professional difficulties. As early as 1970 he was experiencing alcohol and drug problems. A conceptual work, *Suite For Susan Moore And Damion ...* reclaimed something of his former fire but his gifts seemed to desert him following its release. Hardin's high standing as a songwriter has resulted in his work being interpreted by a plethora of artists over the past four decades, including Wilson Phillips and Rod Stewart ('Reason To Believe') and Scott Walker ('The Lady Came From Baltimore'). As Hardin's own songs grew less incisive, he began interpreting the work of other songwriters, including Leonard Cohen, but his resigned delivery, once so alluring, now seemed maudlin. Beset by heroin addiction, his remaining work is a ghost of that early excellence. Tim Hardin died, almost forgotten and totally underrated, in December 1980, of a heroin overdose. Over the past few years Hardin's work has received a wider and more favourable reception. There are enough songs in his catalogue to warrant the term 'great songwriter', certainly a writer of fragile beauty.

● ALBUMS: *Tim Hardin 1* (Verve Forecast 1966) ★★★★, *Tim Hardin 2* (Verve Forecast 1967) ★★★★, *This Is Tim Hardin* (Atco 1967) ★★, *Tim Hardin 3 Live In Concert* (Verve Forecast 1968) ★★★, *Tim Hardin 4* (Verve Forecast 1969) ★★★★, *Suite For Susan Moore And Damion – We Are – One. One, All In One* (Columbia 1969) ★★★, *Golden Archive Series* (MGM 1970) ★★★, *Bird On A Wire* (Columbia 1971) ★★, *Painted Head* (Columbia 1972) ★★, *Archetypes* (MGM 1973) ★★★, *Nine* (GM/Antilles 1974) ★★★, *The Shock Of Grace* (Columbia 1981) ★★★, *The Homecoming Concert* (Line 1981) ★★★★.

● COMPILATIONS: *Best Of Tim Hardin* (Verve Forecast 1969) ★★★★, *Memorial Album* (Polydor 1981) ★★★, *Reason To Believe (The Best Of)* (Polydor 1987) ★★★★, *Hang On To A Dream: The Verve Recordings* (Polydor 1994) ★★★★, *Simple Songs Of Freedom: The Tim Hardin Collection* (Columbia 1996) ★★★★, *Person To Person: The Essential Classic Hardin 1963-1980* (Raven 2000) ★★★★.

HARDY, FRANÇOISE

b. 17 January 1944, Paris, France. After graduating from the Le Bruyère College, Hardy pursued a musical career as a singer/songwriter. Signed to the prestigious French record label Vogue, she had an international million-selling hit in 1962 with the self-composed 'Tous Les Garçons Et Les Filles'. Three years later, she enjoyed her only major UK hit with the softly sung 'All Over The World'. A major star in her home country, she extended her appeal as a result of various modelling assignments and appearances in several movies by Roger Vadim. Her international performing career gradually declined towards the end of the 60s due to stage fright, although she continued to record well-crafted and popular records for her home market. Hardy also set up her own production company, Productions Asparagus, thereby gaining more control over her career. Gradually moving away from the lightweight, quasi-orchestral folk pop sound of her mid-60s heyday, Hardy's sporadic output in subsequent decades established her as one of France's leading MOR entertainers. She returned to recording during the 90s on the Virgin France label, and also appeared on singles by Malcolm McLaren ('The Revenge Of The Flowers') and Air ('Jeanne').

● ALBUMS: *Touts Les Garcons Et Les Filles* aka *The 'Yeh-Yeh' Girl From Paris* (Vogue/Pye/4 Corners 1962) ★★★, *Le Premier Bonheur Du Jour* aka *In Vogue* (Vogue/Pye 1963) ★★★★, *Françoise Hardy Canta Per Voi In Italiano* (Vogue 1963) ★★★, *Mon Amie La Rose* (Vogue 1964) ★★★, *L'Amitie* (Vogue/4 Corners 1965) ★★★,

Françoise Hardy In Deutschland (Bellaphon 1965) ★★★, *Françoise* (Vogue 1966) ★★★, *In English* (Vogue 1966) ★★★, *Ma Jeunesse Fout Le Camp* (Vogue 1967) ★★★★, *Comment Te Dire Adieu* (Vogue 1968) ★★★★, *En Anglais* aka *Loving* (United Artists/Vogue/Reprise 1968) ★★★, *Germinal* (Sonopresse 1970) ★★★, *Soleil* (Sonopresse 1970) ★★★, *One-Nine-Seven-Zero* aka *Alone* (United Artists/Reprise 1970) ★★★, *La Question* (Sonopresse 1971) ★★★★, *L'Eclairage* (Sonopresse 1972) ★★★, *Message Personnel* (WEA 1973) ★★★, *Entr'acte* (WEA 1974) ★★★, *Star* (EMI/Peters Internaional 1977) ★★, *Musique Saoule* (EMI/Peters Internaiona 1978) ★★★, *Gin Tonic* (EMI 1980) ★★, *A Suivre* (Flarenasch 1981) ★★, *Quelqu'un Qui S'En Va* (Flarenasch 1984) ★★, *Decalages* (Flarenasch 1988) ★★★, *Le Danger* (Virgin 1996) ★★★, *Clair-Obscur* (Virgin 2000) ★★★.

● COMPILATIONS: *Golden Hour Presents The Best Of Françoise Hardy* (Golden Hour 1974) ★★★, *L'Integrale Disques Vogue* 4-CD box set (Vogue 1995) ★★★★, *Le Meilleur De Françoise Hardy* (BMG France 2000) ★★★, *The Vogue Years* (Camden 2000) ★★★.

● FILMS: *Château En Suède* aka *Nutty, Naughty Chateau* (1963), *What's New, Pussycat* (1965), *Altissima Pressione* aka *Highest Pressure* (1965), *Masculin, Féminin* aka *Masculine-Feminine* (1966), *Grand Prix* (1966), *Europa Canta* (1967), *Monte Carlo: C'Est La Rose* (1968).

HARMONY GRASS

Formed in Essex, England, in 1968, this close harmony pop group developed from Tony Rivers And The Castaways, a superior beat attraction heavily influenced by the Beach Boys. Longtime associate Ray Brown (bass) joined Rivers (lead vocals) in a venture completed by third former Castaway, Kenny Rowe (second bass), and newcomers Tony Ferguson (lead guitar), Tom Marshall (rhythm guitar/piano) and Bill Castle (drums). Signed to RCA Records, the sextet enjoyed a UK Top 30 hit in 1969 with their debut single, 'Move In A Little Closer', which was produced by Chris Andrews, previously successful with Sandie Shaw and Adam Faith. However, despite recording several equally high class singles, including a cover version of Paul Simon's 'Cecilia', Harmony Grass was unable to consolidate this early commercial promise. Rivers later pursued a career as a successful session singer backing Elton John and Cliff Richard, while the rump of his erstwhile group evolved into Capability Brown and pub band J.J. Foote.

● ALBUMS: *This Is Us* (RCA 1969) ★★.

● COMPILATIONS: *The Collection Vol 1 Castaways* (RPM 1999) ★★★, *The Tony Rivers Collection Volume 2* (RPM 1999) ★★.

HARPERS BIZARRE

Evolving from Santa Cruz band the Tikis, the original Harpers Bizarre emerged in late 1966

ith a line-up comprising lead vocalist/guitarist
:d Templeman (b. Theodore Templeman, 24
:tober 1944, USA), vocalist/guitarist Dick
:oppettone (b. 5 July 1945), vocalist/bass
ayer Dick Young (9 January 1945), vocalist/
uitarist Eddie James and former Beau
'ummels drummer/vocalist John Petersen (b.
January 1942, Rudyard, Michigan, USA). A
rightly cover of Simon And Garfunkel's '59th
reet Bridge Song (Feelin' Groovy)' brought
em a US Top 20 hit and became a perennial
dio favourite. Their first album, boasting the
ranging skills of Leon Russell and the
imposing talents of Randy Newman, backed by
arpers' exceptional vocal talent, proved an
iticing debut. After covering Van Dyke Parks'
ome To The Sunshine', they worked with the
an himself on the hit follow-up, a revival of
ile Porter's 'Anything Goes'. An album of the
me name combined similar standards with
aterial by Parks and Newman. After two more
bums, the group split in 1969 with Templeman
icoming a name staff producer for Warner
'others Records. Three members of the original
1e-up reunited briefly six years later for the
bum *As Time Goes By*.

ALBUMS: *Feelin' Groovy* (Warners 1967) ★★★,
1ything Goes (Warners 1967) ★★, *The Secret*
fe Of Harpers Bizarre (Warners 1968) ★★,
arpers Bizarre 4 (Warners 1969) ★★, *As Time*
1es By (Forest Bay 1976) ★.

COMPILATIONS: *Feelin' Groovy: The Best Of*
arpers Bizarre (Warner Archives 1997) ★★★.

ARRIS, ANITA

3 June 1942, Midsomer Norton, Somerset/
von, England. After winning a talent contest
hen she was only three, Harris learnt to play
e piano and attended the Hampshire School of
·ama. She trained to be a dancer, and, while in
:r teens, performed in Europe and in the
iorus at the El Rancho in Las Vegas. On her
turn to Britain, she sang with the Granadiers
1 television, alongside Gerry Dorsey, who
bsequently found fame and fortune after
ianging his name to Engelbert Humperdinck.
1961, while working with the Cliff Adams
igers, she came to the notice of composer and
indleader John Barry who offered her a
intract with his organization. Her first record
1s a Lionel Bart song, 'I Haven't Got You', on
iich she was accompanied by the John Barry
·chestra. Besides working consistently on
dio, television, and in clubs and theatres
iroughout the UK – including two seasons at
e London Palladium – Harris won the Gold
edal for Britain at the San Remo Song Festival,
d then had a Top 10 hit in 1967 with Tom
ringfield's 'Just Loving You'. This was also the
le of her 1968 Top 30 album which, when released in 1976, is said to have sold over a
illion copies. Her other (minor) singles hits in
e late 60s were 'Playground', 'Anniversary
altz', and 'Dream A Little Dream Of Me'. She

proved to be particularly popular on television
and appeared in *The Saturday Crowd* with Leslie
Crowther, *Magic Box* with David Niven, and
numerous other programmes starring Bernard
Braden, Tommy Cooper, and Morecambe And
Wise. One of her most memorable screen
projects was *Jumbleland*, an innovative
children's programme which was devised by her
writer-director-husband Mike Margolis. In the
70s Harris twice played *Peter Pan* in National
Theatre productions, and established herself as
one of the leading 'principal boys' in traditional
Christmas pantomimes. In the early 80s she
took over the role of Grizabella in Andrew Lloyd
Webber's *Cats*, while her cabaret act continued
to attract excellent reviews, particularly for
several appearances at London's Talk Of The
Town and the Savoy Hotel. In 1982 she was
named Performer Of The Year by the Variety
Club of Great Britain, and two years later
headlined at the Club's Ball Of The Year. In the
90s, as well as continuing to delight cabaret
audiences at venues such as the Pizza On The
Park in London, Harris spent a good deal of her
time starring in provincial productions of two
biographical musicals: *Nightingale*, the story of
'the lady with the lamp', Florence Nightingale;
and *Bertie*, a very different tale about
that debonair man/woman-about-town, the
legendary entertainer, Vesta Tilley.

● ALBUMS: *Just Loving You* (Pye 1967) ★★★★,
Cuddly Toy (CBS 1968) ★★, *Anita Is Peter* (1975)
★★★, *I Love To Sing* (1976) ★★.

● COMPILATIONS: *The Best Of* (1977) ★★★.

HARRIS, JET, AND TONY MEEHAN

Terence 'Jet' Harris (b. 6 July 1939, Kingsbury,
Middlesex, England; guitar) and Tony Meehan
(b. Daniel Joseph Anthony Meehan, 22 March
1943, Hampstead, London, England; drums)
began their partnership in 1959 as members of
the Shadows. Meehan left the group in October
1961 to take up an A&R position at Decca
Records, and the following year Harris began a
solo career with 'Besame Mucho'. 'The Man With
The Golden Arm' gave the guitarist a UK Top 20
hit prior to reuniting with Meehan in 1963. The
duo's debut single, 'Diamonds', was a startling
instrumental composition which topped the UK
charts, while two ensuing releases, 'Scarlett
O'Hara' and 'Applejack', also reached the Top 5.
Each performance matched Harris' low-tuned
Fender Jaguar guitar with Meehan's punchy
drum interjections, and although a bright future
was predicted, a serious car crash undermined
Harris' confidence and the pair split up. Existing
contracts were fulfilled by the Tony Meehan
Combo, although Harris did resume recording
with 'Big Bad Bass'. His subsequent career was
blighted by personal and professional problems,
and successive attempts at rekindling former
glories fell flat. Meehan, meanwhile, enjoyed an
increasingly backroom role as a producer and
arranger.

● COMPILATIONS: *Remembering: Jet Harris And Tony Meehan* (Decca 1976) ★★★★, *Diamonds* (Decca 1983) ★★★, *Diamonds And Other Gems* (Deram 1989) ★★★★, *The Best Of Jet Harris & Tony Meehan* (Spectrum 2000) ★★★.

HARRIS, RICHARD

b. Richard St. John Harris, 1 October 1930, Limerick, Eire. Although better-known as an actor, Harris nonetheless drew praise for his starring role as King Arthur in the film musical *Camelot* in 1967. The following year he began a recording career upon meeting US songwriter Jimmy Webb, the first fruit of which was 'MacArthur Park'. This lengthy, melodramatic composition reached the US and UK Top 5 with sales in excess of 1 million and drew its appeal from a contrast between the singer's cracked vocal and a sweeping, sumptuous backing. The Harris/Webb partnership was maintained on *A Tramp Shining*, and *The Yard Went On Forever*, but subsequent singles, including the haunting 'Didn't We', failed to match the success of the first release. The singer scored a US Top 50 entry with 'My Boy' in 1970, and appeared in the stage production of *Tommy*. Now having concentrated solely on thespian pursuits (and being a reformed alcoholic) he remains a brilliant raconteur.
● ALBUMS: *A Tramp Shining* (Dunhill 1968) ★★★, *The Yard Went On Forever* (Dunhill 1969) ★★★, *Love Album* (Dunhill 1970) ★★, *My Boy* (Dunhill 1971) ★★, *Slides, I, In The Membership Of My Days* (Dunhill 1972) ★★, *Jonathan Livingston Seagull* (Dunhill 1973) ★★, *The Prophet By Kahlil Gibran* (Atlantic 1974) ★.
● COMPILATIONS: *His Greatest Performances* (Dunhill 1979) ★★, *The Webb Sessions 1968-1969* (Raven 1996) ★★★.

HARRISON, NOEL

b. 1934. Harrison's career was furnished with both the best and worst start by the long shadow of Rex Harrison, his famous father. Before capitulating to full-time acting too, Noel – an urbane and accomplished singing guitarist – was well known on the British club circuit before achieving his only hit in 1969. Assisted by its inclusion in *The Thomas Crown Affair* film soundtrack, 'Windmills Of Your Mind' peaked at number 8 in the UK charts, but only 'A Young Girl' elicited further interest. Having tested the thespian water with minor appearances in television's *Man From UNCLE* series, he took over from Tommy Steele in a touring production of *Half A Sixpence*. After several similar starring roles, his talents were directed exclusively towards the theatre.
● ALBUMS: *At The Blue Angel* (Philips 1960) ★★, *The Great Electric Experiment Is Over* (Reprise 1969) ★★.
● COMPILATIONS: *The World Of Noel Harrison* (Decca 1970) ★★★.

HARTLEY, KEEF, BAND

b. 8 March 1944, Preston, Lancashire, England. Together with Colosseum, the Keef Hartle Band of the late 60s, forged jazz and rock mus sympathetically to appeal to the UK progressiv music scene. Drummer Hartley had already ha vast experience in live performances as Ring Starr's replacement in Rory Storm And Th Hurricanes. When Merseybeat died, Hartley wa enlisted by the London-based R&B band th Artwoods, whose line-up included future Dee Purple leader Jon Lord. Hartley was present o their only album *Art Gallery* (now a muc sought-after collector's item). He joined Joh Mayall's Bluesbreakers and was present durir one of Mayall's vintage periods. Both *Crusac* and *Diary Of A Band* highlighted Hartley economical drumming and faultless timing. Th brass-laden instrumental track on John Mayall *Bare Wires* is titled 'Hartley Quits'. The goo natured banter between Hartley and his ex-bo continued onto Hartley's strong debut *Ha Breed*. The opening track 'Hearts And Flower has the voice of Mayall on the telephor officially sacking Hartley, albeit tongue-i cheek, while the closing track 'Sacked' h Hartley dismissing Mayall! The mus intervening features some of the best ever la 60s jazz-influenced blues, and the albu remains an undiscovered classic.
The band for the first album comprised Mill Anderson (b. 12 April 1945, Johnsto Renfrewshire, Scotland; guitar and vocals), Ga Thain (b. 15 May 1948, Wellington, Ne Zealand, d. 19 March 1976; bass), Peter Din (organ) and Spit James (guitar). Later membe to join Hartley's fluid line-up included Mic Weaver (aka Wynder K. Frog) organ, Hen Lowther (b. 11 July 1941, Leicester, Englan trumpet/violin), Jimmy Jewell (saxophone Johnny Almond (flute), Jon Hiseman (wł guested on percussion and congas) and Har Beckett. Hartley, often dressed as an America Indian, sometimes soberly, sometimes in fu headdress and war paint, was a popul attraction on the small club scene. His was o of the few British bands to play the Woodsto Festival, where his critics compared hi favourably with Blood, Sweat And Tears. T *Battle Of NW6* in 1969 further enhanced his cl reputation, although chart success still elud him. By the time of the third album bo Lowther and Jewell had departed, althou Hartley always maintained that his band w like a jazz band, in that musicians could con and go and be free to play with oth aggregations.
Dave Caswell and Lyle Jenkins came in ar made *The Time Is Near*. This albu demonstrated Miller Anderson's fir songwriting ability, and long-time producer Ne Slaven's excellent production. They were just rewarded when the album briefly nudged i way into the UK and US charts. Subseque

albums lost the fire that Hartley kindled on the first three, although the formation of his Little Big Band and the subsequent live album had some fine moments. The recording at London's Marquee club saw the largest ever band assembled on the tiny stage; almost the entire British jazz/rock fraternity seemed to be present, including Chris Mercer, Lynn Dobson, Ray Warleigh, Barbara Thompson, and Derek Wadsworth. By the time *Seventy Second Brave* was released, Anderson had departed having signed a contract as a solo artist. He was clearly the jewel in Hartley's crown (or headgear) and the cohesion that Anderson gave the band as the main songwriter, lead vocalist and lead guitar was instantly lost. Future recordings also lacked Slaven's even production. Hartley and Anderson came together again in 1974 for one album as Dog Soldier but Hartley has been largely inactive in music for many years apart from the occasional tour with John Mayall and sessions with Michael Chapman. In the mid-90s he had a carpentry business in Preston, Lancashire, and although it is alleged that he no longer owns a drumkit attempts were made in the mid-90s to re-form the original line-up. A highly undervalued band requiring reappraisal.

● ALBUMS: *Halfbreed* (Deram 1969) ★★★★, *Battle Of NW6* (Deram 1970) ★★★, *The Time Is Near* (Deram 1970) ★★★★, *Overdog* (Deram 1971) ★★, *Little Big Band* (Deram 1971) ★★★, *Seventy Second Brave* (Deram 1972) ★★, *Lancashire Hustler* (Deram 1973) ★, as Dog Soldier *Dog Soldier* (Deram 1975) ★★.

● COMPILATIONS: *The Best Of Keef Hartley* (Decca 1972) ★★★, *Not Foolish Not Wise* (Mooncrest 1999) ★★.

HARVEY, ALEX

b. 5 February 1935, Gorbals, Glasgow, Scotland, d. 4 February 1982, Zeebruggen, Belgium. Having left school at the age of 15, Harvey undertook a multitude of occupations before opting for music. Inspired by Jimmie Rodgers, Woody Guthrie and Cisco Houston, he became acquainted with several musicians who rehearsed regularly at the city's Bill Patterson Studios. In 1955 Harvey joined saxophonist Bill Patrick in a group that combined rock 'n' roll and traditional jazz. Known jointly as the Clyde River Jazz Band or the Kansas City Skiffle Band, depending on the booking, the unit later evolved into the Kansas City Counts, and joined the Ricky Barnes All-Stars as pioneers of the Scottish rock 'n' roll circuit. By the end of the decade, and with their singer the obvious focal point, the group had became known as Alex Harvey's (Big) Soul Band, the appellation derived from a new form of small group jazz championed by Horace Silver. The band's repertoire consisted of Ray Charles, the Isley Brothers and urban R&B versions, while their innovative use of conga drums and other percussive instruments emphasized the swinging nature of their sound.

Having become popular in Scotland and the north of England, Harvey then moved to Hamburg where he recorded *Alex Harvey And His Soul Band* in October 1963. Curiously, this excellent set did not feature the singer's regular group, but musicians drawn from Kingsize Taylor And The Dominoes. The following year Alex returned to the UK. His group made its London debut on 6 February 1964 and for several months remained a highly popular attraction in the capital. However, another opportunity to capture them on record was lost when *The Blues* consisted of largely solo material with support derived solely from Harvey's younger brother, Leslie. This disparate set included suitably idiosyncratic readings of 'Danger Zone', 'Waltzing Matilda' and 'The Big Rock Candy Mountain'. Despite initial intentions to the contrary, Harvey dissolved the Soul Band in 1965 with a view to pursuing a folk-based direction. However subsequent releases, including 'Agent 00 Soul' and 'Work Song', continued the artist's love of R&B. Having briefly fronted the houseband at Glasgow's Dennistoun Palais, Alex returned to London in 1967 to form the psychedelic Giant Moth. The remnants of this short-lived group – Mox (flute), Jim Condron (guitar/bass) and George Butler (drums) – supported the singer on two invigorating singles, 'Someday Song' and 'Maybe Someday'. Stung by their commercial failure, Harvey took a job in the pit band for the musical *Hair*, which in turn inspired *Hair Rave Up Live From The Shaftesbury Theatre*.

The singer re-established his own career in 1969 with the uncompromising *Roman Wall Blues*. This powerful set included the original version of 'Midnight Moses', a composition that the singer brought to his next substantial group, the Sensational Alex Harvey Band. Galvanized by the tragic death of his brother Leslie while on stage with Stone The Crows, Harvey formed SAHB with Tear Gas, a struggling Glasgow hard rock band. Together they became one of the most popular live attractions of the early 70s until ill health took its toll of their irrepressible leader. He abandoned the group in October 1977 to resume a less frenetic solo career, but *The Mafia Stole My Guitar* failed to recapture former glories. Harvey succumbed to a fatal heart attack on 4 February 1982 in Belgium at the end of a four-week tour of Europe. He was an enigmatic and endearing character who still has stories told about his exploits long after his death.

● ALBUMS: *Alex Harvey And His Soul Band* (Polydor 1964) ★★★, *The Blues* (Polydor 1964) ★★★, *Hair Rave Up Live From The Shaftesbury Theatre* (Pye 1969) ★★, *Roman Wall Blues* (Fontana 1969) ★★, *Alex Harvey Narrates The Loch Ness Monster* (K-Tel 1977) ★★, *The Mafia Stole My Guitar* (RCA 1979) ★★, *The Soldier On The Wall* (Power Supply 1983) ★★★.

● COMPILATIONS: *The Collection* (Castle 1986) ★★★, *Delilah: The Very Best Of Alex Harvey*

(PolyGram 1998) ★★★, *Alex Harvey And His Soul Band* 1963, 1964 recordings (Bear Family 1999) ★★★.

HATCH, TONY

b. 30 June 1939, Pinner, Middlesex, England. After reaching the UK Top 50 under his own name in 1962 with the light orchestral piece, 'Out Of This World', Hatch emerged as a respected songwriter, arranger, and producer of immensely popular hit records. He began taking piano lessons at the age of four, and when he was 10, joined the choir of All Souls Church, Langham Place, in London. While in his teens he worked for a firm of music publishers, before taking a job as assistant producer Top Rank Records. During his National Service in the Army, Hatch was a staff arranger with the Band of the Coldstream Guards, and continued to work part time as a freelance producer with Pye Records and Top Rank. For the latter label he wrote (under the nom de plume of Mark Anthony) and produced Gary Mills' recording of 'Look for A Star', which was a UK and US hit. After his release from the Forces, Hatch joined Pye on a full time basis, and soon had his own roster of artists which included the Brook Brothers, the Viscounts, Emile Ford, the Alexandra Brothers, and the Dagenham Girl Pipers. He also co-wrote and produced several of comedian Benny Hill's popular novelty numbers. In 1963, Hatch introduced the Searchers to Pye, and, after producing their first hit, 'Sweets For My Sweet', wrote (under yet another nom de plume, Fred Nightingale) their follow up, 'Sugar And Spice'.

The following year brought 'Downtown', the first of many numbers of his which became popular for Petula Clark. It boosted her career in the UK and US, and gained her a Grammy Award. She won another one in 1965 for her version of Hatch's 'I Know A Place'. Hatch wrote most of the other chart successes for Clark with Jackie Trent, including 'I Couldn't Live Without Your Love', 'The Other Man's Grass Is Always Greener', Colour My World', and 'Don't Sleep In The Subway'. The duo also wrote the dramatic ballad, 'Where Are You Now (My Love)', which Trent took to the top of the UK chart in 1965 after it had featured in an episode of the Inspector Rose television series, *It's Dark Outside*. In 1967, to mark their wedding day, Pye released Hatch and Trent's version of 'The Two Of Us'. It was the beginning of the couple's highly successful secondary career in cabaret and concerts, although they still continued to write songs, one of which, the lovely ballad 'Joanna', was successful for Scott Walker in 1968. In 1972, Hatch composed the music for George Cukor's film *Travels With My Aunt*, and a year later collaborated with Trent on the score for the West End musical *The Card*, starring Jim Dale and Marti Webb. Among the songs were the lovely 'Opposite Your Smile' and 'I Could Be The One'.

In the 70s, after Hatch had spent some time as a member (an acerbic member) of the panel for the *New Faces* television talent show, he and Trent lived in Southern Ireland for several years in an effort to escape the high rate of taxes in England. Their next move was to Australia, where they have subsequently continued to spend most of each year. In 1985 they wrote the theme song for a new television series, *Neighbours*, which has since become a favourite in the UK. Hatch's other, highly lucrative, small-screen signature tunes have been for UK television programmes such as *Crossroads*, *Man Alive*, *Sportsnight*, *Hadleigh*, *Mr. & Mrs.*, and *Emmerdale Farm*. Each Christmas Hatch plans and produces the spectacular *Carols In The Park* which attracts over 100,000 people to one of Sydney's largest parks. In 1992, Hatch and Trent added the BASCA Award For Services To British Music to their several Ivor Novello Awards, and two years later were in London to supervise a revival of their 1973 show, *The Card*. In 1995, they announced that their marriage was over. Hatch was then based in Minorca, while Trent returned to England to resume her solo career.

● ALBUMS: include *Latin Happening* (Pye 1966) ★★★, *Singers & Swingers* (Pye 1967) ★★★, with Jackie Trent *The Two Of Us* (Pye 1968), with Trent *Live For Life* (Pye 1968), *Latin Velvet* (Pye 1968) ★★★, with Trent *Together Again* (Pye 1969) ★★★, *Cool Latin Sound* (Pye 1968) ★★★, with Trent *Words And Music* (Columbia 1971) ★★★, with Trent *Two For The Show* (Columbia 1972) ★★★, with Trent *Opposite Your Smile* (Pye 1974) ★★, with Trent *Our World Of Music* (Celebrity 1980) ★★★.
● COMPILATIONS: *Golden Hour Of Jackie Trent And Tony Hatch* (Pye 1976) ★★★, *The Best Of Tony Hatch And Jackie Trent* (Sequel 1997) ★★★, *Hatchback* (Sequel 1998) ★★★.
● FURTHER READING: *So You Want To Be In The Music Business*, Tony Hatch.

HATHAWAY, DONNY

b. 1 October 1945, Chicago, Illinois, USA, d. 13 January 1979, New York City, New York, USA. Originally schooled in the gospel tradition, this versatile artist was raised in St. Louis and majored in musical theory at Howard University in Washington DC. He performed in a cocktail jazz trio before gaining employment as a producer with Curtis Mayfield's Curtom Records label. A duet with June Conquest, 'I Thank You Baby', became Hathaway's first hit in 1969. The same year he was signed by Atlantic Records for whom he recorded several imaginative singles, including 'The Ghetto' (1969) and 'Love, Love, Love' (1973). His crafted compositions were recorded by such acts as Aretha Franklin and Jerry Butler, but Hathaway is best remembered for his cool duets with Roberta Flack. Their complementary voices were honed to perfection on 'Where Is The Love' (1972) and 'The Closer I

Get To You' (1978), both of which reached the US Top 5. Why this gifted musician should have taken his own life remains unexplained, but on 13 January 1979, Hathaway threw himself from the fifteenth floor of New York's Essex House hotel. The following year, the singer achieved a posthumous hit in the UK with another Roberta Flack duet, 'Back Together Again', which reached number 3.
● ALBUMS: *Everything Is Everything* (Atco 1970) ★★★, *Donny Hathaway* (Atco 1971) ★★★, *Live* (Atco 1972) ★★, with Quincy Jones *Come Back, Charleston Blue* film soundtrack (Atco 1972) ★★, *Roberta Flack And Donny Hathaway* (Atlantic 1972) ★★★, *Extension Of A Man* (Atco 1973) ★★★, *In Performance* (Atlantic 1977) ★★★, *Roberta Flack Featuring Donny Hathaway* (Atlantic 1980) ★★★.
● COMPILATIONS: *The Best Of Donny Hathaway* (Atco 1978) ★★★, *A Donny Hathaway Collection* (Atlantic 1990) ★★★.

HAVENS, RICHIE
b. Richard Pierce Havens, 21 January 1941, Bedford-Stuyvesant, Brooklyn, New York City, New York, USA. Havens' professional singing career began at the age of 14 as a member of the McCrea Gospel Singers. By 1962 he was a popular figure on the Greenwich Village folk circuit with regular appearances at the Cafe Wha?, Gerdes, and The Fat Black Pussycat. Havens quickly developed a distinctive playing style, tuning his guitar to the open E chord which in turn inspired an insistent percussive technique and a stunningly deft right-hand technique. A black singer in a predominantly white idiom, Havens' early work combined folk material with New York-pop inspired compositions. His soft, yet gritty, voice adapted well to seemingly contrary material and two early releases, *Mixed Bag* and *Something Else Again*, revealed a blossoming talent. However, the artist established his reputation interpreting songs by other acts, including the Beatles and Bob Dylan, which he personalized through his individual technique. Havens opened the celebrated Woodstock Festival and his memorable appearance was a highlight of the film. A contemporaneous release, *Richard P. Havens 1983*, was arguably his artistic apogee, offering several empathic cover versions and some of the singer's finest compositions. He later established an independent label, Stormy Forest, and enjoyed a US Top 20 hit with 'Here Comes The Sun'. A respected painter, writer and sculptor, Havens also enjoys a lucrative career doing voice-overs for US television advertisements.
● ALBUMS: *Mixed Bag* (Verve/Forecast 1967) ★★★★, *Richie Havens Record* (Douglas 1968) ★★, *Electric Havens* (Douglas 1968) ★★, *Something Else Again* (Forecast 1968) ★★★, *Richard P. Havens 1983* (Forecast 1969) ★★★★, *Stonehenge* (Stormy Forest 1970) ★★, *Alarm*

Clock (Stormy Forest 1971) ★★★, *The Great Blind Degree* (Stormy Forest 1971) ★★, *Richie Havens On Stage* (Stormy Forest 1972) ★★★, *Portfolio* (Stormy Forest 1973) ★★★, *Mixed Bag II* (Stormy Forest 1974) ★★, *The End Of The Beginning* (A&M 1976) ★★, *Mirage* (A&M 1977) ★★, *Connections* (Elektra 1980) ★★, *Common Ground* (Connexion 1984) ★★, *Simple Things* (RBI 1987) ★, *Richie Havens Sings The Beatles And Dylan* (Rykodisc 1987) ★★, *Live At The Cellar Door* (Five Star 1990) ★★★, *Now* (Solar/Epic 1991) ★★★, *Cuts To The Chase* (Rhino/Forward 1994) ★★★.
● COMPILATIONS: *Resumé* (Rhino 1993) ★★★★, *The Best Of Richie Havens – The Millennium Collection* (PolyGram 2000) ★★★★.
● FILMS: *Woodstock* (1970), *Catch My Soul* (1974), *Greased Lightning* (1977), *The Boss' Son* (1978), *Hearts Of Fire* (1987), *Street Hunter* (1990).

HAWKINS, EDWIN, SINGERS
As directors of music at their Berkeley church, the Ephresian Church of God in Christ, Edwin Hawkins (b. August 1943, Oakland, California, USA) and Betty Watson began in 1967 to absorb the leading soloists from other San Francisco-based choirs to inaugurate the North California State Youth Choir. In 1969, the 50-strong ensemble recorded an album to boost their funds, and when San Francisco DJ Tom Donahue began playing one of its tracks, 'Oh Happy Day', the assemblage found itself with both a record contract with the Buddah Records label and a surprise international hit. Although renamed the Edwin Hawkins Singers, the featured voice belonged to Dorothy Combs Morrison (b. Longview, Texas, USA) and much of the single's attraction comes from her powerful delivery. The singer subsequently embarked on a solo career which failed to maintain its initial promise while Hawkins, deprived of such an important member, struggled in the wake of this 'novelty' hit, although they enjoyed a period of great demand for session singing. One such session put them back into the US charts in 1970 while guesting on Melanie's Top 10 hit 'Lay Down (Candles In The Rain)'. It was their last chart appearance to date and eventually the group's fortunes faded. The Singers, now somewhat reduced in numbers, continue to tour and occasionally record.
● ALBUMS: include *Let Us Go Into The House Of The Lord* (Pavilion 1968) ★★★★, *Oh Happy Day* (Pavilion 1969) ★★★★, *Peace Is Blowing In The Wind* (Pavilion 1969) ★★★, *I'd Like To Teach The World To Sing* (Buddah 1972) ★★★★, *Live In Atlanta* (PolyGram 1974) ★★★, *Wonderful* (Sounds 1980) ★★★★, *Imagine Heaven* (Birthright 1982) ★★★, *Live With The Oakland Symphony Orchestra* (Birthright 1982) ★★★, *Give Us Peace* (Birthright 1982) ★★★, *Imagine Heaven* (Fixit 1989) ★★★, *Face To Face* (Fixit 1991) ★★★.

● COMPILATIONS: *The Best Of The Edwin Hawkins Singers* (Savoy 1985) ★★★, *The Very Best Of The Edwin Hawkins Singers* (Camden 1998) ★★★.

HAWKINS, RONNIE

b. 10 January 1935, Huntsville, Arkansas, USA. Hawkins, who is rock 'n' roll's funniest storyteller says: 'I've been around so long, I remember when the Dead Sea was only sick.' Hawkins' father played at square dances and his cousin, Dale Hawkins, staked his own claim to rock 'n' roll history with 'Suzie-Q'. Hawkins, who did some stunt diving for Esther Williams' swimming revue, earned both a science and physical education degree at the University of Arkansas, but his heart was in the 'chitlin' starvation circuit' in Memphis. Because the pay was poor, musicians went from one club to another using the 'Arkansas credit card' – a siphon, a rubber hose and a five gallon can. Hawkins befriended Elvis Presley: 'In 1954 Elvis couldn't even spell Memphis: by 1957 he owned it'.

After Hawkins' army service, he followed Conway Twitty's recommendation by working Canadian clubs. While there, he made his first recordings as the Ron Hawkins Quartet, the tracks being included on *Rrrracket Time*. In 1959 Hawkins reached number 45 on the US charts with 'Forty Days', an amended version of Chuck Berry's 'Thirty Days'. He explains, 'Chuck Berry had simply put new lyrics to 'When The Saints Go Marching In'. My record company told me to add ten days. They knew Chess Records wouldn't sue as they wouldn't want to admit it was 'The Saints''. Hawkins' version of Young Jessie's 'Mary Lou' then made number 26 in the US charts. With his handstands and leapfrogging, he became known as Mr. Dynamo and pioneered a dance called the Camel Walk. In 1960 Hawkins became the first rock 'n' roller to involve himself in politics with a plea for a murderer on Death Row, 'The Ballad Of Caryl Chessman', but to no avail. The same year Hawkins with his drummer, Levon Helm, travelled to the UK for the ITV show *Boy Meets Girls*.

He was so impressed by guitarist Joe Brown that he offered him a job, but, on returning home, the Hawks gradually took shape – Levon Helm, Robbie Robertson, Garth Hudson, Richard Manuel and Rick Danko. Their wild 1963 single of two Bo Diddley songs, 'Bo Diddley' and 'Who Do You Love', was psychedelia before its time. 'Bo Diddley' was a Canadian hit, and by marrying a former Miss Toronto, Hawkins made the country his home. He supported local talent and refused, for example, to perform in clubs that did not give equal time to Canadian artists. Meanwhile, the Hawks recorded for Atlantic Records as Levon and the Hawks and were then recruited by Bob Dylan, becoming the Band. The various incarnations of the Hawks have included many fine musicians, notably the pianist Stan Szelest. Hawkins had Canadian Top 10 hits with 'Home From The Forest' and 'Bluebirds Over The Mountain', while his experience in buying a Rolls-Royce was recounted in Gordon Lightfoot's 'Talkin' Silver Cloud Blues'. In 1970 Hawkins befriended John Lennon and Yoko Ono, and the promotional single on which Lennon praises Hawkins' 'Down In The Alley' is a collector's item.

Kris Kristofferson wrote humorous liner notes for Hawkins' album *Rock And Roll Resurrection*, and it was through Kristofferson that Hawkins had a role in the disastrous movie *Heaven's Gate*. Hawkins is better known for his extrovert performance in the Band's *The Last Waltz*. The burly singer has also appeared in Bob Dylan's Rolling Thunder Revue and he has some amusing lines as 'Bob Dylan' in *Renaldo And Clara*; Hawkins' segment with 'happy hooker' Xaviera Hollander includes the line: 'Abraham Lincoln said all men are created equal, but then he never saw Bo Diddley in the shower.' In 1985 Hawkins joined Joni Mitchell, Anne Murray, Neil Young and several others for the Canadian Band Aid record, 'Tears Are Not Enough', by Northern Lights. Hawkins has a regular Canadian television series, *Honky Tonk*, and owns a 200 acre farm and has several businesses. It gives the lie to his colourful quote: '90 per cent of what I made went on women, whiskey, drugs and cars. I guess I just wasted the other 10 per cent.'

● ALBUMS: *Ronnie Hawkins* (Roulette 1959) ★★, *Mr. Dynamo* (Roulette 1960) ★★, *The Folk Ballads Of Ronnie Hawkins* (Roulette 1960) ★★, *Ronnie Hawkins Sings The Songs Of Hank Williams* (Roulette 1960) ★★, *Ronnie Hawkins* (Cotillion 1970) ★★, *Arkansas Rock Pile* (Roulette 1970) ★★, *The Hawk* i (Cotillion 1971) ★★, *Rock 'N' Roll Resurrection* (Monument 1972) ★★, *The Giant Of Rock And Roll* (Monument 1974) ★★, *The Hawk* ii (United Artists 1979) ★★, *Rrrracket Time* (Charly 1979) ★★, *A Legend In His Spare Time* (Quality 1981) ★★, *The Hawk And Rock* (Trilogy 1982) ★★, *Making It Again* (Epic 1984) ★★, *Hello Again ... Mary Lou* (Epic 1987) ★★.
● COMPILATIONS: *The Best Of Ronnie Hawkins & His Band* (Roulette 1970) ★★★, *The Best Of Ronnie Hawkins And The Hawks* (Rhino 1990) ★★★, *The Roulette Years* (Sequel 1994) ★★★.
● VIDEOS: *The Hawk In Concert* (MMG Video 1988), *This Country's Rockin' – Reunion Concert* (1993).
● FURTHER READING: *The Hawk: The Story Of Ronnie Hawkins & The Hawks*, Ian Wallis.
● FILMS: *The Last Waltz* (1978), *Renaldo And Clara* (1978), *Heaven's Gate* (1980), *Meatballs III* (1987), *Boozecan* (1994), *Red Green: Duct Tape Forever* (2001).

HEAD, ROY

b. 1 September 1941, Three Rivers, Texas, USA. This respected performer first formed his group, the Traits, in 1958, after moving to San Marcos.

The line-up included Jerry Gibson (drums), who later played with Sly And The Family Stone. Head recorded for several local labels, often under the supervision of famed Texas producer Huey P. Meaux, but it was not until 1965 that he had a national hit when 'Treat Her Right' reached number 2 on both the US pop and R&B charts. This irresistible song, with its pumping horns and punchy rhythm, established the singer alongside the Righteous Brothers as that year's prime blue-eyed soul exponent. Head's later releases appeared on a variety of outlets, including Dunhill Records and Elektra Records, and embraced traces of rockabilly ('Apple Of My Eye') and psychedelia ('You're (Almost) Tuff'). However, by the 70s he had honed his style and was working as a country singer, and in 1975 he earned a notable US C&W Top 20 hit with 'The Most Wanted Woman In Town'.

● ALBUMS: *Roy Head And The Traits* (TNT 1965) ★★★, *Treat Me Right* (Scepter 1965) ★★★, *A Head Of His Time* (Dot 1968) ★★, *Same People* (Dunhill 1970) ★★, *Dismal Prisoner* (TMT 1972) ★★, *Head First* (Dot 1976) ★★, *Tonight's The Night* (ABC 1977) ★★, *In Our Room* (Elektra 1979) ★★, *The Many Sides Of Roy Head* (Elektra 1980) ★★.

● COMPILATIONS: *Treat Her Right* (Bear Family 1988) ★★★, *Slip Away: His Best Recordings* (Collectables 1993) ★★, *Treat Her Right: Best Of Roy Head* (Varèse Vintage 1995) ★★★★, *White Texas Soul Shouter: The Crazy Cajun Recordings* (Edsel 1998) ★★★.

HEAVY JELLY

The complexities surrounding this intriguing UK progressive band belie its brief lifespan. The name 'Heavy Jelly' first appeared in a fictitious review, run late in 1968 in the London listings magazine, *Time Out*. Interest was such that two labels, Island Records and Head, released singles bearing the name. Island's Heavy Jelly was the rock band Skip Bifferty in disguise, although their lone single, 'I Keep Singing That Same Old Song', achieved a higher profile when it was placed on a popular budget-priced sampler, *Nice Enough To Eat*. The Head release, in the spring of 1969, 'Time Out (The Long Wait)', featured John Moorshead (guitar), Alex Dmochowski (bass) – both from the Aynsley Dunbar Retaliation – drummer Carlo Little and an individual dubbed Rocky. When this single proved popular, the label's managing director, John Curd, registered the Heavy Jelly name and Moorshead and Dmochowski instigated a full-time line-up. Initial album sessions featured Chris Wood and Jim Capaldi from Traffic, but they were later replaced by ex-Animals drummer Barry Jenkins and vocalist Jackie Lomax. Further upheavals followed, the projected album was shelved and the final blow came when Lomax accepted a solo recording deal.

● ALBUMS: *Take Me Down To The Water* (1984) ★★★.

HEBB, BOBBY

b. 26 July 1941, Nashville, Tennessee, USA. An accomplished musician and songwriter, Hebb appeared on the *Grand Ole Opry* at 12 and studied guitar with Chet Atkins. He later moved to New York, ostensibly to play with Mickey And Sylvia. When that duo split, a new combination emerged: Bobby And Sylvia. This short-lived partnership was followed by several solo Hebb releases that culminated in 'Sunny' (1966). Written in memory of his brother Hal, who died the day after the assassination of John F. Kennedy, this simple, melancholic song reached number 2 in the USA and number 12 in the UK. It was recorded by many artists, including Cher and Georgie Fame, whose version reached number 13 in the UK in 1966. Despite his tag as 'the song a day man', Hebb chose the country standard 'A Satisfied Mind' as the follow-up. It fared less well commercially, although the singer later secured a reputation in UK northern soul circles with 'Love Me' and 'Love, Love, Love', which reached the Top 40 in the UK in 1972. Hebb returned to the fringes of the soul chart with 'Sunny 76', a reworking of his best-known moment.

● ALBUMS: *Sunny* (Philips 1966) ★★.

HEDGEHOPPERS ANONYMOUS

Formed in November 1963 and originally known as the Trendsetters, this short-lived quintet consisted of ex-members of the Royal Air Force. Mick Tinsley (b. 16 December 1940), Ray Honeyball (b. 6 June 1941), Leslie Dash (b. 3 April 1943), Alan Laud (b. 13 March 1946) and John Stewart (b. 18 March 1941) were managed by Jonathan King, who wrote and produced their UK Top 5 hit 'It's Good News Week' in 1965. A somewhat contrived cash-in on the then-current 'protest' trend, the single was undeniably catchy, but the group was unable to repeat its success. Although a follow-up, 'Don't Push Me', was given considerable airplay, it failed to chart and the quintet disbanded soon afterwards.

HEINZ

b. Heinz Burt, 24 July 1942, Hargin, Germany, d. 7 April 2000. Bass player Burt was a founder member of the Tornados, a studio group assembled by UK producer Joe Meek. The quintet enjoyed international fame with 'Telstar', but the photogenic dyed-blond Heinz was then groomed for a solo career. Although his debut disc, 'Dreams Do Come True', failed to chart despite magnanimous publicity, the singer later enjoyed a UK Top 5 hit with the 'tribute' to the late Eddie Cochran, 'Just Like Eddie' (1963). An immoderate vocalist, Heinz was bolstered by a crack studio band, the Outlaws, and was accompanied live by the Wild Boys, who included guitarist Ritchie Blackmore. However further minor hits, 'Country Boy' (1963), 'You Were There' (1964), 'Questions I Can't Answer'

(1964), and 'Diggin' My Potatoes' (1965), revealed his limitations and an acrimonious split with Meek ended his chart career. Burt nonetheless remained popular through rock 'n' roll revival shows and cabaret. He died in April 2000 after a long struggle against motor-neurone disease.

● ALBUMS: *Tribute To Eddie* (Decca 1963) ★★.
● COMPILATIONS: *Remembering* (Decca 1977) ★★, *And The Wild Boys* (Rock Machine 1986) ★★, *Dreams Do Come True: The 45s Collection* (Castle 1994) ★★, *The Complete Heinz* (Repertoire 1999) ★★.

HENDRIX, JIMI

b. Johnny Allen Hendrix, 27 November 1942, Seattle, Washington, USA, d. 18 September 1970, London, England. (His father subsequently changed his son's name to James Marshall Hendrix.) More superlatives have been bestowed upon Hendrix than any other rock guitarist. Unquestionably one of music's most influential figures, he brought an unparalleled vision to the art of playing electric guitar. Self-taught (and with the burden of being left-handed with a right-handed guitar), he spent hours absorbing the recorded legacy of southern-blues practitioners, from Robert Johnson to B.B. King. The aspiring musician joined several local R&B bands while still at school, before enlisting as a paratrooper in the 101st Airborne Division. It was during this period that Hendrix met Billy Cox, a bass player with whom he collaborated at several stages during his career. Together they formed the King Kasuals, an in-service attraction later resurrected when both men returned to civilian life. Hendrix was discharged in July 1962 after breaking his right ankle.

He began working with various touring revues, backing, among others, the Impressions, Sam Cooke and the Valentinos. He enjoyed lengthier spells with the Isley Brothers, Little Richard and King Curtis, recording with each of these acts, but was unable to adapt to the discipline their performances required. The experience and stagecraft gained during this formative period proved essential to the artist's subsequent development. By 1965 Hendrix was living in New York. In October he joined struggling soul singer Curtis Knight, signing a punitive contract with the latter's manager, Ed Chalpin. This ill-advised decision returned to haunt the guitarist. In June the following year, Hendrix, now calling himself Jimmy James, formed a group initially dubbed the Rainflowers, then Jimmy James And The Blue Flames. The quartet, which also featured future Spirit member Randy California, was appearing at the Cafe Wha? in Greenwich Village when Chas Chandler was advised to see them. The Animals' bass player immediately recognized the guitarist's extraordinary talent and persuaded him to go to London in search of a more receptive audience.

Hendrix arrived in England in September 1966.

Chandler became his co-manager in partnership with Mike Jeffries (aka Jeffreys), and immediately began auditions for a suitable backing group. Noel Redding (b. 25 December 1945, Folkestone, Kent, England) was selected on bass, having recently failed to join the New Animals, while John 'Mitch' Mitchell (b. 9 July 1947, Ealing, Middlesex, England), a veteran of the Riot Squad and Georgie Fame's Blue Flames, became the trio's drummer. The new group, dubbed the Jimi Hendrix Experience, made its debut the following month at Evereux in France. On returning to England they began a string of club engagements that attracted pop's aristocracy, including Pete Townshend and Eric Clapton. In December the trio released their first single, the understated, resonant 'Hey Joe'. Its UK Top 10 placing encouraged a truly dynamic follow-up in 'Purple Haze'. The latter was memorable for Hendrix's guitar pyrotechnics and a lyric that incorporated the artist's classic line: "Scuse me while I kiss the sky'. On tour, his trademark Fender Stratocaster and Marshall Amplifier were punished night after night, as the group enhanced its reputation with exceptional live appearances. Here Hendrix drew on black culture and his own heritage to produce a startling visual and aural bombardment.

Framed by a halo of long, wiry hair, his slight figure was clad in a bright, rainbow-mocking costume. Although never a demonstrative vocalist, his delivery was curiously effective. Hendrix's playing technique, meanwhile, although still drawing its roots from the blues, encompassed an emotional range far greater than any contemporary guitarist. Rapier-like runs vied with measured solos, matching energy with ingenuity, while a wealth of technical possibilities – distortion, feedback and sheer volume – brought texture to his overall approach. This assault was enhanced by a flamboyant stage persona in which Hendrix used the guitar as a physical appendage. He played his instrument behind his back, between his legs or, in simulated sexual ecstasy, on the floor. Such practices brought criticism from radical quarters, who claimed the artist had become an 'Uncle Tom', employing tricks to ingratiate himself with the white audience – accusations that neglected similar showmanship from generations of black performers, from Charley Patton to 'T-Bone' Walker.

Redding's clean, uncluttered basslines provided the backbone to Hendrix's improvisations, while Mitchell's drumming, as instinctive as his leader's guitar playing, was a perfect foil. Their concessions to the pop world now receding, the Experience completed an astonishing debut album that ranged from the apocalyptic vision of 'I Don't Live Today', to the blues of 'Red House' and the funk of 'Fire' and 'Foxy Lady'. Hendrix returned to America in June 1967 to appear, sensationally, at the Monterey Pop Festival. His performance was a musical and visual feast, culminating in a sequence that saw him playing the guitar with his teeth, and then burning the instrument with lighter fuel. He was now fêted in his homeland, and following an ill-advised tour supporting the Monkees, the Experience enjoyed reverential audiences on the country's nascent concert circuit. *Axis: Bold As Love* revealed a new lyrical capability, notably in the title track and the jazz-influenced 'Up From The Skies'. 'Little Wing', a delicate love song bathed in unhurried guitar splashes, offered a gentle perspective, closer to that of the artist's shy, offstage demeanour.

Released in December 1967, the collection completed a triumphant year, artistically and commercially, but within months the fragile peace began to collapse. In January 1968 the Experience embarked on a gruelling American tour encompassing 54 concerts in 47 days. Hendrix was by this time tiring of the wild-man image that had brought him initial attention, but he was perceived as diffident by spectators anticipating gimmickry. An impulsive artist, he was unable to disguise below-par performances, while his relationship with Redding grew increasingly fraught as the bass player rebelled against the set patterns he was expected to play. *Electric Ladyland*, the last official Experience album, was released in October. This extravagant double set was initially deemed 'self-indulgent', but is now recognized as a major work. It revealed the guitarist's desire to expand the increasingly limiting trio format, and contributions from members of Traffic (Chris Wood and Steve Winwood) and Jefferson Airplane (Jack Casady) embellished several selections. The collection featured a succession of virtuoso performances – 'Gypsy Eyes', 'Crosstown Traffic' – while the astonishing 'Voodoo Chile (Slight Return)', a posthumous number 1 single, showed how Hendrix had brought rhythm, purpose and mastery to the recently invented wah-wah pedal. *Electric Ladyland* included two UK hits, 'Burning Of The Midnight Lamp' and 'All Along The Watchtower'. The latter, an urgent restatement of the Bob Dylan song, was particularly impressive, and received the ultimate accolade when the composer adopted Hendrix's interpretation when performing it live on his 1974 tour.

Despite such creativity, the guitarist's private and professional life was becoming problematic. He was arrested in Toronto for possessing heroin, but although the charges were later dismissed, the proceedings clouded much of 1969. Chas Chandler had, meanwhile, withdrawn from the managerial partnership and although Redding sought solace with a concurrent group, Fat Mattress, his differences with Hendrix were now irreconcilable. The Experience played its final concert on 29 June 1969; Hendrix subsequently formed Gypsies Sons And Rainbows with Mitchell, Billy Cox

(bass), Larry Lee (rhythm guitar), Juma Sultan and Jerry Velez (both percussion). This short-lived unit closed the Woodstock Festival, during which Hendrix performed his famed rendition of the 'The Star-Spangled Banner'. Perceived by some critics as a political statement, it came as the guitarist was increasingly being subjected to pressures from different causes.

In October he formed an all-black group, Band Of Gypsies, with Cox and drummer Buddy Miles, intending to accentuate the African-American dimension in his music. The trio made its debut on 31 December 1969, but its potential was marred by Miles' comparatively flat, pedestrian drumming and unimaginative compositions. Part of the set was issued as *Band Of Gypsies*, but despite the inclusion of the exceptional 'Machine Gun', this inconsistent album was only released to appease former manager Chalpin, who acquired the rights in part-settlement of a miserly early contract. The Band Of Gypsies broke up after a mere three concerts and initially Hendrix confined his efforts to completing the building of his Electric Ladyland recording studio. He then started work on another double set, *First Rays Of The New Rising Sun* (finally released in 1997), and later resumed performing with Cox and Mitchell. His final concerts were largely frustrating, as the aims of the artist and the expectations of his audience grew increasingly separate. His final UK appearance, at the Isle Of Wight festival, encapsulated this dilemma, yet still drew an enthralling performance. The guitarist returned to London following a short European tour. On 18 September 1970, his girlfriend, Monika Dannemann, became alarmed when she was unable to rouse him from sleep. An ambulance was called, but Hendrix was pronounced dead on arrival at a nearby hospital. The inquest recorded an open verdict, with death caused by suffocation due to inhalation of vomit. Eric Burdon claimed at the time to possess a suicide note, but this has never been confirmed.

Two posthumous releases, *Cry Of Love* and *Rainbow Bridge*, mixed portions of the artist's final recordings with masters from earlier sources. These were fitting tributes, but many others were tawdry cash-ins, recorded in dubious circumstances, mispackaged and mistitled. This imbalance has been redressed of late with the release of archive recordings.

In November 1993 a tribute album, *Stone Free*, was released, containing a formidable list of performers including the Pretenders, Eric Clapton, Cure, Jeff Beck, Pat Metheny and Nigel Kennedy, a small testament to the huge influence Hendrix has wielded and will continue to wield as the most inventive rock guitarist of all time. The litigation regarding ownership of his recordings that had been running for many years was resolved in January 1997, when the Hendrix family finally won back the rights from Alan Douglas. This was made possible by the financial weight of Microsoft co-founder Paul Allen, who, in addition to helping with legal expenses, has financed the Jimi Hendrix Museum, which will be located in Seattle. A major reissuing programme took place in 1997, including out-takes from the recording of *Electric Ladyland*. The reissued catalogue on Experience/MCA records is now the definitive and final word. The Hendrix legacy also rests in his prevailing influence on fellow musicians of all ages. Countless guitarists have imitated his technique; few have mastered it, while none at all have matched him as an inspirational player. The electric guitar in the hands of Hendrix was transformed into an extension of his body and as such puts him on an unassailable pedestal.

● ALBUMS: *Are You Experienced?* (Track 1967) ★★★★★, *Axis: Bold As Love* (Track 1967) ★★★★★, *Electric Ladyland* (Track 1968) ★★★★, *Band Of Gypsies* (Track 1970) ★★★, shared with Otis Redding *Monterey International Pop Festival* (Reprise 1970) ★★★★, *Cry Of Love* (Polydor 1971) ★★★, *Experience* (Ember 1971) ★★, *Isle Of Wight* (Polydor 1971) ★★, *Rainbow Bridge* (Reprise 1971) ★★, *Hendrix In The West* (Polydor 1971) ★★★, *More Experience* (Ember 1972) ★, *War Heroes* (Polydor 1972) ★★, *Loose Ends* (Polydor 1974) ★★, *Crash Landing* (Polydor 1975) ★★, *Midnight Lightnin'* (Polydor 1975) ★★, *Nine To The Universe* (Polydor 1980) ★★, *The Jimi Hendrix Concerts* (Columbia 1982) ★★★, *Jimi Plays Monterey* (Polydor 1986) ★★★, *Live At Winterland* (Polydor 1987) ★★★, *Radio One* (Castle 1988) ★★★★, *Live And Unreleased* (Castle 1989) ★★★, *First Rays Of The New Rising Sun* (Experience/MCA 1997) ★★★, *South Saturn Delta* (Experience 1997) ★★★, *Original Soundtrack To The Motion Picture 'Experience'* (Charly 1998) ★★, *Live At The Fillmore East* (MCA 1999) ★★★★, *Live At Woodstock* (MCA 1999) ★★★, *The Albert Hall Experience* (Charly 2001) ★★★.

● COMPILATIONS: *Smash Hits* (Track 1968) ★★★★, *The Essential Jimi Hendrix* (Polydor 1978) ★★★★, *The Essential Jimi Hendrix Volume Two* (Polydor 1979) ★★★, *The Singles Album* (Polydor 1983) ★★★★, *Kiss The Sky* (Polydor 1984) ★★★, *Cornerstones* (Polydor 1990) ★★★, *Blues* (Polydor 1994) ★★★, *Exp Over Sweden* (Univibes 1993) ★★, *Jimi In Denmark* (Univibes 1995) ★★, *BBC Sessions* (Experience/MCA 1998) ★★★★, *Experience Hendrix: The Best Of Jimi Hendrix* (Experience/MCA 1998) ★★★★, *The Jimi Hendrix Experience* 4-CD box set (Experience/MCA 2000) ★★★★, *The Summer Of Love Sessions* (Freud 2001) ★★★, *Voodoo Child: The Jimi Hendrix Collection* (Universal 2001) ★★★★.

● VIDEOS: *Jimi Hendrix Plays Berkeley* (Palace Video 1986), *Jimi Plays Monterey* (Virgin Vision 1986), *Jimi Hendrix* (Warner Home Video 1986), *Experience* (Palace Video 1987), *Rainbow Bridge* (Hendring Video 1988), *Live At The Isle Of Wight 1970* (Rhino Home Video 1990), *Jimi Hendrix*

Live At Monterey (1994), *Jimi At Woodstock* (BMG 1995), *Jimi At The Atlanta Pop Festival* (BMG 1995), *Jimi Hendrix Experience* (BMG 1995), *Jimi Hendrix Plays The Great Pop Festivals* (BMG 1995).

● FURTHER READING: *Jimi: An Intimate Biography Of Jimi Hendrix*, Curtis Knight. *Jimi Hendrix*, Alain Dister. *Jimi Hendrix: Voodoo Child Of The Aquarian Age*, David Henderson. *Scuze Me While I Kiss The Sky: The Life Of Jimi Hendrix*, David Henderson. *Hendrix: A Biography*, Chris Welch. *Hendrix: An Illustrated Biography*, Victor Sampson. *The Jimi Hendrix Story*, Jerry Hopkins. *Crosstown Traffic: Jimi Hendrix And Post-War Pop*, Charles Shaar Murray. *Jimi Hendrix: Electric Gypsy*, Harry Shapiro and Caesar Glebbeek. *Are You Experienced?*, Noel Redding and Carole Appleby. *The Hendrix Experience*, Mitch Mitchell and John Platt. *And The Man With The Guitar*, Jon Price and Gary Geldeart. *The Jimi Hendrix Experience In 1967 (Limited Edition)*, Gerard Mankowitz and Robert Whitaker (photographers). *Jimi Hendrix: A Visual Documentary, His Life, Loves And Music*, Tony Brown. *Jimi Hendrix: Starchild*, Curtis Knight. *Hendrix: Setting The Record Straight*, John McDermott with Eddie Kramer. *The Illustrated Jimi Hendrix*, Geoffrey Guiliano. *Cherokee Mist – The Lost Writings Of Jimi Hendrix*, Bill Nitopi (compiler). *Voodoo Child: The Illustrated Legend Of Jimi Hendrix*, Martin L. Green and Bill Sienkiewicz. *The Ultimate Experience*, Adrian Boot and Chris Salewicz. *The Lost Writings Of Jimi Hendrix*, Jimi Hendrix. *The Complete Studio Recording Sessions 1963-1970*, John McDermott. *Complete Guide To The Music Of*, John Robertson. *The Inner World Of Jimi Hendrix*, Monika Dannemann. *Jimi Hendrix Experience*, Jerry Hopkins. *Jimi Hendrix: Voices From Home*, Mary Willix. *The Man, The Music, The Memorabilia*, Caesar Glebbeek and Douglas Noble. *Eye Witness: The Illustrated Jimi Hendrix Concerts*, Ben Valkhoff. *Hendrix: The Final Days*, Tony Brown. *The Jimi Hendrix Companion*, Chris Potash (ed.). *Through Gypsy Eyes: My Life, The Sixties And Jimi Hendrix*, Kathy Etchingham. *Eyewitness Hendrix*, Johnny Black. *Jimi Hendrix Concert Files*, Tony Brown.

HENRY, CLARENCE 'FROGMAN'

b. 19 March 1937, Algiers, Louisiana, USA. Henry began performing during the 50s with a New Orleans-based R&B group led by Bobby Mitchell. The singer later began work with bandleader Paul Gayten who accompanied him on his 1957 smash 'Ain't Got No Home'. However, it was not until 1961 that 'But I Do' provided a follow-up to this novelty song, earning Henry a US number 4 and UK number 3 hit. Co-written by Bobby Charles, the song featured several seasoned New Orleans musicians, including the young Allen Toussaint, and relaunched Henry's career. The same year a further international success, 'You Always Hurt e One You Love' – previously a hit for the lls Brothers in 1944 – echoed the same fortless style. The following single fared better the UK, with 'Lonely Street'/'Why Can't You' rrowly missing the Top 40, but it was the tist's last substantial hit. He continued to cord for a variety of companies, and a 1969 llection, *Is Alive And Well And Living In New leans*, was acclaimed as a fine example of the escent City' style. Since then, Henry has mained a popular live attraction in his adopted y.

ALBUMS: *You Always Hurt The One You Love* ye 1961) ★★★, *Is Alive And Well And Living In w Orleans* (1969) ★★★, *New Recordings* larence Frogman Henry 1979) ★★, *Little een Frog* (Bear Family 1987) ★★.

COMPILATIONS: *Legendary Clarence ogman' Henry* (Silvertown 1983) ★★★, *But I* (Charly 1989) ★★★★, *I Like That Alligator, by: The Crazy Cajun Recordings* (Edsel 1999) ★★.

ENSKE, JUDY
Chicago, Illinois, USA. This throaty-voiced ger/raconteuse, affectionately known as 'the een of the Beatniks', was a cult hero on the st coast folk scene in the 60s. Henske was sed in the evocatively named Chippewa Falls Wisconsin, leaving to major in voice at sary College in River Forest, Illinois. She bsequently moved to Los Angeles where she ng solo until 1961, when she joined the hiskeyhill Singers. The latter featured former ngston Trio member Dave Guard, David 'Buck' heat, and Cyrus Faryar. The group recorded ly one album, *Dave Guard And The Whiskeyhill gers*, for Capitol Records, before splitting up. e following year, Henske was signed to ektra Records, which released *Judy Henske* and gh Flying Bird. The debut was a live album iich demonstrated that Henske was equally at me as a jazz singer and as a comedy rformer.

e subsequently recorded for Mercury Records d Reprise Records but, despite her dramatic ge presence, commercial success eluded her. e later married former Lovin' Spoonful ember Jerry Yester, with whom she also rformed and recorded as a duo, Henske And ster, releasing *Farewell Aldebaran* on Frank ppa's Straight label. She also played in sebud, a rock band featuring Yester, Henske, ummer John Seiter, bass player David Vaught d pianist Craig Doerge who released a self-led album in 1971. Henske retired from music the early 70s to concentrate on raising her ughter, although she continued writing with erge. The couple later married, and their ngs have been covered by a stellar list of LA-sed musicians, including David Crosby, osby, Stills And Nash and Bette Midler. enske returned to performing in the early 90s, d recorded a new album with Doerge in 1998.

Highly underrated and sadly ignored, this artist has a magnificent voice.

● ALBUMS: *Judy Henske* (Elektra 1963) ★★★★, *High Flying Bird* (Elektra 1963) ★★★★, *Little Bit Of Sunshine ... Little Bit Of Rain* (Mercury 1965) ★★★, *The Death Defying Judy Henske: The First Concert Album* (Reprise 1966) ★★★, with Jerry Yester *Farewell Aldebaran* (Straight 1968) ★★★★, *Loose In The World* (Fair Star 1999) ★★★.

HERD
This UK band originally formed in 1965 as a quintet featuring Terry Clark (vocals), Andy Bown (b. Andrew Bown, 27 March 1946, Beckenham, England; bass), Gary Taylor (guitar) and Tony Chapman (drums). After several line-up shuffles, Bown took over on lead vocals and organ, occasionally relieved by new guitarist Peter Frampton (b. 22 April 1950, Beckenham, Kent, England). In 1967, however, songwriting managers (Ken) Howard And (Alan) Blaikley were taken on in place of Billy Gaff and immediately promoted the reluctant Frampton to centre stage. A near miss with the psychedelic 'I Can Fly' was followed by a portentous adaptation of *Orpheus In The Underworld* (retitled 'From The Underworld'), which became a UK Top 10 hit. Having translated Virgil into pop, Howard And Blaikley next tackled Milton with 'Paradise Lost'. Despite their strange mix of literate pop and jazz rhythms, the Herd were marketed for teenzine consumption and Frampton was voted the 'Face of '68' by *Rave* magazine. Not surprisingly, a more straightforward hit followed with 'I Don't Want Our Loving To Die'. Ambivalent feelings about their pop star status convinced them to dump Howard and Blaikley in favour of the mercurial Andrew Loog Oldham, but their next single, the Frampton-composed 'Sunshine Cottage', missed by a mile. A brief tie-up with yet another manager, Harvey Lisberg, came to nothing and by this time Frampton had left to form Humble Pie. For a brief period, the remaining members struggled on, but to no avail. Bown later teamed up with Andy Fairweather-Low and became a full-time member of Status Quo, while Taylor and Steele guested on various sessions.

● ALBUMS: *Paradise Lost* (Fontana 1968) ★★★, *Lookin' Thru You* US only (Fontana 1968) ★★★, *Nostalgia* (Bumble 1972) ★★★.

● COMPILATIONS: *An Anthology* (Music Club 1998) ★★★, *I Can Fly: The Very Best Of The Herd* (Collectables 1998) ★★★.

HERMAN'S HERMITS
Originally known as the Heartbeats, Herman's Hermits were discovered in 1963 by manager Harvey Lisberg and his partner Charlie Silverman. After restructuring the group, the line-up emerged as Peter Noone (b. 5 November 1947, Manchester, England; vocals), Karl Green

(b. 31 July 1947, Salford, Manchester, England; bass), Keith Hopwood (b. 26 October 1946, Manchester, England; rhythm guitar), Lek Leckenby (b. Derek Leckenby, 14 May 1946, Leeds, England, d. 4 June 1994, Manchester, England; lead guitar) and Barry Whitwam (b. 21 July 1946, Manchester, England; drums – formerly a member of Leckenby's first group, the Wailers). A link with producer Mickie Most and an infectious cover of Earl Jean's US hit, 'I'm Into Something Good' gave the quintet a UK number 1 in 1964. By early 1965, the group had settled into covering 50s songs such as the Rays' 'Silhouettes' and Sam Cooke's 'Wonderful World', when an extraordinary invasion of America saw them challenge the Beatles as a chart act with over 10 million record sales in under 12 months. A stream of non-stop hits over the next two years, including the vaudevillian 'Mrs Brown You've Got A Lovely Daughter' and 'I'm Henry VIII, I Am', effectively transformed them into teen idols. Director Sam Katzman even cast them in a couple of movies, When The Boys Meet The Girls (co-starring Connie Francis) and Hold On!

Although their music-hall-inspired US chart-toppers were not issued as singles in the UK, they enjoyed a run of hits penned by the leading commercial songwriters of the day. 'A Must To Avoid' and 'No Milk Today' were inventive as well as catchy, although by 1968/9 their repertoire had become more formulaic. The hits continued until as late as 1970 when Noone finally decided to pursue a solo career. Thereafter, Herman's Hermits drifted into cabaret. Although a reunion concert did take place at Madison Square Garden in New York in 1973, stage replacements for Noone were later sought, including Peter Cowap, Karl Green, Garth Elliott and Rod Gerrard. Noone eventually settled in California, where he presented his own music show on television, and rekindled an acting career which had begun many years earlier on the top UK soap opera, Coronation Street. Hopwood left the band in 1971 and set up his own company, Pluto Music. Leckenby died in 1994 following a long fight with cancer.
● ALBUMS: Herman's Hermits (Columbia 1965) ★★★, Introducing Herman's Hermits (Columbia 1965) ★★★, Herman's Hermits On Tour (Columbia 1965) ★★★, Hold On! film soundtrack (Columbia 1966) ★★, Both Sides Of Herman's Hermits (Columbia 1966) ★★★, There's A Kind Of Hush (Columbia 1967) ★★★, Mrs Brown You've Got A Lovely Daughter (Columbia 1968) ★★★, Blaze (Columbia 1967) ★★★.
● COMPILATIONS: The Best Of (Columbia 1969) ★★★, The Most Of (MFP 1971) ★★★, The Most Of Volume 2 (MFP 1972) ★★★, Twenty Greatest Hits (K-Tel 1977) ★★★, The Very Best Of (MFP 1984) ★★★, The Collection (Castle 1990) ★★★, The EP Collection (See For Miles 1990) ★★★★, Best Of The EMI Years Volume 1 (EMI 1991) ★★★★, Best Of The EMI Years Volume 2 (EMI

1992) ★★★, Greatest Hits (Prime Cuts 199' ★★★, Golden Legends (Direct Source 200(★★★, Best Of The 60s (Simply The Best 200(★★★★, All The Hits Plus More (Prestige Bi 2001) ★★.
● FILMS: When The Boys Meet The Girls (1965 Hold On! aka There's No Place Like Space (1966)

HESTER, CAROLYN
b. 1936, Waco, Texas, USA. Hester spent h childhood in Austin and Dallas (h grandparents had been folk singers) and the she relocated to New York in 1956 to stud acting with the American Theater Wing. In 19! Hester left to sing in clubs in Cleveland ar Detroit. Her first album was released for Dec(Records' Coral subsidiary in 1958 when Hest was 21. It was produced by Norman Petty, Budd Holly's manager, and Hester soon befriende both Petty and his charge. The recor containing purely traditional material, served a springboard for performances on the New Yo folk network, as Hester became part of a ne wave of acoustic talent who would dominate th 60s (Joan Baez attended an early concert, ar Hester met Bob Dylan at an early show at th famed Gerde's Folk City). Tradition Recor hosted her second album, the first of several be titled simply Carolyn Hester, which wa produced with label owners the Clancy Brother In the UK it was renamed Thursday's Child ar released on Ember Records. It included sever folk club staples of the period such as 'House C The Rising Sun' and 'Go Away From M Window'.
After passing an audition at Columbia Recor for John Hammond her second self-title collection followed, featuring subsequent fello Hammond signing Bob Dylan on harmonica, well as guitarist Bruce Langhorne and Odet bass player Bill Lee (father of film maker Spi Lee). To promote it she came to Englan playing her first UK concerts at the Troubad(Taking a flat in Tregunter Road alongside ne husband Richard Fariña, they became the first a wave of American folk emigrates to ba themselves in London. Rory McEwan booked both for the Edinburgh Festival, but th marital relationship was already failing, despi the fact that Hester was concurrently helpir type Fariña's celebrated book, Been Down Long, It Looks Like Up To Me. Back in the USA sl became a regular on the Hullaballoo televisic series, and renewed acquaintances with Norm; Petty following a second, less successful albu for Columbia. She subsequently recorded tw live albums for Petty's Dot Records, and in th 90s these remain the only Hester material st in print thanks to reissues by Bear Fami Records.
She continued to appear regularly at th Edinburgh Festival and by the late 60s h popularity in the UK outstripped domestic sale This situation was exacerbated by her nob

rganisation of a singers' boycott of ABC
:levision's *Hootenanny* show, following its
:fusal to allow Pete Seeger to perform after he
'as blacklisted as a communist. A second
ntract was then signed with Columbia but no
:leases were forthcoming, aside from a 'best of'
mpilation. Although Hester remained a
opular live attraction, her position in folk's
ierarchy was gradually over-run by Joan Baez
nd Judy Collins. In the late 60s Hester
mbraced a rock-orientated direction with a
roup, the Carolyn Hester Coalition, but it was a
rgely unremarkable flirtation. She then
bandoned music for a full decade while she
rought up her children, though she continued
• perform sporadically. She returned to a more
:tive profile in 1982. In the 90s many were
rawn to her back-catalogue via the testimony of
ong-term fan Nanci Griffith, who featured
[ester on her *Other Voices* album and invited her
• join her for her appearance at the Royal Albert
[all in London. Her recent albums for the Road
oes On Forever label have been well received.
ALBUMS: *Carolyn Hester* (Coral 1957) ★★★,
:arlet Ribbons (Coral 1958) ★★★, *Carolyn
'ester* (Tradition 1960) ★★★, *Carolyn Hester
:olumbia 1961) ★★★, *This Life I'm Living
:olumbia 1963) ★★★, That's My Song* (Dot
)64) ★★★, *Carolyn Hester At The Town Hall
)ot 1965) ★★, The Carolyn Hester Coalition
'ye 1969) ★★★, Thursday's Child Has Far To Go
971) ★★★, Carolyn Hester* (1974) ★★★, *Music
[edicine* (80s) ★★★, *Warriors Of The Rainbow
)0s) ★★, Texas Songbird* (Road Goes On Forever
)94) ★★★, *From These Hills* (Road Goes On
)rever 1996) ★★★, *A Tom Paxton Tribute* (Road
oes On Forever 2000) ★★★★.

[ILL, VINCE

16 April 1937, Coventry, England. A popular
allad singer who has been an enduring
vourite in the UK since the 60s, Hill trained as
aker and worked as a soft drinks salesman and
a colliery, while singing at pubs and clubs in
is spare time. He served in the Royal Signals
uring his period of National Service, and sang
ith the regimental band in Europe and the Far
ast. After demobilization he toured in Leslie
tuart's 19th-century musical comedy *Floradora*,
ter joining trumpeter Teddy Foster's band as
ocalist. After forming the Raindrops vocal
roup with Len Beadle, Jackie Lee and Johnny
orth in 1958, Hill turned solo in 1962 and
:leased 'The River's Run Dry'. He soon found
imself in demand on top television and radio
nows, and his big breakthrough arrived when
e became the resident singer on ITV's *Stars
nd Garters* and radio's *Parade Of the Pops*.
igned to Columbia Records, he enjoyed some
nodest success with 'Take Me To Your Heart
gain', 'Heartaches' and 'Merci Cheri', before
itting the jackpot in 1967 with 'Edelweiss',
hich went to number 2 in the UK chart. He
ntinued to register in the late 60s with a

mixture of old and new ballads, such as 'Roses
Of Picardy', 'Love Letters In The Sand',
'Importance Of Your Love', 'Doesn't Anyone
Know My Name', and 'Little Blue Bird'.
In 1970 Hill gained the Most Popular Singer
Award while representing Britain at the Rio Song
Festival, and a year later had more chart success
with 'Look Around' from the movie *Love Story*.
After guesting on most of the top UK television
variety shows, in 1973 he starred in his own
television series, *They Sold A Million*, which was
enthusiastically received and ran initially for 15
weeks. Since then, he has hosted a 26-week
television series in Canada, and performed his
highly accomplished and extremely entertaining
cabaret act at venues such as The Talk Of The
Town in London, and in several other countries
around the world. He is also much in demand on
cruise ships such as the QE2. In the late 80s and
early 90s he produced and appeared in his own
nostalgia shows which feature music from the
stage and screen, and continues to broadcast
frequently on BBC Radio 2. In addition to writing
and starring as George Loveless, the leader of
the Tolpuddle martyrs in the Radio 4 drama
Tolpuddle, Hill has also played the leading role of
Ivor Novello in the musical *My Dearest Ivor*, and,
in collaboration with Johnny Worth and
playwright Alan Plater, written his own stage
musical, *Zodiac*, based on the life of the
Champagne magnate, Charles Heidseck.
● ALBUMS: *Have You Met* (Columbia 1966)
★★★, *Heartaches* (Columbia 1966) ★★★, *At The
Club* (Columbia 1967) ★★★, *Edelweiss*
(Columbia 1967) ★★★, *Always You And Me*
(Columbia 1968) ★★★, *You Forgot To Remember*
(Columbia 1969) ★★★, *Look Around And You'll
Find Me There* (1971) ★★★, *In My Thoughts Of
You* (1972) ★★★, *They Sold A Million* (1973)
★★★, *Mandy* (1975) ★★★, *Wish You Were Here*
(1975) ★★★, *Midnight Blue* (1976) ★★★, *This Is
My Lovely Day* (1978) ★★★, *While The Feeling's
Good* (1980) ★★★, *That Loving Feeling* (President
1982) ★★★, *Sings The Great Songs Of Today*
(1984) ★★★, *I'm The Singer* (1985) ★★★, *I Will
Always Love You* (1987) ★★★, *Sings The Ivor
Novello Songbook* (1988), *Songs Of My Life 1*
(Prism 2001) ★★★, *That Loving Feeling*
(President 2001) ★★★.
● COMPILATIONS: *The Vince Hill Collection*
(1976) ★★★, *The Very Best Of Vince Hill* (1979)
★★★★, *20 Golden Favourites* (1980) ★★★★,
Greatest Hits: Vince Hill, An Hour Of Hits (1986)
★★★★, *Best Of The EMI Years* (EMI 1992)
★★★★.

HOLLAND/DOZIER/HOLLAND

Brothers Eddie Holland (b. 30 October 1939,
Detroit, Michigan, USA) and Brian Holland (b.
15 February 1941, Detroit, Michigan, USA), and
Lamont Dozier (b. 16 June 1941, Detroit,
Michigan, USA) formed one of the most
successful composing and production teams in
popular music history. Throughout the mid-60s,

they almost single-handedly fashioned the classic Motown Records sound, creating a series of hit singles that revolutionized the development of black music. All three men were prominent in the Detroit R&B scene from the mid-50s, Brian Holland and his brother Eddie with the Fidelatones, and Dozier with the Romeos. By the early 60s, they had all become part of Berry Gordy's Motown concern, working both as performers and as writers/arrangers. After masterminding the Marvelettes' 1961 smash 'Please Mr Postman', Brian Holland formed a production team with his brother Eddie, and Freddy Gorman. In 1963, Gorman was replaced by Dozier, and the trio made their production debut with a disregarded record by the Marvelettes, 'Locking Up My Heart'. Over the next five years, the triumvirate wrote and produced scores of records by almost all the major Motown artists, among them a dozen US number 1 hits.

Although Smokey Robinson can claim to have been the label's first true auteur, Holland/Dozier/Holland created the records that transformed Motown from an enthusiastic Detroit soul label into an international force. Their earliest successes came with Marvin Gaye, for whom they wrote 'Can I Get A Witness?', 'Little Darling', 'How Sweet It Is (To Be Loved By You)' and 'You're A Wonderful One', and Martha And The Vandellas, who had hits with the trio's 'Heat Wave', 'Quicksand', 'Nowhere To Run' and 'Jimmy Mack'. Impressive although these achievements were, they paled alongside the team's run of success with the Supremes. Ordered by Berry Gordy to construct suitable vehicles for the wispy, feminine vocal talents of Diana Ross, they produced 'Where Did Our Love Go?', a simplistic but irresistible slice of lightweight pop-soul. The record reached number 1 in the USA, as did its successors, 'Baby Love', 'Come See About Me', 'Stop! In The Name Of Love' and 'Back In My Arms Again' – America's most convincing response to the otherwise overwhelming success of British beat groups in 1964 and 1965. These Supremes hits charted the partnership's growing command of the sweet soul idiom, combining unforgettable hooklines with a vibrant rhythm section that established a peerless dance groove.

The same process was apparent – albeit with more sophistication – on the concurrent series of hits that Holland/Dozier/Holland produced and wrote for the Four Tops. 'Baby I Need Your Loving' and 'I Can't Help Myself' illustrated their stylish way with up-tempo material; 'It's The Same Old Song' was a self-mocking riposte to critics of their sound, while 'Reach Out, I'll Be There', a worldwide number 1 in 1966, pioneered what came to be known as 'symphonic soul', with a towering arrangement and a melodic flourish that was the peak of their work at Motown. Besides the Supremes and the Four Tops, the trio found success with the Miracles

('Mickey's Monkey' and 'I'm The One You Need' Kim Weston ('Take Me In Your Arms'), and th Isley Brothers ('This Old Heart Of Mine', 'Pu Yourself In My Place' and 'I Guess I'll Alway Love You'). Their long-standing commitment continued to bring them recognition in 1966 an 1967, however, as the Supremes reached the to of the US charts with 'You Can't Hurry Love 'You Keep Me Hangin' On', 'Love Is Here An Now You're Gone', and the mock-psychedeli 'The Happening', and the Four Tops extende their run of success with 'Bernadette' an 'Standing In The Shadows Of Love'.

In 1968, when Holland/Dozier/Hollan effectively commanded the US pop charts, the split from Berry Gordy and Motown, having bee denied more control over their work and mor reward for their labours. Legal disputes officiall kept them out of the studio for several year robbing them of what might have been thei most lucrative period as writers and producer They were free, however, to launch their ow rival to Motown, in the shape of the Hot Wa (June 1969) and Invictus (September 1969 labels. Neither concern flourished until 197(and even then the names of the company founders were absent from the credits of thei records – although there were rumours that th trio were moonlighting under the names of thei employees. On the evidence of Invictus hits b artists such as the Chairmen Of The Board an Freda Payne, the case was convincing, as thei records successfully mined the familiar vein c the trio's Motown hits, at a time when thei former label was unable to recapture that magi without them. Business difficulties, disputes wit their leading artists, and personal conflict gradually wore down the partnership in the earl 70s. A third label, Music Machine, wa unsuccessfully launched in 1972. The followin year Lamont Dozier left the Holland brothers t forge a solo career with ABC Records. Musi Machine was dissolved at the end of the year, an the Holland brothers were forced to undertak production work for their old masters, Motowr Invictus and Hot Wax limped on until 1977. Sinc then there have been only occasional reunion by the trio, none of which have succeeded i rekindling their former artistic fires.

● COMPILATIONS: *Hot Wax Greatest Hits* (H(Wax 1972) ★★★, *The Very Best Of The Invictt Years* (Deep Beats 1997) ★★★, *Invictu Unconquered: The Best Of Invictus Records Vol.* (Deep Beats 1998) ★★★, *Cherish What Is Dear T You: Invictus Unconquered Volume Two* (Dee Beats 1998) ★★★, *Molten Gold: The Best Of H(Wax Records* (Deep Beats 1998) ★★★, *Invictt Chartbusters* (Sequel 1999) ★★★, *Why Can't W Be Lovers* (Castle 2000) ★★★.

HOLLIES

Formed in Manchester, England, in 1962 b childhood friends Allan Clarke (b. Harold Alla Clarke, 5 April 1942, Salford, Lancashire

England; vocals), and Graham Nash (b. 2 February 1942, Blackpool, Lancashire, England; vocals/guitar). They had already been singing together locally for a number of years as a semi-professional duo under a number of names such as the Two Teens, the Levins, the Guytones, the Fourtones, and Ricky And Dane Young. They teamed up with Eric Haydock (b. 3 February 1942, Burnley, Lancashire, England; bass) to form the Deltas, and with the addition of Don Rathbone (drums) and the replacement of guitarist Vic Steele (b. Vic Farrell) by local guitar hero Tony Hicks (b. 16 December 1945, Nelson, Lancashire, England) from Ricky Shaw And The Dolphins, they became the Hollies. Almost immediately they were signed to the same label as the Beatles, the prestigious Parlophone Records. Their first two singles were covers of the Coasters' '(Ain't That) Just Like Me' and 'Searchin'. Both made the UK Top 30 in summer 1963 and the band set about recording their first album.

At the same time Rathbone left to become their road manager and was replaced by Bobby Elliott (b. 8 December 1942, Burnley, Lancashire, England; ex-Ricky Shaw And The Dolphins, Shane Fenton And The Fentones). The band's excellent live performances throughout Britain had already seasoned them for what was to become one of the longest beat group success stories in popular music. Their first two albums contained the bulk of their live act and both albums became long-time residents in the UK charts. Meanwhile, they were enjoying a train of singles hits that continued from 1963-74, and their popularity almost rivalled that of the Beatles and Rolling Stones. Infectious, well-produced hits such as Doris Troy's 'Just One Look', 'Here I Go Again' and the sublime 'Yes I Will' all contained their trademark soaring harmonies. The voices of Clarke, Hicks and Nash combined to make one of the most distinctive sounds to be heard in popular music. As their career progressed the aforementioned trio developed into a strong songwriting team, and wrote most of their own b-sides (under the pseudonym 'L. Ransford'). On their superb third collection, Hollies in 1965, their talents blossomed with 'Too Many People', an early song about over-population. Their first UK number 1 came in 1965 with 'I'm Alive' and was followed within weeks by Graham Gouldman's uplifting yet simple take 'Look Through Any Window'. By Christmas 1965 the band experienced their first lapse when their recording of George Harrison's 'If I Needed Someone' just scraped the UK Top 20 and brought with it some bad press. Both the Hollies and John Lennon took swipes at each other, venting frustration at the comparative failure of a Beatles song. Early in 1966, the band enjoyed a UK number 2 hit with 'I Can't Let Go', which topped the New Musical Express chart jointly with the Walker Brothers' 'The Sun Ain't Gonna

Shine Anymore'. 'I Can't Let Go', co-written by Chip Taylor and originally recorded by Evie Sands, had already appeared on the previous year's Hollies and was one of their finest recordings, combining soaring harmonies with some exceptionally strong, driving guitar work. The enigmatic and troublesome Eric Haydock was sacked in April 1966 and was replaced by Hicks former colleague in the Dolphins, Bernie Calvert (b. 16 September 1942, Nelson, Lancashire, England). The Hollies success continued unabated with Graham Gouldman's 'Bus Stop', the exotic 'Stop Stop Stop', and the poppier 'On A Carousel' and 'Carrie-Anne', all UK Top 5 hits, but also (at last) major Top 10 hits in the US Billboard chart. The Hollies were quick to join the 'flower power' bandwagon, as a more progressive feel had already pervaded their recent album, For Certain Because ..., but with Evolution, their beads and kaftans were everywhere. That same year (1967) the release of the excellent Butterfly showed signs of discontent. Inexplicably, the album failed to make the charts in either the UK or the US. It marked two distinct types of songs from the previously united team of Nash/Clarke/Hicks. On one hand there was a Clarke-influenced song, 'Charley And Fred', and on the other an obvious Nash composition like 'Butterfly'. Nash took a more ambitious route. His style was perfectly highlighted with the exemplary 'King Midas In Reverse', an imaginative song complete with brass and strings. It was, by Hollies standards, a surprising failure (UK number 18).

The following year during the proposals to make Hollies Sing Dylan, Nash announced his departure for Crosby, Stills And Nash. His replacement was Terry Sylvester (b. 8 January 1947, Liverpool, Merseyside, England) of the Escorts. Clarke was devastated by the departure of his friend of more than 20 years and after seven further hits, including the UK Top 5 hits 'Sorry Suzanne' and 'He Ain't Heavy, He's My Brother', decided to leave for a solo career. The band soldiered on with the strange induction of Mikael Rickfors (b. 4 December 1948, Sweden), who sang on Romany and Out On The Road, the latter only being released in Germany. In the USA the million-selling 'Long Cool Woman (In A Black Dress)' narrowly missed the top spot in 1972, ironic also because Allan Clarke was the vocalist on this older number taken from the successful album Distant Light.

Clarke returned in late 1973 after an abortive solo career which included two average albums, My Real Name Is 'Arold and Headroom. The return was celebrated with the worldwide hit, 'The Air That I Breathe', composed by Albert Hammond. Over the next five years the Hollies pursued the supper-club and cabaret circuit as their chart appearances began to dwindle. Although their albums were well produced they were largely unexciting and sold poorly. Clarke left the band in late 1977 to have another stab at a solo career, but rejoined in August 1978 to help record *Five Three One-Double Seven O Four*. In 1981, Sylvester and Calvert left the band, and Alan Coates (b. 26 June 1953, London, England) was drafted in on guitar. Sensing major problems ahead, EMI Records suggested they put together a Stars On 45-type segued single. The ensuing 'Holliedaze' was a UK Top 30 hit, and Graham Nash was flown over for the television promotion. Clarke, Nash, Hicks and Elliott reunited for 1983's *What Goes Around*, which included a minor US hit with the Supremes' 'Stop! In The Name Of Love'. The album was justifiably slammed by the critics, and only made the US charts because of Nash's association.

Following this, the Hollies went back to the oldies path with new members Denis Haines (keyboards) and Steve Stroud (bass). In 1985, Stroud was replaced by Ray Stiles (b. 20 November 1946, Guildford, Surrey, England; ex-Mud). In 1988, the use of 'He Ain't Heavy, He's My Brother' in a television commercial for Miller Lite lager prompted its reissue as a single. The song promptly shot to the top of the UK charts, although a reissue of 'The Air That I Breathe' was less successful. Ian Parker (b. 26 November 1953, Irvine, Ayrshire, England; keyboards) was recruited in 1990, and featured in the stable 90s line-up alongside Clarke, Elliott, Coates, Stiles, and the ever youthful Hicks. In 1993, the Hollies were given an Ivor Novello award in honour of their contribution to British music. Three years later Nash rejoined his old colleagues to help record a version of Buddy Holly's 'Peggy Sue Got Married' for a tribute album. In March 2000 it was announced that Carl Wayne (b. 18 August 1943, Birmingham, England; ex-Move) would be replacing Allan Clarke as lead singer, who had decided to retire. Their longevity is assured as their expertly crafted, harmonic songs represent some of the greatest music to emerge from the mid-60s pop scene.

● ALBUMS: *Stay With The Hollies* (Parlophone 1964) ★★★★, *Here I Go Again* US only (Imperial 1964) ★★★★, *In The Hollies Style* (Parlophone 1964) ★★★★, *Hollies* aka *Reflection* (Parlophone 1965) ★★★★, *Hear! Here!* US only (Imperial 1965) ★★★★, *Beat Group!* US only (Imperial 1966) ★★★★, *Would You Believe?* (Parlophone 1966) ★★★★, *Bus Stop* US only (Imperial 1966) ★★★★, *For Certain Because ... aka Stop! Stop! Stop!* (Parlophone 1966) ★★★★, *Stop! Stop! Stop!* US only (Imperial 1967) ★★★★, *Evolution* aka *The Hollies* (Parlophone/Epic 1967) ★★★, *Butterfly* (Parlophone 1967) ★★★, *Dear Eloise/King Midas In Reverse* US only (Epic 1967) ★★★, *The Hollies Sing Dylan* (UK) *Words And Music By Bob Dylan* (US) (Parlophone/Epic 1969) ★★, *Hollies Sing Hollies* (Parlophone 1969) ★★, *He Ain't Heavy, He's My Brother* US only (Epic 1969) ★★, *Confessions Of The Mind* (Parlophone 1970) ★★, *Moving Finger* US only (Epic 1970) ★★,

Distant Light (Parlophone/Epic 1971) ★★, *Romany* (Polydor/Epic 1972) ★★, *Out On The Road* (Hansa 1973) ★★, *Hollies* (Polydor/Epic 1974) ★★, *Another Night* (Polydor/Epic 1975) ★★, *Write On* (Polydor 1976) ★★, *Russian Roulette* (Polydor 1976) ★★, *Live Hits* (Polydor 1977) ★★, *Clarke, Hicks, Sylvester, Calvert, Elliott* US only (Epic 1977) ★★, *A Crazy Steal* (Polydor/Epic 1978) ★★, *Five Three One-Double Seven O Four* (Polydor 1979) ★★, *Buddy Holly* (Polydor 1980) ★★, *What Goes Around* (WEA/Atlantic 1983) ★★.

● COMPILATIONS: *The Hollies' Greatest Hits* US only (Imperial 1967) ★★★★, *Hollies' Greatest* (Parlophone 1968) ★★★★, *Hollies' Greatest Vol. 2* (Parlophone 1972) ★★★, *The Hollies' Greatest Hits* US only (Epic 1973) ★★★★, *The Very Best Of The Hollies* US only (United Artists 1975) ★★★, *The History Of The Hollies* (EMI 1975) ★★★, *The Hollies Volume 1* US only (Realm 1976) ★★★, *Everything You Always Wanted To Hear By The Hollies But Were Afraid To Ask* US only (Epic 1977) ★★★, *20 Golden Greats* (EMI 1978) ★★★★, *The Best Of The Hollies EP's* (Parlophone 1978) ★★★★, *The Other Side Of The Hollies* (Parlophone 1978) ★★★, *Up Front* (St. Michael 1979) ★★★, *Long Cool Woman In A Black Dress* (MFP 1979) ★★★, *Hollies' Greatest* US only (Capitol 1980) ★★★, *The Air That I Breathe* (Polydor 1980) ★★★, *The Hollies* (MFP 1985) ★★★, *Not The Hits Again* (See For Miles 1986) ★★★★, *All The Hits And More: The Definitive Collection* (EMI 1988) ★★★★, *Rarities* (EMI 1988) ★★★★, *The Hollies* US only (CBS 1989) ★★★, *Love Songs* (MFP 1990) ★★★, *The Hollies Epic Anthology* US only (Epic 1990) ★★★★, *The Air That I Breathe: The Best Of The Hollies* (EMI 1993) ★★★, *30th Anniversary Collection 1963-1993* 3-CD box set (EMI 1993) ★★★★, *Singles A's And B's 1970-1979* (MFP 1993) ★★★★, *Four Hollies Originals* 4-CD box set (EMI 1994) ★★★, *Legendary Top Tens 1963-1988* (Avon 1994) ★★★, *The Best Of The Hollies* (MFP 1995) ★★★, *Four More Hollies Originals* 4-CD box set (EMI 1996) ★★★, *20 Classic Tracks* (EMI 1996) ★★★, *The Best Of The Hollies* (EMI 1997) ★★★★, *At Abbey Road 1963 To 1966* (EMI 1997) ★★★★, *A Special Collection* 3-CD box set (MFP 1997) ★★★, *At Abbey Road 1966 To 1970* (EMI 1998) ★★★★, *The Essential Collection* (MFP 1998) ★★★, *At Abbey Road 1973 To 1989* (EMI 1998) ★★★, *Orchestra Heaven* (EMI 2000) ★★.

● FILMS: *It's All Over Town* (1964).

HOLLOWAY, BRENDA

b. 21 June 1946, Atascadero, California, USA. Brenda Holloway began her recording career with three small Los Angeles labels, Donna, Catch and Minasa, in the early 60s, recording under the aegis of producer Hal Davis. In 1964 Holloway made an impromptu performance at a disc jockeys' convention in California, where she was spotted by a Motown Records talent scout. She signed to the label later that year

becoming its first west coast artist. Her initial Tamla single, 'Every Little Bit Hurts', established her bluesy soul style, and was quickly covered by the Spencer Davis Group in Britain. She enjoyed further success in 1964 with 'I'll Always Love You', and the following year with 'When I'm Gone' and 'Operator'. Her consistent record sales led to her winning a place on the Beatles' 1965 US tour, but subsequent Tamla singles proved less successful. Holloway began to devote increasing time to her songwriting, forming a regular writing partnership with her sister Patrice, and Motown staff producer Frank Wilson. This combination produced her 1968 single 'You've Made Me So Very Happy', a song that proved more successful via the million-selling cover version by the jazz-rock group Blood, Sweat And Tears. In 1968, Holloway's contract with Motown was terminated. The label issued a press release stating that the singer wished to sing for God, although Holloway blamed business differences for the split. She released a gospel album in 1983 and worked with Ian Levine from 1987. She teamed with Jimmy Ruffin in 1989 for a duet, 'On The Rebound', and from time to time returns to the studio to record a new album.
● ALBUMS: *Every Little Bit Hurts* (Tamla 1964) ★★★, *The Artistry Of Brenda Holloway* (Motown 1968) ★★★, *Together* (KRL 1999) ★★★.
● COMPILATIONS: *Greatest Hits & Rare Classics* (Motown 1991) ★★★, *The Very Best Of Brenda Holloway* (Motown 1999) ★★★★.

HOLY MODAL ROUNDERS

Peter Stampfel (b. 1938, Wauwautosa, Wisconsin, USA) and Steve Weber (b. 1942, Philadelphia, Pennsylvania, USA). This on-off partnership was first established in New York's Greenwich Village. The two musicians shared a passion for old-time music and unconventional behaviour, and together they created some of the era's most distinctive records. The duo completed their debut album, *The Holy Modal Rounders* in 1963. It contained several of their finest moments, including the influential 'Blues In The Bottle', which the Lovin' Spoonful, among others, later recorded. The Rounders' second collection, although less satisfying, continued the same cross-section of 20s/30s-styled country and blues. Having accompanied the Fugs on their early releases, Stampfel and Weber broke up; the former began writing for 'alternative' publications. The musicians were reunited in 1967 to complete the experimental, but flawed, *Indian War Whoop*. This often incoherent collection also featured drummer Sam Shepard, an off-Broadway playwright from a parallel Stampfel venture, the Moray Eels. The amalgamation of the two groups led to another album, *The Moray Eels Eat The Holy Modal Rounders*, which was a marked improvement on its predecessor. It featured the sweeping 'Bird Song', later immortalized in the movie *Easy*

Rider. Shepard left the Rounders in 1970, from where he became a successful writer and actor. Three albums of varying quality were then completed until the group, which suffered a plethora of comings and goings, ground to a halt in 1977. Weber and Stampfel were reunited three years later. *Goin' Nowhere Fast* was an excellent set, evocative of the duo's first recordings together, but their revitalized relationship proved temporary. The latter later worked with an all-new group, Pete Stampfel And The Bottlecaps. Another reunion took place in 1996, leading to the warmly received *Too Much Fun!*
● ALBUMS: *The Holy Modal Rounders* (Folklore 1964) ★★★, *The Holy Modal Rounders 2* (Prestige 1965) ★★, *Indian War Whoop* (ESP 1967) ★★, *The Moray Eels Eat The Holy Modal Rounders* (Elektra 1968) ★★★, *Good Taste Is Timeless* (Metromedia 1971) ★★, *Alleged In Their Own Time* (Rounder 1975) ★★, *Last Round* (Adelphi 1978) ★★, as Stampfel And Weber *Goin' Nowhere Fast* (Rounder 1981) ★★★★, *Too Much Fun!* (Rounder 1999) ★★★.
● COMPILATIONS: *I Make A Wish For A Potato* (Rounder 2001) ★★★★.

HONEYBUS

Originally managed by one-time Them drummer Terry Noon, Honeybus was a vehicle for minor hit songwriters Pete Dello and Ray Cane. Following the recruitment of Colin Hare (vocals/guitar) and Peter Kircher (drums), the group was signed to the hip Decca Records subsidiary Deram Records. Their second single, 'Do I Still Figure In Your Life', with its plaintive lyric and striking string arrangement, received extensive airplay but narrowly failed to reach the Top 50. The similarly paced 'I Can't Let Maggie Go' fared better, entering the charts in March 1968 and peaking at number 8. Rather than exploiting the group's success, however, Dello dramatically left Honeybus only months later. Deprived of their main songwriter and gifted arranger, the group failed to escape the one-hit-wonder trap, but almost broke through with 'Girl Of Independent Means'. After advice from their management they folded in 1969. The post-demise release, *Story* (1970), testifies to their fledgling talent. Their single moment of chart glory was later resurrected as the long-running theme for a UK television bread commercial.
● ALBUMS: *Story* (Deram 1970) ★★★.
● COMPILATIONS: *At Their Best* (See For Miles 1989) ★★★, *The Honeybus Story* (Repertoire 1999) ★★★.

HONEYCOMBS

Formed in north London in November 1963, the group was originally known as the Sherabons and comprised: Denis D'ell (b. Denis Dalziel, 10 October 1943, London, England; vocals), Anne 'Honey' Lantree (b. 28 August 1943, Hayes, Middlesex, England; drums), John Lantree (b. 20

August 1940, Newbury, Berkshire, England; bass), Alan Ward (b. 12 December 1945, Nottingham, England; lead guitar) and Martin Murray (rhythm guitar), later replaced by Peter Pye (b. 12 July 1946, London, England). Producer Joe Meek had selected one of their songs as a possible single and the group's chances were enhanced following a management agreement with Ken Howard and Alan Blaikley. Although several record companies passed on the quintet's debut, 'Have I The Right', Pye Records' managing director Louis Benjamin agreed to release the disc. First, however, there was the obligatory name change, with Benjamin selecting Honeycombs after a track by Jimmie Rodgers. The fact that the focus of attention in the group was the red-haired drummer 'Honey' made the renaming even more appropriate. When 'Have I The Right' hit number 1 in the UK in the summer of 1964, the group's pop star future seemed assured. However, a dramatic flop with the follow-up 'Is It Because' caused concern, and although Howard and Blaikley came to the rescue with 'That's The Way', the group faltered amid line-up changes and poor morale, before moving inexorably towards cabaret and the revivalist circuit.

● ALBUMS: *The Honeycombs* (Pye 1964) ★★★, *All Systems Go* (Pye 1965) ★★★, *Here Are The Honeycombs* (Vee Jay 1964) ★★★.
● COMPILATIONS: *Meek And Honey* (PRT 1983) ★★★, *It's The Honeycombs/All Systems Go* (Sequel 1990) ★★★, *The Best Of The Honeycombs* (Sequel 1993) ★★★.

HOOKER, JOHN LEE

b. 22 August 1917, Clarksdale, Mississippi, USA, d. 21 June 2001, Los Altos, California, USA. Dates vary between 1917 to 1920, but due to the age of Hooker's mother when he was born, 1917 is the most likely. He was born into a large family, of between 10 and 12 siblings, who all worked on the fields of a large tenanted agricultural farm. Hooker's first musical experiences, like those of so many other blues singers, were in church. A contrivance made from an inner tube attached to a barn door represented his first makeshift attempts at playing an instrument, but he subsequently learned some guitar from his stepfather William Moore, and they played together at local dances. At the age of 14, he ran away to Memphis, Tennessee, where he met and played with Robert Lockwood.

Two years later he moved to Cincinnati, where he stayed for about 10 years and sang with a number of gospel quartets. In 1943, he moved to Detroit, which was to be his home for many years, and while working during the day as a janitor began playing at night in the blues clubs and bars around Hastings Street, at the heart of that city's black section. Over the years he had developed the unique guitar style that was to make his music so distinctive and compelling. In 1948 he was finally given the chance to record.

Accompanied only by his own electric guitar and constantly tapping foot, 'Boogie Chillen', with its driving rhythm and hypnotic drone of an accompaniment, was a surprise commercial success for Modern Records. The record is rumoured to have sold over a million copies, but this is contested by Hooker as it did not tally with his royalty statement. Over the next few years, they leased a large amount of his material first from Bernie Besman and later from legendary Detroit entrepreneur Joe Von Battle (both of whom also tried a few Hooker issues on their own Sensation and JVB labels, respectively).

Most of these early recordings feature Hooker performing entirely solo; only a few are duets with Eddie Kirkland or another guitarist, and there are one or two with a band. It seems that this solo setting was not typical of his live work at the time, which would have used a small band, probably including piano, second guitar and drums, but his idiosyncratic sense of timing always made him a difficult musician to accompany, and it may be that recording him solo was the most reliable way of ensuring a clean take. Nevertheless, his solo sound on these early records was remarkably self-sufficient. His unique open-tuned guitar enabled him to combine a steady rhythm with inspired lead picking, thereby making full use of his rich, very bluesy baritone vocals. Although this one-man-band format might suggest a throwback to a more down-home ambience, there is a certain hipness and urbane sophistication about these performances that represent a significant departure from the rural background of Hooker's music and contribute very strongly to his characteristic sound. While a solo blues singer was something of an anachronism by this time, there is no doubt that the records sold consistently.

From the late 40s to the early 50s, Hooker recorded prolifically and enjoyed an enormously successful run with Modern, producing such classic records as 'Crawling King Snake', 'In The Mood', 'Rock House Boogie' and 'Shake Holler & Run'. Hooker became increasingly unhappy with the lack of financial reward for his recordings which appeared to sell well. He decided to moonlight, and recorded under a number of different names. Hooker's voice and style of playing is unmistakable and fans had no problem in sussing him out. With tongue firmly in cheek among the many names he adopted were; John Lee Booker, John Lee Cooker, Johnny Williams, Delta John, Sir John Lee Hooker, Little Pork Chops, Texas Slim, Birmingham Sam, John Lee, Boogie Man, Johnny Lee, and John L. Booker. Most of these were also leased from Joe Von Battle.

Hooker's recording success led to tours. He played the R&B circuit across the country and this further developed his popularity with the black American public. In 1955, he severed his connection with Modern and began a long association with Vee Jay Records of Chicago. By his time, the solo format was finally deemed too old-fashioned for the contemporary R&B market and all of these recordings used a tight little band, often including Eddie Taylor on guitar, as well as piano and various combinations of horns. The association with Vee Jay proved very satisfactory, both artistically and commercially, producing a string of hits such as the simplistic but brilliant 'Dimples', 'Maudie' and 'Boom Boom' and promoting further extensive tours. In the late 50s, as the market for R&B was beginning to contract, a new direction opened up for Hooker and he began to appear regularly at folk clubs and folk festivals. He found himself ionized by a new audience consisting mainly of young, white listeners. The folk connection also resulted in new recordings, issued on album by Riverside Records, which reverted to the solo acoustic format. While these recordings lacked the hard edge of the best of his earlier commercial sides, they were fascinating for the fact that the producers encouraged him to dig back into his older repertoire. Several songs reflecting his rural Mississippi background, such as 'Bundle Up And Go' and 'Pea Vine Special' were given his distinctive treatment. These records spread his name more widely when they were released overseas.

In the early 60s his reputation grew considerably as he was often cited by younger pop and rock musicians, in particular the Animals and the Rolling Stones, as a major influence. As a result international tours soon followed. Throughout this period, he continued to release singles and albums on Vee Jay, but records also appeared on other labels. Later in the 60s, he made a number of records for Bluesway, aimed at this younger market. The connection with a new generation of musicians led to various 'super sessions', predictably of varying quality, but bearing fruit most successfully in the early 70s with the release of the stunning Hooker 'N' Heat, in which he played with the American rock blues band Canned Heat. Their famous long improvised boogies clearly owed a great deal to the influence of the older man.

Although the popular enthusiasm for blues waned for a while in the late 70s and early 80s, Hooker's standing rarely faltered and he continued to tour, latterly with the Coast To Coast Blues Band. His early recordings were repackaged and re-released over and over again, with those companies who used him pseudonymously in the early days now proudly taking the opportunity to capitalize on his real name. A remarkable transformation came in 1989 when Hooker recorded The Healer. This superb album featured stellar guest artists on most tracks, including Bonnie Raitt (who is on record as saying that Hooker's guitar sound is one of the most erotic things she has ever heard), Los Lobos, and a duet with Carlos Santana on the title cut. If such a thing as 'Latin blues' existed, this was it. The Healer has gone on to become one of the biggest-selling blues records of all time, and by prompting other older statesmen to record again helped fuel a new blues revival. The 1991 follow-up Mr Lucky reached number 3 in the UK album charts, setting a record for Hooker, at 74, as the oldest artist to achieve that position. On this second guest album he was paired with Ry Cooder, Van Morrison, Albert Collins, and a gamut of other superstars. In his old age, Hooker had begun to fulfil the role of elder statesman of the blues, even appearing in an advertisement for a multinational chemical corporation. The Hooker revival continued right through 1992 with the use of a new version of 'Boom Boom' for a Lee Jeans television advertisement. Both the single and the subsequent album were considerable hits.

Following a hernia operation in 1994 the great man decided to slow down and enjoy his cars and houses. Another fine release, Chill Out, came in 1995. Shortly after its release it was announced that Hooker had retired from performing and was prepared to rest until they 'lowered his bones into the earth'. However, he was back on stage performing in 1996 and released a new album in 1997. Don't Look Back was a Van Morrison production and bore clear signs of his influence; Morrison's 'The Healing Game' and Jimi Hendrix's 'Red House' were the highlights, and 'Don't Look Back' was beautifully understated, with some fine noodling organ and guitar from Charles Brown and Danny Caron respectively. Another reworking of 'Dimples' added nothing to the classic Vee Jay recording. Three years later, Hooker's voice and guitar were cleverly sampled by Ludovic Navarre on the St Germain track, 'Sure Thing'.

Hooker's discography is an absolute minefield; so many tracks have been licensed and re-licensed by so many different labels and much of his regular catalogue is in fact a series of compilations. Goldmine magazine (March 1992) is the best attempt so far. Dozens of his songs have also been issued under alternative titles, with only slight changes in the lyrics. Charles Shaar Murray's labour of love, Boogie Man, is the definitive book on Hooker. This highly readable biography does not patronise one of the key figures of post-war blues, but objectively celebrates and respects the man's massive contribution to his art. Hooker's remarkable voice came from deep within, it was hollow and creamy with a brittle edge. To hear him sing solo (as on 1976's superb Alone) gives the listener an indication of how true he was to his art. This formidable 'cool dude' was the last surviving giant of the real delta folk blues, and therefore, represented a final touchstone with a body of music that is both rich in history and unmatched in its importance. It is a fitting tribute to the

great man that he died peacefully in his sleep.
● ALBUMS: with Sticks McGhee *Highways Of Blues* (Audio Lab 1959) ★★, *The Folk Blues Of John Lee Hooker* (Riverside 1959) ★★★★, *I'm John Lee Hooker* (Vee Jay 1959) ★★★★, *Travelin'* (Vee Jay 1960) ★★★★, *Sings The Blues* (King 1960) ★★★★, *Thats My Story* (Riverside 1960) ★★★★, *House Of The Blues* (Chess 1960) ★★★★, *The Blues* (Crown 1960) ★★★, *The Country Blues Of John Lee Hooker* (Riverside 1960) ★★★★, *The Folk Lore Of John Lee Hooker* (Vee Jay 1961) ★★★★, *Burnin'* (Vee Jay 1962) ★★★, *John Lee Hooker On Campus* (Vee Jay 1963) ★★★, *The Great John Lee Hooker* (Crown 1963) ★★, *The Big Soul Of John Lee Hooker* (Vee Jay 1963) ★★★, *Don't Turn Me From Your Door* (Atco 1963) ★★★, *John Lee Hooker At Newport* (Vee Jay 1964) ★★★★, *Burning Hell* (Riverside/Fontana 1964) ★★★★, *I Want To Shout The Blues* (Stateside 1964) ★★★, *John Lee Hooker And Seven Nights* (Verve/Folkways 1965) ★★★, *Real Folk Blues* (Chess 1966) ★★★★, *It Serve You Right To Suffer* (Impulse! 1966) ★★★, *Live At The Cafe Au Go Go* (Bluesway 1966) ★★★★, *Urban Blues* (Bluesway 1967) ★★★, *Simply The Truth* (Bluesway 1968) ★★★, *You're Leaving Me Baby* (Riverside 1969) ★★★★, *Tupelo Blues* (Riverside 1969), with Earl Hooker *If You Miss 'Im ... I Got 'Im* (Bluesway 1970) ★★★, *Moanin' And Stompin' Blues* (King 1970) ★★★, *That's Where It's At* (Stax 1969) ★★, with Canned Heat *Hooker 'N' Heat* (Liberty 1971) ★★★★, *Endless Boogie* (ABC 1971) ★★★, *Never Get Out Of These Blues Alive* (ABC 1972) ★★★, *Live At Soledad Prison* (ABC 1972) ★★★★, *John Lee Hooker's Detroit* (United Artists 1973) ★★★, *Live At Kabuki Wuki* (Bluesway 1973) ★★, *Mad Man's Blues* (Chess 1973) ★★★, *John Lee Hooker With The Groundhogs* (New World 1973) ★★, *Born In Mississippi, Raised Up In Tennessee* (ABC 1973) ★★, *Whiskey And Wimmen* (Trip 1973) ★★, *Slim's Stomp* (Polydor 1973) ★★, *Mad Man's Blues* (Chess 1973) ★★★, *Free Beer And Chicken* (ABC 1974) ★★, *Blues Before Sunrise* (Bulldog 1976) ★★★, *Alone* (Tomato 1976) ★★★★, *No Friend Around* (Charly 1979) ★★, *This Is Hip* (Charly 1980) ★★★, *Black Snake Blues* (Fantasy 1980) ★★★, *Moanin' The Blues* (Charly 1982) ★★★, *Lonesome Mood* (MCA 1983) ★★★, *Solid Sender* (Charly 1984) ★★, *Jealous* (Pointblank 1986) ★★★, *The Healer* (Chameleon 1989) ★★★★★, *The Detroit Lion* (Demon 1990) ★★, *Boogie Awhile* (Krazy Kat 1990) ★★★, *More Real Folk Blues: The Missing Album* (Chess 1991) ★★★★, *Mr Lucky* (Charisma 1991) ★★★★, *Boom Boom* (Pointblank 1992) ★★★, *Chill Out* (Pointblank 1995) ★★★★, with the Groundhogs *Hooker & The Hogs* 1965 recording (Indigo 1996) ★★, *The First Concert – Alone* 1976 recording (Blues Alliance 1996) ★★★, *Don't Look Back* (Silvertone 1997) ★★★, *The Unknown John Lee Hooker* (Interstate 2000) ★★★.
● COMPILATIONS: *The Best Of John Lee Hooker* (Vee Jay 1962) ★★★, *Collection: John Lee Hooker*

– 20 Blues Greats (Déjà Vu 1985) ★★★, *The Ultimate Collection 1948-1990* (Rhino 1992) ★★★★, *The Best Of John Lee Hooker 1965 To 1974* (MCA 1992) ★★★★, *Blues Brother: Sensation Recordings* (Ace 1992) ★★★★, *The Legendary Modern Recordings 1948-54* (Ace 1993) ★★★★, *Helpless Blues* (Realisation 1994) ★★★, *Original Folk Blues ... Plus* (Ace 1994) ★★★★, *The Rising Sun Collection* (Just A Memory 1994) ★★★, *Live At The Café Au Go Go (And Soledad Prison)* (MCA 1996) ★★★★, *The EP Collection Plus* (See For Miles 1995) ★★★, *The Early Years* (Tomato 1995) ★★★★, *I Feel Good* (Jewel 1995) ★★★, *Alternative Boogie: Early Studio Recordings 1948-1952* (Capitol 1996) ★★★, *The Complete 50's Chess Recordings* (Chess 1998) ★★★★, *Best Of Friends* (Pointblank 1998) ★★★★, *House Rent Boogie* (Ace 2001) ★★★, *Boogie Chillen: The Essential Recordings Of John Lee Hooker* (Indigo 2001) ★★★.
● VIDEOS: *Survivors – The Blues Today* (Hendring Music Video 1989), *John Lee Hooker/Lowell Fulson/Percy Mayfield* (1992), *John Lee Hooker And Friends 1984-1992* (Vestapol Video 1996), *Rare Performances 1960-1984* (Vestapol Video 1996).
● FURTHER READING: *Boogie Chillen: A Guide To John Lee Hooker On Disc*, Les Fancourt. *Boogie Man: The Adventures Of John Lee Hooker In The American Twentieth Century*, Charles Shaar Murray.
● FILMS: *The Blues Brothers* (1980).

HOPKIN, MARY

b. 3 May 1950, Pontardawe, Glamorganshire, Wales. Hopkin's career began while she was still a schoolgirl. Briefly a member of a local folk rock band, she completed several Welsh language releases before securing a slot on the televised talent show, *Opportunity Knocks*. Fashion model Twiggy was so impressed by Hopkin's performance she recommended the singer to Paul McCartney as a prospective signing for the newly formed Apple label. 'Those Were The Days', a traditional song popularized by Gene Raskin of the Limelighters, was selected as the artist's national debut and this haunting, melancholic recording, produced by McCartney, topped both the UK and US charts in 1968. Her follow-up single, 'Goodbye' reached number 2 the following year, but despite its excellent versions of Donovan's 'Happiness Runs' and 'Lord Of The Reedy River', the concurrent *Post Card* showed a singer constrained by often inappropriate material. Nevertheless, the Mickie Most-produced 'Temma Harbour' was another Top 10 hit, while 'Knock Knock Who's There', Britain's entry to the 1970 Eurovision Song Contest, peaked at number 2. 'Think About Your Children', penned by Most protégés Hot Chocolate, was Hopkin's last Top 20 entry, as the singer became increasingly unhappy over the style of her releases. However, a second album *Earth*

Song/Ocean Song, was more representative of Hopkin's talent, and sympathetic contributions from Ralph McTell and Danny Thompson enhanced its enchanting atmosphere. Paradoxically, the set was issued as her contract with Apple expired and, having married producer Tony Visconti, she retired temporarily from recording.

Hopkin resumed her career in 1972 with 'Mary Had A Baby' and enjoyed a minor hit four years later with 'If You Love Me'. The singer also added backing vocals on several sessions, notably David Bowie's Sound And Vision, before joining Mike Hurst (ex-Springfields) and Mike D'Albuquerque (ex-Electric Light Orchestra) in Sundance. Having left this short-lived aggregation, Hopkin resurfaced in 1983 as a member of Oasis (not the UK indie band). Peter Skellern and Julian Lloyd Webber were also members of this act which enjoyed a Top 30 album, but was brought to a premature end when Hopkin was struck by illness. Her subsequent work includes an appearance on George Martin's production of Under Milk Wood, but she remains indelibly linked to her million-selling debut hit.

● ALBUMS: Post Card (Apple 1969) ★★, Earth Song/Ocean Song (Apple 1971) ★★, Those Were The Days (Apple 1972) ★★, The King Of Elfland's Daughter (Chrysalis 1977) ★★, with George Martin Under Milk Wood (EMI 1988) ★★★.

● COMPILATIONS: The Welsh World Of Mary Hopkin (Decca 1979) ★★, Those Were The Days: The Best Of Mary Hopkin (EMI 1995) ★★, Early Recordings (MSI 1998) ★★.

HOPKINS, LIGHTNIN'

b. Sam Hopkins, 15 March 1912, Centreville, Texas, USA, d. 30 January 1982, Houston, Texas, USA. One of the last great country blues singers, Hopkins' lengthy career began in the Texas bars and juke joints of the 20s. Towards the end of the decade he formed a duo with a cousin, Texas Alexander, while his Lightnin' epithet was derived from a subsequent partnership with barrelhouse pianist Thunder Smith, with whom he made his first recordings. Hopkins' early work unveiled a masterly performer. His work first came to prominence when, after being discovered by Sam Charters at the age of 47, The Roots Of Lightnin' Hopkins was released in 1959 and numerous sessions followed. His sparse acoustic guitar and narrated prose quickly made him an important discovery, appealing to the audience of the American folk boom of the early 60s. His harsh, emotive voice and compulsive, if irregular, guitar playing, conveyed an intensity enhanced by the often personal nature of his lyrics.

He became one of post-war blues most prolific talents, completing hundreds of sessions for scores of major and independent labels. This inevitably diluted his initial power, but although Hopkins' popularity slumped in the face of Chicago's electric combos, by the early 60s he was re-established as a major force on the college and concert-hall circuit. In 1967 the artist was the subject of an autobiographical film, The Blues Of Lightnin' Hopkins, which subsequently won the Gold Hugo award at the Chicago Film Festival. Like many other bluesmen finding great success in the 60s (for example, Muddy Waters and John Lee Hooker), he too recorded a 'progressive' electric album: The Great Electric Show And Dance. During the 70s he toured the USA, Canada and, in 1977, Europe, until ill health forced him to reduce such commitments. Hopkins was a true folk poet, embracing social comments with pure blues. He died in 1982, his status as one of the major voices of the blues assured.

● ALBUMS: Strums The Blues (Score 1958) ★★★★, Lightnin' And The Blues (Herald 1959) ★★★, The Roots Of Lightnin' Hopkins (Folkways 1959) ★★★, Down South Summit Meeting (1960) ★★★★, Mojo Hand (Fire 1960) ★★★★, Country Blues (Tradition 1960) ★★★, Lightnin' In New York (Candid 1961) ★★★, Autobiography In Blues (Tradition 1961) ★★★, Lightnin' (Bluesville 1961) ★★★, with Sonny Terry Last Night Blues (Bluesville 1961) ★★★★, Blues In My Bottle (Bluesville 1962) ★★★★, Lightnin' Strikes Again (Dart 1962) ★★★, Sings The Blues (Crown 1962) ★★★, Lightnin' Hopkins (Folkways 1962) ★★★★, Fast Life Woman (Verve 1962) ★★★, On Stage (Imperial 1962) ★★, Walkin' This Street (Bluesville 1962) ★★★★, Lightnin' And Co (Bluesville 1963) ★★★, Smokes Like Lightnin' (Bluesville 1963) ★★★, First Meetin' (World Pacific 1963) ★★★, Lightnin' And The Blues (Imperial 1963) ★★★, Goin' Away (Bluesville 1963) ★★★, Hootin' The Blues (Folklore 1964) ★★★, Down Home Blues (Bluesville 1964) ★★★★, The Roots Of Lightnin' Hopkins (Verve/Folkways 1965) ★★★★, Soul Blues (Prestige 1966) ★★★, Something Blue (Verve/Folkways 1967) ★★★, Free Form Patterns (International Artists 1968) ★★★, California Mudslide (Vault/Rhino 1969) ★★★.

● COMPILATIONS: Legacy Of The Blues Volume Twelve (Sonet 1974) ★★★★, The Best Of Lightnin' Hopkins (Tradition 1964) ★★★, The Gold Star Sessions – Volumes 1&2 (Arhoolie 1990) ★★★★, The Complete Prestige/Bluesville Recordings 7-CD box set (Prestige/Bluesville 1992) ★★★★, The Complete Aladdin Recordings (EMI 1992) ★★★★, Sittin' In With Lightnin' Hopkins (Mainstream 1992) ★★★, Mojo Hand: The Lightnin' Hopkins Anthology (Rhino 1993) ★★★★, Coffee House Blues 1960-62 recordings (Charly 1993) ★★★★, Po' Lightnin' (Arhoolie 1995) ★★★★, Blue Lightnin' (Jewel 1995) ★★★, Hootin' The Blues (Prestige 1995) ★★★★, The Rising Sun Collection (Just A Memory 1995) ★★★★, Autobiography In Blues (Tradition 1996) ★★★★, Country Blues (Tradition 1996) ★★★★, Shake It Baby (Javelin 1996) ★★★, Jake Head Boogie (Ace 1999) ★★★, The Remaining Titles Vol 1: 1950-1961 (Document

1999) ★★★★, *Rainy Day In Houston* (Indigo 2000) ★★★★, *Lightnin' And The Blues: The Herald Sessions* (Buddha 2001) ★★★.
● VIDEOS: *Rare Performances 1960-1979* (Vestapol 1995).
● FURTHER READING: *Lightnin' Hopkins: Blues*, M. McCormick.

HOUR GLASS
Formed in Decatur, Alabama, USA, in 1967 from the ashes of the Allman Joys, the group was fronted by Gregg Allman (b. Gregory Lenoir Allman, 8 December 1947, Nashville, Tennessee, USA; vocals/organ) and his brother Duane Allman (b. 20 November 1946, Nashville, Tennessee, USA, d. 29 October 1971, Macon, Georgia, USA; guitar). Paul Hornsby (keyboards), Mabron McKinney (bass) and Johnny Sandlin completed the original line-up, 'discovered' playing juke-box favourites by the Nitty Gritty Dirt Band and their manager, Bill McEwan. The Hour Glass then moved to California, where they became a popular live attraction. Although their debut album consisted largely of pop/soul cover versions, it did include 'Cast Off All My Fears', an early Jackson Browne composition. However, the set was essentially a vehicle for Gregg's voice, and with session musicians replacing the group proper, the results bore no relation to the quintet's own ambitions. Jesse Willard Carr replaced McKinney for *Power Of Love*, in which several 'southern' soul songs vied with group originals. Once again the album failed to capture their full potential and in a final act of defiance, the Hour Glass booked themselves into the fabled Fame studios, where they completed a searing B.B. King medley. When their label rejected the master as unsuitable, the quintet decided to go their separate ways. Gregg and Duane later formed the Allman Brothers Band, an act later produced by Johnny Sandlin. Hornsby became manager of the group's Capricorn Sound studios while Carr enjoyed a lucrative session career.
● ALBUMS: *Hour Glass* (Liberty 1967) ★★, *The Power Of Love* (Liberty 1968) ★★.
● COMPILATIONS: *Hour Glass 1967-1969* (1973) ★★, *The Soul Of Time* (1985) ★★, *The Best Of The Hour Glass* (EMI 2000) ★★.

HOUSTON, CISSY
b. Emily Drinkard, 1933, Newark, New Jersey, USA. Houston's singing career began in a family gospel group, the Drinkard Singers, which also featured her nieces Dee Dee and Dionne Warwick. The trio was later employed as backing singers for many artists, including Solomon Burke and Wilson Pickett. While Dionne began recording as a solo artist, Houston continued this backroom work. Between 1967 and 1970 she was lead vocalist with the Sweet Inspirations, an impressive quartet who sang on countless releases, primarily for Atlantic Records. Houston's subsequent solo releases included 'I'll Be There' (1970), 'Be My Baby' (1971) and 'Think It Over' (1978), but her career failed to match expectations and was later eclipsed by the success of her daughter Whitney Houston. Cissy has now returned chiefly to the gospel fold, as a major figure in the New Hope Baptist Church Choir of Newark, New Jersey, although in 1992 she shared a secular Shanachie CD with Chuck Jackson.
● ALBUMS: *Presenting Cissy Houston* (Major Minor 1970) ★★★, *The Long And Winding Road* (Pye 1971) ★★, *Cissy Houston* (Private Stock 1977) ★★★, *Think It Over* (Private Stock 1978) ★★, *Warning – Danger* (Private Stock 1979) ★★, *Step Aside For A Lady* (EMI 1980) ★★, with Chuck Jackson *I'll Take Care Of You* (Shanachie 1992) ★★, *Face To Face* (House Of Blues 1996) ★★★, *He Leadeth Me* (House Of Blues 1998) ★★.
● COMPILATIONS: *Mama's Cookin'* (Charly 1987) ★★★, *Midnight Train To Georgia: The Janus Years* (Ichiban 1995) ★★★, *Definitive Collection* (Connoisseur 2000) ★★★.

HOUSTON, THELMA
Thelma Houston left her home town of Leland, Mississippi, USA, in the late 60s to tour with the gospel group the Art Reynolds Singers. Her impassioned vocal style and innate mastery of phrasing brought her to the attention of the prodigal writer/arranger Jimmy Webb in 1969. He composed and produced *Sunshower*, a remarkable song cycle that also included an adaptation of the Rolling Stones' 'Jumping Jack Flash'. The album transcended musical barriers, mixing the fluency of jazz with the passion of soul, and offering Houston the chance to bite into a sophisticated, witty set of lyrics. *Sunshower* won great critical acclaim, and helped her to secure a contract with Motown Records. Initially, the company made inadequate use of her talents, failing to provide material that would stretch her vocal capacities to the full. The stasis was broken in 1976 when Houston reworked 'Don't Leave Me This Way', previously a hit for Harold Melvin And The Bluenotes. Her disco interpretation brought a refreshing touch of class to the genre, and achieved impressive sales on both sides of the Atlantic.
Ever enthusiastic to repeat a winning formula, Motown made several attempts to reproduce the verve of the hit single. Houston issued a series of interesting, if slightly predictable, albums in the late 70s, and also collaborated on two efforts with Jerry Butler, in an attempt to echo Motown's great duets of the 60s. The results were consistent sellers among the black audience, without ever threatening to rival Houston's earlier pop success. A switch to RCA Records failed to alter her fortunes. Houston enjoyed wider exposure in the late 70s with film roles in *Death Scream*, *Norman ... Is That You?* and *The Seventh Dwarf*, and for a while it seemed as if acting would become her main source of

mployment. She retired from recording during he mid-80s, re-emerging in 1987 on MCA with a ritically acclaimed but commercially isappointing album. An album for Reprise ecords in 1990 suffered the same fate. Iouston's inconsistent chart record over the last wo decades belies the impressive calibre of her ocal talents.

● ALBUMS: *Sunshower* (Stateside 1969) ★★, *helma Houston* (Mowest 1973) ★★, *Anyway ou Like It* (Tamla 1976) ★★, with Jerry Butler *helma And Jerry* (Motown 1977) ★★, *The Devil n Me* (Tamla 1977) ★★, with Butler *Two To One* Motown 1978) ★★, *Ready To Roll* (Tamla 1978) ★★, *Ride To The Rainbow* (Tamla 1979) ★★, *reakwater Cat* (RCA 1980) ★★, *Never Gonna Be nother One* (RCA 1981) ★★, *I've Got The Music n Me* (RCA 1981) ★★, *Qualifying Heats* (MCA 987) ★★★, *Throw You Down* (Reprise 1990) ★★.

COMPILATIONS: *Best Of Thelma Houston* Motown 1991) ★★★.

IUMAN BEINZ
his Ohio, USA-based quartet – Richard Belley lead guitar), Ting Markulin (rhythm guitar), 1el Pachuta (bass) and Mike Tatman (drums) – nade their recording debut on the local ;ateway label. Their early releases featured pirited versions of Bob Dylan's 'Times They re A-Changin" and Them's 'Gloria' while other overs revealed an affection for the Who and ardbirds. Signed to Capitol Records in 1967, the einz enjoyed a US Top 10 hit that year with an nterpretation of 'Nobody But Me', originally ecorded by the Isley Brothers. The quartet mbraced a more original direction with he competent *Evolutions*, but disbanded when his brand of superior pop/rock proved nsuccessful.

ALBUMS: *Nobody But Me* (Capitol 1967) ★★, *volutions* (Capitol 1968) ★★.
● COMPILATIONS: *The Human Beinz With The 1ammals* (Capitol 1968) ★★, *The Golden :lassics* (Collectables 1993) ★★.

IUMBLEBUMS
his Scottish folk-singing duo originally onsisted of Tam Harvey (guitar/mandolin) and ;illy Connolly (b. 24 November 1942, nderston, Glasgow, Scotland; guitar/banjo). 'heir debut, *First Collection Of Merry Melodies*, howcased a quirky sense of humour, but it was ot until Harvey was replaced by Gerry Rafferty b. 16 April 1946, Paisley, Scotland), that the act orged an individuality. Rafferty, a former nember of the beat group, Fifth Column, ntroduced a gift for melody and the first release vith Connolly, *The New Humblebums*, featured everal excellent compositions, including 'lease Sing A Song For Us' and 'Her Father)idn't Like Me Anyway'. A further collection,)pen Up The Door, confirmed Rafferty's skills ut the contrast between his Paul McCartney-

influenced compositions ('My Singing Bird') and his partner's lighter, more whimsical offerings was too great to hold under one banner. Connolly returned to the folk circuit, where his between-songs banter quickly became the focal point of his act and introduced a new-found role as a successful comedian. Meanwhile his erstwhile partner began his solo career in 1971 with *Can I Have My Money Back*, before forming a new band, Stealers Wheel.
● ALBUMS: *First Collection Of Merry Melodies* (Transatlantic 1968) ★★★, *The New Humblebums* (Transatlantic 1969) ★★★, *Open Up The Door* (Transatlantic 1970) ★★★.
● COMPILATIONS: *The Complete Humblebums* (Transatlantic 1974) ★★★, *Early Collection* (Transatlantic 1987) ★★★, *Best Of The Humblebums* (BMG 1998) ★★★.

HUMPERDINCK, ENGELBERT
b. Arnold George Dorsey, 2 May 1936, Madras, India. Raised in Leicester, England, and originally known as Gerry Dorsey, this singer had attempted to achieve mainstream success in the UK during the 50s. He was a featured artist on the television series *Oh Boy!*, toured with Marty Wilde and recorded a failed single, 'I'll Never Fall In Love Again'. It was during this period that he first met Gordon Mills, a singer in the Viscounts, who later moved into songwriting and management. By 1963, Dorsey's career had hit rock bottom. The beat boom hampered his singing career and to make matters worse, he fell seriously ill with tuberculosis. Mills, meanwhile, was beginning to win international success for Tom Jones and in 1967 decided to help his old friend Gerry Dorsey. Soon after, the singer was rechristened Engelbert Humperdinck, a name inspired by the composer of the nineteenth-century opera *Hansel And Gretel*, and relaunched as a balladeer. His first single for Decca Records, 'Dommage Dommage', failed to chart, but received considerable airplay. There was no mistake with the follow-up, 'Release Me', which sold a million copies in the UK alone, dominated the number 1 spot for five weeks and, most remarkably, prevented the Beatles from reaching the top with 'Penny Lane'/'Strawberry Fields Forever'. The single also reached number 4 in the *Billboard* Top 200. Humperdinck's follow-up, 'There Goes My Everything', climbed to number 2 in the UK and by the end of the summer he was back at the top for a further five weeks with 'The Last Waltz'. The latter once again sold in excess of a million copies in the UK alone.
In a year dominated by psychedelia and experimentation in rock, Humperdinck was the biggest-selling artist in England. His strong vocal and romantic image ensured regular bookings and brought a further series of UK Top 10 hits including 'Am I That Easy To Forget' (number 3, January 1968), 'A Man Without Love'

(number 2, April 1968), 'Les Bicyclettes De Belsize' (number 5, September 1968), 'The Way It Used To Be' (number 3, February 1969) and 'Winter World Of Love' (number 7, November 1969). Although he faded as a hit-making artist after the early 70s, his career blossomed in America where he took up residence and became a regular on the lucrative Las Vegas circuit. 'After The Lovin'' gave him a number 8 US hit in October 1976. Like his stablemate Tom Jones he went through a long period without recording, which ended in 1987 with the release of a comeback album, *Remember I Love You*, which featured a duet with Gloria Gaynor. In 1990, it was estimated that he had earned 58 Gold records, 18 Platinum albums, and several Grammy Awards. He was still selling plenty of albums, and filling venues such as London's Royal Albert Hall, well into the 90s. Like Jones he has also gained hip credibility in recent years, recording 'Lesbian Seagull' for the cult movie *Beavis And Butthead Do America*, and collaborating with production duo Thunderpuss 2000 on an album of dance remixes. A new version of the evergreen 'Quando Quando Quando' provided Humperdinck with his first UK chart entry since 1973, debuting at number 40 in January 1999.

● ALBUMS: *Release Me* (Decca/Parrot 1967) ★★★, *The Last Waltz* (Decca/Parrot 1967) ★★★, *A Man Without Love* (Decca/Parrot 1968) ★★★, *Engelbert* (Decca/Parrot 1969) ★★★, *Engelbert Humperdinck* (Decca/Parrot 1969) ★★★, *We Made It Happen* (Decca/Parrot 1970) ★★, *Another Time, Another Place* (Decca/Parrot 1971) ★★, *Live At The Riviera, Las Vegas* (Decca/Parrot 1972) ★★★, *In Time* (Parrot 1972) ★★★, *King Of Hearts* (Parrot 1973) ★★, *After The Lovin'* (Epic 1976) ★★★, *Miracles By Engelbert Humperdinck* (Epic 1977) ★★, *Christmas Tyme* (Epic 1977) ★★, *This Moment In Time* (Epic 1979) ★★★, *Merry Christmas* (Epic 1980) ★★★, *Remember I Love You* (White 1987) ★★★, *Live In Concert/All Of Me* (Epic 1989) ★★, *Hello Out There* (Avalanche 1992) ★★★, *The Dance Album* (Interhit 1998) ★★★, *I Want To Wake Up With You* (Universal Music TV 2001) ★★★.

● COMPILATIONS: *Engelbert Humperdinck – His Greatest Hits* (Decca/Parrot 1974) ★★★, *The Engelbert Humperdinck Collection* (Telstar 1987) ★★★, *The Best Of ... Live* (Repertoire 1995) ★★★, *Greatest Songs* (Curb 1995) ★★★, *16 Most Requested Songs* (Columbia 1996) ★★, *The Very Best Of Engelbert Humperdinck* (Heartland 1997) ★★★, *Super Hits* (Epic/Legacy 1998) ★★, *The Collection* (Spectrum 1998) ★★★, *At His Very Best* (Universal 2000) ★★★.

● VIDEOS: *The King Of Romance* (PDC Video 1998), *Blazing A Silver Trail* (Acorn Video 1999).

● FURTHER READING: *Engelbert Humperdinck: The Authorized Biography*, Don Short.

HYLAND, BRIAN

b. 12 November 1943, Woodhaven, Queens, New York, USA. A demonstration disc, recorded with the artist's high school group the Delphis, alerted Kapp Records to Hyland's vocal talent. In 1960 he enjoyed a US chart-topper with 'Itsy Bitsy Teenie Weenie Yellow Polkadot Bikini', one of the era's best-known 'novelty' recordings which subsequently sold over one million copies. Having switched outlets to the larger ABC-Paramount Records, the singer enjoyed further success with 'Let Me Belong To You' (1961 – a US Top 20 hit) 'Ginny Come Lately' (1962 – a UK Top 10 hit), before securing a second gold award for 'Sealed With a Kiss'. Its theme of temporary parting was empathic to the plight of many love-struck teenagers and the song returned to the UK Top 10 in 1975 before being revived in 1990 by Jason Donovan. Hyland continued to enjoy US chart entries, notably with 'The Joker Went Wild' and 'Run, Run, Look And See' (both 1966), but reasserted his career in 1970 with a sympathetic version of the Impressions' 'Gypsy Woman'. This third million-seller was produced by long-time friend Del Shannon, who co-wrote several tracks on the attendant album, but this rekindled success proved short-lived and the artist later ceased recording.

● ALBUMS: *The Bashful Blonde* (Kapp 1960) ★★, *Let Me Belong To You* (ABC 1961) ★★, *Sealed With A Kiss* (ABC 1962) ★★★, *Country Meets Folk* (ABC 1964) ★, *Here's To Our Love* (Philips 1964) ★★, *Rockin' Folk* (Philips 1965) ★★, *The Joker Went Wild* (Philips 1966) ★★★, *Tragedy* (Dot 1969) ★★, *Stay And Love Me All Summer* (Dot 1969) ★★, *Brian Hyland* (Uni 1970) ★★.

● COMPILATIONS: *Greatest Hits* (Rhino 1994) ★★★, *Brian's 21 Big Ones* (Connoisseur 2001) ★★★.

I

IDLE RACE

Dave Pritchard (guitar), Greg Masters (bass) and Roger Spencer (drums) spent several years in the Nightriders, backing Birmingham singer Mike Sheridan. Their frontman left for a solo career in 1966, but with the addition of guitarist/composer Jeff Lynne (b. 30 December 1947, Birmingham, England), the restructured group embarked on an enthralling, independent direction. The quartet took the name the Idle Race in the wake of an unsuccessful debut single released under their former appellation. By 1967 Lynne had become the group's focal point, contributing the bulk of their original material and shaping its sound and direction. *The Birthday Party* showcased his gift for melody and quirky sense of humour, facets prevalent in two of its undoubted highlights, 'Follow Me Follow' and 'The Skeleton And The Roundabout'. The guitarist's grasp on the group was strengthened with their second album, *Idle Race*, which he produced. This evocative selection featured some of Lynne's finest compositions, many of which bore a debt to the Beatles, but without seeming plagiaristic. Any potential, however, was bedevilled by public indifference, and highly commercial pop songs such as 'Come With Me' and 'At The End Of The Road' surprisingly failed to become hits. Repeated overtures to join the Move ultimately proved too strong for Lynne to ignore, and precipitated several changes. Pritchard, Masters and Spencer drafted Mike Hopkins and Roy Collum into the line-up, the latter of whom was then replaced by Dave Walker. This reshaped quintet was responsible for *Time Is*, a progressive rock collection at odds with the erstwhile group's simple pop. Walker then left for Savoy Brown and his place was taken by Birmingham veteran Steve Gibbons. Founder members Pritchard and Spencer abandoned their creation, Bob Lamb and Bob Wilson from Tea And Symphony joined, before a third member of that august ensemble, Dave Carroll, replaced Mike Hopkins. When Greg Masters left the Idle Race in 1971, their link with the past was finally severed and the group became known as the Steve Gibbons Band.

● ALBUMS: *The Birthday Party* (Liberty 1968) ★★★, *Idle Race* (Liberty 1969) ★★★, *Time Is* (Regal Zonophone 1971) ★★.

● COMPILATIONS: *On With The Show* (Sunset 1973) ★★★, *Back To The Story* (Premier 1996) ★★★★.

IFIELD, FRANK

b. 30 November 1937, Coventry, Warwickshire, England. The most successful recording artist in the UK during the early 60s, Ifield is now also one of the most underrated. At the age of nine, his family emigrated to Australia, and Ifield entered showbusiness during his teens. He first came to prominence in Australia during 1957 with 'Whiplash', a song about the 1851 Australian goldrush that was later used as the theme for a long-running television series. After returning to England in the late 50s, Ifield was signed to the EMI Records subsidiary Columbia Records and soon found success working with producer Norrie Paramor. After scoring minor hits with 'Lucky Devil' and 'Gotta Get A Date', he broke through spectacularly with the chart-topping 'I Remember You'. The song had a wonderfully elegiac feel, complemented by Ifield's relaxed vocal and a pleasing harmonica break. The track dominated the UK chart listings, staying at number 1 for a staggering seven weeks and was the first record ever to sell a million copies in England alone. The song also charted in America, a rare feat for a British-based singer in the early 60s. Late in 1962, Ifield was back at the top of the UK charts for a further five weeks with 'Lovesick Blues', which betrayed his love of C&W and emphasized his extraordinary ability as a yodeller. His engaging falsetto became something of a trademark, which differentiated him from other UK vocalists of the period.

A revival of Gogi Grant's 'The Wayward Wind' put Ifield into the record books. No artist in British pop history had previously logged three consecutive number 1 records, but during February 1963 Ifield achieved that honour. Ironically, he shared the number 1 spot jointly with the Beatles' 'Please Please Me', and it was their abrupt rise that year which tolled the death knell for Ifield as a regular chart contender. After stalling at number 4 with 'Nobody's Darlin' But Mine' Ifield experienced his fourth UK chart-topper with the breezy 'Confessin''. His version of the perennial 'Mule Train' added little to the Frankie Laine version and Ifield's last Top 10 hit in the UK was almost an apology for his previous release; the beautifully arranged 'Don't Blame Me'. Thereafter, the material chosen for him seemed weaker and his chart career atrophied. He became the most celebrated victim of the beat boom that was sweeping the UK and never regained the seemingly unassailable position that he enjoyed in the early 60s. He continued his career, playing regularly in pantomime and in stage productions like *Up Jumped A Swagman*, before reverting to cabaret work. During the 80s Ifield concentrated on singing his beloved country music, performing regularly in Australia and the USA. In the 90s following lengthy bouts of ill health, Ifield was residing in Australia, and in 1996 following further illness (an abscess on the lung) his singing was permanently impaired. He now works as a country music radio presenter.

● ALBUMS: *I'll Remember You* (Columbia 1963) ★★★, *Born Free* (Columbia 1963) ★★★, *Blue Skies* (Columbia 1964) ★★★, *Portrait In Song* (Columbia 1965) ★★★, *Up Jumped A Swagman* film soundtrack (Columbia 1965) ★★★, *Someone To Give My Love To* (Spark 1973) ★★, *Barbary Coast* (Fir 1978) ★★, *Sweet Vibrations* (Fir 1980) ★★, *If Love Must Go* (Fir 1982) ★★, *At The Sandcastle* (Fir 1983) ★★.

● COMPILATIONS: *Greatest Hits* (Columbia 1964) ★★★, *Best Of The EMI Years* (Columbia 1991) ★★★★, *The EP Collection* (See For Miles 1991) ★★★★, *Frank Ifield Collection* (HMV Easy 2001) ★★★★.

● FILMS: *Up Jumped A Swagman* (1965).

IKETTES

This female R&B trio was formed by Ike Turner as part of his revue and was used for chorusing. Throughout the 60s and 70s, there were several line-ups of Ikettes, each of which provided a stunning visual and aural complement on stage to the performances of Ike And Tina Turner. Ike Turner occasionally recorded the group, with results that emphasized their tough, soulful R&B sound, much like his work with Tina. The original group was formed from the Artettes – Robbie Montgomery, Frances Hodges and Sandra Harding – who were the backing vocalists for the St. Louis singer Art Lassiter. They provided the chorus sound to Ike And Tina Turner's first hit, 'A Fool In Love.' On the first recordings of the Ikettes in 1962, the group consisted of Delores Johnson (lead), Eloise Hester and 'Joshie' Jo Armstead (b. Josephine Armstead, 8 October 1944, Yazoo City, Mississippi, USA). They recorded the hit 'I'm Blue (The Gong-Gong Song)' (number 3 R&B, number 19 pop) for Atco Records in 1962. The best-known group of Ikettes were Vanetta Fields, Robbie Montgomery and Jessie Smith, a line-up formed in the St. Louis area around 1963. They recorded for the Modern Records label, including the hits 'Peaches 'N' Cream' (number 28 R&B, number 36 pop) and 'I'm So Thankful' (number 12 R&B, number 74 pop), both in 1965. This group left Turner in 1968 and enjoyed a big hit as the Mirettes in 1968 with a remake of the Wilson Pickett hit, 'In The Midnight Hour' (number 18 R&B, number 45 pop). Later line-ups of Ikettes included several singers who developed careers of their own, notably P.P. Arnold, Claudia Lennear and the future Bonnie Bramlett (who formed the duo Delaney And Bonnie).

● ALBUMS: *Soul Hits* (Modern 1965) ★★, *Gold And New* (United Artists 1974) ★★, *Whirlpool* (Uni 1969) ★★.

● COMPILATIONS: *Fine Fine Fine* (Kent 1992) ★★.

ILLINOIS SPEED PRESS

The Chicago-based Illinois Speed Press was originally known as the Gentrys. The quintet – Kal David (vocals, guitar), Paul Cotton (b. 26 February 1943, Los Angeles, California, USA; vocals, guitar), Mike Anthony (organ), Frank Bartoli (bass) and Fred Pappalardo (drums) – was later known as the Rovin' Kind and as such recorded several singles including covers of the Who's 'My Generation' and John Sebastian's 'Didn't Want To Have To Do It'. The group assumed the name Illinois Speed Press in February 1968. Rob Lewine replaced Bartoli prior to recording their first album. This debut showed a promising grasp of melody, but within a year, David and Cotton were the only remaining members. They completed *Duet* together before the latter guitarist accepted an offer to join Poco. His erstwhile colleague was later a founder-member of the Fabulous Rhinestones.

● ALBUMS: *The Illinois Speed Press* (Columbia 1969) ★★, *Duet* (Columbia 1970) ★★★.

IMPRESSIONS

Formed in Chicago in 1957 and originally known as the Roosters, this group comprised Jerry Butler (b. 8 December 1939, Sunflower, Mississippi, USA), Curtis Mayfield (b. 3 June 1942, Chicago, Illinois, USA, d. 26 December 1999), Sam Gooden (b. 2 September 1939, Chattanooga, Tennessee, USA), and brothers Richard Brooks and Arthur Brooks (both born in Chattanooga, Tennessee, USA). Mayfield and Butler first met in the choir of the Travelling Soul Spiritualists Church, from where they formed the Modern Jubilaires and Northern Jubilee Singers. The two teenagers then drifted apart, and while Mayfield was involved in another group, the Alphatones, Butler joined Gooden and the Brooks brothers in the Roosters. Mayfield was subsequently installed as their guitarist. Dubbed the Impressions by their manager, the group's first single for Abner/Falcon, 'For Your Precious Love', was a gorgeous ballad and a substantial hit, reaching number 11 in the US pop chart in June 1958. The label credit, which read 'Jerry Butler And The Impressions', caused internal friction and the two sides split after one more release, 'Come Back My Love'. While Butler's solo career gradually prospered, that of his erstwhile colleagues floundered. He and Mayfield were later reconciled on Butler's 1960 single 'He Will Break Your Heart', the success of which (and of other Mayfield-penned songs) rekindled Impressions' career.

Signed to ABC-Paramount Records in 1961, they had a US number 20 hit with the haunting 'Gypsy Woman'. Subsequent releases were less well received until 'It's All Right' (1963) soared to number 1 in the R&B chart and to number 4 in the pop chart. The group was now a trio of Mayfield, Gooden and Fred Cash, and their hythmic harmonies were set against Johnny ate's stylish arrangements. Magnificent Top 20 ingles – including 'I'm So Proud', 'Keep On ushing', 'You Must Believe Me' (all 1964) and eople Get Ready' (1965) – showed how Mayfield was growing as an incisive composer, reating lyrical songs that were alternately oignant and dynamic. During this period the mpressions had what was to be their last US pop op 10 hit, 'Amen', which was featured in the idney Poitier movie Lilies Of The Field. Mayfield hen set up two short-lived record companies, Windy C in 1966, and Mayfield in 1967. However, it was the singer's third venture, Curtom Records, that proved most durable. In he meantime, the Impressions had emerged rom a period when Motown Records had rovided their prime influence. 'You've Been heatin'' (1965) and 'You Always Hurt Me' 1967), however good in themselves, lacked the ubtlety of their predecessors, but represented a ransition in Mayfield's musical perceptions. tatements that had previously been implicit vere granted a much more open forum. 'This Is My Country' (1968), 'Mighty Mighty Spade And Vhitey' (1969) and 'Check Out Your Mind' (1970) vere tougher, politically based performances, while his final album with the group, the uintessential Young Mods' Forgotten Story, set he framework for his solo work.

Mayfield's replacement, Leroy Hutson, left in 973. Reggie Torian and Ralph Johnson were ubsequently added, and the new line-up topped he R&B chart in 1974 with 'Finally Got Myself ogether (I'm A Changed Man)'. 'First mpressions' (1975) became their only UK hit, ut the following year Johnson left. Although Mayfield, Butler, Cash and Gooden have, on ccasions, re-formed, the latter pair have also ept active their version of the Impressions. ollowing his tragic accident in 1990, which left im as a quadriplegic, Mayfield continued to ecord until his death in 1999. The first four bums by the Impressions represent the very est of sweet soul music; uplifting without accharine.

ALBUMS: The Impressions (ABC-Paramount 963) ★★★★, The Never Ending Impressions ABC-Paramount 1964) ★★★★, Keep On Pushing ABC-Paramount 1964) ★★★★, People Get Ready ABC-Paramount 1965) ★★★★, One By One ABC-Paramount 1965) ★★, Ridin' High (ABC-aramount 1966) ★★★, The Fabulous mpressions (ABC 1967) ★★★, We're A Winner ABC 1968) ★★, This Is My Country (Curtom 968) ★★★, The Young Mods' Forgotten Story urtom 1969) ★★★★, Check Out Your Mind urtom 1970) ★★, Times Have Changed urtom 1972) ★★, Preacher Man (Curtom 1973) ★, Finally Got Myself Together (Curtom 1974) ★, First Impressions (Curtom 1975) ★★★, oving Power (Curtom 1976) ★★, Come To My arty (Curtom 1979) ★★, Fan The Fire (20th entury 1981) ★★.

● COMPILATIONS: The Impressions Greatest Hits (ABC-Paramount 1965) ★★★★, The Best Of The Impressions (ABC 1968) ★★★★, 16 Greatest Hits (ABC 1971) ★★★★, Curtis Mayfield/His Early Years With The Impressions (ABC 1973) ★★★, with Butler and Mayfield solo tracks The Vintage Years – The Impressions Featuring Jerry Butler And Curtis Mayfield (Sire 1977) ★★★, Your Precious Love (Topline 1981) ★★★★, The Definitive Impressions (Kent 1989) ★★★★, The Impressions Greatest Hits (MCA 1989) ★★★★, All The Best (Pickwick 1994) ★★★★, The Very Best Of (Rhino 1997) ★★★, Check Out The Impressions: A Collection 1968-81 (Music Club 1998) ★★★, ABC Rarities (Ace 1999) ★★★.

INCREDIBLE STRING BAND

This UK folk group was formed in 1965 in Glasgow, Scotland, at Clive's Incredible Folk Club by Mike Heron (b. 12 December 1942, Glasgow, Scotland), Robin Williamson (b. 24 November 1943, Edinburgh, Scotland) and Clive Palmer (b. London, England). In 1966 the trio completed The Incredible String Band, a collection marked by an exceptional blend of traditional and original material, but they broke up upon its completion. Heron and Williamson regrouped the following year to record the exceptional 5000 Spirits Or The Layers Of The Onion. On this the duo emerged as a unique and versatile talent, employing a variety of exotic instruments to enhance their global folk palate. Its several highlights included Heron's 'Painting Box' and two of Williamson's most evocative compositions, 'Way Back In The 1960s' and 'First Girl I Loved'. The latter was later recorded by Judy Collins. A de rigueur psychedelic cover encapsulated the era and the pair were adopted by the emergent underground. Two further releases, The Hangman's Beautiful Daughter and Wee Tam And The Big Huge, consolidated their position and saw Williamson, in particular, contribute several lengthy, memorable compositions.

Changing Horses, as its title implies, reflected a growing restlessness with the acoustic format and the promotion of two previously auxiliary members, Licorice McKechnie (vocals, keyboards, guitar, percussion) and Rose Simpson (vocals, bass, violin, percussion), indicated a move to a much fuller sound. The album polarized aficionados with many lamenting the loss of an erstwhile charm and idealism. I Looked Up continued the transformation to a rock-based perspective although U, the soundtrack to an ambitious ballet-cum-pantomime, reflected something of their earlier charm. Liquid Acrobat As Regards The Air in 1971, was stylistically diverse and elegiac in tone. Dancer-turned-musician Malcolm Le Maistre was introduced to the group's circle and, with the departure of both Simpson and McKechnie, a woodwinds/ keyboard player, Gerald Dott, joined the group for No Ruinous Feud. By this point the group owed little to the style of the previous decade although

Williamson's solo, *Myrrh*, invoked the atmosphere of *Wee Tam And The Big Huge* rather than the apologetic rock of *No Ruinous Feud*. The two founding members were becoming estranged both musically and socially and in 1974 they announced the formal end of their partnership.

● ALBUMS: *The Incredible String Band* (Elektra 1966) ★★★, *5000 Spirits Or The Layers Of The Onion* (Elektra 1967) ★★★★, *The Hangman's Beautiful Daughter* (Elektra 1968) ★★★★, *Wee Tam And The Big Huge* (Elektra 1968) ★★★, *Changing Horses* (Elektra 1969), *I Looked Up* (Elektra 1970) ★★, *U* (Elektra 1970) ★★, *Be Glad For The Song Has No Ending* (Island 1971) ★★, *Liquid Acrobat As Regards The Air* (Island 1971) ★★, *Earthspan* (Island 1972) ★★, *No Ruinous Feud* (Island 1973) ★★, *Hard Rope And Silken Twine* (Island 1974) ★★, *In Concert* (Windsong 1992) ★★★, *The Chelsea Sessions* (Pig's Whisker 1997) ★★★, *The First Girl I Loved* (Mooncrest 1998) ★★★.

● COMPILATIONS: *Relics Of The Incredible String Band* (Elektra 1971) ★★★, *Seasons They Change* (Island 1976) ★★★, *The Best Of 1966-1970* (Elektra 2001) ★★★, *'Here Till Here Is There': An Introduction To The Incredible String Band* (Island 2001) ★★★.

● VIDEOS: *Be Glad For The Song Has No Ending* (Island 1994).

INSECT TRUST

One of the most engaging groups to emerge from New York's folk and blues enclaves, the Insect Trust – Luke Faust (banjo, guitar), Bill Barth (d. 13 July 2000, Amsterdam, Holland; guitars), Robert Palmer (woodwind, saxophones), Trevor Koehler (saxophone, upright bass, piano) and Nancy Jeffries (vocals) – were steeped in Greenwich Village heritage (members had played with the Solip Singers and Peter Stampfel of the Holy Modal Rounders). Their eponymous debut album included material from artists as diverse as Gabor Szabo and Skip James, while the quintet's own compositions offered glimpses of traditional American music, which echoed the experimentation found in early Fairport Convention material. A second Insect Trust album, *Hoboken Saturday Night*, was less purposeful; nevertheless, it offered its own share of excellent moments. The use of former John Coltrane drummer Elvin Jones provided an undeniable muscle, but overall the collection lacked the element of surprise which made the group's debut so spellbinding. The group broke up soon after its recording and Koehler's suicide. Palmer subsequently became a respected journalist but although Faust reappeared in the Holy Modal Rounders' circle, the rest of this excellent group failed to maintain a significant career in music.

● ALBUMS: *The Insect Trust* (Capitol 1969) ★★★★, *Hoboken Saturday Night* (Atco 1970) ★★★.

IRON BUTTERFLY

During the progressive music revolution in th late 60s, one of the most surprising success was that of Iron Butterfly. The band was forme by Doug Ingle (b. 9 September 1946, Omah Nebraska, USA; organ, vocals), who added Ro Bushy (b. 23 September 1941, Washington, DC USA; drums), Eric Brann (b. 10 August 195 Boston, Massachusetts, USA; guitar), Le Dorman (b. 19 September 1945, St. Loui Missouri, USA; bass, vocals) and, briefly, Danr Weiss. Together, they were arguably the first t amalgamate the terms 'heavy' and 'rock following the release of their debut in 196 Their second effort, *In-A-Gadda-Da-Vida* ('In Th Garden Of Eden'), became a multi-million-selle and was for a number of years the biggest-sellin item in Atlantic Records' catalogue. The albu also became the record industry's first platinu disc. The 17-minute title-track containe everything a progressive rock fan could want neo-classical organ with Far East undertones, solid beat, screeching guitar parts, barbed-wi feedback and an overlong drum sol Magnificently overwrought at the time, th intervening years have been less kind to i standing.

The follow-up, *Ball*, was less of a success, despi being a better collection of songs, notably th invigorating 'It Must Be Love' and the mo subtle 'Soul Experience'. Brann departed after poor live album and was replaced by tw guitarists: Larry 'Rhino' Rheinhart (b. 7 Jul 1948, Florida, USA) and Mike Pinera (b. 2 September 1948, Florida, USA). However, n further success ensued. *Metamorphosis* was confused collection, recorded when the ban was disintegrating. They re-formed in the mi 70s, delivering two disappointing album Another re-formation, this time in 1992, wa masterminded by Mike Pinera. A new version o 'In-A-Gadda-Da-Vida' was recorded and Pine recruited Dorman and Bushy for extensiv touring in the USA. By 1993, the legendary second album had sold an astonishin 25 million copies and in 1995 the band re formed once more for an anniversary tour.

● ALBUMS: *Heavy* (Atco 1968) ★★★, *In-A Gadda-Da-Vida* (Atco 1968) ★★★★, *Ball* (Atc 1969) ★★★, *Iron Butterfly Live* (Atco 1970) ★ *Metamorphosis* (Atco 1970) ★★, *Scorching Beau* (MCA 1975) ★★, *Sun And Steel* (MCA 197 ★★★.

● COMPILATIONS: *The Best Of Iron Butterfl Evolution* (Atco 1971) ★★★, *Star Collectio* (Atlantic 1973) ★★★, *Light And Heavy: The Be Of Iron Butterfly* (Rhino 1993) ★★★.

IRWIN, BIG DEE

b. DiFosco Ervin, 4 August 1939, New York Cit New York, USA, d. 27 August 1995, Las Vega Nevada, USA. The corpulent R&B singer fir made his mark as lead for the doo-wop group th Pastels, who had successes with two sumptuou ballads, 'Been So Long' (1957) and 'So Far Away' (1958). As a solo artist, he is recalled for a series of tongue-in-cheek singles, the most successful of which was a version of the Bing Crosby hit 'Swinging On A Star' in 1963, an irreverent performance on which he was joined by a perky Little Eva. Irwin's other releases included 'Everybody's Got A Dance But Me', on which he begrudged the dance-based releases of other artists, and 'Happy Being Fat', where Eva, once again, provided the spiky interjections. Irwin later enjoyed intermittent success as a songwriter, including 'What Kind Of Boy', recorded on the Hollies' debut album. He died in 1995 of heart failure.

● COMPILATIONS: *Another Night With Big Dee Irwin* (Westside 1997) ★★★.

IVY LEAGUE
Formed in 1964, the Ivy League was an outlet for songwriters John Carter (b. John Shakespeare, 20 October 1942, Birmingham, England) and Ken Lewis (b. Kenneth James Hawker, 3 December 1942, Birmingham, England). The duo's talent had been established through compositions for several acts, including Mike Sarne's UK novelty hit, 'Will I What', and their own beat group, Carter-Lewis And The Southerners, which featured guitarist Jimmy Page. Perry Ford (b. Bryan Pugh, 1940, Lincoln, England, d. 29 April 1999, England), a former member of Bert Weedon's backing band, completed the Ivy League line-up which had three UK hits in 1965 with 'Funny How Love Can Be' (number 8), 'That's Why I'm Crying' (number 22) and 'Tossing And Turning' (number 3). Their close harmony, falsetto style was modelled on that of the Four Freshmen and Four Seasons and while obviously competent, grew increasingly out-of-step as contemporary pop progressed. The trio reached a creative peak with the atmospheric 'My World Fell Down', but John Carter was now tiring of his creation. Tony Burrows replaced him in 1966 and although Ken Lewis left the group several months later, Perry Ford remained at its helm until the end of the decade, fronting an ever-changing line-up. By then, however, the Ivy League had been surpassed by newer Carter/Lewis projects including the Flowerpot Men and White Plains. Carter's original demos were released in 1998.

● ALBUMS: *This Is The Ivy League* (Pye 1965) ★★★.
● COMPILATIONS: *Sounds Of The Ivy League* (Marble Arch 1967) ★★★, *Tomorrow Is Another Day* (Marble Arch 1969) ★★★,*The Best Of The Ivy League* (1988) ★★★, *Major League* (Sequel 1997) ★★★★.
Solo: John Carter *As You Like It Volume 1: The Denmark Street Demo's 1963-67* (Westside 1998) ★★★, *The Essential Works In The Studios 1963-1982* (EM 2001) ★★★★.

JACKSON, CHUCK
b. 22 July 1937, Latta, South Carolina, USA. Jackson travelled the traditional 50s route into soul music via a spell in the gospel group the Raspberry Singers. In 1957, he joined the hit doo-wop group the Del-Vikings, taking a prominent role on their US Top 10 success 'Whispering Bells'. His strong baritone vocals enabled him to launch a solo career with Beltone Records in 1960, before signing to the more prestigious Wand Records label the following year. Jackson's early 60s singles for Wand epitomized the New York uptown soul style, with sophisticated arrangements – often crafted by Burt Bacharach – supporting his sturdy vocals with female vocalists and orchestras. He enjoyed enormous success in the R&B market for several years with a run of hits that have become soul classics, such as 'I Don't Want To Cry', 'I Wake Up Crying', 'Any Day Now' and 'Tell Him I'm Not Home', although only the majestic 'Any Day Now', co-written by Bacharach, crossed into the US Top 30.
In 1965 he was teamed with Maxine Brown on a revival of Chris Kenner's R&B favourite, 'Something You Got', the first of three hit duets over the next two years. Their partnership was severed in 1967 when Jackson joined Motown Records, a decision he later described as 'one of the worst mistakes I ever made in my life'. Although he notched up a minor hit with Freddie Scott's 'Are You Lonely For Me Baby?' in 1969, the majority of his Motown recordings found him pitched against unsympathetic backdrops in a vain attempt to force him into the label's formula. Jackson left Motown in 1971 for ABC Records, where again he could only muster one small hit, 'I Only Get This Feeling', in 1973. Another switch of labels, to All-Platinum in 1975, produced the chart entry 'I'm Wanting You, I'm Needing You' in his traditional style. In 1980 he joined EMI Records, where his most prominent role was as guest vocalist on two hit albums by Gary 'U.S.' Bonds. In the late 80s Jackson was one of many ex-Motown artists signed to Ian Levine's Motor City label, with whom he released two singles. He released an album with Cissy Houston in 1992.
● ALBUMS: *I Don't Want To Cry* (Wand 1961) ★★★, *Any Day Now* (Wand 1962) ★★★★, *Encore* (Wand 1963) ★★★, *Chuck Jackson On Tour* (Wand 1964) ★★★, *Mr Everything* (Wand 1965) ★★★★, with Maxine Brown *Saying Something* (Wand 1965) ★★★, *A Tribute To Rhythm And Blues* (Wand 1966) ★★★, *A Tribute*

To Rhythm And Blues Vol. 2 (Wand 1966) ★★★, with Maxine Brown Hold On We're Coming (Wand 1966) ★★★, Dedicated To The King (Wand 1966) ★★★, Chuck Jackson Arrives (Motown 1968) ★★★, Goin' Back To Chuck Jackson (Motown 1969) ★★★, Teardrops Keep Falling On My Heart (Motown 1970) ★★★, Through All Times (ABC 1974) ★★★, Needing You, Wanting You (All Platinum 1975) ★★★, The Great Chuck Jackson (Bulldog 1977) ★★★, I Wanna Give You Some Love (EMI America 1980) ★★★, After You (EMI America 1980) ★★, with Cissy Houston I'll Take Care Of You (Shanachie 1992) ★★.
● COMPILATIONS: Chuck Jackson's Greatest Hits (Wand 1967) ★★★★, Mr. Emotion (Kent 1985) ★★★, A Powerful Soul (Kent 1987) ★★★, Good Things (Kent 1991) ★★★, I Don't Want To Cry/Any Day Now (Ace 1993) ★★★★, Encore/Mr Everything (Ace 1994) ★★★, The Great Recordings (Tomato 1995) ★★★★, Bing Bing Bing! (Sequel 1998) ★★.

JAMES, DICK

b. Isaac Vapnick, 1921, London, England, d. 1 February 1986, London, England. Originally a dance band singer under the name of Lee Sheridan, he sang with several of the major bandleaders of the 40s and 50s, including Geraldo and Cyril Stapleton. After changing his name to Dick James he was signed to Parlophone Records label and achieved a memorable UK Top 20 with 'Robin Hood'. The song was commissioned for a long-running television series, The Adventures Of Robin Hood, and a generation of children were entranced by James' lusty, barrel-voiced, perfectly enunciated vocal. The singer enjoyed a further hit with the much-covered 'Garden Of Eden' before retiring from recording, and going into music publishing with Sydney Bron, Eleanor Bron's father. In 1961, he launched his own firm, and in November 1962, to his lasting fortune, was visited by entrepreneur Brian Epstein, and acquired the most lucrative songwriting catalogue of modern times.
With the Beatles, James changed irrevocably Tin Pan Alley music publishing in the UK. Instead of offering the group the traditional 10 per cent retail price of sheet music, he suggested that they form Northern Songs, a separate company that would deal exclusively with the songs of John Lennon and Paul McCartney. The offer was 50/50, half to James and his partner, 20 per cent each to Lennon/McCartney and 10 per cent to Epstein. The success of the Beatles' songwriting team eroded the power of the old Tin Pan Alley songsmiths, but James remained a prominent figure. He had the cream of the Merseybeat groups as part of his company, and also published Manchester's major pop act, the Hollies, and Birmingham's Spencer Davis Group. During the late 60s, he oversaw the publishing side of Larry Page's record company, Page One. After many successful years with the Beatles, James eventually sold his major shareholding in Northern Songs to Lew Grade's ATV company in 1969. His major concern during the early 70s was the extension of Dick James Music into DJM Records, a company in which he was eventually joined by his son Stephen James. As a publisher and record company mogul, he rose to new heights after signing the songwriting team of Elton John and Bernie Taupin. Their catalogue proved one of the most valuable of the era. James finally retired from the business but was forced to return to the fray in 1985 when Elton John belatedly instituted successful legal proceedings to obtain an increased royalty in respect of his compositions from Dick James Music. Some three months after the court case ended, James died at his St John's Wood home.

JAMES, ETTA

b. Jamesetta Hawkins, 25 January 1938, Los Angeles, California, USA. James' introduction to performing followed an impromptu audition for Johnny Otis backstage at San Francisco's Fillmore Auditorium. 'Roll With Me Henry', her 'answer' to the Hank Ballard hit 'Work With Me Annie', was retitled 'The Wallflower' in an effort to disguise its risqué lyric and became an R&B number 1. 'Good Rockin' Daddy' provided another hit, but the singer's later releases failed to chart. Having secured a contract with the Chess Records group of labels, James, also known as Miss Peaches, unleashed a series of powerful songs, including 'All I Could Do Was Cry' (1960), probably the best ever version of 'At Last' (1961), 'Trust In Me' (1961), 'Don't Cry Baby' (1961), 'Something's Got A Hold On Me' (1962), 'Stop The Wedding' (1962) and 'Pushover' (1963). She also recorded several duets with Harvey Fuqua. Heroin addiction sadly blighted both her personal and professional life, but in 1967 Chess took her to the Fame studios. The resultant Tell Mama was a triumph, and pitted James' abrasive voice with the exemplary Muscle Shoals house band. Its highlights included the proclamatory title track, a pounding version of Otis Redding's 'Security' (both of which reached the R&B Top 20) and the despairing 'I'd Rather Go Blind', which was later a UK Top 20 hit for Chicken Shack.
The 1973 album Etta James earned her a US Grammy nomination, despite her continued drug problems, which she did not overcome until the mid-80s. A 1977 album, Etta Is Betta Than Evah, completed her Chess contract, and she moved to Warner Brothers Records. A renewed public profile followed her appearance at the opening ceremony of the Los Angeles Olympics in 1984. Deep In The Night was a critics' favourite. The live Late Show albums, released in 1986, featured Shuggie Otis and Eddie 'Cleanhead' Vinson, and were followed by Seven Year Itch, her first album for Island Records, in 1989. This, and the subsequent

release, *Stickin' To My Guns*, found her back on form, aided and abetted once more by the Muscle Shoals team. She was inducted into the Rock And Roll Hall Of Fame in 1993, prior to her signing a new recording contract with Private Records.

Following the use of her version of Muddy Waters' 'I Just Want To Make Love To You' in a television advertisement, she unexpectedly found herself near the top of the UK charts in 1996, giving this emotional and 'foxy' singer some valuable exposure. All her cover versions, from 'Need Your Love So Bad' to 'The Night Time Is The Right Time', are indelibly stamped by her ability to 'feel' the essence of a lyric and melody, allowing her to take over and shape a song. Her extraordinary voice has been showcased to great effect on her recent Private releases, including *Love's Been Rough On Me*, *Matriarch Of The Blues* and *Blue Gardenia*. The latter, a smooth album demonstrating James' love of jazz ballads, rewarded the singer by rising to the top of the *Billboard* jazz chart.

● ALBUMS: *Miss Etta James* (Crown 1961) ★★★★, *At Last!* (Argo 1961) ★★★★, *Second Time Around* (Argo 1961) ★★★★, *Twist With Etta James* (Crown 1962) ★★★★, *Etta James* (Argo 1962) ★★★★, *Etta James Sings For Lovers* (Argo 1962) ★★★★, *Etta James Top Ten* (Argo 1963) ★★★, *Etta James Rocks The House* (Argo 1964) ★★★, *The Queen Of Soul* (Argo 1965) ★★★★, *Call My Name* (Cadet 1967) ★★★, *Tell Mama* (Cadet 1968) ★★★★★, *Etta James Sings Funk* (Cadet 1970) ★★★, *Losers Weepers* (Cadet 1971) ★★★, *Etta James* (Chess 1973) ★★★, *Come A Little Closer* (Chess 1974) ★★★, *Etta Is Betta Than Evah!* (Chess 1977) ★★★, *Deep In The Night* (Warners 1978) ★★★★, *Changes* (MCA 1980) ★★★, with Eddie 'Cleanhead' Vinson *Blues In The Night: The Early Show* (Fantasy 1986) ★★★, *Blues In The Night: The Late Show* (Fantasy 1986) ★★★, *Seven Year Itch* (Island 1989) ★★★, *Stickin' To My Guns* (Island 1990) ★★★★, *Something's Gotta Hold On Me (Etta James Volume 2)* (Roots 1992) ★★★, *The Right Time* (Elektra 1992) ★★★, *Mystery Lady: Songs Of Billie Holiday* (Private 1994) ★★★, *Love's Been Rough On Me* (Private 1997) ★★★, *Life, Love & The Blues* (Private 1998) ★★★, *12 Songs Of Christmas* (Private 1998) ★★, *Heart Of A Woman* (Private 1999) ★★★, *Matriarch Of The Blues* (Private 2000) ★★★★, *Blue Gardenia* (Private 2001) ★★★★.

● COMPILATIONS: *The Best Of Etta James* (Crown 1962) ★★★★, *The Soul Of Etta James* (Ember 1968) ★★★★, *Golden Decade* (Chess 1972) ★★★★, *Peaches* (Chess 1973) ★★★★, *Good Rockin' Mama* (Ace 1981) ★★★★, *Chess Masters* (Chess 1981) ★★★, *Tuff Lover* (Ace 1983) ★★★★, *Juicy Peaches* (Chess 1985) ★★★, *R&B Queen* (Crown 1986) ★★★, *Her Greatest Sides, Volume One* (Chess/MCA 1987) ★★★★, *R&B Dynamite* reissued as *Hickory Dickory Dock* (Ace 1987) ★★★★, *Rocks The House* (Charly 1987) ★★★★, *The Sweetest Peaches: The Chess Years, Volume 1*

(1960-1966) (Chess/MCA 1988) ★★★★, *The Sweetest Peaches: The Chess Years, Volume 2 (1967-1975)* (Chess/MCA 1988) ★★★★, *Tell Mama* (1988) ★★★★, *Chicago Golden Years* (Vogue 1988) ★★★, *Come A Little Closer* (Charly 1988) ★★★, *Juicy Peaches* (Charly 1989) ★★★★, *The Gospel Soul Of Etta James* (AJK 1990) ★★★, *Legendary Hits* (Jazz Archives 1992) ★★★, *Back In The Blues* (Zillion 1992) ★★★, *The Soulful Miss Peaches* (Charly 1993) ★★★★, *I'd Rather Go Blind – The World Of Etta James* (Trace 1993) ★★★, *Something's Got A Hold* (Charly 1994) ★★★, *Blues In The Night, The Early Show* (Fantasy 1994) ★★★, *Blues In The Night, The Late Show* (Fantasy 1994) ★★★, *Miss Peaches Sings The Soul* (That's Soul 1994) ★★★, *Live From San Francisco '81* (Private Music 1994) ★★★, *The Genuine Article: The Best Of* (MCA/Chess 1996) ★★★★, *Her Best* (MCA/Chess 1997) ★★★★, *The Chess Box* 3-CD box set (MCA 2000) ★★★★, *Love Songs* (Chess 2001) ★★★★, *The Best Of Etta James* (Spectrum 2001) ★★★.

● VIDEOS: *Live At Montreux* (Island Visual Arts 1990), *Live At Montreux: Etta James* (PolyGram Music Video 1992).

● FURTHER READING: *Rage To Survive*, Etta James and David Ritz.

JAMES, TOMMY, AND THE SHONDELLS

Tommy James (b. 29 April 1947, Dayton, Ohio, USA) formed his first group Tommy And The Tornadoes at the age of 13, by which time he had already recorded his debut single, 'Long Pony Tale'. The Shondells comprised James, Larry Coverdale (guitar), Craig Villeneuve (keyboards), Larry Wright (bass) and Jim Payne (drums) and were assembled to fulfil weekend engagements, but they secured a deal with the local Snap label in 1962. Their first release, 'Hanky Panky', was a regional success, but a chance discovery four years later by Pittsburg disc jockey Bob Mack led to its becoming a national number 1 smash, selling in excess of one million copies. Now signed to the Roulette label, James assembled a new Shondells which, following defections, settled around a nucleus of Eddie Gray (guitar), Ronnie Rossman (keyboards), Mike Vale (b. 17 July 1949; bass) and Pete Lucia (drums). The addition of producer/songwriting team Ritchie Cordell and Bo Gentry resulted in a string of classic, neo-bubblegum hits, including 'I Think We're Alone Now', 'Mirage' (both gold discs from 1967) and 'Out Of The Blue' (1968).

The group's effortless grasp of hooklines and melody culminated with the pulsating 'Mony Mony' (1968), a UK number 1 which invoked the style of the classic garage band era. James then assumed complete artistic control of his work, writing, arranging and producing the psychedelic-influenced 'Crimson And Clover'. This haunting, atmospheric piece, described by the singer as 'our second renaissance', topped the US charts and garnered sales of over five million copies. This desire to experiment continued with two further gold-selling singles, 'Sweet Cherry Wine' and 'Crystal Blue Persuasion' (both 1969), and the album *Cellophane Symphony*. In 1970 the group and singer parted on amicable terms, with Lucia and Vale going on to record with rock group Hog Heaven. An exhausted James retired to a farm before launching a solo career. 'Draggin' The Line' (1971) provided a US Top 5 hit although subsequent releases from the early 70s failed to broach the Top 30. In 1980 the singer had another million-seller with 'Three Times In Love', since when he has continued to record, albeit with less success. Tommy James And The Shondells' power was encapsulated in their danceability and bracing fusion of soulful voices, garage group riffs, effervescent pop and occasional bubblegum appeal. This 'pop-pourri' legacy was picked up by younger artists over a decade on when Joan Jett charted with 'Crimson And Clover' and both Billy Joel and Tiffany took Shondells' cover versions back to number 1 in the US charts.

● ALBUMS: *Hanky Panky* (Roulette 1966) ★★★, *It's Only Love* (Roulette 1967) ★★★, *I Think We're Alone Now* (Roulette 1967) ★★★, *Gettin' Together* (Roulette 1968) ★★, *Mony Mony* (Roulette 1968) ★★★, *Crimson & Clover* (Roulette 1968) ★★★, *Cellophane Symphony* (Roulette 1969) ★★, *Travelin'* (Roulette 1970) ★★★.

● COMPILATIONS: *Something Special! The Best Of Tommy James And The Shondells* (Roulette 1968) ★★★, *The Best Of Tommy James And The Shondells* (Roulette 1969) ★★★, *Anthology* (Rhino 1990) ★★★★, *The Best Of Tommy James And The Shondells* (Rhino 1994) ★★★★, *It's A New Vibration: An Ultimate Anthology* (Westside 1997) ★★★★.

JAN AND DEAN

Jan Berry (b. 3 April 1941, Los Angeles, California, USA) and Dean Torrence (b. 10 March 1940, Los Angeles, California, USA). Students at Emerson Junior High School, Berry and Torrence began singing together on an informal basis. They formed an embryonic group, the Barons, with Bruce Johnston and Sandy Nelson, but its members gradually drifted away, leaving Berry, Torrence and singer Arnie Ginsburg to plot a different course. The trio recorded 'Jennie Lee' in 1958. A homage to the subject of Ginsburg's affections, a local striptease artist, the single became a surprise hit, reaching number 8 in the US chart in May. Although featured on the song, Torrence was drafted prior to its success, and the pressing was credited to Jan And Arnie. Subsequent releases failed to achieve success and the pair split up. Berry and Torrence were reunited the following year. They completed several demos in Berry's makeshift studio and, having secured the production and management services of local entrepreneur Lou Adler, the reshaped duo enjoyed a Top 10 entry with 'Baby Talk'. Jan And Dean scored several minor hits

over the ensuing four years until a 1963 release, 'Linda', heralded a departure in their style. Here the duo completed all the backing voices, while the lead was sung in falsetto. The sound was redolent of the Beach Boys and the two performers' immediate future became entwined. Brian Wilson co-wrote 'Surf City', Jan And Dean's first number 1 hit; this glorious summer hit evokes fun, sunshine and 'two girls for every boy'.

The Beach Boys' leader also made telling contributions to several other notable classics, including 'Drag City', 'Dead Man's Curve' and 'Ride The Wild Surf', although Berry's contribution as writer, and later producer, should not be underestimated. However, despite the promise of a television series, and a role in the movie *Easy Come, Easy Go*, relations between he and Torrence became increasingly strained. Dean added fuel to the fire by singing lead on 'Barbara Ann', an international hit pulled from the informal *Beach Boys Party*. The exploitative 'Batman' single, released in January 1966, was the last session the pair recorded together. Within weeks Jan Berry had crashed his sports car receiving appalling injuries. He incurred severe brain damage, but although recovery was slow, the singer did complete a few singles during the early 70s. Torrence kept the Jan And Dean name alive, but failed to recapture the duo's success and subsequently found his true vocation with his highly respected design company, Kittyhawk Graphics. However, the pair were reunited in 1978 when they undertook the support slot for that year's Beach Boys tour.

● ALBUMS: *Jan And Dean* (Dore 1960) ★★★, *Jan And Dean Take Linda Surfin'* (Liberty 1963) ★★★, *Surf City (And Other Swinging Cities)* (Liberty 1963) ★★★, *Drag City* (Liberty 1964) ★★★, *Dead Man's Curve/New Girl In School* (Liberty 1964) ★★★, *Ride The Wild Surf* (Liberty 1964) ★★★, *The Little Old Lady From Pasadena* (Liberty 1964) ★★★, *Command Performance – Live In Person* (Liberty 1965) ★, *Folk 'N Roll* (Liberty 1966) ★★, *Filet Of Soul – A 'Live' One* (Liberty 1966) ★, *Jan And Dean Meet Batman* (Liberty 1966) ★★, *Popsicle* (Liberty 1966) ★★, *Save It For A Rainy Day* (J&D 1967) ★★.

● COMPILATIONS: *Jan And Dean's Golden Hits* (Liberty 1962) ★★★, *Golden Hits Volume 2* (Liberty 1965) ★★★, *Gotta Take That One Last Ride* (One Way 1973) ★★★, *Ride The Wild Surf (Hits From Surf City, USA)* (EMI 1976) ★★★★, *Teen Suite 1958-1962* (Varèse Sarabande 1995) ★★★★, *Surf City (The Very Best Of Jan And Dean)* (EMI 1999) ★★★.

● FURTHER READING: *Jan And Dean*, Allan Clark.

JANSCH, BERT

b. 3 November 1943, Glasgow, Scotland. This highly gifted acoustic guitarist and influential performer learned his craft in Edinburgh's folk circle before being absorbed into London's burgeoning circuit, where he established a formidable reputation as an inventive guitar player. His debut, *Bert Jansch*, is a landmark in British folk music and includes 'Do You Hear Me Now', a Jansch original later covered by Donovan, the harrowing 'Needle Of Death', and an impressive version of Davey Graham's 'Angie'. The artist befriended number of artists starting out in the 60s folk boom, including Robin Williamson and John Renbourn, who played supplementary guitar on Jansch's second selection, *It Don't Bother Me*. The two musicians then recorded the exemplary *Bert And John*, which was released alongside *Jack Orion*, Jansch's third solo album. This adventurous collection featured a nine-minute title track and a haunting version of 'Nottamun Town', the blueprint for a subsequent reading by Fairport Convention. Jansch continued to make exceptional records, but his own career was overshadowed by his participation in the Pentangle alongside Renbourn, Jacqui McShee (vocals), Danny Thompson (bass) and Terry Cox (drums). Between 1968 and 1973 this accomplished, if occasionally sterile, quintet was one of folk music's leading attractions, although the individual members continued to pursue their own direction during this time. The Danny Thompson-produced *Moonshine* marked the beginning of his creative renaissance with delightful sleeve notes from the artist: 'I hope that whoever listens to this record gets as much enjoyment as I did from helping to make it'. *LA Turnaround*, released following the Pentangle's dissolution, was a promising collection and featured assistance from several American musicians including a former member of the Monkees, Michael Nesmith. The album suffered from over production. Although Jansch rightly remains a respected figure, his later work lacks the invention of those early releases. It came to light that much of this lethargy was due to alcoholism, and by his own admission, it took six years to regain a stable condition. In the late 80s he took time out from solo folk club dates to join Jacqui McShee in a regenerated Pentangle line-up, with whom he continues to tour. In the mid-90s he was performing regularly once again with confidence and fresh application. This remarkable reversal after a number of years of indifference was welcomed by his loyal core of fans. *When The Circus Comes To Town* was an album that easily matched his early pivotal work. Not only does Jansch sing and play well but he brilliantly evokes the atmosphere and spirit of the decade in which he first came to prominence. *Live At The 12 Bar* was an excellent example of his sound in the mid-90s, following a successful residency at London's 12 Bar Club. Although the recording quality is poor, another important release came in 1999 when unearthed recordings of some live performances from

1962-64 were transferred to CD and issued by Ace Records' worthy subsidiary, Big Beat. Castle Communications also undertook a fine reissue programme in 2000, and with the publication of Colin Harper's excellent biography, at last Jansch's work has the profile it has warranted for many years. He is a master of British folk/blues with a highly distinctive voice that has improved with age, and is an often breathtakingly fluid and original acoustic guitarist.

● ALBUMS: *Bert Jansch* (Transatlantic 1965) ★★★★, *It Don't Bother Me* (Transatlantic 1965) ★★★★, *Jack Orion* (Transatlantic 1966) ★★★★, with John Renbourn *Bert And John* (Transatlantic 1966) ★★★★, *Nicola* (Transatlantic 1967) ★★★, *Birthday Blues* (Transatlantic 1968) ★★★, with Renbourn *Stepping Stones* (Vanguard 1969) ★★★, *Rosemary Lane* (Transatlantic 1971) ★★★, *Moonshine* (Reprise 1973) ★★★, *LA Turnaround* (Charisma 1974) ★★, *Santa Barbara Honeymoon* (Charisma 1975) ★, *A Rare Conundrum* (Charisma 1978) ★★, *Avocet* (Charisma 1979) ★★★, *Thirteen Down* (Sonet 1980) ★★, *Heartbreak* (Logo 1982) ★★, *From The Outside* (Konexion 1985) ★★★, *Leather Launderette* (Black Crow 1988) ★★, *The Ornament Tree* (Run River 1990) ★★★, *Sketches* (Hypertension 1990) ★★, *When The Circus Comes To Town* (Cooking Vinyl 1995) ★★★★, *Live At The 12 Bar: An Authorized Bootleg* (Jansch 1996) ★★★★, *Toy Balloon* (Cooking Vinyl 1998) ★★★, *Crimson Moon* (When 2000) ★★★, *Downunder* 1996 live recording (Castle 2001) ★★★★, as Loren Auerbach & Bert Jansch *After The Long Night/Playing The Game* (Essential 2001) ★★.

● COMPILATIONS: *Lucky Thirteen* (Vanguard 1969) ★★★, *The Bert Jansch Sampler* (Transatlantic 1969) ★★★★, *Box Of Love* (Transatlantic 1972) ★★★, *The Essential Collection Volume 1 (Strolling Down The Highway)* (Transatlantic 1987) ★★★★, *The Essential Collection Volume 2 (Black Water Side)* (Transatlantic 1987) ★★★, *The Gardener: Essential Bert Jansch 1965-71* (1992) ★★★★, *The Collection* (Castle 1995) ★★★★, *Blackwater Slide* (Recall 1998) ★★★, *Young Man Blues: Live In Glasgow 1962-1964* (Big Beat 1999) ★★★★, *The Pentangle Family* (Transatlantic 2000) ★★★★, *Dazzling Stranger* (Castle 2000) ★★★★.

● FURTHER READING: *Dazzling Stranger: Bert Jansch And The British Folk And Blues Revival*, Colin Harper.

JAY AND THE AMERICANS

This US act was formed in 1961 when former Mystics vocalist John 'Jay' Traynor (b. 2 November 1938) joined ex-Harbor Lites duo Kenny Rosenberg, aka Kenny Vance, and Sandy Yaguda, aka Sandy Deane. Howie Kane (b. Howard Kerschenbaum) completed the line-up, which in turn secured a recording deal through the aegis of the songwriting and production team, Leiber And Stoller. Jay And The Americans scored a US number 5 hit in March 1962 with their second single, the dramatic 'She Cried', but a series of misses exacerbated tension within the group and Traynor left for a low-key solo career. Bereft of a lead vocalist, the remaining trio recruited David 'Jay' Black (b. David Blatt, 2 November 1938) from the Empires. Dubbed 'Jay' to infer continuity, Black introduced fifth member Marty Saunders (guitar) to the line-up, and the following year established his new role with the powerful 'Only In America' (US number 25, August 1963). Initially intended for the Drifters, the song's optimism was thought hypocritical for a black act and the Americans' vocal was superimposed over the original backing track.

In 1964 Artie Ripp assumed the production reins for the quintet's 'Come A Little Bit Closer', a US number 3 in September, followed by 'Let's Lock The Door (And Throw Away The Key)' (US number 11, December 1964). The following year the group was assigned to Gerry Granahan who in turn secured a greater degree of consistency. 'Cara, Mia' (number 4), 'Some Enchanted Evening' (number 13) and 'Sunday And Me' (number 18, and Neil Diamond's first major hit as a songwriter) all reached the US Top 20, and although 'Livin' Above Your Head' was less successful (US number 76, July 1966), this enthralling performance is now recognized as one of the group's finest recordings. The quintet's brand of professional pop proved less popular as the 60s progressed, although revivals of 'This Magic Moment' (number 6, December 1968) and 'Walkin' In The Rain' (number 19, November 1969) were US Top 20 hits. The latter featured the musical talents of Donald Fagen and Walter Becker, later of Steely Dan, but at that point members of the Americans' studio band. By the turn of the decade the group's impetus was waning and with Vance embarking on solo recordings, Sanders writing and Deane producing, Jay Black was granted the rights to the group's name. Further recordings did ensue and he continues to perform on the nostalgia circuit.

● ALBUMS: *She Cried* (United Artists 1962) ★★★, *Jay And The Americans At The Cafe Wha?* (United Artists 1963) ★★, *Come A Little Bit Closer* (United Artists 1964) ★★★, *Blockbusters* (United Artists 1965) ★★, *Sunday And Me* (United Artists 1966) ★★★, *Livin' Above Your Head* (United Artists 1966) ★★★, *Try Some Of This* (United Artists 1967) ★★, *Sands Of Time* (United Artists 1969) ★★, *Wax Museum* (United Artists 1970) ★★.
● COMPILATIONS: *Jay And The Americans' Greatest Hits* (United Artists 1965) ★★★, *Jay And The Americans' Greatest Hits Volume Two* (United Artists 1966) ★★★, *The Very Best Of Jay And The Americans* (United Artists 1975) ★★★, *Come A Little Bit Closer: The Best Of Jay And The Americans* (Capitol 1990) ★★★.

JAY AND THE TECHNIQUES

Formed in Allentown, Pennsylvania, USA, in the mid-60s, Jay And The Techniques were an inter-racial pop group best known for the Top 10 debut single 'Apples, Peaches, Pumpkin Pie' in 1967. The group consisted of vocalist Jay Proctor and six other members: Karl Landis, Ronald Goosly, John Walsh, George Lloyd, Charles Crowl and Dante Dancho. The group built a following in the northeast and was discovered by producer Jerry Ross, who arranged to have them signed to Smash Records, a subsidiary of Mercury Records. 'Apples, Peaches, Pumpkin Pie', was their biggest hit, reaching number 6 in the US in 1967. 'Keep The Ball Rolling', was, like the first, based on a children's game, and it climbed to number 14. The formula held up for one further game-orientated single, 'Strawberry Shortcake', which scraped into the Top 40 in 1968. A final chart success, 'Baby Make Your Own Sweet Music', ended their run on the pop charts in 1968, but a revived Jay And The Techniques placed 'Number Onederful' on the R&B charts in 1976, on Event Records. This was the group's swan song.
● ALBUMS: *Apples, Peaches, Pumpkin Pie* (Smash 1967) ★★, *Love, Lost & Found* (Smash 1968) ★★.
● COMPILATIONS: *Apples, Peaches, Pumpkin Pie* (Collectables 1995) ★★, *The Best Of Jay And The Techniques* (Mercury 1995) ★★.

JAY, PETER, AND THE JAYWALKERS

Originally based in East Anglia, England, the Jaywalkers – Peter Miller (lead guitar), Tony Webster (rhythm guitar), Mac McIntyre (tenor saxophone/flute), Lloyd Baker (piano/baritone saxophone), Geoff Moss (acoustic bass), Johnny Larke (electric bass), and Peter Jay (drums), pre-dated the British beat boom. They scored a minor hit in 1962 with 'Can Can 62', but despite an unquestioned competence, their rather stilted act became increasingly anachronistic. The group attempted a more contemporary image with several R&B-based releases, and in 1966 a restructured line-up emerged under the name Peter Jay And The New Jaywalkers. Now reduced to a quintet, the unit featured vocalist Terry Reid, but despite an impressive appearance on the Rolling Stones' UK tour, they disbanded by the end of that year.

JAYNETTS

Songwriter Zelma 'Zell' Sanders formed this New York-based act around her daughter, Johnnie Louise Richardson, previously half of hit duo Johnnie And Joe. Ethel Davis, Mary Sue Wells, Yvonne Bushnell and Ada Ray completed the line-up featured on 'Sally, Go 'Round The Roses', the quintet's debut single and sole US chart entry. This haunting performance reached number 2 in 1963, and has since become an early classic of the 'girl group' genre, ut the Jaynetts' progress was undermined hen Richardson left following its release. nsuing singles, including 'Keep An Eye On ler' and 'Johnny Don't Cry', were not uccessful, and the group ceased recording in 965. Johnnie Louise Richardson died in 1988.

ALBUMS: *Sally, Go 'Round The Roses* (Tuff 963) ★★.

EFFERSON AIRPLANE

long with the Grateful Dead, Jefferson irplane are regarded as the most successful an Francisco band of the late 60s. The group ere formed in August 1965 by Marty Balin (b. lartyn Jerel Buchwald, 30 January 1942, incinnati, Ohio, USA; vocals, guitar). The ther members in the original line-up were Paul antner (b. 17 March 1941, San Francisco, alifornia, USA; guitar, vocals) and Jorma aukonen (b. 23 December 1940, Washington, C, USA; guitar, vocals). Bob Harvey and Jerry eloquin gave way to Alexander Skip Spence (b. 8 April 1946, Windsor, Ontario, Canada) and igne Anderson (b. Signe Toly Anderson, 15 eptember 1941, Seattle, Washington, USA). heir replacements, Spencer Dryden (b. 7 April 938, New York, USA; drums) and Jack Casady). 13 April 1944, Washington, DC, USA), made p a seminal band that blended folk and rock ito what became known as west coast rock. antner, already a familiar face on the local folk ircuit and Balin, formerly of the Town Criers nd co-owner of the Matrix club, soon became ighly popular locally, playing gigs and benefits rganized by promoter Bill Graham. Eventually iey became regulars at the Fillmore uditorium and the Carousel Ballroom, both a iort distance from their communal home in ie Haight Ashbury district. Anderson departed iortly after the release of their moderately iccessful debut *Jefferson Airplane Takes Off* and as replaced in October 1966 by Grace Slick (b. race Barnett Wing, 30 October 1939, Evanston, linois, USA; vocals).

lick was already well known with her former and, the Great Society, and donated two of ieir songs, 'White Rabbit' and 'Somebody To ove', to the Airplane. Both titles were on their :cond influential collection, *Surrealistic Pillow*, nd both became US Top 10 hits. They have ow achieved classic status as definitive songs om that era. The lyrics of 'White Rabbit' ombined the harmless tale of *Alice In 'onderland* with an LSD trip. Their reputation as enhanced by a strong performance at the :gendary Monterey Pop Festival in 1967. This ational success continued with the erratic fter Bathing At Baxters* and the brilliant *Crown f Creation*. The latter showed the various riters in the band maturing and developing ieir own styles. Balin's 'If You Feel', aukonen's 'Ice Cream Phoenix' and Slick's agi-comic 'Lather' gave the record great ariety. This album also contained 'Triad', a

song their friend David Crosby had been unable to include on a Byrds album. They maintained a busy schedule and released a well-recorded live album, *Bless Its Pointed Little Head*, in 1969. The same year, they appeared at another milestone in musical history: the Woodstock Festival. Later that year they were present at the infamous Altamont Festival, where a group of Hells Angels killed a young spectator and attacked Balin.

Slick and Kantner had now become lovers and their hippie ideals and political views were a major influence on *Volunteers*. While it was an excellent album, it marked the decline of Balin's role in the band. Additionally, Dryden departed and the offshoot Hot Tuna began to take up more of Casady and Kaukonen's time. Wizened fiddler Papa John Creach (b. 28 May 1917, Beaver Falls, Pennsylvania, USA, d. 22 February 1994; violin) joined the band full-time in 1970, although he still continued to play with Hot Tuna. Kantner released a concept album, *Blows Against The Empire*, bearing the name Paul Kantner And The Jefferson Starship. The 'Starship' consisted of various Airplane members, plus Jerry Garcia, David Crosby, Graham Nash, *et al*. This majestic album was nominated for the science fiction Hugo Award. Slick, meanwhile, gave birth to a daughter, China, who later in the year graced the cover of Slick And Kantner's *Sunfighter*. Following a greatest hits selection, *Worst Of*, and the departure of Balin, the band released the cleverly packaged *Bark*. Complete with brown paper bag, the album offered some odd moments, notably Slick's 'Never Argue With A German', sung in spoof German, and new drummer Joey Covington's 50s-sounding *a cappella* 'Thunk'. It also marked the first release on their own Grunt label.

The disappointing *Long John Silver* was followed by a gutsy live outing, *30 Seconds Over Winterland*. This was the last album to bear their name, although an interesting compilation consisting of single releases and studio out-takes later appeared as *Early Flight*. Hot Tuna became Casady and Kaukonen's main interest and Slick and Kantner released further 'solo' albums. The name change evolved without any fuss, and one of the most inventive bands in history prepared for a relaunch as the Jefferson Starship. Kantner, Balin and Casady regrouped briefly as the KBC Band in 1986. The Airplane title was resurrected in 1989 when Slick, Kaukonen, Casady, Balin and Kantner re-formed and released *Jefferson Airplane* to an indifferent audience. By the early 90s Hot Tuna had re-formed, Kantner was rebuilding his Jefferson Starship and Slick had apparently retired from the music business.

● ALBUMS: *Jefferson Airplane Takes Off* (RCA 1966) ★★, *Surrealistic Pillow* (RCA 1967) ★★★★, *After Bathing At Baxter's* (RCA 1967) ★★★, *Crown Of Creation* (RCA 1968) ★★★★,

Bless Its Pointed Little Head (RCA 1969) ★★★, *Volunteers* (RCA 1969) ★★★★, *Bark* (Grunt 1971) ★★★, *Long John Silver* (Grunt 1972) ★★★, *30 Seconds Over Winterland* (Grunt 1973) ★★★, *Jefferson Airplane* (Epic 1989) ★, *Live At The Fillmore East* 1968 recording (RCA 1998) ★★★.
● COMPILATIONS: *Worst Of Jefferson Airplane* (RCA 1970) ★★★, *Early Flight* (Grunt 1974) ★★★, featuring Jefferson Airplane and Jefferson Starship *Flight Log (1966-1976)* (Grunt 1977) ★★★★, *The Best Of Jefferson Airplane* (RCA 1980) ★★★★, *2400 Fulton Street: An Anthology* (RCA 1987) ★★★★, *Collection* (Castle 1988) ★★★, *White Rabbit & Other Hits* (RCA 1990) ★★, *Jefferson Airplane Loves You* 3-CD box set (RCA 1992) ★★★, *Journey: The Best Of Jefferson Airplane* (Camden 1996) ★★★, *Through The Looking Glass* (Almafame 1999) ★★, *Ignition* 4-CD box set (RCA 2001) ★★★★.
● FURTHER READING: *The Jefferson Airplane And The San Francisco Sound*, Ralph J. Gleason. *Grace Slick – The Biography*, Barbara Rowe.

JODY GRIND

UK-based Jody Grind was formed in 1968 by the late pianist/organist Tim Hinkley. Their name was culled from a Horace Silver album title. A veteran of the Bo Street Runners and the Chicago Line Blues Band, he was initially joined by two colleagues, Iav Zagni (guitar) and Barry Wilson (drums). The trio completed an album, *One Step On*, prior to Wilson's departure. He was replaced by Martin Harryman, who in turn made way for Pete Gavin. Guitarist Bernie Holland (who is now an excellent jazz guitarist), meanwhile, took over from Zagni and the restructured line-up recorded *Far Canal* with the help of bass player Louis Cennamo. Jody Grind broke up in March 1970. Hinkley later became part of the *ad hoc* bands Dick And The Firemen and Hinkley's Heroes, while Gavin joined Heads, Hands And Feet. Hinkley produced an album for Chris Farlowe in 1992.
● ALBUMS: *One Step On* (Transatlantic 1969) ★★★, *Far Canal* (Transatlantic 1970) ★★★.

JOHN'S CHILDREN

Formed in Leatherhead, Surrey, England, in 1965, John's Children's earliest antecedent was known as the Clockwork Onions. Louis Grooner (vocals), Andy Ellison (harmonica), Geoff McClelland (guitar), Chris Dorsett (bass) and Chris Townson (drums) made up this short-lived ensemble, with Grooner leaving after one local gig. Ellison stood in as lead singer before Martin Sheller was brought into the line-up, who shortly afterwards changed their name to the Few. Sheller only lasted a few months, with Ellison taking up the vacant lead vocalist slot and Dorsett switching to organ to accommodate new bass player, John Hewlett. Dorsett was the next to leave, following which Ellison, McClelland, Townson and Hewlett renamed themselves the

Silence and recorded a demo tape.
The quartet became John's Children in 196 after meeting manager/producer Simon Napie Bell in San Tropez. They made their debut o the Columbia Records label in October with 'Th Love I Thought I'd Found', an experimenta composition made memorable by a start-stoj staccato tempo. This unusual release wa known by its original title, 'Smashed Blocked', i the USA and Europe. A debut album, entitle *Orgasm*, was then readied for release. The se consisted of rudimentary material overdubbe by fake applause, but was withheld until 1970 i deference to its questionable quality and the controversial title. The band's second singl 'Just What You Want – Just What You'll Get', wa a minor UK hit in early 1967, but marked th departure of McClelland. His replacement wa Napier-Bell protégé and budding singe: songwriter, Marc Bolan, whose spell in John Children, although brief, proved contentiou: His first offering, 'Desdemona', incurred a BB ban over the line 'lift up your skirt and fly', an when a second composition, 'Midsumme Night's Scene', had been recorde unsatisfactorily, Bolan left barely three month after joining to form Tyrannosaurus Rex. Hi former colleagues then released the felicitou flower-power anthem, 'Come And Play With M In The Garden', before exhuming another Bola song, 'Go Go Girl', from an earlier session.
final John's Children line-up – Ellison, Hewlet Townson (now guitar) and Chris Colvill (drums) completed several outstandin engagements before disbanding. Elliso embarked on a brief solo career, later re emerging with Townson in 1975 as Jet and fror there on to Radio Stars. John Hewlett became successful manager with Sparks, while als handling Jook, a less celebrated ensembl which also featured Chris Townson.
The cult status of John's Children continued t grow over the ensuing years, with their musi appearing on several posthumous compilatio albums. They re-formed for a live gig on 23 Ma 1992 in Darmstadt, Germany, following whic Ellison and Townson kept the name going wit the addition of Martin Gordon (bass; ex-Je Radio Stars) and Boz Boorer (guitar; ex-Polecats An EP featuring new material was released i 1999, and a live album recorded the followin year.
● ALBUMS: *Orgasm* (White Whale 1970) ★★★ *The Legendary Orgasm Album* (Cherry Red 198: ★★★, *Music For The Herd Of Herring* (Captai Trip/Blueprint 2001) ★★★.
● COMPILATIONS: *Instant Action* (Hawkey 1984) ★★★, *A Midsummer Night's Scene* (Ba Caruso 1988) ★★★, *Smashed Blocked!* (Burnin Airlines/Get Back! 1998) ★★★, *Jagged Tin Lapse* (Burning Airlines /Get Back! 1998) ★★★
● FURTHER READING: *John's Children*, Dav Thompson.

JOHNNY AND THE HURRICANES

Formed by tenor saxophonist Johnny Paris (b. 1940, Walbridge, Ohio, USA), this instrumental group went through a series of line-up changes from 1957-63. With bass player Lionel 'Butch' Mattice and drummer Tony Kaye, the group recorded the single 'Crossfire' under the name the Orbits in 1959. Under the name Johnny And The Hurricanes, they released the riveting 'Red River Rock', which featured the trademark sound of rasping saxophone, combined with the swirling organ of Paul Tesluk. After enlisting new drummers Don Staczek and Little Bo Savitch along the way, the group continued the hit run in the USA and UK with such instrumentals as 'Reveille Rock', 'Beatnik Fly', 'Down Yonder', 'Rocking Goose' and 'Ja-Da'. In 1963, an entirely new group of Johnny Paris-led Hurricanes toured the UK comprising Eddie Wagenfeald (organ), Billy Marsh (guitar), Bobby Cantrall (bass) and Jay Drake (drums). By this time, however, their instrumental sound was becoming anachronistic and they were soon consumed by the beat boom, which swept the UK and USA. Various line-ups of Hurricanes continued for live performances and cabaret.

● ALBUMS: *Johnny And The Hurricanes* (Warwick 1959) ★★★, *Stormsville* (Warwick 1960) ★★★, *Big Sound Of Johnny And The Hurricanes* (Big Top 1960) ★★★, *Live At The Star Club* (Attila 1965) ★★.

● COMPILATIONS: *The Very Best Of* (Varèse Sarabande 2001) ★★★.

JOHNSON, MARV

b. Marvin Earl Johnson, 15 October 1938, Detroit, Michigan, USA, d. 16 May 1993, Columbia, South Carolina, USA. The gospel training that Johnson received as a teenager in the Junior Serenaders was a major influence on his early R&B releases. In 1958, he formed a partnership with the young Berry Gordy, who was then working as a songwriter and producer for Jackie Wilson. Gordy produced Johnson's earliest releases on Kudo, and launched the Tamla label with Johnson's single 'Come To Me', which became a hit when it was licensed to United Artists. Johnson remained with the label until 1965, scoring a run of chart entries in the early 60s with 'You Got What It Takes', 'I Love The Way You Move' and 'Move Two Mountains' – all produced by Gordy. Johnson's tracks showcased his delicate tenor vocals against a female gospel chorus, and he maintained this style when he signed to Gordy's Motown Records stable in 1965. His initial release on the Gordy Records label, the soul favourite 'I Miss You Baby', was a US hit, although it proved to be a false dawn. His subsequent US releases failed, and Johnson eventually abandoned his recording career in 1968. Ironically, the UK Tamla-Motown label chose this moment to revive Johnson's 1966 recording 'I'll Pick A Rose For My Rose', which became an unexpected Top 20 hit amidst a dramatic revival in the label's popularity in Britain. Johnson quickly travelled to the UK to capitalize on this success, before retiring to become a sales executive at Motown. After almost two decades working behind the scenes in the music business, he returned to performing in 1987, touring with the 'Sounds Of Motown' package and re-recording his old hits for the Nightmare label. He was teamed with Carolyn Gill (of the Velvelettes) by record producer Ian Levine to release 'Ain't Nothing Like The Real Thing' in 1987. He released *Come To Me* on Levine's Motor City label. Johnson collapsed and died at a concert in South Carolina on 16 May 1993.

● ALBUMS: *Marvellous Marv Johnson* (United Artists 1960) ★★★, *More Marv Johnson* (United Artists 1961) ★★, *I Believe* (United Artists 1966) ★★, *I'll Pick A Rose For My Rose* (Motown 1969) ★★, *Come To Me* (Motor City 1990) ★★.

● COMPILATIONS: *The Best Of Marv Johnson – You Got What It Takes* (EMI 1992) ★★★, *The Very Best* (Essential Gold 1996) ★★★★.

JONES, JACK

b. John Allen Jones, 14 January 1938, Los Angeles, California, USA. A popular singer from the early 60s, Jones has one of the finest, and most versatile, light baritone voices in easy listening popular music. The son of actress Irene Hervey and actor/vocalist Allan Jones, Jack studied singing while still at high school. After graduation in 1957, he joined his father's act, making his first appearance at the Thunderbird Hotel, Las Vegas. He left after eight months, and worked in small clubs and lounges, even bowling alleys, and also appeared in the minor musical film *Juke Box Rhythm*. Jones was spotted, third on the bill in a San Francisco club, by arranger-conductor Pete King, who recommended him to Kapp Records. Shortly afterwards, Jones started a six-month stint in the US Air Force, and, during that time, recorded 'Lollipops And Roses', which won him a Grammy in 1962 for Best Performance By A Male Singer. *Cash Box* magazine voted him Most Promising Vocalist in 1962 and 1963; he had a minor hit with 'Call Me Irresponsible', and won another Grammy for 'Wives And Lovers' (1964), which was also the title of a bestselling album, as was 'Dear Heart', 'The Impossible Dream' and 'Lady'. Other 60s chart successes, through until 1967, included 'The Race Is On' and *My Kind Of Town*. Jones also sang the title songs for the movies *Where Love Has Gone* and *Love With A Proper Stranger* and the winning entry of the Golden Globe Awards, 'Life Is What You Make It', from the film *Kotch*. In 1967 he switched from Kapp to RCA Records, and continued to make highly regarded albums, including *Without Her*, the first for his new label. He also appeared frequently on television with artists such as Jerry Lewis and Bob Hope, and was a part of Hope's troupe which entertained the US Forces

in Vietnam in December 1965.
In concert, Jones is an accomplished performer, skilfully mixing old standards such as 'My Romance' and 'People Will Say We're In Love', with more up-to-date songs like 'Light My Fire', 'I Think It's Going To Rain Today', 'What Are You Doing The Rest Of Your Life?' and 'What I Did for Love'. He also has a slick line in patter, for instance, when rejecting the inevitable request for 'The Donkey Serenade' (his father's most famous number): 'We don't have that one, but I'll sing you another song that has a lot of the same notes in it!'. In fact, he will sometimes sing the song, but at a much greater pace than his father ever did, occasionally prefacing it with lines like: 'I don't know if you know this, but my father recorded 'The Donkey Serenade' on the night that I was born. It's true – he was on a very tight schedule!'
Since 1973, Jones has been extremely popular in the UK, and tours regularly. Although to date he has never had a Top 75 single there, he made the charts during the 70s with A Song For You, Breadwinners, Together, Harbour, The Full Life and All To Yourself. Breadwinners, with songs by David Gates, was typical of the way that Jones selected material from the best writers of the 60s and 70s, including Michel Legrand, Alan And Marilyn Bergman, John Lennon and Paul McCartney, Nilsson, Leonard Cohen, Burt Bacharach and Hal David, Randy Newman, Jimmy Webb, Paul Williams, Tony Hatch and Jackie Trent. In the 80s and early 90s he continued to thrive in Las Vegas, at venues such as the Golden Nugget and the Desert Inn. During such performances he added contemporary numbers including 'The Wind Beneath My Wings' and Andrew Lloyd Webber's 'Music Of The Night' to hoary old favourites such as the Love Boat theme. Early in 1991 he played Sky Masterson in a west coast production of Guys And Dolls, and continued with his classy singing act at theatres in several countries, including the London Palladium.
● ALBUMS: Call Me Irresponsible (Kapp 1963) ★★★, Wives And Lovers (Kapp 1963) ★★★★, Bewitched (Kapp 1964) ★★★, Where Love Has Gone (Kapp 1964) ★★★, Dear Heart (Kapp 1965) ★★★★, My Kind Of Town (Kapp 1965) ★★★, There's Love & There's Love & There's Love (Kapp 1965) ★★★, For The 'In' Crowd (Kapp 1966) ★★★, The Impossible Dream (Kapp 1966) ★★★★, Jack Jones Sings (Kapp 1966) ★★★, Lady (Kapp 1967) ★★★★, Our Song (Kapp 1967) ★★★, Without Her (RCA 1967) ★★★, If You Ever Leave Me (RCA 1968) ★★★, Where Is Love? (RCA 1968) ★★, A Time For Us (RCA 1969) ★★, A Song For You (RCA 1972) ★★★, Breadwinners (RCA 1972) ★★★, Together (RCA 1973) ★★★, Write Me A Love Song Charlie (RCA 1974) ★★★, In Person, Sands, Las Vegas (RCA 1974) ★★★, Harbour (RCA 1974) ★★★, The Full Life (RCA 1977) ★★★, All To Yourself (RCA 1977) ★★★, Christmas Album (RCA 1978) ★★, I've Been Here

All The Time (RCA 1980) ★★★, Deja Vu (RCA 1982) ★★★, Fire And Rain (RCA 1985) ★★★, I Am A Singer (USA 1987) ★★★, The Gershwin Album (Columbia 1991) ★★★★, Live At The London Palladium (Coolnote 1996) ★★★, New Jack Swing (Linn 1998), Jack Jones Paints A Tribute To Tony Bennett (One Music 1998) ★★★.
● COMPILATIONS: What The World Needs Now Is Love! (Kapp 1968) ★★★, The Best Of Jack Jones (MCA 1978) ★★★, Magic Moments (MCA 1984) ★★★, Love Songs (MCA 1985) ★★★, Golden Classics (MCA 1986) ★★★, Greatest Hits (MCA 1995) ★★★.

JONES, JANIE
b. Marion Mitchell, Seaham, Co. Durham, England. A former Windmill Theatre girl and sister of vocalist Valerie Mitchell, Janie Jones is more renowned for scandal than her brief recording career. Her several 60s singles included 'Witches Brew' (1965), a minor UK Top 50 hit popularized by pirate radio, but trials for blackmail, prostitution and payola irrevocably linked the singer with scandal. Imprisoned during the 70s, Janie was immortalized in song by the Clash who, as the Lash, provided the requisite backing on her subsequent punk-influenced single, 'House Of The Ju-Ju Queen' (1983).
● COMPILATIONS: I'm In Love With The World Of Janie Jones: The Complete Singles Collection (RPM 1997) ★★.

JONES, JIMMY (R&B)
b. 2 June 1937, Birmingham, Alabama, USA. Jones, who had spent a long apprenticeship singing in R&B doo-wop groups, became a rock 'n' roll star in the early 60s singing 'Handy Man' and other hits with a dramatic and piercingly high falsetto. He began his career as a tap dancer, and in 1955 joined a vocal group, the Sparks Of Rhythm. In 1956 Jones formed his own group, the Savoys, which were renamed the Pretenders in 1956. With all these groups, tracks were recorded in the prevailing doo-wop manner but with no discernible success beyond a few local radio plays in the New York/New Jersey area. Success finally came when Jones launched a solo career, signing with MGM Records' Cub subsidiary in 1959 and hitting his debut, 'Handy Man' (number 3 R&B/number 2 pop chart in 1960). Retaining the same falsetto style, he followed up with 'Good Timin'' (number 8 R&B/number 3 pop chart in 1960), but the decline in sales was considerable for his two other US chart entries, 'That's When I Cried' (number 83 pop chart in 1960) and 'I Told You So' (number 85 pop chart in 1961). In the UK, Jones' chart success was exceptional compared to most of his US contemporaries. In 1960 'Handy Man' reached number 3, 'Good Timin'' number 1, 'I Just Go For You' number 35, 'Ready For Love' number 46 and 'I Told You So' number 33. 'Handy Man'

was revived on the charts twice, by Del Shannon in 1964 and by James Taylor in 1977.

● ALBUMS: *Good Timin'* (MGM 1960) ★★★.

● COMPILATIONS: *Handy Man: The Anthology* (Sequel 2002) ★★★.

JONES, TOM

b. Thomas Jones Woodward, 7 June 1940, Pontypridd, Mid-Glamorgan, Wales. After being seriously ill with TB when he was 12 years old he recovered to become one of the most famous pop singers of the past four decades. Jones began his musical career in 1963 as vocalist in the group Tommy Scott And The Senators. The following year, he recorded some tracks for Joe Meek, which were initially rejected by record companies. He was then discovered by Decca Records A&R producer/scout Peter Sullivan and, following the recommendation of Dick Rowe, was placed in the hands of the imperious entrepreneur Phil Solomon. That relationship ended sourly, after which Scott returned to Wales. One evening, at the Top Hat Club in Merthyr Tydfil, Gordon Mills saw Scott's performance and was impressed. He soon signed the artist and changed his name to Tom Jones. His first single, 'Chills And Fever', failed to chart but, early in 1965, Jones' second release 'It's Not Unusual', composed by Mills and Les Reed, reached number 1 in the UK and in a further 12 countries. The exuberant arrangement, reinforced by Jones' gutsy vocal and a sexy image, complete with hair ribbon, brought him instant media attention. Jones enjoyed lesser hits that year with the ballads 'Once Upon A Time' and 'With These Hands'. Meanwhile, Mills astutely insured that his star was given first choice for film theme songs, and the Burt Bacharach/Hal David composition 'What's New Pussycat?' was a major US/UK hit. By 1966, however, Jones' chart fortunes were in decline and even the title track of a James Bond movie, *Thunderball*, fell outside the UK Top 30. Mills took drastic action by regrooming his protégé for an older market. Out went the sexy clothes in favour of a more mature, tuxedoed image. By Christmas 1966, Jones was effectively relaunched owing to the enormous success of 'Green Green Grass Of Home', which sold over a million copies in the UK alone and topped the charts for seven weeks. Jones retained the country flavour with a revival of Bobby Bare's 'Detroit City' and 'Funny Familiar Forgotten Feelings'. In the summer of 1967, he enjoyed one of his biggest UK hits with the intense 'I'll Never Fall In Love Again', which climbed to number 2. The hit run continued with the restrained 'I'm Coming Home', and the dramatic, swaggering 'Delilah', which added a sense of Victorian melodrama with its macabre line: 'I felt the knife in my hand, and she laughed no more'. In the summer of 1968, Jones again topped the *New Musical Express* charts with 'Help Yourself'.

As the 60s reached their close, Mills put his star on the small screen where he hosted the highly successful show, *This Is Tom Jones*. Unlike similar series, Jones' show attracted some of the best and most critically acclaimed acts of the era. An unusual feature of the show saw Jones duetting with his guests. Some of the more startling vocal workouts occurred when Jones teamed-up with David Crosby during a Crosby, Stills And Nash segment, and on another occasion with Blood, Sweat And Tears' David Clayton-Thomas. Although Jones logged a handful of hits in the UK during the early 70s, he was now an American-based performer, whose future lay in the lucrative Las Vegas circuit he had been playing since the late 60s. Jones became enormously wealthy during his supper-club sojourn and had no reason to continue his recording career, which petered out during the 70s. It was not until after the death of Mills, when his son Mark Woodward took over his management, that the star elected to return to recording. His recording of 'The Boy From Nowhere' (from the musical *Matador*) was perceived as a personal anthem and reached number 2 in the UK in May 1987. It was followed by a re-release of 'It's Not Unusual' which also reached the Top 20.

In 1988, a most peculiar collaboration occurred between Jones and the Art Of Noise on an appealing kitsch version of Prince's 'Kiss'. The song reached the UK Top 5 in October and Jones performed the number at the London Palladium. Soon after, he appeared with a number of other Welsh entertainers on a recording of Dylan Thomas' play for voices *Under Milk Wood*, produced by George Martin. Jones' continued credibility was emphasized once more when he was invited to record some songs written by the mercurial Van Morrison, which appeared on 1991's *Carrying A Torch*. After more than a decade on the Las Vegas circuit, Jones could hardly have hoped for a more rapturous welcome in the UK, both from old artists and the new élite, and he even appeared at 1992's Glastonbury Festival. He entered the digital age with a dance-orientated album produced by various hands including Trevor Horn, Richard Perry, Jeff Lynne and Youth. Jones clearly demonstrated that his voice felt comfortable with songs written by Lynne, the Wolfgang Press and Diane Warren. A new album of duets and collaborations, recorded with a host of popular modern artists, topped the UK charts in October 1999. A cover version of Talking Heads' 'Burning Down The House', recorded with the Cardigans, also broke into the UK Top 10 singles chart. At the beginning of the 21st century, Jones' standing had never been higher.

● ALBUMS: *Along Came Jones* (Decca 1965) ★★★, *It's Not Unusual* US only (Parrot 1965) ★★★, *What's New Pussycat?* US only (Parrot 1965) ★★★, *A-Tom-Ic Jones* (Decca 1966) ★★★★, *Green, Green Grass Of Home*

(Decca/Parrot 1966) ★★★★, *From The Heart* (Decca 1966) ★★★, *Tom Jones Live! At The Talk Of The Town* (Decca/Parrot 1967) ★★★, *13 Smash Hits* (Decca 1967) ★★★, *The Tom Jones Fever Zone* (Parrot 1968) ★★★, *Delilah* (Decca 1968) ★★★, *Help Yourself* (Decca/Parrot 1968) ★★★★, *Tom Jones Live!* (Parrot 1969) ★★★, *This Is Tom Jones* (Decca/Parrot 1969) ★★★, *Tom Jones Live In Las Vegas* (Decca 1969) ★★★, *Tom* (Decca/Parrot 1970) ★★★, *I (Who Have Nothing)* (Decca/Parrot 1970) ★★★, *Tom Jones Sings She's A Lady* (Decca/Parrot 1971) ★★★, *Tom Jones Live At Caesar's Palace, Las Vegas* (Decca/Parrot 1971) ★★★, *Close Up* (Decca/Parrot 1972) ★★★, *The Body And Soul Of Tom Jones* (Decca/Parrot 1973) ★★★, *Something 'Bout You Baby I Like* (Decca 1974) ★★, *Memories Don't Leave Like People Do* (Decca 1975) ★★★, *Say You'll Stay Until Tomorrow* (Epic 1977) ★★, *Do You Take This Man* (EMI 1979) ★★★, *Rescue Me* (Columbia 1980) ★★★, *Darlin'* (Polydor 1981) ★★★, *Matador: The Musical Life Of El Cordobes* cast recording (Epic 1987) ★★★, *At This Moment* (Jive 1989) ★★★, *After Dark* (Stylus 1989) ★★, *Carrying A Torch* (Dover 1991) ★★★, *The Lead And How To Swing It* (ZTT 1994) ★★★★, *Reload* (Gut 1999) ★★★★.

● COMPILATIONS: *Greatest Hits* (Decca/Parrot 1973) ★★★★, *Tom Jones: 20 Greatest Hits* (Decca 1975) ★★★★, *The World Of Tom Jones* (Decca 1975) ★★★★, *Tom Jones Sings 24 Great Standards* (Decca 1976) ★★★★, *What A Night* (EMI 1978) ★★★, *I'm Coming Home* (Lotus 1978) ★★★, *Super Disc Of Tom Jones* (A&M 1979) ★★★, *Tom Jones Sings The Hits* (EMI 1979) ★★★, *The Very Best Of Tom Jones* (EMI 1979) ★★★, *The Golden Hits* (Decca 1980) ★★★, *16 Love Songs* (Contour 1983) ★★★, *The Tom Jones Album* (Decca 1983) ★★★, *The Soul Of Tom Jones* (Decca 1986) ★★★, *Love Songs* (Arcade 1986) ★★★, *The Great Love Songs* (Contour 1987) ★★★, *Tom Jones: The Greatest Hits* (Telstar 1987) ★★★, *It's Not Unusual: His Greatest Hits* (Decca 1987) ★★★★, *The Complete Tom Jones* (The Hit Label 1992) ★★★, *The Ultimate Hit Collection: 1965-1988* (Repertoire 1995) ★★★, *Collection* (Spectrum 1996) ★★★, *In Nashville* (Spectrum 1996) ★★★, *At His Best* (Pulse 1997) ★★★, *The Best Of ... Tom Jones* (Deram 1998) ★★★, *The Ultimate Performance* (Reactive 1998) ★★, *She's A Lady* (Castle 2001) ★★.

● VIDEOS: *One Night Only* (Watchmaker Productions 1997), *The Ultimate Collection* (Prism Leisure Video 1999).

● FURTHER READING: *Tom Jones: Biography Of A Great Star*, Tom Jones. *Tom Jones*, Stafford Hildred and David Griffen. *Tom Jones*, Chris Roberts. *Close Up*, Lucy Ellis and Bryony Sutherland.

JOPLIN, JANIS

b. 19 January 1943, Port Arthur, Texas, USA, d. 4 October 1970, Los Angeles, California, USA. Having made her performing debut in December 1961, this expressive singer subsequently enjoyed a tenure at Houston's Purple Onion club. Drawing inspiration from Bessie Smith and Odetta, Joplin developed a brash, uncompromising vocal style quite unlike accustomed folk Madonnas Joan Baez and Judy Collins. The following year she joined the Waller Creek Boys, an Austin-based act that also featured Powell St. John, later of Mother Earth. In 1963 Janis moved to San Francisco where she became a regular attraction at the North Beach Coffee Gallery. This initial spell was blighted by her addiction to amphetamines and in 1965 Joplin returned to Texas in an effort to dry out. She resumed her university studies, but on recovery turned again to singing. The following year Janis was invited back to the Bay Area to front Big Brother And The Holding Company. This exceptional improvisational blues act was the ideal foil to her full-throated technique and although marred by poor production, their debut album effectively captures an early optimism. Joplin's reputation blossomed following the Monterey Pop Festival, of which she was one of the star attractions. The attendant publicity exacerbated growing tensions within the line-up as critics openly declared that the group was holding the singer's potential in check. *Cheap Thrills*, a joyous celebration of true psychedelic soul, contained two Joplin 'standards', 'Piece Of My Heart' and 'Ball And Chain', but the sessions were fraught with difficulties and Joplin left the group in November 1968. Electric Flag members Mike Bloomfield, Harvey Brooks and Nick Gravenites helped assemble a new act, initially known as Janis And The Joplinaires, but later as the Kozmic Blues Band. Former Big Brother Sam Andrew (guitar, vocals), plus Terry Clements (saxophone), Marcus Doubleday (trumpet), Bill King (organ), Brad Campbell (bass) and Roy Markowitz (drums) made up the band's initial line-up which was then bedevilled by defections. A disastrous debut concert at the Stax Records convention in December 1968 was a portent of future problems, but although *I Got Dem Ol' Kozmic Blues Again Mama* was coolly received, the set nonetheless contained several excellent Joplin vocals, notably 'Try', 'Maybe' and 'Little Girl Blue'. However, live shows grew increasingly erratic as her addiction to drugs and alcohol deepened. When a restructured Kozmic Blues Band, also referred to as the Main Squeeze, proved equally uncomfortable, the singer dissolved the band altogether, and undertook medical advice. A slimmed-down group, the Full Tilt Boogie Band, was unveiled in May 1970. Brad Campbell and latecomer John Till (guitar) were retained from the previous group, while the induction of Richard Bell (piano), Ken Pearson (organ) and Clark Pierson (drums) created a tighter, more intimate sound. In July they toured Canada with the Grateful Dead, before commencing work on a 'debut' album. The sessions were all but complete when, on 4 October 1970, Joplin died of a heroin overdose at her Hollywood hotel.

The posthumous *Pearl* was thus charged with poignancy, yet it remains her most consistent work. Her love of 'uptown soul' is confirmed by the inclusion of three Jerry Ragovoy compositions – 'My Baby', 'Cry Baby' and 'Get It While You Can' – while 'Trust Me' and 'A Woman Left Lonely' show an empathy with its southern counterpart. The highlight, however, is Kris Kristofferson's 'Me And Bobby McGee', which allowed Joplin to be both vulnerable and assertive. The song deservedly topped the US chart when issued as a single and despite numerous interpretations, this remains the definitive version. Although a star at the time of her passing, Janis Joplin has not been accorded the retrospective acclaim afforded other deceased contemporaries. She was, like her idol Otis Redding, latterly regarded as one-dimensional, lacking in subtlety or nuance. Yet her impassioned approach was precisely her attraction – Joplin knew few boundaries, artistic or personal – and her sadly brief catalogue is marked by bare-nerved honesty.

● ALBUMS: *I Got Dem Ol' Kozmic Blues Again Mama!* (Columbia 1969) ★★★, *Pearl* (Columbia 1971) ★★★★, *Janis Joplin In Concert* (Columbia 1972) ★★★, with Big Brother And The Holding Company *Live At Winterland '68* (Columbia 1998) ★★★.

● COMPILATIONS: *Greatest Hits* (Columbia 1973) ★★★★, *Janis* film soundtrack including live and rare recordings (1975) ★★★★, *Anthology* (Columbia 1980) ★★★, *Farewell Song* (Columbia 1982) ★★★, *Janis* 3-CD box-set (Columbia/Legacy 1995) ★★★★, *18 Essential Songs* (Columbia 1995) ★★★, *Box Of Pearls: The Janis Joplin Collection* 5-CD box set (Columbia 1999) ★★★★, *Love, Janis: The Songs, The Letters, The Soul Of Janis Joplin* (Columbia 2001) ★★★★.

● FURTHER READING: *Janis Joplin: Her Life And Times*, Deborah Landau. *Going Down With Janis*, Peggy Caserta as told to Dan Knapp. *Janis Joplin: Buried Alive*, Myra Friedman. *Janis Joplin: Piece Of My Heart*, David Dalton. *Love, Janis*, Laura Joplin. *Pearl: The Obsessions And Passions Of Janis Joplin*, Ellis Amburn. *Scars Of Sweet Paradise: The Life And Times Of Janis Joplin*, Alice Echols.

● FILMS: *American Pop* (1981).

JOURNEYMEN

This US folk trio comprised Scott McKenzie (b. Philip Blondheim, 1 October 1944, Arlington, Virginia, USA; guitar/vocals), Dick Weissman (b. Richard Weissman; banjo/guitar/vocals), and John Phillips (b. 30 August 1935, Parris Island, South Carolina, USA, d. 18 March 2001, USA; guitar/vocals). The group were formed, like many others at the time, as a result of the folk revival of the late 50s and 60s, and featured strong harmonies and a commercial sound that made folk such a saleable commodity at the time. The Journeymen made their debut in 1961 at Gerde's Folk City, New York, and shortly afterwards signed to Capitol Records, releasing *The Journeymen* later the same year. The group's popularity, and commerciality, waned after a relatively short life span, and the members went their separate ways. Phillips attempted to revive the trio's fortunes with the New Journeymen, which featured his wife Michelle Phillips and Marshall Brickman. Phillips went on to form the Mamas And The Papas, while McKenzie found fame as the singer of Phillips composition 'San Francisco (Be Sure To Wear Flowers In Your Hair)'. Weissman continued in the music business, recording *The Things That Trouble My Mind* and *Dick Weissman Sings And Plays Songs Of Protest*.

● ALBUMS: *The Journeymen* (Capitol 1961) ★★★, *Coming Attraction-Live* (Capitol 1962) ★★★, *New Directions* (Capitol 1963) ★★★.

● COMPILATIONS: *The Very Best Of* (Collectables 1998) ★★★.

JOYSTRINGS

'It's An Open Secret', which entered the UK Top 40 in February 1964, remains one of the most unlikely hits of the beat era. The song was written by Joy Webb, a captain in the Salvation Army. Her eight-piece group, the Joystrings, was drawn from the staff of the Army's Training College in London's Denmark Hill. The sole exception was drummer Wyncliffe Noble, an architect by trade. The octet was signed to EMI's Regal Zonophone Records label, following a successful appearance on BBC television's *Tonight* programme, and in December they enjoyed another minor hit with 'A Starry Night'. Despite their seemingly transitory appeal, the Joystrings continued to record for several years, although their novelty aspect quickly waned.

● ALBUMS: *Well Seasoned* (Regal Zonophone 1966) ★★★, *Carols Across The World* (Regal Zonophone 1967) ★★★.

JUNIOR'S EYES

This energetic and musically tight UK progressive rock group was formed in 1968 by Mick Wayne (b. *c.*1946, d. June 1994; guitar/vocals), one-time member of the Outsiders, the Hullaballoos and the Bunch Of Fives with Viv Prince, who eventually changed style and name to the psych band the Tickle. He was joined by John 'Honk' Lodge (bass) and Steve Chapman (drums). Following the release of debut single, 'Mr. Golden Trumpet Player', vocalist Graham Kelly completed the best-known Junior's Eyes line-up. The group was responsible for several excellent records, including the single 'Circus Days'/'Woman Love' and the ambitious, uncompromising, *Battersea Power Station*, released in June 1969. Shortly afterwards, guitarist Tim Renwick (b. 7 August 1949, Cambridge, England) and

drummer John Cambridge joined the group, who went on to back David Bowie on *Man Of Words, Man Of Music* aka *Space Oddity*. Wayne had already added electric guitar to the hit title-track, and played on James Taylor's debut album. Junior's Eyes made their final recordings in August 1969, issuing 'Star Child'/'Sink Or Swim', and played their final live set in February 1970. Cambridge subsequently joined Bowie's short-lived Hype while Renwick and Lodge formed Quiver. Mick Wayne moved to America and worked as a session musician, later resurfacing in the Pink Fairies. He died in a house fire in 1994.
● ALBUMS: *Battersea Power Station* (Regal Zonophone 1969) ★★★.
● COMPILATIONS: *Battersea Power Station – Plus* (Castle 2000) ★★★.

JUSTICE, JIMMY

b. 1940, Carlshalton, Surrey, England. Justice signed to Pye Records in 1960, owing partly to fellow stable-mate singer, Emile Ford, who had spotted Jimmy singing in a coffee-bar. When Justice's first two releases failed in the UK, he relocated to Sweden where his cover of the Jarmels' 'Little Lonely One' charted. In 1962 with the help of producer Tony Hatch, he strung together three UK Top 20 hits: the remarkably fresh cover of the Drifters US hit 'When My Little Girl Is Smiling', 'Ain't That Funny' – an original song penned by Johnny Worth – and 'Spanish Harlem'. Jimmy spent 1962 commuting between England and Sweden (where he had many previous bookings to honour) but managed, together with his group the Excheckers, to join a Larry Parnes UK tour headed by Billy Fury and Joe Brown. This white singer who possessed a mature, soulful voice, was sometimes called 'Britain's Ben E. King', and caused some controversy when he covered King's 'Spanish Harlem' with an uncannily similar vocal style. Justice also recorded for Decca Records in 1969, RCA Records in 1968 and B&C in 1972.
● ALBUMS: *Two Sides Of Jimmy Justice* (Pye 1962) ★★★, *Smash Hits* (Pye 1962) ★★★, *Justice For All* (Kapp 1964) ★★★.
● COMPILATIONS: *Ain't That Funny: The Pye Anthology* (Sequel 2000) ★★★★, *Sings Spanish Harlem* (Castle 2001) ★★★.

K-DOE, ERNIE

b. Ernest Kador Jnr., 22 February 1936, New Orleans, Louisiana, USA, d. 5 July 2001, New Orleans, Louisiana, USA. The ninth of 11 children born to the Reverend Ernest Kador Snr., Ernie began singing at the age of seven in his father's choir. After singing with touring gospel groups, Kador's earliest non-secular recordings were made in the mid-50s as a member of the Blue Diamonds. His first solo record, 'Do Baby Do', was released on Specialty Records in 1956. The singer's biggest hit came on the Minit Records label with the Allen Toussaint song 'Mother-In-Law' (1961), which reached number 1 in the US pop charts. This pointed 'novelty' song was followed by 'Te-Ta-Te-Ta-Ta', and a strong double-sided release, 'I Cried My Last Tear'/'A Certain Girl'. The latter track proved popular in Britain where it was covered by the Yardbirds and the Paramounts. Further K-Doe singles included 'Popeye Joe' and 'I'm The Boss', but it was not until 1967 that he returned to the R&B charts with two singles for the Duke label, 'Later For Tomorrow' and 'Until The Real Thing Comes Along'. K-Doe remained a popular, energetic performer and occasional recording artist in New Orleans, and in 1994 established his own Mother-In-Law Lounge nightclub. He died of liver failure in July 2001.
● ALBUMS: *Mother-In-Law* (Minit 1961) ★★★★, *The Best Of Ernie K-Doe* 1993 live recording (Mardi Gras 1999) ★★★.
● COMPILATIONS: *Burn, K-Doe, Burn!* (Charly 1989) ★★★★, *The Best Of Ernie K-Doe* (Mardi Gras 1999) ★★, *Absolutely The Best* (Fuel 2001) ★★★.

KAEMPFERT, BERT

b. Berthold Kaempfert, 16 October 1923, Hamburg, Germany, d. 21 June 1980, Majorca, Spain. A conductor, arranger, composer, multi-instrumentalist and record producer. Kaempfert played the piano as a child, and later studied at the Hamburg Conservatory of Music. By the time he joined Hans Bussch and his Orchestra during World War II, he was capable of playing a variety of instruments, including the piano, piano-accordion and all the reeds. After the war he formed his own band, and became a big draw in West Germany before joining Polydor Records as a producer, arranger and musical director. In the latter role he had some success with the Yugoslavian Ivor Robic's version of 'Morgen', which made the US Top 20 in 1959, and Freddy Quinn's 'Die Guitarre Und Das Meer'. A year ter he made his own global breakthrough when he topped the US charts with his studio orchestra's recording of 'Wonderland By Night'. It was the precursor to a series of similar recordings in which a solo trumpet (usually Fred Moch) and muted brass were set against a fashion of lush strings and wordless choral effects, all emphasized by the insistent rhythm of a two-beat bass guitar.

This treatment was effectively applied by Kaempfert to several of his own compositions, which were also successful for other artists, such as 'Spanish Eyes' (originally the instrumental 'Moon Over Naples', Al Martino), 'Danke Schoen' (Wayne Newton), 'L-O-V-E' (Nat 'King' Cole), 'A Swingin' Safari' (Billy Vaughn), and 'Wooden Heart', which Elvis Presley sang in his movie, G.I. Blues, and Joe Dowell took to the US number 1 spot in 1961. Two other Kaempfert numbers, 'The World We Knew' (Over And Over)' and 'Strangers In The Night' benefited from the Frank Sinatra treatment. The latter song, part of Kaempfert's score for the James Garner/Melina Mercouri comedy/thriller, A Man Could Get Killed, topped the US and UK charts in 1966. Lyrics for his most successful songs were written by Charles Singleton, Eddie Snyder, Carl Sigman, Kurt Schwabach, Milt Gabler, Fred Wise, Ben Weisman and Kay Twomey. Kaempfert himself had easy listening worldwide hits in his own inimitable style with revivals of 'golden oldies' such as 'Tenderly', Red Roses For A Blue Lady', 'Three O'Clock In The Morning' and 'Bye Bye Blues'. In 1961, Wonderland By Night spent five weeks at number 1 in the US, and Kaempfert continued to chart in the US and UK throughout the 60s, but his records failed to achieve Top 40 status in the 70s, although he still sold a great many, and continued to tour.

Apart from his skill as an arranger and orchestra leader, Bert Kaempfert has another claim to fame in the history of popular music – he was the first person to record the Beatles. While they were playing a club in Hamburg in 1961, Kaempfert hired them to back Tony Sheridan, a singer who had a large following in Germany. After supplying the additional vocals on 'My Bonnie Lies Over The Ocean' and 'When The Saints Go Marching In', Kaempfert allowed Lennon And Co. to record 'Ain't She Sweet' and 'Cry For A Shadow'. When the beat boom got under way, 'My Bonnie', as it was then called, made the US Top 30 in 1964, and 'Ain't She Sweet' became a minor hit in the UK. By the end of the decade the Beatles had broken up, and Kaempfert's best days were behind him, too. In 1980, after completing a successful series of concerts in the UK, culminating in an appearance at the Royal Albert Hall, he was taken ill while on holiday in Majorca, Spain, and died there on 21 June. The 'New Bert Kaempfert Orchestra' was advertising its availability in UK trade papers in the early 90s.

● ALBUMS: Wonderland (Decca 1960) ★★★, Wonderland By Night (Decca 1960) ★★★★, That Happy Feeling (Decca 1962) ★★★, With A Sound In My Heart (Decca 1962) ★★★, That Latin Feeling (Decca 1963) ★★★, Lights Out, Sweet Dreams (Decca 1963) ★★★, Living It Up (Decca 1963) ★★★, Afrikaan Beat (Decca 1964) ★★★, Blue Midnight (Decca 1965) ★★★★, 3 O'Clock In The Morning (Decca 1965) ★★★, The Magic Music Of Far Away Places (Decca 1965) ★★★, Strangers In The Night (Decca 1966) ★★★, Bye Bye Blues (Decca 1966) ★★★, A Swingin' Safari (Decca 1966) ★★★, Relaxing Sound Of Bert Kaempfert (Decca 1966) ★★★, Bert Kaempfert – Best Seller (Decca 1967) ★★★, Hold Me (Decca 1967) ★★★, The World We Knew (Decca 1967) ★★★, Kaempfert Special (Decca 1967) ★★★, Orange Colored Sky (Decca 1971) ★★, Now! (Decca 1971) ★★, A Drop Of Christmas Spirit (MCA 1974) ★★, Everybody Loves Somebody (MCA 1976) ★★★, Swing (MCA 1978) ★★★, Tropical Sunrise (MCA 1978) ★★★, Sounds Sensational (MCA 1980) ★★, Springtime (MCA 1981) ★★★, Moods (MCA 1982) ★★★, Now And Forever (MCA 1983) ★★, Famous Swing Classics (MCA 1984) ★★★, Live In London (MCA 1985) ★★.
● COMPILATIONS: Greatest Hits (Decca 1966) ★★★★, The Very Best Of Bert Kaempfert (Taragon 1995) ★★★★.

KAK

Formed in Sacramento, California, USA at the height of the summer of love in 1967, Kak comprised Dehner C. Patten (guitar/vocals), Gary Yoder (vocals/guitar), Joseph Damrell (bass/guitar/sitar/tambourine) and Christopher Lockhead (drums/keyboards/bass/vocals). The band's sole album, although commercially unsuccessful, has since become a prized collectors' item, showcasing classic west coast melodies and exciting, but never indulgent, guitar work. Much of the music was derivative with some interesting comparisons. Two of the strongest tracks, 'Everything's Changing' and 'Disbelievin'', showed a big Moby Grape influence, while the gentle 'Flowing By' prompted the listener to check the album sleeve to check that it was not Donovan singing. The publicity campaign announced 'Get Kak before Kak gets you'. Kak split up in 1970, after which Yoder, who had previously managed another aspiring act, the Oxford Circle, joined Blue Cheer. Drummer Paul Whaley had been a member of both bands. He participated on Blue Cheer's highly-rated releases, The Original Human Being and Oh! Pleasant Hope. An excellent reissue from Ace Records (Big Beat) added many unissued tracks and supplied detailed and informative background sleeve notes about Kak's brief career.
● ALBUMS: Kak-Ola (Epic 1969) ★★★.
● COMPILATIONS: Kak-Ola (Big Beat 1999) ★★★★.

KALEIDOSCOPE (UK)

Psychedelic pop band Kaleidoscope was formed in west London, England, in 1964 as the Side Kicks. Comprising Eddie Pumer (guitar), Peter Daltrey (vocals/keyboards), Dan Bridgeman (percussion) and Steve Clarke (d. 1 May 1999; bass), they initially worked as an R&B cover band. After changing names to the Key, they switched tempo and style and became Kaleidoscope, and were signed to Fontana Records following the intervention of music publisher Dick Leahy, who became their producer. Their debut single, September 1967's 'Flight From Ashiya', adopted the in-vogue hippie ethos and terminology. Although it failed to chart the subsequent album, *Tangerine Dream*, became a cult success, a position it sustains to this day among fans of 60s psychedelic rock (with a rarity value in excess of £100). Despite a strong underground following, this proved insufficient to launch subsequent singles 'A Dream For Julie' or 'Jenny Artichoke', nor second album *Faintly Blowing*, into the charts. Two further singles, 'Do It Again For Jeffrey' and 'Balloon' in 1969 were issued, but a projected third album was 'lost' when Fontana dropped the band. It was eventually issued in 1991 on the group's own self-titled label. By 1970 the group had transmuted into progressive rock band Fairfield Parlour, whose most vociferous fan was the late UK disc jockey Kenny Everett. Clark died in May 1999 when he was hit by a car.
● ALBUMS: *Tangerine Dream* (Fontana 1967) ★★★, *Faintly Blowing* (Fontana 1969) ★★, *White-Faced Lady* (Kaleidoscope 1991) ★★.
● COMPILATIONS: *Dive Into Yesterday* (Fontana 1997) ★★.

KALEIDOSCOPE (USA)

Formed in 1966, this innovative group owed its origins to California's jug band and bluegrass milieu. Guitarists David Lindley and Chris Darrow were both former members of the Dry City Scat Band, while Solomon Feldthouse (vocals/oud/caz) had performed in the region's folk clubs. John Vidican (drums) and Charles Chester Crill – aka Connie Crill, Max Buda, Fenrus Epp or Templeton Parceley (violin, organ, harmonic, vocals) – completed the line-up which, having flirted with the name Bagdhad Blues Band, then settled on Kaleidoscope. *Side Trips* revealed a group of enthralling imagination, offering a music drawn from the individual members' disparate interests. Blues, jazz, folk and ethnic styles abounded as the quintet forged a fascinating collection, but although the album was comprised of short songs, Kaleidoscope's reputation as a superior live attraction was based on lengthy improvised pieces. The group tried to address this contrast with *A Beacon From Mars*, which contrasted six concise performances with two extended compositions, the neo-Eastern 'Taxim' and the

feedback-laden title track. The album marke[ ] the end of this particular line-up as Darrow opted to join the Nitty Gritty Dirt Band. Vidica[ ] also left the group, and thus newcomers Stua[ ] Brotman (bass) and Paul Lagos (drums) wer[ ] featured on *Incredible Kaleidoscope*, which i[ ] turn offered a tougher, less acid-fol[ ] perspective. There were, nonetheless, sever[ ] highlights, including the expanded 'Seven A[ ] Sweet' and propulsive 'Lie To Me', but th[ ] album was not a commercial success, despit[ ] the publicity generated by the group[ ] sensational appearance at the 1968 Newpo[ ] Folk Festival.

Further changes in the line-up ensued with th[ ] departure of Brotman, who was fired durin[ ] sessions for a prospective fourth album. H[ ] replacement, Ron Johnson, introduced a fun[ ] influenced element to the unit's sound, while[ ] second newcomer, Jeff Kaplan, surprisingl[ ] took most of the lead vocals. Kaleidoscope[ ] muse sadly failed to accommodate thes[ ] changes, and *Bernice* was a marke[ ] disappointment. The late-period group di[ ] complete two excellent songs for the fil[ ] soundtrack of *Zabriskie Point*, but the departure[ ] of Feldthouse and Crill in 1970 signalled the[ ] demise. Despite the addition of Richard Apla[ ] to the line-up, Kaleidoscope dissolved later i[ ] the year in the wake of Kaplan's death from[ ] drugs overdose. David Lindley subsequent[ ] embarked on a career as a session musician an[ ] solo artist, a path Chris Darrow also followe[ ] albeit with less commercial success. The latte[ ] subsequently joined Feldthouse, Brotma[ ] Lagos and Crill in the re-formed un[ ] completing *When Scopes Collide* which, althoug[ ] lacking the innovation of old, was nonethele[ ] entertaining. The same line-up reconvened t[ ] complete 1991's equally meritorious *Greetin[ ] From Kartoonistan ... (We Ain't Dead Yet)*. Suc[ ] sets simply enhanced the Kaleidoscope legen[ ] which was considerably buoyed by a series [ ] excellent compilations. They remain one of th[ ] era's most innovative acts.
● ALBUMS: *Side Trips* (Epic 1967) ★★★, *Beacon From Mars* (Epic 1968) ★★★, *Incredib[ ] Kaleidoscope* (Epic 1969) ★★★, *Bernice* (Ep[ ] 1970) ★★, *When Scopes Collide* (Island 197[ ] ★★★★, *Greetings From Kartoonistan ... (We Air[ ] Dead Yet)* (Curb 1991) ★★★.
● COMPILATIONS: *Bacon From Mars* (Edse[ ] 1983) ★★★, *Rampe Rampe* (Edsel 1984) ★★[ ] *Egyptian Candy* (Legacy 1990) ★★★, *Blues Fro[ ] Baghdad – The Very Best Of Kaleidoscope* (Eds[ ] 1993) ★★★, *Infinite Colours Infinite Patterns: Th[ ] Best Of Kaleidoscope* (Edsel 2000) ★★★.

KANE, EDEN

b. Richard Sarstedt, 29 March 1942, Delhi, Indi[ ] When his family returned to England from Ind[ ] during the mid-50s, Kane became involved i[ ] music, forming a skiffle group with his brother[ ] In 1960, he won a talent contest and cam[ ] nder the wing of managers Michael Barclay nd Philip Waddilove. They changed his name o Eden Kane, inspired by the movie *Citizen ane* and the biblical name Cain. Promoted by he chocolate firm, Cadbury's, Kane's first single 'as 'Hot Chocolate Crazy', which failed to chart. or the follow-up, Kane recorded the catchy, olloquial 'Well I Ask You', which took him to umber 1 in the UK during the summer of 1961.)ver the next year, three more Top 10 hits ollowed: 'Get Lost', 'Forget Me Not' and 'I Don't now Why'. Kane's career suffered a serious etback early in 1963 when Barclay and 'addilove's company Audio Enterprises went nto liquidation. The star's management was assed on to Vic Billings, who persuaded ontana's influential A&R manager Jack averstock to sign him. In early 1964, Kane eturned to the UK Top 10 with 'Boys Cry', which lso proved a major hit in Australia. In the utumn of that year, Kane made the momentous ecision to emigrate to Australia, later relocating o the USA. Although his chart days were over, is younger brothers Peter Sarstedt and Robin arstedt both enjoyed hits in their own right. he brothers combined their talents in 1973 for he album, *Worlds Apart Together*. Thereafter, ane continued to play regularly on the vivalist circuit.

● ALBUMS: *Eden Kane* (Ace Of Clubs 1962) ★★, 's *Eden* (Fontana 1964, reissued as *Smoke Gets Your Eyes* in 1965) ★★, with Peter & Robin arstedt *Worlds Apart Together* (1973) ★★.

COMPILATIONS: *Well I Ask You* (Deram 1999) ★★, *All The Hits Plus More* (Prestige Bite 2001) ★★.

KASENETZ-KATZ SINGING ORCHESTRAL CIRCUS

he brainchild of bubblegum pop producers, erry Kasenetz and Jeff Katz, the Singing rchestral Circus was a sprawling aggregation of ight groups on one record: the Ohio Express, he 1910 Fruitgum Company, Music Explosion, t. Garcia's Magic Music Box, Teri Nelson Group, lusical Marching Zoo, JCW Rat Finks and the t. Louis Invisible Marching Band. Together, ey were responsible for one of ubblegum's more memorable moments with he international hit, 'Quick Joey Small' in 1968. /ith an attendant array of acrobats, clowns, fire-aters and scantily-clad girls, the circus played a oncert at Carnegie Hall with a repertoire which icluded such hits as 'Yesterday', 'We Can Work Out', 'Hey Joe' and 'You've Lost That Lovin' eelin''. The prestige of this event did not revent them from taking their place as one-hit-onders.

KAYE, CAROL

Carol Everett, 1935, Washington, USA. Bass uitarist Kaye was one of the few women usicians, as opposed to vocalists, prospering in he enclosed Los Angeles session fraternity.

During the 60s she joined, among others, Glen Campbell, Tommy Tedesco, Billy Strange (guitars) and Larry Knechtal (piano) as a member of a group affectionately known as Hal Blaine's Wrecking Crew. Kaye contributed to innumerable recordings, the most notable of which were with Phil Spector protégées the Crystals, the Ronettes and Darlene Love. Her bass work also appeared on many west coast Tamla/Motown sessions and, by contrast, *Freak Out*, the first album by the Mothers Of Invention. Her affinity with soul/blues-influenced artists was exemplified in appearances on Joe Cocker's *With A Little Help From My Friends* (1969) and Robert Palmer's *Some People Can Do What They Like* (1976). Classical-styled sessions for David Axelrod contrasted with singer-songwriter work with Dory Previn and exemplified the versatility of this talented and prolific musician. The milestone singles on which Kaye claims to have played (there is some dispute that James Jamerson was on the final mix) are: 'River Deep Mountain High' (Ike And Tina Turner), 'Theme From Shaft' (Isaac Hayes), 'Get Ready' (Temptations), 'Reach Out I'll Be There' (Four Tops), 'I Was Made To Love Her' (Stevie Wonder), 'Everybody's Talkin'' (Nilsson), 'Homeward Bound' (Simon And Garfunkel), 'Good Vibrations' (Beach Boys), 'It's My Party' (Lesley Gore), 'Light My Fire' (Doors), 'You Can't Hurry Love' (Supremes) and 'Young Girl' by Gary Puckett.

KEITH

b. James Barry Keefer, 7 May 1949, Philadelphia, Pennsylvania, USA. Keith was best known for his Top 10 folk rock single '98.6' in January 1967. Keefer started with a band called the Admirations in the early 60s, recording one single for Columbia Records, 'Caravan Of Lonely Men'. He was then discovered by journalist Kal Rudman, who took Keefer to Mercury Records executive Jerry Ross. Signed to that label, and renamed Keith, he recorded his first solo single, 'Ain't Gonna Lie', which narrowly made the US Top 40. '98.6' followed and was his biggest hit, although Keith charted twice in 1967 with lesser hits, 'Tell Me To My Face' and 'Daylight Savin' Time'. He recorded a few more singles for Mercury and two albums, only the first of which made the charts. After spending time in the armed forces, he returned to a changed musical direction, recording a single, 'In And Out Of Love', for Frank Zappa's Discreet label, and singing briefly with Zappa's band (he did not record with them). Keefer recorded one last album, for RCA Records, with no luck, and then left the music business until 1986, when an attempted comeback under his real name proved unsuccessful.

● ALBUMS: *98.6/Ain't Gonna Lie* (Mercury 1967) ★★, *Out Of Crank* (Mercury 1968) ★★, *The Adventures Of Keith* (RCA 1969) ★★.

KIDD, JOHNNY, AND THE PIRATES

Kidd (b. Frederick Heath, 23 December 1939, Willesden, London, England, d. 7 October 1966, England), is now rightly revered as an influential figure in the birth of British rock. Although his backing group fluctuated, this enigmatic figure presided over several seminal pre-Beatles releases. Formed in January 1959, the original line-up consisted of two former members of the Five Nutters skiffle group, Kidd (lead vocals) and Alan Caddy (b. 2 February 1940, Chelsea, London, England, d. 16 August 2000; lead guitar), joined by Tony Docherty (rhythm guitar), Johnny Gordon (bass) and Ken McKay (drums), plus backing singers Mike West and Tom Brown. Their compulsive debut single, 'Please Don't Touch' barely scraped into the UK Top 20, but it remains one of the few authentic home-grown rock 'n' roll performances to emerge from the 50s. Its immediate successors were less original and although they featured session men, most of Kidd's group was then dropped in favour of experienced hands. By 1960, Kidd and Caddy were fronting a new rhythm section consisting of Brian Gregg (bass) and Clem Cattini (b. 28 August 1939, London, England; drums). Their first single, 'Shakin' All Over', was another remarkable achievement, marked by its radical stop/start tempo, Kidd's feverish delivery and an incisive lead guitar solo from session man Joe Moretti.

The song deservedly topped the charts, but its inspiration to other musicians was equally vital. Defections resulted in the formation of a third line-up – Kidd, Johnny Spence (bass), Frank Farley (drums) and Johnny Patto (guitar) – although the last was replaced by Mick Green. Onstage, the group continued to wear full pirate regalia while the singer sported a distinctive eye-patch, but they were under increasing competition from the emergent Liverpool sound. Two 1963 hits, 'I'll Never Get Over You' and 'Hungry For Love', although memorable, owed a substantial debt to Merseybeat at the expense of the unit's own identity. The following year, Green left to join the Dakotas, precipitating a succession of replacements, and although he continued to record, a depressed leader talked openly of retirement. However, the singer re-emerged in 1966, fronting the New Pirates, but Kidd's renewed optimism ended in tragedy when, on 7 October, he was killed in a car crash. This pivotal figure is remembered both as an innovator and for the many musicians who passed through his ranks. John Weider (the Animals and Family), Nick Simper (Deep Purple) and John Moorshead (Aynsley Dunbar Retaliation) are a few of those who donned the requisite costume, while the best-known line-up, Green, Spence and Farley, successfully re-established the Pirates name during the late 70s.

● COMPILATIONS: *Shakin' All Over* (Regal Starline 1971) ★★★, *Johnny Kidd – Rocker* (EMI France 1978) ★★★, *The Best Of Johnny Kidd And The Pirates* (EMI 1978) ★★★, *Rarities* (See For Miles 1983) ★★★, *The Classic And The Rare* (See For Miles 1990) ★★★, *The Complete Johnny Kidd* (EMI 1992) ★★★★, *25 Greatest Hits* (MFP 1998) ★★★★, *The Story* (Erri Plus 2001) ★★★.
● FURTHER READING: *Shaking All Over*, Keith Hunt.

KING CURTIS

b. Curtis Ousley, 7 February 1934, Fort Worth, Texas, USA, d. 13 August 1971, New York City, New York, USA. A respected saxophonist and session musician, Curtis appeared on countless releases, including those as disparate as Buddy Holly and Andy Williams. He is, however, best recalled for his work on Atlantic Records. A former member of Lionel Hampton's band Curtis moved to New York and quickly became an integral part of its studio system. He also scored a number 1 US R&B single, 'Soul Twist' billed as King Curtis And The Noble Knights. The same group switched to Capitol Records, but the leader took a solo credit on later hits 'The Monkey' (1963) and 'Soul Serenade' (1964). Curtis continued his session work with the Coasters, the Shirelles and Herbie Mann, while releases on Atco Records, backed by the Kingpins, progressively established his own career. Several were simply funky instrumental versions of current hits, but his strongest release was 'Memphis Soul Stew' (1967). The saxophonist had meanwhile put together a superb studio group: Richard Tee, Cornell Dupree, Jerry Jemmott and Bernard 'Pretty' Purdie, all of whom contributed to several of Aretha Franklin's finest records. Curtis guested on John Lennon's *Imagine* and was capable of attracting the best session musicians to put in appearances for his own albums, including guitarist Duane Allman on *Instant Groove* and organist Billy Preston on *Live At Fillmore West*. Curtis did venture to the Fame and American studios, but he preferred to work in New York. 'In the south you have to restrain yourself to make sure you come back alive', Ousley said to writer Charlie Gillett. Six months later, in August 1971, he was stabbed to death outside his West 86th Street apartment.

● ALBUMS: *Have Tenor Sax, Will Blow* (Atco 1959) ★★★, *The New Scene Of King Curtis* (New Jazz 1960) ★★★, *Azure* (Everest 1961) ★★★, *Trouble In Mind King Curtis Sings The Blues* (Tru-Sound 1961) ★★★★, *Old Gold* (Tru-Sound 1961) ★★, *Doin' The Dixie Twist* (Tru-Sound 1962) ★★★, *It's Party Time With King Curtis* (Tru-Sound 1962) ★★★★, *Soul Meeting* (Prestige 1962) ★★★, *Arthur Murray's Music For Dancing The Twist* (RCA Victor 1962) ★★, *Soul Twist* (Enjoy 1962) ★★★, *Country Soul* (Capitol 1963) ★★, *The Great King Curtis* (Clarion 1964) ★★, *Soul Serenade* (Capitol 1964) ★★★, *King Curtis Plays The Hits Made Famous By Sam Cooke* (Capitol 1965) ★★★, *That Lovin' Feelin'* (Atco

1966) ★★★, *Live At Small's Paradise* (Atco 1966) ★★★, *Plays The Great Memphis Hits* (Atco 1967) ★★★, *King Size Soul* (Atco 1967) ★★, *Sax In Motion* (Atco 1968) ★★, *Sweet Soul* (Atco 1968) ★★★, *Instant Groove* (Atco 1969) ★★, *Eternally Soul* (Atco 1970) ★★★, *Everybody's Talkin'* (Atco 1970) ★★, *Get Ready* (Atco 1970) ★★★, *Blues At Montreux* (Atco 1970) ★★★, *Live At Fillmore West* (Atco 1971) ★★★, *Mr. Soul* (Ember 1972) ★★★.
● COMPILATIONS: *Best Of King Curtis* (Capitol 1968) ★★★★, *Didn't He Play!* (Red Lightnin' 1988) ★★★, *The Capitol Years 1962-65* (EMI 1993) ★★★★, *Instant Soul: The Legendary King Curtis* (Razor & Tie 1994) ★★★★, *The Best Of King Curtis* (Collectables 1996) ★★★★.

KING, ALBERT

b. Albert Nelson, 23 April 1923 (although three other dates have also been published), Indianola, Mississippi, USA, d. 21 December 1992, Memphis, Tennessee, USA. Despite the fact that his work has been overshadowed by that of his regal namesake B.B. King, this exceptional performer was one of the finest in the entire blues/soul canon. King's first solo recording, 'Bad Luck Blues', was released in 1953, but it was not until the end of the decade that he embarked on a full-time career. His early work fused his already distinctive fretwork to big band-influenced arrangements and included his first successful single, 'Don't Throw Your Love On Me Too Strong'. However, his style was not fully defined until 1966 when, signed to the Stax Records label, he began working with Booker T. And The MGs. This tightly knit quartet supplied the perfect rhythmic punch, a facet enhanced by a judicious use of horns. 'Cold Feet', which included wry references to several Stax stablemates, and 'I Love Lucy', a homage to King's distinctive Gibson 'Flying V' guitar, stand among his finest recordings. However, this period is best remembered for 'Born Under A Bad Sign' (1967) and 'The Hunter' (1968), two performances that became an essential part of many repertoires including those of Free and Cream. King became a central part of the late 60s 'blues boom', touring the college and concert circuit. His classic album, *Live Wire/Blues Power*, recorded at San Francisco's Fillmore Auditorium in 1968, introduced his music to the white rock audience. More excellent albums followed in its wake, including *King Does The King's Thing*, a tribute collection of Elvis Presley material, and *Years Gone By*. His work during the 70s was largely unaffected by prevailing trends. 'That's What The Blues Is All About' borrowed just enough from contemporary styles to provide King with a Top 20 R&B single, but the bankruptcy of two outlets dealt a blow to King's career. A five-year recording famine ended in 1983, and an astute programme of new material and careful reissues kept the master's catalogue alive. King remained a commanding live

performer and an influential figure. A new generation of musicians, including Robert Cray and the late Stevie Ray Vaughan continued to acknowledge his timeless appeal, a factor reinforced in 1990 when King guested on guitarist Gary Moore's 'back-to-the-roots' collection, *Still Got The Blues*. King died late in 1992.
● ALBUMS: *The Big Blues* (King 1962) ★★★, *Born Under A Bad Sign* (Atlantic 1967) ★★★★, *King Of The Blues Guitar* (Atlantic 1968) ★★★★, *Live Wire/Blues Power* (King 1968) ★★★★, with Steve Cropper, 'Pops' Staples *Jammed Together* (Stax 1969) ★★★, *Years Gone By* (Stax 1969) ★★★★, *King, Does The King's Thing* (Stax 1970) ★★★, *Lovejoy* (Stax 1971) ★★, *I'll Play The Blues For You* (Stax 1972) ★★, *Live At Montreux/Blues At Sunrise* (Stax 1973) ★★★, *I Wanna Get Funky* (Stax 1974) ★★, *The Pinch* (Stax 1976) ★★, *Albert* (Utopia 1976) ★★★, *Truckload Of Lovin'* (Utopia 1976) ★★, *Albert Live* (Utopia 1977) ★★★, *King Albert* (1977) ★★★, *New Orleans Heat* (Tomato 1978) ★★★, *San Francisco '83* (Stax 1983) ★★★, *I'm In A 'Phone Booth, Baby* (Stax 1984) ★★★, with John Mayall *The Lost Session* recorded 1971 (Stax 1986) ★★, *Red House* (Essential 1991) ★★★, *Blues At Sunset* (Stax 1996) ★★★, with Stevie Ray Vaughan *In Session* 1983 recording (Fantasy/Stax 1999) ★★★.
● COMPILATIONS: shared with Otis Rush *Door To Door* (Chess 1969) ★★★, *Laundromat Blues* (Edsel 1984) ★★★, *The Best Of Albert King* (Stax 1986) ★★★, *I'll Play The Blues For You: The Best Of Albert King* (Stax 1988) ★★★, *Let's Have A Natural Ball* 1959-63 recordings (Modern Blues Recordings 1989) ★★★, *Wednesday Night In San Francisco (Live At The Fillmore)* and *Thursday Night In San Francisco (Live At The Fillmore)* (Stax 1990) ★★, *Live On Memory Lane* (Monad 1995) ★★★, *Hard Bargain* (Stax 1996) ★★★★, *The Best Of Albert King* (Stax 1998) ★★★, *The Very Best Of Albert King* (Rhino 1999) ★★★★.

KING, BEN E.

b. Benjamin Earl Nelson, 28 September 1938, Henderson, North Carolina, USA. King began his career while still a high-school student singing in a doo-wop group, the Four B's. He later joined the Five Crowns who, in 1959, assumed the name the Drifters. King was the featured lead vocalist and occasional composer on several of their recordings including 'There Goes My Baby' and 'Save The Last Dance For Me' (written by Doc Pomus and Mort Shuman). After leaving the group in 1960, he recorded the classic single 'Spanish Harlem' (1961), which maintained the Latin quality of the Drifters' work and deservedly reached the US Top 10. The follow-up, 'Stand By Me' (1961), was even more successful and was followed by further hits including 'Amor' (1961) and 'Don't Play That Song' (1962). Throughout this period, King's work was aimed increasingly at the pop audience. 'I (Who Have Nothing)' and 'I Could

Have Danced All Night' (both 1963) suggested show business rather than innovation, although Bert Berns' 'It's All Over' (1964) was a superb song. 'Seven Letters' and 'The Record (Baby I Love You)' (both 1965) prepared the way for the rhetorical 'What Is Soul?' (1967), which effectively placed King alongside such soul contemporaries as Otis Redding, Wilson Pickett and Joe Tex.

Unfortunately, King's commercial standing declined towards the end of the 60s when he left the Atlantic Records group of labels. Unable to reclaim his former standing elsewhere, King later re-signed with his former company and secured a US Top 5 hit in 1975 with 'Supernatural Thing Part 1'. In 1977, a collaboration with the Average White Band resulted in two R&B chart entries and an excellent album, *Benny And Us*. King's later recordings, including *Music Trance* (1980) and *Street Tough* (1981), proved less successful, and he briefly joined up with Johnny Moore in a version of the Drifters still plying their trade on the cabaret circuit. In 1986, 'Stand By Me' was included in the movie of the same name, reaching the US Top 10 and number 1 in the UK, thereby briefly revitalizing the singer's autumnal career.

● ALBUMS: *Spanish Harlem* (Atco 1961) ★★★, *Ben E. King Sings For Soulful Lovers* (Atco 1962) ★★★, *Don't Play That Song* (Atco 1962) ★★★, *Young Boy Blues* (Clarion 1964), *Seven Letters* (Atco 1965) ★★★, *What Is Soul?* (Atco 1967) ★★★, *Rough Edges* (Maxwell 1970) ★★★, *Supernatural* (Atco 1975) ★★★, *I Had A Love* (Atco 1976) ★★, with the Average White Band *Benny And Us* (Atlantic 1977) ★★★, *Let Me Live In Your Life* (Atco 1978) ★★, *Music Trance* (Atlantic 1980) ★★, *Street Tough* (Atlantic 1981) ★★, *Save The Last Dance For Me* (EMI 1988) ★★★, *Shades Of Blue* (Half Note 1999) ★★★.

● COMPILATIONS: *Greatest Hits* (Atco 1964) ★★★, *Beginning Of It All* (Mandala 1971) ★★★, *Here Comes The Night* (Edsel 1984) ★★★, *The Ultimate Collection: Ben E. King* (Atlantic 1987) ★★★★, *Anthology One: Spanish Harlem* (RSA 1996) ★★★, *Anthology Two: For Soulful Lovers* (RSA 1996) ★★★, *Anthology Three: Don't Play That Song* (RSA 1996) ★★★, *Anthology Four: Seven Letters* (RSA 1997) ★★★, *Anthology Five: What Is Soul?* (RSA 1997) ★★★, *Anthology Six: Supernatural* (RSA 1997) ★★★, *Anthology Seven: Benny And Us* (RSA 1997) ★★, *The Very Best Of Ben E. King* (Rhino 1998) ★★★★.

● VIDEOS: *The Jazz Channel Presents Ben E. King* (Aviva 2001).

KING, FREDDIE

b. Billy Myles, 3 September 1934, Gilmer, Texas, USA, d. 28 December 1976, Dallas, Texas. Freddie (aka Freddy) was one of the triumvirate of Kings (the others being B.B. and Albert) who ruled the blues throughout the 60s. He was the possessor of a light, laid-back, but not unemotional voice and a facile fast-fingered guitar technique that made him the hero of many young disciples. He learned to play guitar at an early age, being influenced by his mother, Ella Mae King, and her brother Leon. Although forever associated with Texas and admitting a debt to such artists as T-Bone Walker he moved north to Chicago in his mid-teens. In 1950, he became influenced by local blues guitarists Eddie Taylor and Robert Lockwood. King absorbed elements from each of their styles, before encompassing the more strident approaches of Magic Sam and Otis Rush. Here, he began to sit in with various groups and slowly built up the reputation that was to make him a star.

After teaming up with Jimmy Lee Robinson to form the Every Hour Blues Boys he worked and recorded with Little Sonny Cooper's band, Earlee Payton's Blues Cats and Smokey Smothers. These last recordings were made in Cincinnati, Ohio, in August 1960 for Sydney Nathan's King/Federal organization, and on the same day, King recorded six titles under his own name, including the influential instrumental hit 'Hideaway'. He formed his own band and began touring, bolstering his success with further hits, many of them guitar showpieces, some trivialized by titles such as 'The Bossa Nova Watusi Twist', but others showing off his 'crying' vocal delivery. Many, such as '(I'm) Tore Down', 'Have You Ever Loved A Woman' and particularly 'The Welfare (Turns Its Back On You)', became classics of the (then) modern blues. He continued to record for King Federal up until 1966, his career on record being masterminded by pianist Sonny Thompson. He left King Federal in 1966 and took up a short tenure (1968-69) on the Atlantic Records subsidiary label Cotillion.

Ironically, the subsequent white blues-boom provided a new found impetus. Eric Clapton was a declared King aficionado, while Chicken Shack's Stan Webb indicated his debt by including three of his mentor's compositions on his group's debut album. The albums that followed failed to capture the artist at his best. This was not a particularly successful move, although the work he did on that label has increased in value with the passage of time. The same could be said for his next musical liaison, which saw him working with Leon Russell on his Shelter Records label. Much of his work for Russell was over-produced, but King made many outstanding recordings during this period and a re-evaluation of that work is overdue. There was no denying the excitement it generated, particularly on *Getting Ready*, which was recorded at the famous Chess Records studio. This excellent set included the original version of the much-covered 'Going Down'. Live recordings made during his last few years indicate that King was still a force to be reckoned with as he continued his good-natured guitar battles with allcomers, and usually left them far behind. *Burglar* featured a duet with Eric Clapton on 'Sugar Sweet', but the potential of this new relationship was tragically cut short in December 1976 when King died of heart failure at the early age of 43. His last stage appearance had taken place three days earlier in his home town of Dallas.

● ALBUMS: *Freddie King Sings The Blues* (King 1961) ★★★, *Let's Hideaway And Dance Away* (King 1961) ★★★★, *Boy-Girl-Boy* (King 1962) ★★★, *Bossa Nova And Blues* (King 1962) ★★, *Freddie King Goes Surfing* (King 1963) ★★, *Freddie King Gives You A Bonanza Of Instrumentals* (King 1965) ★★★, *24 Vocals And Instrumentals* (King 1966) ★★★, *Hide Away* (King 1969) ★★★★, *Freddie King Is A Blues Master* (Atlantic 1969) ★★★, *My Feeling For The Blues* (Atlantic 1970) ★★★, *Getting Ready* (Shelter 1971) ★★★★, *Texas Cannonball* (Shelter 1972) ★★★, *Woman Across The Water* (Shelter 1973) ★★★, *Burglar* (RSO 1974) ★★★, *Larger Than Life* (RSO 1975) ★★★, *Live At The Electric Ballroom 1974* (Black Top 1996) ★★★.

● COMPILATIONS: *The Best Of Freddie King* (Shelter 1974) ★★★★, *Rockin' The Blues – Live* (Crosscut 1983) ★★★, *Takin' Care Of Business* (Charly 1985) ★★★, *Live In Antibes, 1974* (Concert 1988) ★★★, *Live In Nancy, 1975 Volume 1* (Concert 1989) ★★★, *Blues Guitar Hero: The Influential Early Sessions* (EMI 1993) ★★★, *King Of The Blues* (EMI/Shelter 1996) ★★★★, *Key To The Highway* (Wolf 1995) ★★★, *Stayin' Home With The Blues* RSO material (Spectrum 1998) ★★★, *The Ultimate Collection* (Hip-O 2001) ★★★★.

● VIDEOS: *Freddie King Jan 20 1973* (Vestapol Music Video 1995), *Freddie King In Concert* (Vestapol Music Video 1995), *Freddie King: The !!!!Beat 1966* (Vestapol Music Video 1995), *Live At The Sugarbowl, 1972* (Vestapol Music Video 1998).

KING, SOLOMON

This US singer came to prominence in 1968 with the powerful hit ballad 'She Wears My Ring'. It was based on a classical piece of music called *Golandrina (The Swallow)*. King was signed by manager/entrepreneur Gordon Mills but failed to emulate the phenomenal success of his stablemates Tom Jones and Engelbert Humperdinck. He continued to record well into the 70s, and his version of 'Say A Little Prayer' (1970) is a prized rarity among soul fans.

● ALBUMS: *She Wears My Ring* (Columbia 1968) ★★★, *You'll Never Walk Alone* (Columbia 1971) ★★.

KINGSMEN

Jack Ely (vocals/guitar), Mike Mitchell (guitar) Bob Nordby (bass) and Lynn Easton (drums) began working as the Kingsmen in 1958. Based in Portland, Oregon, USA, they became a staple part of the region's thriving circuit prior to the arrival of Don Gallucci (keyboards) in 1962. The group's debut single, 'Louie Louie', was released the following year. The song was composed and originally recorded by Richard Berry in 1956, and its primitive, churning rhythm was later adopted by several Northwest state bands, including the Wailers and Paul Revere And The Raiders. However, it was the Kingsmen who popularized this endearing composition when it rose to number 2 in the US chart. Its classic C-F-G chord progression, as simple as it was effective, was absorbed by countless 'garage bands', and 'Louie Louie' has subsequently become one of rock's best-known and most influential creations. Indeed, a whole album's worth of recordings of the song by various artists, including the Kingsmen and Richard Berry, was issued by Rhino Records entitled, *The Best Of Louie Louie*. Relations between the individual Kingsmen were sundered on the single's success. Easton informed Ely that he now wished to sing lead, and furthered his argument by declaring himself the sole proprietor of the group's name, having judiciously registered the moniker at their inception. Ely and Norby walked out, although the former won a victory of sorts when a judgement declared that every pressing of the Kingsmen's greatest hit must include the words 'lead vocals by Jack Ely'. His former cohorts added Norm Sundholm (bass) and Gary Abbot (drums), but despite a succession of dance-related releases including 'The Climb', 'Little Latin Lupe Lu' and 'The Jolly Green Giant', the group was unable to maintain a long-term livelihood. Gallucci formed Don And The Goodtimes, Kerry Magnus and Dick Petersen replaced Sundholm and Abbot, but the crucial alteration came in 1967 when Easton left the group. Numerous half-hearted reincarnations aside, his departure brought the Kingsmen to an end.

● ALBUMS: *The Kingsmen In Person* (Wand 1963) ★★, *The Kingsmen, Volume 2 (More Great Sounds)* (Wand 1964) ★★, *The Kingsmen, Volume 3* (Wand 1965) ★★, *The Kingsmen On Campus* (Wand 1965) ★★, *Up Up And Away* (Wand 1966) ★★.

● COMPILATIONS: *15 Great Hits* (Wand 1966) ★★, *The Kingsmen's Greatest Hits* (Wand 1967) ★★, *Louie Louie/Greatest Hits* (Charly 1986) ★★★, *The Very Best Of The Kingsmen* (Varèse Vintage 1998) ★★★.

● FILMS: *How To Stuff A Wild Bikini* (1965).

KINKS

It is ironic that one of Britain's most enduring and respected groups spawned from the beat boom of the early 60s, received, for the best part of two decades, success, adulation and financial reward in the USA. This most 'English' institution were able to fill stadiums in any part of the USA, while in Britain, a few thousand devotees watched their heroes perform in comparatively small clubs or halls.

The Kinks is the continuing obsession of one of Britain's premier songwriting talents, Ray Davies

(b. Raymond Douglas Davies, 21 June 1944, Muswell Hill, London, England; vocals/guitar/piano). Originally known as the Ravens, the Kinks formed at the end of 1963 with a line-up comprising Davies, his brother Dave Davies (b. 3 February 1947, Muswell Hill, London, England; guitar/vocals) and Peter Quaife (b. 31 December 1943, Tavistock, Devon, England; bass), and were subsequently joined by Mick Avory (b. 15 February 1944, London, England; drums). Their first single 'Long Tall Sally' failed to sell, although they did receive a lot of publicity through the efforts of their shrewd managers Robert Wace, Grenville Collins and Larry Page. Their third single, 'You Really Got Me', rocketed to the UK number 1 spot, boosted by an astonishing performance on the UK television show *Ready, Steady, Go!* This and its successor, 'All Day And All Of The Night', provided a blueprint for hard rock guitar playing, with the simple but powerful riffs supplied by the younger Davies. Over the next two years Ray Davies emerged as a songwriter of startling originality and his band were rarely out of the bestsellers list.

Early in 1965, the Kinks returned to the top of the UK charts with the languid 'Tired Of Waiting For You'. They enjoyed a further string of UK hits that year, including 'Everybody's Gonna Be Happy', 'Set Me Free', 'See My Friend' and 'Till The End Of The Day'. Despite the humanity of his lyrics, Ray Davies was occasionally a problematical character, renowned for his eccentric behaviour. The Kinks were equally tempestuous and frequently violent. Earlier in 1965, events had reached a head when the normally placid drummer, Mick Avory, attacked Dave Davies on stage with the hi-hat of his drum kit, having been goaded beyond endurance. Remarkably, the band survived such contretemps and soldiered on. A disastrous US tour saw them banned from that country, however, amid further disputes.

Throughout all the drama, Davies the songwriter remained supreme. He combined his own introspection with humour and pathos. The ordinary and the obvious were spelled out in his lyrics, but, contrastingly, never in a manner that was either. 'Dedicated Follower Of Fashion' brilliantly satirized Carnaby Street narcissism while 'Sunny Afternoon' (another UK number 1) dealt with capitalism and class. 'Dead End Street' at the end of 1966 highlighted the plight of the working class poor: 'Out of work and got no money, a Sunday joint of bread and honey', while later in that same song Davies comments 'What are we living for, two-roomed apartment on the second floor, no money coming in, the rent collector knocks and tries to get in'. All these songs were delivered in Davies' laconic, uniquely English singing voice. The Kinks' albums prior to 1966's *Face To Face* had contained a staple diet of R&B standards and comparatively harmless Davies originals. With *Face To Face* and *Something Else*, however, he set about redefining the English character, with sparkling wit and steely nerve. One of Davies' greatest songs was the final track on the latter; 'Waterloo Sunset' was a simple but emotional *tour de force* with the melancholic singer observing two lovers (many have suggested actor Terence Stamp and actress Julie Christie, but Davies denies this) meeting and crossing over Hungerford Bridge in London. It narrowly missed the top of the charts, as did the follow-up, 'Autumn Almanac', with its gentle chorus, summing up the English working class lifestyle of the 50s and 60s: 'I like my football on a Saturday, roast beef on Sunday is all right, I go to Blackpool for my holiday, sit in the autumn sunlight'.

Throughout this fertile period, Ray Davies, along with John Lennon/Paul McCartney and Pete Townshend, was among Britain's finest writers. But by 1968 the Kinks had fallen from public grace in their home country, despite remaining well respected by the critics. Two superb concept albums, *The Kinks Are The Village Green Preservation Society* and *Arthur (Or The Decline And Fall Of The British Empire)*, failed to sell. This inexplicable quirk was all the harder to take as they contained some of Davies' finest songs. Writing honestly about everyday events seemingly no longer appealed to Davies' public. The former was likened to Dylan Thomas' *Under Milkwood*, while *Arthur* had to compete with Pete Townshend's *Tommy*. Both were writing rock operas without each other's knowledge, but as Johnny Rogan states in his biography of the Kinks: 'Davies' celebration of the mundane was far removed from the studious iconoclasm of *Tommy* and its successors'. The last hit single during this 'first' age of the Kinks was the glorious 'Days'. This lilting and timeless ballad is another of Davies' many classics, and was a major hit for Kirsty MacColl in 1989.

Pete Quaife permanently departed in 1969 and was replaced by ex-Creation member John Dalton. The Kinks returned to the UK bestsellers lists in July 1970 with 'Lola', an irresistible fable of transvestism, which marked the beginning of their breakthrough in the USA by reaching the Top 10. The resulting *Lola Versus Powerman And The Moneygoround, Part One* was also a success there. On this record Davies attacked the music industry and in one track, 'The Moneygoround', openly slated his former managers and publishers, while alluding to the lengthy high court action in which he had been embroiled. The Kinks now embarked on a series of huge US tours and rarely performed in Britain, although their business operation centre and recording studio, Konk, was based close to the Davies' childhood home in north London.

Having signed a new contract with RCA Records in 1971 the band had now enlarged to incorporate a brass section, amalgamating with the Mike Cotton Sound. Following the interesting country-influenced *Muswell Hillbillies*, however, they suffered a barren period. Ray Davies experienced drug and marital problems and their ragged half-hearted live performances revealed a man bereft of his driving, creative enthusiasm. Throughout the early 70s a series of average, over-ambitious concept albums appeared as Davies' main outlet. *Preservation Act 1*, *Preservation Act 2*, *Soap Opera* and *Schoolboys In Disgrace* were all thematic, and *Soap Opera* was adapted for British television as *Starmaker*. At the end of 1976 John Dalton departed, as their unhappy and comparatively unsuccessful years with RCA ended. A new contract with Arista Records engendered a remarkable change in fortunes. Both *Sleepwalker* (1977) and *Misfits* (1978) were excellent and successful albums; Davies had rediscovered the knack of writing short, punchy rock songs with quality lyrics. The musicianship of the band improved, in particular, Dave Davies, who after years in his elder brother's shadow, came into his own with a more fluid style.

Although still spending most of their time playing to vast audiences in the USA, the Kinks were adopted by the British new wave, and were cited by many punk bands as a major influence. Both the Jam ('David Watts') and the Pretenders ('Stop Your Sobbing') provided reminders of Davies' songwriting skill. The UK music press, then normally harsh on rock 'dinosaurs', constantly praised the Kinks and helped to regenerate a market for them in Europe. Their following albums continued the pattern started with *Sleepwalker*, hard-rock numbers with sharp lyrics. Although continuing to be a huge attraction in the USA, the band's UK career remained stubbornly moribund except for regular 'Greatest Hits' packages. Then in 1983, as Ray Davies' stormy three-year relationship with Chrissie Hynde of the Pretenders drew to its close, the Kinks unexpectedly returned to the UK singles chart with the charming 'Come Dancing'. The accompanying video and high publicity profile prompted the reissue of their entire and considerable back catalogue, but following the release of 1984's *Word Of Mouth* the band was released by Arista. They signed a new deal with London Records in the UK and MCA Records in the USA, but their late 80s releases proved disappointing and towards the end of the decade they toured only sporadically amid rumours of a final break-up.

In 1990 the Kinks were inducted into the Rock and Roll Hall of Fame, at the time only the fourth UK band to take the honour behind the Beatles, Rolling Stones and the Who. During the ceremony both Pete Quaife and Mick Avory were present. Later that year they received the Ivor Novello Award for 'outstanding services to British music'. After the comparative failure of *UK Jive* the band left London Records, and after being without a recording contract for some time signed with Sony in 1991. Their debut for that label was *Phobia*, a good album that suffered from lack of promotion (the public still perceiving the Kinks as a 60s act). A prime example was 'Scattered', as good a song as Davies has ever written, which when released was totally ignored apart from a few pro-Kinks radio broadcasters. Following the commercial failure of *Phobia* the band was released from its contract and put out *To The Bone* on their own Konk label. This unplugged session was recorded in front of a small audience at their own headquarters in Crouch End, north London, and contained semi-acoustic versions of some of Davies' finest songs. Both brothers had autobiographies published in the mid-90s. Ray was first with the cleverly constructed *X-Ray*, and Dave responded with *Kink*, a revealing if somewhat pedestrian book.

Whether or not his band can maintain their reputation as a going concern, Ray Davies has made his mark under the Kinks' banner as one of the most perceptive, prolific and popular songwriters of our time. His catalogue of songs is one of the finest available, and he remains one of the most acute observers of the quirks and eccentricities of ordinary life. Much of the Britpop movement from the mid-90s acknowledged a considerable debt to Davies as one of their key musical influences. Bands such as Supergrass, Oasis, Cast, and Damon Albarn of Blur, are some of the Kinks' most admiring students. A long-awaited reissue programme was undertaken by the Castle Communications label in 1998; this was particularly significant as the Kinks catalogue has been mercilessly and often badly reissued for many years. The addition of many bonus tracks on each CD helps make their first five albums even more essential.

● ALBUMS: *Kinks* (UK) *You Really Got Me* (US) (Pye/Reprise 1964) ★★★, *Kinks-Size* US only (Reprise 1965) ★★★, *Kinda Kinks* (Pye/Reprise 1965) ★★★, *Kinkdom* US only (Reprise 1965) ★★★, *The Kink Kontroversy* (Pye/Reprise 1966) ★★★★, *Face To Face* (Pye/Reprise 1966) ★★★★, *Live At Kelvin Hall* (UK) *The Live Kinks* (US) (Pye/Reprise 1968) ★, *Something Else* (Pye/Reprise 1967) ★★★★★, *Are The Village Green Preservation Society* (Pye/Reprise 1968) ★★★★★, *Arthur (Or The Decline And Fall Of The British Empire)* (Pye/Reprise 1969) ★★★★, *Lola Versus Powerman And The Moneygoround, Part One* (Pye/Reprise 1970) ★★★, *Percy* film soundtrack (Pye 1971) ★★, *Muswell Hillbillies* (RCA 1971) ★★★★, *Everybody's In Show-Biz* (RCA 1972) ★★★ *Preservation Act 1* (RCA 1973) ★★, *Preservation Act 2* (RCA 1974) ★★, *Soap Opera* (RCA 1975) ★★, *Schoolboys In Disgrace* (RCA 1975) ★★★, *Sleepwalker* (Arista 1977) ★★★, *Misfits* (Arista 1978) ★★★★, *Low Budget* (Arista 1979) ★★★, *One For The Road* (Arista 1980) ★★★★, *Give The People What They Want* (Arista 1981) ★★★, *State Of Confusion* (Arista

1983) ★★★, *Word Of Mouth* (Arista 1984) ★★, *Think Visual* (London/MCA 1986) ★★, *Live: The Road* (London/MCA 1987) ★★, *UK Jive* (London/MCA 1989) ★★, *Phobia* (Columbia 1993) ★★★, *To The Bone* (UK) (Konk 1994) ★★★★, *To The Bone* (USA) (Guardian 1996) ★★★★.

● COMPILATIONS: *Well Respected Kinks* (Marble Arch 1966) ★★★★, *Greatest Hits!* US only (Reprise 1966) ★★★★, *Then Now And Inbetween* US only (Reprise 1969) ★★★★, *The Kinks* (Pye 1970) ★★★★, *The Kink Kronikles* US only (Reprise 1971) ★★★★, *The Great Lost Kinks Album* US only (Reprise 1973) ★★★, *Lola, Percy And The Apeman Come Face To Face With The Village Green Preservation Society ... Something Else* (Golden Hour 1973) ★★★★, *All The Good Times* 4-LP box set (Pye 1973) ★★★★, *Celluloid Heroes: Greatest Hits* (RCA 1976) ★★★★, *The Kinks File* (Pye 1977) ★★★★, *Second Time Around* US only (RCA 1980) ★★, *Dead End Street: Greatest Hits* (PRT 1983) ★★★★, *Come Dancing With The Kinks* US only (Arista 1986) ★★★, *Are Well Respected Men* (PRT 1987) ★★★★, *Greatest Hits* (Rhino 1989) ★★★★★, *Fab Forty: The Singles Collection: 1964-1970* (Decal 1990) ★★★★, *The EP Collection* (See For Miles 1990) ★★★★, *The EP Collection Vol. Two* (See For Miles 1991) ★★★, *The Complete Collection* (Castle 1991) ★★★★, *Lost & Found (1986-89)* (MCA 1991) ★★, *The Best Of The Ballads* (BMG 1993) ★★★, *Tired Of Waiting For You* (Rhino 1995) ★★★, *Remastered* 3-CD set (Castle 1995) ★★★★, *The Singles Collection/Waterloo Sunset* (Castle 1997) ★★★★★, *Kinks* reissue (Castle 1998) ★★★, *Kinda Kinks* reissue (Castle 1998) ★★★, *The Kink Kontroversy* reissue (Castle 1998) ★★★★, *Face To Face* reissue (Castle 1998) ★★★★, *Something Else* reissue (Castle 1998) ★★★★★, *The Songs We Sang For Auntie: BBC Sessions 1964 > 1977* (Sanctuary 2001) ★★★★, *The Marble Arch Years* 3-CD box set (Castle 2001) ★★★★.

● VIDEOS: *The Kinks: One For The Road* (Time Live 1980), *Come Dancing With The Kinks* (Columbia Pictures Home Video 1986), *Shindig! Presents The Kinks* (Rhino Home Video 1992).

● FURTHER READING: *The Kinks: The Sound And The Fury*, Johnny Rogan. *The Kinks: The Official Biography*, Jon Savage. *The Kinks Part One: You Really Got Me – An Illustrated World Discography Of The Kinks, 1964-1993*, Doug Hinman with Jason Brabazon. *X-Ray*, Ray Davies. *Kink: An Autobiography*, Dave Davies. *The Kinks: Well Respected Men*, Neville Marten and Jeffrey Hudson. *Waterloo Sunset*, Ray Davies. *The Complete Guide To The Music Of The Kinks*, Johnny Rogan.

KIPPINGTON LODGE

Best remembered as the vehicle for the earliest Nick Lowe (b. 24 March 1949, Walton-On-Thames, Surrey, England) recordings, Kippington Lodge stemmed from Lowe's first band, Sounds 4+1, which he formed with school

pal, Brinsley Schwarz. On leaving school, Lowe already used to a nomadic existence as his fathe was in the Royal Air Force, decided to go and se some more of the world, leaving Schwarz t return to his native Tunbridge Wells in Kent Here Schwarz formed Three's A Crowd wh were signed to EMI Records in 1967. Changin their name to Kippington Lodge they release their debut 'Shy Boy' in October. This effectiv pop song was accompanied by the equally goo 'Lady On A Bicycle'. At this point, Lowe returne to England and joined his friends in time for th second single 'Rumours' which was produced b Mark Wirtz. Lowe's arrival fixed the line-up a Schwarz (guitar/vocals), Lowe (bass/vocals) Barry Landerman (organ) and Pete Whal (drums). Landerman soon departed – late resurfacing in Vanity Fare – and was replaced b Bob Andrews (b. 20 June 1949). To supplemen their lack of income from record sales Kippington Lodge became Billie Davies' backin group and released three further singles durin 1968-69. These releases were produced by EM stalwarts such as Mike Collier, Roger Easterb and Des Champ. The last single, a version of th Beatles' 'In My Life', came out in April 1969 anc after doing as poorly as previous efforts, left th group at a loose end. In September they replace Pete Whale with the American drummer Bill Rankin and the name Kippington Lodge wa dropped in favour of that of lead guitaris Brinsley Schwarz.

● COMPILATIONS: *Hen's Teeth* (Edsel 1998 ★★★.

KIRBY, KATHY

b. 20 October 1940, Ilford, Essex, England. He *bel canto* eloquence when in a convent schoc choir had her earmarked for a career in oper until 1956, when an unscheduled performanc with Ambrose And His Orchestra at a loca dancehall precipitated three years as the outfit featured singer – with Ambrose as her mento until his death in 1971. After stints with the b bands of Denny Boyle and Nat Allen, sh headlined seasons in Madrid and Londo nightspots, and won recording contracts on Py and then Decca – but it was only when he strawberry blonde, gloss-lipped appeal wa transferred to UK television in 1963, as a regula on the *Stars And Garters* variety show, that he records started selling. Her biggest UK smashe were with consecutive revivals of Doris Day 'Secret Love' and Teresa Brewer's 'Let Me G Lover', but these were adjuncts to her earning for personal appearances and two BBC serie (*Kathy Kirby Sings*). After a spot on 1965's Roy Command Performance – the apogee of Britis showbusiness – signs of danger were not y perceptible. However, with that year Eurovision Song Contest entry ('I Belong') he Top 40 farewell, and her aspirations to be a fil actress frustrated, Ambrose's manageri arrogance and old-fashioned values upset BB

(and ITV) executives, thus consigning his cocooned client to a cabaret ghost-kingdom. Confused by post-Ambrose administrative chaos, Kirby's prima donna tantrums and failure to honour contracts made her a booker's risk. The 70s were further underscored by a disastrous marriage, bankruptcy, failed comebacks and, in 1979, a spell in a mental hospital following her arrest for an unpaid hotel bill (of which she was innocent). Just as unwelcome was publicity concerning her cohabitation with another woman. When the latter was jailed, the affair ended, and Kirby returned to the stage as an intermission act in a Kent bingo hall. Since then, she has played one-nighters, nostalgia revues and has sold the story of her tragic downfall to a Sunday newspaper. In more recent years Kirby has become a recluse, and speculation as to her whereabouts is constantly being expressed in the UK media. In 1994, 'an exciting new play' entitled *Whatever Happened To Kathy Kirby?*, was presented in the London provinces, while a year later, an unauthorized biography was published.
● ALBUMS: *16 Hits From Stars And Garters* (1964) ★★, *Make Someone Happy* (Decca 1967) ★★★, *My Thanks To You* (Columbia 1968) ★★.
● COMPILATIONS: *The Best Of Kathy Kirby* (Ace of Clubs 1968) ★★★, *The World Of Kathy Kirby* (Decca 1970) ★★★, *Let Me Sing And I'm Happy* (1983) ★★★, *Secret Love* (1989) ★★★, *The Very Best Of Kathy Kirby* (Spectrum 1996) ★★★.
● FURTHER READING: *Kathy Kirby: Is That All There Is?*, James Harman.

KIRK, RAHSAAN ROLAND

b. 7 August 1936, Columbus, Ohio, USA, d. 5 December 1977, Bloomington, Indiana, USA. Originally named 'Ronald', Kirk changed it to 'Roland' and added 'Rahsaan' after a dream visitation by spirits who 'told him to'. Blinded soon after his birth, Kirk became one of the most prodigious multi-instrumentalists to work in jazz, with a career that spanned R&B, bop and the 'New Thing' jazz style. According to Joe Goldberg's sleeve notes for *Kirk's Work* (1961), Kirk took up trumpet at the age of nine after hearing the bugle boy at a summer camp where his parents acted as counsellors. He played trumpet in the school band, but a doctor advised against the strain trumpet-playing imposes on the eyes. At the Ohio State School for the Blind, he took up saxophone and clarinet from 1948. By 1951 he was well-known as a player and was leading his own dance band in the locality. Kirk's ability to play three instruments simultaneously gained him notoriety. Looking through the 'scraps' in the basement of a music store, Kirk found two horns believed to have been put together from different instruments, but which possibly dated from late nineteenth-century Spanish military bands. The manzello was basically an alto saxophone with a 'large, fat, ungainly' bell. The strich resembled 'a larger, more cumbersome soprano'. He found a method

of playing both, plus his tenor, producing a wild, untempered 'ethnic' sound ideal for late-60s radical jazz. He also soloed on all three separately and added flute, siren and clavietta (similar to the melodica used by Augustus Pablo and the Gang Of Four) to his armoury. With all three horns strung around his neck, and sporting dark glasses and a battered top hat, Kirk made quite a spectacle.

The real point was that, although he loved to dally with simple R&B and ballads, he could unleash break-neck solos that sounded like a bridge between bebop dexterity and *avant garde* 'outness'. His debut for a properly distributed label – recorded for Cadet Records in Chicago in June 1960 at the behest of Ramsey Lewis – provoked controversy, some deriding the three-horn-trick as a gimmick, others applauding the fire of his playing. In 1961, he joined the Charles Mingus Workshop for four months, toured California and played on *Oh Yeah!*. He also played the Essen Jazz Festival in Germany. In 1963, he began the first of several historic residencies at Ronnie Scott's club in London. Despite later guest recordings with Jaki Byard (who had played on his *Rip Rig & Panic*) and Mingus (at the 1974 Carnegie Hall concert), Kirk's main focus of activity was his own group, the Vibration Society, with whom he toured the world until he suffered his first stroke in November 1975, which paralysed his right side. With characteristic single-mindedness, he taught himself to play with his left hand only and started touring again. A second stroke in 1977 caused his death.

Long before the 80s 'consolidation' period for jazz, Kirk presented a music fully cognizant of black American music, from Jelly Roll Morton and Louis Armstrong on through Duke Ellington and John Coltrane; he also paid tribute to the gospel and soul heritage, notably on *Blacknuss*, which featured songs by Marvin Gaye, Smokey Robinson and Bill Withers. Several of his tunes – 'The Inflated Tear', 'Bright Moments', 'Let Me Shake Your Tree', 'No Tonic Pres' – have become jazz standards. His recorded legacy is uneven, but it contains some of the most fiery and exciting music to be heard.
● ALBUMS: *Triple Threat* (King 1956) ★★★, with Booker Ervin *Soulful Saxes* (Affinity 1957) ★★★★, *Introducing Roland Kirk* (Argo 1960) ★★★, *Kirk's Work* (Prestige 1961) ★★★★, *We Free Kings* (Mercury 1962) ★★★★, *Domino* (Mercury 1962) ★★★, *Reeds And Deeds* (Mercury 1963) ★★★, *Roland Kirk Meets The Benny Golson Orchestra* (Mercury 1963) ★★★, *Kirk In Copenhagen* (Mercury 1963) ★★★, *Gifts And Messages* (Mercury 1964) ★★★, *I Talk With The Spirits* (Limelight 1964) ★★★, *Rip Rig & Panic* (Limelight 1965) ★★★★, *Slightly Latin* (Limelight 1966) ★★★, *Now Please Don't You Cry, Beautiful Edith* (Verve 1967) ★★★, *Funk Underneath* (Prestige 1967) ★★★, *Here Comes The Whistle Man* (Atlantic 1967) ★★★, *The*

Inflated Tear (Atlantic 1968) ★★★★, _Left And Right_ (Atlantic 1969) ★★★, _Volunteer Slavery_ (Atlantic 1969) ★★★★, _Rahsaan, Rahsaan_ (Atlantic 1970) ★★★, _Natural Black Inventions: Root Strata_ (Atlantic 1971) ★★★, _Blacknuss_ (Atlantic 1972) ★★★★, with Al Hibbler _A Meeting Of The Times_ (Atlantic 1972) ★★★, _Bright Moments_ (Atlantic 1973) ★★★, _Prepare Thyself To Deal With A Miracle_ (Atlantic 1974) ★★★, _The Case Of The Three Sided Dream In Audio Colour_ (Atlantic 1975) ★★★, _The Return Of The 5000 Lb. Man_ (Warners 1975) ★★★, _Kirkatron_ (Warners 1976) ★★★, _Other Folks' Music_ (Warners 1976) ★★★, _Boogie-Woogie String Along For Real_ (Warners 1977) ★★, _Vibration Society_ (Stash 1987) ★★★, _Paris 1976_ (Affinity 1990) ★★★, _Soul Station_ (Affinity 1993) ★★★, _I, Eye, Aye Live At Montreux 1972_ (Rhino 1996) ★★★.
● COMPILATIONS: _The Art Of Rahsaan Roland Kirk (1966-71)_ (Atlantic 1973) ★★★★, _The Man Who Cried Fire_ 1973-77 recordings (Night/Virgin 1990) ★★★★, _Rahsaan: Complete Recordings Of Roland Kirk_ 10-CD box set (Mercury 1991) ★★★★, _Talkin' Verve: Roots Of Acid Jazz_ 1961-67 recordings (Verve 1997) ★★★, _Does Your House Have Lions: The Rahsaan Roland Kirk Anthology_ 1961-76 recordings (Rhino) ★★★★, _Dog Years In The Fourth Ring_ 1965-75 recordings (32 Jazz) ★★★, _Simmer, Reduce, Garnish & Serve_ 1976, 1977 recordings (Warners) ★★★, _Aces Back To Back_ 4-CD set (32 Jazz 1998) ★★★, _A Standing Eight_ 3-CD set (32 Jazz 1999) ★★★.
● VIDEOS: _The One Man Twins_ (Rhino 1997).
● FURTHER READING: _Bright Moments: The Life And Legacy Of Rahsaan Roland Kirk_, John Kruth.

KIRSHNER, DON

b. 17 April 1934, the Bronx, New York, USA. An aspiring songwriter while still in his teens, Kirshner gained early experience penning several naive, and unsuccessful, tracks for Bobby Darin. In an effort to subsidize their careers, the duo composed advertising jingles, one of which was sung by Connie Francis, whom Kirshner later managed. In 1958, he founded Aldon Music with publisher Al Nevins, having convinced the latter of the potential of the burgeoning teen market. The partnership attracted several stellar songwriting teams, including Neil Sedaka and Howard Greenfield, Gerry Goffin and Carole King, and Barry Mann and Cynthia Weil, who composed hits for the Shirelles, Bobby Vee and the Drifters. Kirshner then established Dimension Records as an outlet for his protégés, scored major successes with Little Eva ('The Loco-Motion'), the Cookies ('Chains') and Carole King ('It Might As Well Rain Until September') which was issued on the short-lived Companion subsidiary. In 1963, the Aldon empire was sold to Screen-Gems, of which Kirshner later rose to president. Work for the in-house Colpix label was artistically less satisfying, but established the groundwork for the executive's greatest coup, the Monkees.

His ambitious plan to marry a recording group with a weekly television series was initially a great success, fuelled by material provided by the entrepreneur's staff songwriters, notably Boyce And Hart. However, disputes with the band over royalties, material and the right to perform on record inspired a legal wrangle which ended with Kirshner's departure from the Screen-Gems board. In riposte, he embarked on a similar project, the Archies, but with cartoon characters, rather than temperamental musicians, promoting the songs on the attendant series. New composers, including Andy Kim and Ron Dante, provided a succession of hit songs, including the multi-million selling 'Sugar Sugar'. In 1972, Kirshner began an association with ABC-Television which in turn inspired _Don Kirshner's Rock Concert_, a widely syndicated weekly show which became an integral part of that decade's music presentation. This astute controller successfully guided the career of Kansas under the aegis of his Kirshner record label and has also maintained considerable publishing interests.

KNICKERBOCKERS

The Knickerbockers was formed in 1964 by Buddy Randell (saxophone), a former member of the Royal Teens and Jimmy Walker (drums/vocals). The line-up was completed by the Charles brothers, John (bass) and Beau (lead guitar). Originally known as the Castle Kings, the group took its name from an avenue in their hometown of Bergenfield, New Jersey, USA. Signed to the Challenge label, owned by singing cowboy Gene Autry, the quartet initially forged its reputation recording cover versions, but in 1965 they scored a US Top 20 hit with 'Lies', a ferocious rocker which many listeners assumed was the Beatles in disguise. However, the Knickerbockers were more than mere copyists and later releases, which featured the instrumental muscle of experienced studio hands, established an energetic style which crossed folk rock and the Four Seasons. The group broke up in 1968, unable to rekindle that first flame of success. Randell and Walker both attempted solo careers and for a short time the latter replaced Bill Medley in the Righteous Brothers.
● ALBUMS: _Sing And Sync-Along With Lloyd: Lloyd Thaxton Presents The Knickerbockers_ (Challenge 1965) ★★, _Jerk And Twine Time_ (Challenge 1966) ★★★, _Lies_ (Challenge 1966) ★★★.
● COMPILATIONS: _The Fabulous Knickerbockers_ (Challenge 1988) ★★★, _A Rave-Up With The Knickerbockers_ (Big Beat 1993) ★★★, _Hits, Rarities, Unissued Cuts And More ..._ (Sundazed 1997) ★★★.

KNIGHT, CURTIS

b. Curtis McNear, 9 May 1929, Fort Scott, Kansas, USA, d. 29 November 1999, Amsterdam, the

Netherlands. Having completed his national service, Knight settled in California where he hoped to pursue a career in music. He appeared in a low-budget movie, *Pop Girl*, before relocating to New York during the early 60s. Knight then recorded for several minor labels, but these releases have been eclipsed by the singer's collaborations with Jimi Hendrix, who joined Curtis' group, the Squires, in 1965. Hendrix's tenure there was brief, but the contract he signed with Knight's manager, Ed Chalpin, had unfortunate repercussions, particularly as the guitarist ill-advisedly undertook another recording session in 1967. His spells with Knight yielded 61 songs, 26 studio and 35 live, which have since been the subject of numerous exploitative compilations. Although some of this material is, in isolation, worthwhile, such practices have undermined its value. As Curtis Knight continued to pursue his career throughout the 60s using whatever musicians were available, he increasingly relied on his Hendrix association, and in 1974 published *Jimi*, 'an intimate biography'. By this point Knight was based in London where he led a new group, Curtis Knight – Zeus. This band comprised Eddie Clarke (guitar; later in Motörhead), Nicky Hogarth (keyboards), John Weir (bass) and Chris Perry (drums). They completed two albums, but only one was issued in the UK. The singer undertook a European tour and recorded an unremarkable album before returning to the USA. In the latter part of the decade Knight conceived the black punk-rock band, Pure Hell. He continued to work with a variety of musicians while running his own limousine business. In 1992, Knight relocated to the Netherlands where he continued to record up to his death from cancer in November 1999. He had recently launched the Double Rainbow/Happy Dream label.

ALBUMS: *Get That Feeling* (Decca 1967) ★★★, *Strange Things* (Decca 1968) ★★, *Down In The Village* (Decca 1972) ★★★, *The Second Coming* (Dawn 1974) ★★, with The Midnite Gypsys *Eyes Upon The Sky* (SPV 1989) ★★, *Mean Green Universe* (1995) ★★, *Long Live Rock & Roll* (Golden Sphinx 1996), *On The Road Again* (Columns 1997) ★★, *Blues Root* (Universe 1998) ★★★.

FURTHER READING: *Jimi*, Curtis Knight.

KNIGHT, PETER

b. 23 June 1917, Exmouth, Devon, England, d. 30 July 1985. An arranger, composer and musical director, Knight played the piano by ear as a young child, and studied piano, harmony and counterpoint privately before making his first broadcast on BBC Radio's *Children's Hour* in 1924. After working in semi-professional bands at venues such as London's Gig club, he won the individual piano award with Al Morter's Rhythm Kings in the 1937 *Melody Maker* All London Dance Band Championship. Three years later he

played with the Ambrose Orchestra at the Mayfair Hotel before joining the Royal Air Force for service in World War II. On his discharge, he worked with Sydney Lipton at the Grosvenor House in London for four years before forming a vocal group, the Peter Knight Singers, which became popular on stage and radio. His wife Babs was a founder member and remained with the group for over 30 years. Besides operating the Singers, Knight also worked for Geraldo for a year before becoming a musical director for London West End shows such as *Cockles And Champagne* and *The Jazz Train*, a revue which gave American actress Bertice Reading her first London success. In the late 50s, Knight became musical director for Granada Television, and worked on popular programmes such as *Spot The Tune* and *Chelsea At Nine*. When he resumed freelance work, he arranged and conducted records by artists such as Harry Secombe, Petula Clark, Sammy Davis Jnr. and the Moody Blues (*Days Of Future Passed*). Knight was musical director for a 1964 touring version of Leslie Bricusse and Anthony Newley's show, *The Roar Of The Greasepaint – The Smell Of The Crowd*, and for several series of the extremely popular *Morecambe And Wise Show* on television. In the late 70s, Knight spent some time in Hollywood, and conducted the Los Angeles Philharmonic Orchestra in concerts by the Carpenters. In 1979, he scored and conducted the music for Roman Polanski's Oscar-nominated film *Tess*. His other film credits include the scores for *Sunstruck* (1972) and *Curse Of The Crimson Altar* (1968). Shortly after his death in 1985, Yorkshire television inaugurated the annual Peter Knight Award which 'celebrates and rewards the craft of musical arranging'. Knight rarely put a foot wrong throughout his career and is remembered still with the utmost respect and affection.

● ALBUMS: with the Peter Knight Singers *Vocal Gems From My Fair Lady* (1959) ★★★, with his orchestra *A Knight Of Merrie England* (1960) ★★★, with two pianos and orchestra *The Best Of Ivor Novello And Noël Coward* (1961) ★★★, with the Peter Knight Singers *Voices In The Night* (Deram 1967) ★★★, *Sgt Pepper* (Mercury 1967) ★★, with the Moody Blues *Days Of Future Passed* (Deram 1967) ★★★★, with Bob Johnson *The King Of Elfland's Daughter* (1977) ★★★.

KNIGHT, ROBERT

b. 24 April 1945, Franklin, Tennessee, USA. Knight made his professional vocal debut with the Paramounts, a harmony quintet consisting of schoolfriends. Signed to Dot Records, they recorded 'Free Me' in 1961, a US R&B hit, outselling the cover version by Johnny Preston. After this initial success their subsequent releases flopped and resulted in the group breaking up. Unfortunately, they also broke their contract with Dot and were prevented from recording for four-and-a-half years. Knight continued his studies in chemistry at the

Tennessee State University where he formed vocal trio the Fairlanes. In 1967, Knight was spotted performing with the Fairlanes in Nashville, and was offered a contract as a solo artist by the Rising Sons label. His first recording, 'Everlasting Love', written by label owners Buzz Cason and Mac Gayden, was an immediate success and earned him a US Top 20 hit. This enduring song was an even bigger success in Britain the following year where a cover version by Love Affair reached number 1, and in doing so, kept the singer from progressing further than a Top 40 position. Knight scored two further pop hits at home, 'Blessed Are The Lonely' and 'Isn't It Lonely Together'. In 1973, he overshadowed his previous chart entry in the UK when 'Love On A Mountain Top' reached the Top 10. However, the reissued 'Everlasting Love' went some way to making amends the following year, this time achieving Top 20 status. He continues, perhaps wisely, to advance his career in chemical research, while occasionally performing and recording.
● ALBUMS: *Everlasting Love* (Monument 1967) ★★★, *Love On A Mountain Top* (Monument 1968) ★★★.

KOOBAS

Formed in Liverpool, England, in 1962 and initially known as the Kubas, this superior beat group was comprised of two ex-members of the Midnighters – guitarists Stu Leatherwood and Roy Morris – alongside Keith Ellis (bass) and Tony O'Riley (drums), formerly of the Thunderbeats. The Koobas enjoyed a role in *Ferry Across The Mersey* and in 1965 supported the Beatles on a national tour. The group secured a deal with Pye Records and their debut, 'Take Me For A Little While' (1965), considerable promise. Following 'You'd Better Make Up Your Mind' (1966) the Koobas switched to Columbia Records for the exceptional 'Sweet Music'. A misguided version of Gracie Fields' 'Sally' (1967) undermined the group's growing reputation, as did the equally insubstantial 'Gypsy Fred'. However, they closed their singles career with a superb rendition of Cat Stevens' 'The First Cut Is The Deepest', before completing *The Koobas*. The content of this excellent album ranges from a rendition of Erma Franklin's 'Piece Of My Heart' to the musically complex 'Barricades', one of the finest songs of its era. The group had actually disbanded prior to its release, after which Ellis joined Van Der Graaf Generator.
● ALBUMS: *The Koobas* (Columbia 1969) ★★★.
● COMPILATIONS: *The Koobas* (BGO 2000) ★★★.

KORNER, ALEXIS

b. 19 April 1928, Paris, France, d. 1 January 1984. An inspirational figure in British music circles, Korner was already versed in black music when he met Cyril Davies at the London

Skiffle Club. Both musicians were frustrated by the limitations of the genre and transformed the venue into the London Blues And Barrelhouse Club, where they not only performed together but also showcased visiting US bluesmen. When jazz trombonist Chris Barber introduced an R&B segment into his live repertoire, he employed Korner (guitar) and Davies (harmonica) to back singer Ottilie Patterson. Inspired, the pair formed Blues Incorporated in 1961 and the following year established the Ealing Rhythm And Blues Club in a basement beneath a local cinema. The group's early personnel included Charlie Watts (drums), Art Wood (vocals) and Keith Scott (piano), but later featured Long John Baldry, Jack Bruce, Graham Bond and Ginger Baker in its ever-changing line-up. Mick Jagger and Paul Jones were also briefly associated with Korner, whose continued advice and encouragement proved crucial to a generation of aspiring musicians. However, disagreements over direction led to Davies' defection following the release of *R&B From The Marquee*, leaving Korner free to pursue a jazz-based path. While former colleagues later found success with the Rolling Stones, Manfred Mann and Cream, Korner's excellent group went largely unnoticed by the general public, although he did enjoy a residency on a children's television show backed by his rhythm section of Danny Thompson (bass) and Terry Cox (drums). The name 'Blues Incorporated' was dropped when Korner embarked on a solo career, punctuated by the formation of several temporary groups including Free At Last (1967), New Church (1969) and Snape (1972). While the supporting cast on such ventures remained fluid, including for a short time singer Robert Plant, the last two units featured Peter Thorup who also collaborated with Korner on CCS, a pop-based big band that scored notable hits with 'Whole Lotta Love' (1970), 'Walkin'' and 'Tap Turns On The Water' (both 1971). Korner also derived success from his BBC Radio 1 show that offered a highly individual choice of material. He also broadcast on a long-running programme for the BBC World Service. Korner continued to perform live, often accompanied by former Back Door virtuoso bass player Colin Hodgkinson, and remained a highly respected figure in the music fraternity. He joined Charlie Watts, Ian Stewart, Jack Bruce and Dick Heckstall-Smith in the informal Rocket 88, and Korner's 50th birthday party, which featured appearances by Eric Clapton, Chris Farlowe and Zoot Money, was both filmed and recorded. In 1981, Korner began an ambitious 13-part television documentary on the history of rock, but his premature death from cancer in January 1984 left this and other projects unfulfilled. However, his stature as a vital catalyst in British R&B was already assured.
● ALBUMS: with Blues Incorporated *R&B From The Marquee* (Ace Of Clubs 1962) ★★★★, with Blues Incorporated *Alexis Korner's Blues*

Incorporated (Ace Of Clubs 1964) ★★★, with Blues Incorporated *Red Hot From Alex* aka *Alexis Korner's All Star Blues Incorporated* (Transatlantic 1964) ★★★★, with Blues Incorporated *At The Cavern* (Oriole 1964) ★★★, with Blues Incorporated *Sky High* (Spot 1966) ★★, with Blues Incorporated *Blues Incorporated (Wednesday Night Prayer Meeting)* (Polydor 1967) ★★★★, *I Wonder Who* (Fontana 1967) ★★★, *A New Generation Of Blues* aka *What's That Sound I Hear* (Transatlantic 1968) ★★★, *Both Sides Of Alexis Korner* (Metronome 1969) ★★★, *Alexis* (Rak 1971) ★★★, *Mr. Blues* (Toadstool 1974) ★★★, *Alexis Korner* (Polydor 1974) ★★★, *Get Off My Cloud* (Columbia 1975) ★★★, *Just Easy* (Intercord 1978) ★★★, *Me* (Jeton 1979) ★★★, *The Party Album* (Intercord 1980) ★★★, *Juvenile Delinquent* (1984) ★★, *Live In Paris: Alexis Korner* (Magnum 1988) ★★★; by New Church *The New Church* (Metronome 1970); by Snape *Accidentally Born In New Orleans* (Transatlantic 1973) ★★★, *Snape Live On Tour* (Brain 1974) ★★★.
● COMPILATIONS: *Bootleg Him* (Rak 1972) ★★★, *Profile* (Teldec 1981) ★★★, with Cyril Davies *Alexis 1957* (Krazy Kat 1984) ★★★, with Colin Hodgkinson *Testament* (Thunderbolt 1985) ★★★, *Alexis Korner 1961-1972* (Castle 1986) ★★★, *Hammer And Nails* (Thunderbolt 1987) ★★★, *The Alexis Korner Collection* (Castle 1988) ★★★, *And ....* (Castle 1994) ★★, *On The Move* (Castle 1996) ★★, *The Best Of Alexis Korner* (Castle 2000) ★★★.
● VIDEOS: *Eat A Little Rhythm And Blues* (BBC Video 1988).
● FURTHER READING: *Alexis Korner: The Biography*, Harry Shapiro.

KRAMER, BILLY J., AND THE DAKOTAS

b. William Howard Ashton, 19 August 1943, Bootle, Merseyside, England. Kramer originally fronted Merseybeat combo the Coasters, but was teamed with the Manchester-based Dakotas – Mike Maxfield (b. 23 February 1944; lead guitar), Robin McDonald (b. 18 July 1943; rhythm guitar), Ray Jones (b. 22 October 1939, Oldham, Lancashire, England, d. 20 January 2000; bass) and Elkie Brooks' older brother Tony Mansfield (b. Anthony Bookbinder, 28 May 1943, Salford, Lancashire, England; drums) – upon signing to Brian Epstein's management agency. Having topped the UK charts with the Beatles' 'Do You Want To Know A Secret?' (1963), Kramer's UK chart success was maintained with a run of exclusive John Lennon/Paul McCartney songs, including the chart-topping 'Bad To Me', 'I'll Keep You Satisfied' (number 4) and 'From A Window' (number 10). 'Little Children' (1964), penned by US writers Mort Shuman and John McFarland, gave the group a third number 1 and their first taste of success in the USA, reaching number 7. This was quickly followed by the reissued 'Bad To Me' which also reached the Top 10. Their chart reign ended the following year with the Burt Bacharach-composed 'Trains And

Boats And Planes' peaking at number 12 in the UK. Although subsequent efforts, most notably the lyrical 'Neon City', proved effective, Kramer's career was firmly in the descendent. He embarked on a solo career in January 1967, but having failed to find a new audience, sought solace on the cabaret and nostalgia circuit.
● ALBUMS: *Listen – To Billy J. Kramer* (Parlophone 1963) ★★★, *Little Children* (Imperial 1963) ★★★, *I'll Keep You Satisfied* (Imperial 1964) ★★★, *Trains & Boats & Planes* (Imperial 1965) ★★.
● COMPILATIONS: *The Best Of Billy J. Kramer* (Capitol 1979) ★★★, *The EMI Years* (EMI 1991) ★★★, *The EP Collection* (See For Miles 1995) ★★★, *The Very Best Of* (Erri Gold 1997) ★★★, *At Abbey Road 1963-1966* (EMI 1998) ★★★★, *Golden Legends* (Direct Source 2000) ★★★.

L

LANCE, MAJOR

b. 4 April 1939, Winterville, Mississippi, USA, d. 3 September 1994, Decatur, Georgia, USA. A former amateur boxer and a dancer on the Jim Lounsbury record-hop television show, Lance also sang with the Five Gospel Harmonaires and for a brief period with Otis Leavill and Barbara Tyson in the Floats. His 1959 Mercury Records release, 'I Got A Girl', was written and produced by Curtis Mayfield, a high school contemporary, but Lance's career was not truly launched until he signed with OKeh Records three years later. 'Delilah' opened his account there, while a further Mayfield song, the stylish 'The Monkey Time' in 1963, gave the singer a US Top 10 hit. The partnership between singer and songwriter continued through 1963-64 with a string of US pop chart hits: 'Hey Little Girl', 'Um, Um, Um, Um, Um, Um', 'The Matador' and 'Rhythm'. Although Lance's range was more limited than that of his associate, the texture and phrasing mirrored that of Mayfield's work with his own group, the Impressions. 'Ain't That A Shame', in 1965, marked a pause in their relationship as its commercial success waned.

Although further vibrant singles followed, notably 'Investigate' and 'Ain't No Soul (In These Rock 'N' Roll Shoes)', Lance left OKeh for Dakar Records in 1968 where 'Follow The Leader' was a minor R&B hit. Two 1970 releases on Curtom, 'Stay Away From Me' and 'Must Be Love Coming Down', marked a reunion with Mayfield. From there, Lance moved to Volt, Playboy and Osiris, the last of which he co-owned with Al Jackson, a former member of Booker T. And The MGs. These spells were punctuated by a two-year stay in Britain (1972-74), during which Lance recorded for Contempo and Warner Brothers Records. Convicted of selling cocaine in 1978, the singer emerged from prison to find his OKeh recordings in demand as part of America's 'beach music' craze, where aficionados in Virginia and the Carolinas maintained a love of vintage soul. A heart attack in September 1994 proved fatal for Lance.

● ALBUMS: *Monkey Time* (OKeh 1963) ★★★, *Major Lance's Greatest Hits – Recorded 'Live' At The Torch* (OKeh 1973) ★★, *Now Arriving* (Motown 1978) ★★, *The Major's Back* (1983) ★★, *Live At Hinkley* (1986) ★★.

● COMPILATIONS: *Um Um Um Um Um – The Best Of Major Lance* (OKeh 1964) ★★★, *Major's Greatest Hits* (OKeh 1965) ★★★, *The Best Of Major Lance* (Epic 1976) ★★★, *Monkey Time*

recorded 60s (Edsel 1983) ★★★, *Everybody Loves A Good Time: The Best Of Major Lance* (Columbia 1995) ★★★, *The Best Of Major Lance* (Beat Goes On 1998) ★★★, *The Very Best Of Major Lance* (Sony 2000) ★★★.

LEAVES

Formed in Northridge, California, USA, in 1964, this folk rock group began its career as the Rockwells, a college-based 'frat' band. Founder-members Robert Lee Reiner (guitar) and Jim Pons (bass) were joined by Bill Rinehart (guitar) and Jimmy Kern (drums) in an attraction offering a diet of surf tunes and R&B-styled oldies. By the end of the year vocalist John Beck had been added to the line-up, while Kern was replaced by Tom Ray early in 1965. Having branched into the Los Angeles club circuit, the Rockwells were among the finalists auditioning to replace the Byrds at the fabled Ciro's on Sunset Strip. They duly won the residency whereupon the group took a more contemporary name, the Leaves. Having secured a recording contract with Mira Records via a production deal with singer Pat Boone's Penhouse production company, the Leaves made their recording debut with 'Too Many People' in September 1965. For a follow-up the quintet opted to record 'Hey Joe', a song popularized by the aforementioned Byrds, Love and Music Machine and a subsequent hit for Jimi Hendrix.

Their initial recording was not a success, prompting the departure of Rinehart in February 1966. He later surfaced in the Gene Clark Group and, later, Merry Go Round. Bobby Arlin, veteran of the Catalinas with Leon Russell and Bruce Johnson, took his place. A second version of 'Hey Joe' was released, then withdrawn, before the group proclaimed themselves happy with a third interpretation, which featured fuzz guitar and a vibrant instrumental break. It reached the US Top 40 in May that year, much to the chagrin of those initially playing the song. However, ensuing releases were not well received, placing a strain on the group. Reiner left the line-up, but although the remaining quartet were signed to Capitol Records, further ructions ensued. Pons joined the Turtles during sessions for *All The Good That's Happening*, Ray was fired by the producer, and Beck quit in disgust leaving Arlin to tidy the proceedings. The last-named pair did reunite in 1967 to record a handful of songs, but plans to work as the New Leaves, with the aid of Buddy Sklar (bass) and Craig Boyd (drums), were abandoned when Beck quit. The remaining trio took a new name, Hook. Of the remaining ex-members only Pons retained a high profile as a member of Flo And Eddie and the Mothers Of Invention.

● ALBUMS: *Hey Hoe* (Mira 1966) ★★, *All The Good That's Happening* (Capitol 1967) ★★.

● COMPILATIONS: *The Leaves 1966* (Panda

985) ★★, *The Leaves Are Happening* (Sundazed
000) ★★★.
FILMS: *The Cool Ones* (1967).

LEE, BRENDA

Brenda Mae Tarpley, 11 December 1944,
ithonia, Georgia, USA. Even in early
dolescence, Lee had an adult husk of a voice
at could slip from anguished intimacy through
eepy insinuation to raucous lust, even during
et's Jump The Broomstick', 'Speak To Me
retty' and other jaunty classics that kept her in
e hit parade from the mid-50s to 1965.
hrough local radio and, by 1956, wider
xposure on Red Foley's Ozark Jubilee
roadcasts, 'Little Brenda Lee' was ensured
nough airplay for her first single, a revival of
lank Williams' 'Jambalaya', to crack the US
ountry chart before her *Billboard* Hot 100 debut
ith 1957's 'One Step At A Time'. The novelty of
er extreme youth facilitated bigger triumphs
or 'Little Miss Dynamite' with the million-
elling 'Rockin' Around The Christmas Tree' and
ter bouncy rockers, before the next decade
rought a greater proportion of heartbreak
allads, such as 'I'm Sorry' and 'Too Many
ivers' – plus an acting role in the children's
antasy movie *The Two Little Bears*. 1963 was
nother successful year – especially in the UK
ith the title song of *All Alone Am I*, 'Losing You'
a French translation), 'I Wonder' and 'As Usual'
ach entering the Top 20. While 1964 finished
ell with 'Is It True' and 'Christmas Will Be Just
nother Lonely Day', only minor hits followed.
lthough she may have weathered prevailing
ids, family commitments caused Lee to cut
ack on touring and record only intermittently
fter 1966's appositely titled *Bye Bye Blues*. Lee
esurfaced in 1971 with a huge country hit in
ris Kristofferson's 'Nobody Wins'; this and later
ecordings established her as a star of what was
nen one of the squarest seams of pop. When
ountry gained a younger audience in the mid-
Os, respect for its older practitioners found her
uesting with Loretta Lynn and Kitty Wells on
d. lang's *Shadowland*. – produced in 1988 by
wen Bradley (who had also supervised many
arly Lee records). In Europe, Brenda Lee
emained mostly a memory – albeit a pleasing
ne as shown by Coast To Coast's hit revival of
et's Jump The Broomstick', a high UK placing
or 1980's *Little Miss Dynamite* greatest hits
ollection and Mel Smith And Kim Wilde's
tockin' Around The Christmas Tree'. Lee is
ortunate in having a large rock 'n' roll catalogue
estined for immortality, in addition to her now
igh standing in the country music world. In
993, billed as 'the biggest-selling female star in
op history', Brenda Lee toured the UK and
layed the London Palladium, headlining a
ostalgia package that included Chris Montez,
en Barry and Johnny Tillotson. From her
pening 'I'm So Excited', through to the closing
tockin' All Over The World', she fulfilled all

expectations, and won standing ovations from
packed houses. In keeping with many of their
packages, the Bear Family Records box set is a
superb retrospective.
● ALBUMS: *Grandma, What Great Songs You
Sang* (Decca 1959) ★★, *Brenda Lee* (Decca 1960)
★★★★, *This Is ... Brenda* (Decca 1960) ★★★★,
Miss Dynamite (Brunswick 1961) ★★★★,
Emotions (Decca 1961) ★★★, *All The Way*
(Decca 1961) ★★★, *Sincerely Brenda Lee* (Decca
1962) ★★★★, *Brenda, That's All* (Decca 1962)
★★★★, *All Alone Am I* (Decca 1963) ★★★, *Let
Me Sing* (Decca 1963) ★★★, *Sings Songs
Everybody Knows* (Decca 1964) ★★★, *By Request*
(Decca 1964) ★★★, *Merry Christmas From
Brenda Lee* (Decca 1964) ★★★, *Top Teen Hits*
(Decca 1964) ★★★, *The Versatile Brenda Lee*
(Decca 1965) ★★★, *Too Many Rivers* (Decca
1965) ★★★, *Bye Bye Blues* (Decca 1965) ★★★,
Coming On Strong (Decca 1966) ★★★, *Call Me
Brenda* (Decca 1967) ★★★, *Reflections In Blue*
(Decca 1967) ★★★, *Good Life* (Decca 1967)
★★★, with Tennessee Ernie Ford *The Show For
Christmas Seals* (Decca 1968) ★★★, with Pete
Fountain *For The First Time* (Decca 1968) ★★★,
Johnny One Time (Decca 1969) ★★★, *Memphis
Portrait* (Decca 1970) ★★★, *Let It Be Me*
(Vocalion 1970) ★★★, *A Whole Lotta* (MCA 1972)
★★★, *Brenda* (MCA 1973) ★★★, *New Sunrise*
(MCA 1974) ★★★, *Brenda Lee Now* (MCA 1975)
★★★, *The LA Sessions* (MCA 1977) ★★★, *Even
Better* (MCA 1980) ★★★, *Take Me Back* (MCA
1981) ★★★, *Only When I Laugh* (MCA 1982)
★★★, with Dolly Parton, Kris Kristofferson,
Willie Nelson *The Winning Hand* (Monument
1983) ★★★, *Feels So Right* (MCA 1985) ★★★,
Brenda Lee (Warners 1991) ★★★, *A Brenda Lee
Christmas* (Warners 1991) ★★★, *Greatest Hits
Live* (MCA 1992) ★★★, *Coming On Strong*
(Muskateer 1995) ★★★.
● COMPILATIONS: *10 Golden Years* (Decca
1966) ★★★, *The Brenda Lee Story – Her Greatest
Hits* (MCA 1973) ★★★★, *Little Miss Dynamite*
(MCA 1976) ★★★★, *Greatest Country Hits* (MCA
1982) ★★★, *25th Anniversary* (MCA 1984)
★★★★, *The Early Years* (MCA 1984) ★★★, *The
Golden Decade* (Charly 1985) ★★★★, *The Best Of
Brenda Lee* (MCA 1986) ★★★★, *Love Songs*
(MCA 1986) ★★★, *Brenda's Best* (Ce De 1989)
★★★★, *Very Best Of Brenda Lee Volume 1* (MCA
1990) ★★★★, *Very Best Of Brenda Lee Volume 2*
(MCA 1990) ★★★, *The Brenda Lee Anthology
Volume One, 1956-1961* (MCA 1991) ★★★★, *The
Brenda Lee Anthology Volume Two, 1962-1980*
(MCA 1991) ★★★, *Little Miss Dynamite* 4-CD box
set (Bear Family 1996) ★★★★, *The EP Collection*
(See For Miles 1996) ★★★★, *20th Century
Masters: The Best Of Brenda Lee Millennium
Collection* (MCA 1999) ★★★★.

LEE, LEAPY

b. Lee Graham, 2 July 1942, Eastbourne,
England. One of the troubled stars of British 60s
pop, Lee's career took a surprise upswing when

he moved from Kinks co-manager Robert Wace to the charismatic Gordon Mills. The latter produced the catchy 'Little Arrows', which narrowly failed to reach the UK number 1 spot in 1968. A minor hit with 'Good Morning' and a suitably broad showbusiness repertoire should have served Leapy well, but his waywardness proved his undoing. He began drinking with East End villains and befriended starlet Diana Dors and her husband Alan Lake. One evening at a pub in Sunningdale, Lake and Lee were involved in a fracas during which a publican was slashed across the wrist with a flick knife. Leapy was arrested, charged and suffered the indignity of a jail sentence which seriously put back his career, although Mills occasionally employed him as a producer. Lee eventually left the UK to sing in bars in Majorca, Spain.

LEFT BANKE

Formed in 1965, the Left Banke was the brainchild of pianist/composer Michael Brown (b. Michael Lookofsky, 25 April 1949, New York City, New York, USA). The son of a noted arranger and producer, Brown's early work appeared on releases by Reparata And The Delrons and Christopher And The Chaps, prior to the founding of the Left Banke. Steve Martin (vocals), Tom Finn (bass) and George Cameron (b. London, England; drums) completed the original Left Banke line-up, which scored a US Top 5 hit in 1966 with 'Walk Away Renee'. This gorgeous song adeptly combined elements drawn from the Beatles and baroque, and became a major hit the following year when covered by the Four Tops. The band added Jeff Winfield (guitar) to the line-up and enjoyed further US chart success with 'Pretty Ballerina'. They underwent the first of several personnel changes when Rick Brand replaced Winfield during sessions for an attendant album. Brown retired from touring shortly afterwards, with his place taken by keyboard player Emmett Lake. Internal ructions led to Brown completing a third release, 'Ivy Ivy', with the aid of session musicians, but the band was reunited for 'Desiree', their final chart entry. Brown then abandoned his creation – he later formed Stories – and when Brand also departed, Finn, Cameron and Martin completed *The Left Banke Too* with guitarist Tom Feher. Although bereft of their principal songwriter, the band still captured the spirit of earlier recordings, but broke up in 1969 in the wake of a final single, 'Myrah', which was issued in an unfinished state. They briefly reunited in 1971 for a single on Buddah Records, credited to Steve Martin. A New York independent, Camerica, coaxed Finn, Cameron and Martin back into the studio in 1978. Although initially shelved, the set, which successfully echoed the band's glory days, was belatedly issued eight years later as *Voices Calling* in the UK and *Strangers On A Train* in the USA. Several excellent compilations have

been released since.
● ALBUMS: *Walk Away Renee/Pretty Ballerina* (Smash 1967) ★★★★, *The Left Banke Too* (Smash 1968) ★★, *Voices Calling* UK titl *Strangers On A Train* US title (Barr Caruso/Camerica 1986) ★★★.
● COMPILATIONS: *And Suddenly It's The Le Banke* (Bam-Caruso 1982) ★★★★, *The Histor Of The Left Banke* (Rhino 1985) ★★★★, *Wal Away Renee* mini-album (Bam-Caruso 1986 ★★★, *There's Gonna Be A Storm: The Complet Recordings 1966-1969* (Mercury 1992) ★★★★ *Walk Away From The Left Banke* (See For Mile 1992) ★★★★.

LEMON PIPERS

This New York-based quintet – Ivan Brown (vocals/rhythm guitar), Bill Bartlett (lea guitar), R.G. (Reg) Nave (organ), Stev Walmsley (bass) and Bill Albuagh (drums) made its debut in 1967 with 'Turn Around An Take A Look'. Its rudimentary style was the replaced by the measured approach of aspirin songwriting/production team, Paul Leka an Shelly Pinz. Together they created a distinctiv Lemon Pipers sound, a sparkling mélange c sweeping strings and percussive vibraslap exemplified on the group's million-selling hi 'Green Tambourine'. The attendant albur contained several songs – 'Rice Is Nice 'Shoeshine Boy' – which were recorded in similar style, but the set also contained th startling 'Through With You', an extended tou de force for Bartlett's rampaging guitarwork an a surprise for those anticipating easy-on-the-ea fare. Subsequent recordings failed to matc their early success, and although a secon album, *Jungle Marmalade*, offered severa inventive moments, the Lemon Pipers wer tarred as a bubblegum attraction on the strengt of that first hit. The group broke up in 196! although Bartlett later found success as member of Ram Jam.
● ALBUMS: *Green Tambourine* (Buddah 1967 ★★★, *Jungle Marmalade* (1968) ★★.
● COMPILATIONS: *The Lemon Pipers* (199(★★★, *Golden Classics* (Collectables 1994) ★★★ *Best Of The Lemon Pipers* (Camden 1998) ★★★

LES FLEUR DE LYS

Formed in Southampton, England in 1964, (Les Fleur De Lys initially comprised Frank Smit (guitar/vocals), Alex Chamberlain (keyboards Gary Churchill (bass) and Keith Guster (drums They secured a deal with Andrew Loo Oldham's Immediate Records in 1965. Jimm Page produced and played on their debut, version of Buddy Holly's 'Moondreams', an wrote the b-side, 'Wait For Me'. Chamberlain an Churchill were replaced by Phil Sawyer (guita and Gordon Haskell (bass) for 'Circles', a Pet Townshend song also known as 'Instant Party (Les) Fleur De Lys performed it in creditabl pop art fashion. The line-up then underwer further changes when Smith was replaced by Chris Andrews and Bryn Haworth came in for Phil Sawyer. The group switched labels to Atlantic Records, where they embraced a rock/soul style of music. 'Mud In Your Eye' (1966) was a highly accomplished single and the group was invited to back Donnie Elbert and Sharon Tandy. In 1967, (Les) Fleur De Lys assumed an alias, Rupert's People, for 'Reflections Of Charles Brown', a dreamy single modelled on Procol Harum's 'A Whiter Shade Of Pale'. Its composer, Rod Lynton, formed a 'new' Rupert's People; (Les) Fleur De Lys reverted to their original name. Andrews left for a solo career in 1967, leaving Haworth, Haskell and Guster to work as a trio. Two marvellous singles followed: the haunting 'I Can See A Light' (1967) and hard-rocking 'Gong With The Luminous Nose' (1968), before Haskell was replaced by Tago Byers (bass) and Tony Head (vocals). 'Stop Crossing The Bridge' (1968) and 'Liar' (1969) followed but (Les) Fleur De Lys folded in the wake of the latter release. Haworth became a solo artist during the 70s, while Haskell joined King Crimson and later had huge success in 2001 with a hit single and the album *Harry's Bar*.

LESTER, KETTY

b. Revoyda Frierson, 16 August 1934, Hope, Arkansas, USA. Ketty Lester began her singing career on completing a music course at San Francisco State College. A residency at the city's Purple Onion club was followed by a successful tour of Europe before she joined bandleader Cab Calloway's revue. Later domiciled in New York, Lester's popular nightclub act engendered a recording contract, of which 'Love Letters' was the first fruit. The singer's cool-styled interpretation of this highly popular standard, originally recorded by Dick Haymes, reached the Top 5 in both the USA and UK in 1962, eventually selling in excess of one million copies. The song has been covered many times, with notable successes for Elvis Presley and Alison Moyet. Its attractiveness was enhanced by a memorable piano figure but Lester was sadly unable to repeat the single's accomplished balance between song, interpretation and arrangement. She later abandoned singing in favour of a career as a film and television actress, with appearances in *Marcus Welby MD*, *Little House On The Prairie*, *The Terminal Man* and *The Prisoner Of Second Avenue*, to name but a few. She was later coaxed back into the studio, but only on her stipulation that it would be exclusively to perform sacred music.
● ALBUMS: *Love Letters* (Era 1962) ★★, *Soul Of Me* (RCA Victor 1964) ★★, *Where Is Love* (RCA Victor 1965) ★★, *When A Woman Loves A Man* (Tower 1967) ★★, *I Saw Him* (Mega 1985) ★★.
● COMPILATIONS: *Love Letters: 14 Original Classics* (Collectables 1999) ★★★.

LETTERMEN

This very successful US close-harmony pop trio comprised Bob Engemann (b. 19 February 1936, Highland Park, Michigan, USA), Tony Butala (b. 20 November 1940, Sharon, Pennsylvania, USA) and Jim Pike (b. 6 November 1938, St. Louis, Missouri, USA). Pike, a letterman at Utah's Brigham Young University, released an unsuccessful single on Warner Brothers Records in 1959. In 1960, he and fellow student and ex-Mormon missionary Engemann formed a trio with supper-club singer Butala, who had recorded previously on Topic and Lute. After two unsuccessful singles, they joined Capitol Records and struck gold immediately with 'The Way You Look Tonight'. The smooth ballad singers put an impressive 24 albums in the US chart in the 60s, with 10 of them reaching the Top 40. The popular live act also had another 19 chart singles including the Top 10 hits 'When I Fall In Love' in 1961 and the medley 'Goin' Out Of My Head/Can't Take My Eyes Off You' in 1967. In 1968, Jim's brother Gary replaced Engemann and six years later their brother Donny replaced Jim. In the 70s they were a top-earning club act and were much in demand for television commercial work. The group recorded on their own Alfa Omega label in 1979 and signed with Applause in 1982. This distinctive harmonic vocal group, who have never charted in the UK, have earned nine gold albums to date and sold over $25 million worth of records.
● ALBUMS: *A Song For Young Love* (Capitol 1962) ★★★, *Once Upon A Time* (Capitol 1962) ★★★, *Jim, Tony And Bob* (Capitol 1962) ★★★, *College Standards* (Capitol 1963) ★★★, *The Lettermen In Concert* (Capitol 1963) ★★, *A Lettermen Kind Of Love* (Capitol 1964) ★★, *The Lettermen Look At Love* (Capitol 1964) ★★★, *She Cried* (Capitol 1964) ★★★, *Portrait Of My Love* (Capitol 1965) ★★★, *The Hit Sounds Of The Lettermen* (Capitol 1965) ★★, *You'll Never Walk Alone* (Capitol 1965) ★★★, *More Hit Sounds Of The Lettermen!* (Capitol 1966) ★★, *A New Song For Young Love* (Capitol 1966) ★★★, *For Christmas This Year* (Capitol 1966) ★★, *Warm* (Capitol 1967) ★★★, *Spring!* (Capitol 1967) ★★★, *The Lettermen!!! ... And Live!* (Capitol 1967) ★★, *Goin' Out Of My Head* (Capitol 1968) ★★★, *Special Request* (Capitol 1968) ★★, *Put Your Head On My Shoulder* (Capitol 1968) ★★★, *I Have Dreamed* (Capitol 1969) ★★★, *Hurt So Bad* (Capitol 1969) ★★★, *Traces/Memories* (Capitol 1970) ★★★, *Reflections* (Capitol 1970) ★★, *Everything's Good About You* (Capitol 1971) ★★★, *Feelings* (Capitol 1971) ★★★, *Love Book* (Capitol 1971) ★★★, *Lettermen 1* (Capitol 1972) ★★★, *Alive Again ... Naturally* (Capitol 1973) ★★, *Evergreen* (Alfa Omega 1985) ★★.
● COMPILATIONS: *The Best Of The Lettermen* (Capitol 1966) ★★★, *The Best Of The Lettermen, Vol. 2* (Capitol 1969) ★★★, *All-Time Greatest*

Hits (Capitol 1974) ★★★, Memories: The Very Best Of The Lettermen (Collectables 1999) ★★★.

LEWIS, BARBARA

b. 9 February 1943, Salem, Michigan, USA. Signed to Atlantic Records in 1961, Lewis enjoyed several regional hits before the sensual 'Hello Stranger' established her light but enthralling style. Recorded in Chicago, the performance was enhanced by the vocal support of the Dells. Further singles included the vibrant 'Someday We're Gonna Love Again' (1965), while 'Baby I'm Yours' and 'Make Me Your Baby' (both 1966) maintained her smooth, individual approach. Barbara remained with the label until 1968, but the following year moved to the Stax Records subsidiary Enterprise. Internal problems sadly doomed the album she made there, and having completed a handful of singles, Lewis withdrew from music altogether.
● ALBUMS: Hello Stranger (Atlantic 1963) ★★★, Snap Your Fingers (Atlantic 1964) ★★★, Baby I'm Yours (Atlantic 1965) ★★★, It's Magic (Atlantic 1966) ★★★, Workin' On A Groovy Thing (Atlantic 1968) ★★★, The Many Grooves Of Barbara Lewis (Enterprise 1970) ★★★.
● COMPILATIONS: The Best Of The Best Of Barbara Lewis (Atlantic 1971) ★★★, Hello Stranger (Solid Smoke 1981) ★★★, Golden Classics (Collectables 1987) ★★★, Hello Stranger: The Best Of Barbara Lewis (Rhino/Atlantic 1994) ★★★.

LEWIS, GARY, AND THE PLAYBOYS

One of the most commercially successful US pop groups of the mid-60s, the original Playboys comprised Gary Lewis (b. Gary Levitch, 31 July 1946, New York, USA; vocals/drums), Alan Ramsey (b. 27 July 1943, New Jersey, USA; guitar), John West (b. 31 July 1939, Unrichville, Ohio, USA; guitar), David Costell (b. 15 March 1944, Pittsburgh, Pennsylvania, USA; bass) and David Walker (b. 12 May 1943, Montgomery, Alabama, USA; keyboards). Group leader Gary Lewis was the son of comedian Jerry Lewis and had been playing drums since the age of 14. After appearing at selected Hollywood parties, the ensemble was offered a residency at the Disneyland Park and soon after was signed by Liberty Records and producer Leon Russell. Their debut single, 'This Diamond Ring' (co-written by Al Kooper and originally intended for former idol, Bobby Vee), topped the American charts in February 1965 and spearheaded an remarkable run of Top 10 hits that included 'Count Me In', 'Save Your Heart For Me', 'Everybody Loves A Clown', 'She's Just My Style', 'She's Gonna Miss Her' and 'Green Grass'. The latter, although written by UK composers Cook And Greenaway (alias David And Jonathan), predictably failed to make any impact in the UK market where the group remained virtually unknown.

Undoubtedly the best-selling US group of the mid-60s without a UK hit to their name, they nevertheless enjoyed healthy record sales all over the world, appeared regularly on television, and even participated in a couple of low-budget movies, A Swingin' Summer and Out Of Sight. Their relative decline in 1967 probably had less to do with changing musical fashions than the induction of Gary Lewis to the US Armed Forces. By the time of his discharge in 1968, a set of Playboys were ready to return him to the charts with a remake of Brian Hyland's 'Sealed With A Kiss'. A revival of the Cascades' 'Rhythm Of The Rain' pointed to the fact that the group was running short of ideas while also indicating their future on the revivalist circuit. After disbanding the group at the end of the 60s, Lewis was unsuccessfully relaunched as a singer/songwriter but later assembled a new version of the Playboys for cabaret and festival dates.
● ALBUMS: This Diamond Ring (Liberty 1965) ★★★, Everybody Loves A Clown (Liberty 1965) ★★★, She's Just My Style (Liberty 1966) ★★★★, Hits Again! (Liberty 1966) ★★★, You Don't Have To Paint Me A Picture (Liberty 1967) ★★, New Directions (Liberty 1967) ★★, Now! (Liberty 1968) ★★, Close Cover Before Playing (Liberty 1968) ★★, Rhythm Of The Rain (Liberty 1969) ★★, I'm On The Road Right Now (Liberty 1969) ★★.
● COMPILATIONS: Golden Greats (Liberty 1966) ★★★, More Golden Greats (Liberty 1968) ★★, Twenty Golden Greats (Liberty 1979) ★★★, Greatest Hits: Gary Lewis And The Playboys (Rhino 1986) ★★★, Legendary Masters (Capitol 1990) ★★★, Greatest Hits (Curb 1994) ★★★.

LEWIS, RAMSEY

b. Ramsey Emmanuel Lewis, 27 May 1935, Chicago, Illinois, USA. Lewis started playing piano at the age of six. He graduated from school in 1948, after winning both the American Legion Award as an outstanding scholar and a special award for piano services at the Edward Jenner Elementary School. He began his career as an accompanist at the Zion Hill Baptist Church, an experience of gospel that never left him. He later studied music at Chicago Music College with the idea of becoming a concert pianist, but left at the age of 18 to marry. He found a job working in a record shop and joined the Clefs, a seven-piece dance band. In 1956, he formed a jazz trio with the Clefs' rhythm section (whom he had known since high school) – bass player Eldee Young and drummer Redd Holt. Lewis made his debut recordings with the Argo record label, which later became Chess Records. He also had record dates with prestigious names such as Sonny Stitt, Clark Terry and Max Roach.
In 1959, he played at Birdland in New York City and at the Randall's Island Festival. In 1964, 'Something You Got' was a minor hit, but it was

'The In Crowd', an instrumental cover version of Dobie Gray's hit, that made him famous, reaching number 5 in the US charts and selling over a million copies by the end of 1965. Lewis insisted on a live sound, complete with handclaps and exclamations, an infectious translation of a black church feel into pop. His follow-up, 'Hang On Sloopy', reached number 11 and sold another million. These hits set the agenda for his career. Earnings for club dates increased tenfold. His classic 'Wade In The Water' was a major hit in 1966, and became a long-standing encore number for Graham Bond. The rhythm section of Young and Holt left and resurfaced as a funk outfit in the mid-70s, variously known as Redd Holt Unlimited and Young-Holt Unlimited. Lewis had an astute ear for hip, commercial sounds: his replacement drummer Maurice White left in 1971 to found the platinum mega-sellers Earth, Wind And Fire.

Lewis never recaptured this commercial peak; he attempted to woo his audience by using synthesizers and disco rhythms, and continued securing *Billboard* Top 100 hits well into the 70s. His album success was a remarkable achievement, with over 30 of his albums making the *Billboard* Top 200 listings. *The In Crowd* stayed on the list for almost a year, narrowly missing the top spot. *Mother Nature's Son* was a tribute to the Beatles, while the *Newly Recorded Hits* in 1973 was a dreadful mistake: the originals were far superior. By the 80s he was producing middle-of-the-road instrumental albums and accompanying singers, most notably Nancy Wilson. In the late 90s he was involved with the Urban Knights, a trilogy of releases with Grover Washington Jnr. and Omar Hakim. Nevertheless, it is his 60s hits – simple, infectious and funky – that will long endure.

● ALBUMS: *Down To Earth* (EmArcy 1958) ★★★, *Gentleman Of Swing* (Argo 1958) ★★★, *Gentlemen Of Jazz* (Argo 1958) ★★★, *An Hour With The Ramsey Lewis Trio* (Argo 1959) ★★★, *Stretching Out* (Argo 1960) ★★★, *The Ramsey Lewis Trio In Chicago* (Argo 1961) ★★★, *More Music From The Soil* (Argo 1961) ★★★, *Sound Of Christmas* (Argo 1961) ★★★, *The Sound Of Spring* (Argo 1962) ★★★, *Country Meets The Blues* (Argo 1962) ★★★, *Bossa Nova* (Argo 1962) ★★★, *Pot Luck* (Argo 1962) ★★★, *Barefoot Sunday Blues* (Argo 1963) ★★★, *The Ramsey Lewis Trio At The Bohemian Caverns* (Argo 1964) ★★★, *Bach To The Blues* (Argo 1964) ★★★, *More Sounds Of Christmas* (Argo 1964) ★★★, *You Better Believe It* (Argo 1965) ★★★★, *The In Crowd* (Argo 1965) ★★★★, *Hang On Ramsey!* (Cadet 1965) ★★★★, *Swingin'* (Cadet 1966) ★★★★, *Wade In The Water* (Cadet 1966) ★★★★, *Goin' Latin* (Cadet 1967) ★★, *The Movie Album* (Cadet 1967) ★★, *Dancing In The Street* (Cadet 1967) ★★★, *Up Pops Ramsey Lewis* (Cadet 1968) ★★★, *Maiden Voyage* (Cadet 1968) ★★★, *Mother Nature's Son* (Cadet 1969) ★★,

Another Voyage (Cadet 1969) ★★, *Ramsey Lewis: The Piano Player* (Cadet 1970) ★★★, *Them Changes* (Cadet 1970) ★★★, *Back To The Roots* (Cadet 1971) ★★★, *Upendo Ni Pamoja* (Columbia 1972) ★★★, *Funky Serenity* (Columbia 1973) ★★, *Sun Goddess* (Columbia 1974) ★★★, *Don't It Feel Good* (Columbia 1975) ★★★, *Salongo* (Columbia 1976) ★★★, *Love Notes* (Columbia 1977) ★★★, *Tequila Mockingbird* (Columbia 1977) ★★★, *Legacy* (Columbia 1978) ★★★, *Routes* (Columbia 1980) ★★★, *Three Piece Suite* (Columbia 1981) ★★★, *Live At The Savoy* (Columbia 1982) ★★★, *Chance Encounter* (Columbia 1983) ★★, with Nancy Wilson *The Two Of Us* (Columbia 1984) ★★★, *Reunion* (Columbia 1984) ★★★, *Keys To The City* (Columbia 1987) ★★, *Classic Encounter* (Columbia 1988) ★★, with Billy Taylor *We Meet Again* (Columbia 1989) ★★★, *Urban Renewal* (Columbia 1989) ★★★, *Electric Collection* (Columbia 1991) ★★★, *Ivory Pyramid* (GRP 1992) ★★, *Between The Keys* (GRP 1996) ★★, *Dance Of the Soul* (GRP 1998) ★★★, *Appassionata* (Narada 1999) ★★★★.
● COMPILATIONS: *Choice! The Best Of The Ramsey Lewis Trio* (Cadet 1965) ★★★, *The Best Of Ramsey Lewis* (Cadet 1970) ★★★, *Ramsey Lewis' Newly Recorded All-Time, Non-Stop Golden Hits* (Columbia 1973) ★★★, *The Greatest Hits Of Ramsey Lewis* (Chess 1988) ★★★★, *Collection* (More Music 1995) ★★★, *The Ramsey Lewis Trio In Person 1960-1967* (Chess 1998) ★★★★, *Priceless Jazz Collection* (GRP 1998) ★★★, *This Is Jazz* 80s recordings (Song 1998) ★★★, *Best Of Ramsey Lewis, Millennium Collection* (Chess 2002) ★★★.
● FILMS: *Gonks Go Beat* (1965).

LEYTON, JOHN

b. John Dudley Leyton, 17 February 1939, Frinton-on-Sea, Essex, England. Originally a small-time actor in the television series *Biggles*, Leyton's good looks won him a recording contract with Top Rank Records. Backed by the strong management of Robert Stigwood and talented producer Joe Meek, he recorded 'Tell Laura I Love Her', but lost out to the chart-topping Ricky Valance. A second flop with 'Girl On The Floor Above' was followed by the timely intervention of songwriter Geoff Goddard with the haunting 'Johnny Remember Me'. Stigwood ensured that the song was incorporated into Leyton's latest television role as pop singer Johnny St. Cyr in *Harpers West One*. The nationwide exposure focused attention on the record and its otherworldly ambience and elaborate production were enough to bring Leyton a UK number 1. The Goddard-composed follow-up 'Wild Wind' reached number 2, and there were further minor hits with 'Son This Is She', 'Lone Rider' and 'Lonely City'.

Avoiding the ravages of the beat boom, Leyton continued his acting career in such movies as

The Great Escape (1963) and Von Ryan's Express (1965). After a 10-year recording hiatus, he made a brief comeback in 1974 with an album written entirely by Kenny Young. Thereafter, Leyton concentrated on television work and related business interests. In 2001 Leyton, looking at least ten years younger, began performing again at touring 60s revival shows.
● ALBUMS: The Two Sides Of John Leyton (HMV 1961) ★★★, Always Yours (HMV 1963) ★★, John Leyton (York 1974) ★★.
● COMPILATIONS: Rarities (EMI 1984) ★★, The Best Of John Leyton (Sequel 1988) ★★★, The EP Collection ... Plus (See For Miles 1994) ★★★, Archive (Rialto 1996) ★★★.
● FILMS: It's Trad, Dad! aka Ring-A-Ding Rhythm (1961), The Great Escape (1963), Guns At Batasi (1964), Von Ryan's Express (1965), Every Day's A Holiday aka Seaside Swingers (1965), The Idol (1966), Krakatoa, East Of Java aka Volcano (1969), Fern, The Red Deer (1976), Schizo (1977), Dangerous Davies – The Last Detective (1980).

LIGHTFOOT, TERRY
b. 21 May 1935, Potters Bar, Middlesex, England. Lightfoot made his first appearance on the UK jazz scene as a clarinettist in the early 50s. After leading his own band throughout the 50s, he maintained a band into the next decade, having established a reputation strong enough to shrug off the decline in popularity of his brand of music. During the trad boom of the early 60s he appeared in the film It's Trad Dad. Apart from a brief spell in Kenny Ball's band he continued to lead into the 70s only stepping sideways into hotel management towards the end of the decade. He continued to play however, and by the mid-80s was back in full-time music. Amongst the most polished of British traditional clarinettists, Lightfoot achieved and maintained high standards of performance not only from himself but also from the many fine musicians he employed over the years.
● ALBUMS: Jazz Gumbo Volume 1 (Nixa 1956) ★★★★, Tradition In Colour (Columbia 1958) ★★★★, Trad Parade (Columbia 1961) ★★★, King Kong (1961) ★★★, Lightfoot At Lansdowne (Columbia 1962) ★★★★, Alleycat (Columbia 1965) ★★★, Personal Appearance (1975) ★★★, Terry Lightfoot In Concert (Black Lion 1979) ★★, Clear Round (Plant Life 1981) ★★★, As Time Goes By (PRT 1986) ★★★, At The Jazzband Ball (Bold Reprive 1988) ★★, Stardust (Upbeat 1990) ★★★, New Orleans Jazzmen (Hanover 1990) ★★★, When The Saints (See For Miles 1991) ★★★★, Down On Bourbon Street (Timeless 1994) ★★, Strictly Traditional (Lake 1999) ★★★.

LIMELITERS
The Limeliters were one of the popular forces behind the 60s folk revival in America. The group comprised Lou Gottlieb (b. 10 October 1923, Los Angeles, California, USA, d. 11 July

1996, Sebastopol, California, USA; bass), Alex Hassilev (b. 11 July 1932, Paris, France; guitar/banjo/vocals) and Glenn Yarbrough (b. 12 January 1930, Milwaukee, Wisconsin, USA; guitar/vocals). They formed in Los Angeles in 1959 and took their name from a club, run by Hassilev and Yarbrough, called The Limelite in Aspen, Colorado, USA. Gottlieb was a Doctor of Musicology, having studied under the Austrian composer Arnold Schoenberg, and had previously sung with the Gateway Singers. The group had a minor hit with 'A Dollar Down' in April 1961 on RCA Records, but their albums sold better than singles. Many of their albums were live recordings, including the popular Tonight: In Person, which reached number 5 in the US charts in 1961. The follow-up, The Limeliters, narrowly reached the Top 40 the same year. A third release, The Slightly Fabulous Limeliters made the US Top 10, also in 1961. A series of albums followed, with Sing Out! making the US Top 20 in 1962. Gradually their popularity waned, and when Yarbrough left in November 1963 to pursue a solo career, the group replaced him with Ernie Sheldon. In 1965, Yarbrough, also with RCA, reached the Top 40 in the US album charts with 'Baby The Rain Must Fall'. The title track, taken from a film of the same title, made the Top 20 the same year. In the late 80s Yarbrough re-formed the Limeliters with new members
● ALBUMS: The Limeliters (RCA Victor 1960) ★★★★, Tonight: In Person (RCA Victor 1961) ★★★, The Slightly Fabulous Limeliters (RCA Victor 1961) ★★★, Sing Out! (RCA Victor 1962) ★★★★, Through Children's Eyes (RCA Victor 1962) ★★, Folk Matinee (RCA Victor 1962) ★★★, Our Men In San Francisco (RCA Victor 1963) ★★★, Makin' A Joyful Noise (RCA Victor 1963) ★★★, Fourteen 14K Folk Songs (RCA Victor 1963) ★★★, More Of Everything! (RCA Victor 1964) ★★★, London Concert (RCA Victor 1965) ★★★, The Limeliters Look At Love In Depth (RCA Victor 1965) ★★★, The Original 'Those Were The Days' (RCA Victor 1968) ★★, Time To Gather Seeds (RCA Victor 1970) ★★★, Their First Historic Album (RCA Victor 1986) ★★★★, Alive In Concert (RCA Victor 1988) ★★★.
● COMPILATIONS: The Best Of The Limeliters (RCA Victor 1964) ★★★.

LIND, BOB
b. 25 November 1944, Baltimore, Maryland, USA. Lind is best known for writing and recording the Top 5 folk rock song 'Elusive Butterfly' in 1966. He moved around frequently with his family, and while settled in Denver, Colorado, he began singing folk music in clubs. He moved to the west coast and was signed to World Pacific Records, a division of the larger Liberty Records. Produced by Jack Nitzsche, Lind played guitar on his recordings for the label, while piano was handled by Leon Russell.

His first single, 'Cheryl's Going Home', failed to catch on but was later covered by Cher and the Blues Project. 'Elusive Butterfly' was its b-side and became an international Top 10 hit. Lind was widely touted as 'the new Bob Dylan' and the latest spokesperson for youth during 1966. Despite his pop star looks and sensitive lyrics, however, his subsequent singles failed to reach the charts. *Don't Be Concerned* contained a number of sentimental, but attractive songs. His compositions continued to find interpreters, among them the Turtles, Noel Harrison, Nancy Sinatra and Bobby Sherman. Lind continued to record into the early 70s, switching to Capitol Records without a revival of his commercial fortunes. He was still performing in folk and country music circles in the early 80s.

● ALBUMS: *Don't Be Concerned* (World Pacific 1966) ★★, *The Elusive Bob Lind* (Verve/Forecast 1966) ★★, *Photographs Of Feeling* (World Pacific 1966) ★★, *Since There Were Circles* (Capitol 1971) ★★.

LITTLE ANTHONY AND THE IMPERIALS

Formed in Brooklyn, New York, USA, in 1957, and originally called the Chesters, the group comprised 'Little' Anthony Gourdine (b. 8 January 1940, Brooklyn, New York, USA), Ernest Wright Jnr. (b. 24 August 1941, Brooklyn, New York, USA), Clarence Collins (b. 17 March 1941, Brooklyn, New York, USA), Tracy Lord and Glouster Rogers (b. 1940). A vital link between doo-wop and sweet soul, the Imperials were the prototype for the Delfonics and Stylistics. Gourdine first recorded in 1956 as a member of the Duponts. From there he helped form the Chesters, who became the Imperials on signing to the End label. The 'Little Anthony' prefix was subsequently added at the suggestion of the influential disc jockey Alan Freed. The group's first hit, the haunting Al Lewis-penned 'Tears On My Pillow' (1958), encapsulated the essence of street-corner harmony. Further success came with 'So Much' (1959) and 'Shimmy Shimmy Ko-Ko-Bop' (1960), before Gourdine was persuaded to embark on an ill-fated solo career. In 1964, he formed a 'new' Imperials around Wright, Collins and Sammy Strain (b. 9 December 1940). Their first hit, 'I'm On The Outside (Looking In)', showcased Gourdine's dazzling falsetto, a style continued on 'Goin' Out Of My Head' and 'Hurt So Bad' (both of which reached the US pop Top 10). Complementing these graceful releases were such up-tempo offerings as 'Better Use Your Head' and 'Gonna Fix You Good' (both 1966). The line-up later drifted apart and in 1974 Sammy Strain replaced William Powell in the O'Jays. Three years later, Collins formed his own 'Imperials', touring Britain on the strength of two hit singles, a reissued 'Better Use Your Head', and a new recording, 'Who's Gonna Love Me?'. In the 80s Gourdine released *Daylight* on the religious outlet Songbird.

● ALBUMS: *We Are The Imperials* (End 1959) ★★★, *Shades Of The 40's* (End 1961) ★★★, *I'm On The Outside Looking In* (DCP 1964) ★★★, *Goin' Out Of My Head* (DCP 1965) ★★★, *Paying Our Dues* (Veep 1967) ★★★, *Reflections* (Veep 1967) ★★, *Movie Grabbers* (Veep 1968) ★★, *Out Of Sight, Out Of Mind* (United Artists 1969) ★★, *On A New Street* (Avco 1974) ★★.
Solo: Anthony Gourdine *Daylight* (Songbird 1980) ★★.

● COMPILATIONS: *Little Anthony And The Imperials Greatest Hits* (Roulette 1965) ★★★, *The Best Of Little Anthony And The Imperials* (DCP 1966) ★★★, *The Best Of Little Anthony And The Imperials* (Rhino 1989) ★★★, *25 Greatest Hits* (MFP 1998) ★★★.

LITTLE EVA

b. Eva Narcissus Boyd, 29 June 1943, Bellhaven, North Carolina, USA. Discovered by songwriters Carole King and Gerry Goffin, Little Eva shot to fame in 1962 with the international hit 'The Loco-Motion', a driving, dance-based song. Its ebullient, adolescent approach was muted on a follow-up single, 'Keep Your Hands Off My Baby', but although further releases from the following year, 'Let's Turkey Trot' and 'Old Smokey Locomotion', revived its novelty appeal, they lacked its basic excitement. Eva continued to record until 1965, but her only other substantial hit came with 'Swinging On A Star', a duet with Big Dee Irwin, on which she was, unfortunately, uncredited. She made a UK chart comeback in 1972 with a reissue of 'The Loco-Motion', which peaked at number 11, and the song's lasting appeal was reaffirmed in 1988 when Kylie Minogue emulated Eva's original UK chart position. The following year, Little Eva returned to the recording scene with an album on the Malibu label.

● ALBUMS: *L-L-L-L-Loco-Motion* (Dimension 1962) ★★, *Back On Track* (Malibu 1989) ★★★.

● COMPILATIONS: *Lil' Loco'Motion* (Rock Echoes 1982) ★★, *L L L L Little Eva: The Complete Dimension Recordings* (Westside 1998) ★★★, *The Original* (Disky 1998) ★★★.

LIVERPOOL SCENE

The name 'Liverpool Scene' was derived from a poetry anthology which featured Roger McGough, Adrian Henri (b. 10 April 1932, Birkenhead, England, d. 20 December 2000, Liverpool, England), and Brian Patten. The writers subsequently appeared on UK television's *Look Of The Week*, where their readings were accompanied by guitarist Andy Roberts. McGough and Henri then recorded *The Incredible New Liverpool Scene*, which included definitive performances of their best-known work, including 'Let Me Die A Young Man's Death' (McGough) and 'Tonight At Noon' (Henri). While McGough pursued a career within Scaffold, Henri and Roberts added Mike Hart (guitar/vocals), Mike Evans (saxophone/vocals), Percy Jones (bass) and

Brian Dodson (drums) to create an explicitly rock-based ensemble. UK disc jockey John Peel was an early patron and the group quickly found itself an integral part of music's underground circuit, culminating in their impressive appearance at the 1969 Isle Of Wight Festival. *The Amazing Adventures Of ...* captured the sextet at their most potent, but successive albums, although worthwhile, failed to match the crucial balance between musical and lyrical content and the group broke up in 1970. Hart embarked on a solo career, but while Roberts initially found fame in Plainsong, he was later reunited with both Henri and McGough in Grimms.

● ALBUMS: *The Incredible New Liverpool Scene* (Columbia 1967) ★★, *The Amazing Adventures Of ...* (RCA 1968) ★★★★, *Bread On The Night* (RCA 1969) ★★★, *Saint Adrian Co. Broadway And 3rd* (RCA 1970) ★★★, *Heirloom* (RCA 1970) ★★★.

● COMPILATIONS: *Recollections* (RCA 1972) ★★★.

LOCKLIN, HANK

b. Lawrence Hankins Locklin, 15 February 1918, McLellan, Florida, USA. A farm boy, Locklin worked in the cotton fields as a child and on the roads during the Depression of the 30s. He learned to play the guitar at the age of 10 and was soon performing on local radio and at dances. His professional career started in 1938 and after an interruption for military service, he worked various local radio stations, including WALA Mobile and KLEE Houston. In 1949, he joined the *Louisiana Hayride* on KWKH Shreveport and achieved his first country chart entry with his Four Star recording of his self-penned 'The Same Sweet One'. In 1953, 'Let Me Be The One' became his first country number 1. After moving to RCA Records in the mid-50s, he had Top 10 US country hits with 'Geisha Girl', his own 'Send Me The Pillow You Dream On', both also making the US pop charts, and 'It's A Little More Like Heaven'. His biggest chart success came in 1960, when his million-selling recording of 'Please Help Me, I'm Falling' topped the US country charts for 14 successive weeks and also reached number 8 in the pop charts. It also became one of the first modern country songs to make the British pop charts, peaking at number 9 in a 19-week chart stay. (An answer version by Skeeter Davis called '(I Can't Help You) I'm Falling Too' also became a US country and pop hit the same year.) Locklin became a member of the *Grand Ole Opry* in 1960 and during the next decade, his fine tenor voice and ability to handle country material saw him become one of the most popular country artists.

He registered over 20 US chart entries including 'We're Gonna Go Fishing' and a number 8 hit with what is now a country standard, 'The Country Hall Of Fame', in 1967. He hosted his own television series in Houston and Dallas in the 1970s and during his career has toured

extensively in the USA, Canada and in Europe. He is particularly popular in Ireland, where he has toured many times, and in 1964, he recorded an album of Irish songs. Although a popular artist in Nashville, he always resisted settling there. In the early 60s, he returned to his native Florida and built his home, the Singing L, on the same cotton field where he had once worked as a boy. After becoming interested in local affairs, his popularity saw him elected mayor of his home-town of McLellan. Although Locklin's last chart success was a minor hit in 1971, he remained a firm favourite with the fans and still regularly appeared on the *Opry*. He released a notable new record in 2001 which demonstrated that his voice remains in fine form.

● ALBUMS: *Foreign Love* (RCA Victor 1958) ★★★, *Please Help Me, I'm Falling* (RCA Victor 1960) ★★★, *Encores* (King 1961) ★★, *Hank Locklin* (Wrangler 1962) ★★, *10 Songs* (Design 1962) ★★, *A Tribute To Roy Acuff, The King Of Country Music* (RCA Victor 1962) ★★★, *This Song Is Just For You* (Camden 1963) ★★★, *The Ways Of Life* (RCA Victor 1963) ★★★, *Happy Journey* (RCA Victor 1964) ★★★, *Irish Songs, Country Style* (RCA Victor 1964) ★★★, *Hank Locklin Sings Hank Williams* (RCA Victor 1964) ★★★, *Born To Ramble* (Hilltop 1965) ★★★, *My Kind Of Country Music* (Camden 1965) ★★★, *Down Texas Way* (Metro 1965) ★★★, *Hank Locklin Sings Eddy Arnold* (RCA Victor 1965) ★★★, *Once Over Lightly* (RCA Victor 1965) ★★★, with the Jordanaires *The Girls Get Prettier* (RCA Victor 1966) ★★★, *The Gloryland Way* (RCA Victor 1966) ★★★, *Bummin' Around* (Camden 1967) ★★, *Send Me The Pillow You Dream On* (RCA Victor 1967) ★★★, *Sings Hank Locklin* (1967) ★★★, *Nashville Women* (RCA Victor 1967) ★★★, *Queen Of Hearts* (Hilltop 1968) ★★★, *My Love Song For You* (RCA Victor 1968) ★★★, *Softly – Hank Locklin* (RCA Victor 1969) ★★★, *That's How Much I Love You* (Camden 1969) ★★★, *Wabash Cannonball* (Camden 1969) ★★★, *Best Of Today's Country Hits* (RCA Victor 1969) ★★★, *Lookin' Back* (RCA Victor 1969) ★★★, *Bless Her Heart – I Love Her* (RCA Victor 1970) ★★, *Candy Kisses* (Camden 1970) ★★★, *Hank Locklin & Danny Davis & The Nashville Brass* (RCA Victor 1970) ★★, *The Mayor Of McLellan, Florida* (RCA Victor 1972) ★★★, *There Never Was A Time* (1977) ★★★, with various artists *Carol Channing & Her Country Friends* (1977) ★★, *All Kinds Of Everything* (Topspin 1979) ★★★, *Please Help Me I'm Falling* (Topline 1986) ★★★, *Generations In Song* (Coldwater 2001) ★★★★.

● COMPILATIONS: *The Best Of Hank Locklin* (King 1961) ★★, *The Best Of Hank Locklin* (RCA Victor 1966) ★★★, *Country Hall Of Fame* (RCA Victor 1968) ★★★★, *The First Fifteen Years* (RCA Victor 1971) ★★★, *Famous Country Music Makers* (RCA 1975) ★★, *The Golden Hits* (1977) ★★★, *The Best Of Hank Locklin* (RCA 1979) ★★★, *20 Of The Best* (RCA 1982) ★★★, *Please elp Me I'm Falling* 4-CD box set (Bear Family 995) ★★★★, *Send Me The Pillow That You ream On* 3-CD box set (Bear Family 1997) ★★★, *Please Help Me I'm Falling* (Collectables 998) ★★★, *Masters* (Eagle 1998) ★★★.

LOCOMOTIVE

ormed in Birmingham, England, Locomotive itially achieved fame as a ska/bluebeat band id by the fact that one of their early members, hris Wood had departed in 1967 to join the edgling Traffic. Having made their debut with roken Heart' on the dance-oriented Direction bel, they switched to Parlophone Records for udi's In Love'. This enchanting rock-steady illad reached the UK Top 30 in 1968, but by the llowing year the group had completely ianged its musical direction. Norman Haines uitar/vocals) took control of the band on 'Mr. rmageddon', a haunting progressive rock piece rawing an air of mystery from its pulsating, yet stant, horn section. Mick Taylor (trumpet), Bill adge (saxophone), Mick Hincks (bass) and Bob amb (drums) completed the line-up featured on *e Are Everything You See* which, despite ontemporary commercial indifference, has come one of the era's most fêted releases. ocomotive split up soon after its release, with aines founding the Norman Haines Band. amb, Hincks and associate member Keith Millar ormed the Dog That Bit People. The drummer en went on to join the Steve Gibbons Band.
ALBUMS: *We Are Everything You See* arlophone 1969) ★★★★.

LOMAX, JACKIE

10 May 1944, Wallasey, Merseyside, England. former vocalist with the 60s beat group the ndertakers, Lomax began a new career in merica when this respected Liverpool unit sbanded. Spells with two short-lived bands, the ersey Lads and the Lost Souls, preceded a :turn to England where the singer worked with is own group, the Lomax Alliance, and as a solo :t. Two strong, but unsuccessful, singles llowed before he was signed to the fledgling pple Records but his opening release, 'Sour ilk Sea', written for him by George Harrison, as unfortunately overshadowed by hits for ablemates the Beatles and Mary Hopkin. omax's debut, *Is This What You Want*, featured ontributions from a host of star names cluding Harrison, Paul McCartney, Ringo Starr id Eric Clapton. The artist's stylish ompositions and superb voice were equal to ich esteemed company. Sadly, Apple's internal roblems doomed his undoubted potential and llowing an interlude as part of the elusive eavy Jelly, Lomax returned to America where e completed two more excellent albums, *Home In My Head* and *Three*. In 1973, the singer ined the British-based Badger, a group formed y ex-Yes organist, Tony Kaye. Lomax helped ansform them from a progressive rock band

into a more soulful aggregation, exemplified on *White Lady*, which was produced by Allen Toussaint and consisted solely of Lomax's songs. Badger then split into two factions, with Lomax and bassist Kim Gardner instigating an offshoot unit named after the album. Lomax subsequently resumed his solo career, but the releases that followed were disappointing and the bad luck which had often dogged this worthwhile performer further undermined his career. Lomax did resurface in 1990 as one of several acts contributing to the 'tribute' album *True Voices*, wherein he sang a version of Tim Buckley's 'Devil Eyes'.
● ALBUMS: *Is This What You Want* (Apple 1969) ★★★, *Home Is In My Head* (1971) ★★★, *Three* (1972) ★★, with Badger *White Lady* (1974) ★★, *Livin' For Lovin'* (EMI 1976) ★★★, *Did You Ever Have That Feeling?* (EMI 1977) ★★.

LOPEZ, TRINI

b. Trinidad Lopez III, 15 May 1937, Dallas, Texas, USA. Trini Lopez took folk songs and rocked them up into Latin rhythms, recording 14 chart albums and 13 chart singles between 1963 and 1968. Propelled by a strong R&B-influenced backbeat (usually provided by bass player Dave Shriver and drummer Gene Riggio) and his own incessantly rhythmic guitar, Lopez was at his best when playing live. A number of his nightclub performances were recorded and released as albums. Lopez listened to R&B music while growing up, and formed his first band in Wichita Falls, Texas, at the age of 15. At the recommendation of Buddy Holly, Lopez went to the producer Norman Petty in Clovis, New Mexico, but Lopez did not record with him as Petty wanted to record only instrumental music. In 1958, however, Petty did secure Lopez and his group the Big Beats a contract with Columbia Records, which released the single 'Clark's Expedition'/'Big Boy', ironically, an instrumental. Lopez made his first solo recording, his own composition 'The Right To Rock', for the Dallas-based Volk Records, and then signed with King Records in 1959, recording more than a dozen singles for that label, none of which charted. In late 1962, after the King contract expired, Lopez followed up on an offer by producer Snuff Garrett to join the post-Holly Crickets as vocalist. After a couple of weeks of auditions in Los Angeles that idea did not bear fruit and Lopez formed his own group.
He landed a steady engagement at the nightclub PJ's, where his audience soon grew. He was heard there by Frank Sinatra, who had started his own label, Reprise Records, and who subsequently signed Lopez. He was placed with arranger/producer Don Costa, who wisely chose to record Lopez in concert at the club. His first album, *Trini Lopez At PJ's*, rose to number 2 in the summer of 1963 and stayed in the US charts for nearly two years. The first single from the album, an uptempo party-like version of Pete

Seeger's 'If I Had A Hammer', reached number 3 (number 4 in the UK), out-performing Peter, Paul And Mary's more sedate rendering a year earlier. Lopez's subsequent recordings for Reprise displayed a musical eclecticism – he recorded a folk album, an R&B album, two Latin albums, country, in foreign languages (Spanish and German) and even Broadway show tunes, all in his infectiously simple singalong style. Only one other Top 20 single resulted, 'Lemon Tree' in 1965, and he appeared in a number of films, including *The Dirty Dozen* and *Marriage On The Rocks*, but by the end of the 60s Lopez had largely disappeared from public view. He recorded sporadically in the 70s, including *Viva* and a number of singles for Capitol Records in 1971-72, and *Transformed By Time* for Roulette Records in 1978, and although he continued to sing in Las Vegas during the 80s little has been heard from Lopez since his heyday. There are numerous budget-label album releases of his music available, and several anthologies on European labels.
● ALBUMS: *Teenage Love Songs* (King 1963) ★★, *Trini Lopez At PJ's* (Reprise 1963) ★★★★, *More Of Trini Lopez* (King 1964) ★★, *More Trini Lopez At PJ's* (Reprise 1963) ★★★, *On The Move* (Reprise 1964) ★★★, *The Latin Album* (Reprise 1964) ★★★, *Live At Basin St. East* (Reprise 1964) ★★★, *The Folk Album* (Reprise 1965) ★★, *The Love Album* (Reprise 1965) ★★★, *The Rhythm & Blues Album* (Reprise 1965) ★★, *The Sing-Along World Of Trini Lopez* (Reprise 1965) ★★★, *Trini* (Reprise 1966) ★★★, *24 Songs By The Great Trini Lopez* (King 1966) ★★, *The Second Latin Album* (Reprise 1966) ★★★, *Trini Lopez In London* (Reprise 1967) ★★★, *Now!* (Reprise 1967) ★★★, *It's A Great Life* (Reprise 1968) ★★★, *Trini Country* (Reprise 1968) ★, *Viva* (Reprise 1972) ★★, *Transformed By Time* (Roulette 1978) ★★.
● COMPILATIONS: *Greatest Hits!* (Reprise 1966) ★★★, *La Bamba – His 28 Greatest Hits* (Entertainers 1988) ★★★, *The Very Best Of Trini Lopez* (Disky 1998) ★★★.
● FILMS: *Marriage On The Rocks* (1965), *Poppies Are Also Flowers* aka *Danger Grows Wild* (1966), *The Dirty Dozen* (1967), *Operation Dirty Dozen* (1967), *The Phynx* (1970), *Antonio* (1973), *Social Suicide* (1991).

LORDAN, JERRY

b. Jeremiah Patrick Lordan, 30 April 1934, London, England, d. 24 July 1995. After leaving the Royal Air Force in 1955, Lordan sought work as a comedian before forming a short-lived duo, Lee And Jerry Elvin. During this unsatisfying time he was busy writing songs, and one of his demos, 'A Home, A Car And A Wedding Ring', with Emile Ford guesting on piano, became a minor US hit for Mike Preston. When Anthony Newley took Lordan's 'I've Waited So Long' to number 3 in the UK, the composer was signed as a soloist by Parlophone Records. Five low-ranking Top 50 hits in the first six months of

1960 confirmed Lordan's promise but it was as songwriter for other people that he shone. H biggest solo hit was 'Who Could Be Bluer?' Th shimmering 'Apache' gave the Shadows momentous UK number 1, while Jorge Ingmann almost achieved the same position the USA. Thereafter, Lordan was lauded as th great composer of many instrumentals, enjoyir chart-toppers with the Shadows' 'Wonderf Land', and Jet Harris And Tony Meehan 'Diamonds'. He still wrote lyrics for artists including Cl Laine, Petula Clark, Matt Monro, Shane Fent (I'm A Moody Guy' and 'Walk Away') and on hit-wonder Louise Cordet ('I'm Just A Baby'). the end of the 60s, two more Lordan hits we high in the charts, courtesy of Cilla Blac ('Conversations') and Cliff Richard ('Go Times'). After an all too brief recordin comeback in 1970 with 'Old Man And The Se which was rumoured to have sold only tw hundred copies, Lordan's musical career end and he ceased writing altogether. Following spell as an alcoholic he suffered serious ment problems. During the 70s his financial problem prompted him to sell the copyrights to most his major songs. In the 80s his personal li improved and he started to write songs onc again as a hobby. The Shadows recognized h massive contribution to their career and Bru Welch participated during the memorial servic
● ALBUMS: *All My Own Work* (Parlophone 196 ★★.

LOS BRAVOS

Originally known as Los Sonor, Mike Kogel (b. April 1945, Berlin, Germany; vocals), Anton Martinez (b. 3 October 1945, Madrid, Spai guitar), Manolo 'Manuel' Fernandez (b. September 1943, Seville, Spain, d. 1969; organ Miguel Vicens Danus (b. 21 June 1944, Palma Mallona, Spain; bass) and Pablo 'Gome Samllehi (b. 5 November 1943, Barcelona, Spai drums) were voted Spain's top beat grou following two Top 10 hits in their own countr Kogel had previously recorded as Michael Ar The Firebirds, Mike Keller and Mike And Jc And The Rebel Guys. They achieve international recognition in 1966 when 'Black Black', a song composed by two Englishme Tony Hayes and Steve Wadey, rose to number in the UK charts in the wake of heavy promotic on pirate radio. The song's compulsive hooklir proved equally popular in the USA where reached number 4, but the quintet was sad unable to repeat this success. Despite a series superior pop performances, including a effervescent reading of an Easybea composition, 'Bring A Little Lovin'', 'I Dor Care' (1966) was the group's last UK Top entry. Kogel later recorded as Mike Kennedy.
● ALBUMS: *Black Is Black* (Press 1966) ★★, *L Bravos* aka *Bring A Little Lovin'* (Parrott 196 ★★.

LOTHAR AND THE HAND PEOPLE

Although this splendidly named quintet became fixtures of New York's underground circuit, they were formed in Denver, Colorado, USA, in 1965. College drop-out John Arthur Emelin (vocals/theremin) was initially joined by Richard Lewis (rhythm guitar), Russell 'Rusty' Ford (bass) and Tom Lyle (drums), before William C. Wright (lead guitar) completed the line-up. Lewis and Wright were later replaced by Kim King (guitar) and Paul Conly (keyboards). Much attention to the group was given due to Emelin's use of the theremin, an instrument capable of eerie electronic 'cries' similar to those used in horror movies and previously heard on the Beach Boys' 'Good Vibrations'. Lothar headed east at the behest of the Lovin' Spoonful whom they supported on a provincial tour. The new arrivals quickly secured a recording deal, but the apathy that greeted their first three singles delayed a debut album. *Presenting Lothar And The Hand People* was not issued until late 1968, although its simple, folksy atmosphere recalled a more innocent era. The album was produced by Robert Margouleff who went on to form the experimental Tonto's Expanding Headband. A second collection, *Space Hymn*, followed within a matter of months and showed a group embracing synthesized technology. The set maintained a love of melody, but despite positive reviews, the album was not a commercial success and Lothar And The Hand People broke up in 1971.

● ALBUMS: *Presenting Lothar And The Hand People* (Capitol 1968) ★★, *Space Hymn* (Capitol 1969) ★★.

● COMPILATIONS: *This Is It, Machines* (See For Miles 1986) ★★.

LOUDERMILK, JOHN D.

b. 31 March 1934, Durham, North Carolina, USA. Loudermilk's first musical experience was banging a drum for the Salvation Army; he played various instruments as a child and appeared regularly on the radio from the age of 11. In 1956, George Hamilton IV recorded his song 'A Rose And A Baby Ruth', which went from the local to the national charts, reaching number 6. A few months later, Eddie Cochran made his debut in the US Top 20 with 'Sittin' In The Balcony', another Loudermilk song that he had recorded himself under the pseudonym Johnny D. When Loudermilk moved to Nashville, a stream of hits followed, the UK chart successes being 'Waterloo' (Stonewall Jackson, 1959), 'Angela Jones' (Michael Cox, 1960), 'Tobacco Road' (Nashville Teens, 1964), 'Google Eye' (which was a catfish, Nashville Teens, 1964), 'This Little Bird' (Marianne Faithfull, 1965, and subsequently parodied by the Barron Knights), 'Then You Can Tell Me Goodbye' (Casinos, 1967, and a US country number 1 for Eddy Arnold), 'It's My Time' (the Everly Brothers, 1968), 'Indian Reservation (The

Lament Of The Cherokee Reservation Indian)' (Don Fardon, 1970 and a US number 1 for the Raiders, 1971) and 'Sunglasses' (a revival of a Skeeter Davis record by Tracey Ullman, 1984). His controversial 'death' song, 'Ebony Eyes', was the b-side of the Everly Brothers' 1961 number 1, 'Walk Right Back'. Other successful b-sides include 'Weep No More My Baby' (Brenda Lee's 'Sweet Nothin's'), 'Stayin' In' (Bobby Vee's 'More Than I Can Say'), 'Heaven Fell Last Night' (the Browns' 'The Three Bells') and 'In A Matter Of Moments' (Louise Cordet's 'I'm Just A Baby'). Near misses include 'All Of This For Sally' (Mark Dinning), 'The Guitar Player (Him And Her)' for Jimmy Justice and 'To Hell With Love' for Adam Faith. He arranged an old song, 'Abilene', for George Hamilton IV, which made the US charts in 1963 and became a country standard. His other country music successes include 'Talk Back Trembling Lips' (Ernest Ashworth and Johnny Tillotson), 'Bad News' (Johnny Cash and Boxcar Willie), 'Break My Mind' (George Hamilton IV, Gram Parsons and the Hillsiders), 'You're Ruinin' My Life' (Hank Williams Jnr.) and 'Half-Breed' (Marvin Rainwater). He wrote clever novelty songs for Bob Luman ('The Great Snowman' and 'The File') and for Sue Thompson ('Sad Movies (Make Me Cry)', 'Norman', 'James (Hold The Ladder Steady)' and 'Paper Tiger', all US Top 30 hits). Loudermilk had his own hit with 'The Language Of Love', which made number 13 in the UK in 1962. He made several albums of his own material and they have been collected on two Bear Family compilations, *Blue Train* and *It's My Time*, which contain two previously unreleased tracks in 'The Little Wind Up Doll' and 'Giving You All My Love'. He has often worked in the UK and performs his songs in a similar manner to Burl Ives. He produced Pete Sayers' best album, *Bogalusa Gumbo*, in 1979, but an album that he recorded at the same sessions has not been released. He now spends his time studying ethnomusicology.

● ALBUMS: *The Language Of Love* (RCA Victor 1961) ★★★, *Twelve Sides Of Loudermilk* (RCA Victor 1962) ★★★, *John D. Loudermilk Sings A Bizarre Collection Of Unusual Songs* (RCA Victor 1965) ★★★, *Suburban Attitudes In Country Verse* (RCA Victor 1967) ★★, *Country Love Songs* (RCA Victor 1968) ★★, *The Open Mind Of John D. Loudermilk* (RCA Victor 1969) ★★, *Elloree* (1975) ★★, *Just Passing Through* (1977) ★★.

● COMPILATIONS: *The Best Of John D. Loudermilk* (RCA 1970) ★★★, *Encores* (RCA 1975) ★★★, *Blue Train* (Bear Family 1989) ★★★, *It's My Time* (Bear Family 1989) ★★★, *Sittin' In The Balcony* (Bear Family 1995) ★★★.

LOVE

For many, the doyens of Los Angeles progressive rock in the 60s, brilliantly erratic and producers of one of the finest rock albums ever made: *Forever Changes*. Love were formed in 1965 out of the ashes of the Grass Roots, and comprised former Byrds road manager Bryan MacLean (b. 25 September 1946, Los Angeles, California, USA, d. 25 December 1998, Los Angeles, California, USA; guitar/vocals), Arthur Lee (b. Arthur Taylor Porter, 7 March 1945, Memphis, Tennessee, USA; guitar/vocals), John Echols (b. Memphis, Tennessee, USA; lead guitar). Don Conka (drums) and John Fleckenstein were soon replaced by Alban 'Snoopy' Pfisterer (b. Switzerland) and ex-Surfaris Ken Forssi (b. Cleveland, Ohio, USA, d. 5 January 1998, USA). They become the first rock band to be signed by the expanding Elektra Records, just beating the Doors by a whisker. Their debut single was a cover version of Burt Bacharach and Hal David's 'My Little Red Book', in a different form from the way the writers imagined it. Love were an instant sensation on the LA club scene, outrageous, loud, innovative and stoned. The furiously energetic 'Seven & Seven Is' was released in the summer of 1966 and became their second hit. Line-up changes saw drummer Michael Stuart (ex-Sons Of Adam) and flautist/saxophonist Tjay Cantrelli (b. John Berberis) joining, while Pfisterer moved to harpsichord and organ.

'The Castle' on Da Capo pointed to a new direction, although beautifully crafted songs such as 'Orange Skies' and 'Stephanie Knows Who' were strong tracks. For most listeners 'Revelation', the entire flip side of the album, was a completely self-indulgent exercise in time-wasting and marred a potentially great album. It was Forever Changes, recorded without the departed Pfisterer and Cantrelli, that put them in the history books. That album, 25 years later, is still found on most critics' recommended lists and no comprehensive record collection should be without it. In the All-Time Top 1000 Albums book it is gaining momentum, and is currently number 12. It is a superlative suite of songs, unassumingly brilliant, gentle, biting and full of surprises. It combines the occasional acid guitar solo with gentle acoustic strumming, and is awash with beautiful orchestration. It proved to be Arthur Lee's finest work and marked the end of the partnership with Bryan MacLean.

A new Love, featuring Lee, Frank Fayad (bass), Jay Donnellan (guitar) and the drumming pyrotechnics of George Suranovich and Darren Theaker, recorded the material for Four Sail (on Elektra) and Out Here (on Blue Thumb Records). These records contained rare glimpses of the magic of Forever Changes, but ultimately they were bitter disappointments. Four Sail is notable for the excellent drumming of Suranovich and contains a couple of gems, 'August', and 'I'm With You'. False Start, recorded by Lee, Fayad, Suranovich, Nooney Rickett (rhythm guitar, vocals) and Gary Rowles (guitar), featured few memorable moments, one being the guitar solo from Jimi Hendrix on 'The Everlasting First'.

Lee released a solo album in 1972 before reviving the Love name for the truly wretched Reel To Real. The long-held opinion that Lee had become a casualty of too many chemicals was strengthened throughout subsequent decades with various stories chronicling his erratic and eccentric behaviour.

In 1996 the latest rumours to surface were that Lee and former member Johnny Echols were working together again. Later that year it was confirmed that Lee now suffers from Parkinson's disease. The most astonishing development, though, was Lee's eight-year prison sentence for illegal possession of a firearm. Many attempts to resurrect his career have faltered, although any news of Lee is always greeted with enthusiasm. Like Brian Wilson, Syd Barrett, and Alexander 'Skip' Spence he is another wayward genius who took one trip too many. Forever Changes was reissued in February 2001 with bonus tracks and the legendary single 'Laughing Stock'/'Your Mind And We Belong Together'. The excellent re-mastering was rewarded by an extraordinary wave of music media coverage; not surprisingly the album sneaked into the UK charts for one week. Love's magnificent legacy is a record as important as Pet Sounds, Sgt. Peppers Lonely Hearts Club Band and Kind Of Blue.

● ALBUMS: Love (Elektra 1966) ★★★, Da Capo (Elektra 1967) ★★★★, Forever Changes (Elektra 1967) ★★★★★, Four Sail (Elektra 1969) ★★★★, Out Here (Blue Thumb 1969) ★★, False Start (Blue Thumb 1970) ★★★, Reel To Real (RSO 1974) ★, Love Live 1978 recording (Rhino 1982) ★★, Studio/Live (MCA 1982) ★★, Electrically Speaking: Live In Concert (Yeaah! 2001) ★★, The Last Wall Of The Castle 1966 demos (Deep Six 2001) ★★.

● COMPILATIONS: Revisited (Elektra 1970) ★★★, Masters (Elektra 1973) ★★★, Best Of Love (Rhino 1980) ★★★, Out There (Big Beat 1988) ★★★, Comes In Colours (Big Beat 1993) ★★★★ Love Story: 1966-1972 (Rhino 1995) ★★★★.

● FURTHER READING: Arthur Lee: Love Story Ken Brooks. Arthur Lee: Alone Again Or, Barney Hoskyns.

LOVE AFFAIR

Originally formed in 1966, this London England-based quintet comprised Steve Ellis (vocals), Morgan Fisher (keyboards), Rex Brayley (guitar), Mick Jackson (bass) and Maurice Bacon (drums). Although Ellis was barely 16 years old, the band performed frequently in clubs on a semi-professional basis Fisher was briefly replaced by Lynton Guest and the following year Ellis, backed by session musicians, recorded a sparkling cover version of Robert Knight's 'Everlasting Love' for CBS Records. By January 1968, the single unexpectedly hit number 1 in the UK and Love Affair became instant pop stars with Ellis cherubic looks gracing teen magazines throughout the nation. With Bacon's father Sid overseeing the management, the band resisted the solicitations of more powerful entrepreneurs, yet failed to exploit their potential. Four more Top 20 hits followed, 'Rainbow Valley', 'A Day Without Love', 'One Road' and 'Bringing On Back The Good Times', but by 1969 their lead singer had left to start a solo career. He recorded a few singles and the soundtrack to *Loot* before collaborating with Zoot Money in Ellis, who released two albums for Epic Records (1972's *Riding On The Crest Of A Slump* and 1973's *... Why Not?*). Ellis later sang with Widowmaker, and in 1978 recorded a solo album (*The Last Angry Man*) which was briefly made available on cassette before finally being given a full release in 2000.

The remaining quartet recruited new vocalist Gus Eadon (b. Auguste Eadon; ex- Elastic Band) and began to steer the band in a more progressive direction. The second Love Affair album, released at the beginning of 1971, was credited simply to LA in an attempt to attract a more mature audience. The record was a commercial failure and six months later the band was dropped by CBS. They re-signed to Parlophone Records as Love Affair but were unable to revive their fortunes. Bacon and Fisher left to form Morgan, recording 1973's *Nova Solis* for RCA Records. Fisher later reappeared in Mott The Hoople and the Third Ear Band before releasing some bizarre solo material for Cherry Red Records during the 1980s. Bacon moved into music publishing and management, while Jackson worked his way up to become an important figure in the Alfa Romeo car group. A line-up of the Love Affair featuring no original members went on to issue obscure singles for Pye Records and Creole, before successively plundering the band's name for cabaret/revivalist bookings.

● ALBUMS: *The Everlasting Love Affair* (CBS 1968) ★★★, as LA *New Day* (CBS 1971) ★★, as Steve Ellis' Love Affair *Plugged In: Live At The Cavendish* aka *Love That's Everlasting* (Tring/Javelin 1997) ★★.

● COMPILATIONS: *No Strings* (Angel Air 2001) ★★, *The Best Of The Good Times* (Columbia 2001) ★★★.

LOVE SCULPTURE

Having recorded as the Human Beans, Dave Edmunds (b. 15 April 1944, Cardiff, South Glamorgan, Wales; guitar) and John Williams (bass) formed Love Sculpture in 1967 with Bob 'Congos' Jones (drums). This Cardiff-based trio enjoyed modest airplay with their debut single, 'River To Another Day', before a rousing interpretation of Aram Khachaturian's 'Sabre Dance', initially aired as a radio session by BBC disc jockey John Peel, became a surprising hit single. Its success bestowed a novelty tag on a group already hampered by a lack of musical direction and although their debut album

offered worthy blues interpretations, the psychedelic tinges on a second set were somewhat anachronistic. This impasse led to a split in the original line-up and Mickey Gee (bass) and Terry Williams (drums, later of Man and Dire Straits) joined the guitarist for a final flourish. Edmunds then disbanded the group and embarked on a solo career.

● ALBUMS: *Blues Helping* (Parlophone 1968) ★★★, *Forms And Feelings* (Parlophone 1969) ★★.

● COMPILATIONS: *The Classic Tracks 1968/72* (1974) ★★★, *The Dave Edmunds And Love Sculpture Singles As And Bs* (1990) ★★★, *Premium Gold Collection* (EMI 2000) ★★★.

LOVE, GEOFF

b. 4 September 1917, Todmorden, Yorkshire, England, d. 8 July 1991, London, England. Love was a musical director, arranger, composer and one of the UK's most popular easy-listening music personalities. His father, Kid Love, was World Champion sand dancer, and came to the UK from the USA. Geoff Love learned to play the trombone in his local brass band and made his first broadcast in 1937 on Radio Normandy. He moved to the south of England, and played with violinist Jan Ralfini's Dance Orchestra in London and with the Alan Green Band in Hastings. After six years in the army during World War II, he joined Harry Gold's Pieces Of Eight in 1946, and stayed with them until 1949, providing the vocal on their successful record, 'Blue Ribbon Gal'. In 1955, Love formed his own band for the television show *On The Town*, and soon afterwards started recording for Columbia Records with his Orchestra and Concert Orchestra. He had his first hit in 1958, with a cover-version of Perez Prado's cha-cha-cha 'Patricia', and made several albums including *Enchanted Evenings, Our Very Own* and *Thanks For The Memory (Academy Award Winning Songs)*. In 1959, Love started to release some recordings under the pseudonym, Manuel And His Music Of The Mountains, which proved be immensely successful.

Besides his own orchestral records, Love provided the accompaniment and arrangements on record, and in concert, for many popular artists such as Connie Francis, Russ Conway, Paul Robeson, Judy Garland, Frankie Vaughan, Johnny Mathis, Des O'Connor, Ken Dodd, Marlene Dietrich and Gracie Fields. In the 70s, he formed yet another group, Billy's Banjo Band, later known as Geoff Love's Banjo Band, while still having hits under his own name with *Big War Themes, Big Western Movie Themes* and *Big Love Movie Themes*. He also capitalized on the late 70s dance fad with several volumes of *Geoff Love's Big Disco Sound*, while retaining his more conservative image with *Waltzes With Love* and *Tangos With Love*. He was consistently popular on radio, and on television, where, besides conducting the orchestra, he was especially effective as a comic foil to Max Bygraves on his *Singalongamax*, and similar series. Love's compositions range from the Latin-styled 'La Rosa Negra' to the theme for the hit television situation comedy, *Bless This House*. His prolific album output included mostly film or television themes. His son Adrian (b. 3 August 1944, York, England, d. 10 March 1999, Tunbridge Wells, Kent, England) was a well-known and popular radio broadcaster.

● ALBUMS: recorded variously under names of the Geoff Love Orchestra, Singers, Sound, Ragtime Band, Big Disco Sound, Big Band Dixieland, Banjos, and Mandolins. They are all of a consistently good quality: *Banjo Party Time* (1968) ★★★, *Big Western Movie Themes* (1969) ★★★★, *Great TV Western Themes* (1970) ★★★, *Big War Movie Themes* (1971) ★★★, *Big Western Movie Themes, Number Two* (1971) ★★★, *Big Love Movie Themes* (1971) ★★★, *Banjo Movie Parade* (1971) ★★★, *In Romantic Mood – Love With Love* (1972) ★★★, *Big Concerto Movie Themes* (1972) ★★★, *Your Top TV Themes* (1972) ★★★, *Big Suspense Movie Themes* (1972) ★★★, *Christmas With Love* (1972) ★★★, *Sing-Along Banjo Party* (1973) ★★★, *Melodies That Live Forever* (1973) ★★★, *Somewhere My Love* (1973) ★★★, *Showbusiness* (1973) ★★★, *The Music Of Ennio Morricone* (1973) ★★★, *The Music Of Michael Legrand* (1973) ★★★, *Latin With Love* (1973) ★★★, *Your Favourite TV Themes* (1973) ★★★, *Big Musical Movie Themes* (1973) ★★★, *Mandolin Magic* (1974) ★★★, *Concert Waltzes* (1974) ★★★, *Bridge Over Troubled Water* (1974) ★★, *All-Time Orchestral Hits* (1974) ★★★, *Ragtime With Love* (1974) ★★★, *Sing-Along Minstrel Party* (1974) ★★★, *Sing-Along Western Party* (1974) ★★, *Sing-Along Banjo Party, Number Two* (1975) ★★★, *More Mandolin Magic* (1975) ★★★, *The Golden World Of Puccini* (1975) ★★★, *The Golden World Of Opera* (1975) ★★★, *Big Bond Movie Themes* (1975) ★★★, *Close To You* (1975) ★★★, *Waltzes With Love* (1975) ★★★, *Big Hollywood Movie Themes* (1975) ★★★, *Dreaming With Love* (1976) ★★★, *Big Terror Movie Themes* (1976) ★★★, *The Big, Big Movie Themes* (1976) ★★★, *Magic Mandolins* (1976) ★★★, *A Jolson Sing-Along* (1976) ★★, *Big Band Dixieland* (1976) ★★★, *Geoff Love Plays Elton John* (1976) ★★, *Dance, Dance, Dance* (1976) ★★★, *Take Me Home Country Roads* (1976) ★★, *Very Special Love Songs* (1977) ★★★, *You Should Be Dancing* (1977) ★★, *Geoff Love Plays The Beatles* (1977) ★★, *Star Wars And Other Space Themes* (1978) ★★, *Tangos With Love* (1978) ★★★, *Close Encounters Of The Third Kind And Other Disco Galactic Themes* (1978) ★★★, *South Of The Border* (1978) ★★★, *Big Disco Movie Hits* (1978) ★★, *The Biggest Pub Party In The World* (1979) ★★★, *Music From Mandingo (Tiger In The Night)* (1979) ★★★, *20 Explosive TV Themes* (1979) ★★★, *Gold And Silver* (1979) ★★★, *We're Having A Party* (1979) ★★★, *More Waltzes With Love* (1979) ★★★, *Themes For Super Heroes* (1979) ★★★, *Your 100 Instrumental Favourites, Volume One* (1980) ★★★, *Your 100 Favourite Love Songs, Volume One* (1980) ★★★, *Your 100 Favourite Love Songs, Volume Two* (1980) ★★★★, *Your 100 Instrumental Favourites, Volume Two* (1981) ★★★, *Your 100 Instrumental Favourites, Volume Three* (1981) ★★★, *Your 100 Favourite Love Songs, Volume Three* (1981) ★★★, *Your 100 Instrumental Favourites, Volume Four* (1982) ★★★, *Your 100 Favourite Love Songs, Volume Four* (1982) ★★★, *Your 100 Instrumental Favourites, Volume Five* (1982) ★★★, *Your 100 Favourite Love Songs, Volume Five* (1982) ★★, *A String Of Pearls* (1983) ★★★★, *Sing-Along Banjo Party, Volume Three* (1983) ★★, *Your 100 Instrumental Favourites, Volume Six* (1983) ★★★, *Your 100 Favourite Love Songs, Volume Six* (1983) ★★★, *Your 100 Instrumental Favourites, Volume Seven* (1983) ★★★, *Your 100 Favourite Love Songs, Volume Seven* (1983) ★★★★, *50 Dancing Favourites* (1984) ★★★, *The Best Of British* (1985) ★★★, *An Hour Of Geoff Love's Piano Party* (1987) ★★★, with Shirley Bassey, Howard Keel, Alma Cogan, *Et Al Geoff Love With Friends* (MFP 1993) ★★★.

● FILMS: *It's All Happening* (1963).

LOVIN' SPOONFUL

Few American pop acts have gathered as much universal affection over the years as the brilliant and underrated Lovin' Spoonful. Their back catalogue of hits is constantly repackaged and reissued as their stature increases. They were formed in 1965 by John Sebastian (b. 17 March 1944, New York, USA; vocal/guitar/harmonica/autoharp) and Zalman Yanovsky (b. 19 December 1944, Toronto, Canada; guitar/vocals) following their time together in the Mugwumps (as eulogized in the Mamas And The Papas hit 'Creeque Alley'). The band were completed by Steve Boone (b. 23 September 1943, Camp Lejeune, North Carolina, USA; bass) and Joe Butler (b. 19 January 1943, Long Island, New York, USA; drums/vocals). Their unique blend of jug-band, folk, blues and rock 'n' roll synthesized into what was termed as 'electric good-time music', kept them apart from every other American pop act at that time. In two years they notched up 10 US Top 20 hits, all composed by John Sebastian. The quality of Sebastian's lyrics and melodies help make him one of the finest American songwriters. From the opening strum of Sebastian's autoharp on 'Do You Believe In Magic?' the party began, ranging through the evocative 'You Didn't Have To Be So Nice', the languid singalong 'Daydream', the punchy and lyrically outstanding 'Summer In The City' ('Hot town summer in the city, back of my neck getting dirty and gritty'), to the gentle romanticism of 'Rain On The Roof' ('You and me and the rain on the roof, caught up in a summer shower, drying while it soaks the flowers, maybe we'll be caught for hours').

Their four regular albums were crammed full of

other gems in addition to the hits. Additionally Sebastian wrote the music for two movies, Woody Allen's *What's Up, Tiger Lily?* and Francis Ford Coppola's *You're A Big Boy Now*, the latter featuring the beautiful 'Darling Be Home Soon'. Sadly the non-stop party came to an end in 1967 following the departure of Yanovsky and the arrival, albeit briefly, of Jerry Yester. Sebastian's departure the following year was the final nail in the coffin, although the remaining members squeezed out two minor hit singles before disbanding. In 1991, Steve Boone, Joe Butler and Jerry and Jim Yester announced the re-formation of the band. The latter left in 1993, but with the recruitment of younger members Lena Beckett (keyboards) and Mike Arturi (drums) the band has continued plying their trade on the nostalgia circuit. Without Yanovsky and Sebastian, however, the 'magic' cannot be present.

● ALBUMS: *Do You Believe In Magic* (Kama Sutra 1965) ★★★★, *Daydream* (Kama Sutra 1966) ★★★★★, *What's Up, Tiger Lily?* film soundtrack (Kama Sutra 1966) ★★, *Hums Of The Lovin' Spoonful* (Kama Sutra 1966) ★★★★, *You're A Big Boy Now* film soundtrack (Kama Sutra 1967) ★★, *Everything Playing* (Kama Sutra 1967) ★★★, *Revelation: Revolution '69* (Kama Sutra 1968) ★, *Live At The Hotel Seville* (Varèse Sarabande 1999) ★★.

● COMPILATIONS: *The Best Of The Lovin' Spoonful* (Kama Sutra 1967) ★★★★, *The Best Of The Lovin' Spoonful Volume Two* (Kama Sutra 1968) ★★★, *24 Karat Hits* (Kama Sutra 1968) ★★★, *John Sebastian Song Book Vol. 1* (Kama Sutra 1970) ★★★, *The Very Best Of The Lovin' Spoonful* (Kama Sutra 1970) ★★★★, *Once Upon A Time* (Kama Sutra 1971) ★★★, *The Best ... Lovin' Spoonful* (Kama Sutra 1976) ★★★★, *The Collection* (Castle 1988) ★★★★, *The EP Collection* (See For Miles 1988) ★★★★, *Anthology* (Rhino 1990) ★★★★, *Summer In The City* (Spectrum 1995) ★★★, *The Very Best Of Lovin' Spoonful* (Camden 1998) ★★★★, *Collector's Edition* 3-CD set (Platinum 1999) ★★★.

LULU

b. Marie MacDonald McLaughlin Lawrie, 3 November 1948, Lennox Castle, Glasgow, Scotland. Lulu was originally a beat group vocalist with her own backing group the Luvvers, who comprised Ross Nelson (guitar), Jim Dewar (rhythm guitar), Alec Bell (keyboards), Jimmy Smith (saxophone), Tony Tierney (bass) and David Miller (drums). The 15-year-old singer first came to prominence with a rasping version of the Isley Brothers' 'Shout' in 1964. Under the tutelage of manager Marian Massey she survived a stormy couple of years during which only two of her eight singles charted. Abandoning the Luvvers along the way, she switched record labels from Decca Records to Columbia Records and found a new hitmaker in the form of Mickie Most. A cover of Neil

Diamond's 'The Boat That I Row' saw an upsurge in her career during 1967, which was punctuated by an acting part in the movie *To Sir With Love*. The theme tune from the film gave her a million-selling US number 1, and in the UK it reached number 6, despite being relegated to b-side of the inferior 'Let's Pretend'. Further UK hits followed, notably 'Me, The Peaceful Heart', 'Boy' and 'I'm A Tiger'. Having established herself as an entertainer of wide appeal, Lulu was granted her own television series and later represented Britain in the Eurovision Song Contest. The painfully trite 'Boom-Bang-A-Bang' tied for first place and provided her highest UK chart placing at number 2.

Her brief marriage to Maurice Gibb of the Bee Gees was followed by another switch of labels and musical styles when she worked with famed producer Jerry Wexler on two albums. A lean period of flop singles ended when David Bowie intervened to produce and arrange her hit version of 'The Man Who Sold The World'. During the 70s, she concentrated increasingly on stage work and developed her career as an all-round entertainer, a spin-off of which was becoming the long-standing model/endorser for the Freeman's mail-order catalogue. Appearances in *Guys And Dolls, Song And Dance* and the television programme *The Secret Diary Of Adrian Mole* distracted her from the studio but a disco re-recording of 'Shout', in 1986, repeated the Top 10 success of 22 years before. In 1993, Lulu released *Independence*, an album of 'modern disco-pop with a flavour of classic soul and R&B'. Co-produced by Bobby Womack and London Beat, the title track registered strongly in the UK and US charts, and was followed by another single, 'I'm Back For More', on which Lulu duetted with Womack. She was, by then, creating some of her own material, and one of her songs, 'I Don't Wanna Fight Any More', written with her brother, Billy Laurie, was recorded by Tina Turner.

● ALBUMS: *Something To Shout About* (Decca 1965) ★★★★, *Love Loves To Love Lulu* (Columbia 1967) ★★★, *Lulu's Album* (Columbia 1969) ★★★, *New Routes* (Atco 1970) ★★, *Melody Fair* (Atco 1971) ★★, *Don't Take Love For Granted* (Rocket 1979) ★★★, *Lulu* (Alfa 1981) ★★★, *Take Me To Your Heart Again* (Alfa 1982) ★★★, *Shape Up And Dance With Lulu* (Life Style 1984) ★★, *The Man Who Sold The World* (Start 1989) ★★★, *Independence* (Dome 1993) ★★★.

● COMPILATIONS: *The World Of Lulu* (Decca 1969) ★★★★, *The World Of Lulu Volume 2* (Decca 1970) ★★★, *The Most Of Lulu* (MFP 1971) ★★★★, *The Most Of Lulu Volume 2* (MFP 1972) ★★★, *The Very Best Of Lulu* (Warwick 1980) ★★★★, *Shout* (MFP 1983) ★★★, *I'm A Tiger* (MFP 1989) ★★★, *From Crayons To Perfume: The Best Of ...* (Rhino 1995) ★★★, *Supersneakers* (Sundazed 1997) ★★★, *The Man Who Sold The World* (Sequel 1999) ★★★.

● FILMS: *Gonks Go Beat* (1965).

LUMAN, BOB

b. Robert Glynn Luman, 15 April 1937, Blackjack, near Nacogdoches, Texas, USA, d. 27 December 1978, Nashville, Tennessee, USA. Luman's father, Joe, a school caretaker, bus driver and gifted musician, taught his son country music, but Luman's first love was baseball, which he played on a semi-professional basis until 1959. He was influenced by seeing Elvis Presley in concert, later saying, 'That was the last time I tried to sing like Webb Pierce or Lefty Frizzell'. His band then won a talent contest sponsored by the Texas Future Farmers of America and judged by Johnny Horton. In 1955, Luman recorded the original version of 'Red Cadillac And A Black Moustache' and also a scorching 'Red Hot' for Imperial Records. He joined *The Louisiana Hayride* as replacement for Johnny Cash and came into contact with guitarist James Burton and bass player James Kirkland, whom he recruited for his band. Unfortunately for Luman, Ricky Nelson was so impressed by Luman's musicians that he made them a better offer. After a brief, unsuccessful period with Capitol Records, Luman moved to Warner Brothers Records, who released 'Class Of '59' and 'Dreamy Doll', both featuring Roy Buchanan. He had a transatlantic hit with Boudleaux Bryant's satire on 'death discs' such as 'El Paso' and 'One Of Us (Will Weep Tonight)' in 'Let's Think About Living'. 'If we keep losing our singers like this,' he concluded, 'I'll be the only one you can buy.' He failed to repeat his success, despite such clever novelties as 'The Great Snowman' and 'Private Eye'. After spending part of the early 60s in the army due to the draft laws, he became a member of the *Grand Ole Opry* in 1964 and made many country records for the Hickory label, including John D. Loudermilk's witty 'The File'. He became a big-selling US country artist via his Epic recordings, 'When You Say Love', 'Lonely Women Make Good Lovers' and 'Neither One Of Us (Wants To Be The First To Say Goodbye)', subsequently a pop hit for Gladys Knight And The Pips.

In 1976, he underwent major surgery and then, prompted and produced by Johnny Cash, he recorded *Alive And Well*. Despite the title, he collapsed and died shortly after an appearance at the *Grand Ole Opry*. In recent years, Luman's work has been reassessed with retrospectives and, like Johnny Burnette, it is his early, rockabilly work that most interests collectors. To quote one of his country hits, 'Good Things Stem From Rock 'n' Roll.'

● ALBUMS: *Let's Think About Living* (Warners 1960) ★★★★, *Livin' Lovin' Sounds* (Hickory 1965) ★★★, *Ain't Got Time To Be Unhappy* (Epic 1968) ★★★, *Come On Home And Sing The Blues To Daddy* (Epic 1969) ★★★, *Getting Back To Norman* (Epic 1970) ★★★, *Is It Any Wonder That I Love You?* (Epic 1971) ★★★, *A Chain Don't Talk To Me* (Epic 1971) ★★★, *When You Say Love* (Epic 1972) ★★★, *Lonely Women Make Good*

Lovers (Epic 1972) ★★, *Neither One Of Us* (Epic 1973) ★★, *Red Cadillac And A Black Moustache* (Epic 1974) ★★★, *Still Loving You* (Epic 1974) ★★, *A Satisfied Mind* (Epic 1976) ★★, *Alive And Well* (Polydor 1977) ★★★, *Bob Luman* (Polydor 1978) ★★, *The Pay Phone* (Polydor 1978) ★★, *Try Me* (Rockstar 1988) ★★.

● COMPILATIONS: *The Rocker* (Bear Family 1984) ★★★, *More Of That Rocker* (Bear Family 1984) ★★★, *Still Rockin'* (Bear Family 1984) ★★★, *Carnival Rock* (Bear Family 1988) ★★★, *Wild-Eyed Woman* (Bear Family 1988) ★★★, *American Originals* (Columbia 1989) ★★★★, *Let's Think About Living* (Castle 1994) ★★★, *Luman 1968-1977* 5-CD box set (Bear Family 2000) ★★★★.

● FILMS: *Carnival Rock* (1957).

LUSHER, DON

b. 6 November 1923, Peterborough, Cambridgeshire, England. Lusher grew up in a musical family, his grandfather, father and mother playing and singing in Salvation Army bands. Lusher learned to play trombone and pursued his musical interests at school. At the age of 18, he went into the army but contrived to keep up his playing by joining Salvation Army bands in any town he happened to be near. A visit to a camp he was at by Geraldo And His Orchestra, in whose trombone section was Ted Heath, convinced Lusher that once the war was over that was how he would make his career. In 1947, he left the army, bought a second-hand trombone, and joined a band led by an army friend in Tenby, Wales. He then joined Joe Daniels And His Hot Shots, but only a few weeks later the band folded. Lusher's next professional engagement was with Lou Preager at London's leading dancehall, the Hammersmith Palais. He then worked in a band led by Maurice Winnick at Ciro's Club, following this with important and career-moulding engagements with the Squadronaires and the Ted Heath band, with which he visited the USA. By the 60s Lusher was one of the UK's best-known trombonists, touring extensively with prominent artists, such as Frank Sinatra. Subsequently, Lusher led big bands for special television and radio appearances and for limited concert work, activities which continued into the early 90s. He also established a reputation as an educator, working in this capacity in the USA, Japan and Australia as well as in the UK. Despite his international fame, Lusher has never lost contact with his musical origins and regularly performs and records with brass bands. An outstanding technician, Lusher's flowing, precisely articulated playing style remains an object lesson to fellow trombonists in all areas of music. Throughout the 90s, he led the Ted Heath tribute band for numerous popular reunion concerts.

● ALBUMS: *Lusher & Lusher & Lusher* (1972) ★★★, *Collection* (1976) ★★★, *Don Lusher Big Band* (Chandos 1981) ★★★, *Don Lusher Pays*

ribute To The Great Bands (1986) ★★★, Don usher Pays Tribute To The Great Bands, Volume 2 988) ★★, with Maurice Murphy Just Good riends (1993) ★★.
COMPILATIONS: The Very Best Of Don Lusher ig Band (Nelson 2000) ★★★★.
● FURTHER READING: The Don Lusher Book, on Lusher.

YNCH, KENNY
18 March 1939, Stepney, London, England. ritain's best-known black all-round entertainer as been a television personality for three ecades. The youngest of 13 children, he first ppeared on stage at the age of 12 with his sister, nger Maxine Daniels. At 16 he joined Ed ichol's Band and before going into the national ervice in 1957 worked in a string of bands ncluding Bob Miller's. He was already a roficient jazz singer, singing regularly in the oho clubs and had bit parts in some b-movies ncluding The Criminal. His songwriting talent ad also been recognised by the music publisher reddie Bienstock, who teamed Lynch with one f his Brill Building colleagues Mort Shuman. ynch signed with HMV Records and hit the UK op 40 in 1960 with his debut single, a cover of Aountain Of Love'. He appeared in several urther films and hit his recording peak in 1963 ith two successive Top 10 entries – a cover of Jp On The Roof' and 'You Can Never Stop Me oving You' (which made the US Top 20 when overed by Johnny Tillotson). Over the next 20 ears he was one of the UK's busiest and most opular entertainers and was also awarded an BE. He co-wrote the Small Faces' number 1, ha La La La Lee', and has recorded oasmodically since then on Columbia Records, tlantic Records, Polydor Records, Laser, owerbell and Spartan. In 1983, he had a urprise chart return with a Brit-funk track 'Half he Day's Gone And We Haven't Earned A enny' on Satril. In recent years he has worked s a comedian and has played a lot of golf.
● ALBUMS: Up On The Roof (HMV 1963) ★★★, 'e Like Kenny (MFP 1966) ★★★★, Half The ay's Gone And We Haven't Earned A Penny 983) ★★.
COMPILATIONS: The Very Best Of Kenny ynch (EMI 1987) ★★★.
FILMS: The Criminal (1960).

YNN, BARBARA
Barbara Lynn Ozen, 16 January 1942, eaumont, Texas, USA. Lynn was signed up by roducer Huey P. Meaux after hearing a demo pe and watching her perform in a Texas club. er early records were recorded at Cosimo's ew Orleans studio and leased to the Jamie bel. Composed by Lynn, 'You'll Lose A Good hing' (1962) was an R&B chart-topper and pop op 10 hit in the USA, and was followed by ou're Gonna Need Me' and 'Oh! Baby (We Got Good Thing Goin')'. The last of these was

revived by the Rolling Stones on Out Of Our Heads. Barbara issued several singles on Meaux's own label, Tribe, among which was her version of 'You Left The Water Running' (1966). Subsequent releases for Atlantic Records included 'This Is The Thanks I Get' (1968) and '(Until Then) I'll Suffer' (1972), both of which reached the R&B chart for this accomplished singer, songwriter and guitarist, who continued to tour, including visits to Japan, and also recorded albums for Ichiban and Rounder/Bullseye.
● ALBUMS: You'll Lose A Good Thing (Jamie 1962) ★★★★, Here Is Barbara Lynn (Atlantic 1968) ★★★, You Don't Have To Go (Ichiban 1988) ★★★, Barbara Lynn Live In Japan (1993) ★★★, So Good (Bullseye Blues 1994) ★★, Hot Night Tonight (Texas Music 2000) ★★.
● COMPILATIONS: The Barbara Lynn Story (1965) ★★★, We Got A Good Thing Goin' (1984) ★★, Barbara Lynn (Good Thing 1989) ★★★, You'll Lose A Good Thing (Sound Of The Fifties 1992) ★★★, The Atlantic Years (Ichiban/Soul Classics 1994) ★★★.

LYNN, TAMI
Tami Lynn was one of several New Orleans, Louisiana, USA-based artists who worked for Harold Battiste's AFO (All For One) label during the early 60s. She sang on A Compendium, an album which featured the co-operative's crack houseband, but this phase in her career was forestalled when the company folded. Tami's best-known single, 'I'm Gonna Run Away From You', was originally released in 1967. This powerful Bert Berns composition failed to register in America, but became a belated UK hit in 1971, when it reached number 4. Its popularity was confirmed four years later when it again entered the Top 40. Lynn had meanwhile continued to record, but this excellent performance remains her most lasting legacy.
● ALBUMS: A Compendium (1963) ★★★, Love Is Here And Now You're Gone (1972) ★★★★.

M

MACK, LONNIE
b. Lonnie McIntosh, 18 July 1941, Harrison, Indiana, USA. Lonnie Mack began playing guitar while still a child, drawing early influence from a local blues musician, Ralph Trotts, as well as established figures Merle Travis and Les Paul. He later led a C&W act, Lonnie And The Twilighters, and by 1961 was working regularly with the Troy Seals Band. The following year, Mack recorded his exhilarating instrumental version of Chuck Berry's 'Memphis'. By playing his Gibson 'Flying V' guitar through a Leslie cabinet, the revolving device that gives the Hammond organ its distinctive sound, Mack created a striking, exciting style. 'Memphis' eventually reached the US Top 5, while an equally urgent original, 'Wham', subsequently broached the Top 30. *The Wham Of That Memphis Man* confirmed the artist's vibrant skill, which drew on blues, gospel and country traditions. Several tracks, notably 'I'll Keep You Happy', 'Where There's A Will' and 'Why', also showed Mack's prowess as a soulful vocalist, and later recordings included a rousing rendition of Wilson Pickett's 'I Found A Love'. The guitarist also contributed to several sessions by Freddy King and appeared on James Brown's 'Kansas City' (1967). Mack was signed to Elektra Records in 1968 following a lengthy appraisal by Al Kooper in *Rolling Stone* magazine. *Glad I'm In The Band* and *Whatever's Right* updated the style of early recordings and included several notable remakes, although the highlight of the latter set was the extended 'Mt. Healthy Blues'.

Mack also added bass to the Doors' *Morrison Hotel* (1970) and undertook a national tour prior to recording *The Hills Of Indiana*. This low-key, primarily country album was the prelude to a six-year period of seclusion that ended in 1977 with *Home At Last*. Mack then guested on Michael Nesmith's *From A Radio Engine To The Photon Wing*, before completing *Lonnie Mack And Pismo*, but this regeneration was followed by another sabbatical. He re-emerged in 1985 under the aegis of Texan guitarist Stevie Ray Vaughan, who co-produced the exciting *Strike Like Lightning*. Released on the Alligator Records label, a specialist in modern blues, the album rekindled this talented artist's career, a rebirth that was maintained on the fiery *Second Sight* and *Live! Attack Of The Killer V*.

● ALBUMS: *The Wham Of That Memphis Man* (Fraternity 1963) ★★★★, *Glad I'm In The Band* (Elektra 1969) ★★★, *Whatever's Right* (Elektra 1969) ★★★, *The Hills Of Indiana* (Elektra 1971) ★★★, *Home At Last* (Capitol 1977) ★★, *Lonnie Mack With Pismo* (Capitol 1977) ★★, *Strike Like Lightning* (Alligator 1985) ★★★, *Second Sight* (Alligator 1987) ★★★, *Roadhouses And Dance Halls* (Epic 1988) ★★★, *Live! Attack Of The Killer V* (Alligator 1990) ★★★.
● COMPILATIONS: *For Collectors Only* (Elektra 1970) ★★★, *The Memphis Sound Of Lonnie Mack* (Trip 1974) ★★★★, *Memphis Wham!* (Ace 1999) ★★★★, *From Nashville To Memphis* (Ace 2001) ★★★.

MAD RIVER
Laurence Hammond (vocals, harmonica), David Robinson (lead guitar), Greg Druian (rhythm guitar), Tom Manning (bass) and Greg Dewey (drums) formed the Mad River Blues Band in 1965. Initially based in Yellow Springs, Ohio, USA, the group subsequently moved to California, by which time Druian had been replaced by Rick Bockner. The quintet, now dubbed simply Mad River, initially struggled to assert themselves, but a privately pressed EP helped to secure a series of gigs at prestigious San Franciscan venues. Mad River's debut album was released in 1968. Although mastered too fast owing to a technical error, it remains an enthralling slice of vintage acid rock, where traces of Country Joe And The Fish and Quicksilver Messenger Service blend with Hammond's reedy, quivering voice. A second album, *Paradise Bar And Grill*, was an altogether different affair. A handful of the tracks echoed the style of that first selection while others were indebted to C&W, a genre towards which the singer was increasingly drawn. Two haunting acoustic instrumentals and a cameo appearance by the late writer Richard Brautigan completed one of the late 60s' most engaging collections. Mad River broke up soon after its release. Dewey later joined Country Joe And The Fish, and has subsequently played with numerous Bay Area groups. Hammond pursued his love of country music with his Whiplash Band and recorded an engaging album, *Coyote's Dream*, in 1976. The remainder of the group retired from active performance.
● ALBUMS: *Mad River* (Capitol 1968) ★★★, *Paradise Bar And Grill* (Capitol 1969) ★★★.

MAGIC LANTERNS
Formed in the UK and based in the Manchester area, this soft rock band were formed from the Sabres who were in existence around 1962. At one point the Sabres also included Kevin Godley and Lol Creme, later of 10cc and Godley And Creme. After the temporary title of the Hammers, they became the Magic Lanterns. Their founding members were Jimmy Bilsbury (vocals), Peter Shoesmith (guitar), Ian Moncur (bass) and Allan Wilson (drums). While working in a local nightclub they were

approached by compere Roy Hastings who liked Bilsbury's songs and introduced them to his publisher, Mike Collier. Collier arranged for the band to record a new version of Artie Wayne's US release 'Excuse Me Baby', on the strength of which CBS signed them and released 'Excuse Me Baby' as a single in June 1966. It was a minor hit and was followed by such misses as 'Knight In Rusty Armour', 'Rumplestiltskin', and 'Auntie Griselda', by which time they were sounding increasingly psychedelic. In 1969, Collier switched their management to American Ronnie Oppenheimer who got Steve Rowland (Family Dogg) and Albert Hammond involved. They co-wrote 'Shame, Shame' which became the band's first US hit. Moncur left in 1969 and some time later Shoesmith and Wilson followed suit. The band struggled on for a few more months, but broke up while in Hamburg. The final line-up was Bilsbury, Alistair Beveridge (guitar), Paul Garner (guitar), Mike Osbourne (bass) and Paul Ward (drums). Bilsbury joined the Les Humphries Singers who were popular on the continent and had several singles released in the UK in the 70s. Boney M's Liz Mitchell was a founding member, along with Humphreys.

● ALBUMS: *Lit Up With The Magic Lanterns* (1968) ★★★, *One Night Stand* (Polydor 1971) ★★.

MAMAS AND THE PAPAS

Formed in Los Angeles in 1965, this enthralling harmony act embodied the city's astute blend of folk and pop. John Phillips (b. 30 August 1935, Parris Island, South Carolina, USA, d. 18 March 2001, USA) had been a founder-member of the popular Journeymen, before establishing this new attraction with his wife Michelle Phillips (b. Holly Michelle Gilliam, 4 June 1944, Long Beach, California, USA), and former Mugwumps' members Denny Doherty (b. 29 November 1941, Halifax, Nova Scotia, Canada) and Mama 'Cass' Elliot (b. Ellen Naomi Cohen, 19 September 1941, Baltimore, Maryland, USA, d. 29 July 1974, London, England). Although drawing inspiration from the flourishing milieu of New York's Greenwich Village, the quartet quickly moved to California, where they met producer Lou Adler through the interjection of mutual acquaintance Barry McGuire. The then unnamed Mamas And The Papas contributed backing vocals to the latter's second album, which in turn inspired the band's own career.

Their magnificent debut single, 'California Dreamin'', was originally recorded by McGuire, whose voice was simply erased and replaced by that of Doherty. Penned by Phillips and Gilliam, the song provided a vivid contrast between the cold New York winter and the warmth and security of life on the west coast and effectively established the quartet as arguably the finest vocal ensemble form their era working in the pop field. Their bohemian image was reinforced by their compositional skill and distinctive individual personalities. Visually, they seemed eccentrically contrasting: John, a towering 6 foot 4 inches, thin as a rake, and cast in the role of group intellectual; Denny the 'good-looking Canadian' and master of the sarcastic one-liner; Cass, overweight, uproarious and charming; and Michelle, quiet, beautiful and 'angelic when she wants to be'. With 'California Dreamin'' they infiltrated the US Top 5 and the song became a standard, covered by many artists, most notably Jose Feliciano. The richly-harmonic follow-up, 'Monday, Monday' reached number 1 in the US and also established the quartet in the UK. Further timeless hit singles followed, including the soaring 'I Saw Her Again' and a brilliant revival of the Shirelles 'Dedicated To The One I Love'. Michelle's sensual, semi-spoken introduction, backed by a solitary acoustic guitar remains one of the most classic and memorable openings to any pop recording.

The quartet's albums achieved gold status and while the first was sprinkled with cover versions, the second documented Phillips' development as a songwriter. He was involved in no less than 10 compositions, two of which ('No Salt On Her Tail' and 'Strange Young Girls') were particularly outstanding. Marital problems between John and Michelle eroded the stability of the group and she was fired in 1966 and briefly replaced by lookalike Jill Gibson. The quartet reconvened for *Deliver*, another strong album, which was followed by the autobiographical 'Creeque Alley', which humorously documented their rise to fame.

During the summer of 1967 Phillips organized the Monterey Pop Festival and helped launch the career of former Journeyman Scott McKenzie by writing the chart-topping hippie anthem 'San Francisco (Be Sure To Wear Flowers In Your Hair)'. In the winter of 1967, the quartet arrived in the UK for concerts at London's Royal Albert Hall. After docking at Southampton, Elliot was arrested by police, charged with stealing blankets and keys from the Royal Garden Hotel in Kensington on an earlier visit. The charges were dropped but the concerts were subsequently cancelled, amid rumours of a break-up. The quartet managed to complete one last album, *The Papas & The Mamas*, a superb work that highlighted Phillips' brilliance as a songwriter. 'Safe In My Garden' and the sublime 'Twelve Thirty' were both minor classics, while 'Rooms' and 'Mansions' incisively documented the spiritual isolation that accompanied their rise to international stardom: 'Limousines and laughter, parties ever after/If you play the game you pay the price/purchasing our piece of paradise'. It was a fitting valediction.

After splitting up in 1968, the quartet embarked on solo careers, with varying success. Three years later, they briefly re-formed for *People Like Us*, but their individual contributions were taped separately and the results were disappointing.

Elliot enjoyed the greatest success as a solo artist but her career was tragically cut short by her sudden death in July 1974. Michelle Phillips continued to pursue an acting career, while John plummeted into serious drug addiction, near-death and arrest. He subsequently recovered and in 1982 he and Doherty re-formed the Mamas And The Papas. The new line-up featured Phillips' actress daughter Laura McKenzie (McKenzie Phillips) and Elaine 'Spanky' McFarlane of Spanky And Our Gang. Doherty left when the band began touring full-time, and was replaced by the aforementioned McKenzie for an attraction that steadfastly retains its popularity. The original group was inducted into the Rock And Roll Hall Of Fame in 1998. John Phillips died of heart failure three years later.

● ALBUMS: *If You Can Believe Your Eyes And Ears* (Dunhill/RCA Victor 1966) ★★★★, *The Mamas And The Papas* aka *Cass, John, Michelle, Denny* (Dunhill/RCA Victor 1966) ★★★★, *Deliver* (Dunhill/RCA Victor 1967) ★★★★, *The Papas & The Mamas* (Dunhill/RCA Victor 1968) ★★★★, *People Like Us* (Dunhill 1971) ★.

● COMPILATIONS: *Farewell To The First Golden Era* (Dunhill 1967) ★★★★, *Golden Era Volume 2* (Dunhill 1968) ★★★★, *16 Of Their Greatest Hits* (MCA 1969) ★★★★, *A Gathering Of Flowers* (Dunhill 1971) ★★★, *20 Golden Hits* (Dunhill 1973) ★★★★, *The ABC Collection: Greatest Hits* (ABC 1976) ★★★, *Creeque Alley: The History Of The Mamas And Papas* (MCA 1991) ★★★★, *California Dreamin' – The Very Best Of The Mamas And The Papas* (PolyGram 1995) ★★★★, *All The Leaves Are Brown: The Golden Era Collection* (MCA 2001) ★★★★.

● FURTHER READING: *Papa John*, John Phillips with Jim Jerome. *California Dreamin' – The True Story Of The Mamas And Papas*, Michelle Phillips.

MANCINI, HENRY

b. Enrico Mancini, 16 April 1924, Cleveland, Ohio, USA, d. 14 June 1994, Los Angeles, California, USA. Prompted by his father, a steelworker who loved music, Mancini learned to play several musical instruments while still a small child. As a teenager he developed an interest in jazz and especially music of the big bands. He wrote some arrangements and sent them to Benny Goodman, from whom he received some encouragement. In 1942, he became a student at the Juilliard School of Music, but his career was interrupted by military service during World War II. Immediately following the war he was hired as pianist and arranger by Tex Beneke, who was then leading the Glenn Miller orchestra. Later in the 40s Mancini began writing arrangements for studios, prompted initially by a contract to score for a recording date secured by his wife, singer Ginny O'Connor (of the Mel-Tones). He was also hired to work on films (the first of which was the

Abbott and Costello comedy *Lost In Alaska*), and it was here that his interest in big-band music paid off. He wrote the scores for two major Hollywood biopics, *The Glenn Miller Story* (1954) and *The Benny Goodman Story* (1956), as well as Orson Welles' *Touch Of Evil* classic (1958). Mancini also contributed jazz-influenced scores for television, including those for the innovative *Peter Gunn* series and *Mr Lucky*. His film work continued with scores and songs for such films as *Breakfast At Tiffany's* (1961), from which came 'Moon River' (the Oscar winner that year), and the title songs for *Days Of Wine And Roses* (1962), which again won an Oscar, and *Charade* (1963).

His other film compositions included 'Baby Elephant Walk' from *Hatari!* (1962), the theme from *The Pink Panther* (1964), 'The Sweetheart Tree' from *The Great Race* (1965), and scores for *Man's Favourite Sport?*, *Dear Heart*, *Wait Until Dark*, *Darling Lili*, *Mommie Dearest*, *Victor/Victoria* (1982), for which he won an Oscar for 'Original Song Score' with Leslie Bricusse, *That's Dancing*, *Without A Clue*, *Physical Evidence*, *Blind Date*, *That's Life*, *The Glass Menagerie*, *Sunset*, *Fear*, *Switch*, and *Tom And Jerry: The Movie*, on which he again teamed with Leslie Bricusse. One of the most respected film and television composers – and the winner of 20 Grammy Awards – Mancini acknowledged his greatest legacy to be '. . . my use of jazz – incorporating various popular idioms into the mainstream of film scoring. If that's a contribution, then that's mine.' In addition he also regularly conducted orchestras in the USA and UK in concerts of his music, most of which stood comfortably on its own merits outside the context for which it was originally conceived. In the months prior to his death from cancer, Mancini was working with Leslie Bricusse on the score for the stage adaptation of *Victor/Victoria*.

● ALBUMS: *The Versatile Henry Mancini* (Liberty 1959) ★★★, *March Step In Stereo And Hi-Fi* (Warners 1959) ★★★, *The Music From Peter Gunn* (RCA Victor 1959) ★★★★, *More Music From Peter Gunn* (RCA Victor 1959) ★★★, *The Blues And The Beat* (RCA Victor 1960) ★★★, *The Mancini Touch* (RCA Victor 1960) ★★★★, *Music From Mr Lucky* (RCA Victor 1960) ★★★, *The Original Peter Gunn* (RCA Victor 1960) ★★★★, *Mr Lucky Goes Latin* (RCA Victor 1961) ★★★, *Breakfast At Tiffany's* (1961) ★★★★, *Hatari* (RCA 1962) ★★★, *Combo!* (RCA 1962) ★★★, *Experiment In Terror* (RCA VIctor 1962) ★★, *Uniquely Mancini* (RCA 1963) ★★★, *Our Man In Hollywood* (RCA 1963) ★★★, *The Second Time Around* (1963) ★★★, *Marches* (1963) ★★★, *Charade* (RCA 1963) ★★★★, *The Pink Panther* (RCA 1964) ★★★★, *The Concert Sound Of Henry Mancini* (RCA 1964) ★★★, with his orchestra and chorus *Dear Heart-And Other Songs About Love* (RCA 1965) ★★★, *The Latin Sound Of Henry Mancini* (RCA 1965) ★★★, *The Great Race* (RCA 1965) ★★, *Sounds And Voices* (RCA 1966) ★★★

Arabesque (RCA Victor 1966) ★★★★, *The Academy Award Songs* (RCA 1966) ★★★, *What Did You Do In The War Daddy?* (RCA 1966) ★★, *Music Of Hawaii* (RCA 1966) ★★, *Mancini '67* (RCA 1967) ★★★, *Two For The Road* (RCA 1967) ★★★, *Encore! More Of The Concert Sound Of Henry Mancini* (RCA 1967) ★★★, *A Warm Shade Of Ivory* (RCA 1969) ★★★★, *Six Hours Past Sunset* (RCA 1969) ★★, *Theme From Z And Other Film Music* (RCA 1970) ★★, *Mancini Country* (1970) ★★★, *Themes From Love Story* (RCA 1971) ★★★, *This Is Henry Mancini* (1971) ★★★, *Mancini Concert* (RCA 1971) ★★★, *Big Screen Little Screen* (RCA 1972) ★★, with Doc Severinsen *Brass On Ivory* (RCA 1972) ★★★, *The Mancini Generation* (RCA 1972) ★★, with Severinsen *Brass, Ivory & Strings* (RCA 1973) ★★★, *The Academy Award Winning Songs* (RCA 1975) ★★★, *Symphonic Soul* (RCA 1976) ★★, *A Legendary Performer* (RCA 1976) ★★★, *Mancini's Angels* (RCA 1977) ★★★, *Just You And Me Together Love* (1979) ★★★, *Pure Gold* (1980) ★★★, *Victor/Victoria* (1982) ★★★, *Best Of* (1984) ★★★, *A Man And His Music* (1985) ★★★, with James Galway *In The Pink* (1985) ★★★, *Merry Mancini Christmas* (1985) ★★★, *At The Movies* (1986) ★★★, with Johnny Mathis *The Hollywood Musicals* (Columbia 1987) ★★★, *Henry Mancini And The Royal Philharmonic Pops Orchestra* (1988) ★★★, *Diamond Series* (1988) ★★★, with the Royal Philharmonic Pops Orchestra *Premier Pops* (1988) and *Mancini Rocks The Pops* (1989) ★★★, *Theme Scene* (1989) ★★★, *Mancini In Surround Sound* (1990) ★★★, and various other film and television soundtracks.

COMPILATIONS: *In The Pink: The Ultimate Collection* (RCA Victor 1995) ★★★, *Romantic Movie Themes* (Camden 1997) ★★★, *Martinis With Mancini* (BMG 1998) ★★★, *Henry Mancini Greatest Hits* (RCA 2000) ★★★.

FURTHER READING: *Henry Mancini*, Gene Lees. *Did They Mention The Music?*, Henry Mancini and Gene Lees.

MANFRED MANN

During the UK beat boom of the early 60s, spearheaded by the Beatles, a number of R&B groups joined the tide with varying degrees of achievement. Of these, Manfred Mann had the most commercial success. The band was formed as the Mann-Hugg Blues Brothers by Manfred Mann (b. Manfred Lubowitz, 21 October 1940, Johannesburg, South Africa; keyboards) and Mike Hugg (b. 11 August 1942, Andover, Hampshire, England; drums/vibraphone). They became Manfred Mann shortly after adding Paul Jones (b. Paul Pond, 24 February 1942, Portsmouth, Hampshire, England; harmonica/vocals). The line-up was completed by Mike Vickers (b. 18 April 1941, Southampton, Hampshire, England; flute/guitar/saxophone) and Tom McGuinness (b. 2 December 1941, London, England; bass), following the departure of Dave Richmond. After being signed by a

talent-hungry HMV Records and following one unsuccessful instrumental, they made an impression with the catchy 'Cock-A-Hoop'. The prominent use of Jones' harmonica gave them a distinct sound and they soon became one of Britain's leading groups. No less than two of their singles were used as the theme music to the pioneering British television music programme, *Ready Steady Go.* '5-4-3-2-1' provided the breakthrough Top 10 hit in early 1964. By the summer, the group registered their first UK number 1 with the catchy 'Do Wah Diddy Diddy'.

Over the next two years, they charted regularly with memorable hits such as 'Sha La La', 'Come Tomorrow', 'Oh No Not My Baby' and Bob Dylan's 'If You Got To Go, Go Now'. In May 1966, they returned to number 1 with the sublime 'Pretty Flamingo'. It was to prove the last major hit on which Jones appeared. His departure for a solo career was a potential body blow to the group at a time when personnel changes were regarded as anathema by the pop media and fans. He was replaced by Michael D'Abo (b. 1 March 1944, Betchworth, Surrey, England) recruited from A Band Of Angels, in preference to Rod Stewart, who failed the audition. Mike Vickers had previously departed for a lucrative career as a television composer. He was replaced by Jack Bruce on bass, allowing Tom McGuinness to move to lead guitar, a role with which he was happier. Additionally, Henry Lowther (trumpet) and Lyn Dobson (saxophone) enlarged the line-up for a time and Klaus Voormann replaced Bruce on bass. D'Abo's debut with the group was another hit rendering of a Dylan song, 'Just Like A Woman', their first for the Fontana label. He fitted in astonishingly well with the group, surprising many critics, by maintaining their hit formulae despite the departure of the charismatic Jones. Both 'Semi-Detached Suburban Mr. Jones' and 'Ha! Ha! Said The Clown' were formidable Top 5 hits in the classic Mann tradition.

Along with America's Byrds, they were generally regarded as the best interpreters of Dylan material, a view endorsed by the songwriter himself. This point was punctuated in 1968 when the group registered their third number 1 with the striking reading of his 'Mighty Quinn'. They ended the 60s with a final flurry of Top 10 hits, 'My Name Is Jack', 'Fox On The Run' and 'Raggamuffin Man' before abdicating their pop crown in favour of a heavier approach. Their albums had always been meaty and showed off their considerable dexterity as musicians working with jazz and blues-based numbers. Mann went on to form the jazz/rock band Chapter Three and the highly successful Manfred Mann's Earth Band. In the 90s the majority of the band performed regularly as the Manfreds. Without Manfred Mann they could not use the original name, in his place they recruited Benny Gallagher (bass/vocals) and ex-Family drummer Rob Townsend. Jones and D'Abo perform side by side sharing the spotlight, although Jones' ultimately more pushy personality makes him the star. Still highly respected, Manfred Mann remains one of the finest beat groups of the 60s.

● ALBUMS: *The Manfred Mann Album* (Ascot 1964) ★★★★, *The Five Faces Of Manfred Mann* (HMV 1964) ★★★★, *Mann Made* (HMV 1965) ★★★★, *My Little Red Book Of Winners* (Ascot 1965) ★★★★, *As Is* (Fontana 1966) ★★★, *Pretty Flamingo* (United Artists 1966) ★★★, *What A Mann* (Fontana 1968) ★★★, *The Mighty Garvey* (Fontana 1968) ★★★, as the Manfreds *5-4-3-2-1* (Camden 1998) ★★.

● COMPILATIONS: *Mann Made Hits* (HMV 1966) ★★★★, *Manfred Mann's Greatest Hits* (United Artists 1966) ★★★★, *Soul Of Mann* (HMV 1967) ★★★, *What A Mann* (Fontana 1968) ★★★★, *Semi-Detached Suburban* (EMI 1979) ★★★, *The Singles Plus* (See For Miles 1987) ★★★, *The EP Collection* (See For Miles 1989) ★★★★, *The Collection* (Castle 1990) ★★★, *Ages Of Mann: 22 Classic Hits Of The 60s* (PolyGram 1992) ★★★★, *Best Of The EMI Years* (EMI 1993) ★★★★, *Groovin' With The Manfreds* (EMI 1996) ★★★★, *Singles In The Sixties* (BR Music 1997) ★★★, *The Very Best Of The Fontana Years* (Spectrum 1998) ★★★, *BBC Sessions* (EMI 1998) ★★★, *The Very Best Of Manfred Mann* (MFP 1998) ★★★, *All Manner Of Menn: 1963-1969 And More ...* (Raven 2000) ★★★.

● FURTHER READING: *Mannerisms: The Five Phases Of Manfred Mann*, Greg Russo.

MANN, BARRY

b. Barry Iberman, 9 February 1939, Brooklyn, New York City, New York, USA. One of the leading pop songwriters of his generation. Although trained as an architect, Mann began his career in music following a summer singing engagement in the Catskills resort. He initially composed material for Elvis Presley's publishers Hill & Range, before briefly collaborating with Howie Greenfield. In 1961, he enjoyed a Top 10 hit in his own right with 'Who Put The Bomp (In The Bomp, Bomp, Bomp)', but thereafter it was as a composer that he dominated the *Billboard* Hot 100. During the same year as his solo hit, Mann found a new songwriting partner in Cynthia Weil, whom he soon married. Their first success together was Tony Orlando's 'Bless You' (1961), a simple but effective love song, which endeared them to their new employer, bubblegum genius Don Kirschner, who housed a wealth of songwriting talent in the cubicles of his Brill Building offices. With intense competition from those other husband-and-wife teams Jeff Berry and Ellie Greenwich, and Gerry Goffin and Carole King, Mann and Weil responded with a wealth of classic songs which still sound fresh and impressive to this day.

Like all great songwriters, they adapted well to different styles and themes, and this ensured that their compositions were recorded by a broad range of artists. There was the evocative urban romanticism of the Crystals' 'Uptown' (1962) and the Drifters' 'On Broadway' (1963), novelty teen fodder such as Eydie Gorme's 'Blame It On The Bossa Nova' (1963) and Paul Petersen's 'My Dad' (1963), the desolate neuroticism of Gene Pitney's 'I'm Gonna Be Strong' (1964) and the Righteous Brothers' 'You've Lost That Lovin' Feelin'' (1964), and classic mid-60s protest songs courtesy of the Animals' 'We Gotta Get Out Of This Place', Jody Miller's 'Home Of The Brave', 'Only In America' (Jay And The Americans) and 'Kicks' (Paul Revere And The Raiders)

By the late 60s, Mann and Weil left Kirschner and moved to Hollywood. Throughout this period, they continued to enjoy hit success with Bobby Vinton's 'I Love How You Love Me' (written with Larry Kolber in 1968), Jay And The Americans' 'Walking In The Rain' (1969) and B.J. Thomas' 'I Just Can't Help Believing' (1970). Changes in the pop marketplace subsequently reduced their hit output, but there were some notable successes such as Dan Hill's 'Sometimes When We Touch' (1977). Mann himself still craved recognition as a performer and won a recording contract, but his album work, most notably the aptly titled *Survivor* failed to match the sales of his and his wife's much covered golden hits. *Survivor* was produced by Bruce Johnson and Terry Melcher and was regarded as a leading example of the 70s' singer/songwriter oeuvre. Mann and Weil wrote the original songs for the *Muppet Treasure Island* movie in 1996. *Soul & Inspiration* featured Mann performing new versions of 11 of the duo's greatest hits, with guest singers including Carole King, Bryan Adams, Peabo Bryson, Deana Carter, and Brenda Russell.

● ALBUMS: *Who Put The Bomp* (ABC Paramount 1963) ★★, *Lay It All Out* (New Design 1971) ★★, *Survivor* (RCA 1975) ★★★, *Barry Mann* (Casablanca 1980) ★★, *Soul & Inspiration* (Atlantic 2000) ★★★.

● COMPILATIONS: *Barry Mann Songbook* various artists (Polygram 2001) ★★★.

MANN, MANFRED

(see Manfred Mann)

MAR-KEYS

Formed in Memphis, Tennessee, USA, and originally known as the Royal Spades, the line up comprised Steve Cropper (b. 21 October 1941, Willow Spring, Missouri, USA; guitar), Donald 'Duck' Dunn (b. 24 November 1941, Memphis, Tennessee, USA; bass), Charlie 'Packy' Axton (tenor saxophone), Don Nix (b. 27 September 1941, Memphis, Tennessee, USA; baritone saxophone), Wayne Jackson (trumpet), Charlie Freeman (b. Memphis, Tennessee, USA; guitar), Jerry Lee 'Smoochy' Smith (organ) and

Terry Johnson (drums). Although their rhythmic instrumental style was not unique in Memphis (Willie Mitchell followed a parallel path at Hi Records), the Mar-Keys were undoubted masters. Their debut hit, 'Last Night', reached number 3 in the US *Billboard* pop chart during the summer of 1961, establishing Satellite, its outlet, in the process. Within months, Satellite had altered its name to Stax Records and the Mar-Keys became the label's house band. Initially all-white, two black musicians, Booker T. Jones (organ) and Al Jackson (drums), had replaced Smith and Johnson by 1962. The newcomers, along with Cropper and Dunn, also worked as Booker T. And The MGs. A turbulent group, the Mar-Keys underwent several changes. Freeman left prior to the recording of 'Last Night' (but would later return for live work), Nix and Axton also quit, while Joe Arnold and Bob Snyder joined on tenor and baritone saxophone. They, in turn, were replaced by Andrew Love and Floyd Newman, respectively.

Although commercial success under their own name was limited, the group provided the backbone to sessions by Otis Redding, Sam And Dave, Wilson Pickett, Carla Thomas and many others, and were the pulsebeat to countless classic records. Axton, the son of Stax co-founder Estelle, later fronted the Packers, who had a hit with 'Hole In The Wall' (1965). The single, released on Pure Soul, featured a not-inconspicuous MGs. Line-ups bearing the Mar-Keys' name continued to record despite the desertion of most of the original members. Nix later became part of the Delaney And Bonnie/Leon Russell axis while Charlie Freeman was later part of the Dixie Flyers, one of the last traditional house bands. Both he and Axton died in the early 70s, victims, respectively, of heroin and alcohol abuse. Jackson, Love and Newman, meanwhile, continued the Mar-Keys' legacy with releases on Stax and elsewhere, while simultaneously forging a parallel career as the Memphis Horns.
● ALBUMS: *Last Night* (Atlantic 1961) ★★★, *Do The Popeye With The Mar-Keys* (London 1962) ★★★, *The Great Memphis Sound* (Atlantic 1966) ★★★, with Booker T. And The MGs *Back To Back* (Stax 1967) ★★★, *Mellow Jello* (Atlantic 1968) ★★★, *Damifiknow* (Stax 1969) ★★, *Memphis Experience* (1971) ★★.

MARCELS
The Marcels were one of several doo-wop-influenced American vocal groups to achieve success in the early 60s, despite the passing of the genre's golden age. Cornelius 'Nini' Harp (lead singer), Ronald 'Bingo' Mundy (tenor), Fred Johnson (bass), Gene Bricker (tenor) and Richard Knauss (baritone), all native to Pittsburg, Pennsylvania, USA, achieved fame for their distinctive version of Richard Rodgers/Lorenz Hart's classic 'Blue Moon',

previously a UK Top 10 hit for Elvis Presley in 1956, which topped both the US and UK charts in 1961. Johnson's distinctive bass introduction to the song has remained one of the most enduring vocal phrases of the time. The quartet scored a further US Top 10 hit that year with 'Heartaches', but its personnel was unstable, with Allen Johnson (d. 28 September 1995) replacing Knauss, and Walt Maddox replacing Bricker. Mundy walked out on the group during this same period, which did little to prepare them for the ever-changing trends prevalent during the early 60s, and eventually undermined the Marcels' long-term aspirations.
● ALBUMS: *Blue Moon* (Colpix 1961) ★★★.
● COMPILATIONS: *Heartaches* (Colpix 1987) ★★★, *Rare Items* (Colpix 1988) ★★, *The Best Of The Marcels* (Roulette 1990) ★★★, *The Complete Colpix Sessions* (Sequel 1994) ★★★★.

MARCH, LITTLE PEGGY
b. Margaret Battavio, 7 March 1948, Lansdale, Pennsylvania, USA. A child prodigy, at the age of five, March was a regular cast member of Rex Trailer's television show. She subsequently won a talent contest, before securing a recording deal with RCA Records. The singer secured her sole million-selling disc in 1963 when 'I Will Follow Him' topped the US charts. At the age of 15 she became the youngest person at that time to reach number 1. This memorable song had been adapted from 'Chariot', a gold disc in France for British vocalist Petula Clark the previous year. March enjoyed other minor chart entries, most notably with 'Hello Heartache, Goodbye Love', her sole UK hit, but she is forever linked to her major success. Moving to Germany in the late 60s, she sang frequently on television shows; as a songwriter, she is credited to two European number 1 hits: 'When The Rain Begins To Fall' (Jermaine Jackson and Pia Zadora) and 'Manuel Goodbye' (Audrey Landers). She returned to the USA in the 80s. She performed 'I Will Follow Him' in the 1987 John Waters film, *Hairspray*, a tongue-in-cheek homage to pre-Beatles 60s America.
● ALBUMS: *Little Peggy March* (RCA Victor 1962) ★★★, *I Will Follow Him* (RCA Victor 1963) ★★★, with Bennie Thomas *In Our Fashion* (RCA Victor 1965) ★★, *No Foolin'* (RCA Victor 1968) ★★★.
● COMPILATIONS: *The Very Best Of Little Peggy March* (Taragon 1997) ★★★.

MARMALADE
Originally known as Dean Ford And The Gaylords, this Glasgow-based quintet enjoyed considerable success on the Scottish club circuit between 1961 and 1966. Eventually, they were signed by agent/manager Peter Walsh and, after moving to London, changed their name to Marmalade. The line-up comprised Dean Ford (b. Thomas MacAleese, 5 September 1946, Coatbridge, Glasgow, Scotland; vocals), Graham

Knight (b. 8 December 1946, Glasgow, Scotland; bass), Pat Fairley (b. 14 April 1946, Glasgow, Scotland; rhythm guitar, bass), Junior Campbell (b. William Campbell, 31 May 1947, Glasgow, Scotland; guitar, piano, vocals) and new drummer Alan Whitehead (b. 24 July 1946, Oswestry, Shropshire, England). Signing with CBS Records, the band's first four singles were flops, although 'I See The Rain' was a minor hit in Europe. Toning down their psych-pop leanings for an unpretentious and irresistibly commercial sound, the group reached number 6 in the UK charts in May 1968 with a cover version of the Grass Roots' 'Lovin' Things'. The same December they enjoyed a UK number 1 with an opportunist cover of the Beatles' 'Ob-La-Di, Ob-La-Da'. 'Baby Make It Soon' was their last UK Top 10 hit for CBS in June 1969, after which Walsh negotiated a deal with Decca Records via Dick Rowe.

The moving 'Reflections Of My Life' and 'Rainbow', both UK number 3 singles, were more serious works which ably displayed their underused compositional skills. In 1971, the group suffered a severe setback when Campbell, their producer and main songwriter, quit to attend the Royal College of Music. With replacement Hughie Nicholson (formerly of the Poets), they enjoyed several more UK Top 10 hits, including 'Cousin Norman' (number 6, September 1971), 'Radancer' (number 6, April 1972) and 'Falling Apart At The Seams' (number 9, February 1976). The latter proved a prophetic title, for the group was dogged by line-up changes during the 70s. Changes in the pop marketplace lessened their appeal, and a saucy 'sex on tour' story in the salacious UK Sunday papers caused them considerable embarrassment. With Knight and Whitehead surviving from the original line-up, Marmalade was resuscitated for cabaret purposes later in the decade. There is a fine back catalogue which has stood the test of time.

● ALBUMS: *There's A Lot Of It About* (Columbia 1968) ★★★, *Reflections Of The Marmalade* (Decca 1970) ★★★, *Songs* (Decca 1971) ★★★, *Our House Is Rockin'* (EMI 1974) ★★, *Only Light On My Horizon Now* (Target 1977) ★★, *Doing It All For You* (Skyclad 1979) ★★.

● COMPILATIONS: *The Best Of The Marmalade* (Columbia 1970) ★★★, *The Definitive Collection* (Castle 1996) ★★★★, *I See The Rain: The CBS Years* (Sequel 2000) ★★★★, *Rainbow: The Decca Years* (Sequel 2000) ★★★★, *Reflections Of The Marmalade: The Anthology* (Sanctuary 2001) ★★★★.

MARSDEN, BERYL

b. Beryl Hogg, 1947, Liverpool, England. One of a handful of female singers to emerge during the Mersey boom, Marsden made her debut in January 1963 with the powerful 'I Know'. A vivacious performance earned her the title 'Britain's Brenda Lee', but subsequent releases showed an empathy with soul material and included versions of 'Whenever The Lovelight Starts Shining Through His Eyes' (originally recorded by the Supremes), and 'Break-A-Way', an Irma Thomas song later revived by Tracey Ullman. In 1966, Marsden joined the Shotgun Express, a revue-styled act which initially featured Rod Stewart and Peter Bardens. She appeared on both of the band's singles before joining the She Trinity. She then retired from music for several years but resumed performing in the 70s as a member of Sinbad, a Liverpool outfit which also featured Paddy Chambers (of Paddy, Klaus And Gibson). She later recorded two Peter Bardens' songs, 'I Video'/'Hungry For You', appeared regularly as a Vandella with Martha Reeves and joined fellow-Buddhist Sandie Shaw at several charity concerts.

MARSDEN, GERRY

(see Gerry And The Pacemakers)

MARTHA AND THE VANDELLAS

Martha Reeves (b. 18 July 1941, Alabama, USA), with Annette Sterling Beard, Gloria Williams and Rosalind Ashford, formed the Del-Phis in 1960, one of the scores of female vocal groups then operating in Detroit, Michigan, USA. After Reeves began working as a secretary at Motown Records, they were offered a one-off single release on the label's Melody subsidiary, on which they were credited as the Vels. Gloria Williams left the group when the single flopped, but the remaining trio were allowed a second opportunity, recording 'I'll Have To Let Him Go' in late 1962, when the artist for whom it had been intended, Mary Wells, failed to arrive for the session. Renamed Martha And The Vandellas, the group divided their time between backing other Motown artists and recording in their own right. They were featured on Marvin Gaye's 1962 hit 'Stubborn Kind Of Fellow', before the US Top 30 success of their own release, 'Come And Get These Memories', brought their career as second-string vocalists to an end. Their next single, the dynamic 'Heat Wave', was masterminded by the Holland/Dozier/Holland production team, and epitomized the confidence and verve of the Vandellas' finest work. 'Quicksand' repeated the hit formula with a US Top 10 chart placing, while it was 'Dancing In The Street' that represented the pinnacle of their sound. The song, co-written by Marvin Gaye and Mickey Stevenson, was an invitation to party, given added bite by the tense political situation in the black ghettos. Holland/ Dozier/Holland's production exploited all the potential of the music, using clunking chains to heighten the rhythmic feel, and a majestic horn riff to pull people to their feet. 'Dancing In The Street' was the most exciting record Motown had yet made, and it was a deserved number 2 hit in America. Nothing the Vandellas recorded thereafter eached quite the same peak of excitement, although not for want of trying. 'Nowhere To Run' in 1965 was an irresistible dance hit, which again was given political connotations in some quarters. It introduced a new group member, former Velvelette Betty Kelly, who replaced Annette Sterling Beard. This line-up scored further Top 10 hits with 'I'm Ready For Love' and the infectious 'Jimmy Mack', and celebrated Motown's decision to give Reeves individual credit in front of the group's name with another notable success, 'Honey Chile'. Reeves was taken seriously ill in 1968, and her absence forced the group to disband. By 1970, she was able to resume her career, recruiting her sister Lois and another former Velvelette, Sandra Tilley, to form a new Vandellas line-up. No major US hits were forthcoming, but in Britain they were able to capitalize on the belated 1969 success of 'Dancing In The Street', and had several Top 30 entries in the early 70s. When Motown moved their headquarters from Detroit to Hollywood in 1972, Reeves elected to stay behind. Disbanding the group once again, she fought a lengthy legal battle to have her recording contract annulled, and was eventually free to begin an abortive solo career. Her sister Lois joined Quiet Elegance, while Sandra Tilley retired from the music business, and died in 1982. Motown retained the rights to the Vandellas' name, but chose not to sully the memory of their early 60s hits by concocting a new version of the group without Martha Reeves.

ALBUMS: *Come And Get These Memories* (Gordy 1963) ★★★, *Heat Wave* (Gordy 1963) ★★, *Dance Party* (Gordy 1965) ★★★, *Watchout!* (Gordy 1967) ★★, *Martha & The Vandellas Live!* (Gordy 1967) ★, as Martha Reeves And The Vandellas *Ridin' High* (Gordy 1968) ★★, *Sugar 'n' Spice* (Gordy 1969) ★★, *Natural Resources* (Gordy 1970) ★★, *Black Magic* (Gordy 1972) ★★.

COMPILATIONS: *Greatest Hits* (Gordy 1966) ★★★, *Anthology* (Motown 1974) ★★★★, *Compact Command Performances* (Motown 1992) ★★, *24 Greatest Hits* (Motown 1992) ★★★★, *Live Wire, 1962-1972* (Motown 1993) ★★★★, *Milestones* (Motown 1995) ★★★★, *Early Classics* (Spectrum 1996) ★★★, *The Ultimate Collection* (Motown 1998) ★★★★, *Universal Masters Collection* (Universal 2000) ★★★★.

MARTIN, GEORGE

3 January 1926, London, England. Martin became the world's most famous record producer through his work with the Beatles. Classically trained at London's Guildhall School of Music, he joined EMI Records in November 1950 as a junior A&R man. Five years later, Martin was given charge of the Parlophone Records label where he produced a wide variety of artists. Among them were ballad singers (Shirley Bassey and Matt Monro), skiffle groups (the Vipers), jazz bands (Temperance 7, John Dankworth, Humphrey Lyttelton) and numerous comedy artists. Chief among these were Peter Sellers and Bernard Cribbins, whose 'Right Said Fred' and 'Hole In The Ground' were hits in 1962. By this time, Martin had signed the Beatles to Parlophone and begun a relationship which lasted until their demise in 1970. Apart from insisting that drummer Pete Best be replaced, Martin's main contribution to the group's music lay in his ability to translate their more adventurous ideas into practical terms. Thus, he added classical music touches to 'Yesterday' and 'For No One' and devised the tape loops and studio manipulations that created the stranger sounds on *Revolver* and *Sgt Pepper's Lonely Hearts Club Band*. Martin also made two orchestral albums of Beatles tunes. As Brian Epstein signed Cilla Black, Gerry And the Pacemakers and Billy J. Kramer And the Dakotas to Parlophone, Martin supervised their recordings.

In 1965, he left EMI and set up his own studios, AIR London with fellow producers Ron Richards (Hollies) and John Burgess (Manfred Mann). Four years later the partnership created another studio on the Caribbean island of Montserrat, which became a favoured recording centre for artists including Paul McCartney, Dire Straits and the Rolling Stones. He continued to work with several new EMI artists, notably the Action. In the 70s he produced a series of hit albums by America. During this period he worked with Neil Sedaka, Ringo Starr, Jimmy Webb, Jeff Beck and Stackridge, while producing the soundtrack to the 1978 film of *Sgt Pepper's Lonely Hearts Club Band*. He maintained the Beatles connection, preparing the 1977 release of the live recording *At The Hollywood Bowl*, and produced two of McCartney's solo efforts, *Tug Of War* (1981) and *Pipes Of Peace* (1983). He also produced the soundtrack to McCartney's film musical *Give My Regards To Broad Street*. In the late 70s, AIR was purchased by Chrysalis Records, with Martin becoming a director of the company.

Martin was less prolific as a producer during the late 80s, but created a version of Dylan Thomas' *Under Milk Wood* in 1988 and worked with ex-Dexys Midnight Runners member Andy Leek on his debut solo album. He was awarded a CBE for services to the music industry in 1988. In 1990, he announced plans to replace AIR Studios with a 'state of the art' audio-video complex in north London, and his punctilious attention in remastering the Beatles' entire work for compact disc is demonstrated in the quite remarkable results he achieved. He was instrumental in producing 1992's television documentary to mark the 25th anniversary of *Sgt. Pepper's Lonely Hearts Club Band*. In the mid-90s he was a major part of the Beatles Anthology series, although he was disappointed not to have been asked to produce the two new singles, 'Free As A Bird' and 'Real Love'. This task went to Jeff Lynne, who received some criticism for his production, leading to a number of 'if only George Martin had produced it' comments.

Martin has no worries: his name is firmly in the history books, with an unimpeachable record, his quiet and intelligent persona masking an extraordinary talent. He received the Grammy Trustees Award in 1995, and was rightly awarded a knighthood in 1996 for his services to music, for being such a consistent ambassador and for hardly ever putting a foot wrong. In 1997, Martin staged the Music For Montserrat charity concert, and produced Elton John's 'Candle In The Wind '97', which went on to become the biggest-selling single of all time. In 1998 he released his final album, *In My Life*, a collection of Beatles' cover versions by guest 'vocalists' from music and film including Celine Dion, Jim Carrey, Goldie Hawn and Sean Connery.

● ALBUMS: *Off The Beatle Track* (Parlophone 1964) ★★★, *George Martin* (United Artists 1965) ★★★, *George Martin Scores Instrumental Versions Of The Hits* (1965) ★★★, *Plays Help!* (Columbia 1965) ★★, *Salutes The Beatle Girls* (United Artists) ★★★, *And I Love Her* (Studio Two 1966) ★★★, *By George!* (1967) ★★★, *The Family Way* film soundtrack (1967) ★★★, *British Maid* (United Artists 1968) ★★★, with the Beatles *Yellow Submarine* (Parlophone 1969) ★★★, *Live And Let Die* (United Artists 1973) ★★★, *Beatles To Bond And Bach* (Polydor 1974) ★★★, *In My Life* (Echo 1998) ★★★.

● COMPILATIONS: *Produced By George Martin: 50 Years In Recording* 6-CD box set (EMI 2001) ★★★★.

● FURTHER READING: *All You Need Is Ears*, George Martin. *Summer Of Love: The Making Of Sgt Pepper*, George Martin.

● FILMS: *Give My Regards To Broad Street* (1985).

MARTINDALE, WINK

b. Winston Martindale, 1933, Jackson, Tennessee, USA. A 1959 revival of T. Texas Tyler's 'Deck Of Cards' monologue is as synonymous with this ex-Memphis radio presenter as the pyramids are with Egypt. While studying speech and drama at the state university, he had moonlighted at a city station, working his way up from music librarian. A meeting with Dot Records executive Randy Wood led to the release of 'Deck Of Cards' – a soldier answering a charge of playing cards in church by explaining each one's religious significance – an opus that appealed to Martindale, a former chorister and regular church-goer. Its worldwide success brought far-flung television appearances on Australia's *Bandstand* and UK's *Sunday Night At The London Palladium*, and also caused the artist to migrate to Hollywood, where he hosted the *Teenage Dance Party* television series in the early 60s. 'Deck Of Cards' has been extraordinarily successful in the UK, re-entering the charts on several occasions in the 60s and in 1973. It peaked behind a more recently recorded rival recitation from Max Bygraves.

● ALBUMS: *Wink Martindale* (London 1960) ★ *Deck Of Cards* (Golden Guinea 1963) ★.

MARVELETTES

The Marvelettes' career epitomized th haphazard progress endured by many of th leading girl-groups of the early 60s. Despit enjoying several major US hits, they wer unable to sustain a consistent line-up, and thei constant shifts in personnel made it difficult t overcome their rather anonymous publi image. The group was formed in the late 50s b five students at Inkster High School i Michigan, USA: Gladys Horton, Georgeann Marie Tillman (d. 6 January 1980), Wand Young, Katherine Anderson and Juanita Gran They were spotted at a school talent show b Robert Bateman of the Satintones, wh introduced them to Berry Gordy, head of th fledgling Motown organization. Bateman c produced their early releases with Bria Holland, and the partnership found immediat success with 'Please Mr Postman' – a U number 1 in 1961, and Motown's biggest-sellin record up to that point. This effervescent slic of pop-R&B captivated teenage audiences in th USA, and the song was introduced to an eve wider public when the Beatles recorded faithful cover version on their second album. After a blatant attempt to repeat the winnin formula with 'Twistin' Postman', th Marvelettes made the Top 20 again in 1962 wit 'Playboy' and the chirpy 'Beechwood 4-578' The cycle of line-up changes was alread underway, with Juanita Grant's departur reducing the group to a four-piece. Th comparative failure of the next few singles als took its toll, and by 1965, Tillman had also lef The remaining trio, occasionally augmented b Florence Ballard of the Supremes, was paire with producer/writer Smokey Robinson. H tailored a series of ambitious hit singles for th group, the most successful of which was 'Dor Mess With Bill' in 1966 – although 'The Hunte Gets Captured By The Game' was arguably more significant achievement. Gladys Horto the Marvelettes' usual lead singer, left the grou in 1967, to be replaced by Anne Bogan. The continued to notch up minor soul hits for th remainder of the decade, most notably '(Whe You're) Young And In Love', befor disintegrating in 1970. Wanda Young complete the group's recording commitments with a album, *The Return Of The Marvelettes*, whic saw her supported by session vocalists. In 19 original members Wanda Rogers and Glad Horton, plus Echo Johnson and Jean McLai recorded for Motor City, issuing the disc sounding 'Holding On With Both Hands' ar *Now*. Johnson and McLain were replaced I Jackie and Regina Holleman for subseque releases.

● ALBUMS: *Please Mr Postman* (Tamla 196 ★★★★, *The Marvelettes Sing Smash Hits Of 19*

(Tamla 1962) ★★★, *Playboy* (Tamla 1962) ★★★, *The Marvellous Marvelettes* (Tamla 1963) ★★★★, *Recorded Live: On Stage* (Tamla 1963) ★★, *The Marvelettes* (Tamla 1967) ★★★, *Sophisticated Soul* (Tamla 1968) ★★★, *In Full Bloom* (Motown 1969) ★★, *The Return Of The Marvelettes* (Motown 1970) ★★, *Now* (Motor City 1990) ★★.
● COMPILATIONS: *The Marvelettes Greatest Hits* (Tamla 1963) ★★★★, *Anthology* (Motown 1975) ★★★★, *Compact Command Performances – 23 Greatest Hits* (Motown 1992) ★★★★, *Deliver The Singles 1961-1971* (Motown 1993) ★★★★, *The Very Best* (Essential Gold 1996) ★★★, *The Ultimate Collection* (Motown 1998) ★★★★, *20th Century Masters: The Millennium Collection, The Best Of The Marvelettes* (Motown 2000) ★★★★.

MAUGHAN, SUSAN

b. 1 July 1942, Newcastle-upon-Tyne, Tyne And Wear, England. A popular and vivacious singing star in the UK during the 60s, Susan Maughan began her singing career in 1958 as a member of a popular midland band led by Ronnie Hancock. Their 1961 demonstration disc alerted the Philips label to her talent, and a year in the Ray Ellington Quartet ran concurrently with a nascent recording career, which began with the timely 'Mama Do The Twist'. Maughan enjoyed chart success when the effervescent 'Bobby's Girl' reached the UK Top 3 in 1962, but although 'Hand A Handkerchief To Helen' and 'She's New To You' (both 1963) were minor hits, she was unable to repeat this early triumph. Maughan nonetheless continued to record, and albums featuring a full orchestra (*Swingin' Susan*) or a jazzband (*Hey Look Me Over*) showed her versatility. In 1965, along with a host of other pop stars such as Billy J. Kramer, the Animals, Peter and Gordon, Matt Monro and Herman's Hermits, she appeared in the 'mock concert' film *Pop Gear*, which was hosted by Jimmy Savile. Nearly 30 years later, in 1992, Susan Maughan joined another survivor from those far off days, Jess Conrad, in the UK tour of *The Golden Sounds Of The Sixties*.
● ALBUMS: *I Wanna Be Bobby's Girl But* (Philips 1963) ★★★, *Swingin' Susan* (Philips 1964) ★★★, *Sentimental Susan* (Philips 1965) ★★★, *Hey Look Me Over* (1966) ★★★.
● COMPILATIONS: *Bobby's Girl* (Wing 1966) ★★★.

MAYALL, JOHN

b. 29 November 1933, Macclesfield, Cheshire, England. The career of England's premier white blues exponent and father of British blues has now spanned five decades and much of that time has been unintentionally spent acting as a musical catalyst. Mayall formed his first band in 1955 while at college, and as the Powerhouse Four the group worked mostly locally. Soon afterwards, Mayall enlisted for National Service. He then became a commercial artist and finally moved to London to form his Blues Syndicate, the forerunner to his legendary Bluesbreakers. Along with Alexis Korner, Cyril Davies and Graham Bond, Mayall pioneered British R&B. The astonishing number of musicians who have passed through his bands reads like a who's who. Even more remarkable is the number of names who have gone on to eclipse Mayall with either their own bands or as members of highly successful groups. Pete Frame, author of *Rock Family Trees*, has produced a detailed Mayall specimen, which is recommended.

His roster of musicians included John McVie, Hughie Flint, Mick Fleetwood, Roger Dean, Davey Graham, Eric Clapton, Jack Bruce, Aynsley Dunbar, Peter Green, Dick Heckstall-Smith, Keef Hartley, Andy Fraser, Mick Taylor, Henry Lowther, Tony Reeves, Chris Mercer, Jon Hiseman, Steve Thompson, Colin Allen, Jon Mark, Johnny Almond, Harvey Mandel, Larry Taylor, and Don 'Sugercane' Harris.

His 1965 debut, *John Mayall Plays John Mayall*, was a live album which, although badly recorded, captured the tremendous atmosphere of an R&B club. His first single, 'Crawling Up A Hill', is contained on this set and it features Mayall's thin voice attempting to compete with an exciting, distorted harmonica and Hammond organ. *Bluesbreakers With Eric Clapton* is now a classic, and is highly recommended to all students of white blues. Clapton enabled his boss to reach a wider audience, as the crowds filled the clubs to catch a glimpse of the guitar hero. *A Hard Road* featured some clean and sparing guitar from Peter Green, while *Crusade* offers a brassier, fuller sound. *The Blues Alone* showed a more relaxed style, and allowed Mayall to demonstrate his musical dexterity. *Diary Of A Band Vol. 1* and *Vol. 2* were released during 1968 and capture their sound from the previous year; both feature excellent drumming from Keef Hartley, in addition to Mick Taylor on guitar. *Bare Wires*, arguably Mayall's finest work, shows a strong jazz leaning, with the addition of Jon Hiseman on drums and the experienced brass section of Lowther, Mercer and Heckstall-Smith. The album was an introspective journey and contained Mayall's most competent lyrics, notably the beautifully hymn-like 'I Know Now'. The similarly packaged *Blues From Laurel Canyon* (Mayall often produced his own artwork) was another strong album which was recorded in Los Angeles, where Mayall lived. This marked the end of the Bluesbreakers name for a while, and, following the departure of Mick Taylor to the Rolling Stones, Mayall pioneered a drumless acoustic band featuring Jon Mark on acoustic guitar, Johnny Almond on tenor saxophone and flute, and Stephen Thompson on string bass. The subsequent live album, *The Turning Point*, proved to be his biggest-selling album and almost reached the UK Top 10. Notable tracks are the furious 'Room To Move', with Mayall's finest harmonica solo, and

'Thoughts About Roxanne' with some exquisite saxophone from Almond. The same line-up plus Larry Taylor produced *Empty Rooms*, which was more refined and less exciting. The band that recorded *USA Union* consisted of Americans Harvey Mandel, 'Sugarcane' Harris and Larry Taylor. It gave Mayall yet another success, although he struggled lyrically. Following the double reunion *Back To The Roots*, Mayall's work lost its bite, and over the next few years his output was of poor quality. The halcyon days of name stars in his band had passed and Mayall suffered record company apathy. His last album to chart was *New Year, New Band, New Company* in 1975, featuring for the first time a female vocalist, Dee McKinnie, and future Fleetwood Mac guitarist Rick Vito.

Following a run of albums that had little or no exposure, Mayall stopped recording, playing only infrequently close to his base in California. He toured Europe in 1988 to small but wildly enthusiastic audiences. That same year he signed to Island Records and released *Chicago Line*. Renewed activity and interest occurred in 1990 following the release of his finest album in many years, *A Sense Of Place*. Mayall was interviewed during a short visit to Britain in 1992 and sounded positive, happy and unaffected by years in the commercial doldrums. *Wake Up Call* changed everything once more. Released in 1993, the album is one of his finest ever, and became his biggest-selling disc for over two decades. The 90s have so far been kind to Mayall; the birth of another child in 1995, and a solid new release, *Spinning Coin*. The replacement for the departing Coco Montoya was yet another highly talented guitarist (a fortune with which Mayall is clearly blessed) – Buddy Whittington is the latest, continuing a tradition that started with Clapton and Green. *Blues For The Lost Days* is one of his most important albums lyrically. Many of the songs formed an autobiography and the tone is nostalgic and often sad. *Along For The Ride* is of historical importance, although the pedestrian album cover is off-putting and looks like a Woolworths bargain basement reject. The music within reunited Mayall with several old Bluesbreakers, including Heckstall-Smith, Fleetwood, Peter Green and Mick Taylor, and like-minded musicians such as Gary Moore, Otis Rush, Steve Cropper and Steve Miller.

As the sole survivor from the four 60s UK R&B/blues catalysts, Mayall has played the blues for so long without any deviation that it is hard to think of any other white artist to compare. He has outlived his contemporaries from the early days (Korner, Bond and Davis), and recent reappraisal has put the man back at the top of a genre that he can justifiably claim to have furthered more than any other Englishman.

● ALBUMS: *John Mayall Plays John Mayall* (Decca 1965) ★★★★, *Bluesbreakers With Eric Clapton* (Decca 1966) ★★★★★, *A Hard Road* (Decca 1967) ★★★★, *Crusade* (Decca 1967) ★★★, *The Blues Alone* (Ace Of Clubs 1967) ★★★★★, *Diary Of A Band Vol. 1* (Decca 1968) ★★★, *Diary Of A Band Vol. 2* (Decca 1968) ★★★, *Bare Wires* (Decca 1968) ★★★★★, *Blues From Laurel Canyon* (Decca 1968) ★★★★, *Turning Point* (Polydor 1969) ★★★★, *Empty Rooms* (Polydor 1970) ★★★★, *USA Union* (Polydor 1970) ★★★, *Back To The Roots* (Polydor 1971) ★★★, *Beyond The Turning Point* (Polydor 1971) ★★★, *Memories* (Polydor 1971) ★★★, *Jazz Blues Fusion* (Polydor 1972) ★★★, *Moving On* (Polydor 1973) ★★, *Ten Years Are Gone* (Polydor 1973) ★★, *Down The Line* (London US 1973) ★★, *The Latest Edition* (Polydor 1975) ★★, *New Year, New Band, New Company* (ABC 1975) ★★, *Time Expired, Notice To Appear* (ABC 1975) ★★, *John Mayall* (Polydor 1976) ★★, *A Banquet Of Blues* (ABC 1976) ★★, *Lots Of People* (ABC 1977) ★★, *A Hard Core Package* (ABC 1977) ★★, *Primal Solos* (London 1977) ★★★, *Blues Roots* (Decca 1978) ★★, *Last Of The British Blues* (MCA 1978) ★★, *Bottom Line* (DJM 1979) ★★, *No More Interviews* (DJM 1979) ★★★, *Roadshow Blues* (DJM 1980) ★★, *Last Edition* (Polydor 1983) ★★, *Behind The Iron Curtain* (PRT 1986) ★★, *Chicago Line* (Island 1988) ★★, *Archives To Eighties* (Polydor 1989) ★★★, *A Sense Of Place* (Island 1990) ★★★★, *Wake Up Call* (Silvertone 1993) ★★★★, *The 1982 Reunion Concert* (Repertoire 1994) ★★, *Spinning Coin* (Silvertone 1995) ★★, *Blues For The Lost Days* (Silvertone 1997) ★★★★, *Padlock On The Blues* (Eagle 1999) ★★★, *Rock The Blues* 1970-71 recordings (Indigo 1999) ★, *Along For The Ride* (Eagle 2001) ★★★.

● COMPILATIONS: *Looking Back* (Decca 1969) ★★★★, *World Of John Mayall* (Decca 1970) ★★★★, *World Of John Mayall Volume 2* (Decca 1971) ★★★★, *Thru The Years* (Decca 1971) ★★★, *The John Mayall Story Volume 1* (Decca 1983) ★★★★, *The John Mayall Story Volume 2* (Decca 1983) ★★★, *London Blues 1964-1969* (PolyGram 1992) ★★★★, *Room To Move 1969-1974* (PolyGram 1992) ★★★★, *As It All Began 1964-1969* (Deram 1998) ★★★★, *Silver Tones: The Best Of John Mayall & The Bluesbreakers* (Silvertone 1998) ★★★, *Blues Power* (Snapper 1999) ★★★, *Drivin' On: The ABC Years 1975-1982* (MCA 1999) ★★, *Reaching For The Blues '79 To '81* (Cleopatra 2000) ★★★, *Steppin' Out: An Introduction To John Mayall* (Decca 2001) ★★★.

● VIDEOS: *John Mayall's Bluesbreakers: Blues Alive* (PVE 1995).

● FURTHER READING: *John Mayall: Blues Breaker*, Richard Newman.

MAYFIELD, CURTIS

b. 3 June 1942, Chicago, Illinois, USA, d. 26 December 1999, Roswell, Georgia, USA. As songwriter and vocalist with the Impressions, Mayfield established an early reputation as one of soul music's most intuitive talents. In the decade between 1961 and 1971, he penned a succession of exemplary singles for his group, including 'Gypsy Woman' (1961), 'It's All Right' (1963), 'I'm The One Who Loves You' (1963), 'You Must Believe Me' (1964), 'People Get Ready' (1965), 'We're A Winner' (1968) and 'Choice Of Colors' (1969), the subjects of which ranged from simple, tender love songs to broadsides demanding social and political equality. Years later Bob Marley lifted lines from 'People Get Ready' to populate his own opus, 'One Love'. The independent record companies, Windy C, Mayfield and Curtom Records, emphasized Mayfield's statesman-like role within black music, while his continued support for other artists – as composer, producer or session guitarist – enhanced a virtually peerless reputation. Jerry Butler, Major Lance, Gene Chandler and Walter Jackson were among the many Chicago-based singers benefiting from Mayfield's involvement.

Having parted company with the Impressions in 1970, the singer began his solo career with November's US Top 30 hit '(Don't Worry) If There's A Hell Below We're All Going To Go', a suitably astringent protest song. The following year Mayfield enjoyed his biggest UK success with 'Move On Up', a compulsive dance song that reached number 12 but surprisingly did not chart in the USA. There, the artist's commercial ascendancy was maintained in 1972 with 'Freddie's Dead' (US R&B number 2/number 4 pop hit) and the theme from *Superfly*, a 'blaxploitation' movie that he also scored. Both singles and the attendant album achieved gold status, inspiring further excursions into motion picture soundtracks, including *Claudine*, *A Piece Of The Action*, *Sparkle* and *Short Eyes*, the last of which featured Mayfield in an acting role. However, although the singer continued to prove popular, he failed to sustain this high profile, and subsequent work, including his production of Aretha Franklin's 1978 album, *Almighty Fire*, gained respect rather than commercial approbation.

In 1981, Mayfield joined the Boardwalk label, for which he recorded *Honesty*, his strongest album since the halcyon days of the early 70s. Sadly, the death of the label's managing director Neil Bogart left an insurmountable gap, and Mayfield's career was then blighted by music industry indifference. The singer nonetheless remained a highly popular live attraction, particularly in Britain where '(Celebrate) The Day After You', a collaboration with the Blow Monkeys, became a minor hit.

In 1990, a freak accident, in which part of a public address rig collapsed on top of him during a concert, left Mayfield permanently paralyzed from the neck down. The effects, both personal and professional, proved costly, but not completely devastating in terms of his musical career. The material for *BBC Radio 1*

Live In Concert was gathered from the gig at London's Town And Country Club during Mayfield's 1990 European tour. In 1993, Warner Brothers Records released *A Tribute To Curtis Mayfield* featuring various artists, including Lenny Kravitz, Whitney Houston, Aretha Franklin, Bruce Springsteen, Rod Stewart, Elton John and Steve Winwood. The album was an excellent tribute to the Mayfield songbook. Winwood contributed the highlight, a sparkling version of 'It's All Right'. A year later Charly Records reissued the majority of Mayfield's 70s albums on CD as well as several compilations. The icing on the cake came in 1996 when Rhino Records collated the best material in a three-CD box set. At the end of the same year a new studio album, *New World Order*, was released to excellent reviews. The album stands up to repeated listening, but some particularly enthusiastic critics may have been swayed by their affection for such an important man, together with sympathy for his tragic disability. During the recording Mayfield had to lie on his back in order to give some gravitational power to his singing.

Mayfield's contribution to soul music remains immense, whatever the limitations his disability brought to his last years. He died in hospital on December 26, 1999. The tributes were mighty and genuine; Mayfield had no enemies, only admirers. On his death Aretha Franklin stated he was 'the black Bach'. He was an exemplary songwriter who never descended into cliché, even though most of his work espoused peace, love and freedom. His recorded voice remains with us, perfect, sweet and unique.

● ALBUMS: *Curtis* (Buddah 1970) ★★★, *Curtis/Live!* (Buddah 1971) ★★★, *Roots* (Buddah 1971) ★★★★, *Superfly* film soundtrack (Buddah 1972) ★★★★★, *Back To The World* (Buddah 1973) ★★★★, *Curtis In Chicago* (Buddah 1973) ★★★, *Sweet Exorcist* (Buddah 1974) ★★★, *Got To Find A Way* (Buddah 1974) ★★★, *Claudine* film soundtrack (Buddah 1975) ★★, *Let's Do It Again* (Curtom 1975) ★★★, *There's No Place Like America Today* (Curtom 1975) ★★★, *Sparkle* film soundtrack (Curtom 1976) ★★, *Give, Get, Take And Have* (Curtom 1976) ★★, *Short Eyes* film soundtrack (Curtom 1977) ★★, *Never Say You Can't Survive* (Curtom 1977) ★★, *A Piece Of The Action* film soundtrack (Curtom 1978) ★★, *Do It All Night* (Curtom 1978) ★★★, *Heartbeat* (RSO 1979) ★★★, with Linda Clifford *The Right Combination* (RSO 1980) ★★, *Something To Believe In* (RSO 1980) ★★, *Love Is The Place* (Boardwalk 1981) ★★, *Honesty* (Boardwalk 1983) ★★★★, *We Come In Peace With A Message Of Love* (CRC 1985) ★★★, *Live In Europe* (Ichiban 1988) ★★★, *People Get Ready* (Essential 1990) ★★★, *Take It To The Streets* (Curtom 1990) ★★★★, *BBC Radio 1 Live In Concert* (Windsong 1994) ★★, *New World Order* (Warners 1996) ★★★★, *Live At Ronnie Scott's*

1988 recording (Sanctuary 2000) ★★★.
● COMPILATIONS: *Of All Time* (Curtom 1990)
★★★, *Tripping Out* (Charly 1994) ★★★, *Living
Legend* (Curtom Classics 1995) ★★★, *People Get
Ready: The Curtis Mayfield Story* 3-CD box set
(Rhino 1996) ★★★★, *Love Peace And
Understanding* 3-CD box set (Sequel 1997) ★★★,
Curtis: The Very Best Of (Beechwood 1998)
★★★★, *Gospel* (Rhino 1999) ★★★, *Move On Up:
The Singles Anthology 1970-90* (Sequel 1999)
★★★★.
● VIDEOS: *Curtis Mayfield At Ronnie Scott's*
(Hendring Music Video 1988).
● FILMS: *Superfly* (1972), *The Groove Tube*
(1974).

MC5

Formed in 1964 in Detroit, Michigan, USA, and
originally known as the Motor City Five, the
band was sundered the following year when its
rhythm section left in protest over a new song,
'Back To Comm'. Michael Davis (bass) and
Dennis Thompson (drums) joined founder-
members Rob Tyner (b. Robert Derminer, 12
December 1944, Detroit, Michigan, USA, d. 18
September 1991; vocals), Wayne Kramer (guitar)
and Fred 'Sonic' Smith (b. 1949, d. 4 November
1994; guitar) to pursue the radical direction this
experimental composition offered. By 1967
their repertoire included material drawn from
R&B, soul and *avant garde* jazz, as well as a
series of powerful original songs. Two singles,
'One Of The Guys'/'I Can Only Give You
Everything' (1967) and 'Borderline'/'Looking At
You' (1968), captured their nascent, high-energy
sound as the band embraced the 'street' politics
proselytized by mentor/manager John Sinclair.
Now linked to this former DJ's Trans Love
Commune and White Panther party, the MC5
became Detroit's leading underground act, and
a recording contract with the Elektra Records
label resulted in the seminal *Kick Out The Jams*.
Recorded live at the city's Grande Ballroom,
this turbulent set captured the quintet's
extraordinary sound, which, although loud, was
never reckless.
However, MC5 were dropped from their label's
roster following several disagreements, but later
emerged anew on Atlantic Records. Rock
journalist Jon Landau, later manager of Bruce
Springsteen, was invited to produce *Back In The
USA*, which, if lacking the dissolute thrill of its
predecessor, showed a band able to adapt to
studio discipline. 'Tonight', 'Shakin' Street' and a
remade 'Lookin' At You' are among the
highlights of this excellent set. A third
collection, *High Time*, reasserted a desire to
experiment, and several local jazz musicians
added punch to what nonetheless remains a
curiously ill-focused album on which each
member, bar Davis, contributed material. A
move to Europe, where the band performed and
recorded under the aegis of Rohan O'Rahilly,
failed to halt dwindling commercial prospects,

while the departure of Davis, then Tyner, in
1972, brought the MC5 to an end. Their
reputation flourished during the punk
phenomenon, during which time each former
member enjoyed brief notoriety. Sonic Smith
formed the low-key Sonic's Rendezvous with
Scott Asheton (drums), Scott Morgan (vocals)
and Gary Rasmussen (bass) before marrying
Patti Smith in 1980 (he was heavily featured on
the singer/poet's 'comeback' album, *Dream O
Life*, in 1988). Davis later surfaced in Destroy
All Monsters, while both Kramer and Tyner
attempted to use the MC5 name for several
unrelated projects. They wisely abandoned
such practices, leaving intact the legend of one
of rock's most uncompromising and exciting
acts. In September 1991, Tyner died of a heart
attack in the seat of his parked car in his home
town of Ferndale, Michigan. Smith also passed
away three years later. Kramer, however,
relaunched a solo career in the same year,
enlisting several prominent members of the US
underground/ alternative scene as his new
cohorts.
● ALBUMS: *Kick Out The Jams* (Elektra 1969)
★★★★, *Back In The USA* (Elektra 1970) ★★★
High Time (Elektra 1971) ★★, *Do It* (Revenge
1987) ★★, *Live Detroit 68/69* (Revenge 1988) ★
Motor City Is Burning (Castle 1999) ★.
● COMPILATIONS: *Babes In Arms* cassette only
(ROIR 1983) ★★★, *Looking At You* (Receiver
1994) ★★★, *Power Trip* (Alive 1994) ★★★
Thunder Express (Jungle 1999) ★★★, *'6
Breakout* (Total Energy 1999) ★★, *The Big Bang
Best Of The MC5* (Rhino 2000) ★★★.

McCoys

Formed in Union City, Indiana, USA, in 1962
this beat group initially comprised Rick
Zehringer (b. 5 August 1947, Fort Recovery
Ohio, USA; guitar), his brother Randy (b. 1951
Union City, Indiana, USA; drums) and bass
player Dennis Kelly. Known variously as Rick
And The Raiders or the Rick Z Combo, the
group later added Ronnie Brandon (organ)
becoming the McCoys soon after Randy Hobb
replaced the college-bound Kelly. The quarte
became a highly popular attraction throughou
America's midwest, and were brought to Ber
Berns' Bang label by producers Feldman/
Gottherer/ Goldstein. The group's debut 'Hang
On Sloopy' (1965), topped the US chart and
reached the UK Top 5, but successive releases in
a similar gutsy style fared less well; an early b
side, 'Sorrow', was later adopted by the Merseys
and in turn was covered by David Bowie on his
1973 *Pin-Ups*. The group discarded its
bubblegum image with the progressive *Infinite
McCoys*, and as the house band at New York's
popular Scene club. Owner/entrepreneur Steve
Paul later paired the group with blues protégé
Johnny Winter, whose *Johnny Winter And*
featured the Zehringer siblings and Randy
Hobbs, with Rick, now Rick Derringer, handling

production. When this group was disbanded, Derringer joined Edgar Winter before embarking on a solo career.

● ALBUMS: *Hang On Sloopy* (Bang 1965) ★★★, *You Make Me Feel So Good* (Bang 1966) ★★★, *Infinite McCoys* (Mercury 1968) ★, *Human Ball* (Mercury 1969) ★.

● COMPILATIONS: *Psychedelic Years* (One Way 1994) ★★, *Hang On Sloopy: The Best Of The McCoys* (Legacy 1995) ★★★★.

McDANIELS, GENE

b. Eugene Booker McDaniels, 12 February 1935, Kansas City, Kansas, USA. McDaniels began singing in church as a tiny child and by the age of 11 was a member of a gospel quartet. This was in Omaha, Nebraska, where he was raised and also studied at the Omaha Conservatory of Music. The quartet tried out in New York City where McDaniels was recognized as the pre-eminent singer in the group. In 1954, he relocated to Los Angeles where he swiftly built a reputation singing in jazz clubs. He performed with many noted artists, among them Les McCann, Cannonball Adderley, John Coltrane and Miles Davis. Signed by Liberty Records, he had a US Top 5 hit in 1961 with 'A Hundred Pounds Of Clay' which was followed by another Top 5 single 'Tower Of Strength', and 'Chip Chip', 'Point Of No Return', and 'Spanish Lace', all of which made the charts in the USA. He toured Australia with Dizzy Gillespie and Sarah Vaughan but was becoming dissatisfied with the direction his career was being aimed by his recording company. When his contract ended he went back to New York where he worked with yet more important jazz musicians, such as Herbie Hancock. In 1967, McDaniels went to Europe, remaining there for two years during which time he honed his talents as a songwriter. Back in America, he signed with Atlantic Records as both singer and songwriter. His song, 'Compared To What?' was recorded by McCann and also by Roberta Flack, for whom he then wrote 'Reverend Lee' and the immensely successful 'Feel Like Makin' Love' which reached number 1 on the *Billboard*, *Cash Box* and *Record World* charts in 1974. He also wrote 'Before You Accuse Me', recorded by Creedence Clearwater Revival and covered by Eric Clapton. Between 1974 and 1979 McDaniels was also active as a record producer working with many leading pop artists including Nancy Wilson and Gladys Knight. Another move, this time to Seattle, brought him into contact with Carolyn E. Thompson but it took a few more years before their musical relationship blossomed. Back once again in New York he worked with Michel Legrand on film scores and also wrote songs which have been sung by artists such as Flack, Wilson, Patti Austin and Diane Schuur. It was in 1996 that McDaniels and Thompson formed their own company, Numoon Disc Company, and he entered yet another rewarding and musically fulfilling stage of his packed career. As a singer, McDaniels' strong and commanding voice brought a sense of controlled power to his performances. Despite his considerable success in this area, however, it might well be his later achievements as a songwriter and record producer that will prove to be the most lasting testimony to his stature in the world of popular music.

● ALBUMS: *In Times Like These* (Liberty 1960) ★★★, *Sometimes I'm Happy, Sometimes I'm Blue* (Liberty 1960) ★★★, *A Hundred Pounds Of Clay* (Liberty 1961) ★★★★, *Gene McDaniels Sings Movie Memories* (Liberty 1962) ★★, *Tower Of Strength* (Liberty 1962) ★★★★, *Spanish Lace* (Liberty 1963) ★★, *The Wonderful World Of Gene McDaniels* (Liberty 1963) ★★, *Facts Of Life* (1968) ★★, *Outlaw* (Atlantic 1971) ★★, *Headless Horsemen Of The Apocalypse* (Atlantic 1971) ★★★, *Natural Juices* (1975) ★★.

● COMPILATIONS: *Hit After Hit* (Liberty 1962) ★★★, *Another Tear Falls* (Charly 1986) ★★★, *A Hundred Pounds Of Clay: The Best Of Gene McDaniels* 60s recordings (Collectables 1995) ★★★, *A Hundred Pounds Of Clay/Tower Of Strength* 60s recordings (Beat Goes On 1999) ★★★.

● FILMS: *It's Trad, Dad* aka *Ring A Ding Rhythm* (1962).

McDOWELL, MISSISSIPPI FRED

b. 12 January 1904, Rossville, Tennessee, USA, d. 3 July 1972, Memphis, Tennessee, USA. A self-taught guitarist, McDowell garnered his early reputation in the Memphis area with appearances at private parties, picnics and dances. He later moved to Como, Mississippi, and was employed as a farmer until discovered by field researcher Alan Lomax in 1959. Sessions for Atlantic Records and Prestige confirmed the artist as one of the last great exponents of the traditional bottleneck style and McDowell became a leading light of the 60s blues renaissance. He undertook several recordings with his wife, Annie Mae and, in 1964, appeared at the Newport Folk Festival alongside other major 'rediscoveries' Mississippi John Hurt and Sleepy John Estes; part of his performance was captured on the attendant film. The following year he completed the first of several releases for the California-based Arhoolie Records. These recordings introduced a consistency to his work which deftly combined blues and spiritual material. McDowell also became a frequent visitor to Europe, touring with the American Folk Blues Festival and later appearing in concert in London, where he was supported by Jo Ann Kelly. He appeared on several Dutch television programmes and in two documentary films, *The Blues Maker* (1968) and *Fred McDowell* (1969). The artist was then signed to Capitol Records, for whom he recorded *I Don't Play No Rock 'N' Roll*. Arguably one of the finest releases of its genre, its intimate charm belied the intensity the performer still brought to his work. Despite ailing health McDowell continued to follow a punishing schedule with performances at festivals throughout the USA, but by the end of 1971, such work had lessened dramatically. He died of cancer in July 1972. Although his compositions were not widely covered, the Rolling Stones recorded a haunting version of 'You've Got To Move' on *Sticky Fingers* (1971). McDowell's influence is also apparent in the approach of several artists, notably that of Bonnie Raitt.

● ALBUMS: *Mississippi Delta Blues* (Arhoolie 1964) ★★★★, *My Home Is In The Delta* (Bounty 1964) ★★★, *Amazing Grace* (1964) ★★★, *Mississippi Delta Blues Volume 2* (Arhoolie 1966) ★★★★, *I Do Not Play No Rock 'N' Roll* (Capitol 1969) ★★★★, *Mississippi Fred McDowell And His Blues Boys* (Arhoolie 1969) ★★★, *Steakbone Slide Guitar* (Tradition 1969) ★★★, *Mississippi Fred McDowell In London 1* (Sire/Transatlantic 1970) ★★★, *Mississippi Fred McDowell In London 2* (Transatlantic 1970) ★★★, *Going Down South* (Polydor 1970) ★★★, *Mississippi Fred McDowell* (Arhoolie 1971) ★★★, *The First Recordings* (Rounder 1997) ★★★★, *Levee Camp Blues* (Testament 1998) ★★★★, *Live At The Gaslight* 1972 recording (Live Archive 2001) ★★★.

● COMPILATIONS: *1904-1972* (Xtra 1974) ★★★, with Johnny Woods *Eight Years Ramblin'* (Revival 1977) ★★★, *Keep Your Lamp Trimmed And Burning* (Arhoolie 1981) ★★★, with Jo Ann Kelly *Standing At The Burying Ground* (Red Lightnin' 1984) ★★★★, with Phil Guy *A Double Dose Of Dynamite* (Red Lightnin' 1986) ★★★, *Fred McDowell 1959* (KC 1988) ★★★, *When I Lay My Burden Down* (Blue Moon 1988) ★★★, *1962* (Heritage 1988) ★★★, *The Train I Ride* (1993) ★★★, *Good Morning Little Schoolgirl* (Arhoolie 1994) ★★★, *Ain't Gonna Worry* (Drive Archives 1995) ★★★, *Mississippi Fred McDowell* (Bullseye 1995) ★★★, *I Do Not Play No Rock 'n' Roll* (Capitol 1996) ★★★, *Steakbone Slide Guitar* (Tradition 1998) ★★★★, *Standing At The Burying Ground* 1969 live recording (Sequel 1996) ★★★★, *You Gotta Move* (Arhoolie 2001) ★★★.

McGUIRE, BARRY

b. 15 October 1935, Oklahoma City, Oklahoma, USA. McGuire first came to prominence as a minor actor in *Route 66* before teaming up with singer Barry Kane as Barry And Barry. In 1962, he joined the New Christy Minstrels and appeared as lead singer on several of their hits, most notably, 'Green Green' and 'Saturday Night'. He also sang the lead on their comic but catchy 'Three Wheels On My Wagon'. While still a Minstrel, he composed the hit 'Greenback Dollar' for the Kingston Trio. After leaving the New Christy Minstrels, McGuire signed to Lou Adler's Dunhill Records and was assigned to staff writers P.F. Sloan and Steve Barri. At the peak of the folk-rock boom, they wrote the rabble-rousing protest 'Eve Of Destruction', which

McGuire took to number 1 in the USA, surviving a blanket radio ban in the process. The anti-establishment nature of the lyric even provoked an answer record, 'Dawn Of Correction', written by John Madara and Dave White under the pseudonym the Spokesmen. Ironically, 'Eve Of Destruction' had originally been conceived as a flip-side and at one stage was offered to the Byrds, who turned it down. Coincidentally, both Barry McGuire and Byrds leader Jim (later Roger) McGuinn received a flattering namecheck on the Mamas And The Papas' hit 'Creeque Alley' ('McGuinn and McGuire were just a-getting higher in LA, you know where that's at'). McGuire, in fact, played a significant part in bringing the million-selling vocal quartet to Adler and they later offered their services as his backing singers.

McGuire unsuccessfully attempted to follow up his worldwide hit with other Sloan material, including the excellent 'Upon A Painted Ocean'. He continued to pursue the protest route on the albums *Eve Of Destruction* and *This Precious Time*, but by 1967 he was branching out into acting. A part in *The President's Analyst* led to a Broadway appearance in the musical *Hair*. After the meagre sales of *The World's Last Private Citizen*, McGuire ceased recording until 1971, when he returned with former Mamas And The Papas sideman Eric Hord on *Barry McGuire And The Doctor*. The work featured backing from the cream of the 1965 school of folk rock, including the Byrds' Chris Hillman and Michael Clarke. Soon afterwards, McGuire became a Christian evangelist and thereafter specialized in gospel albums.

● ALBUMS: *The Barry McGuire Album* (Horizon 1963) ★★★, *Star Folk With Barry McGuire* (Surrey 1965) ★★, *Eve Of Destruction* (1965) ★★★, *This Precious Time* (Dunhill 1966) ★★★, *Star Folk With Barry McGuire Vol. 2* (Surrey 1966) ★★, *Star Folk With Barry McGuire Vol. 3* (Surrey 1966) ★★, *Star Folk With Barry McGuire Vol. 4* (Surrey 1966) ★★, *Barry McGuire Featuring Eve of Destruction* (Dunhill 1966) ★★★, *The Eve Of Destruction Man* (Ember 1966) ★, *The World's Last Private Citizen* (Dunhill 1968) ★★, *Barry McGuire And The Doctor* (A&M 1971) ★★, *Seeds* (1973) ★★, *Finer Than Gold* (1981) ★★, *Inside Out* (1982) ★★, *To The Bride* (1982) ★★, *Best Of Barry* (1982) ★★.

● COMPILATIONS: *Anthology* (One Way 1994) ★★★.

McKENZIE, SCOTT

b. Philip Blondheim, 1 October 1944, Arlington, Virginia, USA. McKenzie began his professional career in the Journeymen, a clean-cut folk group. He later recorded some undistinguished solo material before fellow ex-member John Phillips, then enjoying success with the Mamas And The Papas, invited the singer to join him in Los Angeles. Although the folk rock-inspired 'No No No No No' failed to sell, the pairing

ourished spectacularly on 'San Francisco (Be
ure To Wear Some Flowers In Your Hair)'. This
truistic hippie anthem, penned by Phillips,
ncapsulated the innocent wonderment felt by
nany onlookers of the era and the single,
uoyed by an irresistible melody, reached
umber 4 in the US chart, but climbed to the
izzy heights of number 1 in the UK and
aroughout Europe. Meritorious follow-ups,
Like An Old Time Movie' and 'Holy Man', failed
o emulate such success, and although McKenzie
riefly re-emerged with the low-key, country-
nfluenced *Stained Glass Morning*, he remained
ut of the public eye until the 80s, when he
oined Phillips in a rejuvenated Mamas And The
apas.
● ALBUMS: *The Voice Of Scott McKenzie*
Ode/Columbia 1967) ★★, *Stained Glass Morning*
1970) ★★.

1cKUEN, ROD

. Rodney Marvin McKuen, 29 April 1933,
Oakland, California, USA. One of the revered
oets of the late 60s love generation, Rod
1cKuen is also a highly acclaimed singer,
ongwriter and soundtrack composer. He took a
low route to the top, performing various
nanual jobs as a young man and also serving
wo years as an infantryman in Korea. In the
nid-50s McKuen embarked on both a pop career
Happy Is A Boy Named Me' was released in the
JK in 1957) and an attempted acting career,
ombining both by appearing as a musician in
ne rock 'n' roll exploitation movie *Rock, Pretty
aby* in 1956. He also spent a spell as a vocalist
or Lionel Hampton and a nightclub performer,
efore heading to Paris in the 60s. It was here, in
ne company of Jacques Brel and Charles
Aznavour, that he began writing poetry in a free
erse form very typical of the times. Described
y *Newsweek* as 'the king of kitsch', McKuen
ecame one of the few poets able to sell his work
n large volumes, and he became a wealthy man.
His 60s books included *Stanyan Street & Other
orrows*, *Listen To The Warm*, and *Lonesome
ities*.

His musical career continued when he wrote the
core for the 1969 movie adaptation of *The Prime
Of Miss Jean Brodie* including the title song 'Jean'
nd contributed six songs to the soundtrack of
he same year's *A Boy Named Charlie Brown*. He
lso wrote several symphonies, suites and
oncertos during this period, earning a Pulitzer
omination for *The City: A Suite For Narrator
nd Orchestra*. The most interesting of his
umerous pop forays include *McKuen Country*,
n which he enlisted the aid of Glenn Campbell,
ig Jim Sullivan and Barry McGuire in a
erfectly acceptable stab at country rock, and a
eries of bestselling easy listening albums
ecorded with arranger Anita Kerr as the San
ebastian Strings. Among his best remembered
ompositions are 'Love's Been Good To Me'
ecorded by Frank Sinatra on an album of

McKuen songs, *A Man Alone ...*), 'I Think Of You'
(music by Francis Lai and a hit for Perry Como),
'Soldiers Who Want To Be Heroes', 'The World I
Used To Know', 'Jean', 'Doesn't Anybody Know
My Name?', and 'The Importance Of The Rose'.
He also translated/adapted many of Brel's
compositions for English-speaking artists,
producing such well-known songs as 'If You Go
Away', 'Amsterdam', and 'Seasons In The Sun' (a
hit for both the Kingston Trio and Terry Jacks).
McKuen disappeared from the limelight in 1982
after being diagnosed with clinical depression,
but continued to write from his southern
California base. He surfaced occasionally during
the 90s, providing voiceovers for episodes of *The
Little Mermaid* and *The Critic* and appearing at
1997's Carnegie Hall tribute to Frank Sinatra.
● ALBUMS: include *Lazy Afternoon* (Liberty
1956) ★★★, *Summer Love* film soundtrack
(Decca 1958) ★★★, *Anywhere I Wander* (Decca
1958) ★★★, *Alone After Dark* (Decca 1958)
★★★, as the San Sebastian Strings *The Sea*
(Warners 1967) ★★★, *Through European
Windows* (RCA Victor 1967) ★★★, as the San
Sebastian Strings *The Earth* (Warners 1967)
★★★, *Listen To The Warm* (RCA 1968) ★★★, as
the San Sebastian Strings *The Sky* (Warners 1968)
★★★, *Lonesome Cities* (Warners 1968) ★★★,
Joanna film soundtrack (Stateside 1969) ★★, as
the San Sebastian Strings *Home To The Sea*
(Warners 1969) ★★★, *Rod McKuen At Carnegie
Hall* (Warners 1969) ★★★, as the San Sebastian
Strings *For Lovers* (Warners 1969) ★★★, *The
Prime Of Miss Jean Brodie* film soundtrack
(Stateside 1969) ★★★, *New Ballads* (Warners
1970) ★★★, as the San Sebastian Strings *The Soft
Sea* (Warners 1970) ★★★, *Rod McKuen Live In
London!* (Warners 1970) ★★, *Pastorale* (Warners
1971) ★★★★, *Rod McKuen Grand Tour* (Warners
1971) ★★★★, *A Boy Named Charlie Brown* film
soundtrack (Columbia 1971) ★★★, *McKuen
Country* (Columbia 1976) ★★★, *More Rod '77*
(Stanyan 1977) ★★, *Turntable* (Stanyan 1980)
★★, *Rod On Record* (Stanyan 1982) ★★.
● COMPILATIONS: *Greatest Hits Of Rod McKuen*
(Warners 1969) ★★★, *The Best Of Rod McKuen*
(RCA 1969) ★★★, as the San Sebastian Strings
The Complete Sea (Warners 1970) ★★★, *Rod
McKuen's Greatest Hits 2* (Warners 1970) ★★★.
● FURTHER READING: all by Rod McKuen *And
Autumn Came* (poetry). *Stanyan Street & Other
Sorrows* (poetry). *Listen To The Warm* (poetry).
Lonesome Cities (poetry). *In Someone's Shadow*
(poetry). *Twelve Years Of Christmas* (poetry).
Caught In The Quiet (poetry). *Fields Of Wonder*
(poetry). *And To Each Season* (poetry). *Moment
To Moment*. *Come To Me In Silence*
(poetry). *Seasons In The Sun* (novel). *Beyond The
Boardwalk* (poetry). *Celebrations Of The Heart*
(poetry). *The Sea Around Me ...* (poetry). *Alone*
(novel). *Finding My Father: One Man's Search For
Identity* (prose). *Hand In Hand* (novel). *Coming
Close To The Earth* (poetry). *We Touch The Sky*
(poetry). *Love's Been Good To Me* (novel). *The

Power Bright And Shining (poetry). *A Book Of Days* (poetry). *Looking For A Friend* (novel). *An Outstretched Hand* (prose). *The Beautiful Strangers* (poetry). *Book Of Days And A Month Of Sundays* (poetry). *Too Many Midnight's* (novel). *The Sound Of Solitude* (poetry). *Watch For The Wind* (novel). *Suspension Bridge* (poetry). *Intervals* (poetry). *Valentines* (poetry).
● FILMS: *Rock, Pretty Baby* (1956), *Summer Love* (1958), *Wild Heritage* (1958).

McWILLIAMS, DAVID

b. 4 July 1945, Cregagh, Belfast, Northern Ireland. The subject of an overpowering publicity campaign engineered by his manager Phil Solomon, McWilliams was featured on the front, inside and back covers of several consecutive issues of the *New Musical Express*, which extolled the virtues of a new talent. He was incessantly plugged on Radio Caroline. Much was made of his rebellious youth and affinity with Irish music, yet the singer's debut release, 'The Days Of Pearly Spencer'/'Harlem Lady', revealed a grasp of pop's dynamics rather than those of folk. The former song was both impressive and memorable, as was the pulsating follow-up, 'Three O'Clock Flamingo Street', but McWilliams was unable to shake the 'hype' tag which accompanied his launch. His manager believed that Williams a more promising protégé than his other star artist, Van Morrison of Them, but his faith was unrewarded. Williams disliked live performance and failed to show his true talent in front of an audience. Neither single charted and a period of reassessment followed before the artist re-emerged the following decade with a series of charming, folk-influenced collections. In April 1992 Marc Almond took 'The Days Of Pearly Spencer' back into the UK charts.
● ALBUMS: *Singing Songs By David McWilliams* (Major Minor 1967) ★★★, *David McWilliams Vol. 2* (Major Minor 1967) ★★, *Volume III* (Major Minor 1968) ★★, *Lord Offaly* (Dawn/Pye 1972) ★★★, *The Beggar And The Priest* (Dawn 1973) ★★★, *Living's Just A State Of Mind* (Dawn 1974) ★★★, *David McWilliams* (EMI 1977) ★★, *Don't Do It For Love* (EMI 1978) ★★, *Wounded* (Carmel 1982) ★★.
● COMPILATIONS: *The Days Of Pearly Spencer* (Major Minor 1971) ★★★★, *The Best Of The EMI Years* (EMI 1992) ★★★, *The Days Of David McWilliams* (RPM 2001) ★★★★.

MEEK, JOE

b. Robert George Meek, 5 April 1929, Newent, Gloucestershire, England, d. 3 February 1967, London, England. Britain's premier independent record producer of the early 60s, Meek was equally renowned for his pioneering recording techniques and eccentric personality. His career began in 1954, when he joined IBC, the leading independent recording studio of the era. Originally an engineer, he worked on a number of hits, including Lonnie Donegan' 'Cumberland Gap', Frankie Vaughan's 'Gree Door', Johnny Duncan's 'Last Train To Sa Fernando' and Humphrey Lyttelton's 'Ba Penny Blues'. He also turned his hand t songwriting, penning Tommy Steele's 'Put Ring On Her Finger' in 1958. By 1960, he had se up Lansdowne Studios in west London, wher he worked with producer Denis Preston o recordings by various popular jazz artists. An il advised expansion policy encouraged Meek launch Triumph Records, which enjoyed a h with Michael Cox's 'Angela Jones' before rapidl winding down its activities. Thereafter, Mee concentrated on leasing tapes to major label using the title RGM Sound. He worked from converted studio situated above a shop i Holloway Road, north London, and it was her that he created the unusual sounds that were t become his hallmark.

His first major hit as a producer was Joh Leyton's 'Johnny Remember Me', a atmospheric, eerily echo-laden affair whic topped the UK charts in 1961. Leyton followe up with other Meek-produced successes including 'Wild Wind', 'Son, This Is She' an 'Lonely City'. With Geoff Goddard composin suitably ethereal material, Meek enjoye further vicarious chart action with Mike Berr ('Tribute To Buddy Holly') and backing band th Outlaws ('Swingin' Low' and 'Ambush'). B 1962, the increasingly inventive producer ha reached his apogee on the spacey instrumenta 'Telstar', which took the Tornados to the top o the charts on both sides of the Atlantic. He wa now hailed as a genuine original, with a innovative flair unmatched by any of his rival The accolades were to prove short-lived. The mid-60s beat boom spearheaded by the Beatle seriously dented Meek's credibility an commercial standing. His work wa increasingly regarded as novel, rather tha important, and his love for gimmicks too precedence on recordings by Screaming Lor Sutch and others. Meek responded with th much publicized Heinz, who reached the Top 1 in 1963 with the Eddie Cochran tribute, 'Jus Like Eddie'. The same year Meek was arreste for 'importuning' at a public convenience, an at a time when homosexuality was frowne upon Meek's private life remained a dark secret Fortunately, although many of his heterosexua male artists were aware of his penchant fo young men they were loyal to Meek, making i clear that the music was their business.

Meek's commercial fortunes continued t prosper with the swirling 'Have I The Right?', 1964 UK chart-topper for the Honeycombs, bu this was to be his last major success. By 1965, h seemed something of an anachronism, and hi production techniques seemed leaden an predictable rather than startling. The departur of songwriter Geoff Goddard weakened th supply of good material, and a motley series o

flops left record companies disenchanted. Meek's tempestuous personality and often violent behaviour alienated many old friends, while his homosexuality produced feelings of self-loathing and engendered a fear of imminent scandal. His mental instability worsened after experimenting with LSD and there were successive personal and business problems. He became paranoid about his professional work and was also being blackmailed for small amounts of money from past sexual partners. On 3 February 1967, he was involved in a bizarre shooting incident in which he fatally shot his landlady before turning the gun on himself. It was the end of a sometimes brilliant but frustratingly erratic career.
● ALBUMS: with the Blue Men *I Hear A New World* (RPM 1991) ★★★.
● COMPILATIONS: *The Joe Meek Story Volume 1* (Sequel 1992) ★★★★, *It's Hard To Believe It: The Amazing World Of Joe Meek* (Razor & Tie 1995) ★★★, *Joe Meek Presents 304 Holloway Road* (Sequel 1996) ★★★, *Intergalactic Intros* (Diamond 1997) ★★★, *The Joe Meek Story Volume 5: The Early Years* (Sequel 1997) ★★★★, *Joe Meek: Hidden Gems Volume 1* (Diamond 1998) ★★★, *Joe Meek's Groups: Crawdaddy Simone* (RPM 2001) ★★★.
● FURTHER READING: *The Legendary Joe Meek: The Telstar Man*, John Repsch.

MELCHER, TERRY

b. 8 February 1942, New York City, New York, USA. The son of actress/singer Doris Day the artist's early recordings, credited to Terry Day, presaged his period as the youngest ever staff producer with the CBS Records label. He brought singer Bruce Johnston to the company for *Surfin' 'Round The World* (1963), and together the pair oversaw the career of the Rip Chords, before recording a series of excellent singles as Bruce And Terry. Melcher's concurrent productions for Paul Revere And The Raiders proved particularly fruitful, engendering US Top 10 singles 'Kicks', 'Hungry' and 'Good Thing' (all 1966) and a run of eight consecutive albums. However, it is for work with the Byrds that this period is best recalled, and his empathic skills enhanced the band's early folk-rock sets, *Mr Tambourine Man* and *Turn! Turn! Turn!*, as well as later selections, *Ballad Of Easy Rider*, *Untitled* and *Byrdmaniax*. In 1973, band members Roger McGuinn, Chris Hillman and Clarence White joined Johnston and Ry Cooder on *Terry Melcher*, but this introspective set failed to rise above cult status. The artist subsequently set up Equinox, a name derived from an earlier production company. He enjoyed a measure of success with David Cassidy, but Melcher's attempt to rekindle his solo career with *Royal Flush* proved less rewarding. In 1978, Melcher, who many believe was the intended victim of the infamous Sharon Tate murders, left the US

for Britain, reportedly in fear of his life from the remnants of the Charles Manson tribe. He subsequently remained out of the limelight.
● ALBUMS: *Terry Melcher* (CBS 1973) ★★, *Royal Flush* (CBS 1976) ★★.

MERSEYBEATS

Originally called the Mavericks, this Liverpudlian quartet comprised Tony Crane (vocals/lead guitar), Billy Kinsley (vocals/bass), David Ellis (rhythm guitar) and Frank Sloan (drums). In 1962, long before the Beatles put Liverpool on the musical map, they renamed themselves the Merseybeats. Early line-up changes saw Ellis and Sloan replaced by Aaron Williams and John Banks. By mid-1963, Beatlemania had engulfed the UK, and A&R representatives descended upon Liverpool in search of talent. The Merseybeats were scooped up by Fontana and initially signed by Brian Epstein, but left their new mentor within weeks, following an argument over image. Burt Bacharach and Hal David's 'It's Love That Really Counts' gave them a minor hit, but it was the relatively unknown songwriter Peter Lee Stirling (see Daniel Boone) who penned their biggest hit, 'I Think Of You'. Although essentially balladeers on single, the group's EPs had a grittier edge.
The *On Stage* EP, with its use of monochrome photography, was extremely progressive in design terms, as it did not feature the band on the cover, while their debut album included a variety of old musical standards. Pop star pressures prompted founding member Kinsley to leave the group briefly, but he returned in time for their third major hit, 'Wishin' And Hopin''. Other members included Bob Garner, who was himself replaced by Johnny Gustafson from the Big Three. The eclipse of the Mersey Sound eventually took its toll on the group, although a change of management to Kit Lambert brought two more minor hits, 'I Love You, Yes I Do' and 'I Stand Accused'. In January 1966, the group split, paving the way for hit duo the Merseys. In later years, Tony Crane reactivated the group, which still performs regularly on the cabaret circuit.
● ALBUMS: *The Merseybeats* (Fontana 1964) ★★★★.
● COMPILATIONS: *Greatest Hits* (Look 1977) ★★★, *The Merseybeats: Beat And Ballads* (Edsel 1982) ★★★★, *The Very Best Of The Merseybeats* (Spectrum 1997) ★★★★.

MIGHTY BABY

This UK rock group was formed in 1968 around Alan 'Bam' King (b. 18 September 1946, Kentish Town, London, England; guitar), Mike Evans (bass) and Roger Powell (drums), all founder members of the Action, one of London's most exciting Mod groups. Late-period arrivals Martin Stone (guitar, ex-Savoy Brown) and Ian Whiteman (piano, saxophone) completed

Mighty Baby, a name suggested by their manager, John Curd. The quintet's self-titled debut album, released on Curd's self-explanatory Head Records, was a skilful blend of strong melody and instrumental dexterity, exemplified on the opening composition, 'Egyptian Tomb'. Their improvisatory prowess was even greater on live performances, where Stone's imaginative soloing combined with Whiteman's woodwind and keyboard passages, creating a mesmerising sound. The group's second album, *A Jug Of Love*, issued on Mike Vernon's Blue Horizon Records label, captured this spirit of adventure, but Mighty Baby's potential was suddenly shorn when Whiteman, Evans and Powell, who had each accepted the Sufi faith, left to form a new group, the Habibiyya. As such they recorded one album, *If Man But Knew*, in 1972, before pursuing careers as session musicians, notably for Richard Thompson and Sandy Denny. Stone latterly formed Chilli Willi And The Red Hot Peppers with fellow guitarist Phil Lithman, before abandoning music in favour of antiquarian books. King meanwhile joined pub-rock favourites Ace.
● ALBUMS: *Mighty Baby* (Head 1969) ★★★, *A Jug Of Love* (Blue Horizon 1971) ★★★, *Live In The Attic* (Rolled Gold 2001) ★★.
● COMPILATIONS: *Action Speaks Louder Than* credited to the Action (Dojo 1985) ★★.

MIGIL FIVE
Red Lambert (guitar/vocals), Alan Watson (saxophone), Gil Lucas (piano), Lenny Blanche (bass) and Mike Felix (drums/lead vocals) achieved momentary fame when their 'Mockingbird Hill' single reached the UK Top 10 in March 1964, on the strength of a fleeting bluebeat craze. Felix, Blanche and Lucas had previously worked as a jazz trio prior to embracing pop with the addition of Lambert. They recorded as the Migil Four before adding Watson at the suggestion of trumpeter Kenny Ball. Despite inordinate press coverage, the group was unable to repeat this success. They later became stalwarts of the cabaret circuit before disintegrating when Felix began a solo career.
● ALBUMS: *Mockingbird Hill* (Pye 1964) ★★★.
● COMPILATIONS: *Mockin' Bird Hill (The Pye Anthology)* (Sequel 1998) ★★★.

MILLENNIUM
This Los Angeles-based act emerged in 1967, when two former members of Ballroom, producer/songwriter Curt Boettcher (b. 7 January 1944, Eau Claire, Wisconsin, USA, d. 14 June 1987, Los Angeles), and guitarist Lee Mallory, joined forces with singer/guitarist Michael Fennelly b. 1948, New Jersey, New York, USA. Doug Rhodes (organ/bass), Sandy Salisbury (guitar) and Ron Edgar (drums) – all ex-Music Machine – and Joey Stec (guitar) completed the line-up of an act enhanced

considerably by the production skills of Gary Usher. *Begin* offered the sweet, close harmonies of west coast contemporaries the Association and Harper's Bizarre but, despite considerable acclaim, it was not a commercial success, and the unit was officially disbanded soon afterwards. The musicians also contributed to the concurrent Boettcher/Usher project, Sagittarius, while Fennelly, Rhodes and Edgar subsequently formed Bigshot. The UK Poptones label reissued recordings by all the artists connected with this family of musicians.
● ALBUMS: *Begin* (Columbia 1968) ★★★★.
Solo: Joey Stec *Album* 1969 recording (Poptones 2000) ★★★. Sandy Salisbury *Sandy Salisbury* 1969 recording (Poptones 2000) ★★★.
● COMPILATIONS: *Again!* (Poptones 2000) ★★★.

MILLER, MRS
b. Elva Miller, California, USA. Mrs Miller derives her chief notoriety from her popularity among collectors of musical exotica. Her *modus operandi* involves a seasoned although tuneless melodramatic delivery, accompanying whistles and wholly indulgent, untutored phrasing. Her versions of 'Catch A Falling Star' and 'A Hard Day's Night' reveal her as a natural precursor to the worst elements of karaoke, although she did manage chart entries for the atonal splendour of 'Downtown' and 'A Lover's Concerto', in 1966.
● COMPILATIONS: *Greatest Hits* (Capitol 1966) ★★★, *Ultra Lounge: Wild, Cool & Swingin'* (Capitol 1999) ★★★.

MILLER, ROGER
b. 2 January 1936, Fort Worth, Texas, USA, d. 25 October 1992, Los Angeles, California, USA. Miller was brought up in Erick, Oklahoma, and during the late 50s, moved to Nashville, where he worked as a songwriter. His 'Invitation To The Blues' was a minor success for Ray Price, as was '(In The Summertime) You Don't Want Love' for Andy Williams. Miller himself enjoyed a hit on the country charts with the portentously titled 'When Two Worlds Collide'. In 1962, he joined Faron Young's band as a drummer and also wrote 'Swiss Maid', a major hit for Del Shannon. By 1964, Miller was signed to Mercury Records' Smash label, and secured a US Top 10 hit with 'Dang Me'. The colloquial title was reinforced by some humorous, macabre lyrics ('They ought to take a rope and hang me'). The song brought Miller several Grammy Awards, and the following year, he enjoyed an international Top 10 hit with 'King Of The Road'. This stoical celebration of the hobo life, with its jazz-influenced undertones, became his best-known song.
The relaxed 'Engine Engine No. 9' was another US Top 10 hit during 1965, and at the end of the year, Miller once more turned his attention to the UK market with 'England Swings'. This affectionate, slightly bemused tribute to

swinging London at its zenith neatly summed up the tourist brochure view of the city ('bobbies on bicycles two by two . . . the rosy red cheeks of the little children'). Another international hit, the song was forever associated with Miller. The singer's chart fortunes declined the following year, and a questionable cover version of Elvis Presley's 'Heartbreak Hotel' barely reached the US Top 100. In 1968, Miller secured his last major hit with a poignant reading of Bobby Russell's 'Little Green Apples', which perfectly suited his understated vocal style. Thereafter, Miller moved increasingly towards the country market and continued performing regularly throughout America. In 1982, he appeared on the album *Old Friends* with Ray Price and Willie Nelson. Miller's vocals were featured in the Walt Disney cartoon *Robin Hood*, and in the mid-80s he wrote a Broadway musical, *Big River*, based on Mark Twain's *The Adventures Of Huckleberry Finn*. Roger Miller finally lost his battle with cancer when, with his wife Mary and son Roger Jnr. at his bedside, he died on 25 October 1992. A most popular man with his fellow artists, he was also a great humorist and his general outlook was once neatly summed up when he told the backing band on the *Grand Ole Opry*, 'I do this in the key of B natural, which is my philosophy in life.'
● ALBUMS: *Roger Miller* (Camden 1964) ★★★, *Roger And Out* (Smash 1964) ★★★, *Wild Child* aka *The Country Side Of Roger Miller* (Starday 1965) ★★★, *The Return Of Roger Miller* (Smash 1965) ★★★, *The 3rd Time* (Smash 1965) ★★★, *Words And Music* (Smash 1966) ★★★, *Walkin' In The Sunshine* (Smash 1967) ★★★, *A Tender Look At Love* (Smash 1968) ★★★, *Roger Miller* (Smash 1969) ★★★, *Roger Miller* (Smash 1970) ★★, *Waterhole Three* film soundtrack (Columbia 1973) ★★, *Off The Wall* (Windsong 1978) ★★★, *Making A Name For Myself* (20th Century 1980) ★★, *Motive Series* (Mercury 1981) ★★★, with Willie Nelson *Old Friends* (Columbia 1982) ★★★, *The Big Industry* (Fundamental 1988) ★★★.
● COMPILATIONS: *Golden Hits* (Smash 1965) ★★★★, *Little Green Apples* (Pickwick 1976) ★★★★, *Best Of Roger Miller* (Phillips 1978) ★★★★, *Greatest Hits* (RCA 1985) ★★★★, *Best Of Roger Miller, Volume 1: Country Tunesmith* (PolyGram 1991) ★★★★★, *The Best Of Roger Miller, Volume 2: King Of The Road* (Mercury 1992) ★★★★, *King Of The Road* 3-CD box set (Mercury Nashville 1995) ★★★★, *Super Hits* (Epic 1996) ★★, *The Best Of Roger Miller* (Spectrum 1998) ★★★.

MILLIE

b. Millicent Small, 6 October 1942, Clarendon, Jamaica, West Indies. After leaving home at the age of 13 to further her singing career in Kingston, Millie recorded several tracks with producer Coxsone Dodd, who teamed her with Roy Panton. As Roy And Millie, they achieved local success with 'We'll Meet' and 'Oh, Shirley'

and caught the attention of entrepreneur Chris Blackwell. On 22 June 1964, Millie accompanied Blackwell to the UK and recorded Harry Edwards' 'Don't You Know?', before being presented with the catchy 'My Boy Lollipop', formerly a US R&B hit for Barbie Gaye, which became a UK number/US number 2 hit, the first crossover ska record. However, chart fame proved ephemeral. A carbon-copy follow-up, 'Sweet William', was only a minor hit, and 'Bloodshot Eyes' failed to reach the Top 40. Thereafter, she languished in relative obscurity. Even a brief collaboration with Jackie Edwards in Jackie And Millie, and a nude photo-spread in a men's magazine failed to revitalize her career. Ultimately handicapped by her novelty hit, Millie's more serious work, such as the self-chosen *Millie Sings Fats Domino*, was sadly ignored.
● ALBUMS: with Jackie Edwards *Pledging My Love* (1967) ★★★.
● COMPILATIONS: with Jackie Edwards *The Best Of Jackie & Millie* (1968) ★★★, *The Best Of* (Trojan 1970) ★★★.

MILLS, MRS.

b. Gladys Mills, 1922, England, d. 24 February 1978, England. Mills was a popular 50s performer when pianists of the calibre of Winifred Atwell were in vogue. The British wartime spirit of gathering around the 'ol' joanna' to sing songs was a bonding and uplifting tradition. The partygoers of the wartime generation continued the tradition into the 50s and 60s, and judging by the continuing release of albums such as this, into the 70s and 80s. Great for background music at parties, but as concentrated listening, there can be few worse trials of torture. Mills took all the popular tunes of old and ran them together in tinkly piano medleys. Never a massive success chart-wise, her albums sold reasonably well in the UK, and she made countless television appearances, including several on the *Wheeltappers And Shunters Social Club* and the *Billy Cotton Band Show*.
● ALBUMS: *Come To My Party* (1966) ★★★, *Mrs Mills' Party Pieces* (1968) ★★★, *Let's Have Another Party* (1969) ★★★, *I'm Mighty Glad* (1971) ★★★, *All-Time Party Dances* (1978) ★★★, *Piano Party Time* (1984) ★★★, *An Hour Of Mrs Mills* (1987) ★★★.

MIMMS, GARNET, AND THE ENCHANTERS

b. Garrett Mimms, 16 November 1933, Ashland, West Virginia, USA. A former member of Philadelphia-based gospel groups the Evening Stars and the Norfolk Four, Mimms formed a secular quintet, the Gainors, in 1958. The line-up included future soul star Howard Tate, as well as Sam Bell, Willie Combo and John Jefferson. Over the next three years, the Gainors made several singles for Cameo Records, Mercury Records and Tally-Ho which, although

unsuccessful, betrayed a contemporary soul feel. The group subsequently evolved into Garnet Mimms And The Enchanters, where the singer and Sam Bell were joined by Charles Boyer and Zola Pearnell. Signed to United Artists Records in 1963, they came under the tutelage of writer/producer Jerry Ragovoy. His inspired work helped create some of urban R&B's finest moments. The impassioned 'Cry Baby' was an immediate US R&B number 1/pop number 4 hit, while 'Baby Don't You Weep' and 'For Your Precious Love' consolidated their arrival. The group split in 1964, when Mimms embarked on a solo career. Although the Enchanters found a new vocalist and continued to record, they were overshadowed by their former leader. Mimms' subsequent releases, 'Look Away', 'It Was Easier To Hurt Her' and 'I'll Take Good Care Of You', were artistic triumphs, pitting the singer's church roots against Ragovoy's sophisticated backdrop. Such excellent records were not always well received, and in 1967, Mimms was demoted to United Artists' subsidiary Veep. 'My Baby' and 'Roll With The Punches' followed, but the singer's tenuous position was confirmed when the latter was only released in Britain. Ragovoy then took Mimms to Verve Records (where he was also producing Howard Tate), but the four singles that appeared, although good, found little favour. It was not until 1977 that the singer returned to the chart. Credited to Garnet Mimms And The Truckin' Company, 'What It Is' was a minor R&B hit and even clipped the UK chart at number 44. Mimms is now a born-again Christian and has not recorded for many years.
● ALBUMS: with the Enchanters *Cry Baby And 11 Other Hits* (United Artists 1963) ★★★, *As Long As I Have You* (United Artists 1964) ★★★, *Warm And Soulful* (United Artists 1965) ★★★, *I'll Take Good Care Of You* (United Artists 1966) ★★, *Garnet Mimms Live* (United Artists 1967) ★★, *Garnet Mimms Has It All* (Arista 1978) ★★.
● COMPILATIONS: *Roll With The Punches* (Charly 1986) ★★★, *Cry Baby: Garnet Mimms And The Enchanters* (Collectables 1991) ★★★★, *Cry Baby: The Best Of Garnett Mimms* (EMI 1993) ★★★★, *Best Of Garnett Mimms* (Alliance 1997) ★★★.

MINDBENDERS

Originally a backing group for Wayne Fontana, the Mindbenders comprised Eric Stewart (b. 20 January 1945; guitar), Bob Lang (10 January 1946; bass) and Ric Rothwell (b. 11 March 1944; drums). In October 1965, they split with their leader and early the following year enjoyed a transatlantic number 2 hit with the Carole Bayer Sager/Toni Wine composition, 'A Groovy Kind Of Love'. The excellent follow-up, 'Can't Live With You, Can't Live Without You', failed to chart, while its successor 'Ashes To Ashes' was only a minor hit. A cameo appearance in the film *To Sir With Love* maintained the group's profile and they continued to record material by name writers such as Rod Argent and Robert Knight, but to no avail. A brave stab with an average cover of the Box Tops' 'The Letter' scraped into the Top 50, but shortly after the release of 'Uncle Joe The Ice Cream Man' in March 1968, the group dissolved. Eric Stewart and latter-day Mindbender Graham Gouldman went on to form Hotlegs and 10cc, while Bob Lang reappeared in Racing Cars.
● ALBUMS: *The Mindbenders* (Fontana 1966) ★★★, *With Woman In Mind* (Fontana 1967) ★★★.

MINGUS, CHARLES

b. 22 April 1922, Nogales, Arizona, USA, d. 5 January 1979, Cuernavaca, Mexico. Mingus was never allowed the luxury of the feeling of belonging. Reactions to his mixed ancestry (he had British-born, Chinese, Swedish and African-American grandparents) produced strong feelings of anger and reinforced his sense of persecution. However, this alienation, coupled with his own deep sensitivity and tendency to dramatize his experiences, provided substantial fuel for an artistic career of heroic turmoil and brilliance. Formative musical experiences included both the strictures of European classical music and the uninhibited outpourings of the congregation of the local Holiness Church, which he attended with his stepmother. There he heard all manner of bluesy vocal techniques, moaning, audience-preacher responses, wild vibrato and melismatic improvisation, along with the accompaniment of cymbals and trombones – all of it melding into an early gospel precursor of big band that heavily influenced Mingus' mature compositional and performance style. Other influences were hearing Duke Ellington's band, and recordings of Richard Strauss' tone poems and works by Debussy, Ravel, Bach and Beethoven.
Thwarted in his early attempts to learn trombone, Mingus switched from cello to double bass at high school. He studied composition with Lloyd Reese and was encouraged by Red Callender to study bass with Herman Rheimschagen of the New York Philharmonic. He developed a virtuoso bass technique and began to think of the bass finger-board as similar to a piano keyboard. His first professional dates as a bass player included gigs with New Orleans players Kid Ory and Barney Bigard, and then stints with the Louis Armstrong Orchestra (1943-45) and Lionel Hampton (1947), but it was with the Red Norvo Trio (1950) that he first gained national recognition for his virtuosity. Work with other great pioneers of his generation such as Charlie Parker, Miles Davis, Thelonious Monk, Bud Powell, Sonny Stitt, Stan Getz, Lee Konitz, Dizzy Gillespie, Quincy Jones and Teddy Charles continued throughout the 50s. He joined Duke Ellington's band briefly in 1953, but a more artistically profitable association with his

hero occurred with the trio album *Money Jungle*, which they made with Max Roach in 1962. Mingus was a pioneer of black management and artist-led record labels, forming Debut in 1953, and the Charles Mingus label in 1964. His early compositions were varying in success, often due to the difficulty of developing and maintaining an ensemble to realize his complex ideas.

He contributed works to the Jazz Composers' Workshop from 1953 until the foundation of his own workshop ensemble in 1955. Here, he was able to make sparing use of notation, transmitting his intentions from verbal and musical instructions sketched at the piano or on the bass. Mingus' originality as a composer first began to flourish under these circumstances, and with players such as Dannie Richmond, Rahsaan Roland Kirk, Jaki Byard, Jimmy Knepper and Booker Ervin he developed a number of highly evolved works. Crucial among his many innovations in jazz was the use of non-standard chorus structures, contrasting sections of quasi-'classical' composed material with passages of freeform and group improvisations, often of varying tempos and modes, in complex pieces knitted together by subtly evolving musical motifs. He developed a 'conversational' mode of interactive improvisation, and pioneered melodic bass playing. Such pieces as *The Black Saint And The Sinner Lady* (1963) show enormous vitality and a great depth of immersion in all jazz styles, from New Orleans and gospel to bebop and free jazz. Another multi-sectional piece, 'Meditations For A Pair Of Wire Cutters', from the album *Portrait* (1964), is one of many that evolved gradually under various titles. Sections from it can be heard on the 1963 recording *Mingus Plays Piano*, there called 'Myself When I Am Real'. It was renamed 'Praying With Eric' after the tragic death of Eric Dolphy, who made magnificent contributions to many Mingus compositions, but especially to this intensely moving piece.

In the mid-60s, financial and psychological problems began to take their toll, as poignantly recorded in Thomas Reichman's 1968 film *Mingus*. He toured extensively during this period, presenting a group of ensemble works. In 1971, Mingus was much encouraged by the receipt of a Guggenheim fellowship in composition, and the publication of his astonishing autobiography, *Beneath The Underdog*. The book opens with a session conducted by a psychiatrist, and the work reveals Mingus' self-insight, intelligence, sensitivity and tendency for self-dramatization. Touring continued until the gradual paralysis brought by the incurable disease Amyotrophic Lateral Sclerosis prevented him doing anything more than presiding over recordings. His piece 'Revelations' was performed in 1978 by the New York Philharmonic under the direction of Gunther Schuller, who also resurrected *Epitaph* in 1989. Also in 1978, Mingus was honoured at

the White House by Jimmy Carter and an all-star jazz concert. News of his death, aged 56, in Mexico was marked by many tributes from artists of all fields. Posthumously, the ensemble Mingus Dynasty continued to perform his works.

Mingus summed up the preoccupations of his time in a way that transcended racial and cultural divisions, while simultaneously highlighting racial and social injustices. Introducing the first 1964 performance of *Meditations*, Mingus told the audience: 'This next composition was written when Eric Dolphy told me there was something similar to the concentration camps down South, [. . .] where they separated [. . .] the green from the red, or something like that; and the only difference between the electric barbed wire is that they don't have gas chambers and hot stoves to cook us in yet. So I wrote a piece called *Meditations* as to how to get some wire cutters before someone else gets some guns to us.' Off-mike, he can be heard saying to fellow musicians: 'They're gonna burn us; they'll try.' In the turmoil of his life and artistic achievements, and in his painful demise, Mingus became his own artistic creation. A desperate, passionate icon for the mid-twentieth century to which all can relate in some way, he articulated the emotional currents of his time in a way superior to that of almost any other contemporary jazz musician.

● ALBUMS: *Strings And Keys* (Debut 1953) ★★★★, *Intrusions* (Drive Archive 1954) ★★★, with Thad Jones *Jazz Collaborations* 10-inch album (Debut 1954) ★★★★, *Jazz Experiments* (Jazztone 1954) ★★★, *Charlie Mingus* reissued as *Jazz Composers Workshop* (Savoy 1955) ★★★, *Jazzical Moods, Volume 1* 10-inch album (Period 1955) ★★★, *Jazzical Moods Volume 2* 10-inch album (Period 1955) ★★★, *Mingus At The Bohemia* (Debut 1956) ★★★, *The Charles Mingus Quintet Plus Max Roach* (Debut 1956) ★★★, *Pithecanthropus Erectus* (Atlantic 1956) ★★★★, *Scenes In The City* (Affinity 1957) ★★★, *The Clown* aka *Reincarnation Of A Lovebird* (Atlantic 1957) ★★★, *Mingus Three* (Jubilee 1957) ★★★, *East Coasting* (Bethlehem 1958) ★★★★, *A Modern Jazz Symposium Of Music And Poetry* (Bethlehem 1958) ★★★★, *East Coasting* (Bethlehem 1958) ★★★, *Duke's Choice* aka *A Modern Jazz Symposium Of Music And Poetry* (Bethlehem 1958) ★★★, *Wonderland* reissued as *Jazz Portraits* (United Artists 1959) ★★★, *Blues & Roots* (Atlantic 1959) ★★★★★, *Mingus Ah-Um* (Columbia 1959) ★★★★★, *Mysterious Blues* (Candid 1960) ★★★, *Mingus Dynasty* (Columbia 1960) ★★★★, *Pre-Bird* aka *Mingus Revisited* (EmArcy 1960) ★★★, *Mingus At Antibes* (Atlantic 1960) ★★★★, *Charles Mingus Presents Charles Mingus!* (Candid 1960) ★★★★, *Mingus!* (Candid 1960) ★★★★, *Charles Mingus: Mysterious Blues* (Candid 1960) ★★★, *Oh, Yeah!* (Atlantic 1961) ★★★★, *Tonight At Noon* (Atlantic 1961) ★★★, *Chazz!* 1955 recording (Fantasy

1962) ★★★★, with Duke Ellington, Max Roach *Money Jungle* (United Artists 1962) ★★★★, *Town Hall Concert* (United Artists 1963) ★★★, *The Black Saint And The Sinner Lady* (Impulse! 1963) ★★★★★, *Mingus Mingus Mingus Mingus Mingus* (Impulse! 1963) ★★★★, *Paris 1964* (LeJazz/Charly 1964) ★★★, *Live In Stockholm 1964: The Complete Concert* (Royal Jazz 1964) ★★★, *Astral Weeks* (Moon 1964) ★★★, *Revenge* (Revenge 1964) ★★★, *Charlie Mingus Plays Piano* (Impulse! 1964) ★★★★, *The Great Concert Of Charles Mingus* (America/Prestige 1964) ★★★, *Tijuana Moods* 1957 recording (RCA 1964) ★★★★, *Live in Oslo* (Jazz Up 1964) ★★★, *Charles Mingus In Amsterdam Volumes 1 & 2* (Ulysse Musique 1964) ★★★★, *Mingus In Stuttgart Volumes 1 & 2* (Royal Jazz 1964) ★★★, *Mingus In Europe* (Enja 1964) ★★★★, *Right Now: Live At Jazz Workshop* (Fantasy 1964) ★★★★, *Mingus At Monterey* (Charlie Mingus 1964) ★★★★, *Town Hall Concert, Vol. 1* (Charlie Mingus 1965) ★★★★, *Special Music Written For Monterey 1965, But Not Heard* (JWS 1966) ★★★, *My Favourite Quintet* (Charlie Mingus 1966) ★★★★, *Reincarnation Of A Lovebird* (Prestige 1971) ★★★, *With Orchestra* (Denon 1971) ★★, *Let My Children Hear Music* (Columbia 1971) ★★★★, *Charles Mingus And Friends In Concert* (Columbia 1972) ★★★, *Mingus Moves* (Atlantic 1973) ★★★, *Mingus At Carnegie Hall* (Atlantic 1974) ★★★, *Changes One* (Atlantic 1974) ★★★, *Changes Two* (Atlantic 1974) ★★★, *Cumbia And Jazz Fusion* (Atlantic 1977) ★★★, *Three Or Four Shades Of Blues* (Atlantic 1977) ★★★, *Lionel Hampton Presents: The Music Of Charles Mingus* aka *His Final Works* (Gateway 1977) ★★★, *Me, Myself An Eye* (Atlantic 1978) ★★★, *Something Like A Bird* (Atlantic 1978) ★★★, with Joni Mitchell *Mingus* (Asylum 1979) ★★★★, *The Complete Town Hall Concert* 1962 recording (Blue Note 1994) ★★★★.
● COMPILATIONS: *Re-Evaluation: The Impulse! Years* 1963-64 recordings (MCA 1973) ★★★★, *The Art Of Charles Mingus* (Atlantic 1974) ★★★, *Nostalgia In Times Square* 1959 recordings (Columbia 1979) ★★★, *Passions Of A Man: The Complete Atlantic Recordings 1956-1961* 3-LP box set (Atlantic 1979) ★★★★★, *The Complete 1959 CBS Charles Mingus Sessions* 4-LP set (Mosaic 1985) ★★★, *The Young Rebel* 1946-52 recordings (Swingtime 1986) ★★★, *New York Sketch Book 50s* recordings (Charly 1986) ★★★★, *Abstractions* 1954, 1957 recordings (Affinity 1989) ★★★, *Better Git It In Your Soul* 1960 recording (Columbia 1990) ★★★★, *Meditations On Integration* 1964 recording (Bandstand 1990) ★★★, *The Complete Candid Recordings Of Charles Mingus* 4-LP box set (Mosaic 1992) ★★★, *Thirteen Pictures: The Charles Mingus Anthology* 1956-77 recordings (Rhino 1993) ★★★★, *Charles Mingus: The Complete Debut Recordings* 1951-58 recordings 12-CD box set (Debut 1996) ★★★★, *The Legendary Paris Concerts* 1964 recording (Revenge 1996) ★★★, *Passions Of A Man: The*

Complete Atlantic Recordings 1956-1961 6-CD box set (Rhino/Atlantic 1998) ★★★★★, *The Complete 1959 Columbia Sessions* 3-CD box set (Columbia/Legacy 1998) ★★★★★, *The Very Best Of Charles Mingus* (Atlantic 2001) ★★★, *Charles 'Baron' Mingus: West Coast 1945-49* (Uptown 2001) ★★★★.
● VIDEOS: *Charles Mingus Sextet 1964* (Shanachie 1994), *Triumph Of The Underdog* (Academy Video 1998).
● FURTHER READING: *Beneath The Underdog*, Charles Mingus. *Mingus: A Critical Biography*, Brian Priestley. *Revelations*, Charles Mingus. *Charles Mingus, Sein Leben, Seine Musik, Seine Schallplatten*, Horst Weber. *Mingus/Mingus*, Janet Coleman. *Myself When I Am Real: The Life And Music Of Charles Mingus*, Gene Santoro.

MIRACLES

Of all the R&B vocal groups formed in Detroit, Michigan, USA, in the mid-50s, the Miracles proved to be the most successful. They were founded at the city's Northern High School in 1955 by Smokey Robinson (b. William Robinson, 19 February 1940, Detroit, Michigan, USA), Emerson Rogers, Bobby Rogers (b. 19 February 1940, Detroit, Michigan, USA), Ronnie White (b. 5 April 1939, Detroit, Michigan, USA, d. 26 August 1995) and Warren 'Pete' Moore (b. 19 November 1939, Detroit, Michigan, USA). Emerson Rogers left the following year, and was replaced by his sister Claudette, who married Smokey Robinson in 1959. Known initially as the Matadors, the group became the Miracles in 1958, when they made their initial recordings with producer Berry Gordy. He leased their debut, 'Got A Job' (an answer record to the Silhouettes' major hit 'Get A Job'), to End Records, produced a duet by Ron (White) And Bill (Robinson) for Argo, and licensed the classic doo-wop novelty 'Bad Girl' to Chess Records in 1959. The following year, Gordy signed the Miracles directly to his fledgling Motown Records label.
Recognizing the youthful composing talents of Smokey Robinson, he allowed the group virtual free rein in the studio, and was repaid when they issued 'Way Over There', a substantial local hit, and then 'Shop Around', which broke both the Miracles and Motown to a national audience. The song demonstrated the increasing sophistication of Robinson's writing, which provided an unbroken series of hits for the group over the next few years. Their raw, doo-wop sound was further refined on the Top 10 hit 'You Really Got A Hold On Me' in 1962, a soulful ballad that became a worldwide standard after the Beatles covered it in 1963. Robinson was now in demand by other Motown artists: Gordy used him as a one-man hit factory, to mastermind releases by the Temptations and Mary Wells, and the Miracles' own career suffered slightly as a result. They continued to enjoy success in a variety of different styles, mixing dancefloor hits

ch as 'Mickey's Monkey' and 'Going To A Go-
o' with some of Robinson's most durable
llads, such as 'Ooh Baby Baby' and 'The Tracks
f My Tears'. Although Robinson sang lead on
most all the group's recordings, the rest of the
oup provided a unique harmony blend behind
m, while guitarist Marv Tarplin – who co-wrote
veral of their hits – was incorporated as an
nofficial Miracle from the mid-60s onwards.
laudette Robinson stopped touring with the
oup after 1965, although she was still featured
n many of their subsequent releases.
xhausted by several years of constant work,
obinson scaled down his writing commitments
r the group in the mid-60s, when they briefly
orked with Holland/Dozier/Holland and other
otown producers. Robinson wrote their most
mbitious and enduring songs, however,
cluding 'The Tears Of A Clown' in 1966 (a
elated hit in the UK and USA in 1970), 'The
ove I Saw In You Was Just A Mirage', and 'I
econd That Emotion' in 1967. These tracks
pitomized the strengths of Robinson's
ompositions, with witty, metaphor-filled lyrics
ed to aching melody lines and catchy guitar
gures, the latter often provided by Tarplin. Like
any of the veteran Motown acts, the Miracles
ent into a sales slump after 1967 – the year
hen Robinson was given individual credit on
e group's records. Their slide was less
oticeable in Britain, where Motown gained a
op 10 hit in 1969 with a reissue of 'The Tracks
f My Tears', which most listeners imagined was
contemporary record. The success of 'The
ears Of A Clown' prompted a revival in fortune
ter 1970. 'I'm The One You Need' became
nother reissue hit in Britain the following year,
hile 'I Don't Blame You At All', one of their
rongest releases to date, achieved chart
uccess on both sides of the Atlantic.
1 1971, Robinson announced his intention of
aving the Miracles to concentrate on his
osition as vice-president of Motown Records.
is decision belied the title of his final hit with
e group, 'We've Come Too Far To End It Now'
1 1972, and left the Miracles in the unenviable
osition of having to replace one of the most
stinctive voices in popular music. Their choice
as William 'Bill' Griffin (b. 15 August 1950,
etroit, Michigan, USA), who was introduced by
obinson to the group's audiences during a 1972
S tour. The new line-up took time to settle,
hile Smokey Robinson launched a solo career
great acclaim in 1973. The group responded
ith *Renaissance*, which saw them working with
otown luminaries such as Marvin Gaye and
illie Hutch. The following year, they re-
stablished the Miracles as a hit-making force
ith 'Do It Baby' and 'Don'tcha Love It', dance-
rientated singles that appealed strongly to the
oup's black audience. In 1975, 'Love Machine'
ecame the Miracles' first US chart-topper, while
e concept album *City Of Angels* was acclaimed
one of Motown's most progressive releases.

This twin success proved to be the Miracles' last
commercial gasp.
Switching to Columbia Records in 1977, they lost
Billy Griffin, who set out on a little-noticed solo
career. Donald Griffin briefly joined the group in
his place, but the Miracles ceased recording in
1978. Thereafter, Ronnie White and Bill Rogers
steered the outfit into the new decade as a
touring band, before the Miracles disbanded
without any fanfares, only to be re-formed by
Bobby Rogers in 1982. He enlisted Dave Finlay
and Carl Cotton as the new Miracles. Former
members Billy Griffin and Claudette Robinson
(ex-wife of Smokey) recorded solo tracks for Ian
Levine's Motor City label during 1988-91.
Another re-formed group comprising Billy
Griffin, Robinson, Rogers, Donald Griffin, Cotton
and Finlay also recorded for Levine, remaking
'Love Machine' in 1990. White died in 1995 after
losing his battle with leukaemia.
● ALBUMS: *Hi, We're The Miracles* (Tamla 1961)
★★★, *Cookin' With The Miracles* (Tamla 1962)
★★★★, *I'll Try Something New* (Tamla 1962)
★★★, *The Fabulous Miracles* (Tamla 1963) ★★★,
Recorded Live: On Stage (Tamla 1963) ★★,
Christmas With The Miracles (Tamla 1963) ★★,
The Miracles Doin' 'Mickey's Monkey' (Tamla 1963)
★★★, *Going To A Go-Go* (Tamla 1965) ★★★★, *I
Like It Like That* (Tamla 1965) ★★★, *Away We A
Go-Go* (Tamla 1966) ★★★, *Make It Happen*
(Tamla 1967) ★★★, *Special Occasion* (Tamla
1968) ★★★, *Live!* (Tamla 1969) ★★, *Time Out
For Smokey Robinson And The Miracles* (Tamla
1969) ★★★, *Four In Blue* (Tamla 1969) ★★★,
What Love Has Joined Together (Tamla 1970)
★★★, *A Pocket Full Of Miracles* (Tamla 1970)
★★★, *The Season For Miracles* (Tamla 1970)
★★★, *One Dozen Roses* (Tamla 1971) ★★★,
Flying High Together (Tamla 1972) ★★★,
Renaissance (Tamla 1973) ★★★, *Do It Baby*
(Tamla 1974) ★★★, *Don't Cha Love It* (Tamla
1975) ★★, *City Of Angels* (Tamla 1975) ★★★,
The Power Of Music (Tamla 1976) ★★, *Love Crazy*
(Columbia 1977) ★★, *The Miracles* (Columbia
1978) ★★.
● COMPILATIONS: *Greatest Hits From The
Beginning* (Tamla 1965) ★★★★, *Greatest Hits
Volume 2* (Tamla 1968) ★★★★, *1957-72* (Tamla
1972) ★★★★, *Smokey Robinson And The
Miracles' Anthology* (Motown 1973) ★★★★,
Compact Command Performances (Motown 1987)
★★★★, *The Greatest Hits* (Motown 1992)
★★★★, *The 35th Anniversary Collection* 4-CD
box set (Motown Masters 1994) ★★★★, *Early
Classics* (Spectrum 1996) ★★★, *The Ultimate
Collection* (Motown 1998) ★★★★, *Along Came
Love* (Motown 1999) ★★★.
● FURTHER READING: *Smokey: Inside My Life*,
Smokey Robinson and David Ritz.

MISUNDERSTOOD

One of psychedelia's finest bands, the
Misunderstood originated in Riverside,
California, USA, and evolved from a local surfing

outfit, the Blue Notes. Their first line-up – Greg Treadway (guitar), George Phelps (guitar) and Rick Moe (drums) – was augmented by Rick Brown (vocals) and Steve Whiting (bass), before adopting their new name in 1965. Phelps was then replaced by Glenn Ross 'Fernando' Campbell, who played steel guitar. The quintet completed a single, 'You Don't Have To Go'/'Who's Been Talkin'?', before leaving for the UK on the suggestion of UK disc jockey John (Peel) Ravenscroft, then working in San Bernardino, Texas. Treadway was subsequently drafted, and his place was taken by Tony Hill (b. South Shields, Co. Durham, England). The band completed six masters during their London sojourn. 'I Can Take You To The Sun', a hypnotic, atmospheric and ambitious performance, was their only contemporary release, although the rousing 'Children Of The Sun' was issued after their break-up, in 1968. Campbell later re-established the name with several British musicians. Their two blues-cum-progressive singles shared little with the early, trail-blazing unit, and the latter-day version then evolved into Juicy Lucy. Hill meanwhile had departed for High Tide.
● COMPILATIONS: *The Legendary Goldstar Album Plus Golden Glass* (Cherry Red 1984) ★★★, *Before The Dream Faded* (Cherry Red 1992) ★★★★.

MITCHELL, CHAD, TRIO
Chad Mitchell (b. Portland, Oregon, USA), Mike Kobluk and Mike Pugh were students at Gonzaga University in Spokane, Washington, USA, when they formed this influential folk group in 1958. They then crossed America, performing when able, before arriving in New York to secure a recording deal. The following year, Pugh dropped out in favour of Joe Frazier, while the Trio's accompanist, Dennis Collins, was replaced by guitarist Jim McGuinn, who later found fame with the Byrds. The band then embarked on their most successful era, when they became renowned for songs of a satirical or socially-conscious nature. Chad Mitchell left for a solo career in 1965. He was replaced by aspiring songwriter John Denver, but the restructured act, now known as the Mitchell Trio, found it difficult to sustain momentum. Frazier and Kobluk also left the band, which was then sued by its former leader for continuing to use the 'original' name. With the addition of David Boise and Mike Johnson, the new trio was known as Denver, Boise And Johnson, but split up in 1969 when first Johnson, then Denver, left to pursue independent projects. In subsequent years there have been occasional reunions of the original line-up.
● ALBUMS: *The Chad Mitchell Trio Arrives* (Colpix 1960) ★★★, *Mighty Day On Campus* (Kapp 1961) ★★★★, *The Chad Mitchell Trio At The Bitter End* (Kapp 1962) ★★★, *The Chad Mitchell Trio In Action* aka *Blowin' In The Wind*

(Kapp 1962) ★★★, *Singin' Our Mind* (Mercury 1963) ★★★, *The Chad Mitchell Trio In Concert* (Colpix 1964) ★★★, *Reflecting* (Mercury 1964) ★★★, *The Slightly Irreverent Mitchell Trio* (Mercury 1964) ★★★, *Typical American Boys* (Mercury 1965) ★★★, *That's The Way It's Gonna Be* (Mercury 1965) ★★★, *Violets Of Dawn* (Mercury 1966) ★★★, *Mighty Day: The Chad Mitchell Trio Reunion* 1987 recording (Folk Era 1996) ★★★, *The Chad Mitchell Trio Reunion Part 2* 1987 recording (Folk Era 1997) ★★★.
● COMPILATIONS: *The Best Of The Chad Mitchell Trio* (Kapp 1963) ★★★, *The Very Best Of The Chad Mitchell Trio* (Vanguard 1996) ★★, *The Chad Mitchell Trio Collection: The Original Kapp Recordings* (Varèse 1997) ★★★★, *The Best Of The Chad Mitchell Trio: The Mercury Years* (Chronicles/Mercury 1998) ★★★.

MOBY GRAPE
The legend that continues to grow and grow around this late 60s San Francisco rock band is mainly based on their magnificent debut album which fans vainly willed them to repeat. This iconoclastic band was formed in September 1966, with the seminal line-up of Alexander 'Skip' Spence (b. 18 April 1946, Windsor, Ontario, Canada, d. 16 April 1999, Santa Cruz, California, USA; guitar, vocals), Jerry Miller (b. 10 July 1943, Tacoma, Washington, USA; guitar, vocals), Bob Mosley (b. 4 December 1942, Paradise Valley, California, USA; bass, vocals), Don Stevenson (b. 15 October 1942, Seattle, Washington, USA; drums) and Peter Lewis (b. July 1945, Los Angeles, California, USA; guitar, vocals). With record companies queuing up to sign them, they decided to go with CBS Records and became marketing guinea pigs for an unprecedented campaign, whereupon 10 tracks (five singles plus b-sides) were released simultaneously.
Not even the Beatles could have lived up to this kind of launch. Only one of the records dented the US chart, with 'Omaha' reaching a dismal number 88. Had the singles been released in normal sequence, they might all have been hits, as the quality of each song was outstanding. The band fell into immediate disarray, unable to cope with the pressure and hype. The resulting debut, *Moby Grape*, contained all these 10 tracks plus an additional three. The album deservedly reached the US Top 30 album charts, and is now recognized as a classic. The short, brilliantly structured, guitar-based rock songs with fine harmonies still sound fresh in the 90s. The follow-up was a similar success (yet a lesser work) and made the US Top 20 album chart. As with their debut, CBS continued with the ruthless marketing campaign, determined to see a return on their investment, as the band had originally held out for a considerable advance. *Wow* sported a beautiful surrealistic painting collage by Bob Cato, depicting a huge bunch of grapes mixed with an eighteenth-century bear

cene, and came with a free album, *Grape Jam*. Additionally, one of the tracks was recorded at 8 rpm, forcing the listener to get up and change the speed only to hear a spoof item played by Lou Waxman And His Orchestra. Amidst this curious package were some of their finest songs, including Spence's 'Motorcycle Irene', Miller's 'Miller's Blues', Mosley's 'Murder In My Heart For The Judge' and arguably their best track, 'Can't Be So Bad'. Penned by Miller and featuring his stinging guitar solo, this furiously paced heavy rock item is suddenly slowed down and sweetened by an outstanding five-part style harmony. The song failed to chart anywhere.

Spence had departed with drug and mental problems by the time of *Moby Grape '69*, although his ethereal composition 'Seeing' was one of the highlights of an apologetic and occasionally brilliant album (the hype of the past was disclaimed by the 'sincere' sleeve notes). Other notable tracks included Lewis' hymn-like 'I Am Not Willing' and the straightforward rocker 'Truck Driving Man'. A disastrous European tour was arranged, during which the band was constantly overshadowed by the support act Group Therapy. Mosley left on their return to the USA, and allegedly joined the marines. Spence released the extraordinary *Oar*, an album that reflected Spence's condition as a paranoid schizophrenic and subsequently became a cult classic. The rest of the band were forced to fulfil their contract by making a fourth album. The poor-selling and lacklustre *Truly Fine Citizen* was badly received, with most critics having already given up on them. The band then disintegrated, unable to use the name which was and still is owned by their manager, Matthew Katz. The remaining members have appeared as Maby Grope, Mosley Grape, Grape Escape, Fine Vine, the Melvills, the Grape, the Hermans and the Legendary Grape. During one of their many attempts at re-formation, Mosley and Miller actually released a record as Fine Wine. The original five reunited for one more undistinguished album in 1971, *20 Granite Creek*. Out of the mire, only Mosley's 'Gypsy Wedding' showed some promise. Skip Spence delivered the quirky 'Chinese Song', played on a koto, and the silk-voiced Lewis produced 'Horse Out In The Rain' with its unusual timing and extraordinary booming bass.

A live album in 1978 delighted fans, and rumours abounded about various re-formation plans. Some of the band still play together in small clubs and bars, but the magical reunion of the five (just like the five Byrds) can never be. Spence, sadly, was never in any fit state and eventually succumbed to lung cancer in 1999. Unbelievably, it was alleged that Mosley was also diagnosed as a schizophrenic and was living rough on the streets of San Diego. The myth surrounding the band continues to grow as more (outrageous) stories come to light. There is an active fan base on the Internet. Their debut album is one of the true rock/pop classics of the past 30 years (along with Love's *Forever Changes*), and their influence is immense. The 'grape sound' has shown up in many bands over the past 20 years including the Doobie Brothers, R.E.M., the Smithereens, Teenage Fanclub and Weezer, and Robert Plant is a long-term fan. Their appearance at Wetlands, New York, on 6 August 1997 was a delightful surprise. Mosley, Miller and Lewis performed as Moby Grape with ex-Big Brother And The Holding Company Sam Andrew replacing Spence and Randy Guzman replacing Stevenson. Spence died in 1999, leading to a reappraisal of his work by cultists. Moby Grape were, more than any other band from the Bay Area in 1967/8, the true embodiment of the music (but not the culture).

● ALBUMS: *Moby Grape* (Columbia 1967) ★★★★★, *Wow* (Columbia 1967) ★★★, *Grape Jam* (Columbia 1967) ★★★, *Moby Grape '69* (Columbia 1969) ★★★★, *Truly Fine Citizen* (Columbia 1969) ★★★, *20 Granite Creek* (Reprise 1971) ★★★★, *Live Grape* (Escape 1978) ★★★, *Moby Grape* (San Francisco Sound 1983) ★★. Solo: Bob Mosley *Bob Mosley* (Warners 1972) ★★. Peter Lewis *Peter Lewis* (Taxim 1996) ★★★.

● COMPILATIONS: *Great Grape* (Columbia 1973) ★★★, *Vintage Grape* 2-CD box set with unreleased material and alternate takes (Columbia/Legacy 1993) ★★★★★.

MOGG, AMBROSE

b. Andrew Morgan, 1 April 1941, Liverpool, England. Mogg, a catalyst amongst Merseybeat musicians, formed the Caterwaulers in the early 60s and enjoyed local success with 'The Cat Came Back' and other feline songs. He refused to sign with HMV because of the picture of the dog on the label. However, his short time with Decca in 1963 was fraught with problems. Forced to use pugnacious session musicians, Jackie Russell, Gordie Setter and 'Bulldog' Drummer, Mogg's desire to escape from the studio fast turned 'Mean Dog Blues' into a frantic rockabilly classic. Unfortunately for Mogg, the pressing plant was closing for its annual holiday and careless workers approved the record without a hole in its centre. Mogg raged at Decca, who cancelled his contract on grounds of insubordination, saying he should take lessons in manners from the Rolling Stones. A few weeks later, Mogg lost a leg at the Cavern when passionate fans pulled him first one way and then the other. He disappeared into the Catskill Mountains, while 'Mean Dog Blues' became a cult single although the drilling of the holes by collectors is rarely accurate. George Harrison referred to Mogg as an early influence in the biography *The Quiet One* written by Alan Clayson and Mogg's sister Kitty appeared on UK radio during the years he was in exile. Mogg returned to Liverpool in 1989 with nothing in the kitty, but he is clawing his way back into the limelight with sterling work for the Merseycats charity. Music writer Pete Frame and *Record Collector* editor Peter Doggett have both lectured and written about Mogg's standing in the music world. Mogg's reappraisal has been largely due to the writer and broadcaster Spencer Leigh, who has been a major crusader of his work over the past two decades.

● ALBUMS: *Purrfect Alibi* (Whisker 1990) ★★★, *The Litter Tray* (Top-Cat 1996) ★★★, *Plenty Of Pussy* (Purr 2001) ★★★.
● COMPILATIONS: *Four Fingers And A Mogg* (Meeow 1997) ★★★★.

MOJO MEN

This San Francisco-based group – Jimmy Alaimo (vocals/guitar), Paul Curcio (guitar), Don Metchick (organ) and Dennis DeCarr (drums) – was signed to Autumn, the city's leading independent label, in 1965. Here they enjoyed a fruitful artistic relationship with producer Sly Stone, which spawned a minor US hit in 'Dance With Me'. Jan Errico, from stablemates the Vejtables, replaced DeCarr in 1966 as the quartet switched outlets to Reprise Records. The following year they secured a US Top 40 hit with a charming version of Buffalo Springfield's 'Sit Down I Think I Love You', which was engineered and arranged by Van Dyke Parks. The group truncated its name to Mojo in 1968 and, now trimmed to a trio on Metchick's departure, completed the Mojo Magic album before breaking up. Paul Curcio meanwhile founded the Pacific Recording Studio in San Mateo, where Santana recorded their early releases.

● ALBUMS: *Mojo Magic* (Autumn 1968) ★★.
● COMPILATIONS: *Why's Ain't Supposed To Be* (Sundazed 1996) ★★, *Sit Down, It's The Mojo Men* (Sundazed 1996) ★★.

MOJOS

Originally known as the Nomads, this Liverpool beat group was formed in 1962 by Stu James (vocals), Adrian Wilkinson (guitar), Keith Karlson (bass) and John Konrad (drums). They secured early minor fame by winning a songwriting contest that resulted in a recording deal. Pianist Terry O'Toole was added to the line-up prior to the release of the Mojos' debut single, and Nicky Crouch replaced Wilkinson before a follow-up, 'Everything's Alright', was recorded. This energetic 1964 single became a UK Top 10 hit, and the crafted excitement maintained throughout the performance assured its classic status. The group's later releases failed to match this quality, and although a revitalized line-up, consisting of James, Crouch, Lewis Collins (bass) and Aynsley Dunbar (b. 10 January 1946, Liverpool, England; drums) continued as Stu James and the Mojos, they broke up in December 1966. The singer then pursued a career in music publishing and book publishing, while Dunbar joined John Mayall's Bluesbreakers and Collins pursued a acting

career, later starring in the popular UK television series, *The Professionals*.
● COMPILATIONS: *Working* (1982) ★★★.

MONEY, ZOOT

b. George Bruno Money, 17 July 1942, Bournemouth, Dorset, England. A veteran of his hometown's thriving music circuit, Money played in several local rock 'n' roll groups before forming the Big Roll Band in 1961. Its original line-up comprised Roger Collis (guitar), Kevin Drake (tenor saxophone), Johnny King (bass), Peter Brooks (drums) and Zoot on piano and vocals. By 1963, the singer was fronting an all-new line-up of Andy Somers aka Andy Summers (guitar), Nick Newall (saxophone) and Colin Allen (drums), but he left the group for a temporary spot in Alexis Korner's Blue Incorporated. Zoot remained in London when his tenure ended, and his band subsequently joined him there. The Big Roll Band secured a residency at London's prestigious Flamingo Club, and added two new members, Paul Williams (bass/vocals) and Clive Burrow (saxophone), before recording their debut single 'The Uncle Willie'.

In 1965, the group released its first album, *I Should've Been Me*, a compendium of soul and R&B material that enhanced the band's growing reputation. A second album, *Zoot!*, recorded live at Klook's Kleek, introduced newcomer Johnny Almond, who replaced Burrows. This exciting set included a superb James Brown medley and confirmed the group's undoubted strength. However, a devil-may-care attitude undermined their potential, and only one of their excellent singles, 'Big Time Operator' (1966), broached the UK Top 30. Money became famed as much for dropping his trousers onstage as for his undoubted vocal talent, and several of the line-up were notorious imbibers. Yet this lifestyle was reversed in 1967, when Money, Somers and Allen embraced the emergent 'flower-power' movement with Dantalion's Chariot. However, by the following year Zoot had resumed his erstwhile direction with *Transition*, a disappointing release which was pieced together from several sessions.

In 1968, both Money and Somers joined Eric Burdon in his American-based New Animals. Zoot's vocals were heard on a number of tracks with Burdon, notably a lengthy reworking of his Dantalion's Chariot showpiece, 'Madman Running Through The Fields'. Additionally, his spoken dialogue was featured on some of Burdon's more self-indulgent efforts on *Everyone Of Us*. The singer completed *Welcome To My Head* on the group's demise before returning to London for *Zoot Money*. He continued an itinerant path with Centipede, Grimms and Ellis before joining Somers in the Kevin Coyne and Kevin Ayers bands. In 1980, Zoot released the low-key *Mr. Money*, since which he has played on numerous sessions and enjoyed a new career as a character actor in television drama and comedy. In the early 90s he was music controller for Melody Radio, but was back on the road by 1995. The live sound created by the Big Roll Band defined much of the club scene of the mid 60s. A valuable bunch of live tracks were uncovered and released as *Were You There?* in 1999. This splendid collection, although badly recorded, truly captured the smell and heat of those days.

● ALBUMS: *It Should've Been Me* (Columbia 1965) ★★★, *Zoot! Live At Klook's Kleek* (Columbia 1966) ★★★, *Transition* (Direction 1968) ★★, *Welcome To My Head* (1969) ★★, *Zoot Money* (Polydor 1970) ★★, *Mr. Money* (Magic Moon 1980) ★★, with Chris Farlowe *Alexis Korner Memorial Concert Volume 2* (Indigo 1995) ★★★, *Were You There? Live 1966* (Indigo 1999) ★★★★, *Fully Clothed & Naked* (Indigo 2000) ★★.

MONKEES

Inspired by the burgeoning pop phenomena and armed with an advance from Columbia's Screen Gems subsidiary, US television producers Bob Rafelson and Bert Schneider began auditions for a show about a struggling pop band in 1965. When extant acts, including the Lovin' Spoonful, proved inappropriate, an advertisement in the *Daily Variety* solicited 437 applications, including Stephen Stills, Danny Hutton (later of Three Dog Night) and Paul Williams. Following suitably off-beat auditions, the final choice paired two musicians – Michael Nesmith (b. Robert Michael Nesmith, 30 December 1942, Houston, Texas, USA; guitar/vocals) and folk singer Peter Tork (b. Peter Halsten Thorkelson, 13 February 1942, Washington, DC, USA; bass/vocals) – with two budding actors and former child stars – Davy Jones (b. 30 December 1945, Manchester, England; vocals) and ex-*Circus Boy* star Mickey Dolenz (b. George Michael Dolenz, 8 March 1945, Los Angeles, California, USA; drums/vocals).

On 12 September 1966, the first episode of *The Monkees* was aired by NBC-TV and, despite low initial ratings, the show quickly became hugely popular, a feat mirrored when it was launched in the UK. Attendant singles 'Last Train To Clarksville' (US number 1) and 'I'm A Believer' (US and UK number 1), and a million-selling debut album confirmed the band as the latest teenage phenomenon, drawing inevitable comparisons with the Beatles. However, news that the quartet did not play on their records fuelled an already simmering internal controversy. Early sessions had been completed by Boyce And Hart, authors of 'Last Train To Clarksville', and their backing band, the Candy Store Prophets, with the Monkees simply overdubbing vocals. Musical supervision was later handed to Screen Gems executive Don Kirshner, who in turn called in staff songwriters Gerry Goffin and Carole King, Neil Diamond and Jeff Barry to contribute material for the

show. This infuriated the Monkees' two musicians, in particular Nesmith, who described the piecemeal *More Of The Monkees* as 'the worst album in the history of the world'. Sales in excess of five million copies exacerbated tension, but the band won tacit approval from Schneider to complete several tracks under their own devices.

An undeterred Kirshner coaxed Jones to sing on the already-completed backing track to 'A Little Bit Me, A Little Bit You' which was issued, without the band's approval, as their third single. The ensuing altercation saw Kirshner ousted, with the quartet gaining complete artistic freedom. Although not issued as a single in the USA, 'Alternate Title' (aka 'Randy Scouse Git'), Dolenz's ambitious paean to London, reached number 2 in Britain, while two further 1967 singles, 'Pleasant Valley Sunday' and 'Daydream Believer' (composed by John Stewart), achieved gold record status. *Headquarters*, the first Monkees album on which the band played, was a commercial and artistic success, consisting largely of self-penned material ranging from country-rock to vaudevillian pop. *Pisces, Aquarius, Capricorn & Jones Ltd.* featured material drawn from associates Michael Murphy, Nilsson and Chip Martin as the unyielding call on the band's talents continued. This creative drain was reflected in the disappointing *The Birds, The Bees & The Monkees* and its accompanying single, 'Valleri'. The track itself had been recorded in 1966, and was only issued when 'pirate' recordings, dubbed off-air from the television series, attracted considerable airplay. 'The Monkees are dead!', declared an enraged Nesmith, yet the song sold over a million copies, the band's last such success.

The appeal of their series had waned as plots grew increasingly loose, and the final episode was screened in the USA on 25 March 1968. The quartet had meanwhile embarked on a feature movie, *Head*, which contained many in-jokes about their artistic predicaments. Although baffling their one-time teenage audience, it failed to find favour with the underground circuit who still viewed the Monkees as bubblegum. However, *Head* has since been rightly lauded for its imagination and innovation. A dispirited Peter Tork left following its release, but although the remaining trio continued without him, their commercial decline was as spectacular as its ascendancy. Nesmith left for a solo career in 1969, and the following year the Monkees' name was dissolved in the wake of Dolenz/Jones recording *Changes*. However, in 1975, the latter-day duo joined their erstwhile songwriting team in *Dolenz, Jones, Boyce And Hart* which toured under the banner 'The Great Golden Hits Of The Monkees Show'. The project drew cursory interest, but the band's reputation was bolstered considerably during the 80s, when the independent Rhino Records label reissued the entire Monkees back catalogue and the entire series was rescreened on MTV. Although Nesmith demurred, Dolenz, Jones and Tork embarked on a highly successful, 20th anniversary world tour which engendered a live album and a new studio set, *Pool It!*. They then disbanded as members pursued contrasting interests, while attempts to create the New Monkees around Marty Roos, Larry Saltis, Jared Chandler and Dino Kovas in 1987 were aborted. Although reviled by many contemporary critics, the original band's work is now regarded as among the best American pop of its era. Rhino Records released an ambitious 21-volume video collection in 1995 containing all 58 episodes of their television series. The following year's *Justus* was the first recording by the original band (including Nesmith) for over 20 years, and was followed by their first tour of the UK as a quartet.

● ALBUMS: *The Monkees* (Colgems 1966) ★★★★, *More Of The Monkees* (Colgems 1967) ★★★★, *Headquarters* (Colgems 1967) ★★★, *Pisces, Aquarius, Capricorn & Jones Ltd.* (Colgems 1967) ★★, *The Birds, The Bees & The Monkees* (Colgems 1968) ★★, *Head* film soundtrack (Colgems 1968) ★★, *Instant Replay* (Colgems 1969) ★★★, *The Monkees Present* (Colgems 1969) ★★★, *Changes* (Colgems 1970) ★★★, *20th Anniversary Tour 1986* (No Label 1987) ★★, *Live 1967* (Rhino 1987) ★★★, *Pool It!* (Rhino 1987) ★★, *Justus* (Rhino 1996) ★★.

● COMPILATIONS: *Greatest Hits* (Colgems 1969) ★★★★, *Golden Hits* (Colgems 1970) ★★★, *Barrel Full Of Monkees* (Colgems 1970) ★★★★, *Re-focus* (Bell 1973) ★★★, *The Monkees* (Laurie House 1976) ★★★, *Monkeemania: 40 Timeless Hits From The Monkees* Australia only (Arista 1979) ★★★, *Monkeeshines* (Zilch 1981) ★★★, *The Monkees Golden Story* (Arista 1981) ★★★★, *More Greatest Hits Of The Monkees* (Arista 1982) ★★★, *Monkee Business* (Rhino 1982) ★★★, *Tails Of The Monkees* (Silhouette 1983) ★★, *Monkee Flips: Best Of The Monkees, Volume Four – 14 Swinging Songs* (Rhino 1984) ★★★, *Hey-Hey-It's The Monkees: 20 Smash Hits* (Circa 1985) ★★★, *Hit Factory* (Pair 1985) ★★★, *The Best Of The Monkees* (Silver Eagle 1986) ★★★★, *Then & Now ... The Best Of The Monkees* (Arista 1986) ★★★★, *Missing Links* (Rhino 1987) ★★★, *Missing Links Volume Two* (Rhino 1990) ★★★, *Listen To The Band* 4-CD box set (Rhino 1991) ★★★, *Greatest Hits* (Rhino 1995) ★★★★, *Missing Links Volume 3* (Rhino 1996) ★★, *30th Anniversary Collection* (Rhino 1996) ★★★, *Here They Come ... The Greatest Hits Of The Monkees* (Warners/Telstar 1997) ★★★★, *Anthology* (Rhino 1997) ★★★★, *Music Box* 4-CD box set (Rhino 2001) ★★★★, *The Definitive Monkees* 2-CD set (Warners 2001) ★★★★.

● CD ROMS: *Hey Hey We're The Monkees* (nu.millennia 1996).

● VIDEOS: *The Monkees Collection* box set (Rhino 1995), *33 1/3 Revolutions Per Monkee* (Rhino Home Video 1996).

● FURTHER READING: *Love Letters To The Monkees*, Bill Adler. *The Monkees Tale*, Eric Lefcowitz. *The Monkees Scrapbook*, Ed Finn and T. Bone. *Monkeemania*, Glenn A. Baker. *The Monkees: A Manufactured Image*, Ed Reilly, Maggie McMannus and Bill Chadwick. *I'm A Believer: My Life Of Monkees, Music And Madness*, Mickey Dolenz and Mark Bego.

● FILMS: *Head* (1968).

MONRO, MATT

b. Terry Parsons, 1 December 1930, London, England, d. 7 February 1985, Ealing, London, England. This velvet-voiced balladeer first played in bands under the pseudonym Al Jordan before adopting the name Monro, allegedly borrowed from Winifred Atwell's father. Between stints as a bus driver and singer on the UK Camay soap commercial, he recorded for a number of labels, but his choice of material was generally too predictable. His interpretation of 'Garden Of Eden', for example, had to compete with four other versions by hit artists Frankie Vaughan, Gary Miller, Dick James and Joe Valino. Monro's luck changed when producer George Martin asked him to contribute a pseudo-Frank Sinatra version of 'You Keep Me Swingin'' to a Peter Sellers comedy album. This led to a contract with Parlophone Records and a Top 3 hit with 'Portrait Of My Love' (1960).

For the next five years, Monro was a regular chart entrant with his classic up-tempo version of 'My Kind Of Girl' (UK number 5/US number 18, 1961), along with ballads such 'Why Not Now?'/'Can This Be Love', 'Gonna Build A Mountain', 'Softly, As I Leave You', and 'When Love Comes Along'. His excellent interpretation of Lionel Bart's James Bond movie theme 'From Russia With Love', 'Born Free' and the emotive 'Walk Away' (UK number 4/US number 23, 1964) proved particularly successful. The speedy release of a slick adaptation of the Beatles' 'Yesterday' (UK number 8, 1965) underlined the sagacity of covering a song before your competitors. His 1962 album of Hoagy Carmichael songs, with arrangements by his regular musical director Johnny Spence, was right out of the top drawer. A move to the USA in 1965 brought a decline in Monro's chart fortunes in the UK, but he sustained his career as an in-demand nightclub performer. The enduring commercial quality of his voice was recognized by Capitol Records with the Christmas release and television promotion of the compilation album, *Heartbreakers*, in 1980. Ill-health dogged the singer in the early 80s, and he died from cancer in 1985. Ten years later, his son Matt Jnr., who had carved out a career for himself as a golf professional, 'duetted' with his father on an album of some of Matt Snr.'s favourite songs. Since his death, the tag that he was merely a Sinatra copyist has completely reversed, especially in America. Monro's appeal continues and the rich patina of his voice is now seen as original rather than derivative.

● ALBUMS: *Blue And Sentimental* (Decca 1957) ★★★, *Portrait* (Ace Of Clubs 1961) ★★★, *Love Is The Same Anywhere* (Parlophone 1961) ★★★, *My Kind Of Girl* (Parlophone 1961) ★★★★, *Matt Monro Sings Hoagy Carmichael* (Parlophone 1962) ★★★★, *I Have Dreamed* (Parlophone 1965) ★★★, *Walk Away* US only (Liberty 1965) ★★★★, *Hits Of Yesterday* (Parlophone 1965) ★★★★, *This Is The Life!* (Capitol 1966) ★★★★, *Let's Face The Music And Dance* (Capitol 1966) ★★★, *Here's To My Lady* (Capitol 1967) ★★★★, *Invitation To The Movies* (Capitol 1967) ★★★, *Tiempo De Amor* Spanish language (1967) ★★★, *These Years* (Capitol 1967) ★★★, *The Late Late Show* (Capitol 1968) ★★★★, *Invitation To Broadway* (Capitol 1968) ★★★, *Alguien Canto* Spanish language (Capitol 1969) ★★★, *The Southern Star* film soundtrack (RCA Victor 1969), *We're Gonna Change The World* (Capitol 1970) ★★★, *Matt Monro En Espana* Spanish language (1970) ★★★, *For The Present* (Columbia 1973) ★★★, *The Other Side Of The Stars* (Columbia 1975) ★★★, *The Long And Winding Road* (Columbia 1975) ★★★, *If I Never Sing Another Song* (Columbia 1979) ★★★, *Heartbreakers* (EMI 1980) ★★★, *Un Toque De Distincion* Spanish language (RCA 1982) ★★★, *More Heartbreakers* (EMI 1984) ★★★, with Matt Monro Jnr. *Matt Sings Monro* (EMI 1995) ★★★.

● COMPILATIONS: *By Request* (EMI 1987) ★★★, *Softly As I Leave You* (EMI/MFP 1987/1998) ★★★, *A Time For Loving* (EMI/MFP 1989/1998) ★★★, *The EMI Years* (EMI 1990) ★★★★, *The Capitol Years* (EMI 1990) ★★★★, *Matt Monro Sings Don Black* (EMI 1990) ★★★, *Matt Monro Sings* 2-CD set (EMI/MFP 1991) ★★★, *Musica Para Sonar* (EMI Odeon 1991) ★★★, *The Very Best Of Matt Monro* (EMI/MFP 1992) ★★★, *This Is Matt Monro* 2-CD set (EMI/MFP 1993) ★★★, *Through The Years* (EMI 1994) ★★★, *Hollywood & Broadway* (EMI/MFP 1994) ★★★, *The Best Of Matt Monro* (EMI/MFP 1995) ★★★★, *Great Gentlemen Of Song: Spotlight On Matt Monro* (Capitol 1995) ★★★, *Matt Monro* 3-CD box set (EMI 1995) ★★★★, *Complete Heartbreakers* (EMI 1996) ★★★, *Songs Of Love* 3-CD set (EMI/MFP 1997) ★★★, *This Is The Life!/Here's To My Lady* (EMI 1997) ★★★★, *The Singer's Singer* 4-CD box set (EMI 2001) ★★★.

MONTEREY POP FESTIVAL

16-18 June 1967. The burgeoning west coast American music scene was effectively launched at Monterey, California, USA, in 1967. In a transition from 'pop music', performers and bands suddenly found that they were preaching their new music to a like-minded mass audience. The sounds became more adventurous as they explored other musical routes. Blues, jazz and folk became tinged with Eastern and African influences. This galvanization in turn made people more aware and tolerant of these ambitious and different styles. Nevertheless, the music was still labelled 'progressive pop' rather than rock. The festival was the brainchild of John Phillips, Alan Pariser, Paul Simon and Lou Adler, who assembled a board of artists to help stage the event. Derek Taylor, the skilful former press officer of the Beatles and the Byrds, was enrolled. Brian Wilson of the Beach Boys pulled out prior to the event. The Beatles were notably missing. The Rolling Stones, although absent, were there in spirit, with Brian Jones on the advisory board seen wandering in the crowd throughout the proceedings.

The three-day festival was a forerunner to Woodstock, and history has subsequently shown that Monterey was more 'musically' important, although by today's standards it was a comparatively small affair with only 35,000 people present at any one time. The festival gave birth to a movement and introduced major new artists to the general public. It was at Monterey that Jimi Hendrix first attracted mass attention with the public burning of his guitar. Likewise it was Janis Joplin with her band, Big Brother And The Holding Company, who grabbed the audience's imagination with her orgasmic and electrifying performance, as did a quasi-live album by the Mama And The Papas. Otis Redding's accomplishment was memorable in that he brought together black soul and white rock music and became accepted by a predominantly white pop audience. His thrilling and frantic performance broke down all barriers, even although he wore a conservative blue suit instead of the regulation kaftan, beads and flowers. The first major pop music revolution since the Beatles was born at Monterey.

Among other artists who paraded their music at the festival were the Grateful Dead, Electric Flag (featuring the brilliant young Mike Bloomfield), Canned Heat, Buffalo Springfield, the Byrds, the Mamas And The Papas, Eric Burdon And The Animals, Hugh Masekela, Jefferson Airplane, Ravi Shankar, Booker T. And The MGs, the Who, Moby Grape, the Steve Miller Band, Country Joe And The Fish, Simon And Garfunkel, Beverly (Martyn), the Paupers, Lou Rawls, the Association, Johnny Rivers, Quicksilver Messenger Service, Laura Nyro, and the Blues Project. D.A. Pennebaker's 80 minute film *Monterey Pop* captured the event. No official album was ever released although a Jimi Hendrix/Otis Redding album included highlights of their performance. However, the show was broadcast on radio almost in its entirety in 1989 and further extracts from the festival have since been issued on CD.

● COMPILATIONS: *Monterey International Pop Festival* 4-CD box set (Castle 1992) ★★★.

MONTEZ, CHRIS

b. Christopher Montanez, 17 January 1943, Los Angeles, California, USA. Teenage vocalist Montez was discovered by impresario Jim Lee in

1961. Having joined Lee's Monogram label, the singer enjoyed an international hit the following year with 'Let's Dance'. This exciting, Lee-penned single, redolent of the Hispanic 'Latino-rock' style of Ritchie Valens sold over one million copies and climbed to UK number 2/US number 4. A follow-up, 'Some Kinda Fun', reached the UK Top 10 in 1963, but a three-year hiatus ensued before he resurfaced as an easy listening singer on A&M Records in the US, charting with a cover version of 'Call Me'. The charmingly simple 'The More I See You' gave Montez a second UK Top 3 entry in 1966, while minor US successes followed with 'There Will Never Be Another You' and 'Time After Time'. Re-released in the UK in 1972, 'Let's Dance' confirmed its timeless appeal by reaching the UK Top 10. Montez subsequently disappeared into obscurity, although he briefly resurfaced with an album on A&M's Spanish language imprint in the mid-80s.
● ALBUMS: *Let's Dance And Have Some Kinda Fun!!!* (Monogram 1963) ★★★, *The More I See You/Call Me* (A&M 1966) ★★★, *Time After Time* (A&M 1966) ★★★, *Foolin' Around* (A&M 1967) ★★, *Watch What Happens* (A&M 1968) ★★.
● COMPILATIONS: *Let's Dance! All-Time Greatest Hits* (Digital Compact Classics 1991) ★★★, *The Hits* (Repertoire 1999) ★★★.

MONTGOMERY, WES

b. John Leslie Montgomery, 6 March 1923, Indianapolis, Indiana, USA, d. 15 June 1968, Indianapolis, Indiana, USA. Montgomery was inspired to take up the guitar after hearing records by Charlie Christian. Nearly 20 years old at the time, he taught himself to play by adapting what he heard on records to what he could accomplish himself. Guided in part by Christian's example, but also by the need to find a way of playing that did not alienate his neighbours, he evolved a uniquely quiet style. Using the soft part of his thumb instead of a plectrum or the fingers, and playing the melody line simultaneously in two registers, Montgomery was already a distinctive stylist by the time he began to work with local bands. In 1948 he joined Lionel Hampton, touring and recording. In the early 50s he returned to Indianapolis and began playing with his brothers Buddy and Monk Montgomery in the Montgomery-Johnson Quintet (the other members being Alonzo and Robert Johnson). During an after-hours session at a local club, the visiting Cannonball Adderley asked him if he would like a record date. On Adderley's recommendation, Montgomery was recorded by Riverside Records in a series of trio albums that featured artists such as Hank Jones and Ron Carter. These albums attracted considerable attention and Montgomery quickly became one of the most talked about and respected guitarists in jazz. In the early 60s he worked with his brothers in northern California and also played

with John Coltrane. Further recordings, this time with a large string orchestra, broadened Montgomery's horizons and appealed to the non-jazz public. However, despite such commercially successful albums as *Movin' Wes*, *Bumpin'*, *Goin' Out Of My Head* and *A Day In The Life*, he continued to play jazz in small groups with his brothers and with Wynton Kelly, Herb Alpert, Harold Mabern and others. In 1965 he visited Europe, playing club and festival dates in England, Spain and elsewhere. His career was at its height when he died suddenly in June 1968. An outstanding guitarist with an enormous influence upon his contemporaries and countless successors, Montgomery's highly personal style was developed deliberately from Christian, and unwittingly shadowed earlier conceptions by musicians such as Django Reinhardt. In Montgomery's case he stumbled upon these methods not with deliberate intent but through what jazz writer Alun Morgan has described as 'a combination of naïvety and good neighbourliness'.
● ALBUMS: with The Montgomery Brothers *The Montgomery Brothers And Five Others* reissued as *Wes, Buddy & Monk Montgomery* (World Pacific/Pacific Jazz 1957) ★★★, with the Mastersounds *Kismet* (World Pacific 1958) ★★★, with The Montgomery Brothers *Montgomeryland* (Pacific Jazz 1959) ★★★, *New Concepts In Jazz Guitar* (Riverside 1959) ★★★★, *The Incredible Jazz Guitar Of Wes Montgomery* (Riverside 1960) ★★★★★, *Movin' Along* (Riverside 1960) ★★★★, with The Montgomery Brothers *The Montgomery Brothers* (Fantasy 1960) ★★★, with The Montgomery Brothers *The Montgomery Brothers In Canada* (Fantasy 1961) ★★★, with The Montgomery Brothers *Groove Yard* (Riverside 1961) ★★★, with George Shearing *Love Walked In* (Jazzland 1961) ★★★, *So Much Guitar!* (Riverside 1961) ★★★★, *Far Wes* (Pacific 1961) ★★★, *Full House Recorded 'Live' At Tsubo-Berkley, California* (Riverside 1962) ★★★, with Milt Jackson *Bags Meets Wes* (Riverside 1962) ★★★★, *Boss Guitar* reissued as *This Is Wes Montgomery* (Riverside 1963) ★★★★, *Fusion! Wes Montgomery With Strings* reissued as *In The Wee Small Hours* (Riverside 1964) ★★★, *Portrait Of Wes* (Riverside 1964) ★★★★, *Guitar On The Go* (Riverside 1965) ★★★, *Movin' Wes* (Verve 1965) ★★★★, *Bumpin'* (Verve 1965) ★★★★, *Smokin' At The Half Note* (Verve 1965) ★★★★, *Tequila* (Verve 1966) ★★★, *Goin' Out Of My Head* (Verve 1966) ★★★, *California Dreaming* (Verve 1966) ★★★, with Jimmy Smith *Jimmy & Wes The Dynamic Duo* (Verve 1966) ★★★★, with Smith *Further Adventures Of Jimmy And Wes* (Verve 1966) ★★★★, *Easy Groove* (Pacific Jazz 1966) ★★★, with The Montgomery Brothers *Wes' Best* (Fantasy 1967) ★★★, *A Day In The Life* (A&M 1967) ★★★, *Down Here On The Ground* (A&M 1968) ★★, *Road Song* (A&M 1968) ★★, *Willow Weep For Me* 1965 recording (Verve 1969) ★★★, *Eulogy* (Verve 1969) ★★★, *Mood I'm In* (Sunset

969) ★★, *Just Walkin'* 1965/1966 recordings Verve 1971) ★★★, *Impressions* 1965 recording Affinity 1978) ★★★★, *Solitude* 1965 recording Affinity 1978) ★★★★, *Recorded Live At Jorgies Jazz Club* 1961 recording (VGM 1985) ★★★, *Live t Jorgies And More* 1961/1968 recordings (VGM 985) ★★★, *Live In Paris* 1965 recording (France oncert 1988) ★★★★, *Live At Ronnie Scott's* 1965 ecording (DCC 2000) ★★.

COMPILATIONS: *The Best Of Wes Montgomery* Verve 1967) ★★★★, *March 6, 1925 – June 15, 968* (Riverside 1968) ★★★★, *Portrait* (Pacific azz 1968) ★★★★, *Panorama* (Riverside 1969) ★★★, *The Best Of Wes Montgomery, Volume 2* Verve 1969) ★★★★, *The Silver Collection* PolyGram 1984) ★★★★, *Wes Montgomery Plays he Blues* (Verve 1988) ★★★, *Verve Jazz Masters 4: Wes Montgomery* (Verve 1990) ★★★★, *lassics, Vol. 22: Wes Montgomery* (A&M 1991) ★★, *Talkin' Verve: Roots Of Acid Jazz* (Verve 996) ★★★★, *Ultimate Wes Montgomery* (Verve 998) ★★★, *Impressions: The Verve Jazz Sessions* Verve) ★★★★.

FURTHER READING: *Wes Montgomery*, drian Ingram.

MOODY BLUES

he lengthy career of the Moody Blues has come a two distinct phases. The first from 1964-67, hen they were a tough R&B-influenced unit, nd the second from 1967 to the present, where hey are now regarded as rock dinosaurs erforming a blend of melodic pop utilizing ymphonic themes which has been given many bels, among them pomp-rock, classical-rock nd art-rock. The original band was formed in 964 by Denny Laine (b. Brian Hines, 29 ctober 1944, Jersey, Channel Islands; vocals, armonica, guitar), Mike Pinder (b. 12 ecember 1942, Birmingham, England; piano, eyboards), Ray Thomas (b. 29 December 1942, ourport on Severn, England; flute, vocals, armonica), Graeme Edge (b. 30 March 1941, ochester, Staffordshire, England; drums) and lint Warwick (b. 25 June 1940, Birmingham, ngland; bass). During their formative months ley established a strong London club following, nd soon received their big break, as so many hers did, performing live on the influential UK levision show *Ready, Steady, Go!*. Newly signed Decca Records, a few months later their cover ersion of Bessie Banks' 'Go Now!' topped the K charts, complete with its striking piano troduction and solo.

lthough the single made the US Top 10, their ommercial fortunes were on an immediate ecline, although following releases were npeccable. Their excellent debut *The lagnificent Moodies* was a mature effort ombining traditional white R&B standards with riginals. In addition to 'Go Now' they tackled mes Brown's 'I'll Go Crazy' and delivered a enetic version of Sonny Boy Williamson's 'Bye ye Bird'. Laine and Pinder contributed among

others 'Stop' and 'Let Me Go'. Warwick and Laine departed in November 1966 to be replaced by Justin Hayward (b. 14 October 1946, Swindon, Wiltshire, England) and John Lodge (b. 20 July 1945, Birmingham, England). The band signed to Deram Records, Decca's newly-formed progressive outlet. Phase two began with the December 1967 release of Hayward's 'Nights In White Satin', which returned the band to the UK Top 20. (The song has subsequently enjoyed a profitable history, reaching US number 2 in 1972, while further reissues entered the UK Top 10 in 1973 and the Top 20 in 1979).

The accompanying *Days Of Future Passed* was an ambitious orchestral project with Peter Knight conducting the London Festival Orchestra and Tony Clark producing. The album was a massive success and started a run that continued through a further five albums with Knight and Clark (*On The Threshold Of A Dream*, *A Question Of Balance* and *Every Good Boy Deserves Favour* were all UK chart-toppers). The increased use of the mellotron gave an orchestrated feel to much of their work, and while they became phenomenally popular, they also received a great deal of criticism. They enjoyed their greatest success with the single 'Question', which reached number 2 in May 1970. During this period they founded their own record label, Threshold Records, which was based in Cobham, Surrey. Following the US chart-topping *Seventh Sojourn*, the band parted company in 1974 to allow each member to indulge in spin-off projects. Hayward and Lodge became the Blue Jays, enjoying great success with the 'Blue Guitar' single. Thomas (*From Mighty Oaks* and *Hopes Wishes & Dreams*), Lodge (*Natural Avenue*) and Pinder (*The Promise*) released solo albums, while Edge teamed with Adrian Gurvitz for *Kick Off Your Muddy Boots* and *Paradise Ballroom*.

The band reunited for 1978's *Octave*, which became another huge hit, although shortly after its release Pinder decided to leave the music business. Further discontent ensued when Clark resigned. Patrick Moraz (b. 24 June 1948, Morges, Switzerland) from Yes joined the band as Hayward's solo single 'Forever Autumn' hit the UK Top 10 during the summer. This track was taken from Jeff Wayne's epic concept album, *The War Of The Worlds*. The delayed follow-up, 1981's *Long Distance Voyager*, was both an artistic and commercial success, topping the American album chart for three weeks. The band enjoyed another commercial renaissance in 1986, when 'Your Wildest Dreams' and the attendant *The Other Side Of Life* both reached the US Top 10. Moraz left the band in 1990, prior to the recording of *Keys Of The Kingdom*. The Moody Blues have marched on into the new millennium, with the comforting knowledge that they have the ability to fill concert halls and possess a back catalogue that will sell and sell, until the days of future have passed.

● ALBUMS: *The Magnificent Moodies* (UK) *Go*

Now/Moody Blues #1 (US) (Decca/London 1965) ★★★★, *Days Of Future Passed* (Deram 1967) ★★★★, *In Search Of The Lost Chord* (Deram 1968) ★★★, *On The Threshold Of A Dream* (Deram 1969) ★★★★, *To Our Children's Children's Children* (Threshold 1969) ★★★★, *A Question Of Balance* (Threshold 1970) ★★★, *Every Good Boy Deserves Favour* (Threshold 1971) ★★★, *Seventh Sojourn* (Threshold 1972) ★★★★, *Caught Live + 5* (Decca 1977) ★★, *Octave* (Decca 1978) ★★, *Long Distance Voyager* (Threshold 1981) ★★★★, *The Present* (Threshold 1983) ★★★, *The Other Side Of Life* (Polydor 1986) ★★★, *Sur La Mer* (Polydor 1988) ★★★, *Keys Of The Kingdom* (Polydor 1991) ★★, *A Night At Red Rocks With The Colorado Symphony Orchestra* (Polydor 1993) ★★, *Strange Times* (Threshold/Universal 1999) ★★, *Hall Of Fame* (Threshold/Universal 2000) ★★★.
● COMPILATIONS: *This Is The Moody Blues* (Threshold 1974) ★★★★, *Out Of This World* (K-Tel 1979) ★★★, *Voices In The Sky: The Best Of The Moody Blues* (Threshold 1984) ★★★, *Prelude* (Polydor 1987) ★★, *The Magnificent Moodies* expanded edition of debut album (London 1988) ★★★★, *Greatest Hits* (Polydor 1989) ★★★, *Time Traveller* 5-CD box set (Polydor 1994) ★★★, *The Very Best Of The Moody Blues* (PolyGram 1996) ★★★, *The Best Of The Moody Blues* (Polydor 1997) ★★★, *Anthology* (Polydor 1998) ★★★★.
● VIDEOS: *Cover Story* (Stylus 1990), *The Story Of The Moody Blues ... Legend Of A Band* (PolyGram Music Video 1990), *Star Portrait* (Gemini Vision 1991), *A Night At Red Rocks With The Colorado Symphony Orchestra* (PolyGram Music Video 1993).

MOTHER EARTH

Formed in Texas in 1966, Mother Earth was one of several American groups to move to the more liberal San Francisco during the west coast beat boom of the late 60s. The original line-up featured three former members of the Wigs, John 'Toad' Andrews (guitar), Bob Arthur (bass) and George Rains (drums), as well as songwriter R. Powell St. John, who composed several songs for the 13th Floor Elevators. Blues singer Tracy Nelson (b. 27 December 1944, Madison, Wisconsin, USA), was Mother Earth's featured vocalist, while the group was latterly augmented by Mark Naftalin (keyboards) and Martin Fierro (horns). The ensemble made its tentative debut on the soundtrack of the film *Revolution*, before completing a promising debut album in 1968. Nelson's powerful voice enhanced its blues-based foundation, while admirable cameos from guitarist Mike Bloomfield and fiddler Spencer Perkin added to the informal atmosphere. The following year Mother Earth moved to a farm on the outskirts of Nashville. Their music became increasingly country-orientated and by the release of a fourth album, *Satisfied*, only Nelson and Andrews remained from the group's first

release. In 1973 they took the name Tracy Nelson/Mother Earth, but the group was dissolved when the singer's self-titled sole album won critical and commercial plaudits.
● ALBUMS: *Living With The Animals* (Mercury 1968) ★★★, *Make A Joyful Noise* (Mercury 1969) ★★★, *Mother Earth Presents Tracy Nelson Country* (Mercury 1969) ★★, *Satisfied* (Mercury 1970) ★★, *Bring Me Home* (Reprise 1971) ★★, *Mother Earth* (1972) ★★, *Poor Man's Paradise* (1973) ★★★.
● COMPILATIONS: *The Best Of Tracy Nelson And Mother Earth* (Warners 1996) ★★★.

MOTHERS OF INVENTION

This celebrated band was formed in 1964 when guitarist Frank Zappa (b. Frank Vincent Zappa, 21 December 1940, Baltimore, Maryland, USA, d. 4 December 1993, Los Angeles, California, USA) replaced Ray Hunt in the Soul Giants, a struggling R&B-based bar band. Ray Collins (b. 19 November 1937, USA; vocals), Dave Coronado (saxophone), Roy Estrada (b. 17 April 1943, Santa Ana, California, USA; bass) and Jimmy Carl Black (b. 1 February 1938, El Paso, Texas, USA; drums) completed their early line-up, but Coronado abandoned the outfit when the newcomer unveiled his musical strategy. Now renamed the Mothers, the quartet was relocated from Orange County to Los Angeles, where they were briefly augmented by several individuals, including Alice Stuart and Henry Vestine, later guitarist in Canned Heat. Jim Fielder was another bass player who passed through the ranks. He actually joined Buffalo Springfield before he had officially handed in his notice. These temporary additions found Zappa's vision daunting as the Mothers embarked on a disarming mélange of 50s pop, Chicago R&B and *avant garde* music. They were embraced by the city's nascent Underground before an appearance at the famed Whiskey A Go-Go resulted in a recording deal when producer Tom Wilson caught the end of one of their sets.
Now dubbed the Mothers Of Invention, owing to pressure from the record company, the band added guitarist Elliott Ingber (Winged Eel Fingerling) before commencing *Freak Out!*, rock music's first double album. This revolutionary set featured several exceptional pieces, including 'Trouble Every Day', 'Hungry Freaks Daddy' and 'The Return Of The Son Of Monster Magnet', each of which showed different facets of Zappa's evolving tableau. The Mothers' second album, *Absolutely Free*, featured a radically reshaped line-up. Ingber was fired at the end of 1966 while Zappa added a second drummer, Billy Mundi, plus Don Preston (b. 21 September 1932, USA; keyboards), Bunk Gardner (horns) and Jim 'Motorhead' Sherwood (saxophone) to the original nucleus. A six-month residency at New York's Garrick Theatre combined spirited interplay with excellent

material and the set showed growing confidence. Satire flourished on 'Plastic People', America Drinks & Goes Home' and 'Brown Shoes Don't Make It', much of which was inspired by the 'cocktail-bar' drudgery the band suffered in its earliest incarnation.

However, Zappa's ire was more fully flexed on *We're Only In It For The Money*, which featured several barbed attacks on the trappings of 'flower-power'. Housed in a sleeve which cleverly mocked the Beatles' *Sgt. Peppers Lonely Hearts Club Band*, the set included 'The Idiot Bastard Son' ('The father's a Nazi in Congress today, the mother's a hooker somewhere in LA') and 'Who Needs The Peace Corps' ('I'll stay a week and get the crabs and take a bus back home') and indicated Zappa's growing fascination with technology. The album also introduced new member Ian Underwood (saxophone/keyboards), who became an integral part of the band's future work. *Cruising With Ruben & The Jets* was, to quote the liner notes, 'an album of greasy love songs and cretin simplicity'. Despite such cynicism, the band displayed an obvious affection for the 50s doo-wop material on offer, all of which was self-penned and included re-recordings of three songs, 'How Could I Be Such A Fool', 'Any Way The Wind Blows' and 'You Didn't Try To Call Me', first aired on *Freak Out!*. However, the album was the last wholly new set committed by the 'original' line-up. Later releases, *Uncle Meat* (a soundtrack to the then unmade movie), *Burnt Weeny Sandwich* and *Weasels Ripped My Flesh*, were all compiled from existing live and studio tapes as tension within the band pulled it apart. The musicians enjoyed mixed fortunes. Estrada joined newcomer Lowell George in Little Feat, third drummer Arthur Dyre Tripp III switched allegiance to Captain Beefheart, while Jimmy Carl Black formed Geronimo Black with brothers Buzz and Bunk Gardner.

A new Mothers was formed in 1970 from the musicians contributing to Zappa's third solo album, *Chunga's Revenge*, and the scatological on the road' documentary, *200 Motels*. Three former Turtles, Mark Volman (b. 19 April 1947, Los Angeles, California, USA), Howard Kaylan (b. Howard Kaplan, 22 June 1947, the Bronx, New York City, New York, USA) and Jim Pons (b. 14 March 1943, Santa Monica, California, USA; bass) joined Aynsley Dunbar (b. 10 January 1946, Liverpool, England; drums) and long-standing affiliates Ian Underwood and Don Preston in the band responsible for *Live At The Fillmore East, June 1971*. Here, however, the early pot-pourri of Stravinsky, John Coltrane, doo-wop and 'Louie Louie' gave way to condescending innuendo as Zappa threatened to become the person once the subject of his ire. Paradoxically, it became the band's best-selling album to date, setting the tone for future releases and reinforcing the guitarist's jaundiced view of his audience. This period was

brought to a sudden end at London's Rainbow Theatre. A 'jealous' member of the audience attacked the hapless Zappa onstage, pushing him into the orchestra pit where he sustained multiple back injuries and a compound leg fracture. His slow recuperation was undermined when the entire new Mothers, bar Underwood, quit *en masse* to form what became known as Flo And Eddie. Confined to the studio, Zappa compiled *Just Another Band From L.A.* and used the Mothers epithet for the jazz big band on *The Grand Wazoo*. Reverting to rock music, the Mothers' name was re-established with a new, tighter line-up in 1973. However subsequent albums, *Over-Nite Sensation*, *Roxy & Elsewhere* and *One Size Fits All*, were indistinguishable from projects bearing Zappa's name and this now superfluous title was abandoned in 1975, following the release of *Bongo Fury*, a collaboration with Captain Beefheart.

Since Zappa's death a number of biographies have appeared; Neil Slaven's *Electric Don Quixote* is particularly noteworthy. Zappa's entire catalogue has been expertly remastered and reissued with the advent of the compact disc. Rykodisc Records are to be congratulated for their efforts, having purchased the whole catalogue from Gail Zappa for a large, undisclosed sum. The quality of those early Mothers Of Invention recordings are by today's standards quite outstanding.

● ALBUMS: Comprising the entire Frank Zappa catalogue. With The Mothers Of Invention *Freak Out!* (Verve 1966) ★★★★, with The Mothers Of Invention *Absolutely Free* (Verve 1967) ★★★★, with The Mothers Of Invention *We're Only In It For The Money* (Verve 1968) ★★★★, *Lumpy Gravy* (Verve 1968) ★★★★, with The Mothers Of Invention *Cruising With Ruben & The Jets* (Verve 1968) ★★★, with The Mothers Of Invention *Uncle Meat* (Bizarre 1969) ★★★★, *Hot Rats* (Bizarre 1969) ★★★★, with The Mothers Of Invention *Burnt Weeny Sandwich* (Bizarre 1970) ★★★★, with The Mothers Of Invention *Weasels Ripped My Flesh* (Bizarre 1970) ★★★★, *Chunga's Revenge* (Bizarre 1970) ★★★★, with The Mothers *Fillmore East, June 1971* (Bizarre 1971) ★★★, *Frank Zappa's 200 Motels* (United Artists 1971) ★★, with The Mothers *Just Another Band From L.A.* (Bizarre 1972) ★★★, *Waka/Jawaka* (Bizarre 1972) ★★★, with The Mothers *The Grand Wazoo* (Bizarre 1972) ★★★, with The Mothers *Over-Nite Sensation* (DiscReet 1973) ★★★, *Apostrophe (')* (DiscReet 1974) ★★★★, with The Mothers *Roxy & Elsewhere* (DiscReet 1974) ★★★, with The Mothers Of Invention *One Size Fits All* (DiscReet 1975) ★★★★, with Captain Beefheart *Bongo Fury* (DiscReet 1975) ★★★, *Zoot Allures* (Warners 1976) ★★★★, *Zappa In New York* (DiscReet 1978) ★★★, *Studio Tan* (DiscReet 1978) ★★★, *Sleep Dirt* (DiscReet 1979) ★★, *Sheik Yerbouti* (Zappa 1979) ★★★★, *Orchestral Favorites*

(DiscReet 1979) ★★★, *Joe's Garage Act I* (Zappa 1979) ★★★★, *Joe's Garage Acts II & III* (Zappa 1979) ★★★★, *Tinseltown Rebellion* (Barking Pumpkin 1981) ★★★, *Shut Up 'N Play Yer Guitar* (Zappa 1981) ★★★, *Shut Up 'N Play Yer Guitar Some More* (Zappa 1981) ★★★, *Return Of The Son Of Shut Up 'N Play Yer Guitar* (Zappa 1981) ★★★, *You Are What You Is* (Barking Pumpkin 1981) ★★★, *Ship Arriving Too Late To Save A Drowning Witch* (Barking Pumpkin 1982) ★★★, *Baby Snakes* (Barking Pumpkin 1982) ★★★, *The Man From Utopia* (Barking Pumpkin 1983) ★★★, *Baby Snakes* film soundtrack (Barking Pumpkin 1983) ★★, *The London Symphony Orchestra Vol. I* (Barking Pumpkin 1983) ★★★★, *Boulez Conducts Zappa: The Perfect Stranger* (Angel 1984) ★★★, *Them Or Us* (Barking Pumpkin 1984) ★★★, *Thing-Fish* (Barking Pumpkin 1984) ★★★★, *Francesco Zappa* (Barking Pumpkin 1984) ★★★, *Meets The Mothers Of Prevention* (Barking Pumpkin/EMI 1985) ★★★, *Does Humor Belong In Music?* (EMI 1986) ★★★, *Jazz From Hell* (Barking Pumpkin 1986) ★★★, *London Symphony Orchestra Vol. II* (Barking Pumpkin 1987) ★★★, *Guitar* (Barking Pumpkin 1988) ★★★, *Broadway The Hard Way* (Barking Pumpkin 1988) ★★★, *The Best Band You Never Heard In Your Life* (Barking Pumpkin 1991) ★★★★, *Make A Jazz Noise Here* (Barking Pumpkin 1991) ★★★, with The Mothers Of Invention *Ahead Of Their Time* 1968 live recording (Barking Pumpkin 1993) ★★★, with Ensemble Modern *The Yellow Shark* (Barking Pumpkin 1993) ★★★, *Civilization Phaze III* (Barking Pumpkin 1994) ★★★, *Everything Is Healing Nicely* 1991 recording (Barking Pumpkin 1999) ★★★.

Beat The Boots I: with The Mothers Of Invention *'Tis The Season To Be Jelly* 1967 recording (Foo-Eee 1991) ★★★, with The Mothers Of Invention *The Ark* 1969 recording (Foo-Eee 1991) ★★★, *Freaks And Motherf*#@%!* 1970 recordings (Foo-Eee 1991) ★★★, with The Mothers *Piquantique* 1973/1974 recordings (Foo-Eee 1991) ★★★, *Unmitigated Audacity* 1974 recording (Foo-Eee 1991) ★★★, *Saarbrücken 1978* (Foo-Eee 1991) ★★★, *Anyway The Wind Blows* 1979 recording (Foo-Eee 1991) ★★★, *As An Am* 1981/1982 recordings (Foo-Eee 1991) ★★★. Beat The Boots II: *Disconnected Synapses* 1970 recording (Foo-Eee 1992) ★★★, *Tengo Na Minchia Tanta* 1970 recordings (Foo-Eee 1992) ★★★, *Electric Aunt Jemima* 1968 recordings (Foo-Eee 1992) ★★★, *At The Circus* 1978 recording (Foo-Eee 1992) ★★★, *Swiss Cheese/Fire!* 1971 recordings (Foo-Eee 1992) ★★★, *Our Man In Nirvana* 1968 recording (Foo-Eee 1992) ★★★, *Conceptual Continuity* 1976 recording (Foo-Eee 1992) ★★★.

● COMPILATIONS: with The Mothers Of Invention *Mothermania: The Best Of The Mothers* (Verve 1969) ★★★, *The Old Masters Box One* (Barking Pumpkin 1985) ★★★, *The Old Masters Box Two* (Barking Pumpkin 1986) ★★★, *The Old Masters Box Three* (Barking Pumpkin 1987) ★★★, *You Can't Do That On Stage Anymore Vol. 1* (Rykodisc 1988) ★★★★, *You Can't Do That On Stage Anymore Vol. 2: The Helsinki Concert* (Rykodisc 1988) ★★★★, *You Can't Do That On Stage Anymore Vol. 3* (Rykodisc 1989) ★★★★, *You Can't Do That On Stage Anymore Vol. 4* (Rykodisc 1991) ★★★★, *You Can't Do That On Stage Anymore Vol. 5* (Rykodisc 1992) ★★★★, *You Can't Do That On Stage Anymore Vol. 6* (Rykodisc 1992) ★★★★, with The Mothers Of Invention *Playground Psychotics* 1970/1971 recordings (Barking Pumpkin 1992) ★★★, *Strictly Commercial: The Best Of Frank Zappa* (Rykodisc 1995) ★★★, *The Lost Episodes* (Rykodisc 1996) ★★★, *Läther* (Rykodisc 1996) ★★★★, *Plays The Music Of Frank Zappa: A Memorial Tribute* (Barking Pumpkin 1996) ★★★, *Have I Offended Someone?* (Rykodisc 1997) ★★★, *Strictly Genteel: A "Classical" Introduction To Frank Zappa* (Rykodisc 1997) ★★★, *Cheap Thrills* (Rykodisc 1998) ★★★, *Cucamonga* (Del-Fi 1998) ★★, *Mystery Disc* (Rykodisc 1998) ★★, *Son Of Cheep Thrills* (Rykodisc 1999) ★★. The entire reissued catalogue is currently available on Rykodisc.

● VIDEOS: *The Dub Room Special* (Barking Pumpkin 1982), *Frank Zappa's 200 Motels* (Warner Home Video 1984), *Does Humor Belong In Music?* (MPI Home Video 1985), *The Amazing Mr. Bickford* (MPI/Honker Home Video 1987), *Video From Hell* (Honker Home Video 1987), *Uncle Meat: The Mothers Of Invention Movie* (Barfko-Swill 1987), *Baby Snakes* (Honker Home Video 1987), *The True Story Of Frank Zappa's 200 Motels* (Barfko-Swill 1989).

● FURTHER READING: *Frank Zappa: Over Het Begin En Het Einde Van De Progressieve Popmuziek*, Rolf-Ulrich Kaiser. *No Commercial Potential: The Saga Of Frank Zappa & The Mothers Of Invention*, David Walley. *Good Night Boys And Girls*, Michael Gray. *Frank Zappa Et Les Mothers Of Invention*, Alain Dister. *No Commercial Potential: The Saga Of Frank Zappa Then And Now*, David Walley. *Zappalog The First Step Of Zappology*, Norbert Obermanns. *Them Or Us (The Book)*, Frank Zappa. *Mother! Is The Story Of Frank Zappa*, Michael Gray. *Viva Zappa*, Dominique Chevalier. *Zappa: A Biography*, Julian Colbeck. *The Real Frank Zappa Book*, Frank Zappa with Peter Occhiogrosso. *Frank Zappa: A Visual Documentary*, Miles (ed.). *Frank Zappa In His Own Words*, Miles. *Mother! The Frank Zappa Story*, Michael Gray. *Frank Zappa: The Negative Dialectics Of Poodle Play*, Ben Watson. *Being Frank: My Time With Frank Zappa*, Nigey Lennon. *Zappa: Electric Don Quixote*, Neil Slaven. *Frank Zappa: A Strictly Genteel Genius*, Ben Cruickshank. *Cosmik Debris: The Collected History And Improvisations Of Frank Zappa*, Greg Russo. *Necessity Is ... The Early Years Of Frank Zappa & The Mothers Of Invention*, Billy James.

● FILMS: *Head* (1968), *200 Motels* (1971), *Baby Snakes* (1979).

MOTOWN RECORDS

The history of Motown Records remains a paradigm of success for independent record labels, and for black-owned industry in the USA. The corporation was formed in 1959 by Berry Gordy (b. 28 November 1929, Detroit, Michigan, USA), a successful R&B songwriter who required an outlet for his initial forays into production. He used an $800 loan to finance the release of singles by Marv Johnson and Eddie Holland on his Tamla label, one of a series of individual trademarks that eventually included under the Motown umbrella. Enjoying limited local success, Gordy widened his roster, signing acts including the Temptations and Marvelettes in 1960. That year, the Miracles' 'Shop Around' gave the company its first major US hit, followed in 1961 by their first number 1, the Marvelettes' 'Please Mr Postman'. Gordy coined the phrase 'The Sound Of Young America' to describe Motown's output, and his apparently arrogant claim quickly proved well founded. By 1964, Motown was enjoying regular hits via the Supremes and the Four Tops, while Mary Wells' 'My Guy' helped the label become established outside the USA. The label's vibrant brand of soul music, marked by a pounding rhythm and a lightness of touch that appealed to both pop and R&B fans, provided America's strongest response to the massive impact of the British beat group invasion in 1964 and 1965. At the same time, Gordy realized the importance of widening his commercial bases; in 1965, he overtly wooed the middle-of-the-road audience by giving the Supremes a residency at the plush Copa nightclub in New York – the first of many such ventures into traditional showbiz territory. The distance between Motown's original fans and their new surroundings led to accusations that the company had betrayed its black heritage, although consistent chart success helped to cushion the blow.

In 1966, Motown took three steps to widen its empire, snapping up bands such as the Isley Brothers and Gladys Knight And The Pips from rival labels, opening a Hollywood office to double its promotional capabilities, and snuffing out its strongest opposition in Detroit by buying the Golden World and Ric-Tic group of R&B companies. Throughout these years, Gordy maintained a vice-like grip over Motown's affairs; even the most successful staff writers and producers had to submit their work to a weekly quality control meeting, and faced the threat of having their latest creations summarily rejected. Gradually, dissent rose within the ranks, and in 1967 Gordy lost the services of his A&R controller, Mickey Stevenson, and his premier writing/production team, Holland/Dozier/Holland. Two years of comparative failure followed before Motown regained its supremacy in the pop market by launching the career of the phenomenally successful Jackson Five in 1969. Gordy made a bold but ultimately unsuccessful attempt to break into the rock market in 1970 with his Rare Earth label, one of a variety of spin-off companies launched in the early part of the decade. This was a period of some uncertainty for the company; several major acts either split up or chose to seek artistic freedom elsewhere, and the decision to concentrate the company's activities in its California office in 1973 represented a dramatic break from its roots. At the same time, Gordy masterminded the birth of Motown's film division, with the award-winning biopic about Billie Holiday, *Lady Sings The Blues*. The burgeoning artistic and commercial success of Stevie Wonder kept the record division on course, although outsiders noted a distinct lack of young talent to replace the company's original stalwarts.

The mid-70s proved to be Motown's least successful period for over a decade; only the emergence of the Commodores maintained the label as a contemporary musical force. Motown increasingly relied on the strength of its back catalogue, with only occasional releases, such as the Commodores' 'Three Times A Lady' and Smokey Robinson's 'Being With You', rivalling the triumphs of old. The departure of Marvin Gaye and Diana Ross in the early 80s proved a massive psychological blow, and, despite the prominence of Commodores leader Lionel Richie, the company failed to keep pace with the fast-moving developments in black music. From 1986, there were increasing rumours that Berry Gordy was ready to sell the label; these were confirmed in 1988, when Motown was bought by MCA, with Gordy retaining some measure of artistic control over subsequent releases. After more than a decade of disappointing financial returns, Motown remains a record industry legend on the strength of its remarkable hit-making capacities in the 60s. Some realignment was tackled in the 90s by the new label chief Andre Harrell; his brief was to make Motown the leading black music label once again. New releases from Horace Brown, Johnny Gill, Queen Latifah and Boyz II Men started the rebirth. George Jackson became president of the company in November 1997, and helped inaugurate a major remastering program designed to promote the label's 40th anniversary. Late 90s success came with 702, Brian McKnight and a reborn Temptations.

● COMPILATIONS: *Motown Chartbusters Volumes 1 – 10* (Motown 1968-77), *20th Anniversary Album* (Motown 1986) ★★★★, *Hitsville USA: The Motown Singles Collection 1959-1971* 4-CD box set (Motown 1993) ★★★★★, *This Is Northern Soul! 24 Tamla Motown Rarities* (Débutante 1997) ★★★★, *This Is Northern Soul! Volume 2 – The Motown Sound* (Débutante 1998) ★★★, *Tamla Motown Early Classics* (Spectrum 1998) ★★★, *Motown 40 Forever* (Motown 1998) ★★★★, *Motown Celebrates Sinatra* (Motown 1998) ★★.

● VIDEOS: *The Sounds Of Motown* (PMI 1985), *The Sixties* (CIC Video 1987), *Time Capsule Of The 70s* (CIC Video 1987), *Motown 25th: Yesterday, Today, Forever* (MGM/UA 1988).
● FURTHER READING: *Where Did Our Love Go? The Rise And Fall Of The Motown Sound*, Nelson George. *Heat Wave: The Motown Fact Book*, no author listed. *Motown: The History*, Sharon Davis. *To Be Loved: The Music, The Magic, The Memories Of Motown*, Berry Gordy. *Calling Out Around The World: A Motown Reader*, Kingsley Abbott (ed.). *Dancing In The Street*, Suzanne E. Smith.

MOVE

Formed in late 1965 from the ashes of several Birmingham outfits, the original Move comprised Roy Wood (b. Ulysses Adrian Wood, 8 November 1946, Birmingham, England; vocals/guitar), Carl Wayne (b. 18 August 1943, Birmingham, England; vocals), Chris 'Ace' Kefford (bass), Trevor Burton (guitar) and Bev Bevan (b. Beverley Bevan, 25 November 1945, Birmingham, England; drums). Under the guidance of Tony Secunda, they moved to London, signed to Decca Records' hit subsidiary Deram Records, and rapidly established themselves as one of the most inventive and accomplished pop bands on the live circuit. In 1967, their first two UK Top 5 singles, the classically inspired 'Night Of Fear' and upbeat psychedelic 'I Can Hear The Grass Grow' sounded fresh and abrasive and benefited from a series of publicity stunts masterminded by Secunda. Like the Who, the Move specialized in 'auto-destruction', smashing television sets and cars onstage and burning effigies of Adolf Hitler, Ian Smith and Dr Veerwoord. Later in the year, they signed to the reactivated Regal Zonophone Records label which was launched in September with the fashionably titled 'Flowers In The Rain', the first record played on BBC Radio 1. The mischievous Secunda attempted to promote the disc with a saucy postcard depicting Harold Wilson. The Prime Minister promptly sued for libel, thereby diverting Roy Wood's royalties from the UK number 2 hit single to charity. In February 1968, the band returned as strong as ever with the high energy, 50s inspired, 'Fire Brigade', which provided them with their fourth Top 5 single. Soon afterwards, Ace Kefford suffered a nervous breakdown and left the group which continued as a quartet, with Burton switching to bass. The catchy but chaotic 'Wild Tiger Woman' fared less well than expected, as did their bizarrely eclectic EP *Something Else*. Management switches from Tony Secunda to Don Arden and Peter Walsh brought further complications, but the maestro Wood responded well with the evocative 'Blackberry Way', a number 1 on some UK charts. A softening of their once violent image with 'Curly' coincided with Burton's departure and saw Carl Wayne recklessly steering them onto the cabaret circuit. Increasing friction within their ranks culminated in Wayne's departure for a solo career, leaving the Move to carry on as a trio. The heavy rock sound of 'Brontosaurus' and 'When Alice Comes Down To The Farm' supplemented their diverse hit repertoire, and further changes were ahead. The recruitment of Jeff Lynne (b. 30 December 1947, Birmingham, England) from the Idle Race encouraged them to experiment with cellos and oboes while simultaneously pursuing their career as an increasingly straightforward pop act. The final flurry of Move hits ('Tonight', 'Chinatown' and 'California Man') were bereft of the old invention, which was henceforth to be discovered in their grand offshoots, the Electric Light Orchestra (ELO) and Wizzard.
● ALBUMS: *The Move* (Regal Zonophone 1968) ★★★★, *Shazam* (Regal Zonophone 1970) ★★★★, *Looking On* (Fly 1970) ★★★, *Message From The Country* (Harvest 1971) ★★★, *California Man* (Harvest 1974) ★★★.
● COMPILATIONS: *The Collection* (Castle 1986) ★★★, *The Early Years* (Dojo 1992) ★★★, *The BBC Sessions* (Band Of Joy 1995) ★★, *Movements: 30th Anniversary Anthology* 3-CD box set (Westside 1997) ★★★★, *Looking Back ... The Best Of The Move* (Music Club 1998) ★★★, *Omnibus: The 60s Singles As And Bs* (Edsel 1999) ★★★, *Hits & Rarities Singles A's & B's* (Repertoire 1999) ★★★★.

MUDDY WATERS

b. McKinley Morganfield, 4 April 1915, Rolling Fork, Mississippi, USA, d. 30 April 1983, Chicago, Illinois, USA. One of the dominant figures of post-war blues, Muddy Waters was raised in the rural Mississippi town of Clarksdale, in whose juke-joints he came into contact with the legendary Son House. Having already mastered the rudiments of the guitar, Waters began performing and this early, country blues period was later documented by Alan Lomax. Touring the south making field recordings for the Library Of Congress, this renowned archivist taped Waters on three occasions between 1941-42. The following year Waters moved to Chicago where he befriended 'Big' Bill Broonzy, whose influence and help proved vital to the younger performer. Waters soon began using amplified, electric instruments and by 1948 had signed a recording contract with the newly founded Aristocrat label, the name of which was later changed to Chess Records. Waters' second release, 'I Feel Like Goin' Home'/'I Can't Be Satisfied', was a minor R&B hit and its understated accompaniment from bass player Big Crawford set a pattern for several further singles including 'Rollin' And Tumblin'', 'Rollin' Stone' and 'Walkin' Blues'.
By 1951 the guitarist was using a full backing band and among the musicians who passed through its ranks were Otis Spann (piano)

Jimmy Rogers (guitar), Little Walter, Walter 'Shakey' Horton and James Cotton (all harmonica). This pool of talent ensured that the Muddy Waters Band was Chicago's most influential unit and a score of seminal recordings, including 'Hoochie Coochie Man', 'I've Got My Mojo Working', 'Mannish Boy', 'You Need Love' and 'I'm Ready', established the leader's abrasive guitar style and impassioned singing. Waters' international stature was secured in 1958 when he toured Britain at the behest of jazz trombonist Chris Barber. Although criticized in some quarters for his use of amplification, Waters' effect on a new generation of white enthusiasts was incalculable. Cyril Davies and Alexis Korner abandoned skiffle in his wake and their subsequent combo, Blues Incorporated, was the catalyst for the Rolling Stones, the Graham Bond Organisation, Long John Baldry and indeed British R&B itself. Paradoxically, while such groups enjoyed commercial success, Waters struggled against indifference.

Deemed 'old-fashioned' in the wake of soul music, he was obliged to update his sound and repertoire, resulting in such misjudged releases as *Electric Mud*, which featured a reading of the Rolling Stones' 'Let's Spend The Night Together', the ultimate artistic volte-face. The artist did complete a more sympathetic project in *Fathers And Sons* on which he was joined by Paul Butterfield and Mike Bloomfield, but his work during the 60s was generally disappointing. *The London Sessions* kept Waters in the public eye, as did his appearance at the Band's *The Last Waltz* concert, but it was an inspired series of collaborations with guitarist Johnny Winter that signalled a dramatic rebirth. This pupil produced and arranged four excellent albums that recaptured the fire and purpose of Muddy's early releases and bestowed a sense of dignity to this musical giant's legacy. Waters died of heart failure in 1983, his status as one of the world's most influential musicians secured.

● ALBUMS: *Muddy Waters Sings Big Bill Broonzy* (Chess 1960) ★★★, *Muddy Waters At Newport, 1960* (Chess 1963) ★★★★, *Muddy Waters, Folk Singer* (Chess 1964) ★★★★, *Muddy, Brass And The Blues* (Chess 1965) ★★, *Down On Stovall's Plantation* (Testament 1966) ★★★, *Blues From Big Bill's Copacabana* (Chess 1968) ★★★, *Electric Mud* (Cadet 1968) ★★, *Fathers And Sons* (Chess 1969) ★★★, *After The Rain* (Cadet 1969) ★★, *Sail On* (Chess 1969) ★★★, *The London Sessions* (Chess 1971) ★★★, *Live At Mister Kelly's* (1971) ★★★, *Experiment In Blues* (1972) ★★★, *Can't Get No Grindin'* (Chess 1973) ★★★, *Mud In Your Ear* (Musicor 1973) ★★★, *London Revisited* (Chess 1974) ★★, *The Muddy Waters Woodstock Album* (Chess 1975) ★★, *Unk In Funk* (Chess 1977) ★★, *Hard Again* (Blue Sky 1977) ★★★, *I'm Ready* (Blue Sky 1978) ★★★, *Muddy Mississippi Waters Live* (Blue Sky 1979) ★★★, *King Bee* (Blue Sky 1981) ★★★, *Paris 1972* (Pablo 1997)

★★★, *Goin' Way Back* 1967 recording (Just A Memory 1998) ★★★.

● COMPILATIONS: *The Best Of Muddy Waters* (Chess 1957) ★★★★★, *The Real Folk Blues Of Muddy Waters* (Chess 1966) ★★★★, *More Real Folk Blues* (Chess 1967) ★★★★, *Vintage Mud* (Sunnyland 1970) ★★★, *They Call Me Muddy Waters* (Chess 1970) ★★★, *McKinley Morganfield aka Muddy Waters* (Chess 1971) ★★★★, *Back In The Early Days* (Red Lightnin' 1977) ★★★, *Chess Masters* 3 volumes (Chess 1981-83) ★★★★, *Rolling Stone* (Chess 1982) ★★★, *Rare And Unissued* (Chess 1984) ★★★, *Trouble No More: Singles 1955-1959* (Chess/MCA 1989) ★★★, *Muddy Waters* 6-LP box set (Chess 1989) ★★★★★, *The Chess Box 1947-67* 9-CD box set (Chess/MCA 1990) ★★★★★, *Blues Sky* (Columbia/Legacy 1992) ★★★★, *The Complete Plantation Recordings* (Chess/MCA 1993) ★★★★, *The King Of Chicago Blues* (Charly 1995) ★★★★, *His Best: 1947 To 1955* (Chess/MCA 1997) ★★★★, *His Best: 1956 To 1964* (Chess/MCA 1997) ★★★★, *King Of The Electric Blues* (Columbia/Legacy 1998) ★★★, *The Lost Tapes* (Blind Pig 1999) ★★★★, *Best Of Muddy Waters: 20th Century Masters* (MCA 1999) ★★★★, *Mojo: The Live Collection* (MCI 2000) ★★★, *The Best Of Muddy Waters: The Millennium Collection* (MCA 2000) ★★★★, *Rollin' Stone: The Golden Anniversary Collection* (MCA 2000) ★★★★.

● VIDEOS: *Messin' With The Blues* (BMG 1991), *Live* (BMG 1993), *Got My Mojo Working: Rare Performances 1968-1978* (Yazoo 2000).

● FURTHER READING: *The Complete Muddy Waters Discography*, Phil Wight and Fred Rothwell. *Muddy Waters Biographie*, Francis Hofstein. *Muddy Waters: Mojo Man*, Sandra B. Tooze.

N

NAPOLEON XIV

The pseudonym of songwriter, performer and recording engineer Jerry Samuels, Napoleon XIV burst into the US/UK Top 10 in the summer of 1966 with the bizarre 'They're Coming To Take Me Away, Ha-Haaa!'. Although clearly a novelty song, its subject matter, mental illness (brought on by the loss of the singer's dog), prompted a ban on many American radio stations. An attempted follow-up, 'I'm In Love With My Little Red Tricycle' failed to capture the public's imagination and Napoleon's credibility was further dented when it was revealed that the performer undertaking personal appearances to promote the record was not Samuels but a certain Richard Stern. The presence of Napoleon imitator Kim Fowley hardly helped matters. An album based round the hit with lyrics by comedy writer Jim Lehrer was rushed out but in spite of such amusing titles as 'Photogenic, Schizophrenic You', 'The Nuts In My Family Tree' and 'Bats In My Belfry', it failed to sell in vast quantities. Its final track was not even by Napoleon but instead featured the strains of Josephine XV warbling the acerbic 'I'm Happy They Took You Away, Ha-Haaa!'. In 1990, Napoleon's finest moment was given a fresh airing courtesy of former Dead Kennedys vocalist Jello Biafra, whose new group Lard recorded a startling version of the hit.
● ALBUMS: *They're Coming To Take Me Away, Ha-Haaa!* (Warners 1966) ★★.
● COMPILATIONS: *The Second Coming* (Rhino 1996) ★★.

NASHVILLE TEENS

Formed in Weybridge, Surrey, England, in 1962, the Nashville Teens initially comprised vocalists Arthur 'Art' Sharp (b. 26 May 1941, Woking, Surrey, England) and Ray Phillips (b. Ramon John Phillips, 16 January 1944, Tiger Bay, Cardiff, Wales), Michael Dunford (guitar), John Hawken (b. 9 May 1940, Bournemouth, Dorset, England; piano), Pete Shannon (b. Peter Shannon Harris, 23 August 1941, Antrim, Northern Ireland; bass) and Roger Groom (drums). Dunford and Groom left the line-up the following year and the group was completed by John Allen (b. John Samuel Allen, 23 April, 1945, St. Albans, Hertfordshire, England; guitar), Barry Jenkins (b. 22 December 1944, Leicester, England; drums) and third vocalist Terry Crow for a protracted tenure in Hamburg, Germany. This period is chronicled on *Jerry Lee Lewis: Live At The Star Club* on which the septet

backed the veteran rock 'n' roll star. In 1964, and with Crow now absent, the Teens were aligned with producer Mickie Most for a pounding version of 'Tobacco Road', which deservedly climbed to number 6 in the UK. The similarly styled 'Google Eye' also proved popular, reaching the Top 10, but a split with Most ended this brief ascendancy. Collaborations with Andrew Loog Oldham ('This Little Bird') and Shel Talmy ('The Hard Way') were minor hits, but at the expense of the unit's undeniable grasp of R&B. Groom rejoined the line-up in 1966 when Jenkins left for the Animals, but despite excellent versions of Randy Newman's 'The Biggest Night Of Her Life' and Bob Dylan's 'All Along The Watchtower', the Nashville Teens were unable to rekindle former success. A spate of defections – John Hawken later found fame with Renaissance – left Phillips the sole remaining original member. He continues to front this act and concurrently performs with the British Invasion All-Stars, which features musicians drawn from the Downliners Sect, Creation and the Pretty Things.
● ALBUMS: *The Nashville Teens* (New World 1972) ★★, *Live At The Red House* (1984) ★★, *Tobacco Road* 1964 recording (One Way 1997) ★★★.
● COMPILATIONS: *The Best Of* (1993) ★★★.
● FILMS: *Be My Guest* (1965).

NAZZ

Formed in Philadelphia, USA in 1967, the Nazz comprised of Todd Rundgren (b. 22 June 1948, Upper Darby, Philadelphia, Pennsylvania, USA; guitar, vocals), Carson Van Osten (bass, vocals), both ex-members of bar-band Woody's Truck Stop, Robert 'Stewkey' Antoni (lead vocals, keyboards) and Thom Mooney (drums). Although the quartet made its live debut supporting the Doors, manager John Kurland deliberately cultivated an air of exclusivity which ultimately hampered progress. A lucrative recording deal with publishers Screen Gems resulted in *Nazz*, a synthesis of British and US pop invoking the Who, Jimi Hendrix, Buffalo Springfield and Small Faces. However, the unit's anglophilia and mod affectations proved unfashionable in the face of acid-rock which, when coupled with growing internal disharmony, sowed the seeds of their demise. *Nazz Nazz* emphasized the positive elements of its predecessor and although the same influences were still apparent, a sense of individuality was also present. Rundgren's departure for a solo career in 1970 brought the Nazz to an end, and *Nazz III*, compiled from material from the *Nazz Nazz* sessions, was issued posthumously. Stewkey and Mooney were later joined by Rick Nielsen and Tom Petersson (later of Cheap Trick) in Fuse, but only Rundgren achieved lasting success outside the Nazz. Despite negligible commercial gain, his former group's work was later lauded as the precursor to a generation of British-influenced US bands, notably the Raspberries, Stories and Sparks.

● ALBUMS: *Nazz* (SGC 1968) ★★★, *Nazz Nazz* (SGC 1969) ★★★, *Nazz III* (SGC 1970) ★.
● COMPILATIONS: *Best Of The Nazz* (1983) ★★★, *From Philadelphia* (Distortions 1998) ★★★.

NEIL, FRED

b. 1 January 1937, St. Petersburg, Florida, USA, d. 7 July 2001, Summerland Key, Florida, USA. An important figure in America's folk renaissance, Neil's talent first emerged in 1956 when he co-wrote an early Buddy Holly single, 'Modern Don Juan'. He released a few solo singles during the late 50s, often using the name Freddie Neil. By the following decade he was a fixture of the Greenwich Village circuit, both as a solo act and in partnership with fellow singer Vince Martin. The duo embarked on separate careers following the release of *Tear Down The Walls*. Neil's subsequent solo *Bleecker & MacDougal* was an influential collection and contained the original version of 'The Other Side Of This Life', later covered by the Youngbloods, Lovin' Spoonful and the Jefferson Airplane. The singer's deep, resonant voice was equally effective, inspiring the languid tones of Tim Buckley and Tim Hardin.

A reticent individual, Neil waited two years before completing *Fred Neil*, a compulsive selection that featured two of the artist's most famous compositions, 'The Dolphins' and 'Everybody's Talkin''. The latter was adopted as the theme song to *Midnight Cowboy*, the highly successful 1969 movie starring Dustin Hoffman and Jon Voight, although it was a version by Harry Nilsson that became the hit single. Such temporary trappings were of little note to Neil, who preferred the anonymity of his secluded Florida base, from where he rarely ventured. An appearance at the Los Angeles club, the Bitter End, provided the material for *Other Side Of This Life*, an effective resume of his career. This informal performance also contained other favoured material, including 'You Don't Miss Your Water', which featured assistance from country singer Gram Parsons. A major, if self-effacing talent, Fred Neil withdrew from music altogether following this 1971 release. He refused to record or be interviewed and rare live appearances were constrained to benefit events for his charity, Dolphin Project, which he established with marine biologist Richard O'Barry in 1970. Neil died of cancer in July 2001.

● ALBUMS: with Vince Martin *Tear Down The Walls* (Elektra 1964) ★★★, *Bleecker & MacDougal* aka *Little Bit Of Rain* (Elektra 1965) ★★★★, *Fred Neil* aka *Everybody's Talkin'* (Capitol 1966) ★★★, *Sessions* (Capitol 1968) ★★★, *Other Side Of This Life* (Capitol 1971) ★★★.
● COMPILATIONS: *The Very Best Of Fred Neil*

(See For Miles 1986) ★★★★, *The Many Sides Of Fred Neil* (Collector's Choice 1999) ★★★★.

NELSON, RICK

b. Eric Hilliard Nelson, 8 May 1940, Teaneck, New Jersey, USA, d. 31 December 1985, De Kalb, Texas, USA. Nelson came from a showbusiness family. His father, Ozzie Nelson, formed a popular dance band in the 1930s. The band featured singer Harriet Hilliard, who became Ozzie Nelson's wife in 1935. The couple had their own US radio show, *The Adventures Of Ozzie And Harriet*, which transferred to television in 1952. Ricky and his brother David appeared in several episodes of the show. By 1957 Nelson had embarked on his own recording career, with the million-selling, double-sided 'I'm Walking'/'A Teenager's Romance'. A third hit soon followed with 'You're My One And Only Love'. A switch from Verve Records to Imperial Records saw Nelson enjoy further success with the rockabilly 'Be-Bop Baby'. In 1958 Nelson formed a full-time group for live work and recordings, which included James Burton (guitar), James Kirkland (later replaced by Joe Osborn) (bass), Gene Garf (piano) and Richie Frost (drums).

Early that year Nelson enjoyed his first transatlantic hit with 'Stood Up' and, in August, registered the first *Billboard* Hot 100 chart-topper with 'Poor Little Fool'. His early broadcasting experience was put to useful effect when he starred in the Howard Hawks movie western *Rio Bravo* (1959), alongside John Wayne and Dean Martin. Nelson's singles continued to chart regularly and it says much for the quality of his work that the b-sides were often as well known as the a-sides. Songs such as 'Believe What You Say', 'Never Be Anyone Else But You', 'It's Late', 'Sweeter Than You', 'Just A Little Too Much' and 'I Wanna Be Loved' proved that Nelson was equally adept at singing ballads and up-tempo material. One of his greatest moments as a pop singer occurred in the spring of 1961 when he issued the million-selling 'Travelin' Man', backed with the exuberant Gene Pitney composition, 'Hello Mary Lou'. Shortly after the single topped the US charts, Nelson celebrated his 21st birthday in 1961 and announced that he was changing his performing name from Ricky to Rick. Several more pop hits followed, most notably 'Young World', 'Teenage Idol', 'It's Up To You', 'String Along' (his first single for Decca Records), 'Fools Rush In' and 'For You'. With the emergence of the beat boom, Nelson's clean-cut pop was less in demand.

He struggled to find a direction that neither alienated his old fans nor saw him out on a limb. The move to Decca had seen him produce more albums, and the hits slowly dried up. By the time *The Very Thought Of You* and *Spotlight On Rick* were released America was in the grip of Beatlemania; things declined further in 1965 with the disappointing *Best Always* and *Love And*

Kisses. In 1966 he switched to country music. His early albums in this vein featured compositions from such artists as Merle Travis ('Kentucky Means Paradise'), Willie Nelson ('Funny How Time Slips Away') and Hank Williams ('You Win Again'), and it was clear that Nelson seemed to have found a comfortable niche for his voice. By 1967 though, he had ventured further off course and attempted more contemporary songs by writers such as Harry Nilsson ('Without Her'), Paul Simon ('For Emily, Whenever I Find Her') and a clutch of classic Randy Newman songs, none of which were suited to his easy going voice. He ruined the sensitive 'I Think It's Going To Rain Today' and further bad judgements resulted in a dreadful attempt at John Sebastian's 'Daydream'.

He did however manage some beautiful versions of Tim Hardin songs ('Reason To Believe' and 'Don't Make Promises'). After this nadir, in 1969 Nelson formed a new outfit, the Stone Canyon Band, featuring former Poco member Randy Meisner (b. 8 March 1946, Scottsbluff, Nebraska, USA; bass), Allen Kemp (guitar), Tom Brumley (steel guitar) and Pat Shanahan (drums). A credible version of Bob Dylan's 'She Belongs To Me' brought Nelson back into the US charts, and a series of strong, often underrated, albums followed. A performance at Madison Square Garden in late 1971 underlined Nelson's difficulties at the time. Although he had recently issued the accomplished *Rick Sings Nelson*, on which he wrote every track, the audience were clearly more interested in hearing his early 60s hits. Nelson responded by composing the sarcastic 'Garden Party', which reaffirmed his determination to go his own way. The single, ironically, went on to sell a million and was his last hit record. After parting with the Stone Canyon Band in 1974, Nelson's recorded output declined, but he continued to tour extensively. On 31 December 1985, a chartered plane carrying him to a concert date in Dallas caught fire and crashed near De Kalb, Texas. Nelson's work deserves a place in rock history, as he was one of the few 'good-looking kids' from the early 60s who had a strong voice which, when coupled with some exemplary material, remains durable.

● ALBUMS: with various artists *Teen Time* (Verve 1957) ★★, *Ricky* (Imperial 1957) ★★, *Ricky Nelson* (Imperial 1958) ★★, *Ricky Sings Again* (Imperial 1959) ★★, *Songs By Ricky* (Imperial 1959) ★★★, *More Songs By Ricky* (Imperial 1960) ★★, *Rick Is 21* (Imperial 1961) ★★, *Album Seven By Rick* (Imperial 1962) ★★, *Best Sellers By Rick Nelson* (Imperial 1962) ★★, *It's Up To You* (Imperial 1962) ★★★, *A Long Vacation* (Imperial 1963) ★★, *Million Sellers By Rick Nelson* (Imperial 1963) ★★★★, *For Your Sweet Love* (Decca 1963) ★★, *Rick Nelson Sings For You* (Decca 1963) ★★★, *Rick Nelson Sings 'For You'* (Decca 1963) ★★★★, *The Very Thought*

Of You (Decca 1964) ★★, *Spotlight On Ric* (Decca 1964) ★★★, *Best Always* (Decca 1965 ★★, *Love And Kisses* (Decca 1965) ★★, *Brigh Lights And Country Music* (Decca 1966) ★★★★ *On The Flip-Side* film soundtrack (Decca 1966 ★, *Country Fever* (Decca 1967) ★★★★, *Anothe Side Of Rick* (Decca 1968) ★★, *Perspective* (Decc 1968) ★, *Ricky Nelson In Concert* (Decca 1970 ★★★, *Rick Sings Nelson* (Decca 1970) ★★★ *Rudy The Fifth* (Decca 1971) ★★★, *Garden Part* (Decca 1972) ★★★★, *Windfall* (1974) ★★ *Intakes* (Epic 1977) ★★, *Playing To Win* (Capitc 1981) ★★★, *Memphis Sessions* (Epic 1986) ★★★ *Live 1983-1985* (Rhino 1989) ★★★.

● COMPILATIONS: *The Very Best Of Rick Nelso* (Decca 1970) ★★★★, *Legendary Masters* (Unite Artists 1971) ★★★★, *The Singles Album 1963 1976* (United Artists 1977) ★★★★, *The Single Album 1957-63* (United Artists 1977) ★★★★ *Greatest Hits* (Rhino 1984) ★★★, *Rockin' Wit Ricky* (Ace 1984) ★★★★, *String Along With Ric* (Charly 1984) ★★★, *All My Best* (MCA 1985 ★★★★, *Best Of 1963-1975* (MCA 1990) ★★★★ *Best Of Rick Nelson, Volume 2* (Capitol 1991 ★★★★, *1969-1976* (Edsel 1995) ★★★, *The Be* *Of The Later Years 1963-1975* (Ace 1997) ★★★ *25 Greatest Hits* (MFP 1998) ★★★, with th Stone Canyon Band *The Essential Collection* (Ha Moon 1998) ★★★, *Anthology* (Charly 1998 ★★★, *Legacy* 4-CD box set (Capitol 2000 ★★★★.

● FURTHER READING: *The Ricky Nelson Story* John Stafford and Iain Young. *Ricky Nelson: Ide For A Generation*, Joel Selvin. *Ricky Nelson Teenage Idol, Travelin' Man*, Philip Bashe.

NELSON, SANDY

b. Sander L. Nelson, 1 December 1938, Sant Monica, California, USA. Drummer Nelso began his career as a member of the Kip Tyle Band. Appearances in live rock 'n' roll shows le to his becoming an in-demand session musician where he joined an *ad hoc* group of youn aspirants including Bruce Johnston and Ph Spector. Nelson played on 'To Know Him Is T Love Him', a million-selling single written an produced by the latter for his vocal group, th Teddy Bears. Johnston, meanwhile, assisted th drummer on an early demo of 'Teen Beat', powerful instrumental which achieved gol status in 1959 on reaching the Top 10 in both th US and UK. Two years later, Nelson secure another gold disc for 'Let There Be Drums', cc composed with Richie Podolor, who became successful producer with Three Dog Night an Steppenwolf. The pattern was now set for a bev of releases on Imperial Records, each of whic combined a simple guitar melody with Nelson explosive percussion breaks, a style echoing tha of the concurrent surf craze.

Its appeal quickly waned and 'Teen Beat '6 (1964) – recorded in the artist's garage studio was his last chart entry. Guitarists Gle Campbell and Jerry McGee, later of th

Ventures, as well as bass player Carol Kaye were among the musicians contributing to his sessions, but these lessened dramatically towards the end of the decade. During the 70s Nelson was featured in one of impresario Richard Nader's *Rock 'N' Roll Revival* shows, but he retired following the disappointing disco-influenced *Bang Bang Rhythm*. Despite being tempted into occasional, informal recordings, Nelson has remained largely inactive in professional music since 1978, although instrumental aficionados still marvel at the drummer's extensive catalogue.

● ALBUMS: *Teen Beat* (Imperial 1960) ★★★, *He's A Drummer Boy* aka *Happy Drums* (Imperial 1960) ★★★, *Let There Be Drums* (Imperial 1961) ★★★, *Drums Are My Beat!* (Imperial 1962) ★★★, *Drummin' Up A Storm* (Imperial 1962) ★★★, *Golden Hits* retitled *Sandy Nelson Plays Fats Domino* (Imperial 1962) ★★, *On The Wild Side* aka *Country Style* (Imperial 1962) ★★, *Compelling Percussion* aka *And Then There Were Drums* (Imperial/London 1962) ★★★, *Teenage House Party* (Imperial 1963) ★★★, *The Best Of The Beats* (1963) ★★, *Be True To Your School* (1963) ★★, *Live! In Las Vegas* (1964) ★★, *Teen Beat '65* (1965) ★★★, *Drum Discotheque* (1965) ★★, *Drums A Go-Go* (1965) ★★, *Boss Beat* (1966) ★★, *'In' Beat* (1966) ★★, *Superdrums* (Liberty 1966) ★★, *Beat That #!!&** *Drum* (1966) ★★, *Cheetah Beat* (1967) ★★, *The Beat Goes On* (Liberty 1967) ★★, *Souldrums* (Liberty 1968) ★★, *Boogaloo Beat* (Liberty 1968) ★★, *Rock 'N' Roll Revival* (Liberty 1968) ★★, *Golden Pops* (1968) ★★, *Rebirth Of The Beat* (1969) ★★, *Manhattan Spiritual* (1969) ★★, *Groovy!* (Liberty 1969) ★★, *Rock Drum Golden Disc* (1972) ★★, *Keep On Rockin'* (1972) ★★, *Roll Over Beethoven* aka *Hocus Pocus* (1973) ★★, *Let The Good Times Rock* (1974) ★★, *Bang Bang Rhythm* (1975) ★.

● COMPILATIONS: *Beat That Drum* (1963) ★★★, *Sandy Nelson Plays* (1963) ★★★, *The Very Best Of Sandy Nelson* (1978) ★★★, *20 Rock 'N' Roll Hits: Sandy Nelson* (1983) ★★★, *King Of Drums: His Greatest Hits* (See For Miles 1995) ★★★, *Golden Hits/Best Of The Beats* (See For Miles 1997) ★★★.

NEW CHRISTY MINSTRELS

Randy Sparks (b. 29 July 1933, Leavenworth, Kansas, USA), formed this commercialized folk group in 1961. Determined to create a unit that was 'a compromise between the Norman Luboff Choir and the Kingston Trio', he added a popular Oregon quartet, the Fairmount Singers, to his own Randy Sparks Three. A third unit, the Inn Group, which featured Jerry Yester, was absorbed into the line-up, while other Los Angeles-based performers embellished these core acts. Fourteen singers made up the original New Christy Minstrels but although the ensemble was viewed as supplementary to the participants' other careers, interest in the group's debut *Presenting The New Christy*

Minstrels, led to it becoming a full-time venture. Most of these early recruits, including the entire Inn Group, abandoned Sparks' creation at this point, creating the need for further, wholesale changes. New recruits, including Barry McGuire, Barry Kane and Larry Ramos, joined the Minstrels whose next release, *In Person*, documented a successful appearance at the famed Troubador club. The following year (1963) the group secured its first hit single with 'Green Green' which established the ensemble as a leading popular attraction.

The group, however, remained volatile as members continued to come and go. Gene Clark disbanded his Kansas-based trio, the Surf Riders, in order to join the Minstrels, but left after a matter of months, frustrated at the rather conservative material the ensemble recorded. He later formed the Byrds with (Jim) Roger McGuinn and David Crosby. Randy Sparks ended his relationship with the Minstrels in the summer of 1964. Maligned for creating their MOR image, his departure did not result in the more daring direction several members wished to pursue. McGuire, who was increasingly unhappy with such material as 'Three Wheels On My Wagon' and 'Chim Chim Cheree', left the group after seeing several British groups perform during the Minstrels European tour that year. His gravelly rasp was soon heard on his solo international protest hit, 'Eve Of Destruction'. In 1966 Larry Ramos accepted an invitation to join the Association and although several excellent new vocalists, including Kim Carnes and Kenny Rogers, had been absorbed into the Minstrels, their influential days were over. Long-standing members Mike Settle and Terry Williams left when their new ideas were constantly rejected. They formed the First Edition with the equally ambitious Rogers, and subsequently enjoyed the kind of success the parent group previously experienced. Although the New Christy Minstrels continue to exist in some form, singing early hits, show tunes and standards, their halcyon days ended during the mid-60s.

● ALBUMS: *Presenting The New Christy Minstrels* (Columbia 1962) ★★, *The New Christy Minstrels In Person* (Columbia 1962) ★★★, *Tall Tales! Legends & Nonsense* (Columbia 1963) ★★★, *Ramblin' (Featuring Green, Green)* (Columbia 1963) ★★★★, *Merry Christmas!* (Columbia 1963) ★★★, *Today* (Columbia 1964) ★★★, *Land Of Giants* (Columbia 1964) ★★★, *The Quiet Side Of The New Christy Minstrels* (Columbia 1964) ★★★, *Cowboys And Indians* (Columbia 1965) ★★★, *Chim Chim Cheree* (Columbia 1965) ★★, *The Wandering Minstrels* (Columbia 1965) ★★, *In Italy ... In Italian* (Columbia 1966) ★★, *New Kick!* (Columbia 1966) ★★, *Christmas With The Christies* (Columbia 1966) ★★, *On Tour Through Motortown* (Columbia 1968) ★★, *Big Hits From Chitty Chitty Bang Bang* (Columbia 1968) ★★, *You Need Someone To Love* (Gregar 1970) ★★, *The*

Great Soap Opera Themes (1976) ★★. ● COMPILATIONS: *Greatest Hits* (Columbia 1966) ★★★, *The Very Best Of The New Christy Minstrels* (Vanguard 1996) ★★★★, *Golden Classics Edition* (Collectables 1997) ★★★, *Definitive New Christy Minstrels* (Collector's Choice 1998) ★★★, *Coat Your Minds With Honey* (Raven/Topic 1999) ★★★.

NEW VAUDEVILLE BAND

This parodic ensemble initially comprised studio musicians gathered to record a Geoff Stephens composition, 'Winchester Cathedral', a tale of lost love in deepest Hampshire, England, sung in the style of a Bertie Wooster character complete with megaphone vocals. Stephens could not sing and therefore his place was taken by songwriter John Carter. Carter and Stephens worked together on numerous catchy pop songs in the 60s, including the magnificent 'My World Fell Down' recorded by Sagittarius. The need for a permanent line-up arose when in 1966 this contagious single became an international success, to the bizarre extent of winning a Grammy for 'Best Rock And Roll Record'. Having failed to tempt the nascent Bonzo Dog Doo-Dah Band into accepting the role, a group was assembled late in 1966 around Alan Klein aka Tristram, Seventh Earl of Cricklewood (b. 29 June 1942; vocals), Henri Harrison (b. 6 June 1943, Watford, Hertfordshire, England; drums), Stan Haywood (b. 23 August 1947, Dagenham, Essex, England; keyboards), Neil Korner (b. 6 August 1942, Ashford, Kent, England; bass), Mick Wilsher (b. 21 December 1945, Sutton, Surrey, England; guitar), Hugh 'Shuggy' Watts (b. 25 July 1941, Watford, Hertfordshire, England; trombone), Chris Eddy (b. 4 March 1942; bass), and the line-up was completed by Bob Kerr (b. 14 February 1943, London, England; trombone, saxophone), a refugee from the aforementioned Bonzos. The septet continued the 20s style of that debut release and had a second UK Top 10 hit with 'Peek-A-Boo' in 1967. That same year, 'Finchley Central' and 'Green Street Green' also charted in the Top 40, but very soon their novelty appeal waned and the group underwent a gradual process of disintegration while playing out their days on the Las Vegas and English cabaret circuit. Kerr pursued the madcap angle with his new unit, Bob Kerr's Whoopee Band.
● ALBUMS: *Winchester Cathedral* (Fontana 1966) ★★★, *Finchley Central* (Fontana 1967) ★★.

NEWBEATS

This distinctive pop trio featured falsetto Larry Henley (b. 30 June 1941, Arp, Texas, USA) with brothers Marcus 'Marc' Mathis (b. 9 February 1942; bass) and Lewis 'Dean' Mathis (b. 17 March 1939, Hahira, Georgia, USA). Dean had joined Paul Howard's Western Swing Band in 1956 as a pianist and later moved to Dale

Hopkin's Band, with Marc joining shortly afterwards. The Mathis brothers then performed and recorded as Dean And Marc; their version of 'Tell Him No' narrowly missed the US Top 40 in 1959. Henley briefly joined the act before they went their separate ways. After recording as the Brothers on Checker and Argo they also had releases on Check Mate and May before joining Hickory Records, where Henley had been recording fruitlessly as a soloist. Since neither act was successful they decided to record together as the Newbeats. Their first single, 'Bread And Butter', became their biggest hit, shooting to number 2 in the US charts and into the UK Top 20 in 1964. In the USA the shrill-sounding trio kept the Top 40 hits rolling with 'Everything's Alright' in 1964, 'Break Away (From That Boy)' and 'Run Baby Run' (a belated UK Top 10 hit in 1971), the last two in 1965. After a decade on Hickory the trio went to Buddah Records in 1973 and then in 1974 to Playboy. The trio split up that year, with Henley then recording without chart success for Capricorn and later for Atco and Epic. He then turned his attention to songwriting, and has been very successful since. His best-known song was Bette Midler's version of a 1983 country hit, 'The Wind Beneath My Wings'.
● ALBUMS: *Bread & Butter* (Hickory 1964) ★★★, *Big Beat Sounds By The Newbeats* (Hickory 1965) ★★, *Run Baby Run* (Hickory 1966) ★★.
● COMPILATIONS: *The Best Of* (1992) ★★★, *Golden Classics Edition* (Collectables 1995) ★★★.

NEWLEY, ANTHONY

b. George Anthony Newley, 24 September 1931, London, England, d. 14 April 1999, Jensen Beach, Florida, USA. One of the UK's most highly successful songwriters, actors and singers of the 60s. Born in Hackney, east London, Newley was evacuated to Hertfordshire during World War II. He attended the Italia Conti Stage School in London before working as a child actor in several films, including *The Little Ballerina*, *Vice Versa*, and David Lean's acclaimed version of *Oliver Twist* (1948) in which he played the Artful Dodger. A brief spell of national service ended after six weeks on psychiatric grounds. He made his London theatrical debut in John Cranko's revue, *Cranks* in 1955, and had character parts in well over 20 films before he was cast as rock 'n' roll star Jeep Jackson in 1959's *Idle On Parade*. Newley's four-track vocal EP, and his version of the film's hit ballad, Jerry Lordan's 'I've Waited So Long', started a three-year UK chart run that included 'Personality', 'If She Should Come To You', 'And The Heavens Cried', the novelty numbers 'Pop Goes The Weasel' and 'Strawberry Fair' and two UK number 1 hits, 'Why' and Lionel Bart's 'Do You Mind?'. Newley also made the album charts in 1960 with his set of standards, *Love Is A Now And Then Thing*. He made further appearances in the charts with

Tony (1961), and the comedy album *Fool Britannia* (1963), on which he was joined by his wife, Joan Collins, and Peter Sellers. In 1961 Newley collaborated with Leslie Bricusse on the book, music and lyrics for the offbeat stage musical, *Stop The World - I Want To Get Off.* Newley also directed, and played the central role of Littlechap. The show, which stayed in the West End for 16 months, ran for over 500 performances on Broadway, and was filmed in 1966. It produced several hit songs, including 'What Kind Of Fool Am I?', 'Once In A Lifetime' and 'Gonna Build A Mountain'.

In 1964 Bricusse and Newley wrote the lyric to John Barry's music for Shirley Bassey to sing over the titles of the James Bond movie, *Goldfinger.* The team's next musical show in 1965, *The Roar Of The Greasepaint - The Smell Of The Crowd,* with comedian Norman Wisdom in the lead, toured the north of England but did not make the West End. When it went to Broadway Newley took over (co-starring with Cyril Ritchard), but was not able to match the success of *Stop The World,* despite an impressive score that contained such numbers as 'Who Can I Turn To?', 'A Wonderful Day Like Today', 'The Joker', 'Look At That Face' and 'This Dream'. In 1967 Newley appeared with Rex Harrison and Richard Attenborough in the film musical *Doctor Dolittle,* with script and songs by Bricusse. Despite winning an Oscar for 'Talk To The Animals', the film was considered an expensive flop, as was Newley's own movie project in 1969, a pseudo-autobiographical sex-fantasy entitled *Can Hieronymus Merkin Ever Forget Mercy Humppe And Find True Happiness?* Far more successful, in 1971, was *Willy Wonka And The Chocolate Factory,* a Roald Dahl story with music and lyrics by Bricusse and Newley. Sammy Davis Jnr. had a million-selling record with one of the songs, 'The Candy Man'. Bricusse and Newley also wrote several numbers for the 1971 NBC television musical adaptation of *Peter Pan,* starring Mia Farrow and Danny Kaye.

The Good Old Bad Old Days! opened in London in 1972 and had a decent run of 309 performances. Newley sang some of the songs, including 'The People Tree', on his 1972 album, *Ain't It Funny.* In 1989, a London revival of *Stop The World - I Want To Get Off,* directed by Newley, and in which he also appeared, closed after five weeks. In the same year, he was inducted into the Songwriters' Hall Of Fame, along with Leslie Bricusse. In 1991, Newley appeared on UK television with his ex-wife, Joan Collins, in Noël Coward's *Tonight At 8.30,* with its famous 'Red Peppers' segment. In the following year, having lived in California for some years, Newley announced that he was returning to the UK, and bought a house there to share with his 90-year-old mother. In the early 90s he presented *Once Upon A Song,* an anthology of his own material, at the King's Head Theatre in London, and occasionally played the title role in regional productions of the musical *Scrooge,* which Leslie Bricusse had adapted for the stage from his 1970 film. During the remainder of the 90s Newley continued to perform his accomplished cabaret act (in which he amusingly bemoaned the fact that he had not had a hit with one of his own songs) at venues such as the Rainbow & Stars in New York and London's Café Royal. In 1998 he worked in a rather less sophisticated environment when playing crooked car dealer Vince Watson in one of the UK's top-rated television soap operas, *EastEnders.* Tara Newley, the daughter of Newley and Joan Collins, has worked as a radio and television presenter, and in 1994 released her first record entitled 'Save Me From Myself'. Newley lost his battle with cancer and died in April 1999.

● ALBUMS: *Cranks* original cast album (HMV 1956) ★★★, *Love Is A Now And Then Thing* (Decca 1960) ★★★, *Tony* (Decca 1961) ★★★, the London Cast *Stop The World - I Want To Get Off* (Decca 1961) ★★★★, with Joan Collins, Peter Sellers *Fool Britannia* (Ember 1963) ★★★, *In My Solitude* (Decca 1964) ★★★, *Newley Delivered* (Decca 1964) ★★★, the original Broadway Cast recording *The Roar Of The Greasepaint - The Smell Of The Crowd* (RCA Victor 1965) ★★★★, *Who Can I Turn To* (RCA Victor 1965) ★★★★, *Newley Recorded* (RCA Victor 1966) ★★★, *Doctor Dolittle* film soundtrack (Stateside 1967) ★★, *Can Hieronymus Merkin Ever Forget Mercy Humppe And Find True Happiness?* film soundtrack (MCA 1969) ★★, original London Cast recording *The Good Old Bad Old Days!* (EMI 1973) ★★★, *Ain't It Funny* (MGM 1973) ★★★, *The Singer And His Songs* (United Artists 1978) ★★★.

● COMPILATIONS: *The Romantic World Of Anthony Newley* (Decca 1969) ★★★, *The Best Of Anthony Newley* (RCA 1969) ★★★, *The Lonely World Of Anthony Newley* (Decca 1971) ★★★, *Anthony Newley: Mr. Personality* (Decca 1985) ★★★, *Greatest Hits* (Deram 1990) ★★★★, *The Very Best Of Anthony Newley* (Spectrum 1995) ★★★, *Once In A Lifetime: The Anthony Newley Collection* (Razor & Tie 1997) ★★★★, *On A Wonderful Day Like Today: The Anthony Newley Collection* (Camden 2000) ★★★★.

● FILMS: as an actor *Vice Versa* (1948), *The Guinea Pig* (1948), *Oliver Twist* (1948), *Vote For Huggett* (1949), *Don't Ever Leave Me* (1949), *A Boy, A Girl And A Bike* (1949), *Highly Dangerous* (1950), *The Little Ballerina* (1951), *Top Of the Form* (1953), *Up To His Neck* (1954), *The Blue Peter* (1954), *Above Us The Waves* (1955), *High Flight* (1956), *Cockleshell Heroes* (1956), *Port Afrique* (1956), *X The Unknown* (1956), *How To Murder A Rich Uncle* (1957), *Fire Down Below* (1957), *The Man Inside* (1958), *Tank Force* (1958), *The Lady Is A Square* (1959), *Idle On Parade* (1959), *The Heart Of A Man* (1959), *Bandit Of Zhobe* (1959), *Killers Of Killimanjaro* (1959), *Jazz Boat* (1960), *In The Nick* (1960), *The Small World Of Sammy Lee* (1962), *Doctor Dolittle* (1967),

Sweet November (1968), *Can Hieronymus Merkin Ever Forget Mercy Humppe And Find True Happiness?* (1969), *The Old Curiosity Shop* (1975), *It Seemed Like A Good Idea At The Time* (1975), *The Garbage Pail Kids Movie* (1987). As a composer *High Flight* songs (1956), *Jazz Boat* songs (1960), *Stop The World – I Want To Get Off* (1966), *Can Hieronymus Merkin Ever Forget Mercy Humppe And Find True Happiness?* also screenplay, director, producer (1969), *Willy Wonka And The Chocolate Factory* (1971).

NEWTON, WAYNE

b. 3 April 1942, Roanoke, Virginia, USA. Newton began his singing career as a child and later became the most popular and highest-paid star on the Las Vegas nightclub circuit. Inspired by a visit to the *Grand Ole Opry* in Nashville, Newton's first professional singing engagement came at the age of six, when he was paid $5 for a performance. His family relocated to Phoenix, Arizona a few years later, where he learnt to play several instruments, including guitar and piano. He and his brother, Jerry, became a duo and by his early teens Wayne had landed his own television programme on station KOOL in Phoenix. At the age of 16, when the brothers were offered a five-year booking in Las Vegas, the family moved there. The Newton Brothers recorded one single for Capitol Records in 1959, 'The Real Thing'/'I Spy', before recording several singles for the small George Records. In 1962 they were heard by television star Jackie Gleason, who booked them on his programme in September. Wayne was clearly emerging as the star of the act, and brother Jerry dropped out in 1963. By this time he had signed a music publishing contract with Bobby Darin's TM Music and returned to Capitol Records; Darin also oversaw the production of most of Newton's early Capitol recordings. Singing in a Las Vegas-lounge-lizard style, with minor traces of 'safe' rock, Newton's first single to chart was 'Heart (I Hear You Beating)', in 1963. 'Danke Schoen', co-written by Bert Kaempfert, followed and became a Newton trademark which he performed throughout his entire career. Newton's first album, sharing the single's title, was released in the autumn of 1963 and reached number 55.

One notable early single was 1965's 'Comin' On Too Strong', co-written by Gary Usher, who had written some music for the Beach Boys. The song included Bruce Johnston on backing vocals (along with arranger Terry Melcher). Newton continued to record for Capitol until 1967, when he briefly switched to MGM Records before returning to Capitol one last time in 1970. He then proceeded to Chelsea Records, for which he recorded his biggest hit, the number 4 single 'Daddy Don't You Walk So Fast', in 1972. He also charted twice, in 1979 and 1980, on the Aries II label. His total number of chart singles was 17, and 10 albums charted as well, but it became

apparent by the 70s that Newton's strength was in his concert performances in Las Vegas. He not only commanded higher fees for those concerts than any other performer – reportedly $1 million per month – but invested in hotels in that city, becoming wealthy in the process. Newton has also made some nominal film appearances, including 1990's *The Adventures Of Ford Fairlane*.

● ALBUMS: *Danke Schoen* (Capitol 1963) ★★ *Sings Hit Songs* (Capitol 1964) ★★, *In Person* (Capitol 1964) ★★, *Red Roses For A Blue Lady* (Capitol 1965) ★★★, *Summer Wind* (Capitol 1965) ★★, *Wayne Newton – Now!* (Capitol 1966) ★★, *Old Rugged Cross* (Capitol 1966) ★★, *It's Only The Good Times* (Capitol 1967) ★★, *Walking On New Grass* (MGM 1968) ★★, *One More Time* (MGM 1968) ★★, *Daddy Don't You Walk So Fast* (Chelsea 1972) ★★, *Can't You Hear The Song* (Chelsea 1972) ★★, *While We're Still Young* (1973) ★★, *The Best Of Wayne Newton – Live* (1989) ★.

● COMPILATIONS: *The Best Of Wayne Newton* (Capitol 1967) ★★★, *The Artist Collection* (Capitol 1999) ★★★.

NICE

Originally the back-up band to soul singer P.P. Arnold, the Nice became one of the true originators of what has variously been described as pomp-rock, art-rock and classical-rock. The band comprised Keith Emerson (b. 1 November 1944, Todmorden, Yorkshire, England, keyboards), Brian 'Blinky' Davison (b. 25 May 1942, Leicester, England; drums), Lee Jackson (b. 8 January 1943, Newcastle-Upon-Tyne, England; bass, vocals) and David O'List (b. 13 December 1948, Chiswick, London, England, guitar). After leaving Arnold in October 1967 the Nice quickly built a reputation as one of the most visually exciting bands. Emerson's stage act involved, in true circus style, throwing knives into his Hammond Organ, which would emit outrageous sounds, much to the delight of the audience.

Their debut, *The Thoughts Of Emerlist Davjack*, while competent, came nowhere near reproducing their exciting live sound. By the time of the release of its follow-up, *Ars Longa Vita Brevis*, O'List had departed, being unable to compete with Emerson's showmanship and subsequently joined Roxy Music. The album contained their notorious single, 'America', from *West Side Story*. During one performance at London's Royal Albert Hall, they burnt the American flag on stage and were severely lambasted, not only by the Albert Hall authorities, but also by the song's composer, Leonard Bernstein. The band continued their remaining life as a trio, producing their most satisfying and successful work. Both *The Nice* and *Five Bridges* narrowly missed the top of the UK charts, although they were unable to break through in the USA. The former contained an excellent reading of Tim Hardin's 'Hang On To A Dream', with exquisite piano from Emerson. The latter was a bold semi-orchestral suite about working-class life in Newcastle-upon-Tyne. One of their other showpieces was an elongated version of Bob Dylan's 'She Belongs To Me'. *Five Bridges* also contained versions of 'Intermezzo From The Karelia Suite' by Sibelius and Tchaikovsky's 'Pathetique'. Their brave attempt at fusing classical music and rock together with the Sinfonia of London was admirable, and much of what Emerson later achieved with the huge success of Emerson, Lake And Palmer should be credited to the brief but valuable career of the Nice.

With Emerson's departure, Jackson floundered with Jackson Heights, while Davison was unsuccessful with his own band, Every Which Way. Jackson and Davison teamed up again in 1974 to form the ill-fated Refugee. The Nice deserve reappraisal as both their classical rock and psych pop forays were, for the most part, successful, and much of the remastered Immediate Records catalogue reissued by the Sanctuary label stands up well more than 30 years on.

● ALBUMS: *The Thoughts Of Emerlist Davjack* (Immediate 1967) ★★★, *Ars Longa Vita Brevis* (Immediate 1968) ★★★, *The Nice* (Immediate 1969) ★★★★, *Five Bridges* (Charisma 1970) ★★★★, *Elegy* (Charisma 1971) ★★, *The Swedish Radio Sessions* (Castle 2001) ★★.
● COMPILATIONS: *The Best Of The Nice* (Essential 1998) ★★★, *Collection* (Castle 1998) ★★★, *All The Nice* (Repertoire 1999) ★★★, *Here Come The Nice: The Immediate Anthology* 3-CD box set (Castle 2000) ★★★★.

NICHOLLS, BILLY

b. 1950, England. Recorded at the height of ipsy dipsy sunshine pop in 1968, Nicholls' *Would You Believe* became something of a collector's item over the years. Signed to Andrew Loog Oldham's Immediate Records, aspiring songwriter Nicholls had already asked George Harrison for help in starting his career. Oldham financed the recording and enlisted any available Immediate artists to help out. Steve Marriott and Ronnie Lane were available and other session help came from the Apostolic Intervention and the Warm Sounds. The CD reissue enables the listener to hear what is on offer, rather than pay over £1000 for the vinyl original. It is, all said and done, very much a period piece; quaint, melodic, pleasant, but certainly no ground-breaking record like *Pet Sounds*. Nicholls himself is hazy about the project; 'I can't remember anything about these tracks or even being there.' A further album was released in 1974, and another under the name of White Horse in 1977, but both failed to generate any interest. Nicholls received greater acclaim as a hit songwiter in the 70s, and as an occasional musical director to the both the Who

and Pete Townshend.
● ALBUMS: *Would You Believe* (Immediate 1968) ★★★, *Love Songs* (GM 1974) ★★.
● COMPILATIONS: *Snapshot* (Southwest 2000) ★★, *Penumbra Moon* (Southwest 2001) ★★★.

1910 FRUITGUM COMPANY

The aptly named Fruitgum Company were at the forefront of a brief wave of bubblegum-pop in the late 60s. Bubblegum was a form that offered solid dance beats, infantile lyrics and very catchy choruses built around instantly hummable melody lines. The Super K production team of Jeff Katz and Jerry Kasenetz were masters of the form and specialized in studio in-house creations such as the Fruitgum Company. Writer Joey Levine was the voice behind the hits which began with the nursery game anthem 'Simon Says' in 1968 and continued with '1, 2, 3, Red Light', 'Goody Goody Gumdrops', 'Indian Giver' and 'Special Delivery'. Contrary to popular myth, the band did tour and featured Frank Edward Jeckell (b. 10 September 1946, Nanticoke, Pennsylvania, USA) in addition to Levine. By the end of the decade, bubblegum has passed its sell-by date.

●ALBUMS: *Simon Says* (Buddah 1968) ★★, *1, 2, 3 Red Light* (Buddah 1968) ★★, *Indian Giver* (Buddah 1969) ★★, *1910 Fruitgum Company And Ohio Express* (Buddah 1969) ★★★.
● COMPILATIONS: *Best Of The 1910 Fruitgum Company* (Golden Classics 2001) ★★★.

NIRVANA (UK)

Songwriters Patrick Campbell-Lyons (b. Dublin, Eire) and George Alex Spyropoulus (b. Athens, Greece) met in La Gioconda, a legendary coffee bar in Denmark Street, London. Prior to this Campbell-Lyons had been a member of the Teenbeats and had covered the familiar territory of seedy clubs in Holland and Germany. Spyropoulus was working at Kassners music publishers, also in Denmark Street. Having established an instant rapport, the duo formed a group, adding Ray Singer (guitar), Brian Henderson (bass), Michael Coe (viola, French horn) and Sylvia Schuster (cello). The quintet, dubbed Nirvana, secured a recording deal with Island Records after impressing producer Jimmy Miller who in turn influenced Chris Blackwell. They made their official debut in 1967, supporting Traffic, Jackie Edwards and Spooky Tooth at the Saville Theatre, London (owned at that time by Brian Epstein). Their exotic debut, *The Story Of Simon Simopath*, was an episodic fairytale. It emerged in a startlingly colourful cover, featuring a winged child and miniature goddess and centaur, surrounded by stars, planets and three-dimensional block typography. A kitsch concept album that billed itself as a 'science-fiction pantomime', the mock libretto told of the hero's journey from a six-dimensional city to a nirvana filled with sirens. Although the songs generally lacked the weight of their epochal singles, there were some charming moments. It contained the haunting 'Pentecost Hotel', a fragile, orchestrated ballad that brought the group critical approval and was a hit in Europe. The classical gentle mood was perfect for the times. The Alan Bown Set covered the singalong 'We Can Help You', which received considerable airplay, but narrowly failed to chart.

Nirvana themselves were plugged by several discriminating disc jockeys but in spite of the innovative qualities of their singles, the group fell tantalizingly short of a major breakthrough. Campbell-Lyons and Spyropoulus then disbanded the group format and completed a second set as a duo. This melodic collection featured several of Nirvana's finest songs, including 'Tiny Goddess' and 'Rainbow Chaser'. The latter was a powerhouse phased-production, typical of Nirvana's grandiose majesty, and became a minor UK hit in 1968. That same year a strong album followed with *All Of Us*.

The group's career had already begun to falter when Island rejected *Black Flower*, which was subsequently released by Pye Records under the title *To Markos III*. The album was placed with an American company which then went into liquidation. Spyropoulus dropped out of the partnership and moved into film work, leaving his colleague with the rights to the Nirvana trademark. Having completed a fourth album, *Local Anaesthetic*, Campbell-Lyons became a producer with the Vertigo Records label, while recording *Songs Of Love And Praise*, a compendium of new songs and re-recorded Nirvana favourites. This release was the last to bear the group's name. Campbell-Lyons subsequently issued solo albums before reuniting with Spyropoulus for a projected musical, *Blood*. In the 90s the band are very much a cult item, with their original vinyl albums fetching high prices. CD reissues have been released by Edsel Records with fascinating sleeve notes from Campbell-Lyons, largely drawn from his forthcoming autobiography.

● ALBUMS: *The Story Of Simon Simopath* (Island 1968) ★★★, *All Of Us* (Island 1968) ★★, *To Markos 3* (Pye 1969) ★★, *Local Anaesthetic* (Vertigo 1971) ★★★, *Songs Of Love And Praise* (Philips 1972) ★★, *Orange And Blue* (Demon 1996) ★★★.

● COMPILATIONS: *Secret Theatre* (Edsel 1987) ★★, *Chemistry* 3-CD box set (Edsel 1999) ★★★.

NITZSCHE, JACK

b. Bernard Alfred Nitzsche, 22 April 1937, Chicago, Illinois, USA, d. 25 August 2000, Hollywood, California, USA. Nitzsche was raised on a farm near Newaygo, Michigan, but moved to Los Angeles in 1955 to pursue a career as a jazz saxophonist. His long career in pop music began in the late 50s when he joined a cabal of young, Los Angeles-based, aspiring

entrepreneurs including Lee Hazlewood, Lou Adler and Nik Venet. He became acquainted with Sonny Bono, then head of A&R at Specialty Records, who employed him as a music copyist. While at Specialty Nitzsche wrote the novelty hit 'Bongo Bongo Bongo' for Preston Epps, and co-authored, with Bono, 'Needles And Pins', later an international hit for the Searchers. In the early 60s, Nitzsche established his reputation as an arranger through an association with Phil Spector. His contribution to recordings by the Crystals, Ronettes, and Ike And Tina Turner should not be under-emphasized, while a similar relationship with the Rolling Stones resulted in several of the band's classic releases, notably 'The Last Time', '(I Can't Get No) Satisfaction' and 'Get Off Of My Cloud'. Nitzsche also enjoyed success in his own right as a performer with the instrumental hit 'The Lonely Surfer' (1963), before garnering further acclaim for his arranging/production skills for Jackie DeShannon, P.J. Proby and Bob Lind.

In 1966, he co-produced 'Expecting To Fly' for Buffalo Springfield, a track essentially viewed as a solo vehicle for their guitarist Neil Young. The relationship continued when Young opted for a solo career and Nitzsche not only assisted with the recording of *Neil Young* and *Harvest*, but joined his on-tour backing group, Crazy Horse, contributing extensively to their 1970 debut album. Having scored the movie *Performance*, Nitzsche won considerable approbation for similar work on *The Exorcist* and *One Flew Over The Cuckoo's Nest*. The artist also rekindled solo aspirations with the neo-classical orchestral album *St. Giles Cripplegate*, before enjoying further success with arrangements for Mac Davis, Randy Newman and the Tubes. He remained an integral part of the US west coast music industry, and co-authored, with second wife Buffy Sainte-Marie and lyricist Will Jennings, the award-winning 'Up Where We Belong', the theme song to Taylor Hackford's *An Officer And A Gentleman*. In 1991, he audaciously paired Miles Davis and John Lee Hooker on the soundtrack of *The Hot Spot*. Nitzsche died in August 2000 from cardiac arrest brought on by recurrent bronchial infection.

● ALBUMS: *The Lonely Surfer* (Reprise 1963) ★★★, *Dance To The Hits Of The Beatles* (Reprise 1964) ★, *Chopin '66* (Reprise 1966) ★★, *St. Giles Cripplegate* (Warners 1973) ★★★, *The Razor's Edge* (Preamble 1984) ★★.

NYRO, LAURA

b. Laura Nigro, 18 October 1947, The Bronx, New York City, New York, USA, d. 8 April 1997, Danbury, Connecticut, USA. The daughter of an accomplished jazz trumpeter, Nyro was introduced to music at an early age, reputedly completing her first composition when she was only eight years old. Her main influences ranged from Bob Dylan to John Coltrane, but he artist's debut *More Than A New Discovery* aka *The First Songs*) revealed a talent akin to rill Building songwriters Carole King and Ellie Greenwich. Nyro's empathy for soul and R&B nhanced her individuality, although she later isowned the set, claiming its stilted rrangements were completed against her vishes. The set nonetheless contained several ongs which were adapted by other artists, otably 'Stoney End' (Barbra Streisand), 'And Vhen I Die' (Blood, Sweat And Tears) and Wedding Bell Blues' (Fifth Dimension). Nyro vas now managed by David Geffen, and he did nuch to further her own career, although some vould say it was purely to further his own. He ound through Clive Davis and Columbia Records, a sympathetic home for her work. Geffen was also highly active in getting other rtists to record Nyro's songs, although he also ad a financial interest in the music publishing ights. *Eli And The Thirteenth Confession* omplied more closely to Nyro's wishes; while ontaining the highly popular 'Stoned Soul icnic', also a hit for the Fifth Dimension, it evealed the growing sense of introspection that ourished on the following year's *New York endaberry*. Here the singer's dramatic ntonation, capable of sweeping from a whisper o anguished vibrato within a phrase, mphasized a bare emotional nerve exposed on You Don't Love Me When I Cry' and 'Sweet ovin' Baby'. Her frequent jumps in tempo irked ertain critics, but the majority applauded its udacious ambition and peerless fusion of ospel and white soul. The extraordinary Christmas And The Beads Of Sweat, which ncluded the startling 'Christmas Is My Soul', ffered a similar passion while *Gonna Take A Miracle*, a collaboration with producers Gamble nd Huff, acknowledged the music that provided much of the artist's inspiration. Backed y the Sigma Sound Studio house band and inging trio LaBelle, Nyro completed enthralling ersions of uptown R&B and Motown favourites. he then retired from music altogether, but re-merged in 1975 upon the disintegration of her narriage. *Smile* showed the singer's talent had emained intact and included the powerful 'I Am The Blues', while an attendant promotional our spawned *Season Of Lights*. *Nested* was, owever, less impressive and a further domestically inspired hiatus followed. *Mother's piritual* reflected Nyro's reactions to both parenthood and ageing; her comeback was onfirmed in 1988 when she embarked on her irst concert tour in over a decade. *Walk The Dog and Light The Light* was her only new release of he 90s. *Stoned Soul Picnic* was a fitting 34-song etrospective, but only weeks after its release Nyro succumbed to cancer. Laura Nyro will be emembered as a mature songwriter and a ingularly impressive performer, her intonation proving influential on several other female ingers, notably Rickie Lee Jones.

● ALBUMS: *More Than A New Discovery* aka *The First Songs* (Verve/Forecast 1967) ★★★, *Eli And The Thirteenth Confession* (Columbia 1968) ★★★★, *New York Tendaberry* (Columbia 1969) ★★★★, *Christmas And The Beads Of Sweat* (Columbia 1970) ★★★, *Gonna Take A Miracle* (Columbia 1971) ★★★, *Smile* (Columbia 1976) ★★★, *Season Of Lights* (Columbia 1977) ★★★, *Nested* (Columbia 1979) ★★★, *Mother's Spiritual* (Columbia 1985) ★★, *Live At The Bottom Line* (Columbia 1990) ★★, *Walk The Dog And Light The Light* (Columbia 1993) ★★, *Live From Mountain Stage* 1990 recording (Blue Plate 2000) ★★★, *Angel In The Dark* (Rounder 2001) ★★★.
● COMPILATIONS: *Impressions* (Columbia 1980) ★★★★, *Stoned Soul Picnic: The Best Of Laura Nyro* (Columbia/Legacy 1997) ★★★★, various artists *Time And Love: The Music Of Laura Nyro* (Astor Place 1997) ★★★, *Time And Love: The Essential Masters* (Columbia/Legacy 2000) ★★★.

OCHS, PHIL

b. 19 December 1940, El Paso, Texas, USA, d. 9 April 1976, Far Rockaway, New York, USA. A superior singer-songwriter, particularly adept at the topical song, Phil Ochs began his career at Ohio State University. He initially performed in a folk-singing duo, the Sundowners, before moving to New York, where he joined the radical Greenwich Village enclave. Ochs' early work was inspired by Woody Guthrie, Bob Gibson and Tom Paxton, and its political nature led to his involvement with the *Broadside* magazine movement. The singer was signed to the prestigious Elektra Records label, and through his initial work was hailed as a major new talent. He achieved popular acclaim when Joan Baez took one of his compositions, 'There But For Fortune', into the pop charts. Ochs' own version later appeared on his *In Concert*, the artist's best-selling set which also featured the evocative 'When I'm Gone' and the wry 'Love Me I'm A Liberal'. Ochs' move to A&M Records in 1967 signalled a new phase in his career. *Pleasures Of The Harbor*, which included the ambitious 'Crucifixion', emphasized a greater use of orchestration, as well as an increasingly rock-based perspective. He remained a lyrical songwriter; his sense of melody was undiminished, but as the decade's causes grew increasingly blurred, so the singer became disillusioned.

Although *Rehearsals For Retirement* documented the political travails of a bitter 1968, the sardonically titled *Phil Ochs Greatest Hits* showed an imaginative performer bereft of focus. He donned a gold lamé suit in a misguided effort to 'wed Elvis Presley to the politics of Che Guevara', but his in-concert rock 'n' roll medleys were roundly booed by an audience expecting overt social comment. This period is documented on the controversial *Gunfight At Carnegie Hall*. Ochs' later years were marked by tragedy. He was attacked during a tour of Africa and an attempted strangulation permanently impaired his singing voice. Beset by a chronic songwriting block, Ochs sought solace in alcohol and although a rally/concert in aid of Chile, *An Evening With Salvador Allende*, succeeded through his considerable entreaties, he later succumbed to schizophrenia. Phil Ochs was found hanged at his sister's home on 9 April 1976. One of the finest performers of his generation, he was considered, at least for a short time, Bob Dylan's greatest rival.

● ALBUMS: *All The News That's Fit To Sin* (Elektra 1964) ★★★★, *I Ain't Marching An More* (Elektra 1965) ★★★★, *Phil Ochs I Concert* (Elektra 1966) ★★★, *Pleasures Of Th Harbor* (A&M 1967) ★★★★, *Tape Fron California* (A&M 1968) ★★★, *Rehearsals Fo Retirement* (A&M 1969) ★★★★, *Phil Och Greatest Hits* (A&M 1970) ★★★, *Gunfight A Carnegie Hall* (A&M 1971) ★★, *There And Nou Live In Vancouver* (Rhino 1991) ★★★.
● COMPILATIONS: *Phil Ochs - Chords Of Fam* (A&M 1976) ★★★★, *A Toast To Those Who Ar Gone* (Archives Alive 1986) ★★★, *The War I Over: The Best Of Phil Ochs* (A&M 1988) ★★★★ *There But For Fortune* (Elektra 1989) ★★★★ *The Broadside Tapes: 1* (Folkways 1989) ★★★ *American Troubadour* (A&M 1997) ★★★ *Farewells & Fantasies* 3-CD box set (Elektra Rhino 1997) ★★★★, *Live At Newport* 1963 1964/1966 recordings (Vanguard 1998) ★★★ *The Early Years* (Vanguard 2000) ★★★★.
● FURTHER READING: *Phil Ochs: Death Of Rebel*, Marc Elliott. *There But For Fortune: Th Life Of Phil Ochs*, Michael Schumacher.

OHIO EXPRESS

Key players in the bubblegum trend of the lat 60s, the Ohio Express evolved from th Mansfield, Ohio, USA-based group Rare Bree in 1967. The group consisted of Joey Levin (lead vocals), Dale Powers (lead guitar), Dou Grassel (rhythm guitar), Jim Pflaye (keyboards), Dean Krastan (bass) and Tin Corwin (drums). Their first single, 'Beg, Borrov And Steal', had originally been recorded by th group under its old moniker in 1966 before i was reissued the following year by Came Records. There the group teamed up wit producers Jerry Kasenetz and Jeff Katz, an reached number 29 in the autumn of 1967. second Cameo single to chart was 'Try It', song penned by Levine that was later covere by the Standells. In 1968 the Ohio Expres signed with Neil Bogart's Buddah Records an released the bubblegum 'Yummy Yumm Yummy', which became their biggest hit reaching the Top 5 on both sides of the Atlantic By the end of 1969 they had charted on si more occasions, the final time with 'Sausalit (Is The Place To Go)', sung by Graham Gouldman, later of 10cc fame. The Ohi Express released six albums, of which only Ohi Express and Chewy Chewy made any real impac on the US charts. The group carried on unti 1972. Levine played with Reunion in 1974.
● ALBUMS: *Beg, Borrow And Steal* (Came 1968) ★★, *Ohio Express* (Buddah 1968) ★★★ *Salt Water Taffy* (Buddah 1968) ★★, *Chewy Chewy* (Buddah 1969) ★★★, *Mercy* (Budda 1969) ★★.
● COMPILATIONS: *Very Best Of The Ohi Express* (Buddah 1970) ★★★, *The Super k Kollection* (Collectables 1994) ★★★.

OLDHAM, ANDREW LOOG

b. 29 January 1944, Paddington, London, England. His father, an American airman, had already been killed when the young Loog was born. A one-time office junior with designer Mary Quant, Oldham made several attempts at launching a pop career under such aliases as 'Chancery Lane' and 'Sandy Beach'. When these failed he took employment as a publicist for such disparate characters as Don Arden and Brian Epstein. It was during this period that Andrew became acquainted with American producer Phil Spector, who left an indelible mark on his thinking. Having spied a glowing testimony in *Record Mirror*, Oldham watched the Rolling Stones perform at Richmond's Crawdaddy club. Impressed, he persuaded the group to break an unofficial deal with impresario Giorgio Gomelsky and emerged as their manager and producer. Although he initially tried to cultivate a clean-cut image, Oldham quickly abandoned this in favour of a rebellious, unkempt approach that directly pitted his charges against the more sedate Beatles. Copy and publicity was honed for outrage, establishing an impression that haunts the group to this date. Several other charges, including Marianne Faithfull, the Poets and the Mighty Avengers, joined his management stable, and Oldham also began recording in his own right. Clearly still indebted to Phil Spector, he fronted the Andrew Loog Oldham Orchestra over a series of singles and albums which retain a curiosity, rather than musical, value. In 1965, Oldham established the Immediate label with associate Tony Calder. Despite initial success and an impressive roster which included the Small Faces, the Nice, Chris Farlowe and Amen Corner, the company was bankrupt by the end of the decade. Andrew's tenure with the Stones ended in 1967 when he was dismissed following a period of estrangement between the two parties. He later moved to New York, and having established a small office in Broadway's Brill Building, resumed his production career. In 1977 he returned to pop management with the Texan group the Werewolves, and the following year produced their debut album. Oldham latterly married a Colombian film star and now spends several months of the year in Bogota, which he once claimed invokes the atmosphere of 50s London. Still in business with Calder they have recently attempted to resurrect the Immediate label and in 1994 they put their efforts into writing a book on Abba.

● ALBUMS: *16 Hip Hits* (Ace Of Clubs 1964) ★★★, *The Andrew Oldham Orchestra Plays Lionel Bart's Maggie May* (1964) ★★, *East Meets West – Famous Hits Of The Beach Boys And The Four Seasons* (1965) ★★, *The Rolling Stones Songbook* (Decca 1965) ★★, *Gullivers Travels* (Instant 1968) ★★.

● COMPILATIONS: *Rarities* (1984) ★★.

● FURTHER READING: *The Name Of The Game*, A. Oldham, T. Calder and C. Irwin, *Stoned*, Andrew Loog Oldham.

OLDHAM, SPOONER

b. Dewey Linton Oldham, Florence, Alabama, USA. Oldham first came to prominence as an in-house pianist at the Fame recording studio. Here he met Dan Penn and the resultant songwriting partnership was responsible for scores of southern soul compositions, including hits for James And Bobby Purify ('I'm Your Puppet'), Clarence Carter ('She Ain't Gonna Do Right') and Percy Sledge ('Out Of Left Field'). Oldham later moved to California where he became a fixture as a session musician, appearing on albums by Jackson Browne, Maria Muldaur, Linda Ronstadt and the Flying Burrito Brothers. He also maintained his relationship with Penn and the duo subsequently formed an independent production company. During the 70s/80s Oldham appeared with Neil Young as a member of the Gone With The Wind Orchestra and the International Harvesters. In 1999 a live album featuring Oldham performing with Penn was issued. Culled from performances in the UK and Ireland it included many highlights from their magnificent catalogues, including 'Cry Like A Baby' and the classic 'Dark End Of The Street', a song that has been recorded by a wide range of artists from James Carr to Barbara Dickson.

● ALBUMS: with Dan Penn *Moments From This Theatre* (Proper 1999) ★★★★.

ORBISON, ROY

b. 23 April 1936, Vernon, Texas, USA, d. 6 December 1988, Madison, Tennessee, USA. Critical acclaim came too late for one of the leading singers of the 60s. He became the master of the epic ballad of doom-laden despair, possessing a voice of remarkable range and power, and often finding it more comfortable to stay in the high register. The former reluctant rockabilly singer, who worked with Norman Petty and Sam Phillips in the 50s, moved to Nashville and became a staff writer for Acuff-Rose Music. He used his royalties from the success of 'Claudette', recorded by the Everly Brothers, and written for his first wife, to buy himself out of his contract with Sun Records, and signed with the small Monument label. Although his main intention was to be a songwriter, Orbison found himself glancing the US chart with 'Up Town' in 1960. A few months later, his song 'Only The Lonely' was rejected by Elvis Presley and the Everly Brothers, and Orbison decided to record it himself. The result was a sensation: the song topped the UK charts and narrowly missed the top spot in the USA. The trite opening of 'dum dum dum dummy doo wah, yea yea yea yea yeah', leads into one of the most distinctive pop songs ever recorded. It climaxes with a glass-shattering falsetto, and is destined to remain a modern classic.

The shy and quiet-spoken Orbison donned a pair of dark-tinted glasses to cover up his chronic astigmatism, although early publicity photos had already sneaked out. In later years his widow claimed that he was an albino. Over the next five years Orbison enjoyed unprecedented success in Britain and America, repeating his formula with further stylish but melancholy ballads, including 'Blue Angel', 'Running Scared', 'Crying', 'Dream Baby', 'Blue Bayou' and 'In Dreams'. Even during the take-over of America by the Beatles (of whom he became a good friend), Orbison was one of the few American artists to retain his ground commercially. During the Beatles' peak chart year he had two UK number 1 singles, the powerful 'It's Over' and the hypnotic 'Oh Pretty Woman'. The latter has an incredibly simple instrumental introduction with acoustic guitar and snare drum, and it is recognized today by millions, particularly following its use in the blockbuster film *Pretty Woman*. Orbison had the advantage of crafting his own songs to suit his voice and temperament, yet although he continued to have hits throughout the 60s, none except 'It's Too Soon To Know' equalled his former heights; he regularly toured Britain, which he regarded as his second home. He experienced appalling tragedy when, in 1966, his wife Claudette was killed as she fell from the back of his motorcycle, and in 1968, a fire destroyed his home, also taking the lives of his two sons.

In 1967 he starred as a singing cowboy in *The Fastest Guitar Alive*, but demonstrated that he was no actor. By the end of the decade Orbison's musical direction had faltered and he resorted to writing average MOR songs such as the unremarkable 'Penny Arcade'. The 70s were barren times for his career, although a 1976 compilation topped the UK charts. By the end of the decade he underwent open-heart surgery. He bounced back in 1980, winning a Grammy for his duet with Emmylou Harris on 'That Lovin' You Feelin' Again' from the movie *Roadie*, and David Lynch used 'In Dreams' to haunting effect in his chilling *Blue Velvet* in 1986. The following year Orbison was inducted into the Rock And Roll Hall of Fame; at the ceremony he sang 'Oh Pretty Woman' with Bruce Springsteen. With Orbison once again in favour, Virgin Records signed him, and he recorded an album of his old songs using today's hi-tech production techniques. The result was predictably disappointing; it was the sound and production of the classics that had made them great. The video *A Black & White Night* showed Orbison being courted by numerous stars, including Springsteen, Tom Waits and Elvis Costello. This high profile led him to join George Harrison, Bob Dylan, Tom Petty and Jeff Lynne as the Traveling Wilburys. Their splendid debut album owed much to Orbison's major input.

Less than a month after its critically acclaimed release, Orbison suffered a fatal heart attack in Nashville. The posthumously released *Mystery Girl* in 1989 was the most successful album of his entire career, and not merely as a result of morbid sympathy. The record contained a collection of songs that indicated a man feeling happy and relaxed; his voice had never sounded better. The uplifting 'You Got It' and the mellow 'She's A Mystery To Me' were impressive epitaphs to the legendary Big 'O'. His widow Barbara filed a sizeable lawsuit against Sony Records in 1998. She is claiming damages for the underpayment of royalties for Orbison's work with Monument Records over a lengthy period. He possessed one of the best and most distinctive voices in the history of popular music.

● ALBUMS: *Lonely And Blue* (Monument 1961) ★★, *Exciting Sounds Of Roy Orbison (Roy Orbison At The Rockhouse)* (Sun 1961) ★★, *Crying* (Monument 1962) ★★★, *In Dreams* (Monument 1963) ★★★, *Oh Pretty Woman* (1964) ★★★★, *Early Orbison* (Monument 1964) ★★, *There Is Only One Roy Orbison* (MGM 1965) ★★, *Orbisongs* (Monument 1965) ★★, *The Orbison Way* (MGM 1965) ★★, *The Classic Roy Orbison* (MGM 1966) ★★, *Roy Orbison Sings Don Gibson* (MGM 1966) ★★★, *Cry Softly, Lonely One* (MGM 1967) ★★, *The Fastest Guitar Alive* (MGM 1968) ★, *Roy Orbison's Many Moods* (MGM 1969) ★★, *The Big O* (MGM 1970) ★★, *Hank Williams: The Roy Orbison Way* (MGM 1970) ★★, *Roy Orbison Sings* (MGM 1972) ★★, *Memphis* (MGM 1972) ★★, *Milestones* (MGM 1973) ★★, *I'm Still In Love With You* (Mercury 1975) ★★, *Regeneration* (Monument 1976) ★★, *Laminar Flow* (Asylum 1979) ★★, with Johnny Cash, Jerry Lee Lewis, Carl Perkins *The Class Of '55* (1986) ★★★, *Black & White Night* (Virgin 1987) ★★★, *Mystery Girl* (Virgin 1989) ★★★★, *Rare Orbison* (Monument 1989) ★★★, *King Of Hearts* (Virgin 1992) ★★★★, *Combo Concert: 1965 Holland* (Orbison/Demon 1997) ★★★.

● COMPILATIONS: *Roy Orbison's Greatest Hits* (Monument 1962) ★★★★, *More Of Roy Orbison's Greatest Hits* (Monument 1964) ★★★, *The Very Best Of Roy Orbison* (Monument 1965) ★★★★, *The Great Songs Of Roy Orbison* (Monument 1970) ★★★★, *All-Time Greatest Hits Of Roy Orbison, Volumes 1 & 2* (Monument 1976) ★★★, *Golden Days* (Monument 1981) ★★★, *My Spell On You* (Hits Unlimited 1982) ★★★, *Big O Country* (Decca 1983) ★★, *Problem Child* (Zu Zazz 1984) ★★, *In Dreams: The Greatest Hits* (Virgin 1987) ★★★★, *The Legendary Roy Orbison* (Sony 1988) ★★★, *For The Lonely: A Roy Orbison Anthology 1956-1965* (Rhino 1988) ★★★★, *The Classic Roy Orbison (1965-1968)* (Rhino 1989) ★★★, *Sun Years* (Rhino 1989) ★★★★, *Our Love Song* (Monument 1989) ★★★, *Singles Collection* (PolyGram 1989) ★★★, *The Sun Years 1956-58* (Bear Family 1989) ★★★, *The Legendary Roy Orbison* (Columbia 1990) ★★★★, *The Gold Collection* (Tristar 1996) ★★★, *The Very Best Of Roy Orbison* (Virgin 1996) ★★★★, *The Big Roy Orbison: The Original Singles Collection* (Monument 1998) ★★★, *Love Songs* (Virgin

2001) ★★★★, *Orbison 1955-1965* 7-CD box set (Bear Family 2001) ★★★.
● VIDEOS: *A Black & White Night: Roy Orbison And Friends* (Image Entertainment 2001), *Roy Orbison: The Anthology* (Kultur/White Star 1999), *Double Feature: The Man His Music His Life* (Wienerworld 1999).
● FURTHER READING: *Dark Star*, Ellis Amburn. *Only The Lonely: The Roy Orbison Story*, Alan Clayson. *Only The Lonely: The Roy Orbison Story (10th Anniversary Special Edition)*, Alan Clayson.
● FILMS: *The Fastest Guitar Alive* (1966).

ORLONS
A mixture of school friends and neighbours, this Philadelphia-based group was formed by Shirley Brickley (b. 9 December 1944), Steve Caldwell (b. 22 November 1942), Rosetta Hightower (b. 23 June 1944, USA) and Marlena Davis (b. 4 October 1944). Introduced to Cameo Records by the lead singer of the Dovells, Len Barry, the Orlons' first hits, 'The Wah Watusi', 'Don't Hang Up' and 'South Street', cleverly exploited the male/female aspect of the group. Each of these releases reached the US Top 5, but their potential was undermined when 'Cross Fire!' (1963) and 'Rules Of Love' (1964) were only minor hits. Any lingering impetus was lost when Davis and Caldwell left the line-up, but although Audrey Brickley took their place, the Orlons broke up in 1968 when Rosetta Hightower moved to the UK to become a session singer.
● ALBUMS: *The Wah-Watusi* (Cameo 1962) ★★, *All The Hits* (Cameo 1963) ★★, *South Street* (Cameo 1963) ★★★, *Not Me* (Cameo 1964) ★★, *Down Memory Lane* (Cameo 1964) ★★★.
● COMPILATIONS: *Biggest Hits* (Cameo 1963) ★★, *Golden Hits Of The Orlons And The Dovells* (1963) ★★★, *Cameo Parkway Sessions* (London 1978) ★★.

ORPHEUS
Of the three Boston, Massachusetts, USA groups (the others were Ultimate Spinach and the Beacon Street Union) signed to MGM Records in 1968 in an attempt to create a 'Bosstown Sound' to rival San Francisco's scene, Orpheus was the only one to create music still remembered years later. The group formed in the mid-60s and was originally known as the Mods. At that time the members included guitarists/vocalists Bruce Arnold and Jack McKenes, Eric Gulliksen (bass) and Harry Sandler (drums). Preferring a soft-rock sound, the band changed its name to Orpheus and signed to MGM, recording a self-titled album in 1968. Both it and the debut single, 'Can't Find The Time', hit the lower end of the charts, but the single found a home on easy listening radio stations in later years and was still receiving airplay in the early 90s. Orpheus recorded four albums and disbanded in the early 70s.

● ALBUMS: *Orpheus* (MGM 1968) ★★★, *Ascending* (MGM 1968) ★★★, *Joyful* (MGM 1969) ★★, *Orpheus* (MGM 1971) ★★.
● COMPILATIONS: *Orpheus: The Best Of* (Ace 1995) ★★★, *The Very Best Of Orpheus* (Varèse Sarabande 2001) ★★★.

OSBORNE, TONY, SOUND
UK-born Osborne was nominal leader of a traditional jazz outfit whose 'Saturday Jump' was the opening and closing theme to the highly influential BBC Light Programme's *Saturday Club* pop series on which they appeared regularly in the late 50s. By 1960, Osborne had enlisted additional musicians of such exacting calibre that the Tony Osborne Sound was hired frequently as all-purpose accompanists to visiting Americans such as Connie Francis, whose million-selling 'Mama' was recorded in Britain with them. Signed to HMV, the orchestra spent a week in the Top 50 in February 1961 under their own name with the film tune, 'Man From Madrid'. Twelve years later, they notched up a fractionally less minor UK hit – on the Philips label – with 'The Shepherd's Song', featuring vocalist Joanne Brown. Osborne's son Gary has composed numerous songs, most notably with Elton John.

OUTLAWS (UK)
Although officially formed in December 1960, the origins of this group date to the preceding May when Billy Grey (vocals), Billy Kuy (lead guitar), Reg Hawkins (rhythm guitar), Chas Hodges (bass) and Bobby Graham (drums) put together Billy Grey And The Stormers to play at Filey holiday camp. When Grey opted to leave music, the remaining four musicians stayed together as the Outlaws. In 1961 they were signed by producer Joe Meek who employed the group to support vocalist Mike Berry, notably on 'Don't You Think Its Time' and 'Tribute To Buddy Holly'. The Outlaws also recorded instrumentals, most of which were composed by Meek and revolved around cowboy themes. Two 1961 singles, 'Swingin' Low' and 'Ambush', reached the Top 50 of the UK charts, which in turn inspired the release of *Dream Of The West*. By 1962 only Hodges remained from the founding line-up and a reshaped Outlaws was completed by Roger Mingay (lead guitar, ex-Savages), Ken Lundgren (rhythm guitar) and Don Groom (drums). Three further singles, 'Valley Of The Sioux', Ku Pow' and 'Sioux Serande', followed before further changes in personnel. However, by September 1962 the Outlaws had a settled line-up of Hodges, Lundren, Ritchie Blackmore (lead guitar, ex-Savages) and Mick Underwood (drums). They remained a crucial part of Joe Meek's productions, appearing on sessions by John Leyton, Heinz and Glenda Collins, as well as numerous package tours. The Outlaws continued to record under their own name and

the introduction of Blackmore brought more fire to their releases. 'Return Of The Outlaws', 'That Set The West Free' and 'Law And Order' are vibrant singles, but the rise of Merseybeat made Meek's work sound increasingly old-fashioned. The Outlaws' recording career ended with a vocal track, 'Keep A Knockin'', in 1964. Following this Blackmore left to join Heinz's Wild Boys, then Neil Christian's Crusaders. He was replaced by Harvey Hinsley, but in June 1965 the Outlaws split up. Hodges joined Cliff Bennett And The Rebel Rousers, while Underwood joined the embryonic Herd before opting for Episode Six. Lundren emigrated to Canada and Hinsley eventually found a niche as a member of Hot Chocolate.

● ALBUMS: *Dream Of The West* (HMV 1961) ★★.
● COMPILATIONS: *The Outlaws Ride Again (The Singles As And Bs)* (See For Miles 1990) ★★★.

OVERLANDERS

This UK vocal trio – Paul Arnold (aka Paul Friswell), Laurie Mason and Peter Bartholomew – initially pursued a folk-based career, but scored a surprise, if minor, US hit in 1964 with their version of 'Yesterday's Gone'. Buoyed by the addition of Terry Widlake (bass) and David Walsh (drums), they enjoyed a UK number 1 the following year with an opportunistic version of the Beatles' 'Michelle', but the reshaped band was unable to shake off a somewhat anachronistic image. A strong follow-up to their chart-topper, 'My Life', unfortunately failed to chart. Arnold left for a solo career in 1966, but despite the arrival of Ian Griffiths, the Overlanders failed to reap reward from their early success.

● ALBUMS: *Michelle* (Pye 1966) ★★★.
● COMPILATIONS: *Michelle: The Pye Anthology* (Castle 2001) ★★★.

PACIFIC GAS AND ELECTRIC

Formed in Los Angeles, California, USA, in 1968, Pacific Gas And Electric was a quintet that merged blues, gospel, soul, jazz and rock. The members were Charlie Allen (vocals), Glenn Schwartz (lead guitar), Thomas Marshall (rhythm guitar), Brent Black (bass) and Frank Cook (drums), the latter an alumnus of Canned Heat. The group's first album, *Get It On*, was initially issued on the small Bright Orange label and then reissued on the band's own Power Records, scraping into the charts at number 159. An appearance at the Miami Pop Festival in December 1968 was considered a highlight of that event and the group came to the attention of Columbia Records, who subsequently signed them. A self-titled album was released on Columbia in August 1969 and fared somewhat better, reaching number 91. The group's third album, *Are You Ready*, did not fare as well, reaching only number 101, but it did yield their only hit single in the title track, a gospel-influenced rocker that climbed to number 14 in mid-1970. One other album and a couple of further singles were issued but by 1971 the group was in disarray. Various personnel changes, including the addition of a horn section, left Allen the only original member by 1973, when the group's final album was issued on Dunhill Records.

● ALBUMS: *Get It On* (Bright Orange/B&C 1968) ★★★, *Pacific Gas And Electric* (CBS 1969) ★★★, *Are You Ready* (CBS 1970) ★★, *Hard Burn* (CBS 1971) ★★, *PG&E* (1971) ★★, *Pacific Gas And Electric, Starring Charlie Allen* (1973) ★★.
● COMPILATIONS: *The Best Of* (Columbia 1985) ★★★.

PADDY, KLAUS AND GIBSON

Formed in 1965, this Liverpool, England-based 'supergroup' featured Paddy Chambers (b. Patrick John Chambers, 30 April 1944, Liverpool, England, d. 28 September 2000; lead guitar, ex-Big Three and Escorts), Klaus Voormann (b. 29 April 1943, Berlin, Germany; bass) and Gibson Kemp (drums; ex-Kingsize Taylor And The Dominoes). Their three singles included a cover version of Marvin Gaye's 'No Good Without You Baby' and the theme song to British television's *Quick Before They Catch Us*, but despite the patronage of Beatles' manager Brian Epstein, the trio failed to secure commercial success. Plans by Pete Townshend to amalgamate the trio with part of the Who fell apart when tribulations within the latter act were settled. Paddy, Klaus And Gibson embarked on separate careers late in 1966 with Voormann securing subsequent fame as the illustrator of the Beatles' *Revolver* album cover and also as a member of Manfred Mann and the Plastic Ono Band.

PAGE, JIMMY

b. James Patrick Page, 9 January 1944, Heston, Middlesex, England. One of rock's most gifted and distinctive guitarists, Page began his professional career during the pre-beat era of the early 60s. He was a member of several groups, including Neil Christian's Crusaders and Carter Lewis And The Southerners, the latter of which was led by the popular songwriting team Carter And Lewis (John Carter and Ken Lewis). Page played rousing solos on several releases by Carter/Lewis protégés, notably the McKinleys' 'Sweet And Tender Romance', and the guitarist quickly became a respected session musician. He appeared on releases by Lulu, Them, Chris Farlowe, Tom Jones and Dave Berry, as well as scores of less renowned acts such as, Wayne Gibson, the Primitives, First Gear, Gregory Phillips, the Lancastrians, Les Fleur De Lys, the Factotums, Twice As Much, the Masterminds, the Fifth Avenue, but his best-known work was undertaken for producer Shel Talmy. Page appeared on sessions for the Kinks and the Who, joining an élite band of young studio musicians who included Nicky Hopkins, John Paul Jones and Bobby Graham. The guitarist completed a solo single, 'She Just Satisfies', in 1965, and although it suggested a frustration with his journeyman role, he later took up an A&R position with Immediate Records, where he produced singles for Nico and John Mayall. Having refused initial entreaties, Page finally agreed to join the Yardbirds in 1966 and he remained with this groundbreaking attraction until its demise two years later. The guitarist then formed Led Zeppelin, with whom he forged his reputation. His propulsive riffs established the framework for a myriad of tracks – 'Whole Lotta Love', 'Rock 'N' Roll', 'Black Dog', 'When The Levee Breaks' and 'Achilles' Last Stand' – now established as rock classics, while his solos have set benchmarks for a new generation of guitarists. His acoustic technique, featured on 'Black Mountain Side' and 'Tangerine', is also notable, while his work with Roy Harper, in particular on *Stormcock* (1971), was also among the finest of his career. Page's recordings since Led Zeppelin's dissolution have largely been ill-focused. He contributed the soundtrack to Michael Winner's film *Death Wish II*, while the Firm, a collaboration with Paul Rodgers, formerly of Free and Bad Company, was equally disappointing. However, a 1988 release, *Outrider*, did much to re-establish his reputation, with contributions from Robert Plant, Chris Farlowe and Jason Bonham, the son of Zeppelin's late drummer, John. The guitarist then put

considerable effort into remastering that group's revered back-catalogue. *Coverdale/Page* was a successful but fleeting partnership with the former Whitesnake singer in 1993, but it was his reunion with Robert Plant for the *Unledded* project, and an album of new material in 1998, that really captured the public's imagination. Page also achieved an unlikely UK hit single in August 1998, collaborating with Puff Daddy on 'Come With Me', from the *Godzilla* soundtrack. In 2000, Page teamed up with the Black Crowes for a series of highly praised US concerts. The two final shows at the L.A. Amphitheater were captured for posterity on *Live At The Greek*.

● ALBUMS: *Death Wish II* film soundtrack (Swan Song 1982) ★★, with Roy Harper *Whatever Happened To Jugula* (Beggars Banquet 1985) ★★★, *Outrider* (Geffen 1988) ★★, with David Coverdale *Coverdale/Page* (EMI 1993) ★★★, with Robert Plant *Unledded/No Quarter* (Fontana 1994) ★★★★, with Robert Plant *Walking Into Clarksdale* (Atlantic 1998) ★★★★, with The Black Crowes *Live At The Greek* (TVT/SPV 2000) ★★★.
● COMPILATIONS: *Jam Session* (Charly 1982) ★★, *No Introduction Necessary* (Thunderbolt 1984) ★★, *Smoke And Fire* (Thunderbolt 1985) ★★, *Jimmy Page And His Heavy Friends: Hip Young Guitar Slinger* (Sequel 2000) ★★★★, *Guitar For Hire* (Castle 2001) ★★★.
● VIDEOS: with Robert Plant *No Quarter* (Atlantic 1995).
● FURTHER READING: *Mangled Mind Archive: Jimmy Page*, Adrian T'Vell.

PAGE, LARRY

b. Leonard Davies, Hayes, Middlesex, England. While working as a packer at the nearby EMI Records factory, Davies auditioned for his record company and was duly signed. After changing his name to Larry Page in honour of Larry Parks, the star of *The Jolson Story*, the teenager began a brief recording career. Dubbed 'the Teenage Rage' by showbusiness columnist Jack Bentley, Page lived up to his sobriquet with a series of exploits, including a whirlwind romance with a fan leading to a much publicized marriage. With his sharp suits, blue-tinted hair and monotone croon, Page was an unlikely pop star but became one of the first UK performers to cover a Buddy Holly song with 'That'll Be The Day'. After retiring from performance at the end of the 50s, Page joined Mecca Enterprises as a consultant manager and ran the Orchid ballroom in Coventry. This led to a meeting with music publisher Eddie Kassner and the formation of Denmark Productions. With a deal whereby he could select and manage acts, Page launched a selection of minor talent, including Johnny B. Great, the Orchids, Little Lenny Davis and Shel Naylor.

In 1964 Page was approached by two society gentlemen, Robert Wace and Grenville Collins, and offered the chance to co-manage a north

London act known as the Ravens. Page rechristened them the Kinks, helped fashion their image and prevented their imminent dissolution following a notorious quarrel between Dave Davies and Mick Avory, in which the former was hospitalized. An unsatisfactory US tour culminated in a dispute between Page and Ray Davies that festered into a High Court action. Recovering his poise, he promoted a couple of other groups, the Pickwicks and the Riot Squad, before finding another hit artist in the Troggs. On this occasion, Page not only signed the band to a management deal but produced their records and made them the leading lights of Page One (the record company he had formed with publisher Dick James). Remarkably, his association with the Troggs ended in another High Court action yet, in spite of his litigious history, Page was never regarded as one of the unscrupulous managers of the 60s. His name was well known during this period, not only because of frequent appearances in print but the instrumental albums his label released under the self-referential title the Larry Page Orchestra. When Page One ceased operating in the early 70s, Dick James went on to found DJM Records while Larry formed the inauspicious Penny Farthing label. Page rewrote history to some extent in the 1970s and 1980s when he briefly regained managerial control of both the Troggs and the Kinks.
● ALBUMS: *Kinky Music: The Larry Page Orchestra Plays The Music Of The Kinks* (Decca 1965) ★★★, *Executive Suite* (Page One 1968) ★★, *From Larry With Love* (Page One 1968) ★★, *Instumentally Yours* (Page One 1969) ★★, *This Is Larry Page* (Page One 1970) ★★, *Presenting Larry Page* (Page One 1971) ★★.
● COMPILATIONS: *Kinky Music: Mood Mosaic Volume 3* (RPM 2000) ★★★, *Lounge With Larry: Mood Mosaic Volume 4* (RPM 2000) ★★★.

PARAMOUNTS

Formed in Southend, Essex, England, in 1961, the Paramounts evolved out of local beat attraction the Raiders. Comprising Gary Brooker (b. 29 May 1945, Hackney, London, England; keyboards/vocals), Robin Trower (b. 9 March 1945, Catford, London, England; guitar), Chris Copping (b. 29 August 1945, Middleton, Lancashire, England; bass) and Mick Brownlee (drums), the latter replaced by Barrie (B.J.) Wilson (b. Barrie James Wilson, 18 March 1947, Edmonton, London, England, d. 8 October 1990, Oregon, USA) in 1963. The group became one of the region's most popular R&B acts and by 1963 had secured a prestigious deal with EMI Records. Diz Derrick replaced the college-bound Copping prior to recording 'Poison Ivy', the quartet's debut single and sole UK Top 40 entry. Subsequent releases included material drawn from the Coasters, Jackie DeShannon and P.F. Sloan, but despite considerable acclaim, the Paramounts failed to achieve due commercial

success. Later reduced to backing Sandie Shaw and Chris Andrews, they split up in October 1966. Brooker then formed a songwriting team with lyricist Keith Reid which in turn inspired the formation of Procol Harum. By 1969, and in the wake of numerous defections, this attraction contained the same line-up as that of the original Paramounts. Trower and Brooker pursued subsequent solo careers, while the latter also worked with Joe Cocker and Eric Clapton.
● COMPILATIONS: *Whiter Shades Of R&B* (Demon 1983) ★★★, *At Abbey Road (1963-1970)* (EMI 1998) ★★★.

PARTRIDGE, DON

b. 1945, Bournemouth, Dorset, England. Self-styled 'King of the Street Singers', Partridge was discovered busking in London's Berwick Street market by former Viscount Don Paul, who in turn became his manager. 'Rosie', the singer's self-penned debut single, was reputedly recorded for the sum of £8, but became a surprise UK Top 5 hit in 1968. The artist's unconventional lifestyle and penchant for straight-talking resulted in good copy, and engendered greater publicity than his novelty status might otherwise suggest. 'Blue Eyes', Partridge's follow-up single, reached number 3, yet the song is less well recalled than its ebullient predecessor. The singer later supervised *The Buskers*, a various-artists compilation, and enjoyed one further chart entry with 'Breakfast On Pluto' in 1969. After this brief flirtation with fame, Partridge returned to his busking roots and continued to perform into the 90s.
● ALBUMS: *Don Partridge* (Columbia 1968) ★★.

PAXTON, TOM

b. 31 October 1937, Chicago, Illinois, USA. Paxton's interest in folk music developed as a student at the University of Oklahoma. In 1960 he moved to New York and became one of several aspiring performers to frequent the city's Greenwich Village coffee house circuit. Paxton made his professional debut at the Gaslight, the renowned folk haunt that also issued the singer's first album. Two topical song publications, *Sing Out!* and *Broadside*, began publishing his original compositions which bore a debt to the traditional approach of Pete Seeger and Bob Gibson. Paxton also auditioned to join the Chad Mitchell Trio, but although he failed, the group enjoyed a 1963 hit with 'The Marvellous Toy', one of his early songs. The following year Paxton was signed to Elektra Records for whom he recorded his best known work. *Ramblin' Boy* indicated the diversity which marked his recorded career and contained several highly popular performances including 'The Last Thing On My Mind', 'Goin' To The Zoo' and 'I Can't Help But Wonder Where I'm Bound'. Subsequent releases continued this mixture of romanticism, rotest and children's songs, while 'Lyndon Johnson Told The Nation' (*Ain't That News*) and 'Talking Vietnam Pot Luck Blues' (*Morning Again*) revealed a talent for satire and social comment. *The Things I Notice Now* and *#6* enhanced Paxton's reputation as a mature and complex songwriter, yet he remained better known for such simpler compositions as 'Jennifer's Rabbit' and 'Leaving London'.

Paxton left Elektra during the early 70s and though subsequent recordings proved less popular, he commanded a loyal following, particularly in the UK, where he was briefly domiciled. *How Come The Sun* (1971) was the first of three albums recorded during this period and although his work became less prolific, Paxton was still capable of incisive, evocative songwriting, such as 'The Hostage', a track from *Peace Will Come* which chronicled the massacre at Attica State Prison. This powerful composition was also recorded by Judy Collins. Paxton has latterly concentrated in writing songs and books for children. Although he was never fêted in the manner of his early contemporaries Bob Dylan, Phil Ochs and Eric Andersen, his work reveals a thoughtful, perceptive craftsmanship.

ALBUMS: *I'm The Man That Built The Bridges* (Gaslight 1962) ★★, *Ramblin' Boy* (Elektra 1964) ★★★★, *Ain't That News* (Elektra 1965) ★★, *Outward Bound* (Elektra 1966) ★★★, *Morning Again* (Elektra 1967) ★★★, *The Things I Notice Now* (Elektra 1968) ★★★★, *#6* (Elektra 1970) ★★★, *How Come The Sun* (Reprise 1971) ★★, *Peace Will Come* (Reprise 1972) ★★★, *New Songs For Old Friends* (Reprise 1973) ★★★, *Children's Song Book* (Bradleys 1974) ★★, *Something In My Life* (Private Stock 1975) ★★★, *Saturday Night* (MAM 1976) ★★★, *New Songs From The Briarpatch* (Vanguard 1977) ★★★, *Heroes* (Vanguard 1978) ★★★, *Up & Up* (Mountain Railroad 1979) ★★★, *The Paxton Report* (Mountain Railroad 1980) ★★★, *Bulletin* (Hogeye 1983) ★★★, *Even A Gray Day* (Flying Fish 1983) ★★★, *The Marvellous Toy And Other Gallimaufry* (Flying Fish 1984) ★★★, *One Million Lawyers And Other Disasters* (Flying Fish 1985) ★★★, *And Loving You* (Flying Fish 1986) ★★★, *Balloon-Alloon-Alloon* (Sony Kids 1987) ★★★, *Politics Live* (Flying Fish 1988) ★★, *It Ain't Easy* (Flying Fish 1991) ★★★, *A Child's Christmas* (Sony Kids 1992) ★★★, *Peanut Butter Pie* (Sony Kids 1992) ★★★, *Suzy Is A Rocker* (Sony Kids 1992) ★★★, *Wearing The Time* (Sugar Hill 1994) ★★★, *Live For The Record* (Sugar Hill 1996) ★★★, *A Car Full Of Songs* (Sony Kids 1997) ★★★, *Goin' To The Zoo* (Rounder 1997) ★★★, *I've Got A Yo-Yo* (Rounder 1997) ★★★, *Live In Concert* (Strange Fruit 1998) ★★★, *Fun Animal Songs* (Delta 1999) ★★★, *Fun Food Songs* (Delta 1999) ★★★, *A Car Full Of Fun Songs* (Delta 1999) ★★★, *Live From Mountain Stage* (Blue Plate 2001) ★★★, with Anne Hills *Under American Skies*

(Appleseed/Koch 2001) ★★★.
● COMPILATIONS: *The Compleat Tom Paxton* (Elektra 1970) ★★★, *A Paxton Primer* (Pax 1986) ★★★, *The Very Best Of Tom Paxton* (Flying Fish 1988) ★★★, *Storyteller* (Start 1989) ★★★, *I Can't Help But Wonder Where I'm Bound: The Best Of Tom Paxton* (Rhino 1999) ★★★★, *Best Of The Vanguard Years* (Vanguard 2000) ★★★.
● FURTHER READING: *Englebert The Elephant*, Tom Paxton and Steven Kellogg. *Belling The Cat And Other Aesop's Fables*, Tom Paxton and Robert Rayevsky. *The Story Of The Tooth Fairy*, Tom Paxton. *Going To The Zoo*, Tom Paxton.

PEACHES AND HERB

Herb Fame (b. Herbert Feemster, 1 October 1942) and Francine Barker (b. Francine Hurd, 1947). These two Washington-based singers were signed separately to the same record label, Date, and met on a promotional tour. Producer Dave Kapralik put the couple together, and their easy, if unexceptional, voices took 'Close Your Eyes' into the US Top 10 in 1967. The duo continued to figure in the charts with 'United' (1968) and 'When He Touches Me (Nothing Else Matters)' (1969). However, although Barker was featured on these records, she had been replaced for live performances by former session singer Marlene Mack (b. 1945, Virginia, USA). The 'sweethearts of soul' were ostensibly disbanded in July 1970 when a disillusioned Herb Fame left music in favour of the Police Department, although a 'bogus' duo hurriedly stepped in to fill the gap. Herb resumed recording in 1976 with a new 'Peaches', Linda Greene (b. Washington, DC, USA). Following a brief spell at MCA Records, the reconstituted couple moved to Polydor where they enjoyed a major hit with 'Shake Your Groove Thing' (1978). The following year, 'Reunited' reached number 1 in the USA and number 4 in the UK. They continued to enjoy success into the 80s, but these later releases lacked the charm of their early work.
● ALBUMS: *Let's Fall In Love* (Date 1967) ★★★, *For Your Love* (Date 1967) ★★★, *Peaches And Herb* (1977) ★★, *2 Hot!* (Polydor 1978) ★★, *Twice The Fire* (Polydor 1979) ★★, *Worth The Wait* (Polydor 1980) ★★, *Sayin' Something!* (Polydor 1981) ★★, *Remember* (1983) ★★.
● COMPILATIONS: *Peaches And Herb's Greatest Hits* (Date 1968) ★★★, *The Best Of Peaches And Herb* (Mercury 1996) ★★★.

PEANUT BUTTER CONSPIRACY

Originally known as the Ashes, this Los Angeles quintet assumed the above name in 1966. The band, comprising Sandi Robinson (vocals), John Merrill (guitar), Lance Fent (guitar), Al Brackett (bass) and Jim Voigt (drums) made their debut with 'Time Is After You' for the locally based Vault label, before securing a major deal with CBS Records the following year. Here they were united with producer Gary Usher, who sculpted

a harmonious sound redolent of the Mamas And The Papas, Jefferson Airplane and Spanky And Our Gang. *The Peanut Butter Conspiracy Is Spreading* included their anthem-like single, 'It's A Happening Thing' and the haunting 'Then Came Love', but the album failed to make a significant commercial breakthrough. Fent was replaced by Bill Wolff for *The Great Conspiracy* wherein the group showed a greater emphasis on instrumental prowess. 'Turn On A Friend' and 'Time Is After You' confirmed the unit's undoubted potential, but they were dropped from the label following the failure of 'I'm A Fool'/'It's So Hard', a non-album single. A reshaped line-up emerged to complete *For Children Of All Ages* on the Challenge label, but this lacklustre set was a great disappointment and the band then folded. Lance Fent subsequently worked with Randy Meisner, while late-period member Ralph Shuckett (ex-Clear Light) reappeared in Jo Mama.
● ALBUMS: *The Peanut Butter Conspiracy Is Spreading* (Columbia 1967) ★★, *The Great Conspiracy* (Columbia 1968) ★★★, *For Children Of All Ages* (Columbia 1968) ★★.
● COMPILATIONS: *Turn On A Friend* (Edsel 1989) ★★★.

PEDDLERS

Though short of 'teen appeal', this seated, short-haired jazz-styled combo was appreciated by other artists for their stylistic tenacity and exacting technical standards. For much of 1964, the polished jazz-pop concoctions of ex-Tornados Tab Martin (b. 24 December 1944, Liverpool, England; bass), ex-Faron's Flamingos Trevor Morais (b. 16 October 1943, Liverpool, England; drums) and the Dowlands' former backing guitarist Roy Phillips (b. 5 May 1943, Parkstone, Poole, Dorset, England; Hammond organ/vocals) were heard nightly at London's exclusive Scotch of St. James's club – and, the following January, their arrangement of Teddy Randazzo's 'Let The Sunshine In', delivered by Phillips in a blues-tinged snort, slipped fleetingly into the UK Top 50. It took over four years for the three to come up trumps again when an invigorating CBS Records contract launched *Freewheelers* into the album chart. This was the harbinger of a Top 10 strike with the self-penned 'Birth', a stunningly innovative composition. The follow-up, 'Girlie', was a minor success and the Peddlers fared well in the album lists with *Birthday*. The long-term benefits of this commercial Indian summer included the broadening of the group's work spectrum – notably in providing musical interludes for television chat-shows – and the command of larger fees for their stock-in-trade cabaret bookings. When the trio split in the mid-70s, Martin found employment as a session player, Phillips emigrated to Australasia and Morais joined Quantum Jump.
● ALBUMS: *The Fantastic Peddlers* (1966) ★★★,

Live At The Pickwick (Philips 1967) ★★★, *Freewheelers* (Columbia 1968) ★★★★, *Three in A Cell* (Columbia) ★★★, *Birthday* (Columbia 1970) ★★★, *Three For All* (Philips 1970) ★★★, *Georgia On My Mind* (Philips 1971) ★★★, *Suite London* (Philips 1972) ★★.
● COMPILATIONS: *The Best Of The Peddlers* (1974) ★★★, *Part One* (Sony 1997).

PENN, DAN

b. Wallace Daniel Pennington, 16 November 1941, Vernon, Alabama, USA. His reputation as a songwriter was secured when one of his early compositions, 'Is A Bluebird Blue?', was a hit for Conway Twitty in 1960. Penn also led a local group, the Mark V, which included David Briggs (piano), Norbert Putnam (bass) and Jerry Carrigan (drums). Also known as Dan Penn And The Pallbearers, these musicians later formed the core of the first Fame studio house band. Their subsequent departure for a more lucrative career in Nashville left room for a second session group, among whose number was pianist Spooner Oldham. Over the next few years, Penn's partnership with this newcomer produced scores of excellent southern soul compositions, including 'Out Of Left Field', 'I Tears Me Up' (Percy Sledge), 'Slippin' Around' (Clarence Carter) and 'Let's Do It Over' (Joe Simon) and 'The Dark End Of The Street', a classic guilt-laced 'cheating' ballad, first recorded by James Carr. Penn subsequently left Fame to work at the rival American Sound studio where he joined studio-owner Chips Morman, with whom he had also struck up a songwriting partnership (their 'Do Right Woman – Do Right Man' was the b-side of Aretha Franklin's first hit single for Atlantic Records). Later at American Studios, Penn would also be responsible for producing hit group the Box Tops, but in 1969 he broke away to form his own studio, Beautiful Sounds.
The 70s, however, were much less prolific. Having flirted with a singing career with several one-off releases, he finally produced a fine solo album, *Nobody's Fool*, which included the first version of 'I Hate You', later covered by Bobby Bland. Penn also maintained his friendship with Oldham, but by the time the duo formed their own independent production company, the changing face of popular music rendered their talents anachronistic. However, in 1991 Oldham and Penn reunited to appear at the New York Bottom Line's In Their Own Words songwriter series. This live performance of self-penned songs was so successful that it inspired Penn to record a new album of his own work, both old and new, the critically acclaimed *Do Right Man*. To promote the album he played a further series of live dates, including the 1994 Porretta Terme Soul Festival in Italy, and then at London's South Bank Centre as part of a salute to southern songwriters under the banner The American South, which also

included Allen Toussaint and Joe South. A live album recorded in the UK and Ireland with Spooner Oldham was issued in 1999. The following year's *Blue Nite Lounge* was another low-key gem.

ALBUMS: *Nobody's Fool* (Bell 1973) ★★★, *Do Right Man* (Sire/Warners Brothers 1994) ★★★★, with Spooner Oldham *Moments From This Theatre* (Proper 1999) ★★★★, *Blue Nite Lounge* (Tom's Cabin Records 2000) ★★★.

PENTANGLE

Formed in 1967, Pentangle was inspired by *Bert And John*, a collaborative album by folk musicians Bert Jansch (b. 3 November 1943, Glasgow, Scotland) and John Renbourn (b. Torquay, Devon, England). Vocalist Jacqui McShee (b. Catford, South London, England) an established figure on the traditional circuit, joined Danny Thompson (b. April 1939, London, England; bass) and Terry Cox (drums), both of Alexis Korner's Blues Incorporated, in a quintet which also embraced blues and jazz forms. Their respective talents were expertly captured on *The Pentangle*, where the delicate acoustic interplay between Jansch and Renbourn was brilliantly underscored by Thompson's sympathetic support and McShee's soaring intonation. Stylish original material balanced songs pulled from folk's heritage ('Let No Man Steal Your Thyme', 'Brunton Town'), while the inclusion of the Staple Singers' 'Hear My Call' confirmed the group's eclecticism. This feature was expanded on the double-set *Sweet Child*, which included two compositions by jazz bass player Charles Mingus, 'Haitian Fight Song' and 'Goodbye Pork Pie Hat'. The group enjoyed considerable commercial success with *Basket Of Light*, which included 'Light Flight', the theme song to the UK television series, *Take Three Girls*. However, despite an undoubted dexterity and the introduction of muted electric instruments, subsequent releases were marred by a sense of sterility, and lacked the passion of concurrent releases undertaken by the two guitarists.

Pentangle was disbanded in 1972, following which Thompson began a partnership with John Martyn. Cox undertook a lucrative session career before backing French singer Charles Aznavour, and while Jansch continued his solo career, McShee fronted the John Renbourn Band between 1974 and 1981. The original Pentangle reconvened the following year for a European tour and *Open The Door*, although defections owing to outside commitments led to considerable changes. McShee, Cox and Jansch were joined by Nigel Portman-Smith (bass) and Mike Piggott for 1985's *In The Round*. Cox was then replaced by Gerry Conway and Piggott by Rod Clements (ex-Lindisfarne) for 1988's *So Early In The Spring*. *Think Of Tomorrow*, released three years later, saw Clements make way for guitarist Peter Kirtley. The same line-up

also completed 1993's *One More Road* and 1994's *Live*. At this time Jansch once more became distracted by solo projects and the group's later shows saw him replaced by former Cat Stevens' guitarist Alun Davies. In 1995 McShee released her debut solo album (with Conway and John Martyn's ex-keyboard player Spencer Cozens). The following spring Renbourn and McShee celebrated 30 years of playing together with a series of concerts.

● ALBUMS: *The Pentangle* (Transatlantic 1968) ★★★★, *Sweet Child* (Transatlantic 1968) ★★★★, *Basket Of Light* (Transatlantic 1969) ★★★★, *Cruel Sister* (Transatlantic 1970) ★★★, *Reflection* (Transatlantic 1971) ★★★★, *Solomon's Seal* (Reprise 1972) ★★★, *Open The Door* (Making Waves 1983) ★★★, *In The Round* (Making Waves 1985) ★★★, *So Early In The Spring* (Park 1988) ★★★, *Think Of Tomorrow* (Ariola/Hypertension 1991) ★★★, *One More Road* (Permanent 1993) ★★★, *Live At The BBC* (Strange Fruit 1994) ★★★★, *Live 1994* (Hypertension 1995) ★★, *On Air* (Strange Fruit 1998) ★★★, as Jacqui McShee's Pentangle *Passe-Avant* (Park 1998) ★★★, as Jacqui McShee's Pentangle *At The Little Theatre* (Park 2001) ★★★.

● COMPILATIONS: *History Book* (Transatlantic 1972) ★★★★, *Pentangling* (Transatlantic 1973) ★★★★, *The Pentangle Collection* (Transatlantic 1975) ★★★★, *Anthology* (Transatlantic 1978) ★★★★, *The Essential Pentangle Volume 1* (Transatlantic 1987) ★★★★, *The Essential Pentangle Volume 2* (Transatlantic 1987) ★★★, *Early Classics* (Shanachie 1992) ★★★, *People On The Highway 1968 – 1971* (Demon 1993) ★★★★, *Light Flight: The Anthology* (Essential 2000) ★★★, *The Pentangle Family* (Transatlantic 2000) ★★★★.

PETER AND GORDON

Both the sons of doctors and former pupils of the prestigious English public school Westminster Boys, this privileged pair were signed by producer Norman Newell, following a residency at London's Piccadilly Club. Peter Asher (b. 2 June 1944, London, England) and Gordon Waller (b. 4 June 1945, Braemar, Grampian, Scotland), had a crucial advantage over their contemporaries – the priceless patronage of Paul McCartney, who was then dating Peter's sister, Jane. The perfectly enunciated 'A World Without Love' quickly became a transatlantic chart topper and two more 1964 McCartney compositions, 'Nobody I Know' and 'I Don't Want To See You Again', brought further success. The Beatles connection was again evident on 'Woman', which McCartney composed under the pseudonym Bernard Webb. In the meantime, the duo had switched to successful revivals of 50s material, including Buddy Holly's 'True Love Ways' and the Teddy Bears' retitled 'To Know You Is To Love You'. Peter And Gordon's wholesome image was somewhat belied by Waller's appearances in the salacious British Sunday press, but this did little to affect their popularity in the USA. Although the partnership was strained by late 1966, the saucy 'Lady Godiva' provided a new direction and was followed by the similarly quaint novelty numbers 'Knight In Rusty Armour' and 'Sunday For Tea'. One year later, they split. Waller subsequently pursued an unsuccessful solo career and appeared as the Pharoah in *Joseph And The Amazing Technicolor Dreamcoat*. Asher moved to Los Angeles and emerged as a formidable record producer and manager.

● ALBUMS: *Peter & Gordon* (UK) *A World Without Love* (US) (Columbia/Capitol 1964) ★★★, *In Touch With Peter And Gordon* UK only (Columbia 1964) ★★★, *I Don't Want To See You Again* US only (Capitol 1964) ★★★, *I Go To Pieces* (Columbia 1965) ★★★, *True Love Ways* US only (Capitol 1965) ★★★, *Hurtin' 'N' Lovin'* UK only (Columbia 1965) ★★★, *Peter And Gordon Sing And Play The Hits Of Nashville, Tennessee* US only (Capitol 1966) ★★, *Woman* (Capitol/ Columbia 1966) ★★★, *Somewhere* UK only (Columbia 1966) ★★★, *Lady Godiva* (Capitol/ Columbia 1967) ★★, *A Knight In Rusty Armour* (Capitol 1967) ★★, *In London For Tea* (Capitol 1967) ★★, *Hot, Cold And Custard* (Capitol 1968) ★★.

● COMPILATIONS: *Greatest Hits* (Columbia 1966) ★★★, *The Best Of Peter & Gordon* (EMI 1977) ★★★, *The Hits And More* (EMI 1986) ★★★, *Peter & Gordon: The Best Of The EMI Years* (EMI 1991) ★★★, *The Best Of Peter & Gordon* (Rhino 1991) ★★★, *The EP Collection* (See For Miles 1995) ★★★.

PETER, PAUL AND MARY

Peter Yarrow (b. 31 May 1938, New York City, New York, USA), Noel Paul Stookey (b. Paul Stookey, 30 November 1937, Baltimore, Maryland, USA) and Mary Allin Travers (b. 7 November 1937, Louisville, Kentucky, USA) began performing together in the spring of 1961. They were brought together by Albert Grossman, one of folk music's successful entrepreneurs, in an attempt to create a contemporary Kingston Trio. The three singers were already acquainted through the close-knit coffee house circuit, although Dave Van Ronk was briefly considered as a possible member. The group popularized several topical songs, including 'If I Had A Hammer' and were notable early interpreters of Bob Dylan compositions. In 1963 their version of 'Blowin' In The Wind' reached number 2 in the US chart while a follow-up reading of 'Don't Think Twice, It's All Right' also broached the Top 10. They were also renowned for singing children's songs, the most memorable of which was the timeless 'Puff The Magic Dragon'. The trio became synonymous with folk's liberal traditions, but were increasingly perceived as old-fashioned as the

60s progressed. Nonetheless a 1966 selection *Album*, included material by Laura Nyro and featured assistance from Paul Butterfield, Mike Bloomfield and Al Kooper, while the following year's 'I Dig Rock 'N' Roll Music' became their fifth US Top 10 hit. Peter, Paul And Mary enjoyed their greatest success in 1969 with 'Leaving On A Jet Plane'. This melodramatic John Denver song reached number 1 in the US and number 2 in the UK, but by then the individual members were branching out in different directions.

Yarrow had been the primary force behind *You Are What You Eat*, an eccentric hippie movie which also featured Tiny Tim and John Simon and in 1970 he, Travers and Stookey announced their formal dissolution. The three performers embarked on solo careers but were ultimately unable to escape the legacy of their former group. They reunited briefly in 1972 for a George McGovern Democratic Party rally, and again in 1978. Following several albums for the short-lived Gold Castle label in the late 80s, the trio returned to Warner Brothers Records in the 90s. Although criticized for their smooth and wholesome delivery, Peter, Paul And Mary proved to be one of the 60s most distinctive acts and played a crucial bridging role between two contrasting generations of folk music.

● ALBUMS: *Peter, Paul And Mary* (Warners 1962) ★★★★, *Peter, Paul And Mary (Moving)* (Warners 1963) ★★★★, *In The Wind* (Warners 1963) ★★★★, *In Concert* (Warners 1964) ★★★★, *A Song Will Rise* (Warners 1965) ★★★★, *See What Tomorrow Brings* (Warners 1965) ★★★, *Peter, Paul And Mary Album* (Warners 1966) ★★★★, *Album 1700* (Warners 1967) ★★★, *Late Again* (Warners 1968) ★★★, *Peter, Paul And Mommy* (Warners 1969) ★★★, *Reunion* (Warners 1978) ★★★, *Such Is Love* (Warners 1983) ★★, *No Easy Walk To Freedom* (Gold Castle 1986) ★★, *A Holiday Celebration* (Gold Castle 1988) ★★★, *Flowers And Stones* (Gold Castle 1990) ★★, *Peter Paul & Mommy, Too* (Warners 1993) ★★, *LifeLines* (Warners 1995) ★★, *LifeLines Live* (Warners 1996) ★★.

Solo: Paul Stookey *Paul And* (Warners 1971) ★★★, *One Night Stand* (Warners 1973) ★★, *Real ToReel* (1977) ★★, *Something New And Fresh* (1978) ★★, *Band & Bodyworks* (Myrrh 1980) ★★, *Wait'll You Hear This!* (1982) ★★, *State Of The Heart* (1985) ★★, *In Love Beyond Our Lives* (Gold Castle 1990) ★★. Mary Travers *Mary* (Warners 1971) ★★, *Morning Glory* (Warners 1972) ★★, *All My Choices* (Warners 1973) ★★, *Circles* (Warners 1974) ★★, *It's In Everyone Of Us* (Chrysalis 1978) ★★. Peter Yarrow *Peter* (Warners 1972) ★★★, *That's Enough For Me* (Warners 1973) ★★, *Hard Times* (Warners 1975) ★★.

● COMPILATIONS: *(Ten) Years Together: The Best Of Peter, Paul And Mary* (Warners 1970) ★★★★, *Around The Campfire* (Warners 1998) ★★★, *The Collection: Their Greatest Hits & Finest*

Performances (Reader's Digest 1998) ★★★, *Songs Of Conscience & Concern* (Warners 1999) ★★★, *Weave Me This Sunshine* (ABX 1999) ★★★.
● VIDEOS: *25th Anniversary Concert* (Rhino Home Video 1986), *Holiday Concert* (Rhino Home Video 1988), *Peter, Paul & Mommy, Too* (Warner Reprise Video 1993), *LifeLines Live* (Warner Reprise Video 1996).

PHILLIPS, JOHN

b. 30 August 1935, Parris Island, South Carolina, USA, d. 18 March 2001, USA. The son of a marine officer, Phillips studied at George Washington University and briefly attended the US Naval Academy. He relocated to New York in the late 50s to join the Greenwich Village folk scene. Phillips began his recording career in 1960 as a member of pop singing group the Smoothies, but the following year formed the Journeymen with Scott McKenzie and Dick Weissman. This popular harmony folk act completed three albums marked by Phillips' growing songwriting abilities. He relaunched his old group as the New Journeymen with his wife Michelle Phillips and Marshall Brickman. His compositions were by now being recorded by the Kingston Trio, but as traditional folk began embracing elements of rock, so Phillips forged a more contemporary perspective, notably with the Mamas And The Papas. Evocative songs, including 'California Dreamin'', 'Monday, Monday', 'I Saw Her Again' and 'Creeque Alley' helped established this act as one of the finest of its era, while Phillips also penned the anthemic 'San Francisco (Be Sure To Wear Flowers In Your Hair)' for former colleague McKenzie. The artist drew contemporaneous plaudits as chief organizer of the Monterey Pop Festival, but internal disaffection led to the demise of the Mamas And The Papas in 1968.
In 1970 he completed *The Wolfking Of LA*, a superb set and critics favourite, redolent of his erstwhile band but infused with C&W affectations, before completing an ill-fated Mamas And The Papas reunion album. Phillips' recording career waned during the 70s. His third wife, Genevieve Waite, released one album, *Romance Is On The Rise*, which benefited considerably from Phillips' involvement. A solo single, 'Revolution On Vacation', appeared in 1976, but although he produced several tracks for former wife Michelle Phillips' *Victim Of Romance* and assembled the soundtrack for Nicolas Roeg's *The Man Who Fell To Earth*, he fell increasingly under the influence of hard drugs. A projected solo album, with Keith Richards and Mick Jagger assisting, fell apart in a narcotic haze (although the results were finally released in 1998 on Phillips' own Paramour Records). An equally disastrous attempt at a Broadway musical, *Man On The Moon*, further dented Phillips' standing. Convicted of trafficking in narcotics in 1981, he

entered a rehabilitation programme and, following his sentence, re-established the Mamas And The Papas as a touring attraction. His highly-successful autobiography provided a salutary overview of dashed 60s idealism and an extraordinary saga of his gigantic appetite for drugs. In 1988, Phillips joined McKenzie in composing 'Kokomo' which, with additional contributions by Mike Love and Terry Melcher, became a US number 1 hit for the Beach Boys. By 1991 the Mamas And The Papas included Phillips, Scott McKenzie, Elaine 'Spanky' McFarlane and his daughter Laura McKenzie Phillips. Another daughter, Chynna Phillips, was a member of the multi-million selling group Wilson Phillips, and a track about John, written by Chynna is contained on their second album, *Shadows And Light*. Varying line-ups of the Mamas And The Papas, who were inducted into the Rock And Roll Hall Of Fame in 1998, continued touring into the new century. Phillips had completed an album of new material at the time of his death of heart failure in March 2001. Clearly Phillips had lost his muse, and no doubt his former wild lifestyle had taken a lot out of him. However, the body of work he produced between 1966 and 1968 represents some of the best songs of the era. Many of them, already classics, are destined to live on.
● ALBUMS: *The Wolfking Of LA* (Stateside 1970) ★★★★, *Half Stoned* aka *Pay Pack & Follow* (Paramour/Eagle 1998) ★★★, *Phillips 66* (Eagle 2001) ★★.
● FURTHER READING: *Papa John*, John Phillips with Jim Jerome.

PICKETT, WILSON

b. 18 March 1941, Prattville, Alabama, USA. Raised in Detroit, Pickett sang in several of the city's R&B groups. He later joined the Falcons, an act already established by the million-selling 'You're So Fine'. Pickett wrote and sang lead on their 1962 hit 'I Found A Love', after which he launched his solo career. A false start at Correctone was overturned by two powerful singles, 'If You Need Me' and 'It's Too Late', recorded for Lloyd Price's Double L outlet. The former track's potential was undermined by Solomon Burke's opportunistic cover version on Atlantic Records, the irony of which was compounded when Pickett moved to that same label in 1964. An inspired partnership with guitarist Steve Cropper produced the classic standard 'In The Midnight Hour', as well as 'Don't Fight It' (both 1965), '634-5789 (Soulsville, USA)', 'Land Of 1,000 Dances' (written by Chris Kenner), 'Mustang Sally' (all 1966) and 'Funky Broadway' (1967). The singer's other collaborators included erstwhile Falcon Eddie Floyd and former Valentino, Bobby Womack. The latter partnership proved increasingly important as the 60s progressed. A 1968 album, *The Midnight Mover*, contained six songs featuring Womack's involvement. Deprived of the Stax Records house band due to their break with Atlantic, Pickett next recorded at Fame's Muscle Shoals studio. A remarkable version of 'Hey Jude', with Duane Allman on guitar, was the highlight of this period.

A further experiment, this time with producers Gamble And Huff, resulted in two hits, 'Engine Number 9' (1970) and 'Don't Let The Green Grass Fool You' (1971), while a trip to Miami provided 'Don't Knock My Love', his last Top 20 hit for Atlantic. Wilson switched to RCA Records in 1972, but his previous success was hard to regain. A mercurial talent, Pickett returned to Muscle Shoals for *Funky Situation* (1978), issued on his own Wicked label. More recently, he worked alongside Joe Tex, Don Covay, Ben E. King and Solomon Burke in a revamped Soul Clan. Pickett was the invisible figure and role model in the award-winning soul music film *The Commitments* in 1991. Since then, Pickett has found life a struggle and has been arrested and charged with various drug offences. He returned in 1999, however, with his first new studio album in 12 years.

● ALBUMS: *It's Too Late* (Double-L 1963) ★★, *In The Midnight Hour* (Atlantic 1965) ★★★★, *The Exciting Wilson Pickett* (Atlantic 1966) ★★★★, *The Wicked Pickett* (Atlantic 1966) ★★★★, *The Sound Of Wilson Pickett* (Atlantic 1967) ★★★★, *I'm In Love* (Atlantic 1968) ★★★, *The Midnight Mover* (Atlantic 1968) ★★★, *Hey Jude* (Atlantic 1969) ★★★, *Right On* (Atlantic 1970) ★★★, *Wilson Pickett In Philadelphia* (Atlantic 1970) ★★, *If You Need Me* (Joy 1970) ★★, *Don't Knock My Love* (Atlantic 1971) ★★, *Mr. Magic Man* (RCA 1973) ★★, *Miz Lena's Boy* (RCA 1973) ★★, *Tonight I'm My Biggest Audience* (RCA 1974) ★★, *Live In Japan* (1974) ★★, *Pickett In Pocket* (RCA 1974) ★★, *Join Me & Let's Be Free* (RCA 1975) ★★, *Chocolate Mountain* (Wicked 1976) ★★, *A Funky Situation* (Wicked 1978) ★★, *I Want You* (EMI America 1979) ★★, *The Right Track* (EMI America 1981) ★★, *American Soul Man* (Motown 1987) ★★, *It's Harder Now* (Bullseye Blues 1999) ★★★.

● COMPILATIONS: *The Best Of Wilson Pickett* (Atlantic 1967) ★★★★, *The Best Of Wilson Pickett Vol. 2* (Atlantic 1971) ★★★★, *Wilson Pickett's Greatest Hits i* (Atlantic 1973) ★★★★, *Collection* (Castle 1992) ★★★, *A Man And A Half: The Best Of Wilson Pickett* (Rhino/Atlantic 1992) ★★★★★, *Take Your Pleasure Where You Find It: Best Of The RCA Years* (Camden 1998) ★★.

PINKERTON'S ASSORTED COLOURS

Originally known as the Liberators, this Rugby, Warwickshire-based quintet comprised: Samuel 'Pinkerton' Kemp (vocals/autoharp), Tony Newman (guitar), Tom Long (guitar), Barrie Bernard (bass) and Dave Holland (drums). One of the lesser known UK pop groups of the period, they came under the wing of Fortunes manager Reg Calvert, who encouraged them to change their name and to each don a different pastel shade suit. This unusual stress on colour was reflected in various publicity stunts such as polluting the fountains of Trafalgar Square with red dye. The gimmicky use of a kazoo and autoharp, aided by extensive plugging on the pirate radio stations Radio City and Radio Caroline, proved sufficient to break their Decca Records debut single, 'Mirror Mirror'. A minor dispute between their manager and rival Phil Solomon over the ownership of various group names brought them even more publicity than their next single, 'Don't Stop Loving Me Baby', which barely scraped into the Top 50. Stuart Colman replaced Bernard in the line-up, but by that time the group were losing momentum and their prospects were further blighted by the tragic death of their manager. After a lean patch, the group abbreviated their name to Pinkerton's Colours, then Pinkerton and finally evolved into the Flying Machine. That last incarnation brought a happier ending for, in the summer of 1969, the spin-off group achieved a US Top 5 hit with 'Smile A Little Smile For Me'.

PITNEY, GENE

b. 17 February 1941, Hartford, Connecticut, USA. Although Pitney began recording in 1959 ('Classical Rock 'N' Roll' was recorded with Ginny Mazarro as Jamie And Jane), his initial success came as a songwriter, providing the Kalin Twins with 'Loneliness', Roy Orbison with 'Today's Teardrops' and Bobby Vee with 'Rubber Ball'. His solo recording career took off in 1961 with the multi-tracked 'I Wanna Love My Life Away' and the dramatic film themes 'Town Without Pity' and 'The Man Who Shot Liberty Valance'. Throughout this period, he was still writing for other artists, creating big hits for Ricky Nelson ('Hello Mary Lou') and the Crystals ('He's A Rebel'). In 1963, Pitney toured Britain where his 'Twenty Four Hours From Tulsa' reached the Top 10. After meeting the Rolling Stones, he recorded Mick Jagger and Keith Richards' 'That Girl Belongs To Yesterday'. Despite the onslaught of the beat groups, Pitney's extraordinarily impassioned big ballads remained popular in the USA and especially in the UK. Among his hits from this era were Barry Mann and Cynthia Weill's 'I'm Gonna Be Strong' (1964), 'I Must Be Seeing Things' (1965), 'Looking Through The Eyes Of Love' (1965), 'Princess In Rags' (1965), 'Backstage' (1966), Randy Newman's 'Nobody Needs Your Love' (1966), 'Just One Smile' (1966) and 'Something's Gotten Hold Of My Heart' (1967). The controversial 'Somewhere In The Country' (about an unmarried mother) was less successful.

In addition, Pitney recorded albums in Italian and Spanish, with one of his songs, 'Nessuno Mi Puo Guidicare' coming second in the 1966 San Remo Song Festival. There were also country music albums with George Jones and Melba

Montgomery. By the late 60s, his popularity in America had waned but he continued to tour in Europe, having the occasional hit like 'Maria Elena' (1969), 'Shady Lady' (1970) and 'Blue Angel' (1974). In 1989, he had unexpected success when he sang on a revival of 'Something's Gotten Hold Of My Heart' with Marc Almond, which topped the UK charts. He continues to tour regularly, and is especially popular in the UK and Italy. Pitney will be remembered for his impassioned vocals and his almost faultless choice of material throughout the 60s.

● ALBUMS: *The Many Sides Of Gene Pitney* (Musicor 1962) ★★★, *Only Love Can Break A Heart* (Musicor 1962) ★★★, *Gene Pitney Sings Just For You* (Musicor 1963) ★★★, *Gene Pitney Sings World-Wide Winners* (Musicor 1963) ★★★, *Blue Gene* (Musicor 1963) ★★★★, *Gene Pitney Meets The Fair Young Ladies Of Folkland* (Musicor 1964) ★★, *Gene Italiano* (Musicor 1964) ★★, *It Hurts To Be In Love* (Musicor 1964) ★★★★, with George Jones *For The First Time Ever! Two Great Singers* (Musicor 1965) ★★, *I Must Be Seeing Things* (Musicor 1965) ★★★★, *It's Country Time Again!* (Musicor 1965) ★★, *Looking Through The Eyes Of Love* (Musicor 1965) ★★★★, *Espanol* (Musicor 1965) ★★, with Melba Montgomery *Being Together* (Musicor 1965) ★★, *Famous Country Duets* (Musicor 1965) ★, *Backstage (I'm Lonely)* (Musicor 1966) ★★★, *Nessuno Mi Puo Giudicare* (Musicor 1966) ★★, *The Gene Pitney Show* (Musicor 1966) ★★★, *The Country Side Of Gene Pitney* (Musicor 1966) ★, *Young And Warm And Wonderful* (Musicor 1966) ★★★★, *Just One Smile* (Musicor 1967) ★★★★, *Sings Burt Bacharach* (Musicor 1968) ★★★, *She's A Heartbreaker* (Musicor 1968) ★★, *This Is Gene Pitney* (Musicor 1970) ★★, *Ten Years After* (Musicor 1971) ★★, *Pitney '75* (Bronze 1975) ★★, *Walkin' In The Sun* (1979) ★★.

● COMPILATIONS: *Big Sixteen* (Musicor 1964) ★★★★, *More Big Sixteen, Volume 2* (Musicor 1965) ★★★, *Big Sixteen, Volume 3* (Musicor 1966) ★★★, *Greatest Hits Of All Time* (Musicor 1966) ★★★, *Golden Greats* (Musicor 1967) ★★★, *Spotlight On Gene Pitney* (Design 1967) ★★★, *The Gene Pitney Story* double album (Musicor 1968) ★★★, *The Greatest Hits Of Gene Pitney* (Musicor 1969) ★★★★, *The Man Who Shot Liberty Valance* (Music Disc 1969) ★★★, *Town Without Pity* (Music Disc 1969) ★★★, *Twenty Four Hours From Tulsa* (Music Disc 1969) ★★★, *Baby I Need Your Lovin'* (Music Disc 1969) ★★★, *The Golden Hits Of Gene Pitney* (Musicor 1971) ★★★, *The Fabulous Gene Pitney* double album (Columbia 1972) ★★★, *The Pick Of Gene Pitney* (West-52 1979) ★★★, *Anthology 1961-68* (Rhino 1986) ★★★★, *Best Of* (K-Tel 1988) ★★★, *All The Hits* (Jet 1990) ★★★, *Greatest Hits* (Pickwick 1991) ★★★, *The Original Hits 1961-70* (Jet 1991) ★★★, *The EP Collection* (See For Miles 1991) ★★★, *The Heartbreaker* (Repertoire 1994) ★★★, *More Greatest Hits* (Varèse Sarabande 1995)

★★★, *The Gold Collection: 15 Classic Hits* (Summit 1996) ★★★, *The Great Recordings* (Tomato 1996) ★★★, *The Definitive Collection* (Charly 1997) ★★★, *The Hits And More* (Eagle 1998) ★★★★, *25 All-Time Greatest Hits* (Varèse Sarabande 1999) ★★★★, *Being Together/The Country Side Of Gene Pitney* (Sequel 1999) ★★, *Geno Italiano/Nessuno Mi Puo Giudicare* (Sequel 1999) ★★, *Looking Through Gene Pitney: The Ultimate Collection* (Sequel 2000) ★★★★.

PLASTIC PENNY

This immensely talented UK quartet came together in 1968 when three former members of the Universals, Brian Keith (vocals), Paul Raymond (keyboards) and Tony Murray (bass), joined Mick Grabham (lead guitar) and Nigel Olsson (drums) to record for Larry Page's recently launched Page One record label. Their debut was the refreshing and melodic 'Everything I Am', originally recorded by the Box Tops. It became a UK Top 10 hit, but after the failure of the Bill Martin/Phil Coulter composition 'Nobody Knows If', the group drifted into other recording ventures. Singer Brian Keith was the first to quit, leaving before the completion of the group's sole album. One-hit-wonders on paper, Plastic Penny nevertheless established themselves as an excellent musicians' training ground. Grabham founded Cochise and later joined Procol Harum, Murray teamed up with the Troggs, Paul Raymond had spells with Chicken Shack and Savoy Brown, and Olsson collaborated with the Spencer Davis Group and Elton John.

● ALBUMS: *Two Sides Of The Penny* (Page One 1968) ★★★, *Currency* (Page One 1969) ★★, *Heads I Win – Tails You Lose* (Page One 1970) ★★.

POETS

Formed in Glasgow, Scotland in 1961, the Poets were one of Britain's more adventurous acts. Although obliged to play contemporary hits, the group – George Gallagher (vocals), Hume Paton (guitar), Tony Myles (guitar), John Dawson (bass) and Alan Weir (drums) – brought original songs and R&B favourites into their early sets. By 1964 they had become a leading attraction, resplendent in frilled shirts and matching velvet suits. Rolling Stones' manager Andrew Loog Oldham signed the quintet to his management and production company, attracted by their image and self-composed material. The Poets' debut single 'Now We're Thru', reached number 31 in the UK charts. Its ethereal drone and echoed 12-string guitars enhanced Gallagher's nasal delivery and the performance was the template for subsequent releases. Although the group did not secure another hit, their versatile recordings included ballads and uptempo R&B, imbued with their unique approach. The Poets' line-up fragmented and by 1967 none of the original group remained. Andi Mulvey (vocals), Fraser

Watson (guitar), Ian McMillan (guitar), Norrie Maclean (bass) and Jim Breakey completed 'Wooden Spoon', the unit's last official single. Further fragmentation ensued, but the name was retained by McMillan until the early 70s. The core of the group subsequently joined Longdancer, while McMillan formed Blue with late-period member Hughie Nicholson.

POMUS, DOC

b. Jerome Felder, 27 June 1925, Brooklyn, New York, USA, d. 14 March 1991, New York, USA. Doc Pomus wrote the lyrics for several great rock 'n' roll songs of the 60s. With Mort Shuman, who composed the music, Pomus' credits included the Drifters' 'Save The Last Dance For Me', 'This Magic Moment', 'Sweets For My Sweet' and 'I Count The Tears'; Elvis Presley's 'Little Sister', '(Marie's The Name) His Latest Flame', 'Viva Las Vegas', 'Surrender' and others; and Dion's 'A Teenager In Love'. Pomus developed polio at the age of nine and used crutches to walk. (A fall in his adult life left him confined to a wheelchair.) At the age of 15, already playing saxophone and singing at jazz and blues clubs, he changed his name to avoid alerting his parents of his activities – they found out two years later. Pomus recorded a number of blues-influenced singles for independent companies beginning in his late teens, none of which were hits. At that time he also began writing. The first major placement for one of his compositions was 'Boogie Woogie Country Girl', the b-side of Big Joe Turner's 'Corrine Corrina', in 1956. That same year he wrote 'Lonely Avenue', recorded by Ray Charles. In 1957 Pomus teamed up with writers/producers Leiber And Stoller to pen 'Young Blood', a hit for the Coasters, as well as 'She's Not You', a hit for Presley. Pomus and Shuman (who had played piano on some of Pomus' recordings), officially teamed in 1958 and signed to the Hill & Range publishing company in New York.

Although Pomus' first love was blues, he became an adept rock lyricist, and among his earliest hits were such pop songs as Fabian's 'Turn Me Loose', 'I'm A Man' and 'Hound Dog Man'. Pomus and Shuman also wrote the Mystics' 'Hushabye', Bobby Darin's 'Plain Jane', Gary 'U.S.' Bonds' 'Seven Day Weekend', Gene McDaniels' 'Spanish Lace', Terry Stafford's 'Suspicion', Andy Williams' 'Wrong For Each Other' and 'Can't Get Used To Losing You' (later covered by the Beat), and Jimmy Clanton's 'Go, Jimmy, Go'. Presley recorded over 20 of their songs, 'Kiss Me Quick' and 'A Mess Of Blues' being among the other noteworthy titles. Pomus estimated he wrote over one thousand songs during his career. The Pomus-Shuman team separated in 1965 and Pomus kept a low profile throughout much of the late 60s and 70s. In the late 70s he was instrumental in helping assemble the Blues Brothers band and then began writing prolifically again. He co-wrote an album with Mink DeVille's Willy DeVille, two with Dr. John and one with B.B. King, the Grammy-winning There Must Be A Better World Somewhere. Later Pomus co-compositions appeared in the films Cry Baby and Dick Tracy. He remained a champion of the blues and blues musicians until his death and was an often-seen figure at New York clubs where both older and younger blues artists performed. In 1991 Pomus received the Rhythm and Blues Foundation's Pioneer Award, the first white to be so honoured. Pomus died of lung cancer at the age of 65 later that year. He was inducted into the Rock And Roll Hall Of Fame in January 1992.

POOLE, BRIAN, AND THE TREMELOES

Formed in 1958 and fronted by vocalist Brian Poole (b. 2 November 1941, Barking, Essex, England), this UK pop group were initially known as Brian Poole And The Tremilos when they made their debut at the Ilford Palais in 1960. Poole was originally known as a Buddy Holly imitator and even went as far as wearing spectacles filled with plain glass. After his backing musicians reverted to the title Tremeloes, the entire ensemble successfully auditioned for Decca Records on 1 January 1962 and were signed in favour of the Beatles. A cover of the Isley Brothers' 'Twist And Shout' brought them a UK Top 10 hit the following year. The follow-up, a reading of the Contours' 'Do You Love Me?', hit number 1 in the UK and 15 other countries. American success, however, remained frustratingly elusive. Appropriately, the group's manager Peter Walsh recruited Buddy Holly's former mentor Norman Petty to play piano on two further UK smashes, the wistful 'Someone Someone' and mawkish 'The Three Bells'. Thereafter, the group's popularity waned and they seemed increasingly dated in comparison to the more aggressive R&B-based UK pop outfits that emerged in 1964-65. Sensing a crisis, Poole elected to leave the group and branch out into the world of big ballads. He subsequently moved into cabaret, retired to the family butcher business, and later resurfaced with a record and publishing company. Against the odds, it was his backing group, the Tremeloes, that went on to achieve enormous chart success under their own name. In later decades, Poole and most of his original Tremeloes were back ploughing the rich vein of 60s nostalgia tours. In 1996 Poole proved he was no literary slouch with the publication of Talkback: An Easy Guide To British Slang. His two daughters Karen and Shellie found commercial success in the 90s as Alisha's Attic.

● ALBUMS: Twist And Shout With Brian Poole And The Tremeloes (Decca 1963) ★★★★, Big Hits Of '62 (Ace of Clubs 1963) ★, It's About Time (Decca 1965) ★★★.
● COMPILATIONS: Remembering Brian Poole And The Tremeloes (Decca 1977) ★★★★, Twist And Shout (Decca 1982) ★★★, Do You Love Me

Deram 1991) ★★★, *The Very Best Of* (Spectrum 998) ★★★.
● FURTHER READING: *Talkback: An Easy Guide to British Slang*, Brian Poole.

POWER, DUFFY

Power was one of several British vocalists, including Marty Wilde, Billy Fury and Dickie Pride, signed to the Larry Parnes stable. Having completed a series of pop singles, including 'Dream Lover' and 'Ain't She Sweet', the singer embraced R&B in 1963 with a pulsating version of the Beatles' 'I Saw Her Standing There' on which he was backed by the Graham Bond Quartet. Power's later singles included 'Tired, Broke and Busted', which featured support from the Paramounts, but he later supplemented his solo career by joining Alexis Korner's Blues Incorporated. The singer appeared on *Red Hot from Alex* (1964), *Sky High* (1966) and *Blues Incorporated (Wednesday Night Prayer Meeting)* (1967), during which time group members Jack Bruce (bass), Danny Thompson (bass) and Terry Cox (drums) assisted on several informal sessions later compiled on Power's *Innovations* set. Guitarist John McLaughlin also contributed to the album, before joining the vocalist's next project, Duffy's Nucleus. Power resumed his solo career late in 1967 when this short-lived attraction disbanded, but a subsequent fitful recording schedule did little justice to this underrated artist's potential.
ALBUMS: *Innovations* aka *Mary Open The Door* (Transatlantic 1970) ★★★, *Little Boy Blue* (1971) ★, *Duffy Power* (Spark 1973) ★★, *Powerhouse* (Buk 1976) ★★.
COMPILATIONS: *Blues Power* (1992) ★★★.

PRESLEY, ELVIS

Elvis Aaron Presley, 8 January 1935, Tupelo, Mississippi, USA, d. 16 August 1977, Memphis, Tennessee, USA. The most celebrated popular music phenomenon of his era and, for many, the purest embodiment of rock 'n' roll, Elvis Presley's life and career have become part of rock legend. The elder of twins, his younger brother, Jesse Garon, was stillborn, a tragedy that partly contributed to the maternal solicitude dominating his childhood and teenage years. Presley's first significant step towards a musical career took place at the age of eight when he won $5 in a local song contest performing the lachrymose Red Foley ballad, 'Old Shep'. His earliest musical influence came from attending the Pentecostal Church and listening to the psalms and gospel songs. He also had a strong grounding in country and blues and it was the combination of these different styles that was to provide his unique musical identity.
By the age of 13, Presley had moved with his family to Memphis, and during his later school years began cultivating an outsider image, with long hair, spidery sideburns and ostentatious clothes. After leaving school he took a job as a

truck driver, a role in keeping with his unconventional appearance. In spite of his rebel posturing, Presley remained studiously polite to his elders and was devoted to his mother. Indeed, it was his filial affection that first prompted him to visit Sun Records, whose studios offered the sophisticated equivalent of a fairground recording booth service. As a birthday present to his mother, Gladys, Presley cut a version of the Ink Spots' 'My Happiness', backed with the Raskin/Brown/Fisher standard 'That's When Your Heartaches Begin'. The studio manager, Marion Keisker, noted Presley's unusual but distinctive vocal style and informed Sun's owner/producer Sam Phillips of his potential. Phillips nurtured the boy for almost a year before putting him together with country guitarist Scotty Moore and bass player Bill Black. Their early sessions showed considerable promise, especially when Presley began alternating his unorthodox low-key delivery with a high-pitched whine. The amplified guitars of Moore and Black contributed strongly to the effect and convinced Phillips that the singer was startlingly original. In Presley, Phillips saw something that he had long dreamed and spoken of discovering; a white boy who sang like a Negro.
Presley's debut disc on Sun was the extraordinary 'That's All Right (Mama)', a showcase for his rich, multi-textured vocal dexterity, with sharp, solid backing from his compatriots. The b-side, 'Blue Moon Of Kentucky', was a country song, but the arrangement showed that Presley was threatening to slip into an entirely different genre, closer to R&B. Local response to these strange-sounding performances was encouraging and Phillips eventually shifted 20,000 copies of the disc. For his second single, Presley recorded Roy Brown's 'Good Rockin' Tonight' backed by the zingy 'I Don't Care If The Sun Don't Shine'. The more roots-influenced 'Milk Cow Blues Boogie' followed, while the b-side, 'You're A Heartbreaker', had some strong tempo changes that neatly complemented Presley's quirky vocal. 'Baby Let's Play House'/'I'm Left, You're Right, She's Gone' continued the momentum and led to Presley performing on *The Grand Old Opry* and *Louisiana Hayride* radio programmes. A series of live dates commenced in 1955 with drummer D.J. Fontana added to the ranks. Presley toured clubs in Arkansas, Louisiana and Texas billed as 'The King Of Western Bop' and 'The Hillbilly Cat'. Audience reaction verged on the fanatical, which was hardly surprising given Presley's semi-erotic performances. His hip-swivelling routine, in which he cascaded across the stage and plunged to his knees at dramatic moments in a song, was remarkable for the period and prompted near-riotous fan mania. The final Sun single, a cover version of Junior Parker's 'Mystery Train', was later acclaimed by many as the definitive rock 'n' roll single, with its chugging rhythm, soaring

vocal and enticing lead guitar breaks.

It established Presley as an artist worthy of national attention and ushered in the next phase of his career, which was dominated by the imposing figure of Colonel Tom Parker. The Colonel was a former fairground huckster who managed several country artists including Hank Snow and Eddy Arnold. After relieving disc jockey Bob Neal of Presley's managership, Parker persuaded Sam Phillips that his financial interests would be better served by releasing the boy to a major label. RCA Records had already noted the commercial potential of the phenomenon under offer and agreed to pay Sun Records a release fee of $35,000, an incredible sum for the period. The sheer diversity of Presley's musical heritage and his remarkable ability as a vocalist and interpreter of material enabled him to escape the cultural parochialism of his R&B-influenced predecessors. The attendant rock 'n' roll explosion, in which Presley was both a creator and participant, ensured that he could reach a mass audience, many of them newly affluent teenagers.

It was on 10 January 1956, a mere two days after his 21st birthday, that Presley entered RCA's studios in Nashville to record his first tracks for a major label. His debut session produced the epochal 'Heartbreak Hotel', one of the most striking pop records ever released. Co-composed by Hoyt Axton's mother Mae, the song evoked nothing less than a vision of absolute funereal despair. There was nothing in the pop charts of the period that even hinted at the degree of desolation described in the song. Presley's reading was extraordinarily mature and moving, with a determined avoidance of any histrionics in favour of a pained and resigned acceptance of loneliness as death. The economical yet acutely emphatic piano work of Floyd Cramer enhanced the stark mood of the piece, which was frozen in a suitably minimalist production. The startling originality and intensity of 'Heartbreak Hotel' entranced the American public and pushed the single to number 1 for an astonishing eight weeks. Whatever else he achieved, Presley was already assured a place in pop history for one of the greatest major label debut records ever released. During the same month that 'Heartbreak Hotel' was recorded, Presley made his national television debut displaying his sexually enticing gyrations before a bewildered adult audience whose alleged outrage subsequently persuaded producers to film the star exclusively from the waist upwards. Having outsold his former Sun colleague Carl Perkins with 'Blue Suede Shoes', Presley released a debut album that contained several of the songs he had previously recorded with Sam Phillips, including Little Richard's 'Tutti Frutti', the R&B classic 'I Got A Woman' and an eerie, wailing version of Richard Rodgers/Lorenz Hart's 'Blue Moon', which emphasized his remarkable vocal range. Since hitting number 2 in the UK lists with

'Heartbreak Hotel', Presley had been virtually guaranteed European success and his profile was increased via a regular series of releases as RCA took full advantage of their bulging back catalogue. Although there was a danger of overkill, Presley's talent, reputation and immensely strong fanbase vindicated the intense release schedule and the quality of the material ensured that the public was not disappointed. After hitting number 1 for the second time with the slight ballad 'I Want You, Need You, I Love You', Presley released what was to become the most commercially successful double-sided single in pop history, 'Hound Dog'/'Don't Be Cruel'. The former was composed by the immortal rock 'n' roll songwriting team of Leiber And Stoller, and presented Presley at his upbeat best with a novel lyric, complete with a striking guitar solo and spirited hand clapping from his backing group the Jordanaires. Otis Blackwell's 'Don't Be Cruel' was equally effective with a striking melody line and some clever and amusing vocal gymnastics from the hiccuping King of Western Bop, who also received a co writing credit. The single remained at number 1 in the USA for a staggering 11 weeks and both sides of the record were massive hits in the UK. Celluloid fame for Presley next beckoned with *Love Me Tender*, produced by David Weisbert who had previously worked on James Dean's *Rebel Without A Cause*. Presley's movie debut received mixed reviews but was a box-office smash, while the smouldering, perfectly enunciated title track topped the US charts for five weeks. The spate of Presley singles continued in earnest through 1957 and one of the biggest was another Otis Blackwell composition, 'All Shook Up', which the singer used as a cheekily oblique comment on his by now legendary dance movements. By late 1956 it was rumoured that Presley would be drafted into the US Army and, as if to compensate for that irksome eventuality, RCA, Twentieth Century Fox and the Colonel stepped up the work-rate and release schedules. Incredibly, three major films were completed in the next two-and-a-half years. *Loving You* boasted a quasi-auto biographical script with Presley playing a truck driver who becomes a pop star. The title track became the b-side of '(Let Me Be Your) Teddy Bear' which reigned at number 1 for seven weeks. The third movie, *Jailhouse Rock*, was Presley's most successful to date with an excellent soundtrack and some inspired choreography. The Leiber and Stoller title track was an instant classic that again topped the US charts for seven weeks and made pop history by entering the UK listings at number 1.

The fourth celluloid outing, *King Creole* (adapted from the Harold Robbins novel, *A Stone For Danny Fisher*), is regarded by many as Presley's finest film and a firm indicator of his sadly unfulfilled potential as a serious actor. Once more the soundtrack album featured some surprisingly strong material such as the haunting 'Crawfish' and the vibrant 'Dixieland Rock'. By the time *King Creole* was released in 1958, Elvis had already been inducted into the US Forces. A publicity photograph of the singer having his hair shorn symbolically commented on his approaching musical emasculation. Although rock 'n' roll purists mourned the passing of the old Elvis, it seemed inevitable in the context of the 50s that he would move towards a broader base appeal and tone down his rebellious image. From 1958-60, Presley served in the US Armed Forces, spending much of his time in Germany where he was regarded as a model soldier. It was during this period that he first met 14-year-old Priscilla Beaulieu, whom he later married in 1967. Back in America, the Colonel kept his absent star's reputation intact via a series of films, record releases and extensive merchandising. Hits such as 'Wear My Ring Around Your Neck', 'Hard Headed Woman', 'One Night', 'I Got Stung', 'A Fool Such As I' and 'A Big Hunk O' Love' filled the long, two-year gap and by the time Presley reappeared, he was ready to assume the mantle of all-round entertainer. The change was immediately evident in the series of number 1 hits that he enjoyed in the early 60s. The enormously successful 'It's Now Or Never', based on the Italian melody 'O Sole Mio', revealed the King as an operatic crooner, far removed from his earlier raucous recordings. 'Are You Lonesome Tonight?', originally recorded by Al Jolson as early as 1927, allowed Presley to quote some Shakespeare in the spoken-word middle section as well as showing his ham-acting ability with an overwrought vocal.

The new clean-cut Presley was presented on celluloid in *GI Blues*. The movie played upon his recent army exploits and saw him serenading a puppet on the charming chart-topper 'Wooden Heart', which also allowed Elvis to show off his knowledge of German. The grandiose 'Surrender' completed this phase of big ballads in the old-fashioned style. For the next few years Presley concentrated on an undemanding spree of films, including *Flaming Star*, *Wild In The Country*, *Blue Hawaii*, *Kid Galahad*, *Girls! Girls! Girls!*, *Follow That Dream*, *Fun In Acapulco*, *It Happened At The World's Fair*, *Kissin' Cousins*, *Viva Las Vegas*, *Roustabout*, *Girl Happy*, *Tickle Me*, *Harem Scarum*, *Frankie And Johnny*, *Paradise – Hawaiian Style* and *Spinout*. Not surprisingly, most of his album recordings were hastily completed soundtracks with unadventurous commissioned songs. For his singles he relied increasingly on the formidable Doc Pomus/Mort Shuman team who composed such hits as 'Mess Of Blues', 'Little Sister' and 'His Latest Flame'. More and more, however, the hits were adapted from films and their chart positions suffered accordingly. After the 1963 number 1 'Devil In Disguise', a bleak period followed in which such minor songs as 'Bossa Nova Baby', 'Kiss Me

Quick', 'Ain't That Lovin' You Baby' and 'Blue Christmas' became the rule rather than the exception. Significantly, his biggest success of the mid-60s, 'Crying In The Chapel', had been recorded five years earlier, and part of its appeal came from the realization that it represented something ineffably lost.

In the wake of the Beatles' rise to fame and the beat boom explosion, Presley seemed a figure out of time. Nevertheless, in spite of the dated nature of many of his recordings, he could still invest power and emotion into classic songs. The sassy 'Frankie And Johnny' was expertly sung by Presley, as was his moving reading of Ketty Lester's 'Love Letters'. His other significant 1966 release, 'If Everyday Was Like Christmas', was a beautiful festive song unlike anything else in the charts of the period. By 1967, however, it was clear to critics and even a large proportion of his devoted following that Presley had seriously lost his way. He continued to grind out pointless movies such as *Double Trouble*, *Speedway*, *Clambake* and *Live A Little, Love A Little*, even though the box office returns were increasingly poor. His capacity to register instant hits, irrespective of the material was also wearing thin, as such lowly placed singles as 'You Gotta Stop' and 'Long Legged Woman' demonstrated all too alarmingly. However, just as Elvis' career had reached its all-time nadir he seemed to wake up, take stock, and break free from the artistic malaise in which he found himself. Two songs written by country guitarist Jerry Reed, 'Guitar Man' and 'US Male', proved a spectacular return to form for Elvis in 1968, such was Presley's conviction that the compositions almost seemed to be written specifically for him. During the same year, Colonel Tom Parker had approached NBC-TV about the possibility of recording a Presley Christmas special in which the singer would perform a selection of religious songs similar in feel to his early 60s album *His Hand In Mine*. However, the executive producers of the show vetoed that concept in favour of a one-hour spectacular designed to capture Elvis at his rock 'n' rollin' best. It was a remarkable challenge for the singer, seemingly in the autumn of his career, and he responded to the idea with unexpected enthusiasm.

The *Elvis TV Special* was broadcast in America on 3 December 1968 and has since become legendary as one of the most celebrated moments in pop broadcasting history. The show was not merely good but an absolute revelation, with the King emerging as if he had been frozen in time for 10 years. His determination to recapture past glories oozed from every movement and was discernible in every aside. With his leather jacket and acoustic guitar strung casually round his neck, he resembled nothing less than the consummate pop idol of the 50s who had entranced a generation. To add authenticity to the proceedings he was accompanied by his old sidekicks Scotty Moore and D.J. Fontana. There was no sense of self-parody in the show as Presley joked about his famous surly curled-lip movement and even heaped passing ridicule on his endless stream of bad movies. The music concentrated heavily on his 50s classics but, significantly, there was a startling finale courtesy of the passionate 'If I Can Dream' in which he seemed to sum up the frustration of a decade in a few short lines. The critical plaudits heaped upon Elvis in the wake of his television special prompted the singer to undertake his most significant recordings in years. With producer Chips Moman overseeing the sessions in January 1969, Presley recorded enough material to cover two highly praised albums, *From Elvis In Memphis* and *From Memphis To Vegas/From Vegas To Memphis*. The former was particularly strong with such distinctive tracks as the eerie 'Long Black Limousine' and the engagingly melodic 'Any Day Now'. On the singles front, Presley was back in top form and finally coming to terms with contemporary issues, most notably on the socially aware 'In The Ghetto', which hit number 2 in the UK and number 3 in the USA. The glorious 'Suspicious Minds', a wonderful song of marital jealousy, with cascading tempo changes and an exceptional vocal arrangement, gave him his first US chart-topper since 'Good Luck Charm' back in 1962. Subsequent hits such as the maudlin 'Don't Cry Daddy', which dealt with the death of a marriage, ably demonstrated Presley's ability to read a song. Even his final few films seemed less disastrous than expected. In 1969's *Charro*, he grew a beard for the first time in his portrayal of a moody cowboy, while *A Change Of Habit* dealt with more serious subject matter than usual. More importantly, Presley returned as a live performer at Las Vegas, with a strong backing group including guitarist James Burton and pianist Glen D. Hardin. In common with John Lennon, who also returned to the stage that same year with the Plastic Ono Band, Presley opened his set with Carl Perkins' 'Blue Suede Shoes'. His comeback was well received and one of the live songs, 'The Wonder Of You', stayed at number 1 in Britain for six weeks during the summer of 1970. There was also a revealing documentary film of the tour – *That's The Way It Is* – and a companion album that included contemporary cover versions, such as Tony Joe White's 'Polk Salad Annie', Creedence Clearwater Revival's 'Proud Mary' and Neil Diamond's 'Sweet Caroline'.

During the early 70s Presley continued his live performances, but soon fell victim to the same artistic atrophy that had bedevilled his celluloid career. Rather than re-entering the studio to record fresh material he relied on a slew of patchy live albums that saturated the marketplace. What had been innovative and exciting in 1969 swiftly became a tedious routine and an exercise in misdirected potential. The

backdrop to Presley's final years was a sordid slump into drug dependency, reinforced by the pervasive unreality of a pampered lifestyle in his fantasy home, Gracelands. The dissolution of his marriage in 1973 coincided with a further decline and an alarming tendency to put on weight. Remarkably, he continued to undertake live appearances, covering up his bloated frame with brightly coloured jump suits and an enormous, ostentatiously jewelled belt. He collapsed onstage on a couple of occasions and finally on 16 August 1977 his tired body expired. The official cause of death was a heart attack, undoubtedly brought on by barbiturate usage over a long period. In the weeks following his demise, his record sales predictably rocketed and 'Way Down' proved a fittingly final UK number 1.

The importance of Presley in the history of rock 'n' roll and popular music remains incalculable. In spite of his iconographic status, the Elvis image was never captured in a single moment of time like that of Bill Haley, Buddy Holly or even Chuck Berry. Presley, in spite of his apparent creative inertia, was not a one-dimensional artist clinging to history but a multi-faceted performer whose career spanned several decades and phases. For purists and rockabilly enthusiasts it is the early Presley that remains of greatest importance and there is no doubting that his personal fusion of black and white musical influences, incorporating R&B and country, produced some of the finest and most durable recordings of the century. Beyond Elvis 'The Hillbilly Cat', however, there was the face that launched a thousand imitators, that black-haired, smiling or smouldering presence who stared from the front covers of numerous EPs, albums and film posters of the late 50s and early 60s. It was that well-groomed, immaculate pop star who inspired a generation of performers and second-rate imitators in the 60s. There was also Elvis the Las Vegas performer, vibrant and vulgar, yet still distant and increasingly appealing to a later generation brought up on the excesses of 70s rock and glam ephemera. Finally, there was the bloated Presley who bestrode the stage in the last months of his career. For many, he has come to symbolize the decadence and loss of dignity that is all too often heir to pop idolatry. It is no wonder that Presley's remarkable career so sharply divides those who testify to his ultimate greatness and those who bemoan the gifts that he seemingly squandered along the way. Twenty years after his death, in August 1997, there was no waning of his power and appeal. Television, radio, newspapers and magazines all over the world still found that, whatever was happening elsewhere, little could compare to this anniversary.

● ALBUMS: *Elvis Presley* (RCA Victor 1956) ★★★★, *Elvis* (RCA Victor 1956) ★★★★★, *Rock 'N' Roll* UK release (HMV 1956) ★★★★, *Rock 'N'*

Roll No. 2 UK release (HMV 1957) ★★★★, Loving You film soundtrack (RCA Victor 1957) ★★★★, Elvis' Christmas Album (RCA Victor 1957) ★★★, King Creole film soundtrack (RCA Victor 1958) ★★★★, For LP Fans Only (RCA Victor 1959) ★★★★, A Date With Elvis (RCA Victor 1959) ★★★★, Elvis Is Back! (RCA Victor 1960) ★★★★, G.I. Blues film soundtrack (RCA Victor 1960) ★★★, His Hand In Mine (RCA Victor 1961) ★★★, Something For Everybody (RCA Victor 1961) ★★★, Blue Hawaii (RCA Victor 1961) ★★★, Pot Luck (RCA Victor 1962) ★★★, Girls! Girls! Girls! film soundtrack (RCA Victor 1963) ★★★, It Happened At The World's Fair film soundtrack (RCA Victor 1963) ★★, Fun In Acapulco film soundtrack (RCA Victor 1963) ★★, Kissin' Cousins film soundtrack (RCA Victor 1964) ★★, Roustabout film soundtrack (RCA Victor 1964) ★★, Girl Happy film soundtrack (RCA Victor 1965) ★★, Harem Scarum film soundtrack (RCA Victor 1965) ★★, Frankie And Johnny film soundtrack (RCA Victor 1966) ★★, Paradise, Hawaiian Style film soundtrack (RCA Victor 1966) ★★, Spinout film soundtrack (RCA Victor 1966) ★★, How Great Thou Art (RCA Victor 1967) ★★★, Double Trouble film soundtrack (RCA Victor 1967) ★★, Clambake film soundtrack (RCA Victor 1967) ★★, Speedway film soundtrack (RCA Victor 1968) ★★, Elvis – TV Special (RCA Victor 1968) ★★★, From Elvis In Memphis (RCA Victor 1969) ★★★★, From Memphis To Vegas/From Vegas To Memphis (RCA Victor 1969) ★★★, On Stage February 1970 (RCA Victor 1970) ★★★★, Elvis Back In Memphis (RCA Victor 1970) ★★★, That's The Way It Is (RCA 1970) ★★★, Elvis Country (I'm 10,000 Years Old) (RCA 1971) ★★★, Love Letters From Elvis (RCA 1971) ★★★, Elvis Sings The Wonderful World Of Christmas (RCA 1971) ★★★, Elvis Now (RCA 1972) ★★★, He Touched Me (RCA 1972) ★★★, Elvis As Recorded At Madison Square Garden (RCA 1972) ★★★, Aloha From Hawaii Via Satellite (RCA 1973) ★★★, Elvis (RCA 1973) ★★★, Raised On Rock/For Ol' Times Sake (RCA 1973) ★★★, Good Times (RCA 1974) ★★★, Elvis Recorded Live On Stage In Memphis (RCA 1974) ★★★★, Having Fun With Elvis On Stage (RCA 1974) ★, Promised Land (RCA 1975) ★★★, Elvis Today (RCA 1975) ★★★, From Elvis Presley Boulevard, Memphis, Tennessee (RCA 1976) ★★★, Welcome To My World (RCA 1977) ★★★, Moody Blue (RCA 1977) ★★★, Guitar Man (RCA 1980) ★★★, The Ultimate Performance (RCA 1981) ★★★, The Sound Of Your Cry (RCA 1982) ★★★, The First Year (Sun 1983) ★★★, Jailhouse Rock/Love In Las Vegas (RCA 1983) ★★★, Elvis: The First Live Recordings (Music Works 1984) ★★★, The Elvis Presley Interview Record: An Audio Self-Portrait (RCA 1984) ★★, with Carl Perkins and Jerry Lee Lewis The Million Dollar Quartet (RCA 1990) ★★★, The Lost Album (RCA 1991) ★★★, If Every Day Was Like Christmas (RCA 1994) ★★★, Elvis Presley '56 (RCA 1996) ★★★★★, Essential Elvis, Volume 4: A Hundred Years From Now (RCA 1996) ★★★, Essential Elvis, Volume 5: Rhythm And Country (RCA 1998) ★★★, Tiger Man 1968 recording (RCA 1998) ★★★★, Essential Elvis, Volume 6: Such A Night (RCA 2000) ★★★.

● COMPILATIONS: The Best Of Elvis UK release (HMV 1957) ★★★★, Elvis' Golden Records (RCA Victor 1958) ★★★★★, 50,000,000 Elvis Fans Can't Be Wrong: Golden Records, Volume 2 (RCA Victor 1960) ★★★★★, Elvis' Golden Records, Volume 3 (RCA Victor 1963) ★★★★, Elvis For Everyone! (RCA Victor 1965) ★★★, Elvis' Golden Records, Volume 4 (RCA Victor 1968) ★★★★, Elvis Sings 'Flaming Star' And Other Hits From His Movies (RCA Camden 1969) ★★, Let's Be Friends (RCA Camden 1970) ★★★★, Almost In Love (RCA Camden 1970) ★★, Worldwide 50 Gold Award Hits, Volume 1 – A Touch Of Gold 4-LP box set (RCA Victor 1970) ★★★★★, You'll Never Walk Alone (RCA Camden 1971) ★★★, C'mon Everybody (RCA Camden 1971) ★★★, The Other Sides – Worldwide 50 Gold Award Hits, Volume 2 4-LP box set (RCA Victor 1971) ★★★★, I Got Lucky (RCA Camden 1971) ★★★, Elvis Sings Hits From His Movies, Volume 1 (RCA Camden 1972) ★★★, Burning Love And Hits From His Movies, Volume 2 (RCA Camden 1972) ★★★, Separate Ways (RCA Camden 1973) ★★★, Elvis – A Legendary Performer, Volume 1 (RCA 1974) ★★★★, Hits Of The 70s (RCA 1974) ★★★, Pure Gold (RCA 1975) ★★★, Easy Come Easy Go (RCA Camden 1975) ★★★, The U.S. Male (RCA Camden 1975) ★★★, Elvis Presley's Greatest Hits 7-LP box set (Readers Digest 1975) ★★★, Pictures Of Elvis (RCA Starcall 1975) ★★, Elvis – A Legendary Performer, Volume 2 (RCA 1976) ★★★★, Sun Sessions (RCA 1976) ★★★★★, Elvis In Demand (RCA 1977) ★★★, The Elvis Tapes interview disc (Redwood 1977) ★★, He Walks Beside Me (RCA 1978) ★★★, Elvis Sings For Children And Grownups Too! (RCA 1978) ★★★, Elvis – A Canadian Tribute (RCA 1978) ★★★, The '56 Sessions, Volume 1 (RCA 1978) ★★★★, Elvis' 40 Greatest (RCA 1978) ★★★★★, Elvis – A Legendary Performer, Volume 3 (RCA 1979) ★★★★, Our Memories Of Elvis (RCA 1979) ★★★, Our Memories Of Elvis Volume 2 (RCA 1979) ★★★, The '56 Sessions, Volume 2 (RCA 1979) ★★★★, Elvis Presley Sings Leiber And Stoller (RCA 1979) ★★★★, Elvis – A Legendary Performer, Volume 4 (RCA 1980) ★★★★, Elvis Aaron Presley 8-LP box set (RCA 1980) ★★★, This Is Elvis (RCA 1981) ★★★, Elvis – Greatest Hits, Volume 1 (RCA 1981) ★★, The Elvis Medley (RCA 1982) ★★★, I Was The One (RCA 1983) ★★★★, Elvis' Golden Records, Volume 5 (RCA 1984) ★★★★, Elvis: A Golden Celebration 6-LP box set (RCA 1984) ★★★, Rocker (RCA 1984) ★★★★, Reconsider Baby (RCA 1985) ★★★★, A Valentine Gift For You (RCA 1985) ★★★, Always On My Mind (RCA 1985) ★★★★, Return Of The Rocker (RCA 1986) ★★★, The Number One Hits (RCA 1987) ★★★★★, The Top Ten Hits (RCA 1987) ★★★★, The Complete Sun Sessions (RCA 1987) ★★★★★, Essential Elvis (RCA 1988)

★★★★, *Stereo '57 (Essential Elvis Volume 2)* (RCA 1988) ★★★★, *Known Only To Him: Elvis Gospel: 1957-1971* (RCA 1989) ★★★★, *Hits Like Never Before: Essential Elvis, Volume 3* (RCA 1990) ★★★, *Collector's Gold* (RCA 1991) ★★★★, *The King Of Rock 'n' Roll: The Complete '50s Masters* 5-CD box set (RCA 1992) ★★★★★, *From Nashville To Memphis: The Essential '60s Masters* 5-CD box set (RCA 1993) ★★★★★, *Amazing Grace: His Greatest Sacred Songs* (RCA 1994) ★★★★, *Heart And Soul* (RCA 1995) ★★, *Walk A Mile In My Shoes: The Essential '70s Masters* 5-CD box set (RCA 1995) ★★★★, *Presley – The All Time Greats* (RCA 1996) ★★★★, *Great Country Songs* (RCA 1997) ★★★, *Platinum: A Life In Music* 4-CD box set (RCA 1997) ★★★★, *Love Songs* (Camden 1999) ★★★★, *Sunrise* (RCA 1999) ★★★★, *Suspicious Minds: The Memphis 1969 Anthology* (RCA 1999) ★★★★, *The Home Recordings* (RCA 1999) ★★, *Artist Of The Century* 3-CD set (RCA 1999) ★★★★★, *Can't Help Falling In Love: The Hollywood Hits* (RCA 1999) ★★★, *The Legend Begins* (Manifest 2000) ★★, *Peace In The Valley* 3-CD box set (RCA 2000) ★★★★, *The 50 Greatest Hits* (RCA 2000) ★★★★★, *The Live Greatest Hits* (RCA 2001) ★★★★, *Elvis: Live In Las Vegas* 4-CD box set (RCA 2001) ★★★★.

● VIDEOS: *Elvis On Tour* (MGM/UA 1984), *Elvis Presley In Concert* (Mountain Films 1986), *68 Comeback Special* (Virgin Vision 1986), *One Night With You* (Virgin Vision 1986), *Aloha From Hawaii* (Virgin Vision 1986), *'56 In the Beginning* (Virgin Vision 1987), *Memories* (Vestron Music Video 1987), *This Is Elvis* (Warner Home Video 1988), *Graceland* (Video Gems 1988), *Great Performances Volume 1* (Buena Vista 1990), *Great Performances Volume 2* (Buena Vista 1990), *Young Elvis* (Channel 5 1990), *Sun Days With Elvis* (MMG Video 1991), *Elvis: A Portrait By His Friends* (Qube Pictures 1991), *The Lost Performances* (BMG 1992), *Private Elvis* (1993), *Elvis In Hollywood* (1993), *The Alternate Aloha Concert* (Lightyear 1996), *Elvis 56 – The Video* (BMG 1996), *Elvis – That's The Way It Is* (1996), *Private Moments* (Telstar 1997), *The Great Performances* (Wienerworld 1997), *The Legend Lives On* (Real Entertainment 1997), *Collapse Of The Kingdom* (Real Entertainment 1997), *The King Comes Back* (Real Entertainment 1997), *Wild In Hollywood* (Real Entertainment 1997), *Rocket Ride To Stardom* (Real Entertainment 1997), *Elvis: All The Kings Men* (Real Entertainment 1997), *NBC T.V. Special* (Lightyear 1997).

● FURTHER READING: To begin to wade through the list of books about Elvis is daunting. Many are appalling, some are excellent. In reality you only need two, and both were written in recent years by Peter Guralnick. *Last Train To Memphis* and *Careless Love* are historically accurate, objective and beautifully written.

I Called Him Babe: Elvis Presley's Nurse Remembers, Marian J. Cocke. *The Three Loves Of*

Elvis Presley: The True Story Of The Presley Legend, Robert Holmes. *A Century Of Elvis*, Albert Hand. *The Elvis They Dig*, Albert Hand. *Operation Elvis*, Alan Levy. *The Elvis Presley Pocket Handbook*, Albert Hand. *All Elvis: An Unofficial Biography Of The 'King Of Discs'*, Philip Buckle. *The Elvis Presley Encyclopedia*, Roy Barlow. *Elvis: A Biography*, Jerry Hopkins. *Meet Elvis Presley*, Favius Friedman *Elvis Presley*, Paula Taylor. *Elvis*, Jerry Hopkins. *The Elvis Presley Scrapbook 1935-1977*, James Robert Paris *Elvis And The Colonel*, May Mann. *Recording Sessions 1954-1974*, Ernst Jorgensen and Erik Rasmussen. *Elvis Presley: An Illustrated Biography*, W.A. Harbinson. *Elvis: The Films And Career Of Elvis Presley*, Steven Zmijewsky and Boris Zmijewsky. *Presley Nation*, Spencer Leigh *Elvis*, Peter Jones. *Presley: Entertainer Of The Century*, Antony James. *Elvis And His Secret*, Maria Gripe. *On Stage, Elvis Presley*, Kathleen Bowman. *The Elvis Presley American Discography*, Ron Barry. *Elvis: What Happened*, Red West, Sonny West and Dave Hebler. *Elvis: Tribute To The King Of Rock*, Dick Tatham. *Elvis Presley*, Todd Slaughter. *Elvis: Recording Sessions* Ernst Jorgensen, Erick Rasmussen and Johnny Mikkelsen. *The Life And Death Of Elvis Presley*, W.A. Harbinson. *Elvis: Lonely Star At The Top* David Hanna. *Elvis In His Own Words*, Mick Farren and Pearce Marchbank. *Twenty Years Of Elvis: The Session File*, Colin Escott and Martin Hawkins. *Starring Elvis*, James W. Bowser. *My Life With Elvis*, Becky Yancey and Cliff Lindecker. *The Real Elvis: A Good Old Boy*, Vince Staten. *The Elvis Presley Trivia Quiz Book*, Helen Rosenbaum. *A Presley Speaks*, Vester Presley *The Graceland Gates*, Harold Lloyd. *The Boy Who Dared To Rock: The Definitive Elvis*, Paul Lichter. *Eine Illustrierte Dokumentation*, Bernd King and Heinz Plehn. *Elvis Presley Speaks*, Hans Holzer *Elvis: The Legend Lives! One Year Later*, Martin A. Grove. *Private Elvis*, Diego Cortez. *Bill Adler's Love Letters To Elvis*, Bill Adler. *Elvis: His Life And Times In Poetry And Lines*, Joan Buchanan West *Elvis '56: In The Beginning*, Alfred Wertheimer *Elvis Presley: An Illustrated Biography*, Rainer Wallraf and Heinz Plehn. *Even Elvis*, Mary Ann Thornton. *Elvis: Images & Fancies*, Jac L. Tharpe *Elvis In Concert*, John Reggero. *Elvis Presley: A Study In Music*, Robert Matthew-Walker. *Elvis Portrait Of A Friend*, Marty Lacker, Patsy Lacker and Leslie E. Smith. *Elvis Is That You?*, Holly Hatcher. *Elvis: Newly Discovered Drawings Of Elvis Presley*, Betty Harper. *Trying To Get To You: The Story Of Elvis Presley*, Valerie Harms. *Love Of Elvis*, Bruce Hamilton and Michael L. Liben. *Elvis With Love*, Lena Canada. *The Truth About Elvis*, Jess Stearn. *Elvis: We Love You Tender*, Dee Presley, David Rick and Billy Stanley *Presleyana*, Jerry Osborne and Bruce Hamilton *Elvis: The Final Years*, Jerry Hopkins. *When Elvis Died*, Nancy Gregory and Joseph. *All About Elvis* Fred L. Worth and Steve D. Tamerius. *Elvis Presley: A Reference Guide And Discography*, John

A. Whisle. *The Illustrated Discography*, Martin Hawkins and Colin Escott. *Elvis: Legend Of Love*, Marie Greenfield. *Elvis Presley: King Of Rock 'N' Roll*, Richard Wooton. *The Complete Elvis*, Martin Torgoff. *Elvis Special 1982*, Todd Slaughter. *Elvis*, Dave Marsh. *Up And Down With Elvis Presley*, Marge Crumbaker with Gabe Tucker. *Elvis For The Record*, Maureen Covey. *Elvis: The Complete Illustrated Record*, Roy Carr and Mick Farren. *Elvis Collectables*, Rosalind Cranor. *Jailhouse Rock: The Bootleg Records Of Elvis Presley 1970*, Lee Cotten and Howard A. DeWitt. *Elvis The Soldier*, Rex and Elisabeth Mansfield. *All Shook Up: Elvis Day-By-Day, 1954-1977*, Lee Cotten. *Elvis*, John Townson, Gordon Minto and George Richardson. *Priscilla, Elvis & Me*, Michael Edwards. *Elvis On The Road To Stardom: 1955-1956*, Jim Black. *Return To Sender*, Howard F. Banney. *Elvis: His Life From A To Z*, Fred L. Worth and Steve D. Tamerius. *Elvis And The Colonel*, Dirk Vallenga with Mick Farren. *Elvis: My Brother*, Bill Stanley with George Erikson. *Long Lonely Highway: 1950's Elvis Scrapbook*, Ger J. Rijff. *Elvis In Hollywood*, Gerry McLafferty. *Reconsider Baby: Definitive Elvis Sessionography*, E. Jorgensen. *Elvis '69, The Return*, Joseph A. Tunzi. *The Death Of Elvis: What Really Happened*, Charles C. Thompson and James P. Cole. *Elvis For Beginners*, Jill Pearlman. *Elvis, The Cool King*, Bob Morel and Jan Van Gestel. *The Elvis Presley Scrapbooks 1955-1965*, Peter Haining (ed.). *The Boy Who Would Be King. An Intimate Portrait Of Elvis Presley By His Cousin*, Earl Greenwood and Kathleen Tracy. *Elvis: The Last 24 Hours*, Albert Goldman. *The Elvis Files*, Gail Brewer-Giorgio. *Elvis, My Dad*, David Adler and Ernest Andrews. *The Elvis Reader: Texts And Sources On The King Of Rock 'n' Roll*, Kevin Quain (ed.). *Elvis Bootlegs Buyer's Guide, Pts 1 & 2*, Tommy Robinson. *Elvis: The Music Lives On - The Recording Sessions 1954-1976*, Richard Peters. *The King Forever*, no author listed. *Dead Elvis: A Chronicle Of A Cultural Obsession*, Greil Marcus. *Elvis People: Cult Of The King*, Ted Harrison. *In Search Of The King*, Craig Gelfand, Lynn Blocker-Krantz and Rogerio Noguera. *Aren Med Elvis*, Roger Ersson and Lennart Svedberg. *Elvis And Gladys*, Elaine Dundy. *King And I: Little Gallery of Elvis Impersonators*, Kent Barker and Karin Pritikin. *Elvis Sessions: The Recorded Music Of Elvis Aaron Presley 1953-1977*, Joseph A. Tunzi. *Elvis: The Sun Years*, Howard A. DeWitt. *Elvis In Germany: The Missing Years*, Andreas Schroer. *Graceland: The Living Legend Of Elvis Presley*, Chet Flippo. *Elvis: The Secret Files*, John Parker. *The Life And Cuisine Of Elvis Presley*, David Adler. *Last Train To Memphis: The Rise Of Elvis Presley*, Peter Guralnick. *In His Own Words*, Mick Farren. *Elvis: Murdered By The Mob*, John Parker. *The Complete Guide To The Music Of ...*, John Robertson. *Elvis' Man Friday*, Gene Smith. *The Hitchhiker's Guide To Elvis*, Mick Farren. *Elvis, The Lost Photographs 1948-1969*, Joseph Tunzi and O'Neal. *Elvis Aaron Presley:*

Revelations From The Memphis Mafia, Alanna Nash. *The Elvis Encyclopaedia*, David E. Stanley. *E: Reflections On The Birth Of The Elvis Faith*, John E. Strausbaugh. *Elvis Meets The Beatles: The Untold Story Of Their Entangled Lives*, Chris Hutchins and Peter Thompson. *Elvis, Highway 51 South, Memphis, Tennessee*, Joseph A. Tunzi. *Elvis In The Army*, William J. Taylor Jnr. *Everything Elvis*, Pauline Bartel. *Elvis In Wonderland*, Bob Jope. *Elvis: Memories And Memorabilia*, Richard Bushkin. *Elvis Sessions II: The Recorded Music Of Elvis Aaron Presley 1953-1977*, Joseph A. Tunzi. *The Ultimate Album Cover Book*, Paul Dowling. *The King Of The Road*, Robert Gordon. *That's Alright, Elvis*, Scotty Moore and James Dickerson. *Raised On Rock: Growing Up At Graceland*, David A. Stanley and Mark Bego. *Elvis: In The Twilight Of Memory*, June Juanico. *The Rise And Fall And Rise Of Elvis*, Aubrey Dillon-Malone. *In Search Of Elvis: Music, Race, Art, Religion*, Vernon Chadwick (editor). *The Complete Idiot's Guide To Elvis*, Frank Coffey. *The Elvis Encyclopedia: An Impartial Guide To The Films Of Elvis*, Eric Braun. *Essential Elvis*, Peter Silverton. *Talking Elvis*, Trevor Cajiao. *A Life In Music: The Complete Recording Sessions*, Ernst Jorgensen. *Careless Love: The Unmaking Of Elvis Presley*, Peter Guralnick. *Elvis For CD Fans Only*, Dale Hampton. *Double Trouble: Bill Clinton And Elvis Presley In The Land Of No Alternatives*, Greil Marcus. *A Life In Music: The Complete Recording Sessions*, Ernst Jorgensen. *Elvis Day By Day: The Definitive Record Of His Life And Music*, Peter Guralnick and Ernst Jorgensen. *Elvis: The King On Film*, Chutley Chops (ed.). *Colonel Tom Parker: The Curious Life Of Elvis Presley's Eccentric Manager*, James L. Dickerson.

● FILMS: *Love Me Tender* (1956), *Loving You* (1957), *Jailhouse Rock* (1957), *King Creole* (1958), *G.I. Blues* (1960), *Flaming Star* (1960), *Wild In The Country* (1961), *Blue Hawaii* (1961), *Kid Galahad* (1962), *Girls Girls Girls* (1962), *Follow That Dream* (1962), *It Happened At The World's Fair* (1963), *Fun In Acapulco* (1963), *Roustabout* (1964), *Viva Las Vegas* (1964), *Kissin' Cousins* (1964), *Tickle Me* (1965), *Harem Scarum* aka *Harem Holiday* (1965), *Girl Happy* (1965), *Spinout* (1966), *Paradise Hawaiian Style* (1966), *Frankie And Johnny* (1966), *Easy Come Easy Go* (1967), *Clambake* (1967), *Live A Little Love A Little* (1968), *Speedway* (1968), *Stay Away Joe* (1968), *Double Trouble* (1968), *The Trouble With Girls* (1969), *Charro!* (1969), *Change Of Habit* (1969), *This Is Elvis* compilation (1981).

PRESTON, JOHNNY

b. John Preston Courville, 18 August 1939, Port Arthur, Texas, USA. This pop ballad and rock singer first performed in the Lamar University (Beaumont, Texas) group the Shades, in 1957, and was brought to the attention of Mercury Records by disc jockey and singer, the Big Bopper (Jape Richardson). Among the tracks

Richardson wrote and produced for him was the novelty 'Running Bear', a sad tale of Red Indian love gone wrong. The record took four months to chart Stateside but it then went on to became a chart-topper in the US and UK during 1959/60 (after Richardson's tragic death in the plane crash with Buddy Holly). Despite a disastrous UK tour (cut three weeks short due to poor houses), he had transatlantic Top 20 successes with the follow-ups 'Cradle Of Love' and a revival of Shirley And Lee's 'Feel So Fine'. He later recorded for Imperial, TCF Hall (including 'Running Bear '65'), ABC and Hallway, but never graced the charts again.

● ALBUMS: *Running Bear* (Mercury 1960) ★★★, *Come Rock With Me* (Mercury 1961) ★★, *Johnny Preston Sings* (Mercury 1960) ★★★.

● COMPILATIONS: *Running Bear* (Collectables 1995) ★★★.

PRESTON, MIKE

b. Jack Davis, 14 May 1934, Hackney, London, England. The ex-boxer and cartoon cameraman was discovered singing in a small club in London's West End by noted agent Dennis Preston. He was given his stage name in a competition by readers of Patrick Doncaster's pop music column in the *Daily Mirror* newspaper. This pop ballad singer's first single was 'A House, A Car And A Wedding Ring', a Jerry Lordan composition with musical direction from Harry Robinson. The Decca release failed to create much interest in the UK but charted in the US in early 1958. This led to his visiting America for promotion and appearing on the shows of Alan Freed and Dick Clark amongst others. Preston continued to work as a cameraman, until he had his biggest UK hit in 1959 with a cover of the Fleetwoods' 'Mr. Blue', which narrowly missed the Top 10. He later appeared in the film *Climb Up The Wall* with Craig Douglas and Russ Conway. In all, he had four UK Top 40 singles, the last, 'Marry Me' which peaked at number 14, was the winning song from the 1961 ITV television *Song Contest*. After leaving Decca he recorded without success on Emerald.

PRETTY THINGS

One of England's seminal R&B bands, the Pretty Things were formed at Sidcup Art College, Kent, England, in September 1963. The original line-up featured a founder-member of the Rolling Stones, Dick Taylor (b. 28 January 1943, Dartford, Kent, England; guitar), plus Phil May (b. 9 November 1944, Dartford, Kent, England; vocals), Brian Pendleton (b. 13 April 1944, Wolverhampton, West Midlands, England, d. 25 May 2001, Maidstone, Kent, England; rhythm guitar), John Stax (b. 6 April 1944, Crayford, Kent, England; bass) and Peter Kitley (drums), although the latter was quickly replaced by Viv Andrews. The band secured a recording contract within months of their inception. Their label then insisted that the luckless Andrews be removed in favour of Viv Prince (b. Loughborough, Leicestershire, England), an experienced musician and ex-member of Carter-Lewis And The Southerners. The Pretty Things' debut single, 'Rosalyn', scraped into the UK Top 50, but its unfettered power, coupled with the group's controversial, unkempt appearance, ensured maximum publicity. Their brash, almost destructive, approach to R&B flourished with two exciting UK Top 20 singles, 'Don't Bring Me Down' and 'Honey I Need'. The unit's exuberant first album offered much of the same. Skip Alan (b. Alan Skipper, 11 June 1948, London, England) replaced the erratic Prince in November 1965. Although the Pretty Things' commercial standing had declined, subsequent singles, 'Midnight To Six Man' and 'Come See Me', were arguably their finest works, combining power with purpose. However, first Pendleton, then Stax, left the band and sessions for a third album, *Emotions*, were completed with two former members of the Fenmen, Wally Allen (bass/vocals) and John Povey (b. 20 August 1944, London, England; keyboards/vocals). Initially hired on a temporary basis, the duo proved crucial to the Pretty Things' subsequent development.

By late 1967 the quintet was immersed in the emergent underground scene. Their music combined harmonies with experimentation, and two exceptional singles, 'Defecting Grey' and 'Talking About The Good Times', are definitive examples of English 'flower-power' pop. The group's new-found confidence flourished on 1968's *S.F. Sorrow*, an ambitious concept album that reportedly influenced the Who's *Tommy*. The set was not a commercial success, and a recurring instability – Skip Alan was replaced by former Tomorrow drummer John 'Twink' Alder – only to rejoin again, also proved detrimental. Dick Taylor's departure in November 1969 was highly damaging, and although the group's subsequent album, *Parachute*, was lauded in *Rolling Stone* magazine, his distinctive guitar sound was notably absent. The Pretty Things collapsed in 1971, but re-formed under a core of May, Povey and Skip Alan to complete *Freeway Madness*. This trio remained central through the band's subsequent changes until May embarked on a solo career in 1976. Two years later the *Emotions* line-up – May, Taylor, Povey, Allen and Alan – was reunited. The same quintet, plus guitarist Peter Tolson (b. 10 September 1951, Bishops Stortford, Hertfordshire, England), completed a studio album, *Cross Talk* in 1980.

In 1990 a revitalized unit released a rousing version of Barry McGuire's 1965 US number 1 'Eve Of Destruction'. By the mid-90s they were still gigging, now under the watchful eye of manager Mark St. John. He had successfully on them back rights to songs and royalties. In 996 after dozens of changes of personnel and mage the line-up was the same as the unit that ecorded the stunning 'Come See Me'; May, aylor, Alan, Allan and Povey. *S.F. Sorrow* was iven its live premiere at Abbey Road studios in eptember 1998, with Dave Gilmour guesting on uitar. A new studio album followed in 1999 ogether with a fine remastering and reissue rogramme from Snapper Music.

ALBUMS: *The Pretty Things* (Fontana 1965) ★★★, *Get The Picture?* (Fontana 1965) ★★★★, *motions* (Fontana 1967) ★★, *S.F. Sorrow* (EMI 968) ★★★★, *Parachute* (Harvest 1970) ★★★★, *reeway Madness* (Warners 1972) ★★★, *Silk orpedo* (Swan Song 1974) ★★★, *Savage Eye* Swan Song 1976) ★★★, *Live '78* (Jade 1978) ★★, *ross Talk* (Warners 1980) ★★, *Live At The Ieartbreak Hotel* (Ace 1984) ★★, *Out Of The sland* (Inak 1988) ★★, *On Air* (Band Of Joy 992) ★★, *Rage Before Beauty* (Madfish 1999) ★★, *Resurrection* (Worldwidetribe 1999) ★★★. he group also completed several albums of ackground music suitable for films: *Electric anana* (De Wolfe 1967) ★★, *More Electric anana* (De Wolfe 1968) ★★, *Even More Electric anana* (De Wolfe 1969) ★★, *Hot Licks* (De Wolfe 973) ★★, *Return Of The Electric Banana* (De Volfe 1978) ★★.

COMPILATIONS: *Greatest Hits 64-67* (Philips 975) ★★★★, *The Vintage Years* (Sire 1976) ★★★, *Singles A's And B's* (Harvest 1977) ★★★, *lectric Banana: The Seventies* (Butt 1979) ★★, *lectric Banana: The Sixties* (Butt 1980) ★★, *The retty Things 1967-1971* (See For Miles 1982) ★★★, *Cries From The Midnight Circus: The Best f The Pretty Things 1968-1971* (Harvest 1986) ★★, *Let Me Hear The Choir Sing* (Edsel 1986) ★★, *Closed Restaurant Blues* (Bam Caruso 987) ★★★, *Unrepentant* 2-CD box set (Fragile 995) ★★★, *Latest Writs Greatest Hits: The Best f Pretty Things* (Snapper 2000) ★★★★.

● FURTHER READING: *The Pretty Things: Their wn Story And The Downliners Sect Story*, Mike ax.

RINCE BUSTER

Cecil Bustamante Campbell, 28 May 1938, ingston, Jamaica, West Indies. Buster was amed after Alexandra Bustamante, the leader f the Jamaican Labour Party, and began his areer as a boxer, but soon found his pugilistic lents being put to use as a bouncer/strong-arm an and minder for Coxsone Dodd's Down Beat ound system. Competition was fierce in the arly days, with fights frequently breaking out etween the supporters of rival sounds, and with ires (and people) being cut regularly; Buster till carries the scars (literally). He claims, like many others, personally to have invented the ka sound, and he was certainly involved from e very early stages – at first, with his work for odd, and after they had parted company, with is own Voice Of The People sound system,

record label and shop. His very first recording session produced one of the all-time classics of Jamaican music, 'Oh Carolina', with vocals by the Folkes Brothers and musical accompaniment from Count Ossie. Inventive and innovative at the time, the record still sounds every bit as exciting. Buster released countless records both by himself and other top acts on his Wild Bells, Voice Of The People and Buster's Record Shack labels, which were subsequently released in the UK on Blue Beat Records. They proved as popular there as they had been in Jamaica, firstly with the Jamaican community and secondly with the mods, who took Buster to their hearts with songs such as 'Al Capone' and 'Madness'. He toured the UK in the mid-60s to ecstatic crowds and appeared on the hugely popular *Ready, Steady, Go!* television show.

He recorded in many different styles but his talking records were the most popular, including the hilarious 'Judge Dread', in which he admonishes rude boys, the wildly misogynistic 'Ten Commandments', the evocative 'Ghost Dance' – a look back at his early Kingston dancehall days, the confused and confusing 'Johnny Cool', and the less well-known but equally wonderful 'Shepherd Beng Beng'. He also claims to have taught Georgie Fame to play ska and he influenced other white pop acts – Madness named themselves after his song (debuting with a tribute, 'The Prince') – and he inspired doorman/bouncer Alex Hughes to adopt the name Judge Dread and have UK chart hits with variations on Prince Buster's lewd original, 'Big Five'. Towards the end of the 60s, Buster tended towards 'slack' or rude records that were only mildly risqué compared with what was to follow; nevertheless, they caused a sensation at the time. He wisely invested his money in record shops and juke-box operations throughout the Caribbean, and in the early 70s, he took to recording many top names, including Big·Youth, Dennis Alcapone, John Holt, Dennis Brown and Alton Ellis, with varying degrees of success. He soon realized that his older recordings consistently outsold his newer efforts and he turned to re-pressing his extensive back catalogue on single and releasing his old albums both in Jamaica and the UK. He also put together some excellent compilations where the superb sleeve-notes, written by the Prince himself, attack in no uncertain terms the music of the day: 'They have used guns to spoil the fun and force tasteless and meaningless music upon the land.'

Throughout the rest of the 70s and on into the 80s he lived on his shops, his juke-boxes and his past glories, but he returned to live work in the latter half of the 80s. He has become a crowd-puller again, for, as he says: 'The people know my songs and loved them.' In 1992, he even started, for the first time in years, to record new music again. 'Whine & Grine' was used as a soundtrack to a Levi's commercial, resulting in a return to the UK charts in April 1998. Regardless of the quality of his more recent work, Prince Buster's music has already inspired generations of performers. He is respected abroad – probably more than in his native Jamaica – but he will always retain his place as one of the few Jamaican artists to reach directly to the international audience. Many more have played their part indirectly, but his name was known both through his own recordings ('Al Capone' reached the lower regions of the UK national charts) and his work with other people. It is unlikely that any other Jamaican artist (apart from Bob Marley) still has his records so regularly played in clubs and dances throughout the world. In 2000, Guinness used Prince Buster's 'Burkes Law' in a television commercial.

● ALBUMS: with various artists *I Feel The Spirit* (Blue Beat 1963) ★★★★, with various artists *Pain In My Belly* (Islam/Blue Beat 1966) ★★★★, *On Tour* (1966) ★★★, *Judge Dread Rock Steady* (Blue Beat 1967) ★★★, *Wreck A Pum Pum* (Blue Beat 1968) ★★★★, *She Was A Rough Rider* (Melodisc 1969) ★★★★, *Big Five* (Melodisc 1972) ★★★.

● COMPILATIONS: *Prince Buster's Fabulous Greatest Hits* (Fab 1967) ★★★★, *Original Golden Oldies Volumes 1 & 2* (Prince Buster 1989) ★★★★, *Fabulous Greatest Hits* (Diamond Range 1998) ★★★★.

PROBY, P.J.

b. James Marcus Smith, 6 November 1938, Houston, Texas, USA. This iconoclastic singer spent his early career in Hollywood, recording demos for song publishing houses. Several low-key singles ensued, credited to Jett Powers and a number of bit parts as an actor ensued, before the Proby appellation surfaced on 'So Do I' (1963). 'Powers' had already demonstrated a songwriting talent, his most notable composition being 'Clown Shoes' for Johnny Burnette in 1962. The artist came to Britain the following year, at the behest of producer Jack Good, to appear on the *Around The* Beatles television special. An ebullient revival of 'Hold Me', originally a gentle ballad, brought Proby a UK Top 3 hit, while the similarly raucous 'Together' reached number 8. Proby completely changed direction following a move to Liberty Records and, again, reached the UK Top 10 with a memorable version of 'Somewhere' from *West Side Story*. This record started a series of epic ballads featuring Proby's strong but affected vocal. Both 'I Apologise' (complete with Billy Eckstine paraphrasing) and 'Maria' (again from *West Side Story*) became big hits. Proby's biggest hit, however, was with the popular UK press. Following a 'split trousers' incident, Proby was accused of obscenity. He then made an act of regularly splitting his crushed blue velvet jumpsuit. He completed his attire during the mid-60s with a Tom Jones wig and black bow tie

and baggy nightshirts. Prior to 'Maria' (4 month earlier) his chart career suddenly floundered with John Lennon and Paul McCartney's 'Tha Means A Lot', and although further immaculate productions followed after 'Maria' with 'To Make A Big Man Cry' and the Righteous Brothers sounding 'I Can't Make It Alone', Proby wa relegated to the cabaret circuit. Although he continued to record, the press were more interested in his tax problems and subsequent bankruptcy. *Three Week Hero* won retrospective acclaim when the singer's backing group achieved fame as Led Zeppelin. In 1970, Proby took the role of Iago in *Catch My Soul*, forme mentor Good's rock adaptation of *Othello* Proby's subsequent work was more sporadic; he appeared on the UK nightclub circuit, played Elvis Presley in the stage production *Elvis Or Stage* until he was sacked, and continued to court publicity for erratic behaviour. In 1985 he completed two suitably eccentric versions of 'Tainted Love', previously a hit for Soft Cell which became the first of a series of contentious singles for Manchester-based independent label Savoy Records. Recreations of songs by Joy Division ('Love Will Tear Us Apart') and David Bowie ('Heroes') followed, but further release were marred by poor production and the artist often incoherent intonation.

Although years of apparent self-abuse ha robbed the singer of his powers of old, he retained the ability to enthral and infuriate. In 1993 Proby made an unannounced appearance in Jack Good's *Good Rockin' Tonite* at the Liverpool Empire. Further Proby sightings wer made in June 1995 when he began a 15-minute spot during each performance of the London production of the Roy Orbison musical *Only The Lonely*. In late 1996, in a major interview with *Q* magazine, Proby once again squared up for another comeback. This came in muted form with a minor hit collaboration with Marc Almond on a cover version of Cupid Inspiration's 'Yesterday Has Gone'. Proby remains a wonderfully unpredictable eccentric

● ALBUMS: *I Am P.J. Proby* (Liberty 1964) ★★★★, *P.J. Proby* (Liberty 1965) ★★★★, *P.J. Proby In Town* (Liberty 1965) ★★★, *Enigma* (Liberty 1966) ★★★, *Phenomenon* (Liberty 1967) ★★, *Believe It Or Not* (Liberty 1968) ★★, *Three Week Hero* (Liberty 1969) ★★, *I'm Yours* (Ember 1973) ★★, *The Hero* (Palm 1981) ★★, *Clown Shoes* (1987) ★★, *The Savoy Sessions* (Savoy 1995) ★★, *Legend* (EMI 1996) ★★, *Lord Horror* (Savoy 1999) ★★.

● COMPILATIONS: as Jet Powers *Californi License* (Liberty 1969) ★, *Somewhere* (Sunset 1975) ★★★, *The Legendary P.J. Proby At His Very Best* (See For Miles 1986) ★★★★, *The Legendary P.J. Proby At His Very Best, Volume 2* (See Fo Miles 1987) ★★★★, *The EP Collection* (See Fo Miles 1996) ★★★★, *The Very Best Of P.J. Prob* (EMI 1998) ★★★★.

PROCOL HARUM

This soulful progressive rock band was originally formed in Essex, England following the demise of the R&B pop unit, the Paramounts. Gary Brooker (b. 29 May 1945, Hackney, London, England; piano/vocals), Matthew Fisher (b. 7 March 1946, Addiscombe, Croydon, Surrey, England; organ), Bobby Harrison (b. 22 June 1939, East Ham, London, England; drums), Ray Royer (b. 8 October 1945, the Pinewoods, Essex, England; guitar) and Dave Knights (b. David John Knights, 28 June 1945, Islington, London, England; bass) made their debut with the ethereal 'A Whiter Shade Of Pale', one of the biggest successes of 1967. The single has now achieved classic status with continuing sales which now run to many millions. The long haunting Bach-influenced introduction takes the listener through a sequence of completely surreal lyrics, which epitomized the 'Summer Of Love'. 'We skipped the light fandango, turned cart-wheels across the floor, I was feeling kind of seasick, the crowd called out for more'. It was followed by the impressive Top 10 hit 'Homburg'. By the time of the hastily thrown together album (only recorded in mono), the band were falling apart. Harrison and Royer departed to be replaced with Brooker's former colleagues B.J. Wilson (b. Barrie James Wilson, 18 March 1947, Edmonton, London, England, d. 8 October 1990, Oregon, USA) and Robin Trower (b. 9 March 1945, Catford, London, England), respectively.

The other unofficial member of the band was lyricist Keith Reid (b. 10 October 1946, England), whose penchant for imaginary tales of seafaring appeared on numerous albums. The particularly strong *A Salty Dog*, with its classic John Player cigarette pack cover, was released to critical acclaim. The title track and 'The Devil Came From Kansas' were two of their finest songs. Fisher and Knights departed and the circle was completed when Chris Copping (b. 29 August 1945, Middleton, Lancashire, England; organ/bass) became the last remaining former member of the Paramounts to join. On *Broken Barricades*, in particular, Trower's Jimi Hendrix-influenced guitar patterns began to give the band a heavier image which was not compatible with Reid's introspective fantasy sagas. This was resolved by Trower's departure, to join Frankie Miller in Jude, and following the recruitment of Dave Ball (b. 30 March 1950, Handsworth, Birmingham, West Midlands, England) and the addition of Alan Cartwright (b. 10 October 1945, England; bass), the band pursued a more symphonic direction. The success of *Live In Concert With The Edmonton Symphony Orchestra* was unexpected. It marked a surge in popularity, not seen since the early days. The album contained strong versions of 'Conquistador' and 'A Salty Dog', and was a Top 5, million-selling album in the USA. Further line-up changes ensued with Ball departing and

Mick Grabham (b. 22 January 1948, Sunderland, Tyne & Wear, England; ex-Cochise) joining in 1972. This line-up became their most stable and they enjoyed a successful and busy four years during which time they released three albums. *Grand Hotel* was the most rewarding, although both the following had strong moments. 'Nothing But The Truth' and 'The Idol' were high points of *Exotic Birds And Fruit*, while 'Pandora's Box' was the jewel in *Procol's Ninth*, giving them another surprise hit single. By the time *Something Magic* was released in 1977 the musical climate had dramatically changed and Procol Harum were one of the first casualties of the punk and new wave movement. Having had a successful innings Gary Brooker initiated a farewell tour and Procol Harum quietly disappeared.

In August 1991, Brooker, Trower, Fisher and Reid got back together, with Mark Brzezicki (b. 21 June 1957, Slough, Buckinghamshire, England; ex-Big Country) replacing the recently deceased Wilson. Unlike many re-formed 'dinosaurs' the result was a well-received album *The Prodigal Stranger*, which achieved minimal sales. Brooker has continued to lead various line-ups of Procol Harum ever since.

● ALBUMS: *Procol Harum* aka *A Whiter Shade Of Pale* (Deram/A&M 1967) ★★★, *Shine On Brightly* (Regal Zonophone/A&M 1968) ★★★, *A Salty Dog* (Regal Zonophone/A&M 1969) ★★★★, *Home* (Regal Zonophone/A&M 1970) ★★★, *Broken Barricades* (Chrysalis/A&M 1971) ★★★, *Live In Concert With The Edmonton Symphony Orchestra* (Chrysalis/A&M 1972) ★★★★, *Grand Hotel* (Chrysalis 1973) ★★★, *Exotic Birds And Fruit* (Chrysalis 1974) ★★★, *Procol's Ninth* (Chrysalis 1975) ★★★, *Something Magic* (Chrysalis 1977) ★★, *The Prodigal Stranger* (Zoo 1991) ★★★, with various artists *The Long Goodbye* aka *Symphonic Music Of Procol Harum* (RCA Victor 1995) ★★.

● COMPILATIONS: *The Best Of Procol Harum* (A&M 1972) ★★★★, *Platinum Collection* (Cube 1981) ★★★★, *The Collection* (Castle 1985) ★★★★, *The Chrysalis Years 1973-1977* (Chrysalis 1989) ★★★★, *Chapter One: Turning Back The Page 1967-1991* (Zoo 1991) ★★★★, *The Early Years* (Griffin 1992) ★★★, *Homburg And Other Hats: Procol Harum's Best* (Essential 1995) ★★★★, *Halycon Daze* (Music Club 1997) ★★★, *30th Anniversary Anthology* 3-CD set (Westside 1998) ★★★★.

● FURTHER READING: *Beyond The Pale*, Claes Johansen.

PUCKETT, GARY, AND THE UNION GAP

Originally known as the Outcasts, a San Diego act renowned for cover versions, this popular group took the name Union Gap in January 1967. Although burdened by a passé image – they dressed in American Civil War uniforms – 'General' Gary Puckett (b. 17 October 1942, Hibbing, Minnesota, USA; vocals), 'Sergeant'

Dwight Benett (b. December 1945, San Diego, California, USA; tenor saxophone), 'Corporal' Kerry Chater (b. 7 August 1945, Vancouver, British Columbia, Canada; bass), 'Private' Gary 'Mutha' Withem (b. 22 August 1946, San Diego, California, USA; woodwind/piano) and 'Private' Paul Whitbread (b. 8 February 1946, San Diego, California, USA; drums) enjoyed considerable success through their relationship with songwriter/producer Jerry Fuller. 'Woman Woman' achieved gold status in 1967, and the following year the quintet scored three more million-sellers with 'Young Girl', a chart-topper in the US and UK, 'Lady Willpower' and 'Over You', each of which were marked by Puckett's soaring vocal line. However, the formula appeal of their highly polished sound gradually waned and the group disbanded in 1971. Puckett continues as a solo artist endlessly recycling his past hits. In 1996 *As It Stands* was issued and featured some re-recordings of 'Lady Willpower', 'Young Girl' and others, together with new songs such as 'As It Stands' and 'I Ain't Got Noth'n But The Blues'.

● ALBUMS: *Woman Woman* (Columbia 1968) ★★★, *Young Girl* (Columbia 1968) ★★★, *Incredible* (Columbia 1968) ★★★, *The New Gary Puckett And The Union Gap Album* (1970) ★★. Solo: Gary Puckett *The Gary Puckett Album* (1971) ★★, *As It Stands* (Juslor 1996) ★★.

● COMPILATIONS: *Gary Puckett And The Union Gap's Greatest Hits* (Columbia 1970) ★★★, *Looking Glass* (Columbia 1995) ★★★, *A Golden Classics Edition* (Collectables 1997) ★★★, *Super Hits* (Sony 1999) ★★★.

PURIFY, JAMES AND BOBBY

Formed in 1965, this high-powered soul duo consisted of James Purify (b. 12 May 1944, Pensacola, Florida, USA) and Robert Lee Dickey (b. 2 September 1939, Tallahassee, Florida, USA). Unfairly tarnished as a surrogate Sam And Dave, the duo's less frenetic style was nonetheless captivating. During the early 60s Dickey worked as a singer/guitarist in the Dothan Sextet, a group fronted by Mighty Sam McClain. When Florida disc jockey 'Papa' Don Schroeder offered Sam a solo career, Dickey introduced his cousin, James Purify, as a replacement. Their onstage duets became so popular that Schroeder added them to his fast-growing roster. Their first single, 'I'm Your Puppet', was recorded at Fame in Muscle Shoals and released on Bell. Written by Dan Penn and Spooner Oldham, this simple, poignant ballad became the duo's only US Top 10 hit in September 1966. Rather than follow their own path, the cousins were tempted towards cover versions including 'Shake A Tail Feather' and 'I Take What I Want'. In spite of the undoubted quality of these releases, many critics dubbed them 'contrived'. In 1967 'Let Love Come Between Us' became their last US Top 30 hit, although several strong records followed. When Dickey retired in 1970 James found another 'Bobby' in Ben Moore and it was this new combination that secured a 1976 British hit with a remake of 'I'm Your Puppet'. Unable to sustain this rejuvenation, the duo parted, although Moore resurfaced in 1979 with a solo album, *Purified*. The pick of the original duo's Bell recordings can be found on *100% Purified Soul*.

● ALBUMS: *James And Bobby Purify* (Bell 1967) ★★★, *The Pure Sound Of The Purifys* (Bell 1968) ★★★, *You And Me Together Forever* (Casablanca 1978) ★★.

● COMPILATIONS: *100% Purified Soul* (Charly 1988) ★★★★, *Keep Pushin'* (Camden 1998) ★★★.

PURPLE GANG

Formed in Manchester, England, the original line-up consisted of Lucifer (b. Peter Walker; vocals/kazoo), Deejay Robinson (harmonica/mandolin), Ank Langley (jug), Geoff Bourjer (piano/washboard) and James 'Joe' Beard (guitar). All were students at Stockport College of Art. They achieved notoriety when their debut, 'Granny Takes A Trip', was adopted by the English 'underground' as an unofficial anthem. Although a happy, jugband song, the 'trip' reference was taken to be about LSD, despite fervent claims by the group that this was not their intention. It was finally banned by the BBC, and foiled UK presenter John Peel's valiant attempts to break the single. Joe Beard (12-string guitar), Gerry Robinson (mandolin), Geoff Bowyer (keyboards) and Lucifer completed an attendant album in the space of two days, but had split up by the time of its release. 'Kiss Me Goodnight Sally Green' failed miserably as their brand of jug-band music could never compete with phased effects and sitars which were the order of the day in 1968. Continued interest in their anthemic single inspired a re-formation in 1969, but with George Janken (bass) and Irish Alex (washboard/drums) replacing Lucifer. However, the heavy style embraced by the new unit failed to generate interest.

● ALBUMS: *The Purple Gang Strikes* (Transatlantic 1968) ★★★.

AND THE MYSTERIANS

Originally formed in Saginaw, Michigan, USA in 1963 as XYZ, ? and the Mysterians entered rock 'n' roll immortality as the band which first popularized the punk-rock classic '96 Tears'. ? (Question Mark) was vocalist Rudy Martinez (b. Mexico) and, after numerous line-up changes, the Mysterians became Frankie Rodriguez, Jnr. b. 9 March 1951, Crystal City, Texas, USA; keyboards), Robert Lee 'Bobby' Balderrama (b. Mexico; lead guitar), Francisco Hernandez 'Frank' Lugo (b. 15 March 1947, Welasco, Texas, USA; bass) and Eduardo Delgardo 'Eddie' Serrato b. Mexico; drums). '96 Tears' was initially intended as the b-side of their debut single, first issued on the tiny Pa-Go-Go label. However, disc jockeys in Michigan, where the band had now settled, turned it over and began playing the three-chord rocker with the now-infamous lead organ line (played on a Vox, not Farfisa as legend dictates). The record was sold to the Cameo label and re-released, whereupon it became a number 1 single in September. The band's name invited further publicity, with ? (Martinez had changed his name legally) refusing to divulge his true identity and opaque sunglasses shielding him from recognition. They charted with three more Cameo singles of which only 'I Need Somebody', in 1966, made any significant impact, reaching number 22 in the US charts. Despite success with these singles and their first album, ? And The Mysterians never again came close to recapturing their brief moment of fame. A second album appeared on Cameo, before the band released one-off singles or Capitol Records and Ray Charles' Tangerine label. Further low-key releases appeared sporadically through the 70s and 80s, and in 1997 the band re-formed to re-record the best of their classic 60s material for the Collectables label.

'96 Tears' was incorporated into the live sets of countless 'garage bands' during the 60s, and was later revived by such artists as Eddie And The Hot Rods (1976), Garland Jeffreys (1981) and the Stranglers (1990). The 'cheesy' organ sound the band used in most of their material has become synonymous with many 60s outfits, but arguably, this band have first claim, if not for their timing, but for their overall sound; pure 60s.

● ALBUMS: 96 Tears (Cameo 1966) ★★★, Action (Cameo 1967) ★★★, Dallas Reunion Tapes

cassette only (ROIR 1984) ★★, Question Mark & The Mysterians (Collectables 1997) ★★★, More Action (Cavestomp 1999) ★★★.
● COMPILATIONS: Feel It! The Very Best Of ? And The Mysterians (Varèse Vintage 2001) ★★★.

QUICKSILVER MESSENGER SERVICE

Of all the bands that came out of the San Francisco area during the late 60s Quicksilver typified most the style, attitude and sound of that era. The original band in 1964 comprised: Dino Valenti (b. 7 October 1943, Danbury, Connecticut, USA, d. 16 November 1994, Santa Rosa, California, USA; vocals), John Cipollina (b. 24 August 1943, Berkeley, California, USA, d. 29 May 1989; guitar), David Freiberg (b. 24 August 1938, Boston, Massachusetts, USA; bass, vocals), Jim Murray (vocals, harmonica), Casey Sonoban (drums) and, very briefly, Alexander 'Skip' Spence (b. 18 April 1946, Windsor, Ontario, Canada; guitar, vocals), before being whisked off to join the Jefferson Airplane as drummer. Another problem that later proved to be significant in Quicksilver's development was the almost immediate arrest and imprisonment of Valenti for a drugs offence. He did not rejoin the band until late 1969. In 1965 the line-up was strengthened by the arrival of Gary Duncan (b. Gary Grubb, 4 September 1946, San Diego, California, USA; guitar) and, replacing Sonoban, Greg Elmore (b. 4 September 1946, San Diego, California, USA). Murray departed soon after their well-received appearance at the Monterey Pop Festival in 1967.

The quartet of Cipollina, Duncan, Elmore and Freiberg recorded the first two albums; both are important in the development of San Francisco rock music, as the twin lead guitars of Cipollina and Duncan made them almost unique. The second collection, Happy Trails, is now regarded as a classic. George Hunter and his Globe Propaganda company were responsible for some of the finest album covers of the 60s and Happy Trails is probably their greatest work. The live music within showed a spontaneity that the band were never able to recapture on subsequent recordings. The side-long suite of Bo Diddley's 'Who Do You Love' has some incredible dynamics and extraordinary interplay between the twin guitarists. Duncan departed soon afterwards and was replaced by UK session pianist and ex-Steve Miller Band member, Nicky Hopkins (b. 24 February 1944, London, England, d. 6 September 1994, California, USA). His contributions breathed some life into the disappointing Shady Grove, notably with the frantic 'Edward, The Mad Shirt Grinder'. Just For Love showed a further decline, with Valenti, now back with the band, becoming overpowering and self-indulgent. 'Fresh Air' gave them a Top 50 US hit in 1970. Cipollina departed, as did Freiberg following his arrest in 1971 for drug possession (he found a lucrative career later with Jefferson Starship). Various incarnations have appeared over the years with little or no success. As recently as 1987, Gary Duncan recorded an album carrying the Quicksilver name, but by then old fans were more content to purchase copies of the first two albums on compact disc.

● ALBUMS: *Quicksilver Messenger Service* (Capitol 1968) ★★★★, *Happy Trails* (Capitol 1969) ★★★★★, *Shady Grove* (Capitol 1969) ★★, *Just For Love* (Capitol 1970) ★★, *What About Me* (Capitol 1971) ★★, *Quicksilver* (Capitol 1971) ★★, *Comin' Thru* (Capitol 1972) ★★, *Solid Silver* (Capitol 1975) ★★, *Maiden Of The Cancer Moon* 1968 recording (Psycho 1983) ★★, *Peace By Piece* (Capitol 1987) ★★.

● COMPILATIONS: *Anthology* (Capitol 1973) ★★★, *The Best Of Quicksilver Messenger Service* (Capitol 1990) ★★★, *Sons Of Mercury (1968-1975)* (Rhino 1991) ★★★★, *The Best Of Quicksilver Messenger Service* (CEMA 1992) ★★★.

QUIET FIVE

The UK-based Quiet Five had nothing to do with Bradford's Quiet Three. Kris Ife (guitar), Roger McKew (guitar), John Howell (keyboards), Richard Barnes (bass) and Roger Marsh (drums) backed Bournemouth singer Patrick Dane before Barnes assumed lead vocals framed by lush harmonies reminiscent of the Searchers. Released by Parlophone Records in May 1965, the Five's 'When The Morning Sun Dries The Dew' – co-written by Ife – and its follow-up (a 1966 arrangement of Paul Simon's 'Homeward Bound') were both minor UK hits but a cover of a Rolling Stones album track, 'I Am Waiting', was a flop – as was 1967's 'Goodnight Sleep Tight', a one-shot single on CBS Records. With the group's consequent split, Barnes recorded several solo singles for Philips Records, of which two ('Take To The Mountains' and 'Go North') crept into 1970's Top 40.

RAWLS, LOU

b. Louis Allen Rawls, 1 December 1935, Chicago, Illinois, USA. Briefly a member of the acclaimed gospel group the Pilgrim Travellers, this distinctive singer began forging a secular career following his move to California in 1958. An association with Sam Cooke culminated in 'Bring It On Home To Me', where Rawls' throaty counterpoint punctuated his colleague's sweet lead vocal. Rawls' own recordings showed him comfortable with either small jazz combos or cultured soul, while an earthier perspective was shown on his mid-60s release, *Lou Rawls Live*. He achieved two Top 20 singles with 'Love Is A Hurtin' Thing' (1966) and 'Dead End Street' (1967), and enjoyed further success with a 1969 reading of Mable John's 'Your Good Thing (Is About To End)'. Several attempts were made to mould Rawls into an all-round entertainer, but while his early 70s work was generally less compulsive, the singer's arrival at Philadelphia International Records signalled a dramatic rebirth. 'You'll Never Find Another Love Like Mine', an international hit in 1976, matched the classic Philly sound with Rawls' resonant delivery, and prepared the way for a series of exemplary releases including 'See You When I Git There' (1977) and 'Let Me Be Good To You' (1979). The singer maintained his association with producers Gamble And Huff into the next decade. His last chart entry, 'I Wish You Belonged to Me', came in 1987 on the duo's self named label, since which time he has recorded for the jazz outlet Blue Note Records and released his first solo gospel album, *I'm Blessed*. Rawls has also pursued an acting career and provided the voice for several Budweiser beer commercials.

● ALBUMS: *Black And Blue* (Capitol 1963) ★★★, *Tobacco Road* (Capitol 1963) ★★★, *Nobody But Lou Rawls* (Capitol 1965) ★★★, *Lou Rawls And Strings* (Capitol 1965) ★★, *Lou Rawls Live* (Capitol 1966) ★★★, *Lou Rawls Soulin'* (Capitol 1966) ★★★, *Lou Rawls Carryin' On!* (Capitol 1967) ★★★, *Too Much!* (Capitol 1967) ★★★, *That's Lou* (Capitol 1967) ★★★, *Merry Christmas Ho! Ho! Ho!* (Capitol 1967) ★, *Feeling Good* (Capitol 1968) ★★★, *You're Good For Me* (Capitol 1968) ★★★, *The Way It Was – The Way It Is* (Capitol 1969) ★★★, *Close-Up* (Capitol 1969) ★★★, *Your Good Thing* (Capitol 1969) ★★★, *You've Made Me So Very Happy* (Capitol 1970) ★★, *Natural Man* (MGM 1971) ★★, *Silk And Soul* (MGM 1972) ★★, *All Things In Time* (Philadelphia International 1976) ★★★

Unmistakably Lou (Philadelphia International 1977) ★★★★★, *When You Hear Lou, You've Heard It All* (Philadelphia International 1977) ★★★★, *Lou Rawls Live* (Philadelphia International 1978) ★★★, *Let Me Be Good To You* (Philadelphia International 1979) ★★★★, *Sit Down And Talk To Me* (Philadelphia International 1980) ★★★, *Shades Of Blue* (Philadelphia International 1981) ★★★, *Now Is The Time* (Portrait 1982) ★★★, *When The Night Comes* (Epic 1983) ★★★, *Close Company* (Epic 1984) ★★★, *Love All Your Blues Away* (Epic 1986) ★★★, *At Last* (Blue Note 1989) ★★★, *Portrait Of The Blues* (Capitol 1992) ★★★, *Christmas Is The Time* (Blue Note 1993) ★★★, *Seasons 4 U* (Rawls & Brokaw 1998) ★★★, *I'm Blessed* (Malaco 2001) ★★★.

● COMPILATIONS: *The Best Of Lou Rawls: The Capitol/Blue Note Years* (Capitol 1968) ★★★, *Soul Serenade* (Stateside 1985) ★★★, *Stormy Monday* (See For Miles 1985) ★★★, *Classic Soul* (Blue Moon 1986) ★★★, *Greatest Hits* (Curb 1990) ★★★, *The Philly Years* (Repertoire 1995) ★★★★, *Love Is A Hurtin' Thing: The Silk & Soul Of Lou Rawls* (EMI 1997) ★★★★, *The Best Of Lou Rawls: The Classic Philadelphia Recordings* (Music Club 1998) ★★★★, *Anthology* (The Right Stuff/Capitol 2000) ★★★★.

● VIDEOS: *The Jazz Channel Presents Lou Rawls* (Aviva International 2000).

● FILMS: *Angel, Angel, Down We Go* aka *Cult Of The Damned* (1970), *Lookin' Italian* aka *Showdown* (1994), *Leaving Las Vegas* (1995), *The Prince* (1996), *Driven* (1996), *Wildly Available* (1996), *Livers Ain't Cheap* aka *The Real Thing* (1997), *The Price Of Kissing* (1997), *Motel Blue* (1997), *After The Game* (1997), *Blues Brothers 2000* (1998), *Watchers Reborn* (1998), *The Rugrats Movie* voice only (1998), *Still Breathing* (1998), *Everything's Jake* (2000), *Bel Air* (2000), *The Code Conspiracy* (2001).

REDDING, OTIS

b. 9 September 1941, Dawson, Georgia, USA, d. 10 December 1967, Lake Monona, Madison, Wisconsin, USA. The son of a Baptist minister, Redding assimilated gospel music during his childhood and soon became interested in jump blues and R&B. After resettling in Macon, he became infatuated with local luminary Little Richard, and began singing on a full-time basis. A high-school friend and booking agent, Phil Walden, then became his manager. Through Walden's contacts Redding joined Johnny Jenkins And The Pinetoppers as a sometime singer and occasional driver. Redding also began recording for sundry local independents, and his debut single, 'She's Alright', credited to Otis And The Shooters, was quickly followed by 'Shout Ba Malama'. Both performances were firmly in the Little Richard mould. The singer's fortunes blossomed when one of his own songs, 'These Arms Of Mine', was picked up for the Stax Records subsidiary Volt. Recorded at the tail end of a Johnny Jenkins session, this aching ballad crept into the American Hot 100 in May 1963. Further poignant releases, 'Pain In My Heart', 'That's How Strong My Love Is' and 'I've Been Loving You Too Long', were balanced by brassy, up-tempo performances including 'Mr. Pitiful', 'Respect' and 'Fa-Fa-Fa-Fa-Fa (Sad Song)'. He remained something of a cult figure until 1965, although he had already released a series of excellent albums.

It was the release of the magnificent *Otis Blue* that triggered off a major appreciation, in which original material nestled beside cover versions of the Rolling Stones' '(I Can't Get No) Satisfaction' and two songs by another mentor, Sam Cooke ('Wonderful World and 'A Change Is Gonna Come'). His version of the Temptations' 'My Girl' then became a UK hit. *Complete & Unbelievable: The Otis Redding Dictionary Of Soul* contained a stunning version of 'Try A Little Tenderness'. This song was written in 1933 by Harry Woods, James Campbell and Reginald Connelly, yet Redding turns it into an aching contemporary soul ballad. Meanwhile the singer's popularity was further enhanced by the tour of the *Hit The Road Stax* revue in 1967. 'Tramp', a duet with Carla Thomas, also provided success, while Redding's production company, Jotis, was responsible for launching the career of Arthur Conley. A triumphant appearance at the legendary 1967 Monterey Pop Festival suggested that Redding was about to attract an even wider following. He appeared on stage completely out of fashion with the colourful beads and bells of the audience, wearing one of his familiar dark blue silk and mohair suits, with tie and smart shoes. His explosive set was, along with that of Jimi Hendrix, the highlight of the festival. More importantly, he unified the 'love crowd' like never before. He brought his music of black origin into the hearts of white hippies (many of them middle-class kids who had never heard soul music). A few months later tragedy struck. On 10 December 1967, a light aircraft in which he was travelling plunged into Lake Monona, Madison, Wisconsin, killing the singer, his valet, the pilot and four members of the Bar-Kays.

The wistful '(Sittin' On) The Dock Of The Bay', a song Redding had recorded just three days earlier, became his only million-seller and US pop number 1. The single's seeming serenity about sitting on a jetty in San Francisco's harbour, as well as several posthumous album tracks, suggested a sadly unfulfilled maturity. Although some critics now point to Redding's limited vocal range, few could match his guttural sounding voice, which, at any volume, could send shivers into the spine. Such was his emotional drive, and his distinctive sound remains immediately compelling. There is no doubt that Redding matched the smooth vocal intensity of artists such as Marvin Gaye, Curtis Mayfield and Al Green. What should also be acknowledged is the considerable amount of classic songs he wrote, often with guitarist Steve Cropper. They stand as some of the most enduring moments of the golden age of soul music. Redding should be regarded as a giant of the genre.

● ALBUMS: *Pain In My Heart* (Atco 1964) ★★★★, *The Great Otis Redding Sings Soul Ballads* (Volt 1965) ★★★★, *Otis Blue/Otis Redding Sings Soul* (Volt 1965) ★★★★★, *The Soul Album* (Volt 1966) ★★★★, *Complete And Unbelievable: The Otis Redding Dictionary Of Soul* (Volt 1966) ★★★★, with Carla Thomas *The King & Queen* (Stax 1967) ★★★★, *Live In Europe* (Volt 1967) ★★★★, *The Dock Of The Bay* (Volt 1968) ★★★, *The Immortal Otis Redding* (Atco 1968) ★★★, *In Person At The Whisky A Go Go* (Atco 1968) ★★★, *Love Man* (Atco 1969) ★★★★, *Tell The Truth* (Atco 1970) ★★★, shared with Jimi Hendrix *Monterey International Pop Festival* (Reprise 1970) ★★★★, *Live Otis Redding* (Atlantic 1982) ★★★, *Good To Me: Recorded Live At The Whiskey A Go Go, Vol. 2* (Stax 1993) ★★★.

● COMPILATIONS: *The History Of Otis Redding* (Volt 1967) ★★★★, *Here Comes Some Soul From Otis Redding And Little Joe Curtis* pre-1962 recordings (Marble Arch 1968) ★, *Remembering* (Atlantic 1970) ★★★, *The Best Of Otis Redding* (Atco 1972) ★★★★, *Pure Otis* (Atlantic 1979) ★★★, *Come To Me* (Charly 1984) ★★, *Dock Of The Bay: The Definitive Collection* (Atlantic 1987) ★★★★, *The Otis Redding Story* 4-LP box set (Atlantic 1989) ★★★★, *Remember Me* US title *It's Not Just Sentimental* UK title (Stax 1992) ★★★, *Otis!: The Definitive Otis Redding* 4-CD box set (Rhino 1993) ★★★★★, *The Very Best Of Otis Redding* (Rhino 1993) ★★★★, *The Very Best Of Otis Redding, Vol. 2* (Rhino 1995) ★★★, *Love Songs* (Rhino 1998) ★★★★, *Dreams To Remember: The Anthology* (Rhino 1998) ★★★★.

● VIDEOS: *Remembering Otis* (Virgin 1990).

● FURTHER READING: *The Otis Redding Story*, Jane Schiesel.

REEVES, JIM

b. James Travis Reeves, 20 August 1923, Galloway, Texas, USA, d. 31 July 1964 (Reeves' plaque in the Country Music Hall Of Fame mistakenly gives his date of birth as 1924). Reeves' father died when he was 10 months old and his mother was left to raise nine children on the family farm. Although only aged five, Reeves was entranced when a brother brought home a gramophone and a Jimmie Rodgers record, 'Blue Yodel No. 5'. When aged nine, he traded stolen pears for an old guitar he saw in a neighbour's yard. A cook for an oil company showed him the basic chords and when aged 12, he appeared on a radio show in Shreveport, Louisiana. By virtue of his athletic abilities, he won a scholarship to the University of Texas. However, he was shy, largely because of a stammer, which he managed to correct while at university (Reeves' records are known for perfect diction and

delivery). His first singing work was with Moon Mullican's band in Beaumont, Texas, and he worked as an announcer and singing disc jockey at KGRI in Henderson for several years (Reeves eventually bought the station in 1959). He recorded two singles for a chain store's label in 1949. In November 1952 Reeves moved to KWKH in Shreveport, where his duties included hosting the *Louisiana Hayride*. He stood in as a performer when Hank Williams failed to arrive and was signed immediately to Abbott Records. In 1953, Reeves received gold discs for two high-voiced, country novelties, 'Mexican Joe' and 'Bimbo'. In 1955 he joined the *Grand Ole Opry* and started recording for RCA Records in Nashville, having his first hit with a song based on the 'railroad, steamboat' game, 'Yonder Comes A Sucker'. Chet Atkins considered 'Four Walls' a 'girl's song', but Reeves persisted and used the song to change his approach to singing. He pitched his voice lower and sang close to the microphone, thus creating a warm ballad style which was far removed from his hillbilly recordings. 'Four Walls' became an enormous US success in 1957, crossing over to the pop market and becoming a template for his future work. From then on, Atkins recorded Reeves as a mellow balladeer, giving him some pop standards and replacing fiddles and steel guitar with piano and strings (exceptions include an album of narrations, *Tall Tales And Short Tempers*).

Reeves had already swapped his western outfit for a suit and tie, and, in keeping with his hit 'Blue Boy', his group, the Wagonmasters, became the Blue Boys. He always included a religious section in his stage show and also sang 'Danny Boy' to acknowledge his Irish ancestry. 'He'll Have To Go' topped the US country charts for 14 weeks and made number 2 in the US pop charts. In this memorable song, Reeves conveyed an implausible lyric with conviction, and it has now become a country standard. A gooey novelty, 'But You Love Me Daddy', recorded at the same session with Steve, the nine-year-old son of bass player Bob Moore, was a UK Top 20 hit 10 years later. Having established a commercial format, 'Gentleman Jim' had success with 'You're The Only Good Thing', 'Adios Amigo', 'Welcome To My World' (UK number 6) and 'Guilty', which features French horns and oboes. His records often had exceptional longevity; 'I Love You Because' (number 5) and 'I Won't Forget You' (number 3) were on the UK charts for 39 and 25 weeks, respectively. He became enormously popular in South Africa, recording in Afrikaans, and making a light-hearted film there, *Kimberley Jim*, which became a local success. Reeves did not like flying but after being a passenger in a South African plane that developed engine trouble, he obtained his own daytime pilot's licence.

On 31 July 1964 pilot Reeves and his pianist/manager, Dean Manuel, died when their ingle-engine plane ran into difficulties during a torm and crashed into dense woods outside ashville. The bodies were not found until 2 ugust despite 500 people, including fellow country singers, being involved in the search. eeves was buried in a specially landscaped rea by the side of Highway 79 in Texas, and his ollie, Cheyenne, was buried at his feet in 1967. eeves continued to have hits with such ironic tles as 'This World Is Not My Home' and the elf-penned 'Is It Really Over?'. Although Reeves ad not recorded 'Distant Drums' officially – the ong had gone to Roy Orbison – he had made a demo for songwriter Cindy Walker. ccompaniment was added and, in 1966, Distant Drums' became Reeves' first UK umber 1. He had around 80 unreleased tracks nd his widow Mary Reeves followed a brilliant, uncharitable, marketing policy whereby nheard material would be placed alongside reviously issued tracks to make a new album. ometimes existing tracks were remastered and uets were constructed with Deborah Allen and he late Patsy Cline. Reeves became a estselling album artist to such an extent that *40 Golden Greats* topped the album charts in 1975. oth the Blue Boys and his nephew John Rex eeves have toured with tribute concerts, and uch of Reeves' catalogue is still available. eeves' relaxed style has influenced Don Villiams and Daniel O'Donnell, but the ombination of pop balladry and country music s more demanding than it appears, and Reeves emains its father figure. Mary Reeves, who did o much to keep his name alive, died on 11 November 1999.

ALBUMS: *Jim Reeves Sings* (Abbott 1956) ★★, *inging Down The Lane* (RCA Victor 1956) ★★★, *imbo* (RCA Victor 1957) ★★★, *Jim Reeves* (RCA ictor 1957) ★★★, *Girls I Have Known* (RCA 'ictor 1958) ★★★, *God Be With You* (RCA Victor 958) ★★★, *Songs To Warm The Heart* (RCA ictor 1959) ★★★, *He'll Have To Go* (RCA Victor 960) ★★★★, *According To My Heart* (Camden 960) ★★★, *The Intimate Jim Reeves* (RCA Victor 960) ★★★★, *Talking To Your Heart* (RCA Victor 961) ★★★, *Tall Tales And Short Tempers* (RCA ictor 1961) ★★★, *The Country Side Of Jim eeves* (RCA Victor 1962) ★★★, *A Touch Of elvet* (RCA Victor 1962) ★★★, *We Thank Thee* RCA Victor 1962) ★★★, *Good 'N' Country* Camden 1963) ★★★★, *Diamonds In The Sand* Camden 1963) ★★★, *Gentleman Jim* (RCA ictor 1963) ★★★★, *The International Jim eeves* (RCA Victor 1963) ★★★, *Twelve Songs Of hristmas* (RCA Victor 1963) ★★★, *Moonlight nd Roses* (RCA Victor 1964) ★★★★, *Have I Told ou Lately That I Love You?* (RCA Victor 1964) '★★, *Kimberley Jim* (RCA Victor 1964) ★★, *The m Reeves Way* (RCA Victor 1965) ★★★, *Distant Drums* (RCA Victor 1966) ★★★★, *Yours incerely, Jim Reeves* (RCA Victor 1966) ★★★, *lue Side Of Lonesome* (RCA Victor 1967) ★★★, *ly Cathedral* (RCA Victor 1967) ★★★, *A Touch*

of Sadness (RCA Victor 1968) ★★★, *Jim Reeves On Stage* (RCA Victor 1968) ★★★, *Jim Reeves – And Some Friends* (RCA Victor 1969) ★★★, *Jim Reeves Writes You A Record* (RCA Victor 1971) ★★★, *Something Special* (RCA Victor 1971) ★★★, *Young And Country* (RCA Victor 1971) ★★★, *My Friend* (RCA Victor 1972) ★★★, *Missing You* (RCA Victor 1972) ★★★, *Am I That Easy To Forget* (RCA Victor 1973) ★★★, *Great Moments With Jim Reeves* (RCA Victor 1973) ★★, *I'd Fight The World* (RCA Victor 1974) ★★★, *Songs Of Love* (RCA Victor 1975) ★★, *I Love You Because* (RCA Victor 1976) ★★, *It's Nothin' To Me* (RCA Victor 1977) ★★★★, *Jim Reeves* (RCA Victor 1978) ★★★, with Deborah Allen *Don't Let Me Cross Over* (RCA Victor 1979) ★★, *There's Always Me* (RCA Victor 1980) ★★, with Patsy Cline *Greatest Hits* (RCA Victor 1981) ★★, *Dear Hearts & Gentle People* (1992) ★★★, *Jim Reeves* (Summit 1995) ★★★.

● COMPILATIONS: *The Best Of Jim Reeves* (RCA Victor 1964) ★★★, *The Best Of Jim Reeves, Volume 2* (RCA Victor 1966) ★★★, *The Best Of Jim Reeves, Volume 3* (RCA Victor 1969) ★★★, *The Best Of Jim Reeves Sacred Songs* (RCA Victor 1975) ★★★, *Abbott Recordings, Volume 1* (1982) ★★★, *Abbott Recordings, Volume 2* (1982) ★★, *Live At The Grand Ole Opry* (CMF 1987) ★★★, *Four Walls – The Legend Begins* (RCA 1991) ★★★★, *The Definitive Jim Reeves* (RCA 1992) ★★★, *Welcome To My World: The Essential Jim Reeves Collection* (RCA 1993) ★★★★, *Welcome To My World* 16-CD box set (Bear Family 1994) ★★★★, *The Essential Jim Reeves* (RCA 1995) ★★★★, *The Ultimate Collection* (RCA 1996) ★★★★, *Jim Reeves And Friends Radio Days Volume 1* 4-CD box set (Bear Family 1998) ★★★★, *The Unreleased Hits Of Jim Reeves* (BMG 2000) ★★★, *Jim Reeves And Friends Radio Days Volume 2* 4-CD box set (Bear Family 2001) ★★★.

● FURTHER READING: *The Saga Of Jim Reeves: Country And Western Singer And Musician*, Pansy Cook. *Like A Moth To A Flame: The Jim Reeves Story*, Michael Streissguth.

REPARATA AND THE DELRONS

Schoolfriends Mary Aiese, Nanette Licari, Anne Fitzgerald and Regina Gallagher began performing together in 1962. Dubbed the Del-Rons in honour of the Dell-Vikings and Del-Satins, they appeared at dances in their Brooklyn neighbourhood before Mary realigned the group around Carol Drobinicki, Sheila Reille, Kathy Romeo and Margi McGuire. The last was asked to leave when the group acquired a recording deal which in turn engendered 'Whenever A Teenager Cries'. This light, but plaintive offering topped the local New York chart, but although it only rose to number 60 nationally, the single – credited to Reparata And The Delrons – nonetheless secured the trio's reputation. With Mary taking the lead spot, the group underwent further alterations when original member Licari and newcomer Lorraine

Mazzola replaced Reille and Romeo. Although commercial success eluded them, the revitalized trio recorded a series of excellent singles, including the Jeff Barry-penned 'I'm Nobody's Baby Now' and 'I Can Hear The Rain', which featured Melba Moore on backing vocals. Despite continued apathy at home the trio enjoyed a major UK hit when the excellent 'Captain Of Your Ship' reached number 13 in 1968. Paradoxically the vocal line featured Mazzola, who assumed the name Reparata when Mary Aiese retired in 1970. Mazzola, Licari and newcomer Cookie Sirico completed the concept album, *1970 Rock 'N' Roll Revolution*, which contained various 'girl-group' classics, before disbanding in 1973. Mazzola later appeared in Lady Flash, the backing group to Barry Manilow, but her continued use of the name Reparata was challenged by Aiese who reclaimed the appellation for a series of solo singles, of which 'Shoes' reached the UK Top 50 in 1975.

● ALBUMS: *Whenever A Teenager Cries* (World Artists 1965) ★★, *1970 Rock 'N' Roll Revolution* (1970) ★★.

REVERE, PAUL, AND THE RAIDERS

Formed in Portland, Oregon, USA, in 1961, when pianist Revere added Mark Lindsay (b. 9 March 1942, Cambridge, Idaho, USA; vocals/saxophone) to the line-up of his club band, the Downbeats. Drake Levin (guitar), Mike Holliday (bass) and Michael Smith (drums) completed a group later known as Paul Revere And The Nightriders, before settling on their Raiders appellation. Several locally issued singles ensued, including 'Beatnik Sticks' and 'Like Long Hair', the latter of which rose into the US Top 40. Group manager and disc jockey Roger Hart then financed a demonstration tape which in turn engendered a prestigious recording deal with CBS Records. Their version of bar band favourite 'Louie Louie' was issued in 1963, but although highly successful regionally, was outsold by local rivals the Kingsmen who secured the national hit. A year passed before the Raiders recorded a new single, during which time Phil Volk had replaced Holliday. 'Louie Go Home' showed their confidence remained undiminished, but it was 1965 before the Raiders hit their commercial stride with the punky 'Steppin' Out'. By this point the band was the resident act on *Where The Action Is*, Dick Clark's networked, daily television show. The attendant exposure resulted in a series of classic pop singles, including 'Just Like Me' (1965) 'Kicks', 'Hungry', 'Good Things' (all 1966) and 'Him Or Me – What's It Gonna Be?' (1967), each of which were impeccably produced by Terry Melcher. However, the Raiders' slick stage routines and Revolutionary War garb – replete with thigh-boots, tights, frilled shirts and three-cornered hats – was frowned upon by the emergent underground audience.

The departures of Smith, Levin and Volk made little difference to the Raiders' overall sound, enhancing suspicion that session musician were responsible for the excellent studio sound Later members Freddy Weller (guitar), Keith Allison (bass) and Joe (Correro) Jnr. (drums were nonetheless accomplished musicians, and thus enhanced the professional approach marking *Hard 'N' Heavy (With Marshmallow)* and *Collage*. Despite inconsistent chart places, the group maintained a high television profile a hosts of *Happening 68*. In 1969 Lindsay embarked on a concurrent solo career, bu although 'Arizona' sold over one million copies later releases proved less successful. Two year later the Raiders scored an unexpected US chart topper with 'Indian Reservation (The Lament O The Cherokee Reservation Indian)', previously a UK hit for Don Fardon, but it proved their fina Top 20 hit. Although Weller forged a new caree in country music, Revere and Lindsay struggled to keep the band afloat, particularly whe dropped by their long-standing label. Lindsay departed in 1975, but Revere became the act' custodian, presiding over occasional releases fo independent outlets with a stable line-up comprising Doug Heath (guitar), Ron Foos (bass and Omar Martinez (drums). The Raider flourished briefly during the US Bicentennia celebrations, before emerging again in 198. mixing old favourites and new songs on thei Raiders America label. This regeneration prove short-lived, although Revere still fronts the ban on the nostalgia circuit, with additional long serving members Danny Krause (keyboards and Carl Driggs (lead vocals).

● ALBUMS: *Like, Long Hair* (Gardena 1961 ★★★, *Paul Revere And The Raiders* aka *In Th Beginning* (Jerden 1961) ★★, *Here They Come* (Columbia 1965) ★★★, *Just Like Us!* (Columbi 1966) ★★★, *Midnight Ride* (Columbia 1966 ★★★, *The Spirit Of '67* aka *Good Thing* (Columbi 1967) ★★★, *Revolution!* (Columbia 1967) ★★★ *A Christmas Present ... And Past* (Columbia 1967 ★★★, *Goin' To Memphis* (Columbia 1968) ★★★ *Something Happening* (Columbia 1968) ★★★ *Hard 'N' Heavy (With Marshmallow)* (Columbia 1969) ★★, *Alias Pink Puzz* (Columbia 1969) ★★★ *Collage* (Columbia 1970) ★★★, *India Reservation* (Columbia 1971) ★★★, *Country Win* (Columbia 1972) ★★, *We Gotta All Get Togethe* (Realm 1976) ★★, *Featuring Mark Lindsay' Arizona* (Realm 1976) ★★.

● COMPILATIONS: *Greatest Hits* (Columbi 1967) ★★★, *Greatest Hits, Vol. 2* (Columbia 1971 ★★★, *All-Time Greatest Hits* (Columbia 1972 ★★★, *Kicks* (Edsel 1983) ★★★, *The Legend O Paul Revere* (Columbia/Legacy 1990) ★★★★ *The Essential Ride '63-'67* (Columbia/Legacy 1995) ★★★★, *Mojo Workout!* (Sundazed 2000 ★★★.

RHINOCEROS

A rock band that promised more than it was abl to deliver, Rhinoceros was an Elektra Record

signing of the late 60s. The group looked a formidable line-up on paper with Michael Fonfara (ex-Electric Flag; keyboards), Billy Mundi (ex-Buffalo Springfield; drums), Doug Hastings (ex-Buffalo Springfield; guitar), Danny Weis (ex-Iron Butterfly; guitar) and John Finlay (vocals). The spectacular fold-out cover artwork on their debut by G. Sazaferin showed a brightly colourful, beaded Rhinoceros. Unfortunately the music was disappointing; only the Buddy Miles-influenced 'You're My Girl (I Don't Want To Discuss It)' and their 'greatest hit', the instrumental 'Apricot Brandy', stood out. The BBC adopted the latter as a Radio 1 theme. Two more albums followed, but by now the ponderous Rhinoceros had turned into a dodo.
● ALBUMS: *Rhinoceros* (Elektra 1968) ★★★, *Satin Chickens* (Elektra 1969) ★★, *Better Times Are Coming* (Elektra 1970) ★.

RICHARD, CLIFF

b. Harry Roger Webb, 14 October 1940, Lucknow, India. One of the most popular and enduring talents in the history of UK show business, Webb began his career as a rock 'n' roll performer in 1957. His fascination for Elvis Presley encouraged him to join the Dick Teague Skiffle Group and several months later he teamed up with drummer Terry Smart and guitarist Norman Mitham to form the Drifters. They played at various clubs in the Cheshunt/ Hoddesdon area of Hertfordshire before descending on the famous 2I's coffee bar in London's Soho. There, they were approached by lead guitarist Ian Samwell and developed their act as a quartet. In 1958, they secured their big break in the unlikely setting of a Saturday morning talent show at the Gaumont cinema in Shepherd's Bush. It was there that the senatorial theatrical agent George Ganyou recognized Webb's sexual appeal and singing abilities and duly financed the recording of a demonstration tape of 'Breathless' and 'Lawdy Miss Clawdy'. A copy reached the hands of EMI Records producer Norrie Paramor who was impressed enough to grant the ensemble an audition. Initially, he intended to record the newly christened Cliff Richard as a solo artist backed by an orchestra, but the persuasive performer insisted upon retaining his own backing group.

With the assistance of a couple of session musicians, the unit recorded the American teen ballad 'Schoolboy Crush' as a projected first single. An acetate of the recording was paraded around Tin Pan Alley and came to the attention of the influential television producer Jack Good. It was not the juvenile 'Schoolboy Crush' that captured his attention, however, but the Ian Samwell b-side 'Move It'. Good reacted with characteristically manic enthusiasm when he heard the disc, rightly recognizing that it sounded like nothing else in the history of UK pop. The distinctive riff and unaffected vocal seemed authentically American, completely at odds with the mannered material that usually emanated from British recording studios. With Good's ceaseless promotion, which included a full-page review in the music paper *Disc*, Richard's debut was eagerly anticipated and swiftly rose to number 2 in the UK charts. Meanwhile, the star made his debut on Good's television showcase *Oh Boy!*, and rapidly replaced Marty Wilde as Britain's premier rock 'n' roll talent. The low-key role offered to the Drifters persuaded Samwell to leave the group to become a professional songwriter and producer, and by the end of 1958 a new line-up emerged featuring Hank B. Marvin and Bruce Welch. Before long, they changed their name to the Shadows, in order to avoid confusion with the black American R&B group, the Drifters. Meanwhile, Richard consolidated his position in the rock 'n' roll pantheon, even outraging critics in true Elvis Presley fashion. The *New Musical Express* denounced his 'violent, hip-swinging' and 'crude exhibitionism' and pontificated: 'Tommy Steele became Britain's teenage idol without resorting to this form of indecent, short-sighted vulgarity'. Critical mortification had little effect on the screaming female fans who responded to the singer's boyish sexuality with increasing intensity.

1959 was a decisive year for Richard and a firm indicator of his longevity as a performer. With management shake-ups, shifts in national musical taste and some distinctly average singles his career could easily have been curtailed, but instead he matured and transcended his Presley-like beginnings. A recording of Lionel Bart's 'Living Doll' provided him with a massive UK number 1 and three months later he returned to the top with the plaintive 'Travellin' Light'. He also starred in two films, within 12 months. *Serious Charge*, a non-musical drama, was banned in some areas as it dealt with the controversial subject of homosexual blackmail. The Wolf Mankowitz-directed *Expresso Bongo*, in which Richard played the delightfully named Bongo Herbert, was a cinematic pop landmark, brilliantly evoking the rapacious world of Tin Pan Alley. It remains one of the most revealing and humorous films ever made on the music business and proved an interesting vehicle for Richard's varied talents. From 1960 onwards Richard's career progressed along more traditional lines leading to acceptance as a middle-of-the-road entertainer. Varied hits such as the breezy, chart-topping 'Please Don't Tease', the rock 'n' rolling 'Nine Times Out Of Ten' and reflective 'Theme For A Dream' demonstrated his range, and in 1962 he hit a new peak with 'The Young Ones'. A glorious pop anthem to youth, with some striking guitar work from Hank Marvin, the song proved one of his most memorable number 1 hits.

The film of the same name was a charming period piece, with a strong cast and fine score. It broke box office records and spawned a series of similar movies from its star, who was clearly following Elvis Presley's cinematic excursions as a means of extending his audience. Unlike the King, however, Richard supplemented his frequent movie commitments with tours, summer seasons, regular television slots and even pantomime appearances. The run of UK Top 10 hits continued uninterrupted until as late as mid-1965. Although the showbiz glitz had brought a certain aural homogeneity to the material, the catchiness of songs such as 'Bachelor Boy', 'Summer Holiday', 'On The Beach' and 'I Could Easily Fall' was undeniable. These were neatly, if predictably, complemented by ballad releases such as 'Constantly', 'The Twelfth Of Never' and 'The Minute You're Gone'. The formula looked likely to be rendered redundant by the British beat boom, but Richard expertly rode that wave, even improving his selection of material along the way. He bravely, although relatively unsuccessfully, covered a Rolling Stones song, 'Blue Turns To Grey', before again hitting top form with the beautifully melodic 'Visions'. During 1966, he had almost retired after converting to fundamentalist Christianity, but elected to use his singing career as a positive expression of his faith. The sparkling 'In The Country' and gorgeously evocative 'The Day I Met Marie' displayed the old strengths to the full, but in the swiftly changing cultural climate of the late 60s, Richard's hold on the pop charts could no longer be guaranteed.

The 1968 Eurovision Song Contest offered him a chance of further glory, but the jury placed him a close second with the 'oom-pah-pah'-sounding 'Congratulations'. The song was nevertheless a consummate Eurovision performance and proved one of the biggest UK number 1s of the year. Immediately thereafter, Richard's chart progress declined and his choice of material proved at best desultory. Although there were a couple of solid entries, Raymond Froggatt's 'Big Ship' and a superb duet with Hank Marvin, 'Throw Down A Line', Richard seemed a likely contender for Variety as the decade closed.

The first half of the 70s saw him in a musical rut. The chirpy but insubstantial 'Goodbye Sam, Hello Samantha' was a Top 10 hit in 1970 and heralded a notable decline. A second shot at the Eurovision Song Contest with 'Power To All Our Friends' brought his only other Top 10 success of the period and it was widely assumed that his chart career was over. However, in 1976 there was a surprise resurgence in his career when Bruce Welch of the Shadows was assigned to produce his colleague. The sessions resulted in the bestselling album I'm Nearly Famous, which included two major hits, 'Miss You Nights' and 'Devil Woman'. The latter was notable for its decidedly un-Christian imagery and the fact that it gave Richard a rare US chart success. Although Welch remained at the controls for two more albums, time again looked as though it would

kill off Richard's perennial chart success. A string of meagre singles culminated in the dull 'Green Light', which stalled at number 57, his lowest chart placing since he started singing. Coincidentally, his backing musicians, Terry Britten and Alan Tarney, had moved into songwriting and production at this point and encouraged him to adopt a more contemporary sound on the album Rock 'N' Roll Juvenile. The most startling breakthrough, however, was the attendant single 'We Don't Talk Anymore', written by Tarney and produced by Welch. An exceptional pop record, the song gave Richard his first UK number 1 hit in over a decade and also reached the Top 10 in the USA.

The 'new' Richard sound, so refreshing after some of his staid offerings in the late 70s, brought further well-arranged hits, such as 'Carrie' and 'Wired For Sound', and ensured that he was a chart regular throughout the 80s. Although he resisted the temptation to try anything radical, there were subtle changes in his musical approach. One feature of his talent that emerged during the 80s was a remarkable facility as a duettist. Collaborations with Olivia Newton-John, Phil Everly, Sarah Brightman, Sheila Walsh, Elton John and Van Morrison added a completely new dimension to his career. It was something of a belated shock to realize that Richard may be one of the finest harmony singers working in the field of popular music. His perfectly enunciated vocals and the smooth texture of his voice have the power to complement work that he might not usually tackle alone. The possibility of his collaborating with an artist even further from his sphere than Van Morrison remains a tantalizing challenge.

Throughout his six decades in the pop charts, Richard has displayed a valiant longevity. He parodied one of his earliest hits with comedy quartet the Young Ones and registered yet another number 1, while still singing religious songs on gospel tours. He appeared in Time and in John Farrar and Tim Rice's hugely successful Heathcliff (his own Songs From Heathcliff was drawn from the show). He sued the New Musical Express for an appallingly libellous review, far more vicious than their acerbic comments back in 1958. He celebrated his 50th birthday with a move into social commentary with the anti-war hit 'From A Distance'. He was nominated to perform at the celebrations for VE day in 1995, appearing with Vera Lynn, and has now been adopted as her male equivalent. It was no surprise, therefore, to learn that he was to be knighted for his services to popular music in May 1995. Richard's long-held belief that most UK pop radio stations have an official veto on his tracks seemed to be proven in September 1998, when he distributed a heavily remixed promo of his soon-to-be-released single, 'Can't Keep This Feeling In', under the pseudonym Blacknight. It was instantly playlisted by youth-orientated stations all over the country, and went to number 10 in the singles chart the following month. The singer was further angered when DJ Chris Evans, owner of Virgin Radio, announced that he wanted the station's entire stock of Richard's records 'thrown out'. In an unprecedented move, BBC Radio 1 responded by clearing its morning schedules for a four-hour tribute 'Stand Up For Cliff Day' hosted by Jill Dando. Such was the demand for tickets to his November/December 1998 Royal Albert Hall concerts celebrating 40 years in showbusiness, that a further 12 performances were scheduled for March 1999. At the end of the year he was criticised for being opportunistic when he combined the 'Lord's Prayer' and 'Auld Lang Syne' into 'The Millennium Prayer'. Tacky though it was it still reached number 1 in the UK. So he goes on – Sir Cliff Richard has outlasted every musical trend of the past four decades with a sincerity and commitment that may well be unmatched in his field. He is British pop's most celebrated survivor.

● ALBUMS: *Cliff* (Columbia 1959) ★★★, *Cliff Sings* (Columbia 1959) ★★★★, *Me And My Shadows* (Columbia 1960) ★★★★, *Listen To Cliff* (Columbia 1961) ★★★, *21 Today* (Columbia 1961) ★★★, *The Young Ones* (Columbia 1961) ★★★, *32 Minutes And 17 Seconds With Cliff Richard* (Columbia 1962) ★★★★, *Summer Holiday* (Columbia 1963) ★★★, *Cliff's Hit Album* (Columbia 1963) ★★★★, *When In Spain* (Columbia 1963) ★★★, *Wonderful Life* (Columbia 1964) ★★★, *Aladdin And His Wonderful Lamp* (Columbia 1964) ★★★, *Cliff Richard* (Columbia 1965) ★★★, *More Hits By Cliff* (Columbia 1965) ★★★, *When In Rome* (Columbia 1965) ★★, *Love Is Forever* (Columbia 1965) ★★★, *Kinda Latin* (Columbia 1966) ★★★, *Finders Keepers* (Columbia 1966) ★★, *Cinderella* (Columbia 1967) ★★, *Don't Stop Me Now* (Columbia 1967) ★★★, *Good News* (Columbia 1967) ★★★, *Cliff In Japan* (Columbia 1968) ★★★, *Two A Penny* (Columbia 1968) ★★★, *Established 1958* (Columbia 1968) ★★★, *Sincerely Cliff* (Columbia 1969) ★★★, *It'll Be Me* (Regal Starline 1969) ★★★, *Cliff 'Live' At The Talk Of The Town* (Regal Starline 1970) ★★★, *All My Love* (MFP 1970) ★★★, *About That Man* (Columbia 1970) ★★★, *Tracks 'N' Grooves* (Columbia 1970) ★★★, *His Land* (Columbia 1970) ★★★, *Cliff's Hit Album* stereo reissue of 1963 album (EMI 1971) ★★★★, *Take Me High* (EMI 1973) ★★★, *Help It Along* (EMI 1974) ★★★, *The 31st Of February Street* (EMI 1974) ★★★, *Everybody Needs Someone* (MFP 1975) ★★★, *I'm Nearly Famous* (EMI 1976) ★★★, *Cliff Live* (MFP 1976) ★★★, *Every Face Tells A Story* (EMI 1977) ★★★, *Small Corners* (EMI 1977) ★★★, *Green Light* (EMI 1978) ★★★, *Thank You Very Much* (EMI 1979) ★★★, *Rock 'N' Roll Juvenile* (EMI 1979) ★★★, *Rock On With Cliff* (MFP 1980) ★★★, *Listen To Cliff* (MFP 1980) ★★★, *I'm No Hero* (EMI 1980) ★★★, *Love Songs* (EMI 1981) ★★★, *Wired For Sound* (EMI 1981) ★★★, *Now You See Me, Now You Don't* (EMI 1982) ★★★,

Dressed For The Occasion (EMI 1983) ★★★, *Silver* (EMI 1983) ★★★, *Cliff In The 60s* (MFP 1984) ★★★, *Cliff And The Shadows* (EMI 1984) ★★★, *Thank You Very Much* (MFP 1984) ★★★, *The Rock Connection* (EMI 1984) ★★★, *Walking In The Light* (Myrrh 1985) ★★★, *Time* (EMI 1986) ★★★, *Hymns And Inspirational Songs* (Word 1986) ★★★, *Always Guaranteed* (EMI 1987) ★★★, *Stronger* (EMI 1989) ★★★, *From A Distance ... The Event* (EMI 1990) ★★★, *Together With Cliff* (EMI 1991) ★★★, *The Album* (EMI 1993) ★★★, *Songs From Heathcliff* (EMI 1995) ★★★, *Real As I Wanna Be* (EMI 1998) ★★★, *Wanted* (Papillon 2001) ★★★.

● COMPILATIONS: *The Best Of Cliff* (Columbia 1969) ★★★★, *The Best Of Cliff Volume 2* (Columbia 1972) ★★★★, *The Cliff Richard Story* 6-LP box set (WRC 1972) ★★★, *40 Golden Greats* (EMI 1979) ★★★★, *The Cliff Richard Songbook* 6-LP box set (WRC 1980) ★★★★, *Private Collection 1979-1988* (EMI 1988) ★★★, *20 Original Greats* (EMI 1989) ★★★, *The Hit List* (EMI 1994) ★★★★, *At The Movies 1959-1974* (EMI 1996) ★★★, *The Rock 'N' Roll Years 1958-1963* 4-CD box set (EMI 1997) ★★★, *On The Continent* 5-CD box set (Bear Family 1998) ★★★, *1960s* (EMI 1998) ★★★, *1970s* (EMI 1998) ★★★, *1980s* (EMI 1998) ★★★, *The Whole Story: His Greatest Hits* (EMI 2000) ★★★★.

● VIDEOS: *Two A Penny* (1978), *The Video Connection* (PMI 1984), *Together* (PMI 1984), *Thank You Very Much* (Thorn-EMI 1984), *Rock In Australia* (PMI 1986), *We Don't Talk Anymore* (Gold Rushes 1987), *Video EP* (PMI 1988), *The Young Ones* (1988), *Summer Holiday* (1988), *Wonderful Life* (1988), *Take Me High* (Warner Home Video 1988), *Private Collection* (PMI 1988), *Always Guaranteed* (PMI 1989), *Live And Guaranteed* (PMI 1989), *From A Distance ... The Event Volumes 1 and 2* (PMI 1990), *Together With Cliff Richard* (PMI 1991), *Expresso Bongo* (1992), *Cliff-When The Music Stops* (1993), *Access All Areas* (1993), *The Story So Far* (1993), *The Hit List* (PMI 1995), *The Hit List Live* (PMI 1995), *Finders Keepers* (1996), *Cliff At The Movies* (PolyGram Music Video 1996), *The 40th Anniversary Concert* (VCI 1998), *An Audience With* (VCI 2000).

● FURTHER READING: *Driftin' With Cliff Richard: The Inside Story Of What Really Happens On Tour*, Jet Harris and Royston Ellis. *Cliff, The Baron Of Beat*, Jack Sutter. *It's Great To Be Young*, Cliff Richard. *Me And My Shadows*, Cliff Richard. *Top Pops*, Cliff Richard. *Cliff Around The Clock*, Bob Ferrier. *The Wonderful World Of Cliff Richard*, Bob Ferrier. *Questions: Cliff Answering Reader And Fan Queries*, Cliff Richard. *The Way I See It*, Cliff Richard. *The Cliff Richard Story*, George Tremlett. *New Singer, New Song: The Cliff Richard Story*, David Winter. *Which One's Cliff?*, Cliff Richard with Bill Latham. *Happy Christmas From Cliff*, Cliff Richard. *Cliff In His Own Words*, Kevin St. John. *Cliff*, Patrick Doncaster and Tony Jasper. *Cliff Richard*, John Tobler. *Silver Cliff: A 25 Year Journal 1958-1983*, Tony Jasper. *Cliff*

Richard, Single-Minded, no author listed. *Cliff Richard: The Complete Recording Sessions, 1958-1990*, Peter Lewry and Nigel Goodall. *Cliff: A Biography*, Tony Jasper. *Cliff Richard, The Complete Chronicle*, Mike Read, Nigel Goodall and Peter Lewry. *Cliff Richard: The Autobiography*, Steve Turner. *Ultimate Cliff*, Peter Lewry and Nigel Goodall. *A Celebration: The Official Story Of 40 Years In Show Business*, André Deutsch.

● FILMS: *Serious Charge* (1959), *Expresso Bongo* (1960), *The Young Ones* (1961), *Summer Holiday* (1962), *Wonderful Life* (1964), *Thunderbirds Are Go!* (1966), *Finders Keepers* (1966), *Two A Penny* (1968), *Take Me High* (1973).

RIGHTEOUS BROTHERS

Despite their professional appellation, Bill Medley (b. 19 September 1940, Santa Ana, California, USA) and Bobby Hatfield (b. 10 August 1940, Beaver Dam, Wisconsin, USA) were not related. They met in 1962 at California's Black Derby club, where they won the approbation of its mixed-race clientele. By blending Medley's sonorous baritone with Hatfield's soaring high tenor, this white duo's vocal style invoked that of classic R&B, and a series of excellent singles, notably 'Little Latin Lupe Lu', followed. They achieved national fame in 1964 following several appearances on US television's highly popular *Shindig*. Renowned producer Phil Spector then signed the act to his Philles label and proceeded to mould his 'Wagnerian' sound to their dramatic intonation. 'You've Lost That Lovin' Feelin'' justifiably topped the US and UK charts and is rightly lauded as one the greatest pop singles of all time. A similar passion was extolled on 'Just Once In My Life' and 'Ebb Tide', but the relationship between performer and mentor rapidly soured. The Righteous Brothers moved outlets in 1966, but despite gaining a gold disc for '(You're My) Soul And Inspiration', a performance modelled on their work with Spector, the duo was unable to sustain the same success. They split in 1968, with Medley beginning a solo career and Hatfield retaining the name with new partner Jimmy Walker, formerly of the Knickerbockers. This short-lived collaboration ended soon afterwards, but the original pair were reunited in 1974 for an appearance on *The Sonny And Cher Comedy Hour*. They scored a US Top 3 hit that year with the maudlin 'Rock 'n' Roll Heaven', but were unable to regain former glories and have subsequently separated and re-formed on several occasions. In 1987 Medley enjoyed an international smash with '(I've Had) The Time Of My Life', a duet with Jennifer Warnes taken from the film *Dirty Dancing*, while a reissue of 'Unchained Melody', a hit for the Righteous Brothers in 1965, topped the UK chart in 1990 after it featured in the movie *Ghost*.

● ALBUMS: *The Righteous Brothers – Right Now!* (Moonglow 1963) ★★, *Some Blue-Eyed Soul* (Moonglow 1965) ★★, *You've Lost That Lovin' Feelin'* (Philles 1965) ★★★★, *Just Once In My Life* (Philles 1965) ★★★★, *Back To Back* (Philles 1965) ★★★★, *This Is New!* (Moonglow 1965) ★★, *In Action* (Sue 1966) ★★, *Soul And Inspiration* (Verve 1966) ★★★★, *Go Ahead And Cry* (Verve 1966) ★★★, *Sayin' Somethin'* (Verve 1967) ★★★, *Souled Out* (Verve 1967) ★★★, *Standards* (Verve 1967) ★★★, *One For The Road* (Verve 1968) ★★★, *Rebirth* (Verve 1970) ★★, *Give It To The People* (Haven 1974) ★★, *The Sons Of Mrs Righteous* (Haven 1975) ★★, *Reunion* (Hit 1999) ★★★.

● COMPILATIONS: *The Best Of The Righteous Brothers* (Moonglow 1966) ★★, *Greatest Hits* (Verve 1967) ★★★★, *Greatest Hits Volume 2* (Verve 1969) ★★★, *2 By 2* (MGM 1973) ★★★, *Best Of The Righteous Brothers* (Verve 1987) ★★★★, *Anthology (1962-1974)* (Rhino 1989) ★★★★, *Best Of The Righteous Brothers* (Curb 1990) ★★★, *Unchained Melody: The Very Best Of The Righteous Brothers* (PolyGram 1990) ★★★★, *The Moonglow Years* (PolyGram 1991) ★★★.

● VIDEOS: *21st Anniversary Celebration* (Old Gold 1990).

● FILMS: *Beach Ball* (1964).

RISING SONS

One of the most legendary unrecorded groups, the Rising Sons consisted of Taj Mahal (b. Henry Saint Clair Fredericks, 17 May 1940, New York City, New York, USA; vocals, guitar), Ry Cooder (vocals, guitar), Gary Marker (bass), Ed Cassidy (drums) and Jesse Lee Kincaid (vocals, guitar). Kevin Kelley also deputized on drums during their brief recording period when Cassidy injured his wrist playing a frenetic version of 'Blind' Willie McTell's 'Statesboro Blues'. Formed in Los Angeles, California, USA, in 1965, the group was signed to Columbia Records but their album was never issued. One single, 'Candy Man'/'The Devil's Got My Woman', did surface, but the group had by then disbanded. Mahal became a prominent blues/folk performer, Cooder made his name playing sessions and later recorded successfully under his own name. Kelley briefly joined the Byrds and Cassidy became a mainstay in Spirit. Marker became a renowned journalist. Sessions from the album, produced by Byrds/Paul Revere associate Terry Melcher, became widely bootlegged due to interest in the various participants, and nearly two decades later they were given an official release by Columbia Records. Mahal contributed three new vocal takes for this project, but its patchwork quality finally laid to rest one of the great mysteries of the 60s.

● ALBUMS: *Rising Sons Featuring Taj Mahal And Ry Cooder* (Columbia/Legacy 1993) ★★★.

RIVERS, JOHNNY

b. John Ramistella, 7 November 1942, New York City, New York, USA. Johnny Rivers enjoyed a succession of pop hits in the 60s and 70s, initially by remaking earlier R&B songs and eventually with his own compositions. His singles were spirited creations, some recorded live in front of an enthusiastic, hip Los Angeles audience. His father moved the family to Baton Rouge, Louisiana, in 1945, where Rivers began playing guitar at the age of eight. By the age of 13, having become enamoured of the local rock 'n' roll and R&B artists, he was fronting his own group. In 1958, he ventured to New York to make his first recording. Top disc jockey Alan Freed met the singer and gave him his new name, Johnny Rivers, and also recommended to the local Gone Records label that they sign Rivers. They did, and his first single, 'Baby, Come Back', was issued that year. At 17 Rivers moved to Nashville, where he wrote songs with another aspiring singer, Roger Miller, and recorded demo records for Elvis Presley, Johnny Cash and others, including Ricky Nelson, who recorded Rivers' 'Make Believe' in 1960. Rivers relocated to Los Angeles at that time. Between 1959 and his 1964 signing to Imperial Records he recorded singles for small labels such as Guyden, Cub and Dee Dee, as well as the larger Chancellor, Capitol Records, MGM Records, Coral Records and United Artists Records, none with any chart success.

In late 1963 Rivers began performing a three-night stand at the LA club Gazzari's, which was so successful it was extended for weeks. He then took up residency at the popular discotheque the Whisky A-Go-Go, where his fans began to include such stars as Johnny Carson, Steve McQueen and Rita Hayworth. His first album for Imperial, *Johnny Rivers At The Whisky A Go Go*, was released in the summer of 1964 and yielded his first hit, Chuck Berry's 'Memphis', which reached number 2. Further hits during 1964-65 included Berry's 'Maybellene', Harold Dorman's 'Mountain Of Love', the traditional folk song 'Midnight Special', Willie Dixon's 'Seventh Son' and Pete Seeger's 'Where Have All The Flowers Gone', each delivered in a rousing, loose interpretation that featured Rivers' nasal vocal, his concise, soulful guitar-playing and sharp backing musicians. Relentlessly rhythmic, the tracks were produced by Lou Adler, working his way towards becoming one of the city's most formidable hitmakers. Rivers started 1966 with 'Secret Agent Man', the theme song from a popular television spy thriller. Later that year he achieved his only number 1 record with his own 'Poor Side Of Town' (co-written with Adler), an uncharacteristic ballad using top studio musicians such as Hal Blaine, James Burton and Larry Knechtal.

Rivers also launched his own Soul City record label in 1966, signing the popular 5th Dimension, who went on to have four Top 10 singles on the label. Retreating from the party atmosphere of his earlier recordings for Imperial, Rivers had hits in 1967 with two Motown Records cover versions, the Four Tops' 'Baby I Need Your Lovin'' and Smokey Robinson's 'The Tracks Of My Tears'. Following an appearance at the Monterey Pop Festival, another soulful ballad, the James Hendricks-penned 'Summer Rain', became Rivers' last major hit of the 60s. The latter also appeared on Rivers' bestselling album, *Realization*. Early 70s albums such as *Slim Slo Slider*, *Home Grown* and *LA Reggae* were critically lauded but not commercially successful, although the latter gave Rivers a Top 10 single with Huey 'Piano' Smith's 'Rockin' Pneumonia And The Boogie Woogie Flu'. A version of the Beach Boys' 'Help Me Rhonda' (with backing vocal by Brian Wilson) was a minor success in 1975, and two years later Rivers landed his final Top 10 single, 'Swayin' To The Music (Slow Dancin')'. Rivers recorded a handful of albums in the 80s, including a live one featuring the old hits.

● ALBUMS: *Johnny Rivers At The Whisky A Go Go* (Imperial 1964) ★★★★, *The Sensational Johnny Rivers* (Capitol 1964) ★★★★, *Go, Johnny, Go* (1964) ★★★, *Here We A-Go-Go Again* (Imperial 1964) ★★★, *Johnny Rivers In Action!* (Imperial 1965) ★★★, *Meanwhile Back At The Whisky A Go Go* (Imperial 1965) ★★★★, *Johnny Rivers Rocks The Folk* (Imperial 1965) ★★, *And I Know You Wanna Dance* (Imperial 1966) ★★★, *Changes* (Imperial 1966) ★★★, *Rewind* (Imperial 1967) ★★★, *Realization* (Imperial 1968) ★★★, *Johnny Rivers* (Sunset 1968) ★★★, *A Touch Of Gold* (Imperial 1969) ★★★, *Slim Slo Slider* (Imperial 1970) ★★★, *Rockin' With Johnny Rivers* (Sunset 1971) ★★★, *Non-Stop Dancing At The Whisky A Go Go* (United Artists 1971) ★★★, *Home Grown* (United Artists 1971) ★★★, *L.A. Reggae* (United Artists 1972) ★★★, *Johnny Rivers* (United Artists 1972) ★★★, *Blue Suede Shoes* (United Artists 1973) ★★★, *Last Boogie In Paris* (Atlantic 1974) ★★★, *Rockin' Rivers* (1974) ★★★, *Road* (Atlantic 1975) ★★★, *New Lovers And Old Friends* (Epic 1975) ★★★, *Help Me Rhonda* (Epic 1975) ★★★, *Wild Night* (United Artists 1976) ★★★, *Outside Help* (Big Tree 1978) ★★, *Borrowed Time* (RSO 1980) ★★, *The Johnny Rivers Story* (1982) ★★★, *Portrait Of* (1982) ★★★, *Not A Through Street* (Priority 1983) ★★.

● COMPILATIONS: *Johnny Rivers' Golden Hits* (Imperial 1966) ★★★, *The History Of Johnny Rivers* (Liberty 1971) ★★★, *Go Johnny Go* (Hallmark 1971) ★★★, *Greatest Hits* re-recordings (MCA 1985) ★★, *The Best Of Johnny Rivers* (EMI America 1987) ★★★, *Anthology 1964-1977* (Rhino 1991) ★★★★.

ROBINSON, SMOKEY

b. William Robinson, 19 February 1940, Detroit, Michigan, USA. A founding member of the Miracles at Northern High School, Detroit, in 1955, Robinson became one of the leading figures in the local music scene by the end of the decade. His flexible tenor voice, which swooped easily into falsetto, made him the group's obvious lead vocalist, and by 1957 he was composing his own variations on the R&B hits of the day. That year he met Berry Gordy, who was writing songs for R&B star Jackie Wilson, and looking for local acts to produce. Vastly impressed by Robinson's affable personality and promising writing talent, Gordy took the teenager under his wing. He produced a series of Miracles singles in 1958 and 1959, all of which featured Robinson as composer and lead singer, and leased them to prominent R&B labels. In 1960 he signed the Miracles to his Motown Records stable, and began to groom Robinson as his second-in-command.

In Motown's early days, Robinson was involved in every facet of the company's operations, writing, producing and making his own records, helping in the business of promotion and auditioning many of the scores of young hopefuls who were attracted by Gordy's growing reputation as an entrepreneur. Robinson had begun his career as a producer by overseeing the recording of the Miracles' 'Way Over There', and soon afterwards he was charged with developing the talents of Mary Wells and the Supremes. Wells soon became Robinson's most successful protégé: Robinson wrote and produced a sophisticated series of hit singles for her between 1962 and 1964. These records, such as 'You Beat Me To The Punch', 'Two Lovers' and 'My Guy', demonstrated his growing confidence as a writer, able to use paradox and metaphor to transcend the usual banalities of the teenage popular song. A measure of Robinson's influence over Wells' career is the fact that she was unable to repeat her chart success after she elected to leave Motown, and Robinson, in 1964. Although Robinson was unable to turn the Supremes into a hit-making act, he experienced no such failure in his relationship with Motown's leading male group of the mid-60s, the Temptations. Between 1964 and 1965, Robinson was responsible for the records that established their reputation, writing lyrical and rhythmic songs of a calibre that few writers in pop music have equalled since. 'The Way You Do The Things You Do' set the hit sequence in motion, followed by the classic ballad 'My Girl' (later equally popular in the hands of Otis Redding), the dance number 'Get Ready', 'Since I Lost My Baby' and the remarkable 'It's Growing', which boasted a complex lyric hinged around a series of metaphorical images. During the same period, Robinson helped to create two of Marvin Gaye's most enduring early hits, 'Ain't That Peculiar' and 'I'll Be Doggone'. Throughout the 60s, Smokey Robinson combined this production and A&R work with his own career as leader of the Miracles. He married fellow group member Claudette Rogers in 1959, and she provided the inspiration for Miracles hits such as 'You've Really Got A Hold On Me' and 'Ooh Baby Baby'. During the mid-60s, Robinson was apparently able to turn out high-quality songs to order,

working with a variety of collaborators including fellow Miracle Ronnie White, and Motown guitarist Marv Tarplin.

As the decade progressed, Bob Dylan referred to Robinson apparently without irony, as 'America's greatest living poet'; as if to justify this assertion, Robinson's lyric-writing scaled new heights on complex ballads such as 'The Love I Saw In You Was Just A Mirage' and 'I Second That Emotion'. From 1967 onwards, Robinson was given individual credit on the Miracles' releases. For the next two years, their commercial fortunes went into a slide, which was righted when their 1965 recording of 'The Tracks Of My Tears' became a major hit in Britain in 1969, and the four-year-old 'The Tears Of A Clown' achieved similar success on both sides of the Atlantic in 1970. At the end of the decade, Robinson briefly resumed his career as a producer and writer for other acts, collaborating with the Marvelettes on 'The Hunter Gets Captured By The Game', and the Four Tops on 'Still Water (Love)'. Business concerns were occupying an increasing proportion of his time, however, and in 1971 he announced that he would be leaving the Miracles the following year, to concentrate on his role as Vice-President of the Motown corporation.

A year after the split, Robinson launched his solo career, enjoying a hit single with 'Sweet Harmony', an affectionate tribute to his former group, and issuing the excellent Smokey. The album included the epic 'Just My Soul Responding', a biting piece of social comment about the USA's treatment of blacks and American Indians. Robinson maintained a regular release schedule through the mid-70s, with one new album arriving every year. Low-key and for the most part lushly produced, they made little impact, although Robinson's songwriting was just as consistent as it had been in the 60s. He continued to break new lyrical ground, striking the banner for non-macho male behaviour on 1974's 'Virgin Man', and giving name to a new style of soft soul on 1975's A Quiet Storm. Singles such as 'Baby That's Backatcha' and 'The Agony And The Ecstasy' sold well on the black market, but failed to achieve national airplay in the USA, while in the UK Robinson was regarded as a remnant from the classic era of Motown. His first film soundtrack project, Big Time, in 1977, won little praise, and it appeared as if his creative peak was past. Instead, he hit back in 1979 with 'Cruisin'', his biggest chart success since 'The Tears Of A Clown' nine years earlier. A sensuous ballad in the musical tradition of his 60s work, the record introduced a new eroticism into his writing, and restored faith in his stature as a contemporary performer.

Two years later, he gained his first UK number 1 with 'Being With You', a touching love song that came close to equalling that achievement in the USA. 'Tell Me Tomorrow' enjoyed more Stateside access in 1982, and Robinson settled into another relaxed release schedule that saw him ride out the 80s on a pattern of regular small hits and consistent album sales. Robinson was contributing significantly less new material, however, and his 1988 autobiography, *Smokey*, revealed that he had been battling against cocaine addiction for much of the decade. Although his marriage to Claudette failed, he returned to full health and creativity, and enjoyed two big hits in 1987, 'Just To See Her' and 'One Heartbeat'. He was voted into the Rock and Roll Hall Of Fame in 1988, and returned to the Motown stable in the late 90s after a brief tenure with SBK at the start of the decade. Smokey Robinson is now one of the senior figures in popular music, a writer and producer still best remembered for his outstanding work in the 60s, but who has seldom betrayed the responsibility of that legacy since then.

ALBUMS: *Smokey* (Tamla 1973) ★★★, *Pure Smokey* (Tamla 1974) ★★★, *A Quiet Storm* (Tamla 1975) ★★★, *Smokey's Family Robinson* (Tamla 1976) ★★★, *Deep In My Soul* (Tamla 1977) ★★★, *Big Time* (Tamla 1977) ★★★, *Love Breeze* (Tamla 1978) ★★★, *Smokin'* (Tamla 1978) ★★, *Where There's Smoke* (Tamla 1979) ★★★, *Warm Thoughts* (Tamla 1980) ★★★, *Being With You* (Tamla 1981) ★★★★, *Yes It's You Lady* (Tamla 1982) ★★★, *Touch The Sky* (Tamla 1983) ★★, *Blame It On Love* (Tamla 1983) ★★★, *Essar* (Tamla 1984) ★★★, *Smoke Signals* (Tamla 1985) ★★★, *One Heartbeat* (Motown 1987) ★★, *Love, Smokey* (Motown 1990) ★★★, *Double Good Everything* (SBK 1991) ★★, *Intimate* (Motown 1999) ★★★.

COMPILATIONS: with the Miracles *The Greatest Hits* (Motown 1992) ★★★★, with the Miracles *The 35th Anniversary Collection* 4-CD box set (Motown Masters 1994) ★★★★, *Early Classics* (Spectrum 1996) ★★★★, *The Ultimate Collection* (Motown 1998) ★★★.

FURTHER READING: *Smokey: Inside My Life*, Smokey Robinson and David Ritz.

ROCKIN' BERRIES

This early 60s UK pop quintet comprised Clive Lea (b. 16 February 1942, Birmingham, England; vocals), Geoffrey Turton (b. 11 March 1944, Birmingham, England; guitar), Bryan Charles 'Chuck' Botfield (b. 14 November 1943, Birmingham, England; guitar), Roy Austin (b. 27 December 1943, Birmingham, England; guitar) and Terry Bond (b. 22 March 1943, Birmingham, England; drums). After beginning as an R&B cover group, they fell under the spell of visiting American Kim Fowley, who suggested they cover the Tokens' US hit 'He's In Town'. The song hit the Top 5 in late 1964 and was followed by two other hits, 'What In The World's Come Over You' (not to be confused with the Jack Scott million-seller of the same name) and an excellent reading of the Reflections' 'Poor Man's Son', with Lea and Turton on counter vocals.

Like several of their contemporaries, the Berries quickly laid the foundations for a career in cabaret by including comedy sketches and parodic impressions of other artists into their act. A minor hit with 'The Water Is Over My Head' in July 1966 concluded their chart run. By 1968 Turton had embarked on a solo career as Jefferson, while the group continued on the timeless supper-club circuit.

● ALBUMS: *In Town* (Piccadilly 1964) ★★★, *Life is Just A Bowl Of Berries* (Piccadilly 1964) ★★★, *Black Gold* (Satril 1976) ★★.
● COMPILATIONS: *Bowl Of The Rockin' Berries* (1988) ★★★, *They're In Town (The Pye Anthology)* (Sequel 1998) ★★★.

ROCKIN' VICKERS

Formed in Blackpool, England in 1963, around Harry Feeny (vocals), Ian Holdbrook (guitar/harmonica), Steven (Vickers) Morris (bass) and Cyril 'Ciggy Shaw' (drums), this R&B group was originally billed 'the Reverend Black And The Rocking Vicars'. Having encountered problems over bookings, Feeny, who acted as the group's agent, changed their name to the Rockin' Vickers. The band became one of the North of England's most popular acts, and they secured a deal with Decca Records in 1964. The Rockin' Vickers' version of Neil Sedaka's 'I Go Ape', was modelled on the gutsy sound of the Big Three and Undertakers but it was not a hit. When Decca dropped the group, Holdbrook left the line-up. He was replaced by Ian Willis aka Ian Kilminster, now better known as Lemmy of Motörhead. He introduced a hybrid pop-art sound to the group although this was not apparent on their next single, 'Zing! Went The Strings Of My Heart', a hit in Finland, but not issued in the UK. In 1966 the Rockin' Vickers signed a production deal with Shel Talmy who recorded the group for CBS Records. Their first single for the label was 'It's Alright', a Pete Townshend composition later rewritten as 'The Kids Are Alright'. The Rockin' Vickers followed this with a version of the Kinks 'Dandy' which, despite an undeniable charm, failed to chart. The disillusioned group split up in 1967 after which Lemmy joined numerous groups, including Sam Gopal and Hawkwind, before becoming a successful heavy metal legend with Motörhead.
● COMPILATIONS: *The Complete Rockin' Vickers Collection* (RPM/Retro 1995) ★★★, *The Complete: It's Alright* (RPM 1999) ★★★.

ROE, TOMMY

b. 9 May 1942, Atlanta, Georgia, USA. Vocalist Roe began his career with high school act, the Satins. The group performed several of his compositions, notably 'Sheila', which they recorded in 1960. The single was unsuccessful, but Roe revived the song two years later upon securing a solo deal. This Buddy Holly-influenced rocker topped the US chart, and

reached the Top 3 in Britain where the artist enjoyed considerable popularity. Roe scored two Top 10 hits in 1963 with 'The Folk Singer' and 'Everybody' and, although not a major chart entry, 'Sweet Pea' garnered considerable airplay through the auspices of pirate radio. The song reached the US Top 10, as did its follow-up, 'Hooray For Hazel', but Roe's biggest hit came in 1969 when 'Dizzy' topped the charts on both sides of the Atlantic. The singer enjoyed further success with 'Heather Honey' and 'Jam Up Jelly Tight', but for much of the 70s he opted to pursue a low-key career in his home state. Roe did attempt a 'comeback' with *Energy* and *Full Bloom*, but subsequently plied the nostalgia circuit. Memories of his past success were resurrected when 'Dizzy' returned to the top of the UK charts in 1992 in a version by the Wonder Stuff and alternative comedian Vic Reeves.
● ALBUMS: *Sheila* (ABC 1962) ★★★, *Something For Everybody* (ABC 1964) ★★★, *Everybody Likes Tommy Roe* (HMV 1964) ★★★, *Ballads And Beat* (HMV 1965) ★★★, *It's Now Winters Day* (ABC 1967) ★★, *Phantasy* (ABC 1967) ★★, *Dizzy* (ABC 1969) ★★★, *We Can Make Music* (ABC 1970) ★★, *Beginnings* (ABC 1971) ★★, *Energy* (Monument 1976) ★★, *Full Bloom* (Monument 1977) ★★.
● COMPILATIONS: *Sweet Pea* (ABC 1966) ★★★, *12 In A Roe: A Collection Of Tommy Roe's Greatest Hits* (ABC 1970) ★★★, *Tommy Roe's Greatest Hits* (Stateside 1970) ★★★, *16 Greatest Hits* (ABC 1971) ★★★, *Greatest Hits* (MCA 1993) ★★★, *Greatest Hits* (Curb 1994) ★★, *Dizzy: The Best Of Tommy Roe* (Music Club 1998) ★★★, *Tommy's 22 Big Ones* (Connoisseur 2001) ★★★.

ROGERS, JULIE

b. Julie Rolls, 6 April 1943, London, England. She left her Bermondsey secondary school in 1959 for a long working holiday as a dancer in Spain. Next, she worked as a secretary and then a ship's stewardess before becoming singer with a middle-of-the-road band led by Teddy Foster with whom she later functioned in a cabaret duo and, under a new stage surname, made a radio debut in 1962 on the BBC Light Programme's *Music With A Beat*. Following an audition for Philips A & R manager Johnny Franz, she recorded her first single 'It's Magic', in 1963. Her recording career touched its zenith the following year when 'The Wedding' – an orchestrated translation of a song (by Argentinian Joaquin Prieto) which she had first heard in Spain – rose to a UK number 3, triggered by an initial plug on the ITV television regional magazine, *Day By Day*. As well as generating huge sheet music sales, it also disturbed the US Top Ten, despite two previous hit versions in 1961 by Anita Bryant and Malcolm Vaughan. The yuletide follow-up, 'Like A Child' and 1965's 'Hawaiian Wedding Song' were only minor hits, but Rogers remained in

demand on the variety circuit for the rest of the decade.
● ALBUMS: *The Sound Of Julie* (Mercury 1965) ★★★, *Contrasts* (Mercury 1966) ★★, *Songs Of Inspiration* (Mercury 1967) ★★★.
● COMPILATIONS: *The Wedding* (Polygram 1999) ★★★.

ROLLING STONES

Originally billed as the Rollin' Stones, the first line-up of this immemorial English 60s group was a nucleus of Mick Jagger (b. Michael Philip Jagger, 26 July 1943, Dartford, Kent, England; vocals), Keith Richard (b. Keith Richards, 18 December 1943, Dartford, Kent, England; guitar), Brian Jones (b. Lewis Brian Hopkin-Jones, 28 February 1942, Cheltenham, Gloucestershire, England, d. 3 July 1969, Sussex, England; rhythm guitar) and Ian Stewart (b. 1938, d. 12 December 1985; piano). Jagger and Richard were primary school friends who resumed their camaraderie in their closing teenage years after finding they had a mutual love for R&B and particularly the music of Chuck Berry, Muddy Waters and Bo Diddley. Initially, they were teamed with bass player Dick Taylor (later of the Pretty Things) and before long their ranks extended to include Jones, Stewart and occasional drummer Tony Chapman. Their patron at this point was the renowned musician Alexis Korner, who had arranged their debut gig at London's Marquee club on 21 July 1962. In their first few months the group met some opposition from jazz and blues aficionados for their alleged lack of musical 'purity' and the line-up remained unsettled for several months.
In late 1962 bass player Bill Wyman (b. William George Perks, 24 October 1936, Penge, Kent, England) replaced Dick Taylor while drummers came and went including Carlo Little (from Screaming Lord Sutch's Savages) and Mick Avory (later of the Kinks, who was billed as appearing at their debut gig, but didn't play). It was not until as late as January 1963 that drummer Charlie Watts (b. Charles Robert Watts, 2 June 1941, Wembley, Middlesex, England) reluctantly surrendered his day job and committed himself to the group. After securing a residency at Giorgio Gomelsky's Crawdaddy Club in Richmond, the Stones' live reputation spread rapidly through London's hip cognoscenti. One evening, the flamboyant Andrew Loog Oldham (b. 29 January 1944, Paddington, London, England), appeared at the club and was so entranced by the commercial prospects of Jagger's sexuality that he wrested them away from Gomelsky and, backed by the financial and business clout of agent Eric Easton, became their manager. Within weeks Oldham had produced their first couple of official recordings at IBC Studios. By this time record company scouts were on the prowl with Decca Records' Dick Rowe leading the march

and successfully signing the group.

After re-purchasing the IBC demos, Oldham selected Chuck Berry's 'Come On' as their debut. The record was promoted on the prestigious UK television pop programme *Thank Your Lucky Stars* and the Stones were featured sporting matching hounds-tooth jackets with velvet collars. This was to be one of Oldham's few concessions to propriety for he would soon be pushing the boys as unregenerate rebels. Unfortunately, pianist Ian Stewart was not deemed sufficiently pop star-like for Oldham's purpose and was unceremoniously removed from the line-up, although he remained road manager and occasional pianist. After supporting the Everly Brothers, Little Richard, Gene Vincent and Bo Diddley on a Don Arden UK package tour, the Stones released their second single, a gift from John Lennon and Paul McCartney entitled 'I Wanna Be Your Man'. The disc fared better than its predecessor climbing into the Top 10 in January 1964. That same month the group enjoyed their first bill-topping tour supported by the Ronettes.

The early months of 1964 saw the Stones catapulted to fame amid outrage and controversy about the surliness of their demeanour and the length of their hair. This was still a world in which the older members of the community were barely coming to terms with the Beatles neatly-groomed mop tops. While newspapers asked 'Would you let your daughter marry a Rolling Stone?', the quintet engaged in a flurry of recording activity which saw the release of an EP and an album both titled *The Rolling Stones*. The discs consisted almost exclusively of extraneous material and captured the group at their most derivative stage. Already, however, there were strong signs of an ability to combine different styles. The third single, 'Not Fade Away', saw them fuse Buddy Holly's quaint original with a chunky Bo Diddley beat that highlighted Jagger's vocal to considerable effect. The presence of Phil Spector and Gene Pitney at these sessions underlined how hip the Stones had already become in the music business after such a short time. With the momentum increasing by the month, Oldham characteristically over-reached himself by organizing a US tour which proved premature and disappointing. After returning to the UK, the Stones released a decisive cover of the Valentinos' 'It's All Over Now', which gave them their first number 1.

A best-selling EP, *Five By Five*, cemented their growing reputation, while a national tour escalated into a series of near riots with scenes of hysteria wherever they played. There was an ugly strain to the Stones' appeal which easily translated into violence. At the Winter Gardens Blackpool the group hosted the most astonishing rock riot yet witnessed on British soil. Frenzied fans displayed their feelings for the group by smashing chandeliers and demolishing a Steinway grand piano. By the end of the evening

over 50 people were escorted to hospital for treatment. Other concerts were terminated within minutes of the group appearing on-stage and the hysteria continued throughout Europe. A return to the USA saw them disrupt the stagey *Ed Sullivan Show* prompting the presenter to ban rock 'n' roll groups in temporary retaliation. In spite of all the chaos at home and abroad, America remained resistant to their appeal, although that situation would change dramatically in the New Year.

In November 1964, 'Little Red Rooster' was released and entered the *New Musical Express* chart at number 1, a feat more usually associated with the Beatles and, previously, Elvis Presley. The Stones now had a formidable fan base and their records were becoming more accomplished and ambitious with each successive release. Jagger's accentuated phrasing and posturing stage persona made 'Little Red Rooster' sound surprisingly fresh while Brian Jones' use of slide guitar was imperative to the single's success. Up until this point, the group had recorded cover versions as a-sides, but manager Andrew Oldham was determined that they should emulate the example of Lennon/McCartney and locked them in a room until they emerged with satisfactory material. Their early efforts, 'It Should Have Been You' and 'Will You Be My Lover Tonight?' (both recorded by the late George Bean) were bland, but Gene Pitney scored a hit with the emphatic 'That Girl Belongs To Yesterday' and Jagger's girlfriend Marianne Faithfull became a teenage recording star with the moving 'As Tears Go By'. 1965 proved the year of the international breakthrough and three extraordinary self-penned number 1 singles. 'The Last Time' saw them emerge with their own distinctive rhythmic style and underlined an ability to fuse R&B and pop in an enticing fashion. America finally succumbed to their spell with '(I Can't Get No) Satisfaction', a quintessential pop lyric with the still youthful Jagger sounding like a jaundiced roué. Released in the UK during the 'summer of protest songs', the single encapsulated the restless weariness of a group already old before its time. The distinctive riff, which Keith Richard invented with almost casual dismissal, became one of the most famous hook lines in the entire glossary of pop and was picked up and imitated by a generation of garage groups thereafter.

The 1965 trilogy of hits was completed with the engagingly surreal 'Get Off Of My Cloud' in which Jagger's surly persona seemed at its most pronounced to date. As well as the number 1 hits of 1965, there was also a celebrated live EP, *Got Live If You Want It* which reached the Top 10 and, *The Rolling Stones No. 2* that continued the innovative idea of not including the group's name on the front of the sleeve. There was also some well documented bad boy controversy when Jagger, Jones and Wyman were arrested and charged with urinating on the wall of an East London petrol station. Such scandalous behaviour merely reinforced the public's already ingrained view of the Stones as juvenile degenerates.

With the notorious Allen Klein replacing Eric Easton as Oldham's co-manager, the Stones consolidated their success by renegotiating their Decca contract. Their single output in the USA simultaneously increased with the release of a couple of tracks unavailable in single form in the UK. The sardonic put-down of suburban Valium abuse, 'Mother's Little Helper' and the Elizabethan-styled 'Lady Jane', complete with atmospheric dulcimer, displayed their contrasting styles to considerable effect. Both these songs were included on their fourth album, *Aftermath*. A breakthrough work in a crucial year, the recording revealed the Stones as accomplished rockers and balladeers, while their writing potential was emphasized by Chris Farlowe's chart-topping cover of 'Out Of Time'. There were also signs of the Stones' inveterate misogyny particularly on the cocky 'Under My Thumb' and an acerbic 'Stupid Girl'. Back in the singles chart, the group's triumphant run continued with the startlingly chaotic '19th Nervous Breakdown' in which frustration, impatience and chauvinism were brilliantly mixed with scale-sliding descending guitar lines. 'Paint It, Black' was even stronger, a raga-influenced piece with a lyric so doom-laden and defeatist in its imagery that it is a wonder that the angry performance sounded so passionate and urgent.

The Stones' nihilism reached its peak on the extraordinary 'Have You Seen Your Mother Baby, Standing In The Shadow?', a scabrous-sounding solicitation taken at breathtaking pace with Jagger spitting out a diatribe of barely coherent abuse. It was probably the group's most adventurous production to date, but its acerbic sound, lengthy title and obscure theme contributed to rob the song of sufficient commercial potential to continue the chart-topping run. Ever outrageous, the group promoted the record with a photo session in which they appeared in drag, thereby adding a clever, sexual ambivalence to their already iconoclastic public image. 1967 saw the Stones' anti-climactic escapades confront an establishment crackdown. The year began with an accomplished double a-sided single, 'Let's Spend The Night Together'/'Ruby Tuesday' which, like the Beatles' 'Penny Lane'/'Strawberry Fields Forever', narrowly failed to reach number 1 in their home country. The accompanying album, *Between The Buttons*, trod water and also represented Oldham's final production. Increasingly alienated by the Stones' bohemianism, he would move further away from them in the ensuing months and surrender the management reins to his partner Klein later in the year. On 12 February, Jagger and Richard

were arrested at the latter's West Wittering home 'Redlands' and charged with drugs offences. Three months later, the home of increasingly unstable Brian Jones was raided and he was charged with similar offences.

The Jagger/Richard trial in June was a cause célèbre which culminated in the notorious duo receiving heavy fines and a salutary prison sentence. Judicial outrage was tempered by public clemency, most effectively voiced by *The Times*' editor William Rees-Mogg who, borrowing a phrase from Pope, offered an eloquent plea in their defence under the leader title, 'Who Breaks A Butterfly On A Wheel?' Another unexpected ally was rival group the Who, who rallied to the Stones' cause by releasing a single coupling 'Under My Thumb' and 'The Last Time'. The sentences were duly quashed on appeal in July, with Jagger receiving a conditional discharge for possession of amphetamines. Three months later, Brian Jones tasted judicial wrath with a nine-month sentence and suffered a nervous breakdown before seeing his imprisonment rescinded at the end of the year.

The flurry of drug busts, court cases, appeals and constant media attention had a marked effect on the Stones' recording career which was severely curtailed. During their summer of impending imprisonment, they released the fey 'We Love You', complete with slamming prison cell doors in the background. It was a weak, flaccid statement rather than a rebellious rallying cry. The image of the cultural anarchists cowering in defeat was not particularly palatable to their fans and even with all the publicity, the single barely scraped into the Top 10. The eventful year ended with the Stones' apparent answer to *Sgt Peppers Lonely Hearts Club Band* – the extravagantly-titled *Their Satanic Majesties Request*. Beneath the exotic 3-D cover was an album of psychedelic/cosmic experimentation bereft of the R&B grit that had previously been synonymous with the Stones' sound. Although the album had some strong moments, it had the same inexplicably placid inertia of 'We Love You', minus notable melodies or a convincing direction. The overall impression conveyed was that in trying to compete with the Beatles' experimentation, the Stones had somehow lost the plot. Their drug use had channelled them into laudable experimentation but simultaneously left them open to accusations of having 'gone soft'. The revitalization of the Stones was demonstrated in the early summer of 1968 with 'Jumping Jack Flash', a single that rivalled the best of their previous output. The succeeding album, *Beggars Banquet*, produced by Jimmy Miller, was also a return to strength and included the socio-political 'Street Fighting Man' and the brilliantly macabre 'Sympathy For The Devil', in which Jagger's seductive vocal was backed by hypnotic Afro-rhythms and dervish yelps.

While the Stones were re-establishing themselves, Brian Jones was falling deeper into drug abuse. A conviction in late 1968 prompted doubts about his availability for US tours and in the succeeding months he contributed less and less to recordings and became increasingly jealous of Jagger's leading role in the group. Richard's wooing and impregnation of Jones' girlfriend Anita Pallenberg merely increased the tension. Matters reached a crisis point in June 1969 when Jones officially left the group. The following month he was found dead in the swimming pool of the Sussex house that had once belonged to writer A.A. Milne. The official verdict was 'death by misadventure'. A free concert at London's Hyde Park two days after his death was attended by a crowd of 250,000 and became a symbolic wake for the tragic youth. Jagger released thousands of butterflies and narrated a poem by Shelley for Brian. Three days later, Jagger's former love Marianne Faithfull attempted suicide. This was truly the end of the first era of the Rolling Stones.

The group played out the last months of the 60s with a mixture of vinyl triumph and further tragedy. The sublime 'Honky Tonk Women' kept them at number 1 for most of the summer and few would have guessed that this was to be their last UK chart topper. The new album, *Let It Bleed* (a parody of the Beatles' *Let It Be*) was an exceptional work spearheaded by 'Gimme Shelter' and revealing strong country influences ('Country Honk'), startling orchestration ('You Can't Always Get What You Want') and menacing blues ('Midnight Rambler'). It was a promising debut from John Mayall's former guitarist Mick Taylor (b. Michael Kevin Taylor, 17 January 1948, Welwyn Garden City, Hertfordshire, England) who had replaced Jones only a matter of weeks before his death. Even while *Let It Bleed* was heading for the top of the album charts, however, the Stones were singing out the 60s to the backdrop of a Hells Angels' killing of a black man at the Altamont Festival in California. The tragedy was captured on film in the grisly *Gimme Shelter* movie released the following year. After the events of 1969, it was not surprising that the group had a relatively quiet 1970. Jagger's contrasting thespian outings reached the screen in the form of *Performance* and *Ned Kelly* while Jean-Luc Goddard's tedious portrait of the group in the studio was delivered on *One Plus One*. For a group who had once claimed to make more challenging and gripping films than the Beatles and yet combine artistic credibility with mass appeal, it all seemed a long time coming.

After concluding their Decca contract with a bootleg-deterring live album, *Get Yer Ya-Ya's Out!*, the Stones established their own self-titled label. The first release was a three track single, 'Brown Sugar'/'Bitch'/'Let It Rock', which contained some of their best work, but narrowly failed to reach number 1 in the UK. The lead track contained a quintessential Stones riff: insistent, undemonstrative and stunning, with the emphatic brass work of Bobby Keyes

embellishing Jagger's vocal power. The new album, *Sticky Fingers,* was as consistent as it was accomplished, encompassing the bluesy 'You Gotta Move', the thrilling 'Moonlight Mile', the wistful 'Wild Horses' and the chilling 'Sister Morphine', one the most despairing drug songs ever written. The entire album was permeated by images of sex and death, yet the tone of the work was neither self-indulgent nor maudlin. The group's playful fascination with sex was further demonstrated on the elaborately designed Andy Warhol sleeve which featured a waist-view shot of a figure clad in denim, with a real zip fastener which opened to display the lips and tongue motif that was shortly to become their corporate image. Within a year of *Sticky Fingers*, the group returned with a double album, *Exile On Main Street*. With Keith Richard firmly in control, the group were rocking-out on a series of quick-fire songs. The album was severely criticized at the time of its release for its uneven quality but was subsequently re-evaluated favourably, particularly in contrast to their later work.

The Rolling Stones' soporific slide into the 70s mainstream probably began during 1973 when their jet-setting was threatening to upstage their musical endeavours. Jagger's marriage and Richard's confrontations with the law took centre stage while increasingly average albums came and went. *Goat's Head Soup* was decidedly patchy but offered some strong moments and brought a deserved US number 1 with the imploring 'Angie'. 1974's 'It's Only Rock 'n' Roll' proved a better song title than a single, while the undistinguished album of the same name saw the group reverting to Tamla/Motown Records for the Temptations' 'Ain't Too Proud To Beg'. The departure of Mick Taylor at the end of 1974 was followed by a protracted period in which the group sought a suitable replacement. By the time of their next release, *Black And Blue*, former Faces guitarist Ron Wood (b. Ronald David Wood, 1 June 1947, Hillingdon, Middlesex, England) was confirmed as Taylor's successor. The album showed the group seeking a possible new direction playing variants on white reggae, but the results were less than impressive.

By the second half of the 70s the gaps in the Stones' recording and touring schedules were becoming wider. The days when they specially recorded for the singles market were long past and considerable impetus had been lost. Even big rallying points, such as the celebrated concert at Knebworth in 1976, lacked a major album to promote the show and served mainly as a greatest hits package. By 1977, the British music press had taken punk to its heart and the Stones were dismissed as champagne-swilling old men, who had completely lost touch with their audience. The Clash effectively summed up the mood of the time with their slogan 'No Elvis, Beatles, Stones' in '1977'. Against the odds, the Stones responded to the challenge of their younger critics with a comeback album of remarkable power. *Some Girls* was their most consistent work in years, with some exceptional high-energy workouts, not least the breathtaking 'Shattered'. The disco groove of 'Miss You' brought them another US number 1 and showed that they could invigorate their repertoire with new ideas that worked. Jagger's wonderful pastiche of an American preacher on the mock country 'Far Away Eyes' was another unexpected highlight. There was even an attendant controversy thanks to some multi-racist chauvinism on the title track, not to mention 'When The Whip Comes Down' and 'Beast Of Burden'. Even the cover jacket had to be re-shot because it featured unauthorized photos of the famous, most notably actresses Lucille Ball, Farrah Fawcett and Raquel Welch.

To conclude a remarkable year, Keith Richard escaped what seemed an almost certain jail sentence in Toronto for drugs offences and was merely fined and ordered to play a couple of charity concerts. As if in celebration of his release and reconciliation with his father, he reverted to his original family name Richards. In the wake of Richards' reformation and Jagger's much-publicized and extremely expensive divorce from his model wife Bianca, the Stones reconvened in 1980 for *Emotional Rescue*, a rather lightweight album dominated by Jagger's falsetto and over-use of disco rhythms. Nevertheless, the album gave the Stones their first UK number 1 since 1973 and the title track was a Top 10 hit on both sides of the Atlantic. Early the following year a major US tour (highlights of which were included on *Still Life*) garnered enthusiastic reviews, while a host of repackaged albums reinforced the group's legacy. 1981's *Tattoo You* was essentially a crop of old outtakes but the material was anything but stale. On the contrary, the album was surprisingly strong and the concomitant single 'Start Me Up' was a reminder of the Stones at their 60s best, a time when they were capable of producing classic singles at will. One of the Stones' cleverest devices throughout the 80s was their ability to compensate for average work by occasional flashes of excellence. The workmanlike *Undercover*, for example, not only boasted a brilliantly menacing title track ('Undercover Of The Night') but one of the best promotional videos of the period. While critics continually questioned the group's relevance, the Stones were still releasing worthwhile work, albeit in smaller doses.

A three-year silence on record was broken by *Dirty Work* in 1986, which saw the Stones sign to CBS Records and team up with producer Steve Lillywhite. Surprisingly, it was not a Stones original that produced the expected offshoot single hit, but a cover of Bob And Earl's 'Harlem Shuffle'. A major record label signing often coincides with a flurry of new work, but the Stones were clearly moving away from each other creatively and concentrating more and more on individual projects. Wyman had already tasted some chart success in 1983 with the biggest solo success from a Stones' number, 'Je Suis Un Rock Star' and it came as little surprise when Jagger issued his own solo album, *She's The Boss*, in 1985. A much publicized-feud with Keith Richards led to speculation that the Rolling Stones story had come to an anti-climactic end, a view reinforced by the appearance of a second Jagger album, *Primitive Cool*, in 1987. When Richards himself released the first solo work of his career in 1988, the Stones' obituary had virtually been written. As if to confound the obituarists, however, the Stones reconvened in 1989 and announced that they would be working on a new album and commencing a world tour. Later that year the hastily-recorded *Steel Wheels* appeared and the critical reception was generally good. 'Mixed Emotions' and 'Rock And A Hard Place' were radio hits while 'Continental Drift' included contributions from the master musicians of Joujouka, previously immortalized on vinyl by the late Brian Jones. After nearly 30 years in existence, the Rolling Stones began the 90s with the biggest grossing international tour of all time, and ended speculation about their future by reiterating their intention of playing on indefinitely. Wyman officially resigned in 1993, however, and was replaced by the highly experienced Darryl Jones (b. 11 December 1961, Chicago, Illinois, USA). *Voodoo Lounge* was one of their finest latterday recordings, sounding both lyrically daring and musically fresh. They sounded charged up and raring to go for the 1995 USA tour. Monies taken at each gig could almost finance the national debt and provided confirmation (as if it were needed) that they are still the world's greatest rock band, a title that is likely to stick. Riding a crest after an extraordinarily active 1995 *Stripped* was a dynamic semi-plugged album. Fresh sounding and energetic acoustic versions of 'Street Fighting Man', 'Wild Horses' and 'Let It Bleed' among others, emphasized just how great the Jagger/Richards songwriting team is. The year was marred however by some outspoken comments by Keith Richards on R.E.M. and Nirvana. These clumsy comments did not endear the grand old man of rock to a younger audience, which was all the more surprising as the Stones had appeared to be in touch with contemporary rock music. Citing R.E.M. as 'wimpy cult stuff' and Kurt Cobain as 'some prissy little spoiled kid' were, at best, ill-chosen words. *Bridges To Babylon* was a particularly fresh-sounding album, with Charlie Watts anchoring the band's sound like never before. His drumming was not only exceptional, but was mixed to the foreground, giving the record a much cleaner and funkier sound. No other rock band in history has been able to grow old so well, and so disgracefully.

● ALBUMS: *The Rolling Stones* (London/Decca

1964) ★★★★, *12X5* (London 1964) ★★★★, *The Rolling Stones* (London/Decca 1965) ★★★★, *The Rolling Stones Now!* (London 1965) ★★★★, *December's Children (And Everybody's* (London 1965) ★★★★, *Out Of Our Heads* (Decca/London 1965) ★★★★, *Aftermath* (Decca/London 1966) ★★★★, *Got Live If You Want It* (London 1966) ★★★, *Between The Buttons* (London/Decca 1967) ★★★, *Their Satanic Majesties Request* (Decca/London 1967) ★★★, *Flowers* (London 1967) ★★★, *Beggars Banquet* (London 1968) ★★★★★, *Let It Bleed* (London/Decca 1969) ★★★★★, *'Get Yer Ya-Ya's Out!'* (Decca/London 1970) ★★★★, *Sticky Fingers* (Rolling Stones 1971) ★★★★, *Exile On Main Street* (Rolling Stones 1972) ★★★★★, *Goat's Head Soup* (Rolling Stones 1973) ★★★, *It's Only Rock 'N' Roll* (Rolling Stones 1974) ★★★, *Black And Blue* (Rolling Stones 1976) ★★★, *Love You Live* (Rolling Stones 1977) ★★★, *Some Girls* (Rolling Stones 1978) ★★★, *Emotional Rescue* (Rolling Stones 1980) ★★, *Tattoo You* (Rolling Stones 1981) ★★★, *Still Life (American Concerts 1981)* (Rolling Stones 1982) ★★, *Undercover* (Rolling Stones 1983) ★★, *Dirty Work* (Rolling Stones 1986) ★★★, *Steel Wheels* (Rolling Stones 1989) ★★★, *Flashpoint* (Rolling Stones 1991) ★★★, *Voodoo Lounge* (Virgin 1994) ★★★★, *Stripped* (Virgin 1995) ★★★, *Bridges To Babylon* (Virgin 1997) ★★★★, *No Security* (Virgin 1998) ★★★★.
● COMPILATIONS: *Big Hits (High Tide And Green Grass)* (London 1966) ★★★★, *Through The Past, Darkly* (London 1969) ★★★★, *Hot Rocks 1964-1971* (London 1972) ★★★★, *More Hot Rocks (Big Hits And Fazed Cookies)* (London 1972) ★★★★, *The Rolling Stones Singles Collection: The London Years* 3-CD box set (Abko/London 1989) ★★★★★, *Jump Back: The Best Of The Rolling Stones 1971-1993* (Virgin 1993) ★★★★. Many other compilation and archive albums have also been issued.
● CD ROM: *Voodoo Lounge* (Virgin 1995).
● VIDEOS: *The Stones In The Park* (BMG 1993), *Gimme Shelter* (1993), *Live At The Max* (PolyGram Music Video 1994), *25 x 5 The Continuing Adventures Of The Rolling Stones* (1994), *Sympathy For The Devil* (BMG 1995), *Voodoo Lounge* (Game Entertainment 1995), *One Plus One* (Connoisseur 1998), *Bridges To Babylon 1998: Live In Concert* (Game Entertainment 1998).
● FURTHER READING: *The Rolling Stones File*, Tim Hewat. *The Stones*, Philip Carmelo Luce. *Uptight With The Rolling Stones*, Richard Elman. *Rolling Stones: An Unauthorized Biography In Words, Photographs And Music*, David Dalton. *Mick Jagger: The Singer Not The Song*, J. Marks. *Mick Jagger: Everybody's Lucifer*, Anthony Scaduto. *A Journey Through America With The Rolling Stones*, Robert Greenfield. *Les Rolling Stones*, Philippe Contantin. *The Rolling Stones Story*, George Tremlett. *The Rolling Stones*, Cindy Ehrlich. *The Rolling Stones*, David Dalton. *The Rolling Stones: A Celebration*, Nik Cohn. *The*

Rolling Stones, Tony Jasper. *The Rolling Stones: An Illustrated Record*, Roy Carr. *The Rolling Stones*, Jeremy Pascall. *The Rolling Stones On Tour*, Annie Leibowitz. *Up And Down With The Rolling Stones*, Tony Sanchez with John Blake. *The Rolling Stones: An Annotated Bibliography*, Mary Laverne Dimmick. *Keith Richards*, Barbara Charone. *Rolling Stones In Their Own Words*, Rolling Stones. *The Rolling Stones: An Illustrated Discography*, Miles. *The Rolling Stones In Their Own Words*, David Dalton and Mick Farren. *The Rolling Stones: The First Twenty Years*, David Dalton. *Mick Jagger In His Own Words*, Miles. *The Rolling Stones In Concert*, Linda Martin. *The Rolling Stones: Live In America*, Philip Kamin and Peter Goddard. *Death Of A Rolling Stone: The Brian Jones Story*, Mandy Aftel. *Jagger*, Carey Schofield. *The Rolling Stones: The Last Tour*, Philip Kamin and James Karnbac. *The Rolling Stones A To Z*, Sue Weiner and Lisa Howard. *The Rolling Stones*, Robert Palmer. *The Stones*, Philip Norman. *Satisfaction: The Rolling Stones*, Gered Mankowitz. *The Rolling Stones*, Dezo Hoffman. *On The Road With The Rolling Stones*, Chet Flippo. *The True Adventures Of The Rolling Stones*, Stanley Booth. *Heart Of Stone: The Definitive Rolling Stones Discography*, Felix Aeppli. *Yesterday's Papers: The Rolling Stones In Print*, Jessica MacPhail. *The Life And Good Times Of The Rolling Stones*, Philip Norman. *Stone Alone*, Bill Wyman and Ray Coleman. *The Rolling Stones 25th Anniversary Tour*, Greg Quill. *Blown Away: The Rolling Stones And The Death Of The Sixties*, A.E. Hotchner. *The Rolling Stones: Complete Recording Sessions 1963-1989*, Martin Elliott. *The Rolling Stones Story*, Robert Draper. *The Rolling Stones Chronicle: The First Thirty Years*, Massimo Bonanno. *Rolling Stones: Images Of The World Tour 1989-1990*, David Fricke and Robert Sandall. *The Rolling Stones' Rock 'N' Roll Circus*, no author listed. *The Rolling Stones: Behind The Buttons (Limited Edition)*, Gered Mankowitz and Robert Whitaker (Photographers). *Golden Stone: The Untold Life And Mysterious Death Of Brian Jones*, Laura Jackson. *Rolling Stones: Das Weissbuch*, Dieter Hoffmann. *Not Fade Away: Rolling Stones Collection*, Geoffrey Giuliano. *Keith Richards: The Unauthorised Biography*, Victor Bockris. *The Rolling Stones: The Complete Works Vol.1 1962-75*, Nico Zentgraf. *Street Fighting Years*, Stephen Barnard. *Paint It Black: The Murder Of Brian Jones*, Geoffrey Giuliano. *Brian Jones: The Inside Story Of The Original Rolling Stone*, Nicholas Fitzgerald. *Who Killed Christopher Robin*, Terry Rawlings. *A Visual Documentary*, Miles. *Not Fade Away*, Chris Eborn. *Complete Guide To The Music Of*, James Hector. *The Stones By Krüger*, Stefan Krüger. *The Rolling Stones 1962-1995: The Ultimate Guide*, Felix Aeppli. *The Rolling Stones Chronicle*, Massimo Bonanno. *Good Times Bad Times: The Definitive Diary Of The Rolling Stones 1960-1969*, Terry Rawlings and Keith Badman. *It's Only Rock 'N' Roll*, Steve Appleford. *The*

Rolling Stones: A Life On The Road. Pleased To Meet You, Michael Putland (photographer). *Brian Jones: The Last Decadent*, Jeremy Reed. *The Murder Of Brian Jones: The Secret Story Of My Love Affair With The Murdered Rolling Stone*, Anna Wohlin with Christine Lindsjöo. *Rock On Wood: The Origin Of A Rock & Roll Face*, Terry Rawlings.

RONETTES

Veronica 'Ronnie' Bennett (b. 10 August 1943, New York, USA), her sister Estelle (b. 22 July 1944, New York, USA) and cousin Nedra Talley (b. 27 January 1946, New York, USA) began their career as a dance act, the Dolly Sisters. By 1961 they had become the resident dance troupe at the famed Peppermint Lounge, home of the twist craze, and having taken tuition in harmony singing, later secured a recording contract. The trio's first single, 'I Want A Boy', was credited to Ronnie And The Relatives, but when 'Silhouettes' followed in 1962, the Ronettes appellation was in place. They recorded four singles for the Colpix/May group and appeared on disc jockey Murray The K's *Live From The Brooklyn Fox* before a chance telephone call resulted in their signing with producer Phil Spector. Their first collaboration, the majestic 'Be My Baby' defined the girl-group sound as Spector constructed a cavernous accompaniment around Ronnie's plaintive, nasal voice. The single reached the Top 5 in the USA and UK before being succeeded by the equally worthwhile 'Baby I Love You', another Top 20 entrant in both countries. The producer's infatuation with Ronnie – the couple were later married – resulted in some of his finest work being reserved for her, and although ensuing singles, including 'The Best Part of Breaking Up', 'Walking In The Rain' (both 1964) and 'Is This What I Get For Loving You' (1965), failed to recapture the Ronettes' early success, they are among the finest pop singles of all time. Following their 1966 offering, 'I Can Hear Music', the group's career was shelved during Spector's mid-60s 'retirement'.

The Ronettes name re-emerged in 1969 on A&M Records with 'You Came, You Saw, You Conquered!'. Credited to 'The Ronettes Featuring The Voice Of Veronica' (effectively Ronnie and session singers), this excellent single was nonetheless commercially moribund and Ronnie's aspirations were again sublimated. She released a one-off single for Apple Records in 1971, which marked the recording debut of the Ronnie Spector stage name. She separated from Spector in 1973 and joined Buddah Records, founding a new group with vocalists Diane Linton (later replaced by Denise Edwards) and Chip Fields. Ronnie And The Ronettes made their debut that year with 'Lover Lover', before changing their name to Ronnie Spector and the Ronettes for 'I Wish I Never Saw The Sunshine', an impassioned remake of a

song recorded by the original line-up, but which remained unissued until 1976. The group's name was then dropped as its lead singer pursued her solo ambitions. The long-running litigation between the Ronettes and Phil Spector came to a close in July 2000, when they were finally awarded $2.6 million in overdue payment of royalties dating back to 1963.

● ALBUMS: *Presenting The Fabulous Ronettes Featuring Veronica* (Philes 1964) ★★★.
● COMPILATIONS: *The Ronettes Sing Their Greatest Hits* (Phil Spector International 1975) ★★★, *Their Greatest Hits – Volume II* (1981) ★★, *The Colpix Years 1961-63* (Murray Hill 1987) ★★★, *The Best Of* (ABKCO 1992) ★★★, *The Ultimate Collection* (Marginal 1997) ★★★★.

ROOFTOP SINGERS

Cashing in on the folk music revival of the early 60s, the Rooftop Singers were a trio specifically assembled for the purpose of recording a single song, 'Walk Right In', originally recorded in 1930 by Gus Cannon And The Jugstompers. The Rooftop Singers consisted of Erik Darling (b. 25 September 1933, Baltimore, Maryland, USA), Bill Svanoe and former Benny Goodman band vocalist, Lynne Taylor. Darling had played in folk groups called the Tune Tellers and the Tarriers, the latter including future actor Alan Arkin, and replaced Pete Seeger in the Weavers in 1958, remaining with them for four years. In 1962 he heard 'Walk Right In' and adapted the lyrics for a more modern sound, utilizing two 12-string guitars and an irresistible rhythm; he then assembled the trio and signed with Vanguard Records. 'Walk Right In' became that label's, and the group's, only number 1 record. The Rooftop Singers placed one album and two other folk songs in the US charts: 'Tom Cat' and 'Mama Don't Allow'. The group disbanded in 1967 and Taylor died the same year; Darling and Svanoe subsequently retired from the music business.

● ALBUMS: *Walk Right In!* (Vanguard 1963) ★★★★, *Goodtime* (Vanguard 1964) ★★★, *Rainy River* (Vanguard 1965) ★★★.
● COMPILATIONS: *The Best Of Rooftop Singers* (Vanguard 1992) ★★★★.

ROSE, TIM

b. 23 September 1940, USA. A one-time student priest and navigator for the USAF Strategic Air Command, Rose began his professional music career playing guitar with the Journeymen, a folk group active in the early 60s which featured John Phillips and Scott McKenzie. He subsequently joined 'Mama' Cass Elliot and James Hendricks in another formative attraction, the Big Three. Although initially based in Chicago, the trio later moved to New York, where Rose forged a career as a solo singer on the group's disintegration in 1964. A gruff stylist and individual, he was turned down by Elektra Records and Mercury Records before securing a contract with Columbia Records. A series of majestic singles then followed, including 'Hey Joe' (1966) and 'Morning Dew' (1967). Rose's slow, brooding version of the former was the inspiration for that of Jimi Hendrix, while the latter, written by Rose and folk singer Bonnie Dobson, was the subject of cover versions by, among others, Jeff Beck and the Grateful Dead.

Tim Rose was assembled from several different sessions, but the presence of several crack session musicians – Felix Pappalardi (bass/piano), Bernard Purdie (drums) and Hugh McCracken (guitar) – provided a continuity. The set included a dramatic reading of 'I'm Gonna Be Strong', previously associated with Gene Pitney, and the haunting anti-war anthem 'Come Away Melinda', already recorded by the Big Three, on which Rose's blues-soaked, gritty voice was particularly effective. The singer's next release, 'Long Haired Boys', was recorded in the UK under the aegis of producer Al Kooper, before Rose returned to the USA to complete *Through Rose Coloured Glasses* (1969). This disappointing album lacked the strength of its predecessor and the artist was never again to scale the heights of his early work.

He switched outlets to Capitol Records for *Love – A Kind Of Hate Story*, before the disillusioned performer abandoned major outlets in favour of the Playboy label where his manager's brother was employed. The promise of artistic freedom was fulfilled when Gary Wright of Spooky Tooth, a group Rose revered, produced the ensuing sessions. The album, also entitled *Tim Rose*, contained a version of the Beatles' 'You've Got To Hide Your Love Away' performed at a snail's pace. It was not a commercial success and the singer again left for the UK where he believed audiences were more receptive. Resident in London, Rose undertook a series of live concerts with fellow exile Tim Hardin, but this ill-fated partnership quickly collapsed. *The Musician*, released in 1975, revealed a voice which retained its distinctive power, but an artist without definite direction. In 1976 Rose was recording a new album with help from Andy Summers, Snowy White, Raphael Ravenscroft, B.J. Cole and Michael D'Alberquerque. This country-tinged album was finally released on President in 1991 as *The Gambler*. Rose moved back to New York in the late 70s. In 1997 he resurfaced with an excellent new album, *Haunted*, mixing old material with recent interpretations. His voice has not lost any of its power and it is a mystery why an artist of his calibre had spent recent times demonstrating carrot-slicing machines in Bloomingdales store in New York.

● ALBUMS: *Tim Rose* (Columbia 1967) ★★★★, *Through Rose Coloured Glasses* (Columbia 1969) ★★, *Love – A Kind Of Hate Story* (Capitol 1970) ★★, *Tim Rose* (Dawn 1972) ★★, *The Musician* (Atlantic 1975) ★★, *The Gambler* (President

1991) ★★, *Tim Rose/Through Rose Coloured Glasses* (BGO 1998) ★★★★, *Haunted* (Best Dressed 1997) ★★★★.
● COMPILATIONS: *Hide Your Love Away* (Flying Thorn 1998) ★★★.

ROULETTES
Formed in London, England in 1962, the Roulettes made their recording debut that year with 'Hully Gully Slip And Slide', released on Pye Records. The single was not a success but the group was saved from obscurity in 1963 when they were invited to back singer Adam Faith. By this point their line-up comprised Russ Ballard (b. 31 October 1945, Waltham Cross, Hertfordshire, England; lead guitar), Peter Thorpe (b. 25 May 1945, Hertfordshire, England; rhythm guitar), John Rodgers (bass) and Bob Henrit (b. 2 May 1944, Waltham Cross, Hertfordshire, England; drums). Ballard and Henrit had previously worked together as members of the Daybreakers. The Roulettes were featured on all of Faith's singles until May 1965, including the hits 'The First Time' and 'We Are In Love'. They also played on his 1964 album *On The Move*. The Roulettes rekindled their own recording career in 1963 with 'Soon You'll Be Leaving Me'. It was the first of a series of superior beat singles they recorded for Parlophone Records including 'Bad Time', 'I'll Remember Tonight' (both 1964) and the excellent 'The Long Cigarette' (1965). By that point John 'Mod' Rogan (b. 3 February 1944, West Hartlepool, Yorkshire, England), had replaced John Rodgers, who died in a car crash in 1964. The Roulettes momentum faltered upon breaking from Faith. They split up in 1967, having completed two memorable singles, 'Rhyme Boy Rhyme' and 'Help Me To Help Myself', for Fontana Records. Ballard and Henrit switched to Unit Four Plus Two with whom they already enjoyed a close association, as leader 'Buster' Meikle had also been a member of the Daybreakers. Indeed Ballard played guitar on Unit Four Plue Two's 1965 hit, 'Concrete And Clay' and both musicians were featured on several subsequent recordings. Following a period of inactivity after Unit Four Plus Two's demise, Ballard and Henrit returned in Argent.
● ALBUMS: *Stakes And Chips* (Parlophone 1965) ★★★.
● COMPILATIONS: *Stakes And Chips* (BGO 1992) ★★★.

ROUTERS
A US instrumental group formed in the early 60s in the Los Angeles area, the original Routers were not the same musicians that eventually secured the group's only hit in 1962 with 'Let's Go (Pony)'. The original group consisted of musicians Mike Gordon, Al Kait, Bill Moody, Lynn Frazier and a fifth musician (unknown).

Signed to Warner Brothers Records, the group was assigned to producer Joe Saraceno, who then proceeded to use studio musicians and not the actual group on the recording of 'Let's Go (Pony)'. The single reached the US charts at number 19 and *Let's Go With The Routers*, was released, but it too was apparently recorded by session musicians such as Hal Blaine and Plas Johnson. Warner Brothers continued to issue singles under the name Routers, one of which, 'Sting Ray', reached the charts in 1963. There were three other Warner albums, followed by later Routers singles on RCA Records and Mercury Records (which also released an album) as late as 1973, after which the name was apparently shelved and the remaining members disbanded. Probably unknown to the band and the composers of the song 'Let's Go' was that this chorus was adopted by UK football fans in the mid-60s. The handclapping is followed by the chant of the 'let's go' lyric, which is replaced by the name of the team in question. Football historians have deemed that West Ham supporters were the first to use it, later imitated by other London clubs. It is now a universal chant. If the composers were entitled to a performing royalty they would be billionaires many times over.
● ALBUMS: *Let's Go With The Routers* (Warners 1963) ★★★, *The Routers Play 1963's Great Instrumental Hits* (Warners 1963) ★★, *Charge!* (Warners 1964) ★★, *Go Go Go With The Chuck Berry Songbook* (Warners 1965) ★★.

RUBY AND THE ROMANTICS
Edward Roberts (first tenor), George Lee (second tenor), Ronald Mosley (baritone) and Leroy Fann (bass) had been working as the Supremes prior to the arrival of Ruby Nash Curtis (b. 12 November 1939, New York City, New York, USA) in 1962. Curtis had met the group in Akron, Ohio, and took on the role as their lead singer. They subsequently secured a contract with the New York label Kapp and at the suggestion of the company, changed their name to Ruby And The Romantics. By the following year they had taken the evocative 'Our Day Will Come' to the top of the US pop chart, earning them a gold disc. Over the next 12 months the group enjoyed a further six hits including the original version of 'Hey There Lonely Boy' which, with a change of gender, was later revived by Eddie Holman. After three years at Kapp, the group signed to the ABC Records label. In 1965 'Does He Really Care For Me?', the Romantics' last chart entry, preceded a wholesale line-up change. Ruby brought in a new backing group; Richard Pryor, Vincent McLeod, Robert Lewis, Ronald Jackson and Bill Evans, but in 1968 the forthright Curtis replaced this version with Denise Lewis and Cheryl Thomas.
● ALBUMS: *Our Day Will Come* (Kapp 1963) ★★★, *Till Then* (Kapp 1963) ★★★, *Ruby And*

The Romantics (ABC 1967) ★★, *More Than Yesterday* (ABC 1968) ★★.
● COMPILATIONS: *Greatest Hits Album* (Kapp 1966) ★★★, *The Very Best Of ...* (Target 1995) ★★★.

RUSH, TOM
b. 8 February, 1941, Portsmouth, New Hampshire, USA. Tom Rush began performing in 1961 while a student at Harvard University. Although he appeared at clubs in New York and Philadelphia, he became a pivotal figure of the Boston/New England circuit and such haunts as the Cafe Yana and the Club 47. The self-released *Live At The Unicorn*, culled from two sets recorded at another of the region's fabled coffee houses, was poorly distributed but its competent mixture of traditional songs, blues and Woody Guthrie compositions was sufficient to interest the renowned Prestige Records label. *Got A Mind To Ramble* and *Blues Songs And Ballads*, completed over three days, showcased an intuitive interpreter. Rush's exemplary versions of 'Barb'ry Allen' and 'Alabama Bound' were enough to confirm his place alongside Dave Van Ronk and Eric Von Schmidt, the latter of whom was an important influence on the younger musician. *Tom Rush*, his first release on the Elektra Records label, was one of the era's finest folk/blues sets. The artist had developed an accomplished bottleneck guitar style that was portrayed to perfection on 'Panama Limited', an eight-minute compendium comprising several different songs by Bukka White. *Take A Little Walk With Me* contained the similarly excellent 'Galveston Flood', but its high points were six electric selections drawn from songs by Bo Diddley, Chuck Berry and Buddy Holly. Arranged by Al Kooper, these performances featured musicians from Bob Dylan's ground-breaking sessions and helped transform Rush from traditional to popular performer. This change culminated in *The Circle Game*, which contained material by Joni Mitchell, James Taylor and Jackson Browne, each of whom had yet to record in their own right. The recording also included the poignant 'No Regrets', the singer's own composition, which has since become a pop classic through hit versions by the Walker Brothers (1976) and Midge Ure (1982).
Tom Rush, the artist's first release for CBS Records, introduced his long-standing partnership with guitarist Trevor Veitch. Once again material by Jackson Browne and James Taylor was to the fore, but the album also contained compositions by Fred Neil and Murray McLaughlin's beautiful song of leaving home, 'Child's Song', confirming Rush as having immaculate taste in choice of material. However, two subsequent releases, *Wrong End Of The Rainbow* and *Merrimack County*, saw an increased emphasis on material Rush either wrote alone, or with Veitch. By contrast a new version of 'No Regrets' was the sole original or

Ladies Love Outlaws, a collection which marked a pause in Rush's recording career. It was 1982 before a new set, *New Year*, was released. Recorded live, it celebrated the artist's 20th anniversary while a second live album, *Late Night Radio*, featured cameos from Steve Goodman and Mimi Fariña. Both were issued on Rush's Night Light label on which he also repackaged his 1962 debut. In 1990 his New Hampshire home and recording studio were totally destroyed by fire. This cultured artist subsequently moved to Wyoming, but little was heard from him during the rest of the 90s. The owner of one of music's most expressive voices returned to the recording studio at the end of the decade to record a new track, 'River Song', for a CD retrospective of his career.

● ALBUMS: *Live At The Unicorn* (Own Label 1962) ★★, *Got A Mind To Ramble* aka *Mind Rambling* (Folklore 1963) ★★, *Blues Songs And Ballads* (Prestige 1964) ★★, *Tom Rush* (Elektra 1965) ★★★★, *Take A Little Walk With Me* aka *The New Album* (Elektra 1966) ★★★★, *The Circle Game* (Elektra 1968) ★★★★, *Tom Rush* (Columbia 1970) ★★★★, *Wrong End Of The Rainbow* (Columbia 1970) ★★★, *Merrimack County* (Columbia 1972) ★★★, *Ladies Love Outlaws* (Columbia 1974) ★★★, *New Year* (Night Light 1982) ★★, *Late Night Radio* (Night Light 1984) ★★.

● COMPILATIONS: *Classic Rush* (Elektra 1970) ★★★★, *The Best Of Tom Rush* (Columbia 1975) ★★★★, *The Very Best Of Tom Rush: No Regrets* (Sony 1999) ★★★★.

RYAN, PAUL AND BARRY

b. Paul and Barry Sapherson, 24 October 1948, Leeds, England (Paul d. 29 November 1992). The twin sons of popular singer Marion Ryan, Paul and Barry were launched as a clean-cut act to attendant showbusiness publicity. Their debut single, 'Don't Bring Me Your Heartaches' reached the UK Top 20 in 1965, and over the ensuing months the siblings enjoyed respectable, if unspectacular, chart placings with 'Have Pity On The Boy' and 'I Love Her'. The Ryans shifted away from their tailored image with 'Have You Ever Loved Somebody' (1966) and 'Keep It Out Of Sight' (1967), penned, respectively, by the Hollies and Cat Stevens, but such releases were less successful. They split amicably in 1968 with Paul embarking on a songwriting career while Barry recorded as a solo act. Together they created 'Eloise', the latter's impressive number 2 hit and subsequent million seller, but ensuing singles failed to emulate its popularity. Paul's compositions included 'I Will Drink The Wine', which was recorded by Frank Sinatra, but neither brother was able to sustain initial impetus. During 1969 Barry had an accident which caused serious burns to his face. In the 70s Paul moved to the USA, but later left the music business and opened a chain of hairdressing salons.

● ALBUMS: *The Ryans Two Of A Kind* (Decca 1967) ★★★, *Paul And Barry Ryan* (MGM 1968) ★★★.

● COMPILATIONS: *The Best Of Paul & Barry Ryan* (Popumentary 1998) ★★★.

RYDELL, BOBBY

b. Robert Ridarelli, 26 April 1942, Philadelphia, Pennsylvania, USA. Probably the most musically talented of the late 50s Philadelphia school of clean-cut teen-idols, Rydell first performed in public as a drummer at the age of seven. At nine he debuted on Paul Whiteman's *Teen Club* amateur television show and was the show's regular drummer for three years. He attended the same boys club as Fabian and Frankie Avalon, formed a duo with Avalon in 1954 and shortly afterwards, they both joined local group Rocco And The Saints. After several rejections from labels, he recorded his first solo single 'Fatty Fatty' for his manager's Veko label. In 1958 he joined Cameo-Parkway and his fourth release for that label, 'Kissin' Time' (which owed something to 'Sweet Little Sixteen'), became the first of his 18 US Top 40 hits over the next four years. The photogenic pop/rock singer's best-known transatlantic hits are 'Wild One', 'Sway' and 'Volare' (only two years after the song first topped the charts) all in 1960 and 'Forget Him', a song written and produced in Britain by Tony Hatch in 1963. Rydell, whose ambition was always to be an all-round entertainer, starred in the movie *Bye Bye Birdie* and quickly, and initially successfully, moved into the cabaret circuit. The arrival of the British groups in 1964 was the final nail in his chart coffin. He later recorded without success for Capitol, Reprise, RCA, Perception and Pickwick International. Rydell has continued to work the club and oldies circuit and had some recognition for his role in rock when the high school in the hit 70s musical *Grease* was named after him. He returned to the studio in 1995 to re-record all his greatest hits as *The Best Of Bobby Rydell*.

● ALBUMS: *We Got Love* (Cameo 1959) ★★★, *Bobby Sings* (Cameo 1960) ★★, *Bobby Rydell Salutes The Great Ones* (Cameo 1961) ★★, *Rydell At The Copa* (Cameo 1961) ★★, *Bobby Rydell/Chubby Checker* (Cameo-Parkway 1961) ★★★, *Bye Bye Birdie* (Cameo 1963) ★★, *Wild Wood Days* (Cameo 1963) ★★, *The Top Hits Of 1963* (Cameo 1964) ★★, *Forget Him* (Cameo 1964) ★★.

● COMPILATIONS: *Bobby's Biggest Hits* (Cameo 1961) ★★★, *All The Hits* (Cameo 1962) ★★★, *Biggest Hits, Volume 2* (Cameo 1962) ★★, *16 Golden Hits* (Cameo 1965) ★★, *Greatest Hits* (1993) ★★, *Best Of Bobby Rydell* (K-Tel 1995) ★★, *The Best Of Bobby Rydell* (Prestige 2000), *The Complete Bobby Rydell On Capitol* (Collectors Choise 2001)

● FILMS: *Because They're Young* (1960).

RYDER, MITCH, AND THE DETROIT WHEELS

b. William Levise Jnr., 26 February 1945, Detroit, Michigan, USA. An impassioned singer, bearing an aural debt to Little Richard, Mitch Ryder spent his formative years frequenting the clubs on Woodward Avenue, watching many of Tamla/Motown's star attractions. Having outgrown two high school bands, Levise formed Billy Lee And The Rivieras in 1963. Jim McCarty (lead guitar – later of Buddy Miles Express and Cactus), Joe Cubert (rhythm guitar), Earl Elliott (bass) and 'Little' John Badanjek (drums) completed the group's early line-up, which recorded two singles for local labels prior to their 'discovery' by producer Bob Crewe. The quintet was then given a sharper name – Mitch Ryder And The Detroit Wheels – and in 1965 secured their biggest hit with the frenzied 'Jenny Take A Ride', a raw and earthy performance which set new standards in 'blue-eyed' soul. Uninhibited at a time of increasing sophistication, Ryder successfully captured the power of his black inspirations. Subsequent releases showed a similar verve, but the group reached its zenith with the exceptional medley of 'Devil With A Blue Dress On' and 'Good Golly Miss Molly'. From there, however, the formula became predictable and more studied recreations failed to emulate its fire. The Wheels were summarily fired in 1967 as the singer was coaxed towards safer fare. He and Crewe split up in rancorous circumstances but a union with guitarist Steve Cropper resulted in the excellent *Detroit-Memphis Experiment*.

In 1971 Levise formed Detroit, a hard-edged rock band of great promise which disintegrated prematurely. The singer then abandoned music, nursing a throat ailment that threatened his one-time livelihood. He resumed performing in the late 70s and although later releases lack the overall passion of those initial recordings, there are moments when that erstwhile strength occurs. In the 90s Mitch Ryder is still a major concert attraction. A primary influence on Bruce Springsteen, the architect of Detroit's 'high-energy' performers, the MC5 and the Stooges, Ryder's talent should not be under-estimated.

● ALBUMS: with the Detroit Wheels *Take A Ride* (New Voice 1966) ★★★★, *Breakout ... !!!* (New Voice 1966) ★★★, *Sock It To Me!* (New Voice 1967) ★★★.

Mitch Ryder solo *What Now My Love?* (Dyno Voice 1967) ★★, *Mitch Ryder Sings The Hits* (New Voice 1968) ★★, *The Detroit-Memphis Experience* (Dot 1969) ★★★, *How I Spent My Vacation* (Line 1979) ★★★, *Naked But Not Dead* (Line 1980) ★★★, *Live Talkies* (Line 1981) ★★★, *Got Change For A Million* (Line 1981) ★★★, *Smart Ass* (Line 1982) ★★★, *Never Kick A Sleeping Dog* (Line 1983) ★★★, *Red Blood, White Mink* (Line 1988) ★★★, *In The China Shop* (Line 1988) ★★★, *La Gash* (Line 1992) ★★, *Rite Of Passage* (Line 1994) ★★.

● COMPILATIONS: *All Mitch Ryder Hits!* (New Voice 1967) ★★★, *All The Heavy Hits* (Crewe 1967) ★★★, *Mitch Ryder And The Detroit Wheels' Greatest Hits* (Bellaphon 1972) ★★★, *Rev Up: The Best Of Mitch Ryder And The Detroit Wheels* (Rhino 1990) ★★★, *Detroit Breakout! An Ultimate Anthology* (Westside 1997) ★★★.

rejoined the original members to record one more single on Valient under the name of Suddens, but after that record failed the members left the music business.

SADLER, BARRY, STAFF SGT.
b. 1 November 1940, Carlsbad, New Mexico, USA, d. 5 November 1989, Tennessee, USA. While stationed at Fort San Houston, Texas, Staff Sergeant Barry Sadler spent his spare time composing a number of songs and, after serving in Vietnam, decided to complete a lyric dedicated to his regiment, the US Army Special Forces, aka the Green Berets. The result was submitted to a publisher who passed the composition on to author Robin Moore whose book, *The Green Berets*, was a bestseller. Together, Sadler and Moore refashioned the song into 'The Ballad Of The Green Berets' which, following its release on RCA Records surprisingly dominated the US number 1 position for an astonishing five weeks in 1966. Sadler's repertoire was limited, but he managed to complete a follow-up, 'The "A" Team' and a bestselling album. His career thereafter was stormy and controversial. After re-enlisting in the Army and briefly pursuing an acting career, he was charged and acquitted of the murder of Nashville songwriter Lee Emerson Bellamy. Three years later, in 1981, he was found not guilty of a charge of shooting his former business partner. It was an extraordinary dénouement to the career of one of the most unlikely chart-topping artists of all time. In 1988, he was shot in the head during a robbery attempt at his Guatemala home. He suffered brain damage and died of heart failure the following year.
● ALBUMS: *Ballads Of The Green Berets* (RCA 1966) ★★, *The "A" Team* (RCA 1966) ★.

SAFARIS
A rock 'n' roll vocal group from Los Angeles, California, USA. The Safaris typified the best of white vocal group rock n' roll of the early 60s, the marriage of soulful vocals and the perfect feeling of teen angst. Members were lead Jim Stephens, Sheldon Breier, Richard Clasky, and Marv Rosenberg. Their splendid ballad, 'Image Of A Girl' (number 6 pop), from 1960, was their only hit record, making the group a one-hit-wonder. The record was a huge international hit, and made a significant enough impact in the UK to generate two cover versions, by Mark Wynter (number 11) and Nelson Keene (number 37). The Safaris had one weak follow-up, 'The Girl With The Story In Her Eyes' (number 85 pop) and then broke up. Stephens continued the group's name with three new members, but could not make a return to the charts. Stephens

SAGITTARIUS
Formed in Los Angeles, California, USA in 1967, Sagittarius was a studio group created by singer-songwriter Curt Boettcher and Byrds' producer Gary Usher. Its close-knit harmony sound and lush orchestration was similar to that of the Millennium, a concurrent project whose members provided the instrumental backing on *Present Tense*. Bruce Johnston and Terry Melcher added their vocals to a set best recalled for 'My World Fell Down', a gorgeous pop song reminiscent of the Beach Boys, written by the British team of John Carter (b. John Shakespeare, 20 October 1942, Birmingham, England) and Ken Lewis (b. James Hawker, 3 December 1942, Birmingham, England), for their own group, the Ivy League. The Sagittarius version drew considerable acclaim, but failed to chart when issued as a single. *The Blue Marble*, issued on the Usher/Boettcher outlet Together, continued in the vein of its predecessor, but when it too failed to reap due commercial rewards, the concept was discontinued. Poptones have reissued their small but interesting catalogue.
● ALBUMS: *Present Tense* (Columbia 1968) ★★★, *The Blue Marble* (Together 1969) ★★★★.

SAINTE-MARIE, BUFFY
b. 20 February 1941, Piapot Reserve, Saskatchewan, Canada. Adopted and raised in Maine and Massachusetts, Sainte-Marie received a PhD in Fine Art from the University of Massachusetts, but eschewed a teaching career in favour of folk singing. She was signed to Vanguard Records in 1964, following her successful performances at Gerde's Folk City. Her debut *It's My Way!* introduced a remarkable compositional and performing talent. Sainte-Marie's impassioned plea for Indian rights, 'Now That The Buffalo's Gone', reflected her native-American parentage and was one of several stand-out tracks, along with 'Cod'ine' and 'The Universal Soldier'. The latter was recorded, successfully, by Donovan, which helped to introduce her to a wider audience. Her second selection included 'Until It's Time For You To Go', a haunting love song that was later recorded by Elvis Presley. However, Sainte-Marie was also a capable interpreter of other writers' material, as her versions of songs by Bukka White, Joni Mitchell and Leonard Cohen showed. Her versatility was also apparent on a superb C&W collection, *I'm Gonna Be A Country Girl Again*, and on *Illuminations*, which featured an electronic score on several tracks. A tireless campaigner for American Indian rights, Sainte-Marie secured an international hit in 1971 with the theme song to the movie *Soldier Blue*, but

subsequent releases failed to capitalize on this success. Temporarily bereft of direction, Sainte-Marie returned to the Indian theme with *Sweet America*, but with the collapse of the ABC Records label, she retired to raise her family and concentrate on her work for children's foundations, which included regular appearances on *Sesame Street*. Her later credits included co-composing, with lyricist Will Jennings, the 1982 Joe Cocker/Jennifer Warnes' hit, 'Up Where We Belong' which featured in the movie *An Officer And A Gentleman*. Her welcome return to the music scene in 1992, following her signing with Chrysalis Records, produced the warmly received *Coincidence And Likely Stories*, which displayed her interest in computer technology (Sainte-Marie is a prominent digital artist). *Up Where We Belong*, released in February 1996, included several new recordings of her old material.

● ALBUMS: *It's My Way!* (Vanguard 1964) ★★★, *Many A Mile* (Vanguard 1965) ★★★★, *Little Wheel Spin And Spin* (Vanguard 1966) ★★★, *Fire & Fleet & Candlelight* (Vanguard 1967) ★★★, *I'm Gonna Be A Country Girl Again* (Vanguard 1968) ★★★★, *Illuminations* (Illuminations 1969) ★★★, *She Used To Wanna Be A Ballerina* (Vanguard 1971) ★★★★, *Moonshot* (Vanguard 1972) ★★★, *Quiet Places* (Vanguard 1973) ★★, *Buffy* (MCA 1974) ★★, *Changing Woman* (MCA 1975) ★★, *Sweet America* (ABC 1976) ★★, *Coincidence And Likely Stories* (Chrysalis 1992) ★★★, *Up Where We Belong* (EMI 1996) ★★★.

● COMPILATIONS: *The Best Of Buffy Sainte-Marie* (Vanguard 1970) ★★★★, *Native North American Child: An Odyssey* (Vanguard 1974) ★★★, *The Best Of Buffy Sainte-Marie, Volume 2* (Vanguard 1974) ★★★.

SAM AND DAVE

Samuel David Moore (b. 12 October 1935, Miami, Florida, USA) and David Prater (b. 9 May 1937, Ocilla, Georgia, USA, d. 9 April 1988). Sam And Dave first performed together in 1961 at Miami's King Of Hearts club. Moore originally sang in his father's Baptist church before joining the Melonaires, while Prater, who had worked with the Sensational Hummingbirds, was also gospel-trained. Club-owner John Lomelo became the duo's manager and was instrumental in securing their contract with Roulette. Five singles and one album subsequently appeared between 1962 and 1964, produced by R&B veteran Henry Glover, but it was not until Jerry Wexler signed Sam And Dave to Atlantic Records that their true potential blossomed. For political reasons, their records appeared on Stax Records; they used the Memphis-based house band, while many of their strongest moments came from the Isaac Hayes/David Porter staff writing team. 'You Don't Know Like I Know', 'Hold On I'm Comin' (both 1966), 'Soul Man' (1967) and 'I Thank You' (1968), featuring Prater's gritty delivery and

Moore's higher interjections, were among the genre's finest.

When Stax and Atlantic separated in 1968, Sam And Dave reverted to the parent company, but a disintegrating personal relationship seemed to mirror their now decaying fortune. The amazing 'Soul Sister, Brown Sugar' (1969) delayed the slide, but the duo split briefly the next year when Sam Moore began his own career. Three solo singles followed, but the pair were reunited by a contract with United Artists Records. A renewed profile, on the strength of the Blues Brothers' success with 'Soul Man', faltered when the differences between the two men proved irreconcilable. By 1981, Moore was again pursuing an independent direction, but his sole chart success came when he was joined by Lou Reed for a remake of 'Soul Man' six years later. Prater found a new foil in the 'Sam' of Sam And Bill, but before they were able to consolidate this new partnership, Prater died in a car crash on 9 April 1988. Sam Moore in the meantime has been working consistently all over the world, notably on luxury cruise-liners. In 2001 some master tapes of his solo material were discovered and issued the following year. The best duo in the history of soul music, Sam And Dave released records that combined urgency with an unbridled passion.

● ALBUMS: *Sam And Dave* i (Roulette/King 1966) ★★, *Hold On, I'm Comin'* (Stax 1966) ★★★★, *Double Dynamite* (Stax 1967) ★★★★, *Soul Men* (Stax 1967) ★★★★, *I Thank You* (Atlantic 1968) ★★★, *Double Trouble* (Stax 1969) ★★★, *Back At 'Cha* (United Artists 1976) ★★, *Sam And Dave* ii 1962-63 recordings (Edsel 1994) ★★.

● COMPILATIONS: *The Best Of Sam And Dave* (Atlantic 1969) ★★★★, *Can't Stand Up For Falling Down* (Edsel 1984) ★★★, *Greatest Hits* (Castle 1986) ★★★, *Wonderful World* (Topline 1987) ★★★, *Sweet Funky Gold* (Gusto 1988) ★★★, *Sweat 'N' Soul: Anthology 1968 - 1971* (Rhino 1993) ★★★★, *The Very Best Of ...* (Rhino 1995) ★★★★.

SAM THE SHAM AND THE PHARAOHS

b. Domingo Samudio aka Sam Samudio, Dallas, Texas, USA. Although drawing inspiration from the Tex-Mex tradition, Sam's initial releases were made for Memphis-based outlets. Backed by the Pharaohs, which comprised Ray Stinnet (guitar), Butch Gibson (saxophone), David Martin (bass) and Jerry Patterson (drums), he had a US chart-topper in 1965 with 'Wooly Bully', a pulsating novelty dance song that achieved immortality as a staple part of aspiring bar band repertoires. The single became the act's sole UK Top 20 hit, but they enjoyed further success in the USA with 'Lil' Red Riding Hood', which reached number 2 the following year. The group later mutated into the Sam The Sham Revue, but the singer dissolved the venture in 1970 to embark on a solo career under his own name. Although

Hard And Heavy featured support from guitarist Duane Allman, the set was marred by inconsistency and failed to establish its proponent's talent. Domingo subsequently contributed to the soundtrack of the 1982 movie *The Border* and remains a popular talent in his native state.

● ALBUMS: *Sam The Sham And Wooly Bully* (MGM 1965) ★★★, *Their Second Album* (MGM 1965) ★★, *Sam The Sham And The Pharaohs On Tour* (MGM 1966) ★★, *Lil' Red Riding Hood* (MGM 1966) ★★, *The Sam The Sham Revue/Nefertiti* (MGM 1967) ★★, *Ten Of Pentacles* (MGM 1968) ★★.

● COMPILATIONS: *The Best Of Sam The Sham And The Pharoahs* (MGM 1967) ★★★, *Pharaohization: The Best Of Sam The Sham And The Pharaohs* (Rhino 1999) ★★★.

● FILMS: *The Fastest Guitar Alive* (1966).

SARSTEDT, PETER

b. December 1941 New Delhi, India, but moved to England in 1954. Brother of 60s pop idol Eden Kane (playing briefly as his bass player) this singer-songwriter was a denizen of the British folk scene when the hunt was on for a native riposte to Bob Dylan. Sarstedt was not chosen but, growing a luxuriant black moustache, he cultivated the image of a suave wanderer of global bohemia. Recording for United Artists Records, his 'I Am A Cathedral' was an airplay hit on pirate radio and university juke-boxes, but it was not until 1969 that he restored family fortunes with a UK number 1, 'Where Do You Go To My Lovely', which has since attained status as a pop classic (sharing the Ivor Novello Award for 1969 with David Bowie's 'Space Oddity') and is a perennial on 'gold' format radio stations. That year, both an album and another single ('Frozen Orange Juice') also sold well throughout Europe. Yet, although a forerunner of the early 70s 'self-rock' school, his style was not solemn enough for its collegian consumers. In 1973, he teamed up on *Worlds Apart Together* with Kane and another sibling, Robin Sarstedt. Then came the resumption of his solo career with the issue of further albums, which was accompanied by the unexpected BBC airplay for 'Beirut' from *PS ...*, and 'Love Among The Ruins' almost charting in 1982. Based in Copenhagan for several years, he settled down with his American wife, Joanna, on a Wiltshire farm. In the early 90s he was seen on 60s nostalgia shows, often supporting Gerry And The Pacemakers. He returned to recording in the late 90s with *England's Lane*, with further assistance from Kane.

● ALBUMS: *Peter Sarstedt* (United Artists 1969) ★★, *As Though It Were A Movie* (United Artists 1969) ★★, *Every Word You Say Is Written Down* (United Artists 1971) ★★★, with Eden Kane, Robin Sarstedt *Worlds Apart Together* (Regal Zonophone 1973) ★★, *Tall Tree* (Warners 1975) ★★, *PS ...* (Ariola 1979) ★★★, *Update* (Ariola 1982) ★★★, with Clive Sarstedt *Asia Minor* (Music Master 1985) ★★★, *Never Say Goodbye* (1987) ★★★, *England's Lane* (Round Tower 1998) ★★.

● COMPILATIONS: *The Best Of Peter Sarstedt: Where Do You Go To My Lovely?* (EMI 1996) ★★★, *Peter Sarstedt Collection* (HMV Easy 2001) ★★★.

SCAFFOLD

Formed in Liverpool, England, in 1962, the Scaffold was the unlikely confluence of two concurrent 'booms' – satire and Merseybeat. Poet Roger McGough (b. 9 November 1937) and humorist John Gorman (b. 4 January 1937) joined Mike McGear (b. Michael McCartney, 7 January 1944), younger brother of Paul McCartney, to create an act not solely reliant on pop for success. They contributed material to *Gazteet*, a late-night programme on ABC-Television and following an acclaimed residency at London's Establishment club, took their 'Birds, Marriages and Deaths' revue to the 1964 Edinburgh Festival, where they later returned on several occasions. Although the trio enjoyed major hits with 'Thank U Very Much' (1967) and 'Lily The Pink' (1968) – the latter of which was a massive Christmas UK number 1 – these tongue-in-cheek releases contrasted the group's in-concert revues and albums. Here McGough's poetry and Gorman's comedy routines were of equal importance and their versatility was confirmed on their first two albums The schoolboy-ish 'Gin Gan Goolie' gave the group a minor chart entry in 1969, before the unit was absorbed by Grimms, a larger, if similarly constituted, act which also featured members of the Liverpool Scene.

On its demise McGear recorded *Woman*, before agreeing to resurrect Scaffold for *Fresh Liver* on which Zoot Money (keyboards) and Ollie Halsall (guitar) joined the Average White Band horn section to help bring a rock-based perspective to the trio's work. The haunting 'Liverpool Lou' provided another UK Top 10 hit in 1974, but the founder members embarked on separate paths following *Sold Out*. McGear resumed his solo career, and became a credible photographer, while McGough returned to writing poetry. Gorman pursued a career in television, principally on the cult UK television children's show *Tiswas* and was back in the UK charts alongside Sally James, Chris Tarrant and Lenny Henry as the Four Bucketeers with 'The Bucket Of Water Song' in 1980.

● ALBUMS: *An Evening With The Scaffold* (Parlophone 1968) ★★★, *Lily The Pink* (Parlophone 1969) ★★★, *An Evening With* (Parlophone 1968) ★★, *Fresh Liver* (Island 1973) ★★, *Sold Out* (Warners 1975) ★★.

● COMPILATIONS: *The Singles A's And B's* (See For Miles 1982) ★★★, *The Best Of The EMI Years* (EMI 1992) ★★★, *At Abbey Road 1966-1971* (EMI 1998) ★★★.

SCOTT, RONNIE

b. Ronald Schatt, 28 January 1927, London, England, d. 23 December 1996, London, England. Scott began playing on the soprano saxophone but switched to tenor in his early teens. After playing informally in clubs he joined the Johnny Claes band in 1944, before spells with Ted Heath, Bert Ambrose and other popular British dance bands. Scott also played on transatlantic liners in order to visit the USA and hear bebop at first hand. By the late 40s he was a key figure in the London bop scene, playing at the Club Eleven, of which he was a co-founder. During the 50s he led his own band and was also co-leader with Tubby Hayes of the Jazz Couriers. In 1959, he opened his own club in Gerrard Street, London, later moving to Frith Street. During the 60s he divided his time between leading his own small group and running the club, but also found time to play with the Clarke-Boland Big Band. The decade of the 60s was a milestone for popular music; for high-quality jazz there was only one place in London to visit – Ronnie's.

In the 70s and 80s he continued to lead small bands, usually a quartet, occasionally touring but most often playing as the interval band between sessions by the modern American jazz musicians he brought to the club. As a player, Scott comfortably straddles the mainstream and modern aspects of jazz. His big tone lends itself to a slightly aggressive approach, although in his ballad playing he displays the warmth that characterized the work of Zoot Sims and late-period Stan Getz, musicians he admires, but does not imitate. Although a gifted player, Scott's greatest contribution to jazz was in his tireless promotion of fine British musicians and in his establishment of his club, booking the best American talent. His venue has become renowned throughout the world for the excellence of its setting and the artists on display. In 1981, Scott was awarded an OBE in recognition of his services to music. Following a bout of depression he was found dead at his London flat in December 1996.

In the twenty-first century, the Frith Street club, under the direction of Scott's long-time partner, Pete King, retains its status as the city's leading jazz venue.

● ALBUMS: *Battle Royal* (Esquire 1951) ★★★, *The Ronnie Scott Jazz Group* i (Esquire 1952) ★★★★, *The Ronnie Scott Jazz Group* ii (Esquire 1953) ★★★, *The Ronnie Scott Jazz Group* iii (Esquire 1954) ★★★, *The Ronnie Scott Jazz Group* iv (Esquire 1954) ★★★, *At The Royal Festival Hall* (Decca 1956) ★★★, *Presenting The Ronnie Scott Sextet* (Philips 1957) ★★★, *The Jazz Couriers In Concert* (1958) ★★★, *The Last Word* (1959) ★★★, *The Night Is Scott And You're So Swingable* (Fontana 1966) ★★★, *Ronnie Scott & The Band Live At Ronnie Scott's* (CBS Realm 1968) ★★★★, *Scott At Ronnie's* (1973) ★★★, *Serious Gold* (1977) ★★★, *Great Scott* (1979) ★★★, with various artists *Ronnie Scott's 20th Anniversary Album* (Ronnie Scott's Jazz House 1979) ★★★, *Never Pat A Burning Dog* (Ronnie Scott's Jazz House 1990) ★★★, *When I Want Your Opinion, I'll Give It To You* 1963, 1964 recordings (Ronnie Scott's Jazz House 1998) ★★★★, with Sonny Stitt *The Night Has A Thousand Eyes* 1964 recordings (Ronnie Scott's Jazz House 1998) ★★★.

● FURTHER READING: *Jazz At Ronnie Scott's*, Kitty Grime (ed.). *Let's Join Hands And Contact The Living*, John Fordham. *Jazz Man: The Amazing Story Of Ronnie Scott And His Club*, John Fordham. *The Story Of Ronnie Scott's*, John Fordham. *A Fine Kind Of Madness: Ronnie Scott Remembered*, Rebecca Scott with Mary Scott.

SEARCHERS

One of the premier beat groups from the mid-60s Merseybeat explosion, the Liverpool-based Searchers were formed in 1960 by Chris Curtis (b. Christopher Crummey, 26 August 1941, Oldham, Lancashire, England; drums), Mike Pender (b. Michael John Prendergast, 3 March 1942, Liverpool, England; lead guitar), Tony Jackson (b. 16 July 1940, Liverpool, England; vocals, bass) and John McNally (b. 30 August 1941, Liverpool, England; rhythm guitar). Having previously backed Liverpool singer Johnny Sandon, they broke away and took their new name from the 1956 John Ford western, *The Searchers*. During 1962, they appeared in Hamburg and, after sending a demo tape to A&R representative Tony Hatch, they were signed to Pye Records the following year. Their Doc Pomus/Mort Shuman debut, 'Sweets For My Sweet', was a memorable tune with strong harmonies and a professional production. By the summer of 1963 it had climbed to number 1, establishing the Searchers as rivals to Brian Epstein's celebrated stable of Liverpool groups. *Meet The Searchers* was swiftly issued and revealed the band's R&B pedigree on such standards as 'Farmer John' and 'Love Potion Number 9'. Meanwhile, Tony Hatch composed a catchy follow-up single, 'Sugar And Spice', which just failed to reach number 1. It was their third single, however, that won them international acclaim.

The Jack Nitzsche/Sonny Bono composition 'Needles And Pins' was a superb melody, brilliantly arranged by the Searchers and a striking chart-topper of its era. It also established them in the USA, reaching the Top 20 in March 1964. It was followed that same year by further US Hot 100 successes with 'Ain't That Just Like Me', 'Sugar And Spice', and 'Someday We're Gonna Love Again'. Earlier that year the band released their superbly atmospheric cover version of the Orlons' 'Don't Throw Your Love Away', which justifiably gave them a third UK number 1 single and reached the US Top 20. The pop world was shocked by the abrupt departure of bass player Tony Jackson, whose falsetto vocals had contributed much to the group's early sound and identity. He was replaced in the autumn by Frank Allen (b. Francis Renaud

McNeice, 14 December 1943, Hayes, Middlesex, England), a former member of Cliff Bennett And The Rebel Rousers and close friend of Chris Curtis.

A strident reading of Jackie DeShannon's 'When You Walk In The Room' was another highlight of 1964 and showed their rich Rickenbacker guitar work to notable effect. The Malvina Reynolds protest song, 'What Have They Done To The Rain', indicated their folk-rock potential, but its melancholic tune and slower pace was reflected in a lower chart placing. A return to the 'old' Searchers sound, with the plaintive 'Goodbye My Love', took them back into the UK Top 5 in early 1965, but the number 1 days were over. For a time, it seemed that the Searchers might not slide as inexorably as rivals Billy J. Kramer And The Dakotas and Gerry And The Pacemakers. They had enjoyed further US success in late 1964 with their Top 5 cover version of the Clovers' 'Love Potion Number 9', and the following year 'Bumble Bee' and 'What Have They Done To The Rain' also reached the Top 30. The Curtis/Pender hit, 'He's Got No Love' (UK number 12) showed that they could write their own hit material but this run could not be sustained. The release of P.F. Sloan's 'Take Me For What I'm Worth' suggested that they might become linked with the Bob Dylan-inspired folk-rock boom. Instead, their commercial fortunes rapidly declined and after Curtis was replaced by John Blunt (b. Croydon, Surrey, England), they were finally dropped by Pye.

Their last UK hit was a cover version of the Hollies' 'Have You Ever Loved Somebody'; this proved to be their penultimate success in the USA, which ended with 'Desdemona' (number 94) in 1971. Cabaret stints followed but the Searchers continued playing and in the circumstances underwent minimal line-up changes, with Billy Adamson (b. Scotland) replacing Blunt in 1969. They threatened a serious resurgence in 1979 when Sire Records issued a promising comeback album. The attempt to reach a new wave audience was ultimately unsuccessful, however, and after the less well-received Play For Today (titled Love's Melodies in the USA), the group stoically returned to the cabaret circuit. Pender left in December 1985 to set up his own rival outfit, Mike Pender's Searchers. He was replaced by Spencer James, who had previously played with various bands including First Class. James adopted the lead vocalist role on Hungry Hearts, a brand new album recorded for the Coconut label in 1989. The same year they supported Cliff Richard at Wembley Stadium in front of record audiences.

The band continues to ply their trade to appreciative audiences on the lucrative nostalgia circuit. To their credit, the Searchers' act does not dwell on 60s hits and they remain one of the most musically competent and finest surviving performing bands from the 60s' golden age. Ex-

member Jackson was imprisoned in 1997 for making threats with an offensive weapon. The following year Adamson retired from music, and was replaced by Eddie Rothe. A full reappraisal for the Searchers is long overdue. Their choice of material was both daring and intelligent, and they have rarely been cited with being pioneering or original. For a brief while they most certainly were.

● ALBUMS: Meet The Searchers (UK) (Pye 1963) ★★★★, Meet The Searchers/Needles And Pins (US) (Kapp 1963) ★★★, Sugar And Spice (UK) (Pye 1963) ★★★, Hear! Hear! (US) (Mercury 1964) ★★★, It's The Searchers (UK) (Pye 1964) ★★★, Bumble Bee: The New Searchers LP (US) (Kapp 1964) ★★★, This Is Us (US) (Kapp 1964) ★★★, Sounds Like Searchers (UK) The Searchers No. 4 (US) (Pye/Kapp 1965) ★★★, Take Me For What I'm Worth (Pye/Kapp 1965) ★★★, Second Take (RCA 1972) ★★, The Searchers (Sire 1979) ★★★, Play For Today aka Love's Melodies (Sire 1981) ★★, Hungry Hearts (Coconut 1989) ★★.
● COMPILATIONS: Greatest Hits (Rhino 1985) ★★★★, Silver Searchers (PRT 1986) ★★★★, The Searchers Hit Collection (Castle 1987) ★★★★, The EP Collection (See For Miles 1989) ★★★★, 30th Anniversary Collection (Sequel 1992) ★★★★, The EP Collection Volume 2 (See For Miles 1992) ★★★, Rare Recordings (See For Miles 1993) ★★★, The Definitive Collection (Castle 1998) ★★★, The Pye Anthology 1963-1967 (Sequel 2000) ★★★★.
● FURTHER READING: Travelling Man – On The Road With The Searchers, Frank Allen.

SEDAKA, NEIL

b. 13 March 1939, Brooklyn, New York City, New York, USA. Pianist Sedaka began his songwriting career with lyricist Howard Greenfield in the early 50s. During this high school period, Sedaka dated Carol Klein (later known as Carole King). For a brief period, Sedaka joined the Tokens, then won a scholarship to New York's Juilliard School of Music. In 1958, the pianist joined Don Kirshner's Brill Building school of instant songwriters. Sedaka's first major hit success came with 'Stupid Cupid', which was an international smash for Connie Francis. The following year, Sedaka signed to RCA Records as a recording artist and enjoyed a minor US hit with 'The Diary'. The frantic follow-up, 'I Go Ape', was a strong novelty record, which helped establish Sedaka. This was followed by one of his most famous songs, 'Oh Carol', a lament directed at his former girlfriend Carole King, who replied in kind with the less successful 'Oh Neil'. Sedaka's solid voice and memorable melodies resulted in a string of early 60s hits, including 'Stairway To Heaven', 'Calendar Girl', 'Little Devil', 'King Of Clowns', 'Happy Birthday Sweet Sixteen' and 'Breaking Up Is Hard To Do'. These songs summed up the nature of Sedaka's lyrical appeal. The material subtly dramatized the trials and rewards of teenage life and the emotional upheavals resulting from birthdays, break-ups and incessant speculation on the qualities of a loved one.

Such songs of neurotic love had their distinct time in the early 60s, and with the decline of the clean-cut teen balladeer and the emergence of groups, there was an inevitable lull in Sedaka's fortunes. He abandoned the pop star role but continued writing a fair share of hits over the next 10 years, including 'Venus In Blue Jeans' (Jimmy Clanton/Mark Wynter), 'Working On A Groovy Thing' (5th Dimension), 'Puppet Man' (Tom Jones) and 'Is This The Way To Amarillo?' (Tony Christie). In 1972, Sedaka effectively relaunched his solo career with *Emergence* and relocated to the UK. By 1973, he was back in the British charts with 'That's When The Music Takes Me'. *The Tra-La Days Are Over* was highly regarded and included 'Our Last Song Together', dedicated to Howard Greenfield. With *Laughter In The Rain*, Sedaka extended his appeal to his homeland. The title track topped the US charts in 1975, completing a remarkable international comeback. That same year, the Captain And Tennille took Sedaka's 'Love Will Keep Us Together' to the US number 1 spot and the songwriter followed suit soon after with 'Bad Blood'. The year ended with an excellent reworking of 'Breaking Up Is Hard To Do' in a completely different arrangement which provided another worldwide smash. He enjoyed his last major hit during 1980 in the company of his daughter Dara on 'Should've Never Let You Go'. Sedaka still tours and records on a regular basis.

● ALBUMS: *Neil Sedaka* (RCA Victor 1959) ★★★★, *Circulate* (RCA Victor 1961) ★★★, *Sings Little Devil And His Other Hits* (RCA Victor 1961) ★★★★, *Sings His Greatest Hits* (RCA Victor 1962) ★★★★, *Emergence* (Kirshner 1971) ★★★, *The Tra-La Days Are Over* (MGM 1973) ★★★★, *Solitaire* (Kirshner 1974) ★★★, *Laughter In The Rain* (Polydor 1974) ★★★, *Live At The Royal Festival Hall* (Polydor 1974) ★★★, *Overnight Success* (Polydor 1975) ★★, *The Hungry Years* (Rocket 1975) ★★, *On Stage* (RCA 1976) ★★, *Steppin' Out* (Rocket 1976) ★★, *A Song* (Elektra/Polydor 1977) ★★, *All You Need Is The Music* (Elektra 1978) ★★, *In The Pocket* (Elektra 1980) ★★, *Now* (Elektra/Polydor 1981) ★★, *Come See About Me* (MCA 1984) ★★, *The Good Times* (PRT 1986) ★★, *Love Will Keep Us Together: The Singer And His Songs* (Polydor 1992) ★★★, *Classically Sedaka* (Telstar 1995) ★★★, *Tales Of Love And Other Passions* (Artful 1998) ★★★.

● COMPILATIONS: *Sedaka's Back* (Rocket 1974) ★★★★, *Laughter And Tears: The Best Of Neil Sedaka Today* (Polydor 1976) ★★★, *Me And My Friends* (Polydor 1986) ★★★, *Timeless: The Very Best Of Neil Sedaka* (Polydor 1991) ★★★, *Laughter In The Rain: The Best Of Neil Sedaka 1974-1980* (Varèse Vintage 1994) ★★★★, *Tuneweaver* (Varèse Vintage 1995) ★★★★.

● FURTHER READING: *Breaking Up Is Hard To Do*, Neil Sedaka.

● FILMS: *Sting Of Death* (1965), *Playgirl Killer* aka *Portrait Of Fear* (1966).

SEEDS

Formed in 1965, the Seeds provided a pivotal link between garage/punk rock and the emergent underground styles. They were led by Sky Saxon (b. Richard Marsh, USA), a charismatic figure already established on the fringes of a budding Los Angeles scene through a handful of low-key releases. Jan Savage (guitar), Darryl Hooper (keyboards) and Rick Andridge (drums) completed his newest venture that had a US hit the following year with the compulsive 'Pushin' Too Hard'. Its raw, simple riff and Saxon's howling, half-spoken intonation established a pattern that remained almost unchanged throughout the group's career. The Seeds enjoyed minor chart success with 'Mr. Farmer' and 'Can't Seem To Make You Mine', while their first two albums, *The Seeds* and *A Web Of Sound*, were also well received. The latter featured the 14-minute 'Up In Her Room', in which Saxon's free-spirited improvisations were allowed to run riot. The quartet embraced 'flower-power' with *Future*. Flutes, tablas, cellos and tubas were added to the basic Seeds riffs while such titles as 'March Of The Flower Children' and 'Flower Lady And Her Assistant' left little doubt as to where Saxon's sympathies lay. This release was followed by a curious interlude wherein the group, now dubbed the Sky Saxon Blues Band, recorded *A Full Spoon Of Seedy Blues*. This erratic and rather unsatisfactory departure came replete with a testimonial from Muddy Waters, but it later transpired that the project was a failed ploy by the group to escape their recording contract. Their last official album, *Raw And Alive At Merlin's Music Box*, marked a return to form. Subsequent singles charted a collapsing unit and psyche, although Saxon later re-emerged as Sky Sunlight, fronting several aggregations known variously as Stars New Seeds or the Universal Stars Band. Jan Savage, meanwhile, joined the Los Angeles Police Department.

● ALBUMS: *The Seeds* (Crescendo 1966) ★★★, *A Web Of Sound* (Crescendo 1966) ★★★, *Future* (Crescendo 1967) ★★, *A Full Spoon Of Seedy Blues* (Crescendo 1967) ★★, *Raw And Alive At Merlin's Music Box* (Crescendo 1967) ★★★.

● COMPILATIONS: *Fallin' Off The Edge* (GNP 1977) ★★★, *Evil Hoodoo* (Bam Caruso 1988) ★★★, *A Faded Picture* (Diablo 1991) ★★★, *Flower Punk* 3-CD set (Demon 1996) ★★★, *Raw & Alive & Rare Seeds* (Diablo 2001) ★★★.

SEEKERS

Founded in Australia in 1963, the original Seekers comprised Athol Guy (b. 5 January 1940, Victoria, Australia; vocals, double bass)

Keith Potger (b. 2 March 1941, Columbo, Sri Lanka; vocals, guitar), Bruce Woodley (b. 25 July 1942, Melbourne, Australia; vocals, guitar) and Ken Ray (lead vocals, guitar). After a year with the above line-up, Athol Guy recruited Judith Durham (b. 3 July 1943, Melbourne, Australia) as the new lead singer and it was this formation that won international success. Following a visit to London in 1964, the group were signed to the Grade Agency and secured a prestigious guest spot on the televised *Sunday Night At The London Palladium*. Tom Springfield, of the recently defunct Springfields, soon realized that the Seekers could fill the gap left by his former group and offered his services as songwriter/producer. Although 1965 was one of the most competitive years in pop, the Seekers strongly challenged the Beatles and the Rolling Stones as the top chart act of the year. A trilogy of folk/pop smashes, 'I'll Never Find Another You', 'A World Of Our Own' and 'The Carnival Is Over', widened their appeal, leading to lucrative supper-club dates and frequent television appearances. Aside from Tom Springfield's compositions, such as 'Walk With Me', they also scored a massive chart hit with Malvina Reynolds' 'Morningtown Ride' and gave Paul Simon his first UK success with a bouncy adaptation of 'Someday One Day'. Meanwhile, Bruce Woodley teamed up with Simon to write some songs, including the Cyrkle hit 'Red Rubber Ball'. In early 1967, the breezy 'Georgy Girl' (written by Tom Springfield and Jim Dale) was a transatlantic Top 10 hit but thereafter, apart from 'When Will The Good Apples Fall' and 'Emerald City', the group were no longer chart regulars. Two years later they bowed out in a televised farewell performance, and went their separate ways. Keith Potger oversaw the formation of the New Seekers before moving into record production; Bruce Woodley became a highly successful writer of television jingles; Athol Guy spent several years as a Liberal representative in the Victoria parliament; and Judith Durham pursued a solo singing career. She had a minor UK hit in 1967 with 'Olive Tree', and her 1973 album, *Here I Am*, contained songs by Rod McKuen, Nilsson and Elton John, as well as some folksy and jazz material.

In 1975, the Seekers briefly re-formed with teenage Dutch singer Louisa Wisseling replacing Judith Durham. They enjoyed one moment of chart glory when 'The Sparrow Song' topped the Australian charts. In 1990 Judith Durham was involved in a serious car crash and spent six months recovering. The experience is said to have inspired her to reunite the original Seekers, and they played a series of 100 dates across Australia and New Zealand, before appearing in several 1994 Silver Jubilee Reunion Concerts in the UK at venues that included London's Royal Albert Hall and Wembley Arena. The quartet has continued to tour throughout the world and also recorded

their first studio album for 30 years, *Future Road*.
● ALBUMS: *Introducing The Seekers* aka *The Seekers* (W&G/Decca 1963) ★★★, *The Seekers* aka *Roving With The Seekers* (W&G 1964) ★★★, *Hide & Seekers* aka *The Four And Only Seekers* (WRC 1965) ★★★, *A World Of Our Own* (EMI 1965) ★★★, *Come The Day* aka *Georgy Girl* (EMI/Capitol 1966) ★★★, *Seen In Green* (EMI/Capitol 1967) ★★★, *Live At The Talk Of The Town* (EMI 1968) ★★, *Future Road* (EMI 2000) ★★.
● COMPILATIONS: *The Best Of The Seekers* (EMI 1968) ★★★, *Golden Collection* aka *The Seekers Sing* (Philips 1969) ★★★, *A World Of Their Own* (EMI 1969) ★★★, *The Seekers Greatest Hits* (EMI 1988) ★★★, *A Carnival Of Hits* (EMI 1994) ★★★.
● FURTHER READING: *Colours Of My Life*, Judith Durham.

SHADES OF BLUE

From Detroit, Michigan, USA, Shades Of Blue are known for just one hit, 'Oh How Happy', which, with its singalong simplicity and good cheer, raced up the chart in 1966, reaching number 12. The members of the group were Nick Marinelli, Linda Allan, Bob Kerr and Ernie Dernai. They were discovered and produced by soul singer Edwin Starr, who was looking for a white group to record 'Oh How Happy', a song he had written years earlier. After the group were turned down by another Detroit company, Starr took them to Harry Balk's small Impact operation, and with 'Oh How Happy', Impact achieved its only national hit. The group could not give Balk another big record, as their two subsequent records in 1966 – 'Lonely Summer' and 'Happiness' – stalled on the lower reaches of the charts.
● ALBUMS: *Happiness Is The Shades of Blue* (Impact 1966) ★★.

SHADOWS

Always to be remembered as the UK's premier instrumental group, the Shadows evolved from the Five Chesternuts to become Cliff Richard's backing group, the Drifters. By late 1958 the line-up had settled and under their new name the Shadows, the group comprised: Hank B. Marvin (b. Brian Robson Rankin, 28 October 1941, Newcastle-upon-Tyne, England; lead guitar), Bruce Welch (b. 2 November 1941, Bognor Regis, Sussex, England; rhythm guitar), Jet Harris (b. Terence Hawkins, 6 July 1939, London, England; bass) and Tony Meehan (b. Daniel Meehan, 2 March 1943, London, England; drums). Soon after backing Cliff Richard on his first single, they were signed as a group by EMI Records' A&R manager Norrie Paramor. After two singles under their old name, the Drifters, they issued the vocal 'Saturday Dance', which failed to sell. An abrupt change of fortune came in 1960 when they met singer/songwriter Jerry Lordan, who presented them with 'Apache'. Their instrumental was one of the finest of its era and dominated the UK number 1 position for six weeks, as well as being voted single of the year in several music papers. It was duly noted that they had knocked their singer's 'Please Don't Tease' off the top of the charts and, in doing so, firmly established themselves as important artists in their own right.

The Shadows' influence on the new generation of groups that followed was immense. Marvin was revered as a guitarist, and although the group was firmly part of the British showbusiness establishment, their musical credibility was beyond question. A wealth of evocative instrumentals followed, including 'FBI', 'The Frightened City', 'The Savage' and 'Guitar Tango'. These Top 10 singles were interspersed with four formidable UK number 1 hits: 'Kon-Tiki', 'Wonderful Land', 'Dance On' and 'Foot Tapper'. Despite such successes, the group underwent personnel shifts. Both Tony Meehan and Jet Harris left the group to be replaced by drummer Brian Bennett (b. 9 February 1940, London, England). Ironically, the Shadows soon found themselves competing against the combined forces of Jet Harris And Tony Meehan, who recorded some startling instrumentals in their own right, including the chart-topping 'Diamonds'. Bass player Brian Locking quit to commit himself to his Jehovah's Witness faith, and was replaced by ex-Interns bass player John Rostill (b. 16 June 1942, Birmingham, West Midlands, England, d. 26 November 1973).

The Shadows continued to chart consistently during 1963/4 with 'Atlantis', 'Shindig', 'Geronimo', 'Theme For Young Lovers' and 'The Rise And Fall Of Flingel Bunt', but it was clear that the Mersey beat boom had lessened their appeal. Throughout this period, they continued to appear in films with Cliff Richard and undertook acting and musical roles in *Aladdin And His Wonderful Lamp* at the London Palladium, which spawned the hit 'Genie With The Light Brown Lamp'. An attempted change of direction was notable in 1965 with the minor vocal hits, 'The Next Time I See Mary Ann' and 'Don't Make My Baby Blue'. Further movie and pantomime appearances followed, amid a decline in chart fortunes. At the end of 1968, the group announced that they intended to split up. In late 1969, a streamlined Shadows featuring Marvin, Rostill, Bennett and pianist Alan Hawkshaw toured Japan. Marvin then pursued some solo activities before reuniting with Welch for the Crosby, Stills And Nash-influenced Marvin, Welch And Farrar. The early 70s coincided with numerous personal dramas. Marvin became a Jehovah's Witness, Welch had a tempestuous relationship with singer Olivia Newton-John and Rostill was fatally electrocuted while playing his guitar. In 1974, the Shadows

reconvened for *Rockin' With Curly Leads*, on which they were joined by bass player/producer Alan Tarney. Several live performances followed before the group was offered the opportunity to represent the United Kingdom in the Eurovision Song Contest. They achieved second place with 'Let Me Be The One', which also provided them with their first UK Top 20 hit in 10 years. The stupendous success of an accompanying *20 Golden Greats* compilation effectively revitalized their career. By 1978, they were back in the UK Top 10 for the first time since 1965 with an instrumental reading of 'Don't Cry For Me Argentina'. That feat was repeated several months later with 'Theme From The Deer Hunter (Cavatina)'. Regular tours and compilations followed and in 1983, the group received an Ivor Novello Award from the British Academy of Songwriters, Composers and Authors to celebrate their 25th anniversary. Long regarded as one of the great institutions of UK pop music, the Shadows have survived a generation of musical and cultural changes in fashion yet continue to please audiences with their instrumental abilities. It is, however, for their massive influence of five decades over budding young guitarists, ready to afford a Fender Stratocaster, that they will be remembered. No UK 'beat combo' has ever been or is ever likely to be more commercially successful.

● ALBUMS: *The Shadows* (Columbia 1961) ★★★★, *Out Of The Shadows* (Columbia 1962) ★★★★, *Dance With The Shadows* (Columbia 1964) ★★★★, *The Sound Of The Shadows* (Columbia 1965) ★★★★, *Shadow Music* (Columbia 1966) ★★★, *Jigsaw* (Columbia 1967) ★★★, *From Hank, Bruce, Brian And John* (Columbia 1967) ★★★, with Cliff Richard *Established 1958* (Columbia 1968) ★★★, *Shades Of Rock* (Columbia 1970) ★★★, *Rockin' With Curly Leads* (EMI 1973) ★★★, *Specs Appeal* (EMI 1975) ★★★, *Live At The Paris Olympia* (EMI 1975) ★★, *Tasty* (EMI 1977) ★★★, with Cliff Richard *Thank You Very Much* (EMI 1979) ★★★, *Change Of Address* (Polydor 1980) ★★, *Hits Right Up Your Street* (Polydor 1981) ★★, *Life In The Jungle/Live At Abbey Road* (Polydor 1982) ★★, *XXV* (Polydor 1983) ★★★, *Guardian Angel* (Polydor 1984) ★★, *Moonlight Shadows* (Polydor 1986) ★★★, *Simply Shadows* (Polydor 1987) ★★★, *Steppin' To The Shadows* (Roll Over Records 1989) ★★★, *Reflections* (Polydor 1991) ★★★.

● COMPILATIONS: *The Shadows' Greatest Hits* (Columbia 1963) ★★★★, *More Hits!* (Columbia 1965) ★★★★, *Somethin' Else* (Regal Starline 1969) ★★★, *20 Golden Greats* (EMI 1977) ★★★★, *The Shadows At The Movies* (MFP 1978) ★★★, *String Of Hits* (EMI 1979) ★★★★, *Rock On With The Shadows* (MFP 1980) ★★, *Another String Of Hot Hits* (EMI 1980) ★★★, *The Shadows 6-LP box set* (WRC 1981) ★★★★, *The Shadows Live!* (MFP 1981) ★★★, *The Shadows' Silver*

Album (Tellydisc 1983) ★★★, *The Shadows'
Vocals* (EMI 1984) ★★★, *At Their Very Best*
(Polydor 1989) ★★★★, *Themes And Dreams*
(Roll Over Records 1991) ★★★, *The Early Years
1959-1966* 6-CD box set (EMI 1991) ★★★★, *The
Best Of Hank Marvin And The Shadows* (Polydor
1994) ★★★, *The First 20 Years At The Top* (EMI
1995) ★★★★, *Hank Marvin And The Shadows
Play The Music Of Andrew Lloyd Webber And Tim
Rice* (Polydor 1997) ★★★, *The Very Best Of Hank
Marvin & The Shadows: The First 40 Years*
(Polydor 1998) ★★★★, *50 Golden Greats* (EMI
2000) ★★★, *The Shadows Collection* (HMV Easy
2001) ★★★.
● FURTHER READING: *The Shadows By
Themselves*, Shadows. *Foot Tapping: The Shadows
1958-1978*, George Thomson Geddes. *The
Shadows: A History And Discography*, George
Thomson Geddes. *The Story Of The Shadows: An
Autobiography*, Shadows as told to Mike Reed.
*Rock 'N' Roll: I Gave You The Best Years Of My Life:
A Life In The Shadows*, Bruce Welch. *Funny Old
World: The Life And Times Of John Henry Rostill*,
Rob Bradford. *A Guide To The Shadows And Hank
Marvin On CD*, Malcolm Campbell. *The Shadows
At EMI: The Vinyl Legacy*, Malcolm Campbell.
● FILMS: *Carnival Rock* (1957), *Expresso Bongo*
(1960), *Finders Keepers* (1966).

SHADOWS OF KNIGHT
Formed in Chicago in 1965, the original line-up
comprised Jim Sohns (vocals), Warren Rogers
(lead guitar), Jerry McGeorge (rhythm guitar),
Norm Gotsch (bass) and Tom Schiffour (drums).
As the house band at the city's Cellar club, the
Shadows were already highly popular when they
secured a recording contract. Their debut single,
a cover version of the classic Them track,
'Gloria', written by a youthful Van Morrison, was
the climax to the quintet's stage act, but when
the group toned down its mildly risqué lyric,
they were rewarded with a US Top 10 hit. By this
point Gotsch had been replaced by Joe Kelly,
with Rogers switching to bass to accommodate
the changing instrument role of Kelly. Their
best-known line-up now established, the
Shadows Of Knight enjoyed another minor chart
entry with 'Oh Yeah', before completing their
debut album. *Gloria* consisted of several Chicago
R&B standards which, paradoxically, were
patterned on UK interpretations of the same
material. Two excellent group originals, 'Light
Bulb Blues' and 'It Happens That Way', revealed
an emergent, but sadly under used, talent.
Back Door Men offered a slightly wider
perspective with versions of 'Hey Joe' and
'Tomorrow's Gonna Be Just Another Day' (also
recorded by the Monkees), but the highlight was
an inspired interpretation of 'Bad Little Woman',
originally recorded by Irish group the Wheels.
Dave 'The Hawk' Wolinski replaced Warren
Rogers when the latter was drafted in late 1966.
This was the prelude to wholesale changes
when, on 4 July 1967, Sohns fired the entire

group. The singer subsequently reappeared
fronting a new line-up – John Fisher, Dan
Baughman, Woody Woodfuff and Kenny Turkin –
and a new recording deal with the bubblegum
Super K label. 'Shake' gave the group a final US
Top 50 entry, but its unashamed pop approach
owed little to the heritage of the 'old'. Further
releases for the same outlet proved equally
disappointing, while an attempt at recreating
the past with 'Gloria 69' was unsuccessful. Sohns
has led several versions of his group over the
ensuing years, McGeorge found fleeting
notoriety as a member of H.P. Lovecraft, while
Wolinski found fame as a member of Rufus and
his work with Michael Jackson.
● ALBUMS: *Gloria* (Dunwich 1966) ★★★, *Back
Door Men* (Dunwich 1967) ★★★, *The Shadows Of
Knight* (Super-K 1969) ★★★.
● COMPILATIONS: *Gee-El-O-Are-I-Ay (Gloria)*
(Radar 1979) ★★★, *Raw And Alive At The Cellar:
1966* (1992) ★★, *Dark Sides: The Best Of The
Shadows Of The Knight* (Rhino 1994) ★★★.

SHANGRI-LAS
Late entrants in the early 60s school of 'girl
groups', the Shangri-Las comprised two pairs of
sisters, Mary-Ann and Margie Ganser (d. August
1996) and Betty and Mary Weiss. During 1963
they were discovered by Shadow Morton and
recorded two singles under the name Bon Bons
before signing to the newly formed Red Bird
Records label. Relaunched as the Shangri-Las,
they secured a worldwide hit with 'Remember
(Walkin' In The Sand)', a delightful arrangement
complete with the sound of crashing waves and
crying seagulls. It was the sound-effect of a
revving motorbike engine which opened their
distinctive follow-up, 'Leader Of The Pack',
which was even more successful and a prime
candidate for the 'death disc' genre with its
narrative of teenage love cut short because of a
motorcycle accident. By 1966, Margie Ganser
had left the group, although this had little effect
on their popularity or output. They had already
found a perfect niche, specializing in the
doomed romanticism of American teenage life
and unfolding a landscape filled with
misunderstood adolescents, rebel boyfriends,
disapproving parents, the foreboding threat of
pregnancy and, inevitably, tragic death. This hit
formula occasionally wore thin but Shadow
Morton could always be relied upon to engineer
a gripping production. During their closing hit
phase in 1966/7, the group recorded two songs,
'I Can Never Go Home Anymore' and 'Past
Present And Future', which saw the old teenage
angst transmogrified into an almost tragic,
sexual neuroticism. The enduring commercial
quality of their best work was underlined by
consistent repackaging and the successive chart
reappearances of the biker anthem, 'Leader Of
The Pack'.
● ALBUMS: *Leader Of The Pack* (Red Bird 1965)
★★★, *'65* (Red Bird 1965) ★★★.

● COMPILATIONS: *Golden Hits* (Mercury 1966) ★★★, *The Best Of the Shangri-La's* (Bac-Trac 1985) ★★★, *16 Greatest Hits* (1993) ★★★, *Myrmidons Of Melodrama* (RPM 1995) ★★★, *The Best Of* (Mercury 1996) ★★★.
● FURTHER READING: *Girl Groups: The Story Of A Sound*, Alan Betrock.

SHANNON, DEL

b. Charles Westover, 30 December 1934, Coopersville, Michigan, USA, d. 8 February 1990, Santa Clarita, California, USA. From the plethora of clean, American, post doo-wop male vocalists to find enormous success in the early 60s, only a small handful retained musical credibility. Shannon was undoubtedly from this pedigree. More than 30 years after his chart debut, Shannon's work is still regularly played. His early musical interests took him under the country influence of the legendary Hank Williams. Shannon's first record release, however, was pure gutsy pop; the infectious melody was written by accident while rehearsing in the local Hi-Lo club with keyboard player Max Crook (Maximillian). The song was 'Runaway', a spectacular debut that reached the top of the charts in the USA and UK, and was subsequently recorded by dozens of admiring artists. The single, with its shrill sounding Musitron (an instrument created by Crook) together with Shannon's falsetto, was irresistible. Johnny Bienstock, who was running Big Top Records in New York, received a telephone order following a Miami radio station's playing of the track. The order was for an unprecedented 39,000 copies. At that stage Bienstock knew he had unleashed a major star. What is not generally known is that Shannon sang flat on all the recordings of the song. Bienstock and a colleague went into the studio overnight, and sped up and redubbed the master tape so that Shannon's voice was at the correct pitch. The record was released a full 10 seconds shorter, and nobody else, including Shannon, ever noticed.

He succeeded, however, where others failed, due to his talent as a composer and his apparent maturity, appealing to the public with a clear youthful strident voice. This paradox was cleared up many years later, when it was discovered that he was five years older than stated. Had this come out in 1961, it is debatable whether he would have competed successfully alongside his fresh-faced contemporaries. His teenage tales of loneliness, despair, broken hearts, failed relationships, infidelity and ultimate doom, found a receptive audience; Shannon rarely used the word 'love' in his lyrics. Even the plaintive, almost happy, 1962 hit 'Swiss Maid' combined his trademark falsetto with yodelling, ending with the heroine dying, forlorn and unhappy. Over the next three years Shannon continued to produce and write his own material with great success, especially in

Britain, where his run of 10 consecutive hits ended with 'Sue's Gotta Be Mine' in October 1963. In the interim, he had produced several memorable Top 10 successes, including the bitingly acerbic 'Hats Off To Larry' and 'Little Town Flirt', which betrayed an almost misogynistic contempt. The reworked themes of his songs were now beginning to pale, and together with the growth of Merseybeat, Shannon's former regular appearances in the charts became sporadic, even although he was the first American artist to record a Beatles song, 'From Me To You'.

Shannon worked steadily for the next 25 years, enjoying a few more hit singles including a cover version of Bobby Freeman's 'Do You Wanna Dance', followed by 'Handy Man', formerly a hit for Jimmy Jones, from whom he 'borrowed' his famous falsetto. In 1965 'Keep Searchin'' was Shannon's last major success. The song had an elegiac feel, recalling an era of innocence already passed. Throughout the 60s and 70s Shannon was a regular visitor to Britain where he found a smaller but more appreciative audience. He acquired many professional admirers over the years including Jeff Lynne, Tom Petty and Dave Edmunds, who variously helped him rise above his sad decline into a nether world of alcohol and pills. The 1981 Petty-produced *Drop Down And Get Me* was critically well-received but sold poorly. Ironically, he received a belated hit in America with 'Sea Of Love', which found favour in 1982. This led to a brief renaissance for him in the USA, with a minor country hit ('In My Arms Again') in 1985 for Warner Brothers Records. In 1987 he recorded an unreleased album with Petty, who recruited Lynne and George Harrison to sing backing vocals on the Australian single 'Walk Away'. Although Shannon was financially secure through wise property investment, he still performed regularly. Ultimately, however, he was branded to rock 'n' roll revival tours that finally took their toll on 8 February 1990, when a severely depressed Shannon pointed a .22 calibre rifle to his head and pulled the trigger, ending the misery echoed in his catalogue of hits. *Rock On!* collects the material Shannon had been recording prior to his death.
● ALBUMS: *Runaway* (Big Top/London 1961) ★★★★, *Hats Off To Del Shannon* (London 1963) ★★★★, *Little Town Flirt* (Big Top 1963) ★★★★, *Handy Man* (Amy 1964) ★★★★, *Del Shannon Sings Hank Williams* (Amy 1965) ★★, *One Thousand Six Hundred Sixty Seconds With Del Shannon* (Amy 1965) ★★★, *This Is My Bag* (Liberty 1966) ★★, *Total Commitment* (Liberty 1966) ★★, *The Further Adventures Of Charles Westover* (Liberty 1968) ★★★, *Del Shannon Live In England* (United Artists 1973) ★★, *Drop Down And Get Me* (Network 1981) ★★★, *Rock On!* (Silvertone 1991) ★★.
● COMPILATIONS: *The Best Of Del Shannon*

(Dot 1967) ★★★★, *The Vintage Years* (Sire 1975) ★★★★, *The Del Shannon Collection* (Line 1987) ★★★★, *Runaway Hits* (Edsel 1990) ★★★★, *I Go To Pieces* (Edsel 1990) ★★★★, *Looking Back, His Biggest Hits* (Connoisseur 1991) ★★★★, *Greatest Hits* (Charly 1993) ★★★★, *A Complete Career Anthology 1961-1990* (Raven 1998) ★★★★, *The Definitive Collection* (Recall 1998) ★★★★, *The EP Collection* (See For Miles 1998) ★★★, *The Best Of Del Shannon* (Repertoire 1999) ★★★, *Definitive Collection* (Recall 2000) ★★★, *25 All Time Greatest Hits* (Varèse Sarabande 2001) ★★★★.
● FILMS: *It's Trad, Dad* aka *Ring-A-Ding Rhythm* (1962).

SHAPIRO, HELEN

b. 28 September 1946, Bethnal Green, London, England. Helen Shapiro drew considerable attention when, as a 14-year-old schoolgirl, she scored a UK Top 3 hit with 'Don't Treat Me Like A Child'. A deep intonation belied her youth, and by the end of 1961 the singer had scored two chart-topping singles with 'You Don't Know' and 'Walkin' Back To Happiness'. This success was maintained the following year with 'Tell Me What He Said' (number 2) and 'Little Miss Lonely' (number 8), as Shapiro won concurrent polls as Best British Female Singer and was voted Best Newcomer by the Variety Club of Great Britain. However, having recorded the original version of 'It's My Party' during an artistically fruitful session in Nashville, Helen was disappointed when an acetate reached Lesley Gore, who enjoyed a massive international hit using a similar arrangement. Shapiro's producer, Norrie Paramor, also vetoed the opportunity to record 'Misery', composed with Shapiro in mind by John Lennon and Paul McCartney. Indeed the advent of the Beatles helped to undermine the singer's career.

Despite being younger than many beat group members, Shapiro was perceived as belonging to a now outmoded era and despite a series of excellent singles, was eclipsed by 'newcomers' Cilla Black and Dusty Springfield. The late 60s proved more fallow still and, barring one pseudonymous release, Shapiro did not record at all between 1970 and 1975. A Russ Ballard song, 'Can't Break The Habit', became a minor hit in Europe during 1977 and in turn engendered *All For The Love Of The Music*, a set sadly denied a UK release. Six years later Shapiro resurfaced on writer Charlie Gillett's Oval label. *Straighten Up And Fly Right* showed the singer had lost none of her early power and this excellent collection of standards was rightly acclaimed. An equally confident collaboration with jazz musician Humphrey Lyttelton ensued, since which Helen Shapiro has maintained a high profile through radio, television and live appearances, singing jazz-influenced big-band material and gospel songs. She also made an impressive London cabaret debut at the Café Royal in 1995.

● ALBUMS: *Tops With Me* (Columbia 1962) ★★★★, *Helen's Sixteen* (Columbia 1963) ★★★★, *Helen In Nashville* (Columbia 1963) ★★, *Helen Hits Out* (Columbia 1964) ★★★, *All For The Love Of The Music* (1977) ★★★, *Straighten Up And Fly Right* (Oval 1983) ★★★, *Echoes Of The Duke* (1985) ★★★, *The Quality Of Mercer* (Calligraph 1987) ★★★★, *Nothing But The Best* (1995) ★★★, *Sing, Swing Together* (Calligraph 1999) ★★★.
● COMPILATIONS: *Hits And A Miss Helen Shapiro* (Encore 1965) ★★★, *Twelve Hits And A Miss Shapiro* (Encore 1967) ★★★, *The Very Best Of Helen Shapiro* (Columbia 1974) ★★★★, *The 25th Anniversary Album* (MFP 1986) ★★★★, *The EP Collection* (See For Miles 1989) ★★★★, *Sensational! The Uncollected Helen Shapiro* (RPM 1995) ★★★★, *Original Hits* (Musicrama 1997) ★★★, *Abbey Road 1961-1967* (EMI 1998) ★★★★.
● FURTHER READING: *Walking Back To Happiness*, Helen Shapiro. *Helen Shapiro: Pop Princess*, John S. Janson.
● FILMS: *It's Trad, Dad* aka *Ring-A-Ding Rhythm* (1962).

SHAW, SANDIE

b. Sandra Goodrich, 26 February 1947, Dagenham, Essex, England. Discovered by singer Adam Faith, Shaw was taken under the imperious wing of his manager Eve Taylor and launched as a teenage pop star in 1964. Her first single, 'As Long As You're Happy', proved unsuccessful but the follow-up, an excellent reading of Burt Bacharach and Hal David's '(There's) Always Something There To Remind Me' reached number 1 in the UK. A striking performer, known for her imposing height, model looks and bare feet, Shaw's star shone for the next three years with a series of hits, mainly composed by her songwriter/producer Chris Andrews. His style, specializing in abrupt, jerky, oom-pah rhythms and plaintive ballads, served Sandie well, especially on the calypso-inspired 'Long Live Love', which provided her second UK number 1 in 1965. By the following year, Shaw's chart placings were slipping and Taylor was keen to influence her towards cabaret. Chosen to represent Britain in the 1967 Eurovision Song Contest, Shaw emerged triumphant with the Bill Martin/Phil Coulter-composed 'Puppet On A String', which gave her a third UK number 1. After one further Martin/Coulter hit, 'Tonight In Tokyo', she returned to Andrews with only limited success.

By 1969 she was back on the novelty trail with Peter Callender's translation of the French 'Monsieur Dupont'. Attempts to launch Shaw as a family entertainer were hampered by salacious newspaper reports and during the 70s, troubled by a failed marriage to fashion entrepreneur Jeff Banks, she effectively retired. In the early 80s she was rediscovered by Heaven 17 offshoots BEF, and recorded a middling version of 'Anyone Who Had A Heart', previously a number 1 for her old rival Cilla Black. The Shaw resurgence was completed when she was heavily promoted by Smiths vocalist Morrissey, one of whose compositions, 'Heaven Knows I'm Miserable Now' was clearly inspired by the title of Shaw's failed 60s single, 'Heaven Knows I'm Missing You Now'. With instrumental backing from the Smiths, Shaw enjoyed a brief chart comeback with 'Hand In Glove' in 1984. In 1986, she reached the lower regions of the UK chart with a cover of Lloyd Cole's 'Are You Ready To Be Heartbroken?' Her comeback album, on Rough Trade Records, featured songs by Morrissey, the Smiths and the Jesus And Mary Chain. In 1996, Shaw withdrew from performing and recording to set up the Arts Clinic. This specialist counselling service, run by Shaw under her married name of Powell, uses her experience in the music business to help artists combat problems of stress, drug dependency and eating disorders.

● ALBUMS: *Sandie Shaw* (Pye 1965) ★★★, *Me* (Pye 1965) ★★★, *Puppet On A String* (Pye 1967) ★★, *Love Me, Please Love Me* (Pye 1967) ★★, *The Sandie Shaw Supplement* (Pye 1968) ★★, *Reviewing The Situation* (Pye 1969) ★★, *Hello Angel* (Rough Trade 1988) ★★.

● COMPILATIONS: *Golden Hits Of Sandie Shaw* (Golden Guinea 1965) ★★★★, *Sandie Sings* (Golden Guinea 1967) ★★★★, *The Golden Hits Of Sandie Shaw* (Marble Arch 1968) ★★★★, *A Golden Hour Of Sandie Shaw – Greatest Hits* (Golden Hour 1974) ★★★★, *20 Golden Pieces* (Bulldog 1986) ★★★, *The Sandie Shaw Golden CD Collection* (K-Tel 1989) ★★★, *The EP Collection* (See For Miles 1991) ★★★★, *Nothing Less Than Brilliant: The Best Of Sandie Shaw* (Virgin 1994) ★★★★, *Cover To Cover* (Emporio 1995) ★★★, *Cool About You – The BBC Sessions 1984/88* (RPM 1998) ★★★, *Princess Of Britpop* (Sequel 1998) ★★★, *The Pye Anthology 64/67* (Sequel 2000) ★★★★.

● VIDEOS: *Live In London* (Channel 5 1989).

● FURTHER READING: *The World At My Feet*, Sandie Shaw.

SHERIDAN, TONY

b. Anthony Sheridan McGinnity, 21 May 1940, Norwich, Norfolk, England. Sheridan formed his first band, the Saints, in 1955, before moving to London. There he joined Vince Taylor And The Playboys in early 1959, with whom he played a residency in Hamburg, Germany. A popular attraction at clubs such as the Kaiserkeller with the Jets, that group soon evolved into the Beat Brothers with a line-up of Sheridan (vocals/guitar), Ken Packwood (guitar), Rick Richards (guitar), Colin Melander (bass), Ian Hines (keyboards) and Jimmy Doyle (drums), although their various formations changed almost constantly. Some of the more interesting personnel to pass through the Beat Brothers in these nebulous days at the Kaiserkeller were John Lennon, Paul McCartney, George Harrison, Stuart Sutcliffe and Pete Best. This line-up undertook a recording session in 1961 with producer Bert Kaempfert at the controls, recording 'My Bonnie' and 'The Saints' among other songs. By the following year, the Beat Brothers had been joined by Ringo Starr, Roy Young (keyboards) and Rikky Barnes (saxophone).

Sheridan's first appearance at the infamous Star Club arrived on 12 May 1962, fronting the Tony Sheridan Quartet, who were later retitled the Star Combo. By 1964 he had teamed up with Glaswegian expatriates Bobb Patrick Big Six. However, with the Hamburg beat boom all but over by 1964, Sheridan travelled to Vietnam to play US army bases, accompanied by Volker Tonndorf (bass), Jimmy Doyle (drums) and vocalist Barbara Evers. He eventually returned to Hamburg to turn solo in 1968, where his cult status endured into the following decades. Sheridan then converted to the Sannyasin religion and renamed himself Swami Probhu Sharan, living with his family in Ottersberg near Bremen, Germany.

● ALBUMS: *My Bonnie* (Polydor 1962) ★★, *The Beatles' First Featuring Tony Sheridan* (Polydor 1964) ★★, *Just A Little Bit Of Tony Sheridan* (Polydor 1964) ★★, *The Best Of Tony Sheridan* (Polydor 1964) ★★, *Meet The Beat* (Polydor 1965) ★★, *Rocks On* (Metronome 1974) ★★, *Worlds Apart* (Antagon 1978) ★★.

● FURTHER READING: *Hamburg: The Cradle Of British Rock*, Alan Clayson.

SHIRELLES

Formed in Passaic, New Jersey, USA, the Shirelles are arguably the archetypal 'girl-group'; Shirley Owens (b. 10 June 1941), Beverly Lee (b. 3 August 1941), Doris Kenner (b. Doris Coley, 2 August 1941, North Carolina, USA, d. 5 February 2000, Sacramento, California, USA) and Addie 'Micki' Harris (b. 22 January 1940, d. 10 June 1982) were initially known as the uncomfortably named Poquellos. School friends for whom singing was simply a pastime, the quartet embarked on a professional career when a classmate, Mary Jane Greenberg, recommended them to her mother. Florence Greenberg, an aspiring entrepreneur, signed them to her Tiara label, on which the resultant single, 'I Met Him On A Sunday', was a minor hit. This inspired the inauguration of a second outlet, Scepter Records, where the Shirelles secured pop immortality with 'Will You Love Me Tomorrow'. Here, Alston's tender, aching vocal not only posed the crucial question, but implied that she already had decided 'yes' to her personal dilemma. One of pop's most treasured recordings, it was followed by a series of exceptional singles, 'Mama Said' (1961), 'Baby It's You' (1962) and 'Foolish Little Girl' (1963), which confirmed their exemplary position.

The Shirelles' influence on other groups, including those in Britain, is incalculable, and the Beatles, the Merseybeats and Manfred Mann are among those who covered their work. The quartet's progress was dealt a crucial setback when producer and arranger Luther Dixon left to take up another post. Newer Scepter acts, including Dionne Warwick, assumed the quartet's one-time prime position, while a punitive record contract kept the group tied to the label. By the time the Shirelles were free to move elsewhere, it was too late to enjoy a contemporary career and the group was confined to the 'oldies' circuit. Alston left for a solo career in 1975. Harris died of a heart attack in June 1982 following a performance in Atlanta. By combining sweetening strings with elements of church music and R&B, the Shirelles exerted an unconscious pivotal influence on all female vocal groups. They were inducted into the Rock And Roll Hall Of Fame in 1996.

● ALBUMS: *Tonight's The Night* (Scepter 1961) ★★★, *The Shirelles Sing To Trumpets And Strings* (Scepter/Top Rank 1961) ★★★, *Baby It's You* (Scepter/Stateside 1962) ★★★★, *Twist Party* (Scepter 1962) ★★★, *Foolish Little Girl* (Scepter 1963) ★★★, *It's A Mad Mad Mad Mad World* (Scepter 1963) ★★, *The Shirelles Sing The Golden Oldies* (Scepter 1964) ★, with King Curtis *Eternally Soul* (Wand 1970) ★★★, *Tonight's The Night* (Wand 1971) ★★★, *Happy In Love* (RCA 1971) ★★, *The Shirelles* (RCA 1973) ★★, *Let's Give Each Other Love* (RCA 1976) ★★, *Spontaneous Combustion* (Scepter 1997) ★★.
Solo: Shirley Alston [Owens] *With A Little Help From My Friends* (Strawberry 1975) ★★, *Lady Rose* (Strawberry 1977) ★★.

● COMPILATIONS: *The Shirelles Hits* (Scepter/Stateside 1963) ★★★★, *The Shirelles Greatest Hits Volume 2* (Scepter 1967) ★★★, *Remember When Volume 1* (Wand 1972) ★★★, *Remember When Volume 2* (Wand 1972) ★★★, *Golden Hour Of The Shirelles* (Golden Hour 1973) ★★★, *Juke Box Giants* (Audio Fidelity 1981) ★★★, *The Shirelles Anthology (1959-1967)* (Rhino 1984) ★★★★, *Soulfully Yours* (Kent/Ace 1985) ★★★, *Sha La La* (Impact/Ace 1985) ★★★, *The Shirelles Anthology (1959-1964)* (Rhino 1986) ★★★★, *Lost And Found* (Impact/Ace 1987) ★★★, *Greatest Hits* (Impact/Ace 1987) ★★★★, *16 Greatest Hits* (Gusto 1988) ★★★★, *The Collection* (Castle 1990) ★★★★, *The Best Of* (Ace 1992) ★★★★, *Lost And Found: Rare And Unissued* (1994) ★★★, *The Very Best Of The Shirelles* (Rhino 1994) ★★★★, *The World's Greatest Girls Group* (Tomato/Rhino 1995) ★★★★, *The EP Collection* (See For Miles 1999) ★★★.

● FURTHER READING: *Girl Groups: The Story Of A Sound*, Alan Betrock.

SHUMAN, MORT

b. 12 November 1936, Brooklyn, New York City, New York, USA, d. 3 November 1991, London, England. After studying music, Shuman began writing songs with blues singer Doc Pomus in 1958. Early in 1959 two of their songs were Top

40 hits: 'Plain Jane' for Bobby Darin, and Fabian's 'I'm A Man'. During the next six years, their catalogue was estimated at over 500 songs, in a mixture of styles for a variety of artists. They included 'Surrender', 'Viva Las Vegas', 'Little Sister' and 'Kiss Me Quick' (Elvis Presley), 'Save The Last Dance For Me', 'Sweets For My Sweet' and 'This Magic Moment' (the Drifters), 'A Teenager In Love' (Dion And The Belmonts), 'Can't Get Used To Losing You' (Andy Williams), 'Suspicion' (Terry Stafford), 'Seven Day Weekend' (Gary 'U.S.' Bonds) and 'Spanish Lace' (Gene McDaniels). Around the time of the team's break-up in 1965, Shuman collaborated with several other writers. These included John McFarland for Billy J. Kramer's UK number 1, 'Little Children', Clive Westlake for 'Here I Go Again' (the Hollies), ex-pop star Kenny Lynch, for 'Sha La La La Lee' (Small Faces), 'Love's Just A Broken Heart' (Cilla Black), producer Jerry Ragovoy for 'Get It While You Can' and 'Look At Granny Run, Run' (Howard Tate).
Subsequently, Shuman moved to Paris, where he occasionally performed his own one-man show, and issued solo albums such as *My Death* and *Imagine ...*, as well as writing several songs for Johnny Halliday. In 1968 Shuman translated the lyrics of French composer Jacques Brel; these were recorded by many artists including Dusty Springfield, Scott Walker and Rod McKuen. Together with Eric Blau, he devised, adapted and wrote lyrics for the revue *Jacques Brel Is Alive And Well And Living In Paris*. Shuman also starred in the piece, which became a worldwide success. In October 1989, *Budgie*, a musical set in London's Soho district, with Shuman's music and Don Black's lyrics, opened in the West End. It starred former pop star, turned actor and entrepreneur, Adam Faith, and UK soap opera actress, Anita Dobson. The show closed after only three months, losing more than £1,000,000. Shuman wrote several other shows, including *Amadeo, Or How To Get Rid Of It*, based on an Ionesco play, a Hong Kong portrayal of *Madame Butterfly* and a reworking of Bertolt Brecht and Kurt Weill's opera *Aufstieg Und Fall Der Stadt Mahogonny*. None has yet reached the commercial theatre. After undergoing a liver operation in the spring of 1991, he died in London.

● ALBUMS: *My Death* (Reprise 1969) ★★★, *Amerika* (Philips 1972) ★★★, *Mort Shuman* (Philips 1973) ★★★, *Voila Comment* (Philips 1973) ★★★, *Imagine ...* (Philips 1976) ★★★, *My Name Is Mortimer* (Philips 1977) ★★★, *Distant Drum* (Atlantic 1991) ★★★, *Ses Plus Belles Chansons* (Polydor 1997) ★★★.

SIMON AND GARFUNKEL

This highly successful folk-rock duo first played together during their early years in New York. Paul Simon (b. Paul Frederic Simon, 13 October 1941, Newark, New Jersey, USA) and Art Garfunkel (b. Arthur Garfunkel, 5 November

1941, Queens, New York City, New York, USA) were initially inspired by the Everly Brothers and under the name Tom And Jerry enjoyed a US Top 50 hit in 1957 with the rock 'n' roll styled 'Hey, Schoolgirl'. They also completed an album which was later reissued after their rise to international prominence in the 60s. Garfunkel subsequently returned to college and Simon pursued a solo career before the duo reunited in 1964 for *Wednesday Morning, 3AM*. A strong, harmonic work, which included an acoustic reading of 'The Sound Of Silence', the album did not sell well enough to encourage the group to stay together. While Simon was in England the folk-rock boom was in the ascendant and producer Tom Wilson made the presumptuous but prescient decision to overdub 'The Sound Of Silence' with electric instrumentation. Within weeks, the song (retitled 'The Sounds Of Silence') was number 1 in the US charts, and Simon and Garfunkel were hastily reunited. An album titled after their million-selling single was rush-released early in 1966 and proved a commendable work. Among its major achievements was 'Homeward Bound', an evocative and moving portrayal of life on the road, which went on to become a transatlantic hit. The solipsistic 'I Am A Rock' was another international success with such angst-ridden lines as, 'I have no need of friendship, friendship causes pain'. In keeping with the social commentary that permeated their mid-60s' work, the group included two songs whose theme was suicide: 'A Most Peculiar Man' and 'Richard Cory'.

Embraced by a vast following, especially among the student population, the duo certainly looked the part with their college scarves, duffel coats and cerebral demeanour. Their next single, 'The Dangling Conversation', was their most ambitious lyric to date and far too esoteric for the Top 20. Nevertheless, the work testified to their artistic courage and boded well for the release of a second album within a year: *Parsley, Sage, Rosemary And Thyme*. The album took its title from a repeated line in 'Scarborough Fair', which was their excellent harmonic weaving of that traditional song and another, 'Canticle'. An accomplished work, the album had a varied mood from the grandly serious 'For Emily, Whenever I May Find Her' to the bouncy 'The 59th Street Bridge Song (Feelin' Groovy)' (subsequently a hit for Harpers Bizarre). After two strong but uncommercial singles, 'At The Zoo' and 'Fakin' It', the duo contributed to the soundtrack of the 1968 movie, *The Graduate*. The key song was 'Mrs. Robinson' which provided the duo with one of their biggest international sellers. That same year saw the release of *Bookends*, a superbly-crafted work, ranging from the serene 'Save The Life Of My Child' to the personal odyssey 'America' and the vivid imagery of 'Old Friends'. *Bookends* is still felt by many to be their finest work.

In 1969 the duo released 'The Boxer', a long, wordy track that nevertheless found commercial success on both sides of the Atlantic. This classic single reappeared on the duo's next album, the celebrated *Bridge Over Troubled Water*. One of the bestselling albums of all time (303 weeks on the UK chart), the work's title track became a standard with Garfunkel's angelic vocal set perfectly matched to the lush, orchestral arrangement and contrasting tempo. Heavily gospel-influenced, the album includes several well-covered songs such as 'Keep The Customer Satisfied', 'Cecilia' and 'El Condor Pasa'. While at the peak of their commercial success, with an album that dominated the top of the chart listings for months, the duo became irascible and their partnership abruptly ceased. The release of a *Greatest Hits* package in 1972 included four previously unissued live tracks and during the same year the duo performed together at a benefit concert for Senator George McGovern. A further reunion occurred on the hit single 'My Little Town' in 1975. Six years later they performed in front of half a million fans at New York's Central Park (the results were captured on *The Concert In Central Park*). Although another studio album was undertaken, the sessions broke down and Simon transferred the planned material to his 1983 solo *Hearts And Bones*. In the autumn of 1993 Paul Simon and Art Garfunkel settled their differences long enough to complete 21 sell-out dates in New York.

● ALBUMS: *Wednesday Morning, 3AM* (Columbia 1965) ★★, *The Sound Of Silence* (Columbia 1966) ★★★★, *Parsley, Sage, Rosemary And Thyme* (Columbia 1966) ★★★★, *The Graduate* film soundtrack (Columbia 1968) ★★, *Bookends* (Columbia 1968) ★★★★, *Bridge Over Troubled Water* (Columbia 1970) ★★★★, *The Concert In Central Park* (Warners 1982) ★★★.

● COMPILATIONS: *Simon And Garfunkel's Greatest Hits* (Columbia 1972) ★★★★, *The Simon And Garfunkel Collection* (Columbia 1981) ★★★★, *The Definitive Simon And Garfunkel* (Columbia 1992) ★★★★, *Old Friends* 4-CD box set (Columbia 1997) ★★★★, *The Very Best Of Simon & Garfunkel: Tales From New York* (Columbia 1999) ★★★★, *Two Can Dream Alone* (Burning Airlines 2000) ★★★, *The Columbia Studio Recordings 1964-1970* 5-CD box set (Columbia/Legacy 2001) ★★★★.

● FURTHER READING: *Simon & Garfunkel: A Biography In Words & Pictures*, Michael S. Cohen. *Paul Simon: Now And Then*, Spencer Leigh. *Paul Simon*, Dave Marsh. *Simon And Garfunkel*, Robert Matthew-Walker. *Bookends: The Simon And Garfunkel Story*, Patrick Humphries. *The Boy In The Bubble: A Biography Of Paul Simon*, Patrick Humphries. *Paul Simon*, Patrick Humphries. *Simon And Garfunkel: Old Friends*, Joseph Morella and Patricia Barey. *Simon And Garfunkel: The Definitive Biography*, Victoria Kingston.

SIMONE, NINA

b. Eunice Waymon, 21 February 1933, Tyron, North Carolina, USA. An accomplished pianist as a child, Simone later studied at New York's Juilliard School Of Music. Her jazz credentials were established in 1959 when she secured a hit with an emotive interpretation of George Gershwin's 'I Loves You Porgy'. Her influential 60s work included 'Gin House Blues', 'Forbidden Fruit' and 'I Put A Spell On You', while another of her singles, 'Don't Let Me Be Misunderstood', was later covered by the Animals. The singer's popular fortune flourished upon her signing with RCA Records. 'Ain't Got No – I Got Life', a song lifted from the musical *Hair*, was a UK number 2, while her searing version of the Bee Gees' 'To Love Somebody' reached number 5. In America, her own composition, 'To Be Young, Gifted And Black', dedicated to her late friend, the playwright Lorraine Hansberry, reflected Simone's growing militancy. Releases then grew infrequent as her political activism increased.

A commanding, if taciturn, live performer, Simone's appearances became increasingly focused on benefits and rallies, although a fluke UK hit, 'My Baby Just Cares For Me', a resurrected 50s master, pushed the singer, momentarily, into the commercial spotlight when it reached number 5 in 1987. Tired of an America she perceived as uncaring, Simone has settled in France where her work continues to flourish. An uncompromising personality, Nina Simone's interpretations of pop, soul, jazz, blues and standards are both compulsive and unique.

● ALBUMS: *Little Girl Blue* (Bethlehem 1959) ★★, *Nina Simone And Her Friends* expanded reissue of first album (Bethlehem 1959) ★★, *The Amazing Nina Simone* (Colpix 1959) ★★★★, *Nina Simone At The Town Hall* (Colpix 1959) ★★★, *Nina Simone At Newport* (Colpix 1960) ★★★★, *Forbidden Fruit* (Colpix 1961) ★★★, *Nina Simone At The Village Gate* (Colpix 1961) ★★★, *Nina Simone Sings Ellington* (Colpix 1962) ★★★, *Nina's Choice* (Colpix 1963) ★★★, *Nina Simone At Carnegie Hall* (Colpix 1963) ★★★★, *Folksy Nina* (Colpix 1964) ★★★, *Nina Simone In Concert* (Philips 1964) ★★★, *Broadway ... Blues ... Ballads* (Philips 1964) ★★★, *I Put A Spell On You* (Philips 1965) ★★★, *Tell Me More* (Philips 1965) ★★★, *Pastel Blues* (Philips 1965) ★★★, *Let It All Out* (Philips 1966) ★★★, *Wild Is The Wind* (Philips 1966) ★★★, *Nina With Strings* (Colpix 1966) ★★★, *High Priestess Of Soul* (Philips 1966) ★★★★, *Nina Simone Sings The Blues* (RCA Victor 1967) ★★★★, *Silk And Soul* (RCA Victor 1967) ★★★, *'Nuff Said* (RCA Victor 1968) ★★★, *Black Gold* (RCA 1969) ★★★, *Nina Simone And Piano!* (RCA Victor 1969) ★★★, *To Love Somebody* (RCA 1971) ★★★, *Here Comes The Sun* (RCA 1971) ★★★, *Heart And Soul* (RCA 1972) ★★★,

Emergency Ward (RCA 1973) ★★★, *It Is Finished* (RCA 1974) ★★★, *Gifted And Black* (Mojo 1974) ★★★, *I Loves You Porgy* (CBS 1977) ★★★, *Baltimore* (CTI 1978) ★★★, *Cry Before I Go* (Manhattan 1980) ★★★, *Nina Simone* (Dakota 1982) ★★★, *Fodder On My Wings* (IMS 1982) ★★★, *Nina's Back* (VPI 1985) ★★★, *Live At Vine Street* (Verve 1987) ★★★, *Live At Ronnie Scott's* (Windham Hill 1988) ★★★, *Live* (Zeta 1990) ★★, *The Blues* (Novus/RCA 1991) ★★★, *A Single Woman* (Elektra 1993) ★★★, *The Great Show Of Nina Simone: Live In Paris* (Accord 1996) ★★.

● COMPILATIONS: *The Best Of Nina Simone* (Philips 1966) ★★★★, *The Best Of Nina Simone* (RCA 1970) ★★★★, *Fine And Mellow* (Golden Hour 1975) ★★★, *The Artistry Of Nina Simone* (RCA 1982) ★★★, *Music For The Millions* (Phillips 1983) ★★★, *My Baby Just Cares For Me* (Charly 1984) ★★★★, *Lady Midnight* (Connoisseur 1987) ★★★, *The Nina Simone Collection* (Deja Vu 1988) ★★★★, *The Nina Simone Story* (Deja Vu 1989) ★★★, *16 Greatest Hits* (1993) ★★★★, *Anthology: The Colpix Years* (Rhino 1997) ★★★★, *Saga Of The Good Life And Hard Times* 1968 sessions (RCA 1997) ★★★★, *The Great Nina Simone* (Music Club 1997) ★★★, *Ultimate Nina Simone* (Verve 1997) ★★★★, *Blue For You: The Very Best Of Nina Simone* (Global 1998) ★★★★, *Sugar In My Bowl: The Very Best Of 1967-1972* (RCA 1998) ★★★★, *At Newport, At The Village Gate, And Elsewhere ...* (Westside 1999) ★★★★, *Nina Simone's Finest Hour* (Verve 2000) ★★★, *Gin House Blues: Nina Simone In Concert* (Castle Pie 2000) ★★★.

● VIDEOS: *Live At Ronnie Scott's* (Hendring Music Video 1988).

● FURTHER READING: *I Put A Spell On You: The Autobiography Of Nina Simone*, Nina Simone with Stephen Cleary.

SINATRA, NANCY

b. 8 June 1940, Jersey City, New Jersey, USA. Determined not to rest on the laurels of famous father, Frank Sinatra, Nancy spent several years taking lessons in music, dance and drama. She made an impressive appearance on the Frank Sinatra/Elvis Presley television special (1959), and two years later made her recording debut with 'Cuff Links And A Tie Clip'. From 1960-65, she was married to pop singer Tommy Sands. Further releases were combined with a budding acting career until 1966 when, having teamed with producer/songwriter Lee Hazlewood, Nancy enjoyed an international smash with the sultry number 1 'These Boots Are Made For Walkin''. It's descending bass line on every verse made it one of the most recognisable hits of 1966. 'How Does That Grab You, Darlin'', 'Friday's Child', and 'Sugar Town', all entered the US Top 40, before 'Somethin' Stupid', a duet with her father, gave the singer a second UK and US chart topper.

Her other mostly country-styled record hits

during the 60s included 'Love Eyes', 'Jackson' and 'Lightning's Girl' (both with Hazlewood), 'Lady Bird', 'Highway Song', and 'Some Velvet Morning'. In 1971, she joined Hazlewood again for the slightly risqué 'Did You Ever'. She also made nightclub appearances, and starred in television specials and feature films such as *Get Yourself A College Girl*, *The Wild Angels* and Elvis Presley's *Speedway*, and sang the theme song to the James Bond movie *You Only Live Twice*. After spending some years away from the limelight, during which she concentrated on bringing up her two daughters by choreographer Hugh Lambert, in 1985 she published a biography entitled *Frank Sinatra: My Father*. A decade later she embarked on a major comeback, releasing her first solo album for more than 15 years, and posing *au naturel* for a six-page pictorial in *Playboy* magazine.

● ALBUMS: *Boots* (Reprise 1966) ★★★, *How Does That Grab You?* (Reprise 1966) ★★★, *Nancy In London* (Reprise 1966) ★★, *Sugar* (Reprise 1967) ★★★, *Country, My Way* (Reprise 1967) ★★★, *Movin' With Nancy* (Reprise 1968) ★★★★, with Lee Hazlewood *Nancy & Lee* (Reprise 1968) ★★★, *Nancy* (Reprise 1969) ★★, *Woman* (Reprise 1970) ★★★, *This Is Nancy Sinatra* (RCA 1971) ★★, with Lee Hazlewood *Did You Ever* (RCA Victor 1972) ★★.

● COMPILATIONS: *Nancy's Greatest Hits* (Reprise 1970) ★★★, *One More Time* (Cougar 1995) ★★★, *Sheet Music: A Collection Of Hits* (DCC 1998) ★★★, *You Go-Go Girl!* (Varèse Sarabande 1999) ★★★★.

● VIDEOS: *Movin' With Nancy* (Aviva 2000).

● FILMS: *Get Yourself A College Girl* aka *The Swinging Set* (1964), *For Those Who Think Young* (1964), *Marriage On The Rocks* (1965), *The Wild Angels* (1966), *The Oscar* (1966), *The Last Of The Secret Agents?* (1966), *The Ghost In The Invisible Bikini* (1966), *Movin' With Nancy* (1967), *Speedway* (1968), *Nancy & Lee In Las Vegas* (1975).

SINGING NUN

b. Jeanine Deckers, 17 October 1933, Belgium, d. 31 March 1985, Wavre, Belgium. Better known as Sister Luc Gabrielle of the Fichermont convent in Waterloo, Belgium, this guitar-playing vocalist came to prominence after signing to Philips Records in 1961. Their Belgium branch issued her album *Soeur Sourire* (Sister Smile), which sold well on the continent. One of the songs, the French sung 'Dominique', a breezy tribute to the founder of the Dominican order, captured the imagination of the international record-buying public and became a worldwide hit, reaching number 1 in the USA during Christmas 1963. Her album also reached the top of the US charts in the same month and she received the Grammy Award for 'Best Gospel Or Religious Recording' of 1963. Revenue for the sales of her work was contributed to foreign missions. Although the Singing Nun appeared on the

prestigious *Ed Sullivan Show*, she failed to secure a hit follow-up. However, Debbie Reynolds starred in a biopic of the nun's life and the movie was advertised with a shot of Soeur Sourire riding a scooter and playing an acoustic guitar. Worldly trappings eventually enticed Deckers from the convent in October 1966. She changed her name to Luc Dominique and recorded the controversial 'Glory Be To God For The Golden Pill'. She later set up a school for autistic children with her friend Annie Pescher, but in March 1985 the pair took a fatal overdose of alcohol and barbiturates. At the time they owed $63,000 in back taxes for money earned during Deckers' singing career, despite the fact that all proceeds had gone to the convent.

● ALBUMS: *Soeur Sourire* aka *The Singing Nun* (Philips 1962) ★★★, *Her Joy, Her Songs* (Philips 1963) ★★★, *I Am Not A Star* (Philips 1967) ★★★.

SINGING POSTMAN

One of the most implausible stars of the swinging 60s, the Singing Postman (aka Allan Smethurst, b. 19 November 1927, Sheringham, Norfolk, England, d. 22 December 2000, Grimsby, Lincolnshire, England) nevertheless crafted one of the better examples of the novelty pop song in 'Hev Yew Gotta Loight, Boy?'. A legend on his own delivery route, Smethurst was an authentic Norfolk postie, who extolled life's simple pleasures and misfortunes with judicious stressing of the East Anglia country vernacular. Tracks on his recordings were all notated in the relevant 'patois', 'Oi Can't Git A Noice Loaf Of Bread', 'They're Orl Playing' Dommies In The Bar' and 'A Miss From Diss' offering huge insights into the life cycle of the Fenland citizen. Many were written from the point of view of a bygone wartime era, as Smethurst moved between Norfolk and Grimsby during World War II. He became a favourite on local BBC radio in the early 60s. Such mildly comic, rural anecdotage may have forever remained a secret to the listeners of Norfolk had it not been for the merest brush with the pop charts. 'Hev Yew Gotta Light, Boy?', included on the *First Delivery* EP, picked up radio play in the mid-60s, and the Singing Postman was soon engaged in promotional duties on popular UK television shows such as *Nationwide*, *Crackerjack* and the *Des O'Connor Show*. Astonishingly, the track won the Ivor Novello award for Best Novelty Song in 1966 and the EP broke into the UK Top 10. Sadly, what otherwise might have been a long, if somewhat secular career, was hampered by celebrity. Smethurst continued to release records but by the start of the 70s he was penniless, his name had been dragged through the courts via an alleged assault, and he had developed a serious drinking problem. Forced to give up his career in 1970 after his fingers became arthritic, Smethurst made an abortive comeback in 1977 with the 'Fertilising Lisa' single. That may very well have been that, until, in 1994, a television advertisement for Ovaltine Light used 'Hev Yew Gotta Light, Boy?' as its soundtrack. Sadly for Smethurst the attention arrived a little late in the day. His royalty cheque was eventually posted to a Salvation Army hostel in Grimsby, where reporters discovered him. Smethurst remained at the hostel until his death in December 2000.

● ALBUMS: *Recorded Delivery* (Parlophone 1966) ★★★, *The Singing Postman's Year* (Parlophone 1968) ★★★★.

SIR DOUGLAS QUINTET

Formed in 1964, the quintet was fashioned by a Houston-based producer, Huey P. Meaux, and former teenage prodigy, Doug Sahm (b. 6 November 1941, San Antonio, Texas, USA, d. 18 November 1999, Taos, New Mexico, USA). The name, Sir Douglas Quintet, first used on 'Sugar Bee' (1964), was fashioned to suggest Anglo credentials in the midst of the British Invasion, but Sahm's southern accent soon belied the attempted deception. Augie Meyers (b. 31 May 1940; organ), Francisco (Frank) Morin (b. 13 August 1946; horns), Harvey Kagan (b. 18 April 1946; bass) and John Perez (b. 8 November 1942; drums) completed the line-up which had an international hit with 'She's About A Mover', an infectious blend of Texas pop and the Beatles' 'She's A Woman', underscored by Meyers' simple, insistent keyboards. This charming style continued on several further singles and the band's debut album, prematurely entitled *The Best Of Sir Douglas Quintet*.

In keeping with several Texans, including Janis Joplin and the 13th Floor Elevators, the Quintet sought the relaxed clime of San Francisco following an arrest on drugs charges in 1966. However, it was two years before the band resumed recording, although only Sahm and Morin were retained from the earlier unit which was bolstered by other Lone Star state exiles Wayne Talbert (piano), Martin Fierro (horns) and George Rains (drums). The original Quintet was reconstituted for *Mendocino*. This superb selection remains their finest offering and includes the atmospheric 'At The Crossroads', a fiery remake of 'She's About A Mover' and the compulsive title track, which became the band's sole million-seller when released as a single. This commercial peak was not sustained and despite delivering several other excellent albums, the unit broke up in 1972 when Sahm embarked on a solo career. It was, however, a temporary respite and, after re-forming in 1976, the band was resurrected on several occasions, in part to tour and capitalize on a continued European popularity. Sahm suffered a fatal heart attack in a New Mexico motel room in November 1999.

● ALBUMS: *The Best Of Sir Douglas Quintet* (Tribe 1965) ★★★, *Sir Douglas Quintet + 2 =*

Honkey Blues (Smash 1968) ★★★, *Mendocino* (Smash 1969) ★★★★, *Together After Five* (Smash 1970) ★★★, *1+1+1 = 4* (Philips 1970) ★★, *The Return Of Doug Saldaña* (Philips 1971) ★★★, as Doug Sahm With The Sir Douglas Quintet *Rough Edges* (Mercury 1973) ★★, as the Sir Douglas Band *Texas Tornado* (Atlantic 1973) ★★, with Freddy Fender *Re-union Of The Cosmic Brothers* (Crazy Cajun 1976) ★★★, as Sir Douglas Quintet, Doug Sahm And Augie Meyers *Live Love* reissued as *Wanted Very Much Alive* (TRC 1977) ★★★, *The Tracker* (Crazy Cajun 1977) ★★, *Border Wave* (Takoma 1981) ★★★, *Quintessence* (Sonet/Varrick 1982) ★★, *Back To The 'Dillo* (Sonet 1983) ★★★, *Midnight Sun* (Sonet/Stony Plain 1983) ★★★, *Live: Texas Tornado* (Takoma 1983) ★★★, *Rio Medina* (Sonet/Stony Plain 1984) ★★, *Luv Ya' Europa* (Sonet 1985) ★★★, *Day Dreaming At Midnight* (Elektra 1994) ★★★★.

● COMPILATIONS: *The Best Of The Sir Douglas Quintet* (Takoma 1980) ★★★★, *The Collection* (Castle 1986) ★★★★, *Sir Doug's Recording Trip* (Edsel 1989) ★★★, *The Best Of Doug Sahm And The Sir Douglas Quintet* (Mercury 1990) ★★★★, *The Crazy Cajun Recordings* (Crazy Cajun 1998) ★★★, *San Antonio Rock: The Harlem Recordings 1957-1961* (Norton 2000) ★★.

SKIP BIFFERTY

John Turnbull (guitar/vocals), Mickey Gallagher (keyboards), Colin Gibson (bass) and Tommy Jackman (drums) were all members of the Chosen Few, a popular beat group initially based in Newcastle-upon-Tyne, England. Vocalist Graham Bell was added to the line-up which assumed the name Skip Bifferty in the spring of 1966. The quintet made their energetic debut in August the following year with the excellent 'On Love', a song from their previous incarnation's repertoire. It was followed by two memorable examples of pop psychedelia, the last of which, 'Man In Black', was produced by the Small Faces team of Steve Marriott and Ronnie Lane. Skip Bifferty's first album continued the melodic craftsmanship of those singles. Bell's assured voice soared over a rich tapestry of sound, resulting in one of the late 60s' most rewarding collections. The band's potential withered under business entanglements and an astonishing conflict with their proprietorial manager Don Arden. Although they tried to forge an alternative career as Heavy Jelly, litigation over the rights to the name brought about their demise. Bell, Turnbull and Gallagher were later reunited in Bell And Arc, but while the singer then embarked on an ill-fated solo career, his former colleagues found success in Ian Dury's Blockheads. The band have subsequently become a cult item for UK record collectors, with their lone album fetching very high prices.

● ALBUMS: *Skip Bifferty* (RCA 1968) ★★★★.

SLEDGE, PERCY

b. 25 November 1941, Leighton, Alabama, USA. An informal, intimate singer, former hospital nurse Sledge led a popular campus attraction, the Esquires Combo, prior to his recording debut. Recommended to Quin Ivy, owner of the Norala Sound studio, Sledge arrived with a rudimentary draft of 'When A Man Loves A Woman'. A timeless single, its simple arrangement hinged on Spooner Oldham's organ sound and the singer's homely, nasal intonation. Released in 1966, it was a huge international hit, setting the tone for Sledge's subsequent path. A series of emotional, poignant ballads followed, poised between country and soul, but none achieved a similar commercial profile. 'It Tears Me Up', 'Out Of Left Field' (both 1967) and 'Take Time To Know Her' (1968) nonetheless stand among southern soul's finest achievements. Having left Atlantic Records, Sledge re-emerged on Capricorn in 1974 with *I'll Be Your Everything*, which included the R&B Top 20 title track. Two 80s collections of re-recorded hits, *Percy* and *Wanted Again*, confirm the singer's intimate yet unassuming delivery. Released in Britain following the runaway success of a resurrected 'When A Man Loves A Woman' (the song reached number 2 in 1987 after featuring in a Levi's advertisement), they are not diminished by comparison. In 1994 Sledge recorded his first all-new set for some time, the excellent *Blue Night* on Sky Ranch, which capitalized on the Sledge 'strong suit', the slow-burning countrified soul-ballad, even though the sessions were recorded in Los Angeles. The appearance of musicians such as Steve Cropper and Bobby Womack helped to ensure the success of the album.

● ALBUMS: *When A Man Loves A Woman* (Atlantic 1966) ★★★★, *Warm And Tender Soul* (Atlantic 1966) ★★★★, *The Percy Sledge Way* (Atlantic 1967) ★★★, *Take Time To Know Her* (Atlantic 1968) ★★★, *I'll Be Your Everything* (Capricorn 1974) ★★★, *If Loving You Is Wrong* (Charly 1986) ★★★, *Percy!* (Monument 1987) ★★★, *Wanted Again* (Demon 1989) ★★, *Blue Night* (Sky Ranch 1994) ★★★★.

● COMPILATIONS: *The Best Of Percy Sledge* (Atlantic 1969) ★★★★, *The Golden Voice Of Soul* (Atlantic 1975) ★★★, *Any Day Now* (Charly 1984) ★★★, *Warm And Tender Love* (Blue Moon 1986) ★★★, *When A Man Loves A Woman (The Ultimate Collection)* (Atlantic 1987) ★★★★, *It Tears Me Up: The Best Of Percy Sledge* (Rhino 1992) ★★★★, *The Very Best Of Percy Sledge* (Rhino 1998) ★★★★, *All Time Greatest Hits* (Cleopatra 2001) ★★★.

SLOAN, P.F.

b. Phillip Gary Schlein, 1944, New York City, New York, USA. Sloan moved to Los Angeles as a teenager and in 1959 recorded his first single, 'All I Want Is Loving', for the ailing Aladdin Records. When a second release, 'If You Believe In Me' failed to sell, Sloan began a career as a contract songwriter. In 1964 he joined Lou Adler's Trousdale Music where he was teamed with fellow aspirant Steve Barri. Together they wrote singles for Shelley Fabares, Bruce And Terry and Terry Black, as well as Adler protégés, Jan And Dean. Sloan and Barri composed several of the duo's hits and contributed backing harmonies under a pseudonym, the Fantastic Baggys. The pair recorded the much-prized surf album *Tell 'Em I'm Surfin'* under this sobriquet.

The emergence of folk rock had a profound influence on Sloan. By 1965 he was writing increasingly introspective material. The Turtles recorded three of his songs, 'You Baby', 'Let Me Be' and 'Can I Get To Know You Better', but passed on 'Eve Of Destruction', which became a US number 1 for the gruff-voiced Barry McGuire, despite an extensive radio ban. Folk purists balked at Sloan's perceived opportunism, but he was embraced by many as the voice of youth and a spokesman for a generation. The singer rekindled his own recording career with 'The Sins Of A Family' and the brilliant *Songs Of Our Times*. His poetic lyrics and love of simile provoked comparisons with Bob Dylan, but Sloan's gift for pop melody was equally apparent. The set included 'Take Me For What I Am Worth', later a hit for the Searchers. *Twelve More Times* featured a much fuller sound and featured two of Sloan's most poignant compositions, 'This Precious Time' and 'I Found a Girl'. He also enjoyed success, with Barri, as part of another 'backroom' group, the Grass Roots. When 'Where Were You When I Needed You' reached the US Top 30 in 1966, the pair put an official band together to carry on the name. By this point the more altruistic Sloan was growing estranged from his commercially minded partner and they drifted apart the following year. 'Karma (A Study Of Divination's)', credited to Philip Sloan, showed an artist embracing the trinkets of 1967, although the subsequent *Measure Of Pleasure* was rather bland. A lengthy break ensued, broken only by the singer/songwriter-styled *Raised On Records*.

Without a contract, he wound down music business commitments, prompting no less a personage than Jim Webb to mourn his absence with the moving tribute 'P.F. Sloan' from the 1977 album, *El Mirage*. Sloan re-emerged from seclusion in 1985 with an appearance at New York's Bottom Line club. Here he was supported by Don Ciccone (ex-Critters; Four Seasons) and future Smithereens' member Dennis Diken in 1990 the singer rewrote 'Eve Of Destruction' as 'Eve Of Destruction, 1990 (The Environment)', which was recorded by the equally reclusive Barry McGuire. In November that year Sloan played at the annual National Academy Of Songwriters' convention. He received a standing ovation from an audience comprised of the best-known songwriters of a generation. In 1993

Sloan recorded his first album in over 20 years, *(Still On The) Eve Of Destruction*. It was initially released only in Japan.
● ALBUMS: *Songs Of Our Times* (Dunhill 1965) ★★★, *Twelve More Times* (Dunhill 1966) ★★★, *Measure Of Pleasure* (Atco 1968) ★★, *Raised On Records* (Mums 1972) ★★, *(Still On The) Eve Of Destruction* (All The Best 1993) ★★.
● COMPILATIONS: *The Best Of P.F. Sloan (1965-1966)* (Rhino 1986) ★★★★, *Anthology* (One Way 1993) ★★★★, *Child Of Our Times: The Trousdale Demo Sessions, 1965-67* (Varèse Sarabande 2001) ★★★.
● FURTHER READING: *Travelling Barefoot On A Rocky Road*, Stephen J. McParland.

SLY AND THE FAMILY STONE

This US group was formed in San Francisco, California, in 1967 by Sly Stone (b. Sylvester Stewart, 15 March 1944, Dallas, Texas, USA), Freddie Stone (b. 5 June 1946, Dallas, Texas, USA; guitar), Rosie Stone (b. Rosemary Stewart, 21 March 1945, Vallejo, California, USA; piano), Cynthia Robinson (b. 12 January 1946, Sacramento, California, USA; trumpet), Jerry Martini (b. 1 October 1943, Colorado, USA; saxophone), Larry Graham (b. 14 August 1946, Beaumont, Texas, USA; bass) and Greg Errico (b. 1 September 1946, San Francisco, California, USA; drums). Sly Stone's recording career began in 1948. A child prodigy, he drummed and added guitar to 'On The Battlefield For My Lord', a single released by his family's group, the Stewart Four. At high school he sang harmony with the Vicanes, but by the early 60s he was working the bars and clubs on San Francisco's North Beach enclave. Sly learned his trade with several bands, including Joe Piazza And The Continentals, but he occasionally fronted his own. 'Long Time Away', a single credited to Sylvester Stewart, dates from this period. He also worked as a disc jockey at stations KSOL and KDIA.
Sly joined Autumn Records as a songwriter/house-producer, and secured a 1964 success with Bobby Freeman's 'C'mon And Swim'. His own opportunistic single, 'I Just Learned How To Swim', was less fortunate, a fate that also befell 'Buttermilk Pts 1 & 2'. Stone's production work, however, was exemplary; the Beau Brummels, the Tikis and the Mojo Men enjoyed a polished, individual sound. In 1966 Sly formed the Stoners, a short-lived group that included Cynthia Robinson. The following year Sly And The Family Stone made its debut on the local Loadstone label with 'I Ain't Got Nobody'. The group was then signed to Epic, where their first album proclaimed itself *A Whole New Thing*. However, it was 1968 before 'Dance To The Music' became a Top 10 single in the USA and UK. 'Everyday People' topped the US chart early the following year, but Sly's talent was not fully established until a fourth album, *Stand!*, was released. Two million copies were sold, while

tracks including the title song, 'I Want To Take You Higher' and 'Sex Machine', transformed black music forever. Rhythmically inventive, the whole band pulsated with a crazed enthusiasm that pitted doo-wop, soul, the San Francisco sound, and more, one on top of the other. Contemporaries, from Miles Davis to George Clinton and the Temptations, showed traces of Sly's remarkable vision. A sensational appearance at the Woodstock Festival reinforced his popularity.
The new decade began with a double-sided hit, 'Thank You (Falettinme Be Mice Elf Agin)'/'Everybody Is A Star', an R&B and pop number 1, but the optimism suddenly clouded. Sly began missing concerts; those he did perform were often disappointing and when *There's A Riot Goin' On* did appear in 1971, it was dark, mysterious and brooding. This introverted set nevertheless reached number 1 in the US chart, and provided three successful singles, 'Family Affair' (another US R&B and pop number 1), 'Running Away' and 'Smilin'', but the joyful noise of the 60s was now over. *Fresh* lacked Sly's erstwhile focus while successive releases, *Small Talk* and *High On You*, reflected a waning power. The Family Stone was also crumbling: Larry Graham left to form Graham Central Station, Rosie Stone recorded a solo album as Rose Banks, while Andy Newmark replaced Greg Errico. However, the real undermining factor was the leader's drug dependency, a constant stumbling block to Sly's recurrent 'comebacks'. A 1979 release, *Back On The Right Track*, featured several original members, but later tours were dogged by Sly's addiction problem. Jailed for possession of cocaine in 1987, this innovative artist closed the decade fighting further extradition charges and there was little of any note heard of Stone in the 90s.
● ALBUMS: *A Whole New Thing* (Epic 1967) ★★★, *Dance To The Music* (Epic 1968) ★★★★, *Life* (USA) *M'Lady* (UK) (Epic/Direction 1968) ★★★★, *Stand!* (Epic 1969) ★★★★★, *There's A Riot Going On* (Epic 1971) ★★★★★, *Fresh* (Epic 1973) ★★★, *Small Talk* (Epic 1974) ★★★, *High On You* (Epic 1975) ★★, *Heard Ya Missed Me, Well I'm Back* (Epic 1976) ★★, *Back On The Right Track* (Warners 1979) ★★★, *Ain't But The One Way* (Warners 1982) ★★.
● COMPILATIONS: *Greatest Hits* (Epic 1970) ★★★★, *High Energy* (Epic 1975) ★★★★, *Ten Years Too Soon* (Epic 1979) ★★, *Anthology* (Epic 1981) ★★★★, *Takin' You Higher: The Best Of Sly And The Family Stone* (Sony 1992) ★★★★, *Precious Stone: In The Studio With Sly Stone 1963-1965* (Ace 1994) ★★, *Three Cream Crackers And A Dog Biscuit* (Almafame 1999) ★★.

SMALL FACES

Formed in London during 1965, this mod-influenced group initially comprised Steve Marriott (b. 30 January 1947, London, England, d. 20 April 1991, Essex, England; vocals, guitar),

Ronnie 'Plonk' Lane (b. 1 April 1946, Plaistow, London, England, d. 4 June 1997, Trinidad, Colorado; bass), Jimmy Winston (b. James Langwith, 20 April 1945, Stratford, London, England; organ) and Kenny Jones (b. 16 September 1948, Stepney, London, England; drums). Fronted by former child actor Marriott, the group signed to Don Arden's Contemporary Records management and production and their product was licensed to Decca Records. Their debut, 'Whatcha Gonna Do About It', an in-house composition/production by Ian Samwell (formerly of Cliff Richard's Drifters) was a vibrant piece of Solomon Burke-influenced R&B that brought them into the UK Top 20. Within weeks of their chart entry, organist Winston was replaced by Ian McLagan (b. 12 May 1945, Hounslow, Middlesex, England; organ/piano), a former member of the Muleskinners and Boz And The Boz People. While their first release had been heavily hyped, the second, 'I Got Mine', surprisingly failed to chart. Arden responded to this setback by recruiting hit songwriters Kenny Lynch and Mort Shuman, whose catchy 'Sha La La La Lee' gave the group a UK Top 3 hit. The Marriott/Lane-composed 'Hey Girl' reinforced their chart credibility, which reached its apogee with the striking Arden-produced 'All Or Nothing'. The latter was their most raucous single to date; its strident chords and impassioned vocal from Marriott ensuring the disc classic status in the annals of mid-60s UK white soul. The festive 'My Mind's Eye' brought a change of style, which coincided with disagreements with their record company.

By early 1967, they were in litigation with their manager and found themselves banned from the prestigious UK television programme Top Of The Pops after Marriott insulted its producer. A final two singles for Decca, 'I Can't Make It' and 'Patterns', proved unsuccessful. Meanwhile, the group underwent a series of short-term management agreements with Harold Davison, Robert Wace and Andrew Loog Oldham. The Rolling Stones' manager signed them to his label Immediate Records and this coincided with their metamorphosis into a quasi-psychedelic ensemble. The drug-influenced 'Here Comes The Nice' was followed by the experimental and slightly parodic 'Itchycoo Park'. With their Top 10 status reaffirmed, the group returned to their blues style with the powerful 'Tin Soldier', which featured P.P. Arnold on backing vocals and a lengthy moody intro, combining McLagen's organ and wurlitzer piano. For 'Lazy Sunday' the group combined their cockney charm with an alluring paean to hippie indolence; it was a strange combination of magnificent working-class music-hall wit and drug-influenced mind expansion. Those same uneasy elements were at work on their chart-topping Ogden's Nut Gone Flake, which won several design awards for its innovative round cover in the shape of a tobacco tin. They also enlisted the bizarre nonsense

wordsmith Stanley Unwin for the links. For their final single, the group bowed out with the chaotic 'The Universal' and the posthumous hit 'Afterglow Of Your Love'.

In February 1969, Marriott decided to join Peter Frampton of the Herd in a new group, which emerged as Humble Pie. The Small Faces then disbanded only to re-emerge as the Faces. Successful reissues of 'Itchycoo Park' and 'Lazy Sunday' in the mid-70s persuaded Marriott, Jones, McLagan and new boy Rick Wills to revive the Small Faces name for two albums, neither of which was well received. Subsequently, Jones joined the Who, Wills teamed up with Foreigner, McLagan played live with the Rolling Stones and Marriott reverted to playing small pubs in London. In 1989, Marriott recorded 30 Seconds To Midnight, but was unable to forge a fully successful solo career. He perished in a fire in his Essex home in 1991. Lane was slowly deteriorating with multiple sclerosis from his base in the USA.

Over the past three decades, the Small Faces, probably more than any other band, have been victims of ruthless reissues. Using inferior master tapes, reduced in quality by generation upon generation of duplicating, a superb catalogue of songs (that the band does not own) has been passed like a hot potato between just about every mid-price record company in existence. During the 'Britpop' explosion of the mid-90s, the band was favourably reappraised. Much of the chirpy exuberance of bands such as Blur, Supergrass, Cast and the Candyskins is indebted to the Small Faces. In 1995 Jones started litigation, attempting to recover substantial missing and unpaid royalties from the previous 25 years. The same year, a UK television documentary and a box set, The Immediate Years, were produced. Bowing to public (or at least music business) pressure, Castle Communications paid a six-figure sum to the members of the band in 1996, together with a future royalty stream. Ian McLagan's book All The Rage is an excellent starting point for newcomers.

● ALBUMS: The Small Faces (Decca 1966) ★★★, Small Faces (Immediate 1967) ★★★, There Are But Four Faces US only (Immediate 1968) ★★★, Ogden's Nut Gone Flake (Immediate 1968) ★★★★, Playmates (Atlantic 1977) ★★, 78 In The Shade (Atlantic 1978) ★.
● COMPILATIONS: From The Beginning (Decca 1967) ★★★, The Autumn Stone (Immediate 1969) ★★★★, In Memoriam (Small Faces Live) Germany only (Immediate 1969) ★★★, Archetypes US only (MGM 1970) ★★★, Wham Bam (Immediate 1970) ★★★, Early Faces US only (Pride 1972) ★★★, The History Of Small Faces US only (Pride 1972) ★★★, Magic Moments (Immediate/Nems 1976) ★★★, Rock Roots: The Decca Singles (Decca 1977) ★★★, Greatest Hits (Immediate/Nems 1978) ★★★, Profile (Teldec 1979) ★★★, Small Faces, Big Hits (Virgin 1980) ★★★, For Your Delight, The Darlings Of Wapping Wharf

Launderette (Virgin 1980) ★★★, *Sha La La La Lee* (Decca 1981) ★★★, *Historia De La Musica Rock* (Decca Spain 1981) ★★★, *By Appointment* (Accord 1982) ★★★, *Big Music: A Compleat Collection* (Compleat 1984) ★★, *Sorry She's Mine* (Platinum 1985) ★★, *The Collection* (Castle 1985) ★★★, *Quite Naturally* (Castle 1986) ★★★, *20 Greatest Hits* (Big Time 1988) ★★, *Nightriding: Small Faces* (Knight 1988) ★★, *The Ultimate Collection* (Castle 1990) ★★★, *Singles A's And B's* (See For Miles 1990) ★★★★, *Lazy Sunday Success* 1990) ★★, *25 Greatest Hits* (Repertoire 1992) ★★, *It's All Or Nothing* (Spectrum 1993) ★★, *Itchycoo Park* (Laserlight 1993) ★★★, *Small Faces' Greatest Hits* (Charly 1993) ★★★, *Here Comes The Nice* (Laserlight 1994) ★★★, *Greatest Hits* (Arc 1994) ★★, *The Best Of The Small Faces Summit* 1995) ★★, *The Small Faces Boxed: The Definitive Anthology* (Repertoire 1995) ★★★★, *The Immediate Years* 4-CD box set (Charly 1995) ★★★★, *The Very Best Of The Small Faces* (Charly 1998) ★★★, *The Singles Collection* 6-CD box set (Castle 1999) ★★★★, *The Darlings Of Wapping Wharf Launderette: The Immediate Anthology Sequel* 1999) ★★★★, *Me You And Us Too: Best Of The Immediate Years* (Repertoire 1999) ★★★.
● VIDEOS: *Big Hits* (Castle 1991).
● FURTHER READING: *The Young Mods' Forgotten Story*, Paolo Hewitt. *Happy Boys Happy*, Roland Schmidt and Uli Twelker. *Quite Naturally*, Keith Badman and Terry Rawlins. *A Fortnight Of Furore: The Who And The Small Faces Down Under*, Andrew Neil. *All The Rage*, Ian McLagan. *Rock On Wood: The Origin Of A Rock & Roll Face*, Terry Rawlings.
FILMS: *Dateline Diamonds* (1965).

SMITH, JIMMY

b. James Oscar Smith, 8 December 1925, Norristown, Pennsylvania, USA. The sound of the Hammond Organ in jazz was popularized by Smith, often using the prefix 'the incredible' or 'the amazing'. Smith has become the most famous jazz organist of all times and arguably the most influential. Brought up by musical parents, he was formally trained on piano and bass and combined the two skills with the Hammond while leading his own trio. He was heavily influenced by Wild Bill Davis. By the mid-50s Smith had refined his own brand of smoky soul jazz, which epitomized laid-back 'late night' blues-based music. His vast output for the 'soul jazz' era of Blue Note Records led the genre and resulted in a number of other Hammond B3 maestros' appearing, notably, Jimmy McGriff, 'Brother' Jack McDuff, 'Big' John Patten, Richard 'Groove' Holmes and 'Baby Face' Willette. Smith was superbly complemented by outstanding musicians. Although Art Blakey played with Smith, Donald Bailey remains the definitive Smith drummer, while Smith tackled the bass notes on the Hammond.
The guitar was featured prominently throughout the Blue Note years and Smith used the talents of Eddie McFadden, Quentin Warren and Kenny Burrell. Further immaculate playing came from Stanley Turrentine (tenor saxophone), Lee Morgan (trumpet) and Lou Donaldson (alto saxophone). Two classic albums from the late 50s were *The Sermon* and *Houseparty*. On the title track of the former, Smith and his musicians stretch out with majestic 'cool' over 20 minutes, allowing each soloist ample time. In 1962 Jimmy moved to Verve Records where he became the undisputed king, regularly crossing over into the pop bestsellers and the singles charts with memorable titles such as 'Walk On The Wild Side', 'Hobo Flats' and 'Who's Afraid Of Virginia Woolf'. These hits were notable for their superb orchestral arrangements by Oliver Nelson, although they tended to bury Smith's sound. However, the public continued to put him into the charts with 'The Cat', 'The Organ Grinder's Swing' and, with Smith on growling vocals, 'Got My Mojo Working'. His albums at this time also made the bestseller lists, and between 1963 and 1966 Smith was virtually ever-present in the album charts with a total of 12 albums, many making the US Top 20. Smith's popularity had much to do with the R&B boom in Britain during the early 60s. His strong influence was found in the early work of Steve Winwood, Georgie Fame, Zoot Money, Graham Bond and John Mayall.

Smith's two albums with Wes Montgomery were also well received; both allowed each other creative space with no ego involved. As the 60s ended Smith's music became more MOR and he pursued a soul/funk path during the 70s, using a synthesizer on occasion. Organ jazz was in the doldrums for many years and although Smith remained its leading exponent, he was leader of an unfashionable style. After a series of low-key and largely unremarkable recordings during the 80s, Smith delivered the underrated *Off The Top* in 1982. Later in the decade the Hammond organ began to come back into favour in the UK with the James Taylor Quartet and the Tommy Chase Band, and in Germany with Barbara Dennerlein. Much of Smith's seminal work has been remastered and reissued on compact disc since the end of the 80s, almost as vindication for a genre that went so far out of fashion, it disappeared. A reunion with Kenny Burrell produced a fine live album, *The Master*, featuring reworkings of classic trio tracks; further renewed interest in his career came in 1995 when he returned to Verve for *Damn!*, the home of his most commercial work. On this album he was joined by some of the finest young jazz players, many of whom were barely born at the time of Smith's 60s heyday. The stellar line-up on this, one of the finest albums of his career, comprised Roy Hargrove (trumpet), Mark Turner (saxophone), Ron Blake (saxophone), Nicholas Payton (trumpet), Abraham Burton (saxophone), Art Taylor (drums), Tim Warfield (saxophone), Mark Whitfield (guitar), Bernard Purdie (drums) and Christian McBride (bass). *Dotcom Blues* enlisted the likes of B.B. King, Taj Mahal, Dr. John and Keb Mo, turning the session into a blues vocal album. Smith was only occasionally allowed to show his prowess. Now enjoying a major renaissance, Smith is the Frank Sinatra of the jazz organ, being both the instrument's greatest ambassador and its finest interpreter.

● ALBUMS: *Jimmy Smith At The Organ Volume 1* (Blue Note 1956) ★★★★, *Jimmy Smith At The Organ Volume 2* (Blue Note 1956) ★★★★, *The Incredible Jimmy Smith At The Organ Volume 3* (Blue Note 1956) ★★★, *The Incredible Jimmy Smith At Club Baby Grand Volume 1* (Blue Note 1956) ★★★, *The Incredible Jimmy Smith At Club Baby Grand Volume 2* (Blue Note 1956) ★★★, *The Champ* (Blue Note 1956) ★★★, *A Date With Jimmy Smith Volume 1* (Blue Note 1957) ★★★, *A Date With Jimmy Smith Volume 2* (Blue Note 1957) ★★★, *The Sounds Of Jimmy Smith* (Blue Note 1957) ★★★, *Plays Pretty Just For You* (Blue Note 1957) ★★★, *House Party* (Blue Note 1957) ★★★★, *Groovin' At Small's Paradise Volume 1* (Blue Note 1958) ★★★★, *Groovin' At Small's Paradise Volume 2* (Blue Note 1958) ★★★, *The Sermon* (Blue Note 1958) ★★★★, *Cool Blues* (Blue Note 1958) ★★★★, *Home Cookin'* (Blue Note 1958) ★★★★, *Crazy! Baby* (Blue Note 1960) ★★★★, *Midnight Special* (Blue Note 1960) ★★★★, *Open House* (Blue Note 1960) ★★★★, *Back At The Chicken Shack* (Blue Note 1960) ★★★★, *Jimmy Smith Plays Fats Waller* (Blue Note 1962) ★★★, *Bashin': The Unpredictable Jimmy Smith* (Verve 1962) ★★★★, *Hobo Flats* (Verve 1963) ★★★, *I'm Movin' On* (Blue Note 1963) ★★★★, *Rockin' The Boat* (Blue Note 1963) ★★★, *Any Number Can Win* (Verve 1963) ★★★, with Kenny Burrell *Blue Bash!* (Verve 1963) ★★★★, *Prayer Meetin'* (Blue Note 1964) ★★★★, *Who's Afraid Of Virginia Woolf* (Verve 1964) ★★★★, *The Cat* (Verve 1964) ★★★★, *Christmas '64* (Blue Note 1964) ★★, *Organ Grinder's Swing* (Verve 1965) ★★★★★, *Softly As A Summer Breeze* (Blue Note 1965) ★★★, *Monster* (Verve 1965) ★★, *'Bucket'!* (Blue Note 1966) ★★★★, *Got My Mojo Workin'* (Verve 1966) ★★★★, *Hoochie Coochie Man* (Verve 1966) ★★★★, *Peter And The Wolf* (Verve 1966) ★★★, with Wes Montgomery, *Jimmy & Wes The Dynamic Duo* (Verve 1966) ★★★★, with Montgomery *Further Adventures Of Jimmy And Wes* (Verve 1966) ★★★★, *Christmas Cookin'* (Verve 1966) ★★, *Respect* (Verve 1967) ★★★, *Stay Loose* (Verve 1968) ★★★, *Livin' It Up* (Verve 1968) ★★★, featuring George Benson *The Boss* (Verve 1969) ★★★, *Groove Drops* (Verve 1970) ★★★, *Root Down* (Verve 1972) ★★★, *Bluesmith* (Verve 1972) ★★★★, *Portuguese Soul* (Verve 1973) ★★, *I'm Gonna Git Myself Together* (MGM 1973) ★★, *Other Side Of Jimmy Smith* (MGM 1973) ★★, *It's Necessary* (Mercury 1977) ★★★, *Confirmation* 1957/1958 recordings (Blue Note 1979) ★★★, *The Cat Strikes Again* (Laserlight 1980) ★★★, *On The Sunny Side* 1958 recording (Blue Note 1981) ★★★, *Off The Top* (Elektra Musician 1982) ★★★, *Keep On Comin'* (Elektra Musician 1983) ★★★, *Lonesome Road* 1957 recording (Blue Note) ★★★★, *Go For Whatcha Know* (Blue Note 1986) ★★★, *Prime Time* (Milestone 1990) ★★★, *Fourmost* (Milestone 1991) ★★★, *Sum Serious Blues* (Milestone 1993) ★★★, *The Master* (Somethin' Else/Blue Note 1994) ★★★, *The Master II* (Somethin' Else/Blue Note 1997) ★★, *Damn!* (Verve 1995) ★★★★, with Eddie Harris *All The Way Live* 1981 recording (Milestone 1996) ★★★, *Jimmy Smith And His Trio* 1965 recording (RTE 1996) ★★★, *Angel Eyes: Ballads & Slow Jams* (Verve 1996) ★★★★, *Standards* 1958 recordings (Blue Note 1998) ★★, with Joey DeFrancesco *Incredible!* (Concord Jazz 2000) ★★★, *DotCom Blues* (Blue Thumb 2001) ★★★.

● COMPILATIONS: *Best Of Jimmy Smith* (Verve 1967) ★★★★, *Best Of Jimmy Smith II* (Verve 1967) ★★★, *Jimmy Smith's Greatest Hits* 1956-63 recordings (Blue Note 1968) ★★★★, *The Best Of Jimmy Smith* (Blue Note 1988) ★★★★, *Compact Jazz: Jimmy Smith Plays The Blues* (Verve 1988) ★★★★, *Walk On The Wild Side: The Best Of The Verve Years* 1962-73 recordings (Verve 1995) ★★★★, *The Complete February 1957 Jimmy Smith Blue Note Sessions* 5-LP/3-CD box set (Mosaic) ★★★★, *Jazz 'Round Midnight* 1963-72 recordings (Blue Note) ★★★, *Talkin' Verve: Roots Of Acid Jazz* 1963-72 recordings (Verve 1996) ★★★★, *A New Sound, A New Star: Jimmy Smith At The Organ, Vols. 1-2* 1956 recordings (Capitol 1997) ★★★★, *Ultimate Jimmy Smith* (Verve 1999) ★★★★, *JS:B.3: The Very Best Of Jimmy Smith* (Verve 2001) ★★★★.

SMOKE

Mick Rowley (vocals), Mal Luker (lead guitar), Phil Peacock (rhythm guitar), John 'Zeke' Lund (bass) and Geoff Gill (drums) were initially known as the Shots. This Yorkshire, England group was groomed for success by Alan Brush, a gravel pit owner and self-made millionaire who harboured dreams of pop management. His ambitions faltered when the Shots' lone single 'Keep A Hold Of What You've Got', failed to sell. Phil Peacock then dropped out of the line-up, but within months the remaining quartet approached producer Monty Babson with several new demos. The most promising song, 'My Friend Jack', was released in February 1967 under the group's new name, the Smoke. Although irresistibly commercial, problems arose when the line 'my friend Jack eats sugar lumps' was construed as celebrating drug abuse. The record was banned in Britain, but became a massive hit on the continent and on the pirate radio ships, inspiring a release for the group's only album, *It's Smoke Time*. Later singles continued their quirky-styled pop, but they failed to garner a significant breakthrough. Having toyed with yet another appellation,

Chords Five, Lund, Luker and Gill began work as resident musicians at Babson's Morgan Sound studios. Several more singles, credited to the Smoke, appeared on various labels during the late 60s/early 70s. These often throwaway efforts featured sundry variations on the above triumvirate, accompanied by any other backroom staff present.

● ALBUMS: *It's Smoke Time* (1967) ★★★.
● COMPILATIONS: *My Friend Jack* (1988) ★★★.

SOFT MACHINE

Founded in 1966, the original line-up was Robert Wyatt (b. 28 January 1945, Bristol, Avon, England; drums, vocals), Kevin Ayers (b. 16 August 1944, Herne Bay, Kent, England; vocals), Daevid Allen, Mike Ratledge and, very briefly, guitarist Larry Nolan. By autumn 1967 the classic line-up of the Soft Machine's art-rock period (Ayers, Wyatt and Ratledge) had settled in. They toured with Jimi Hendrix, who, along with his producer, ex-Animals member Chas Chandler, encouraged them and facilitated the recording of their first album. (There had been earlier demos for Giorgio Gomelsky's Marmalade label, but these were not issued until later, and then kept reappearing in different configurations under various titles.) From the end of 1968, when Ayers left, until February 1970, the personnel was in a state of flux (Lyn Dobson, Marc Charig and Nick Evans were members for a while), and the music was evolving into a distinctive brand jazz-rock.
The band's second and third long-playing releases, *Volume Two* and *Third*, contain their most intriguing and exciting performances. Highlighted by Wyatt's very English spoken/sung vocals, the group had still managed to inject some humour into their work. The finest example is Wyatt's mercurial 'The Moon In June'. By mid-1970 the second definitive line-up (Ratledge, Wyatt, bass player Hugh Hopper and saxophonist Elton Dean) was finally in place. It was this band that Tim Souster showcased when he was allowed a free hand to organize a late-night Promenade Concert in August 1970. In autumn 1971, Wyatt left to form Matching Mole (a clever pun on the French translation of Soft Machine; Machine Molle), and Phil Howard came in on drums until John Marshall became the permanent drummer. For the next few years, through a number of personnel changes (farewell Dean and Hopper, welcome Karl Jenkins, Roy Babbington) the Soft Machine were, for many listeners, the standard against which all jazz-rock fusions, including most of the big American names, had to be measured. However, with Ratledge's departure in January 1976 the group began to sound like a legion of other guitar-led fusion bands, competent and craftsmanlike, but, despite the virtuosity of guitarists Allan Holdsworth and John Etheridge, without the edge of earlier incarnations, and certainly without the dadaist elements of Wyatt's time.
In 1984, Jenkins and Marshall brought together a new edition of the band (featuring Dave Macrae, Ray Warleigh and a number of new Jenkins compositions) for a season at Ronnie Scott's club. Various line-ups carried on playing as the Soft Machine into the following decade, albeit with little success and even less panache. Jenkins subsequently embarked on a highly successful career composing advertising jingles, including work for Renault, Levi's and Jaguar cars. His composition for Delta Airlines, 'Adiemus', was released as a single and became a hit in Germany. Soft Machine's first three albums contain the best of their work, clearly showing they were one of the most adventurous and important progressive bands of the late 60s, one that gently led their followers to understand and appreciate jazz.
● ALBUMS: *Soft Machine* (Probe 1968) ★★★, *Volume Two* (Probe 1969) ★★★★, *Third* (CBS 1970) ★★★★, *Fourth* (CBS 1971) ★★★, *Fifth* (CBS 1972) ★★★, *Six* (CBS 1973) ★★★, *Seven* (CBS 1973) ★★, *Bundles* (Harvest 1975) ★★★, *Softs* (Harvest 1976) ★★, *Alive & Well Recorded In Paris* (Harvest 1978) ★★, *Land Of Cockayne* (EMI 1981) ★★, *Live At The Proms 1970* (Reckless 1988) ★★, *The Peel Sessions* (Strange Fruit 1990) ★★★★, *BBC Radio 1 Live In Concert* 1971 recording (Windsong 1993) ★★★, *BBC Radio 1 Live In Concert* 1972 recording (Windsong 1994) ★★★, *Rubber Riff* (Voiceprint 1994) ★★, *Live In France* (One Way 1995) ★★, *Live At The Paradiso 1969* (Voiceprint 1995) ★★, *Spaced* 1968 recording (Cuneiform 1996) ★★★, *Virtually* (Cuneiform 1997) ★★, *Live 70* (Blueprint 1998) ★★★, *Noisette* 1970 live recording (Cuneiform 2000) ★★★, *Turns On Volume 1* (Voiceprint 2001) ★★, *Turns On Volume 2* (Voiceprint 2001) ★★.
● COMPILATIONS: *Faces & Places Vol. 7* 1967 recordings (BYG 1972) ★★★, *Triple Echo* 3-LP box set (Harvest 1977) ★★★, *Jet Propelled Photographs* 1967 recordings (Get Back 1989) ★★★, *The Best Of Soft Machine: Harvest Years* (See For Miles 1995) ★★★, *Man In A Deaf Corner: Anthology 1963-1970* (Mooncrest 2001) ★★★.
● FURTHER READING: *Gong Dreaming*, Daevid Allen.

SONNY AND CHER

Although touted as the misunderstood young lovers of 1965 folk rock Sonny Bono (b. Salvatore Bono, 16 February 1935, Detroit, Michigan, USA, d. 15 January 1998, Lake Tahoe, California, USA) and Cher (b. Cherilyn Sarkisian La Pierre, 20 May 1946, El Centro, California, USA) were not as fresh and naïve as their image suggested. Bono already had a chequered history in the music business stretching back to the late 50s when he wrote and produced records by artists such as Larry Williams, Wynona Carr and Don And Dewey. He also recorded for several small labels under an array of aliases such as Don Christy, Sonny Christy and Ronny Sommers. In 1963, he came under the aegis of producer Phil

Spector at the Philles label, working as a PR man and studio assistant at the Goldstar Studios. Teaming up with Spector's engineer and arranger Jack Nitzsche, Bono co-wrote 'Needles And Pins', a UK number 1 for the Searchers in 1964. He also became romantically attached to Cher, who began session work for Spector as a backing singer.

Although the duo recorded a couple of singles under the exotic name Caesar And Cleo, it was as Sonny And Cher that they found fame with 1965's transatlantic number 1, 'I Got You Babe'. Arranged by the underrated Harold Battiste, the single was a majestic example of romanticized folk rock and one of the best-produced discs of its time. Bono's carefree, bohemian image obscured the workings of a music business veteran and it was no coincidence that he took full advantage of the pair's high profile. During late 1965, they dominated the charts as both a duo and soloists with such hits as 'All I Really Want To Do' (US number 15; UK number 9), 'Laugh At Me' (US number 10; UK number 9), 'Baby Don't Go' (US number 8; UK number 11), 'Just You' (US number 20), and 'But You're Mine' (US number 15; UK number 17). Although their excessive output resulted in diminishing returns, their lean periods were still punctuated by further hits, most notably 'Little Man' (UK number 4, September 1966) and 'The Beat Goes On' (US number 6, January 1967). By the late 60s they had fallen from critical grace, but starred in the low budget movie *Good Times*, while Cher appeared in *Chastity*. A brief resurgence as MOR entertainers in the 70s brought them their own television series, *The Sonny & Cher Comedy Hour*, and hits with 'All I Ever Need Is You' (US number 7, October 1971; UK number 8, January 1972) and 'A Cowboys Work Is Never Done' (US number 8, February 1972), although by 1974 they had divorced. Extra-curricular acting activities ended their long-standing musical partnership.

While Cher went on to achieve a phenomenally successful acting and singing career, Bono also continued to work as an actor, but adopted a completely different role in 1988 when he was voted mayor of Palm Springs, California, and was later elected to the House of Representatives. He was killed in a skiing accident in January 1998.

● ALBUMS: *Look At Us* (Atco 1965) ★★, *The Wondrous World Of Sonny & Cher* (Atco 1966) ★★, *In Case You're In Love* (Atco 1967) ★★, *Good Times* (Atco 1967) ★★, *Sonny & Cher Live* (Kapp 1971) ★, *All I Ever Need Is You* (Kapp 1972) ★★, *Mama Was A Rock And Roll Singer, Papa Used To Write All Her Songs* (MCA 1973) ★, *Live In Las Vegas Vol. 2* (MCA 1973) ★.

● COMPILATIONS: *Greatest Hits* (Atco 1967) ★★★, *Greatest Hits* (MCA 1974) ★★★, *All I Ever Need: The Kapp/MCA Anthology* (MCA 1996) ★★★.

● FURTHER READING: *Sonny And Cher*, Thomas Braun.

● FILMS: *Good Times* (1967), *Chastity* (1969).

SOPWITH CAMEL

Formed in San Francisco, California in 1965, Sopwith Camel originally consisted of Peter Kraemer (guitar/vocals), Terry McNeil (guitar/keyboards), Rod Albin (bass) and Fritz Kasten (drums). This embryonic line-up faltered with the loss of its rhythm section, but the arrival of William Sievers (guitar), Martin Beard (bass) and former Mike Bloomfield drummer Norman Mayell heralded the beginning of the group's most successful era. Their debut single, 'Hello Hello', reached the US Top 30 in January 1967, and its charming simplicity recalled the good-time music of the Lovin' Spoonful. The two groups shared the same label and Sopwith Camel were promoted as a surrogate, denying them the guitar-based direction their live show offered. *Sopwith Camel* was, nonetheless, a fine collection, highlighted by the enthralling 'Frantic Desolation'. The group broke up, however, when the record was not as successful as they had hoped. However, in 1972 the 'hit' line-up, bar Sievers, was reunited for *The Miraculous Hump Returns From The Moon*. This showcased a jazz-based emphasis, but failed to rekindle past glories and in 1974 the band split again. Kraemer did attempt to resurrect the name three years later, but when a van containing all of their equipment was destroyed by fire, Sopwith Camel was officially grounded.

● ALBUMS: *Sopwith Camel* reissued in 1986 with one extra track as *Frantic Desolation* (Kama Sutra 1967) ★★★, *The Miraculous Hump Returns From The Moon* (Reprise 1972) ★★★.

SORROWS

Formed in Coventry, England, in 1963, the Sorrows consisted of Don Maughn (vocals), Pip Whitcher (lead guitar), Wez Price (rhythm guitar), Philip Packham (bass) and Bruce Finley (drums). They achieved minor fame with 'Take A Heart', a pulsating, brooding performance wherein a rolling drum pattern and throbbing bass created a truly atmospheric single. Their fusion of R&B and mod-pop continued on several ensuing releases, but the quintet was unable to secure consistent success. Maughn, who was later known as Don Fardon, left the group for a solo career in 1967. A restructured Sorrows, Price, Packham, Finley and Chris Fryers (vocals/organ/guitar), then moved to Italy where 'Take A Heart' had become a substantial hit. The group completed several further recordings exclusive to that country, before breaking up at the end of the decade.

● ALBUMS: *Take A Heart* (Piccadilly 1965) ★★★, *Old Songs New Songs* (1968) ★★.

● COMPILATIONS: *Pink Purple Yellow And Red* (1987) ★★★.

SOUL, JIMMY

b. James McCleese, 24 August 1942, Weldon, North Carolina, USA, d. 25 June 1988. A former boy preacher, McCleese acquired his 'Soul' epithet from his congregations. He subsequently toured southern US states as a member of several gospel groups, including the famed Nightingales, wherein Soul was billed as 'The Wonder Boy', before discovering a forte for pop and R&B. He became a popular attraction around the Norfolk area of Virginia where he was introduced to songwriter/producer Frank Guida, who guided the career of Gary 'U.S.' Bonds. Soul joined Guida's S.P.Q.R. label and enjoyed a Top 20 US R&B hit with his debut single, 'Twistin' Matilda', before striking gold with his second release, 'If You Wanna Be Happy', which topped the US pop chart in 1963. Both songs were remakes of popular calypso tunes, reflecting Guida's passion for West Indian music. The song also became a minor hit in Britain, and was latterly covered by the Peter B's, a group that included Peter Bardens, Peter Green and Mick Fleetwood. It proved to be Soul's final chart entry although he remained a popular entertainer until his death in June 1988.
● ALBUMS: *If You Wanna Be Happy* (S.P.Q.R. 1963) ★★★, *Jimmy Soul And The Belmonts* (S.P.Q.R. 1963) ★★★.
● COMPILATIONS: *If You Wanna Be Happy: The Very Best Of* (Ace 1996) ★★★.

SPANKY AND OUR GANG

The original line-up of this engaging US harmony group – Elaine 'Spanky' McFarlane (tambourine/washboard), Nigel Pickering (12-string guitar) and Oz Bach (stand-up bass/kazoo) – began performing together in Chicago's folk clubs. Within months they were joined by Malcolm Hale (guitar/vocals) and John George Seiter (drums) and this restructured line-up had a US Top 10 hit with its debut release, 'Sunday Will Never Be The Same'. This evocative song bore traces of the Mamas And The Papas and the more conservative Seekers, a style maintained on its follow-up, 'Lazy Day'. Bach was then replaced by Geoffrey Myers, who in turn made way for Kenny Hodges. Sixth member Lefty Baker (vocals/guitar) expanded the group's harmonic range, but while the haunting 'Like To Get To Know You' suggested a more mature direction, Spanky And Our Gang seemed more content with a bubbly, good-time, but rather lightweight approach. The premature death of Hale in 1968 undermined the group's inner confidence, and any lingering momentum faltered when 'Give A Damn', a campaign song for the Urban Coalition League, incurred an airplay ban in several states. The remaining quintet broke up in 1969 although McFarlane and Pickering retained the name for the country-influenced *Change*. In 1981 the former joined a rejuvenated Mamas

And The Papas, before touring with an all-new Spanky And Our Gang.
● ALBUMS: *Spanky And Our Gang* (Mercury 1967) ★★★, *Like To Get To Know You* (Mercury 1968) ★★★, *Anything You Choose/Without Rhyme Or Reason* (Mercury 1969) ★★, *Spanky And Our Gang Live* (1970) ★★, *Change* (1975) ★★.
● COMPILATIONS: *Spanky's Greatest Hits* (1969) ★★★, *The Best Of Spanky And Our Gang* (Rhino 1986) ★★★, *Greatest Hits* (Mercury 1999) ★★★.

SPECTOR, PHIL

b. Harvey Phillip Spector, 26 December 1940, the Bronx, New York City, New York, USA. Arguably pop's most distinctive record producer. Spector became involved in music upon moving to Fairfax, California, in 1953. While there, he joined a loosely knit community of young aspirants, including Lou Adler, Bruce Johnson and Sandy Nelson, the last of whom played drums on Spector's debut recording, 'To Know Him Is To Love Him'. This million-selling single for the Teddy Bears – Spector, Annette Kleibard and Marshall Leib – topped the US chart in 1958, but further releases by the group proved less successful. The artist's next project, the Spectors Three, was undertaken under the aegis of local entrepreneurs Lee Hazlewood and Lester Sill, but when it, too, reaped little commercial reward, the latter recommended Phil's talents to New York production team Leiber And Stoller. In later years Spector made extravagant claims about his work from this period which have been rebuffed equally forcibly by his one-time mentors. He did contribute greatly as a composer, co-writing 'Spanish Harlem' and 'Young Boy Blues' for Ben E. King, while adding a notable guitar obligato to the Drifters' 'On Broadway'. His productions, although less conspicuous, included releases by LaVern Baker, Ruth Brown and Billy Storm, as well as the Top Notes' original version of the seminal 'Twist And Shout'. Spector's first major success as a producer came with Ray Petersen's version of 'Corrina Corrina', a US Top 10 in 1960, and Curtis Lee's 'Pretty Little Angel Eyes', which reached number 7 the following year. Work for the Paris Sisters not only engendered a Top 5 hit, ('I Love How You Love Me') but rekindled an association with Lester Sill, with whom Spector formed Philles Records in 1961. Within months he bought his partner out to become sole owner; this autocratic behaviour marked all subsequent endeavours. It nonetheless resulted in a string of classic recordings for the Crystals and Ronettes including 'He's A Rebel' (1962), 'Then He Kissed Me', 'Be My Baby' and 'Baby I Love You' (all 1963), which were not only substantial international hits, but defined the entire 'girl-group' genre. Imitative releases supervised by David Gates, Bob Crewe and Sonny Bono, although excellent in their own right, failed to recapture Spector's dense production technique, later dubbed the 'wall of sound', which relied on lavish orchestration, layers of percussion and swathes of echo. Recordings were undertaken at the Gold Star studio in Los Angeles where arranger Jack Nitzsche and engineer Larry Levine worked with a team of exemplary session musicians, including Tommy Tedesco (guitar), Larry Knechtal (piano/bass), Harold Battiste, Leon Russell (keyboards) and Hal Blaine (drums).

Although ostensibly geared to producing singles, Spector did undertake the ambitious *A Christmas Gift For You*, on which his label's premier acts performed old and new seasonal favourites. Although not a contemporary success – its bonhomie was made redundant following the assassination of President Kennedy – the set is now rightly regarded as a classic. Spector's releases also featured some of the era's finest songwriting teams – Goffin And King, Barry And Greenwich and Barry Mann and Cynthia Weil – the last of which composed 'You've Lost That Lovin' Feelin'' for the Righteous Brothers, the producer's stylistic apogee. Several critics also cite 'River Deep Mountain High', a 1966 single by Ike And Tina Turner as Spector's greatest moment. It represented Spector's most ambitious production, but although his efforts were rewarded with a UK Top 3 hit, this impressive release barely scraped the US Hot 100 and a dispirited Spector folded his label and retired from music for several years.

He re-emerged in 1969 with a series of releases for A&M Records which included 'Black Pearl', a US Top 20 hit entry for Sonny Charles And The Checkmates. Controversy then dogged his contribution to the Beatles' *Let It Be* album. Spector assembled the set from incomplete tapes, but his use of melancholic orchestration on 'The Long And Winding Road' infuriated the song's composer, Paul McCartney, who cited this intrusion during the group's rancorous break-up. Spector nonetheless became installed at their Apple label, where he produced albums by John Lennon (*The Plastic Ono Band*, *Imagine*, *Sometime In New York City*), George Harrison (*All Things Must Pass* and the commemorative *Concert For Bangla Desh*). However, his behaviour grew increasingly erratic following the break-up of his marriage to former Ronette Ronnie Spector, and his relationship with Lennon was severed during sessions for the nostalgic *Rock 'N' Roll* album (1974).

In the meantime Spector had established the Warner-Spector outlet which undertook new recordings with, among others, Cher and Nilsson, as well as several judicious re-releases. A similar relationship with UK Polydor Records led to the formation of Phil Spector International, on which contemporary singles by Dion, Darlene Love and Jerri Bo Keno vied with 60s recordings and archive material. As the 70s progressed so Spector became a recluse, although he emerged to produce albums by

Leonard Cohen (*Death Of A Ladies Man* – 1977) and the Ramones (*End Of The Century* – 1980), the latter of which included a revival of 'Baby I Love You', the group's sole UK Top 10 hit. Despite undertaking abortive sessions with the Flamin' Groovies, Spector remained largely detached from music throughout the 80s, although litigation against Leiber and Stoller and biographer Mark Ribowsky kept his name in the news. Spector was inducted into the Rock And Roll Hall Of Fame in 1989, and having adopted Allen Klein as representative, completed negotiations with EMI Records for the rights to his extensive catalogue. The interest generated by this acquisition is a tribute to the respect afforded this producer whose major achievements were contained within a brief three-year period. In June 2000 the long-running litigation with his former wife Ronnie was resolved. The Ronettes were awarded back royalties of $2.6 million.

● COMPILATIONS: *Today's Hits* (Philles 1963) ★★★, *A Christmas Gift For You* (Philles 1963) ★★★★, *Phil Spector Wall Of Sound, Volume 1: The Ronettes* (Phil Spector International 1975) ★★★★, *Phil Spector Wall Of Sound, Volume 2: Bob B. Soxx And The Blue Jeans* (Phil Spector International 1975) ★★★★, *Phil Spector Wall Of Sound, Volume 3: The Crystals* (Phil Spector International 1975) ★★★★, *Phil Spector Wall Of Sound, Volume 4: Yesterday's Hits Today* (Phil Spector International 1976) ★★★★, *Phil Spector Wall Of Sound, Volume 5: Rare Masters* (Phil Spector International 1976) ★★★, *Phil Spector Wall Of Sound, Volume 6: Rare Masters Volume 2* (Phil Spector International 1976) ★★★, *The Phil Spector Story* (1976) ★★★, *Echoes Of The Sixties* (1977) ★★★, *Phil Spector 1974-1979* (1979) ★★★★, *Wall Of Sound* (1981) ★★★, *Phil Spector: The Early Productions 1958-1961* (Rhino 1984) ★★★, *Twist And Shout: Twelve Atlantic Tracks Produced By Phil Spector* (1989) ★★★, *Back To Mono* 4-CD box set (Rhino 1991) ★★★★★.

● FURTHER READING: *The Phil Spector Story: Out Of His Head*, Richard Williams. *The Phil Spector Story*, Rob Finnis. *He's A Rebel: Phil Spector, Rock And Roll's Legendary Producer*, Mark Ribowsky. *Collecting Phil Spector: The Man, The Legend, The Music*, Jack Fitzpatrick and James E. Fogerty.

SPINNERS

This popular UK folk group was formed in 1958 by Tony Davis (b. 24 August 1930, Blackburn Lancashire, England; banjo, tin whistle, guitar, kazoo), Mick Groves (b. 29 September 1936, Salford, Lancashire, England; guitar), Hughie Jones (b. Hugh E. Jones, 21 July 1936, Liverpool, England; guitar, harmonica, banjo) and Cliff Hall (b. 11 September 1925, Oriente Pourice, Cuba; guitar, harmonica). Hall was born to Jamaican parents who returned to Jamaica in 1939. He came to England after joining the Royal Air Force in 1942. The group was often augmented in concert by 'Count' John McCormick (double bass), generally regarded as the fifth 'Spinner'. Occasionally rebuked by folk 'purists' as bland and middle-of-the-road, the Spinners nevertheless introduced many people to folk music. The regular sell-out attendances at their concerts were a testimony to this, and songs that are now covered by other performers and often mistakenly referred to as 'traditional' are in fact Hughie Jones originals: 'The Ellan Vannin Tragedy', 'The Marco Polo' and 'The Fairlie Duplex Engine'. After a 30-year career, the Spinners decided to call it a day with the release of the double album *Final Fling*. Since retiring, the group has made a number of reunion tours, proving that the public's enthusiasm for them has not waned. Davis and Jones continued to perform and record as solo artists, while Groves is Chair of Education on Wirral Borough Council. Hall is now retired.

● ALBUMS: *Quayside Songs Old And New* (EMI 1962) ★★★, *The Spinners* (Fontana 1963) ★★★, *Folk At The Phil!* (Fontana 1964) ★★★, *More Folk At The Phil* (Fontana 1965) ★★★, *Another LP By The Spinners* (Fontana 1966) ★★★, *The Family Of Man* (Philips 1966) ★★★, *Live Performance* (Contour 1967) ★★★, *Another Spinner From The Spinners* (Fontana 1967) ★★★, *The Singing City* (Philips 1967) ★★★, *Clockwork Storybook* aka *Stop, Look, Listen* (Fontana 1969) ★★★, *Not Quite Folk* (Fontana 1969) ★★★, *The Spinners Are In Town* (Fontana 1970) ★★★, *Love Is Teasing* (Columbia 1972) ★★★, *At The London Palladium* (EMI 1974) ★★★, *Sing Out, Shout With Joy* (EMI 1975) ★★, *English Collection* (EMI 1976) ★★★, *All Day Singing* (EMI 1977) ★★★, *Sing Songs Of The Tall Ships* (EMI 1978) ★★★, *By Arrangement* aka *Everybody Loves Saturday Night* (MFP 1979) ★★★, *Around The World And Back Again* (Dingle's 1981) ★★★, *Here's To You ... From The Spinners* (PRT 1982) ★★★, *In Our Liverpool Home* (PRT 1983) ★★, *Last Night We Had A Do* (PRT 1984) ★★, *Your 20 Favourite Christmas Carols* (Capitol 1985) ★★, *Final Fling* (EMI 1988) ★★★.

● COMPILATIONS: *16 Startracks* (Philips 1967) ★★★, *Spotlight On The Spinners* (Philips 1969) ★★★, *Collection* (Contour 1970) ★★★, *10 Of The Best* (Fontana 1970) ★★★, *18 Golden Favourites* (Note 1979) ★★★, *20 Golden Folk Songs* (EMI 1979) ★★★, *Caribbean Sunshine Hits* (One-Up 1981) ★★★, *Here's To The Spinners* (MFP 1982) ★★★, *The Best Of The Spinners* aka *Maggie May* (Castle 1992) ★★★★.

● FURTHER READING: *The Spinners*, David Stuckey.

SPIRIT

'Out of Topanga Canyon, from the Time Coast' stated the CBS Records publicity blurb for one of their finest acts of the late 60s. The rock band with a hint of jazz arrived with their self-titled debut album. Evolving out of Spirits Rebellious, the new band was formed by Randy California (b. Randolph Wolfe, 20 February 1951, Los Angeles, California, USA, d. 2 January 1997; guitar), Ed 'Mr Skin' Cassidy (b. 4 May 1931, Chicago, Illinois, USA; drums), John Locke (b. 25 September 1943, Los Angeles, California, USA; keyboards), Jay Ferguson (b. John Ferguson, 10 May 1947, Burbank, California, USA; vocals) and Mark Andes (b. 19 February 1948, Philadelphia, Pennsylvania, USA; bass). Media interest was assured when it was found out that not only had the band a shaven-headed drummer who had played with many jazz giants including Gerry Mulligan, Cannonball Adderley and Thelonious Monk, but that he was also the guitarist's father (later amended to stepfather). The quality of the music, however, needed no hype. The album's tasteful use of strings mixed with Locke's stunning electric piano blended well with California's mature hard-edged guitar. Ferguson's lyrics were quirky and brilliant. 'Fresh Garbage', for example, contained the lines: 'Well look beneath your lid some morning, see the things you didn't quite consume, the world's a can for your fresh garbage.' The album reached number 31 in the US chart and stayed for over seven months.

The following year's *The Family That Plays Together* in 1969, was a greater success and spawned a US Top 30 hit single, 'I Got A Line On You'. Ferguson had to share the songwriting credits with the fast-developing California. The Lou Adler-produced set flowed with perfect continuity and almost 30 years later, the album sounds fresh. *Clear* contained Locke's instrumental music for the movie *The Model Shop*, including the beautifully atmospheric 'Ice'. As a touring band they were most impressive, with Cassidy's massive drum kit sometimes dwarfing the stage. California would often use a clear perspex Stratocaster, while tinkering with his echoplex device which emitted the most colourful sound. The band's fourth collection, *Twelve Dreams Of Dr Sardonicus*, was arguably their finest work, with Ferguson and California's songwriting reaching a peak. Although it was their lowest charting album to date (failing to make the Top 50 in the USA), it has subsequently and deservedly become their bestselling record. California's awareness for environmental and ecological issues was cleverly linked into his song 'Nature's Way', while Ferguson put in strong contributions including 'Animal Zoo'. The tensions within the band were mounting, however, and Ferguson and Andes left to form Jo Jo Gunne (the former later enjoyed great success as a solo artist, while Andes went on to join Firefall). John Arliss (bass) briefly came into the line-up, but then California also departed to be replaced by Al and Christian Staehely.

The John Locke-dominated *Feedback* was not a commercial or critical success. The remains of Spirit disintegrated, although Locke and the Staehely brothers kept the name alive until the mid-70s with a variety of drummers, including Stu Perry. The Staehely brothers continue to work in the business, Christian as a session musician and Al as one of the leading music business lawyers in the USA. Randy California attempted a solo career under the Kaptain Kopter moniker, recruiting Cassidy and bass player Larry 'Fuzzy' Knight. The Spirit moniker was subsequently revived by first California and then Cassidy, despite the fact that the Staehely brothers were still touring under the name. During this period, Cassidy and California had their legendary album *Potatoland* rejected (it was eventually released after active petitioning from the UK rock magazine, *Dark Star*). The effect on California's health meant he was forced to leave the band, although Cassidy and Knight continued to tour as Spirit with new members Steven Lyle (vocals, keyboards), Steve Edwards (guitar), and Scott Shelley (guitar).

Spirit returned with a new recording contract in 1975 and a rejuvenated California. The new nucleus of California, Cassidy and bass player Barry Keene, with regular contributions from Locke and Andes, toured widely and built up a loyal following in Britain and Germany. The albums, while delighting the fans, sold poorly and the band became despondent. Nevertheless, there were some spectacular highlights, most notably the stunning yet perplexing double album *Spirit Of '76*. The 1976 release *Farther Along* was a virtual reunion album, with Cassidy and California joined by Locke, Andes and the latter's brother, Matt. The adventurous *Future Games*, meanwhile, featured samples of music and dialogue from television shows such as *Star Trek* and *The Muppet Show*. A depressed California, interviewed in London in 1978-79, stated that Spirit would not rise and that he would *never* play with Ed Cassidy again. Fortunately California was wrong, as the original five were back together in 1984 for *The Thirteenth Dream*. They attempted reworkings of vintage Spirit numbers and sadly the album failed.

California attempted to keep the Spirit name alive with various assorted line-ups, usually together with the fatherly hand of Ed Cassidy, and with Locke occasionally on board. Both *Rapture In the Chambers* and *Tent Of Miracles* (with new bass player Mike Nile) were disappointing works. Cassidy and California continued into the 90s using the Spirit moniker with varied line-ups. At the time of California's tragic death the band had only just released *California Blues*, which featured Andes back in the line-up, and were due to undertake a lengthy tour of Europe where they retained a strong following. On 2 January 1997 California and his 12-year-old son were swimming in Hawaii when a freak wave engulfed them. California was able to push his son to safety but was dragged back by the undertow. His body was never found. Ironically, it is only California

who could have continued as the moral owner of the name, as he was and always has been the true spirit of the band. Spirit's imagination and intuitive grasp of melody put them head and shoulders above most of the bands they shared a stage with.

● ALBUMS: *Spirit* (Ode 1968) ★★★★, *The Family That Plays Together* (Ode 1969) ★★★★, *Clear* (Ode 1969) ★★★, *Twelve Dreams Of Dr. Sardonicus* (Epic 1970) ★★★★★, *Feedback* (Epic 1972) ★★, *Spirit Of '76* (Mercury 1975) ★★★★, *Son Of Spirit* (Mercury 1975) ★★★, *Farther Along* (Mercury 1976) ★★★, *Future Games (A Magical Kahuna Dream)* (Mercury 1977) ★★★★, *Live Spirit* (Potato 1978) ★★★, *The Adventures Of Kaptain Kopter & Commander Cassidy In Potatoland* 1974 recording (Rhino/Beggars Banquet 1981) ★★★, *The Thirteenth Dream* aka *Spirit Of '84* (Mercury 1984) ★★, *Rapture In The Chambers* (I.R.S. 1989) ★★, *Tent Of Miracles* (Dolphin 1990) ★★, *Live At La Paloma* (W.E.R.C. C.R.E.W. 1995) ★★★, *California Blues* (W.E.R.C. C.R.E.W. 1996) ★★★, *Live At The Rainbow 1978* (Past & Present 1999) ★★.

● COMPILATIONS: *The Best Of Spirit* (Epic 1973) ★★★, *Time Circle (1968-1972)* (Epic/Legacy 1991) ★★★★, *Chronicles 1967-1992* (W.E.R.C. C.R.E.W. 1991) ★★★★, *The Mercury Years* (Mercury 1997) ★★★★, *Cosmic Smile* (Phoenix Media 2000) ★★★, *The Very Best Of Spirit: 100% Proof* (Sony 2000) ★★.

SPOOKY TOOTH

Formed in 1967 as a blues outfit, Spooky Tooth quickly moved into progressive rock during the heady days of the late 60s. Formerly named Art, they released a ponderous cover version of Buffalo Springfield's 'For What It's Worth' as 'What's That Sound'. The original band comprised Gary Wright (b. 26 April 1945, Englewood, New Jersey, USA; keyboards, vocals), Mike Kellie (b. 24 March 1947, Birmingham, West Midlands, England; drums), Luther Grosvenor (b. 23 December 1949, Evesham, Worcestershire, England; guitar), Mike Harrison (b. 3 September 1945, Carlisle, Cumberland, England; vocals) and Greg Ridley (b. 23 October 1947, Cumberland, England; bass). Their hard work on the English club scene won through, although their only commercial success was in the USA. They combined hard-edged imaginative versions of non-originals with their own considerable writing abilities. *It's All About* was a fine debut; although not a strong seller it contained their reading of 'Tobacco Road', always a club favourite, and their debut single, 'Sunshine Help Me', which sounded uncannily similar to early Traffic.

It was *Spooky Two*, however, that put them on the map; eight powerful songs with a considerable degree of melody, this album remains as one of the era's finest heavy rock albums. Their self-indulgent excursion with

Pierre Henry on *Ceremony* was a change of direction that found few takers, save for the superb cover painting by British artist John Holmes. *The Last Puff* saw a number of personnel changes: Ridley had departed for Humble Pie, Gary Wright left to form Wonderwheel and Grosvenor later emerged as Ariel Bender' in Stealers Wheel and Mott The Hoople. Three members of the Grease Band joined; Henry McCullough (b. Portstewart, Ireland), Chris Stainton and Alan Spenner. The album contained a number of non-originals, notably David Ackles' 'Down River' and a superb version of 'Son Of Your Father'. The band broke up shortly after its release, although various members, including Foreigner's Mick Jones, Bryson Graham (drums), Mike Patto and Ian Herbert (bass) eventually regrouped for three further albums which, while competent, showed no progression and were all written to a now dated rock formula. Judas Priest later recorded 'Better By You, Better Than Me', which resulted in a court case following the deaths of two fans. The band was accused of inciting violence, causing the two fans to shoot themselves. The original line-up of Spooky Tooth, minus Gary Wright, regrouped in 1999 to record a worthy album for the German Ruf label. *Cross Purpose* featured a new version of 'That Was Only Yesterday', while other strong tracks included Mike Kellie's 'How' and Karl Wallinger's 'Sunshine'.

ALBUMS: *It's All About* (UK) *Tobacco Road* (US) Island/Mala 1968) ★★★, *Spooky Two* Island/A&M 1969) ★★★★, with Pierre Henry *Ceremony* (Island/A&M 1970) ★★, *The Last Puff* Island/A&M 1970) ★★★★, *You Broke My Heart So I Busted Your Jaw* (Island/A&M 1973) ★★, *Witness* (Island 1973) ★★, *The Mirror* (Good Ear/Island 1974) ★★, *Cross Purpose* Ruf/Brilliant 1999) ★★★.
● COMPILATIONS: with Gary Wright *That Was Only Yesterday* (Island/A&M 1976) ★★★, *The Best Of Spooky Tooth* (Island 1976) ★★★★.

SPOTNICKS

A Swedish instrumental group of the late 50s and early 60s, their career actually continued well into the 90s. Originally they comprised Bo Winberg (b. 27 March 1939, Gothenburg, Sweden; lead guitar), Bob Lander (b. Bo Starander, 11 March 1942, Sweden; rhythm guitar, vocals), Björn Thelin (b. 11 June 1942, Sweden; bass) and Ove Johannsson (b. Sweden; drums). They were assembled by Winberg in 1957 as the Frazers, with Lander on guitar and vocals, Thelin on bass, Johannsson on drums, with Winberg himself playing lead guitar and building most of the band's equipment; including a guitar transmitter that allowed primitive flex-free playing. Spotted by Roland F. Ferneborg in 1960 they became the Spotnicks in 1961 and had several hit singles in their homeland. They were signed to Oriole Records

in the UK in 1962 and toured the country, gaining instant notoriety for their gimmick of wearing spacesuits on stage.
The Spotnicks played a mixture of instrumentals and Lander vocals, and first hit with 'Orange Blossom Special' in 1962. That same year they toured Russia and were introduced to cosmonaut Yuri Gagarin. They had further UK hits with 'Rocket Man', 'Hava Nagila' and 'Just Listen To My Heart' during 1962-63. In 1963 they made their cinematic debut in the pop film *Just For Fun*. A cover version of the Tornados' 'Telstar' was released in Sweden under the pseudonym the Shy Ones. Johannsson left in 1963 to become a priest and was replaced by Derek Skinner (b. 5 March 1944, London, England). In 1965 they added organist Peter Winsnes to the line-up and in September Skinner left to be replaced by Jimmy Nicol. Nicol was the drummer famed for having deputized for Ringo Starr on a 1964 Beatles World Tour, when he was hospitalized after having collapsed with tonsillitis. Nicol had also played with the Blue Flames and his own band the Shubdubs. After much touring Nicol left in early 1967 and was replaced by Tommy Tausis (b. 22 March 1946). In October Thelin was called up for National Service and replaced by Magnus Hellsberg. Two years later Göran Samuelsson replaced Winsnes.
The group eventually broke up in 1970, but Winberg was persuaded to re-form the band the following year to record the Japanese album *Ame No Ballad*. Several further line-up changes occurred over the following years as the band continued to tour and record prolifically in Europe. Winberg was the only constant member although Lander was normally in the band until he left to form the Viking Truckers. Various line-ups of the band were still active well into the 90s.
● ALBUMS: *Out-A Space: In London* (Karusell 1962) ★★★, *In Paris: Dansons Avec Les Spotnicks* (Karusell 1963) ★★★, *In Spain: Bailemos Con Los Spotnicks* (SweDisc 1963) ★★★, *In Stockholm* (SweDisc 1964) ★★★, *In Berlin* (SweDisc 1964) ★★★, *At Home In Gothenburg* (SweDisc 1965) ★★, *In Tokyo* (SweDisc 1966) ★★, *Around The World* (SweDisc 1966) ★★★, *In Winterland* (SweDisc 1966) ★★, *Live In Japan* (SweDisc 1967) ★★, *In Acapulco, Mexico* (SweDisc 1967) ★★★, *In The Groove* (SweDisc 1968) ★★★, *By Request* (SweDisc 1968) ★★, *Back In The Race* (Polydor 1970) ★★, *Ame No Ballad* (Canyon 1971) ★★, *Something Like Country* (Polydor 1972) ★★★, *Bo Winberg & The Spotnicks Today* (Polydor 1973) ★★★, *Live In Berlin '74* (Polydor 1974) ★★, *Feelings – 12 Brand New Songs* (Polydor 1976) ★★, *Charttoppers Recorded 77* (Polydor 1977) ★★, *The Great Snowman* (Marianne 1978) ★★, *Never Trust Robots* (Polydor 1978) ★★, *Saturday Night Music* (Marianne 1979) ★★, *Pink Lady Super Hits* (SweDisc 1979) ★★, *20th Anniversary Album* (Polydor 1980) ★★, *We Don't Wanna Play Amapola No More* (Mill 1982) ★★, *In The Middle Of The Universe* (Mill 1983) ★★, *Highway Boogie*

(Mill 1985) ★★, *In Time* (Mill 1986) ★★, *Love Is Blue* (Europa 1987) ★★, *Happy Guitar* (Imtrat 1987) ★★, *Unlimited* (Mill 1989) ★★, *The Spotnicks/Bo Winberg #1* (BMG 1993) ★★, *Tracks* (BMG 1995) ★★★, *The Spotnicks 1997* (Riverside 1997) ★★★.

● COMPILATIONS: *The Best Of The Spotnicks* (Chrysalis 1978) ★★★, *The Very Best Of The Spotnicks* (Air 1981) ★★★, *16 Golden World Hits* (Koch 1987) ★★★.

● FILMS: *Just For Fun* (1963).

SPRINGFIELD, DUSTY

b. Mary Isabel Catherine Bernadette O'Brien, 16 April 1939, Hampstead, London, England, d. 2 March 1999, Henley-on-Thames, Oxfordshire, England. A long-standing critical favourite but sadly neglected by the mass public from the early 70s until the end of the 80s, the career of the greatest white soul/pop singer the UK has ever produced was a turbulent one. Formerly referred to as 'the White Negress', Springfield began as a member of the cloying pop trio the Lana Sisters in the 50s, and moved with her brother Tom (Dion O'Brien, b. 2 July 1934, Hampstead, London, England), and Tim Field into the Springfields, one of Britain's top pop/folk acts of the early 60s. During the Merseybeat boom, she took a bold step by going solo. Her debut in late 1963 with 'I Only Want To Be With You' (the first ever song performed on the long-running UK television programme *Top Of The Pops*) removed any doubts the previously shy convent girl may have had; this jaunty, endearing song is now a classic of 60s pop. She joined the swinging London club scene and became a familiar icon for teenage girls, with her famous beehive blonde hairstyle and her dark 'panda' eye make-up. Over the next three years Springfield was constantly in the bestselling singles chart with a string of unforgettable hits, and consistently won the top female singer award in the UK, beating off stiff opposition from Lulu, Cilla Black and Sandie Shaw. During this time she campaigned unselfishly on behalf of the then little-known black American soul, R&B and Motown Records artists; her mature taste in music differentiated her from many of her contemporaries. Her commitment to black music carried over into her tour of South Africa in 1964, when she played in front of a mixed audience and was immediately deported.

Springfield's early albums were strong sellers, although they now appear to have been rushed works. Her own doubts about the finished product at the time, showed her up to be a fussy perfectionist. Three decades later it is clear that she was absolutely correct, they could have been perfected with more time, and her own high artistic standards would have been satisfied. Her pioneering choice of material by great songwriters such as Burt Bacharach, Hal David, Randy Newman and Carole King was exemplary. The orchestral arrangements by Ivor Raymonde and Johnny Franz, however, often drowned Springfield's voice, and her vocals sometimes appeared thin and strained due to insensitive production. She made superb cover versions of classics such as 'Mockingbird', 'Anyone Who Had A Heart', 'Wishin' And Hopin'', 'La Bamba', and 'Who Can I Turn To'. Her worldwide success came when her friend Vicki Wickham and Simon Napier-Bell added English words to the Italian hit 'Io Che Non Vivo (Senzate)', thereby creating 'You Don't Have To Say You Love Me'. This million-selling opus became her sole UK chart-topper in 1966. At the end of a turbulent year she had an altercation with temperamental jazz drummer Buddy Rich, with whom she was scheduled to play at New York's prestigious Basin Street East club. The music press reported that she had pushed a pie in his face, but years later Springfield revealed the true story; the often outspoken Rich was allegedly resentful at not receiving top billing and caused difficulties when she asked to rehearse her show with the (his) band. Rich was heard to respond 'you fucking broad, who do you think you fucking are, bitch?'; Springfield retaliated by punching him in the face.

By the end of the following year (1967), she was becoming disillusioned with the showbusiness carousel on which she found herself trapped. She appeared out of step with the summer of love and its attendant psychedelic music. Her BBC television series attracted healthy viewing figures, but it was anathema to the sudden change in the pop scene. The comparatively progressive and prophetically titled *Where Am I Going?* attempted to redress this. Containing a jazzy, orchestrated version of Bobby Hebb's 'Sunny' and Jacques Brel's 'If You Go Away' (English lyrics by Rod McKuen), it was an artistic success but flopped commercially (or, in the words of biographer Lucy O'Brien, was 'released to stunning indifference'). The following year a similar fate awaited the excellent *Dusty ... Definitely*. On this she surpassed herself with her choice of material from the rolling 'Ain't No Sunshine Since You've Been Gone' to the aching emotion of Randy Newman's 'I Think It's Gonna Rain Today', but her continuing good choice of songs was no longer attracting fans.

In 1968, as Britain was swamped by the progressive music revolution, the uncomfortable split between what was underground and hip, and what was pop and unhip, became prominent. Springfield, well aware that she could be doomed to the variety club chicken-in-a-basket circuit in the UK, departed for Memphis, Tennessee, one of the music capitals of the world, and immediately succeeded in recording a stunning album and her finest work, *Dusty In Memphis*. The expert production team of Tom Dowd, Jerry Wexler and Arif Mardin were the first people to recognize that her natural soul voice should be placed at the fore, rather than competing with full and overpowering string arrangements. The album remains a classic and one of the finest records of the 60s. The single 'Son Of A Preacher Man' became a major hit, but the album failed in the UK and only reached a derisory number 99 in the US chart.

Following this bitter blow, Springfield retreated and maintained a lower profile, although her second album for Atlantic Records, *A Brand New Me*, was a moderate success. Released in the UK as *From Dusty With Love*, the Thom Bell/Kenny Gamble-credited production boosted her waning popularity in her homeland, where she still resided, although she spent much of her time in the USA. *Cameo*, from 1973, exuded class and featured a superlative cover version of Van Morrison's 'Tupelo Honey', but sold little and yielded no hit singles. Springfield had, by this time, disappeared from the charts, and following a veiled admission in an interview with Ray Coleman for London's *Evening Standard* in 1975 that she was bisexual, moved to Los Angeles. For the next few years she recorded sporadically, preferring to spend her time with friends such as Billie Jean King and to campaign for animal rights (she was an obsessive cat lover). Additionally, she succumbed to pills and alcohol abuse, and even attempted suicide.

Following the release of the inappropriately titled *It Begins Again* some five years after her previous release, she was propelled towards a comeback, which failed, although the album did garner respectable sales. Notable tracks were the Carole Bayer Sager gem 'I'd Rather Leave While I'm In Love', and a Barry Manilow song, 'Sandra', featuring a lyric that addressed chillingly similar events to her own life. The follow-up, *Living Without Your Love*, was poorly received; it contained an indifferent version of the Miracles' 'You Really Got A Hold On Me'. 'Baby Blue' became a minor hit in 1979 but the comeback was over. Springfield went to ground again, even although one unsuccessful single in 1980, 'Your Love Still Brings Me To My Knees', remains an undiscovered nugget. In the early 80s she relocated to Toronto and resurfaced in 1982 with the energetic, disco-influenced *White Heat*. Featuring ex-Hookfoot guitarist Caleb Quaye and Nathan East (bass), it was her best album during these musically barren years, yet it failed to gain a release outside the USA. Two years later she duetted with Spencer Davis on Judy Clay and William Bell's 'Private Number', which, although an excellent choice of song, merely served to highlight Davis' limited vocal range. A further attempt to put her in the public eye was orchestrated by club owner Peter Stringfellow in 1985. He contracted her to his record label. After one single, 'Just Like Butterflies', she fluttered out of sight again. Her phoenix-like return towards the end of the

80s was due entirely to Neil Tennant and Chris Lowe of the Pet Shop Boys, who persuaded her to duet with them on their hit single 'What Have I Done To Deserve This?' in 1987. They then wrote the theme for the film *Scandal*, which Springfield took into the bestsellers; 'Nothing Has Been Proved' was an ideal song, the lyrics cleverly documenting an era that she knew only too well. She followed this with another of their compositions, 'In Private', which, although a lesser song lyrically, became a bigger hit. The subsequent album, *Reputation*, became her most successful for over 20 years. In the early 90s she moved back from America and for a time resided in the Netherlands with her beloved cats. Having returned to the UK, in 1994 she underwent chemotherapy for breast cancer. This delayed the release and promotion of her long-awaited new album with Columbia Records. *A Very Fine Love* arrived in the wake of the single 'Wherever Would I Be'; this Diane Warren big production ballad featured a duet with Daryl Hall. The rest of the album proved that Springfield retained a singing voice that could chill the spine and warm the heart, and with the aid of modern recording techniques she could make any song sound good.

Springfield was inducted into the Rock And Roll Hall Of Fame in 1999, too late and too ill to attend. She was also awarded an OBE in the 1999 New Year Honours list, but barely four weeks after receiving the honour at a private gathering in the Royal Marsden Hospital she finally succumbed to cancer. Her greatest asset, in addition to her voice, was her devilish sense of humour and her remarkable ability to recognize a good songwriter; her choice of material over the years was consistently good. A diva who was able to cross over into every gender genre, adored by gays and straights. No female singer has ever commanded such love and respect. 'Unique' can be bestowed upon her with confidence. She was the best female vocalist Britain has ever produced, and unlikely to be bettered.

● ALBUMS: *A Girl Called Dusty* (Philips 1964) ★★★★, *Ev'rything's Coming Up Dusty* (Philips 1965) ★★★★, *Where Am I Going* (Philips 1967) ★★★★, *Dusty ... Definitely* (Philips 1968) ★★★★, *Dusty In Memphis* (Philips 1969) ★★★★★, *A Brand New Me (From Dusty With Love)* (Philips 1970) ★★★★, *See All Her Faces* (Philips 1972) ★★★, *Cameo* (Philips 1973) ★★★, *Dusty Sings Burt Bacharach And Carole King* (Philips 1975) ★★★, *It Begins Again* (Mercury 1978) ★★★, *Living Without Your Love* (Mercury 1979) ★★★, *White Heat* (Casablanca 1982) ★★★★, *Reputation* (Parlophone 1990) ★★★, *A Very Fine Love* (Columbia 1995) ★★.

● COMPILATIONS: *Golden Hits* (Philips 1966) ★★★★, *Stay Awhile* (Wing 1968) ★★★★, *This Is Dusty Springfield* (Philips 1971) ★★★★, *This Is Dusty Springfield Volume 2: The Magic Garden* (Philips 1973) ★★★★, *Greatest Hits* (Philips

1979) ★★★★, *The Very Best Of Dusty Springfield* (K-Tel 1981) ★★★★, *Dusty: Love Songs* (Philips 1983) ★★★★, *The Silver Collection* (Philips 1988) ★★★★★, *Dusty's Sounds Of The 60's* (Pickwick 1989) ★★★★, *Love Songs* (Pickwick 1989) ★★★★, *Dusty Springfield Songbook* (Pickwick 1990) ★★★★★, *Blue For You* (1993) ★★★★, *Goin' Back: The Very Best Of Dusty Springfield* (Philips 1994) ★★★★★, *Dusty, The Legend Of Dusty Springfield* 4-CD box set (Philips 1994) ★★★★, *Something Special* (Mercury 1996) ★★★★, *Songbooks* (Philips 1998) ★★★★, *The Very Best Of Dusty Springfield* (Mercury 1998) ★★★★, *Simply Dusty: The Definitive Dusty Springfield Collection* 4-CD box set (Mercury 2000) ★★★★★.
● FURTHER READING: *Dusty*, Lucy O'Brien. *Scissors And Paste: A Collage Biography*, David Evans. *Dancing With Demons*, Penny Valentine and Vicki Wickham.

SPRINGFIELDS

Formed in 1960, this popular UK folk-based attraction was based around singer/songwriter Dion O'Brien (b. 2 July 1934, Hampstead, London, England,) and his sister Mary Isabel Catherine Bernadette (b. 16 April 1939, Hampstead, London, England, d. 2 March 1999, Henley-on-Thames, Oxfordshire, England), who accompanied him on guitar. Better known as Tom and Dusty Springfield, the duo was later joined by the former's partner, Tim Field, and the following year the revitalized unit became one of Britain's top vocal groups. The trio enjoyed UK Top 5 singles with 'Island Of Dreams' (1962) and 'Say I Won't Be There' (1963), by which time Field had been replaced by Mike Longhurst-Pickworth, who took the less cumbersome professional name Mike Hurst. The Springfields enjoyed success in America with 'Silver Threads And Golden Needles', a country standard that paradoxically failed to chart in Britain. However, although the single went on to sell in excess of one million copies, it was the group's only substantial US hit. The group split up in 1963 with each member then pursuing solo ventures. Dusty Springfield became the UK's leading female singer, brother Tom continued his songwriting career, while Hurst established himself as a leading pop producer through his work with Cat Stevens.
● ALBUMS: *Kinda Folksy* (Philips 1961) ★★★, *Folk Songs From The Hills* (Philips 1963) ★★.
● COMPILATIONS: *The Springfields Story* (Philips 1964) ★★★★, *Sing Again* (Fontana 1969) ★★★, *Island Of Dreams* (Contour 1971) ★★★.
● FILMS: *It's All Over Town* (1964).

SQUIRES, ROSEMARY

b. Joan Rosemary Yarrow, 7 December 1928, Bristol, Avon, England. This civil servant's daughter took vocal, piano and guitar lessons before and during study at Salisbury's St Edmund's Girls School. In 1940, a broadcast on the BBC Home Service's *Children's Hour* created demand for her in local venues that embraced US army bases. With an endearing west country burr, she sang in various combos formed within these camps, as well as in the Polish Military Band while employed in an antique bookshop and then an office. After becoming a professional performer, she was employed by Ted Heath, Geraldo, Cyril Stapleton and other big band conductors as well as smaller jazz bands led by Max Harris, Kenny Baker and Alan Clare – with whose trio she appeared at a BBC Festival of Jazz at the Royal Albert Hall. She has long been known to Britain at large, having been omnipresent since the late 40s on BBC Radio light entertainment programmes – including *Melody Time*, *Workers' Playtime* and many of her own series. In 1962, she hovered just outside the UK chart with a version of 'The Gypsy Rover'. Currently reported to be living again in Salisbury, she remains an active musician, with Tibetan culture among her extra-mural interests. She was secretary of Britain's Tibet Society from 1972-75. In 1991, she surprised her friends (and herself) by marrying for the first time, although it was far from being the first occasion on which she has changed her name. She recorded one of her most successful titles, 'Frankfurter Sandwiches', under the *nom de plume* of Joanne And The Streamliners, and in the 90s she still continues with her 'second career' – singing for television jingles. She is also DJ on her own Sunday afternoon programme on Radio Wiltshire.
● ALBUMS: *My One And Only* (C5 1989) ★★, *A Time For Rosemary* (1993) ★★★.

STANDELLS

Tony Valentino (guitar/vocals) and Larry Tamblyn (organ) formed the Standells in 1962. The early line-up included drummer Gary Leeds (b. 3 September 1944, Glendale, California, USA), who later found fame in the Walker Brothers, Gary Lane (bass) and former Mouseketeer Dick Dodd (drums). The quartet became a leading teen-based attraction in plush Los Angeles nightspots. This conformist image was shattered on their association with producer Ed Cobb, who fashioned a series of angst-cum-protest punk anthems in 'Sometimes Good Guys Don't Wear White', 'Why Pick On Me?' and the exceptional 'Dirty Water', a US number 11 hit in 1966. In 1966, Gary Lane left the band during a tour of Florida. He was succeeded by Dave Burke, who in turn was replaced the following year by John Fleck (né Fleckenstein). The latter, who co-wrote 'Can't Explain' on Love's debut album, went on to become a leading cinematographer. The Standells also appeared in 1967's exploitation movie, *Riot On Sunset Strip*, but by this time their career was waning. Unfashionable in the face of San Francisco's acid-rock, the band's career was confined to the cabaret circuit as original members drifted away. Lowell George, later of Frank Zappa's Mothers Of Invention and Little Feat, briefly joined their ranks, but by 1970 the Standells had become an oldies attraction. Several members re-formed in 1999 for a live show at the Cavestomp festival, later released as *Ban This!*

● ALBUMS: *The Standells Live At PJs* (Liberty 1964) ★★★, *Live And Out Of Sight* (Sunset 1966) ★★★, *Dirty Water* (Tower 1966) ★★★, *Why Pick On Me* (Tower 1966) ★★, *The Hot Ones* (Tower 1966) ★★, *Try It* (Tower 1967) ★★, *Ban This! (Live From Cavestomp)* (Varèse Sarabande 2000) ★★.

● COMPILATIONS: *The Best Of The Standells* (Rhino 1984) ★★★, *Very Best Of The Standells* (Hip-O 1998) ★★★.

● FILMS: *Get Yourself A College Girl* (1964), *Riot On Sunset Strip* (1967).

STAPLE SINGERS

This well-known US family gospel group was formed in 1951 by Pops Staples (b. Roebuck Staples, 28 December 1914, Winona, Mississippi, USA, d. 19 December 2000, Dolton, Illinois, USA) and four of his children, Mavis Staples (b. Chicago, Illinois, USA), Cleotha Staples and Pervis Staples, who was later replaced by Yvonne Staples. The group fused an original presentation of sacred music, offsetting Mavis Staples' striking voice against her father's lighter tenor, rather than follow the accustomed 'jubilee' or 'quartet' formations, prevalent in the genre. Pops' striking guitar work, reminiscent of delta-blues, added to their inherent individuality. Singles such as 'Uncloudy Day', 'Will The Circle Be Unbroken' and 'I'm Coming Home', proved especially popular, while an original song, 'This May Be The Last Time', provided the inspiration for the Rolling Stones' hit 'The Last Time'.

During the early half of the 60s, the group tried to broaden its scope. Two singles produced by Larry Williams, 'Why (Am I Treated So Bad)' and 'For What It's Worth', a Stephen Stills composition, anticipated the direction the Staples would take on signing with Stax Records in 1967. Here they began recording material contributed by the label's established songwriters, including Homer Banks and Bettye Crutcher, which embraced a moral focus, rather than a specifically religious one. Reduced to a quartet following the departure of Pervis, a bubbling version of Bobby Bloom's 'Heavy Makes You Happy' (1970) gave the group their first R&B hit. This new-found appeal flourished with 'Respect Yourself' (1971) and 'I'll Take You There' (1972 – a US pop number 1), both of which expressed the group's growing confidence. Their popularity was confirmed with 'If You're Ready (Come Go With Me)' (1973), 'City In The Sky' (1974), and by appearances in two movies, *Wattstax* and *Soul*

To Soul. The Staple Singers later moved to the Curtom label where they had an immediate success with two songs from a Curtis Mayfield-penned film soundtrack, 'Let's Do It Again' (another US pop number 1) and 'New Orleans'. These recordings were the group's last major hits although a series of minor R&B chart places between 1984 and 1985 continued the Staples' long-established ability to be both populist and inspirational.

● ALBUMS: *Uncloudy Day* (Vee Jay 1959) ★★★, *Swing Low Sweet Chariot* (Vee Jay 1961) ★★★★, *Gospel Program* (Epic 1961) ★★★, *Hammers And Nails* (Epic 1962) ★★★, *Great Day* (Epic 1963) ★★★, *25th Day Of December* (Epic 1963) ★★★, *Spirituals* (Epic 1965) ★★★, *Amen* (Epic 1965) ★★★, *Freedom Highway* (Epic 1965) ★★★★, *Why* (Epic 1966) ★★★, *This Little Light* (Epic 1966) ★★★, *For What It's Worth* (Epic 1967) ★★★, *Amen* (Epic 1967) ★★★, *Pray On* (Stax 1968) ★★★, *Soul Folk In Action* (Stax 1968) ★★★, *We'll Get Over* (Stax 1970) ★★★, *I Had A Dream* (Stax 1970) ★★★, *Heavy Makes You Happy* (Stax 1971) ★★★, *The Staple Swingers* (Stax 1971) ★★★★, *Bealitude: Respect Yourself* (Stax 1972) ★★★★, *Be What You Are* (Stax 1973) ★★★, *Use What You Got* (Stax 1973) ★★★, *City In The Sky* (Stax 1974) ★★★, *Let's Do It Again* film soundtrack (Curtom 1975) ★★★, *Pass It On* (Curtom 1976) ★★★, *Family Tree* (Warners 1977) ★★, *Unlock Your Mind* (Warners 1978) ★★, *Hold On To Your Dream* (20th Century 1981) ★★, *Turning Point* (Private I 1984) ★★★, *Are You Ready* (Private I 1985) ★★★.

● COMPILATIONS: *The Best Of The Staple Singers* (Stax 1975) ★★★★, *Stand By Me* (DJM 1977) ★★★, *Respect Yourself: The Best Of The Staple Singers* (Stax 1988) ★★★★, *The Very Best Of The Staple Singers Live: Volume One* (Collectables 1998) ★★★.

● FILMS: *Soul To Soul* (1971), *Wattstax* (1973), *The Last Waltz* (1978).

STARR, EDWIN

b. Charles Hatcher, 21 January 1942, Nashville, Tennessee, USA. The brother of soul singers Roger and Willie Hatcher, Edwin Starr was raised in Cleveland, where he formed the Future Tones vocal group in 1957. They recorded one single for Tress, before Starr was drafted into the US Army for three years. After completing his service, he toured for two years with the Bill Doggett Combo, and was then offered a solo contract with the Ric Tic label in 1965. His first single, 'Agent Double-O-Soul', was a US Top 30 hit and Starr exploited its popularity by appearing in a short promotional film with actor Sean Connery, best known for his role as James Bond. 'Stop Her On Sight (S.O.S.)' repeated this success, and brought Starr a cult following in Britain, where his strident, gutsy style proved popular in specialist soul clubs.

When Motown Records took over the Ric Tic

catalogue in 1967, Starr was initially overlooked by the label's hierarchy. He re-emerged in 1969 with '25 Miles', a Top 10 hit that owed much to the dominant soul style of the Stax Records label. An album of duets with Blinky brought some critical acclaim, before Starr resumed his solo career with the strident, politically outspoken 'War', a US number 1 in 1970. Teamed with writer/producer Norman Whitfield, Starr was allowed to record material that had been earmarked for the Temptations, who covered both of his subsequent Motown hits, 'Stop The War Now' and 'Funky Music Sho Nuff Turns Me On'. Starr's own credentials as a writer had been demonstrated on 'Oh How Happy', which had become a soul standard since he first recorded it in the late 60s. He was given room to blossom on the 1974 soundtrack *Hell Up In Harlem*, which fitted into the 'blaxploitation' mould established by Curtis Mayfield and Isaac Hayes. Tantalized by this breath of artistic freedom, Starr left the confines of Motown in 1975, recording for small labels in Britain and America before striking a new commercial seam in 1979 with two major disco hits, 'Contact' and 'HAPPY Radio'. In the 80s, Starr was based in the UK, where he collaborated with the Style Council on a record in support of striking coal miners, and enjoyed a run of club hits on the Hippodrome label, most notably 'It Ain't Fair' in 1985. Between 1989 and 1991, Starr worked with Ian Levine's Motor City Records, recording a remake of '25 Miles' in a modern style and releasing *Where Is The Sound*.

● ALBUMS: *Soul Master* (Gordy 1968) ★★★, *25 Miles* (Gordy 1969) ★★★, with Blinky *Just We Two* (Gordy 1969) ★★★, *War And Peace* (Gordy 1970) ★★★, *Involved* (Gordy 1971) ★★★, *Hell Up In Harlem* film soundtrack (Gordy 1974) ★★★, *Free To Be Myself* (1975) ★★★, *Edwin Starr* (1977) ★★, *Afternoon Sunshine* (GTO 1977) ★★★, *Clean* (20th Century 1978) ★★, *HAPPY Radio* (20th Century 1979) ★★★, *Stronger Than You Think I Am* (20th Century 1980) ★★, *Where Is The Sound* (Motor City 1991) ★★.

● COMPILATIONS: *The Hits of Edwin Starr* (Tamla Motown 1972) ★★★, *20 Greatest Motown Hits* (Motown 1986) ★★★, *Early Classics* (Spectrum 1996) ★★★, *The Essential Collection* (Spectrum 2001) ★★★.

STEPPENWOLF

Although based in southern California, Steppenwolf evolved out of a Toronto act, the Sparrow. John Kay (b. Joachim F. Krauledat, 12 April 1944, Tilsit, Germany; vocals), Michael Monarch (b. 5 July 1950, Los Angeles, California, USA; lead guitar), Goldy McJohn (b. 2 May 1945; keyboards), Rushton Moreve (bass) and Jerry Edmonton (b. 24 October 1946, Canada; drums) assumed their new name in 1967, inspired by the novel by cult author Herman Hesse. John Morgan replaced Moreve

prior to recording. The band's exemplary debut album included 'Born To Be Wild' which reached number 2 in the US charts. This rebellious anthem was written by Dennis Edmonton (aka Mars Bonfire), guitarist in Sparrow and brother of drummer Jerry. It was featured in the famous opening sequence of the movie *Easy Rider*, and has since acquired classic status (the song achieved its highest UK chart position, number 18, when it was re-released in February 1999). Steppenwolf actively cultivated a menacing, hard rock image, and successive collections mixed this heavy style with blues. 'Magic Carpet Ride' and 'Rock Me' were also US Top 10 singles yet the group deflected the criticism attracted by such temporal success by addressing contemporary issues such as politics, drugs and racial prejudice. Newcomers Larry Byrom (guitar) and Nick St. Nicholas (b. 28 September 1943, Hamburg, Germany; bass), former members of Time, were featured on *Monster*, Steppenwolf's most cohesive set. A concept album based on Kay's jaundiced view of contemporary (1970) America, it was a benchmark in the fortunes of the group. Continued personnel changes undermined their stability, and later versions of the band seemed content to further a spurious biker image, rather than enlarge on earlier achievements. Kay dissolved the band in 1972, but his solo career proved inconclusive and within two years he was leading a reconstituted Steppenwolf. The singer has left and re-formed his creation several times over the ensuing years, but has been unable to repeat former glories.

● ALBUMS: *Steppenwolf* (Dunhill 1968) ★★★, *The Second* (Dunhill 1968) ★★★, *Steppenwolf At Your Birthday Party* (Dunhill 1969) ★★★, *Early Steppenwolf* (Dunhill 1969) ★★★, *Monster* (Dunhill 1969) ★★★★, *Steppenwolf 'Live'* (Dunhill 1970) ★★, *Steppenwolf 7* (Dunhill 1970) ★★, *For Ladies Only* (Dunhill 1971) ★★★, *Slow Flux* (Mums 1974) ★★, *Hour Of The Wolf* (Epic 1975) ★★, *Skullduggery* (Epic 1976) ★★, *Live In London* (Attic 1982) ★★, *Wolf Tracks* (Attic 1982) ★★, *Rock & Roll Rebels* (Qwil 1987) ★★, *Rise And Shine* (I.R.S. 1990) ★★. Solo John Kay: *The Lost Heritage Tapes* (Macola 1998) ★★, *Heretics And Privateers* (Cannonball 2001) ★★★.

● COMPILATIONS: *Steppenwolf Gold* (Dunhill 1971) ★★★, *Rest In Peace* (Dunhill 1972) ★★★, *16 Greatest Hits* (Dunhill 1973) ★★★★, *Masters Of Rock* (Dunhill 1975) ★★★, *Golden Greats* (MCA 1985) ★★★, *Born To Be Wild: Retrospective* (MCA 1991) ★★★, *All Time Greatest Hits* (MCA 1999) ★★★★.

STORM, RORY

b. Alan Caldwell, 1940, Liverpool, England, d. 28 September 1972. Vocalist Caldwell began performing as a member of the Texan Skiffle Group, before forming one of the city's first beat groups with Johnny Byrne alias Johnny Guitar (b. 4 December 1939, d. 18 August 1999), Lou Walters, Ty Brian and Ritchie Starkey, later known as Ringo Starr. The quintet employed several names – the Raving Texans, Al Caldwell And His Jazzmen – before becoming Rory Storm And The Hurricanes in 1960, with Caldwell assuming the lead persona. They enjoyed a fervent local popularity, in part because of the singer's showmanship, and were placed third behind the Beatles and Gerry And The Pacemakers in a poll undertaken by the *Mersey Beat* newspaper in 1962. Starr's switch to the Beatles in August that year precipitated a recurrent drumming problem, and a stand-in was required on the Hurricanes' contributions to *This Is Merseybeat*. Spirited but unoriginal, the three tracks they completed revealed a barely adequate vocalist, while a later version of 'America', produced by Brian Epstein, failed to capture an in-concert fire. The premature death of Ty Brian and the departure of Lou Walters ended any lingering potential, and the Hurricanes were disbanded in 1966 following their appearance at the last night of the famed Cavern club. Rory then pursued a career as a disc jockey but, increasingly prone to ill-heath, he died following an accidental overdose of alcohol and medication. His grief-stricken mother committed suicide on discovering his body. Byrne became a technician in the Merseyside ambulance service, although he later formed the New Hurricanes to perform at commemorative events. He died in 1999 from motor neurone disease.

STRAWBERRY ALARM CLOCK

Based in California and originally known as the Sixpence, the Strawberry Alarm Clock enjoyed a US number 1 in 1967 with the memorable 'Incense And Peppermints'. This euphoric slice of 'flower-power' bubblegum was initially intended as a b-side and the featured voice was that of a friend on hand during the session, rather than an official member. The group – Mark Weitz (organ), Ed King (lead guitar), Lee Freeman (rhythm guitar), Gary Lovetro (bass) and Randy Seol (drums) – added a second bass player, George Bunnell, prior to recording a debut album. The new arrival was also an accomplished songwriter, and his contributions enhanced a set that coupled hippie trappings with enchanting melodies and some imaginative instrumentation. Such features were maintained on successive Strawberry Alarm Clock albums, while 'Tomorrow' and 'Sit With The Guru' continued their reign as chart contenders. The group supplied much of the music for the film *Psyche-Out*, in which they also appeared. Gary Lovetro left the line-up prior to *Wake Up It's Tomorrow*, and several subsequent changes undermined the band's direction. *Good Morning Starshine*, released in 1969, introduced a reshaped band where Jimmy

Pitman (guitar) and Gene Gunnels (drums) joined Weitz and King, the latter of whom was relegated to bass. Although undoubtedly professional, this particular quartet lacked the innovation of its predecessor and although they remained together until 1971, the Strawberry Alarm Clock was unable to regain its early profile. Ed King later joined Lynyrd Skynyrd, while several of his erstwhile colleagues were reunited during the 80s for a succession of 'summer of love revisited' tours. 'Incense And Peppermints' was featured in the first *Austin Powers* movie in 1997.
● ALBUMS: *Incense And Peppermints* (Uni 1967) ★★★, *Wake Up It's Tomorrow* (Uni 1967) ★★, *The World In A Seashell* (Uni 1968) ★★, *Good Morning Starshine* (Uni 1969) ★★.
● COMPILATIONS: *The Best Of The Strawberry Alarm Clock* (Uni 1970) ★★★, *Changes* (Vocalion 1971) ★★.

STRAY

Originally formed in 1966, as the Stray, they metamorphosed as a formidable UK hard rock act in 1969/70. Stray was comprised of Del Bromham (b. London, England; guitar/vocals/keyboards) Steve Gadd (guitar/harmonica/vocals), Gary Giles (bass) and Ritchie Cole (drums) replacing Steve Crutchley. They were signed by Transatlantic Records soon after inception as the label sought to expand its previously folk-based roster. *Stray* captured the band at the height of its powers, notably on the exciting 'All In Your Mind' and 'Taken All The Good Things'. Subsequent albums followed in a similar vein but, despite a prolific output, Stray were unable to break free from the shackles of their rather limited style. They did, however, achieve momentary notoriety when briefly managed by Charlie Kray, brother of the notorious Kray twins. Peter Dyer (guitar/vocals) replaced Gadd prior to recording *Houdini*, but this made little impact on Stray's dwindling fortunes. They split up in 1977, after which Bromham embarked on a short-lived solo career, recording for Gull Records, among others. With Dusty Miller (bass), and Phil McKee (drums) Bromham resurrected the band in the mid-90s and showed that his guitar technique is as sharp as ever. In the late 60s the first wave of heavy guitar idols were usually Jimmy Page, Eric Clapton and Jeff Beck. Bromham's past work should be reappraised as he clearly slipped through the net. His playing on the live portion of *Dangerous Games* is often quite stunning.
● ALBUMS: *Stray* (Transatlantic 1970) ★★★★, *Suicide* (Transatlantic 1971) ★★★, *Saturday Moving Pictures* (Transatlantic 1972) ★★, *Mundaz* (Transatlantic 1973) ★★, *Move It* (Transatlantic 1974) ★★, *Tracks* (Transatlantic 1975) ★★★, *Stand Up And Be Counted* (Dawn 1975) ★★, *Houdini* (Pye 1976) ★★, *Hearts Of Fire* (Pye 1976) ★★, *Live At The Marquee* (Mystic

1996) ★★, as Del Bromham's Stray *Alive And Gigging* (Mystic 1997) ★★, *Dangerous Games* (Receiver 2001) ★★★★.

SUPREMES

America's most successful female vocal group of all time was formed by four Detroit schoolgirls in the late 50s. Diana Ross (b. 26 March 1944, Detroit, Michigan, USA), Betty Hutton, Florence Ballard (b. 30 June 1943, Detroit, Michigan, USA, d. 22 February 1976) and Mary Wilson (b. 6 March 1944, Greenville, Mississippi, USA) named themselves the Primettes in tribute to the local male group, the Primes – who themselves found fame in the 60s as the Temptations. Having issued a solitary single on a small local label, the Primettes were signed to Berry Gordy's Motown Records stable, where they initially found public acceptance hard to find. For more than two years, they issued a succession of flop singles, despite the best efforts of top Motown writer/producer Smokey Robinson to find them a suitable vehicle for their unsophisticated talents. Only when Diana Ross supplanted Florence Ballard as the group's regular lead vocalist, at Gordy's suggestion, did the Supremes break into the US charts. The dynamic 'When The Lovelight Starts Shining In His Eyes', modelled on the production style of Phil Spector, was the group's first hit in 1963.

The follow-up single flopped, so Gordy handed over the group to the newly formed Holland/Dozier/Holland writing and production team. They concocted the slight, but effervescent, 'Where Did Our Love Go' for the Supremes, which topped the US charts and was also a major hit in Britain. This achievement inaugurated a remarkable run of successes for the group and their producers, as their next four releases – 'Baby Love', 'Come See About Me', 'Stop! In The Name Of Love' and 'Back In My Arms Again' – all topped the US singles charts, while 'Baby Love' became the only record by an American group to reach number 1 in Britain during the beat-dominated year of 1964. All these singles were hinged around insistent, very danceable rhythms with repetitive lyrics and melodies, which placed no great strain on Ross' fragile voice. With their girl-next-door looks and endearingly unsophisticated demeanour, the Supremes became role models for young black Americans and their name was used to promote a range of merchandising, even (ironically) a brand of white bread. The rather perfunctory 'Nothing But Heartaches' broke the chart-topping sequence, which was immediately restored by the more ambitious 'I Hear A Symphony'. As Holland/Dozier/Holland moved into their prime, and Ross increased in confidence, the group's repertoire grew ever more mature. They recorded albums of Broadway standards, played residencies at expensive nightclubs, and were expertly groomed by Motown staff as all-round entertainers. Meanwhile, the hits kept coming, with four more US number 1 hits in the shape of 'You Can't Hurry Love', 'You Keep Me Hanging On', 'Love Is Here And Now You're Gone' and 'The Happening' – the last of which was a blatant attempt to cash in on the psychedelic movement.

Behind the scenes, the group's future was in some jeopardy; Florence Ballard had grown increasingly unhappy in the supporting role into which Berry Gordy had coerced her, and her occasionally erratic and troublesome behaviour was ultimately used as an excuse to force her out of the group. Without fanfare, Ballard was ousted in mid-1967, and replaced by Cindy Birdsong; most fans simply did not notice. At the same time, Ross' prime position in the group's hierarchy was confirmed in public, when she was given individual credit on the group's records, a move that prompted a flurry of similar demands from the lead singers of other Motown groups. 'Reflections', an eerie, gripping song that was one of Motown's most adventurous productions to date, introduced the new era. Motown's loss of Holland/Dozier/Holland slowed the group's progress in 1968, before they bounced back with two controversial slices of overt social commentary, 'Love Child' and 'I'm Livin' In Shame', the first of which was yet another US number 1. The Supremes also formed a successful recording partnership with the Temptations, exemplified by the hit single 'I'm Gonna Make You Love Me'. During 1969, there were persistent rumours that Berry Gordy was about to launch Diana Ross on a solo career. These were confirmed at the end of the year, when the Supremes staged a farewell performance, and Ross bade goodbye to the group with the elegiac 'Someday We'll Be Together' – a US chart-topper on which, ironically, she was the only member of the Supremes to appear. Ross was replaced by Jean Terrell, sister of heavyweight boxer Ernie Terrell. The new line-up, with Terrell and Mary Wilson alternating lead vocal duties, gained immediate success with 'Up The Ladder To The Roof' in early 1970, while 'Stoned Love', the group's biggest UK hit for four years, revived memories of their early successes with its rhythmic base and repetitive hook. The Supremes also tried to revive the atmosphere of their earlier recordings with the Temptations on a series of albums with the Four Tops. Gradually, their momentum was lost, and as Motown shifted its centre of activity from Detroit to California, the Supremes were left behind.

Lynda Laurence replaced Cindy Birdsong in the line-up in 1972; Birdsong returned in 1974 when Laurence became pregnant. The latter move coincided with the departure of Jean Terrell, whose place was taken by Scherrie Payne (b. 14 November 1944, Detroit, Michigan, USA). With the group recording only rarely, Birdsong quit again, leaving Mary Wilson – at last established as the unchallenged leader – to recruit Susaye Greene in her place. This trio recorded the self-explanatory *Mary, Scherrie And Susaye* in 1976, before disbanding the following year. Mary Wilson attempted to assemble a new set of Supremes for recording purposes, and actually toured Britain in 1978 with Karen Rowland and Karen Jackson in the line-up. The termination of her Motown contract stymied this move, however, and since then the use of the Supremes' name has legally resided with Motown. They have chosen not to sully the memory of their most famous group by concocting an ersatz Supremes to cash in on their heritage. Jean Terrell, Scherrie Payne and Lynda Laurence won the rights to use the Supremes' name in the UK. Payne began recording disco material with producer Ian Levine in 1989, for the Nightmare and Motor City labels. Levine also signed Laurence, Wilson and ex-Supreme Susaye Greene to solo contracts and recorded Terrell, Lawrence and Greene for a remake of 'Stoned Love'. The career of Mary Wilson has also continued with a starring role in the Toronto, Canada production of the stage musical *The Beehive* in 1989 and the publication of the second volume of her autobiography in 1990. In 1988, the Supremes were inducted into the Rock And Roll Hall Of Fame.

● ALBUMS: *Meet The Supremes* (Motown 1963) ★★★, *Where Did Our Love Go?* (Motown 1964) ★★★, *A Bit Of Liverpool* (Motown 1964) ★★, *The Supremes Sing Country, Western And Pop* (Motown 1964) ★, *We Remember Sam Cooke* (Motown 1965) ★★★, *More Hits By The Supremes* (Motown 1965) ★★★, *Merry Christmas* (Motown 1965) ★★★, *The Supremes At The Copa* (Motown 1965) ★★★, *I Hear A Symphony* (Motown 1966) ★★★, *The Supremes A-Go-Go* (Motown 1966) ★★★, *The Supremes Sing Holland, Dozier, Holland* (Motown 1967) ★★★★, *The Supremes Sing Rodgers And Hart* (Motown 1967) ★★, *Right On* (Motown 1970) ★★★, with the Four Tops *The Magnificent Seven* (Motown 1970) ★★★★, *New Ways But Love Stays* (Motown 1970) ★★★, *Touch* (Motown 1971) ★★, with the Four Tops *The Return Of The Magnificent Seven* (Motown 1971) ★★, with the Four Tops *Dynamite* (Motown 1971) ★★★, *Floy Joy* (Motown 1972) ★★★, *The Supremes* (Motown 1975) ★★, *High Energy* (Motown 1976) ★★, *Mary, Scherrie And Susaye* (Motown 1976) ★★★. As Diana Ross And The Supremes: *Reflections* (Motown 1968) ★★★, *Diana Ross And The Supremes Sing And Perform 'Funny Girl'* (Motown 1968) ★, *Diana Ross And The Supremes Live At London's Talk Of The Town* (Motown 1968) ★★★, with the Temptations *Diana Ross And The Supremes Join The Temptations* (Motown 1968) ★★★, *Love Child* (Motown 1968) ★★★, with the Temptations *TCB* (Motown 1968) ★★★, *Let The Sunshine In*

(Motown 1969) ★★, with the Temptations *Together* (Motown 1969) ★★★, *Cream Of The Crop* (Motown 1969) ★★, with the Temptations *Diana Ross And The Supremes On Broadway* (Motown 1969) ★★, *Farewell* (Motown 1970) ★★.

● COMPILATIONS: *Diana Ross And The Supremes Greatest Hits* (Motown 1967) ★★★★, *Diana Ross And The Supremes Greatest Hits, Volume 2* (Motown 1967) ★★★★, *Diana Ross And The Supremes Greatest Hits, Volume 3* (Motown 1969) ★★★, *Anthology 1962-69* (Motown 1974) ★★★★, *Supremes At Their Best* (Motown 1978) ★★★, *20 Greatest Hits* (Motown 1986) ★★★★, *25th Anniversary* (Motown 1986) ★★★★, *Early Classics* (Spectrum 1996) ★★★, *The Ultimate Collection* (Motown 1998) ★★★★, *The Supremes* 5-CD box set (Motown 2000) ★★★★.

● FURTHER READING: *Reflections*, Johnny Bond. *Dreamgirl: My Life As A Supreme*, Mary Wilson. *Supreme Faith: Someday We'll Be Together*, Mary Wilson with Patricia Romanowski. *All That Glittered: My Life With The Supremes*, Tony Turner and Barbara Aria.

● FILMS: *Beach Ball* (1965).

SURFARIS

Formed in Glendora, California, in 1962, the Surfaris – Jim Fuller (lead guitar), Jim Pash (guitar), Bob Berryhill (guitar), Pat Connolly (bass) and Ron Wilson (drums) – achieved international success the following year with 'Wipe Out'. This frantic yet simplistic instrumental, originally envisaged as a throwaway b-side, is recognized as one of the definitive surfing anthems. Controversy arose when the Surfaris discovered that the music gracing their debut album was, in fact, played by a rival group, the Challengers. However, despite their understandable anger, such backroom machinations remained rife throughout the quintet's career. Their third album, *Hit City '64*, introduced a partnership with producer Gary Usher, who employed a team of experienced session musicians on ensuing Surfaris' releases. In 1965 the group abandoned beach and hot-rod themes for folk rock. Wilson had developed into an accomplished lead singer and with Ken Forssi (b. Cleveland, Ohio, USA, d. 5 January 1998, USA) replacing Connolly on bass, the Surfaris completed the promising *It Ain't Me Babe*. The contract with Usher ended and the group broke up when the last remaining original member, Jim Pash, left the line-up. Newcomer Forssi then joined Love, and although no other member achieved similar success, the Surfaris' name was resurrected in 1981 when they performed at Disneyland.

● ALBUMS: *Wipe Out* (Dot 1963) ★★★, *The Surfaris Play Wipe Out And Others* (Decca 1963) ★★★, *Hit City '64* (Decca 1964) ★★★, *Fun City, USA* (Decca 1964) ★★, *Hit City '65* (Decca 1965) ★★, *It Ain't Me Babe* (Decca 1965) ★★★, *Surfaris*

Live (1983) ★★.
● COMPILATIONS: *Yesterday's Pop Scene* (Coral 1973) ★★★, *Surfers Rule* (Decca 1976) ★★★, *Gone With The Wave* (Decca 1977) ★★★, *Wipe Out! The Best Of The Surfaris* (Varèse Sarabande 1994) ★★★, *Surfaris Stomp* (Varèse Sarabande 1995) ★★★.

SUTCH, SCREAMING LORD
b. David Sutch, 10 November 1940, Harrow, Middlesex, England, d. 16 June 1999. Sutch rose to prominence in 1960 as the first long-haired pop star, with tresses in excess of 18 inches. His recording career peaked with such early releases as 'Til The Following Night', 'Jack The Ripper' and 'I'm A Hog For You', all produced by the late Joe Meek. Although he never registered a chart entry, Sutch boasted one of the most accomplished live acts of the era in the Savages, whose ranks included such luminaries as Ritchie Blackmore, Nicky Hopkins and Paul Nicholas. For nearly 40 years, Sutch sustained his flagging recording career with a plethora of publicity stunts ranging from dramatic marriage proposals to standing for Parliament and founding his own radio station. In 1970, he enjoyed some minor success in the US album charts with *Lord Sutch And Heavy Friends*, which featured Blackmore, Hopkins, Jimmy Page, Jeff Beck, Keith Moon, Noel Redding and John Bonham. He became better known for his appearances at countless election result events, usually in front of a television camera. He founded the Monster Raving Loony Party and enjoyed a degree of fame for many years. Musically he had little to offer. He was found dead in 1999.
● ALBUMS: *Lord Sutch And Heavy Friends* (Atlantic 1970) ★, *Hands Of Jack The Ripper* (Atlantic 1972) ★, *Alive And Well* (Babylon 1980) ★, *Rock & Horror* (Ace 1982) ★, *Murder In The Graveyard* (Fury 1992) ★, *Live Manifesto* (Jet 1992) ★,
● COMPILATIONS: *The Screaming Lord Sutch Story* (Skull N'Bones 1991) ★, *Munster Rock* (Munster 2001) ★.
● FURTHER READING: *Life As Sutch: The Official Autobiography Of Monster Raving Loony*, Lord David Sutch with Peter Chippindale.

SWINGING BLUE JEANS
Determined to concentrate on rock 'n' roll, several leading figures in Liverpool's skiffle scene founded the Bluegenes in 1958. They were singer and lead guitarist Ray Ennis (b. 26 May 1942), rhythm guitarist Ray Ellis (b. 8 March 1942), bass player Les Braid (b. 15 September 1941), drummer Norman Kuhlke (b. 17 June 1942) and Paul Moss (banjo), all born in Liverpool. Minus Moss, the group became one of the leading attractions in the Merseyside beat group scene and also played in Hamburg. Following the Beatles' first successes, the Swinging Blue Jeans (as they had been

renamed) signed a recording deal with the HMV Records label. The Beatles-sounding 'It's Too Late Now', was a minor hit the following year, but it was the group's third single, 'Hippy Hippy Shake', that provided their biggest success when it reached number 2. This rasping rendition of a Chan Romero song remains one of the era's finest performances, invoking a power the Blue Jeans never quite recaptured. Their version of 'Good Golly Miss Molly' nonetheless peaked at number 11, while the reflective rendition of Betty Everett's soul ballad 'You're No Good' reached number 3. An excellent reading of Dionne Warwick's hit 'Don't Make Me Over' stalled outside the Top 30. It was, however, the quartet's last substantial hit despite a series of highly polished singles, including 'Promise You'll Tell Her' (1964), 'Crazy 'Bout My Baby' (1965). The Blue Jeans were unfairly dubbed anachronistic. Several personnel changes also ensued, including the induction of two former Escorts, Terry Sylvester and Mike Gregory, but neither this, nor a brief change of name to Music Motor, made any difference to their fortunes. In 1968, the band was briefly renamed Ray Ennis And The Blue Jeans but when Sylvester was chosen to replace Graham Nash in the Hollies, the remaining members decided to split up.
The revival of interest in 60s music persuaded Ennis to re-form the Swinging Blue Jeans in 1973. He re-recorded 'Hippy Hippy Shake' for an album on Dart Records and continued leading the band on the UK scampi-and-chips revival circuit for the next two decades. A 1992 reissue album included nine previously unreleased tracks; among them, versions of Little Richard's 'Ready Teddy' and 'Three Little Fishes', the novelty song first recorded in 1939 by US bandleader Kay Kyser. They continue to regularly work the 60s nostalgia circuit with considerable success.
● ALBUMS: *Blue Jeans A' Swinging* aka *Swinging Blue Jeans* aka *Tutti Frutti* (HMV 1964) ★★★, *The Swinging Blue Jeans: La Voce Del Padrone* (HMV 1966) ★★★, *Hippy Hippy Shake* (Imperial 1973) ★★★, *Brand New And Faded* (Dart 1974) ★★, *Live Sharin'* (Prestige 1990) ★★.
● COMPILATIONS: *Shake: The Best Of The Swinging Blue Jeans* (EMI 1986) ★★★, *All The Hits Plus More* (Prestige 1992) ★★★, *The EMI Years* (EMI 1992) ★★★★, *At Abbey Road* (EMI 1998) ★★★.

SYNDICATE OF SOUND
Formed in San Jose, California, USA, in 1964, the Syndicate Of Sound were known for one classic garage band/punk single, 'Little Girl', a US Top 10 hit on Bell Records in 1966. The group consisted of Don Baskin (b. 9 October 1946, Honolulu, Hawaii, USA; vocals/saxophone), John Sharkey (b. 8 June 1946, Los Angeles, California, USA; guitar/keyboards), Jim Sawyers (lead guitar), Bob Gonzales (bass/

and John Duckworth (b. 18 November 1946, Springfield, Missouri, USA; drums). After an unsuccessful single for the Scarlet label, they recorded 'Little Girl' for the local Hush Records. It was a regional hit and picked up for national distribution by Bell, for which the group also recorded an album. The group placed two other minor singles on the charts, one later that year for Bell and another in 1970 on Buddah Records. They also recorded unsuccessfully for Capitol Records before disbanding in 1970.

● ALBUMS: *Little Girl* (Bell 1966) ★★.
● COMPILATIONS: *Little Girl* (Sundazed 1997) ★★.

T-BONES

A studio instrumental group of Liberty Records based in Los Angeles, California, USA, the T-Bones represent an era when many instrumentals were recorded by house-band session members and released on the unsuspecting public as being recordings by a real rock 'n' roll live ensemble. The T-Bones represented a variety of studio sessionmen under the production aegis of Joe Saraceno (b. 16 May 1937, Utica, New York, USA), who had previous experience with another studio instrumental hitmaker, the Routers (of 'Let's Go' fame). The mainstays of the band were guitarist Don Hamilton (originally from Wetnatchee, Washington), bassist Joe Frank Carollo (from Leland, Mississippi), and drummer/steel drummer Tommy Reynolds (from New York City). The first LPs by the T-Bones, *Boss Drag* and *Boss Drag At The Beach*, were released in 1964 to exploit the craze for instrumentals evoking surf and hot-rod themes. *Doin' The Jerk* followed in 1965 to exploit a huge west coast dance craze, The Jerk. The T-Bones became a notable one-hit-wonder act in late 1965 with a huge hit, 'No Matter What Shape (Your Stomach's In)' (number 3 pop), a composition by Sascha Burland based on an Alka-Seltzer commercial. An album of the same name became the group's only chart entry, at number 75 in the pop chart. A follow-up, 'Sippin' And Chippin'', which was based on a Nabisco jingle, only reached number 62, and the album of the same name did not chart at all. The last T-Bones album was *Everyone's Gone To The Moon*, late in 1966. Hamilton, Frank and Reynolds went on to become a notable rock act in the 70s as Hamilton, Joe Frank And Reynolds.

● ALBUMS: *Boss Drag* (Liberty 1964) ★★, *Boss Drag At The Beach* (Liberty 1964) ★, *Doin' The Jerk* (Liberty 1965) ★, *No Matter What Shape* (Liberty 1966) ★★, *Sippin' And Chippin'* (Liberty 1966) ★, *Everyone's Gone To The Moon* (Liberty 1966) ★★.

TAMS

This US group was formed in 1952 as the Four Dots in Atlanta, Georgia, USA. Their line-up featured Joseph Pope (b. 6 November 1933, d. 16 March 1996), Charles Pope (b. 7 August 1936), Robert Lee Smith (b. 18 March 1936) and Horace Kay (b. 13 April 1934). Although such an early origin suggests longevity, it was not until 1960 that the group emerged with a single on Swan. Now dubbed the Tams (derived by their wearing of Tam O'Shanter hats on stage), they added a further member, Floyd Ashton (b. 15 August 1933), prior to signing with Bill Lowery, an Atlanta song publisher and entrepreneur. Among those already on his books were Joe South and Ray Whitley, two musicians who would work closely with the group. 'Untie Me', a South composition, was recorded at Fame and leased to Philadelphia's Arlen Records. The song became a Top 20 US R&B hit, but follow-up releases failed until 1963 when Lowery secured a new deal with ABC-Paramount Records. The Tams' first single there, 'What Kind Of Fool (Do You Think I Am?)', reached the US Top 10 and established a series of Whitley-penned successes. His compositions included 'You Lied To Your Daddy' and 'Hey Girl Don't Bother Me', ideal material for Joe Pope's ragged lead and the group's unpolished harmonies.

After 1964, the group preferred Atlanta's Master Sound studio, by which time Albert Cottle (b. 1941, Washington, DC, USA) had replaced Ashton. South and Whitley continued their involvement, writing, playing on and producing various sessions, but the Tams had only one further US hit in 1968 with the bubbling 'Be Young, Be Foolish, Be Happy', which peaked on the *Billboard* R&B chart at 26 and reached the UK Top 40 in 1970. By the end of the 60s their mentors had moved elsewhere while the Master Sound house band was breaking up. Dropped by ABC, the Tams unsuccessfully moved to 1-2-3 and Capitol Records until a chance reissue of 'Hey Girl Don't Bother Me' became a surprise UK number 1 in 1971. They were not to chart again until 16 years later when their association with the Shag, a dance craze and subsequent 80s film, secured a further lifeline to this remarkable group, giving the group a UK Top 30 hit with 'There Ain't Nothing Like Shaggin''.

● ALBUMS: *Presenting The Tams* (ABC 1964) ★★★, *Hey Girl Don't Bother Me* (ABC 1964) ★★★★, *Time For The Tams* (ABC 1967) ★★★, *A Portrait Of The Tams* (ABC 1969) ★★, *Be Young, Be Foolish, Be Happy* (Stateside 1970) ★★.

● COMPILATIONS: *A Little More Soul* (ABC 1968) ★★★★, *The Best Of The Tams* (Capitol 1971) ★★★, *The Mighty Mighty Tams* (Sounds South 1978) ★★★, *Greatest Hits – Beach Party Vol. 1* (Carousel South 1981) ★★★, *Atlanta Soul Connection* (Charly 1983) ★★★, *Beach Music From The Tams* (Compleat 1983) ★★★, *Reminiscing* (Wonder 1982) ★★★, *There Ain't Nothing Like ... The Tams* (Virgin 1987) ★★★, *The Best Of (Hey Girl Don't Bother Me)* (Half Moon 1998) ★★★.

TATE, HOWARD

b. Macon, Georgia, USA. A former member of the Gainors with Garnet Mimms, Tate also sang with Bill Doggett's band. A solo act by 1962, he (like Mimms) was guided by producer/songwriter Jerry Ragovoy. Between 1966 and 1968, Howard secured four US R&B hits on Verve Records including 'Ain't Nobody Home', 'Look At Granny Run, Run' (later covered by Ry Cooder) and 'Stop' (later covered by Mike Bloomfield and Al Kooper). Tate's work provided material for several acts, most notably Janis Joplin, who recorded 'Get It While You Can'. After releasing two singles on the Turntable label, 'There Are The Things That Make Me Know You're Gone' (1969) and 'My Soul's Got A Hole In It' (1970), Tate moved to Atlantic Records where he enjoyed the production assistance of former mentor Ragovoy. From there he moved on to various other labels, but sadly, with little success, and he left music to work as an insurance salesman. Longstanding Tate fans were delighted with the news in August 2001 that, after far too long, the singer was going back into the recording studio with Ragovoy. Tate possesses a fabulous voice of great tone and range, and it remains a mystery why he has not been more successful or prolific. His late 60s material was the same class as Sam Cooke, Marvin Gaye and Johnnie Taylor. His reissued material is crying out to be heard.

● ALBUMS: *Get It While You Can* (Verve 1967) ★★★★, *Howard Tate* (Atlantic 1972) ★★★.

● COMPILATIONS: *Get It While You Can: The Legendary Sessions* (Mercury 1995) ★★★★.

TAYLOR, DEREK

b. 7 May 1932, Liverpool, England, d. 7 September 1997. As a London *Daily Express* show-business correspondent, he was briefed to do a 'hatchet job' on the Beatles' agreement to appear on 1963's Royal Variety Show but he could only praise them. Another *Express* commission to collate George Harrison's weekly ruminations for 12 Fridays (Harrison was paid £150 for each one) was the foundation of a lasting friendship with the guitarist, strengthened when Taylor was put on the group's payroll as Brian Epstein's personal assistant and ghost writer of his *Cellarful Of Noise* autobiography. In October 1964, he became the Beatles' press officer after his predecessor's outraged resignation. Conflicts with Epstein hastened Taylor's own exit in 1965. Emigrating to California, he gained employment as publicist for the Byrds, the Beach Boys, the Mamas And The Papas, Buffalo Springfield and other acts, and was on the steering committee of the celebrated Monterey Pop Festival in 1967. The following year found him back in London as the obvious choice to organize the Beatles' Apple Corps publicity department, his urbane, sympathetic manner winning many important contacts. While at Apple, he attempted to compose a stage musical with Harrison, but a more tangible legacy was his *As Time Goes By* memoir of two years 'in a bizarre royal court in a strange fairy tale'. Following Apple's collapse Taylor moved to Los Angeles as Head of Special Projects for Warner-Reprise Records (later WEA Records) before transfer to Europe as the label's general manager. Further musical chairs ensued and then promotion to Vice-President of Creative Services back in Hollywood, where he was honoured with a *This Is Your Life*-type citation, with Harrison and Ringo Starr among other leading entertainers walking on to tell some funny story from the past. By autumn 1979, the mercurial Taylor had gravitated back to England after Harrison's HandMade film company cried out for his unique skills. Extra-mural duties included penning scene-setting commentaries to the ex-Beatle's taped reminiscences for publication as *I Me Mine*. Happy with the result, Harrison interceded on his hireling's behalf to convince Genesis Publications that Taylor's idiosyncratic account of his own life would be viable. In 1985, therefore, 2,000 hand-tooled copies of Taylor's witty yarn, *Fifty Years Adrift*, went on sale at £148 each. His sparkling book, *It Was Twenty Years Ago Today* was accompanied by an engaging television film. They both brilliantly encapsulated the essence of the 'summer of love'. Among Taylor's later projects was the narrative to a collection of the late Michael Cooper's photographs. He also worked occasionally for British regional television – and on Apple Records' reissue programme. He was a major consultant to the *Anthology* television and album series in 1996. Taylor was a gentle soul who was deeply respected and is crucial to any student of the Beatles and music of the 60s. Writer and editor Chris Charlesworth stated after Taylor's death in 1997, 'He was the most diplomatic person I ever met, he should have been an ambassador for Britain, and could have solved something like the Arab-Israeli conflict by bringing the two sides together. He was that good.'

● FURTHER READING: *As Time Goes By*, Derek Taylor. *Fifty Years Adrift (In An Open-Necked Shirt)*, Derek Taylor. *It Was Twenty Years Ago Today*, Derek Taylor.

TAYLOR, FELICE

b. 29 January 1948, Richmond, California, USA. Felice emerged from the burgeoning Los Angeles girl-group scene where she recorded with the Sweets, a trio which also featured her sisters Darlene and Norma. Signed as a solo act to the Mustang label, Taylor's three 1967 singles there were each produced and co-written by Barry White. 'It May Be Winter Outside (But In My Heart It's Spring)' was an R&B hit although the beatier 'I'm Under The Influence Of Love' unaccountably failed to chart. White later re-recorded both songs with Love Unlimited. Taylor meanwhile scored a substantial UK hit with her third release, 'I Feel Love Comin' On'. She then moved labels to Kent, but stripped of White's imaginative arrangements, her adenoidal delivery tended to grate. Her best latter-day offering was 'All I Want To Do Is Love

You'. Recorded in Britain, it was written by Derv Gordon and arranged by Eddy Grant, two former members of the Equals.

TAYLOR, JOHNNIE

b. 5 May 1938, Crawfordsville, Arkansas, USA, d. 31 May 2000, Dallas, Texas, USA. Having left home at the age of 15, Taylor surfaced as part of several gospel groups, including the Five Echoes and the Highway QCs. In 1956 he joined the Soul Stirrers, replacing Sam Cooke on the latter's recommendation. Taylor switched to secular music in 1961; releases on Cooke's Sar and Derby labels betrayed his mentor's obvious influence. In 1965 he signed with Stax Records and had several R&B hits before 'Who's Making Love' (1968) crossed over into *Billboard*'s pop Top 5. Further releases, including 'Take Care Of Your Homework' (1969), 'I Believe In You (You Believe In Me)' and 'Cheaper To Keep Her' (both 1973), continued this success. The albums *Wanted: One Soul Singer, Who's Making Love ...* and *Taylored In Silk* best illustrate his lengthy period at Stax. Taylor maintained his momentum on a move to Columbia Records. The felicitous 1976 US chart-topper, 'Disco Lady', was the first single to be certified platinum by the R.I.A.A., but although subsequent releases reached the R&B chart they fared less well with the wider audience. Following a short spell with Beverly Glen, the singer found an ideal niche on Malaco Records, a bastion for traditional southern soul. Taylor's first album there, 1984's *This Is The Night*, reaffirmed his gritty, blues-edged approach, a feature consolidated on *Wall To Wall, Lover Boy* and *Crazy 'Bout You*. In 1996, Taylor experienced something of a revival when his Malaco album *Good Love!* became a huge hit and reached the top of the *Billboard* blues chart. Taylor, dubbed the 'Philosopher Of Soul', had one of the great voices of the era: expressive graceful and smooth, and yet it is a mystery why he failed to reach the heights attained by the likes of Otis Redding, Marvin Gaye and Wilson Pickett. Taylor's early work on Sar can be found on *The Roots Of Johnnie Taylor*.

● ALBUMS: *Wanted: One Soul Singer* (Stax 1967) ★★★★, *Who's Making Love ...* (Stax 1968) ★★★★, *Raw Blues* (Stax 1968) ★★★, *The Johnnie Taylor Philosophy Continues* (Stax 1969) ★★★, *Rare Stamps* (Stax 1970) ★★★, *One Step Beyond* (Stax 1971) ★★★, *Taylored In Silk* (Stax 1973) ★★★★, *Super Taylor* (Stax 1974) ★★★, *Eargasm* (Columbia 1976) ★★★, *Rated Extraordinaire* (Columbia 1977) ★★, *Disco 9000* (Columbia 1977) ★★, *Ever Ready* (Columbia 1978) ★★, *Reflections* (Columbia 1979) ★★, *She's Killing Me* (Columbia 1979) ★★, *A New Day* (Columbia 1980) ★★, *Just Ain't Good Enough* (Beverly Glen 1982) ★★★, *This Is Your Night* (Malaco 1984) ★★★, *Wall To Wall* (Malaco 1985) ★★★, *Lover Boy* (Malaco 1987) ★★★, *In Control* (Malaco 1988) ★★, *Crazy 'Bout You*

(Malaco 1989) ★★★, *I Know It's Wrong, But I ... Just Can't Do Right* (Malaco 1991) ★★★, *Real Love* (Malaco 1994) ★★★, *Good Love!* (Malaco 1996) ★★★★, *Taylored To Please* (Malaco 1998) ★★★, *Gotta Get The Groove Back* (Malaco 1999) ★★★★.
● COMPILATIONS: *The Roots Of Johnnie Taylor* (Sar 1969) ★★★, *Johnnie Taylor's Greatest Hits Vol. 1* (Stax 1970) ★★★★, *The Johnnie Taylor Chronicle (1968-1972)* (Stax 1978) ★★★★, *The Johnnie Taylor Chronicle (1972-1974)* (Stax 1978) ★★★, *The Best Of Johnnie Taylor* (Columbia 1981) ★★, *Little Bluebird* (Stax 1991) ★★★, *The Best Of Johnnie Taylor ... On Malaco Vol. 1* (Malaco 1994) ★★★, *The Best Of Johnnie Taylor: Rated X-Traordinaire* (Columbia/Legacy 1996) ★★★, *Funksoulbrother* (Fuel 2000) ★★★, *Lifetime* 3-CD box set (Stax 2000) ★★★★.

TEMPERANCE 7

Formed in 1955 to play 20s-style jazz, the Temperance 7 consisted at various times of Whispering Paul McDowell (vocals), Captain Cephas Howard (trumpet, euphonium and various instruments), Joe Clark (clarinet), Alan Swainston-Cooper (pedal clarinet, swanee whistle), Philip 'Finger' Harrison (banjo, alto and baritone saxophone), Canon Colin Bowles (piano, harmonica), Clifford Beban (tuba), Brian Innes (drums), Dr. John Grieves-Watson (banjo), Sheik Haroun el John R.T. Davies (trombone, alto saxophone) and Frank Paverty (sousaphone). Their debut single, 'You're Driving Me Crazy' (producer George Martin's first number 1), was followed by three more hits in 1961, 'Pasadena', 'Hard Hearted Hannah'/'Chili Bom Bom', and 'Charleston'. In 1963 they appeared in the play *The Bed Sitting Room* written by John Antrobus and Spike Milligan. They split in the mid-60s, but their spirit resurfaced in groups such as the Bonzo Dog Doo-Dah Band and the New Vaudeville Band. The Temperance 7 were re-formed in the 70s by Ted Wood, brother of the Rolling Stones' Ron Wood. Colin Bowles is reported to have died several years ago, but the other original members are said to be pursuing a variety of interests, including publishing, film set and graphic designing, acting and antiques.
● ALBUMS: *Temperance 7* (Parlophone 1961) ★★★★, *Temperance 7 Plus One* (Argo 1961) ★★★, *Hot Temperance 7* (1987) ★★★, *Tea For Eight* (1990) ★★★, *33 Not Out* (1990) ★★★.
● COMPILATIONS: *Pasadena & The Lost Cylinders* (Lake 1997) ★★★.

TEMPO, NINO, AND APRIL STEVENS

Nino Tempo (b. 6 January 1935, Niagara Falls, New York, USA) forged a career as session musician and arranger/composer for Rosemary Clooney and Steve Lawrence, before forming a duo with sister April Stevens (b. 29 April, Niagara Falls, New York, USA). The latter had already enjoyed minor success as a solo act with 'Teach Me Tiger', but the siblings scored a major hit in 1963 when their revival of 'Deep Purple' topped the US charts and secured a Grammy award as that year's Best Rock 'N' Roll Recording. They also held the record for many years with the longest title; the b-side of 'Deep Purple' was 'I've Been Carrying A Torch For You For So Long That It's Burned A Great Big Hole In My Heart'. Reworkings of 'Whispering' and 'Star Dust' also reached the bestsellers but Tempo achieved a more contemporary outlook following backroom and compositional work with Phil Spector. He and Stevens embraced a folk-rock/girl group direction with 'All Strung Out' and 'I Can't Go On Living (Without You Baby)' which the former co-wrote with Jerry Riopelle. An excellent attendant album contained compositions by David Gates and Warren Zevon, but the couple's passé image hindered potential interest. They later embarked on separate paths with Tempo resuming his association with Spector during the 70s, particularly with new protégé Jerri Bo Keno.
● ALBUMS: *Deep Purple* (Atco 1963) ★★★, *Nino & April Sing The Great Songs* (Atlantic 1964) ★★★, *Hey Baby* (Atco 1966) ★★★, *Nino Tempo, April Stevens Programme* (60s), *All Strung Out* (White Whale 1967) ★★.
● COMPILATIONS: *Sweet And Lovely: The Best Of ...* (Varèse Sarabande 1996) ★★★.

TEMPTATIONS

The most successful group in black music history was formed in 1961 in Detroit, Michigan, USA, by former members of two local R&B outfits. Eddie Kendricks (b. 17 December 1939, Union Springs, Alabama, USA) and Paul Williams (b. 2 July 1939, Birmingham, Alabama, USA, d. 17 August 1973) both sang with the Primes; Melvin Franklin (b. David English, 12 October 1942, Montgomery, Alabama, USA, d. 23 February 1995, Los Angeles, California, USA), Eldridge Bryant and Otis Williams (b. Otis Miles 30 October 1941, Texarkana, Texas, USA) came from the Distants. Initially known as the Elgins, the quintet were renamed the Temptations by Berry Gordy when he signed them to Motown Records in 1961. After issuing three singles on the Motown subsidiary Miracle Records, one of them under the pseudonym of the Pirates, the group moved to the Gordy label. 'Dream Come Home' provided their first brief taste of chart status in 1962, although it was only when they were teamed with writer, producer and performer Smokey Robinson that the Temptations achieved consistent success.
The group's classic line-up was established in 1963, when Eldridge Bryant was replaced by David Ruffin (b. 18 January 1941, Meridian, Mississippi, USA, d. 1 June 1991). His gruff baritone provided the perfect counterpoint to Kendricks' wispy tenor and falsetto, a contrast

that Smokey Robinson exploited to the full. Over the next two years, he fashioned a series of hits in both ballad and dance styles, carefully arranging complex vocal harmonies that hinted at the group's doo-wop heritage. 'The Way You Do The Things You Do' was the Temptations' first major hit, a stunningly simple rhythm number featuring a typically cunning series of lyrical images. 'My Girl' in 1965, the group's first US number 1, demonstrated Robinson's graceful command of the ballad idiom, and brought Ruffin's vocals to the fore for the first time (this track, featured in the movie *My Girl*, was reissued in 1992 and was once again a hit). 'It's Growing', 'Since I Lost My Baby', 'My Baby' and 'Get Ready' continued the run of success into 1966, establishing the Temptations as the leaders of the Motown sound. 'It's Growing' brought a fresh layer of subtlety into Robinson's lyric writing, while 'Get Ready' embodied all the excitement of the Motown rhythm factory, blending an irresistible melody with a stunning vocal arrangement. Norman Whitfield succeeded Robinson as the Temptations' producer in 1966 – a role he continued to occupy for almost a decade. He introduced a new rawness into their sound, spotlighting David Ruffin as an impassioned lead vocalist, and creating a series of R&B records that rivalled the output of Stax Records and Atlantic Records for toughness and power.

'Ain't Too Proud To Beg' introduced the Whitfield approach, and while the US Top 3 hit 'Beauty Is Only Skin Deep' represented a throwback to the Robinson era, 'I'm Losing You' and 'You're My Everything' confirmed the new direction. The peak of Whitfield's initial phase with the group was 'I Wish It Would Rain', a dramatic ballad that the producer heightened with delicate use of sound effects. The record was another major hit, and gave the Temptations their sixth R&B number 1 in three years. It also marked the end of an era, when David Ruffin first requested individual credit before the group's name; when this was refused, he elected to leave for a solo career. He was replaced by ex-Contours member Dennis Edwards (b. 3 February 1943, Birmingham, Alabama, USA), whose strident vocals fitted perfectly into the Temptations' harmonic blend. Whitfield chose this moment to inaugurate a new production style. Conscious of the psychedelic shift in the rock mainstream, and the inventive soul music being created by Sly And The Family Stone, he joined forces with lyricist Barrett Strong to pull Motown brutally into the modern world. The result was 'Cloud Nine', a record that reflected the increasing use of illegal drugs among young people, and shocked some listeners with its lyrical ambiguity. Whitfield created the music to match, breaking down the traditional barriers between lead and backing singers and

giving each of the Temptations a recognizable role in the group.

Over the next four years, Whitfield and the Temptations pioneered the concept of psychedelic soul, stretching the Motown formula to the limit, introducing a new vein of social and political comment, and utilizing many of rock's experimental production techniques to hammer home the message. 'Runaway Child, Running Wild' examined the problems of teenage rebellion; 'I Can't Get Next To You' reflected the fragmentation of personal relationships (and topped the US charts with the group's second number 1 hit); and 'Ball Of Confusion' bemoaned the disintegrating fabric of American society. These lyrical tracts were set to harsh, uncompromising rhythm tracks, seeped in wah-wah guitar and soaked in layers of harmony and counterpoint. The Temptations were greeted as representatives of the counter-culture, a trend that climaxed when they recorded Whitfield's outspoken protest against the Vietnam War, 'Stop The War Now'.

The new direction alarmed Eddie Kendricks, who felt more at home on the series of collaborations with the Supremes that the group also taped in the late 60s. He left for a solo career in 1971, after recording another US number 1, the evocative ballad 'Just My Imagination'. He was replaced first by Richard Owens, then later in 1971 by Damon Harris. This line-up recorded the 1972 number 1, 'Papa Was A Rolling Stone', a production *tour de force* which remains one of Motown's finest achievements, belatedly winning the label its first Grammy Award. After that, everything was an anti-climax. Paul Williams left the group in 1971, to be replaced by another former Distants member, Richard Street; Williams shot himself in 1973, after years of depression and drug abuse. Whitfield's partnership with Strong was broken the same year, and although he continued to rework the 'Papa Was A Rolling Stone' formula, the commercial and artistic returns were smaller. The Temptations still had hits, and 'Masterpiece', 'Let Your Hair Down' (both 1973) and 'Happy People' (1975) all topped the soul charts, but they were no longer a leading force in black music.

Whitfield left Motown in 1975; at the same time, Glenn Leonard replaced Damon Harris in the group. After struggling on for another year, the Temptations moved to Atlantic Records for two albums, which saw Louis Price taking the place of Dennis Edwards. When the Atlantic partnership brought no change of fortunes, the group returned to Motown, and to Dennis Edwards. *Power* in 1980 restored them to the charts, before Rick James engineered a brief reunion with David Ruffin and Eddie Kendricks for a tour, an album, and a hit single, 'Standing On The Top'. Ruffin and Kendricks then left to form a duo, Ron Tyson replaced Glenn Leonard, and Ali-Ollie Woodson took over the role of lead vocalist from Edwards. Woodson brought with him a song called 'Treat Her Like A Lady', which became their biggest UK hit in a decade. Subsequent releases confirmed the quality of the current line-up, although without a strong guiding hand they are unlikely to rival the achievements of the late 60s and early 70s line-ups, who represented the culmination of Motown's classic era. Franklin's death in February 1995 left Otis Williams as the sole remaining founder-member. Astonishingly, 1998's *Phoenix Rising* provided the group with their first ever platinum album. In the autumn of 2000, the Temptations, with a line-up comprising Williams, Terry Weeks, Ron Tyson, Harry McGillberry and Barrington Henderson, celebrated a formidable 40 years in the business, with Otis Williams wearing the broadest grin.

● ALBUMS: *Meet The Temptations* (Gordy 1964) ★★★★, *The Temptations Sing Smokey* (Gordy 1965) ★★★★, *Temptin' Temptations* (Gordy 1965) ★★★★, *Gettin' Ready* (Gordy 1966) ★★★★, *Temptations Live!* (Gordy 1967) ★★, *With A Lot O' Soul* (Gordy 1967) ★★★, *The Temptations In A Mellow Mood* (Gordy 1967) ★★★, *Wish It Would Rain* (Gordy 1968) ★★★★, *Diana Ross And The Supremes Join The Temptations* (Motown 1968) ★★★, with Diana Ross And The Supremes *TCB* (Motown 1968) ★★★, *Live At The Copa* (Gordy 1968) ★★, *Cloud Nine* (Gordy 1969) ★★★★, *The Temptations' Show* (Gordy 1969) ★★★, *Puzzle People* (Gordy 1969) ★★★, with Diana Ross And The Supremes *Together* (Motown 1969) ★★★, with Diana Ross And The Supremes *On Broadway* (Motown 1969) ★★★, *Psychedelic Shack* (Gordy 1970) ★★★★, *Live At London's Talk Of The Town* (Gordy 1970) ★★★, *The Temptations Christmas Card* (Gordy 1970) ★, *Sky's The Limit* (Gordy 1971) ★★★, *Solid Rock* (Gordy 1972) ★★★, *All Directions* (Gordy 1972) ★★★, *Masterpiece* (Gordy 1973) ★★★, *1990* (Gordy 1973) ★★★, *A Song For You* (Gordy 1975) ★★★, *House Party* (Gordy 1975) ★★, *Wings Of Love* (Gordy 1976) ★★, *The Temptations Do The Temptations* (Gordy 1976) ★★, *Hear To Tempt You* (Atlantic 1977) ★★, *Bare Back* (Atlantic 1978) ★★, *Power* (Gordy 1980) ★★, *Give Love At Christmas* (Gordy 1980) ★, *The Temptations* (Gordy 1981) ★★, with Jimmy Ruffin, Eddie Kendricks *Reunion* (Gordy 1982) ★★★, *Surface Thrills* (Gordy 1983) ★★, *Back To Basics* (Gordy 1984) ★★★, *Truly For You* (Gordy 1984) ★★, *Touch Me* (Gordy 1985) ★★, *To Be Continued ...* (Gordy 1986) ★★★, *Together Again* (Motown 1987) ★★★, *Special* (Motown 1989) ★★, *Milestone* (Motown 1991) ★★, *Phoenix Rising* (Motown 1998) ★★★★★, *Ear-Resistable* (Motown 2000) ★★★, *Awesome* (Motown 2001) ★★★.

● COMPILATIONS: *The Temptations Greatest Hits* (Gordy 1966) ★★★★, *Temptations Greatest Hits, Volume 2* (Gordy 1970) ★★★★, *Anthology* (Motown 1973) ★★★★, *All The Million Sellers* (Gordy 1981) ★★★, *Best Of The Temptations* (Telstar 1986) ★★, *25 Anniversary* (Motown 1986) ★★★★, *Compact Command Performances* (Motown 1989) ★★★, *Hum Along And Dance: More Of The Best 1963-1974* (Rhino 1993) ★★★, *The Original Lead Singers Of The Temptations* (1993) ★★★, *Emperors Of Soul* 5-CD box set (Motown 1994) ★★★★, *Early Classics* (Spectrum 1996) ★★★, *The Ultimate Collection* (Motown 1998) ★★★★, *You've Got To Earn It* (Motown 1999) ★★★, *Psychedelic Soul* (Spectrum 2000) ★★★★, *At Their Very Best* (Universal 2001) ★★★.

● VIDEOS: *Get Ready* (PMI 1988), *Temptations And The Four Tops* (Video Collection 1988), *Live In Concert* (Old Gold 1990).

● FURTHER READING: *Temptations*, Otis Williams with Patricia Romanowski.

TEN YEARS AFTER

Formed in Nottingham, England, as the Jaybirds in 1965, they abandoned their pedestrian title for a name that slotted in with the booming underground progressive music scene. The quartet of Alvin Lee (b. 19 December 1944, Nottingham, England; guitar, vocals), Chick Churchill (b. 2 January 1949, Mold, Flint/Clwyd, Wales; keyboards), Ric Lee (b. 20 October 1945, Cannock, Staffordshire, England; drums) and Leo Lyons (b. 30 November 1943, Bedford, England; bass) played a mixture of rock 'n' roll and blues that distinguished them from the mainstream blues of Fleetwood Mac, Chicken Shack and Savoy Brown. Their debut album was largely ignored and it took months of gruelling club work to establish their claim. The superb live *Undead*, recorded at Klook's Kleek club, spread the word that Lee was not only an outstanding guitarist, but he was the fastest by a mile. Unfortunately for the other three members, Lee overshadowed them to the extent that they became merely backing musicians in what was described as the Alvin Lee show. The band began a series of US tours that gave them the record of more US tours than any other UK band. Lee's furious performance of 'Goin' Home' at the Woodstock Festival was one of the highlights, although that song became a millstone for them. Over the next two years they delivered four solid albums, which all charted in the UK and the USA.

Sssssh, with its Graham Nash cover photography, was the strongest. 'Stoned Woman' epitomized their sound and style, although it was 'Love Like A Man' from *Cricklewood Green* that gave them their only UK hit (number 10, June 1970). *A Space In Time* saw them briefly relinquish guitar-based pieces in favour of electronics. By the time of *Rock 'N' Roll Music To The World* the band were jaded and they rested from touring to work on solo projects. This resulted in Lee's *On The Road To Freedom* with gospel singer

Mylon LeFevre and a dull album from Chick Churchill, *You And Me*. When they reconvened, their spark and will had all but gone and remaining albums were poor. After months of rumour, Lee admitted that the band had broken up. In 1978 Lee formed the trio Ten Years Later, with little reaction, and in 1989 the original band re-formed and released *About Time*, but only their most loyal fans were interested. The band remained active in the following decade.

● ALBUMS: *Ten Years After* (Deram 1967) ★★★, *Undead* (Deram 1968) ★★★★, *Stonedhenge* (Deram 1969) ★★★, *Ssssh* (Deram 1969) ★★★★, *Cricklewood Green* (Deram 1970) ★★★★, *Watt* (Deram 1970) ★★★, *A Space In Time* (Chrysalis 1971) ★★★, *Rock 'N' Roll Music To The World* (Chrysalis 1972) ★★, *Recorded Live* (Chrysalis 1973) ★★, *Positive Vibrations* (Chrysalis 1974) ★★, *About Time* (Chrysalis 1989) ★★, *Live 1990* (Demon 1994) ★★, *Live At The Fillmore East 1970* (EMI 2001) ★★★★.
● COMPILATIONS: *Alvin Lee & Company* (Deram 1972) ★★★, *Goin' Home! – Their Greatest Hits* (Deram 1975) ★★★, *The Essential* (Chrysalis 1992) ★★★★, *Solid Rock* (Chrysalis 1997) ★★★.
● FURTHER READING: *Alvin Lee & Ten Years After: A Visual History*, Herb Staehr.

TERRELL, TAMMI

b. Thomasina Montgomery, 29 April 1945, Philadelphia, Pennsylvania, USA, d. 16 March 1970, USA. Tammi Terrell began recording for Scepter/Wand Records at the age of 15, before touring with the James Brown Revue for a year. In 1965, she married heavyweight boxer Ernie Terrell, the brother of future Supreme Jean Terrell. Terrell's warm, sensuous vocals won her a contract with Motown Records later that year, and in 1966 she enjoyed a series of R&B hits, among them a soulful rendition of 'This Old Heart Of Mine'. In 1967, she was selected to replace Kim Weston as Marvin Gaye's recording partner. This inspired teaming produced Gaye's most successful duets, and the pair issued a stream of hit singles between 1967 and 1969. 'Ain't No Mountain High Enough' and 'You're All I Need To Get By' epitomized their style, as Gaye and Terrell wove around each other's voices, creating an aura of romance and eroticism that led to persistent rumours that they were lovers. From the beginning, their partnership was tinged with unhappiness, Terrell collapsing in Gaye's arms during a performance in 1967. She was diagnosed as suffering from a brain tumour, and despite a series of major operations over the next three years, her health steadily weakened. By 1969, she was unable to perform in public, and on several of the duo's final recordings, their producer, Valerie Simpson, controversially claims to have taken her place. Ironically, one of these tracks, 'The Onion Song', proved to be the most successful of the Gaye/Terrell singles

in the UK. Tammi Terrell died on 16 March 1970, her burial service attracting thousands of mourners, including many of her Motown colleagues. Her death has been the subject of much speculation, centred on rumours that her brain disorders were triggered by alleged beatings administered by a member of the Motown hierarchy. These accusations were given voice in *Number One With A Bullet*, a novel by former Gaye aide Elaine Jesmer, which included a character clearly based on Terrell.

● ALBUMS: with Marvin Gaye *United* (Tamla 1967) ★★★, with Gaye *You're All I Need* (Tamla 1968) ★★★, with Gaye *Easy* (Tamla 1969) ★★★, *Early Show* (1969) ★★★, *Irresistible Tammy* (Motown 1969) ★★★.
● COMPILATIONS: *Marvin Gaye & Tammi Terrell: Greatest Hits* (Tamla 1970) ★★★, *The Essential Collection* (Spectrum 2001) ★★★.

TEX, JOE

b. Joseph Arrington Jnr., 8 August 1933, Rogers, Texas, USA, d. 13 August 1982, Navasota, Texas, USA. The professional career of this popular singer began onstage at the Apollo. He won first place in a 1954 talent contest and duly secured a record deal. Releases on King Records, Ace Records and the Anna labels were derivative and disappointing, but Tex meanwhile honed his songwriting talent. James Brown's version of 'Baby You're Right' (1962) became a US R&B number 2, after which Tex was signed by Buddy Killen, a Nashville song publisher, who in turn established Dial as a recording outlet. Although early releases showed promise, it was not until 1965 that Tex prospered. Recorded at Fame and distributed by Atlantic Records, 'Hold On To What You've Got' was a US Top 5 hit. The first of several preaching singles, its homely values were maintained on 'A Woman Can Change A Man' and 'The Love You Save (May Be Your Own)'. However, Joe was equally comfortable on uptempo songs, as 'S.Y.S.L.J.F.M. (The Letter Song)' (1966) and 'Show Me' (1967) proved. Later releases were less successful and although 'Skinny Legs And All' and 'Men Are Gettin' Scarce' showed him still capable of major hits, the singer seemed unsure of his direction.

A fallow period ended with 'I Gotcha' (1972), an irresistibly cheeky song, but Tex chose this moment to retire. A convert to the Muslim faith since 1966, he changed his name to Yusuf Hazziez, and toured as a spiritual lecturer. He returned to music in 1975. Two years later he enjoyed a 'comeback' hit with the irrepressible 'Ain't Gonna Bump No More (With No Big Fat Woman)'. By the 80s, however, Tex had withdrawn again from full-time performing. He devoted himself to Islam, his Texas ranch and the Houston Oilers football team. He was tempted into a Soul Clan reunion in 1981, but

in August 1982 he died following a heart attack.
● ALBUMS: *Hold On* (Checker 1964) ★★★, *Hold What You've Got* (Atlantic 1965) ★★★, *The New Boss* (Atlantic 1965) ★★★★, *The Love You Save* (Atlantic 1966) ★★★, *I've Got To Do A Little Better* (Atlantic 1966) ★★★★, *Live And Lively* (Atlantic 1968) ★★, *Soul Country* (Atlantic 1968) ★★★, *You Better Believe It* (Atlantic 1969) ★★★, *Buying A Book* (Atlantic 1969) ★★★, *Sings With Strings And Things* (Atlantic 1970) ★★★, *From The Roots Came The Rapper* (Atlantic 1972) ★★, *I Gotcha* (Dial 1972) ★★, *Spills The Beans* (Dial 1973) ★★, *Another Man's Woman* (Powerpak 1974) ★★, *Bumps And Bruises* (Epic 1977) ★★, *Rub Down* (Epic 1978) ★★, *He Who Is Without Funk Cast The First Stone* (Dial 1979) ★★.
● COMPILATIONS: *The Best Of Joe Tex* (King 1965) ★★★, *The Very Best Of Joe Tex* (Atlantic 1967) ★★★★, *Greatest Hits* (Atlantic 1967) ★★★★, *The Very Best Of Joe Tex – Real Country Soul ... Scarce As Hen's Teeth* (Rhino 1988) ★★★, *I Believe I'm Gonna Make It: The Best Of Joe Tex 1964-1972* (Rhino 1988) ★★★★, *Different Strokes* (Charly 1989) ★★★, *I Gotcha (His Greatest Hits)* (BMG 1993) ★★★, *Skinny Legs And All: The Classic Early Dial Sides* (Kent 1994) ★★★, *You're Right Joe Tex!* (Kent 1995) ★★★, *25 All Time Greatest Hits* (Varèse Sarabande 2000) ★★★.

THEM

Formed in Belfast, Northern Ireland, in 1963, Them's tempestuous career spawned some of the finest records of the era. The original line-up – Van Morrison (b. 31 August 1945, Belfast, Northern Ireland; vocals, harmonica), Billy Harrison (guitar), Eric Wrixen (keyboards), Alan Henderson (bass) and Ronnie Millings (drums) – were stalwarts of the city's Maritime Hotel, where they forged a fiery, uncompromising brand of R&B. A demo tape featuring a lengthy version of 'Lovelight' engendered a management agreement with the imposing Phil Solomon, who persuaded Dick Rowe to sign the group to Decca Records. The group then moved to London and issued their debut single, 'Don't Start Crying Now', which flopped. Brothers Patrick and Jackie McAuley had replaced Wrixen and Millings by the time Them's second single, 'Baby Please Don't Go', was released. Although aided by session musicians, the quintet's performance was remarkable, and this urgent, exciting single – which briefly served as the theme song to the influential UK television pop programme *Ready Steady Go* – deservedly reached the UK Top 10. It was backed by the Morrison-penned 'Gloria', a paean to teenage lust hinged to a hypnotic riff, later adopted by aspiring bar bands.
The follow-up, 'Here Comes The Night', was written and produced by R&B veteran Bert Berns. It peaked at number 2, and although it suggested a long career, Them's internal disharmony undermined progress. Peter Bardens (b. 19 June 1945, Westminster, London,

England) replaced Jackie McAuley for the group's debut album, which matched brooding original songs, notably the frantic 'Mystic Eyes' and 'You Just Can't Win', with sympathetic cover versions. Further defections ensued when subsequent singles failed to emulate their early success and by the release of *Them Again*, the unit had been recast around Morrison, Henderson, Jim Armstrong (guitar), Ray Elliott (saxophone, keyboards) and John Wilson (drums). This piecemeal set nonetheless boasted several highlights, including the vocalist's impassioned reading of the Bob Dylan composition, 'It's All Over Now, Baby Blue'. Dave Harvey then replaced Wilson, but this version of Them disintegrated in 1966 following a gruelling US tour and a dispute with Solomon. Posthumous releases included the extraordinary 'The Story Of Them', documenting the group's early days at the Maritime in Belfast.
Morrison then began a highly prolific solo career, leaving behind a period of confusion that saw the McAuley brothers re-emerge with a rival unit known variously as 'Them', 'Them Belfast Gypsies', the 'Freaks Of Nature', or simply the 'Belfast Gypsies'. Meanwhile, ex-Mad Lads singer Kenny McDowell joined Henderson, Armstrong, Elliott and Harvey in a reconstituted Them, who moved to Los Angeles following the intervention of producer Ray Ruff. *Now And Them* combined garage R&B with the *de rigueur* west coast sound exemplified by the lengthy 'Square Room', but the new line-up found it hard to escape the legacy of its predecessors. Elliott left the group in 1967, but the remaining quartet completed the psychedelic *Time Out, Time In For Them* as a quartet before McDowell and Armstrong returned to Belfast to form Sk'Boo. Henderson then maintained the Them name for two disappointing albums, on which he was supported by anonymous session musicians, before joining Ruff for a religious rock-opera, *Truth Of Truths*. He subsequently retired from music altogether, but renewed interest in his old group's heritage prompted a reunion of sorts in 1979 when the bass player recruited Billy Harrison, Eric Wrixen, Mel Austin (vocals) and Billy Bell (drums) for *Shut Your Mouth*. True to form, both Harrison and Wrixen were fired prior to a tour of Germany, after which the Them appellation was again laid to rest.
● ALBUMS: *Them* aka *The Angry Young Them* (Decca 1965) ★★★★, *Them Again* (Decca 1966) ★★★★, *Now And Them* (Tower 1968) ★★★, *Time Out, Time In For Them* (Tower 1968) ★★★, *Them* (Happy Tiger 1970) ★★★, *In Reality* (Happy Tiger 1971) ★★★, *Shut Your Mouth* (Teldec 1979) ★★★.
Solo: Billy Harrison *Billy Who?* (Vagabound 1980) ★★.
● COMPILATIONS: *The World Of Them* (Decca 1970) ★★★★, *Them Featuring Van Morrison,*

Lead Singer (Decca 1973) ★★★, *Backtrackin' With Them* (London 1974) ★★★, *Rock Roots: Them* (Decca 1976) ★★★★, *One More Time* (Decca 1984) ★★★, *The Them Collection* (Castle 1986) ★★★, *The Singles* (See For Miles 1987) ★★★★, *The Story Of Them* (Deram 1997) ★★★★.
● FURTHER READING: *Van Morrison: A Portrait Of The Artist*, Johnny Rogan.

THIRD EAR BAND

Described by founder Glenn Sweeney as 'electric-acid-raga', the music of the UK-based Third Ear Band employed the drone-like figures and improvisatory techniques beloved by fellow pioneers the Soft Machine and Terry Riley. However, the esoteric, almost preternatural sweep of their work gave the band its originality as they studiously invoked an aura of ley-lines, druids and cosmology. Sweeney (drums, percussion) had been part of London's free-jazz circle prior to forming two *avant garde* ensembles, the Sun Trolly and the Hydrogen Juke-Box. Paul Minns (oboe, recorder), Richard Coff (violin) and cellist Mel Davis completed the line-up on the Third Ear Band's 1969 debut, *Alchemy*. The band found the hazy summers of the late 60s an ideal setting for their always original ideas. They were the ideal act to open an open air festival, setting the tone for whatever progressive rock band would follow. Ursula Smith replaced Davis on the band's self-titled second album, which featured four long and strikingly eclectic tracks. The unit was then commissioned to compose the soundtrack to a German television film about the doomed lovers Pierre Abélard and Héloise Fulbert, which was finally made available on the Blueprint label in 1999. Smith was replaced in the line-up by three new members, Paul Buckmaster, Simon House (ex-High Tide) and Denim Bridges, for the Third Ear Band's soundtrack work on Roman Polanski's adaptation of *Macbeth* (released on vinyl as *Music From Macbeth*). However, although their ethereal music provided the ideal accompaniment to this remarkable project, the band's highly stylized approach proved too specialized for mainstream acceptance. Unless the listener was prepared to 'get their ear in', the band would find their worthy sounds being treated as ideal for background, and not, as they intended, listened to with genuine concentration.
The Third Ear Band performed only sporadically during the rest of the decade, before Sweeney and Minns instigated a more permanent reunion in 1988. Featuring new members Allen Samuel (violin) and Mick Carter (guitar), *Live Ghosts* revealed that the passage of time had not dimmed the band's vision. Minns and Samuel were replaced by Neil Black (violin) and Lyn Dobson (saxophone, flute) on the subsequent studio release, *Magic Music*.

Sweeney continues to lead the Third Ear Band into the new millennium.
● ALBUMS: *Alchemy* (Harvest 1969) ★★★★, *Third Ear Band* aka *Elements* (Harvest 1970) ★★★★, *Music From Macbeth* (Harvest 1972) ★★★, *Live Ghosts* (Materiali Sonori 1988) ★★★, *Magic Music* (Materiali Sonori 1990) ★★★, *Brain Waves* (Materiali Sonori 1993) ★★★, *Live* (Voiceprint 1996) ★★★, *Magic Music* aka *New Age Magical Music* (Blueprint 1997) ★★★, *Abelard And Heloise* 1970 recording (Blueprint 1999) ★★★.
● COMPILATIONS: *Experiences* (Harvest 1976) ★★★, *Hymn To The Sphinx* (Mooncrest 2001) ★★★.

THIRD RAIL (60s)

A studio group comprised of Artie Resnick (writer of the Young Rascals' 'Good Lovin''), his wife Kris and Joey Levine, the Third Rail recorded their first single, 'R Subway Train That Came To Life', in 1966 for Cameo Records. Switching to Epic Records the following year, they recorded an album, *Id Music*, which included a song called 'Run Run Run' which commented on the futility of the urban rat race to a punky psychedelic sound. That single became a minor chart hit and was later rediscovered via the classic *Nuggets* compilation. The Third Rail released four more singles but failed to realize any further hits. Levine joined the Ohio Express in 1968.
● ALBUMS: *Id Music* (Epic 1967) ★★★.

13TH FLOOR ELEVATORS

Formed in Austin, Texas, USA in 1965, this influential psychedelic rock band evolved from the nucleus of the Lingsmen, a popular local attraction. The original line-up included Stacey Sutherland (guitar), Benny Thurman (bass), John Ike Walton (drums) and Max Rainey (vocals), but the latter was replaced by Roky Erickson (b. Roger Erkynard Erickson, 15 July 1947, Dallas, Texas, USA; vocals, guitar). The quartet retained their anachronistic name until adding lyricist and jug player Tommy Hall (b. 21 September 1943, USA), whose wife Clementine, suggested their more intriguing appellation.
The 13th Floor Elevators made their recording debut with 'You're Gonna Miss Me'. Erickson had recorded this acerbic composition with an earlier outfit, the Spades, but his new colleagues added an emphatic enthusiasm missing from the original version. Hall's quivering jug interjections, unlikely in a rock setting, suggested a taste for the unusual enhanced by the band's mystical air. Their 1966 debut, *The Psychedelic Sounds Of The 13th Floor Elevators*, combined this offbeat spiritualism with crude R&B to create some of the era's most compulsive music. However, the band's overt drug culture proselytization led to inevitable confrontations with the conservative Texan authorities. Several arrests ensued, the band's

live appearances were monitored by the state police, while a management dispute led to the departure of Walton and new bass player Ronnie Leatherman (who had replaced Thurman after the release of 'You're Gonna Miss Me').

The Elevators broke up briefly during the summer of 1967, but Hall, Erickson and Sutherland regrouped around a new rhythm section of Dan Galindo (b. San Antonio, Texas, USA, d. May 2001, Austin, Texas, USA) and Danny Thomas. A second album, *Easter Everywhere*, maintained the high quality of its predecessor, but external pressures proved too strong to repel. Studio outtakes were overdubbed with fake applause to create the implausible *Live*, and the band finally disintegrated in late 1968 when Erickson and Sutherland were both busted for drug offences. To avoid being sent to prison, Erickson claimed to be a Martian and was committed to Rusk State Hospital for the criminally insane. Sutherland was not so lucky and was imprisoned in Huntsville, the Texas state prison. A final collection, *Bull Of The Woods*, coupled partially completed performances with older, unissued masters.

Erickson was released from Rusk State in 1972, and made an abortive attempt to re-form the 13th Floor Elevators with Walton and other musicians. His solo career and numerous reissues and archive compilations have furthered this seminal band's reputation, but their tragic history culminated in 1978 when Sutherland was shot dead by his wife.

● ALBUMS: *The Psychedelic Sounds Of The 13th Floor Elevators* (International Artists 1966) ★★★★, *Easter Everywhere* (International Artists 1967) ★★★, *Live* (International Artists 1968) ★, *Bull Of The Woods* (International Artists 1968) ★★, *I've Seen Your Face Before* live recording (Big Beat 1988) ★★★, *Out Of Order: Live At The Avalon Ballroom* 1966 recording (Magnum 1993) ★★★.
● COMPILATIONS: *Epitaph For A Legend* (International Artists 1980) ★★★, *Fire In My Bones* (Texas Archive 1985) ★★, *Elevator Tracks* (Texas Archive 1987) ★★, *The Original Sound Of The 13th Floor Elevators* (USA) *Demos Everywhere* (UK) (13th Hour 1988) ★, *The Collection* 4-CD set (Decal 1991) ★★★, *The Interpreter* (Thunderbolt 1996) ★★★, *The Best Of ... Manicure Your Mind* (Eva 1997) ★★★, *All Time Highs* (Music Club 1998) ★★★, *The Legendary Group At Their Best* (Collectables 2001) ★★★.

THOMAS, CARLA

b. 21 December 1942, Memphis, Tennessee, USA. The daughter of Rufus Thomas, Carla first performed with the Teen Town Singers. "Cause I Love You', a duet with her father, was released on Satellite (later Stax Records) in 1960, but the following year she established herself as a solo

act with 'Gee Whiz (Look At His Eyes)'. Leased to Atlantic Records, the song became a US Top 10 hit. 'I'll Bring It On Home To You' (1962 – an answer to Sam Cooke), 'What A Fool I've Been' (1963) and 'Let Me Be Good To You' (1965) then followed. 'B-A-B-Y', written by Isaac Hayes and David Porter, reached the US R&B Top 3, before a series of duets with Otis Redding proclaimed her 'Queen of Soul'. An excellent version of Lowell Fulson's 'Tramp' introduced the partnership. 'Knock On Wood' and 'Lovey Dovey' followed before Redding's premature death. Thomas' own career was eclipsed as Aretha Franklin assumed her regal mantle. Singles with William Bell and Johnnie Taylor failed to recapture past glories, although the singer stayed with Stax until its bankruptcy in 1975. Since then Thomas has not recorded, although she tours occasionally with the Stax revival shows, and she appeared, along with her father, at the Porretta Terme Soul Festival in 1991.

● ALBUMS: *Gee Whiz* (Atlantic 1961) ★★★, *Comfort Me* (Stax 1966) ★★★★, *Carla* (Stax 1966) ★★★★, with Otis Redding *King And Queen* (Stax 1967) ★★★★, *The Queen Alone* (Stax 1967) ★★★★, *Memphis Queen* (Stax 1969) ★★★, *Love Means Carla Thomas* (Stax 1971) ★★.
● COMPILATIONS: *The Best Of Carla Thomas* (Atlantic 1969) ★★★★, *Hidden Gems* (Stax 1992) ★★★, *Gee Whiz: The Best Of Carla Thomas* (Rhino 1994) ★★★★.

THOMAS, IRMA

b. Irma Lee, 18 February 1941, Ponchatoula, Louisiana, USA. The 'Soul Queen Of New Orleans' was discovered in 1958 by bandleader Tommy Ridgley. Her early records were popular locally, but an R&B hit came in 1960 with '(You Can Have My Husband But Please) Don't Mess With My Man'. The following year Thomas rejoined producer/writer Allen Toussaint, with whom she had worked on her first recordings. This reunion resulted in two of Irma's finest singles, 'It's Raining' and 'Ruler Of My Heart' (1962), the latter a prototype for Otis Redding's 'Pain In My Heart'. After signing with the Imperial Records label in 1963 she recorded 'Wish Someone Would Care' (1964), which reached the US Top 20, while the follow-up, 'Anyone Who Knows What Love Is (Will Understand)', also entered the national chart. This single is better recalled for its b-side, 'Time Is On My Side', which was successfully covered by the Rolling Stones. Thomas continued to record excellent singles without achieving due commercial success. Her final hit was a magnificent interpretation of 'Good To Me' (1968), recorded at Muscle Shoals and issued on Chess Records. She then moved to Canyon, Roker and Cotillion, before appearing on Swamp Dogg's short-lived Fungus label with *In Between Tears* (1973). Irma has continued to record fine albums for the Rounder Records label and she remains a highly popular live attraction. Her career has continued into the new millennium with regular studio albums and a planned biography.

● ALBUMS: *Wish Someone Would Care* (Imperial 1964) ★★★★, *Take A Look* (Imperial 1968) ★★★★, *In Between Tears* (Fugus 1973) ★★★, *Irma Thomas Live* (Island 1977) ★★, *Soul Queen Of New Orleans* (Maison De Soul 1978) ★★★, *Safe With Me* (Paula 1979) ★★★, *The New Rules* (Rounder 1986) ★★, *The Way I Feel* (Rounder 1988) ★★★★, *Simply The Best* (Rounder 1991) ★★★, *True Believer* (Rounder 1992) ★★★, *Walk Around Heaven: New Orleans Gospel Soul* (Rounder 1994) ★★★, *The Story Of My Life* (Rounder 1997) ★★, with Marcia Ball, Tracy Nelson *Sing It!* (Rounder 1998) ★★★, *My Heart's In Memphis: The Songs Of Dan Penn* (Rounder 2000) ★★, *If You Want It Come And Get It* (Rounder 2001) ★★★★.

● COMPILATIONS: *Time Is On My Side* (Kent 1983) ★★★, *The Best Of Irma Thomas: Break-A-Way* (EMI 1986) ★★★, *Something Good: The Muscle Shoals Sessions* (1989) ★★★, *Ruler Of Hearts* (Charly 1989) ★★★, *Time Is On My Side: The Best Of Vol. 1* (EMI 1992) ★★★★, *The Soul Queen Of New Orleans* (Razor & Tie 1993) ★★★, *Time Is On My Side* (Kent 1996) ★★★★, *The Irma Thomas Collection* (Razor & Tie 1997) ★★★★.

THOMAS, RUFUS

b. 26 March 1917, Cayce, Mississippi, USA, d. 15 December 2001, Memphis, Tennessee, USA. A singer, dancer and entertainer, Thomas learned his trade as a member of the Rabbit Foot Minstrels, a vaudeville-inspired touring group. By the late 40s he was performing in several Memphis nightclubs and organizing local talent shows. B.B. King, Bobby Bland and Little Junior Parker were discovered in this way. When King's career subsequently blossomed, Thomas replaced him as a disc jockey at the black-owned radio station WDIA and remained there until 1974, fronting the influential shows *House Of Happiness* and *Special Delivery* and acting as a mentor to many of the city's blues, soul and rock musicians.

Thomas began recording in the early 40s, and several releases appeared on Star Talent, Chess Records and Meteor before 'Bear Cat' became a Top 3 US R&B hit. An answer to Big Mama Thornton's 'Hound Dog', it was released on Sun Records in 1953. Thomas remained a local celebrity until 1960 when he recorded with his daughter, Carla Thomas. Their duet, "Cause I Love You', was issued on the fledgling Satellite (later Stax Records) label where it became a regional hit. Thomas secured his reputation with a series of infectious singles; 'Walking The Dog' (1963) was a US Top 10 entry, while several of his other recordings, notably 'Jump Back' and 'All Night Worker' (both in 1964), were beloved

by aspiring British groups. His later success with novelty numbers – 'Do The Funky Chicken' (1970), '(Do The) Push And Pull, Part 1' (1970) and 'Do The Funky Penguin (Part 1)' (1971) – has obscured the merits of less brazen recordings. 'Sophisticated Cissy' (1967) and 'Memphis Train' (1968) are prime 60s R&B.

Thomas stayed with Stax until its 1975 collapse, from where he moved to AVI. His releases there included *If There Were No Music* and *I Ain't Getting Older, I'm Gettin' Better*. In 1980 Thomas re-recorded several of his older songs for a self-named collection on Gusto. In the 80s he abandoned R&B and recorded some rap with *Rappin' Rufus*, on the Ichiban Records label, and tackled blues with *That Woman Is Poison*, on the Alligator Records label. Bob Fisher's Sequel Records released a new album from Thomas in 1996. *Blues Thang!* proved to be an unexpected treat from a man celebrating his 79th birthday at the time of release. Two years later he received an award from the Rock And Roll Hall Of Fame for five decades promoting black music on radio. Thomas continued to record and perform regularly before open-heart surgery curtailed his activities. The 'crown prince of Memphis soul' aka 'the world's oldest teenager' died of heart failure in December 2001.

● ALBUMS: *Walking The Dog* (Stax 1963) ★★★★, *Do The Funky Chicken* (Stax 1970) ★★★★, *Doing The Push And Pull Live At PJ's* (Stax 1971) ★★★, *Did You Hear Me?* (Stax 1972) ★★★, *Crown Prince Of Dance* (Stax 1972) ★★★, *Blues In The Basement* (Artists Of America 1975) ★★★, *If There Were No Music* (Avid 1977) ★★★, *I Ain't Gettin' Older, I'm Gettin' Better* (Avid 1977) ★★★, *Rufus Thomas* (Gusto 1980) ★★, *Rappin' Rufus* (Ichiban 1986) ★★★, *That Woman Is Poison!* (Alligator 1988) ★★★, *Blues Thang!* (Sequel 1996) ★★★, *Rufus Live* 1996 recording (Ecko 1998) ★★, *Swing Out* (High Stacks 1999) ★★★.

● COMPILATIONS: *Jump Back: A 1963-67 Retrospective* (Edsel 1984) ★★★, *Can't Get Away From This Dog* (Stax 1992) ★★★, *The Best Of: The Singles* (Ace/Stax 1993) ★★★★, *The Best Of Rufus Thomas: Do The Funky Somethin'* (Rhino 1996) ★★★★, *Memories* (MCA 1998) ★★★, *Funky Chicken* (Metro 2000) ★★★.

● FILMS: *Wattstax* (1973), *Great Balls Of Fire!* (1989), *Mystery Train* (1989), *Saturday Night, Sunday Morning: The Travels Of Gatemouth Moore* (1992), *A Family Thing* (1996), *Cookie's Fortune* (1999).

THUNDERCLAP NEWMAN

Although singer/composer Speedy Keen (b. John Keen, 29 March 1945, Ealing, London, England) wrote much of this short-lived group's material, its impact was derived from the quirky, old-fashioned image of pianist Andy Newman. Guitarist Jimmy McCulloch (b. 4 June 1953, d. 27 September 1979) completed the original line-up responsible for 'Something In

The Air', a soaring, optimistic song which was a dramatic UK number 1 hit in the summer of 1969. The song was produced by Pete Townshend. *Hollywood Dream* bode well for the future, highlighting Keen's surreal vision and Newman's barrelhouse piano fills, but a long delay in selecting a follow-up single undermined the band's standing. The eventual choice, 'Accidents', was another excellent composition, but lacked the immediacy of its predecessor. Despite the addition of two new members – Jim Pitman-Avory (bass) and Jack McCulloch (drums) – Thunderclap Newman were unable to achieve a satisfactory live sound and, bereft of chart success, broke up. Speedy Keen and Andy Newman began solo careers, Jack McCulloch joined Andwella's Dream, while Jimmy McCulloch joined Stone The Crows and, later, Wings.

● ALBUMS: *Hollywood Dream* (Track 1970) ★★★.

TILLOTSON, JOHNNY

b. 20 April 1939, Jacksonville, Florida, USA. Tillotson's father was a country music disc jockey and Johnny himself was appearing on local radio from the age of nine. His parents encouraged his talent by giving him first a ukulele and then a guitar, and he was influenced by the singing cowboys (Gene Autry, Roy Rogers) and country singer Hank Williams. He appeared regularly on Tom Dowdy's television show, from which he was recommended to Archie Bleyer, the owner of Cadence Records. His first single in 1958, recorded while he was completing his BSc in Journalism And Communications, combined the teen ballad 'Dreamy Eyes' with the up-tempo 'Well, I'm Your Man'. Although his roots were in country music, he was encouraged to revive the R&B ballads 'Never Let Me Go', 'Pledging My Love' and 'Earth Angel'. In 1960 he released the classic teen-ballad 'Poetry In Motion', which went to number 2 in the USA and number 1 in the UK. The b-side, 'Princess, Princess', was popular in its own right and the equal of many of his later hits. Tillotson's follow-up, 'Jimmy's Girl', was less successful but he went to number 3 in the USA with 'It Keeps Right On A-Hurtin', a self-penned country ballad. The song has been recorded by over 100 performers including Elvis Presley.

Tillotson's baby-face and slight frame made him an ideal teen-idol for the early 60s, but his musical preference was country music. He had further success by reviving the country songs 'Send Me The Pillow You Dream On' and 'I Can't Help It (If I'm Still In Love With You)'. In the movie *Just For Fun* he sang 'Judy, Judy, Judy', which he wrote with Doc Pomus and Mort Shuman. His ballad 'You Can Never Stop Me Loving You' was a US Top 20 hit, but Kenny Lynch's version was preferred by UK record-buyers. A spell in the US Army prevented Tillotson from capitalizing on his success, but when he signed with MGM Records he was determined to become a country performer. 'Talk Back Trembling Lips' was a country and pop hit, but his subsequent records – 'Worried Guy', 'I Rise, I Fall', 'She Understands Me', 'Heartaches By The Number' – only reached the Top 40. Tillotson moved to California in 1968, and during the 70s recorded for the Ampex, Buddah Records and United Artists Records labels. He also became a regular on the lounge circuit in Las Vegas, hence a single of 'Cabaret'. Tillotson also remains popular on US army bases in Europe and he has had several hits in Japan following successful appearances there. The 30-track compilation *All His Early Hits – And More!!!!*, which was released in the UK by Ace Records in 1990, is the best introduction to his work and includes an early version of 'Poetry In Motion'.

● ALBUMS: *Johnny Tillotson's Best* (Cadence 1962) ★★★, *It Keeps Right On A-Hurtin'* (Cadence 1962) ★★★, *You Can Never Stop Me Loving You* (Cadence 1963) ★★★, *Talk Back Trembling Lips* (MGM 1964) ★★★, *The Tillotson Touch* (MGM 1964) ★★★, *She Understands Me* (MGM 1965) ★★, *That's My Style* (MGM 1965) ★★★, *Our World* (MGM 1966) ★★★, *No Love At All* (MGM 1966) ★★★, *The Christmas Touch* (MGM 1966) ★★, *Here I Am* (MGM 1967) ★★★, *Tears On My Pillow* (Ampex 1970) ★★★, *Johnny Tillotson* (Buddah 1972) ★★★, *Johnny Tillotson* (United Artists) ★★★.

● COMPILATIONS: *Scrapbook* (Bear Family 1984) ★★★, *All His Early Hits: And More!!!!* (Ace 1990) ★★★★, *Poetry In Motion* (Varèse Sarabande 1996) ★★★★, *It Keeps Right On A Hurtin': The MGM Years* (Varèse Vintage 1999) ★★★★, *The EP Collection ... Plus* (See For Miles 2000) ★★★★.

● FILMS: *Just For Fun* (1963), *The Fat Spy* (1965).

TINY TIM

b. Herbert Khaury, 12 April 1930, New York, USA, d. 30 November 1996, Minneapolis, USA. Eccentric entertainer Tiny Tim played regularly on the New York Greenwich Village circuit during the early/mid-60s. With his warbling voice, long scraggly hair and camp mannerisms, he specialized in show tunes dating back to the musicals of the 20s. Following an appearance in the movie *You Are What You Eat*, he secured a regular spot on the highly rated *Rowan And Martin's Laugh-In* comedy series. The comic incongruity of this middle-aged man, who sang in a cracked falsetto and played the ukulele, proved novel enough to warrant a Top 20 US hit in 1968 with 'Tip Toe Through The Tulips With Me'. Several albums and tours followed and at the height of his media fame he attracted a mass audience for his live television marriage on Johnny Carson's *The Tonight Show* to the young girl he called 'Miss Vicky' (Victoria May Budinger). His professed celibacy and highly moral sexual standpoint created instant copy and the controversial marriage was well chronicled, from the birth of baby Tulip, to the divorce court.

By the early 70s the Tiny Tim fad had passed, and having lost his contract with Reprise Records he continued to issue singles on small independent labels, to little success. In the late 80s Tim completed a cassette-only release, *The World's Longest Non-Stop Singing Record*, which was recorded live in Brighton, England. He subsequently moved to Australia where he became acquainted with graphic artist Martin Sharp, who designed Cream's distinctive *Wheels Of Fire* sleeve as well as several covers of *Oz* magazine. Sharp's work graced *Tiny Tim Rocks*, a disappointing mélange of the singer's high falsetto and ill-fitting hard rock, but his version of AC/DC's 'Highway To Hell' achieved modest sales. During the 90s, known as Mr. Tim, the singer returned to the USA to live in Des Moines, Iowa, 'because it's clean'. In 1993 he married for a third time, and lived in Minneapolis with 'Miss Sue' until his death in 1996.

● ALBUMS: *God Bless Tiny Tim* (Reprise 1968) ★★★, *Tiny Tim's Second Album* (Reprise 1969) ★★★, *For All My Little Friends* (Reprise 1969) ★★, *With Love And Kisses: A Concert from Fairyland* (Bouquet 1968) ★★, *Tiny Tim, Michelle Ramos And Bruce Haack* (Ra-Jo International 1986) ★★, *Rock* (Regular 1993) ★★, *I Love Me* (Seeland 1995) ★★, *Live In Chicago* (Bughouse 1995) ★★, *Songs Of An Impotent Troubadour* (Durtro 1995) ★★, *Tiny Tim's Christmas Album* (Durtro 1995) ★★★, *Unplugged* (Tomanna 1996) ★★, with Brave Combo *Girl* (Rounder 1996) ★★.

● FURTHER READING: *Tiny Tim*, Harry Stein.

TOKENS

Formed in 1955 in Brooklyn, New York, USA, the Tokens were one of the most successful white harmony groups of the early 60s, best known for their 1961 number 1 single 'The Lion Sleeps Tonight' (number 11 in the UK). The group was originally called the Linc-Tones (taken from Lincoln High School, which the original members all attended) and consisted of tenor vocalist Hank Medress (b. 19 November 1938, Brooklyn, New York, USA), Neil Sedaka (b. 13 March 1939, Brooklyn, New York, USA), Eddie Rabkin and Cynthia Zolitin. The following year Rabkin left and was replaced by Jay Siegel (b. 20 October 1939, Brooklyn, New York, USA). With that line-up the group recorded 'I Love My Baby' for the Melba label, with no success. The next change came in 1958 when Sedaka departed for a hugely successful solo career as a performer and songwriter. Zolitin also left in 1958 and the remaining duo carried on for a year with other singers as Darrell And The Oxfords, recording two singles for Roulette Records.

Twelve-year-old Mitch Margo (b. 25 May 1947,

Brooklyn, New York, USA) and his brother Phil (b. 1 April 1942, Brooklyn, New York, USA) joined Medress and Siegel in December 1959 and the group changed its name to the Tokens. This was the most successful and stable line-up of the Tokens. Their first recording as such was the 1961 self-penned 'Tonight I Fell In Love', which the Tokens sold to the small Warwick Records. Following the record's rise to number 15 in the USA, the Tokens forged a creative partnership with producers and songwriters Hugo Peretti and Luigi Creatore at RCA Records. That pair, along with songwriter George Weiss, reworked the folk song 'Wimoweh', itself reworked by the folk group the Weavers from a 30s South African song called 'Mbube', into 'The Lion Sleeps Tonight'. After the single peaked at the top of the US charts (number 11 in the UK), the quartet took on another vocalist, Joseph Venneri, for live performances (he later appeared on recordings, and was replaced in the mid-60s by Brute Force (b. Stephen Friedland), who went on to record two solo albums under the Brute Force pseudonym after leaving the Tokens in 1970). In early 1962 the Tokens branched out from recording under their own name by signing a production deal with Capitol Records and establishing Big Time Productions in New York. During 1962, they attempted to repeat the success of their number 1 record by reworking other songs, including another African folk song, 'B'wa Nina (Pretty Girl)', and the Ritchie Valens hit 'La Bomba' (with a slight spelling change), itself an old Mexican folk song. The Tokens never recaptured the success they enjoyed with 'The Lion Sleeps Tonight', although they appeared on the US singles chart regularly until the beginning of the 70s on a succession of record labels, including their own BT Puppy Records, which they formed in 1964 (the label's greatest success was with the group the Happenings, who released two Top 5 singles on the label, produced by the Tokens). Among their other notable releases were 'He's In Town' in 1964, 'I Hear Trumpets Blow' in 1966 and 'Portrait Of My Love' in 1967.

Meanwhile, their production career took off in 1963 with the success of 'He's So Fine', a number 1 single by the girl group the Chiffons. Members of the Tokens also sang on many sessions for other artists at this time, including Bob Dylan (*Highway 61 Revisited*) and the Blues Project. In 1967 the Tokens signed with Warner Brothers Records (which refused to release a concept album they had recorded entitled *Intercourse*, which the group released itself in 1971) and two years later switched over to Buddah Records. By then their reign as hitmakers was long over, and the group began splintering. Mitch Margo spent 1969-71 in the Army and Medress departed the group in October 1970 to produce. His most successful venture was as co-producer of Tony Orlando and Dawn, one of the bestselling pop groups of the 70s. Medress also produced a 1972 remake of 'The Lion Sleeps Tonight' by Robert John, which reached number 3 in the USA, and produced records by singer Dan Hill and New York rocker/cabaret singer Buster Poindexter, a pseudonym for ex-New York Dolls singer David Johansen. The Tokens carried on without Medress until 1973, when the remaining trio changed its name to Cross Country and signed to Atco Records. As such, they placed one single on the US chart, a remake of the Wilson Pickett hit 'In The Midnight Hour' which reached number 30 in 1973. The group finally split in 1974, although they cut a single together, 'A Tribute To The Beach Boys '76', in 1976. A reunion concert in New York in 1981 featured the Margo brothers, Siegel and Medress. Some of the group members, particularly Mitch Margo, attempted to keep the Tokens name alive by forming new groups into the 80s, and one even re-recorded 'The Lion Sleeps Tonight' in 1988 for the small Downtown label. Phil Margo went on to become a manager of rock bands. Jay Siegel became owner/manager of a recording studio in New York.

● ALBUMS: *The Lion Sleeps Tonight* (RCA Victor 1961) ★★★★, *We, The Tokens, Sing Folk* (RCA Victor 1962) ★★★★, *Wheels* (RCA Victor 1964) ★★★, *Again* (RCA Victor 1966) ★★★, *King Of The Hot Rods* (Diplomat 1966) ★★★, *I Hear Trumpets Blow* (BT Puppy 1966) ★★, with the Happenings *Back To Back* (1967) ★★, *It's A Happening World* (Warners 1967) ★★, *Life Is Groovy* (1970) ★★, *Tokens Of Gold* (BT Puppy 1969) ★★★, *December 5th* (BT Puppy 1971) ★★, *Both Sides Now* (1971) ★★, *Intercourse* (BT Puppy 1971) ★★, *Cross Country* (1973) ★★.

● COMPILATIONS: *Greatest Moments* (BT Puppy 1970) ★★★, *Very Best Of The Tokens* (Buddah 1971) ★★★, *The All Time Greatest Hits* (Taragon 1998) ★★★.

TOMORROW

Formed in 1967, Tomorrow evolved when former mod-influenced group the In Crowd embraced the emergent psychedelic/'flower-power' trend. Keith West (b. Keith Hopkins, 6 December 1943, Dagenham, Essex, England; vocals), Steve Howe (b. Stephen James Howe, 8 April 1947, Holloway, London, England; guitar), John 'Junior' Wood (bass) and Twink (b. John Alder, 1944, Colchester, Essex, England; drums) became a regular feature of London's 'underground' clubs before securing pop fame with the quirky 'My White Bicycle'. This simple but enduring song was successfully resurrected by Nazareth, reaching UK number 14 in June 1975. Tomorrow's lone album mixed Syd Barrett-styled whimsy with faerie-inspired rock, but their progress was undermined by singer West's concurrent solo career as part of the projected *Teenage Opera*, and the attendant UK hit single 'Excerpt From A Teenage Opera'

(number 2, August 1967). The group completed a cameo part in the film, *Smashing Time*, before breaking up in April 1968, after which Twink joined the Pretty Things. Steve Howe later found fame in Yes.

● ALBUMS: *Tomorrow* (Parlophone 1968) ★★★.
● COMPILATIONS: *50 Minute Technicolor Dream* (RPM 1998) ★★.

TORNADOS

The only serious challengers to the Shadows as the UK's top instrumental unit, the Tornados merely lasted as long as their console svengali, independent record producer Joe Meek. In 1961, he assembled the quintet initially as house band at his Holloway, London studio, to back solo performers such as Don Charles, John Leyton and Billy Fury. The latter was namechecked in the title of the Tornados' debut single, 'Love And Fury'. From Colin Hicks and his Cabin Boys, Meek had drawn guitarist Alan Caddy (b. 2 February 1940, Chelsea, London, England, d. 16 August 2000, England) and drummer Clem Cattini (b. 28 August 1939, London, England), both of whom had also played with Johnny Kidd And The Pirates. Rhythm guitarist George Bellamy (b. 8 October 1941, Sunderland, England) and keyboard player Roger Lavern (b. Roger Jackson, 11 November 1938, Kidderminster, England) were session players, although Norman Hale actually played organ on 'Love And Fury'. Bass player Heinz Burt (b. 24 July 1942, Hargin, Germany, d. 7 April 2000), meanwhile, was one of Meek's own protégés. In their own right, the Tornados made the big time with their second single, the otherworldly 'Telstar'.

Composed by Meek with his creative confrère Geoff Goddard deputizing for Lavern on clavioline, this quintessential 60s instrumental anticipated many of the electronic ventures of a subsequent and less innocent pop generation. Moreover, in 1962 it topped the domestic hit parade and unbelievably did likewise in the USA, where no UK group, not even the Shadows, had made much headway. Although a capitalizing tour of North America was unwisely cancelled, Meek's boys played 'Eric The Red' to Britain's invasion of US charts two years later. 1963 was another good year for the Tornados with 'Globetrotter', 'Robot' and 'The Ice Cream Man' – all with catchy juxtapositions of outer space aetheria and funfair vulgarity – cracking the UK Top 20. Flattering too were those myriad copyist combos in their artistic debt, notably the Volcanos with 'Polaris'. Danger, however, became apparent in the comparative failure of 'Dragonfly' shortly after the exit of Burt for a solo career (his last recorded appearance with the band had actually been on 'Globetrotter'). Burt was replaced by Tab Martin, Brian Gregg and Ray Randall in quick succession, but the absence of his blond Norse radiance onstage, coupled with the levelling blow of the beat boom and its emphasis on vocals had rendered the Tornados passé. Lavern and Bellamy had also jumped ship by the time 'Dragonfly' was released. Worse, new ideas were thin on the ground. The 'Robot' b-side, 'Life On Venus', for instance, almost repeated the 'Telstar' melody.

Following the departure of Cattini, the last original Tornado, there came further desperate strategies, with 1965's 'Early Bird' (which featured a young Ritchie Blackmore on guitar) and 'Stingray' again harking back to the million-selling sound of 'Telstar'. The penniless Meek's suicide in 1967 coincided with the outfit's interrelated disbandment. In the mid-70s, Bellamy, Burt, Cattini and Lavern – as 'The Original Tornados' – managed some nostalgia revues and a remake of 'Telstar' before going their separate ways. Nevertheless, with a new Tornados, Cattini tried again in 1989. While this line-up features a female singer, the loudest cheers are reserved for the ancient instrumentals, especially Meek's eerie US number 1.

● ALBUMS: *Away From It All* (Decca 1963) ★★★.

● COMPILATIONS: *The World Of The Tornados* (Decca 1972) ★★★, *Remembering ... The Tornados* (Decca 1976) ★★★, *The Original 60s Hits* (Music Club 1994) ★★★, *The EP Collection* (See For Miles 1996) ★★★★, *The Very Best Of The Tornados* (Music Club 1997) ★★★, *Telstar: The Complete* (Repertoire 1998) ★★★, *Satellites And Sound Effects* (Connoisseur 2000) ★★★.

Toys

Three high-school friends, Barbara Harris (b. 18 August 1945, Elizabeth City, North Carolina, USA), Barbara Parritt (b. 1 October 1944, Wilmington, North Carolina, USA) and June Montiero (b. 1 July 1946, New York City, USA) formed the Toys in Jamaica, New York. The group is best recalled for their 1965 hit 'A Lover's Concerto', a Supremes-influenced performance adapted from Bach's 'Minuet In G'. 'Attack', another piece appropriated from a classical theme, also reached the US and UK charts but further releases, 'May My Heart Be Cast To Stone' and 'Baby Toys' were only minor US pop hits. Although a 1968 single, 'Sealed With A Kiss' returned them to the US soul Top 50, the trio split up soon afterwards.

● ALBUMS: *The Toys Sing 'A Lover's Concerto' And 'Attack'* (1966) ★★.

● FILMS: *It's A Bikini World* (1967).

Traffic

Formed in 1967, this stellar UK group comprised Steve Winwood (b. 12 May 1948, Birmingham, England; keyboards, guitar, bass, vocals), Chris Wood (b. 24 June 1944, Birmingham, England, d. 12 July 1983; saxophone, flute), Jim Capaldi (b. 24 August 1944, Evesham, Worcestershire, England; drums, percussion, vocals) and Dave Mason (b. 10 May 1945, Worcester, England; guitar, vocals). Winwood had conceived, plotted and formed Traffic just prior to his departure from the Spencer Davis Group. Traffic were archetypes of psychedelic Britain in 1967 in dress, attitude and music. They were the originators of the 'getting it together in the country cottage' syndrome, which found so many followers. Their potpourri of musical styles was innovative and daring, created in the communal atmosphere of their cottage in Berkshire. Their first single, 'Paper Sun', with its infectious sitar opening was an instant hit, closely followed by 'Hole In My Shoe' (parodied in a 1984 number 2 UK hit by Neil the hippie, from BBC Television's *The Young Ones*) and the film theme 'Here We Go Round The Mulberry Bush'. Mason left at the end of an eventful year, just as the first album, *Mr. Fantasy* was released. From then on Traffic ceased to be a singles band, and built up a large following, especially in the USA.

Their second album, *Traffic*, showed refinement and progression. Dave Mason had returned briefly and two of his songs were particularly memorable, 'You Can All Join In' and 'Feelin' Alright' (later covered by Joe Cocker). In 'Who Knows What Tomorrow May Bring?', Winwood sings, 'We are not like all the rest, you can see us any day of the week, come around, sit down, take a sniff, fall asleep, baby you don't have to speak'. This lyric perfectly encapsulated the hippie lifestyle of the late 60s. Another outstanding song, 'Forty Thousand Headmen' combined a lyrical tale of pure fantasy with lilting flute and jazz tempo. *Last Exit* was a fragmented affair and during its recording Mason departed once more. The second side consisted of just two tracks recorded live with the band as a trio. Winwood bravely attempted to hold the ensemble together by singing and playing Hammond organ in addition to using the bass pedals to compensate for the lack of a bass guitar. At this point the band disintegrated leaving Winwood to wander into Blind Faith. The others teamed up once again with Dave Mason to form the short-lived Mason, Capaldi, Wood and Frog. The Frog was Mick Weaver (aka Wynder K. Frog). Neither band lasted; the former made one highly successful album and the latter were never committed to vinyl.

Following a brief spell as a member of Ginger Baker's Airforce, Winwood embarked on a solo project, to be called Mad Shadows. He enlisted the help of Wood and Capaldi, and to the delight of the music press this became Traffic once again. The resulting album was the well-received *John Barleycorn Must Die*. Rick Grech, formerly of Family, Blind Faith and Airforce, also joined the band. In 1971 *Welcome To The Canteen* appeared with Dave Mason rejoining for a third time. This disappointing live album contained an overlong version of 'Gimme Some Lovin'' from Winwood's days in the Spencer Davis Group. Ironically it was Mason who shone, with two tracks from his superb *Alone Together* album. Drummer Jim Gordon (from Derek And The Dominos) and Reebop Kwaku Baah (b. 1944, Lagos, Nigeria; d. 1982) joined in 1971, allowing Capaldi to take the role as frontman. The excellent *The Low Spark Of High Heeled Boys* (1971) was followed by *Shoot Out At The Fantasy Factory* in 1973. The latter saw the substitution of David Hood and Roger Hawkins for Grech and Gordon. Both albums achieved gold status in the USA. Throughout their turbulent career Traffic were never able to reproduce their inventive arrangements on stage. Witnesses would concur that Traffic were erratic when playing live. This trait was highlighted on their penultimate album, *On The Road*.

The final Traffic album was *When The Eagle Flies* in 1974, another fine collection with Rosko Gee on bass and 'Gentleman' Jim Capaldi back behind the drum kit. Traffic did not so much break up as fizzle out, although they did record together again when Capaldi became involved on Winwood's later solo work. Traffic had already left an indelible mark as creators of inventive and sometimes glorious music and it was a delight that 20 years after they dissolved, the name was born again with Capaldi and Winwood attempting to recreate their unique sound. The album *Far From Home* was warmly rather than ecstatically received and they followed it with a major tour of the USA supporting the Grateful Dead and then a short European tour. The album was a true joint effort, but the strong structured soul sound of the record erred towards a Winwood solo outing rather than the wandering and ethereal beauty of Traffic. Outstanding tracks include the funky 'Here Comes The Man', and 'Some Kinda Woman' and the almost Traffic-like 'State Of Grace', with its spiritual feel complemented by the rousing gospel piano introduction for the glorious 'Every Night, Every Day'.

● ALBUMS: *Mr. Fantasy* (Island 1967) ★★★★, *Traffic* (Island 1968) ★★★★★, *Last Exit* (Island 1969) ★★, *John Barleycorn Must Die* (Island 1970) ★★★★, *Welcome To The Canteen* (Island 1971) ★★★, *The Low Spark Of High Heeled Boys* (Island 1971) ★★★★, *Shoot Out At The Fantasy Factory* (Island 1973) ★★★, *On The Road* (Island 1973) ★★, *When The Eagle Flies* (Island 1974) ★★★, *Far From Home* (Virgin 1994) ★★★.

● COMPILATIONS: *Best Of Traffic* (Island 1970) ★★★★, *Heavy Traffic* (Island 1975) ★★★★, *More Heavy Traffic* (Island 1975) ★★★, *Smiling Phases* 2-CD set (Island 1991) ★★★★, *Heaven Is In Your Mind: An Introduction To Traffic* (Island 1998) ★★★, *The Best Of Traffic* (Spectrum 2001) ★★★.

● FURTHER READING: *Keep On Running: The Steve Winwood Story*, Chris Welch. *Back In The High Life: A Biography Of Steve Winwood*, Alan Clayson.

TREMELOES

When UK chart-toppers Brian Poole And The Tremeloes parted company in 1966 few would have wagered that the backing group would outdo the lead singer. Remarkably, however, the relaunched Tremeloes went on to eclipse not only Poole, but the original hit-making act. At the time of their reconvening in 1966, the line-up comprised Rick West (b. Richard Westwood, 7 May 1943, Dagenham, Essex, England; guitar), Alan Blakley (b. 1 April 1942, Dagenham, Essex, England, d. 1995; rhythm guitar), Dave Munden (b. 2 December 1943, Dagenham, Essex, England; drums) and Alan Howard (b. 17 October 1941, Dagenham, Essex, England; bass). In May of 1966 Howard was replaced by Mike Clark; however, a mere three months later his spot was taken by Len 'Chip' Hawkes (b. 11 November 1946, London, England), whose lead vocals and boyish looks gave the group a stronger visual identity. In order to keep up with the times, the group abandoned their stage suits in favour of Carnaby Street garb and fashionably longer hair. Their second generation debut for Decca Records was a cover of Paul Simon's 'Blessed', which proved unsuccessful. Seeking more commercial material they moved to CBS Records and covered 'Good Day Sunshine' from the Beatles' *Revolver*. In spite of radio play it too failed to chart, but their third release 'Here Comes My Baby' (a Cat Stevens composition) smashed into the Top 20 on both sides of the Atlantic.

An astute follow-up with 'Silence Is Golden', previously the flip-side of the Four Seasons' 'Rag Doll', proved a perfect vehicle for the Tremeloes' soft harmonic style and gave them their only UK number 1 and their highest US chart entry (number 11). Having established themselves as a hit act, they notched up an impressive run of hits during the late 60s including 'Even The Bad Times Are Good', 'Suddenly You Love Me', 'Helule Helule' and 'My Little Lady'. At the end of the decade, the group seemed weary of their role in the pop world and broke away from their usual Tin Pan Alley songsmiths to write their own material. Their first attempt, '(Call Me) Number One', was an impressive achievement, arguably superior to the material that they had recorded since 1967. When it reached number 2 in the charts, the group convinced themselves that a more ambitious approach would bring even greater rewards. Overreacting to their dream start as hit writers, they announced that they were 'going heavy' and suicidally alienated their pop audience by dismissing their earlier record-buying fans as 'morons'.

Their brief progressive phase was encapsulated

in the album *Master*, which won no new fans but provided a final Top 20 single, 'Me And My Life'. Thereafter, they turned increasingly to cabaret where their strong live performances were well appreciated. In 1974 Chip Hawkes went to Nashville, USA, to pursue an ultimately unsuccessful solo career (his son Chesney Hawkes would enjoy a brief moment in the spotlight in the late 80s). Blakley left the following January, and Aaron Woolley and Bob Benham were brought in as replacements. The Tremeloes continued to record on an occasional basis, with albums being released by DJM Records and their old label CBS. They were still active in the new millennium, with Munden and West joined by Joe Gillingham (keyboards, vocals) and Davey Freyer (bass, vocals).

● ALBUMS: *Here Comes The Tremeloes* (CBS 1967) ★★★★, *Chip, Dave, Alan And Rick* (CBS 1967) ★★★, *Here Comes My Baby* US only (Epic 1967) ★★★★, *Even The Bad Times Are Good* US only (Epic 1967) ★★★, *Suddenly You Love Me* US only (Epic 1968) ★★★, *World Explosion 58/68* US only (Epic 1968) ★★★, *Live In Cabaret* (CBS 1969) ★★, *Master* (CBS 1970) ★★, *Shiner* (DJM 1974) ★★, *Don't Let The Music Die* (DJM 1976) ★★, *May Morning* 1970 film soundtrack (Castle 2000) ★★★.

● COMPILATIONS: *Greatest Hits* (Pickwick 1981) ★★★, *The Ultimate Collection* (Castle 1990) ★★★, *The Best Of The Tremeloes* (Rhino 1992) ★★★★, *Silence Is Golden* (Spectrum 1995) ★★★, *Tremendous Hits* (Music Club 1997) ★★★, *The Definitive Collection* (Castle 1998) ★★★, *Good Day Sunshine: Singles A's & B's* (Castle 1999) ★★★★.

TRENT, JACKIE

b. Jacqueline Trent, 6 September 1940, Newcastle-Under-Lyme, Staffordshire, England. A singer and lyricist who has achieved much of her success in collaboration with her husband, Tony Hatch. After performing in amateur productions from an early age, Trent started singing with local bands at the age of 13, and turned professional when she was 17. She toured parts of Europe and the Middle East, and played in cabaret in London, and traditional seaside shows. In the early 60s she recorded for the Oriole label before successfully auditioning for Pye Records producer Tony Hatch in 1964. Hatch had already written several successful compositions, including the theme to the television UK soap opera, *Crossroads*. Together, they wrote the melodic 'Where Are You Now? (My Love)', which Trent took to number 1 in the UK chart in 1965. During the late 60s they composed several major hits for Petula Clark, including 'Don't Sleep In The Subway', 'The Other Man's Grass', 'I Couldn't Live Without Your Love', and 'Colour My World'. Scott Walker also made the chart with their 'Joanna' in 1968. For their wedding day in 1967, Pye issued 'The Two Of Us', an incidental item they had

recorded months before. Its success, particularly in Australia, caused them to form a double act for cabaret, and make frequent trips to the Antipodes. In 1970 Trent starred as Nell Gwynne in the regional musical *Nell!*, with Hatch as co-producer and musical director. Two years later, the couple wrote the score for Cameron Mackintosh's first West End production, *The Card*, a musical adaptation of Arnold Bennett's novel, which starred Jim Dale, Marti Webb, Eleanor Bron and Millicent Martin. The songs included 'I Could Be The One', 'That's The Way The Money Goes' and 'Opposite Your Smile'. Another project, *Rock Nativity* (1974), proved to be 'one biblical musical too many'. Around the same time they released *Two For The Show*. Since 1982, Hatch and Trent have spent the majority of each year living and working in Australia, and in 1986 they wrote the theme song for *Neighbours*, a television soap set in Melbourne. Its success spread to the UK, and it was even introduced into the USA in 1991. They have composed several other UK television themes, including *Mr & Mrs*. Hatch and Trent's most successful stage project, *The Card*, was revived at the Open Air Theatre in London's Regent Park in 1992. In the same year the couple celebrated their 25th wedding anniversary, and also received the British Association of Songwriters Authors and Publishers' prestigious Award for Services to British Music, to add to their several Ivor Novello Awards. After their marriage ended in 1995, Trent returned to England to pick up her solo career, and in 1996 was touring with a provincial production of the musical *High Society*.

● ALBUMS: *The Magic Of Jackie Trent* (Pye 1965) ★★★★, *Once More With Feeling* (Pye 1967) ★★★, *Stop Me And Buy One* (Pye 1967) ★★★, *Yesterdays* (Pye 1968) ★★★★, *The Night, The Music And...* (1979) ★★★, with Tony Hatch *Two For The Show* (1973) ★★★, with Hatch *Our World Of Music* (1980) ★★★.

● COMPILATIONS: *The Best Of Jackie Trent* (1973) ★★★★, *Golden Hour Of Jackie Trent And Tony Hatch* (Pye 1976) ★★★★, *Where Are You Now My Love: The Pye Anthology* (Sequel 2000) ★★★★.

TROGGS

The original Troglodytes were an ill-starred early 60s UK band from Andover who suddenly found themselves reduced to two members: vocalist Dave Wright and bass player Reginald Ball (b. 12 June 1943, Andover, Hampshire, England). Another local outfit, Ten Feet Five, were suffering similar personnel upheavals with bass player Peter Staples (b. 3 May 1944, Andover, Hampshire, England) and guitarist Chris Britton (b. 21 January 1945, Watford, Hertfordshire, England) surviving the purge. At the suggestion of their respective managers, the two acts amalgamated, with Ball surprisingly emerging as the new lead vocalist. On the advice of *New Musical Express* journalist Keith Altham, Ball later changed his name to Reg Presley in the hope of attracting some attention from Elvis fans. Wright, meanwhile, had moved on to another Hampshire band, the Loot, while the revitalized and renamed Troggs found a drummer, Ronnie Bond (b. Ronald Bullis, 4 May 1943, Andover, Hampshire, England, d. 13 November 1992).

In 1966, after signing with producer/manager Larry Page, the band recorded a one-off single for CBS Records, 'Lost Girl'. Their debut flopped but after switching to Larry's new label Page One (distributed by Fontana Records), they found success with a cover of Chip Taylor's 'Wild Thing', which reached number 2 in the UK in May 1966. The follow-up, 'With A Girl Like You', went one better, establishing the Troggs as one of the most popular acts in the country. Stateside success was equally impressive with 'Wild Thing' topping the charts. Unfortunately, due to a misunderstanding with Sonny And Cher's managers Charlie Greene and Brian Stone (who had organized a re-recording of the disc), 'Wild Thing' was released on two different labels, Atco Records and Mercury Records. To make matters worse, the flip-side of the Atco version was the scheduled follow-up, 'With A Girl Like You'.

While their prospects in America waned, the band enjoyed an affectionate notoriety at home where their provincial politeness and inane naïvety contrasted markedly with the forced sexiness of songs such as 'I Can't Control Myself' and 'Anyway That You Want Me'. Although they boasted three songwriters and potential solo artists whose work was covered by others, the Troggs were never taken seriously by the press or pop élite. While clearly at home with basic rockers like 'Give It To Me', the band also tinkered with counter-culture subject matter on 'Night Of The Long Grass' and 'Love Is All Around', and their albums also occasionally veered towards the psychedelic market. Any hopes of sustaining their hit career were lost when they fell out with Larry Page in a High Court action that made case law. Thereafter they became predominantly a touring band, with Presley infrequently abetted by Britton, Bond and Tony Murray (from Plastic Penny).

During the 70s they achieved a certain cult status thanks to the hilarious 'Troggs Tapes', a notorious bootleg recording of an abortive session, consisting mainly of a stream of swear words. Later that decade they reunited with Page for an odd reworking of the Beach Boys' 'Good Vibrations' and recorded a live album at Max's Kansas City. Two-and-a-half decades on, the band still perform with their credibility growing rather than shrinking. Their R.E.M.-linked *Athens Andover* took people by surprise, utilizing Presley songs (and one from Chip Taylor) and blending the raw Troggs sound with contributions from Peter Buck and Mike Mills. The album was a clear indication that after being the butt of jokes for many years the Troggs are one of the finest ever 60s pop bands, a fact that was confirmed when Wet Wet Wet's cover version of 'Love Is All Around' took up residence at the head of the UK listings for over three months in 1994. Reg Presley, now an enthusiastic crop-circle investigator and UFO watcher, can at last look forward to a long and financially comfortable retirement, although, with Britton, he has kept the Troggs going as a live act.

● ALBUMS: *From Nowhere ... The Troggs* (Fontana 1966) ★★★★, *Trogglodynamite* (Page One 1967) ★★★★, *Cellophane* (Page One 1967) ★★★★, *Mixed Bag* (Page One 1968) ★★★, *Trogglomania* (Page One 1969) ★★★, *Contrasts* (DJM 1970) ★★, *With A Girl Like You* (DJM 1975) ★★, *The Original Troggs Tapes* (DJM 1976) ★, *Live At Max's Kansas City* (President 1981) ★, *Black Bottom* (RCA 1982) ★★, *Rock It Up* (Action Replay 1984) ★★, *Au* (New Rose 1989) ★★, *Athens Andover* (Page One 1992) ★★★.

● COMPILATIONS: *The Best Of The Troggs* (Page One 1967) ★★★★, *The Best Of The Troggs Volume 2* (Page One 1968) ★★★, *Wild Things* (DJM 1975) ★★★, *14 Greatest Hits* (Spectrum 1988) ★★★★, *The Troggs Hit Singles Anthology* (Fontana 1991) ★★★, *Archaeology 1966 – 1976* (Fontana 1992) ★★★, *Greatest Hits* (PolyGram 1994) ★★★★, *The EP Collection* (See For Miles 1996) ★★★★.

● FURTHER READING: *Rock's Wild Things: The Troggs Files*, Alan Clayson and Jacqueline Ryan.

TROY, DORIS

b. Doris Higginsen, 6 January 1937, New York City, USA. The daughter of a Baptist preacher, Doris abandoned her gospel beginnings in favour of a jazz group, the Halos. She recorded as half of Jay And Dee and soon also began making her mark as a songwriter, using her grandmother's name of Payne as a *nom de plume*. In 1960 Dee Clark recorded her song 'How About That?' for Vee Jay, while Troy cut a lone single for Everest before concentrating on background singing, with ex-Drinkard Singers Dionne and Dee Dee Warwick and their aunt Cissy Houston, behind many acts including the Drifters, Solomon Burke and Chuck Jackson. Then in 1963 Troy co-penned 'Just One Look', and when Juggy Murray of Sue Records 'sat on' a demo of it, she took a copy to Jerry Wexler at Atlantic Records, who promptly released it exactly as recorded and watched it become a US Top 10 hit. It was covered the following year by the Hollies, and reached the UK number 2 slot. Other releases included the equally insistent 'What'cha Gonna Do About It?', which reached the UK Top 40 in 1964, but failed to succeed in her home country. Later singles for Capitol and Calla were equally underrated. After settling in London in 1969, she recorded a self-titled album for the Beatles' label Apple, with the help of George Harrison and Eric Clapton. Troy also recorded for People and Polydor and later worked as a session singer, contributing to a number of albums including Pink Floyd's *Dark Side Of The Moon*. From the mid-80s to 1991 Troy performed in an off-Broadway musical about her life, *Mama, I Want To Sing*, and again when it opened in London in February 1995.

● ALBUMS: *Just One Look* (Atlantic 1963) ★★★, *Doris Troy* (Apple 1970) ★★★, *Rainbow Testament* (1972) ★★, *Stretching Out* (1974) ★★★, *Mama, I Want To Sing* (1986) ★★★.
● COMPILATIONS: *Just One Look: The Best Of ...* (Ichiban 1994) ★★★★.

TUCKER, TOMMY

b. Robert Higginbotham, 5 March 1933, Springfield, Ohio, USA, d. 22 January 1982. Renowned as an R&B performer, Tucker began his career as a jazz musician playing piano and clarinet for the Bob Woods Orchestra. He led his own group, the Dusters, recorded under the name Tee Tucker for Atco Records in 1961 and worked with saxophonist Roland Kirk prior to recording 'Hi-Heel Sneakers' in 1964. This simple, but compulsive, 12-bar blues song established the singer's reputation when it was consistently covered by other acts. This one song contained a pot-pourri of references, including the bizarre 'hi-heel sneakers' and 'wig hats on her head'. Further excellent singles in a similar style, including 'Long Tall Shorty', were less successful and forced Tucker to revert to club work. He visited Britain during the 70s as part of the *Blues Legends* package and, inspired by an enthusiastic response, began recording again. This irrepressible performer, sadly, died from poisoning in 1982.

● ALBUMS: *Greatest Twist Hits (Rock And Roll Machine)* (Atlantic 1961) ★★★, *Hi-Heel Sneakers & Long Tall Shorty* (Checker 1964) ★★★★, *Mother Tucker* (Red Lightnin' 1974) ★★★, *Rocks Is My Pillow, Cold Ground Is My Bed* (Red Lightnin' 1982) ★★, *Memphis Badboy* (Zu Zazz 1987) ★★★, *Tommy Tucker And His Californians* (Circle 1988) ★★, *Tommy Tucker And His Orchestra* (Circle 1988) ★★★.

TURNER, IKE AND TINA

Ike Turner (b. Izear Luster Turner Jnr., 5 November 1931, Clarksdale, Mississippi, USA) and Tina Turner (b. Annie Mae Bullock, 26 November 1938, Brownsville, Tennessee, USA). The commercial rebirth of singer Tina Turner, coupled with revelations about her ex-husband's unsavoury private life, has obscured the important role Ike Turner played in the development of R&B. A former piano player with Sonny Boy Williamson and Robert Nighthawk, Turner formed his Kings Of Rhythm during the late 40s. This influential group was responsible for 'Rocket 88', a 1950 release often named as the first rock 'n' roll recording but confusingly credited to its vocalist, Jackie Brenston. Turner then became a talent scout for Modern Records where he helped develop the careers of Bobby Bland, B.B. King and Howlin' Wolf. Now based in St. Louis, his Kings Of Rhythm were later augmented by a former gospel singer, Annie Mae Bullock. Originally billed as 'Little Ann', she gradually became the core of the act, particularly following her marriage to Ike in 1958.

Their debut release as Ike And Tina Turner came two years later. 'A Fool In Love', a tough, uncompromising release featuring Tina's already powerful delivery, preceded several excellent singles, the most successful of which was 'It's Gonna Work Out Fine' (1961). Highlighted by Ike's wry interjections, this superior performance defined the duo's early recordings. Although their revue was one of the leading black music touring shows, the Turners were curiously unable to translate this popularity into record sales. They recorded for several labels, including Sue Records, Kent and Loma, but a brief spell with Philles was to prove the most controversial. Here, producer Phil Spector constructed his 'wall-of sound' around Tina's impassioned voice, but the resultant single, 'River Deep – Mountain High', was an unaccountable miss in the USA, although in the UK charts it soared into the Top 3. Its failure was to have a devastating effect on Spector. Ike, unhappy at relinquishing the reins, took the duo elsewhere when further releases were less successful.

A support slot on the Rolling Stones' 1969 North American tour introduced the Turners to a wider, generally white, audience. Their version of John Fogerty's 'Proud Mary' was a gold disc in 1971, while the autobiographical 'Nutbush City Limits' (1973) was also an international hit. The group continued to be a major in-concert attraction, although Tina's brazen sexuality and the show's tired formula ultimately paled. The Turners became increasingly estranged as Ike's character darkened; Tina left the group in the middle of a tour and the couple were finally divorced in 1976. Beset by problems, chemical or otherwise, Ike spent some 18 months in prison, a stark contrast to his ex-wife's very public profile. In *What's Love Got To Do With It?* (1993), a film biography of Tina Turner, Ike was portrayed as a 'vicious, womanising Svengali'. Since his return Turner has attempted to redress the balance of his past with little success.

● ALBUMS: *The Soul Of Ike And Tina Turner* (Sue 1960) ★★, *Dance With The Kings Of Rhythm* (Sue 1960) ★★★, *Dance With Ike And Tina Turner* (Sue 1962) ★★★, *Festival Of Live Performances* (Kent 1962) ★★, *Dynamite* (Sue 1963) ★★★★, *Don't Play Me Cheap* (Sue 1963)

★★★, *It's Gonna Work Out Fine* (Sue 1963) ★★★★, *Please Please Please* (Kent 1964) ★★★, *The Soul Of Ike And Tina Turner* (Kent 1964) ★★★, *The Ike And Tina Show Live* (Loma 1965) ★★★★, *The Ike And Tina Turner Show Live* (Warners 1965) ★★★★, *River Deep – Mountain High* (London 1966) ★★★★, *So Fine* (Pompeii 1968) ★★★★, *In Person* (Minit 1968) ★★★★, *Cussin', Cryin' And Carrying On* (Pompeii 1969) ★★★, *Get It Together!* (Pompeii 1969) ★★★★, *A Black Man's Soul* (Pompeii 1969) ★★★, *Outta Season* (Liberty 1969) ★★★, *In Person* (Minit 1969) ★★★, *River Deep – Mountain High* (A&M/London 1969) ★★★★, *Come Together* (Liberty 1970) ★★★, *The Hunter* (Harvest 1970) ★★★★, *Workin' Together* (Liberty 1971) ★★★, *Her Man, His Woman* (Capitol 1971) ★★★, *Live In Paris* (Liberty 1971) ★★★★, *Live At Carnegie Hall – What You Hear Is What You Get* (Liberty 1971) ★★★, *'Nuff Said* (United Artists 1972) ★★, *Feel Good* (United Artists 1972) ★★, *Let Me Touch Your Mind* (United Artists 1973) ★★, *Nutbush City Limits* (United Artists 1973) ★★★★, *Strange Fruit* (1974) ★★★, *Sweet Island Rhode Red* (United Artists 1974) ★★, *Delilah's Power* (United Artists 1977) ★★, *Airwaves* (1978) ★★.
● COMPILATIONS: *Ike And Tina Turner's Greatest Hits* (Sue 1965) ★★★, *Ike And Tina Turner's Greatest Hits* (Warners 1969) ★★★★, *Tough Enough* (Liberty 1984) ★★★, *Fingerpoppin' -The Warner Brothers Years* (Warners 1988) ★★★, *Proud Mary: The Best Of Ike And Tina Turner* (EMI 1991) ★★★★, *Feel It!* (Carlton 1998) ★★★.
● FURTHER READING: *I Tina*, Tina Turner with Kurt Loder. *The Tina Turner Experience*, Chris Welch. *Takin' Back My Name*, Ike Turner with Nigel Cawthorne.

TURTLES

Having begun their career playing in college-based surf instrumental groups, the Nightriders and the Crossfires, this Westchester, Los Angeles-based sextet abruptly switched to beat music during 1964 in imitation of the Beatles. The line-up consisted of Howard Kaylan (b. Howard Kaplan, 22 June 1947, the Bronx, New York, USA; vocals, saxophone) and Mark Volman (b. 19 April 1947, Los Angeles, California, USA; vocals, saxophone), backed by Al Nichol (b. 31 March 1945, North Carolina, USA; piano, guitar), Jim Tucker (b. 17 October 1946, Los Angeles, California, USA; guitar), Chuck Portz (b. 28 March 1945, Santa Monica, California, USA; bass) and Don Murray (b. 8 November 1945, Los Angeles, California, USA, d. 22 March 1996; drums). By the summer of 1965 they found themselves caught up in the folk rock boom and, impressed by the success of local rivals the Byrds, elected to call themselves the Tyrtles. That idea was soon dropped, but as the Turtles they slavishly followed the Byrds blueprint, covering a Bob Dylan song, 'It Ain't Me Babe' to considerable effect (the song reached US number 8 in autumn 1965).

After rejecting 'Eve Of Destruction' as a possible follow-up, they used the services of its composer, the new 'king of protest' P.F. Sloan. His pen provided two further US hits, 'Let Me Be' (number 29, October 1965) and 'You Baby' (number 20, February 1966) before their commercial appeal wilted. The psychedelic boom of 1967 saw a change in the band's image and coincided with line-up fluctuations resulting in the induction of drummer John Barbata and successive bass players Chip Douglas and Jim Pons (ex-Leaves). The exuberant 'Happy Together' revitalized their chart fortunes, hitting the number 1 spot in the US in February 1967, and providing the band with their first UK hit when it reached number 12 in March. The song has now achieved classic status and is a perennial turntable hit. The follow-up 'She'd Rather Be With Me' (US number 3/UK number 4) was another zestful singalong establishing the Turtles, now minus Tucker, as expert pop craftsmen.

The mid-tempo 'You Know What I Mean' (US number 12) and 'Elenore' (US number 6/UK number 7) were also impressive, with the usual sprinkling of affectionate parody that worked against the odds. The Turtles hardly looked like pop stars but sang delightfully anachronistic teen ballads and ended their hit career by returning to their folk-rock roots, courtesy of 'You Showed Me' (US number 6, January 1969), first recorded by the Byrds in 1964. With a final touch of irony their record company issued the once rejected 'Eve Of Destruction' as one of their final singles. After the band dissolved, Kaylan and Volman (with Pons) joined Frank Zappa and his Mothers Of Invention and later emerged as Flo And Eddie, recording solo albums and offering their services as producers and backing singers to a number of prominent artists. Volman and Kaylan later revived the band, as the Turtles ... Featuring Flo And Eddie, for touring purposes. Don Murray died following complications during surgery in 1996.
● ALBUMS: *It Ain't Me Babe* (White Whale 1965) ★★★, *You Baby* (White Whale 1966) ★★★, *Happy Together* (White Whale 1967) ★★★, *The Battle Of The Bands* (White Whale 1968) ★★★, *Turtle Soup* (White Whale 1969) ★★, *Wooden Head* (White Whale 1971) ★★, *Happy Together Again* (Sire 1974) ★★.
● COMPILATIONS: *Golden Hits Vol. I* (White Whale 1967) ★★★, *Golden Hits Vol. II* (White Whale 1970) ★★★, *20 Greatest Hits* (Rhino 1983) ★★★★, *20 Golden Classics* (Mainline 1990) ★★★, *Happy Together: The Very Best Of The Turtles* (Music Club 1991) ★★★, *Happy Together: 30 Years Of Rock & Roll* 5-CD box set (Laserlight 1995) ★★★.

TWICE AS MUCH

Songwriters David Skinner and Andrew Rose formed this UK group in 1965. The duo was managed by Andrew Loog Oldham, who also signed them to his Immediate Records label/ publishing empire. Their material, in many ways reminiscent of the classic Brill Building style, was recorded by several artists, including Del Shannon, Chris Farlowe and P.P. Arnold, and the pair also recorded several excellent singles. Twice As Much enjoyed their greatest success with 'Sittin' On A Fence', a Jagger/Richard original rejected from the Rolling Stones' *Aftermath* sessions. Skinner and Rose took the song to number 25 in the UK, a position their own compositions failed to emulate. David Skinner later joined Uncle Dog, Clancy and Phil Manzanera's 801, before replacing Paul Carrack in Roxy Music.

● ALBUMS: *Own Up* (Immediate 1966) ★★★, *That's All* (Immediate 1969) ★★.

● COMPILATIONS: *Sittin' On A Fence: The Immediate Anthology* (Sequel 1999) ★★★.

TWINKLE

b. Lynn Annette Ripley, 15 July 1947, Surbiton, Surrey, England. Unlike her mid-60s female contemporaries, Twinkle actually wrote her own hits, a feat that should not be underestimated. After traipsing around Denmark Street, the Tin Pan Alley of British pop, the 16-year-old was auditioned by producer Tommy Scott and placed in the hands of manager Phil Solomon. Like most of the Solomon stable she was signed to Decca Records by Dick Rowe and her records were arranged by Phil Coulter. 'Terry', a biker anthem similar in theme to the contemporaneous Shangri-Las' hit 'Leader Of The Pack', was a Top 3 smash in early 1965. The song's morbid theme provoked a moral backlash, and it was banned by the BBC as debates raged in the press about the corrupting influence of so-called 'death discs'. The teenager soon made her first public appearance supporting Jerry Lee Lewis at Brighton and prepared her next release, the charming 'Golden Lights', which proved only a minor hit. Although she wrote several other songs, including 'Boy That I Once Knew', 'Saturday Nights' and 'Unhappy Boy', no further success was forthcoming. Her main frailty was a lack of vocal power which prevented her building a following on the live circuit. After retiring to become a housewife, marrying the actor spotlighted in the 'And all because the lady loves Milk Tray' advertising campaign, she returned briefly in 1972 with a cover of the Monkees' 'I'm A Believer'. More recently, her work was introduced to a younger audience thanks to the Smiths' cover version of 'Golden Lights'.

● COMPILATIONS: *Golden Lights: The Twinkle Story* (1993) ★★.

TYRANNOSAURUS REX

Formed in 1967 by singer/guitarist Marc Bolan, Tyrannosaurus Rex was originally envisioned as an electric sextet until a hire purchase company repossessed their equipment. Bolan was then joined by percussionist Steve 'Peregrine' Took (b. 28 July 1949, Eltham, South London, England, d. 27 October 1980) in an acoustic-based venture that combined his love of classic rock 'n' roll with an affection for faerie mythology. Marc's unusual quivering vocal style rendered most of his lyrics incomprehensible, but the effect was genuinely enchanting and the duo were quickly adopted by the emergent 'underground'. BBC disc jockey John Peel became a tireless promoter of the group, which shared billings on his roadshow and was featured heavily on his radio programme *Top Gear*. Tyrannosaurus Rex enjoyed three minor hit singles with 'Debora', 'One Inch Rock' and 'King Of The Rumbling Spires', and achieved notable success with their albums, of which *My People Were Fair And Had Sky In Their Hair But Now They're Content To Wear Stars On Their Brows* and *Unicorn* reached the UK Top 20. The latter set showed a marked departure from previous stark accompaniment, adding harmonium, bass and piano to their lexicon. Their partnership was sundered in 1969 following an acrimonious US tour and Bolan was joined by Mickey Finn, late of Hapshash And The Coloured Coat for *A Beard Of Stars*. Here the unit's transformation was complete and this electric set, although still encompassing chimerical fables, was the natural stepping-stone for Bolan's transformation into a fully fledged pop idol with T. Rex.

● ALBUMS: *My People Were Fair And Had Sky In Their Hair But Now They're Content To Wear Stars On Their Brows* (Regal Zonophone 1968) ★★★★, *Prophets, Seers, Sages, The Angels Of The Ages* (Regal Zonophone 1968) ★★★★, *Unicorn* (Regal Zonophone 1969) ★★★, *A Beard Of Stars* (Regal Zonophone 1970) ★★★.

● COMPILATIONS: *The Best Of T. Rex* (Fly 1971) ★★★★, *The Definitive Tyrannosaurus Rex* (Sequel 1993) ★★★★, *BBC Radio 1 Live In Concert* (Windsong 1993) ★★★★, *A BBC History* (Band Of Joy 1996) ★★★★.

● FURTHER READING: *Tyrannosaurus Rex*, Ray Stevenson.

ULTIMATE SPINACH

One of three bands from Boston, Massachusetts, USA, signed to MGM Records in an attempt to create a Bosstown Sound to rival San Francisco's music scene (the others were Orpheus and Beacon Street Union), Ultimate Spinach recorded three albums in a two-year period before fading away. The band, originally called Underground Cinema, comprised Ian Bruce-Douglas (vocals, keyboards – also the group's songwriter and arranger), Keith Lahteinen (vocals, drums), Geoffrey Winthrop (lead guitar, sitar, vocals), Barbara Hudson (vocals, guitar) and Richard Ness (bass). Their self-titled 1968 album was the highest-charting of any of the 'Bosstown' albums, reaching number 34 in the USA. The record was typically pseudo-psychedelic for the period, both lyrically and musically. It was followed later that year with *Behold & See* and in 1969 by a third release, which sported an entirely new line-up save for Hudson. Among the new members in that second line-up was Jeff 'Skunk' Baxter on guitar, later of Steely Dan and the Doobie Brothers.

● ALBUMS: *Ultimate Spinach* (MGM 1968) ★★★, *Behold & See* (MGM 1968) ★★★, *III* (MGM 1969) ★.

● COMPILATIONS: *The Box* 3-CD box set (Akarma 2001) ★★★.

UNDERTAKERS

Formed in Wallasey, Merseyside, in 1961, the Undertakers were initially known as the Vegas Five, but assumed their new sobriquet when a printer's error advertised them as such in a local newspaper. Their original line-up featured Jimmy McManus (vocals), Chris Huston (lead guitar), Geoff Nugent (guitar/vocals), Brian 'Boots' Jones (saxophone/vocals), Dave 'Mushy' Cooper (bass) and Bob Evans (drums), but within 18 months the core of Jones, Huston and Nugent had been joined by Jackie Lomax (b. 10 May 1944, Wallasey, Merseyside, England; bass/vocals) and Bugs Pemberton (drums). The quintet completed four singles between 1963 and 1964, including versions of material by the Shirelles ('Everybody Loves A Lover'), Solomon Burke ('Stupidity') and Roscoe Gordon ('Just A Little Bit'). Adequate rather than urgent, these releases lacked the passion of corresponding live performances where, bedecked in black frock coats, the Undertakers added a strong visual approach to their brand of driving R&B led by a powerful saxophone sound. An album

entitled *Undertakers* was recorded for Pye Records in 1964, but was not released until the mid-90s. The group attempted to update their image by truncating their name to the 'Takers, but split up in 1965 following a chaotic spell domiciled in New York. Jackie Lomax then pursed an intermittently successful career both as a solo and as a session vocalist.

● COMPILATIONS: *Unearthed* (Big Beat 1996) ★★★.

UNIT FOUR PLUS TWO

Formed in Hertfordshire, England, this aptly named 60s pop sextet comprised: Buster Meikle (b. David Meikle, 1 March 1942, vocals, guitar), Tommy Moeller (b. 23 February 1945; vocals, tambourine, piano, guitar), Peter Moules (b. 14 October 1944; vocals/autoharp, guitar, banjo), Rodney Garwood (b. 27 March 1944; bass) and Hugh Halliday (b. 12 December 1944; drums). Originally Unit Four, a folk quartet, they extended their ranks to six in January 1962. The folk element remained in their repertoire with such standards as 'Cottonfields' and 'La Bamba', while their first two Decca Records singles, 'Green Fields' and 'Sorrow And Rain', were out of keeping with the prevalent beat scene. With the assistance of Russ Ballard and Bob Henrit of the Roulettes (who later joined the group), they recorded the rhythmic 'Concrete And Clay', which brought them to number 1 in the UK in 1965. The follow-up, 'You've Never Been In Love Like This Before', reached the Top 20, but after a couple of further minor hits with 'Baby Never Say Goodbye' and 'Hark!', their lightweight pop style proved insufficient for chart success. In 1969, with the beat boom long forgotten, they disbanded.

● ALBUMS: *Unit Four Plus Two – First Album* (Decca/London 1965) ★★, *Unit Four Plus Two* (Fontana 1969) ★★.

● COMPILATIONS: *Remembering* (1977) ★★, *Concrete And Clay* (Repertoire 1994) ★★★.

UNITED STATES OF AMERICA

Formed in 1967 by New York-born electronics composer Joseph Byrd (b. Tucson, Arizona, USA). The rest of the line-up comprised University of California Los Angeles students Dorothy Moskowitz (vocals), Gordon Marron (electric violin), Rand Forbes (bass) and Craig Woodson (drums). The quintet's lone, self-titled album, a biting satire on contemporary America, featured several haunting compositions including 'Love Song For The Dead Che' and 'The Garden Of Earthly Delights'. The humorous 'I Won't Leave My Wooden Wife For You Sugar' received most airplay as disc jockeys found them hard to categorize. At times reminiscent of Jefferson Airplane, the innovative use of electronic effects gave the collection its chilling factor and it remains one of the era's more lasting works. Byrd was also responsible for arranging Phil

Ochs' powerful composition 'Pleasures Of The Harbor' and later formed a new group, the Field Hippies. However, the resultant *The American Metaphysical Circus* lacked the discipline of his first release. Moscovitz subsequently re-emerged in Country Joe McDonald's All Star Band while Byrd was responsible for producing Ry Cooder's 1978 release, *Jazz*, and recording two quirky synthesizer solo albums.

● ALBUMS: *The United States Of America* (Columbia 1968) ★★★.

VALANCE, RICKY

b. David Spencer, *c.*1939, Ynytsdou, Wales. After singing in local clubs for a couple of years, Valance was discovered by an A&R representative from EMI Records and placed in the hands of producer Norrie Paramor. At the first recording session, Valance was given the chance of covering Ray Peterson's US hit, 'Tell Laura I Love Her'. A wonderfully enunciated reading was rewarded with a number 1 hit in September 1960, thanks to airplay on Radio Luxembourg, but none of Valance's follow-ups, including 'Movin' Away', 'Jimmy's Girl', 'Bobby' and 'Try To Forget Her', created any interest, and even with a move to Decca Records the dismal 'Six Boys' flopped. He continues playing clubs and the revival circuit.

VAN RONK, DAVE

b. 30 June 1936, Brooklyn, New York, USA. Van Ronk was a leading light of the Greenwich Village folk scene in the 60s, acting as a mentor to the young Bob Dylan. After a spell in the merchant marines Van Ronk became a professional performer in the mid-50s. Highly proficient on the guitar and banjo, his first love was New Orleans jazz and he began his musical career playing in jazz groups. His initial involvement with folk music did not come about until 1957 when he worked with Odetta. From this, his interest in blues grew, inspired by Josh White. A regular at Greenwich Village's Washington Square, Van Ronk's reputation for playing blues, together with his distinctive gruff voice, grew until he was signed by Folkways Records in 1959. His first album, however, appeared during the same year on the Lyrichord label. After a couple of releases he moved to Prestige Records in 1962, and from the mid-60s concentrated more on jazz and jug band music. He formed a band called the Ragtime Jug Stompers, and in 1964 signed to Mercury Records. He continued playing concerts both in the USA and abroad and in 1965 played the Carnegie Hall as part of the New York Folk Festival. Van Ronk reduced his work rate during the 70s, but still released several well-received albums for Philo Records. In 1974 he took the stage with Dylan and Phil Ochs at *An Evening With Salvador Allende*, performing a closing version of the former's 'Blowin' In The Wind'. Van Ronk has continued to record for various labels and remains a tireless live performer.

● ALBUMS: *Dave Van Ronk Sings Ballads, Blues*

And Spirituals (Folkways 1959) ★★★★ reissued as *Gambler's Blues* (Verve/Folkways 1965) and *Black Mountain Blues* (Folkways 1968), *Dave Van Ronk Sings Earthy Ballads And Blues* (Folkways 1961) ★★★★, *Inside* (Prestige/Folklore 1962) ★★★, *Folksinger* (Prestige 1963) ★★★★, with the Red Onion Jazz Band *In The Tradition* (Prestige 1964) ★★★, *Just Dave Van Ronk* (Mercury 1964) ★★★, *Dave Van Ronk And The Ragtime Jug Stompers* (Mercury 1964) ★★★, *Dave Van Ronk Sings The Blues* (Verve/Folkways 1965) ★★★★, *No Dirty Names* (Verve/Forecast 1966) ★★★, *Dave Van Ronk And The Hudson Dusters* (Verve/Forecast 1968) ★★★★, *Van Ronk* (Polydor 1971) ★★★, *Songs For Ageing Children* (Chess/Cadet 1973) ★★★, *Sunday Street* (Philo 1976) ★★★★, with Frankie Armstrong *Let No One Deceive You: Songs Of Bertolt Brecht* (Aural Tradition 1978) ★★★, *Somebody Else, Not Me* (Philo 1980) ★★★, *Your Basic Dave Van Ronk Album* (Kicking Mule/Sonet 1982) ★★★, *St. James Infirmary* reissued as *Statesboro Blues* (Paris 1983) ★★★, *Going Back To Brooklyn* (Reckless 1985) ★★★, *Dave Van Ronk Presents Peter And The Wolf* (Alacazam 1990) ★★, *Hummin' To Myself* (Gazell 1990) ★★★, *To All My Friends In Far-Flung Places* (Gazell 1994) ★★★, *From ... Another Time & Place* (Alcazar 1995) ★★★, *Live At Sir George Williams University* (Just A Memory 1997) ★★.
● COMPILATIONS: *Hesitation Blues* (Big Beat 1988) ★★★★, *The Folkways Years, 1959-1961* (Smithsonian/Folkways 1991) ★★★★, *A Chrestomathy* (Gazell 1992) ★★★★.

VANILLA FUDGE

This US rock group was formed in December 1966 and comprised Mark Stein (b. 11 March 1947, New Jersey, USA; organ), Vince Martell (b. 11 November 1945, Bronx, New York, USA; guitar), Tim Bogert (b. 27 August 1944, Richfield, New Jersey, USA; bass) and Joey Brennan (drums). All were previously members of the Pigeons, a New York-based group modelled on the Young Rascals. Brennan was latterly replaced by Carmine Appice (b. 15 December 1946, Staten Island, New York, USA), and having established a style in which contemporary songs were imaginatively rearranged, the unit was introduced to producer Shadow Morton, who had a reputation for melodramatic pop with the Shangri-Las. Dubbed Vanilla Fudge by their record label, the quartet scored an immediate success with an atmospheric revival of the Supremes' hit, 'You Keep Me Hangin' On'. The slowed tempo, studious playing and mock-gospel harmonies set a precedent for the group's debut album, which featured similarly operatic versions of the Impressions' 'People Get Ready', Sonny And Cher's 'Bang Bang' and the Beatles' 'Eleanor Rigby' and 'Ticket To Ride'. The audacity of this first selection was impossible to repeat. A

flawed concept album, *The Beat Goes On*, proved overambitious, while further selections showed a group unable to create original material of the calibre of the first album. Subsequent records relied on simpler, hard-edged rock. When Vanilla Fudge split in 1970, the bass player and drummer remained together in Cactus before abandoning their creation in favour of Beck, Bogert And Appice. Stein worked with Tommy Bolin and Alice Cooper before forging a new career composing advertising jingles, while Martell later appeared in the Good Rats, a popular Long Island bar-band. The group briefly re-formed in 1983, releasing *Mystery* which failed to make any impact.
● ALBUMS: *Vanilla Fudge* (Atco 1967) ★★★, *The Beat Goes On* (Atco 1968) ★★, *Renaissance* (Atco 1968) ★★, *Near The Beginning* (Atco 1969) ★★, *Rock & Roll* (Atco 1970) ★★, *Mystery* (Atco 1984) ★★, *Live: The Best Of The Vanilla Fudge* (Rhino 1991) ★.
● COMPILATIONS: *The Best Of The Vanilla Fudge* (Atco 1982) ★★, *Psychedelic Sundae – The Best Of* (Rhino 1993) ★★★.

VANITY FARE

This late 60s British pop quintet, which took its name (respelled) from Thackeray's famous novel, comprised: Dick Allix (b. 3 May 1945, Gravesend, Kent, England; drums), Trevor Brice (b. 12 February 1945, Rochester, Kent, England; vocals), Tony Goulden (b. 21 November 1944, Rochester, Kent, England; guitar), Tony Jarrett (b. 4 September 1944; double bass and guitar) and Barry Landeman (b. 25 October 1947, Woodbridge, Suffolk, England; keyboards). Managed by Roger Easterby and signed to Larry Page's Page One label, the clean-cut Vanity Fare hit the UK Top 20 in the summer of 1968 with the appropriately titled 'I Live For The Sun'. It was almost a year and another summer before they returned to the charts with 'Early In The Morning', this time abandoning their suits in favour of neckerchiefs and Carnaby Street garb. Although they claimed they could only chart in summer, their final success, 'Hitchin' A Ride', was a surprise festive hit.
● ALBUMS: *The Sun, The Wind And Other Things* (Page One 1969) ★★.

VEE, BOBBY

b. Robert Thomas Velline, 30 April 1943, Fargo, North Dakota, USA. Vee's first exposure to the rock 'n' roll scene occurred in macabre circumstances when his group, the Shadows, deputized for Buddy Holly after the singer was killed in an air crash. Soon after, Vee's group were discovered by famed producer Tommy 'Snuff' Garrett and saw their record 'Suzie Baby' released on a major label, Liberty Records. Vee rapidly became a solo artist in his own right. One of his first recordings was a cover of Adam Faith's 'What Do You Want?', which failed to emulate the British artist's UK chart-topping success. Vee was subsequently groomed as a soloist, his college-boy looks and boy-next-door persona cleverly combined with a canon of teenage anthems provided by Brill Building songwriters.

After charting with a revival of the Clovers' 1956 hit 'Devil Or Angel', Vee found transatlantic success via the infectious, if lyrically innocuous, 'Rubber Ball'. Between 1961 and 1962, he peaked with a series of infectious hits including 'More Than I Can Say', 'How Many Tears', 'Take Good Care Of My Baby' (a US number 1), 'Run To Him', 'Please Don't Ask About Barbara', 'Sharing You' and 'A Forever Kind Of Love'. The imaginatively titled 'The Night Has A Thousand Eyes' proved his most enduring song. Like many American teen-orientated artists, Vee's appeal waned following the arrival of the Beatles and the beat group explosion. He did manage a couple of film appearances (*Play It Cool* and *Just For Fun*) before the hit bubble burst. While Beatlemania raged, he reverted to the work of his original inspiration, Buddy Holly. Both *Bobby Vee Meets The Crickets* and *Bobby Vee Meets The Ventures* were promoted by touring. In 1967 Vee returned to the US Top 10 with 'Come Back When You Grow Up'. An attempt to fashion a more serious image prompted Vee to revert to his real name for *Nothing Like A Sunny Day*. The experiment was short-lived, however, and Vee later contented himself with regular appearances at rock 'n' roll revival shows.

● ALBUMS: *Bobby Vee Sings Your Favorites* (Liberty 1960) ★★, *Bobby Vee* (Liberty 1961) ★★★, *Bobby Vee With Strings And Things* (Liberty 1961) ★★★, *Bobby Vee Sings Hits Of The Rockin' '50s* (Liberty 1961) ★★★, *Take Good Care Of My Baby* (Liberty 1961) ★★★★, *Bobby Vee Meets The Crickets* (Liberty 1962) ★★★★, *A Bobby Vee Recording Session* (Liberty 1962) ★★★★, *Merry Christmas From Bobby Vee* (Liberty 1962) ★★, *The Night Has A Thousand Eyes* (Liberty 1963) ★★★, with the Ventures *Bobby Vee Meets The Ventures* (Dolton 1963) ★★★, *I Remember Buddy Holly* (Liberty 1963) ★★★, *Bobby Vee Sings The New Sound From England!* (Liberty 1964) ★★, *30 Big Hits From The 60s* (Liberty 1964) ★★★, *Bobby Vee Live On Tour* (Liberty 1965) ★, *C'mon Let's Live A Little* film soundtrack (1966) ★★, *Look At Me Girl* (Liberty 1966) ★★★, *Come Back When You Grow Up* (Liberty 1967) ★★, *Just Today* (Liberty 1968) ★★, *Do What You Gotta Do* (Liberty 1968) ★★★, *Gates, Grills And Railings* (1969) ★★, *Nothing Like A Sunny Day* (1972) ★★, with the Shadows *The Early Rockin' Years* (K-Tel 1995) ★★, *Down The Line* 1996 recording (Rollercoaster 2001) ★★★.

● COMPILATIONS: *Bobby Vee's Golden Greats* (Liberty 1962) ★★★★, *Bobby Vee's Golden Greats, Volume Two* (Liberty 1966) ★★★, *A Forever Kind of Love* (Sunset 1969) ★★★, *Legendary Masters* (United Artists 1973) ★★★★, *The Bobby Vee Singles Album* (1980) ★★★★, *The EP Collection* (See For Miles 1991) ★★★★, *The Very Best Of* (1993) ★★★★, *Bobby Vee Greatest Hits* (Warners 1994) ★★★★, *Favorites* (Masters 1997) ★★★★.

● FILMS: *C'mon Let's Live A Little* (1967).

VELVELETTES

Two pairs of sisters, Millie and Cal Gill, and Bertha and Norma Barbee, formed the original Velvelettes line-up in 1961 at Western Michigan State University. After recording a one-off single, 'There He Goes', for IPG Records in 1963, they were signed to Motown Records, where they were placed in the hands of fledgling producer Norman Whitfield. This partnership spawned three classic singles, 'Needle In A Haystack', 'He Was Really Sayin' Something' and 'These Things Will Keep Me Lovin' You', which epitomized Motown's approach to the all girl-group sound. A flurry of personnel changes effectively halted the Velvelettes' progress in 1965: Millie Gill and the Barbee sisters left, to be replaced briefly by two future members of Martha And The Vandellas, Sandra Tilley and Betty Kelly, and Annette McMullen. This line-up also dissolved after a few months. In 1970, 'These Things Will Keep Me Loving You' became a belated UK hit, confirming the Velvelettes' cult status among British soul fans. The original line-up regrouped in 1984 to play revival shows, and re-recorded their hits for Nightmare Records. The original line-up of Carolyn Gill-Street, Bertha Barbee-McNeal, Norma Barbee-Fairhurst and Millie Gill-Arbour recorded a disco version of 'Needle In A Haystack' for Ian Levine's label in 1987, and continue recording to the present day. *One Door Closes* consisted half of old hits and half of new material, recorded in an updated Motown style.

● ALBUMS: *One Door Closes* (Motor City 1990) ★★.

● COMPILATIONS: *The Very Best Of The Velvelettes* (Motown 1999) ★★★.

VELVET OPERA

This popular UK act, which adeptly mixed soul and psychedelic/progressive styles, evolved from Jaymes Fenda And The Vulcans, one of several bands to secure a recording deal following their appearance in the televised contest, *Ready Steady Win*. Former Vulcan songwriter John Ford (b. 1 July 1948, Fulham, London, England; bass) was subsequently joined by Elmer Gantry (vocals), Colin Forster (guitar) and Richard Hudson (b. Richard William Stafford Hudson, 9 May 1948, London, England; drums) in a group initially dubbed Elmer Gantry's Velvet Opera. Their excellent debut album included the pulsating 'Flames', which, despite regular appearances on BBC Radio 1's *Top Gear*, failed to become a hit. In

1968 Forster was replaced by Paul Brett who then left to join Fire. Gantry also abandoned the group, which then truncated their name to Velvet Opera. Colin Forster rejoined Ford, Hudson and new vocalist John Joyce for *Ride A Hustler's Dream*, but this lacked the purpose of its predecessor, save for the excellent 'Anna Dance Square'. The quartet fell apart when Hudson and Ford joined the Strawbs, with whom they remained until 1973. Having written several of the group's most commercial offerings, the duo then left to pursue their own career as Hudson-Ford. By 1974, Gantry was fronting a band which, until checked by litigation, accepted illicit bookings as 'Fleetwood Mac' while the genuine article were off the road. A year later, Gantry emerged once more as singer on Stretch's solitary UK chart entry, 'Why Did You Do It'.

● ALBUMS: *Elmer Gantry's Velvet Opera* (CBS 1967) ★★★, *Ride A Hustler's Dream* (CBS 1969) ★★★.

● COMPILATIONS: *The Very Best Of Elmer Gantry* (See For Miles 1996) ★★★.

VELVET UNDERGROUND

The antithesis of late-60s west coast love and peace, New York, USA's the Velvet Underground portrayed a darker side to that era's hedonism. Their pulsating drive married with intellectual precision and resulted in one of rock's most innovative and lasting catalogues. Lou Reed (b. 2 March 1942, Freeport, Long Island, New York, USA; guitar, vocals) and John Cale (b. 9 March 1942, Garnant, West Glamorgan, Wales; viola, bass, organ) provided a contrast in personality and approach that ensured the band's early notoriety. Reed was a contract songwriter and performer at Pickwick Records, responsible for a series of budget-priced recordings issued under several names, the best-known of which was the Primitives. Cale, a classically trained child prodigy, had secured a scholarship to study in America, but was drawn into the band's nascent circle when he contributed a viola passage to Reed's anti-dance composition 'The Ostrich'. A third member of the Primitives, Walter De Maria, was quickly replaced by Sterling Morrison (b. 29 August 1942, East Meadow, Long Island, New York, USA, d. 30 August 1995, Poughkeepsie, New York, USA; guitar), who had studied creative writing with Reed at Syracuse University. The reshaped unit was completed by drummer Angus MacLise (d. Nepal 1979) who suggested they adopt the name 'The Velvet Underground', the title of a contemporary pulp paperback. MacLise was also instrumental in securing the band's first gigs at multimedia events and happenings, but left when they began accepting fees. He was replaced by Maureen 'Mo' Tucker (b. 1945, New Jersey, USA), sister of a friend of Sterling Morrison. The band met pop-art celebrity Andy Warhol in 1965 following an appearance at the Cafe Bizarre. He invited them to join the Exploding Plastic Inevitable, a theatrical mixture of music, films, light-shows and dancing, and also suggested adding actress/singer Nico (b. Christa Paffgen, 16 October 1938, Cologne, Germany, d. 18 July 1988) to the line-up. The band recorded their debut album in the spring of 1966 but the completed master was rejected by several major companies, fearful of both its controversial content and lengthy tracks. *The Velvet Underground & Nico* was eventually issued by Verve Records the following year. Infamous for Warhol's prominent involvement – he designed the distinctive peel-off banana screen print featured on its sleeve and is credited as producer – this powerful collection introduced Reed's decidedly urban infatuations, a fascination for street culture and amorality bordering on voyeurism.

Reed's talent, however, was greater than mere opportunism. His finely honed understanding of R&B enhanced a graphic lyricism whereby songs about drugs ('I'm Waiting For The Man', 'Heroin'), sado-masochism ('Venus In Furs') or sublimation ('I'll Be Your Mirror') were not only memorable for their subjects, but also as vibrant pop compositions. These skills were intensified by Cale's haunting, graphic viola work, Nico's gothic intonation and the band's combined sense of dynamism, which blended Tucker's relentless pulse with some of rock's most inspired sonic experimentation. Now rightly regarded as a musical milestone, *The Velvet Underground & Nico* was generally reviled on release. Contemporary radio shunned its stark ugliness and subject matter, while the disparate counter-cultures of Los Angeles and San Francisco abhorred the dank underbelly that this uncompromising band had revealed as a challenge to their floral dreams.

Nico left for a solo career in 1967 and the remaining quartet then parted from Warhol's patronage. Sessions for a second album, *White Light/White Heat*, exacerbated other internal conflicts and its six compositions were marked by a raging intensity. While the title track and the relentless 'I Heard Her Call My Name' suggested an affinity to 'I'm Waiting For The Man', two extended pieces, 'The Gift' and 'Sister Ray', caught the Velvet Underground at its most radical. The latter performance, a grinding, remorseless, sexual cacophony, was recorded live in the studio at maximum volume, and although Reed later suggested he was trying to approximate the free-jazz of Ornette Coleman, this 17-minute *tour de force* offers some of John Cale's most inspired atonal instrumental work. This pivotal figure was then removed from the band and replaced by an orthodox bass player, former Grass Menagerie member Doug Yule. A third album, entitled simply *The Velvet Underground*, unveiled a pastoral approach, gentler and more subtle, retaining the chilling, disquieting aura of previous releases. Now firmly within Reed's grasp, the quartet were implicit rather than direct, although moments of their previous fury were apparent on several interludes. *Loaded*, an album of considerable commercial promise, emphasized their new-found perspective. Released in 1970, this unfettered collection contained one of Reed's most popular compositions, 'Sweet Jane', and in celebrating pop's rich heritage, offered an optimism rarely heard in previous work. Paradoxically, by the time *Loaded* was issued, Lou Reed had abandoned the group he had created and Doug Yule, who had encouraged the commercial aspect of the album, now took control, leading several variations on the Velvet Underground name. A poorly received album, *Squeeze*, confirmed that the definitive unit ended with Reed's departure, so much so that the album is not generally perceived to be part of the band's discography.

Despite the tribulations endured during its brief life span, the Velvet Underground has since become regarded as one of rock music's most influential acts, particularly during the 80s when a new generation of performers, from Joy Division to Jesus And Mary Chain, declared their indebtedness. A series of archive releases, including *1969: Velvet Underground Live*, *VU* and *Another View*, add further fuel to the talent and insight that lay within the Velvet Underground and enhance their legendary status. A rumour, followed by an announcement in 1993 that the band, without Doug Yule, had re-formed for a major tour, was greeted with anxious excitement. The subsequent performances delighted thousands of fans, with a vast percentage barely born when the band had last performed. Old wounds were opened between Cale and Reed and no further plans were imminent other than a one-off appearance together following their induction to the Rock And Roll Hall Of Fame in 1996. Sadly, Sterling Morrison died only a few months before the latter event.

● ALBUMS: *The Velvet Underground & Nico* (Verve 1967) ★★★★★, *White Light/White Heat* (Verve 1968) ★★★★, *The Velvet Underground* (MGM 1969) ★★★★, *Loaded* (Cotillion/Atlantic 1970) ★★★★, *Live At Max's Kansas City* (Cotillion/Atlantic 1972) ★, *Squeeze* (Polydor 1973) ★★, *1969: Velvet Underground Live* (Mercury 1974) ★★★, *Live MCMXCIII* (Sire/Warners 1993) ★★★, *Loaded (Fully Loaded)* (Rhino 1997) ★★★★.

● COMPILATIONS: *Velvet Underground* (Golden Archive Series 1970) ★★★, *Andy Warhol's Velvet Underground Featuring Nico* (MGM 1971) ★★★★, *Lou Reed And The Velvet Underground* aka *That's The Story Of My Life* (Pride 1973) ★★★, *Velvet Underground* (MGM Special 1976) ★★★, *VU* (Verve PolyGram 1985) ★★★, *Another View* (Verve PolyGram 1986) ★★, *The Velvet Underground* 5-LP box set (Polydor 1986) ★★★, *The Best Of The Velvet Underground* (Verve 1989) ★★★★, *The Best Of Lou Reed & The Velvet Underground* (Global Television 1995) ★★★★, *Peel Slowly And See* 5-CD box set (Polydor 1995) ★★★★, *The Best Of The Velvet Underground: The Millennium Collection* (Polydor 2000) ★★★★, *Rock & Roll: An Introduction To The Velvet Underground* (Polydor 2001) ★★★★, *Bootleg Series Volume 1: The Quine Tapes* 3-CD set (Polydor 2001) ★★★, *Final V.U. 1971-1973* 4-CD box set (Captain Trip 2001) ★★.

● VIDEOS: *Velvet Redux – Live MCMXCIII* (Warner Music Vision 1993).

● FURTHER READING: *Lou Reed & The Velvets*, Nigel Trevena. *The Velvet Underground & Lou Reed*, Mike West. *Up-Tight: The Velvet Underground Story*, Victor Bockris & Gerard Malanga. *Lou Reed & The Velvet Underground*, Diana Clapton. *Beyond The Velvet Underground*, Dave Thompson. *The Velvet Underground Handbook*, M.C. Kostek. *Warhol's Factory: The Velvet Years 1965-1967*, Stephen Shore & Lynne Tillman. *'69 On The Road: Velvet Underground Photographs*, Doug Yule. *The Velvet Underground Companion: Four Decades Of Commentary*, Albin Zak III. *The Complete Guide To The Music Of The Velvet Underground*, Peter Hogan.

● FILMS: *Venus In Furs* (1965), *Andy Warhol's Exploding Plastic Inevitable* (1966), *The Velvet Underground And Nico (A Symphony Of Sound)* (1966), *Walden* aka *Diaries, Notes And Sketches* (1968), *Scenes From The Life Of Andy Warhol* (1990).

VELVETT FOGG

This UK, Midlands-based attraction was one of several acts launched by the Pye Records label in 1969 during a belated attempt to enter the progressive rock market. *Velvett Fogg*, replete with BBC disc jockey John Peel's glowing testimony, revealed an organ-based sound redolent of the Nice and Spooky Tooth. 'Come Away Melinda', popularized by Tim Rose and the Bee Gees' 'New York Mining Disaster, 1941', contrasted several original songs, the most interesting of which, 'Lady Caroline' and 'Wizard Of Gobsolob', were penned by guitarist Paul Eastment. The line-up also included Frank Wilson (keyboards) and Keith Law. The band also completed a non-album single, 'Telstar '69', in which they reconstructed the famed Tornados classic. Velvett Fogg disbanded soon afterwards, although Eastment quickly reappeared in cult favourites, the Ghost, while Wilson joined Warhorse.

● ALBUMS: *Velvett Fogg* (Pye 1969) ★★★.

VENTURES

This pivotal instrumental group was formed in Tacoma, Washington, USA, in 1959 when workmates Don Wilson (b. 10 February 1937, USA; rhythm guitar) and Bob Bogle (b. 16 January 1937, USA; lead guitar) discovered a mutual interest in music. They began performing together as the Impacts, using a pick-up rhythm section, before Nokie Edwards (b. 9 May 1939, USA; bass) and Skip Moore (drums) completed a line-up redubbed the Ventures. The quartet made its debut with 'Cookies And Coke', released on their own Blue Horizon label, before discovering Johnny Smith's 'Walk, Don't Run' on Chet Atkins' *Hi-Fi In Focus* album. Initially a jazz instrumental, it nonetheless lent itself to a simplified chord structure and by emphasizing its beat, the Ventures constructed a powerful, compulsive sound that not only became their trademark, but was echoed in the concurrent surfing style. The single, re-released on the Dolton Records label, reached number 2 in the US charts (number 8 UK) with sales in excess of one million copies, a distinction matched by its follow-up, 'Perfidia'. At this point Moore had been replaced by Howie Johnson (d. 1988), who in turn retired following a major car accident. Drummer Mel Taylor (b. 1934, New York City, New York, USA, d. 11 August 1996, Los Angeles, California, USA) was then added to the group. Other notable Ventures singles included 'The 2,000 Pound Bee (Part 2)' (1962), which featured the then revolutionary fuzz-guitar, 'The Savage' (1963), originally recorded by the Shadows, and 'Diamond Head' (1965), later immortalized by the Beach Boys. The Ventures' continued appeal lay in an ability to embrace contemporary fashion, as evinced on *Play The "Batman" Theme* (1966), *Super Psychedelics* (1967) and *Underground Fire* (1969), without straying too far from their established format. They also survived several personnel changes; Nokie traded roles with Bogle in 1963 before leaving altogether five years later. He was replaced by session guitarist Gerry McGee, whose numerous credits include Elvis Presley, the Monkees and Kris Kristofferson, and organist Sandy Lee, although the latter was in turn supplanted by Johnny Durrill, formerly of the Five Americans. In 1969 the Ventures had their last major US hit when 'Hawaii Five-O', the theme tune to a popular detective series, reached number 4.

They remained a popular attraction, particularly in Japan, where the group is the subject of almost fanatical reverence and the group is among the Top 10 composers in Japanese history. Annual tours throughout the 70s were supplemented by many exclusive recordings, and several tracks were hits twice: once as instrumentals and again with lyrics courtesy of local composers and singers. The group withstood the loss of Taylor, McGee and Durrill (Edwards returned to the line-up in 1972); the remaining trio added new drummer Jo Barile and, buoyed by a succession of keyboard players and vocalists, they continued their highly lucrative career. Musically, the Ventures continued to court contemporary trends, including disco and reggae, while assuming greater artistic control with the

founding of their Tridex label. Mel Taylor rejoined Bogle, Wilson and Edwards in 1979 as the unit attempted to rekindle their reputation at home. The latter stayed five years before being replaced by the returning McGee. They continue to attract loyal support in Europe and Japan (where they have released over 200 albums), and during the 90s the UK label See For Miles Records launched an excellent reissue series. The death of Taylor from cancer in 1996 led to his son, Leon, joining Bogle, McGee and Wilson in the new line-up. The Ventures remain one of the world's most respected instrumental units.

● ALBUMS: *Walk, Don't Run* (Dolton 1960) ★★★★, *The Ventures* (Dolton 1961) ★★★★, *Another Smash* (Dolton 1961) ★★★, *The Colorful Ventures* (Dolton 1961) ★★★, *Twist With The Ventures aka Dance* (Dolton 1962) ★★★, *Twist Party Volume 2* aka *Dance With The Ventures* (Dolton 1962) ★★★, *Mashed Potatoes And Gravy* aka *The Ventures' Beach Party* (Dolton 1962) ★★★, *Going To The Ventures' Dance Party* (Dolton 1962) ★★★, *The Ventures Play 'Telstar' And 'Lonely Bull'* (Dolton 1963) ★★, with Bobby Vee *Bobby Vee Meets The Ventures* (Liberty 1963) ★★★, *Surfin'* (Dolton 1963) ★★★, *The Ventures Play The Country Classics* aka *I Walk The Line* (Dolton 1963) ★★, *Let's Go!* (Dolton 1963) ★★★★, *In Space* (Dolton 1964) ★★, *The Fabulous Ventures* (Dolton 1964) ★★, *Walk, Don't Run, Volume 2* (Dolton 1964) ★★★, *Knock Me Out!* (Dolton 1965) ★★★, *In Japan* (Liberty 1965) ★★★, *On Stage* (Dolton 1965) ★★★, *A-Go-Go* (Dolton 1965) ★★★, *The Christmas Album* (Dolton 1965) ★★★, *Adventures In Paradise* aka *White Album* (Ventures 1965) ★★★, *Play Guitar With The Ventures* (Dolton 1965) ★★★, *Where The Action Is* (Dolton 1966) ★★★, *Play The "Batman" Theme* (Dolton 1966) ★★★, *In Japan, Volume 2* (Liberty 1966) ★★★, *All About The Ventures Live* (Liberty 1966) ★★★, *Go With The Ventures* (Dolton 1966) ★★★, *Wild Thing!* (Dolton 1966) ★★★, *Blue Sunset* (Liberty 1966) ★★★, *On Stage Encore* (Liberty 1967) ★★★, *Guitar Freakout* aka *Revolving Sounds* (Dolton 1967) ★★★, *Wonderful Ventures* (Liberty 1967) ★★★, *Super Psychedelics* aka *Changing Times* (Liberty 1967) ★★★, *Pops In Japan* (Liberty 1967) ★★★, *Ventures Deluxe* (Liberty 1967) ★★★, *$1,000,000 Weekend* (Liberty 1967) ★★, *The Versatile Ventures* (Liberty 1967) ★★★, *Live Again* (Liberty 1968) ★★★, *Flights Of Fantasy* (Liberty 1968) ★★★, *Pops In Japan No. 2* (Liberty 1968) ★★★, *Pops Sound* (Liberty 1968) ★★★, *The Horse* aka *On The Scene* (Liberty 1968) ★★★, *Best Of Surfing* (Liberty 1968) ★★★, *In Tokyo '68* (Liberty 1968) ★★★, *Underground Fire* (Liberty 1969) ★★★, *Hawaii Five-O* (Liberty 1969) ★★, *Colourful Ventures* (Liberty 1969) ★★★, *Journey To The Moon* (Liberty 1969) ★★★, *Swamp Rock* (Liberty 1969) ★★★, *10th Anniversary Album* (Liberty 1970) ★★★, *Golden Pops* (Liberty 1970) ★★★, *Live*

(Liberty 1970) ★★★, *New Testament* (United Artists 1971) ★★, *Pops In Japan '71* (Liberty 1971) ★★★, *On Stage '71* (Liberty 1971) ★★★, *Theme From "Shaft"* (United Artists 1972) ★★, *Pops In Japan '71* (Liberty 1971) ★★★, *Joy: The Ventures Play The Classics* (United Artists 1972) ★★★, *Rock And Roll Forever* (United Artists 1972) ★★★, *On Stage '72* (Liberty 1972) ★★★, *Pops In Japan '73* (Liberty 1973) ★★★, *On Stage '73* (Liberty 1973) ★★★, *Only Hits* (United Artists 1973) ★★★, *The Jim Croce Songbook* (United Artists 1974) ★★, *On Stage '74* (Liberty 1974) ★★★, *Play The Carpenters* (United Artists 1974) ★★, *On Stage '75* (Liberty 1975) ★★★, *Hollywood: Yuya Uchida Meets The Ventures* (Liberty 1976) ★★★, *On Stage '76* (Liberty 1976) ★★★, *Rocky Road: The New Ventures* (United Artists 1976) ★★, *TV Themes* (United Artists 1977) ★★, *Live In Japan '77* (King 1977) ★★★, *In Space '78* (King 1978) ★★, *Surfin' USA '78* (King 1978) ★★, *Pops Best 20* (King 1978) ★★, *On Stage '78* (King 1978) ★★, *Latin Album* (King 1979) ★★, *Surfin' '79* (King 1979) ★★, *Original Four* (East World 1979) ★★★, *Chameleon* (East World 1980) ★★, *Super Live '80* (East World 1980) ★★★, *'60s Pops* (East World 1981) ★★★, *Pops In Japan '81* (East World 1981) ★★★, *St Louis Memory* (East World 1982) ★★, *The Ventures Today* (Valentine 1983) ★★★, *Surfin' Deluxe* (EMI 1984) ★★, *Radical Guitars* (Iloki 1987) ★★★, *Best Hit Collection* (Teichiku 1989) ★★★, *Play Southern All Stars* (Toshiba 1990) ★★, *Live In Japan '90* (Toshiba 1990) ★★★, *Flyin' High* (Toshiba 1992) ★★★, *Wild Again: The Ventures Play Heavy Hitters* (Toshiba 1996) ★★★, *Wild Again II: Tribute To Mel Taylor* (Toshiba 1997) ★★★, *Wild Again Concert '97* (Toshiba 1998) ★★★, *V-Gold* (M&I 1999) ★★★, *Walk, Don't Run 2000* (M&I 1999) ★★★, *V-Gold Live '99* (M&I 1999) ★★★, *V-Gold II* (M&I 2000) ★★, *Acoustic Rock* (M&I 2000) ★★, *In Japan Live 2000* (M&I 2000) ★★★, *V-Gold III* (M&I 2001) ★★, *Play Southern All Stars – Tsunami* (M&I 2001) ★★★.
● COMPILATIONS: *Original Hits* (Liberty 1964) ★★★, *Best Of The Ventures* (Liberty 1965) ★★★, *Best Of The Ventures, Volume 2* (Liberty 1966) ★★★, *Running Strong* (Sunset 1966) ★★★, *Golden Greats* (Liberty 1967) ★★★, *Golden Original Hits* (Liberty 1967) ★★★, *Guitar Genius Of The Ventures* (Sunset 1968) ★★★, *Deluxe Double, Volume 1* (Liberty 1968) ★★★, *Deluxe Double, Volume 2* (Liberty 1969) ★★★, *This Is The Ventures, Volume 1* (Liberty 1969) ★★★, *This Is The Ventures, Volume 2* (Liberty 1969) ★★★, *Super Group* (Sunset 1969) ★★★, *More Golden Greats* (Liberty 1970) ★★★, *A Decade With The Ventures* (Liberty 1971) ★★★, *Superpak* (United Artists 1971) ★★★, *Very Best Of The Ventures* (United Artists 1975) ★★★, *15 Years Of Japanese Pop* (Liberty 1975) ★★★, *Now Playing* (United Artists 1975) ★★★, *Early Sounds* (Liberty 1976) ★★★, *20 Greatest Hits* (Tee Vee 1977) ★★★★, *Special Deluxe Edition 8-LP set* (United Artists 1979) ★★★, *Greatest Hits* (Tridex 1980) ★★★, *Rare Collection* (King 1980) ★★★, *Walk, Don't Run: The Best Of The Ventures* (EMI 1990) ★★★★, *The Collection: Ventures Forever* (East World 1981) ★★★, *Best Of Live '65-'69* (Toshiba 1991) ★★★, *Live Box, Volume 1* 4-CD box set (Toshiba 1992) ★★★, *History Box, Volume 1* 4-CD box set (Toshiba 1992) ★★★, *History Box, Volume 2* 4-CD box set (Toshiba 1992) ★★★, *History Box, Volume 3* 4-CD box set (Toshiba 1992) ★★★, *History Box, Volume 4* 4-CD box set (Toshiba 1992) ★★★, *History Box, Volume 5* 4-CD box set (Toshiba 1992) ★★★, *Live Box, Volume 2* 4-CD box set (Toshiba 1992) ★★★, *Pops In Japan Box* 4-CD box set (Toshiba 1992) ★★★, *Live Box, Volume 3* 4-CD box set (Toshiba 1993) ★★★, *EP Box* 4-CD box set (Toshiba 1994) ★★★, *In The Vaults* (Ace 1997) ★★★, *In The Vaults, Volume 2* (Ace 1999) ★★★, *Best Collection Box Set* 8-CD box set (EMI 2000) ★★★, *The Ultimate Collection* (See For Miles 2001) ★★★.

VERNONS GIRLS

The group sponsored by UK's Vernon's football pools started with 70 members singing songs such as 'Nymphs And Shepherds'. This choir was reduced to 16 by the late 50s and was regularly seen on pop television shows like *Oh Boy*. They recorded for Parlophone Records without success between 1958 and 1961. Their only hits appeared on Decca Records when they were reduced to the trio of Maureen Kennedy, Jean Owen and Frances Lee. Their first and biggest hit was a cover of Clyde McPhatter's 'Lover Please', which reached the UK Top 20 in 1962. The b-side, the Liverpudlian-sung 'You Know What I Mean', also hit the charts as did covers of 'The Loco-Motion' and 'Do The Bird' and their original song 'Funny All Over'. The Vernons Girls group of the 50s also spawned solo hit maker Lyn Cornell and groups the Ladybirds, the Breakaways and the Two-Tones. With frequently changing personnel, the group continued for many more years, playing the UK cabaret circuit and recording (sometimes simply as the Vernons) on labels like Pye and Galaxy. One member, Joyce Baker, later married singer Marty Wilde. Members of the original television group have been frequently seen backing artists on UK television and stage and been heard singing backing vocals on countless hit records.
● ALBUMS: *The Vernons Girl* (Parlophone 1958) ★★★.

VINTON, BOBBY

b. Stanley Robert Vinton, 16 April 1935, Canonsburg, Pennsylvania, USA. Born of Polish extraction, Vinton was one of the more enduring boy-next-door pop idols who sprang up in the early 60s. He began as a trumpeter before agreeing to front his high school band as featured vocalist. A tape of one such performance reached Epic Records, who signed him in 1960. Composed by Al Byron and Paul Evans, 'Roses Are Red (My Love)' was Vinton's first national smash but it was overtaken in Britain by Ronnie Carroll's Top 10 cover version. Despite a much-publicized arrival in London for his cameo in the teen-exploitation movie, *Just For Fun*, a second US number 1, 'Blue Velvet', was initially ignored in the UK, although another American smash, a revival of Vaughn Monroe's 'There! I've Said It Again', made number 34 in 1963.

Vinton continued playing in supper clubs until 1968, when a policy of revamping hits by old rivals put his arrangements of Jimmy Crawford's 'I Love How You Love Me', Bobby Vee's 'Take Good Care Of My Baby' and the Teddy Bears' retitled 'To Know Her Is To Love Her' high up the Hot 100. This formula worked again in 1972 with Brian Hyland's 'Sealed With A Kiss', but it was 1974's 'My Melody Of Love', a new song co-written by Vinton himself, that gave him one more US chart-topper. Vinton also hosted his own television series during the mid-70s. His version of 'Blue Moon' was heard on the soundtrack of *An American Werewolf In London* in 1981 but it was the use of 'Blue Velvet' in both the 1989 movie of the same name and a television commercial that brought about a huge 1991 windfall in Britain. Vinton became omnipresent until the song's fall from the charts and the failure of 'Roses Are Red', which was reissued as the follow-up.

● ALBUMS: *Dancing At The Hop* (Epic 1961) ★★★, *Young Man With A Big Band* (Epic 1961) ★★★, *Roses Are Red* (Epic 1962) ★★★, *Sings The Big Ones* (Epic 1962) ★★★, *The Greatest Hits Of The Greatest Groups* (Epic 1963) ★★, *Blue On Blue* (Epic 1963) ★★★, *Blue Velvet* (Epic 1963) ★★★, *There! I've Said It Again* (Epic 1964) ★★★, *My Heart Belongs To Only You* (Epic 1964) ★★★, *Tell Me Why* (Epic 1964) ★★★, *Mr. Lonely* (Epic 1964) ★★★, *Sings For Lonely Nights* (Epic 1965) ★★★, *Laughing On The Outside (Crying On The Inside)* (Epic 1965) ★★★, *Drive-In Movie Time* (Epic 1965) ★★, *Satin Pillows And Careless* (Epic 1966) ★★★, *Please Love Me Forever* (Epic 1967) ★★★, *Take Good Care Of My Baby* (Epic 1968) ★★★, *I Love How You Love Me* (Epic 1968) ★★★, *Vinton* (Epic 1969) ★★★, *My Elusive Dreams* (Epic 1970) ★★★, *Ev'ry Day Of My Life* (Epic 1972) ★★★★, *Sealed With A Kiss* (Epic 1972) ★★★, *Melodies Of Love* (ABC 1974) ★★★, *With Love* (Epic 1974) ★★★, *Heart Of Hearts* (ABC 1975) ★★★, *The Bobby Vinton Show* (ABC 1975) ★★★, *The Name Is Love* (ABC 1977) ★★★, *Mr Lonely: Greatest Songs Today* (Warners 1991) ★★★, *Greatest Polka Hits Of All Time* (Warners 1991) ★★, *Kissin' Christmas* (Epic 1995) ★★.

● COMPILATIONS: *Bobby Vinton's Greatest Hits* (Epic 1964) ★★★, *Bobby Vinton's Greatest Hits Of Love* (Epic 1969) ★★★, *Bobby Vinton's All-Time Greatest Hits* (Columbia 1972) ★★★, *Sings The Golden Decade Of Love – Songs Of The 50s*

(Epic 1975) ★★★, *16 Most Requested Songs* (Columbia/Legacy 1991) ★★★★, *The Essence Of Bobby Vinton* (Epic/Legacy 1995) ★★★★.

● FURTHER READING: *The Polish Prince*, Bobby Vinton.

● FILMS: *Surf Party* (1964), *Big Jake* aka *The Million Dollar Kidnapping* (1971), *The Train Robbers* (1973).

VIPs

Formed in Carlisle, England, this blues/soul quintet comprised Mike Harrison (b. 3 September 1945, Carlisle, Cumberland, England; vocals), Jimmy Henshaw (guitar), Frank Kenyon (rhythm guitar), Greg Ridley (b. 23 October 1947, Cumberland, England; bass) and Walter Johnstone (drums). Signed to RCA Records in 1964, they released the Jimmy Reed-influenced 'Don't Keep Shouting At Me' before moving to CBS Records for 'Wintertime', which was curiously credited to the VIPPS. Ploughing similar ground to the Spencer Davis Group, they found a new home at Island Records where Chris Blackwell produced their exuberant reading of Joe Tex's 'I Wanna Be Free'. Several singles followed, but line-up changes gradually took their toll. Harrison, Ridley, guitarist Luther Grosvenor (b. 23 December 1949, Evesham, Worcestershire, England), drummer Mike Kellie (b. 24 March 1947, Birmingham, England) and keyboardist Keith Emerson (b. 1 November 1944, Todmorden, Lancashire, England) recorded *Supernatural Fairy Tales* with producer Guy Stevens, though by this time they had changed their name to Art. After further false starts, Ridley, Grosvenor, Kellie and Harrison formed Spooky Tooth.

VOGUES

This US vocal group was formed in Turtle Creek, near Pittsburgh, Pennsylvania, by schoolfriends Bill Burkette (lead baritone), Don Miller (baritone), Hugh Geyer (first tenor) and Chuck Blasko (second tenor). They began singing as the Val-Aires in 1960, but took the above name prior to signing with the tiny Co & Ce label. In 1965 the Vogues scored two US number 4 singles with 'You're The One' and 'Five O'Clock World', the latter of which was a majestic slice of east coast harmony pop, reminiscent of Jay And The Americans or the Four Seasons at their best. The quartet continued to enjoy minor success, but it was not until they joined Reprise Records that the group enjoyed another significant hit. 'Turn Around, Look At Me' (US number 7, June 1968) was the Vogues' only million-selling release and the prelude to a decidedly MOR direction when they took the 1957 Bobby Helms hit, 'My Special Angel', into the Top 10 in September 1968. Their later work lacked the earthy enthusiasm of those early offerings, although its professionalism secured a place with adult audiences.

● ALBUMS: *Meet The Vogues* (Co&Ce 1965) ★★★, *You're The One* (Ling 1966) ★★★, *Five O'Clock World* (Co&Ce 1966) ★★★, *Turn Around, Look At Me* (Reprise 1968) ★★★, *Till* (Reprise 1969) ★★, *Memories* (Reprise 1969) ★★.

● COMPILATIONS: *The Vogues' Greatest Hits* (1969) ★★★, *You're The One: The Best Of The Vogues: The Co & Ce Sessions* (Varèse Vintage 1996) ★★★.

WALKER BROTHERS

Hailing from America but transposed to England in the mid-60s, this hit trio comprised Scott Walker (b. Noel Scott Engel, 9 January 1943, Hamilton, Ohio; USA), John Walker (b. John Maus, 12 November 1943, New York; USA) and Gary Walker (b. Gary Leeds, 3 September 1944, Glendale, California; USA). Leeds, an ex-member of the Standells, had discovered former session bass player Engel appearing with Maus in an ensemble called the Dalton Brothers. In 1964, the trio changed their name to the Walker Brothers and following a false start at home decided to relocate to the UK. After arriving in February 1965, they fell into the hands of manager Maurice King and were soon signed to Philips Records. Their debut, 'Pretty Girls Everywhere', featured Maus as lead vocalist, but it was the Engel-voiced follow-up, 'Love Her', which cracked the UK Top 20 in May 1965. By this time, Scott was the chosen 'a-side' main vocalist, with Maus providing the strong high harmony.

The group neatly slotted into the gap left by Phil Spector's protégés the Righteous Brothers, who had topped the charts earlier in the year but failed to sustain their impact in the UK. As well as emulating their rivals' vocal power, the Walkers boasted film star looks and swiftly emerged as pin-up idols with a huge teenage following. On album, the trio played a contrasting selection of ballads, soul standards and occasional upbeat pop, but for the singles they specialized in high melodrama, brilliantly augmented by the string arrangements of Johnny Franz, with accompaniment directed by either Ivor Raymonde or Reg Guest. The lachrymose Burt Bacharach/Hal David ballad 'Make It Easy On Yourself' (originally a US hit for Jerry Butler) gave them a UK chart number 1, while the similarly paced 'My Ship Is Coming In' reached the Top 3. Their neurotic romanticism reached its apogee on the Bob Crewe/Bob Gaudio composition, 'The Sun Ain't Gonna Shine Anymore', in which Scott's deep baritone was wonderfully balanced by John's Four Seasons-styled soaring harmony. The song topped the UK listings for a month and gave them their second and last US Top 20 hit. Thereafter, there was immense friction in the Walker Brothers' camp and their second EP *Solo Scott, Solo John* (1967) neatly summarized their future intentions.

Although they continued to chart in the UK between 1965 and 1967, the quality of their material was generally less impressive. Pete Autell's '(Baby) You Don't Have To Tell Me' seemed a weak follow-up to their grandiose number 1 and commenced their gradual commercial decline. Another Bacharach/David composition, 'Another Tear Falls', fared little better at number 12, while the film theme, 'Deadlier Than The Male' could only scrape the Top 30. The much-covered Bert Berns composition 'Stay With Me Baby' retained the melodrama, but there was no emphatic comeback and in early 1967 the group elected to break up. The emotional impact on their loyal fanbase should have pushed their farewell single, 'Walking In The Rain', to the upper echelons of the chart but as the *New Musical Express* reviewer Derek Johnson sadly noted: 'Walkers Last Not So Great'.

As soloists, the Walker Brothers suffered mixed fortunes with only Scott troubling the charts, but it was still a surprise when the trio reunited in 1975. Their comeback album, *No Regrets*, consisted largely of extraneous material, but the classy Tom Rush title track returned the group to the Top 10 for the first time since 'The Sun Ain't Gonna Shine Anymore', released nearly a decade before. A follow-up album, *Lines*, was similar in style to its predecessor, but for their swan song, the self-penned *Nite Flights*, the trio produced a brave, experimental work, with oblique, foreboding lyrics and unusual arrangements (most notably on 'The Electrician'). The album was a commercial failure, but by the time the initial sales figures had been computed, John, Gary and Scott had returned to their individual ventures and concomitant obscurity, although the latter remains a cult figure in the UK and Europe.

● ALBUMS: *Take It Easy With The Walker Brothers* (Philips 1965) ★★★★, *Portrait* (Philips 1966) ★★★★, *Images* (Philips 1967) ★★★, *No Regrets* (GTO 1975) ★★★, *Lines* (GTO 1977) ★★, *Nite Flights* (GTO 1978) ★★★★, *The Walker Brothers In Japan* 1968 recording (Bam Caruso 1987) ★★.

● COMPILATIONS: *After The Lights Go Out: The Best Of 1965-1967* (Fontana 1990) ★★★★, *No Regrets: The Best Of The Walker Brothers* (Fontana 1991) ★★★★, *The Collection* (Spectrum 1996) ★★★★, *If You Could Hear Me Now* (Sony 2001) ★★★.

● FILMS: *Beach Ball* (1965).

WALKER, JOHN

b. John Maus, 12 November 1943, New York, USA. Originally a child actor, Maus moved to the west coast to pursue a career as a musician and in the early 60s formed the Dalton Brothers with Scott Engel. By 1964, Gary Leeds joined the duo who soon changed their name to the Walker Brothers, relocating to England the following year. Throughout his period with the Walker Brothers, Maus retained a second pseudonym, John Stewart, which can be seen on the b-side of

many of the trio's recordings. Interestingly, it was Maus who sang lead on the Walker Brothers' debut 'Pretty Girls Everywhere', but once the follow-up, 'Love Her', became a hit, Scott Walker enjoyed the prestige of singing on all future a-sides. Maus nevertheless proved himself an excellent high harmony singer and his six feet 4 inches height and sports-star frame made him an obvious sex symbol counterpoint to the sensual 'little boy lost' appeal of his partner. Disputes between the 'brothers' ended their collaboration in 1967 but Maus soon returned with the minor hit 'Annabella'. Unable to match the level of fame he enjoyed as a Walker Brother, Maus eventually returned to Los Angeles. With his solo career on ice, he, not surprisingly, accepted Scott Walker's invitation to resurrect the Walker Brothers name in 1975. The reunion lasted until 1978 and three albums were issued. Early in the 80s, Scott was supposedly producing an album for Maus and his wife Brandy, but the project failed to reach fruition. Having built his own studio, Maus studied to become a recording engineer and set up the publishing company Arena Artistes Association. He elected to record some of the songs he had stockpiled, resulting in the pleasant soft rock collection *You*.

● ALBUMS: *You* (Arena 2000) ★★★.

WALKER, JUNIOR, AND THE ALL STARS

b. Autry DeWalt II, 14 June 1931, Blytheville, Arkansas, USA, d. 23 November 1995, Battle Creek, Michigan, USA. His record label, Motown Records, stated that he was born in 1942. Walker was inspired to take up the saxophone by the jump blues and R&B bands he heard in the early 50s. In his mid-teens, he formed his first instrumental group, the Jumping Jacks, adopting the stage name Junior Walker after a childhood nickname. By 1961 he had achieved a prominent local reputation, which reached the ear of label owner and former Moonglow, Harvey Fuqua. He signed Walker to his Harvey label, allowing him free rein to record a series of raw saxophone-led instrumentals. In 1964 Walker followed Fuqua to Motown, where he perfected a blend of raunchy R&B and Detroit soul typified by his 1965 hit, 'Shotgun'. With its repeated saxophone riffs and call-and-response vocals, it established Walker as the label's prime exponent of traditional R&B, a reputation that was confirmed by later hits like 'Shake And Fingerpop' and 'Road Runner'. The latter was produced by Holland/Dozier/Holland, who also encouraged Walker to record instrumental versions of hits they had written for other Motown artists.

Walker's style became progressively more lyrical in the late 60s, a development that reached its peak on the 1969 US Top 5 hit, 'What Does It Take (To Win Your Love)?' This also marked the pinnacle of his commercial success, as subsequent attempts to repeat the winning formula were met with growing public indifference, and from 1972 onwards the All Stars recorded only sporadically. *Hot Shot* in 1976, produced by Brian Holland, marked a move towards the burgeoning disco market, which was confirmed on two further albums that year, Walker's first as a solo artist. In 1979, he was one of several Motown artists to move to Whitfield Records. Finding his career deadlocked, Walker returned to Motown in 1983, issuing *Blow The House Down*, an exercise in reclaiming lost ground. The novelty single 'Sex Pot' rekindled memories of his classic hits, although Walker's greatest commercial success in the 80s came when he guested with Foreigner and played the magnificent saxophone solo on their hit single 'Urgent'. He lost a two-year battle with cancer in November 1995.

● ALBUMS: *Shotgun* (Soul/Tamla Motown 1965) ★★★★, *Soul Session* (Tamla Motown 1966) ★★★★, *Road Runner* (Tamla Motown 1966) ★★★★, *Live!* (Tamla Motown 1967) ★★★, *Home Cookin'* (Tamla Motown 1969) ★★★, *Gotta Hold On To This Feeling* (Soul 1969) ★★★, *What Does It Take To Win Your Love?* (Soul 1969) ★★★, *A Gassssssss* (Soul 1970) ★★★, *Rainbow Funk* (Soul 1971) ★★★, *Moody Jr.* (Soul 1971) ★★★, *Peace And Understanding Is Hard To Find* (Soul 1973) ★★, *Hot Shot* (Soul 1976) ★★, *Sax Appeal* (Soul 1976) ★★★, *Whopper Bopper Show Stopper* (Soul 1976) ★★, *Smooth* (Soul 1978) ★★, *Back Street Boogie* (Whitfield 1979) ★★, *Blow The House Down* (Motown 1983) ★★.

● COMPILATIONS: *Greatest Hits* (Soul 1969) ★★★★, *Anthology* (Motown 1981) ★★★★, *Junior Walker's Greatest Hits* (Motown 1982) ★★★★, *19 Greatest Hits* (Motown 1987) ★★★★, *Shake And Fingerpop* (Blue Moon 1989) ★★★, *Compact Command Performance – 19 Greatest Hits* (Motown 1992) ★★★★, *The Ultimate Collection* (Motown 1997) ★★★★, *20th Century Masters: The Millennium Collection* (Motown 2000) ★★★★.

WALKER, SCOTT

b. Noel Scott Engel, 9 January 1943, Hamilton, Ohio, USA. After relocating to New York during childhood, this precocious talent initially pursued a career as an actor, and also briefly recorded in 1957 under the name Scotty Engel. Moving to Hollywood, he worked on sessions with arranger Jack Nitzsche before joining the Routers in 1961 as a bass player. He next teamed up with singer John Maus as the Dalton Brothers, which gradually evolved into the Walker Brothers with the addition of drummer Gary Leeds. The trio moved to England and found themselves fêted as teen-idols, with a string of hits that established them as one of the most successful UK-based groups of the mid-60s. The group broke up in May 1967 at a time when Scott was still regarded as a sex symbol and potential solo superstar. Yet there was something contradictory about the singer's image. Ridden with angst during the Walker Brothers' teen-idol peak, he was known for his moody reclusiveness, tendency to wear dark glasses and stay in curtain-closed rooms during daylight hours. The classic pop existentialist, Walker was trapped in a system that regarded him as a contradiction.

His manager Maurice King encouraged a straightforward showbusiness career involving regular television appearances and even cabaret. Walker, meanwhile, had become a devotee of French composer Jacques Brel and included several of his songs on his debut solo album, *Scott*. There is no finer example of the contradiction that Walker faced than the incongruous image of the singer performing Brel's 'My Death' on BBC television's chirpy *Billy Cotton Band Show*. Walker's quirky and stylistically diverse vision juxtaposed the brutal visions of Brel with contemporary MOR standards such as Tony Bennett's 'When Joanna Loved Me'. Walker was also displaying immense talent as a songwriter in his own right with poetic, brooding songs, such as 'Such A Small Love' and 'Always Coming Back To You'. Eschewing young, modern producers, Walker stuck with the lush, orchestral arrangements of Johnny Franz, Reg Guest, Peter Knight and Wally Stott on his subsequent self-titled albums. The results were rendered unique by Walker's distinctive, deep, crooning tone and strong vibrato.

On the strength of the Walker Brothers' dedicated audience, Scott's solo albums were chart successes in the UK, but as an artist he remained the great contradiction. Singer/songwriter, MOR entertainer, Brel interpreter and television personality, his entire career dramatized a constant clash between pop star trappings and artistic endeavour. Even his similarly titled hit singles emphasized the grand contradiction: 'Jackie' was a racy Brel song that mentioned 'authentic queers and phoney virgins' and was banned by the BBC; 'Joanna' was pure schmaltz, written by the Tin Pan Alley husband and wife team Tony Hatch and Jackie Trent. Walker's uneasiness about his career was emphasized in a number of confusing decisions and record releases. At one point, he reverted to his real surname Engel, and announced that he would no longer be issuing singles.

While 1969's brilliant *Scott 4* at last contained solely original material and might have heralded the re-evaluation of Walker as a serious songwriter, the BBC chose that very same period to issue the MOR *Scott Walker Sings Songs From His TV Series*. Undervalued and apparently uncertain about his direction, Walker's muse grew increasingly weary after the 60s. Reissued in 1996, *'Til The Band Comes In*, his 1970 collaboration with manager and songwriter Ady Semel however, is a joy of discovery. Released a year after the Woodstock Festival, Walker could not have been more out of step with musical fashion, yet more than 25 years later the quality of the songs stands up, and above all they feature a voice to weep to. By 1972 he seemed to bow to popular demand by recording an album of cover versions, *The Moviegoer*. A shift towards country music followed before Scott reunited with Maus and Leeds in the mid-70s for a series of Walker Brothers albums. Thereafter he retreated from the music business. His enigmatic career, remarkable voice and intense songwriting continued to inspire a new generation of performers, however, including Julian Cope (who selected 1981's *Fire Escape In The Sky: The Godlike Genius Of Scott Walker*), Marc Almond (who provided sleevenotes for 1990's *Boy Child*) and a number of deep, crooning vocalists, who attempted to replicate that unique vibrato.

Walker returned to the studio to record 1984's critically acclaimed but commercially unsuccessful *Climate Of Hunter*, a complex and difficult collection of songs that proved too challenging for many ears. After its release Walker returned to his second love, painting, and retreated from the public eye once more. Then, in 1992, he surprised everyone by signing a major recording contract. Three years later he delivered *Tilt*, the most ear-challenging work he has recorded to date. The album found two distinct camps: one that criticized him for not delivering the smooth ballads of old and the other (a much younger audience) who found this difficult, semi-operatic work intriguing. The record company showed a great sense of humour when they released the title track as a single. In the late 90s, Walker contributed new recordings to several movie soundtracks, including a cover version of Bob Dylan's 'I Threw It All Away' for *To Have And To Hold*, and 'Only Myself To Blame' for the James Bond movie *The World Is Not Enough*. He also composed the soundtrack for Leos Carax's *Pola X*, and in June 2000 organised the South Bank's Meltdown Festival.

● ALBUMS: *Scott* (Philips 1967) ★★★, *Scott 2* (Philips 1968) ★★★★, *Scott 3* (Philips 1969) ★★★★, *Scott Walker Sings Songs From His TV Series* (Philips 1969) ★★, *Scott 4* (Philips 1969) ★★★★★, *'Til The Band Comes In* (Philips 1970) ★★★, *The Moviegoer* (Philips 1972) ★★, *Any Day Now* (Philips 1973) ★★, *Stretch* (CBS 1973) ★★★, *We Had It All* (CBS 1974) ★★, *Climate Of Hunter* (Virgin 1984) ★★★★, *Tilt* (Fontana/ Drag City 1995) ★★★.

● COMPILATIONS: *Looking Back With Scott Walker* (Ember 1968) ★★★, *The Romantic Scott Walker* (Philips 1969) ★★★, *The Best Of Scott Walker* (Philips 1970) ★★★, *This Is Scott Walker* (Philips 1971) ★★★★, *This Is Scott Walker, Volume 2* (Philips 1972) ★★★, *Spotlight On Scott Walker* (Philips 1976) ★★★, *Fire Escape In The Sky: The Godlike Genius Of Scott Walker* (Zoo

1981) ★★★★, *Scott Walker Sings Jacques Brel* (Philips 1981) ★★★★, *Boy Child: The Best Of 1967-1970* (Fontana 1990) ★★★★, *When Is A Boy A Man? Early Years Of Scott Walker* (A-Side 1995) ★★, *It's Raining Today: The Scott Walker Story (1967-70)* (Razor & Tie 1996) ★★★★.

● FURTHER READING: *Scott Walker: A Deep Shade Of Blue*, Mike Watkinson and Pete Anderson. *Butterfly: The Music Of Scott Walker*. *Another Tear Falls*, Jeremy Reed. *Scott Walker*, Ken Brooks.

WARWICK, DIONNE

b. Marie Dionne Warrick, 12 December 1940, East Orange, New Jersey, USA. One of the truly sophisticated voices over the past three decades of soul influenced pop, Warwick first sang in Newark's New Hope Baptist Church choir. She played piano with the Drinkard Singers, a gospel group her mother managed, and studied at Connecticut's Hart School of Music. During the same period, Warwick also formed the Gospelaires with her sister, Dee Dee and aunt Cissy Houston. Increasingly employed as backing singers, the trio's voices appeared on records by the Drifters and Garnet Mimms. Through such work Warwick came into contact with songwriters Burt Bacharach and Hal David. Her first solo single, on the Scepter label, 'Don't Make Me Over' (1963), was a fragile slice of 'uptown R&B' and set the tone for such classic collaborations as 'Anyone Who Had A Heart' and 'Walk On By'. Bacharach's sculpted, almost grandiose compositions were the perfect setting for Warwick's light yet perfect phrasing, delicate almost to the point of vulnerability. 'You'll Never Get To Heaven (If You Break My Heart)', 'Reach Out For Me' (both 1964) and 'Are You There (With Another Girl)' (1966) epitomized the style. Although many of her singles charted, few were Top 10 hits, and the soulful edge, prevalent for the first two years, was gradually worn away.

As her songwriters moved ever closer to the mainstream, so Warwick too embraced a safer, albeit classier, approach with such successes as the uplifting 'I Say A Little Prayer' (1967) and 'Do You Know The Way To San Jose?' (1968). In 1971, Warwick abandoned both her label and mentors for Warner Brothers Records, but despite several promising releases, the relationship floundered. Around this time she also added an extra 'e' to the end of her name, on advice given to her by an astrologer. Her biggest hit came with the (Detroit) Spinners on the Thom Bell-produced 'Then Came You' (1974). Warwick moved to Arista Records in 1979 where work with Barry Manilow rekindled her commercial standing. *Heartbreaker*, her collaboration with the Bee Gees, resulted in several hit singles while a pairing with Luther Vandross on 'How Many Times Can We Say Goodbye?' was also a success. 'That's What Friends Are For' pitted Dionne with Elton John,

Gladys Knight and Stevie Wonder, and became a number 1 in both the US R&B and pop charts. Duets with Jeffrey Osborne, Kashif and Howard Hewitt, of Shalamar, maintained this newly-rediscovered profile in subsequent decades.

● ALBUMS: *Presenting Dionne Warwick* (Scepter 1963) ★★★, *Anyone Who Had A Heart* (Scepter 1964) ★★★★, *Make Way For Dionne Warwick* (Scepter 1964) ★★★★, *The Sensitive Sound Of Dionne Warwick* (Scepter 1965) ★★★★, *Here I Am* (Scepter 1966) ★★★★, *Dionne Warwick In Paris* (Scepter 1966) ★★★, *Here Where There Is Love* (Scepter 1967) ★★★, *Dionne Warwick Onstage And In The Movies* (Scepter 1967) ★★★, *The Windows Of The World* (Scepter 1968) ★★★, *Dionne In The Valley Of The Dolls* (Scepter 1968) ★★★★, *The Magic Of Believing* (Scepter 1968) ★★★, *Promises Promises* (Scepter 1968) ★★★★, *Soulful* (Scepter 1969) ★★★, *Dionne Warwick's Greatest Motion Picture Hits* (Scepter 1969) ★★★, *I'll Never Fall In Love Again* (Scepter 1970) ★★★, *Very Dionne* (Scepter 1970) ★★, *The Love Machine* (Scepter 1971) ★★★★, *The Dionne Warwick Story - Live* (Scepter 1971) ★★, *From Within* (Scepter 1972) ★★, *Dionne* (Warners 1972) ★★, *Just Being Myself* (Warners 1973) ★★, *Then Came You* (Warners 1975) ★★★, *Track Of The Cat* (Warners 1975) ★★★, with Isaac Hayes *A Man And A Woman* (HBS 1977) ★★★, *Only Love Can Break A Heart* (Musicor 1977) ★★★, *Love At First Sight* (Warners 1979) ★★★, *Dionne* (Arista 1979) ★★★★, *No Night So Long* (Arista 1980) ★★, *Hot! Live And Otherwise* (Mobile Fidelity 1981) ★★★, *Friends In Love* (Arista 1982) ★★★, *Heartbreaker* (Arista 1982) ★★★, *How Many Times Can We Say Goodbye* (Arista 1983) ★★, *Friends* (Arista 1985) ★★★, *Finder Of Lost Loves* (Arista 1985) ★★★ *Without Your Love* (Arista 1985) ★★★, *Reservations For Two* (Arista 1988) ★★★, *Dionne Warwick Sings Cole Porter* (Arista 1989) ★★★, *Friends Can Be Lovers* (Arista 1993) ★★★, *Aquarela Do Brazil* (Arista 1995) ★★★, *Dionne Sings Dionne* (River North 1998) ★★★.

● COMPILATIONS: *Dionne Warwick's Golden Hits, Part 1* (Scepter 1967) ★★★★, *Dionne Warwick's Golden Hits, Part 2* (Scepter 1969) ★★★★, *The Best Of Dionne Warwick* (Pye 1983) ★★★★, *The Dionne Warwick Collection: Her All-Time Greatest Hits* (Rhino 1989) ★★★★★, *Greatest Hits 1979-1990* (Arista 1989) ★★★★, *The Essential Collection* (Global 1996) ★★★★, *Walk On By: The Definitive Dionne Warwick Collection* (Warners 2000) ★★★★.

WASHINGTON, GENO (AND THE RAM JAM BAND)

b. Indiana, USA. Washington was in the US Air Force, stationed in East Anglia, England, when he initiated his singing career by climbing onstage to join a local band for an impromptu performance. On leaving the services, he remained in Britain and headed for London where he fronted the Ram Jam Band which

comprised Pete Gage (guitar), Lionel Kingham (tenor saxophone), Buddy Beadle (baritone saxophone), Jeff Wright (organ), John Roberts (bass) and Herb Prestige (drums). The group adopted a fast-paced, almost frantic style which pitched one soul favourite after another, deliberately leaving the audience with little time to breathe, or to question the ensemble's lack of subtlety. Although none of Washington's singles reached the UK Top 30, his fervent in-concert popularity ensured that the first two albums charted, both reaching the UK Top 10. The formula was repeated on later collections, but by 1968 the mixture was growing ever more anachronistic as progressions elsewhere in music left the Ram Jam Band behind. Peter Gage went on to join Vinegar Joe. They disbanded by the end of the decade and Geno's several comebacks notwithstanding, the group remained fixed to a particular mid-60s era. Although immortalized in the 1980 UK number 1 hit, 'Geno' by Dexys Midnight Runners, Washington was more of a footnote than innovator. He continues to record sporadically, performing the occasional London club date and tour and by the mid-90s had seemingly reinvented himself as a blues singer. Part of his current act incorporates, with audience participation, Washington's musical talents with hypnotism.

● ALBUMS: *Hand Clappin' - Foot Stompin' - Funky Butt - Live!* (Piccadilly 1966) ★★★, *Hipsters, Flipsters, Finger Poppin' Daddies* (Piccadilly 1967) ★★, *Shake A Tail Feather* (Piccadilly 1968) ★★, *Running Wild - Live* (Pye 1969) ★★, *Up Tight* (Marble Arch 1969) ★★, *Geno's Back* (DJM 1976) ★★, *Live* (DJM 1976) ★★, *That's Why Hollywood Loves Me* (DJM 1979) ★★, *Put Out The Cat* (Teldec 1981) ★★, *Live Sideways* (Ammunition 1986) ★★, *Take That Job And Stuff It* (1987) ★★, *Loose Lips* (Uncensored 1995) ★★, *What's In The Pot?* (Sound FX 1997) ★★.

● COMPILATIONS: *My Bombers, My Dexys, My High: The Sixties Studio Sessions* (Sequel 1998) ★★★, *Geno! Geno! Geno!: Live In The Sixties* 3-CD set (Sequel 1998) ★★★.

WELLS, MARY

b. 13 May 1943, Detroit, Michigan, USA, d. 26 July 1992, Los Angeles, California, USA. At the age of 17, Mary Wells composed 'Bye Bye Baby', a song which she offered to R&B star Jackie Wilson. His producer, Berry Gordy, was sufficiently impressed to offer her a contract with the newly formed Motown Records label, and Wells' rendition of her song became one of the company's first Top 50 hits in 1960. Gordy entrusted her career to Smokey Robinson, who masterminded all her subsequent Motown releases. Robinson composed a remarkable series of clever, witty soul songs, full of puns and unexpected twists, and set to irresistible melody lines. Wells responded with the fluency of the natural vocalist and the results were Motown's most mature and adventurous records of the early 60s. 'The One Who Really Loves You' set the pattern as a Top 10 hit in 1962, while 'You Beat Me To The Punch' and 'Two Lovers' matched that success and offered two of Robinson's more subtle lyrics. 'What's Easy For Two Is So Hard For One' was Wells' answer to the predominant New York girl-group sound, and another Top 30 hit in 1964. The pinnacle of the Robinson/Wells partnership, however, was 'My Guy', a US number 1 and UK Top 5 contender in 1964. Sophisticated and assured, it introduced the Motown sound to a worldwide audience, and marked out Wells as America's most promising soul vocalist.

At the same time, Berry Gordy encouraged her to record an album of duets with Motown's top male star, Marvin Gaye, from which 'Once Upon A Time' was pulled as another major hit single. Just as Well's career reached its peak, she chose to leave Motown, tempted by an offer from 20th Century Fox that included the promise of film work. Without the guidance of Smokey Robinson, she was unable to capture her hit form, and she left the label the following year.

In 1966, she married Cecil Womack of the Valentinos, and moved to Atco Records, where she scored three further minor hits with 'Dear Lover', 'Such A Sweet Thing' and 'The Doctor'. That marked the end of her chart career: subsequent sessions for a variety of US labels proved less than successful, and after a long period without a contract she was reduced to re-recording her Motown hits for Allegiance in the early 80s. Despite being diagnosed as having throat cancer she continued touring during the late 80s. Wells signed to Ian Levine's Motor City label in 1987 and released *Keeping My Mind On Love* in 1990. She lost her battle against her illness on 26 July 1992.

● ALBUMS: *Bye Bye Baby, I Don't Want To Take A Chance* (Motown 1961) ★★★, *The One Who Really Loves You* (Motown 1962) ★★★, *Two Lovers And Other Great Hits* (Motown 1963) ★★★, *Recorded Live On Stage* (Motown 1963) ★★★, *Second Time Around* (Motown 1963) ★★★, with Marvin Gaye *Together* (Motown 1964) ★★★, *Mary Wells Sings My Guy* (Motown 1964) ★★★★, *Mary Wells* (20th Century 1965) ★★★, *Mary Wells Sings Love Songs To The Beatles* (20th Century 1965) ★★★, *Vintage Stock* (Motown 1966) ★★★, *The Two Sides Of Mary Wells* (Atco 1966) ★★★, *Ooh!* (Movietone 1966) ★★★, *Servin' Up Some Soul* (Jubilee 1968) ★★, *In And Out Of Love* (EPK 1981) ★★, *Keeping My Mind On Love* (Motor City 1990) ★★.

● COMPILATIONS: *Greatest Hits* (Motown 1964) ★★★, *The Old, The New And The Best Of Mary Wells* (Allegiance 1984) ★★★, *Compact Command Performances* (Sequel 1993) ★★★, *The Complete Jubilee Sessions* (Sequel 1993) ★★★, *Ain't It The Truth: The Best Of Mary Wells*

1964-82 (Varèse Sarabande 1993) ★★★, *Looking Back 1961-64* (Motown 1993) ★★★, *Dear Lover: The Atco Sessions* (Ichiban 1995) ★★★, *Early Classics* (Spectrum 1996) ★★★, *Never, Never Leave Me: The 20th Century Sides* (Ichiban 1997) ★★★, *20th Century Masters: The Millennium Collection* (Motown 1999) ★★★★.

● FILMS: *Catalina Caper* (1967).

WEST, KEITH

b. Keith Hopkins, 6 December 1943, Dagenham, Essex, England. Lead vocalist with the In Crowd and Tomorrow, West embarked on a concurrent solo career while still a member of the latter group. His debut single written with Mark Wirtz, 'Excerpt From A Teenage Opera', was a UK number 2 hit in August 1967, but when 'Sam', another song from the same project, failed to emulate its predecessor, West withdrew from further involvement. Tomorrow broke up in 1968 and West temporarily abandoned performing when 'On A Saturday' failed to chart. He resumed recording in 1973 with two low-key singles, before founding Moonrider with ex-Animals guitarist John Weider. In the 90s West can fondly hark back to the ambitions of record producer Wirtz and the potentially endless stream of material for various Teenage Operas. West is now a director of Burns Guitars.

● COMPILATIONS: *Excerpts From ... Keith West: Groups And Sessions 65-74* (RPM 1995) ★★, *A Teenage Opera* (RPM 1996) ★★★.

WESTON, KIM

b. Agatha Natalie Weston, 20 December 1939, Detroit, Michigan, USA. Kim Weston received her musical education with the Wright Specials gospel group, an influence that survived throughout her subsequent career. Torn between pursuing music or acting, she was persuaded to join the Motown label in the early 60s by Johnny Thornton, the cousin of two of the label's top producers, Eddie and Brian Holland. After a minor hit with 'Love Me All The Way' in 1963, Weston joined Marvin Gaye's soul revue, forming a partnership that was captured on record in 1964 and again in 1967. In the interim, Weston was produced by Holland/Dozier/ Holland on a series of classic dance records that highlighted her versatile, gospel-tinged vocals. 'Take Me In Your Arms' was a substantial soul hit in 1965, followed the next year by the equally fluent 'Helpless'. In 1967, she and Gaye recorded 'It Takes Two', one of the finest of Motown's love duets. That same year, Weston married Motown producer Mickey Stevenson, who encouraged her to join him in a new venture at MGM Records. The move proved a commercial disappointment, and later releases on People and Pride failed to restore Weston to the charts. In the 70s, she devoted much time to community projects and art groups, besides finding time to record an album of jazz standards with the Hastings Street Jazz Experience. More recently, she was one of several Motown artists to re-record her hits on Ian Levine's Nightmare label. In 1987 she became the first ex-Motown artist to work with producer Ian Levine, who proceeded to sign virtually every Motown act during the next three years. Weston teamed up with Marvin Gaye's brother Frankie for a remake of 'It Takes Two' in 1989. She has so far released two new albums which mix new material with fresh versions of 60s Motown hits.

● ALBUMS: with Marvin Gaye *Take Two* (Tamla 1966) ★★★, *For The First Time* (MGM 1967) ★★★, *This Is America* (MGM 1968) ★★★, *Kim Kim Kim* (Volt 1970) ★★, *Investigate* (Motor City 1990) ★★, *Talking Loud* (Motor City 1992) ★★.

● COMPILATIONS: *The Very Best* (Essential Gold 1996) ★★★, *The Very Best Of The Motor City Recordings* (Hot 1996), *Greatest Hits & Rare Classics* (Spectrum 1998) ★★★.

WHO

Formed in Shepherd's Bush, London, England in 1964, the Who evolved out of local youth club band the Detours. Pete Townshend (b. 19 May 1945, Chiswick, London, England; guitar/vocals), Roger Daltrey (b. 1 March 1944, Shepherd's Bush, London, England; vocals) and John Entwistle (b. John Alec Entwistle, 9 October 1944, Chiswick, London, England; bass) founded this attraction, and having jettisoned Colin Dawson (vocals) and Doug Sanden (drums), recruited Keith Moon (b. 23 August 1946, Wembley, London, England, d. 7 September 1978, England) as a replacement for the latter. The restructured quartet was adopted by manager/publicist Peter Meadon, who changed their name to the High Numbers, dressed them in stylish clothes and determinedly courted a mod audience. Their sole single, 'I'm The Face', proclaimed this allegiance although Meadon shamelessly purloined its melody from Slim Harpo's 'Got Love If You Want It'. Two budding film directors, Kit Lambert and Chris Stamp, then assumed management responsibilities and having reverted to their Who sobriquet, the band assiduously began courting controversial publicity.

Townshend's guitar pyrotechnics were especially noteworthy; the instrument was used as an object of rage as he smashed it against floors and amplifiers in simulation of painter Gustav Metzke's auto-destructive art, although the origins of the act derived from when Townshend accidentally broke the neck of his guitar in a low-ceilinged club to the perverse delight of the crowd. Their in-person violence matched an anti-social attitude and despite a highly successful residency at the famed Marquee club, the Who were shunned by major labels. They eventually secured a deal through Shel Talmy, an independent producer who placed the group with American Decca Records. Their recordings were then sub-contracted through UK subsidiary, Brunswick Records, a perilous arrangement bearing later repercussions. 'I Can't Explain', released in January 1965, rose to the UK Top 10 on the strength of appearances on television's *Ready, Steady, Go!* and *Top Of The Pops*, the latter transpiring when another act dropped out. Written by Townshend, already the band's established composer, but modelled on the Kinks, the song's formal nature surprised those expecting a more explosive performance. Such hopes were answered by the innovative 'Anyway, Anyhow, Anywhere' and 'My Generation', the latter of which encapsulated the frustrations of an amphetamine-charged adolescent, both in its stuttered intonation and smash-and-grab instrumental section. This pivotal release, one of the benchmarks of British 60s pop served as the title track to the Who's debut album, the release of which was delayed to accommodate new Townshend originals at the expense of now *passé* cover versions. 'The Kids Are Alright' and 'Out In The Street' articulated a sense of cultural affinity and if the songwriter's attachment to the mod phenomenon was undoubtedly expedient, the cult held a lasting fascination for him.

However, despite artistic and commercial success, the Who wished to sever their punitive contract with Talmy. When he refused to renegotiate their terms of contract, the band simply refused to honour it, completing a fourth single, 'Substitute', for a new label and production company. The ensuing wrangle was settled out of court, but although the unit achieved their freedom, Talmy retained five percent royalty rights on all recordings made until the end of the decade. The Who continued to enjoy chart success, adeptly switching subject matter from a parochial clique to eccentric characterizations involving transvestism ('I'm A Boy') and masturbation ('Pictures Of Lily'). Townshend's decidedly English perceptions initially precluded a sustained international success. *A Quick One* and *The Who Sell Out*, the latter of which was, in part, programmed as a homage to pirate radio, thus proved more acceptable to the UK audience. The Who's popularity in the USA flourished only in the wake of their appearance at the 1967 Monterey Pop Festival.

They returned to the UK Top 10 in the winter of 1967 with the powerful 'I Can See For Miles'. Despite their strength as a singles act, however, the band failed to achieve a number 1 hit on either side of the Atlantic. They embraced the album market fully with *Tommy*, an extravagant rock opera which became a staple part of their increasingly in-demand live appearances. The set spawned a major hit in 'Pinball Wizard' but, more crucially, established the band as a serious act courting critical respectability. *Tommy* was later the subject of a film, directed by the suitably eccentric Ken Russell, as well as an orchestrated interpretation, recorded under the aegis of impresario Lou Reizner. This over-exposure undermined the power of the original, and fixed a musical albatross around its creator's neck. The propulsive *Live At Leeds* was a sturdy concert souvenir (regarded by many as one the best live albums ever recorded), while Townshend created his next project, *Lighthouse*, but this ambitious work was later aborted, with several of its songs incorporated into the magnificent classic *Who's Next*. Here the Who asserted their position as one of rock's leading attractions by producing an album that contained 'Baba O'Riley' and 'Won't Get Fooled Again', two epic anthems destined to form an integral part of the band's 70s lexicon. The latter reached the UK Top 10 and was the prelude to a series of specifically created singles – 'Let's See Action' (1971), 'Join Together' (1972), 'Relay' (1973) – which marked time as Townshend completed work on *Quadrophenia*. This complex concept album was a homage to the mod sub-culture which provided the artist with his first inspiration. Although compared unfavourably with *Tommy*, the set's plot and musical content, while stylistically the antithesis of the band's early outburst, has shown a greater longevity and was the subject of a commercially successful film, featuring future stars Toyah and Sting. Commitments to solo careers undermined the parent unit's progress and *The Who By Numbers*, although a relevant study of the ageing rock star, was deemed low-key in comparison with earlier efforts.

Another hiatus ensued, during which the ever self-critical Townshend reassessed his progress in the light of punk. The quartet re-emerged with the confident *Who Are You*, but its release was sadly overshadowed when, on 23 August 1978, Keith Moon died following an overdose of medication taken to alleviate alcohol addiction. His madcap behaviour and idiosyncratic, exciting drumming had been an integral part of the Who fabric and rumours of a permanent split abounded. A retrospective film, *The Kids Are Alright*, enhanced a sense of finality, but the band resumed recording in 1979 having added former Small Faces/Faces drummer Kenny Jones (b. 16 September 1948, Stepney, London, England) to the line-up. However, any new-found optimism was undermined that year when 11 fans were killed prior to a concert at the Cincinnati Riverfront Colosseum in Ohio during a rush to secure prime vantage points, and neither *Face Dances* nor *It's Hard* recaptured previous artistic heights, although the former contained the fiery 'You Better You Bet', which restored them to the UK Top 10. A farewell tour was undertaken in 1982-83 and although the band did reunite for an appearance at Live Aid, they remained estranged until the end of the decade. Townshend's reluctance to tour – he now suffered from tinnitus – and his much-publicized period of heroin addiction, were major stumbling blocks, but in 1989 he agreed to undertake a series of US dates to celebrate the band's 25th anniversary (with Simon Phillips on drums). Townshend, Daltrey and Entwistle were augmented by a large ensemble of supporting musicians for a set indebted to nostalgia, which culminated in Hollywood with an all-star gala rendition of *Tommy*. As such, the tour confirmed the guitarist's fears – a request to include material from his concurrent solo album *The Iron Man* was vetoed.

Townshend's desire to progress and challenge preconceptions has marked the very best of the Who's extensive and timeless catalogue. In 1993, over 25 years after its original release as an album, a production of *Tommy*, retitled *The Who's Tommy*, was staged on Broadway, and won five Tony Awards. The Who's star continued to rise in 1994 with the sympathetically packaged *Thirty Years Of Maximum R&B* CD box set, and was maintained with the reissued *Live At Leeds* with many extra tracks added from that memorable gig. The recording recalls a period that showed Townshend's playing at its most fluid and Daltrey's vocals strong and effortless. Further reissues in the mid-90s included *The Who Sell Out*, *Who's Next* and *A Quick One*, all of which were expertly remastered and contain many extra tracks, including the legendary *Ready Steady Who* EP. From these albums it is clear from where 90s bands such as Dodgy, Blur, and Swervedriver derive their 'Cockney' rock. Released three decades too late for most Who fans, the *Live At The Isle Of Wight Festival* set demonstrates (as does *Live At Leeds*) what an astonishing live band they were (and are). The quality of the Isle Of Wight concert recording is surprisingly good, and is a welcome windfall to their (still) considerable following.

In June 1996 the band appeared at London's Hyde Park, performing *Quadrophenia* in front of 200,000 people. Further performances were given in the USA and the UK later that year. The drummer for this latest re-formation was Zak Starkey (b. 13 September 1965, London, England), son of Ringo Starr. The Who's major tour in 2000 (with Starkey and John 'Rabbit' Bundrick) was remarkable. Keith Moon would have been proud of the younger Starkey's uncanny ability to 'play in the style of'. Townshend appeared to enjoy playing onstage and relations on and off stage with Daltrey were highly amiable. The music at most concerts was stunning, and belied the ages of the three senior members. They are unquestionably one of the finest acts of the rock generation, and they continue to be one of the most influential and exciting.

● ALBUMS: *My Generation* (Brunswick 1965) ★★★★, *The Who Sings My Generation* (Decca 1966) ★★★★, *A Quick One* (Reaction 1966)

★★★, *The Who Sell Out* (Track 1967) ★★★★, *Happy Jack* (Decca 1967) ★★★, *Magic Bus – The Who On Tour* (Decca 1968) ★★★, *Tommy* (Track 1969) ★★★★, *Live At Leeds* (Track 1970) ★★★★★, *Who's Next* (Track 1971) ★★★★★, *Quadrophenia* (MCA 1973) ★★★★, *The Who By Numbers* (Polydor 1975) ★★★, *Who Are You* (Polydor 1978) ★★, *The Kids Are Alright* film soundtrack (Polydor 1979) ★★★, *Quadrophenia* film soundtrack (Polydor 1979) ★★★★, *Face Dances* (Polydor 1981) ★★, *It's Hard* (Polydor 1982) ★★, *Join Together* (Virgin 1990) ★★★, *Live At The Isle Of Wight Festival 1970* (Essential 1996) ★★★★, *Live At Leeds Deluxe Edition* (Polydor 2001) ★★★★★.

● COMPILATIONS: *Magic Bus* (Decca 1967) ★★★, *Direct Hits* (Decca 1968) ★★★, *Meaty, Beaty, Big & Bouncy* (Polydor 1971) ★★★★★, *Odds & Sods* (Track 1974) ★★★★, *The Story Of The Who* (Polydor 1976) ★★★, *Hooligans* (MCA 1981) ★★★, *Rarities Volume 1 (1966-1968)* (Polydor 1983) ★★★, *Rarities Volume 2 (1970-1973)* (Polydor 1983) ★★★, *The Singles* (Polydor 1984) ★★★, *Who's Last* (MCA 1984) ★★, *Who's Missing* (MCA 1985) ★★, *Who's Better Who's Best* (Polydor 1988) ★★★★, *The Who Collection* (Stylus 1988) ★★★, *Thirty Years Of Maximum R&B* 4-CD box set (Polydor 1994) ★★★★★, *My Generation – The Very Best Of The Who* (Polydor 1996) ★★★★★, *BBC Sessions* (Polydor 2000) ★★★★.

● VIDEOS: *The Kids Are Alright* (PolyGram Music Video 1984), *Thirty Years Of Maximum R&B Live* (PolyGram Music Video 1994), *The Who Live At The Isle Of Wight Festival 1970* (Warner Music Vision 1996), *Live, Featuring The Rock Opera Tommy* (Sony Music Video 1996), *Classic Albums: Who's Next* (Eagle Rock 1999), *The Who & Special Guests Live At The Royal Albert Hall* (Aviva International 2001).

● FURTHER READING: *The Who*, Gary Herman. *The Who*, Jeff Stein and Chris Johnston. *Les Who*, Sacha Reins. *The Who ... Through The Eyes Of Pete Townshend*, Conner McKnight and Caroline Silver. *The Who*, George Tremlett. *The Who: Ten Great Years*, Cindy Ehrlich. *The Who Generation*, Nik Cohn. *A Decade Of The Who: An Authorized History In Music, Paintings, Words And Photo*, Steve Turner. *The Story Of Tommy*, Richard Barnes and Pete Townshend. *Whose Who? A Who Retrospective*, Brian Ashley and Steve Monnery. *Keith Moon: The Life And Death Of A Rock Legend*, Ivan Waterman. *The Who: Britain's Greatest Rock Group*, John Swenson. *The Who File*, Pearce Marchbank. *Quadrophenia*, Alan Fletcher. *The Who In Their Own Words*, Steve Clarke. *Mods!*, Richard Barnes. *The Who*, Paul Sahner and Thomas Veszelits. *The Who*, Giacomo Mazzone. *The Who: An Illustrated Discography*, Ed Hanel. *Moon The Loon: The Amazing Rock And Roll Life Of Keith Moon, Late Of The Who*, Dougal Butler with Chris Trengove and Peter Lawrence. *The Who: The Illustrated*

Biography, Chris Charlesworth. *Full Moon: The Amazing Rock & Roll Life Of Keith Moon, Late Of The Who*, Dougal Butler. *The Who Maximum R & B: An Illustrated Biography*, Richard Barnes. *Before I Get Old: The Story Of The Who*, Dave Marsh. *The Who: The Farewell Tour*, Philip Kamin and Peter Goddard. *The Complete Guide To The Music Of ...*, Chris Charlesworth. *The Who In Sweden*, Ollie Lunden (ed.). *The Who Concert File*, Joe McMichael and Irish Jack Lyones. *Dear Boy: The Life Of Keith Moon*, Tony Fletcher. *A Fortnight Of Furore: The Who And The Small Faces Down Under*, Andrew Neil. *Meaty, Beaty, Big And Bouncy*, John Perry. *The Who On Record: A Critical History 1963-1998*, John Atkins. *Eyewitness The Who*, Johnny Black.

● FILMS: *Tommy* (1975), *The Kids Are Alright* (1978), *Quadrophenia* (1979).

WILLIAMS, ANDY

b. Howard Andrew Williams, 3 December 1928, Wall Lake, Iowa, USA. Williams began his singing career in the local church choir with his three brothers. The quartet became popular on their own radio shows from Cincinnati, Des Moines and Chicago. They backed Bing Crosby on his Oscar-winning 'Swinging On A Star', from the 1944 movie *Going My Way*, and in the same year appeared in the minor musical film *Kansas City Kitty*. He also Williams dubbed Lauren Bacall's singing voice in her first film with Humphrey Bogart, *To Have And Have Not*. From 1947-48 the Williams Brothers worked with top pianist/singer Kay Thompson in nightclubs and on television. Williams went solo in 1952, and featured regularly on Steve Allen's *Tonight Show* for over two years. Signed to the Cadence label, Williams had his first success in 1956 with 'Canadian Sunset', which was followed by a string of Top 20 entries, including 'Butterfly' (number 1), 'I Like Your Kind Of Love' (a duet with Peggy Powers), 'Lips Of Wine', 'Are You Sincere?', 'Promise Me, Love', 'Hawaiian Wedding Song', 'Lonely Street' and 'The Village Of St. Bernadette'. In 1961, Williams moved to Columbia Records, and had his first big hit for the label with the Doc Pomus/Mort Shuman composition, 'Can't Get Used To Losing You', which went to number 2 in the US charts in 1963. From then, until 1971 when the singles hits dried up, he was in the US Top 20 with 'Hopeless', 'A Fool Never Learns', and '(Where Do I Begin) Love Story'. Williams reached number 4 in the UK in 1973 with Neil Sedaka's 'Solitaire', but it was in the album charts that he found greater success.

By the early 70s it was estimated that he had received 13 worldwide gold disc awards for chart albums such as *Moon River & Other Great Movie Themes*, *Days Of Wine And Roses* (a US number 1), *The Wonderful World Of Andy Williams*, *Dear Heart*, *Born Free*, *Love Andy* (a

UK number 1), *Honey, Happy Heart, Home Loving Man* (another UK number 1) and *Love Story*. The enormous sales were no doubt assisted by his extremely successful weekly variety showcase that ran from 1962-71, and won an Emmy for Best Variety Show. It also gave the Osmond Brothers nationwide exposure. In 1964, Williams made his solo film debut in *I'd Rather Be Rich*, which starred Maurice Chevalier, Robert Goulet, Sandra Dee and Hermione Gingold. It was a remake of the 1941 comedy *It Started With Eve*, and Williams sang the Jerry Keller/Gloria Shayne number, 'Almost There', which just failed to reach the top of the UK chart in 1965. Despite the lack of consistent television exposure in the late 70s, Williams still sold a remarkable number of albums, particularly in the UK where his *Solitaire, The Way We Were*, and *Reflections*, all made the Top 10. In 1984, the album *Greatest Love Classics* featured Williams singing contemporary lyrics to classical themes, accompanied by the Royal Philharmonic Orchestra.

In the early 90s, Williams became the first non-country entertainer to build his own theatre along Highway 76's music-theatre-strip in Branson, Missouri. The $8 million 2,000-seater Andy Williams Moon River Theatre is part of a complex that includes a 250-room hotel and restaurant. Williams headlines there himself for nine months each year, and remains one of America's most popular singers, still renowned for his smooth vocal texture and relaxed approach. In 1999, cashing in on the 'lounge music' vogue, he released a new compilation and the double a-sided single, 'Music To Watch Girls By'/'Can't Take My Eyes Off You'. Both tracks were featured in UK television commercials.

● ALBUMS: *Andy Williams Sings Steve Allen* (Cadence 1957) ★★, *Andy Williams* (Cadence 1958) ★★, *Andy Williams Sings Rodgers And Hammerstein* (Cadence 1959) ★★★, *Lonely Street* (Cadence 1959) ★★★, *The Village Of St. Bernadette* (Cadence 1960) ★★, *Two Time Winners* (Cadence 1960) ★★★, *To You Sweetheart, Aloha* reissued as *Hawaiian Wedding Song* (Cadence 1960) ★★, *Under Paris Skies* (Cadence 1961) ★★★, *Danny Boy And Other Songs I Like To Sing* (Columbia 1962) ★★★, *Moon River & Other Great Movie Themes* (Columbia 1962) ★★★★, *Warm And Willing* (Columbia 1962) ★★★, *Million Seller Songs* (Cadence 1963) ★★★, *Days Of Wine And Roses* (Columbia 1963) ★★★★, *The Andy Williams Christmas Album* (Columbia 1963) ★★★, *The Wonderful World Of Andy Williams* (Columbia 1964) ★★★, *The Academy Award Winning 'Call Me Irresponsible'* (Columbia 1964) ★★★, *The Great Songs From 'My Fair Lady' And Other Broadway Hits* (Columbia 1964) ★★★★, *Dear Heart* (Columbia 1965) ★★★★, *Almost There* (Columbia 1965) ★★★★, *Can't Get Used To Losing You* (Columbia 1965) ★★★★, *Merry Christmas* (Columbia 1965) ★★★, *The Shadow Of Your Smile* (Columbia 1966) ★★★, *May Each Day* (Columbia 1966) ★★★, *In The Arms Of Love* (Columbia 1967) ★★★, *Born Free* (Columbia 1967) ★★★★, *Love, Andy* (Columbia 1967) ★★★★, *Honey* (Columbia 1968) ★★★★, *Happy Heart* (Columbia 1969) ★★★★, with the Osmonds *Get Together With Andy Williams* (Columbia 1969) ★★, *Can't Help Falling In Love* (Columbia 1970) ★★★★, *Raindrops Keep Falling On My Head* (Columbia 1970) ★★★, *The Andy Williams' Show* (Columbia 1970) ★★★, *Home Loving Man* (Columbia 1971) ★★★★, *Love Story* (Columbia 1971) ★★★, *You've Got A Friend* (Columbia 1971) ★★★, *The Impossible Dream* (Columbia 1972) ★★★★, *Love Theme From 'The Godfather'* (Columbia 1972) ★★★, *A Song For You* (Columbia 1972) ★★★, *Alone Again (Naturally)* (Columbia 1972) ★★★, *The First Time Ever I Saw Your Face* (Columbia 1973) ★★★, *Solitaire* (Columbia 1973) ★★★, *The Way We Were* (Columbia 1974) ★★★, *You Lay So Easy On My Mind* (Columbia 1974) ★★★, *An Evening With Andy Williams, Live In Japan* (Columbia 1975) ★★★, *The Other Side Of Me* (Columbia 1975) ★★★, *Showstoppers* (Embassy 1977) ★★★, *Let's Love While We Can* (Columbia 1980) ★★★, *Wedding And Anniversary Album* (Columbia 1981) ★★★, with the Royal Philharmonic Orchestra *Greatest Love Classics* (EMI 1984) ★★★, *Close Enough For Love* (Warners 1986) ★★★.

● COMPILATIONS: *Andy Williams' Best* reissued as *Canadian Sunset* (Cadence 1962) ★★★, *Andy Williams' Newest Hits* (Columbia 1966) ★★★, *The Andy Williams Sound Of Music* (Columbia 1969) ★★★, *Andy Williams' Greatest Hits* (Columbia 1970) ★★★, *Andy Williams' Greatest Hits, Volume Two* (Columbia 1973) ★★★, *Reflections* (Columbia 1978) ★★★, *Great Songs Of The Seventies* (Columbia 1979) ★★★, *Great Songs Of The Sixties* (Columbia 1980) ★★★, *Collection* (Pickwick 1980) ★★★, *The Very Best Of Andy Williams* (Hallmark 1984) ★★★, *16 Most Requested Songs* (Columbia/Legacy 1986) ★★★★, *Andy Williams Collection* (Castle 1987) ★★★, *Portrait Of A Song Stylist* (Masterpiece 1989) ★★★, *The Best Of Andy Williams* (Columbia 1996) ★★★, *In The Lounge With ... Andy Williams* (Columbia 1999) ★★★, *(I Think) I Love The 70s* (Columbia 2001) ★★★, *Music To Fall In Love By: A New Collection Of Live Recordings* (Music Club 2001) ★★★, *Sings House Of Bamboo* (Castle 2001) ★★★.

● FILMS: with William Brothers Group *Kansas City Katie* (1944), with William Brothers Group *Janie* (1944), *I'd Rather Be Rich* (1964).

WILLIAMS, DANNY

b. 7 January 1942, Port Elizabeth, South Africa. Williams started singing professionally at the age of 13 and was spotted by producer Norman Newell when touring England in *The Golden*

City Dixies show in 1959. The ultra-smooth ballad singer, often called 'Britain's Johnny Mathis', joined HMV Records and released his first single, 'Tall A Tree', in 1959. A regular on the television pop show *Drumbeat*, he had two minor hits with 'We Will Never Be This Young Again' and 'The Miracle Of You', before his version of the much-recorded 'Moon River' shot to number 1 in 1961. Follow-ups 'Jeannie' (co-written by Russ Conway) and a cover of Andy Williams' 'Wonderful World Of The Young', also made the UK Top 10 in 1962. In 1964 'White On White', a UK flop, gave him a US Top 10 hit. For the next decade he worked the clubs, and recordings on Deram and Philips meant little. In 1977, he briefly returned to the Top 40 with 'Dancin' Easy', a re-working of a Martini television commercial. Despite continued success in various countries, especially the Middle East, in the early 80s Williams quit showbusiness and concentrated on his business interests. He made a comeback, touring with Eartha Kitt in 1989, and two years later starred in a concert at London's Strand Theatre. Since then, he has continued to sing at various venues throughout the UK, including the popular holiday-camp circuit.

● ALBUMS: *White On White* (1964) ★★★, *I'm A Song – Sing Me* (1973) ★★★, *Any Time, Any Place, Anywhere* (1977) ★★.

● COMPILATIONS: *Moon River And Other Great Songs* (EMI 1977) ★★★★, *EMI Years* (EMI 1993) ★★★★.

● FILMS: *It's All Happening* (1963).

WILLIAMS, MASON

b. 24 July 1936, Abilene, Texas, USA. This Oklahoma City University mathematics student was a self-taught guitarist who, after moonlighting in local venues, toured North America with the Wayfarers Trio before enlistment in the US Navy. On demobilization, he peddled topical tunes on the Los Angeles folk club circuit where he met the Limeliters' Glenn Yarbrough who introduced him to the Smothers Brothers. When this comedy duo began performing his compositions on their nationally broadcast television series, other acts – among them the Kingston Trio and Petula Clark – began recording his material. His most lucrative song was the 1968 novelty UK number 1 'Cinderella Rockefella', (with Nancy Ames) for Esther And Abi Ofarim. That year, he enjoyed a million-seller in his own right with the Grammy-winning 'Classical Gas', an orchestrated instrumental (from The Mason Williams Phonograph Record song cycle). A one-hit-wonder, he nevertheless protracted a prolific recording career into the 70s with accompaniment by such LA session colleagues as Hal Blaine, Ron Tutt, Milt Holland and Al Casey. He also achieved success as a poet, author, cabaret entertainer and concept artist with one of his exhibitions at Pasadena Arts Museum the subject of a feature in *Life* magazine. A reissue of 'Classical Gas' in 1978 met with further success, as did his collaboration with Mannheim Steamroller for their album *Classical Gas* in 1987.

● ALBUMS: *Them Poems And Things* (Vee Jay 1968) ★★★, *The Mason Williams Phonograph Record* (1968) ★★★, *The Mason Williams Ear Show* (1968) ★★★, *Music By Mason Williams* (1969) ★★★, *Hand Made* (1970) ★★, *Improved* (1971) ★★★, with Mannheim Steamroller *Classical Gas* (American Gramophone 1987) ★★★.

WILLIAMS, MAURICE, AND THE ZODIACS

This R&B vocal group from Lancaster, South Carolina, USA, was led by Maurice Williams (b. 26 April 1938, Lancaster, South Carolina, USA; pianist/songwriter). The hit record 'Stay', which went to number 3 R&B and number 1 pop in 1960, immortalized the Zodiacs as a one-hit-wonder group. (In the UK 'Stay' went to number 14 in 1961.) Williams, however, had a long history before and after the hit, forming his first group, the Gladiolas, in 1955. Besides Williams, the group consisted of Earl Gainey (tenor), William Massey (tenor/baritone), Willie Jones (baritone), and Norman Wade (bass). Their one hit for the Nashville-based Excello Records was 'Little Darlin'', which went to number 11 R&B and number 41 pop in 1957. The record was covered with greater success by the Canadian group, the Diamonds. In 1960 Williams formed the Zodiacs, consisting of Wiley Bennett (tenor), Henry Gaston (tenor), Charles Thomas (baritone), Albert Hill (double bass), and Little Willie Morrow (drums). After the unforgettable 'Stay' the group honoured themselves with many outstanding compositions, most notably 'I Remember' (number 86 pop in 1961), 'Come Along' (number 83 pop in 1961), and 'May I' (1966), but nothing close to a hit resulted. The latter song was re-recorded in 1969 by Bill Deal And The Rhondels who had a Top 40 national hit with it. The most frequently remade Williams song was 'Stay', which the Hollies in the UK (1963), the Four Seasons (1964), and Jackson Browne (1978) all placed on the charts. Its timeless lyric of teenage lust and angst has been passed through the decades: 'Well your mama don't mind, well your papa don't mind', leading to the punch line, 'Oh won't you stay, just a little bit longer'. During subsequent decades Williams sustained a career with a new group of Zodiacs, playing their classic catalogue to the Beach Music club circuit in the Carolinas.

● ALBUMS: *Stay* (Herald 1961) ★★★★, *At The Beach* (Snyder 1965) ★★★ *Maurice Williams And The Zodiacs* (Ripete 1988) ★★★, *Back To Basics* (EMN 2000) ★★.

● COMPILATIONS: *The Best Of Maurice Williams & the Zodiacs* i (Relix 1989) ★★★★,

The Best Of Maurice Williams & The Zodiacs ii (Collectables 1991) ★★★★, *Anthology* (Ripete 1994) ★★★★.

WILSON, JACKIE

b. Jack Leroy Wilson, 9 June 1934, Detroit, Michigan, USA, d. 21 January 1984, Mount Holly, New Jersey, USA. When parental pressure thwarted his boxing ambitions, Wilson took to singing in small local clubs. He sang with the Thrillers (a predecessor group to the Royals) and recorded some solo tracks for Dizzy Gillespie's Dee Gee label as Sonny Wilson, before replacing Clyde McPhatter in Billy Ward And The Dominoes. Wilson joined this notable group in 1953, but embarked on a solo career four years later with Brunswick Records. His first single for that label was the exuberant 'Reet Petite', a comparative failure in the USA where it crept to a lowly pop position and missed the R&B lists altogether. In the UK, however, it soared to number 6, thereby establishing Wilson in the minds of the British pop-purchasing audience. 'Reet Petite' had been written by Berry Gordy and Tyran Carlo (Roquel 'Billy' Davis), who went on to compose several of Wilson's subsequent releases, including the hits 'Lonely Teardrops' (1958), 'That's Why (I Love You So)' (1959) and 'I'll Be Satisfied' (1959).

In 1960, Wilson enjoyed two R&B number 1 hits with 'Doggin' Around' and 'A Woman, A Lover, A Friend'. His musical direction then grew increasingly erratic, veering from mainstream to pseudo-opera. There were still obvious highlights such as 'Baby Workout' (1963), 'Squeeze Her Please Her' (1964), 'No Pity (In The Naked City)' (1965), but all too often his wonderfully fluid voice was wasted on cursory, quickly dated material. The artist's live appearances, however, remained both exciting and dramatic, capable of inspiring the ecstasy his sometimes facile recordings belied. Wilson's career was rejuvenated in 1966. Abandoning his New York recording base, he moved to Chicago, where he worked with producer Carl Davis. He offered a more consistent empathy and 'Whispers (Gettin' Louder)' (1966), '(Your Love Keeps Lifting Me) Higher And Higher' (1967) and the sublime 'I Get The Sweetest Feeling' (1968) stand among his finest recordings. However, it did not last; 'This Love Is Real (I Can Feel Those Vibrations)' (1970) proved to be Wilson's last Top 10 R&B entry, by which time his work was influenced by trends rather than setting them. In September 1975, while touring with the Dick Clark revue, Wilson suffered a near-fatal heart attack onstage at New Jersey's Latin Casino. He struck his head on falling and the resulting brain damage left him comatose. He remained hospitalized until his death on 21 January 1984.

Wilson's career remains a puzzle; he never did join Berry Gordy's Motown Records empire, despite their early collaboration and friendship.

Instead, the singer's legacy was flawed – dazzling in places, disappointing in others. Immortalized in the Van Morrison song 'Jackie Wilson Said (I'm In Heaven When You Smile)', which was also a UK Top 5 hit for Dexys Midnight Runners in 1982, his name has remained in the public's eye. Fate provided a final twist in 1987, when an imaginative video (which some claimed belittled the singer's memory), using Plasticene animation, propelled 'Reet Petite' to number 1 in the UK charts. He was inducted into the Rock And Roll Hall Of Fame the same year.

● ALBUMS: *He's So Fine* (Brunswick 1958) ★★★, *Lonely Teardrops* (Brunswick 1959) ★★★★, *Doggin' Around* (Brunswick 1959) ★★★, *So Much* (Brunswick 1960) ★★★, *Night* (Brunswick 1960) ★★★, *Jackie Wilson Sings The Blues* (Brunswick 1960) ★★★★, *A Woman A Lover A Friend* (Brunswick 1961) ★★★★, *Try A Little Tenderness* (Brunswick 1961) ★★★, *You Ain't Heard Nothing Yet* (Brunswick 1961) ★★★, *By Special Request* (Brunswick 1961) ★★★, *Body And Soul* (Brunswick 1962) ★★★, *Jackie Wilson At The Copa* (Brunswick 1962) ★★★, *Jackie Wilson Sings The World's Greatest Melodies* (Brunswick 1962) ★★★, *Baby Workout* (Brunswick 1963) ★★★★, *Merry Christmas From Jackie Wilson* (Brunswick 1963) ★★, with Linda Hopkins *Shake A Hand* (Brunswick 1963) ★★, *Somethin' Else* (Brunswick 1964) ★★★★, *Soul Time* (Brunswick 1965) ★★★★, *Spotlight On Jackie Wilson* (Brunswick 1965) ★★★, *Soul Galore* (Brunswick 1966) ★★★, *Whispers* (Brunswick 1967) ★★★, *Higher And Higher* (Brunswick 1967) ★★★★, with Count Basie *Manufacturers Of Soul* (Brunswick 1968) ★★★, *I Get The Sweetest Feeling* (Brunswick 1968) ★★★★, *Do Your Thing* (Brunswick 1970) ★★★, *This Love Is Real* (Brunswick 1970) ★★★, *You Got Me Walking* (Brunswick 1971) ★★, *Beautiful Day* (Brunswick 1973) ★★, *Nowstalgia* (Brunswick 1974) ★★, *Nobody But You* (Brunswick 1976) ★★.

● COMPILATIONS: *My Golden Favourites* (Brunswick 1960) ★★★, *My Golden Favourites – Volume 2* (Brunswick 1964) ★★★, *Jackie Wilson's Greatest Hits* (Brunswick 1969) ★★★, *It's All Part Of Love* (Brunswick 1969) ★★★, *Classic Jackie Wilson* (Skratch 1984) ★★★, *Reet Petite* (Ace 1985) ★★★★, *The Soul Years* (Kent 1985) ★★★★, *The Soul Years Volume 2* (Kent 1986) ★★★, *Higher And Higher* i (Kent 1986) ★★★, *Through The Years* (Rhino 1987) ★★★, *The Very Best Of Jackie Wilson* (Ace 1987) ★★★, *Mr Excitement!* 3-CD box set (Rhino 1992) ★★★★★, *The Very Best Of Jackie Wilson* (Rhino 1994) ★★★★, *A Portrait Of Jackie Wilson* (Essential Gold/Pickwick 1995) ★★★★, *Higher And Higher* ii (Rhino 1995) ★★★★, *The Hit Collection* (Carlton 1997) ★★★, *The Titan Of Soul* 3-CD box set (Edsel 1998) ★★★★, *Sweetest Feelin': The Very Best Of Jackie Wilson* (Music Club 1999) ★★★.

● FURTHER READING: *Lonely Teardrops: The Jackie Wilson Story*, Tony Douglas.
● FILMS: *Go Johnny Go* (1958).

WILSON, NANCY

b. 20 February 1937, Chillicothe, Ohio, USA. Wilson began singing in clubs in and around Columbus, Ohio. She attracted attention among jazz musicians, made her first records in 1956, and in the late 50s toured with a band led by Rusty Bryant. At the end of the decade she sang with George Shearing, with whom she recorded, and Cannonball Adderley. It was at Adderley's insistence that she went to New York, where she was soon signed by Capitol Records. During the next few years Wilson made numerous albums, toured extensively, and built a substantial following among the popular audience but always retained a connection, if sometimes tenuously so, with jazz. She also hosted a variety series for NBC, *The Nancy Wilson Show*. In the early 80s she was again working more closely with jazz musicians, including Hank Jones, Art Farmer, Benny Golson and Ramsey Lewis. Later in the decade she was active around the world, performing at major concert venues and singing in a style that revealed that the long years in the more flamboyant atmosphere of popular music had given her a taste for slightly over-dramatizing songs. Nevertheless, when backed by top-flight musicians she could still deliver a rhythmic and entertaining performance. During the 90s her work successfully crossed over to the New Adult Contemporary market.
● ALBUMS: *Like Love* (Capitol 1959) ★★★★, *Something Wonderful* (Capitol 1960) ★★★★, *Nancy Wilson With Billy May's Orchestra* (Capitol 1959) ★★★★, with George Shearing *The Swingin's Mutual* (Capitol 1961) ★★★★, *Nancy Wilson With Gerald Wilson's Orchestra* (Capitol 1961) ★★★, with Cannonball Adderley *Nancy Wilson/Cannonball Adderley* (Capitol 1962) ★★★★, *Hello Young Lovers* (Capitol 1962) ★★★★, *Broadway: My Way* (Capitol 1963) ★★★★, *Hollywood: My Way* (Capitol 1963) ★★★, *Nancy Wilson With Jimmy Jones's Orchestra* (Capitol 1963) ★★★★, *Yesterday's Love Songs, Today's Blues* (Capitol 1963) ★★★★, *Today, Tomorrow, Forever* (Capitol 1964) ★★★, *Nancy Wilson With Kenny Dennis's Group* (Capitol 1964) ★★★, *How Glad I Am* (Capitol 1964) ★★★, *The Nancy Wilson Show!* (Capitol 1965) ★★★★, *Today: My Way* (Capitol 1965) ★★★, *Gentle Is My Love* (Capitol 1965) ★★★, *From Broadway With Love* (Capitol 1966) ★★★★, *A Touch Of Today* (Capitol 1966) ★★★, *Tender Loving Care* (Capitol 1966) ★★★, *Nancy Wilson With Oliver Nelson's Orchestra* (Capitol 1967) ★★★★, *Nancy – Naturally* (Capitol 1967) ★★★, *Just For Now* (Capitol 1967) ★★★, *Nancy Wilson With H.B. Barnum's Orchestra* (Capitol 1967) ★★★, *Lush Life* aka *The Right To Love* (Capitol 1967) ★★★★, *Welcome To My Love* (Capitol 1968) ★★★★, *Easy* (Capitol 1968) ★★★, *The Sound Of Nancy Wilson* (Capitol 1968) ★★★★, *Nancy Wilson With The Hank Jones Quartet* (Capitol 1969) ★★★, *Nancy* (Capitol 1969) ★★★, *Son Of A Preacher Man* (Capitol 1969) ★★★, *Hurt So Bad* (Capitol 1969) ★★★, *Can't Take My Eyes Off You* (Capitol 1970) ★★★★, *Now I'm A Woman* (Capitol 1970) ★★★, *But Beautiful* (Capitol 1971) ★★★, *Kaleidoscope* (Capitol 1971) ★★★, *All In Love Is Fair* (Capitol 1974) ★★★, *Come Get To This* (Capitol 1975) ★★★, *This Mother's Daughters* (Capitol 1976) ★★★, *I've Never Been To Me* (Capitol 1977) ★★★, *Life, Love And Harmony* (Capitol 1979) ★★★, with Ramsey Lewis *The Two Of Us* (Capitol 1984) ★★★, *Keep You Satisfied* (Columbia 1985) ★★★, *Forbidden Lover* (Columbia 1987) ★★★★, *Nancy Now!* (Columbia 1989) ★★★, *Lady With A Song* (Columbia 1990) ★★★, *With My Lover Beside Me* (Columbia 1991) ★★★, *Love, Nancy* (Columbia 1994) ★★★, *If I Had My Way* (Columbia 1997) ★★★, *A Nancy Wilson Christmas* (Manchester Craftsman's Guild 2001) ★★★.
● COMPILATIONS: *The Best Of Nancy Wilson* (Capitol 1968) ★★★★, *Nancy Wilson's Greatest Hits* (Capitol 1988) ★★★★, *The Capitol Years* (Capitol 1992) ★★★★, *Spotlight On Nancy Wilson* (Capitol 1995) ★★★★, *The Best Of The Jazz And Blues Sessions* (Blue Note 1996) ★★★★, *Greatest Hits* (Columbia 1999) ★★★★, *Anthology* (The Right Stuff/Capitol 2000) ★★★★.

WONDER, STEVIE

b. Steveland Judkins, 13 May 1950, Saginaw, Michigan, USA. Born Judkins, Wonder now prefers to be known as Steveland Morris after his mother's married name. Placed in an incubator immediately after his birth, baby Steveland was given too much oxygen, causing Steveland to suffer permanent blindness. Despite this handicap, Wonder began to learn the piano at the age of seven, and had also mastered drums and harmonica by the age of nine. After his family moved to Detroit in 1954, Steveland joined a church choir, the gospel influence on his music balanced by the R&B of Ray Charles and Sam Cooke being played on his transistor radio. In 1961, he was discovered by Ronnie White of the Miracles, who arranged an audition at Motown Records. Berry Gordy immediately signed Steveland to the label, renaming him Little Stevie Wonder (the 'Little' was dropped in 1964). Wonder was placed in the care of writer/producer Clarence Paul, who supervised his early recordings. These accentuated his prodigal talents as a multi-instrumentalist, but did not represent a clear musical direction. In 1963, however, the release of the ebullient live recording 'Fingertips (Part 2)' established his commercial success, and Motown quickly marketed him on a series of albums as 'the 12-year-old genius' in an attempt to link him with the popularity of 'the genius', Ray Charles. Attempts to repeat the success of 'Fingertips' proved abortive, and Wonder's career was placed on hold during 1964 while his voice was breaking. He re-emerged in 1965 with a sound that was much closer to the Motown mainstream, scoring a worldwide hit with the dance-orientated 'Uptight (Everything's Alright)', which he co-wrote with Henry Cosby and Sylvia Moy. This began a run of US Top 40 hits that continued unbroken (apart from seasonal Christmas releases) for over six years.

From 1965-70, Stevie Wonder was marketed like the other major Motown stars, recording material that was chosen for him by the label's executives, and issuing albums that mixed conventional soul compositions with pop standards. His strong humanitarian principles were allowed expression on his version of Bob Dylan's 'Blowin' In The Wind' and Ron Miller's 'A Place In The Sun' in 1966. He co-wrote almost all of his singles from 1967 onwards, and also began to collaborate on releases by other Motown artists, most notably co-writing Smokey Robinson And The Miracles' hit 'The Tears Of A Clown', and writing and producing the (Detroit) Spinners' 'It's A Shame'.

His contract with Motown expired in 1971; rather than re-signing immediately, as the label expected, Wonder financed the recording of two albums of his own material, playing almost all the instruments himself, and experimenting for the first time with more ambitious musical forms. He pioneered the use of the synthesizer in black music, and also widened his lyrical concerns to take in racial problems and spiritual questions. Wonder then used these recordings as a lever to persuade Motown to offer a more open contract, which gave him total artistic control over his music, plus the opportunity to hold the rights to the music publishing in his own company, Black Bull Music. He celebrated the signing of the deal with the release of the solo recordings, *Where I'm Coming From* and *Music Of My Mind*, which despite lukewarm critical reaction quickly established him at the forefront of black music.

Talking Book in 1972 combined the artistic advances of recent albums with major commercial success, producing glorious hit singles with the polyrhythmic funk of 'Superstition' and the crafted ballad, 'You Are The Sunshine Of My Life'. Wonder married fellow Motown artist Syreeta on 14 September 1970; he premiered many of his new production techniques on *Syreeta* (1972) and *Stevie Wonder Presents Syreeta* (1974), for which he also wrote most of the material. *Innervisions* (1973) consolidated his growth and success with *Talking Book*, bringing further hit singles with the socially aware 'Living For The City' and 'Higher

Ground'. Later that year, Wonder was seriously injured in a car accident; his subsequent work was tinged with the awareness of mortality, fired by his spiritual beliefs. The release of *Fulfillingness' First Finale* in 1974 epitomized this more austere approach. The double album *Songs In The Key Of Life* (1976) was widely greeted as his most ambitious and satisfying work to date. It showed a mastery and variety of musical forms and instruments, offering a joyous tribute to Duke Ellington on 'Sir Duke', and heralding a pantheon of major black figures on 'Black Man'. This confirmed Wonder's status as one of the most admired musicians and songwriters in contemporary music.

Surprisingly, after this enormous success, no new recordings surfaced for over three years, as Wonder concentrated on perfecting the soundtrack music to the documentary film, *The Secret Life Of Plants*. This primarily instrumental double album was greeted with disappointing reviews and sales. Wonder quickly delivered the highly successful *Hotter Than July* in 1980, which included a tribute song for the late Dr. Martin Luther King, 'Happy Birthday', and a notable essay in reggae form on 'Masterblaster (Jamming)'. The failure of his film project brought an air of caution into Wonder's work, and delays and postponements were now a consistent factor in his recording process. After compiling the retrospective double album *Stevie Wonder's Original Musiquarium I* in 1982, which included four new recordings alongside the cream of his post-1971 work, Wonder scheduled an album entitled *People Move Human Play* in 1983. This never appeared; instead, he composed the soundtrack music for the movie *The Woman In Red*, which included his biggest-selling single to date, the sentimental ballad 'I Just Called To Say I Loved You'. The album on which he had been working since 1980 eventually appeared in 1985 as *In Square Circle*. Like his next project, *Characters* in 1987, it heralded a return to the accessible, melodic music of the previous decade, but the unadventurous nature of both projects, and the heavy expectations engendered by the delay in their release, led to a disappointing reception from critics and public alike.

Wonder's status as an elder statesman of black music, and a champion of black rights, was boosted by his campaign in the early 80s to have the birthday of Dr. Martin Luther King celebrated as a national holiday in the USA. This request was granted by President Reagan, and the first Martin Luther King Day was celebrated on 15 January 1986 with a concert at which Wonder topped the bill. Besides his own recordings, Wonder has been generous in offering his services as a writer, producer, singer or musician to other performers. His most public collaborations included work with Paul McCartney, which produced a cloying but enormous hit, 'Ebony And Ivory', Gary Byrd,

Michael Jackson, and Eurythmics, and on the benefit records by USA For Africa and Dionne Warwick And Friends. *Conversation Peace* in 1995 was an average album with no outstanding songs, but our expectation of Wonder is different to that of most other artists. He could release 10 indifferent, poor, weak or spectacular records over the next 20 years and nothing would change our fixed perception of him and of the body of outstanding music he has produced since 1963.

● ALBUMS: *Tribute To Uncle Ray* (Tamla 1962) ★★★, *The Jazz Soul Of Little Stevie* (Tamla 1962) ★★★, *The 12-Year-Old Genius Recorded Live* (Tamla 1963) ★★★, *With A Song In My Heart* (Tamla 1963) ★★, *Stevie At The Beach* (Tamla 1964) ★★, *Up-Tight (Everything's Alright)* (Tamla 1966) ★★★, *Down To Earth* (Tamla 1966) ★★★, *I Was Made To Love Her* (Tamla 1967) ★★★★, *Someday At Christmas* (Tamla 1967) ★★, *For Once In My Life* (Tamla 1968) ★★★★, *My Cherie Amour* (Tamla 1969) ★★★★, *Stevie Wonder Live* (Tamla 1970) ★★, *Stevie Wonder Live At The Talk Of The Town* (Tamla 1970) ★★★, *Signed Sealed & Delivered* (Tamla 1970) ★★★★, *Where I'm Coming From* (Tamla 1971) ★★★★, *Music Of My Mind* (Tamla 1972) ★★★★, *Talking Book* (Tamla Motown 1972) ★★★★★, *Innervisions* (Tamla Motown 1973) ★★★★★, *Fulfillingness' First Finale* (Tamla Motown 1974) ★★★, *Songs In The Key Of Life* (Motown 1976) ★★★★★, *Stevie Wonder's Journey Through The Secret Life Of Plants* (Motown 1979) ★★, *Hotter Than July* (Motown 1980) ★★★, *The Woman In Red* soundtrack (Motown 1984) ★★, *In Square Circle* (Motown 1985) ★★, *Characters* (Motown 1987) ★★, *Conversation Peace* (Motown 1995) ★★, *Natural Wonder* (Motown 1995) ★★.

● COMPILATIONS: *Greatest Hits* (Tamla 1968) ★★★★, *Greatest Hits Vol. 2* (Tamla 1971) ★★★★, *Anthology* aka *Looking Back* 1962-71 recordings (Motown 1977) ★★★★, *Stevie Wonder's Original Musiquarium I* (Motown 1982) ★★★★, *Song Review: A Greatest Hits Collection* (Motown 1998) ★★★, *At The Close Of A Century* 4-CD box set (Motown 1999) ★★★★, *Ballad Collection* (Motown 2000) ★★★.

● FURTHER READING: *Stevie Wonder*, Sam Hasegawa. *The Story Of Stevie Wonder*, Jim Haskins. *Stevie Wonder*, Ray Fox-Cumming. *Stevie Wonder*, Constanze Elsner. *The Picture Life Of Stevie Wonder*, Audrey Edwards. *Stevie Wonder*, C. Dragonwagon. *Stevie Wonder*, Beth P. Wilson. *The Stevie Wonder Scrapbook*, Jim Haskins with Kathleen Benson. *Stevie Wonder*, Rick Taylor. *Innervisions: The Music Of Stevie Wonder*, Martin E. Horn.

● FILMS: *Bikini Beach* (1964).

WOODSTOCK FESTIVAL

If the Monterey Pop Festival in 1967 was the birth of the new music revolution, Woodstock was its coming of age. The original Woodstock Art and Music Fair was forcibly moved from its planned location after protest from local townsfolk of Wallkill, New York State, USA. Their opposition to 'long-haired weirdos' was typical of 1969. The new location was 40 miles away at a 600-acre dairy farm in Bethel owned by Max Yasgur. A steady trail of spectators arrived up to a week before the event, which took place on 15, 16 and 17 August 1969, to make sure they had a reasonable chance to catch a glimpse of at least one of the dozens of stars scheduled to appear. The line-up was intimidating in its scale: the Who, Jimi Hendrix, Crosby, Stills, Nash And Young, John Sebastian, Jefferson Airplane, Grateful Dead, Santana, Joe Cocker, Sly And The Family Stone, Country Joe And The Fish, Ten Years After, the Band, Johnny Winter, Blood, Sweat And Tears, the Paul Butterfield Blues Band, Sha Na Na, Janis Joplin, Ravi Shankar, the Keef Hartley Band, the Incredible String Band, Canned Heat, Melanie, Tim Hardin, Joan Baez, Arlo Guthrie, Richie Havens, Creedence Clearwater Revival, and Sweetwater. Estimates vary but it was generally felt that no less than 300,000 spectators were present at any one time, sharing 600 portable lavatories and inadequate water facilities. Nobody was prepared for the wave of bodies that formed, choking the highways from all directions. The world press which had previously scorned the popular hippie movement and the power of their musical message, were at last speaking favourably, as one. It was possible for vast amounts of youngsters to congregate for a musical celebration, without violence and regimented supervision. Joni Mitchell (who was not present) was one of the artists who eulogized the event in her song 'Woodstock': 'I'm going down to Yasgur's Farm, I'm gonna join in a rock 'n' roll band, I'm gonna camp out on the land and set my soul free'. Michael Wadleigh's groundbreaking movie and the subsequent live albums have insured Woodstock's immortality, and although there are some critics of the 'love generation' few can deny that Woodstock was a milestone in musical history. It is no exaggeration to claim that the festival totally changed the world's attitude towards popular music.

How much that attitude had changed was reflected in two attempts to recreate the original festival during the 90s. The first event was held at Saugerties, New York, on 12, 13 and 14 August 1994, with a line-up mixing contemporary artists with acts who appeared at the original festival. The weekend passed off with relatively little trouble despite several stage invasions, although many commentators bemoaned the stifling corporate atmosphere and the loss of the original festival's spirit. Five years later a three day festival was organised at Griffiss Park, a former air base, by John Scher and Michael Lang, the latter one of the organisers of the original 1969 event. The event ended in violence on Sunday night, with festival-goers setting fire to several refrigeration trailers and causing extensive damage. As recriminations began, many people blamed the previous night's aggressive nu metal line-up for inflaming the crowd. The biggest irony was that the police, the counter-culture's sworn enemy at the original event, were congratulated by the organisers for ensuring that no greater damage or harm was caused.

● COMPILATIONS: Woodstock (Atco 1969) ★★★★, Woodstock II (Atco 1970) ★★★, Woodstock: Three Days Of Peace And Music: The 25th Anniversary Collection (Atlantic 1994) ★★★, Woodstock '94 (A&M 1994) ★★★, Woodstock '99 (Sony 1999) ★★★.

● VIDEOS: Woodstock '94 (PolyGram Music Video 1995).

● FURTHER READING: Woodstock: Festival Remembered, Jean Young. Woodstock Festival Remembered, Michael Lang. Woodstock Vision, Elliott Landy. Woodstock: An Oral History, Joel Makowers.

● FILMS: Woodstock (1970).

WYNTER, MARK

b. Terence Lewis, 29 January 1943, Woking, Surrey, England. Wynter was one of several UK heart-throbs in the early 60s who took their cue from the USA. Once the extrovert champion of many a school sports day, he was serving in a general store by day, and sang with the Hank Fryer Band in Peckham Co-op Hall, London in the evening, when his well-scrubbed, good looks betrayed star potential to Ray Mackender, a Lloyds underwriter who dabbled in pop management. As 'Mark Wynter', the boy was readied for his new career with vocal exercises, tips on stage demeanour from a RADA coach, and advice about a middle-of-the-road repertoire from Lionel Bart. After exploratory intermission spots in metropolitan palais, he was signed to Decca Records, and had UK chart entries until 1964 – beginning with 'Image Of A Girl' (1960) at number 11. At the height of his fame two years later, he reached the Top 10 with covers of Jimmy Clanton's 'Venus In Blue Jeans' and Steve Lawrence's 'Go Away Little Girl'. From then on, he resorted to a-side revivals of such 50s chestnuts as 'It's Almost Tomorrow' and 'Only You', but was overcome, like so many others, by the burgeoning beat boom. He did play a major role in the lightweight beat movie Just For Fun, but the poor script did not flatter Wynter's abilities. He then turned his attention to the theatre, both straight and musical. He played the leading role in Conduct Unbecoming for more than a year at the Queen's Theatre in London, and for six months in Australia. He appeared with Evelyn Laye and Stanley Baxter in the musical Phil The Fluter, with Julia McKenzie in On The Twentieth Century, and in Charley's Aunt. He also starred in Side By Side By Sondheim in Toronto, Chichester, and on the UK tour. In the 1982 Chichester Festival season he

acted in several plays including On The Rocks and Henry V, and also sang in Valmouth. Wynter played the male lead in Sheridan Morley's Noël And Gertie in London, Hong Kong, and New York. His other work in musicals during the 80s included the role of the King in a revival of The King And I, the title roles in Hans Andersen and Barnum, the 1986 revival of Charlie Girl with Cyd Charisse and Paul Nicholas in London, and the part of Robert Browning in Robert And Elizabeth. During the 90s Wynter spent two years on that famous rubbish dump in the New London Theatre which is inhabited by Andrew Lloyd Webber's Cats, and was also seen as the Phantom and M. Andre in The Phantom Of The Opera, and starred as Vittorio opposite Bonnie Langford in the 1998 West End revival of Sweet Charity. He has appeared frequently in the provinces and portrayed Emile de Becque in a national tour of South Pacific. For BBC Radio 2, Wynter narrated The Danny Kaye Story, and his UK television work has included a series with Dora Bryan – According To Dora, as well as Tale Of Two Rivers with Petula Clark, his own series Call In On Wynter, A Tribute To Terence Rattigan, Cedar Tree, Sally Ann, Once Upon A Time, Sounds Like A Story, Just For Fun, The Haunted House Of Horrors, Red, The Jealous Mirror, and Superman.

● ALBUMS: The Warmth Of Wynter (Decca 1961) ★★, Mark Wynter (Golden Guinea 1964) ★★★, Mark Wynter (Ace Of Clubs 1965) ★★★, Recollected (Sequel 1991) ★★★.

● COMPILATIONS: Go Away Little Girl: The Pye Anthology (Sequel 2000) ★★★.

● FILMS: Just For Fun (1964).

YARDBIRDS

This pivotal UK R&B group was formed in London in 1963 when Keith Relf (b. 22 March 1943, Richmond, Surrey, England, d. 14 May 1976; vocals, harmonica) and Paul Samwell-Smith (b. 8 May 1943, Richmond, Surrey, England; bass), both members of semi-acoustic act the Metropolis Blues Quartet, joined forces with Chris Dreja (b. 11 November 1944, Surbiton, Surrey, England; rhythm guitar), Tony 'Top' Topham (lead guitar) and Jim McCarty (b. 25 July 1943, Liverpool, England; drums). Within months Topham had opted to continue academic studies and was replaced in October by Eric Clapton (b. Eric Clapp, 30 March 1945, Ripley, Surrey, England). The reconstituted line-up forged a style based on classic Chicago R&B and quickly amassed a following in the nascent blues circuit. They succeeded the Rolling Stones as the resident band at Richmond's popular Crawdaddy club, whose owner, Giorgio Gomelsky, then assumed the role of group manager. Two enthusiastic, if low-key singles, 'I Wish You Would' and 'Good Morning Little Schoolgirl', attracted critical interest, but the quintet's fortunes flourished with the release of Five Live Yardbirds. Recorded during their tenure at the Marquee club, the set captured an in-person excitement and was marked by an exceptional rendition of Howlin' Wolf's 'Smokestack Lightning'.

Clapton emerged as the unit's focal point, but a desire for musical purity led to his departure in March 1965 in the wake of a magnificent third single, 'For Your Love'. Penned by Graham Gouldman, the song's commerciality proved unacceptable to the guitarist despite its innovative sound. Clapton later resurfaced in John Mayall's Bluesbreakers and Derek And The Dominos before establishing a highly successful solo career. Jeff Beck (b. 24 June 1944, Surrey, England), formerly of the Tridents, joined the Yardbirds as the single rose to number 1 in the UK's New Musical Express chart. Gouldman provided further hits in 'Heartful Of Soul' and 'Evil Hearted You', the latter of which was a double-sided chart entry with the band-penned 'Still I'm Sad'. Based on a Gregorian chant, the song indicated a desire for experimentation prevailing in the raga-rock 'Shapes Of Things', the chaotic 'Over Under Sideways Down' and the excellent Roger The Engineer. By this point Simon Napier-Bell had assumed management duties, while disaffection with touring, and the unit's

sometimes irreverent attitude, led to the departure of Samwell-Smith in June 1966. Respected session guitarist Jimmy Page (b. James Patrick Page, 9 January 1944, Heston, Middlesex, England) was brought into a line-up that, with Dreja switching to bass, now adopted a potentially devastating twin-lead guitar format. The experimental 'Happenings Ten Years Time Ago' confirmed such hopes, but within six months Beck had departed during a gruelling USA tour. The Yardbirds remained a quartet but, despite a growing reputation on the American 'underground' circuit, their appeal as a pop attraction waned. Despite late-period collaborations with the commercially minded Mickie Most, singles, including 'Little Games' (1967) and 'Goodnight Sweet Josephine' (1968), failed to chart. The disappointing Little Games was denied a UK release but found success in the USA. They followed with two bizarre successes in America: 'Ha Ha Said The Clown' and Nilsson's 'Ten Little Indians'. When Relf and McCarty announced a desire to pursue a folk-based direction, the band folded in July 1968. Page subsequently founded Led Zeppelin, Dreja became a highly successful photographer while the remaining duo forged a new career, firstly as Together, then Renaissance.

The legacy of the Yardbirds has refused to die, particularly in the wake of the fame enjoyed by its former guitarists. Relf was fatally electrocuted in 1976, but the following decade McCarty and Dreja joined Samwell-Smith – now a respected record producer – in Box Of Frogs. When this short-lived attraction folded, the former colleagues reverted to their corresponding careers, with McCarty remaining active in music as a member of the British Invasion All-Stars and the Yardbirds Experience. In 1992, McCarty and Dreja performed a series of reunion concerts in London to commemorate the Yardbirds election to the Rock And Roll Hall Of Fame. The two men reunited once more in 1996, this time on a more permanent basis. The allure of the Yardbirds still flourishes and they remain acclaimed as early practitioners of technical effects and psychedelic styles. The 'blueswailing' Yardbirds have maintained enormous credibility as true pioneers of British R&B, classic experimental pop and early exponents of heavy rock.

● ALBUMS: Five Live Yardbirds (Columbia 1964) ★★★★, For Your Love US only (Epic 1965) ★★★, Having A Rave Up With The Yardbirds US only (Epic 1966) ★★★, Roger The Engineer aka Over Under Sideways Down (Epic 1966) ★★★, Little Games (Epic 1967) ★★★, The Yardbirds Reunion Concert (Renaissance 1992) ★★★.

● COMPILATIONS: The Yardbirds With Sonny Boy Williamson 1963 recordings (Fontana 1966) ★★★, The Yardbirds' Greatest Hits (Epic 1967) ★★★, The Yardbirds Featuring Performances By Jeff Beck, Eric Clapton, Jimmy Page (Epic 1970)

★★★, *Remember The Yardbirds* (Regal 1971) ★★★★, *Live Yardbirds* (Epic 1971) ★★★, *Yardbirds Featuring Eric Clapton* (Charly 1977) ★★★, *Yardbirds Featuring Jeff Beck* (Charly 1977) ★★★, *Shapes Of Things (Collection 1964-1966)* (Charly 1978) ★★★, *The First Recordings* (Charly 1982) ★★★, *Shapes Of Things* 7-LP box set (Charly 1984) ★★★, *The Studio Sessions* (Charly 1989) ★★★, *Yardbirds ... On Air* (Band Of Joy 1991) ★★, *Smokestack Lightning* (Sony 1991) ★★★★, *Blues, Backtracks And Shapes Of Things* (Sony 1991) ★★, *Train Kept A Rollin': The Complete Giorgio Gomelsky Recordings* 4-CD box set (Charly 1993) ★★★★, *Honey In Your Hips 1963-66 recordings* (Charly 1994) ★★★, *The Best Of The Yardbirds* (Rhino 1994) ★★★, *Good Morning Little Schoolgirl* (Essential Gold 1995) ★★★, *Where The Action Is!* (New Millennium/Caroline 1997) ★★★, *The Complete BBC Sessions* (Get Back 1998) ★★★, *The Best Of The Yardbirds* (Charly 1998) ★★★★, *The Ultimate Collection* (Recall 1999) ★★★, *Cumular Limit* (Burning Airlines 2000) ★★★, *Ultimate!* (Rhino 2001) ★★★★.

● VIDEOS: *Yardbirds* (Delilah Music Pictures 1991).

● FURTHER READING: *Blues In The Night: The Yardbirds' Story*, James White. *Yardbirds*, John Platt. *Yardbirds World*, Richard MacKay and Michael Ober. *Yardbirds: The Ultimate Rave-up*, Greg Russo.

YOUNG RASCALS

This expressive act, one of America's finest pop/soul ensembles, made its debut in a New Jersey club, the Choo Choo in February 1965. Felix Cavaliere (b. 29 November 1943, Pelham, New York, USA; organ, vocals), Eddie Brigati (b. 22 October 1946, New York City, USA; vocals, percussion) and Dino Danelli (b. 23 July 1945, New York City, USA; drums) were each established musicians on the city's R&B circuit, serving time in several popular attractions, including Joey Dee And The Starliters. It was here that the trio encountered Gene Cornish (b. 14 May 1946, Ottawa, Canada; vocals, guitar), who became the fourth member of a breakaway act, initially dubbed Felix And The Escorts, but later known as the Young Rascals. The quartet enjoyed a minor hit with 'I Ain't Gonna Eat Out My Heart Anymore' before securing a US number 1 with the energetic 'Good Lovin''. Despite a somewhat encumbering early image – knickerbockers and choir boy shirts – the band's soulful performances endeared them to critics and peers, earning them a 'group's group' sobriquet.

Now established as one of the east coast's most influential attractions, spawning a host of imitators from the Vagrants to Vanilla Fudge, the Young Rascals secured their biggest hit with 'Groovin''. This melancholic performance became an international hit, signalling a lighter, more introspective approach, and although Brigati was featured on the haunting 'How Can I Be Sure?', a US Top 5 entry, Cavaliere gradually became the band's focal point. In 1968 the band dropped its 'Young' prefix and enjoyed a third US number 1 with 'People Got To Be Free'. An announcement that every Rascals live appearance must also include a black act enforced their commitment to civil rights, but effectively banned them from southern states. The quartet later began exploring jazz-based compositions, and although remaining respected, lost much of their commercial momentum. Brigati and Cornish left in 1971, and although newcomers Buzzy Feiten (guitar), Ann Sutton (vocals) and Robert Popwell (drums) contributed to final albums, *Peaceful World* and *The Island Of Real*, the Rascals were clearly losing momentum and broke up the following year. Felix Cavaliere then enjoyed a moderate solo career while Danelli and Cornish formed Bulldog and Fotomaker. The three musicians were reunited in 1988 for an extensive US tour.

● ALBUMS: *The Young Rascals* (Atlantic 1966) ★★★, *Collections* (Atlantic 1966) ★★★, *Groovin'* (Atlantic 1967) ★★★★, as The Rascals *Once Upon A Dream* (Atlantic 1968) ★★★, as The Rascals *Freedom Suite* (Atlantic 1969) ★★★, as The Rascals *Search And Nearness* (Atlantic 1969) ★★, as The Rascals *See* (Atlantic 1970) ★★, as The Rascals *Peaceful World* (Columbia 1971) ★★, as The Rascals *The Island Of Real* (Columbia 1972) ★★.

● COMPILATIONS: *Timepeace: The Rascals' Greatest Hits* (Atlantic 1968) ★★★★, *Star Collection* (WEA 1973) ★★★, *Searching For Ecstasy: The Rest Of The Rascals 1969-1972* (Rhino 1988) ★★★★, *Anthology (1965-1972)* (Rhino 1992) ★★★★, *The Very Best Of The Rascals* (Rhino 1994) ★★★★, *All I Really Need: The Atlantic Recordings 1965-1971* (Rhino Handmade 2000) ★★★★.

YOUNGBLOODS

Formed in 1965 in Boston, Massachusetts, the Youngbloods evolved from the city's thriving traditional music circuit. The band was formed by folk singers Jesse Colin Young (b. Perry Miller, 11 November 1944, New York City, New York, USA) and Jerry Corbitt (b. Tifton, Georgia, USA) who together completed a single, 'My Babe', prior to the arrival of aspiring jazz drummer Joe Bauer (b. 26 September 1941, Memphis, Tennessee, USA) and guitarist/pianist Lowell Levinger III, better known simply as Banana (b. Cambridge, Massachusetts, USA). Young began playing bass when several candidates, including Felix Pappalardi and Harvey Brooks, proved incompatible, and the quartet took the name 'Youngbloods' from the singer's second solo album. Having secured a residency at New York's famed Cafe Au Go Go, the band established itself as a leading folk rock-cum-good time attraction. Their debut, *The*

Youngbloods, captures this formative era and mixes excellent original songs, including the ebullient 'Grizzly Bear', with several choice cover versions. The band's reading of Dino Valenti's 'Get Together' subsequently became a hit in California where it was adopted as a counter-culture anthem. The lyric: 'Come on now people, smile on your brother, everybody get together, try and love one another right now', perfectly captured the mood of late-60s Californian rock music.

The Youngbloods then settled on the west coast. *Elephant Mountain*, their most popular album, reflected a new-found peace of mind and included several of the band's best-known songs, including 'Darkness, Darkness' and 'Sunlight'. Jerry Corbitt had left the line-up during the early stages of recording allowing Bauer and Banana space to indulge in improvisational interludes. The Youngbloods gained complete artistic freedom with their own label, Raccoon. However releases by Bauer, Banana and Young dissipated the strengths of the parent unit, whose final releases were marred by inconsistency. A friend from the Boston days, Michael Kane, joined the band in the spring of 1971, but they split the following year when Young resumed his solo career. Banana, Bauer and Kane continued as Banana And The Bunch, but this occasional venture subsequently folded. In 1984 Levinger reappeared in the Bandits, before retiring from music to run a hang-gliding shop.

● ALBUMS: *The Youngbloods* (RCA 1966) ★★★, *Earth Music* (RCA 1967) ★★★, *Elephant Mountain* (RCA 1968) ★★★★, *Rock Festival* (Raccoon 1970) ★★★, *Ride The Wind* (Raccoon 1971) ★★★, *Good 'N' Dusty* (Raccoon 1971) ★★, *High On A Ridgetop* (Raccoon 1972) ★★.
● COMPILATIONS: one side only *Two Trips* (Mercury 1970) ★★, *The Best Of The Youngbloods* (RCA 1971) ★★★, *Sunlight* (RCA 1971) ★★, *Get Together* (RCA 1971) ★★★, *This Is The Youngbloods* (RCA 1972) ★★★, *Point Reyes Station* (Edsel 1987) ★★, *From The Gaslight To The Avalon* (Decal 1988) ★★★, *Euphoria 1965-1969* (Raven/Topic 1999) ★★★★.

Z

ZOMBIES

Rod Argent (b. 14 June 1945, St. Albans, Hertfordshire, England; piano), Colin Blunstone (b. 24 June 1945, St. Albans, Hertfordshire, England; vocals), Paul Atkinson (b. 19 March 1946, Cuffley, Hertfordshire, England; guitar), Paul Arnold (bass) and Hugh Grundy (b. 6 March 1945, Winchester, Hampshire, England; drums) formed the Zombies in 1963, although Chris White (b. 7 March 1943, Barnet, Hertfordshire) replaced Arnold within weeks of their inception. This St. Albans-based quintet won the local Herts Beat competition, the prize for which was a recording deal with Decca Records. The Zombies' debut single, 'She's Not There', rose to number 12 in the UK, but proved more popular still in America, where it reached number 2. Blunstone's breathy voice and Argent's imaginative keyboard arrangement provided the song's distinctive features and the group's crafted, adventurous style was then maintained over a series of excellent singles. Sadly, this diligence was not reflected in success, and although 'Tell Her No' was another US Top 10 entrant, it fared much less well at home while later releases, including 'Whenever You're Ready' and 'Is This The Dream' unaccountably missed out altogether.

The group, not unnaturally, grew frustrated and broke up in 1967 on completion of *Odessey & Oracle*. The promise of those previous releases culminated in this magnificent collection which adroitly combined innovation, melody and crafted harmonies. Its closing track, 'Time Of The Season', became a massive US hit, but despite several overtures, the original line-up steadfastly refused to reunite. Argent and Grundy were subsequently joined by ex-Mike Cotton bass player Jim Rodford (b. 7 July 1941, St. Albans, Hertfordshire, England) and Rick Birkett (guitar) and this reshaped ensemble was responsible for the Zombies' final single, 'Imagine The Swan'. Despite the label credit, this release was ostensibly the first recording by the keyboard player's new venture, Argent. Colin Blunstone, meanwhile, embarked on a stop-start solo career.

The band reconvened to record *New World* in 1991, which on release received respectable reviews. An ambitious and expertly produced CD box set was released in 1997 by Ace Records, with alternate takes and unissued material. At the launch party in London the original five members played together for the first time in over 25 years. Four years later Argent and

Blunstone reconvened to record the duo album, *Out Of The Shadows*. The Zombies' work is overdue for serious reappraisal, in particular the songwriting talents of Argent and White.

● ALBUMS: *Begin Here* (Decca 1965) ★★★, *Odessey & Oracle* (Columbia 1968) ★★★★, *Early Days* (London 1969), ★★ *The Zombies Live On The BBC 1965-1967* (Rhino 1985) ★★★, *Meet The Zombies* (Razor 1989) ★★★, *Five Live Zombies* (Razor 1989) ★★★, *New World* (JSE 1991) ★★.

● COMPILATIONS: *The World Of The Zombies* (Decca 1970) ★★★★, *Time Of The Zombies* (Epic 1973) ★★★, *Rock Roots* (Decca 1976) ★★★, *The Best And The Rest Of The Zombies* (Back Trac 1984) ★★★, *Greatest Hits* (DCC 1990) ★★★, *Best Of The Zombies* (Music Club 1991) ★★★, *The EP Collection* (See For Miles 1992) ★★★★, *The Zombies 1964-67* (More Music 1995) ★★★, *Zombie Heaven* 4-CD box set (Ace 1997) ★★★★.

● FURTHER READING: *The Zombies: Hung Up On A Dream*, Claes Johansen.

INDEX

A

A Band Of Angels, 7, 150, 329
A.B. Skhy, 7, 224
Abba, 69, 375
Abbot, Gary, 299
Abbott And Costello, 328
Abbott, George, 57
Abrahams, Mick, 123
Abshire, Nathan, 31
AC/DC, 192
Academy, 7 and *passim*
Accent, 7 and *passim*
Accents, 7-8
Ace, Johnny, 71
Aces, 165
Ackles, David, 196
Acklin, Barbara, 8, 115
Action, 8 and *passim*
Acuff, Roy, 316
Acuff-Rose Music, 375
Acutt, John, 207
Ad Libs, 8
Adam, Mike And Tim, 9
Adamo, 9
Adams Singers, 251
Adams, Bryan, 330
Adams, Cliff, 251
Adams, David, 5
Adams, Derroll, 197
Adams, Pete, 197
Adams, Ray, 25
Adamson, Billy, 429
Adderley, Cannonball, 9, 133, 157, 339, 356, 451, 505
Adderley, Nat, 9, 91
Adler, Lou, 9, 12, 36, 205, 282, 327, 355, 372, 411, 449
Adnopoz, Elliott Charles, 197
Africa Brass, 133
After Tea, 10, 163
Aguilar, Dave, 122
Aiese, Mary, 405-406
Air Supply, 20
Airey, Don, 131
Aitken, Laurel, 10-11
Akens, Jewel, 11
Alaimo, Jimmy, 352
Alan Brown, 82
Alan, Carl, 32
Albarn, Damon, 301
Albin, Peter, 63, 139
Albin, Rod, 448
Albuagh, Bill, 310
Alcapone, Dennis, 397
Alder, John, 207, 396, 476

Aldridge, Alan, 49
Alex, George, 371
Alexander, Arthur, 11
Alexander, Gary, 22
Alexander, George, 241
Alexander, J.W., 136
Alexander, James, 33-34
Alexander, Richard, 11
Alford, John, 12
Alfredo, Giovanni, 123
Alice Cooper, 486
Alisha's Attic, 388
Allan, Jack, 287
Allchin, Barry, 204
Allen, Barbara, 8
Allen, Charles, 33
Allen, Charlie, 378
Allen, Colin, 153, 335, 352
Allen, Daevid, 447
Allen, Deborah, 405
Allen, Frank, 53, 428-429
Allen, Jack, 187
Allen, Jeff, 50, 192
Allen, John, 287, 364
Allen, Johnny, 196, 258
Allen, Mark, 335
Allen, Mick, 187
Allen, Mike, 447
Allen, Nat, 302
Allen, Paul, 260
Allen, Peter, 27
Allen, Rick, 83, 234
Allen, Robert, 183
Allen, Rod, 219
Allen, Steve, 502
Allen, Terry, 6
Allen, Wally, 197, 396
Allen, Yvonne, 196
Allensby, Derek, 219
Allin, Mary, 384
Allison, Bob, 12
Allison, Jerry, 145
Allison, Keith, 406
Allison, Mose, 11-12, 209-210
Allisons, 12
Allix, Dick, 486
Allman Brothers Band, 272
Allman, Duane, 236, 272, 296, 386, 427
Allman, Gregg, 272
Allman, Kurt, 58
Almond, Johnny, 252, 335, 352
Almond, Marc, 342, 387, 398, 496
Alpert, Herb, 9, 12-13, 22, 27, 70, 156, 356
Alston, Barbara, 148
Alston, Shirley, 437

Altamont Festival, 13, 285, 417
Altham, Keith, 480
Alvin, Johnny, 209
Amboy Dukes, 14, 227
Ambrose, 122, 302, 305, 351, 428
Amburn, Ellis, 291, 377
Amen Corner, 14, 20, 375
American Breed, 14
American Flyer, 76
American Hot Wax, 60
Ames Brothers, 15, 26, 222
Ames, Ed, 15
Amoo, Eddie, 116
Amorphous, 242
Amory Kane, 15, 210
Anders And Poncia, 73, 146
Andersen, Eric, 130, 381
Andersen, Terry, 7
Anderson, Edward, 58
Anderson, Gary, 78
Anderson, Katherine, 334
Anderson, Miller, 92, 163, 252
Anderson, Pete, 35, 496
Anderson, Pink, 35
Anderson, Terry, 26
Andersson, Benny, 69
Andes, Mark, 451
Andrew, Sam, 63, 290, 351
Andrews, Bob, 302, 358
Andrews, Chris, 15, 208, 250, 311, 380, 435
Andrews, Julie, 86
Andrews, Viv, 396
Andridge, Rick, 430
Andrijasevich, Gary, 122
Andromeda, 15, 24
Andwella's Dream, 15, 474
Animals, 16-17 and *passim*
Ankrah, Roy, 116
Annette, 17 and *passim*
Anthony, John, 82
Anthony, Mike, 276
Anthony, Paul, 170
Anthony, Ray, 107
Anthony, Richard, 17
Anthrax, 74
Aorta, 18
Aphrodite's Child, 18
Aplan, Richard, 294
Apostol, John, 105
Appice, Carmine, 73, 486
Applejacks, 18-20
Appletree Theatre, 19

Aquarian Age, 260
Arbus, Dave, 192
Arcadium, 19
Archies, 19, 148, 167, 304
Arden, Don, 14, 19, 362, 375, 415, 441
Ardley, Neil, 20
Area Code 615, 20
Argent, 421, 511-512
Argent, Rod, 346, 511
Arkin, Alan, 420
Arland, Henry, 70
Arlen, Harold, 54
Arlin, Bobby, 308
Armstead, 'Joshie' Jo, 276
Armstrong, Bob, 112
Armstrong, Frankie, 486
Armstrong, Jim, 470
Armstrong, Louis, 32, 303, 346
Arnaz, Alberto, IV, 170
Arnaz, Desi, 170
Arnold, Billy Boy, 168-169
Arnold, Bob, 331
Arnold, Bruce, 377
Arnold, Eddy, 162, 206, 316, 390
Arnold, Jerry, 67
Arnold, Joe, 331
Arnold, P.P., 20-21, 276, 370, 444, 483
Arnold, Patricia, 20
Arnold, Paul, 378, 511
Arnone, Mike, 183
Arrington, Joseph, Jnr., 469
Ars Nova, 21
Art, 21 and *passim*
Art Ensemble Of Chicago, 38
Art Of Noise, 193, 289
Arthur, Bob, 358
Arthur, J., 126
Arthur, Jean, 58
Arturi, Mike, 323
Asher, Peter, 383
Asheton, Scott, 338
Ashford And Simpson, 231
Ashford, Rosalind, 332
Ashley, Steve, 501
Ashton, Floyd, 464
Ashton, Gardner And Dyke, 66
Asleep At The Wheel, 53
Association, 22 and *passim*
Astaire, Fred, 126

Asylum Choir, 22
Atkins, Chet, 22-24, 142, 162, 257, 404
Atkins, Jim, 22
Atkins, John, 501
Atkinson, Bill, 235
Atkinson, Craig, 139
Atkinson, Paul, 511
Atlanta Rhythm Section, 128
Atomic Rooster, 15, 24, 62, 87, 212
Attack, 24 and *passim*
Attenborough, Richard, 369
Atwell, Winifred, 345
Au Go-Go Singers, 24, 94
Auger, Brian, 30, 95, 181, 237
Aum, 24
Austin Powers, 28, 459
Austin, Dallas, 262
Austin, Danny, 8
Austin, Mel, 470
Austin, Patti, 339
Austin, Roy, 413
Autosalvage, 24
Autry, Gene, 304
Avalon, Frankie, 17, 423
Average White Band, 193, 298, 427
Avon Sisters, 24
Avons, 24-25
Avory, Mick, 300-301, 380, 414
Axelrod, David, 195, 295
Ayers, Kevin, 352, 447
Aykroyd, Dan, 146
Azevedo, Walter, 102
Aznavour, Charles, 25-26, 68, 341, 383

B

B. Bumble And The Stingers, 26, 224
B., Stevie, 505
B.B. Blunder, 74
Baah, Reebop Kwaku, 478
Bacharach, Burt, 26-28, 62, 83, 156, 167, 225, 233, 279, 288-289, 320, 343, 387, 435, 454-455, 493, 496
Bachelors, 28-29
Bacon, Francis, 106
Bacon, Maurice, 320
Bad Company, 379
Badanjek, John, 424
Badfinger, 48
Baez, Joan, 29-30, 184, 187, 191, 211-212, 234, 263, 290, 374, 507
Bagdasarian, Ross, 121-122
Baggott, Martin, 18

Bailey, Bill, 154
Bailey, Donald, 445
Bailey, Pearl, 54
Bailey, Pete, 40
Baja Marimba Band, 166
Baker Gurvitz Army, 247
Baker, Arthur, 188
Baker, Butch, 36
Baker, David, 7
Baker, Ginger, 71, 77-78, 142, 247, 306
Baker, Jack, 77
Baker, John, 7, 36
Baker, Joyce, 491
Baker, Keith, 30
Baker, Kenny, 32, 456
Baker, LaVern, 449
Baker, Lloyd, 284
Baker, Maury, 21
Baker, Peter, 142
Bakerloo, 30
Baldry, Long John, 30-31, 157, 181, 306, 363
Balfa Brothers, 31
Balfa, Dewey, 31-32
Balin, Marty, 13, 285
Balk, Harry, 64
Ball, Dave, 62, 399
Ball, Dennis, 62
Ball, George, 32
Ball, Kenny, 32, 65, 344
Ball, Lucille, 170, 418
Ball, Marcia, 473
Ball, Michael, 69
Ball, Reginald, 479
Ballard, Florence, 32, 334, 460
Ballard, Hank, 119, 280
Ballard, Russ, 421, 435, 484
Ballinger, Dave, 36
Banana And The Bunch, 511
Band Of Gypsies, 259-260
Banks, Darrell, 33
Banks, Homer, 33, 457
Banks, Rose, 443
Bar-Kays, 33-34, 403
Barbarians, 34
Barbata, John, 482
Barbee, Norma, 487
Barber, Adrian, 63
Barber, Chris, 32, 65, 306, 363
Barclay, Michael, 295
Bardens, Peter, 120, 332, 449, 470
Bardot, Brigitte, 66, 230
Bare, Bobby, 162-163
Barefoot Jerry, 20
Bargeron, Dave, 72
Barile, Jo, 490
Barker, Francine, 381
Barnard, Bob, 32
Barnes, J.J., 34
Barnes, James Jay, 34
Barnes, Ken, 44

Barnes, Mike, 106
Barnes, Richard, 402, 501
Barnes, Ricky, 253
Barnett, Grace, 245, 285
Barrett, Fanita, 74
Barrett, Roger, 34
Barrett, Syd, 34-35, 320
Barri, Steve, 10, 36, 92, 210, 241, 340, 442
Barrie, J.J., 380
Barrie, James, 380, 399
Barris, Chuck, 104
Barron Knights, 36
Barry, Jeff, 19, 36, 41, 56, 62, 73, 86, 172, 245, 353
Barry, John, 5, 66, 69, 82, 251
Barry, Len, 37, 178, 309, 377
Barry, Paul, 423
Barry, Sandra, 8
Bart, Lionel, 37-38, 209, 251, 508
Barth, Bill, 278
Barthol, Bruce, 139
Bartholomew, Dave, 59
Bartholomew, Peter, 378
Bartlett, Bill, 310
Bartoli, Frank, 276
Barton, Gordon, 15
Basie, Count, 54, 161, 504
Baskin, Don, 462
Bass, Colin, 306
Bass, Fontella, 38, 167
Bass, Ralph, 88, 120
Bassey, Shirley, 37-39, 69, 85, 322, 369
Bateman, Robert, 33, 334
Bates, Django, 158
Batt, Mike, 249
Battavio, Margaret, 331
Battered Ornaments, 39-40, 91
Battin, Clyde, 99
Battin, Skip, 99, 223-224
Battiste, Harold, 40, 448, 450
Bauer, Joe, 510
Baughman, Dan, 433
Bauldie, John, 5, 190
Baverstock, Jack, 12, 155, 210, 218, 295
Baxter, Les, 166
Baxter, Stanley, 508
Bay City Rollers, 113, 138, 233
Beach Boys, 4, 17, 40-44, 47, 59, 61, 92, 148-149, 151, 221, 250, 282, 355, 370, 375, 385, 425, 464, 476, 490
Beach, Alan, 140
Beacon Street Union, 44, 213
Beadle, Len, 263

Beard, Joe, 400
Beard, Martin, 448
Beatles, 4, 11, 14, 17, 23, 34, 37, 41, 44-50, 53, 56, 59, 61, 68, 74, 80, 86, 94, 97-100, 115-117, 122, 124-125, 142, 149, 165-167, 183, 185, 199-200, 208, 213-215, 221, 223, 234, 238, 255, 262, 265, 273, 275, 280, 293, 301, 304, 306, 310, 313, 317, 322, 329, 333-334, 342-343, 348, 350, 353, 355, 372, 375-376, 383, 388, 395, 398, 415, 417, 431, 434-436, 453, 459, 465, 482, 487, 498
Beatmasters, 21
Beatstalkers, 50
Beau Brummels, 50-51, 251, 443
Beaver, Dave, 233
Bécaud, Gilbert, 107
Beck, Bogert And Appice, 486
Beck, Don, 169
Beck, Jeff, 24, 62, 66, 173, 216, 246, 259, 333, 421, 459, 462, 509-510
Beck, John, 308
Becker, Walter, 284
Beckett, Barry, 188
Beckett, Harry, 20, 252
Beckett, Lena, 323
Bedlam, 63
Bedrocks, 51
Bee Gees, 62, 323, 496
Been, Michael, 18, 247
Beetham, Pete, 7
Beethoven, 67, 346, 367
Beggars Opera, 51
Begleiter, Lionel, 37
Behan, Dominic, 181
Bel Canto, 302
Bel-Airs, 52
Belafonte, Harry, 52-53, 126, 184
Belfast Gypsies, 224
Bell And Arc, 441
Bell, Alec, 323
Bell, Billy, 470
Bell, Graham, 441
Bell, Jimmy, 323
Bell, Johnnie, 472
Bell, Madeline, 156
Bell, Richard, 290
Bell, Sam, 198, 345-346
Bell, Thom, 455
Bell, William, 128, 472
Bellamy, George, 476
Belle Stars, 198
Belley, Richard, 273
Belmonts, 53, 104, 170-171, 449
Belshaw, Brian, 74
Belsky, Harold Simon, 70

Belushi, John, 146
Belvin, Jesse, 56
Beneke, Tex, 328
Benett, Dwight, 400
Benjamin, Louis, 268
Bennett, Anthony, 53
Bennett, Brian, 432
Bennett, Cliff, 53, 150, 378, 429
Bennett, Don, 122
Bennett, Duster, 53
Bennett, John, 32
Bennett, Patricia, 121
Bennett, Tony, 54-55, 288
Bennett, Veronica, 420
Bennett, Wiley, 503
Benno, Marc, 22
Benny, Jack, 160
Benoit, David, 246
Benson, Bruce, 34
Benson, George, 446
Benson, John, 32
Benson, Kathleen, 507
Benson, Renaldo, 222
Benson, Robby, 233
Benton, Brook, 55-56
Beradis, Luke 'Babe', 179
Bergman, Alan And Marilyn, 288
Berigan, Bunny, 134
Berlin, Irving, 81
Berline, Byron, 169-170
Bernard, Barrie, 386
Bernhardt, Warren, 21
Bernhart, Milt, 57
Berns, Bert, 56, 96, 180, 204, 218, 226, 325, 470, 494
Bernstein, Elmer, 56, 69-70
Bernstein, Leonard, 57-58, 370
Bernstein, Louis, 57
Bernstein, Peter, 58
Berry, Chuck, 16, 45, 47-48, 58-60, 67, 120, 169, 212, 392, 414, 422
Berry, Dave, 60-61, 379
Berry, Jan, 282
Berry, Jeff, 330
Berry, Mike, 61, 113, 342, 377
Berry, Richard, 61, 299
Berryhill, Bob, 461
Bertrand, Eddie, 52
Besman, Bernie, 268
Best, George, 211
Best, Graham, 19
Best, Jerry, 97
Best, John, 31, 133, 207, 227, 270, 314, 319, 336
Best, Johnny, 111, 296, 411, 474
Best, Pat, 82
Best, Pete, 44-45, 49-50, 61, 149, 199, 319, 333, 436

Best, Tony, 55, 254, 436
Betrock, Alan, 434, 437
Bettis, John, 28
Bevan, Beverley, 362
Beveridge, Alistair, 327
Biafra, Jello, 364
Bialablow, Tom, 183
Bickerton, Wayne, 61, 149
Bidwell, Dave, 120
Bienstock, Freddy, 62
Bienstock, Johnny, 62, 64, 434
Bifferty, Skip, 20, 257, 441
Big Audio Dynamite, 38
Big Bertha, 62-63
Big Bopper, 92, 395
Big Brother And The Holding Company, 63, 139, 240, 290-291, 355
Big Three, 63, 196, 199, 201, 213, 343, 378, 413, 420-421
Big Top Records, 62, 64, 434
Bigard, Barney, 346
Bikel, Theodore, 64-65
Bilk, Acker, 32, 65-66, 164
Bill Deal And The Rhondels, 503
Billings, Vic, 295
Billingslea, Joe, 135
Billups, Viola, 217
Billy The Kid, 187, 190-191
Bilsbury, Jimmy, 326
Birds, 66 and passim
Birdsong, Cindy, 460
Birkett, Rick, 7, 511
Birkin, Jane, 66, 230
Birmingham Sam, 268
Birrell, Pete, 227
Bishop, Elvin, 7, 97
Bishop, Sid, 168
Bjorn, Frank, 55
Black Cat Bones, 67
Black Crowes, 379
Black Flag, 201
Black Grape, 174
Black Lace, 67
Black Pearl, 34
Black Sabbath, 20
Black Slacks, 83
Black Velvet Flag, 201
Black, Bill, 67, 389
Black, Bill, Combo, 67
Black, Brent, 378
Black, Cilla, 27, 45, 67-68, 83, 156, 199-200, 318, 333, 435-436, 454
Black, David, 284
Black, Don, 57, 68-70, 355
Black, Jay, 284
Black, Jim, 395
Black, Jimmy Carl, 88, 358-359

Black, Johnny, 5, 112, 260, 501
Black, Neil, 471
Black, Roy, 70
Black, Terry, 36, 442
Blackfoot, 33
Blackford, Andy, 17, 95, 115
Blackhawk, 159
Blackjack, 324
Blackmore, Ritchie, 61, 81, 123, 129, 141, 257, 377, 462, 477
Blackwell, Chris, 10, 163, 194, 345, 371, 492
Blackwell, Otis, 221, 390
Blackwell, Robert 'Bumps', 136
Blackwood, Lloyd, 141
Blaikley, Alan, 268
Blaikley, Howard, 155, 261, 268
Blaine, Hal, 70-71, 244, 411, 422, 450, 503
Blair, William, 131
Blake, John, 49, 419
Blake, Ron, 445
Blake, William, 175, 228
Blakely, Paul, 105
Blakely, Ronee, 187
Blakey, Art, 445
Blakley, Alan, 478
Bland, Bobby, 7, 36, 61, 71, 382, 473, 481
Bland, Robert Calvin, 71
Blasko, Chuck, 492
Blau, Eric, 437
Bledsoe, Fern, 213
Bleyer, Archie, 474
Blind Faith, 71-72, 145, 163, 477
Blockheads, 441
Blonde On Blonde, 72, 185-187, 190
Blondheim, Philip, 291, 340
Blood, Sweat And Tears, 42, 72, 76, 94, 110, 236, 252, 267, 507
Bloom, Bobby, 73
Bloomfield, Mike, 73, 97, 150, 195, 236, 290, 358, 363, 384, 448, 464
Blossom Toes, 74, 181, 213, 237
Blossoms, 74, 77
Blow Monkeys, 337
Blow, Will, 296
Blue Angel, 65, 201, 252
Blue Blood Group, 7
Blue Cheer, 74-75, 293
Blue Jays, 61, 223, 357
Blue Mink, 156
Blue Velvets, 144, 237
Blue, David, 75, 196
Blue, Jimmy, 446
Blues Brothers, 78, 80, 88,

90, 117-118, 146-147, 225-226, 270, 329, 388, 403
Blues Magoos, 75-76
Blues Project, 72, 76, 315, 355, 475
Bluesbreakers, 53, 142, 235, 252, 335-336, 352, 509
Blumenfeld, Roy, 76
Blunder, B.B., 74
Blunstone, Colin, 511
Bo Street Runners, 76, 120, 286
Bob And Earl, 76-77
Bob B. Soxx And The Blue Jeans, 74, 77, 450
Bock, Jerry, 160
Bockner, Rick, 326
Bockris, Victor, 419, 489
Boettcher, Curt, 22, 77, 344, 425
Bogart, Humphrey, 501
Bogart, Neil, 337
Bogert, Tim, 486
Bogguss, Suzy, 23
Bogle, Bob, 489
Boisot, Louise, 137
Bolan, Marc, 74, 286, 483
Bolin, Tommy, 486
Bolton, Pete, 112
Bond, Graham, 16, 40, 77-78, 91-92, 142, 157, 205, 306, 313, 335, 363, 389, 445
Bond, Johnny, 461
Bond, Ronnie, 480
Bond, Terry, 413
Bonds, Gary 'U.S.', 78, 279, 449
Bonham, 379, 462
Bonham, Jason, 379
Bonham, John, 462
Bonney, Graham, 78
Bono, Sonny, 40, 79, 372, 428, 447, 449
Bonzo Dog Doo-Dah Band, 79, 368, 466
Boogie Jake, 271
Bookbinder, Anthony, 150, 307
Booker T. And The MGs, 33, 80, 146, 217-218, 297, 308, 331, 355
Booker, John Lee, 268
Boone, Daniel, 15
Boone, Debby, 81
Boone, Pat, 80-82
Boone, Skip, 24
Boone, Steve, 24, 322-323
Boones, 81
Boot, Adrian, 260
Booth, Stanley, 419
Booth, Tim, 179
Borisoff, Leonard, 37, 178
Bosstown Sound, 484
Bostic, Earl, 131

Boston Dexters, 82
Bourjer, Geoff, 400
Bourke, Ciaran, 181
Bow Wow Wow, 56
Bowden, Ron, 32
Bowen, Frank, 149
Bowie, David, 50, 84, 292, 323, 338, 398
Bowie, Lester, 38
Bowles, Bruce, 233
Bowman, Don, 162-163
Bown, Alan, 82, 372
Bown, Andy, 14, 261
Bowyer, Geoff, 400
Box Of Frogs, 509
Box Tops, 82-83, 234, 382, 387
Boyce And Hart, 83, 304, 353
Boyce, Tommy, 83
Boyd, Craig, 308
Boyd, Eddie, 119
Boyd, Eva Narcissus, 315
Boyd, Jenny, 173
Boyer, Charles, 346
Boylan, Terence, 19
Boyle, Denny, 302
Boyz II Men, 239, 361
Boyzone, 139
Brackett, Al, 381
Braddock, Bessie, 116
Braden, Bernard, 251
Braden, Tommy, 251
Bradley, Owen, 309
Braff, Ruby, 54
Bramlett, Bonnie, 276
Brand, Rick, 310
Brando, Marlon, 58, 126
Brandon, Ronnie, 338
Bratton, Creed, 241
Braun, Eric, 395
Brautigan, Richard, 326
Brave Combo, 475
Brayley, Rex, 320
Bread, 196
Breakaways, 83, 491
Breau, Lenny, 23
Brecht, Bertolt, 130, 153, 175, 208, 437, 486
Brecht, Kurt, 130, 153, 175, 208, 437
Brecker, Michael, 132
Brecker, Randy, 72
Breier, Sheldon, 425
Brel, Jacques, 83-84, 130, 341, 437, 495-496
Brenda And The Tabulations, 84
Brennan, Joey, 486
Brennan, Walter, 84
Brenston, Jackie, 481
Brett, Paul, 488
Brian, Eddie, 498
Brian, Lewis, 414
Brian, Ty, 459
Brice, Trevor, 486
Bricker, Gene, 331

Brickley, Audrey, 377
Brickley, Shirley, 377
Brickman, Marshall, 291, 385
Bricusse, Leslie, 85, 161, 305, 328, 369
Bridgeman, Dan, 294
Brigati, Eddie, 164, 510
Briggs, David, 20, 382
Briggs, Vic, 16
Bright, Ronnie, 149
Brightman, Sarah, 70, 408
Brill Building, 56, 62, 86, 148, 167, 325, 330, 373, 375, 429, 483, 487
Brinsley Schwarz, 194, 302
Britt, Mai, 161
Britten, Terry, 408
Britton, Chris, 479
Britton, Geoff, 192
Brogues, 86
Bromham, Del, 459
Bron, Eleanor, 280, 479
Bronco, 82
Brook Brothers, 86-87, 254
Brook, Geoffrey, 86
Brook, Ricky, 86
Brooker, Gary, 380, 399
Brooklyn Bridge, 87
Brooks, Arthur, 96, 276, 320
Brooks, Danny, 178
Brooks, Derek, 67
Brooks, Elkie, 150
Brooks, Garth, 189
Brooks, Harvey, 185, 195, 290, 510
Brooks, Peter, 352
Brooks, Richard, 276
Brooks, Stuart, 67
Broonzy, 'Big' Bill, 362
Brotherhood Of Man, 217
Brothers Johnson, 422
Brotman, Stuart, 294
Broussard, Austin, 31
Broussard, Grace, 150
Brown Brothers, 90
Brown, Alan, 82
Brown, Andy, 220
Brown, Arthur, 87-88, 249
Brown, Billy, 449
Brown, Bobby, 88
Brown, Charles, 117, 269
Brown, Charlie, 246, 341
Brown, Clarence 'Gatemouth', 104
Brown, Dennis, 397
Brown, Henry, 260
Brown, Horace, 361
Brown, James, 80, 87-90, 166, 225, 352, 469
Brown, Jane, 87
Brown, Joe, 83, 90, 229, 256, 292
Brown, John, 80, 132, 196

Brown, Marion, 132
Brown, Maxine, 90-91, 279-280
Brown, Michael, 310
Brown, Oscar, Jnr., 91
Brown, Paul, 5
Brown, Pete, 39-40, 78, 91, 143, 205
Brown, Peter, 49
Brown, Phil, 91
Brown, Ray, 250
Brown, Rick, 350
Brown, Roger, 90
Brown, Ruth, 178, 449
Brown, Sally, 11
Brown, Sam, 21, 90
Brown, Sandy, 122
Brown, Tom, 296
Brown, Tony, 5, 260
Brown, Vincent, 87
Browne, Ivan, 310
Browne, Jackson, 19, 29, 272, 375, 422, 503
Browning, Robert, 508
Brownlee, Mick, 380
Browns, 90
Brox, Annette, 182
Brox, Victor, 182
Bruce And Terry, 92, 330, 343, 425, 442
Bruce, Ed, 92
Bruce, Edwin, 92
Bruce, Jack, 77-78, 142-143, 182, 306, 329, 335, 389
Bruce, Tommy, 92
Bruce-Douglas, Ian, 484
Bruisers, 93
Brumley, Tom, 366
Brush, Alan, 446
Bryant, Anita, 93, 414
Bryant, Boudleaux, 162, 202
Bryant, Eldridge, 466
Bryant, Rusty, 505
Bryson, Peabo, 330
Brzezicki, Mark, 399
Bubble Puppy, 93
Buchanan, Roy, 324
Buchwald, Martyn Jerel, 285
Buck, Alan, 220
Buck, Mike, 480
Buck, Peter, 480
Buckinghams, 93
Buckley, Tim, 196, 365
Buckmaster, Paul, 471
Buda, Max, 294
Budd, Eric, 215
Budgie, 69, 208, 437
Buffalo Springfield, 24, 62, 94-95, 147, 150, 170, 355, 358, 364, 372, 464
Bullet, Jim, 22
Bunch Of Fives, 291
Bunn, Alan, 123

Bunnell, George, 459
Burch, Johnny, 142
Burdon, Eric, 9, 16-17, 95, 117, 153, 259, 352, 355
Burgess, John, 333
Burgess, Michael, 5
Burgess, Paul, 5
Burke, Dave, 456
Burke, Pat, 220
Burke, Solomon, 56, 95-96, 140, 272, 386, 480, 484
Burke, Tony, 5
Burkette, Bill, 492
Burnette, Johnny, 324, 398
Burns, Eddie, 35
Burns, Ken, 133
Burns, Paddy, 101
Burns, Ralph, 74
Burns, Tito, 12
Burrell, Kenny, 133, 445-446
Burrito Brothers, 13, 99-100, 138, 169, 375
Burrows, Clive, 123, 352
Burrows, Tony, 217, 279
Burt, David, 225
Burt, Heinz, 257, 476
Burton, Abraham, 445
Burton, James, 324, 365, 392, 411
Burton, John, 6
Burton, Trevor, 362
Bush, Richard, 17
Bushnell, Yvonne, 284
Bushy, Ron, 278
Bussch, Hans, 292
Bustamante, Alexandra, 397
Butala, Tony, 311
Butler, Billy, 96
Butler, Chris, 501
Butler, Floyd, 227
Butler, Jerry, 96-97, 115, 202, 254, 272-273, 276-277, 323, 337
Butler, Joe, 322-323
Butterfield Blues Band, 73, 97, 185, 195-196, 507
Butterfield, Billy, 134
Butterfield, Paul, 73, 97, 185, 195-196, 363, 384, 507
Butts Band, 176
Byard, Jaki, 303, 347
Bygraves, Max, 65, 85, 321, 334
Byrd, Bobby, 76, 88
Byrd, Gary, 506
Byrd, Joseph, 484
Byrds, 22, 46-47, 66, 70, 92, 94, 97-100, 132, 147-148, 167, 169-170, 206, 224, 285, 308, 320, 329, 340, 343, 350, 355,

367, 410, 464, 482
Byrne, Johnny, 459
Byrne, Sean, 139
Byrom, Larry, 458
Bystanders, 100-101, 113

C

C, Roy, 56, 101
Caddy, Alan, 296, 476
Cadets, 40, 101, 138
Cahill, Patricia, 29
Caiola, Al, 102
Calder, Tony, 375
Caldwell, Al, 459
Caldwell, Ronnie, 33
Caldwell, Steve, 377
Cale, John, 178, 246, 488
California, Randy, 258,
   451-452
Callender, Red, 346
Calvert, Bernie, 265
Calvert, Reg, 220, 386
Cambridge, John, 292
Cameron, Dave, 76, 197,
   216
Cameron, George, 310
Cammarata, Frank, 179
Camp, Bob, 234
Campbell, Alan, 50
Campbell, Alex, 102
Campbell, Brad, 290
Campbell, Cecil, 397
Campbell, Eddie, 50
Campbell, Glen, 41, 81,
   233, 295, 366
Campbell, Ian, Folk
   Group, 102-103
Campbell, James, 403
Campbell, Junior, 219,
   332
Campbell, Lorna, 102
Campbell, Rick, 86
Campbell, Tommy, 295
Campbell, William, 219,
   332
Campbell-Lyons, Patrick,
   371
Candoli, Conte, 246
Candoli, Pete, 57
Candy Flip, 89
Candyskins, 444
Cane, Ray, 267
Canetti, Jacques, 84
Cann, John, 15, 24
Canned Heat, 103-104,
   269-270, 355, 358, 378,
   507
Cannon, Ace, 67
Cannon, Freddy, 104-105
Cannon, Gus, 420
Cannonball, Wabash, 316
Cantrall, Bobby, 287
Cantrelli, Tjay, 320
Canzano, Dominic, 179
Capaldi And Frog, 477

Capaldi, Jim, 224, 257,
   477-478
Capitols, 105
Capris, 105
Captain And Tennille, 70,
   430
Captain Beefheart, 105-
   106, 227, 359
Caravelles, 106
Carey, Mariah, 226
Cargman, Jerry, 210
Carless, Mick, 249
Carlisle, Bill, 22
Carlos, Don, 141
Carlton, Larry, 158
Carman, Brian, 116
Carmichael, Hoagy, 209,
   354-355
Carnegie, Dale, 108
Carnes, Kim, 367
Carollo, Joe Frank, 463
Carpenter, Mary-Chapin,
   30
Carpenters, 13, 70, 135,
   305, 491
Carr, David, 220
Carr, Ian, 20, 158-160
Carr, James, 106-107, 375,
   382
Carr, Jesse Willard, 272
Carr, Mike, 20
Carr, Patrick, 112
Carr, Roy, 49, 395, 419
Carr, Tony, 49
Carr, Vikki, 107
Carr, Wynona, 447
Carrack, Paul, 483
Carreras, José, 26
Carrigan, Jerry, 382
Carrington, Jack, 172
Carroll, Dave, 275
Carroll, Hattie, 184
Carson, Johnny, 411
Carson, Terry, 165
Carter And Lewis, 107-
   108, 217, 379
Carter Family, 22, 109-110
Carter, Benny, 9, 122, 157
Carter, Betty, 118
Carter, Carlene, 110
Carter, Clarence, 375
Carter, Deana, 330
Carter, Jimmy, 64, 347
Carter, John, 107, 109,
   217, 279, 368, 425
Carter, Johnny, 111
Carter, June, 109, 111
Carter, Maybelle, 22
Carter, Peter, 219
Carter, Ray, 118
Carter, Ron, 158, 356
Carthy, Martin, 184
Cartwright, Alan, 399
Caryl, Ronnie, 216
Casady, Jack, 285
Cascades, 108
Casey, Al, 503

Cash, Fred, 276
Cash, Jack, 108
Cash, John R., 111
Cash, Johnny, 108-112,
   186, 197, 324, 376, 411
Cash, Peter, 112
Cash, Philip, 18
Cash, Rosanne, 108, 110
Cashman And West, 112
Cashman, Terry, 112
Casinos, 112
Cass And The
   Cassanovas, 63
Cassavetes, John, 57
Cassidy, David, 141, 149,
   343
Cassidy, Ed, 410, 452
Castaways, 112-113, 240,
   250
Castells, 113
Castle, Bill, 250
Castro, Peppy, 75
Casuals, 101, 113
Caswell, Dave, 252
Catchpole, Tony, 82
Cathedral, Grace, 246
Cato, Bob, 350
Cattini, Clem, 113, 296,
   476
Cauchi, Les, 87
Cauley, Ben, 33
Causi, Jerry, 34
Cavaliere, Felix, 164, 510
Cavallari, Tony, 247
CCS, 306
Ceballos, Wayne, 24
Cennamo, Louis, 286
Centipede, 352
Chad And Jeremy, 114
Chairmen Of The Board,
   264
Challenger, Reg, 51
Chalpin, Ed, 258, 305
Chamberlain, Alex, 310
Chamberlain, Richard,
   114
Chambers Brothers, 114-
   115, 238
Chambers, Joe, 157
Chambers, John, 213, 378
Chambers, Paddy, 63,
   201, 213, 332, 378
Chambers, Paul, 132, 157
Chameleons, 154
Chance, Larry, 191
Chandler, Bryan James,
   16, 115
Chandler, Chas, 16, 115,
   194, 258-259, 447
Chandler, Gene, 8, 96-97,
   115, 337
Chaney, Roy, 139
Channel, Bruce, 115
Channing, Carol, 316
Chantays, 116, 152
Chants, 116, 207
Chapin, Harry, 196

Chaplin, Blondie, 42
Chaplin, Charles, 126
Chapman, Michael, 253
Chapman, Mike, 31
Chapman, Philip, 241
Chapman, Roger, 212
Chapman, Steve, 291
Chapman, Tony, 261, 414
Charig, Marc, 447
Charisse, Cyd, 508
Charlatans, 116-117
Charles, Bobby, 120, 260
Charles, Bryan, 413
Charles, David, 26, 118
Charles, Don, 476
Charles, Jimmy, 196
Charles, Ray, 16, 54, 117-
   118, 137, 154, 178, 197,
   238, 245, 253, 388, 505-
   506
Charles, Sonny, 450
Charles, Teddy, 159, 346
Charters, Sam, 271
Chas And Dave, 61
Chase, Tommy, 77, 445
Chater, Kerry, 400
Chatton, Brian, 216
Checker, Chubby, 78, 118-
   119, 179, 423
Cheech And Chong, 10
Cher, 40, 70, 76, 79, 98,
   202, 238, 257, 315, 410,
   447-448, 450
Cherry, Don, 133-134
Chess Records, 59, 96,
   119-120, 138, 212, 222,
   231, 256, 280, 298, 312,
   348, 362, 472-473
Chess, Leonard, 120
Chess, Philip, 119
Chessmen, 120
Chevalier, Maurice, 502
Chevrons, 112
Cheynes, 120
Chi-Lites, 8
Chicago Line Blues Band,
   76, 286
Chicago Loop, 236
Chicken Shack, 120-121,
   280, 387, 446, 468
Chiffons, 121, 475
Chilli Willi And The Red
   Hot Peppers, 344
Chilliwack, 129
Chilton, Alex, 82
Chimes, 121
Chipmunks, 121-122
Chisholm, George, 32,
   122
Chocolate Watch Band,
   86, 122-123
Chodorov, Jerome, 58
Chordaires, 7
Christian, Charlie, 59,
   356
Christian, Neil, 20, 123
Christian, Rick, 5

Christie, Julie, 300
Christie, Lou, 123
Christy, Don, 79, 447
Christy, Sonny, 79, 447
Churchill, Chick, 468-469
Churchill, Gary, 310
Ciconne, Don, 146
Ciner, Al, 14
Cipollina, John, 401
Circus, 123 and passim
City Of Angels, 349
Claes, Johnny, 428
Clague, Dave, 79
Clancy Brothers, 262
Clancy Brothers And
    Tommy Makem, 123-
    124, 181
Clancy, Tom, 124
Clapton, Eric, 47, 62, 71,
    142, 178, 258-259, 298-
    299, 306, 317, 335-336,
    339, 380, 459, 481, 509-
    510
Clare, Alan, 456
Clarion Skiffle Group, 102
Clark And Hillman, 100
Clark, Alan, 466
Clark, Andy, 261
Clark, B., 125-126
Clark, Brian, 102
Clark, Chris, 124
Clark, Christine, 124
Clark, Dave, 6, 36, 124-
    125, 135
Clark, Dave, Five, 36,
    124-125, 135
Clark, Dee, 125-126, 480
Clark, Delecta, 125
Clark, Dick, 104, 118, 396,
    504
Clark, Gene, 97-98, 100,
    169-170, 308, 367
Clark, Harold Eugene, 97,
    169
Clark, Joe, 466
Clark, Mike, 478
Clark, Pete, 201
Clark, Petula, 126-127,
    177, 230, 254, 305, 318,
    331, 479, 503, 508
Clark, Sonny, 312
Clark, Tony, 357
Clarke, Allan, 264-266
Clarke, Eddie, 305
Clarke, Gussie, 141
Clarke, Mark, 131
Clarke, Michael, 97, 99-
    100, 340
Clarke, Ross, 177
Clarke, Steve, 294, 501
Clarke-Boland Big Band,
    428
Clasky, Richard, 425
Class, Barry, 220
Classics IV, 127-128
Claunch, Quinton, 106-107
Clay, Judy, 128, 455

Clayson, Alan, 5, 50, 84,
    164, 351, 377, 436, 478,
    480
Clayton-Thomas, David,
    72, 289
Cleaves, Jessica, 227
Clement, Jack, 92, 108
Clements, Rod, 383
Clements, Terry, 290
Clempson, Dave, 30, 131
Clemson, Terry, 178
Cliff, Jimmy, 165
Cliff, Tony, 409-410
Clifford, Doug, 144, 237
Clifford, Linda, 337
Cline, Patsy, 142, 405
Clinton, Bill, 243, 395
Clinton, George, 34, 443
Clooney, Rosemary, 134,
    466
Clouds, 129
Clowney, David Cortez,
    137
Cluskey, Conleth, 28
Clyde, Jeremy, 114
Coasters, 178, 296, 307,
    380, 388
Coates, Maurice, 84
Cobain, Kurt, 418
Cobb, Ed, 122, 456
Cobb, James, 128
Cobb, Jimmy, 157
Cobby, Richard, 7
Cobham, Billy, 158
Cocco, Lenny, 121
Cochise, 387
Cochran, Eddie, 257, 319,
    342
Cocker, Joe, 13, 113, 117,
    380, 426, 507
Cockney Rebel, 74
Coe, Michael, 371
Coeds And The Playgirls,
    74
Coff, Richard, 471
Cogan, Alma, 27, 37, 56,
    322
Cohen, David, 75, 84,
    139, 245
Cohen, Leonard, 84, 130,
    171, 214, 249, 288, 425,
    450
Cohen, Paul, 438
Cohn, Al, 12, 159
Cohn, Nik, 56, 419, 501
Colbert, Charles, 14
Cole, B.J., 421
Cole, Bill, 133, 160
Cole, Gary, 86
Cole, Michael, 421
Cole, Nat 'King', 55, 59,
    117, 136, 231
Cole, Natalie, 96
Cole, Ritchie, 459
Coleman, Cy, 54, 161
Coleman, Ornette, 106,
    488

Coleman, Ray, 49, 200,
    234, 419, 455
Coles, Brian, 22
Collier, Mike, 302, 327
Collins, Albert, 269
Collins, Bootsy, 88
Collins, Clarence, 315
Collins, Dennis, 350
Collins, Frances, 148
Collins, Glenda, 129-130,
    377
Collins, Grenville, 300,
    379
Collins, Joan, 234, 369
Collins, John, 123
Collins, Judy, 130, 196,
    234, 245, 263, 277, 290,
    381
Collins, Larry, 300
Collins, Lewis, 352
Collins, Mel, 123
Collins, Peter, 369
Collins, Phil, 216
Collins, Ray, 206, 358
Collins, Tom, 196
Collis, Roger, 352
Collum, Roy, 275
Colman, Stuart, 386
Colomby, Bobby, 72
Colon, August, 166
Colosseum, 30, 78, 131,
    212, 252, 500
Coltrane, John, 131-133,
    157-160, 278, 303, 339,
    356, 359, 372
Colville, Chris, 286
Colyer, Ken, 65
Combo, Willie, 345
Combustible Edison, 201
Comden, Betty, 57
Comerford, Paul, 201
Commodores, 361
Common, Bob, 45
Como, Perry, 23, 148
Condron, Jim, 253
Conka, Don, 320
Conley, Arthur, 133-134,
    140, 403
Conly, Paul, 319
Connelly, Reginald, 403
Connery, Sean, 334, 457
Conniff, Ray, 134-135
Connolly, Billy, 138, 273
Connor, Cecil Ingram, 99
Connors, Carol, 36
Conrad, Jess, 135, 166,
    335
Conroy, Dennis, 148
Constanten, Tom, 242
Conti, Bill, 28
Contours, 124, 135, 209,
    238
Conway, Gerry, 193, 383
Conway, Russ, 321, 396
Cooder, Ry, 193, 269, 343,
    410
Cook And Greenaway,

155, 180, 210, 312
Cook, Barbara, 58
Cook, Frank, 103, 378
Cook, Roger, 90, 155, 180,
    210
Cook, Stu, 144, 237
Cooke, Sam, 10, 16, 70,
    119, 135-137, 225, 258,
    296, 402-403, 461, 464-
    465, 505
Cooker, John Lee, 268
Cookies, 137, 304
Coonce, Erik Michael,
    241
Coonce, Rick, 241
Cooper, Andy, 32
Cooper, Dave, 484
Cooper, Mike, 182
Cooper, Mushy, 213
Cooper, Tommy, 251
Cooper, Tony, 182
Cope, Julian, 496
Copland, Aaron, 57
Copping, Chris, 380, 399
Corbitt, Jerry, 510-511
Corcoran, Bryan, 204
Cord, Joe, 148
Cordell, Ritchie, 281
Cordet, Helene, 137
Cordet, Louise, 137, 318
Corea, Chick, 158
Corneal, Jon, 169
Cornell, Lynn, 137
Cornish, Gene, 164, 510
Coronado, Dave, 358
Corsairs, 137
Cortez, Dave 'Baby', 137-
    138
Corvettes, 138
Coryell, Larry, 19
Cosby, Henry, 506
Costa, Don, 317
Costell, David, 312
Costello, Elvis, 28, 54, 376
Cottle, Albert, 464
Cotton, Billy, 345, 495
Cotton, James, 363
Cotton, Mike, 16, 300
Cotton, Paul, 276
Cougars, 138
Coulter, Phil, 138-139,
    387, 483
Council, Floyd, 35
Count Bishops, 179
Count Five, 139
Count Ossie, 218, 397
Count Talent And The
    Originals, 73
Country Joe And The
    Fish, 63, 139-140, 245,
    326, 355, 507
Countrymen, 140
Covay, Don, 140, 231, 386
Coventry, Alan, 82
Coverdale Page, 379
Coverdale, David, 379
Coverdale, Larry, 281

Cowan, Dennis, 79
Cowap, Peter, 262
Coward, Noël, 172, 208, 305
Cowsills, 141, 213
Cox, Billy, 258-259
Cox, John, 383
Cox, Michael, 141
Cox, Mike, 194
Cox, Neil, 103
Cox, Terry, 283, 306, 383, 389
Coxsone, Lloyd, 141
Coyne, Kevin, 352
Craig, Judy, 121
Craine, Don, 178
Cramer, Floyd, 23, 141-142, 162, 390
Crane, Tony, 343
Crane, Vincent, 87-88
Craswell, Denny, 112-113
Crawford, Dave, 129
Crawford, Jack, 57
Crawford, Joan, 57
Crawford, Michael, 69
Crawford, Randy, 140
Cray, Robert, 140, 297
Crazy Elephant, 236
Crazy Horse, 372
Cream, 142-143 and *passim*
Creation, 143 and *passim*
Creatore, Luigi, 475
Creedence Clearwater Revival, 24, 144-145, 237, 339, 507
Cregan, Jim, 74
Creme, Lol, 326
Crewe, Bob, 104, 145, 221, 424, 449, 493
Crewsdon, Roy, 227
Cribbins, Bernard, 333
Crickets, 145-146, 317, 487
Crill, Connie, 294
Criss, Sonny, 246
Criterions, 112
Critters, 146, 167
Croce, Jim, 112, 491
Croce, Joe, 121
Crocitto, Margo, 236
Crome Cyrcus, 146
Cropper, Steve, 80, 140, 146, 297, 330, 336, 385, 404, 424, 442
Crosby And Nash, 98, 147, 206, 240, 242, 261, 265, 289
Crosby, Bing, 32, 203, 279, 501
Crosby, David, 13, 94, 97-98, 147, 261, 285, 289, 367
Crosby, Stills And Nash, 98, 206, 242, 261, 265, 289
Crosby, Stills, Nash And

Young, 13, 94, 100, 129, 147, 240, 507
Crouch, Nicky, 212, 352
Crow, Terry, 364
Crowell, Rodney, 110
Crowl, Charles, 284
Crowther, Bruce, 5
Crowther, Leslie, 251
Cruise, Tom, 43
Crumb, Ann, 69
Crummey, Christopher, 428
Crusaders, 123, 378-379
Crutcher, Bettye, 33, 457
Crutchley, Steve, 459
Cruzados, 188
Cryan' Shames, 148
Crystals, 148 and *passim*
Cubert, Joe, 424
Cuckoo Patrol, 227
Cuff Links, 148
Cuffley, John, 219
Cunningham, Billy, 82
Cunningham, Carl, 33
Cupid's Inspiration, 148
Curcio, Paul, 352
Curd, John, 257, 344
Curtis, Adrian, 247
Curtis, Chris, 428-429
Curtis, Lee, And The All-Stars, 61, 149, 213
Curtis, Paul, 247
Curtis, Phil, 216
Curtis, Sam, 247
Curtis, Sonny, 145
Cymbal, Johnny, 149
Cyrkle, 149, 431

D

D'Abo, Michael, 7, 150, 220, 329
D'Arby, Terence Trent, 163
Dacres, Desmond, 164
Daily Flash, 150
Daisley, Bob, 121
Daking, Geoff, 75
Dakotas, 27, 150, 199, 296, 307, 333, 429
Dale And Grace, 150
Dale, Bobby, 173
Dale, Dick, 151-152
Dale, Glen, 219-220
Dale, Jim, 152, 254, 479
Dalton, David, 209, 244, 291, 419
Dalton, John, 143, 300-301
Daltrey, Peter, 294
Daltrey, Roger, 208, 499
Dalziel, Denis, 267
Damone, Vic, 26
Damrell, Joseph, 293
Dana, Vic, 153
Dancho, Dante, 284
Dando, Jill, 409

Dane Stephens And The Deepbeats, 207
Dane, Barbara, 115
Dane, Patrick, 402
Daniels, Billy, 161
Daniels, Eddie, 11
Daniels, Joe, 324
Daniels, Maxine, 325
Danko, Rick, 185, 256
Dankworth, Johnny, 137
Dantalion's Chariot, 352
Dante, Ron, 19, 148, 167, 304
Danus, Vicens, 318
Darin, Bobby, 62, 153-154, 245, 249, 304, 437
Darling, Erik, 420
Darrell And The Oxfords, 475
Darren, James, 154-155, 205
Darron, Benny, 22
Darrow, Chris, 138, 294
Darway, Chris, 146
Dash, Leslie, 257
Daughtry, Dean, 128
Dave Dee, Dozy, Beaky, Mick And Tich, 155, 210, 216
Davenport, Darius LaNoue, 24
Davenport, Lester, 168
David And Jonathan, 155-156
David, Charles, 26, 118
David, Hal, 27-28, 156, 225, 233, 288-289, 454, 493, 496
David, Kal, 276
David, Mack, 26, 57
Davidson, Brian 'Blinky', 24
Davidson, Jim, 135
Davidson, Lenny, 124
Davies, Alan, 7
Davies, Alun, 383
Davies, Cyril, 77, 97, 157, 306-307, 335, 363
Davies, Dave, 300-302, 380
Davies, Douglas, 62, 300
Davies, Graham, 72, 335
Davies, Hunter, 49-50
Davies, John R.T., 466
Davies, Leonard, 84, 379
Davies, Mansell, 103
Davies, Megan, 18
Davies, Ray, 62, 84, 109, 175, 299-302, 380
Davies, Trevor, 155
Davis Sisters, 162-163
Davis, Barry, 160
Davis, Bill, 160, 445
Davis, Billie, 157, 204
Davis, Billy, 215
Davis, Carl, 8, 115, 504
Davis, Charles, 135

Davis, Clive, 373
Davis, Danny, 23, 142, 316
Davis, Don, 33-34
Davis, Gary, 160
Davis, Georgia, 162
Davis, Hal, 266
Davis, Jack, 160, 162, 396
Davis, Joe, 284
Davis, Mac, 372
Davis, Mark, 157
Davis, Marlena, 377
Davis, Mary, 284
Davis, Mel, 471
Davis, Michael, 338
Davis, Miles, 131, 133, 157-160, 240, 339, 346, 372, 443
Davis, Milt, 159
Davis, Newman, 210, 372
Davis, Paul, 160
Davis, Richard, 160
Davis, Sammy, Jnr., 86, 136, 153, 160-161, 305, 369
Davis, Skeeter, 162-163, 316, 319
Davis, Spencer, Group, 10, 33, 163-164, 194, 267, 280, 387, 477-478, 492
Davis, Tim, 7
Davis, Wild Bill, 445
Davis, Willie, 164
Davison, Harold, 444
Davison, Wild Bill, 122
Dawes, Tom, 149
Dawson, Alan, 148
Dawson, Colin, 499
Dawson, John, 387
Dawson, Johnny, 196
Day, Alice, 60
Day, Bob, 12
Day, Bobby, 76
Day, Doris, 92, 343
Day, Jimmy, 101
Day, Mark, 49
Day, Terry, 343
Day, Wyatt, 21
Daybreakers, 421
Daylighters, 202
De Cocq, Jim, 210
De La Barreda, Antonio, 104
De La Parra, Adolfo, 103
De La Parra, Fito, 103-104
De Maria, Walter, 488
De Paris, Wilbur, 178
De Paul, Lynsey, 20
De Veuve, Doreen, 210
De Vore, Darrell, 116
de Young, Cliff, 129
Deacon Blue, 28
Dead Kennedys, 364
Dean, James, 127, 161, 183
Dean, Johnny, 36

Dean, Paul, 170
Dean, Roger, 335
Deane, Sandy, 283
DeCarr, Dennis, 352
Decker, Jack, 146
Dee, Alan, 120, 164
Dee, Dave, 155, 210, 216
Dee, David, 155, 394
Dee, Jay, 77, 480
Dee, Joey, And The
    Starliters, 164, 510
Dee, Sandra, 154, 502
Deene, Carol, 164
Deep Purple, 21, 199,
    217, 252, 466
DeFrancesco, Joey, 446
DeJohnette, Jack, 158
Dekker, Desmond, 164-
    165
Del Din, Robert, 191
Del-Satins, 87, 405
Del-Vikings, 279
Delaney And Bonnie, 331
Delaney, Eric, 32
Delfonics, 315
Dell-Vikings, 405
Dello, Pete, 267
Dells, 312
Delvy, Richard, 52
Dennerlein, Barbara, 445
Dennis, Denny, 44
Dennis, Mike, 178
Dennisons, 165
Dennistoun, 253
Denny, David, 228
Denny, John, 166, 328
Denny, Martin, 165-166
Denny, Sandy, 344
Densmore, John, 175,
    177
Denton, Mickey, 112
Denver, John, 70, 350,
    384
Denver, Karl, 166
DePrisco, Pat, 121
Derek And The Dominos,
    62, 509
Derrick, Diz, 380
Derringer, Rick, 338
Des Barres, Michael, 246
DeSanto, Sugar Pie, 38,
    166-167
DeShannon, Jackie, 27,
    79, 146, 156, 167, 372,
    380
Desi And Billy, 170
Desmond, Norma, 126
Destroy All Monsters,
    338
Detergents, 167
Devey, Willie, 101
Deviants, 168
DeVille, Willy, 388
DeVito, Nick, 221
DeVito, Tommy, 221
Devotions, 168
Dewar, Jim, 323

Dewey, Greg, 139, 326
Dexys Midnight Runners,
    497, 504
Dey, Tony, 150
Diamond Head, 155
Diamond, Neil, 27, 37,
    56, 70, 213, 353
Diamonde, Dick, 192
Diaz, Herman, 201
Dick And Dee Dee, 168
Dick, Michael, 97
Dickey, Robert Lee, 400
Dickinson, Angie, 27
Dickon, Richie, 75
Dickson, Barbara, 375
Dickson, Jim, 97
Diddley, Bo, 60, 120, 168-
    169, 231, 256, 414-415,
    422
Dietrich, Marlene, 26,
    208, 321
DiGilio, Frank, 179
Diken, Dennis, 442
Dillard And Clark, 100,
    169
Dillard, Doug, 169-170
Dillard, George, 169
Dillard, Rodney, 170
Dillards, 169-170
Dillon, Eric, 214
Dillon, Paul, 192
Diltz, Henry, 147
Dimino, Rick, 148
DiMucci, Dion, 53, 170-
    171
Dines, Peter, 252
Dino, Desi And Billy, 170
Dion And The Belmonts,
    170-171
Dion, Celine, 226, 334
Dire Straits, 188, 333
Disco Tex And The Sex-
    O-Lettes, 145
DiScuillo, Hank, 191
Disney, Walt, 17, 345
Distel, Sacha, 230
Dixie Cups, 37, 171-172
Dixie Flyers, 331
Dixon, Eugene, 115
Dixon, Luther, 213, 437
Dmochowski, Alex, 123,
    182, 257
Dobson, Anita, 69, 437
Dobson, Bonnie, 421
Dobson, Lyn, 329, 471
Docherty, Tony, 296
Doctor West's Medicine
    Show And Jug Band,
    172
Dodd, Coxsone, 345
Dodd, Dick, 52, 456
Dodd, Ken, 172, 218, 321
Dodgy, 500
Dodson, Brian, 315
Dodson, Larry, 33
Doe, John, 85
Dog Soldier, 253

Doggett, Bill, 457
Doggett, Peter, 5, 50, 352
Doherty, Denny, 197, 327
Dolan, Michael, 249
Dolan, Steve, 249
Dolby, Ray, Dr., 172
Dolby, Thomas, 173
Dolenz, Mickey, 83, 353-
    354
Dolinger, Jim, 247
Dolphy, Eric, 132-133,
    347
Dominic, John, 76
Domino, Fats, 81, 118,
    345, 367
Dominoes, 253, 504
Don And Dewey, 447
Don And The Goodtimes,
    299
Donahue, Tom, 50, 255
Donaldson, Lou, 445
Donaldson, Pat, 153
Doncaster, Patrick, 49, 61,
    409
Donegan, Lonnie, 32, 208
Donegan, Norman, 8
Donen, Stanley, 58
Donlinger, Jim, 18
Donlinger, Tom, 18
Donna, Jim, 112
Donnellan, Jay, 320
Donner, Ral, 173
Donovan, 29, 173-174,
    208, 283, 293, 425
Donovan, Jason, 274
Doobie Brothers, 351, 484
Doonican, Val, 174-175
Doors, 175-177 and
    passim
Dorman, Lee, 278
Dors, Diana, 310
Dorsett, Chris, 286
Dorsey, Lee, 40, 177
Dorsey, Tommy, 153
Dothan Sextet, 400
Dott, Gerald, 277
Doubleday, Marcus, 195,
    290
Douglas, Alan, 259
Douglas, Chip, 482
Douglas, Craig, 177, 396
Douglas, Jim, 482
Douglas, Josephine, 237
Douglas, Kirk, 110
Douglas, Paul, 51
Douglas, Steve, 193
Douglas, Tony, 505
Dovells, 37, 178-179, 377
Dowd, Tom, 62, 178, 454
Dowell, Joe, 293
Dower, David, 119
Downes, Bob, 15, 113
Downliners Sect, 178-179,
    364, 397
Doyle, Jimmy, 436
Dozier, Lamont, 263-264
Dr. Feelgood, 179

Dr. John, 21, 40, 73, 388,
    446, 466
Dr. Strangely Strange,
    179, 219
Drachen Theaker, 87
Dragon, Daryl, 42
Drake, Charlie, 135, 153
Drake, Jay, 287
Drake, John, 14
Drake, Kevin, 352
Draper, Robert, 419
Dread, Blacker, 141
Dreamers, 7, 61, 74, 179,
    210, 227
Dreamlovers, 179
Dreja, Chris, 509
Drew, Ronnie, 181
Drifters, 27, 53, 178-181,
    284, 292, 297-298, 304,
    407, 431, 480, 496
Driscoll, Julie, 181, 237
Drobinicki, Carol, 405
Druckman, Joel, 79
Druian, Greg, 326
Drummond, Tim, 158
Dry City Scat Band, 294
Dryden, Spencer, 285
Dubliners, 138, 181-182
Duddy, Lyn, 205
Dudley, John, 313
Duffy's Nucleus, 389
Duffy, Raymond, 219
Dulfer, Candy, 158
Dummer, John, Blues
    Band, 182
Dunbar, Aynsley,
    Retaliation, 123, 182,
    257, 335, 352, 359
Duncan, Gary, 86, 401-
    402
Duncan, Kirk, 90
Dundas, David, 70
Dundy, Elaine, 395
Dunford, Michael, 364
Dunkerley, John, 102-103
Dunn, James, 179
Dupree, Champion Jack,
    53, 67
Dupree, Cornell, 296
Dupree, Simon, 182
Dupree, Simon, And The
    Big Sound, 182
Duprees, 183
Durante, Jimmy, 160
Dure, Mike, 210
Durham, Judith, 431
Durrant, Elmy, 216
Durrill, Johnny, 490
Dwyer, Bernie, 227
Dyer, Peter, 459
Dylan, Bob, 3, 30, 45, 47,
    73, 75, 86, 98-99, 103,
    109, 171, 183-191, 193,
    197, 211-212, 234, 236,
    240, 243, 249, 255-256,
    259, 262, 266, 372, 376,
    381, 384, 412, 427, 442,

470, 475, 482, 485
Dymond, John, 155
Dyre, Arthur, 359

E

E Street Band, 78
Eadon, Gus, 321
Eagles, 19, 75, 164, 169
Earl Sixteen, 141
Earl, James, 115
Earl-Jean, 137
Earls, 191
Earth Band, 329
Earth Opera, 191-192, 196
Earth, Wind And Fire, 313
East Of Eden, 50, 192
East, Nathan, 455
Easterby, Roger, 302, 486
Easton, Elliot, 144
Easton, Eric, 240, 414, 416
Easybeats, 192-193, 241, 318
Eaton, Roger, 75
Eaton, Wally, 128
Echols, John, 320
Eckstine, Billy, 19, 157, 398
Eclection, 193
Eddie And The Hot Rods, 401
Eddy, Chris, 368
Eddy, Duane, 53, 74, 193
Eden, John, 5
Edgar, Ron, 344
Edge, Graeme, 357
Edison Lighthouse, 217
Edmonton Symphony Orchestra, 399
Edmonton, Dennis, 458
Edmonton, Jerry, 458
Edmunds, Dave, 321, 434
Edsels, 194
Edward, Charles, 58
Edward, Jim, 177
Edwards, Dennis, 135, 467
Edwards, Earl, 115
Edwards, George, 247
Edwards, Jackie, 10, 194, 345, 371
Edwards, Millard, 201
Edwards, Nokie, 490
Edwards, Steve, 452
Edwards, Tommy, 222
Edwards, Wilfred, 194
Einarson, John, 95
Eire Apparent, 194
El Dorados, 81
Elbert, Donnie, 194-195, 311
Electric Flag, 73, 195, 236, 290, 355
Electric Light Orchestra,

20, 362
Electric Prunes, 195
Elektra Records, 21, 64, 75, 97, 130, 170, 175, 196, 257, 261, 320, 326, 338, 374, 380, 406, 420, 422
Elgins, 196, 466
Eliot, T.S., 232
Ellington, Duke, 12, 20, 54, 132-133, 157, 162, 303, 347, 506
Ellington, Ray, 335
Elliot, 'Mama' Cass, 196, 420
Elliot, Mike, 220
Elliott, Bern, And The Fenmen, 197
Elliott, Earl, 424
Elliott, Garth, 262
Elliott, Jack, 187
Elliott, Marc, 374
Elliott, Ramblin' Jack, 30, 197-198
Elliott, Ron, 50
Ellis, Alfred, 88
Ellis, Alton, 397
Ellis, David, 343
Ellis, Glyn, 218
Ellis, Hortense, 194
Ellis, Ian, 129
Ellis, Keith, 306
Ellis, Ray, 462
Ellis, Shirley, 198
Ellis, Steve, 320
Ellis, Vivian, 70
Ellison, Andy, 286
Ellison, Lorraine, 56, 198
Ellwood, Alan, 19
Ellwood, Robert, 19
Elmore, Greg, 86, 401
Elsdon, Alan, 32, 219
Elston, Harry, 227
Ely, Jack, 299
Emerson, Keith, 21, 370, 492
Emerson, Lake And Palmer, 371
Emery, Ralph, 162
Emma, John, 5
Endino, Jack, 74
Engber, Evan, 172
Engel, Scott, 493-495
Engemann, Bob, 311
England, John, 16, 119, 267, 476
England, Paul, 423, 511
Engle, Butch, And The Styx, 51
English, Michael, 21, 249
English, Scott, 8
Ennis, Ray, 462
Eno, Brian, 7
Enthoven, David, 7
Entire Sioux Nation, 205
Entner, Warren, 241
Entwistle, John, 499

Episode Six, 63, 198-199, 378
Epp, Fenrus, 294
Epps, Preston, 372
Epstein, Brian, 37, 44, 47, 49, 63, 68, 149, 199-200, 223, 238, 280, 333, 343, 375, 378, 459
Equals, 200, 465
Ercolani, James, 154
Erickson, Roky, 471
Errico, Greg, 443
Errico, Jan, 352
Erskine, Marshall, 51
Ertegun, Ahmet, 94, 147, 178
Ervin, Booker, 303, 347
Ervin, DiFosco, 278
Escorts, 200-201, 265, 462, 510
Escott, Colin, 394-395
Eskerson, Dave, 63
ESP, 28, 228
Esposito, Mike, 75
Esquires, 201, 442
Esquivel, 166, 201
Essex, 201-202 and passim
Estefan, Gloria, 226
Estes, Sleepy John, 339
Estrada, Roy, 358
Etheridge, John, 447
Eubanks, Darrell, 33
Eurythmics, 506
Evans, Bill, 54-55, 157-158, 422
Evans, Bob, 484
Evans, Chris, 409
Evans, David, 456
Evans, Ernest, 118
Evans, Gil, 20, 157, 160
Evans, John, 82
Evans, Keith, 178
Evans, Maureen, 202
Evans, Mike, 8, 315, 343
Evans, Nick, 447
Evans, Paul, 90, 492
Evans, Tommy, 180
Evans, Tornado, 123
Even Dozen Jug Band, 191
Everett, Betty, 96, 202
Everett, Kenny, 294
Everett, Rupert, 188
Everly Brothers, 12, 51, 87, 110, 113, 202-204, 233, 319, 375, 415, 438
Everly, Don, 202-204
Everly, Phil, 113, 204, 408
Evers, Barbara, 436
Everything But The Girl, 235
Exciters, 36, 56, 204, 245
Eyes, 204-205 and passim
Eyes Of Blue, 205
Eyre, Mickey, 214
Eyre, Tommy, 182

F

Fabares, Shelley, 155, 205, 442
Fabray, Nanette, 205
Fabric, Bent, 55
Fabulous Rhinestones, 276
Factotums, 379
Fagen, Donald, 284
Fagin, Joe, 90
Fahey, John, 206-207
Fairfield Parlour, 294
Fairies, 207 and passim
Fairley, Pat, 219, 332
Fairport Convention, 103, 278, 283
Fairs, Jim, 148
Fairweather-Low, Andy, 14, 261
Faith, Adam, 15, 69, 207-208, 250, 319, 421, 435, 437
Faith, Percy, 54, 102
Faithfull, Marianne, 113, 137, 167, 208-209, 375, 415, 417
Falcons, 209, 217, 385
Fame, Georgie, 12, 91, 177, 209-210, 257, 397, 445
Fame, Herb, 381
Family Dogg, 15, 210
Family Tree, 86, 210
Fandango, 13, 399
Fann, Leroy, 422
Fanny, 219
Fantastic Baggys, 36, 210-211, 442
Fardon, Don, 211, 406, 448
Farina, Richard, 29, 75, 130
Farinas, 212, 224
Farley, Frank, 150, 296
Farlowe, Chris, 76, 131, 212, 286, 306, 353, 375, 379, 483
Farmer, Art, 505
Farmer, Steve, 14
Farnon, Robert, 54
Faron's Flamingos, 135, 212-213
Farr, Gary, 213
Farrar, John, 408
Farrell, Brian, 247
Farrell, Louie, 247
Farrell, Wes, 213
Farren, Mick, 168, 394-395, 419
Farrow, Mia, 86, 369
Faryar, Cyrus, 234, 261
Fascinations, 213
Fat Mattress, 213-214, 217, 259
Faust, Luke, 278

Favio, Tony, 167
Fayad, Frank, 320
Feemster, Herbert, 381
Feeny, Harry, 413
Feiten, Buzzy, 510
Felder, Jerome, 388
Feldthouse, Solomon, 294
Felix, Julie, 214
Felix, Mike, 344
Fenda, Jaymes, And The Vulcans, 487
Fender, Freddy, 441
Fender, Leo, 151
Fendermen, 214
Fennelly, Michael, 344
Fenner, John, 32
Fenton, Shane, 214, 265, 318
Fentones, 214-215
Fenwick, Ray, 10, 163
Ferguson, Jay, 451
Ferguson, John, 451
Ferguson, Michael, 116
Ferguson, Tony, 250
Ferneborg, Roland F., 453
Ferrara, Fred, 87
Fever Tree, 215
Fielder, Jim, 72, 94, 358
Fields, Dorothy, 161
Fields, Gracie, 321
5th Dimension, 215
Figueiredo, Larry, 191
Finlay, Dave, 349
Finlay, John, 407
Finley, Bruce, 448
Finn, Mickey, 483
Finnegan, John, 75
Finnegan, Mike, 63
Finnie, Lance, 209
Finnis, Rob, 450
Fireballs, 215-216, 235
Fish, C.J., 139-140
Fisher, Bobby, 233
Fisher, Eddie, 19, 69
Fisher, John, 433
Fisher, Martin, 192
Fisher, Matthew, 15, 179, 399
Fisher, Morgan, 320
Fito, Alfredo, 19
Fitzgerald, Anne, 405
Fitzgerald, Ella, 132
Fitzpatrick, James, 450
Five Americans, 490
Five Echoes, 465
Flack, Roberta, 27, 254-255, 339
Flamin' Groovies, 450
Flaming Star, 391, 395
Flaming Youth, 216
Flamingos, 81, 135, 212-213, 382
Flanagan, Kevin, 178
Flanagan, Ralph, 102
Flanagan, Tommy, 132
Flanders, Tommy, 76
Flatt And Scruggs, 109

Fleck, John, 456
Flee-Rekkers, 216
Fleerackers, Peter, 216
Fleetwood Mac, 42, 53, 120, 336, 468
Fleetwood, Mick, 76, 120, 335, 449
Fleetwoods, 153
Fleming, Robert, 196
Fletcher, Tony, 501
Flint, Hughie, 335
Flippo, Chet, 395, 419
Flirtations, 61, 217
Flo And Eddie, 237, 308, 359, 482
Floating Bridge, 217
Flock, 217
Flores, Bill, 122
Flowerpot Men, 108, 214, 217, 279
Floyd, Eddie, 209, 217-218, 385
Flying Burrito Brothers, 13, 99-100, 138, 169, 375
Fogerty, John, 96, 144, 237
Fogerty, Tom, 144, 237
Foley, Ellen, 246
Foley, Red, 81, 389
Folkes Brothers, 218, 397
Folschow, Bob, 112
Folwell, Bill, 21
Fonda, Jane, 87
Fonfara, Mike, 195
Fontana, D.J., 67, 218, 389, 392
Fontana, Wayne, 218, 346
Fontenot, Hadley, 31
Foos, Ron, 406
Forbes, Rand, 484
Ford, Aiden, 103
Ford, Clinton, 218-219
Ford, Dean, And The Gaylords, 219, 331
Ford, Emile, And The Checkmates, 219, 254, 292, 318
Ford, Ernie, 309
Ford, John, 428, 487
Ford, Mary, 219
Ford, Perry, 108, 279
Ford, Richard, 209
Ford, Robben, 209
Ford, Russell, 319
Ford, Tennessee Ernie, 309
Fordham, John, 5, 428
Forest, 219 and passim
Formby, George, 223
Forssi, Ken, 320, 461
Forster, Colin, 487-488
Forsyth, Bruce, 86
Fortunes, 219-220 and passim
Foster, Joe, 6
Foster, John, 201

Foster, Julia, 221
Foster, Stephen, 98
Foster, Teddy, 414
Fotheringay, 153, 193
Foundations, 220 and passim
Fountain, Pete, 309
Four Brothers, 114
Four Bucketeers, 427
Four Freshmen, 40, 279
Four Pennies, 36, 220
Four Seasons, 145-146, 149, 221-222, 241, 279, 304, 375, 492, 503
Four Tops, 135, 222-223, 249, 264, 310, 361, 412, 460-461, 468
Four Tunes, 11
Fourmost, 45, 199, 223, 446
Fowler, Mick, 241
Fowley, Kim, 7, 26, 212, 223, 364, 413
Foxx, Inez And Charlie, 224
Frame, Pete, 5, 335, 351
Frampton, Peter, 261, 444
Francis, Connie, 68, 304, 321, 377, 429
Francis, John, 139
Francis, Ritchie, 205
Franco, Joe, 237
Francois, Claude, 230
Frank, Edward, 371
Frank, Jackson C., 214
Frank, Joe, 168, 463
Frank, Johnny, 112
Franklin, Aretha, 62, 91, 136, 140, 156, 178, 224-226, 254, 337, 472
Franklin, Bruce, 337
Franklin, C.L., Rev., 224
Franklin, Erma, 56, 226
Franklin, Mark, 226
Franklin, Melvin, 466
Franz, Johnny, 414, 454, 493, 495
Fraser, Andy, 335
Fraser, Ian, 86
Fraternity Of Man, 206, 226-227
Fratto, Russ, 59
Frazier, Joe, 350
Frazier, Lynn, 421
Fred, John, And His Playboy Band, 227
Freddie And The Dreamers, 210, 227
Freed, Alan, 59, 315, 396, 411
Freeman, Charlie, 330-331
Freeman, Ernie, 26
Freeman, Gerry, 18
Freeman, Lee, 459
Freiberg, David, 401
French, Pete, 62

Freyer, Davey, 479
Fricke, David, 419
Friedman, Myra, 291
Friends Of Distinction, 227-228
Frost, Max, 18
Frost, Richie, 365
Frumious Bandersnatch, 228
Fry, Royston, 76
Fryer, Fritz, 220
Fryer, Hank, 508
Fryers, Chris, 448
Fugs, 168, 228, 267
Full Tilt Boogie Band, 290
Fuller, Bobby, 228-229
Fuller, Jerry, 400
Fuller, Jim, 228, 461
Fulson, Lowell, 270
Funicello, Annette, 17
Funkadelic, 88
Fuqua, Harvey, 231, 280, 494
Furay, Richie, 24, 94-95
Fureys, 138
Fury, Billy, 166, 214, 229, 292, 389, 476
Fuzzy Duck, 15

G

G-Clefs, 104
Gabler, Milt, 293
Gadd, Steve, 209, 459
Gadenwitz, Peter, 58
Gaff, Billy, 261
Gage, Pete, 497
Gaines, Steven, 44, 49
Gainey, Earl, 503
Gainsbourg, Serge, 66, 230
Galahad, Kid, 391, 395
Gale, Eric, 19
Gall, France, 230
Gallagher, Benny, 330
Gallagher, George, 387
Gallagher, Mickey, 441
Gallagher, Noel, 28
Gallagher, Regina, 405
Gallucci, Don, 299
Galway, James, 139, 329
Gamble And Huff, 62, 373, 386, 402
Gamble, R.C., 26
Gandy, Fred, 207
Ganser, Margie, 433
Gantry, Elmer, 487-488
Ganyou, George, 407
Garbarek, Jan, 132
Garborit, John, 146
Garcia, Jerry, 7, 241, 244, 285
Garcia, Juan, 201
Gardiner, Ricky, 51
Gardner, Bunk, 358-359

Gardner, Kim, 66, 143, 317
Gardner, Mike, 233
Gardner, Morris, 179
Garf, Gene, 365
Garforth, Richard, 219
Garfunkel, Art, 437-438
Garland, Judy, 37, 321
Garland, Red, 132, 157
Garner, Bob, 143, 343
Garner, James, 92, 293
Garner, Paul, 327
Garon, Jesse, 389
Garrett, Bobby, 77
Garrett, Pat, 187, 190-191
Garrett, Snuff, 317
Garrett, Tommy, 486
Garrick, David, 231
Garrison, Jimmy, 132
Garrity, Freddie, 227
Garwood, Rodney, 484
Gary, John, 494
Gaston, Henry, 503
Gates, David, 202, 288, 449, 466
Gateway Singers, 314
Gatlin, Larry, 109
Gaudio, Bob, 221, 493
Gavin, Mike, 5
Gavin, Pete, 286
Gayden, Mac, 20, 306
Gaydon, John, 7
Gaye, Barbie, 345
Gaye, Ellie, 245
Gaye, Marvin, 34, 140, 231-233, 238, 264, 303, 332, 349, 361, 464-465, 469, 498-499
Gayle, Crystal, 109
Gaynor, Gloria, 274
Gayten, Paul, 260
Gee, Mickey, 321
Gee, Rosko, 478
Geffen, David, 187, 373
General, Mikey, 141
Genesis, 166, 209, 216, 235, 465
Gentle Giant, 183, 205
Gentle Soul, 465
Gentle, Johnny, 44, 113
Gentry, Bobbie, 233
Gentry, Ruby, 233
Gentrys, 233-234, 276
George, Barbara, 40, 134
George, Lowell, 206, 226, 242, 246, 359, 457
George, Nelson, 239, 362
George, Samuel, 105
George, Terry, 32
Geraldo, 280, 305, 324, 456
Geronimo Black, 359
Gerrard, Rod, 262
Gerry And The Pacemakers, 137, 165, 199, 234, 333, 427, 429, 459

Getz, Dave, 63, 139
Getz, Stan, 12, 132, 234-235, 346, 428
Geyer, Dennis, 7
Gibb, Barry, 221
Gibb, Maurice, 323
Gibbons Band, 275, 317
Gibbons, Steve, 275, 317
Gibbs, Mike, 20
Gibson, Bob, 234, 374, 380
Gibson, Butch, 426
Gibson, Colin, 441
Gibson, Don, 23, 376
Gibson, James, 209
Gibson, Jerry, 257
Gibson, Jill, 327
Gibson, Terry, 178
Gibson, Wayne, 379
Giguere, Russ, 22
Gilbert, Ronnie, 75
Gilberto, Astrud, 234-235
Gilberto, João, 234-235
Giles, Gary, 459
Gill, Andy, 190
Gill, Bob, 148
Gill, Cal, 487
Gill, Carolyn, 287
Gill, Geoff, 446
Gill, Johnny, 239, 361
Gill, Millie, 487
Gillan, Ian, 198-199
Gillespie, Dizzy, 131, 157, 159, 339, 346
Gillett, Charlie, 296
Gilliam, Holly Michelle, 327
Gillingham, Joe, 479
Gilmer, Jimmy, And The Fireballs, 216, 235
Gilmour, David, 34
Gingold, Hermione, 502
Ginsberg, Allen, 30, 187
Ginsburg, Arnie, 282
Girard, Chuck, 113
Giuliano, Geoffrey, 49, 419
Glascock, Brian, 235
Glascock, John, 121, 235
Glass Menagerie, 235, 328
Gleason, Jackie, 370
Gleason, Ralph J., 286
Glen, Beverly, 465
Glickstein, Fred, 217
Glover, Henry, 426
Glover, Roger, 198-199
Goddard, Geoff, 61, 313, 342, 476
Godding, Brian, 74
Godfrey, Arthur, 93
Godley And Creme, 326
Godley, Kevin, 326
Gods, 24, 49, 235
Goffin, David, 91
Goffin, Gerry, 99, 145, 235, 304, 315, 330, 353
Goffin/King, 45, 145,

236, 450
Goins, Herbie, 236
Goldberg, Barry, 73, 195, 236
Goldie And The Gingerbreads, 236
Goldman, Albert, 395
Goldner, George, 172
Goldsboro, Bobby, 90
Goldstein, Harvey, 195
Golliwogs, 144, 237
Golson, Benny, 303, 505
Gomelsky, Giorgio, 181, 237, 375, 509-510
Gomez, Tony, 220
Good Rats, 237, 486
Good, Jack, 135, 141, 166, 237, 398, 407
Gooden, Sam, 96, 276
Goodhand-Tait, Philip, 123
Goodies, 25, 168
Goodman, Benny, 58, 161, 328, 420
Goodman, Jerry, 217
Goodman, Steve, 423
Goodsall, John, 82
Goosly, Ronald, 284
Gopal, Sam, 413
Gordon, Billy, 135
Gordon, Derv, 465
Gordon, Jim, 478
Gordon, John, 395
Gordon, Johnny, 296
Gordon, Lincoln, 200
Gordon, Martin, 286
Gordon, Michael, 33
Gordon, Mike, 421
Gordon, Robert, 395
Gordy, Anna, 232
Gordy, Berry, 32, 222, 231, 238-239, 264, 287, 334, 348, 361-362, 412, 460, 466, 497-498, 504-505
Gore, Lesley, 239, 435
Gorka, Kenny, 146
Gorman, Freddy, 264
Gorman, John, 427
Gottleib, Lou, 314
Gould, Don, 18
Goulden, Tony, 486
Goulding, Tim, 179
Gouldman, Graham, 218, 346, 374, 509
Goulet, Robert, 239-240, 502
Gourdine, Anthony, 315
Grabham, Mick, 387, 399
Graham Central Station, 443
Graham, Bill, 188, 240, 285
Graham, Bobby, 377, 379
Graham, Bruce, 142, 306
Graham, Bryson, 453
Graham, Davey, 335

Graham, Ernie, 194
Graham, John, 5, 240
Graham, Larry, 443
Graham, Lee, 146, 309
Graham, Mike, 453
Grainer, Ron, 69
Granahan, Gerry, 284
Grand Funk Railroad, 236
Granito, Carmine, 19
Grant, Al, 126
Grant, Eddy, 200, 465
Grant, Juanita, 334
Grant, Julie, 83, 240
Grant, Keith, 178
Grant, Marshall, 108
Grapefruit, 240-241
Grass Roots, 10, 36, 70, 211, 241, 320, 442
Grateful Dead, 7, 13, 41, 99, 189-190, 228, 240-244, 285, 291, 355, 421, 478, 507
Gravenites, Nick, 63, 97, 195, 290
Gray, Dobie, 244-245
Gray, Eddie, 281
Gray, Michael, 190, 360
Gray, Owen, 10, 218
Gray, Roger, 148
Graziano, Lee, 14
Grease Band, 182, 194, 208, 453
Great Awakening, 245
Great Guitars, 60, 169
Great Society, 245, 285
Grebb, Marty, 93, 247
Grech, Ric, 71, 73, 145, 212
Gréco, Juliette, 230
Green, Adolph, 57
Green, Al, 80, 167, 404
Green, Alan, 321
Green, Bill, 260
Green, Dick, 335
Green, Doc, 180
Green, Doc, Jnr., 180
Green, Jerome, 168
Green, Jerry, 135
Green, John, 53
Green, Karl, 262
Green, Mick, 150, 296, 336, 449
Green, Peter, 53, 92, 182, 335-336, 449
Green, Tony, 150
Greenaway, Roger, 155, 180, 210
Greenbaum, Norman, 172
Greenberg, Florence, 436
Greene, Brian, 480
Greene, Charlie, 480
Greene, Linda, 381
Greene, Richard, 76
Greene, Susaye, 461
Greenfield, Howard, 304, 330, 429-430

Greenfield, Robert, 240, 244, 419
Greenslade, Dave, 131, 212
Greenwich, Ellie, 19, 36, 41, 62, 86, 245-246, 330, 373
Greenwood, Nick, 87
Gregg, Brian, 296, 476
Gregory, John, 76
Gregory, Mike, 200, 462
Grey, Billy, 377
Griffin, Billy, 349
Griffin, Donald, 349
Griffith, Nanci, 197, 263
Griffiths, Brian, 63
Griffiths, Derek, 21
Griffiths, Ian, 378
Griffiths, Martin, 51
Grifters, 57
Grill, Rob, 241
Grind, Jody, 286
Grisman, David, 191
Groom, Don, 377
Groom, Roger, 364
Grooner, Louis, 286
Grossman, Albert, 63, 184, 384
Grosvenor, Luther, 21, 452, 492
Groundhogs, 270
Groves, Mick, 450
Grubb, Gary, 86, 401
Grundy, David Holgate, 60
Grundy, Hugh, 511
GTOs, 246
Guaraldi, Vince, 246
Guard, Dave, 261
Guercio, James William, 42
Guercio, Jim, 93
Guest, Reg, 493, 495
Guida, Frank, 78, 449
Guillory, Isaac, 148
Guinness, Alec, 126
Guitar Slim, 117
Gulliksen, Eric, 377
Gummoe, John, 108
Gun, 247
Gunn, Peter, 328
Gunnell, Rik, 212
Gunnels, Gene, 459
Guralnick, Peter, 134, 394-395
Gurley, James, 63
Gurvitz, Adrian, 247, 357
Gurvitz, Paul, 247
Gustafson, John, 63, 199
Guster, Keith, 310
Guthrie, Arlo, 197, 507
Guthrie, Woody, 183, 186, 197-198, 253, 374, 422
Guy, Athol, 430-431
Guy, Buddy, 120
Guy, Phil, 340
Guzman, Randy, 351
Gypsy Kings, 29

H

H.P. Lovecraft, 18, 247, 433
Habibiyya, 344
Hackett, Bobby, 54
Hadley, Mike, 103
Hage, Martin, 10
Hague, Ian, 212
Haines, Norman, 317
Hakim, Omar, 313
Haldane, Stan, 82
Hale, Malcolm, 449
Haley, Bill, 392
Hall, Adrian, 244
Hall, Bob, 182, 243
Hall, Cliff, 450
Hall, Clifton, 220
Hall, Daryl, 455
Hall, Dave, 182
Hall, John, 200
Hall, Kelvin, 301
Hall, Rick, 225
Hall, Robert, 241
Hall, Tommy, 471
Hall, Willie, 33, 80
Hallam, Jesse, 110
Halliday, Hugh, 484
Halligan, Dick, 72
Hallowell, John, 145
Hallyday, Johnny, 230, 247-248
Hallyday, Lee, 247
Halperin, Jerry, 7
Halsall, Ollie, 427
Hamilton, Andy, 5
Hamilton, Don, 463
Hamilton, Frank, 463
Hamilton, George, IV, 162-163, 319
Hamilton, Joe, 463
Hamilton, John, 197
Hamilton, Mark, 5
Hamilton, Roy, 55
Hamilton, Tim, 197
Hamlisch, Marvin, 70
Hammock, Cleveland, Jnr., 179
Hammond, Albert, 156, 210, 265, 327
Hammond, John, 73, 184-185, 225, 262
Hammond, Laurence, 326
Hammond, Roy, 101
Hammond, Steve, 214
Hampton, Carl, 33
Hampton, Christopher, 70
Hampton, Lionel, 9, 341, 346, 348, 356
Hancock, Herbie, 158, 339
Hancock, Wayne, 158
Hancox, Paul, 121
Handley, Jerry, 105
Hanna, Jeff, 138

Hansberry, Lorraine, 439
Happy Mondays, 166, 173
Hapshash And The Coloured Coat, 21, 249, 483
Harburg, E.Y. 'Yip', 126
Hard Meat, 249
Harder, Eddie, 191
Hardin And York, 163
Hardin, Alan, 116
Hardin, Eddie, 163
Hardin, Glen D., 145, 392
Hardin, Tim, 29, 154, 197, 208, 235, 245, 249-250, 365-366, 421, 507
Harding, John Wesley, 186, 190
Harding, Sandra, 276
Hardy, Damon J., 7
Hardy, Françoise, 250
Hare, Colin, 267
Harem Scarum, 391, 393, 395
Hargrove, Roy, 445
Harkleroad, Bill, 106
Harman, David, 155
Harman, James, 303
Harmony Grass, 250
Harper, Colin, 283
Harper, Roy, 379
Harpers Bizarre, 51, 149, 250-251
Harrell, Andre, 239, 361
Harris, Anita, 251
Harris, Barbara, 477
Harris, Bob, 6
Harris, Bobby, 56
Harris, Damon, 467
Harris, Danny, 8
Harris, David, 29
Harris, Eddie, 446
Harris, Emmylou, 109-110, 169, 197, 248, 376
Harris, Hugh, 8
Harris, Jet, 157, 251-252, 318, 409, 431-432
Harris, Jet, And Tony Meehan, 251-252, 432
Harris, John, 252
Harris, Kenny, 456
Harris, Max, 456
Harris, Peter Shannon, 364
Harris, Richard, 10, 138, 252
Harris, Tim, 220
Harrison, Bobby, 399
Harrison, George, 23, 44, 46, 48, 70, 83, 189, 193, 317, 351, 371, 376, 434, 436, 450, 481
Harrison, Henri, 368
Harrison, Mike, 21, 452, 492
Harrison, Noel, 252, 315

Harrison, Rex, 86, 252, 369
Harry, Bill, 49-50
Harryman, Martin, 286
Hart, Bobby, 83, 233
Hart, Charles, 69
Hart, Charlie, 40
Hart, Gerry, And The Hartbeats, 204
Hart, Jimmy, 233
Hart, Les, 219
Hart, Lorenz, 85
Hart, Mickey, 242, 244
Hart, Mike, 315
Hart, Peter, 219
Hart, Roger, 406
Hartford, John, 170
Hartley, Keef, 335
Hartley, Keef, Band, 21, 92, 252, 507
Hartman, John, 133
Hartman, Johnny, 133
Harvey, Alex, 84, 253-254
Harvey, Bob, 285
Harvey, Dave, 470
Harvey, Tam, 273
Haseman, Vikki, 83
Haskell, Gordon, 149, 310
Haskins, Jim, 507
Hassilev, Alex, 314
Hastings, Doug, 94, 150, 407
Hastings, Roy, 327
Hatch, Tony, 83, 87, 116, 126-127, 216, 254, 288, 292, 423, 428, 479, 495
Hatcher, Charles, 457
Hatcher, Willie, 457
Hatfield, Bobby, 410
Hathaway, Donny, 254-255
Hatton, Billy, 223
Hauser, Tim, 112
Havens, Richie, 249, 255, 507
Hawken, John, 364
Hawker, James, 107, 217, 279, 425
Hawker, Kenneth, 107, 217, 279
Hawkes, Chesney, 479
Hawkes, Chip, 479
Hawkins, 'Screamin' Jay', 87
Hawkins, Barbara Ann, 171
Hawkins, Bill, 112
Hawkins, Coleman, 122, 157
Hawkins, Dale, 120, 256
Hawkins, Edwin, Singers, 255-256
Hawkins, Jamesetta, 280
Hawkins, John, 256
Hawkins, Martin, 394-395
Hawkins, Reg, 377
Hawkins, Roger, 478

Hawkins, Ron, 256
Hawkins, Ronnie, 256
Hawkins, Rosa Lee, 171
Hawkins, Terence, 431
Hawks, Howard, 365
Hawkshaw, Alan, 219, 432
Hawksworth, Mick, 15
Hawkwind, 413
Hawn, Goldie, 334
Haworth, Bryn, 311
Haydock, Eric, 265
Hayes, David, 33, 426, 472
Hayes, Helen, 123
Hayes, Isaac, 33, 426, 458, 472, 497
Hayes, Steve, 318
Hayes, Tony, 318
Hayes, Tubby, 428
Haymes, Dick, 311
Hayward, Justin, 357
Hayward, Lawrence, 226
Hayward, Richard, 206, 226
Hayworth, Rita, 411
Hazelwood, Mike, 210
Hazlewood, Lee, 193, 233, 372, 439-440, 449
Hazziez, Yusuf, 469
Head, Roy, 256-257
Heads, Hands And Feet, 286
Heath, Frederick, 296
Heath, Percy, 157
Heath, Ted, 324, 428, 456
Heathcliff, 408-409
Heatly, Phil, 204
Heaven 17, 435
Heavy Jelly, 257, 317, 441
Heavy Metal Kids, 249
Hebb, Bobby, 257
Hebron, John, 7
Heckstall-Smith, Dick, 77-78, 131, 306, 335
Hedgehoppers Anonymous, 257
Hedges, Carol, 157
Heinz, 257-258, 342, 377, 394, 476
Hellsberg, Magnus, 453
Helm, Levon, 185, 256
Helms, Bobby, 492
Henderson, Alan, 470
Henderson, Barrington, 468
Henderson, Bill, 129
Henderson, Brian, 371
Henderson, David, 260
Henderson, Dickie, 174
Henderson, Dorris, 193
Henderson, Gerry, 24
Henderson, Harvey, 33
Henderson, Joe 'Mr Piano', 68
Henderson, Michael, 371
Henderson, Stewart, 34

Hendricks, Bobby, 180
Hendricks, James, 196, 420
Hendricks, Jon, 137, 209
Hendrickse, Margorie, 137
Hendrix, Jimi, 16, 74, 93, 115, 129, 132, 142, 147, 158, 164, 194, 213, 249, 258-260, 305, 308, 320, 355, 364, 403-404, 421, 447, 507
Hendrix, Margie, 137
Hendryx, Nona, 128, 246
Henley, Larry, 368
Henri, Adrian, 315
Henrit, Bob, 421, 484
Henry, Clarence 'Frogman', 260-261
Henry, Dolores, 148
Henry, John, 212, 433
Henry, Lenny, 427
Henry, Pierre, 452-453
Henry, Stuart, 358
Henry, Thomas, 103
Henry, Tony, 260, 335
Henshaw, Jimmy, 492
Henske, Judy, 196, 261
Hensley, Ken, 235
Hensley, Roy, 112
Herbert, Bongo, 407
Herbert, Ian, 453
Herd, 210, 216, 261, 378, 444
Herman's Hermits, 36, 90, 113, 205, 231, 261-262, 335
Herman, Gary, 501
Herman, William, 18
Herman, Woody, 9
Heron, Mike, 277
Hertha, Kurt, 70
Hervey, Irene, 287
Hesse, Herman, 458
Hester, Carolyn, 184, 211, 262-263
Hester, Eloise, 276
Hewitt, Howard, 497
Hewlett, John, 286
Hi-Lo's, 40
Hibbler, Al, 304
Hicks, Colin, 113, 220, 476
Hicks, Dan, 116-117
Hicks, Les, 72
Hicks, Tom, 113
Hicks, Tony, 265
Higginbotham, Robert, 481
Higgins, Henry, 114, 200
High Llamas, 43
Hightower, Rosetta, 377
Highwaymen, 110
Hildred, Stafford, 290
Hill, Albert, 503
Hill, Billie, 202
Hill, Dan, 476

Hill, Harold, 152
Hill, Tony, 350
Hill, Vince, 263
Hilliard, Bob, 27
Hilliard, Harriet, 365
Hillman, Chris, 94, 97, 340, 343
Hinchcliffe, Tony, 214
Hincks, Mick, 317
Hine, Eric, 183
Hines, Brian, 357
Hines, Ian, 436
Hinkley, Tim, 76, 286
Hinsley, Harvey, 378
Hinson, Arthur, 135
Hiseman, Jon, 77, 131, 252, 335
Hite, Bob, 104
Hixon, William, 51
Hoagland, Dan, 18
Hobbs, Randy, 338
Hodge, Keith, 15
Hodges, Chas, 61, 377
Hodges, Eddie, 87
Hodges, Frances, 276
Hodges, Johnny, 131
Hodges, Kenny, 449
Hodgkinson, Colin, 306-307
Hodkinson, Mark, 5, 209
Hoellerich, Gerd, 70
Hoffman, Dustin, 365
Hogan, Carl, 59
Hogan, Don, 179
Hogarth, Nicky, 305
Hoggs, Billy, 135
Holdbrook, Ian, 413
Holden, Randy, 74
Holdsworth, Allan, 447
Holiday, Billie, 54-55, 136, 238, 281, 361
Holland, Bernie, 286
Holland, Brian, 263-264, 334, 495, 498
Holland, Dave, 158, 386
Holland, Eddie, 238, 263, 361
Holland, Milt, 503
Holland/Dozier/Holland, 196, 222, 263-264, 332, 349, 361, 460-461, 494, 498
Holleman, Regina, 334
Holler, Dick, 171
Holliday, Michael, 27
Holliday, Mike, 406
Hollies, 147, 201, 203, 264-266, 280, 423, 462, 480, 503
Hollis, Peter, 120
Holloway, Brenda, 8, 266-267
Holloway, Stanley, 69
Hollowell, Alton, 209
Holly, Buddy, 45, 162-163, 216, 266, 296, 317, 365, 379, 388, 392, 422,

486-487
Hollywood Argyles, 223
Hollywood Blue Jays, 61
Hollywood Flames, 76
Holm, Paul, 179
Holman, Eddie, 422
Holmes, Christine, 210
Holmes, John, 453
Holmes, Richard 'Groove', 445
Holmes, Robert, 394
Holofcener, Larry, 160
Holt, Dennis, 397
Holt, John, 397
Holt, Redd, 312-313
Holtzman, Vivian, 215
Holy Modal Rounders, 228, 267
Holzman, Jac, 175, 196
Homer And Jethro, 22
Hondells, 113
Honey Cone, 74
Honeyball, Ray, 257
Honeybus, 267
Honeycombs, 155, 267-268, 342
Honeydrippers, 61
Hood, David, 478
Hood, Roger, 478
Hooker, Earl, 270
Hooker, John Lee, 103-104, 120, 158, 168, 182, 184, 268-270, 372
Hooper, Darryl, 430
Hope, Bob, 54, 160
Hope, Elmo, 132
Hopkin, Mary, 270-271, 317
Hopkins, Jerry, 177, 260, 394
Hopkins, Keith, 476, 498
Hopkins, Lightnin', 271-272
Hopkins, Linda, 504
Hopkins, Mike, 275
Hopkins, Nicky, 157, 379, 401, 462
Hopkins, Richard, 72
Hopkins, Sam, 271
Hopper, Dennis, 158
Hopper, Hugh, 35, 447
Hopwood, Keith, 262
Hord, Eric, 340
Horn, Jim, 193
Horn, Trevor, 289
Horne, Lena, 52
Hornsby, Bruce, 243
Hornsby, Clive, 165
Hornsby, Paul, 272
Hornsby, Vince, 243
Horton, Gladys, 334
Horton, Johnny, 324
Horton, Walter 'Shakey', 363
Hot Butter, 167
Hot Chocolate, 69, 270, 378

Hot Tuna, 285
Hotchner, A.E., 419
Hour Glass, 272
House, Simon, 471
House, Son, 103, 362
Houston, Cisco, 253
Houston, Cissy, 128, 272, 279-280, 480, 496
Houston, Dale, 150
Houston, Thelma, 97, 272-273
Houston, Whitney, 225, 230, 272, 337
Hovorka, Bob, 168
Howard And Blaikley, 155, 261, 268
Howard, Alan, 155, 216, 268, 478
Howard, Bob, 191
Howard, John, 214
Howard, Ken, 216, 268
Howe, Steve, 476
Howell, John, 402
Howlin' Wolf, 97, 119-120, 136, 182, 238, 481
Hudson, Barbara, 484
Hudson, Garth, 185, 256
Hudson, Richard, 256, 487
Hudson-Ford, 488
Hugg, Mike, 329
Hughes, Alex, 397
Hughes, Harry, 129
Hughes, Lynne, 117
Hughes, Mike, 5
Hullaballoos, 291
Hultgren, Georg, 193
Human Beinz, 273
Humble Pie, 35, 261, 444, 453
Humblebums, 273
Humes, Anita, 201-202
Humperdinck, Engelbert, 113, 251, 273-274, 299
Humphrey, John, 333
Humphrey, Phil, 214
Humphries, John, 190
Humphries, Patrick, 190, 438
Hunt, Joe, 21
Hunt, Ray, 358
Hunter, George, 116, 401
Hunter, Ivory Joe, 81
Hunter, Meredith, 13
Hunter, Robert, 242, 244
Hunter, Russell, 168
Hurd, Francine, 381
Hurst, Mike, 271, 456
Hurt, Mississippi John, 339
Huston, Chris, 484
Hutch, Willie, 349
Hutchinson, Johnny, 63
Hutchinson, Nigel, 76
Hutson, Leroy, 277
Hutton, Betty, 460
Hutton, Danny, 353

Huxley, Rick, 124
Hyland, Brian, 148, 274
Hyman, Jerry, 72
Hynde, Chrissie, 301
Hynes, Dave, 90

I

Idle Race, 74, 275, 362
Ifield, Frank, 275-276
Iglesias, Julio, 156, 245
Ikettes, 20, 276
Illinois Speed Press, 276
Impressions, 276-277 and passim
Incredible String Band, 179, 196, 219, 277-278, 507
Ingber, Elliot, 226
Ingmann, Jorgen, 318
Ingram, Adrian, 357
Ingram, Luther, 33
Innes, Brian, 466
Innes, Neil, 79
Innocents, 223
Insect Trust, 278
Instant Action Jug Band, 139
Iron Butterfly, 62, 278
Irvine, Andy, 179
Irving, Bill, 219
Irving, Don, 51
Irwin, Big Dee, 278-279, 315
Isley Brothers, 56, 87, 119, 138, 253, 258, 264, 273, 361
Italiano, Gene, 387
Ives, Burl, 319
Ivy League, 9, 108, 113, 279, 425
Ivy, Quin, 442

J

J.J. Foote, 250
Jack, Betty, 162
Jackie And Millie, 345
Jackman, Tommy, 441
Jacks, Terry, 84
Jackson Five, 361
Jackson Heights, 371
Jackson, Al, 18, 33, 80, 146, 308, 331
Jackson, Arthur, 5
Jackson, Ben, 140
Jackson, Blair, 244
Jackson, Carl, 33
Jackson, Charlie, 330
Jackson, Chuck, 91, 96, 140, 272, 279-280, 480
Jackson, David, 169
Jackson, Eddie, 84
Jackson, George, 361
Jackson, J.J., 279

Jackson, Karen, 461
Jackson, Lee, 370
Jackson, Mahalia, 91, 225
Jackson, Mark, 5
Jackson, Maurice, 84
Jackson, Michael, 48, 69, 433, 506
Jackson, Mick, 320
Jackson, Millie, 33
Jackson, Paul, 157
Jackson, Raymond, 33
Jackson, Roger, 476
Jackson, Tony, 53, 428
Jackson, Walter, 337
Jackson, Wayne, 330
Jacobs, David, 199
Jacobsen, Erik, 172
Jacquet, Illinois, 157
Jaeger, Rick, 7
Jagger, Mick, 13, 20, 205, 208, 212, 306, 385-386, 414, 419
Jah Screechy, 141
Jamerson, James, 295
James, Barry, 295
James, Billy, 106, 360
James, Chris, 427
James, David, 281
James, Dick, 45, 47, 199, 280, 354, 380
James, Eddie, 251
James, Elmore, 119
James, Etta, 120, 167, 280-281
James, Fanita, 74, 77
James, Harry, 134, 403
James, Jesse, 135
James, Jimmy, 258, 379, 445, 449
James, Joni, 183, 422
James, Larry, 281
James, Lewis, 352, 425
James, Marcus, 398
James, Michael, 141
James, Paul, 44, 205
James, Ray, 179
James, Richard, 83, 87
James, Rick, 467
James, Sally, 427
James, Shirley, 115
James, Skip, 206, 278
James, Stu, 352
James, Tommy, And The Shondells, 281-282
Jamison, Roosevelt, 106-107
Jan And Arnie, 282
Jan And Dean, 9, 12, 36, 40, 70, 210, 282, 442
Janken, George, 400
Jans, Tom, 211
Jansch, Bert, 208, 282-283, 383
Jansen, Hans, 10
Jardell, Robert, 31
Jardine, Al, 40, 43

Jarrett, Keith, 158
Jarrett, Tony, 486
Jay And The Americans, 8, 213, 283-284, 492
Jay And The Techniques, 284
Jay, Peter, And The Jaywalkers, 284
Jayne, Mitch, 170
Jaynetts, 284
Jeckell, Frank Edward, 371
Jefferson Airplane, 13, 240, 245, 259, 285-286, 355, 365, 382, 401, 484, 507
Jefferson Starship, 285-286
Jefferson, John, 345, 507
Jeffrey, Mike, 19
Jeffreys, Garland, 401
Jeffries, Mike, 115, 258
Jeffries, Nancy, 278
Jelfs, Ian, 123
Jellybread, 7
Jemmott, Jerry, 296
Jenkins, Barry, 16, 257, 364
Jenkins, Johnny, 403
Jenkins, Karl, 447
Jenkins, Lyle, 252
Jennings, Waylon, 23, 92, 110-111, 162
Jennings, Will, 28, 372, 426
Jerome, Jim, 328, 385
Jesmer, Elaine, 469
Jesus And Mary Chain, 436, 489
Jethro Tull, 238
Jewel And Eddie, 11
Jewell, Jimmy, 252
Jewry, Bernard, 214
Jive Five, 124
Jo Jo Gunne, 451
Jo Mama, 382
Joan Marie, 171
Joanne And The Streamliners, 456
Jody Grind, 286
Joel, Billy, 282
Johannsson, Ove, 453
Johansen, David, 476
John And Johnny, 133, 268
John's Children, 286
John, Chris, 212
John, Clive, 100
John, Elton, 28, 31, 80, 123, 225, 250, 280, 322, 337, 377, 387, 408, 431, 497
John, Graham, 5, 240
John, Little Willie, 89
John, Richard, 72, 252, 409, 445
John, Robert, 476

Johnnie And Joe, 284
Johnny And John, 133, 268
Johnny And June, 111
Johnny And The Hurricanes, 62, 64, 216, 287
Johnny And The Moondogs, 44
Johnson, 'Blind' Willie, 206
Johnson, Allen, 331
Johnson, Bob, 305
Johnson, Bruce, 308, 330, 449
Johnson, Carol, 204
Johnson, Delores, 276
Johnson, Derek, 494
Johnson, Earl, 287
Johnson, Echo, 334
Johnson, Eddie, 238, 361
Johnson, Fred, 331
Johnson, Gareth, 72
Johnson, Gene, 331
Johnson, Howie, 490
Johnson, Hubert, 135
Johnson, J.J., 9, 157
Johnson, Jack, 159
Johnson, Jimmy, 233
Johnson, Joe, 217
Johnson, Johnnie, 59
Johnson, Marv, 238, 287, 361
Johnson, Marvin, 287
Johnson, Michael, 217
Johnson, Mike, 350
Johnson, Paul, 52
Johnson, Plas, 422
Johnson, Ralph, 277
Johnson, Richard, 52, 72
Johnson, Robert, 258
Johnson, Ron, 294
Johnson, Rudolph, 201
Johnson, Syl, 80
Johnson, Tommy, 103, 179
Johnson, William, 179
Johnson, Willie, 206
Johnston, Bruce, 41-43, 92, 282, 343, 366, 370, 425
Johnstone, Walter, 492
Jolson, Al, 62, 391
Jones Brothers, 156
Jones, Alan, 14
Jones, Allan, 287
Jones, Billy, 212
Jones, Bob, 287, 321
Jones, Bobby, 18, 379
Jones, Booker T., 80, 146, 331
Jones, Brian, 355, 414, 416, 418-420, 484
Jones, Chris, 290
Jones, Chuck, 63
Jones, Darryl, 418
Jones, Davy, 83, 353

Jones, Eddie, 84
Jones, Elvin, 132, 278
Jones, George, 134, 194, 387
Jones, Glenn, 206-207
Jones, Gloria, 74
Jones, Graham, 453
Jones, Hank, 356, 505
Jones, Hughie, 450-451
Jones, Jack, 25, 27, 143, 287-288
Jones, Janie, 288
Jones, Jeff, 100
Jones, Jerry, 84
Jones, Jimmy, 87, 288, 434
Jones, Joe, 157, 172
Jones, John, 20, 192, 379
Jones, John Paul, 20, 192, 379
Jones, Kenny, 444, 500
Jones, Lee, 121, 373
Jones, Malcolm, 35
Jones, Mark, 5
Jones, Max, 5
Jones, Michael, 18
Jones, Mick, 453
Jones, Mickey, 83, 100, 185
Jones, Mike, 100
Jones, Neil, 14
Jones, Paul, 7, 20, 150, 192, 306, 329, 379
Jones, Percy, 315
Jones, Peter, 394
Jones, Phalon, 33
Jones, Philly Joe, 157
Jones, Quincy, 69, 159-160, 205, 239, 255, 346
Jones, Ray, 150, 307
Jones, Rickie Lee, 373
Jones, Rob, 330
Jones, Ron, 356
Jones, Shirley, 115
Jones, Simon, 5
Jones, Thad, 347
Jones, Willie, 503
Jook, 286
Joplin, Janis, 56, 63, 139, 198, 226, 290-291, 355, 441, 464, 507
Jordan, Al, 354
Jordan, Clay, 146
Jordan, Danny, 167
Jordan, John, 168
Jordan, Louis, 168
Jordan, Ronny, 158
Jordan, Tommy, 167
Jordanaires, 316, 390
Joseph, Patrick, 120
Journeymen, 291, 327, 340, 385, 420
Joy Division, 398, 489
Joyce, John, 488
Joyce, Teddy, 122
Joystrings, 291
Judas Jump, 14

Judas Priest, 453
Judge Dread, 397-398
Judge, Alan, 197
Juicy Lucy, 169, 350
Jumping Jacks, 494
Junior's Eyes, 291-292
Junior, Guitar, 332
Justice, Jimmy, 83, 292, 319

K

K-Doe, Ernie, 292
Kabuki, 270
Kador, Ernest, Jnr., 292
Kaempfert, Bert, 292-293, 370, 436
Kagan, Harvey, 441
Kait, Al, 421
Kak, 74, 293
Kalb, Danny, 76
Kaleidoscope, 20, 66, 104, 294, 505
Kalin Twins, 90, 167, 386
Kane, Amory, 15, 210
Kane, Barry, 340, 367
Kane, Eden, 294-295, 427
Kane, Howie, 283
Kane, Michael, 511
Kantner, Paul, 285
Kaplan, Howard, 359, 482
Kaplan, Jeff, 294
Kapner, Mark, 139
Kapralik, Dave, 381
Karloff, Boris, 58
Karlson, Keith, 352
Karmen, Janice, 122
Karmon, Freddy, 104
Kasenetz, Jerry, 295, 371, 374
Kasenetz-Katz Singing Orchestral Circus, 295
Kassner, Eddie, 379
Kasten, Fritz, 448
Katz, Jeff, 295, 371, 374
Katz, Matthew, 351
Katz, Steve, 72, 76
Katzman, Sam, 262
Kaukonen, Jorma, 285
Kay, Horace, 463
Kay, John, 458
Kaye, Carol, 244, 295, 367
Kaye, Danny, 86, 369, 508
Kaye, Ian, 7
Kaye, Larry, 244
Kaye, Sammy, 156
Kaye, Tony, 287, 317
Kaylan, Howard, 359, 482
Kaz, Eric, 75
Keel, Howard, 322
Keen, John, 473
Keen, Speedy, 473-474
Keene, Barry, 452
Keene, Nelson, 425
Kefford, Ace, Stand, 62

Kefford, Chris 'Ace', 362
Keisker, Marion, 389
Keith, 295-296 and passim
Keith, Brian, 387
Keith, Jeff, 462
Keith, Michael, 5
Keliehor, Jon, 150
Keller, Dennis, 215
Keller, Jack, 235
Keller, Jerry, 502
Keller, Mike, 318
Kelley, Kevin, 99, 410
Kellie, Mike, 21, 452, 492
Kellogg, Burns, 74
Kelly, Betty, 333, 487
Kelly, Dave, 182
Kelly, Dennis, 338
Kelly, Gene, 57
Kelly, Jo Ann, 182, 339-340
Kelly, Joe, 113, 433
Kelly, Luke, 181
Kelly, Mike, 182
Kelly, Ned, 417
Kelly, Wynton, 157, 356
Kemp, Allen, 366
Kemp, Gibson, 378
Kendall, Alan, 235
Kendricks, Eddie, 466-468
Kennedy, Jimmy, 70
Kennedy, John, 257
Kennedy, Maureen, 491
Kennedy, Mike, 6, 318
Kennedy, Nigel, 259
Kennedys, 364
Kenner, Chris, 119
Kenner, Doris, 436
Kennibrew, Dee Dee, 148
Kenny And The Cadets, 40
Keno, Jerri Bo, 450, 466
Kenton, Stan, 102
Kenyon, Dave, 5
Kenyon, Frank, 492
Keresman, Mark, 5-6
Kerley, Lenny, 148
Kern, Jimmy, 308
Kerr, Anita, 341
Kerr, Bob, 79, 368, 431
Kerrison, John, 199
Kerslake, Lee, 235
Kestrels, 156
Keyes, Bobby, 248, 417
Keys, Cherry, 140
Khan, George, 40
Khan, Steve, 116
Khaury, Herbert, 474
Khouri, Ken, 10
Kibbee, Martin, 206, 226
Kid Galahad, 391, 395
Kidd, Johnny, And The Pirates, 113, 296, 476
Kilgore, Merle, 109
Killen, Buddy, 469
Killen, Louis, 124
Kilmer, Val, 176
Kilminster, Ian, 413

Kim, Andy, 19, 37, 304
Kincaid, Jesse Lee, 410
Kincaid, Mark, 195
King Bee, 363
King Cool, 395
King Crimson, 7, 123, 149, 235, 311
King Curtis, 258, 296-297, 437
King Diamond, 353
King Kasuals, 258
King Kolax, 131
King Of The Wheels, 229
King, Alan, 8, 343
King, Albert, 147, 297
King, B.B., 7, 71, 240, 258, 272, 296-298, 388, 446, 473, 481
King, Ben E., 56, 140, 180, 297-298, 386, 449
King, Bill, 290
King, Billie Jean, 455
King, Bob, 29, 395
King, Bobby, 7, 140, 473
King, Carole, 10, 13, 86, 91, 129, 137, 145, 155, 235, 304, 315, 330, 353, 373, 429, 454-455
King, Dave, 27
King, Denis, 69
King, Ed, 459
King, Freddie, 21, 120, 227, 298-299
King, Freddy, 326
King, Jackson, 228
King, Jean, 74, 455
King, Jim, 212
King, Jimmy, 26, 33
King, Johnny, 352
King, Jonathan, 257
King, Kim, 319
King, Martin Luther, 52, 171, 243, 506
King, Maurice, 493, 495
King, Mick, 53
King, Pete, 287, 428
King, Peter, 352
King, Reg, 8
King, Reggie, 8
King, Robert, 298
King, Solomon, 96, 299, 386
King, Steve, 10
Kingham, Lionel, 497
Kings Of Rhythm, 481
Kingsmen, 299, 406
Kingston Trio, 84, 234, 261, 340-341, 384-385, 503
Kinks, 61-62, 113, 143, 169, 175, 231, 237, 299-302, 310, 379-380, 413-414, 499
Kinrade, John, 200
Kinsley, Billy, 343
Kippington Lodge, 302
Kirby, John, 119

Kirby, Kathy, 25, 302-303
Kirchherr, Astrid, 44
Kirchin, Tim, 212
Kirk, James, 303
Kirk, John, 304
Kirk, Rahsaan Roland, 303-304, 347
Kirke, Simon, 67
Kirkland, Eddie, 268
Kirkland, Frank, 168
Kirkland, James, 324, 365
Kirshner, Don, 19, 86, 153, 235, 304, 353
Kitley, Peter, 396
Kitt, Eartha, 503
Klaus And Gibson, 378-379
Klein, Alan, 368
Klein, Allen, 47, 136, 416, 450
Klein, Carol, 429
Klein, Warren, 206, 226
Knauss, Richard, 331
Knechtel, Larry, 193
Knepper, Jimmy, 347
Knickerbockers, 304, 410, 510
Knight, Curtis, 258, 260, 304-305
Knight, Gladys, 28, 140, 231, 324, 339, 361, 497
Knight, Graham, 219, 331
Knight, Larry, 452
Knight, Peter, 305, 357, 495
Knight, Robert, 305, 346
Knopfler, Mark, 23, 188
Knust, Michael, 215
Kobluk, Mike, 350
Koblun, Ken, 94
Koehler, Trevor, 278
Koerner, John, 198
Koerner, Ray And Glover, 196
Kogel, Mike, 318
Kolber, Larry, 330
Kong, Leslie, 10, 164
Konikoff, Sandy, 185
Konitz, Lee, 157, 159, 346
Konrad, John, 352
Koobas, 306
Kool Gents, 125
Kooper, Al, 72-73, 76, 185-186, 195, 219, 312, 326, 384, 421-422
Kootch, Danny, 228
Korner, Alexis, 77, 123, 157, 306-307, 335, 353, 363, 414
Korner, Neil, 368
Kornfeld, Artie, 141
Kortchmar, Danny, 129
Kossoff, Paul, 67
Kotch, 287
Kotke, Lenny, 237
Kottke, Leo, 206-207
Koussevitzky, Serge, 57

Kovas, Dino, 354
Kraemer, Peter, 448
Kramer, Billy J. And The Dakotas, 27, 199, 307, 333, 429
Kramer, Eddie, 260
Kramer, John, 166
Kramer, Wayne, 338
Krastan, Dean, 374
Krauledat, Joachim F., 458
Kravitz, Lenny, 337
Kretmar, Don, 76
Kretzmer, Herbert, 25
Kreutzmann, Bill, 241
Krikorian, Steve, 145
Kristofferson, Kris, 109-111, 256, 309, 490
Krupa, Gene, 155
Kubas, 306
Kula Shaker, 88
Kulberg, Andy, 76
Kulberberg, Tuli, 228
Kurland, John, 364
Kuy, Billy, 377
Kyser, Kay, 462

L

La Pierre, Cherilyn, 79, 447
LaBelle, 28, 145, 373
LaBelle, Patti, 28
LaCroix, Jerry, 72
Lady Flash, 406
Lagos, Paul, 294
Lahteinen, Keith, 484
Lai, Francis, 69, 341
Laine, Cleo, 118, 318
Laine, Denny, 357
Laine, Frankie, 275
Laing, Dave, 5
Lake, Alan, 310
Lake, Greg, 235
Lake, Steve, 5
Lalor, Steve, 150
Lamb, Bob, 275, 317
Lambert, Kit, 343, 499
Lana Sisters, 454
Lancastrians, 379
Lance, Major, 218, 308, 337
Landau, Jon, 338
Lander, Bob, 453
Lander, Tony, 198
Landerman, Barry, 302
Landis, Karl, 284
Landon, Neil, 213, 217
Landy, Eugene, 42-43
Lane, Gary, 456
Lane, Lois, 106
Lane, Ronnie, 371, 441, 443
Lane, Rosemary, 283
Lang, Bob, 346
lang, k.d., 54

Lang, Peter, 207
Langford, Bonnie, 508
Langford, Peter, 36
Langhorne, Bruce, 262
Langley, Ank, 400
Langwith, James, 444
Lanois, Daniel, 189
Lantree, John, 267
LaPore, Dennis, 75
Lark, Stan, 215
Larkey, Charles, 228
Lasker, Jay, 10
Lasman, Mike, 7
Lassiter, Art, 276
Last, James, 83, 235
Latham, Billy Rae, 170
Latham, Chris, 6
Latouche, John, 58
Lauber, Ken, 20
Laud, Alan, 257
Lauder, Andrew, 6
Laundau, Bill, 113
Lauper, Cyndi, 246
Laurel Canyon Ballet Company, 246
Laurence, Lynda, 460-461
Laurents, Arthur, 58
Laurie, Billy, 323
Lavern, Roger, 476
Lawrence, Claire, 129
Lawrence, Steve, 26, 466
Layden, Graham, 40
Laye, Evelyn, 508
Lea, Clive, 413
Leadon, Bernie, 138, 169
Leaf, David, 44
Leahy, Dick, 294
Leapy Lee, 309
Leatherman, Ronnie, 472
Leatherwood, Stu, 306
Leaves, 308-309 and *passim*
Leavill, Otis, 308
Leckenby, Lek, 262
Led Zeppelin, 20, 210, 379, 398, 509
Ledigo, Hugh, 32
Lee, Albert, 123, 145, 203, 212
Lee, Alvin, 15, 468-469
Lee, Arthur, 320
Lee, Barbara, 121
Lee, Barry, 330
Lee, Bernie, 149
Lee, Bert, 174
Lee, Beverly, 436
Lee, Bill, 262
Lee, Billy, And The Rivieras, 424
Lee, Bob, 190
Lee, Brenda, 96-97, 108, 167, 309
Lee, Bunny, 11
Lee, C.P., 190
Lee, Charles, 159
Lee, Curtis, 61, 149, 213
Lee, Dave, 212

Lee, Frances, 491
Lee, Frankie, 186
Lee, George, 422
Lee, Graham, 146, 309
Lee, Irma, 472
Lee, Jackie, 77, 263
Lee, Jim, 355
Lee, Jimmy, 298
Lee, John, 103-104, 120, 158, 168, 182, 184, 268-271, 372
Lee, Johnny, 263, 268
Lee, Larry, 259
Lee, Laura, 120
Lee, Peggy, 161
Lee, Peter, 343
Lee, Phil, 203
Lee, Ric, 468
Lee, Roberta, 233
Lee, Sammy, 85, 369
Lee, Sandy, 490
Lee, Sharon, 167
Lee, Stan, 346
Leeds, Gary, 456, 493-495
Leeman, Mark, Five, 91, 120
Lees, Gene, 329
Lefevre, Mylon, 469
Left Banke, 310
Legrand, Michel, 69, 159, 288, 339
Lehrer, Jim, 364
Leib, Marshall, 206, 449
Leiber And Stoller, 45, 56, 64, 86, 172, 178, 180, 204, 283, 388, 390, 393, 449-450
Leiber, Jerry, 172
Leigh, Carolyn, 54
Leigh, Paul, 438
Leigh, Spencer, 5, 49-50, 61, 352, 394, 438
Leillo, John, 75
Lejeune, Louis, 31
Leka, Paul, 310
Lemon Pipers, 310
Lennear, Claudia, 276
Lennon, John, 19, 44, 49, 70, 98, 116, 149, 199, 223, 241, 243, 256, 265, 280, 288, 300, 307, 392, 398, 415, 435-436, 450
Lennox, Annie, 225
Lennox, Davie, 50
Lenoir, Phil, 67
Leonard, Chuck, 107
Leonard, Deke, 101
Leonard, Glenn, 467
Leonard, Roger, 101
Lerner, Alan Jay, 58, 69
(Les) Fleur De Lys, 120, 149, 310-311, 379
Lesh, Phil, 241
Lester, Eddie, 32
Lester, Ketty, 311
Lettermen, 311-312
Levin, Drake, 406

Levine, Ian, 124, 127, 196, 267, 287, 461, 499
Levine, Irwin, 219
Levine, Joey, 371, 374, 471
Levine, Larry, 450
Levinger, Lowell, III, 510
Levise, William, Jnr., 423
Levitt And McClure, 51
Levitt, Dan, 51
Levy, Harry, 19
Levy, Jacques, 187
Lewis, Barbara, 56, 312
Lewis, Bob, 287
Lewis, Bunny, 177
Lewis, Dave, 15
Lewis, Denise, 422
Lewis, Gary, And The Playboys, 22, 70, 312
Lewis, Graham, 5
Lewis, Huey, 240
Lewis, James, 352, 425
Lewis, Jerry Lee, 103, 108-109, 111, 238, 364, 376, 393, 483
Lewis, John, 107, 157
Lewis, Ken, 107, 217, 279, 425
Lewis, Peter, 350-351
Lewis, Ramsey, 303, 312-313, 505
Lewis, Richard, 319
Lewis, Robert, 422
Lewis, Rudy, 180
Lewis, Terence, 508
Lewisohn, Mark, 49-50
Leyton, John, 313-314, 377, 476
Libert, David, 248
Liberto, Vivian, 108
Licari, Nanette, 405
Liggins, Joe, 61
Lightfoot, Gordon, 130
Lightfoot, Terry, 32, 220, 314
Lillie, Beatrice, 85
Lillywhite, Steve, 418
Limeliters, 314
Lind, Bob, 314-315, 372
Linde, Sam, 116
Lindley, David, 294
Lindsay, Jimmy, 141
Lindsay, Mark, 406
Lipman, Maureen, 58
Lipsius, Fred, 72
Lipton, Sydney, 305
Lisberg, Harvey, 261
Litherland, James, 131
Lithman, Phil, 344
Little Anthony And The Imperials, 83, 148, 315
Little Big Band, 253
Little Eva, 137, 279, 304, 315
Little Feat, 206, 226, 246, 359, 457
Little Joe, 404

Little John, 89
Little Milton, 38, 167
Little Pork Chops, 268
Little Richard, 81, 87, 140, 258, 403, 415, 423
Little Sonny, 119, 298
Little Walter, 97, 119, 363
Little, Carlo, 217, 257, 414
Little, Joe, 404
Liverpool Scene, 315-316, 427
Lloyd Webber, Andrew, 39, 69, 433
Lloyd Webber, Julian, 271
Lloyd, Charles, 284
Lloyd, George, 284
Lloyd, Patrick, 200
Lock, Graham, 5
Locke, John, 451
Locke, Sondra, 203
Lockhead, Christopher, 293
Locking, Brian, 432
Locklin, Danny, 316
Locklin, Hank, 162, 316
Locks, Fred, 141
Lockwood, Robert, 268, 298
Locomotive, 317
Loder, Kurt, 482
Lodge, John, 291, 357
Lofgren, Nils, 21
Loggins And Messina, 94
Loggins, Kenny, 94
Loizzo, Gary, 14
Lomax, Alan, 339, 362
Lomax, Jackie, 257, 317, 484
London, Eric, 212
London, John, 138
London, Mark, 53, 69
Lone Star, 441
Long, George, 395
Long, Joe, 221
Long, Shorty, 481
Long, Steve, 36
Long, Tom, 386
Longdancer, 388
Longhurst-Pickworth, Mike, 456
Loomis, Mark, 122
Loose Gravel, 117
Lopez, Trini, 317-318
Lorber, Rick, 14
Lord, Jon, 21, 217, 252
Lord, Tracy, 315
Lordan, Jerry, 137, 318, 396, 432
Los Angeles Philharmonic Orchestra, 305
Los Bravos, 318
Los Lobos, 269
Lothar And The Hand People, 319

Loudermilk, John D., 164, 319
Louisiana Hayride, The, 116, 316, 324, 404
Lounsbury, Jim, 308
Louvin Brothers, 22
Louvin, Charlie, 92
Love, 319-320 and passim
Love Affair, 320-321 and passim
Love Jones, 113
Love Sculpture, 321
Love Unlimited, 465
Love, Andrew, 331
Love, Barbara Jean, 227
Love, Darlene, 77, 295, 450
Love, Geoff, 172, 321-322
Love, John, 49
Love, Larry, 380
Love, Laura, 36, 291, 313, 485
Love, Mike, 40-43, 385
Love, Steve, 321
Lovegrove, Chris, 204
Lovetro, Gary, 459
Lovin' Spoonful, 22, 24, 261, 267, 319, 322-323, 353, 365, 448
Lowe, Chris, 455
Lowe, Earl, 115
Lowe, James, 115
Lowe, Jim, 195
Lowe, Nick, 110, 302
Lowery, Bill, 127, 464
Lowther, Henry, 252, 329, 335
Loxender, Dave, 148
Luboff, Norman, 367
Lucas, Gil, 344
Lucas, Robert, 104
Lucas, Trevor, 193
Lucasta, Anna, 161
Lucia, Pete, 281
Lucky 13, 175
Luker, Mal, 446
Lulu, 56, 68, 323, 379, 454
Luman, Bob, 319, 324
Lund, John 'Zeke', 446
Lundgren, Ken, 377
Lunny, Donal, 124
Lusher, Don, 324-325
Lutton, Dave, 194
Lydon, Michael, 118
Lyle, Steven, 452
Lyle, Tom, 319
Lyles, Pat, 137
Lynch, Bob, 181
Lynch, David, 376
Lynch, Eddie, 120
Lynch, John, 6
Lynch, Kenny, 325, 437, 444
Lynn, Barbara, 325
Lynn, Chris, 253
Lynn, Loretta, 309

Lynn, Tami, 325
Lynn, Vera, 408
Lynne, Jeff, 48, 189, 193, 275, 289, 333, 362, 376, 434
Lynton, Rod, 311
Lynyrd Skynyrd, 459
Lyons, Leo, 468
Lyttelton, Humphrey, 66, 435

M

Mabern, Harold, 356
Macauley, Tony, 31, 150, 156, 180, 193, 220
Macbeth, Peter, 220
MacColl, Kirsty, 300
MacDonald, Ian, 49-50
Mack, Bob, 281
Mack, Lonnie, 326
Mack, Marlene, 381
Mack, Ted, 81
Mackender, Ray, 508
MacKenna, Barney, 181
Mackintosh, Cameron, 38, 69
MacLaine, Shirley, 161
Maclean, Bryan, 320
MacLean, Dougie, 102
Maclean, Norrie, 388
MacLeod, John, 220
MacLise, Angus, 488
Macrae, Dave, 447
Mad River, 326
Madara, John, 340
Maddox, Walt, 331
Madge, Bill, 317
Madisons, 198
Mae, Annie, 339, 481
Maestro, Johnny, 87
Magic Lanterns, 210, 326-327
Magic Sam, 136, 298
Magma, 237
Magnum, 217
Magnus, Kerry, 299
Maguire, Les, 234
Maharishi Mahesh Yogi, 41, 47, 200
Mahavishnu Orchestra, 217
Mair, Alan, 50
Majewski, Hank, 221
Makeba, Miriam, 52
Makem, Tommy, 123-124, 181
Malara, Bob, 179
Male, Kerilee, 193
Mallett, Saundra, 196
Mallory, Lee, 344
Mamas And The Papas, 10, 70, 197, 291, 322, 327-328, 340-341, 355, 382, 385, 449, 464
Mamas Boys, 464

Manassas, 100, 129, 147, 206
Mancha, Steve, 34
Mancini, Henry, 328-329
Mandel, Harvey, 103, 335-336
Mandrell, Barbara, 134
Manfred Mann, 7, 36, 91, 120, 142, 150, 169, 183, 306, 329-330, 379, 437
Manfred Mann's Earth Band, 329
Manhattan Transfer, 8, 112
Manhattans, 90
Manilow, Barry, 167, 406, 455, 496
Mann, Barry, 86-87, 129, 155, 235, 304, 330, 386, 450
Mann, Herbie, 296
Mann, Kal, 118
Mann, Manfred, 7, 36, 91, 120, 142, 150, 169, 183, 306, 329-330, 379, 437
Manne, Shelly, 57
Mannheim Steamroller, 503
Manning, Tom, 326
Mansfield, Tony, 150, 307
Manson, Charles, 41, 47, 228, 343
Manuel And His Music Of The Mountains, 321
Manuel, Bobby, 80
Manuel, Dean, 404
Manuel, Richard, 185, 256
Manzarek, Ray, 175, 177
Mar-Keys, 80, 146, 217, 330-331
Marcels, 194, 331
March, Little Peggy, 331
Marchello, Mickey, 237
Marcos, Ferdinand, 46
Marcotte, Jim, 7
Marcus, Greil, 186, 395
Mardin, Arif, 454
Margo, Mitch, 475-476
Margo, Phil, 476
Margolis, Mike, 251
Margouleff, Robert, 319
Marinelli, Michael, 217
Marion, Ronald, 216
Marionette, 186
Mark Four, 143
Mark IV, 101
Mark, Jon, 335
Mark, Louisa, 141
Marker, Gary, 410
Markowitz, Roy, 290
Marks, David, 40
Markulin, Ting, 273
Marley, Bob, 165, 337
Marmalade, 331-332 and *passim*
Marriott, Steve, 371, 441, 443

Marron, Gordon, 484
Marsden, Beryl, 332
Marsden, Freddie, 234
Marsden, Gerry, 137, 234, 332
Marsh, Dave, 395, 438, 501
Marsh, Richard, 430
Marsh, Roger, 402
Marshall, Bob, 116
Marshall, Grant, 108
Marshall, John, 447
Marshall, Thomas, 378
Marshall, Tom, 250
Martell, Vince, 486
Martha And The Vandellas, 213, 264, 332-333, 487
Martin, Anthony, Jnr., 170
Martin, Bill, 82, 138, 387, 435
Martin, Chip, 353
Martin, David, 426
Martin, Dean, 110, 160-161, 170, 365
Martin, Dewey, 94, 170
Martin, George, 8, 45-49, 68, 152, 199, 223, 271, 289, 333-334, 354
Martin, Larry, 24
Martin, Linda, 419
Martin, Mary, 64, 185
Martin, Millicent, 479
Martin, Paul, 170
Martin, Steve, 310
Martin, Vince, 365
Martindale, Wink, 334
Martinez, Antonio, 318
Martinez, Rudy, 401
Martini, Jerry, 443
Martino, Al, 149
Martyn, John, 383
Marvelettes, 264, 334-335, 361, 412
Marvelows, 201
Marvin, Hank B., 407, 431
Marvin, Welch And Farrar, 432
Masekela, Hugh, 13, 98, 355
Mason, Barry, 9, 92, 125
Mason, Dave, 197, 224, 477
Mason, Laurie, 378
Mason, Wood, Capaldi And Frog, 477
Massey, Calvin, 132
Massey, Marian, 323
Massey, William, 503
Massi, Nick, 221
Masters, Greg, 275
Mastin, Will, 160
Mastrangelo, Carlo, 53, 170
Mastrangelo, John, 87
Matching Mole, 447
Mathews, Tom, 112

Mathis, Johnny, 167, 245, 321, 329
Maughan, Susan, 335
Maughn, Don, 211, 448
Mauldin, Joe B., 145
Maus, John, 493-495
Mavericks, 343
Max Frost And The Troopers, 18
Maxfield, Mike, 150, 307
May, Annie, 135
May, Billy, 57, 377
May, Dave, 5
May, Phil, 396
May, Simon, 69
Mayall, John, 12, 21, 97, 104, 120, 131, 153, 182, 253, 297, 335-336, 379, 445
Mayfield, Curtis, 96, 213, 276-277, 308, 336-338, 404, 458
Mayfield, Percy, 270
Mazarro, Ginny, 386
Mazer, Elliot, 20
Mazzola, Lorraine, 405
MC5, 35, 196, 338, 424
McAleer, Dave, 5
McAuley, Jackie, 470
McAuley, Jackie, 470
McBride, Christian, 446
McCann, Jim, 182
McCann, Les, 339
McCartney, Michael, 49, 427
McCartney, Paul, 19, 44, 53, 68, 79, 110, 193, 199, 201, 223, 270, 280, 288, 300, 307, 317, 333, 383, 415, 427, 435-436, 450, 506
McCarty, Jim, 424, 509
McClain, Charly, 134
McClain, Mighty Sam, 400
McClane, Ian, 15
McClean, Norbert, 196
McCleese, James, 449
McClelland, Geoff, 286
McClinton, Delbert, 116
McCloud, Brewster, 10
McClure, Bobby, 38
McCoo, Marilyn, 215
McCoy, Charlie, 20
McCoy, Van, 202
McCoys, 56, 85, 338-339
McCracken, Charlie, 74, 163
McCracken, Hugh, 421
McCulloch, Danny, 16
McCulloch, Gordon, 102
McCulloch, Jack, 16, 474
McCulloch, Jimmy, 473-474
McCullough, Henry, 194, 453
McDaniels, Gene, 27, 56, 339

McDermott, Jack, 104
McDermott, John, 260
McDonald, Carol, 236
McDonald, Country Joe, 139
McDonald, Kathi, 63
McDonald, Robin, 150, 307
McDougall, Dave, 15
McDougall, Richard, 105
McDowell, Kenny, 470
McDowell, Mississippi Fred, 339-340
McEwan, Bill, 272
McFadden, Eddie, 445
McFarland, John, 307, 437
McFarland, Spanky, 234
McGear, Mike, 427
McGee, Bobby, 198
McGee, Jerry, 366
McGeorge, Jerry, 247, 433
McGhee, Sticks, 270
McGillberry, Harry, 468
McGough, Roger, 315, 427
McGovern, George, 384, 438
McGregor, Craig, 190
McGriff, Jimmy, 445
McGuinn, Clark And Hillman, 100
McGuinn, Jim, 97, 130, 350
McGuinn, Roger, 42, 187, 234, 343, 367
McGuinness Flint, 235
McGuinness, Tom, 329
McGuire, Barry, 10, 36, 327, 340-341, 367, 442
McGuire, Margi, 405
McGuire, Pat, 121
McGurk, Tommy, 149
McIntyre, Mac, 284
McJohn, Goldy, 458
McKay, Ken, 296
McKechnie, Licorice, 277
McKee, Phil, 459
McKenzie, Ali, 66
McKenzie, Angus, 166
McKenzie, Julia, 508
McKenzie, Laura, 328, 385
McKenzie, Scott, 291, 327, 340-341, 385, 420
McKew, Roger, 90, 402
McKinleys, 108
McKinney, Mabron, 272
McKinnie, Dee, 336
McKnight, Brian, 361
McKuen, Rod, 341, 431, 437
McLagan, Ian, 188, 444-445
McLain, Jean, 334
McLaren, Malcolm, 250
McLaren, Steve, 165

McLaughlin, John, 77, 158, 217, 389
McLaughlin, Ollie, 105
Mclean, Norman, 196
McLemore, Lamont, 215
McLeod, Alice, 132
McLeod, John, 31
McLeod, Vincent, 422
McManus, Jimmy, 484
McMichael, Joe, 501
McMillan, Ian, 388
McMullen, Annette, 487
McNally, John, 428
McNaughton, Toto, 82
McNeil, Terry, 448
McPhatter, Clyde, 55, 179-180, 504
McPhee, Skip, 204
McPhee, Tony, 182, 249
McQueen, Steve, 411
McRae, Barry, 160
McRae, Carmen, 161
McShee, Jacqui, 283, 383
McTavish, Dave, 62
McTell, Ralph, 270
McVay, Ray, 113
McVie, Christine, 42
McVie, John, 53, 335
McWilliams, David, 342
Meadon, Peter, 499
Meagher, Ron, 50
Meaux, Huey P., 257, 325, 441
Medley, Bill, 304, 410
Medley, John, 235
Medley, Phil, 56
Medress, Hank, 475
Meehan, Tony, 137, 251-252, 431-432
Meek, Joe, 53, 129, 216, 257, 268, 289, 313, 342-343, 377, 462, 476
Meek, Robert George, 342
Meikle, Buster, 484
Meikle, David, 484
Meisner, Randy, 366, 382
Mel And Kim, 309
Melander, Colin, 436
Melanie, 507
Melcher, Terry, 92, 98, 330, 343, 385, 406, 410, 425
Mellers, Wilfred, 49
Melton, Barry, 139-140
Members, Dave, 479
Memphis Horns, 116, 331
Memphis Slim, 53, 104
Menard, D.L., 31
Mendes, Sergio, 13
Mercer, Chris, 253, 335
Mercer, Johnny, 154
Mercer, Pat, 84
Mercouri, Melina, 293
Merrill, John, 381
Merryweather, Neil, 236
Merseybeats, 63, 143, 343, 437

Messina, Jim, 94
Metchick, Don, 352
Metheny, Pat, 259
Metzner, Doug, 139
Meyers, Augie, 441
Michael And The Firebirds, 318
Michael, George, 89, 225, 353
Michael, Peter, 6
Michaels, David, 247
Michaels, Lee, 210
Michalski, John, 139
Mickey And Sylvia, 257
Midler, Bette, 28, 156, 261
Midnight Runners, 333, 497, 504
Mighty Avengers, 375
Mighty Baby, 8, 213, 343-344
Mighty Sam, 400
Migil Five, 344
Mike And Joe And The Rebel Guys, 318
Mike And The Utopians, 7
Mikey General, 141
Milano, Freddie, 53, 170
Miles, Barry, 160
Miles, Buddy, 195, 259, 424
Miles, George, 195
Miles, John, 159
Miles, Richard, 160
Milkwood, 300
Miller, Andy, 344
Miller, Cleo, 196
Miller, David, 323
Miller, Don, 492
Miller, Dusty, 459
Miller, Elva, 344
Miller, Frankie, 399
Miller, Gary, 27, 354
Miller, Glenn, 129, 328
Miller, Harry, 181
Miller, Jerry, 123, 350
Miller, Jimmy, 371, 416
Miller, Jonathan, 58
Miller, Mitch, 54, 134
Miller, Mrs, 344
Miller, Paul, 6
Miller, Perry, 181, 510
Miller, Peter, 284
Miller, Robert, 196
Miller, Roger, 344-345, 411
Miller, Ronnie, 140
Miller, Steve, 7, 59, 228, 236, 336, 355
Millie, 194, 345
Milligan, Spike, 466
Mills Brothers, 261
Mills, Freddie, 237
Mills, Gary, 135
Mills, Gladys, 345
Mills, Gordon, 273, 289, 299, 310
Mills, Leroy, 51

Mills, Mike, 480
Mills, Mrs., 345
Mimms, Garnet, And The Enchanters, 56, 198, 345-346, 464, 496
Mincelli, Mike, 105
Mindbenders, 218, 346
Mingay, Roger, 377
Mingus Dynasty, 347
Mingus, Charles, 303, 346-348, 383
Minnelli, Liza, 161
Minns, Paul, 471
Minogue, Dennis, 112
Minogue, Kylie, 315
Minott, Sugar, 141
Miracles, 349 and passim
Miranda, Bob, 248
Miss Christine, 246
Miss Cynderella, 246
Miss Lucy, 246
Miss Mercy, 246
Miss Pamela, 246
Miss Sandra, 246
Miss Sparky, 246
Misunderstood, 349 and passim
Mitchell, Billy, 259
Mitchell, Bob, 50, 299
Mitchell, Bobby, 260
Mitchell, Chad, Trio, 52, 350, 380
Mitchell, Guy, 134
Mitchell, James, 422
Mitchell, Joni, 130, 171, 256, 348, 422, 425, 507
Mitchell, Leonard, 171, 425
Mitchell, Liz, 327
Mitchell, Marion, 288
Mitchell, Mike, 299
Mitchell, Mitch, 115, 260
Mitchell, Valerie, 288
Mitham, Norman, 407
Mitropoulos, Dimitri, 57
Mittell, Lynn, 100
Moby Grape, 93, 123, 247, 293, 350-351, 355
Moe, Rick, 350
Moeller, Tommy, 484
Mogg, Ambrose, 351
Mojo Men, 352, 443
Mojos, 119, 352
Molten, 'Moulty', 34
Moman, Chips, 392
Monarch, Michael, 458
Moncur, Ian, 326
Money, Zoot, 16, 153, 306, 321, 352-353, 427, 445
Monger, Alan, 216
Monk, Jack, 35
Monk, Thelonious, 12, 132-133, 157, 159, 346, 451
Monkees, 70, 73, 83, 103, 142, 238, 259, 283, 304, 353-354, 490

Monro, Matt, 25, 68-69, 85, 318, 335, 354-355
Monroe, James, 209
Monroe, Marilyn, 80, 151
Montanez, Christopher, 355
Monte Carlo, 85, 250
Montez, Chris, 309, 355
Montgomery Brothers, 356
Montgomery, Bob, 145
Montgomery, Buddy, 356
Montgomery, John, 356
Montgomery, Melba, 387
Montgomery, Monk, 356
Montgomery, Robbie, 276
Montgomery, Thomasina, 469
Montgomery, Wes, 356-357, 445-446
Montiero, June, 477
Montoya, Coco, 336
Moody Blues, 72, 201, 222, 305, 357-358
Moody, Bill, 421
Moody, Ron, 86
Moon, Charley, 85
Moon, Doug, 105
Moon, Keith, 462, 499-501
Moon, Tony, 501
Moondog, 112
Mooney, Thom, 364
Moonglows, 231
Moonrider, 498
Moore, Ben, 400
Moore, Bob, 404
Moore, David, 426
Moore, Gary, 131, 179, 336
Moore, Gatemouth, 473
Moore, James, 395
Moore, Melba, 406
Moore, Mike, 6
Moore, Robin, 425
Moore, Sam, 426
Moore, Scotty, 67, 389, 391, 395
Moore, Stan, 70
Moore, William, 268
Moorer, Alvis, 201
Moorer, Betty, 201
Moorer, Gilbert, 201
Moorshead, John, 182, 257, 296
Morais, Trevor, 382
Moraz, Patrick, 357
Moreira, Airto, 158
Morgan, Adrian, 138
Morgan, Alun, 356
Morgan, Andrew, 351
Morgan, John, 458
Morgan, Lee, 445
Morgan, Mark, 195
Morgan, Ron, 195
Morganfield, McKinley, 362-363
Morias, Trevor, 212

Morningstar, Marjorie, 205
Morricone, Ennio, 322
Morris, Jeff, 34
Morris, Roy, 306
Morris, Steven, 413
Morrison, Bob, 177
Morrison, Dorothy Combs, 255
Morrison, James, 175, 177
Morrison, Jim, 175-177, 470
Morrison, Patricia, 177
Morrison, Sterling, 488-489
Morrison, Van, 12, 56, 117, 209-210, 240, 269, 289, 342, 408, 433, 470-471, 504
Morrissey, 436
Morrow, Little Willie, 503
Morton, Jelly Roll, 303
Morton, Lionel, 220
Morton, Rockette, 105
Morton, Shadow, 245, 433, 486
Mosley, Bob, 350-351
Mosley, Ronald, 422
Moss, Geoff, 284
Moss, Jerry, 12
Moss, Paul, 462
Moss, Wayne, 20
Most, Mickie, 16, 19, 119, 214, 262, 323, 364, 509
Mother Earth, 290, 358
Motherlode, 89
Mothers Of Invention, 88, 94, 103, 206, 224, 246, 295, 308, 358-360, 457, 482
Motörhead, 205, 413
Motown Records, 34, 36, 96, 120, 124, 135, 144, 196, 215, 221-223, 231, 238, 264, 266, 272, 277, 279, 287, 332, 348-349, 361, 411-412, 417, 454, 458, 460, 466, 469, 487, 494, 497, 504-505
Mott The Hoople, 321, 453
Moules, Peter, 484
Mountain, Valerie, 164
Mouskouri, Nana, 52
Move, 358 and passim
Moy, Sylvia, 506
Moyet, Alison, 311
Mr Brown, 91
Mr C, 122
Muddy Waters, 59, 97, 119, 168-169, 240, 271, 362-363, 414, 430
Mudlarks, 24
Mugwumps, 197, 322
Muldaur, Maria, 375
Muldoon, Clive, 168
Mulligan, Declan, 50

Mulligan, Gerry, 12, 157, 451
Mulvey, Andi, 387
Munden, Dave, 478
Mundi, Billy, 358, 407
Munroe, Pete, 168
Munroe, Tony, 66
Murdoch, Bruce, 75
Murphy, Bernard, 84
Murphy, Kevin, 14
Murphy, Michael, 353
Murray, Anne, 256
Murray, Charles Shaar, 260, 270
Murray, Dee, 163
Murray, Don, 482
Murray, Jim, 401
Murray, Martin, 268
Murray, Neil, 131, 256, 422
Murray, Tony, 387, 480
Musique, 206, 250, 348
Musselwhite, Charlie, 236
Mydland, Brent, 242
Myers, Mike, 28
Myers, Paul, 58
Myers, Stanley, 69
Myles, Billy, 298
Myles, John, 387
Myles, Tony, 387
Myman, Bob, 210
Mynah Birds, 94
Myrick, Weldon, 20
Mystics, 283

N

Nacardo, Vinny, 105
Naftalin, Mark, 97, 358
Nagy, John, 191
Napier-Bell, Simon, 286, 454, 509
Napoleon XIV, 224, 364
Nash, David, 147
Nash, Graham, 147, 150, 201, 265-266, 285, 462, 468
Nashville Teens, 16, 19, 91, 179, 319, 364
Navarre, Ludovic, 269
Navarro, Fats, 159
Naylor, Shel, 379
Nazareth, 476
Nazz, 364-365
Neal, Bob, 390
Neal, Pat, 233
Neil, Barry, 86
Neil, Chris, 5
Neil, Fred, 196, 365, 422
Nelson, Albert, 297
Nelson, Earl, 76, 180, 297
Nelson, Eric Hilliard, 365
Nelson, George, 239, 362
Nelson, Jim, 323
Nelson, John, 366
Nelson, Lee, 76

Nelson, Oliver, 445
Nelson, Ozzie, 365
Nelson, Pete, 217
Nelson, Phil, 366
Nelson, Rick, 365-366
Nelson, Ross, 323
Nelson, Sandy, 223, 282, 366-367, 449
Nelson, Teri, Group, 295
Nelson, Tracy, 358, 473
Nelson, Willie, 92, 110-111, 309, 345, 366
Nesmith, Michael, 283, 353
Ness, Richard, 484
Nevins, Al, 304
New Christy Minstrels, 24, 340, 367-368
New Colony Six, 18
New Jazz Orchestra, 20
New Riders Of The Purple Sage, 224
New Seekers, 196, 431
New Vaudeville Band, 79, 368, 466
Newbeats, 368
Newell, Norman, 38, 172, 383, 502
Newley, Anthony, 37, 85, 126, 161, 174, 318, 368-369
Newman, Andy, 473-474
Newman, David, 288, 454
Newman, Floyd, 331
Newman, Randy, 51, 167, 181, 251, 288, 366, 372, 454
Newman, Richard, 336
Newman, Tom, 386
Newman, Tony, 155, 386
Newmark, Andy, 443
Newton, Paul, 235
Newton, Wayne, 370
Newton-John, Olivia, 408, 432
Ney, Michael, 129
Nice, 370-371 and passim
Nichol, Al, 482
Nicholas, Frank, 179
Nicholas, Paul, 462, 508
Nicholson, Geoff, 192
Nicholson, Hughie, 332, 388
Nick And The Nomads, 207
Nico, 379, 419, 488-489
Nicol, Jimmy, 453
Nicols, Maggie, 181
Nielsen, Rick, 364
Nighthawk, Robert, 119, 481
Nilsson, Harry, 365-366
1910 Fruitgum Company, 295, 371
Nirvana, 371 and passim
Nitty Gritty Dirt Band, 138, 272, 294

Nitzsche, Jack, 79, 167, 314, 372, 428, 448, 450, 495
Niven, David, 251
Nix, Don, 330
Nix-Nomads, 207
Nolan, Larry, 447
Nolder, Terry, 204
Noon, Terry, 267
Noone, Peter, 261
Nordby, Bob, 299
Norman, Dave, 8
Norman, Philip, 49, 419
Norvo, Red, 9, 346
Novello, Ivor, 65, 69-70, 85, 156, 254, 263, 266, 301, 305, 427, 432, 440, 479
NRBQ, 162-163
Nugent, Geoff, 484
Nugent, Ted, 14
Nunlee, Darrel, 135
Nyholt, Jim, 18
Nyro, Laura, 215, 355, 372-373, 384

O

O'Barry, Richard, 365
O'Brien, Lucy, 454, 456
O'Connor, Des, 321, 440
O'Connor, Michael, 89
O'Connor, Sinead, 139
O'Donnel, Michael, 178
O'Donnell, Daniel, 405
O'Jays, 315
O'Rahilly, Ronan, 16, 62
O'Riley, Tony, 306
O'Rourke, Jim, 206
O'Toole, Peter, 126
Oakley, Annie, 205
Oakley, Vic, 100
Obispo, Luis, 195
Ocean Colour Scene, 21
Ochs, Phil, 29, 75, 196-197, 374, 381, 485
Odetta, 52, 124, 183, 262, 290, 485
Ofarim, Esther And Abi, 503
Ogg, Alex, 5
Ohio Express, 295, 371, 374, 471
Ohio Knox, 129
Ohio Players, 209
Ohio Untouchables, 209
Oldham, Andrew Loog, 208, 237, 261, 364, 375, 387, 414, 444, 482
Oldham, Dewey Linton, 375
Oldham, Spooner, 375, 382-383, 400
Oliver, Sy, 119
Olsen, Keith, 77, 242
Olsen, Mike, 210

Olsen, Richard, 116
Olsson, Nigel, 163, 387
Ono, Yoko, 47-48, 256
Oppenheimer, Ronnie, 210, 327
Orbison, Roy, 108, 111, 113, 142, 189, 375-377, 386, 398, 405
Orlando, Tony, 213, 475
Orlons, 178, 377
Ornadel, Cyril, 68, 85
Orpheus, 44, 246, 261, 377, 484
Orr, Don, 26
Ory, Kid, 346
Osborn, Joe, 245
Osborne, Jeffrey, 497
Osborne, Tony, Sound, 377
Osbourne, Ozzy, 20
Oskar, Lee, 95
Osmond, Marie, 151
Osmonds, 502
Otis And The Shooters, 403
Otis, Clyde, 55
Otis, Johnny, 166, 169, 280
Otis, Shuggie, 280
Ott, Horace, 140
Ousley, Curtis, 296
Outlaws, 377 and *passim*
Overlanders, 156, 378
Overnall, Harry, 212
Owens, Jimmy, 21
Owens, Richard, 467
Owens, Shirley, 436-437
Owsley, Stanley, 241
Oxford Circle, 293

P

Pablo, Augustus, 303
Pace, Ronnie, 204
Pace, Sam, 201
Pachuta, Mel, 273
Pacific Gas And Electric, 378
Paddy, Klaus And Gibson, 378-379
Paffgen, Christa, 488
Page, Jimmy, 107, 123, 143, 167, 212, 279, 310, 379, 459, 462, 509-510
Page, Ken, 379
Page, Larry, 78, 300, 379-380, 480, 486
Page, Patti, 70
Paige, Elaine, 69, 126
Palance, Jack, 57
Paley, Andy, 43
Palmer, Alan, 82
Palmer, Bruce, 94
Palmer, Carl, 87, 212
Palmer, Clive, 277
Palmer, Dave, 14

Palmer, Earl, 70
Palmer, John, 74, 193
Palmer, Michael, 141
Palmer, Richard, 36
Palmer, Robert, 82, 278, 419
Palumbo, Larry, 191
Panebianco, Ginger, 236
Panton, Roy, 345
Papalia, Giovanni, 21
Pappalardi, Felix, 421, 510
Pappalardo, Fred, 276
Paradons, 223
Paramor, Norrie, 24, 92, 138, 219, 275, 407, 431, 435, 485
Paramount Jazz Band, 65-66
Paramounts, 292, 305, 380, 389, 399
Parcel Of Rogues, 182
Pardo, Joe, 168
Paris Sisters, 449
Paris, Johnny, 64, 287
Pariser, Alan, 355
Park, Alan, 51
Parker, Billy, 188
Parker, Charlie, 12, 157, 346
Parker, David, 35
Parker, Ian, 266
Parker, John, 19, 395
Parker, Junior, 71, 473
Parker, Maceo, 88
Parker, Robert, 141
Parks, Larry, 379
Parks, Van Dyke, 41-42, 130, 352
Parnell, Val, 174
Parnes, Larry, 44, 93, 113, 209, 292, 389
Parritt, Barbara, 477
Parry, Eddie, 165
Parsons, Eugene Victor, 99
Parsons, Gene, 99
Parsons, Gram, 99-100, 169, 319, 365
Parsons, Terry, 354
Parton, Dolly, 162, 309
Partridge Family, 70, 141, 213
Partridge, Don, 380
Partridge, John, 70
Pash, Jim, 461
Paton, Hume, 387
Patrick, Bill, 253
Patrick, Charles, 80
Patrick, James, 379, 509
Patrick, John, 213, 378, 409
Patrick, Phil, 167
Patten, Brian, 315
Patten, Dehner C., 293
Patten, John, 445
Patterson, Bill, 253
Patterson, Jerry, 426

Patterson, Joe, 112
Patterson, Linnie, 82
Patterson, Ottilie, 306
Patto, Johnny, 296
Patto, Mike, 76, 453
Patton, Charley, 206, 258
Paul, Clarence, 505
Paul, Dean, 170
Paul, Don, 380
Paul, Frankie, 141
Paul, Les, 23, 219, 326
Paul, Mike, 384
Paul, Steve, 5, 338
Paupers, 355
Paverty, Frank, 466
Pawle, Ivan, 179
Paxton, Gary S., 223
Paxton, Tom, 75, 196, 214, 216, 234, 263, 374, 380-381
Payne, Bill, 226
Payne, Freda, 264
Payne, Gordon, 145
Payne, Jim, 281
Payne, Scherrie, 460-461
Payton, Brenda, 84
Payton, Denis, 124
Payton, Nicholas, 445
Peaches And Herb, 381
Peacock, Phil, 446
Peacock, Roger, 120
Peanut Butter Conspiracy, 129, 381-382
Pearce, Earnestine, 217
Pearson, Ken, 290
Pearson, Noel, 120
Peaston, David, 38
Peay, Benjamin Franklin, 55
Peck, Ged, 217
Peck, Gregory, 108
Peddlers, 213, 382
Pedersen, Herb, 100
Peel, Dave, 5
Peel, John, 120, 219, 316, 321, 483
Pegg, Dave, 103
Peloquin, Jerry, 285
Pelosi, Jeff, 146
Pelsia, J.W., 31
Pemberton, Bugs, 484
Pender, Mike, 428
Pendleton, Brian, 396
Penn, Dan, 375, 382, 400, 473
Pentangle, 283, 383
Peretti, Hugo, 475
Perez, John, 441
Perfect, Christine, 120
Perkins, Carl, 45, 92, 108-109, 111, 376, 390, 393
Perkins, Jerry, 393
Perkins, Luther, 108
Perkins, Polly, 7
Perkins, Terence, 177
Perks, William, 414

Perry, Bill, 240
Perry, Chris, 305
Perry, Jimmy, 279
Perry, John, 240, 501
Perry, Lee, 11
Perry, Richard, 289
Perry, Stu, 452
Pet Shop Boys, 455
Peter And Gordon, 45, 114, 229, 335, 383-384
Peter, Paul And Mary, 184, 234, 384
Peters, Bernadette, 69
Peters, Jeff, 90
Peters, Richard, 395
Petersen, Dick, 299
Petersen, John, 50, 251
Petersen, Paul, 155, 205
Peterson, Dickie, 74
Peterson, Ralph, 74
Peterson, Ray, 36
Peterson, Sylvia, 121
Petersson, Tom, 364
Petters, John, 122
Petty, Norman, 145, 216, 262, 317, 375, 388
Petty, Tom, 188-189, 376, 434
Peyser, Joan, 58
Peyton, Lawrence, 222
Pflayer, Jim, 374
Phay, Danny, 122
Phelps, George, 350
Phenomena, 353
Phil The Fluter, 508
Phillips, Chynna, 385
Phillips, Dave, 102
Phillips, Eddie, 143
Phillips, Gregory, 379
Phillips, Jim, 328, 385
Phillips, John, 291, 327-328, 340, 355, 364, 385, 420
Phillips, McKenzie, 385
Phillips, Michelle, 291, 327-328, 385
Phillips, Ray, 364
Phillips, Roy, 382
Phillips, Scott, 385, 420
Phillips, Sid, 53
Phillips, Simon, 500
Phillips, Utah, 198
Piaf, Edith, 25, 126
Piazza, Joe, 443
Piblokto!, 40, 91
Picariello, Freddy, 104
Pickens, Earl, 149
Pickering, Nigel, 449
Pickett, Kenny, 143
Pickett, Wilson, 140, 209, 272, 276, 298, 331, 385-386, 465, 476
Pickford Hopkins, Gary, 205
Pierce, Webb, 324
Pierson, Clark, 290
Pierson, Jon, 21

Piggott, Mike, 383
Pike, Jim, 311
Pilloud, Rod, 146
Pinder, Mike, 357
Pinera, Mike, 278
Pink Fairies, 35, 168, 205, 207, 246, 292
Pink Floyd, 35
Pinkerton's Assorted Colours, 386
Pinkney, Bill, 180
Pinz, Shelly, 310
Pistilli, Gene, 112
Piston, Walter, 57
Pitman, Jimmy, 459
Pitman-Avory, Jim, 474
Pitney, Gene, 27, 149, 156, 167, 365, 386-387, 415, 421
Pitt, Ken, 50
Pixies, 196
Plainsong, 316
Plant, Robert, 306, 351, 379
Planxty, 138
Plaster Casters, 246
Plastic Ono Band, 379, 392, 450
Plastic Penny, 121, 387
Plater, Alan, 5, 263
Platt, John, 260, 510
Player, John, 286, 399, 432
Pockriss, Lee, 148, 167, 205
Poco, 94, 276, 366
Podolor, Richie, 366
Poets, 387-388 and *passim*
Pogues, 182
Poindexter, Buster, 476
Poison, 473
Poitier, Sidney, 277
Polci, Gerry, 221
Pollack, Lew, 29
Pomus, Doc, 62, 86, 171, 297, 388, 391, 428, 437, 474, 501
Pond, Paul, 329
Pons, Jim, 308, 359, 482
Pool, Malcolm, 21
Poole, Brian, And The Tremeloes, 45, 56, 124, 135, 213, 388, 478
Poole, Mac, 62
Poole, Terry, 30
Pope, Charles, 463
Pope, Joseph, 463
Popsicle, 282
Porter, Cole, 497
Porter, David, 33, 426, 472
Portman-Smith, Nigel, 383
Portz, Chuck, 482
Posa, Frank, 217
Potger, Keith, 431
Potter, Butch, 40

Potts, Sylvester, 135
Poulos, Jon Jon, 93
Povey, Jon, 197
Powell, Bud, 346
Powell, Clive, 209
Powell, Cozy, 62
Powell, Dick, 31, 146
Powell, Robert, 86
Powell, Roger, 8, 343
Powell, William, 315
Power Station, 292
Power, Duffy, 214, 389
Power, Will, 20
Powers, Dale, 374
Powers, Toni, 245
Prater, David, 426
Preager, Lou, 324
Premru, Raymond, 20
Prescod, Frank, 138
Prescott, Betty, 83
Presley, Elvis, 23, 62, 67, 70, 80, 107-109, 126, 142, 162, 173, 202, 205, 219, 238, 243, 248, 256, 293, 297, 311, 324, 331, 374-375, 389-395, 398, 407, 411, 415, 425, 439, 474, 490
Presley, Reg, 480
Preston, Billy, 47, 296
Preston, Denis, 342
Preston, Dennis, 396
Preston, Don, 358-359
Preston, Johnny, 305, 395-396
Preston, Mike, 318, 396
Pretty Things, 35, 168, 178, 197, 207, 364, 396-397, 476
Previn, Dory, 295
Price, Alan, 16, 209-210, 237
Price, Jim, 248
Price, Kenny, 92
Price, Lloyd, 219
Price, Louis, 467
Price, Rod, 67
Pride, Charley, 23
Pride, Dickie, 113, 389
Priestley, Brian, 133, 348
Primes, 460, 466
Primettes, 32, 460
Primitives, 379, 488
Prince Buster, 397
Prince La La, 40
Prince, Hal, 58
Prince, Rod, 93
Prince, Viv, 291, 396
Pritchard, Barry, 219
Pritchard, Dave, 275
Proby, P.J., 37, 108, 113, 210, 219, 224, 238, 372, 398
Procol Harum, 62, 179, 380, 387, 399
Propellerheads, 39
Pryce, Jonathan, 38

Pryor, Richard, 422
Psyche-Out, 459
Public Enemy, 89
Puckett, Gary, And The Union Gap, 128, 295, 399-400
Puff Daddy, 379
Pugh, Bryan, 108, 279
Pugh, Mike, 350
Pumer, Eddie, 294
Purdie, Bernard, 91, 296, 421, 446
Purify, Bobby, 375, 400
Purify, James, 400
Purify, James And Bobby, 375, 400
Purple Gang, 400
Putnam, Norbert, 20, 382
Pye, Peter, 268

Q

Quaife, Peter, 300
Quant, Mary, 375
Quantrell, Margot, 83
Quarry Men, 44
Quaye, Caleb, 455
Queen Latifah, 239, 361
Queen, B.B., 281
? And The Mysterians, 401
Quickly, Tommy, 199
Quicksilver Messenger Service, 86, 169, 240, 326, 355, 401-402
Quiet Five, 402
Quill, Greg, 419
Quincy, Dave, 76
Quinichette, Paul, 133
Quinn, Derek, 227
Quintessence, 441
Quirico, DeWayne, 228

R

R.E.M., 28, 351, 418, 480
Rabbit Foot Minstrels, 473
Rabkin, Eddie, 475
Raelettes, 137
Rafelson, Bob, 353
Rafferty, Gerry, 273
Ragovoy, Jerry, 56, 198, 218, 291, 346, 437, 464
Rainbow Bridge, 259-260
Rainey, Chuck, 19
Rainey, Max, 471
Rains, George, 358, 441
Raitt, Bonnie, 140, 269, 340
Ram Jam, 212, 310, 497
Ramistella, John, 410
Ramones, 450
Ramos, Larry, 367
Ramsey, Alan, 312

Randall, Freddy, 32
Randell, Buddy, 304
Rankin, Billy, 302
Rankin, Brian, 431
Ransley, Tony, 183
Rare Earth, 361
Raskin, Gene, 270
Raskin, Jonathan, 21
Raspberry Singers, 279
Rathbone, Don, 265
Ratledge, Mike, 35, 447
Rattigan, Terence, 508
Rattles, 248
Ravel, Chris, 15
Ravenscroft, Raphael, 421
Rawls, Lou, 12, 355, 402-403
Ray, Ada, 284
Ray, Anthony, 107
Ray, Dave, 447
Ray, James, 179
Ray, Johnnie, 69, 134, 160
Ray, Johnny, 245
Ray, Ken, 431
Ray, Tom, 308
Raymond, Paul, 121, 387
Raymonde, Ivor, 229, 454, 493
Rea, Chris, 39
Read, Mike, 410
Reading, Bertice, 305
Rebennack, Mac, 40
Record, Eugene, 8
Red Cadillac And A Black Moustache, 324
Redding, David, 213
Redding, Noel, 115, 213, 258, 260, 462
Redding, Otis, 96, 128, 133, 136, 178, 194, 260, 291, 298, 331, 355, 403-404, 465, 472
Reed, Jerry, 23, 109, 391
Reed, Jimmy, 16
Reed, John, 5, 178
Reed, Les, 9, 125, 289
Reed, Lou, 178, 426, 488-489
Rees, Wyndham, 205
Rees-Mogg, William, 416
Reese, Jim, 228
Reese, Lloyd, 346
Reeves, Barry, 74
Reeves, James Travis, 404
Reeves, Jim, 23, 142, 404-405
Reeves, John Rex, 405
Reeves, Martha, 213, 332-333
Reeves, Mary, 405
Reeves, Tony, 131, 335
Reeves, Vic, 414
Regan, Joan, 164
Reid, Duke, 10, 141, 164
Reid, Eileen, 101
Reid, Keith, 380, 399

Reid, Terry, 284
Reilly, Maggie, 354
Reiner, Fritz, 57
Reiner, Robert Lee, 308
Reinhardt, Django, 356
Reins, Frank, 105
Relf, Bob, 76
Relf, Keith, 509
Renaldo And Clara, 30, 75, 187, 191, 256
Renbourn, John, 193, 283, 383
Rendell, Don, 20
Renwick, Tim, 292
Reparata And The Delrons, 310, 405
Repsch, John, 343
Resnick, Artie, 471
Revere, Paul, And The Raiders, 61, 92, 299, 343, 406
Revolutionaries, 247
Reynolds, Debbie, 440
Reynolds, Malvina, 429
Reynolds, Tommy, 463
Rheimschagen, Herman, 346
Rheinhart, Larry 'Rhino', 278
Rhinoceros, 406-407
Rhodes, Doug, 344
Rhodes, Emitt, 77
Rhodes, Robert, 44
Rhythm Factory, 467
Ribowsky, Mark, 450
Rice, Larry, 100
Rice, Mack, 209
Rice, Tim, 21, 433
Rich, Buddy, 454
Rich, Charlie, 109
Rich, Herbie, 195
Richard, Cliff, 34, 37, 62, 83, 87, 113, 203, 207, 214, 238, 248, 250, 318, 407-410, 429, 431-432
Richard, Ervin 'Dick', 31
Richards, Billy, 169
Richards, Keith, 60, 169, 188, 385, 414, 418-419
Richards, Rick, 436
Richards, Ron, 333
Richardson, Joe, 138
Richie, Lionel, 238, 361
Richmond, Dannie, 347
Richmond, Dave, 329
Rick And The Ravens, 175
Rickett, Nooney, 320
Ricks, Tommy, 179
Ridarelli, Robert, 423
Riddell, Kirk, 123
Riddle, Nelson, 38
Ridgley, Tommy, 472
Ridley, Greg, 21, 452, 492
Righteous Brothers, 70, 238, 257, 304, 410, 450, 493

Riley, Terry, 471
Rimbaud, Arthur, 185
Rinehart, Bill, 308
Riopelle, Jerry, 466
Riot Squad, 78, 258, 380
Rip Chords, 92, 343
Ripp, Artie, 73, 284
Rising Sons, 306, 410
Ritchie, Brian, 459
Ritter, Preston, 195
Ritz, David, 118, 226, 233, 281, 349, 413
Rivers, Johnny, 9, 36, 70, 355, 410-411
Rivers, Tony, And The Castaways, 240, 250
Rivingtons, 223
Rizzo, Pat, 148
Rizzo, Rick, 148
Roach, Max, 157, 312, 347
Roaring Sixties, 212
Robbins, Harold, 390
Robbins, Jerome, 57-58
Robbins, Marty, 27, 134
Robert And Elizabeth, 508
Robert, Alan, 175
Robert, George, 342
Roberts, Alan, 102
Roberts, Andy, 315
Roberts, Bobby, 10
Roberts, Doug, 216
Roberts, Jim, 52
Roberts, John, 497
Roberts, Mike, 315
Robertson, John, 50, 260, 395
Robertson, Liz, 86
Robertson, Robbie, 185, 256
Robeson, Paul, 321
Robey, Don, 71
Robinson, Arnett, 209
Robinson, Bill 'Bojangles', 160
Robinson, Claudette, 349
Robinson, Cynthia, 443
Robinson, David, 326, 349, 413
Robinson, Earl, 131
Robinson, Harry, 12, 396
Robinson, Jimmy Lee, 298
Robinson, John, 381
Robinson, Lee, 298
Robinson, Peter, 199
Robinson, R.B., 135
Robinson, Sandi, 381
Robinson, Smokey, 136, 222, 238, 264, 303, 334, 348-349, 411-413, 460, 466-467, 497-498, 506
Robinson, Spike, 122
Robinson, Tom, 209
Robinson, William, 348, 411
Roche, Pierre, 25
Rock, Tommy, 501

Rockin' Berries, 224, 413
Rockin' Vickers, 413
Rocky Sharpe And The Replays, 194
Roden, Jess, 82
Roderick, David, 220
Rodford, Jim, 511
Rodgers, John, 421
Rodgers, Paul, 379
Rodgers, Richard, 85, 126, 331, 390
Rodney, Don, 156
Rodzinski, Artur, 57
Roe, Tommy, 77, 128, 413-414
Rogan, Johnny, 5, 20, 94, 98, 100, 147, 169, 300, 302, 471
Rogers, Bill, 349
Rogers, Bobby, 348-349
Rogers, Claudette, 412
Rogers, Emerson, 348
Rogers, Glouster, 315
Rogers, Jimmy, 119, 197, 363
Rogers, Julie, 414
Rogers, Kenny, 367
Rogers, Pete, 57
Rogers, Roy, 158
Rogers, Shorty, 57
Rogers, Wanda, 334
Rogers, Warren, 433
Rolling Stones, 3, 11, 13, 17, 19, 34, 36-37, 45-46, 48, 59, 66, 79-80, 98, 120, 162, 168, 188, 195, 197, 205, 213, 231, 237, 240, 265, 269, 301, 306, 325, 333, 335, 340, 351, 355, 363, 372, 375, 386, 396, 402, 408, 414-419, 431, 444, 472, 509
Rollins, Sonny, 132, 157, 159
Rolls, Julie, 414
Romanowski, Patricia, 461, 468
Romantics, 422
Romeo, Kathy, 405
Romero, Chan, 462
Ronettes, 37, 70, 148, 164, 172, 245, 295, 372, 415, 420, 449-450
Ronson, Mick, 187
Ronstadt, Linda, 19, 138, 375
Rooftop Singers, 420
Rooney, Herb, 204
Roos, Marty, 354
Rory Storm And The Hurricanes, 45, 252, 459
Rose, Andrew, 482
Rose, Cynthia, 90
Rose, Fred, 22
Rose, Tim, 196, 420-421, 489

Rosen, Mike, 193
Rosenberg, Kenny, 283
Rosenberg, Marv, 425
Rosolino, Frank, 246
Ross, Adam, 113
Ross, Andy, 198
Ross, Annie, 209-210
Ross, Diana, 32, 128, 232, 236, 238, 264, 361, 460-461, 468
Ross, Glenn, 350
Ross, Jerry, 284, 295
Ross, Margaret, 137
Rossman, Ronnie, 281
Rostill, John, 432-433
Rothchild, Paul A., 21, 176
Rotolo, Suze, 184
Roulettes, 18, 208, 421, 484
Roussos, Demis, 18
Roustabout, 391, 393, 395
Routers, 421-422, 463, 495
Routh, J.W., 110
Rowan, Peter, 191
Rowberry, Dave, 16
Rowe, Barbara, 245, 286
Rowe, Dick, 28, 45, 199, 289, 332, 414, 470, 483
Rowland, Karen, 461
Rowland, Steve, 15, 155, 210, 327
Rowley, Mick, 446
Roxy Music, 7, 63, 370, 483
Royal Teens, 221, 304
Royal, Billy Joe, 128
Royaltones, 90
Royer, Ray, 399
Rubettes, 61
Rubin, Rick, 110
Ruby And The Romantics, 422
Rudolph, Paul, 168
Ruff, Ray, 470
Ruffin, David, 466-467
Ruffin, Jimmy, 267, 468
Rugge-Price, James, 7
Runaways, 224
Rundgren, Todd, 140, 364
Rupe, Art, 136
Rupert's People, 311
Rush, Otis, 120, 297-298, 336
Rush, Tom, 169, 196-197, 422-423, 494
Russell, Brenda, 330
Russell, Brian, 129
Russell, Dave, And The Renegades, 204
Russell, George, 157
Russell, Jackie, 351
Russell, Jeff, 49
Russell, Ken, 500
Russell, Leon, 13, 22, 251,

298, 308, 312, 314, 331, 450
Russell, Rosalind, 58
Russo, Bill, 20
Ryan, Barry, 423
Ryan, Don, 146
Ryan, Jim, 146
Ryan, Marion, 423
Ryan, Mick, 124
Ryan, Paul, 423
Ryan, Paul And Barry, 423
Ryan, Phil, 92, 205
Rydell, Bobby, 87, 119, 423
Ryder, Jean, 83
Ryder, Mitch, And The Detroit Wheels, 236, 424

S

Sade, 235
Sadler, Barry, Staff Sgt., 425
Safaris, 425
Sager, Carole Bayer, 27, 225, 346, 455
Sagittarius, 425 and passim
Sahm, Doug, 441
Sain, Oliver, 38
Sainte-Marie, Buffy, 372, 425-426
Salewicz, Chris, 260
Salgues, Y., 26
Saltis, Larry, 354
Salvato, John, 183
Sam And Bill, 426
Sam And Dave, 96, 331, 400, 426
Sam Gopal, 413
Sam The Sham And The Pharaohs, 426-427
Sam The Soul, 135
Sambora, Richie, 169
Samudio, Domingo, 426
Samudio, Sam, 426
Samuel, Allen, 364, 471
Samuels, Jerry, 364
Samwell, Ian, 407, 444
Samwell-Smith, Paul, 509
San Sebastian Strings, 341
Sanborn, David, 97
Sanchez, Ray, 168
Sanchez, Tony, 419
Sanden, Doug, 499
Sanders, Ed, 228
Sanders, Pharoah, 132
Sanderson, Duncan, 168
Sandler, Harry, 377
Sandlin, Johnny, 272
Sandon, Johnny, 428
Sands, Evie, 265
Sands, Tommy, 70, 83, 439

Santana, 188, 240, 269, 352, 507
Santana, Carlos, 269
Santollo, Joe, 183
Sapherson, Barry, 423
Saraceno, Joe, 422, 463
Sarne, Mike, 108, 157
Sarstedt, Peter, 295, 427
Sarstedt, Richard, 294
Sarstedt, Robin, 295, 427
Satintones, 334
Saunders, Marty, 284
Saunders, Mike, 9
Saunders, Red, 125
Saunders, Tim, 9
Savage, Jon, 302
Savile, Jimmy, 335
Savoy Brown, 121, 275, 387, 468
Savoy, Mark, 31
Sawyer, Phil, 120, 163, 310-311
Sawyer, Tom, 84-85
Sawyers, Jim, 462
Sax Appeal, 495
Saxon, Sky, 430
Saxon, Stan, 124
Sayer, Leo, 208
Sazaferin, G., 407
Scaduto, Anthony, 190, 419
Scaffold, 315, 427
Scaggs, Boz, 209
Scala, Ralph, 75
Scales, Harvey, 201
Schachner, Robert, 194
Scheck, George, 153
Scheer, Ireen, 210
Schiffour, Tom, 433
Schneider, Bert, 353
Schoen, Danke, 370
Schoenberg, Arnold, 314
Schofield, Willie, 209
Schuller, Gunther, 347
Schuster, Sylvia, 371
Schuur, Diane, 339
Schwabach, Kurt, 293
Schwartz, Glenn, 378
Schwartz, Peter, 31
Schwarz, Brinsley, 194, 302
Scofield, John, 158
Scoppettone, Dick, 251
Scott, David, 8
Scott, Freddy, 56
Scott, Jack, 413
Scott, Joe, 71
Scott, John, 493
Scott, Keith, 306
Scott, Ken, 496
Scott, Mary, 428
Scott, Noel, 493, 495
Scott, Rebecca, 428
Scott, Ronnie, 428
Scott, Tommy, 289, 483
Scotty And Bill, 67
Screaming Blue

Messiahs, 196
Seal, Bob, 129
Seals, Troy, 326
Searchers, 36, 50, 53, 61, 79, 148, 167, 180, 254, 372, 402, 428-429, 442, 448
Seatrain, 76, 192
Sebastian, John, 146, 322-323, 507
Secombe, Harry, 85-86, 305
Secunda, Tony, 362
Sedaka, Neil, 86, 137, 304, 333, 429-430, 475
Sedgewick, Mike, 9
Sedgewick, Peter 'Adam', 9
Seeds, 430 and passim
Seeger, Pete, 214, 263, 380, 420
Seekers, 196, 430-431, 449
Segarini, Bob, 210
Seger, Bob, 169
Sehorn, Marshall, 177
Seiter, George, 449
Seiter, John, 261, 449
Sellar, Gordon, 51
Sellers, Peter, 333, 354, 369
Selvin, Joel, 366
Sensational Alex Harvey Band, 253
Senzan, Allan, 7
Seol, Randy, 459
Sergides, Miguel, 19
Settle, Mike, 367
Severinsen, Doc, 329
Seville, David, 121
Sewell, Marshall, 194
Sha Na Na, 507
Shades Of Blue, 120, 431
Shadows, 431-433 and passim
Shadows Of Knight, 433
Shakespeare, John, 107, 217, 279, 425
Shakespeare, William, 192
Shakin' Stevens, 163, 238
Shalamar, 497
Shanahan, Pat, 366
Shangri-Las, 37, 167, 245, 433, 486
Shankar, Ravi, 46, 240, 355, 507
Shannon, Del, 62, 64, 123, 274, 289, 344, 434-435, 483
Shannon, Pete, 364
Shapiro, Harry, 78, 260, 307
Shapiro, Helen, 167, 177, 435
Shapiro, Nat, 84
Sharkey, John, 462
Sharon, Ralph, 54

Sharp, Cecil, 181
Sharp, Dee Dee, 179
Shaw, Artie, 134
Shaw, Chris, 380
Shaw, Robin, 217
Shaw, Sandie, 15, 27, 68, 156, 250, 332, 380, 435-436, 454
Shayne, Gloria, 502
Shazam, 362
She Trinity, 332
Shearing, George, 356, 505
Sheeley, Sharon, 167
Sheen, Bobby, 77
Sheffler, Ted, 146
Shehan, John, 181
Sheldon, Ernie, 314
Shelley, Paul, 155
Shelley, Scott, 452
Shelton, Robert, 184, 190
Shepard, Sam, 188, 190, 267
Shepp, Archie, 132-133
Sheppard, Andy, 132
Sheridan, Lee, 280
Sheridan, Mike, 275
Sheridan, Tony, 44, 48, 143, 293, 436
Sherley, Glen, 109
Sherman, Bobby, 315
Sherman, Joe, 85
Sherman, Richard, 15, 24
Shetler, Tom, 209
Shields, Harvey, 198
Shirelles, 169, 213, 296, 304, 327, 436-437, 484
Shirley, Jerry, 35
Shirley, John, 198
Shoesmith, Peter, 326
Sholes, Steve, 22
Shore, Dinah, 102
Short, Brian, 67, 274
Shorter, Wayne, 158
Shotgun Express, 182, 332
Showaddywaddy, 56, 83, 116, 191
Shriver, Dave, 317
Shuckett, Ralph, 129, 382
Shulman, Derek, 182-183
Shuman, Mort, 62, 84, 86, 171, 307, 325, 388, 391, 428, 437, 444, 474, 501
Shusha, 53
Sideras, Lucas, 18
Sidran, Ben, 7, 12, 210
Siegel, Jay, 475-476
Siegel, Peter, 191
Sievers, William, 448
Sigman, Carl, 293
Sill, Lester, 449
Silver, Cliff, 409
Silver, Horace, 157, 253, 286
Silverhead, 246
Silverman, Charlie, 261

Silverstein, Shel, 109
Simmons, Gene, 67
Simon And Garfunkel, 29, 70, 103, 149, 355, 437-438
Simon, Carly, 196
Simon, John, 384
Simon, Paul, 29, 140, 149, 214, 355, 366, 431, 437-438, 471
Simone, Nina, 9, 16, 245, 439
Simper, Nick, 217, 296
Simpson, Andrea, 106
Simpson, Rose, 277
Simpson, Valerie, 469
Sims, Zoot, 12, 428
Sinatra, Frank, 22, 32, 57, 70, 153, 161, 245, 293, 317, 324, 341, 423, 439-440, 446
Sinatra, Nancy, 70, 85, 315, 439-440
Sinclair, John, 338
Sing, Will, 288
Singer, Ray, 371
Singers, Gateway, 314
Singing Nun, 440
Singing Postman, 440
Singleton, Charles, 293
Sinks, Earl, 145
Sir Douglas Quintet, 441
Sirico, Cookie, 406
Sivuca, 91
Skellern, Peter, 271
Skhy, A.B., 7, 224
Skinner, David, 482-483
Skinner, Derek, 216, 453
Skip And Flip, 223
Skip Bifferty, 20, 257, 441
Skipper, Alan, 396
Skitter, 218
Sklar, Buddy, 308
Sky, Patrick, 75
Slade, 115
Slapp Happy, 113
Slater, Rodney, 79
Slaven, Neil, 5, 360
Slay, Frank, 104
Sledge, Percy, 375, 442
Slick, Grace, 94, 245, 285-286
Sloan, Frank, 343
Sloan, P.F., 10, 36, 92, 210, 241, 340, 380, 442-443, 482
Sloan, Philip, 442
Sloman, Larry, 190
Sly And The Family Stone, 257, 443, 467, 507
Small Faces, 19-20, 24, 214, 364, 375, 441, 443-445, 500-501
Small, Millie, 194
Smart, Terry, 407
Smeda, Nat, 116

Smet, Jean-Philippe, 247
Smethurst, Allan, 440
Smiley Culture, 158
Smith, Andy, 103
Smith, Bernadine Boswell, 213
Smith, Bessie, 290
Smith, Bobby, 173
Smith, Brian, 216
Smith, Carl, 109
Smith, Chris, 5
Smith, Earl, 97
Smith, Frank, 34, 310
Smith, Fred, 338
Smith, G.E., 189
Smith, Gordon, 216
Smith, Graham, 77
Smith, Ian, 362
Smith, James Marcus, 398
Smith, James Oscar, 445
Smith, Jerry, 217
Smith, Jessie, 276
Smith, Jim, 152
Smith, Jimmy, 131, 323, 356, 445-446
Smith, John L., 112
Smith, Kim, 309
Smith, Larry, 79
Smith, Mel, 309
Smith, Michael, 406
Smith, Mike, 14, 18, 124, 150
Smith, Nigel, 15
Smith, Norman, 51
Smith, Patti, 338
Smith, Paul, 97
Smith, Ray, 173
Smith, Robert Lee, 463
Smith, Ronnie, 50
Smith, Steve, 5
Smith, Stewart, 34
Smith, Tony, 323
Smith, Ursula, 471
Smith, Warren, 108
Smithereens, 351
Smiths, 436
Smoke, 446-447 and passim
Smothers Brothers, 503
Smythe, Danny, 82
Snow, Hank, 23, 390
Snyder, Bob, 331
Snyder, Dave, 108
Snyder, Eddy, 108
Soft Cell, 74, 398
Soft Machine, 35, 181, 194, 224, 249, 447, 471
Sohns, Jim, 433
Solley, Pete, 212
Soloff, Lew, 72
Solomon, Andy, 14
Solomon, Dorothy, 29
Solomon, Phil, 28, 66, 138, 181, 289, 342, 386, 470, 483
Somers, Andy, 153, 352

Sommers, Ronny, 79, 447
Sondheim, Stephen, 58
Sone, Ray, 178
Sonny And Cher, 40, 79, 238, 410, 447-448
Sonny Red, 12, 394
Sonoban, Casey, 401
Sopwith Camel, 172, 448
Sorrow, S.F., 396-397
Sorrows, 448 and passim
Soul Of Man, 71
Soul Sisters, 38, 167
Soul Stirrers, 135-136, 465
Soul, David, 38
Soul, Jimmy, 449
Sound 5, 450
Sounds Orchestral, 246
Souster, Tim, 447
South, Harry, 209
South, Joe, 383, 464
Southern Pacific, 144
Sovine, Red, 22
Spampinato, Sal, 50
Spanky And Our Gang, 112, 328, 382, 449
Spann, Otis, 168, 363
Sparks, Randy, 367
Spear, Roger Ruskin, 79
Spearhead, 45
Spector, Abner, 137
Spector, Larry, 99
Spector, Phil, 22, 36, 40-41, 48, 62, 70, 74, 77, 79, 148, 171, 180, 222, 245, 295, 366, 372, 375, 410, 415, 420, 447, 449-450, 460, 466, 481
Spector, Ronnie, 420, 450
Spedding, Chris, 40, 91, 113
Speer, Steve, 233
Spence, Johnny, 296, 354
Spence, Skip, 285, 351
Spencer, David, 485
Spencer, Herbert, 86
Spencer, Mike, 5, 275
Spencer, Paul, 438
Spencer, Pete, 50, 61
Spencer, Roger, 275
Spenner, Alan, 453
Sperling, Dee Dee, 168
Spicher, Buddy, 20
Spickard, Bob, 116
Spinella, Bob, 146
Spirit, 451-452 and passim
Spirits Rebellious, 451
Spooky Tooth, 21, 371, 421, 452-453, 489, 492
Spoons, Sam, 79
Spotnicks, 453-454
Springfield, Dusty, 27-28, 68, 83, 113, 156, 178, 435, 437, 454-456
Springfield, Tom, 431
Springfields, 431, 454, 456
Springsteen, Bruce, 78, 171, 337-338, 376, 424

Squadronaires, 122, 324
Squier, Billy, 129
Squires, Rosemary, 456
St John Gostine, Dick, 168
St. Clair, Alex, 105
St. Cyr, Johnny, 313
St. Germain, 269
St. John, Mark, 396
St. John, Powell, 290, 358
St. Nicholas, Nick, 458
Stable, Simon, 217
Stackridge, 333
Staczek, Don, 287
Staehely, Christian, 451
Stafford, Jo, 183
Stainton, Chris, 453
Stamp, Chris, 499
Stamp, Terence, 300
Stampfel, Pete, And The Bottlecaps, 267
Stampfel, Peter, 228, 267, 278
Standells, 52, 122, 206, 374, 456-457, 493
Stanley, Bob, 145
Stanley, George, 395
Stanshall, Vivian, 79
Staple Singers, 33, 457
Staples, Mavis, 457
Staples, Pervis, 457
Staples, Peter, 479
Staples, Pops, 457
Staples, Yvonne, 457
Stapleton, Cyril, 280, 456
Starander, Bo, 453
Starchild, 260
Stardust, Alvin, 214
Starfighters, 192
Starkey, John, 500
Starkey, Ritchie, 459
Starkey, Zak, 500
Starliters, 164, 510
Starr, Edwin, 34, 431, 457-458
Starr, Kay, 81
Starr, Ringo, 45, 61, 70, 199, 201, 317, 333, 436, 453, 459, 465, 500
Starrs, Mike, 131
State, Wayne, 441
Statler Brothers, 109
Status Quo, 261
Stax, John, 396
Stealers Wheel, 273, 453
Steam Packet, 30, 181
Steampacket, 237
Steel, John, 16
Steele, Tommy, 37, 126, 220, 252
Steely Dan, 201, 284, 484
Stein, Chris, 501
Stein, Mark, 486
Steinberg, Lewis, 80
Stephens, Bruce, 74
Stephens, Dane, 207

Stephens, Geoff, 69-70, 368
Stephens, Jim, 425
Stephens, Leigh, 74
Steppenwolf, 36, 366, 458
Stereolab, 201
Sterling, Annette, 332-333
Stern, Richard, 364
Stevens, April, 466
Stevens, Cat, 20, 136, 224, 423, 456, 478
Stevens, Dave, 108
Stevens, Guy, 21, 249, 492
Stevens, Shakin', 163, 238
Stevenson, Bill, 191-192
Stevenson, Don, 350
Stevenson, Mickey, 332, 361, 498
Stewart, Billy, 140, 167, 231
Stewart, Chaz, 52
Stewart, Chris, 194
Stewart, Diane, 78
Stewart, Eric, 346
Stewart, Ian, 306, 414-415
Stewart, John, 257, 337, 494
Stewart, Rod, 30-31, 33, 74, 91, 136, 150, 178, 181-182, 216, 249, 329, 332, 337
Stewart, Rosemary, 443
Stewart, Sylvester, 50, 443
Stewart, Winston, 33
Stigwood, Robert, 157, 200, 313
Stiles, Ray, 266
Still, Bob, 398
Stills, Stephen, 24, 73, 94, 130, 147, 195, 353, 457
Stinnet, Ray, 426
Stipe, Michael, 28
Stirling, Peter Lee, 343
Stitt, Sonny, 312, 346, 428
Stokes, John, 28-29
Stokes, Sean James, 28
Stokes, Terry, 119
Stoller, Mike, 172
Stone Canyon Band, 366
Stone The Crows, 153, 253, 474
Stone, Brian, 419, 480
Stone, Freddie, 443
Stone, Gerry, 148
Stone, Joe, 507
Stone, Martin, 8, 343
Stone, Mary, 205
Stone, Rosie, 443
Stone, Sly, 50, 225, 352, 443
Stonebridge, Lou, 235
Stooges, 196, 424
Stookey, Paul, 384
Stopford-Harrison, Ian George, 218

Storball, Donald, 105
Storm, Billy, 449
Storm, Rory, 45, 252, 458-459
Stott, Wally, 495
Strain, Sammy, 315
Strange, Billy, 295
Strangeloves, 56
Stranglers, 401
Strawberry Alarm Clock, 459
Strawbs, 14, 488
Stray, 459-460
Strazza, Peter, 195
Streamliners, 456
Street, Richard, 467
Streeter, Roberta Lee, 233
Streisand, Barbra, 70
Stringfellow, Peter, 455
Strong, Barrett, 467
Strouse, Charles, 161
Struthers, Dave, 16
Stuart, Alice, 358
Stuart, Barry, 11
Stuart, Fred, 6
Stuart, Michael, 320
Stubblefield, Clyde, 88
Stubbs, Joe, 135, 209
Stubbs, Levi, 209, 222
Stuckey, David, 451
Style Council, 235, 458
Stylistics, 315
Styne, Jule, 69
Styx, 51
Sugerman, Danny, 177
Sullivan, Barry, 341
Sullivan, Big Jim, 341
Sullivan, Ed, 45, 125, 151, 184, 239, 415, 440
Sullivan, Jim, 341
Sullivan, Niki, 145
Sullivan, Peter, 289
Summers, Andy, 16, 153, 352, 421
Summers, Jerry, 178
Sun Ra, 131
Sundholm, Norm, 299
Sundowners, 374
Sundquist, Jim, 214
Sunnyland Slim, 119
Supergrass, 301, 444
Supertramp, 82
Supremes, 32-33, 70, 128, 217, 222-223, 238, 264, 334, 361, 412, 422, 460-461, 467-468
Suranovich, George, 320
Surfaris, 461-462
Sutch, Screaming Lord, 342, 462
Sutcliffe, Pauline, 50
Sutcliffe, Stuart, 44-45, 436
Sutton, Johnny, 178
Svanoe, Bill, 420
Swamp Dogg, 96, 134
Swarbrick, Dave, 102-103
Sweeney, Glenn, 471

Sweeny, Vic, 82
Sweet Inspirations, 128, 272
Sweetenham, Geoff, 241
Sweetenham, Pete, 241
Sweetman, Dave, 219
Swervedriver, 500
Swinging Blue Jeans, 201, 462
Sylvester, Mike, 462
Sylvester, Terry, 200, 265, 462
Symposium, 347
Syndicate Of Sound, 462
Syreeta, 506
Szabo, Gabor, 278
Szelest, Stan, 256

T

T. Rex, 483
Tait, Rob, 40
Taj Mahal, 158, 446
Talley, Gary, 82
Talley, Nedra, 420
Talmy, Shel, 29, 83, 143, 165, 192, 364, 379, 413, 499
Tamblyn, Larry, 456
Tampa Red, 12
Tams, 128, 463-464
Tandy, Sharon, 311
Tangerine Dream, 294
Tanner, Dave, 138
Tarantino, Quentin, 152
Tarbutton, Jimmy, 233
Tarney, Alan, 408, 432
Tarplin, Marv, 349, 412
Tarrant, Chris, 427
Tarriers, 420
Tartachny, Paul, 44
Tarwater, 150
Tate, Howard, 198, 345, 464
Tatman, Mike, 273
Taupin, Bernie, 280
Tausis, Tommy, 453
Taylor, Alan, 113, 397
Taylor, Alistair, 49
Taylor, Allan, 397
Taylor, Art, 132, 445
Taylor, Arthur, 320
Taylor, Bill, 317
Taylor, Billy, 313
Taylor, Bob, 178
Taylor, Chip, 247, 265
Taylor, Clive, 14
Taylor, Dallas, 95, 129, 147, 206
Taylor, Derek, 49, 355, 464-465
Taylor, Dick, 396, 414
Taylor, Eddie, 269, 298
Taylor, Eric, 95
Taylor, Eve, 15, 435
Taylor, Felice, 465

Taylor, Gary, 129, 261
Taylor, James, 42, 289, 422, 445
Taylor, John, 235
Taylor, John T., 8
Taylor, Johnnie, 33, 136, 464-466, 472
Taylor, Kingsize, And The Dominoes, 253
Taylor, Larry, 103-104, 335-336
Taylor, Lynne, 420
Taylor, Mel, 490-491
Taylor, Michael, 235, 417
Taylor, Mick, 188, 235, 317, 335-336, 417
Taylor, Neil, 14
Taylor, Rick, 507
Taylor, Robert, 298
Taylor, Rodney, 201
Taylor, Shawn, 201
Taylor, Tim, 445
Taylor, Vince, 436
Taylor, William, 395
Te Kanawa, Kiri, 58
Teagarden, Jack, 122
Tebb, Johnny, 113
Tedesco, Tommy, 295, 450
Tee, Richard, 91, 209, 296
Teenage Fanclub, 351
Tegza, Michael, 247
Temperance 7, 466
Temple, Jerry, 212
Templeman, Ted, 251
Tempo, Nino, and April Stevens, 466
Temptations, 466-468 and *passim*
10cc, 326, 346, 374
Ten Feet Five, 479
10,000 Maniacs, 196
Ten Years After, 15, 468-469, 507
Tennant, Neil, 455
Terra Firma, 93
Terrell, Ernie, 460, 469
Terrell, Jean, 460-461, 469
Terrell, Tammi, 231-233, 469
Terry, Clark, 261, 312
Terry, Sonny, 271
Tesluk, Paul, 287
Tex, Joe, 140, 298, 386, 469-470
Texas Slim, 268
Thain, Gary, 252
Tharp, Chuck, 215
Thaxton, Lloyd, 304
Them, 470-471 and *passim*
Thibodeaux, Gladius, 31
Third Ear Band, 321, 471
Third Rail, 471
Thirteenth Floor Elevators, 441

Thomas, B.J., 60, 156
Thomas, Carla, 112, 128, 331, 403-404, 472-473
Thomas, Charles, 503
Thomas, Charlie, 180
Thomas, Cheryl, 422
Thomas, Danny, 472
Thomas, Dave, 72
Thomas, Gary, 76
Thomas, Glyn, 76
Thomas, Henry, 103
Thomas, Irma, 120, 332, 472-473
Thomas, Leon, 240
Thomas, Mary, 8, 148
Thomas, Mary Ann, 8
Thomas, Ray, 357
Thomas, Robert, 486
Thomas, Rufus, 472-473
Thompson, Barbara, 20, 131, 253
Thompson, Bobby, 20
Thompson, Carolyn E., 339
Thompson, Danny, 270, 283, 306, 383, 389
Thompson, Dave, 286, 489
Thompson, Dennis, 338
Thompson, Derek, 253
Thompson, James, 395
Thompson, Kay, 501
Thompson, Lucky, 157
Thompson, Mick, 143
Thompson, Randall, 57
Thompson, Richard, 22, 213, 344
Thompson, Sonny, 298
Thompson, Steve, 335
Thompson, Sue, 319
Thomson, Liz, 190
Thorkelson, Peter Halsten, 353
Thornbury, James, 104
Thornton, Johnny, 498
Thorpe, Peter, 421
Thorup, Peter, 306
Thrasher, Andrew, 180
Three Dog Night, 36, 366
Throbbing Gristle, 166
Thunder Alley, 17
Thunderbeats, 306
Thunderclap Newman, 473-474
Thurman, John, 471
Tickner, George, 228
Tidmarsh, Christopher, 123
Tierney, Tony, 323
Tiffen, Harry, 140
Tijuana Brass, 12-13
Tikis, 51, 250, 443
Till, John, 290
Tiller, Paul, 179
Tilley, Sandra, 333, 487
Tilley, Vesta, 251
Tillman, Georgeanna

Marie, 334
Tillman, Keith, 182
Tillotson, Johnny, 309, 474
Timebox, 76
Tiny Tim, 246, 384, 474-475
Tippett, Keith, 181
Tippetts, Julie, 181
Tjader, Cal, 246
Tobler, John, 5, 44, 177, 409
Toe Fat, 53, 235
Tokens, 166, 248, 429, 475-476
Tolson, Peter, 396
Tom And Jerry, 328, 438
Tommis, Colin, 103
Tommy And Jimmy, 180
Tommy And The Tornadoes, 281
Tomorrow, 476 and *passim*
Tomsco, George, 215-216
Tongue And Groove, 117
Tonkin, Garfield, 149
Tonto's Expanding Headband, 319
Topham, Tony, 509
Torian, Reggie, 277
Tork, Peter, 353
Tornados, 113-114, 229, 257, 342, 476-477, 489
Torney, Ned, 122
Toto, 82
Touch, Peter, 384
Toussaint, Allen, 40, 177, 260, 292, 317, 383, 472
Townsend, Rob, 330
Townshend, Pete, 12, 258, 300, 310, 371, 378, 413, 474, 499, 501
Townson, Chris, 286
Toyah, 500
Toys, 199, 477
Tracey, Stan, 65
Tracy, Dick, 388
Traffic, 477-478 and *passim*
Trammell, Danny, 215
Trancynger, John 'Buddy', 179
Traveling Wilburys, 189, 376
Travers, Mary, 384
Travis, Betty, 32
Travis, Merle, 23, 326, 366
Treadway, Greg, 350
Treadwell, George, 180
Tremeloes, 45, 124, 135, 388, 478-479
Trent D'Arby, Terence, 163
Trent, Jackie, 126, 254, 288, 479, 495
Trent, Jacqueline, 479

Trevor, Kip, 6
Troggs, 247, 380, 387, 479-480
Trotts, Ralph, 326
Troupe, Quincy, 160
Trovajoli, Armando, 86
Trower, Robin, 380, 399
Troy, Doris, 480-481
Tucker, Bob, 67
Tucker, Jim, 482
Tucker, Maureen 'Mo', 488
Tucker, Tommy, 481
Tufano, Dennis, 93
Tulin, Mark, 195
Turnbull, John, 82, 441
Turner, Alan, 76
Turner, Bobby, 116
Turner, Charles, 178
Turner, Chris, 482
Turner, Ike, 276, 481-482
Turner, Ike And Tina, 37, 245, 276, 372, 450, 481-482
Turner, Joe, 137, 178
Turner, Mark, 445
Turner, Ray, 178
Turner, Rick, 24
Turner, Sammy, 62
Turner, Steve, 50, 233, 410, 501
Turner, Tina, 37, 245, 276, 323, 372, 450, 481-482
Turney, Ross, 129
Turrentine, Stanley, 235, 445
Turtles, 36, 206, 308, 315, 359, 442, 482
Tutt, Ron, 503
Tuttle, John, 215
Twain, Mark, 52
Twain, Shania, 226
Twiggy, 270
Twinkle, 138, 483
Twitch, Elmer, 90, 123
Twitty, Conway, 382
Twomey, Kay, 293
Tyler, Kip, 366
Tyner, McCoy, 132
Tyner, Rob, 338
Tyrannosaurus Rex, 286, 483
Tyson, Barbara, 308
Tyson, Ron, 467-468

U

Ulaky, Wayne, 44
Ullman, Tracey, 319, 332
Ulmer, Charles, 25
Ultimate Spinach, 44, 377, 484
Ulvaeus, Bjorn, 69
Undertakers, 317, 413, 484

Underwood, Ian, 359
Underwood, Mick, 199, 377
Unit Four Plus Two, 76, 421, 484
United States Of America, 484-485
Unwin, Stanley, 444
Upchurch, Phil, 125, 178
Upsetters, 140, 165
Ure, Midge, 422
Uriah Heep, 30, 235
Usher, Gary, 17, 77, 99, 114, 344, 370, 425, 461
Ussery, Bob, 113
Uzzell, James, 137
Uzzell, Jay 'Bird', 137

V

Vadim, Roger, 87, 250
Valance, Ricky, 36, 313, 485
Vale, Jerry, 68
Vale, Mike, 281
Valens, Ritchie, 356, 475
Valenti, Dino, 401
Valentine, Davy, 148
Valentine, Hilton, 16
Valentine, Steve, 205
Valentines, 50, 137
Valentino, Bobby, 385
Valentino, Sal, 50
Valentino, Tony, 456
Valentinos, 136, 258, 498
Valino, Joe, 354
Vallee, Rudy, 172
Vallenga, Dirk, 395
Valli, Frankie, 123, 221-222
Vallory, Ross, 228
Van Der Graaf Generator, 306
Van Dyke, Dick, 114
Van Osten, Carson, 364
Van Ronk, Dave, 75, 384, 422, 485-486
Van Vliet, Jan, 106
Vance, Kenny, 283
Vance, Paul, 148, 167
Vanda And Young, 192, 241
Vanda, Harry, 192, 241
Vandenberg, 192
Vandergelder, Peter, 245
Vandross, Luther, 225, 496
Vandyke, Les, 207
Vangelis, 18
Vanilla Fudge, 486, 510
Vanity Fare, 302, 486
Vapnick, Isaac, 280
Vartan, Sylvie, 248
Vaughan, Frankie, 321, 354
Vaughan, Jimmie, 169

Vaughan, Malcolm, 414
Vaughan, Sarah, 339
Vaughan, Stevie Ray, 152, 297, 326
Vee, Bobby, 4, 145-146, 167, 304, 386, 486-487, 490
Veitch, Trevor, 422
Vejtables, 352
Velez, Jerry, 259
Velez, Martha, 53
Velvelettes, 487
Velvet Opera, 487-488
Velvet Underground, 178, 488-489
Velvett Fogg, 489
Venable, Kim, 128
Venet, Nik, 40, 372
Vengerova, Isabella, 57
Venneri, Joseph, 475
Ventures, 489-491 and *passim*
Venus And The Razorblades, 224
Vera, Billy, 128-129, 140
Vermouth, Apollo C., 79
Vernieri, Larry, 164
Vernon, Mike, 7, 53, 67, 120
Vernons Girls, 83, 137, 491
Vestine, Henry, 103, 206, 358
Vickers, Howie, 129
Vickers, Mike, 329
Vickers, Walter, 201
Vidican, John, 294
Villeneuve, Craig, 281
Vincent, Gene, 32, 224, 415
Vinegar Joe, 82, 497
Vinson, Eddie 'Cleanhead', 131, 280-281
Vinton, Bobby, 491-492
Visconti, Tony, 271
Viscounts, 254, 273
Vito, Rick, 336
Vliet, Don Glen, 105
Vogues, 492-493
Voight, Jon, 365
Voigt, Jim, 381
Volk, Phil, 406
Volman, Mark, 359, 482
Von Battle, Joe, 268
Von Schmidt, Eric, 211-212, 422
Voormann, Klaus, 329, 378

W

Wace, Robert, 300, 310, 379, 444
Waddell, Bugs, 212
Waddilove, Philip, 295

Waddington, Tony, 61, 149
Wade, Brett, 195
Wade, Norman, 503
Wadeson, Pete, 5
Wadey, Steve, 318
Wadsworth, Derek, 253
Wagenfeald, Eddie, 287
Wagoner, Porter, 162
Wailers, 299
Waite, David, 140
Waite, Genevieve, 385
Waits, Tom, 197, 376
Walden, Narada Michael, 28, 225
Walden, Phil, 403
Waldman, Brian, 82
Wales, Howard, 7
Walker Brothers, 27, 83, 156, 422, 456, 493-496
Walker, Cindy, 405
Walker, Dave, 275
Walker, David, 312
Walker, Gary, 456, 493
Walker, Jimmy, 304, 410
Walker, John, 493-494
Walker, Johnnie, 6, 193
Walker, Junior, And The All Stars, 238, 494
Walker, Lillian, 204
Walker, Peter, 400
Walker, Scott, 84, 249, 254, 437, 479, 493-496
Walker, Shirley, 213
Walker, T-Bone, 298
Wall, Larry, 233
Wallach, Bonnie, 172
Waller, Fats, 32, 92, 122, 446
Waller, Gordon, 383
Waller, Mickey, 157, 216
Walley, David, 360
Wallis, Larry, 205
Walmsley, Steve, 310
Walsh, David, 378
Walsh, John, 284, 408
Walsh, Peter, 20, 331, 362, 388
Walsh, Sheila, 408
Walter, Dick, 7
Walter, Dominique, 230
Walters, Lou, 459
Ward, Alan, 268
Ward, Billy, 504
Ward, Clara, 225
Ward, Ed, 74
Ward, Paul, 327
Ward, Robert, 209
Ware, John, 138
Warfield, Tim, 445
Warhol, Andy, 417, 488-489
Warhorse, 489
Warleigh, Ray, 253, 447
Warlocks, 241
Warner, Alan, 220
Warner, Jimmy, 228

Warnes, Jennifer, 410
Warren, Diane, 289, 455
Warren, Frank, 5
Warren, George, 206
Warren, Quentin, 445
Warwick, Clint, 357
Warwick, Dee Dee, 480
Warwick, Dionne, 8, 27, 91, 128, 156, 230, 272, 437, 496-497, 507
Was, Don, 51, 122, 203
Washburn, Donna, 169
Washington, Dinah, 55
Washington, Geno (And The Ram Jam Band), 236, 497
Washington, George, 385
Washington, Grover, Jnr., 313
Waters, John, 21, 271, 331
Waters, Roger, 21, 34
Waters, Warren, 116
Watson, Alan, 344
Watson, Ben, 5, 360
Watson, Doc, 23
Watson, Fraser, 387
Watson, Johnny 'Guitar', 169
Watson, Junior, 104
Watson, Mike, 8
Watt, Norman, 8
Watts, Charlie, 306, 414, 418
Watts, George, 103
Waxman, Lou, 351
Way, Pete, 286
Wayfarers, 503
Waymon, Eunice, 439
Wayne, Bob, 218
Wayne, Carl, 266, 362
Wayne, John, 365
Wayne, Mick, 291-292
Wayne, Rick, 218
Weakley, Michael, 195
Weathers, John 'Pugwash', 205
Weaver, Blue, 14
Weaver, Ken, 228
Weaver, Mick, 207, 214, 252, 477
Weavers, 166, 420, 475
Webb Brothers, 121
Webb, Bernard, 383
Webb, David, 106
Webb, Harry Roger, 407
Webb, Jimmy, 87, 215, 235, 252, 272, 288, 333
Webb, Marti, 69, 254, 479
Webb, Paul, 288
Webb, Roy Dean, 170
Webb, Stan, 120-121, 298
Webb, Tom, 217
Weber, Steve, 228, 267
Webster, Tony, 284
Wechter, Julius, 166
Weeks, Terry, 468
Weezer, 351

Weider, John, 16, 296, 498
Weil, Cynthia, 16, 86, 129, 304, 330, 450
Weill, Kurt, 130, 153, 208
Weir, Alan, 387
Weir, Bob, 241, 243
Weis, Danny, 407
Weisberg, Richard, 44
Weisbert, David, 390
Weisbrod, Bob, 168
Weisman, Ben, 293
Weiss, George, 160, 475
Weiss, Shelly, 7
Weissman, Dick, 291, 385
Weitz, Mark, 459
Welby, Marcus, 311
Welch, Bruce, 318, 407-408, 431, 433
Welch, Chris, 143, 164, 260, 478, 482
Welch, Raquel, 418
Welham, Hadrian, 219
Weller, Freddy, 406
Weller, Paul, 21, 28
Welles, Orson, 123
Wells, Chris, 124
Wells, Kitty, 202, 309
Wells, Mary, 231-232, 284, 332, 348, 412, 497-498
Wells, Mary Sue, 284
Welnick, Vince, 243
Welsh, Alex, 220
Welsh, Bob, 116
Wertheimer, Alfred, 394
Wesley, Fred, 88
Wesley, John, 186, 190
Wesselman, Tom, 249
West Coast Pop Art Experimental Band, 198
West, Alex, 102
West, Keith, 476, 498
West, Mike, 296, 489
West, Richard, 478
West, Rick, 478
West, Robert, 209
West, Sonny, 394
West, Tommy, 112
Westbrook, Mike, 20
Western Flyer, 249
Westlake, Clive, 437
Westlake, Kevin, 74, 213
Weston, Bob, 174
Weston, Kim, 231-232, 264, 469, 498
Westover, Charles, 64, 434
Westwood, Richard, 478
Wet Wet Wet, 480
Wexler, Jerry, 56, 62, 128, 188, 225, 323, 426, 454, 480
Weymouth, Nigel, 21, 249
Whale, Pete, 302
Whaley, Paul, 74, 293
Wheels, Dave, 433
Whetstone, Richard, 195

While, Chris, 91
Whiskeyhill Singers, 261
Whitbread, Paul, 400
Whitcher, Pip, 448
White Plains, 108, 217, 279
White, Andy, 137
White, Barry, 465
White, Bill, 14, 349
White, Bukka, 206, 422, 425
White, Chris, 511
White, Clarence, 99-100, 343
White, Dave, 340
White, George, 47, 169
White, James, 510
White, John, 133, 510
White, Josh, 124, 485
White, Maurice, 313
White, Nathaniel Andrew, 133
White, Priscilla, 67
White, Ray, 112
White, Roger, 204
White, Ronnie, 348-349, 412, 505
White, Snowy, 421
White, Tam, 82
White, Ted, 225
White, Timothy, 44
Whitehead, Alan, 24, 332
Whiteman, Ian, 8, 343
Whitesnake, 131, 379
Whitfield, Mark, 445
Whitfield, Norman, 458, 467, 487
Whiting, Steve, 350
Whitley, Ray, 464
Whitney, Charlie, 212
Whitsett, Carson, 80
Whittington, Bill, 86, 210
Whitwam, Barry, 262
Who, 501 and passim
Wickham, Vicki, 454, 456
Widlake, Terry, 378
Widowmaker, 321
Wilcox, Jerry, 214
Wilde, Marty, 141, 214, 238, 273, 389, 407, 491
Wilde, Oscar, 176
Wildhorn, Frank, 86
Wilhelm, Mike, 116
Wilkinson, David, 7
Wilkinson, Keith, 352
Wilkinson, Lois, 106
Willard, Glen, 123
Williams Brothers, 501
Williams, Aaron, 343
Williams, Allan, 44, 49
Williams, Andy, 114, 238, 296, 344, 501-502
Williams, Annette, 74
Williams, Danny, 502
Williams, Dave, 6
Williams, Don, 405
Williams, George, 486

Williams, Gloria, 332
Williams, Hank, 110-111, 142, 151, 183, 206, 256, 316, 366, 376, 404, 434, 474
Williams, Johnny, 268
Williams, Kenneth, 121
Williams, Larry, 79, 123, 447, 457
Williams, Mason, 503
Williams, Maurice, And The Zodiacs, 503
Williams, Miller, 344
Williams, Nanette, 74
Williams, Otis, 81, 466, 468
Williams, Paul, 190, 244, 288, 352-353, 466-467
Williams, Phil, 450
Williams, Ray, 100, 205
Williams, Richard, 160, 450, 467
Williams, Roy, 376
Williams, Simon, 5
Williams, Steve, 502
Williams, Terry, 321, 367, 468
Williams, Tony, 90, 158, 288
Williamson, 'Tudge', 50
Williamson, John, 283
Williamson, Robin, 277, 283
Williamson, Sonny Boy 'Rice Miller', 12, 16, 237
Willie And The Poor Boys, 144
Willis, Alan, 165
Willis, Bobby, 68
Willis, Carolyn, 74
Willis, Chuck, 137
Willis, Ian, 413
Willmer, Eric, 197
Wills, Martin, 67
Wills, Rick, 444
Wilmer, Valerie, 133
Wilsh, Mike, 220
Wilsher, Mick, 368
Wilson Phillips, 249, 385
Wilson, Alan, 103
Wilson, Allan, 326
Wilson, B.J., 399
Wilson, Barrie, 76, 380, 399
Wilson, Barry, 5, 286
Wilson, Bob, 275
Wilson, Brian, 5, 17, 40-44, 92, 282, 320, 355
Wilson, Carl, 40, 42-43
Wilson, Charlie, 74
Wilson, Dennis, 40-44
Wilson, Don, 489
Wilson, Frank, 222, 267, 489
Wilson, Gerald, 505
Wilson, Harold, 120, 362

Wilson, J., 380, 399
Wilson, Jackie, 8, 135, 238, 287, 412, 497, 504-505
Wilson, Jim, 74
Wilson, Jimmy, 505
Wilson, Joe, 128, 140
Wilson, John, 470
Wilson, Mary, 32, 460-461
Wilson, Michael, 155
Wilson, Nancy, 313, 339, 505
Wilson, Patricia, 461
Wilson, Raymond, 51
Wilson, Ron, 461
Wilson, Smokey, 222
Wilson, Sonny, 504
Wilson, Terry, 116
Wilson, Tom, 185, 358, 438
Wilson, Tony, 505
Wilson, Willie, 35
Wimmer, Kevin, 31
Winberg, Bo, 453-454
Winding, Kai, 157
Wine, Toni, 19, 346
Winfield, Chuck, 72
Winfield, Jeff, 310
Wing, Barnett, 245, 285
Winged Eel Fingerling, 227
Winkelman, Bob, 228
Winnick, Maurice, 324
Winsnes, Peter, 453
Winston, Jimmy, 444
Winter, Edgar, 338
Winter, Johnny, 338, 363, 507
Winterhalter, Hugo, 102
Winters, Ricky, 53
Winwood, Mervyn, 163
Winwood, Muff, 163
Winwood, Steve, 71, 117, 163-164, 337, 445, 477-478
Wirtz, Mark, 302, 498
Wisdom, Norman, 85, 369
Wisdom, Owen, 51
Wisdom, Trevor, 51
Wise, Fred, 293
Wise, Nick, 44
Wisseling, Louisa, 431
Withers, Bill, 303
Withers, Pick, 188
Witherspoon, Jimmy, 95
Wolfe, Randolph, 451
Wolff, Bill, 382
Wolfgang Press, 289
Womack And Womack, 323, 442
Womack, Bobby, 136, 140, 323, 385, 442
Womack, Cecil, 498
Wombles, 249
Wonder Stuff, 414
Wonder, Stevie, 231, 238, 361, 497, 505-507

Wood, Art, 306
Wood, Arthur, 21
Wood, Chris, 120, 257, 317, 477
Wood, Colin, 466
Wood, David, 66, 417
Wood, John 'Junior', 476
Wood, Randy, 334
Wood, Ron, 21, 66, 143, 188, 417, 466
Wood, Roy, 53, 113, 362
Wood, Ted, 466
Woodfuff, Woody, 433
Woodley, Bruce, 149, 431
Woods, Bob, 481
Woods, Harry, 403
Woods, Johnny, 340
Woodson, Craig, 484
Woodward, Mark, 289
Woody, Dan, 433
Wooler, Bob, 213
Wooster, Bertie, 368
Wooten, George, 137
Worth, Johnny, 263, 292
Wray, John, 191
Wren, Christopher S., 112
Wright, Darlene, 74, 77, 148
Wright, Dave, 479
Wright, Edna, 74
Wright, Ernest, Jnr., 315
Wright, Gary, 21, 248,

421, 452-453
Wright, Ian, 6
Wright, Jeff, 497
Wright, John, 497
Wright, John Lincoln, 44
Wright, Larry, 281
Wright, Pat, 148
Wright, Rick, 35
Wright, Steve, 192
Wright, Tim, 6
Wright, William C., 319
Wrixen, Eric, 470
Wyatt, Robert, 35, 447
Wycherley, Ronald, 229
Wyman, Bill, 210, 414, 419
Wymer, Nick, 207
Wynette, Tammy, 245
Wynn, Tommy, 167
Wynter, Mark, 425, 508

Y

Yaguda, Sandy, 283
Yana, 422
Yancey, Marvin, 96
Yanovsky, Zalman 'Zally', 197
Yarbrough, Glenn, 314, 503
Yardbirds, 46, 120, 169,

179, 213, 237, 273, 292, 379, 509-510
Yarrow, Peter, 384
Yasgur, Max, 507
Yazoo, 276
Yearwood, Trisha, 189
Yello, 39
Yester, Jerry, 22, 261, 323, 367
Yester, Jim, 22, 323
Yoder, Gary, 74, 293
York, George, 450
York, John, 99
York, Keith, 60
York, Paul, 170, 437
York, Pete, 163
Yost, Dennis, 128
Young Disciples, 298
Young Rascals, 164, 486, 510
Young, Ally, 31
Young, Bill, 158
Young, Bob, 485
Young, Cliff, 129, 409
Young, Colin, 220, 510
Young, Dick, 31, 251
Young, Eldee, 312
Young, George, 192, 241
Young, Greg, 510
Young, Jesse Colin, 510
Young, Kenny, 314
Young, Leon, 65
Young, Lester, 131

Young, Neil, 80, 94, 147, 150, 256, 372, 375
Young, Nelson, 366
Young, Paul, 163
Young, Reggie, 67
Young, Richard, 122, 409
Young, Vicki, 70
Young, Wanda, 334
Young-Holt Unlimited, 313
Youngbloods, 162, 365, 510-511
Yule, Doug, 488-489
Yuma, Johnny, 110

Z

Zabo, Dave, 108
Zagni, Iav, 286
Zappa, Frank, 105-106, 206, 358-360, 482
Zawinul, Joe, 158
Zehringer, Rick, 338
Zelkowitz, Genya, 236
Zephyrs, 169
Zevon, Warren, 224, 466
Zimmer, Dave, 94, 147
Zimming, Bernie, 168
Zolitin, Cynthia, 475
Zombies, 7, 511-512
ZZ Top, 93